17)

THIs book belongs
to :

Clara

Stoughton

Clara :

Yay! ♡

Oxford
Illustrated
Children's
Dictionary

OXFORD

UNIVERSITY PRESS

eggs

lips

OXFORD
UNIVERSITY PRESS

Great Clarendon Street, Oxford OX2 6DP

Oxford University Press is a department of the University of Oxford.
It furthers the University's objective of excellence in research, scholarship,
and education by publishing worldwide in

Oxford   New York

Auckland   Cape Town   Dar es Salaam   Hong Kong   Karachi
Kuala Lumpur   Madrid   Melbourne   Mexico City   Nairobi
New Delhi   Shanghai   Taipei   Toronto
With offices in
Argentina   Austria   Brazil   Chile   Czech Republic   France   Greece
Guatemala   Hungary   Italy   Japan   Poland   Portugal   Singapore
South Korea   Switzerland   Thailand   Turkey   Ukraine   Vietnam

Oxford is a registered trade mark of Oxford University Press
in the UK and in certain other countries

leaves

colours

First published 2010
This edition 2017

cockroaches

British Library Cataloguing in Publication Data

Data available

ISBN: 978-0-19-911993-6

Oxford Illustrated Children's Dictionary & Thesaurus
2017 revised edition ISBN: 978-0-19-276394-5

1 3 5 7 9 10 8 6 4 2

Printed in China

clown

buzzard

film

The Publishers would like to thank Shutterstock and
Wikipedia for permission to use their material. Every care has
been taken to trace copyright holders. However, if there have
been unintentional omissions or failure to trace copyright
holders, we apologize, and will, if informed, endeavour to
make corrections in any future edition.

How to Use your Dictionary

Dictionary entries
The words defined are headwords, and they are arranged in alphabetical order. The words derived from each word (derivatives) are at the end of an entry, sometimes with short definitions, sometimes grouped together. Words with the same spelling but with a different meaning or origin (homographs) are given separate entries and numbered with a raised figure, e.g. **lean**[1] (bend your body) and **lean**[2] (not fat).

Pronunciation
Help is given with pronouncing words when they are difficult in some way, when two words with the same spelling are pronounced differently (such as several words spelled **bow**), and when the same word is pronounced differently in its different word classes or parts of speech (as with **record**).

The pronunciation is given in brackets, introduced by '*rhymes with...*' (when possible) or '*say...*' followed by a simple scheme that uses ordinary letters, e.g.

bow[1] noun (*rhymes with* **cow**)
apostrophe noun (say a-**pos**-tro-fi)

frog

Words are divided into syllables, and the main stress is shown by bold type (thick black letters).

The following sounds should be noted:
oo shows the sound as in s**oo**n
uu shows the sound as in b**oo**k
th shows the sound as in **th**in
th shows the sound as in *th*is
zh shows the sound as in vi**s**ion

Word classes
Word classes are printed in italics (e.g. *noun, adjective, adverb*) after the word and before its definition.

Inflections and plurals
The parts of verbs, plurals of nouns, and some comparatives and superlatives and adverbs are given after the word class when they are irregular, e.g.

break verb (**breaking, broke, broken**)
good adjective (**better, best**)

Meanings
Many words have more than one meaning. Each meaning is numbered separately.

Labels
Words or meanings that are only used informally or in spoken English are marked informal. Subject labels are given for certain meanings that are used in, say, grammar, mathematics, or science.

Examples
Examples of words in use are given in italic or sloping print *like this* to help make a meaning clearer.

Oxford Children's Corpus
All the text has been backed by the Oxford Children's Corpus, which is a large unique electronic database of language written for and by children. It is resourced from a variety of children's literature and select websites, and consists of 300 million words and is growing!

Dictionary features

pronunciation help

label

headword

alphabet tab

inflections

word class

plural

word origin

Guide a member of the Girl Guides Association, an organization for girls

guide *verb*
to guide someone is to show them the way or help them do something

guide dog *noun*
a dog specially trained to lead a blind person

guidelines *plural noun*
guidelines are rules and information about how to do something

guillotine *noun (say* gil-o-teen*)*
1 a machine once used in France for beheading people **2** a device with a sharp blade for cutting paper

guilt *noun*
1 guilt is an unpleasant feeling you have when you have done something wrong **2** a person's guilt is the fact that they have done something wrong • *Everyone was convinced of his guilt.*

guilty *adjective (***guiltier, guiltiest***)*
1 someone is guilty when they have done wrong **2** someone feels guilty when they know they have done wrong

guinea pig *noun*
1 a small furry animal without a tail, kept as a pet **2** a person who is used in an experiment

guitar *noun*
a musical instrument played by plucking its strings
guitarist *noun* someone who plays the guitar

gulf *noun*
a large area of sea partly surrounded by land

gull *noun*
a seagull

gullet *noun*
the tube from the throat to the stomach

gullible *adjective*
someone is gullible when they can be easily fooled about something

gully *noun (***gullies***)*
a narrow channel that carries water

gulp *verb*
1 to gulp something is to swallow it quickly or greedily **2** to gulp is to make a loud swallowing noise, especially out of fear
gulp *noun*
a loud swallowing noise

gum¹ *noun*
the firm fleshy part of the mouth that holds the teeth

gum² *noun*
1 a sticky substance used as glue **2** chewing gum **gummy** *adjective* sticky like gum
gum² *verb (***gumming, gummed***)*
to gum something is to cover it or stick it with gum

gun *noun*
1 a weapon that fires shells or bullets from a metal tube **2** a pistol fired to signal the start of a race
gun *verb (***gunning, gunned***)*
to gun someone down is to shoot them with a gun

gunfire *noun*
gunfire is the firing of guns, or the noise they make

gunman *noun (***gunmen***)*
a man armed with a gun

gunpowder *noun*
gunpowder is a type of explosive

gurdwara *noun*
a building where Sikhs worship

gurgle *verb*
to gurgle is to make a bubbling sound • *Water gurgled down the pipe.*

guru *noun*
1 a Hindu religious teacher **2** a wise and respected teacher

Guru Granth Sahib *noun*
the holy book of the Sikh religion

gush *verb*
1 to gush is to flow quickly **2** to gush is also to talk quickly and with excitement

gust *noun*
a sudden rush of wind or rain **gusty** *adjective*

gut *noun*
the lower part of the digestive system; the intestine
gut *verb (***gutting, gutted***)*
1 to gut a dead fish or animal is to remove its insides before cooking it **2** to gut a place is to remove or destroy the inside of it • *The fire gutted the house.*

guts *plural noun*
1 the insides of a person or animal, especially the stomach and intestines **2** *(informal)* courage and determination

gutter *noun*
a long narrow channel at the side of a street or along the edge of a roof, to carry away rainwater

guy¹ *noun*
1 a figure in the form of Guy Fawkes, burnt on or near 5 November in memory of the Gunpowder Plot to blow up Parliament in 1605 **2** *(informal)* a man

guzzle *verb*
to guzzle food or drink is to eat or drink it greedily

gym *noun (say* jim*) (informal)*
1 a gym is a gymnasium
2 gym is gymnastics

gymkhana *noun (say* jim-**kah**-na*)*
a show of horse-riding contests and other events

gymnasium *noun*
a place equipped for gymnastics

gymnast *noun*
a person who does gymnastics

gymnastics *plural noun*
gymnastics are exercises and movements that show the body's agility and strength

gypsy *noun* **gymnast** *(***gypsies***)*
a member of a community of people, also called **travellers**, who live in caravans or similar vehicles and travel from place to place

gyroscope *noun*
a device used in navigation, that keeps steady because of a heavy wheel spinning inside it

WORD ORIGIN
The word *gyroscope* comes from a Greek word *gyros* meaning 'a ring or circle'.

H'h

habit *noun*
something that you do often and almost without thinking **habitual** *adjective* something is habitual when you do it regularly, as a habit **habitually** *adverb*

habitat *noun*
an animal's or plant's habitat is the place where it naturally lives or grows

hack *verb*
to hack something is to chop or cut it roughly

hacker *noun*
someone who uses a computer to get access to a company's or government's computer system without permission

hacksaw *noun*
a saw with a thin blade for cutting metal

A B C D E F G H I J K L M N O P Q R S T U V W X Y Z

guide words

haddock noun (**haddock**)
a sea fish used for food

hag noun
an ugly old woman

haggard adjective
looking ill or very tired

haggis noun
a Scottish food made from some of the inner parts of a sheep mixed with oatmeal

haggle verb
to haggle is to argue about a price or agreement

haiku noun (**haiku**) (say hy-koo)
a Japanese short poem, with three lines and 17 syllables in the pattern 5,7,5

hail¹ noun
frozen drops of rain

hail¹ verb
it hails or it is hailing when hail falls

hail² verb
to hail someone is to call out or wave to them to get their attention

hailstone noun
a piece of hail

hair noun
1 hair is the soft covering that grows on the heads and bodies of people and animals 2 a hair is one of the fine threads that makes up this soft covering

hairbrush noun
a brush for tidying your hair

haircut noun
cutting a person's hair when it gets too long; the style into which it is cut

hairdresser noun
someone whose job is to cut and arrange people's hair

hair-raising adjective
terrifying or dangerous

hairstyle noun
a way or style of arranging your hair

hairy adjective (**hairier, hairiest**)
having a lot of hair

Hajj noun
the Hajj is the journey to Mecca that all Muslims try to make at least once in their lives

hake noun (**hake**)
a sea fish used for food

halal adjective
halal meat is prepared according to Muslim law

half noun (**halves**)
each of the two equal parts that something is or can be divided into

half adverb
partly; not completely • This meat is only half cooked.

half-hearted adjective
not very enthusiastic
half-heartedly adverb not very enthusiastically

half-mast noun
a flag is at half-mast when it is lowered to halfway down its flagpole, as a sign that someone important has died

half-term noun
a short holiday from school in the middle of a school term

half-time noun
a short break in the middle of a game

halfway adverb, adjective
at a point half the distance or amount between two places or times

hall noun
1 a space or passage inside the front door of a house 2 a very large room for meetings, concerts, or other large gatherings of people 3 a large important building or house, such as a town hall

hallo exclamation
a word used to greet someone or to attract their attention

Hallowe'en noun
the night of 31 October, when people used to think that ghosts and witches might appear

hallucination noun
something you think you can see or hear when it isn't really there

halo noun (**haloes**)
a circle of light, especially one shown round the head of a saint or angel in a painting

halt verb
to halt is to stop
halt noun
to call a halt is to stop something to come to a halt is to stop

halter noun
a rope or strap put round a horse's head so that it can be controlled

halve verb
1 to halve something is to divide it into halves 2 to halve something is to reduce to half its size or amount • If the shop had another checkout it would halve the queues.

ham noun
ham is meat from a pig's leg

hamburger noun
a round flat cake of minced beef that is fried and usually eaten in a bread roll

hammer noun
a tool with a heavy metal head at the end of a handle, used for hitting nails in or beating out things
hammer verb
1 to hammer something is to hit it with a hammer 2 to hammer is to knock loudly • We heard someone hammering on the door. 3 (informal) to hammer someone in a game or contest is to defeat them completely

hammock noun
a bed made of a strong net or piece of cloth hung up above the ground or floor

hamper¹ noun
a large box-shaped basket with a lid
hamper² verb
to hamper someone or something is to get in their way or make it difficult for them to work

words with the same spelling but different meaning (homographs)

hamster noun
a small furry animal with cheek pouches, often kept as a pet

hand noun
1 the part of your body at the end of your arm 2 a pointer on a clock or watch 3 the cards held by one player in a card game 4 a worker, especially a member of a ship's crew 5 side or direction • the right-hand side • on the other hand at hand near or close by to give someone a hand is to help them on hand ready and available to get out of hand is to get out of control
hand verb
to hand something to someone is to give or pass it to them something is handed down when it is passed on from one generation to the next

handbag noun
a small bag for holding money, keys, and other personal items

handcuffs plural noun
a pair of metal rings joined by a chain, used for locking a person's wrists together

handful noun
1 as much as you can carry in one hand 2 a small number of people or things • There were only a handful of people in the audience. 3 (informal) a troublesome person

example sentence

handicap noun
a disadvantage

handicraft noun
artistic work done with your hands, such as woodwork and pottery

numbered meanings

a b c d e f g h i j k l m n o p q r s t u v w x y z

robots

Grammar

Words belong to various **word classes** (also called **parts of speech**). Knowing about word classes helps you to understand how words work and helps you to use them correctly and creatively.

nouns
Nouns are used to name people, places, or things and tell you who or what a sentence is about.
common nouns refer to people or things in general: for example, *dancer, lizard, sandwich,* and *television.* They can be divided into concrete nouns, which we can see, touch, taste, smell, or hear (e.g. *baby, penguin, explosion, aroma, telescope*), and abstract nouns, which describe ideas (e.g. *beauty, horror, mystery*).
proper nouns give the name of a specific person, place, or thing, for example *Shakespeare, Antarctica, Hallowe'en.* Proper nouns always begin with a capital letter.

verbs
A verb can describe an action or process (e.g. *dive, chew, heal, thaw*), a feeling or state of mind (e.g. *worry, think, know, believe*), or a state (e.g. *be, remain*). A sentence usually contains at least one verb.

adjectives
Adjectives give us more information about nouns e.g. *tall, pale, delicious, jagged, untrue.* They can come before a noun (e.g. a *tall* giraffe, a *jagged* cliff), or they can come after a verb like *be, become,* or *grow* (e.g. The soup will be *delicious*; My companion became *pale*; The weather grew *cold*). Some adjectives can only be used in one position: *afraid* can only be used after a verb, and *utter* only before a noun. You can say *The crew were afraid* but not *an afraid crew*; and you can say *It was an utter disaster* but not *The disaster was utter.*

adverbs
Adverbs answer questions such as *when?, where?, why?, how?,* and *how much?* A few adverbs modify adjectives: for example *The map is **very** old* tells you how old the map is, and *a **fairly** expensive car* describes a car that is quite (but not very) expensive. Most adverbs tells us more about verbs: for example, *The troll ate **ravenously*** tells you how the troll was eating, *It rains here **frequently*** tells you how often it rains, and *Hammering was heard **downstairs*** tells you where hammering was heard. Adverbs like these are often formed by adding -*ly* to an adjective e.g. *ravenously, frequently.* Notice that adverbs can also go with other adverbs: *Sam smiled **rather** sheepishly.*

pronouns
Pronouns are used to replace a noun or noun phrase in a sentence or clause, and help to avoid repeating words. There are several types of pronoun:
personal pronouns: *I, you, he, she, it, we, they, me, you, him, her, it, us, them*
reflexive prounouns: *myself, yourself, himself, herself, itself, ourselves, yourselves, themselves*
relative pronouns: *what, who, whom, whose, which, that*
interrogative pronouns: *what, who, whom, whose*
demonstrative pronouns: *this, that, these, those*

tarantula

prepositions

Prepositions show how a noun or pronoun relates to the other words in a sentence or clause. They can show:
• the position or direction of a person or thing:
*The spider scurried **along** the wall, **across** the carpet, **through** the doorway, **down** the stairs, **past** the cat, **up** the curtain, **out** of the window, and **into** the garden.*
• the time something happens or lasts:
*Can you come to my house **on** Tuesday **around** five o'clock?*
*We were in Athens **in** August, **during** the Olympics.*
• the connection between people of things:
*Inspector McBride was always grumbling **about** something.*
*Does this dress go better **with** the red shoes or the brown?*

conjunctions

Conjunctions are used to join words, phrases, or clauses in a sentence. *And, but, for, or, neither, nor, yet, although, because, if, until, unless, when, where, while,* and *whereas* are all conjunctions.
Words like these are used to link ideas in a piece of writing.

exclamations

These are words such as *ah!, oh!,* and *ouch!* that are typically written with an exclamation mark.

beads

Punctuation

Punctuation is the use of special marks to make a piece of writing easier to read and understand. Punctuation marks show divisions and connections between sentences, clauses or individual words: for example, a full stop (.) marks the end of a sentence; a comma (,) separates clauses or items in a list; a question mark (?) indicates a question; and quotation marks (" ") show direct speech (the actual words someone speaks). Other types of punctuation are the use of capital letters at the start of a sentence or a proper noun, and the use of an apostrophe to show possession (the cat's bowl) or to indicate a missing letter (don't, I've).

violin

mummy

a b c d e f g h i j k l m n o p q r s t u v w x y z

A
B
C
D
E
F
G
H
I
J
K
L
M
N
O
P
Q
R
S
T
U
V
W
X
Y
Z

Commonly misspelled words

i before e
chief
niece
pierce
priest
siege
yield
achievement
mischievous
wield

e before i
eight
height
seize
weird
deceive
foreign
receive

words including u
gauge
guard
juice
guarantee
nuisance
pronunciation
sausage

silent letters
knife
psychic
receipt
write

eed or ede
precede
proceed

double or single letters
accommodate
accommodation
address
aggressive
beginning
cassette
colossal
committee
disappear
disappearance
disappoint
disappointment
dissect
embarrass
embarrassment
exaggerate
harass
install
instalment
millennium
millionaire
necessary
parallel
questionnaire
recommend
skilful
threshold
unnecessary
withhold

other difficult spellings
answer
conscientious
cylinder
desperate
ecstasy
extraordinary
extravagant
February
government
length
library
responsible
rhythm
sandwich
scavenge
secretary
separate
sergeant
signature
strength
twelfth
unconscious
vengeance
Wednesday

leopard

Aa

a *determiner* (called the *indefinite article*)
1 one; any • *I would like a holiday.* **2** each; every • *I go there twice a month.*

aback *adverb*
to be taken aback is to be surprised and slightly shocked by something someone says or does • *We were taken aback by this silly idea.*

abacus *noun*
a frame with rows of beads that slide on wires, used for counting and doing sums

abacus

abandon *verb*
to abandon something or someone is to go away and leave them, without intending to go back for them
• *Someone abandoned these poor kittens on the street.* **abandon ship** passengers abandon a sinking ship when they get into the lifeboats to save their lives

abbey *noun*
a place where monks or nuns live and work

abbey

abbreviation *noun*
a word or group of letters that is a shorter form of something longer
• *BBC is an abbreviation of 'British Broadcasting Corporation'.*

abdomen *noun*
1 the part of the human body where the stomach is **2** the back part of the body of an insect or spider

abide *verb*
you cannot abide something or someone when you don't like them at all • *I can't abide blackcurrants.*

ability *noun* (**abilities**)
1 ability is the skill or talent to do something • *They have a lot of ability at games.* **2** an ability is a special skill or talent
• *a person of many abilities*

able *adjective*
1 having the power or skill or opportunity to do something • *They were not able to find our house.*
2 having a special talent or skill
• *John is a very able musician.* **ably** *adverb* to do something ably is to do it well and use skill or talent

abnormal *adjective*
unusual or peculiar, not normal
abnormality *noun* something unusual or abnormal
• *a physical abnormality*

aboard *adverb, preposition*
someone is aboard when they have got on a train, ship, or aircraft • *The passengers were now all aboard.* • *It's time to get aboard the train.*

abolish *verb*
to abolish a rule or custom is to get rid of it • *Some people would like to abolish homework.*

abolition *noun*
(*say* ab-o-**lish**-on)
getting rid of something

abominable *adjective*
very shocking, dreadful • *It was an abominable crime.*

aboriginal *noun*
one of the original inhabitants of a country. When **Aboriginal** refers to Australia you spell it with a capital A.

Aborigines *plural noun*
(*say* ab-er-**ij**-in-eez)
the people who lived in Australia before the European settlers arrived there

about *preposition*
1 to do with, connected with
• *The story is about animals.*
2 approximately, roughly
• *She's about five feet tall.*

about *adverb*
1 in various directions or places
• *They were running about.*
2 somewhere near by • *There were wild animals about.* **to be about to do something** is to be just going to do it • *He was about to leave.*

above *preposition*
1 higher than, over • *There was a window above the door.* **2** more than • *The temperature was just above freezing.*

above *adverb*
at a higher point, or to a higher point • *Look at the stars above.*

abreast *adverb*
side by side • *They walked three abreast.*

abroad *adverb*
in a foreign country • *They live abroad now.*

abrupt *adjective*
1 sudden and unexpected
• *The van came to an abrupt halt.*
2 rude and unfriendly
• *He gave an abrupt reply.*

abscess *noun*
a painful swelling on the body containing pus

abseil *verb*
to abseil is to lower yourself down a steep cliff or rock by sliding down a rope

absence *noun*
not being in a place where you are expected, for example school or work

absent *adjective*
not present; away

absentee *noun*
someone who is away, for example not at school or work

absent-minded *adjective*
forgetting things easily
absent-mindedly *adverb*

absolute *adjective*
total, complete • *For a moment there was absolute silence.*

absolutely *adverb*
1 completely **2** (*informal*) definitely
• *'Are you going to Beth's party?' 'Absolutely!'*

absorb *verb*
1 to absorb something like liquid is to soak it up **2** to be absorbed in something is to be interested in it and give it all your attention • *He was very absorbed in his book.*

absorbent *adjective*
an absorbent material soaks up liquid easily

abstract *adjective*
to do with ideas and not with physical things • *abstract patterns*

absurd *adjective*
silly or ridiculous • *It was an absurd thing to say.* **absurdity** *noun* something that is silly or ridiculous

abundant *adjective*
large in amount, plentiful
abundance *noun* a large amount, plenty • *There was an abundance of good things.*

abuse *verb* (*say* a-**bewz**)
1 to abuse something is to treat

a
b
c
d
e
f
g
h
i
j
k
l
m
n
o
p
q
r
s
t
u
v
w
x
y
z

it badly and harm it **2** to abuse someone is to say unpleasant things about them **3** to abuse someone also means to hurt them or treat them cruelly

abuse *noun* (say a-**bewss**)
1 treating something badly
2 unpleasant words said about someone • *She got a lot of abuse from her so-called friends.*
3 physical harm or cruelty done to someone

abusive *adjective*
saying unpleasant things about someone

academic *adjective*
to do with learning in a school or university • *an academic subject*

academy *noun* (**academies**)
a college or school

accelerate *verb*
to accelerate is to go faster
acceleration *noun* an increase in speed, going faster

accelerator *noun*
a pedal that you press down to make a motor vehicle go faster

accent *noun*
1 your accent is the way you pronounce words, which shows where you are from • *He has a Yorkshire accent.* **2** a special mark put over a letter, usually when it's a foreign word, to show its pronunciation • *The word 'resumé' has an accent on the second 'e'.*

accept *verb*
1 to accept something is to take it when someone offers it to you **2** to accept an invitation is to say 'yes' to it **3** to accept an idea or suggestion is to agree that it is true or worth thinking about **acceptance** *noun* taking something that someone offers you

acceptable *adjective*
good enough, satisfactory • *Their behaviour was not acceptable.*

access *noun*
a way to reach a place • *This road is the only access to the house.*

access *verb*
(in ICT) to access data is to find it on a computer and be able to use it

accessible *adjective*
easy to reach or approach

accident *noun*
something unexpected that happens, especially when something is broken, or someone is hurt or killed
by accident by chance, not intentionally

accidental *adjective*
something is accidental when it happens by chance and not because someone wants it to happen
• *accidental damage* **accidentally** *adverb* to do something accidentally is to do it by mistake or without meaning to • *David accidentally dropped a tin on his foot.*

accommodate *verb*
to accommodate someone or something is to provide them with a place to stay or find space for them

accommodation *noun*
accommodation is a place to live or stay • *They were looking for cheap accommodation.*

accompaniment *noun*
the music played on a piano or another instrument while a singer sings

accompany *verb* (**accompanies, accompanying, accompanied**)
1 to accompany someone is to go somewhere with them **2** to accompany a singer is to play the piano or another instrument while they sing

accomplish *verb*
to accomplish something is to do it successfully **accomplished** *adjective* good at doing something, skilful **accomplishment** *noun* something you do well

accord *noun*
to do something of your own accord is to do it willingly and without being told to

accordingly *adverb*
1 consequently; therefore
2 in a way that is suitable
• *You are older now and must behave accordingly.*

according to *preposition*
1 You say **according to someone** to show where a piece of information comes from • *According to Katie, there is a party tomorrow.* **2** You say **according to something** when you are comparing two things • *The shop has priced the apples according to their size.*

accordion
noun
a portable musical instrument like a large concertina with a set of keys like a piano's at one end

accordion

account *noun*
1 a description or story about something that happened
2 an amount of money someone has in a bank or building society
3 a statement of the money someone owes or has received, a bill **on account of something** because of it **to take something into account** is to consider it along with other things

account *verb*
to account for something is to be or give an explanation of it • *How do you account for these marks?*

accountant *noun*
a person whose job is to write and organize the money accounts of a person or organization
accountancy *noun* accountancy is the job an accountant does

accumulate *verb*
1 to accumulate things is to collect them or pile them up
2 things accumulate when they form a heap or pile **accumulation** *noun*

accuracy *noun*
accuracy is being exactly right or correct

accurate *adjective*
done exactly and carefully • *She does accurate work.* **accurately** *adverb* to do something accurately is to do it carefully and exactly
• *You have to measure the room accurately.*

accuse *verb*
to accuse someone is to say that they did something wrong
accusation *noun* a statement accusing someone of something

accustomed *adjective*
to be accustomed to something is to be used to it • *She was not accustomed to being treated so rudely.*

ace *noun*
1 the four aces in a pack of cards are the cards with an A in the corner and a large emblem of the suit in the centre
2 someone or something very clever or skilful

ache *noun*
a dull steady pain

ache *verb*
to ache is to feel a dull steady pain

achieve *verb*
to achieve something is to succeed in doing it or getting it **achievement** *noun* something you succeed in doing • *Winning the prize was a fine achievement.*

acid noun
a substance that contains hydrogen and causes chemical change. Acids are the opposite of alkalis.

acid adjective
sour or bitter to taste **acidic** adjective containing a lot of acid **acidity** noun the level of acid in a substance

acid rain noun
rain that contains harmful acids because it has mixed with waste gases from the air

acknowledge verb
1 to acknowledge something is to admit that it is true
2 to acknowledge a letter is to say that you have received it
3 to acknowledge a debt or favour is to say you are grateful for it **acknowledgement** noun

acne noun (say **ak**-ni)
a skin disease with red pimples on the face

acorn noun
the seed of an oak tree. It is oval with a stem ending in the shape of a cup.

acoustics plural noun
(say a-**koo**-stiks)
1 the acoustics of a place are the qualities that make it good or bad for sound **2** (singular noun) the science of sound

acquaint verb
1 to acquaint someone with something is to tell them something about it, so they know what it is
2 to be acquainted with someone is to know them slightly

acquaintance noun
someone you know slightly
to make someone's acquaintance is to get to know them

acquire verb
to acquire something is to obtain it, usually with some effort or difficulty

acquit verb (**acquitting, acquitted**)
to acquit someone is to decide that they are not guilty of a crime, especially in a law trial

acre noun (say **ay**-ker)
an acre is the area of a piece of land containing 4,840 square yards (0.4 hectare)

acrobat noun (say **ak**-ro-bat)
an entertainer who gives displays of jumping and balancing **acrobatic** adjective to do with an acrobat; like what an acrobat does • They were amazed at her acrobatic skills.

acrobatics plural noun
exercises of jumping and balancing that an acrobat does.

acronym noun (say **ak**-ro-nim)
a word or name that is formed from the first letters of other words, for example UFO is an acronym of unidentified flying object

across adverb, preposition
1 from one side of something to the other • The table measures 1.5 metres across. **2** to the other side of something • How can we get across the busy road?

act noun
1 something that someone does **2** an individual performance in a programme of entertainment, for example a juggling act or a comic act **3** one of the main sections of a play or opera **4** a new law that a government makes **to put on an act** is to show off or pretend to be something you are not

act verb
1 to do something useful or necessary • We need to act straight away. **2** to behave in a certain way • She's been acting very strangely recently. **3** to act in a play or film is to take part in it

action noun
1 an action is something that someone does **2** action is fighting in a battle • He was killed in action. **out of action** not working properly **to take action** is to do something decisive

activate verb
to activate a machine or device is to start it working

active adjective
1 busy, taking part in lots of activities **2** doing things, working • an active volcano

activity noun (**activities**)
1 activity is doing things **2** an activity is something special that someone does • They enjoy outdoor activities.

actor noun
someone who takes part in a play or film

actress noun
a girl or woman who takes part in a play or film

actual adjective
really there or really happening

actually adverb
really, in fact • Actually, I think you are wrong.

acupuncture noun
acupuncture is a way of curing disease or taking away pain by pricking parts of the body with needles

acute adjective
1 sharp or intense • She has an acute pain. **2** severe • The explorers were suffering from an acute shortage of food. **3** clever, quick to understand something **4** an acute accent is the mark put over a letter, as in resumé **5** an acute angle is an angle of less than 90 degrees

AD
short for Anno Domini, used with dates that come after the birth of Jesus Christ, for example AD 1492 is the year Columbus reached America

adapt verb
1 to adapt something is to change it so you can use it for something different **2** to adapt to something is to make yourself cope with it • They adapted to life in the country very quickly. **adaptation** noun an adaptation is something someone has adapted, for example a book they have made into a film

adaptor noun
a device for connecting different pieces of equipment

add verb
1 to add one number to another is to put them together to get a bigger number **2** to add one thing to another is to mix them together, for example the different things in a recipe **to add up** is what numbers do to make a bigger number, called a total **to add numbers up** is to make them into a bigger number

adder noun
a small poisonous snake

addict noun
someone with a habit they can't give up, for example taking drugs or drinking alcohol **addicted** adjective someone who is addicted to a habit can't give it up **addiction** noun a habit that someone can't give up

addition noun
1 addition is the process of adding numbers together, or adding other things **2** an addition is something or someone that has been added • James is an addition to the class. **in addition** also, as well

additional adjective
extra, added on

acrobat

adder

a b c d e f g h i j k l m n o p q u v w x y z

additive noun
something that is added to food, for example as a flavouring

address noun
1 the details of the place where someone lives • *My address is 29 High Street, Newtown.* **2** (in computing) a set of words and symbols that tells you where you can find something using a computer, for example on the Internet • *What's your email address?* **3** a speech

address verb
1 to address a letter or parcel is to write the address on it before sending it **2** to address a person or a group of people is to make an important remark or speech to them • *The judge addressed the prisoner.*

adenoids plural noun
your adenoids are the spongy flesh at the back of your nose, which can become swollen making it difficult to breathe

adequate adjective
enough, sufficient

adhesive noun
something such as glue that you use to stick things together

adhesive adjective
causing things to stick together

Adi Granth noun
(*say* ah-di **grunt**)
the holy book of the Sikhs

adjacent adjective
near or next to something • *Her house is adjacent to the shop.*

adjective noun
a word that describes a noun or adds to its meaning, for example *big, honest, red*

adjust verb
1 to adjust something is to change it slightly or change its position **2** to adjust to something is to try to get used to it • *They found it hard to adjust to life in the city.*
adjustment noun a small change you make to something

administration noun
administration is running a business or governing a country
administrator noun someone who helps to run a business or organization

admirable adjective
worth admiring; excellent • *You have done an admirable piece of work.* **admirably** adverb in an admirable way • *The note is written in admirably clear handwriting.*

admiral noun
an officer of the highest rank in the navy

admiration noun
admiration is a feeling you have for someone or something when you think they are very good or very beautiful • *He was filled with admiration for his sister.*

admire verb
1 to admire someone or something is to think they are very good or very beautiful **2** to admire something is also to look at it and enjoy it • *They went to the top of the hill to admire the view.* **admirer** noun • *Adele has many admirers.*

admission noun
1 admission is being allowed to go into a place • *Admission to the show is by ticket only.* **2** an admission is something that someone admits or confesses • *He is guilty by his own admission.*

admit verb (**admitting, admitted**)
1 to admit someone is to let them come into a place **2** to admit something is to say that it has happened or that you have done it

admittance noun
admittance is being allowed to go into a private place

admittedly adverb
although it is true; without denying it • *Admittedly I was teasing the dog, but I didn't expect it to bite.*

ado noun
without more ado without wasting any more time

adolescent noun
a young person who is older than a child and not yet an adult, from about 15 to 18 **adolescence** noun the time between being a child and being an adult

adopt verb
1 to adopt a child is to take them into your family and bring them up as your own **2** to adopt a system or method is to start using it
adoption noun adoption is adopting someone or something
adopted adjective an adopted child is one that someone has adopted **adoptive** adjective adoptive parents are parents who have adopted a child

adorable adjective
lovely, worth adoring

adore verb
to adore someone or something is to love them or admire them very much **adoration** noun adoration is adoring someone or something

adorn verb
to adorn something is to decorate it or make it pretty **adornment** noun

adornment is making something pretty

adrenalin noun
a hormone that stimulates your nervous system and makes you feel ready to do something

adrift adverb, adjective
something such as a boat is adrift when it is loose and drifting about

adult noun
a fully grown person or animal

adultery noun (*say* a-**dul**-ter-i)
adultery is having a lover in addition to a husband or wife

advance noun
1 an advance is a forward movement **2** advance is improvement or progress **3** an advance of money is a loan **4** an advance warning is a warning given beforehand
in advance beforehand

advance verb
1 to advance is to move forward **2** to advance is also to make progress

advanced adjective
1 a long way forward **2** an advanced course or exam is one at a higher level

advantage noun
something useful or helpful
to take advantage of someone is to treat them unfairly when they are not likely to complain
to take advantage of something is to make good use of it

Advent noun
in the Christian Church, the period before Christmas

adventure noun
an adventure is an exciting, dangerous, or interesting event or journey **adventurous** adjective an adventurous person likes to do interesting or exciting things

adverb noun
a word that tells you how or when or where or why something happens. In these sentences, the words in italics are adverbs: They moved *slowly.* Come back *soon.* I *only* want a drink.

advert noun
(informal) an advertisement

advertise verb
to advertise something that you do or that you have made is to praise it in a newspaper or on television so that people will want it

advertisement noun
a public notice or short television film that tries to persuade people to buy something

advice noun
advice is something you say to someone to help them decide what to do

advisable adjective
sensible, worth doing

advise verb
to advise someone is to tell them what you think they should do

aerial noun
a wire or metal rod for receiving or sending radio or television signals

aerial adjective
from or in the air, or from aircraft • *They showed us an aerial photograph of our school.*

aerobatics plural noun
an exciting display by flying aircraft **aerobatic** adjective to do with aerobatics • *They went to see an aerobatic display.*

aeroplane noun
a flying machine with wings

aeroplane

aerosol noun
a device that holds a liquid under pressure and lets it out in a fine spray

affair noun
1 something interesting that happens, an event
2 someone's affairs are their private business • *Keep your nose out of my affairs.*

affect verb
to affect someone or something is to cause them to change or to harm them • *The dampness might affect his health.*

affection noun
love or fondness • *I have a great affection for my nephew.* **affectionate** adjective showing love or fondness

afflict verb
to be afflicted by something unpleasant, like an illness, is to suffer from it **affliction** noun a great illness or problem that makes someone suffer

afford verb
1 to be able to afford something is to have enough money to pay for it
2 to be unable to afford the time to

do something is not to have enough time for it

afforestation noun
the process of covering an area of land with trees

afloat adjective, adverb
floating; on a boat • *Do you enjoy life afloat?*

afraid adjective
frightened **I'm afraid** I am sorry; I regret • *I'm afraid I've burnt the cakes.*

after preposition, adverb
meaning 'later' or 'later than' • *Come after dinner.* • *I'll do it after.*

afternoon noun
the time from midday or lunchtime until evening

afterwards adverb
at a later time

again adverb
1 once more; another time
2 as before • *You will soon be well again.* **again and again** lots of times

against preposition
1 touching or hitting • *He was leaning against the wall.*
2 opposed to, not liking • *Are you against smoking?*

age noun
1 your age is how old you are
2 an age is a period of history • *the Elizabethan age*
ages (informal) a long time • *We've been waiting ages.*

age verb
to age is to become old

aged adjective
1 (say ayjd) having the age of • *The girl was aged 9.* **2** (say ay-jid) very old • *We saw an aged man.*

agent noun
1 someone whose job is to organize things for other people • *We sold our flat through an estate agent.* **2** a spy • *He is a secret agent.* **agency** noun an agent's office or business

aggravate verb
1 to aggravate something is to make it worse **2** (informal) to aggravate someone is to annoy them **aggravation** noun

aggression noun
starting a war or attack; being aggressive **aggressor** noun someone who starts an attack

aggressive adjective
1 an aggressive person or group of people is one that is likely to attack or use violence **2** an aggressive activity is one that people do with energy and that has a strong effect

• *They began an aggressive sales campaign.*

agile adjective
able to move quickly and easily **agility** noun agility is being agile

agitated adjective
worried and anxious • *Why are you getting so agitated?* **agitation** noun agitation is getting worried or anxious • *He could not hide his agitation.*

ago adverb
in the past • *She died long ago.*

agonizing adjective
1 an agonizing pain is one that hurts terribly **2** an agonizing choice or decision is one that you find very difficult to make

agony noun (**agonies**)
severe pain or suffering

agree verb
1 to agree with someone is to think the same as them **2** to agree to do something is to say that you are willing to • *She agreed to go with him.* **3** something agrees with someone when it suits them or does them good • *Spicy food doesn't agree with her.*

agreeable adjective
1 willing to do something that someone suggests • *We shall go if you are agreeable.* **2** (rather old use) pleasant • *It is a very agreeable little place.*

agreement noun
1 agreement is thinking the same • *Are we in agreement?*
2 an agreement is an arrangement that people have agreed on

agriculture noun
agriculture is farming, or growing food on the land

agricultural adjective
to do with agriculture

aground adverb
stuck on the bottom of a river or the sea in shallow water • *The ship has run aground.*

ahead adverb
forwards, in front • *Sheila went ahead to show us the way.*

aid noun
1 aid is help you give someone **2** aid is also money or food or other help that a country sends to a poorer country **3** an aid is something that helps someone to do something better • *He was wearing a hearing aid.* **in aid of something** or **someone** so as to help them

aid verb
to aid someone is to help them

a
b
c
d
e
f
g
h
i
j
k
l
m
n
o
p
q
r
s
t
u
v
w
x
y
z

AIDS noun
a disease caused by a virus, which destroys the body's immunity to other diseases

AIDS virus

ailment noun
a minor illness

aim verb
1 to aim a gun at someone or something is to point it at them so as to shoot them 2 to aim something like a ball is to throw it or kick it in a particular direction 3 to aim to do something is to try to do it

aim noun
1 a person's aim is what they intend to do 2 aim is also pointing a weapon in a particular direction

aimless adjective
not having any definite aim or purpose • He led an aimless life.
aimlessly adverb

air noun
1 air is the mixture of gases which surrounds the earth and which everyone breathes 2 an air is a tune 3 an air of mystery or secrecy is a feeling that things are mysterious or secret **to go by air** is to travel in an aeroplane **to be on the air** is to be on the radio or television

air verb
1 to air clothes or washing is to put them in a warm place to finish drying 2 to air a room is to let fresh air into it 3 to air views or opinions is to say them so that people know them

airborne adjective
1 flying in an aircraft 2 carried by the air • an airborne virus

aircraft noun
an aeroplane or a helicopter • The two aircraft passed each other over the Atlantic.

air force noun
the part of a country's fighting force that uses aircraft

airline noun
a company that takes people to places by aircraft

airliner noun
a large aircraft for carrying passengers

airlock noun
1 a bubble of air that forms in liquid and stops it flowing through a pipe 2 a compartment with airtight doors at each end

airmail noun
airmail is mail that is sent by air

airport noun
a place where aircraft land and take off, with passenger terminals and other buildings

air raid noun
an attack by bombs dropped from aircraft

airship noun
a large balloon with engines, designed to carry passengers or cargo

airtight adjective
not letting air get in or out

airy adjective (**airier, airiest**)
1 with plenty of fresh air
2 like air **airily** adverb to do something airily is to do it in a casual or light-hearted way • He replied airily that he didn't want to know.

aisle noun (rhymes with **mile**)
a passage between or beside rows of seats in a church, theatre, or cinema, or on an aeroplane

ajar adverb, adjective
slightly open • Please leave the door ajar.

alarm verb
to alarm someone is to make them frightened or anxious

alarm noun
1 a warning sound or signal 2 a feeling of fear or anxiety • He cried out in alarm. 3 an alarm clock

alarm clock noun
a clock with a loud ring or bleep, which can be set to wake you up

alas exclamation
(old use) something you say when you are sad

albatross noun
a large seabird with long wings

album noun
1 a book in which you keep things like photographs or stamps or autographs 2 a collection of songs on a CD, record, or digital download

alcohol noun
1 a colourless liquid made by fermenting sugar or starch
2 drinks containing this liquid (for example beer, wine, gin), which affects people's behaviour and can make them drunk if they have too much

alcoholic adjective
containing alcohol
alcoholic noun
someone who is constantly ill from drinking too much alcohol

alcove noun
a part of a room where the wall is set back from the main part

alert adjective
watching for something; ready to act

alert verb
to alert someone to a danger or problem is to warn them about it

alert noun
an alarm **on the alert** on the lookout for danger or attack

A level noun
a higher standard of examination that is taken after the GCSE, especially by pupils who want to go to university

algebra noun (say al-ji-bra)
mathematics in which letters and symbols are used to represent numbers

WORD ORIGIN

The word **algebra** comes from an Arabic word al-jabr meaning 'putting broken parts together', which was the title of a book on mathematics by an Arab mathematician.

alias noun (say ay-li-as)
a false or different name that someone uses instead of their real name
alias adverb
also named • Clark Kent, alias Superman

alibi noun (say al-i-by)
evidence that someone accused of a crime was not there when the crime was committed

alien noun (say ay-li-en)
1 someone who is not a citizen of the country where they are living
2 in science fiction, a being from another world

alien adjective
1 foreign 2 not in keeping, quite unlike • Lying was alien to his nature.

alight adjective
on fire, burning

alike adjective
similar, like each other
alike adverb
in the same way • He treats everybody alike.

alive adjective
living, existing • Is he alive?

alkali noun (**alkalis**)
(say al-ka-ly)
a substance that neutralizes acids or

that combines with acids to form salts
alkaline adjective containing an alkili

all determiner, adverb, noun
meaning 'everything' or 'everyone'
• *That is all I know.*
• *All my books are in the desk.*
• *She was dressed all in white.*

Allah
the Muslim name of God

allegation noun
(say a-li-**gay**-shun)
you make an allegation when you
accuse someone of doing something
wrong

allege verb (say a-**lej**)
to allege that someone has done
something is to accuse them of it,
usually without proof • *He alleged
that I stole his ring.*

allegiance noun (say a-**lee**-jans)
loyalty shown to a person or
organization

allergy noun
a condition that some people have
that makes their body react badly to
things they eat or drink or touch or
breathe in, for example dust, milk, or
some kinds of food **allergic** adjective
someone is allergic to something if
they become ill or uncomfortable
when they eat it or touch it • *She must
be allergic to goat's milk.*

alley noun
1 a narrow street or passage
2 a place where you can
play at skittles or tenpin bowling

alliance noun
an agreement between countries
to support each other and have the
same enemies

allied adjective
having an alliance; on the same side
• *The allied countries declared war.*

alligator noun
a large reptile like a crocodile

allotment noun
a small rented piece of ground used
for growing vegetables

allow verb
1 to allow someone to do something
is to let them do it • *We will allow
you to leave now.* • *Smoking is not
allowed.* **2** to allow an amount of
money is to provide it for some reason
• *She was allowed £10 for books.*

allowance noun
a sum of money given regularly to
someone **to make allowances** is
to be considerate • *We must make
allowances for his age.*

alloy noun
a metal formed from a mixture of
other metals

all right adjective
satisfactory; in good condition • *She
fixed my bike, so it's all right.*

ally noun (**allies**) (say **al**-I)
1 a country in alliance with another
country **2** a person who helps or
cooperates with you

almighty adjective
1 having a lot of power
2 (informal) very great • *They were
making an almighty din.*

almond noun (say **ah**-mond)
an oval nut that you can eat

almost adverb
very close to but not quite
• *I am almost ready.*

alone adjective, adverb
without any other people or other
things; on your own • *He soon
discovers that he is not alone on the
island.*

along preposition, adverb
1 from one end of something to the
other **2** on; onwards • *Move along,
please!* **3** accompanying someone
• *I have brought my brother along.*

alongside preposition, adverb
next to something

aloud adverb
in a voice that can be heard

alphabet noun
the letters used in a language,
usually arranged in a set order
alphabetical adjective to do
with the alphabet **alphabetically**
adverb something is arranged
alphabetically when it is in the order
of the alphabet

alphabet

already adverb
by or before now
• *I've already told you once.*

also adverb
as an extra, besides • *We also need
some bread.*

altar noun
a table or raised surface used in
religious ceremonies

alter verb
to alter something is to change it
alteration noun a change you
make to something

alternate adjective
(say ol-ter-nat)
1 happening on every other one • *My
sister and I take the dog for a walk
on alternate days.*
2 coming in turns, one after the
other • *alternate laughter and tears*
alternately adverb one after the
other in turn • *The weather was
alternately fine* **alternate** verb (say
ol-ter-**nayt**) to alternate is to happen
in turns

alternative noun
(say ol-**ter**-na-tiv)
something you can choose instead of
something else • *If you don't like this
book there is an alternative.*
alternative adjective
for you to choose instead of
something else • *The cafe has an
alternative menu for vegetarians.*

although conjunction
in spite of the fact that • *Although
the sun was shining, it was still cold.*

altitude noun
the height of something, especially
above sea level

alto noun
1 a female singer with a low voice;
also called a contralto **2** a male
singer with a voice higher than a
tenor's

altogether adverb
1 completely • *He is altogether
wrong.* **2** on the whole • *Altogether, it
wasn't a bad holiday.*

aluminium noun
a silver-coloured metal that is light
in weight

always adverb
1 all the time, at all times
2 often, constantly • *You are always
crying.* **3** whatever happens • *You
can always sleep on the floor.*

a.m.
short for Latin *ante meridiem* which
means 'before midday'

amateur noun (say **am**-a-ter)
someone who does something
because they like it, without being
paid for it

amaze verb
to amaze someone is to surprise
them greatly **amazement** noun
amazement is a feeling of great
surprise

ambassador noun
someone sent to a foreign country to
represent their own government

amber noun
1 a hard, clear, yellowish
substance used for making
ornaments **2** a yellowish colour, the

one used in traffic lights as a signal for caution

ambiguous *adjective*
having more than one possible meaning, uncertain • *His reply was ambiguous.*

ambition *noun*
1 ambition is a strong desire to be successful in life **2** an ambition is something you want to do very much • *His ambition is to run his own airline.* **ambitious** *adjective* an ambitious person wants very much to be successful in life

amble *verb*
to amble along is to walk slowly

ambulance *noun*
a vehicle for carrying sick or injured people

ambush *noun*
a surprise attack from a hidden place

ambush *verb*
to ambush someone is to attack them suddenly from a hidden place

amend *verb*
to amend something like a piece of writing is to change or improve it **amendment** *noun* a change to a piece of writing or a law

amiable *adjective*
friendly, good-tempered **amiability** *noun* friendliness **amiably** *adverb*

amid or **amidst** *preposition*
in the middle of, among

ammonia *noun*
a gas or liquid with a strong smell, used to make cleaning liquids

ammunition *noun*
bullets, bombs, and other explosive objects used in fighting

amnesty *noun* (**amnesties**)
a decision to pardon people who have broken the law

amoeba *noun* (*say* a-**mee**-ba)
a tiny creature made of one cell. It can change shape and split itself in two.

among or **amongst** *preposition*
1 surrounded by, in the middle of • *She was hiding among the bushes.* **2** between • *Let's divide the money amongst ourselves.*

amount *noun*
a quantity or total

amount *verb*
to amount to something is to reach it as a total • *The bill amounted to £55.*

amphibian *noun*
an animal that can live on land and in water **amphibious** *adjective* an amphibious animal is able to live on land and in water

ample *adjective*
1 large, having plenty of space • *This car has an ample boot.* **2** more than enough • *We had ample provisions.* **amply** *adverb* generously; with as much as you need or even more • *They were amply rewarded.*

amplifier *noun*
an electronic device for making music or other sounds louder

amplify *verb* (**amplifies, amplifying, amplified**)
to amplify sounds is to make them louder or stronger **amplification** *noun* amplification is making voices or other sounds louder

amputate *verb*
to amputate an arm or a leg is to cut it off when it is diseased **amputation** *noun* amputation is cutting off an arm or a leg

amuse *verb*
1 to amuse someone is to make them laugh or smile **2** to amuse yourself is to find pleasant things to do

amusement *noun*
1 an amusement is something that amuses you **2** amusement is being amused; laughing or smiling

amusing *adjective*
making you laugh or smile • *It was an amusing story.*

an *adjective* (called the *indefinite article*)
a word used instead of **a** when the next word begins with a vowel-sound or a silent **h** • *Take an apple.* • *You can hire boats for £5 an hour.*

anaemia *noun* (*say* a-**nee**-mi-a)
a poor condition of the blood that makes someone look pale **anaemic** *adjective* an anaemic person suffers from anaemia

anaesthetic *noun*
(*say* an-iss-**thet**-ik)
a drug or gas that makes you unable to feel pain

anagram *noun*
a word or phrase made by

rearranging the letters of another word or phrase, for example *carthorse* is an anagram of *orchestra*

analyse *verb*
1 to analyse something is to examine it carefully **2** to analyse a substance is to divide it into its parts

analysis *noun* (**analyses**)
a detailed study or examination of something

anarchy *noun*
1 anarchy is having no government or controls, leading to a breakdown in law and order **2** complete disorder or confusion **anarchist** *noun* someone who thinks that government and laws are bad and should be abolished

anatomy *noun*
the study of the parts of the body **anatomical** *adjective* to do with anatomy

ancestor *noun*
a person who lived in the past and was in the same family as someone alive now **ancestry** *noun* a person's ancestry is the list of all their ancestors

anchor *noun*
a heavy object joined to a ship by a chain or rope and dropped to the bottom of the sea to stop the ship from moving

ancient *adjective*
1 belonging to times that were long ago **2** very old • *They came from an ancient family.*

and *conjunction*
linking words and phrases
• *We had cakes and lemonade.*
• *Touch that and you'll get burnt.*
• *Go and buy a pen.*

anecdote *noun*
a short amusing or interesting story about a real person or thing

anemone *noun*
(*say* a-**nem**-on-i)
1 a small flower with the shape of a cup **2** a sea anemone

angel *noun*
1 a being that some people believe in, who is a messenger or attendant of God **2** a very kind or beautiful person

anger *noun*
a strong feeling that you do not like what someone

has said or done, making you want to quarrel or fight with them

angle noun
1 the space between two lines or surfaces that meet 2 a point of view • What is your angle on this?

angle verb
to angle something is to put it in a slanting position

angler noun
someone who fishes with a fishing rod **angling** noun the sport of fishing with a fishing rod

angry adjective (**angrier, angriest**)
feeling or showing anger **angrily** adverb

anguish noun
great suffering or unhappiness **anguished** adjective suffering or unhappy

animal noun
a living thing that can move and feel, such as a horse, snake, fish, bird, or insect

animated adjective
an animated film is one made by photographing a series of still pictures and showing them rapidly one after another, so they appear to move **animation** noun a way of making films from still pictures so they appear to move

aniseed noun
a seed with a strong sweet taste like liquorice

ankle noun
the part of your leg where it is joined to your foot

annihilate verb (say a-**ny**-il-ayt)
to annihilate something is to destroy it completely **annihilation** noun annihilation is destroying something completely

anniversary noun (**anniversaries**)
a day when you remember something special that happened on the same date in an earlier year

announce verb
to announce something is to say it publicly **announcer** noun someone who announces something, especially on radio or television

announcement noun
something that is made known publicly, especially in a newspaper or on radio or television

annoy verb
to annoy someone is to give them a feeling of not being pleased

annoyance noun
1 annoyance is the feeling of being annoyed 2 an annoyance is something that annoys you • Wasps are a great annoyance at a picnic.

annual adjective
happening or coming every year **annually** adverb once every year • A new book comes out annually.

annual noun
a children's book of stories or comic strips that comes out once a year

anonymous adjective
an anonymous book or letter is one with the name of the writer unknown **anonymously** adverb with the name unknown

anorak noun
a thick warm jacket with a hood

anorexia noun
(say an-er-**eks**-ee-a)
an illness that makes someone not want to eat **anorexic** adjective an anorexic person is suffering from anorexia • She has an anorexic daughter.

another determiner, pronoun
a different person or thing • Have another look. • May I have another?

answer noun
1 an answer is what you say when someone asks you a question 2 the answer to a problem is something that solves it

answer verb
1 to answer someone is to give them an answer 2 to answer a telephone is to pick it up when it rings **to answer back** is to say something rude or cheeky as an answer

ant noun
a tiny insect that lives in large groups

antelope noun
an animal like a deer, that lives in Africa and parts of Asia

antenna noun
1 (**antennae**) a long thin feeler on the head of an insect or shellfish 2 (**antennas**) an aerial

anthem noun
a religious or patriotic song, usually sung by a choir or group of people

anthology noun (**anthologies**)
a collection of poems, stories, or songs in one book

antibiotic noun
a drug that kills bacteria. Penicillin is an antibiotic.

anticipate verb
1 to anticipate something

is to expect it and be ready for it • The police were anticipating trouble. 2 to anticipate someone is to act before they do • They anticipated us in getting the early train.

anticipation noun
looking forward to doing something

anticlimax noun
a disappointing ending or result after something exciting

anticlockwise adverb, adjective
moving in the opposite direction to the hands of a clock

anticyclone noun
an area where air pressure is high, usually causing fine weather

antidote noun
something which takes away the bad effects of a poison or disease

antiquated adjective
old-fashioned

antique noun (say an-**teek**)
something that is valuable because it is very old

antiseptic noun
a chemical that kills germs

antler noun
the horn of a deer, which divides into several branches

antonym noun (say **ant**-o-nim)
a word that is opposite in meaning to another • 'Soft' is an antonym of 'hard'.

anvil noun
a large block of iron on which a blacksmith hammers metal into shape

anxiety noun (**anxieties**)
1 anxiety is a feeling of being worried 2 an anxiety is something that worries you

anxious adjective
1 worried and nervous 2 eager to do something • They were anxious to help us.

any determiner
1 one or some • Have you any wool? 2 no matter which • Come any day you like. 3 every • Any fool knows that!

any adverb
at all; in some degree • Is it any good?

anybody noun, pronoun
anyone

anyhow adverb
1 anyway 2 (informal) carelessly, without much thought • Books were placed anyhow on the shelves.

anyone noun, pronoun
any person

anything noun, pronoun
any thing

anyway *adverb*
whatever happens; whatever the situation may be • *If it rains, we'll go anyway.*

anywhere *adverb*
in any place or to any place

apart *adverb*
1 away from each other; separately • *Keep your desks apart.*
2 into pieces • *It fell apart.*

apartment *noun*
1 a set of rooms
2 (*in America*) a flat

ape *noun*
a monkey without a tail, such as a gorilla or a chimpanzee

ape

aphid or **aphis** *noun*
a tiny insect that sucks juices from plants

apologetic *adjective*
saying you are sorry for something
apologetically *adverb* in a way that shows you are sorry • *He replied apologetically.*

apologize *verb*
to apologize to someone is to tell them you are sorry

apology *noun*
a statement that you are sorry for doing something wrong

apostle *noun*
in Christianity, one of the twelve men sent out by Christ to tell people about God

apostrophe *noun*
(*say* a-**pos**-tro-fi)
a punctuation mark (') used to show that letters have been left out, as in *can't* and *he'll.* It is also used with *s* to show who owns something, as in

the boy's books (one boy), *the boys' books* (more than one boy).

appal *verb* (**appalling, appalled**)
to appal someone is to shock them a lot • *The violence appalled everyone.*

appalling *adjective*
dreadful, shocking • *The room was in an appalling mess.*

apparatus *noun*
an apparatus is a set of equipment for a special use

apparent *adjective*
1 clear, obvious • *He burst out laughing for no apparent reason.*
2 appearing to be true • *They were not put off by their apparent failure.*

apparently *adverb*
as it seems, so it appears
• *The door had apparently been locked.*

appeal *verb*
1 to appeal for something is to ask for it when you need it badly • *They are appealing for money to rebuild the church roof.* 2 to appeal to someone is to interest or attract them • *The cover of the book really appeals to me.* 3 to appeal against a decision is to ask for it to be changed • *He decided to appeal against his prison sentence.*

appeal *noun*
1 an appeal is asking for something you need 2 appeal is what makes something interesting • *Adventure stories have a lot of appeal for older children.* 3 an appeal is asking for a decision to be changed

appear *verb*
1 to appear is to become visible
2 to appear is also to seem • *They appeared very anxious.* 3 to appear in a film or play is to take part in it

appearance *noun*
1 coming into sight 2 taking part in a play, film, show, etc. 3 what someone looks like 4 what something seems to be

appendicitis *noun*
an inflammation or disease of the appendix

appendix *noun*
1 (**appendixes**) a small tube leading off from the intestines in the body 2 (**appendices**) an extra section at the end of a book

appetite *noun*
a desire for something, especially for food

appetizing *adjective*
looking good to eat

applaud *verb*
to applaud someone or something is to show that you like them, especially by clapping

applause *noun*
clapping or cheering after someone has given a speech or given a performance

apple *noun*
a round fruit with skin that is red, green, or yellow

appliance *noun*
a device or gadget

application *noun*
1 an application is a letter or form you use to ask for something important, such as a job
2 application is when you make a lot of effort to do something

applied *adjective*
used for something practical
• *Engineering is an applied science.*

apply *verb* (**applies, applying, applied**)
1 to apply something is to put it on something else • *You need to apply a patch to the puncture.* 2 to apply for a job is to write formally and ask for it 3 to apply to someone is to concern them • *These rules apply to everybody.* 4 to apply yourself to something is to give it all your attention

appoint *verb*
to appoint someone is to choose them for a job

appointment *noun*
1 an arrangement to meet or visit someone 2 a job or position

appreciate *verb*
1 to appreciate something is to enjoy or value it 2 to appreciate a fact is to understand it • *You don't seem to appreciate how lucky we are.* 3 to appreciate is to increase in value

appreciation *noun*
1 appreciation is showing that you enjoy or value something
2 appreciation is also an increase in the money value of something, such as a house or a work of art

appreciative *adjective*
an appreciative person or group shows how much they enjoy or value something • *I enjoy playing to an appreciative audience.*

apprehension *noun*
nervous fear or worry
apprehensive *adjective* nervous and worried

apprentice *noun*
someone who is learning a trade or craft **apprenticeship** *noun* the

A B C D E F G H I J K L M N O P Q R S T U V W X Y Z

time when someone is an apprentice

approach *verb*
1 to approach a place is to come near to it **2** to approach someone is to go to them with a request or offer **3** to approach a problem or difficulty is to start solving it

approach *noun*
1 coming near to a place **2** a way of tackling a problem **3** a way or road leading up to a building • *The approach to the house had trees on each side.* **4** the final part of an aircraft's flight as it comes in to land

approachable *adjective*
friendly and easy to talk to

appropriate *adjective*
suitable

approval *noun*
thinking well of someone or something

approve *verb*
to approve of someone or something is to think they are good or suitable

approximate *adjective*
roughly correct but not exact • *The dates in brackets are approximate only.* **approximately** *adverb* roughly but not exactly • *It will cost approximately twenty pounds.*

approximation *noun*
something that is a rough estimate and not exact

apricot *noun*
a juicy, orange-coloured fruit like a small peach, with a stone in it

apricots

April *noun*
the fourth month of the year

apron *noun*
a piece of clothing worn over the front of your body to protect your clothes

apt *adjective*
1 likely to do something • *He is apt to be careless.* **2** suitable • *I need to find an apt quotation.*

aptitude *noun*
a natural ability to do something well

aquarium *noun*
a tank or building for keeping live fish

aquatic *adjective*
to do with water and swimming • *They enjoy aquatic sports.*

aqueduct *noun*
a bridge that carries water across a valley

arabic figures or **arabic numerals** *plural noun*
the figures 1, 2, 3, 4, and so on (compare *Roman numerals*)

arable *adjective*
to do with the growing of crops

arbitrary *adjective* (say ar-bi-trer-i)
done or chosen at random or without a proper reason • *It was an arbitrary decision.*

arc *noun*
part of the circumference of a circle, a curve

arcade *noun*
a covered place to walk, with shops down each side

arch *noun*
a curved structure that helps to support a bridge or building
arch *verb*
to make a curved shape • *The cat arched its back.*

archaeology *noun*
(say ar-ki-ol-o-ji) the study of ancient people from the remains of their buildings **archaeological** *adjective* an archaeological site or discovery is one to do with people from the ancient past **archaeologist** *noun* someone who studies archaeology

archbishop *noun*
the chief bishop of a region

archer *noun*
someone who shoots with a bow and arrows

archery *noun*
the sport of shooting with a bow and arrows

architect *noun* (say ar-ki-tekt)
someone whose work is to design buildings

architecture *noun*
1 the work of designing buildings **2** a style of building • *Victorian architecture*

area *noun*
1 part of a country, place, surface, etc. **2** the space occupied by something • *The area of this room is 20 square metres.*

arena *noun* (say a-**ree**-na)
a place where a sports event takes place

argue *verb*
1 to argue with someone is to quarrel with them **2** to argue is also to give reasons for something • *She argued that flying is safer than going by train.*

argument *noun*
1 a quarrel **2** a reason or set of reasons someone gives to try to convince someone about something

arise *verb* (**arising, arose, arisen**)
1 to arise is to appear or to come into existence • *All kinds of different problems arise through the story.* **2** (old meaning) to rise; to stand up

aristocracy *noun* (**aristocracies**)
the aristocracy are the people from important families who often have titles like *Lord* and *Lady*

aristocrat *noun* (say a-ris-to-krat)
a nobleman or noblewoman **aristocratic** *adjective* to do with aristocrats

arithmetic *noun*
the study of using numbers and working things out with them **arithmetical** *adjective* to do with arithmetic, or using arithmetic

ark *noun*
1 in the Bible, the ship in which Noah and his family escaped the Flood **2** a model of Noah's ark

arm *noun*
1 the part of your body between your shoulder and your hand **2** the sleeve of a coat or dress **3** the side part of a chair, on which you can rest your arm

arm *verb*
1 to arm people is to give them weapons **2** to arm is to prepare for war

armada *noun* (say ar-**mah**-da)
a fleet of warships, especially the Spanish Armada which attacked England in 1588

armadillo *noun*
a South American animal whose body is covered with a shell of bony plates

armchair *noun*
a chair with parts on either side to rest your arms on

armed forces *plural noun*
the army, navy, and air force of a country

armistice *noun*
an agreement to stop fighting in a war or battle

armour noun
armour is a metal suit or covering to protect people or equipment in battle
armoured adjective having armour

armpit noun
the hollow part under your arm at your shoulder

archer

arms plural noun
weapons • Lay down your arms.

army noun (**armies**)
1 a large number of soldiers ready to fight 2 a large group • They had an army of supporters.

aroma noun
(say a-**roh**-ma)
a pleasant smell, for example of food
aromatic adjective having a pleasant smell

around adverb, preposition
1 round • They stood around the pond. 2 about • Stop running around.

arouse verb
1 to arouse someone is to make them wake up 2 to arouse feelings in someone is to cause them to have those feelings

arrange verb
1 to arrange things is to put them all in the position you want 2 to arrange a meeting or event is to organize it 3 to arrange to do something is to make sure someone does it

arrangement noun
1 arrangement is how you arrange or display something, for example flowers or a table setting
2 an arrangement is something you agree with someone else • We made an arrangement to meet at the clock tower.

arrest verb
to arrest someone is to take hold of them by the power of the law because they may have committed a crime

arrest noun
taking hold of someone by the power of the law

arrival noun
1 an arrival is when someone or something arrives at a place
2 an arrival is also someone who is new or has just arrived • Have you met the new arrivals?

arrive verb
1 to arrive at a place is to get there at the end of a journey
2 to arrive is also to happen
• The great day arrived.

arrogant adjective
an arrogant person is unpleasantly proud and thinks they are more important than anyone else
arrogance noun a feeling someone has that they are more important than anyone else

arrow noun
1 a pointed stick shot from a bow 2 a sign used to show direction or position

arsenal noun
a place where bullets, shells, and weapons are made or stored

arsenic noun
a strong poison made from a metallic element and used in insecticides

arson noun
the crime of deliberately setting fire to a building

art noun
1 art is producing something by drawing or painting or sculpture
2 the arts are subjects such as history and languages, as distinct from the sciences such as physics and chemistry 3 an art is also a special skill in something, such as sewing or public speaking

artery noun (**arteries**)
a tube carrying blood from the heart to parts of the body

arthritis noun (say arth-**ry**-tiss)
a disease that makes joints in the body painful and stiff **arthritic** adjective (say arth-**rit**-ik) suffering from arthritis

article noun
1 an object or thing that you can touch or pick up
2 a piece of writing published in a newspaper or magazine
3 (in grammar) the word 'a' or 'an' (called the indefinite article) or the word 'the' (called the definite article)

articulate adjective
(say ar-**tik**-yoo-lat)
an articulate person is able to speak clearly and fluently

articulated lorry noun (**articulated lorries**)
a large lorry with a cab that is connected to the main part by a joint that bends, so that it can turn more easily

artificial adjective
made by human beings and not by nature **artificially** adverb

artillery noun (**artilleries**)
1 artillery is a collection of large guns 2 the artillery is the part of the army that uses large guns

artist noun
1 someone who produces art, especially a painter 2 an entertainer **artistry** noun the skill of an artist • The carving showed great artistry.

artistic adjective
1 to do with art and artists
2 showing skill and beauty
• an artistic flower arrangement

as conjunction, adverb, preposition
linking words and phrases
• As you were late, you had better stay behind. • Leave it as it is. • She slipped as she got off the bus. • It is not as hard as you think. • He was dressed as a sailor.

asbestos noun
a fireproof material that is made up of fine soft fibres

ascend verb
to ascend something like a hill or staircase is to go up it

ascent noun
an ascent is a climb, usually a hard or long one

ash¹ noun
ash is the powder that is left after something has been burned

ash² noun
an ash or ash tree is a tree with silvery bark and winged seeds

ashamed adjective
feeling guilty or upset about something you have done

ashore adverb
on the shore

aside adverb
to or at one side; away
• Step aside and let them pass.

ask verb
1 to ask someone something is to speak to them so as to find out or get something 2 to ask someone to something like a party is to invite them

asleep adverb, adjective
sleeping

aspect *noun*
one way of looking at a problem or situation • *Perhaps the worst aspect of winter is the dark mornings.*

asphalt *noun* (*say* **ass**-falt)
a sticky black stuff like tar. It is mixed with gravel to make a surface for roads and areas such as playgrounds.

aspirin *noun*
a drug used to relieve pain or reduce fever

ass *noun*
a donkey

assassinate *verb*
to assassinate someone such as a ruler or leader is to murder them to stop them having power **assassin** *noun* a person who assassinates someone **assassination** *noun* the murder of a ruler or leader

assault *noun*
a violent or illegal attack on someone

assault *verb*
to assault someone is to attack them violently

assemble *verb*
1 to assemble people or things is to bring them together in one place
2 to assemble something is to make it by putting the parts together
3 to assemble is to come together in one place • *Please assemble in the playground.*

assembly *noun*
1 an assembly is when a lot of people come together and someone speaks to them, for example in a school
2 an assembly is also a group of people who meet together, such as a parliament
3 assembly of a machine or piece of furniture is putting the parts together to make it

WORD ORIGIN

The words **assemble** and **assembly** come from Latin words *ad* meaning 'to' or 'towards' and *simul* meaning 'together'.

assert *verb*
to assert something is to say it strongly and clearly **assertion** *noun* something you say clearly and strongly

assess *verb*
to assess someone or something is to decide how good or useful they are **assessment** *noun* an opinion about something after thinking about it carefully

asset *noun*
something useful or valuable to someone

assign *verb*
to assign something to someone is to give it to them as their share or duty • *A different teacher is assigned to each subject.*

assignment *noun*
a piece of work that someone is given to do

assist *verb*
to assist someone is to help them, usually in a practical way

assistance *noun*
help someone gets when they need information or support

assistant *noun*
1 someone whose job is to help another person in their work
2 someone who serves in a shop

associate *verb*
(*say* a-**soh**-shi-ayt)
to associate one thing with another is to connect them in your mind • *I associate Christmas with ice and snow.*

association *noun*
an association is an organization for people sharing an interest or doing the same work

assorted *adjective*
of various kinds; mixed and different

assortment *noun*
a mixture of different things or people

assume *verb*
to assume something is to think it is true or likely without being sure of it • *I assume you will be coming tomorrow.* **assumed** *adjective* an assumed name is one that is not the person's real name

assumption *noun*
something you assume or take for granted

assurance *noun*
1 an assurance is a promise or guarantee **2** assurance is confidence in yourself

assure *verb*
to assure someone is to tell someone something definite • *I can assure you that we will make every effort to help.*

asterisk *noun*
a star-shaped sign * used in printing and writing to draw attention to something

asteroid *noun*
one of the small planets found mainly between the orbits of Mars and Jupiter

asthma *noun* (*say* **ass**-ma)
a disease which makes breathing difficult

asthmatic *adjective*
suffering from asthma

asthmatic *noun*
someone who is suffering from asthma

astonish *verb*
to astonish someone is to surprise them very much **astonishment** *noun* a feeling of great surprise

astound *verb*
to astound someone is to amaze or shock them very much

astrology *noun*
astrology is studying how the planets and stars may affect people's lives **astrological** *adjective* to do with astrology **astrologer** *noun* someone who studies astrology

astronaut *noun*
someone who travels in a spacecraft

astronomical *adjective*
1 to do with astronomy
2 (*informal*) extremely large • *The cost of the party was astronomical.*

astronomy *noun*
astronomy is studying the sun, moon, planets, and stars **astronomer** *noun* someone who studies astronomy

at *preposition*
showing where someone or something is • *I was at the hospital.* • *They are looking at their new books.*

atheist *noun*
someone who does not believe in a God **atheism** *noun* a belief that there is no God

athlete *noun*
someone who is good at athletics or other sports

athletic *adjective*
1 to do with athletics • *an athletic competition*
2 good at sports; strong

athletics *plural noun*
physical exercises and sports such as running and jumping

atlas *noun*
a book of maps

WORD ORIGIN

Atlas was a Titan in Greek mythology who offended the gods and was punished by having to support the universe on his shoulders. A picture of him was often put at the beginning of old atlases, and this is how they got their name.

a
b
c
d
e
f
g
h
i
j
k
l
m
n
o
p
q
r
s
t
u
v
w
x
y
z

atmosphere noun
1 the earth's atmosphere is the air around it 2 an atmosphere is a feeling you get in a room or at a place • *The atmosphere of the house was cheerful and friendly.*

atmospheric adjective
1 to do with the earth's atmosphere 2 having a strong atmosphere

atom noun
the smallest possible part of a chemical element

atom bomb or **atomic bomb** noun
a bomb that uses atomic energy to make the explosion, and has nuclear fallout

atomic adjective
involving atoms; nuclear

atrocious adjective
(*say* a-**troh**-shus) awful, terrible

attach verb
to attach one thing to another is to fix or fasten it

attached adjective
to be attached to someone is to be fond of them

attachment noun
1 an extra part you fix to a device so that it can do a special kind of work • *The garden hose has an attachment for washing cars.* 2 a fondness or friendship • *The boys felt a real attachment to their pet hamster.* 3 (*in computing*) a document that you send to someone with an email message

attack noun
1 an attempt to hurt someone with violence 2 an attempt to harm someone or something by using unfriendly words 3 a sudden illness or pain

attack verb
to attack someone is to try to hurt them with violence, or to harm them with unfriendly words

attain verb
to attain something is to reach or achieve it • *I have attained Grade 3 on the violin.* **attainment** noun
something you have achieved

attempt verb
to attempt to do something is to make an effort to do it

attempt noun
an attempt at something is making an effort to do it

attend verb
1 to attend something like a meeting or a wedding is to be there 2 to attend school or college is to be a pupil or student there 3 to attend

to someone is to look after them, especially when they are ill 4 to attend to something is to spend time dealing with it • *She had some business to attend to.*

attendance noun
1 attendance is being somewhere where you are supposed to be 2 the attendance at an event is the number of people who are there to see it

attendant noun
someone who helps or goes with another person

attention noun
giving care or thought to someone or something
to stand to attention is to stand with your feet together and your arms straight down, like soldiers on parade

attic noun
a room or space under the roof of a house

attitude noun
your attitude is the way you think or feel about something, and the way you behave

attract verb
1 to attract someone is to seem pleasant to them and get their attention or interest 2 to attract something unwelcome is to make it come • *Empty bottles of drink attract wasps.* 3 to attract something is also to pull it by a physical force like magnetism • *Magnets attract metal pins.*

attraction noun
1 attraction is the power to attract someone 2 an attraction is something pleasant that visitors to a place like to see, such as a fair or a museum

attractive adjective
1 pleasant, good-looking 2 interesting or welcome • *They made us an attractive offer of a free holiday.*

auburn adjective
auburn hair is a reddish-brown colour

auction noun
a sale at which things are sold to the person who offers the most money for them **auctioneer** noun an official in charge of an auction

audible adjective
loud enough to be heard

audience noun
the people who have come to see or hear an event like a concert or film

audition noun
a test to see if a performer is suitable to act in a play or sing in a choir

auditorium noun
(*say* aw-dit-**or**-i-um) the part of a theatre or concert hall where the audience sits

August noun
the eighth month of the year

aunt noun
1 the sister of your mother or father 2 your uncle's wife

auntie or **aunty** noun (**aunties**)
(*informal*) an aunt

au pair noun (*say* oh-**pair**)
a person from another country, usually a girl or young woman, who works for a time in someone's home

authentic adjective
real, genuine **authenticity** noun
being authentic

author noun
the writer of a book or something like a poem or story

authority noun (**authorities**)
1 authority is the power to give orders to other people 2 the authorities are the people who have the power to make decisions 3 an authority on a subject is an expert on it or it is a book that gives you reliable information about it

autistic adjective
having a disability that makes it difficult for someone to communicate with other people **autism** noun

autobiography noun (**autobiographies**)
the story of someone's life that they have written themselves **autobiographical** adjective
autobiographical writing is written by a person about their own life

autograph noun
the signature of a famous person

automatic adjective
1 an automatic process is one that works on its own, without needing attention or control by humans 2 an automatic action is one that you do without specially thinking about it **automatically** adverb by automatic means; without having to use controls all the time

automobile noun
(*in America*) a motor car

autumn noun (*say* **aw**-tum)
the season when leaves fall off the trees, between summer and winter

available *adjective*
able to be found or used • *The theme music is now available.*
availability *noun* availability is how easily you can find or get something

avalanche *noun* (say **av**-a-lahnsh)
a sudden heavy fall of snow and ice down the side of a mountain

avenue *noun*
a wide street, usually with trees along each side

average *noun*
1 an average is the number you get by adding several amounts together and dividing the total by the number of amounts • *The average of 2, 4, 6, and 8 is 5.* **2** the average is the usual or ordinary standard • *Their work is well above the average.* **average** *adjective* of the usual or ordinary standard

average *verb*
to average is to have as an average • *In the rainforest the rainfall can average more than 2500mm a year.*

aviary *noun* (**aviaries**)
a place where birds are kept

aviation *noun*
aviation is flying in aircraft

avid *adjective*
keen, eager • *She is an avid reader.*

avoid *verb*
1 to avoid something or someone is to keep yourself away from them • *She swerved in time to avoid a tree.* **2** to avoid something is also to find a way of not doing it • *They wanted to avoid extra homework.* **avoidance** *noun* avoidance is avoiding something

awake *adjective*
not sleeping
awake *verb* (**awaking, awoke, awoken**)
to awake is to wake up

award *noun*
something such as a prize given to a person who has done something successful
award *verb*
to award something to someone is to give it to them as an award

aware *adjective*
to be aware of something is to know about it or realize it is there • *They soon became aware of the danger.* **awareness** *noun* awareness is knowing about something

away *adverb*
at a distance or somewhere else • *I wish those people would go away.* • *The ice cream melted so I threw it away.*

away *adjective*
an away match is one that is played at the opponents' ground

awe *noun*
fear and wonder • *The mountains filled him with awe.* **awed** *adjective* filled with fear and wonder

awful *adjective*
1 (*informal*) very bad; very great • *I've been an awful fool.* **2** causing fear or horror • *It was an awful sight.* **awfully** *adverb* (*informal*) very, extremely • *It's awfully hot in June.*

awhile *adverb*
for a short time

awkward *adjective*
1 difficult to use or cope with • *The box was an awkward shape.* **2** embarrassed and uncomfortable • *She felt awkward and shy in his presence.*

axe *noun*
a tool for chopping

axis *noun* (**axes**)
a line through the centre of a spinning object • *The earth rotates on its axis once every 24 hours.*

axle *noun*
the rod through the centre of a wheel, on which it turns

Bb

babble *verb*
1 to babble is to talk quickly, without making much sense **2** to babble is also to make a murmuring or bubbling sound • *They came across a babbling brook.*

baboon *noun*
a large kind of monkey with a long muzzle and a tail

baby *noun* (**babies**)
a very young child

babysit *verb* (**babysitting, babysat**)
to babysit is to look after a child while its parents are out **babysitter** *noun* someone who babysits

bachelor *noun*
a man who has not married

back *noun*
1 the part of your body between your shoulders and your bottom **2** the upper part of a four-legged animal's body **3** the part of a thing that is furthest away from the front • *The back of the house faces a river.*
back *adjective*
placed at or near the back • *Let's sit in the back row.*
back *adverb*
1 backwards or towards the back • *Go back!* **2** to where someone or something was before • *When will you be coming back?* **3** to an earlier time • *Think back to when you were little.*
back *verb*
1 to back a vehicle is to move it backwards **2** to back someone is to support them or give them help **to back down** is to admit you were wrong about something **to back out** is to decide not to get involved in something

backbone *noun*
your backbone is your spine

background *noun*
1 the background of a picture or view is the part that is farthest away from you, behind the main subject **2** the background to an event or situation is all the things that help to explain why it happened **3** a person's background is their family, education, and what they have done in their life

backing *noun*
1 backing is support or help • *Our firm will give you financial backing.* **2** the backing on a pop song is the music that is played or sung to support the main singer or tune

baboon

a
b
c
d
e
f
g
h
i
j
k
l
m
n
o
p
q
r
s
t
u
v
w
x
y
z

backstroke noun
a stroke you use when swimming on your back

backward adjective
1 facing or aimed towards the back • She walked past him without a backward glance.

backward adverb
backwards

backwards adverb
1 towards the back 2 with the back end going first 3 in the opposite order to the usual one • Can you say the alphabet backwards?

backyard noun
an open area at the back of a building

bacon noun
smoked or salted meat from the back or sides of a pig

bacteria plural noun
tiny organisms that can cause diseases **bacterial** adjective to do with bacteria

bad adjective (**worse, worst**)
1 not good or well done • We were watching a very bad film on television.
2 someone who is bad is wicked or naughty 3 someone is bad at something when they can't do it very well • Tracy is bad at maths.
4 harmful to your health • Eating fatty foods is bad for you. **not bad** fairly good, all right

badge noun
a small piece of metal, plastic, or cloth that you pin or sew on your clothes to tell people something about you

badger noun
a grey animal with a black and white head, which lives underground and comes out at night to feed

badger verb
to badger someone is to keep asking them to do something • He's been badgering his mum for weeks for a new bike.

badly adverb
1 not well • They did the work badly.
2 seriously • He was badly wounded.
3 very much • I need a drink badly. **badly off** poor or unfortunate

badminton noun
a game in which players use rackets to hit a light object called a *shuttlecock* backwards and forwards across a high net

bad-tempered adjective
a bad-tempered person is one who often becomes angry

baffle verb
to baffle someone is to puzzle or confuse them completely

bag noun
a container made of soft material, for holding or carrying things **bags of something** (informal) plenty • There's bags of room.

bag verb (**bagging, bagged**)
to bag something is to get hold of it or take it • I bagged the best seat.

baggage noun
baggage is the suitcases and bags you take on a journey

baggy adjective (**baggier, baggiest**)
baggy clothes hang loosely from your body

bagpipes plural noun
bagpipes are a musical instrument you play by squeezing air out of a bag into a set of pipes

bail[1] noun
bail is money that has to be paid or promised so that a person accused of a crime will not be kept in prison before their trial

bail[2] noun
bails are the two small pieces of wood placed on top of the stumps in cricket

bail verb
to bail water out of a boat is to scoop it over the side

Bairam noun (say **by**-ram)
either of two Muslim festivals, one in the tenth month and one in the twelfth month of the Islamic year

Baisakhi noun
a Sikh festival held in April

bait noun
bait is a small amount of food put on a hook or in a trap to catch fish or animals

bait verb
to bait a hook or trap is to put the bait on it or in it, to catch fish or animals

bake verb
1 to bake food is to cook it in an oven, especially bread or cakes 2 to bake something like clay is to make it hard by heating it in an oven 3 to bake is to become very hot, especially in the sun

baker noun
someone who makes or sells bread and cakes

bakery noun
a place where bread is made or sold

balance noun
1 a person's balance is their feeling of being steady • He lost his balance and fell over. 2 a balance is a device for weighing things, with two trays hanging from the ends of a horizontal bar 3 the balance of a bank account is the difference between the money paid into it and the money taken out of it 4 a balance is also an amount of money that someone owes • I will pay you the balance on Saturday.

balance verb
to balance something is to keep it steady • He was balancing a tray on one hand.

balcony noun (**balconies**)
1 a platform built out from the wall of a building, with a railing round it 2 the upstairs part of a cinema or theatre

bald adjective
a bald person does not have much hair or any hair on their head

bale[1] noun
a large bundle of something like hay or straw, usually tied up tightly

bale[2] verb
to bale out is to jump out of an aircraft with a parachute

ball noun
1 a round object used in many games 2 anything that is made into a round shape • a ball of string 3 a grand or formal party where people dance

balloon

ballad noun
a simple song or poem that tells a story

ballerina noun (say bal-e-**ree**-na)
a female ballet dancer

ballet noun (say **bal**-ay)
a form of dancing in which a group of dancers perform special steps and movements to tell a story to music

balloon noun
1 a small rubber pouch that you fill up with air or gas and use as a toy or for decoration 2 a large round or pear-shaped bag filled with a light gas or hot air, so that it can

carry people into the air **3** an outline in a strip cartoon containing the words the characters are saying

ballot noun (say **bal**-ot)
a method of voting in secret by making a mark on a piece of paper and putting it into a box

ballpoint noun
a pen with a tiny ball at the tip, round which the ink flows

ballroom noun
a large room where dances are held

balsa noun (say **bol**-sa)
a kind of lightweight wood used to make models

bamboo noun
a tall tropical plant with hard hollow stems, used for making furniture

ban verb (**banning, banned**)
to ban something is to forbid people to do it

bamboo

banana noun
a long curved fruit with a yellow skin

band noun
1 a group of people playing music together **2** an organized group of people doing something together **3** a circular strip of something

band verb
to band together is to join together to form an organized group

bandage noun (say **ban**-dij)
a strip of material that you wrap round a wound to protect it

bandit noun
a member of a gang of robbers who attack travellers

bandstand noun
a platform for a band playing music outdoors, usually in a park

bandy adjective (**bandier, bandiest**)
bandy legs curve outwards at the knees

bang noun
1 a sudden loud noise **2** a heavy blow or knock

bang verb
1 to bang something is to hit or shut it noisily • *Don't bang the door when you go out.* **2** to bang something is to knock it hard against something else • *She banged her knee on the desk.*

banish verb
to banish someone is to punish them by sending them away and ordering them not to return • *The emperor banished him to a remote island.*
banishment noun banishment is being banished

banisters plural noun
banisters are a rail with upright supports at the side of a staircase

banjo noun
a musical instrument like a small guitar with a round body

bank noun
1 a business which looks after people's money **2** the ground beside a river or lake **3** a piece of raised or sloping ground **4** a place where something is stored and collected • *a blood bank* **5** a bank of clouds is a mass of them **6** a bank of lights or switches is a row of them

bank verb
1 to bank money is to put it in a bank **2** to bank is to lean over while changing direction • *The plane banked as it turned to land.* to bank on something is to rely on it • *We're banking on the weather being good.*

bank holiday noun
a public holiday, when the banks are closed

bankrupt adjective
not able to pay your debts
bankruptcy noun bankruptcy is when a person or business can't pay their debts

banner noun
a large strip of cloth with writing on it, carried on a pole or between two poles in a procession or demonstration

banquet noun (say **bank**-wit)
a large formal dinner, often with speeches

baptism noun
baptism is the ceremony of baptizing someone

baptize verb
to baptize someone is to sprinkle them with water, or dip them in

water, in a ceremony welcoming them into the Christian Church

bar noun
1 a long piece of something hard **2** a counter or room where drinks and refreshments are served **3** one of the small equal sections into which music is divided • *A waltz has three beats in a bar.*
bar verb (**barring, barred**)
1 to bar something is to fasten it with a bar **2** to bar someone from something is to prevent them from taking part in it **3** to bar someone's way is to stop them getting past

barbarian noun
an uncivilized or savage person

barbaric or **barbarous** adjective
savage and cruel **barbarity** noun savage cruelty

barbecue noun
1 a metal frame used for grilling food over a charcoal fire outdoors **2** a party at which food is cooked outdoors on a barbecue

barbed wire noun
wire with sharp twisted spikes on it, used to make fences

barber noun
someone whose job is to cut men's hair

bar code noun
a set of black lines that are printed on goods, library books, etc. so that they can be identified by a computer

bare adjective
1 not covered with anything • *The trees were bare.* **2** empty or almost empty • *The cupboard was bare.* **3** only just enough • *They just had the bare necessities of life.*

barely adverb
only just; with difficulty • *They were barely able to see in the fog.*

bargain noun
1 something that you buy cheaply **2** an agreement between two people to do something for each other • *I expect you to keep your side of the bargain.*
bargain verb
to bargain over something is to argue over its price

barge noun
a long flat-bottomed boat used especially on canals
barge verb
to barge into someone is to bump clumsily into them or push them out of the way

bark noun
1 a bark is the sound made by a dog or a fox **2** bark is the outer covering of a tree's branches or trunk

banjo

A
B
C
D
E
F
G
H
I
J
K
L
M
N
O
P
Q
R
S
T
U
V
W
X
Y
Z

bark verb
1 a dog or fox barks when it makes its special sound
2 you can say a person barks when they speak loudly or sharply

barley noun
a kind of grain which is used for food and to make beer

bar mitzvah noun
a religious ceremony for Jewish boys who have reached the age of 13, when they accept some of the responsibilities of an adult. The ceremony for a girl is called a **bat mitzvah.**

barn noun
a building on a farm used to store things such as grain or hay

barnacle noun
a shellfish that attaches itself to rocks and the bottoms of ships

barometer noun (say ba-**rom**-it-er)
an instrument that measures air pressure, used in forecasting the weather

baron noun
a member of the lowest rank of noblemen

baroness noun
a female baron or a baron's wife

barracks noun
the buildings where soldiers live

barrage noun (say ba-rahzh)
1 heavy gunfire 2 a large amount of something • We received a barrage of complaints. 3 a dam or barrier built across a river to make the water deeper

barrel noun
1 a large container for liquids, with curved sides and flat ends
2 the metal tube of a gun, through which the shot is fired

barren adjective
barren land or plants cannot produce any crops or fruit

barricade noun
a barrier, especially one put up quickly to block a street

barricade verb
to barricade a place is to block or defend it with a barrier

barrier noun
a fence or wall put up to stop people getting past

barrister noun
a lawyer who argues legal cases in the higher courts

barrow noun
1 a small cart 2 an ancient mound of earth over a grave

barter verb
to barter is to exchange goods for other goods, without using money

base noun
1 the lowest part of something, or the part on which something stands 2 a place from which an organization like an army or business is controlled

base verb
to base one thing on another thing is to use the second thing as the starting point for the first • She based the story on an event in her own childhood.

baseball noun
1 baseball is an American game like rounders, in which the players hit a ball and run round a series of four 'bases' to score points 2 a baseball is the ball used in this game

basement noun
a room or part of a building below ground level

bash verb
(informal) to bash someone or something is to hit them hard

bashful adjective
shy

basic adjective
forming the first or most important part • He has a basic knowledge of French. • Food is a basic human need.

basically adverb
in the most important ways; essentially • She is basically lazy.

basin noun
1 a deep bowl for mixing food in 2 a large container to hold water for washing your face and hands in 3 a river basin is the area of land where the river's water comes from

basis noun (**bases**)
1 the basis of something is what you start from or add to • These players will be the basis of a new team.
2 a basis is the way in which something is arranged or organized • You will be paid on a monthly basis.

bask verb
to bask is to lie or sit comfortably warming yourself in the sun

basket noun
a container made of strips of wood, cane, or wire woven together

basketball noun
1 basketball is a team game in which players try to throw a large ball through a high net hanging from a hoop 2 a basketball is the ball used in this game

bass adjective (say bayss)
forming the lowest sounds in music

bass noun (say bayss)
a bass singer or instrument

bassoon noun
a woodwind instrument that plays low notes

bat[1] noun
a shaped piece of wood used to hit the ball in cricket, baseball, and other games

bat[1] verb (**batting, batted**)
to bat is to take a turn at using a bat in cricket, baseball, and other games

bat[2] noun
a flying mammal that looks like a mouse with wings. Bats come out at night to feed.

bat

batch noun
a set of things made at one time or dealt with together

bated adjective
with bated breath waiting anxiously

bath noun
1 a bath is a large container you fill with water and get into to wash yourself 2 a bath sometimes means the water in a bath • Your bath is getting cold. 3 the baths are also a public swimming pool

bath verb
1 to bath someone is to give them a bath 2 to bath is to have a bath

bathe verb
1 to bathe is to go swimming in the sea or a river 2 to bathe a sore part of your body is to wash it gently

bathe noun
a bathe is a swim

bathroom noun
a room for having a bath or wash in

bat mitzvah noun
a religious ceremony for Jewish girls who have reached the age of 12, when they accept some of the responsibilities of an adult. The ceremony for a boy is called a **bar mitzvah.**

baton noun
a short stick, especially one you use to conduct an orchestra or in a relay race

batsman noun (**batsmen**)
a player who uses a bat in cricket

batter verb
to batter someone or something is to hit them hard and often • *The huge waves battered the rocks.*

batter noun
batter is a mixture of flour, eggs, and milk beaten together and used to make pancakes or to coat food before you fry it

battery noun (**batteries**)
1 a portable device for storing and supplying electricity 2 a series of cages in which animals are kept close together on a farm • *Free-range hens are not kept in batteries.* 3 a set of devices that are used together, especially a group of large guns

battle noun
1 a fight between two armies 2 a struggle

battlefield noun
a place where a battle is or was fought

battlements plural noun
the top of a castle wall, usually with gaps for firing arrows

battleship noun
a large warship armed with powerful guns

bawl verb
to bawl is to shout or cry loudly

bay noun
1 a place by the sea or a lake where the shore curves inwards 2 an area that is marked out to be used for parking vehicles, storing things, etc. **to keep someone at bay** is to prevent them from coming near you

bayonet noun
a steel blade that can be fixed to the end of a rifle and used for stabbing

bazaar noun
1 a sale held to raise money for charity 2 a covered market in an Eastern country

BC
short for *before Christ*, used with dates that come before the birth of Jesus Christ • *Julius Caesar came to Britain in 55 BC.*

be verb (**I am**; **you are**; **he, she,** or **it is**; **they are**; **I, he, she,** or **it was**, **you were**, **they were**; **I, you,** or **they have been**; **he, she,** or **it has been**)
1 to be is to exist or happen • *There is a bus stop at the corner.* • *The final is on Saturday.* 2 to be someone or something is to have that position or quality • *She is my teacher.* • *You are very tall.*

beach noun
the strip of pebbles or sand close to the sea

beacon noun
a light or fire used as a warning signal

bead noun
1 a small piece of glass, wood, or plastic with a hole through it, threaded on a string or wire to make a necklace or bracelet 2 a small drop of liquid • *She had beads of sweat on her face.*

beads

beady adjective (**beadier, beadiest**)
beady eyes are small and bright

beak noun
the hard, horny part of a bird's mouth

beaker noun
1 a tall drinking mug, usually without a handle 2 a glass container used for pouring liquids in a science laboratory

beam noun
1 a long, thick bar of wood or metal 2 a ray of light or other radiation

beam verb
1 to beam is to send out a beam of light or radio waves
2 you can say a person beams when they smile very happily

bean noun
1 a kind of plant with seeds growing in pods 2 the seed or pod of this kind of plant, eaten as food

bear[1] verb (**bore, born** or **borne**)
1 to bear something is to carry or support it 2 to bear something is to put up with it or suffer it • *I can't bear all this noise.* 3 a woman bears children when she gives birth to them • *She has borne three sons.*

bear[2] noun
a large heavy animal with thick fur and sharp hooked claws

bearable adjective
something that is bearable is something you are able to put up with • *His toothache was hardly bearable.*

beard noun
hair on the lower part of a man's face **bearded** adjective a bearded man is a man with a beard

bearing noun
1 your bearing is the way you stand and walk 2 the direction or position of something in relation to something else **to lose your bearings** is to forget where you are in relation to other things

beast noun
1 any large four-footed animal 2 (*informal*) a person you think is cruel or unkind

beat verb (**beating, beat, beaten**)
1 to beat someone or something is to hit them repeatedly, especially with a stick 2 to beat someone in a game or match is to do better than them and win it 3 to beat a cooking mixture is to stir it quickly so that it becomes thicker 4 to beat something is to shape or flatten it by hitting it many times 5 to beat is also to make regular movements like your heart does **to beat someone up** is to attack them very violently

beat noun
1 a regular rhythm or stroke, like your heart makes 2 a strong rhythm in pop music 3 the regular route of a police officer

beautiful adjective
very pleasing to look at or listen to **beautifully** adverb

beauty noun (**beauties**)
1 beauty is a quality that gives delight or pleasure, especially to your senses • *They enjoyed the beauty of the sunset.* 2 a beauty is a particularly beautiful person or thing

beaver noun
1 a brown furry animal with strong teeth and a long flat tail, which builds dams in rivers 2 a member of the most junior section of the Scout Association

because conjunction
for the reason that • *We were happy because it was a holiday.* **because of someone** or **something** for that reason; on account of them • *He limped because of his bad leg.*

beckon verb
to beckon to someone is to make a sign asking them to come to you

become verb (**becoming, became, become**)
to become something is to start being something described • *It gradually became darker.*

bed noun
1 a bed is a piece of furniture for sleeping on 2 bed is the place where you sleep • *I'm going to bed now.* 3 a bed is also a part of a garden where plants are grown 4 the bed of the sea

a
b
c
d
e
f
g
h
i
j
k
l
m
n
o
p
q
r
s
t
u
v
w
x
y
z

or of a river is the bottom of it

bedclothes *plural noun*
sheets, blankets, and duvets for using on a bed

bedding *noun*
things for making a bed, such as sheets, blankets, and duvets

bedraggled *adjective*
(say bi-**drag**-uld) wet and dirty

bedroom *noun*
a room where you sleep

bedside *noun*
the space beside a bed, especially the bed of someone who is ill • *He sat by his son's bedside all night.*

bedspread *noun*
a covering put over the top of a bed

bedtime *noun*
the time when you are supposed to go to bed

bee *noun*
a stinging insect that makes honey

beech *noun*
a tree with smooth bark and glossy leaves

bees

beef *noun*
the meat of an ox, bull, or cow

beefburger *noun*
a hamburger

beehive *noun*
a container for bees to live in

beer *noun*
beer is an alcoholic drink made from malt and hops

beet *noun* (**beet** or **beets**)
beet is a plant used as a vegetable or for making sugar

beetle *noun*
an insect with hard, shiny covers over its wings

beetroot *noun* (**beetroot**)
the dark red root of beet used as a vegetable

before *adverb, preposition*
1 earlier, or earlier than • *Have you been here before?* • *They came the day before yesterday.* **2** in front of • *He stood up before the whole school.*

beforehand *adverb*
earlier, or before something else happens • *She had tried to phone me beforehand.* • *Let me know beforehand if you want to come on the picnic.*

beg *verb* (**begging, begged**)
1 to beg is to ask people to give you money or food **2** to beg someone is to ask them seriously or desperately • *He begged me not to tell the teacher.*

beggar *noun*
someone who lives by begging in the street

begin *verb* (**beginning, began, begun**) to begin something is to start doing it **beginner** *noun* someone who is just starting to learn or is still learning a subject

beginning *noun*
the start of something

behalf *noun*
on behalf of something to help a cause • *They were collecting money on behalf of cancer research.* on someone's behalf for them or in their name • *Will you accept the prize on my behalf?*

behave *verb*
1 to act in a certain way • *My sister has been behaving very strangely recently.* **2** to show good manners • *Why can't you behave?*

behaviour *noun*
1 your behaviour is the way you behave **2** animal behaviour is the way animals normally behave and treat one another

behind *adverb, preposition*
1 at or to the back • *The others are a long way behind.* • *She hid behind a tree.* **2** not making good progress • *He's behind the rest of the class in French.* **3** supporting or encouraging • *We're all behind you.* behind someone's back without them knowing about it

behind *noun*
your behind is your bottom • *He kicked me on the behind.*

beige *noun, adjective* (say bayzh)
a light yellowish-brown colour

being *noun*
a being is a person or creature of any kind

belch *verb*
1 to belch is to make a noise by letting air come up from your stomach through your mouth **2** a chimney or factory belches smoke or fumes when it sends out thick smoke or fumes into the air

belch *noun*
the act or sound of belching

belfry *noun* (**belfries**)
the top part of a tower or steeple, in which bells hang

belief *noun*
1 a belief is something you believe • *They have very few beliefs.* **2** belief

is when you believe something

believe *verb*
1 to believe something is to think that it is true **2** to believe someone is to think that they are telling the truth **3** to believe in something is to think it is real or important • *Do you believe in ghosts?*
believable *adjective* something is believable when you are able to believe it **believer** *noun* someone who believes in God

bell

bell *noun*
a device that makes a ringing sound, especially a cup-shaped metal object that rings when it is struck

bellow *verb*
to bellow is to roar or shout loudly and deeply

bellows *plural noun*
bellows are a device for blowing out air, especially into a fire to make it burn more strongly

belly *noun* (**bellies**)
1 the abdomen or the stomach of a human **2** the part underneath the body of a four-legged animal

belong *verb*
1 to belong to someone is to be their property • *The pencil belongs to me.*
2 to belong to a club or group is to be a member of it • *We both belong to the tennis club.*
3 to belong somewhere is to have a special place where it goes • *The butter belongs in the fridge.*

belongings *plural noun*
your belongings are the things that you own

beloved *adjective*
(say bi-**luvd** or say bi-**luv**-id)
greatly loved

below *preposition*
lower than, under • *We have nice neighbours in the flat below us.*

below *adverb*
at a lower point, or to a lower point • *I'll have the top bunk, and you can sleep below.*

belt *noun*
1 a strip of material, often leather or cloth, that you wear round your waist **2** a long narrow area • *The path ran through a belt of woodland.*

belt *verb*
(*informal*) **1** to belt someone is to hit them hard **2** to belt along is to move very fast

bench *noun*
1 a long seat **2** a long table for working at

bend *verb* (**bending, bent**)
1 to bend something is to make it curved or crooked **2** to bend is to become curved or crooked • *The trees were bending in the wind.* **3** to bend is also to move the top of your body downwards • *She bent down to pick up the cat.*

bend *noun*
a part where something curves or turns

beneath *preposition, adverb*
under • *Beneath the soil there is clay.*

benefit *noun*
1 a benefit is something that is useful or helpful • *Television is one of the benefits of modern science.* **2** benefit is money that the government pays to help people who are poor, sick, or out of work **to give someone the benefit of the doubt** is to believe them even though you cannot be sure

benefit *verb*
you benefit from something, or it benefits you, when it helps you

bent *adjective*
1 curved or crooked **2** (*slang*) dishonest

bequeath *verb*
(*rhymes with* **breathe**)
to bequeath something to someone is to leave it to them in a will

bequest *noun*
a gift of money or property that someone leaves to a person in their will

bereaved *adjective*
a bereaved person is someone with a close relative who has recently died **bereavement** *noun* someone suffers bereavement when a close relative dies

beret *noun* (*say* **bair**-ay)
a soft, round, flat cap

berry *noun* (**berries**)
a small, juicy fruit

berserk *adjective*
to go berserk is to become extremely angry or lose control • *The man went berserk and started flinging things around.*

berth *noun*
1 a sleeping place on a ship or train **2** a place where a ship is tied up

beside *preposition*
next to; close to • *The little house stood beside a lake.* **to be beside yourself** is to be very excited or upset • *He was beside himself with anger.*

besides *preposition*
in addition to • *Who came besides you?*

besides *adverb*
also; in addition to this • *The coat cost too much. Besides, it's the wrong colour.*

besiege *verb* (*say* bi-**seej**)
to besiege a place is to surround it until the people inside surrender

best *adjective*
most excellent; most able to do something • *She's the best swimmer in the class.*

best *adverb*
1 in the best way; most • *We'll do what suits you best.* **2** most usefully; most wisely • *He is best ignored.*

best *noun*
the best person or thing, or the best people or things • *She was the best at tennis.* • *These apples are the best you can buy.* **to do your best** is to do as well as you can **to make the best of something** is to accept it and enjoy it as much as you can, even though it is not very good

best man *noun*
someone who helps the bridegroom at his wedding

bestseller *noun*
a book or other product that has sold in very large numbers

bet *noun*
1 an agreement that you will receive money if you are correct in choosing the winner of a race or in saying something will happen, and will lose money if you are not correct **2** the money you risk losing in a bet

bet *verb* (**betting, bet** or **betted**)
1 to bet, or to bet money, is to make a bet **2** (*informal*) to bet something is to say you are sure about it • *I bet I'm right.*

betray *verb*
1 to betray someone is to do them harm when they are expecting your support **2** to betray something you are trying to keep hidden is to reveal it • *The look on her face betrayed her surprise.* **betrayal** *noun* betrayal is betraying someone

better *adjective*
1 more excellent • *I need a better bike.* **2** to be better is to feel well again after an illness • *Are you better?*

better *noun*
a better person or thing **to get the better of someone** is to defeat or outwit them

better *adverb*
in a better way • *Try to do it better next time.* **to be better off** is to be more fortunate in some way, for example by having more money

better *verb*
to better something is to improve on it • *She hopes to better her own record time.*

between *preposition, adverb*
within two or more points; among • *Call me between Tuesday and Friday.* • *The train runs between London and Glasgow.* • *What is the difference between butter and margarine?* • *Divide the sweets between the children.* • *The two houses are side by side with a fence between.*

beware *verb* (**beware**)
a warning to be careful • *Beware of pickpockets.*

bewilder *verb*
to bewilder someone is to puzzle them completely **bewilderment** *noun* bewilderment is being bewildered or puzzled

bewitch *verb*
to bewitch someone is to put a spell on them

beyond *preposition, adverb* farther on • *Don't go beyond the end of the street.* • *You can see the next valley and the mountains beyond.*

bias *noun*
bias is a strong feeling in favour of one person or side and against another • *The referee was accused of bias.* **biased** *adjective* someone is biased when they show that they prefer one person or side over another

bib *noun*
a piece of cloth or plastic you put under a baby's chin during meals to protect its clothes from stains

Bible *noun*
the holy book of Christianity and Judaism **biblical** *adjective* to do with the Bible

bicycle *noun*
a two-wheeled vehicle that you ride by pushing down on pedals with your feet

bicycle

bid *noun*
1 offering an amount you will pay for something, especially at an auction **2** an attempt • *He will make a bid for the world record tomorrow.*

bid *verb* (**bidding, bid**)
to bid an amount of money is to offer it for something at an auction

bide *verb*
to bide your time is to wait, expecting something to happen that will help you

big *adjective* (**bigger, biggest**)
1 more than the normal size; large **2** important • *This is a big decision.* **3** elder • *Have you met my big sister?*

bike *noun*
(*informal*) a bicycle or motorcycle

bikini *noun*
a woman's two-piece swimsuit

bilingual *adjective*
speaking two languages well

bill¹ *noun*
1 a piece of paper that tells you how much money you owe for something **2** a plan for a new law in parliament **3** a poster

bill² *noun*
a bird's beak

billiards *noun*
a game played with long sticks (called *cues*) and three balls on a cloth-covered table

billion *noun*
a thousand million (1,000,000,000) **billionth** *adjective, noun* a thousand-millionth

billow *verb*
to billow is to rise up or move like waves on the sea • *Her cloak billowed out behind her.*

bin *noun*
a large or deep container, especially one that you put rubbish or litter in

binary *adjective*
having two parts • *a binary star*

binary system *noun*
a system of expressing numbers by using the digits 0 and 1 only. For example, 21 is written 10101.

bind *verb* (**binding, bound**)
1 to bind things is to tie them up or tie them together **2** to bind something is to wrap a piece of material round it **3** to bind a book is to fasten the pages inside a cover **4** to bind someone is to make them do something or promise something

bingo *noun*
a game played with cards with numbered squares. These are covered or crossed out as the numbers are called out, and the first person to complete the card wins the game

binoculars *plural noun*
a device with lenses for both eyes, for making distant objects seem nearer

biodegradable *adjective*
able to be broken down by bacteria in the environment • *All our packaging is biodegradable.*

biography *noun* (**biographies**)
the story of a person's life **biographer** *noun* someone who writes a biography **biographical** *adjective* a biographical story or history is one that is about a person's life

biology *noun*
the science or study of living things **biological** *adjective* to do with biology **biologist** *noun* a person who studies biology

birch *noun*
a thin tree with shiny bark and slender branches

bird *noun*
a feathered animal with two wings, two legs, and a beak

bird of prey *noun*
a bird that feeds on animal flesh, such as an eagle or hawk

birth *noun*
birth is the beginning of a person's or animal's life, when they come out of their mother's body

birthday *noun*
the anniversary of the day on which you were born

birthmark *noun*
a coloured mark which has been on someone's skin since they were born

birthplace *noun*
the place where someone was born

biscuit *noun*
a small flat kind of cake that has been baked until it is hard

bishop *noun*
1 a senior priest in the Christian Church who is in charge of all the churches in a city or district **2** a chess piece shaped like a bishop's hat

bison *noun* (**bison**)
a wild ox with shaggy hair

bit *noun*
1 a small piece or amount of something **2** the part of a horse's bridle that is put into its mouth **3** the part of a tool that cuts or grips **4** (*in computing*) the smallest unit of data or memory **a bit** slightly • *I'm a bit worried.* **bit by bit** gradually

bitch *noun*
a female dog, fox, or wolf

bite *verb* (**biting, bit, bitten**)
1 to bite something is to cut it or hold it with your teeth **2** to sting or hurt • *a biting wind*

bite *noun*
1 to give a person or animal a bite is to bite them **2** a mark or spot made by biting • *He was covered in insect bites.* **3** a snack • *Would you like a bite?*

bitter *adjective*
1 tasting sour and unpleasant **2** feeling angry and resentful because you are disappointed about something • *She is very bitter about losing her place in the team.* **3** extremely cold • *There was a bitter wind.*

black *adjective* ●
1 of the darkest colour, like coal or soot **2** having dark skin **3** dismal; not hopeful • *The outlook is black.* **4** very dirty

black *noun*
a black colour

blackberry *noun* (**blackberries**)
a sweet black berry

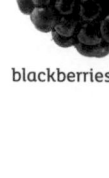

blackberries

blackbird *noun*
a dark European songbird

blackboard *noun*
a dark board for writing on with chalk

blacken *verb*
1 to blacken something is to make it black **2** to blacken someone's name is to say bad things about them

black eye *noun*
an eye with heavy bruises round it

black hole *noun*
a region in space with such strong gravity that no light escapes

blackmail *verb*
to blackmail someone is to get money from them by threatening to tell people something that they want to keep secret

blackout *noun*
1 when a person becomes unconscious for a short time **2** a time when lights are kept hidden or turned off

blacksmith *noun*
someone who makes and repairs things made of iron, and fits shoes on horses

bladder *noun*
your bladder is the bag-like part of your body where urine collects

blade *noun*
1 the sharp part of a device for cutting, such as a knife or sword **2** the flat, wide part of an oar or propeller **3** a long narrow leaf of grass

blame *verb*
to blame someone is to say that they have done something wrong • *My brother broke the window but they blamed me.*

blame *noun*
to get the blame for something is to be blamed for it **to be to blame** is to be the person who has done something wrong

blancmange *noun* (say bla-**monj**)
blancmange is a pudding like a jelly made with milk

blank *adjective*
1 not written, drawn, or printed on • *The piece of paper was blank.* **2** showing no expression or interest • *His face looked blank.* **to go blank** is to suddenly forget everything • *When he asked me the way, my mind went blank.*

blank *noun*
1 an empty space **2** a cartridge for a gun which makes a noise but does not fire a bullet

blanket *noun*
a large piece of thick cloth, used as a warm covering for a bed

blare *verb*
to blare is to make a harsh, loud sound

blasphemous *adjective*
(say **blas**-fe-mus)
disrespectful about God or a religion
blasphemy *noun* talking without respect about God or a religion

blast *noun*
1 a strong rush of wind or air **2** a sharp or loud noise • *The referee gave a long blast of his whistle.*

blast *verb*
to blast something is to blow it up with explosives

blast-off *noun*
the launch of a spacecraft

blaze *noun*
1 a very bright fire **2** a very bright colour or light

blaze *verb*
1 to blaze is to burn or shine brightly **2** to blaze with a feeling is to feel it very strongly • *He was blazing with anger.*

blazer *noun*
a kind of jacket, often with a badge on the front

bleach *noun*
a substance used to clean things or make clothes white

bleach *verb*
to bleach something is to make it white

bleak *adjective*
1 bare and cold • *No trees grew on this bleak hillside.* **2** dreary and miserable • *The future looks bleak.*

bleary *adjective* (**blearier, bleariest**) bleary eyes are tired and do not see clearly

bleat *noun*
the cry of a sheep or goat

bleat *verb*
a sheep or goat bleats when it makes a bleat

bleed *verb* (**bleeding, bled**)
to bleed is to lose blood from your body, for example if you are injured

bleep *noun*
a small, high sound like the sound some digital watches make

blemish *noun*
1 a mark or stain on something **2** a fault or weakness

blend *verb*
to blend things is to mix them together smoothly or easily

blend *noun*
a smooth mixture

bless *verb*
1 to bless someone is to wish or bring them happiness **2** to bless someone is also to ask God to look after them

blessing *noun*
1 a prayer or act of blessing someone **2** something you are glad of or happy about • *It's a blessing that they are safe.*

blight *noun*
1 blight is a plant disease **2** a blight is a thing that spoils or damages something

blind *adjective*
1 not able to see **2** without thought or understanding

blind *verb*
1 to blind someone is to make them blind **2** a bright light blinds you when it makes you unable to see for a time

blind *noun*
a screen for a window

blindfold *noun*
a piece of cloth used to cover someone's eyes so that they cannot see

blindfold *verb*
to blindfold someone is to cover their eyes with a blindfold

blink *verb*
to blink is to shut and open your eyes quickly

bliss *noun*
bliss is great happiness
blissful *adjective* very happy
blissfully *adverb* very happily

blister *noun*
a swelling like a bubble on your skin

blitz *noun*
a sudden violent attack, especially from aircraft

WORD ORIGIN

The word **blitz** is a shortening of the German word *Blitzkrieg*, which means 'lightning war'.

blizzard *noun*
a severe snowstorm

bloated *adjective*
swollen or puffed out

blob *noun*
a small round lump of something like paint or ice cream

block *noun*
1 a solid piece of something hard such as wood **2** a large building or group of buildings with streets all around it **3** something that stops people getting through • *They came to a road block and had to turn back.*

block *verb*
1 to block something is to get in the way of it • *Tall buildings blocked our view.* **2** to block something like a pipe or drain is to prevent water flowing through it

blockade *noun*
when a city or port is surrounded to stop people or goods from getting in or out

blockage *noun*
1 something that stops up a pipe or drain **2** a blocked state • *Roadworks are causing blockages in the traffic.*

block capitals or **block letters** *plural noun*
large capital letters

blog *noun*
a website on which someone writes regularly about their own life or opinions

blond or **blonde** *adjective*
fair-haired

blonde *noun*
a fair-haired girl or woman

blood *noun*
the red liquid that flows through your veins and arteries

bloodhound *noun*
a large breed of dog which can track people over long distances by following their scent

bloodshed *noun*
bloodshed is the killing and injuring of people

bloodshot *adjective*
eyes are bloodshot when they are streaked with red from being strained or tired

a b c d e f g h m n o p q r s t u v w x y z

bloodstream noun
the bloodstream is the blood flowing round your body

bloodthirsty adjective (**bloodthirstier, bloodthirstiest**)
enjoying killing and violence

bloody adjective
1 bleeding, or covered in blood 2 a bloody fight or battle is one in which a lot of people are killed or badly hurt

bloom verb
to bloom is to produce flowers • Look! The roses have bloomed!

blossom

bloom noun
a bloom is a flower in bloom trees and plants are in bloom when they are producing flowers

blossom noun
1 a blossom is a flower, especially on a fruit tree 2 blossom is a mass of flowers on a tree

blossom verb
1 a tree or bush blossoms when it produces flowers 2 to blossom is also to develop into something very fine or good • She has blossomed into a lovely singer.

blot noun
1 a spot or blob of ink 2 a flaw or fault

blot verb (**blotting, blotted**)
to blot something is to make a blot on it to blot something out is to remove it or make it invisible

blotch noun
an untidy patch of colour **blotchy** adjective having lots of blotches

blouse noun
a loose piece of clothing like a shirt that girls and women wear

blow noun
1 a hard knock or hit 2 a shock or disappointment • The news came to her as a terrible blow. 3 the action of blowing

blow verb (**blowing, blew, blown**)
1 to blow is to force out air from your mouth or nose • He blew on his cold hands to warm them up. 2 to move in the wind • Her hat blew off. 3 to blow something is to form it by blowing • Let's blow bubbles. 4 to blow something such as a whistle is to make a sound with it to blow something up is to destroy it with an explosion to

blow up is to be destroyed in an explosion

blue adjective
1 of the colour of a bright cloudless sky 2 sad and miserable • I'm feeling blue.

blue noun
a blue colour out of the blue with no warning • My friend turned up out of the blue.

bluebottle noun
a large blue fly that makes a loud buzz

blues plural noun
blues is a type of music that is often sad to get the blues is to feel sad and miserable

bluff verb
to bluff someone is to make them think that you will do something that you don't intend to do or that you know something that you don't really know

bluff noun
a bluff is something that someone says or does to bluff someone else, for example an empty promise or threat • He said he'd report us, but that was just a bluff. to call someone's bluff is to challenge them to do what they have threatened to do

blunder noun
a careless mistake

blunt adjective
1 having an edge that is smooth and not good for cutting 2 saying what you mean without trying to be polite or tactful

blur verb (**blurring, blurred**)
to blur something is to make it unclear or smeared

blur noun
an unclear shape with no definite outline • Without her glasses on, everything was a blur.

blurt verb
to blurt something out is to say it suddenly, without thinking

blush verb
to blush is to have a strong pink tinge in your face because you are embarrassed or ashamed

bluster verb
to bluster is to boast or make threats that don't mean very much

boa or **boa constrictor** noun
a large South American snake that coils round its prey and crushes it

boar noun
1 a wild pig 2 a male pig

board noun
1 a board is a flat piece of wood, used in building 2 a board is also a flat piece of wood or cardboard used to play games with, for example a dartboard or a chess board 3 a board is a group of people who run a company or organization 4 board is daily meals supplied in return for money or work • The price of the holiday includes full board. on board aboard a ship

board verb
1 to board a ship or train or aircraft is to get on it for a journey 2 to board is to get meals and accommodation to board something up is to cover it with boards

boarder noun
1 a child who lives at a boarding school during the term 2 a lodger

boarding school noun
a school in which the pupils live during the term

boast verb
to boast about something that you own or that you have done is to talk proudly about it, often in order to impress people

boastful adjective
a boastful person likes to talk a lot about the things they own or the things they have done **boastfully** adverb

boat noun
a vehicle designed to float and travel on water

bob verb (**bobbing, bobbed**)
to bob is to move gently up and down, like something floating on water

bobble noun
a small round ball of something soft such as wool, used as a decoration on a hat or clothing

bobsleigh or **bobsled** noun
a large sledge with two sets of runners

bodice noun
the upper part of a woman's dress

body noun (**bodies**)
1 the body is the flesh and bones and other parts of a person or animal 2 a body is a dead person or corpse 3 the body of something is the main part of it 4 a body of people is a group of them in one place 5 a body is a distinct object or piece of matter • Stars and planets are heavenly bodies.

bodyguard noun
a guard who protects someone from being attacked

bog *noun*
bog or a bog is an area of wet, spongy ground **boggy** *adjective* boggy ground is wet and spongy

bogus *adjective*
false; not real or genuine
• *He gave a name that turned out to be bogus.*

boil[1] *verb*
1 to boil a liquid is to heat it until it starts to bubble and give off vapour **2** to boil is to start bubbling, like water **3** to boil food is to cook it in boiling water **to be boiling** (*informal*) is to be very hot, like the weather • *It's boiling outside.*

boil[2] *noun*
a painful red swelling on the skin

boiler *noun*
a container for heating water or making steam

boiling point *noun*
the temperature at which something boils

boisterous *adjective*
noisy and lively

bold *adjective*
1 brave and adventurous **2** clear and easy to see

bollard *noun*
a short thick post put up on a road, used to keep out traffic

bolt *noun*
1 a sliding bar for fastening a door or window **2** a thick metal pin for fastening things together **3** a flash of lightning

bolt *verb*
1 to bolt a door or window is to fasten it with a bolt **2** to bolt is to run away in panic, as a horse does **3** to bolt food is to swallow it too quickly

bomb *noun*
a container with explosives, which blows up when it is detonated

bomb *verb*
to bomb a place is to attack it with bombs

bombard *verb*
1 to bombard a place is to attack it with heavy gunfire **2** to bombard someone with questions or complaints is to direct a large number of questions or complaints at them **bombardment** *noun* a heavy attack with guns

bomber *noun*
1 an aircraft built to drop bombs **2** a person who plants or sets off a bomb

bond *noun*
1 a shared experience or feeling that brings people close together **2** bonds are ropes or chains used to tie people up

bondage *noun*
bondage is being a slave

bone *noun*
a bone is one of the hard pieces of a skeleton

bonfire *noun*
a large fire lit out of doors

bonnet *noun*
1 the hinged cover over the front part of a car **2** a baby's or woman's hat with strings that tie under the chin

bonus *noun*
1 an extra payment that someone gets for their work **2** an extra advantage or reward

bony *adjective* (**bonier, boniest**)
1 bony people or animals have bones without much flesh on them **2** full of bones **3** thin and hard, like a bone

boo *verb*
to boo is to shout out that you don't like what someone has said or done, like an angry audience in a theatre

book *noun*
a set of sheets of paper, usually with printing or writing on, fastened together inside a cover

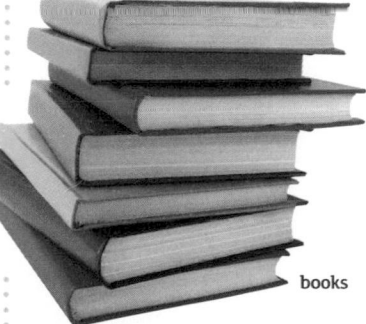

books

book *verb*
1 to book something such as a seat in a theatre or on a train, or a room in a hotel, is to arrange for it to be kept for you **2** to book something is to record it in a book or list

bookcase *noun*
a piece of furniture with shelves for holding books

booklet *noun*
a small book with paper covers

bookmaker *noun*
a person whose business is taking bets, especially bets made on horse races

bookmark *noun*
something you use to mark a place in a book

boom *noun*
1 a deep hollow sound **2** a time when people are well off **3** a long pole at the bottom of a sail to keep it stretched

boom *verb*
1 to boom is to make a deep hollow sound, like a heavy gun **2** to boom is also to speak in a loud deep voice **3** to boom is also to grow quickly or be prosperous • *Business is booming.*

boomerang *noun*
a curved stick which moves in a curve and comes back to you when you throw it

boost *verb*
to boost something is to increase its size or value or power • *Being in the drama group has really boosted his confidence.* **booster** *noun*

boomerang

boot *noun*
1 a heavy shoe that covers the ankle and sometimes part of your leg **2** the space for luggage at the back of a car

boot *verb*
1 to boot someone is to kick them hard **2** to boot up a computer is to switch it on and start it

booth *noun*
a small compartment for a special purpose, such as making a telephone call or having your photo taken

border *noun*
1 the border between two countries is the line where they meet • *We're about to cross the Scottish border.* **2** an edge • *There is a black border around the poster.* **3** a flower bed

bore *verb*
1 to bore someone is to make them feel tired and uninterested **2** to bore a hole is to drill it through something

bore *noun*
a dull or uninteresting person or thing

boredom *noun*
a feeling of tiredness and lack of interest

boring *adjective*
dull and uninteresting
• *The book was really boring.*

born *adjective*
to be born is to start your life
• *My little brother was born on the 17th of December.*

borough *noun* (say **bu**-ro)
an important town or district with its own local council

borrow *verb*
to borrow something is to have it for a time and then return it to its owner

a
b
c
d
e
f
l
m
n
o
p
q
r
s
t
u
v
w
x
y
z

bosom *noun*
a woman's breasts

boss *noun*
(*informal*) a person who is in charge of a business or group of workers

boss *verb*
(*informal*) to boss someone is to order them around

bossy *adjective* (**bossier, bossiest**)
(*informal*) a bossy person is fond of ordering people about

botany *noun*
botany is the study of plants
botanist *noun* someone who studies botany **botanical** *adjective* to do with botany or plants

both *determiner, pronoun*
the two of them, not just one • *I want them both in the team.*

both *adverb*
you use **both** with **and** to say two things about something or someone • *He is both friendly and helpful.*

bother *verb*
1 to bother someone is to cause them trouble or worry 2 to be bothered to do something is to take trouble over it

bother *noun*
bother is trouble or worry

bottle *noun*
a glass or plastic container with a narrow neck for holding liquids

bottle *verb*
to bottle something is to put it in a bottle **to bottle something up** is to keep something you are worried about to yourself

bottle bank *noun*
a large tank or drum for putting glass bottles and jars in for recycling

bottom *noun*
1 the bottom of something is its lowest point 2 the bottom of a garden is the farther end of it, away from the house 3 your bottom is the part of you that you sit on, also called your buttocks

bough *noun* (*rhymes with* **cow**)
a large branch of a tree that reaches out from the trunk

boulder *noun*
a very large smooth stone

bounce *verb*
1 to bounce is to spring back when thrown against something, like a rubber ball 2 to bounce something like a ball is to throw it so that it bounces

bounce *noun*
1 a bounce is the action of bouncing 2 bounce is liveliness, such as a young child or puppy has

bouncy *adjective*
a bouncy person is lively and full of energy

bound[1] *adjective*
to be bound for a place is to be travelling towards it • *This train is bound for London.* **to be bound to do something** is to have to do it or be likely to do it • *He is bound to come.*

bound[2] *verb*
to bound is to leap or to run with leaping steps

bound[3] *noun*
a leaping movement

boundary *noun*
(**boundaries**)
1 a line that marks a limit 2 a hit to the outer edge of a cricket field

bounds *plural noun*
a place that is **out of bounds** is somewhere you are not allowed to go • *The teachers' common room is out of bounds to pupils.*

bouquet *noun*
(*say* boo-**kay** or *say* boh-**kay**)
an attractively arranged bunch of flowers

bout *noun* (*say* bowt)
1 a period of illness • *I've just had a bout of flu.* 2 a boxing or wrestling fight

bow[1] *noun* (*rhymes with* **go**)
1 a knot made with loops 2 the stick used for playing a stringed musical instrument such as a violin or cello 3 a long curved piece of wood with a tight string joining its ends, used for shooting arrows

bow[2] *noun* (*rhymes with* **cow**)
the front part of a ship

bow[3] *verb* (*rhymes with* **cow**)
to bow is to bend your body forwards to show respect or as a greeting

bow[3] *noun* (*rhymes with* **cow**)
a movement of bowing your body • *The pianist stood up to take a bow.*

bowels *plural noun*
your bowels are the long tubes in your body that carry waste food for passing out of the body

bowl[1] *noun*
1 a deep round dish for eating from 2 a heavy ball used in the game of bowls or tenpin bowling

bowl[2] *verb*
(*in cricket*) 1 to bowl is to send the ball towards the batsman 2 to bowl someone is to get them out by hitting the wicket with the ball

bowler *noun*
1 someone who bowls in cricket 2 a

hat with a rounded top and a narrow brim

bowling *noun*
1 bowling is the game of bowls 2 bowling is also another game, in which you have to knock down skittles with a ball you roll down an alley 3 the action of throwing a cricket ball

bowls *plural noun*
a game played on a smooth piece of grass, in which you roll heavy balls towards a small target ball called the 'jack'

bounce

bow tie *noun*
a tie in the form of a bow, worn by men as part of formal dress

box *noun*
1 a container made of wood or cardboard, often with a lid 2 a small rectangle that you fill in on a form or computer screen 3 a special compartment or booth, such as a theatre box or a witness box in a lawcourt

box *verb*
1 to box is to fight with the fists 2 to box something is to put it into a box

boxer *noun*
1 someone who boxes 2 a breed of dog that looks like a bulldog

Boxing Day *noun*
the first weekday after Christmas Day

box office *noun*
a place where you can buy seats for the theatre or cinema

boy *noun*
a male child **boyhood** *noun* the time when a man was a boy **boyish** *adjective* looking or behaving like a boy

boycott *verb*
to boycott something is to refuse to buy it or have anything to do with it • *They boycotted the buses when the fares went up.*

boyfriend *noun*
someone's boyfriend is the male friend they have a romantic relationship with

bra *noun*
a piece of underwear women wear to support their breasts

brace *noun*
1 a device for holding something in place 2 a wire device for straightening the teeth

bracelet *noun*
a small band or chain you wear round your wrist

braces *plural noun*
braces are a pair of stretching straps worn over the shoulders to hold trousers up

bracket *noun*
1 a kind of punctuation mark used in pairs round words or figures to separate them from what comes before and after. Brackets are round () or square []. 2 a support attached to a wall to hold up a shelf or screen

brag *verb* (**bragging, bragged**)
to brag is to boast

braid *noun*
1 a plait 2 a decorative ribbon or band

braille *noun*
braille is a system of writing or printing using raised dots, which blind people can read by touch

---

WORD ORIGIN

Braille is named after a French teacher called Louis Braille, who was blind from the age of three and invented the system. He died in 1852.

---

brain *noun*
1 your brain is the part inside the top of your head that controls your body 2 brain also means a person's mind or intelligence • *He's got a good brain.*

brainy *adjective* (**brainier, brainiest**) (*informal*) clever, intelligent • *She's the brainiest child in the school.*

brake *noun*
a device for making a vehicle stop or slow down

bramble *noun*
a bramble is a blackberry bush or a prickly bush like it

branch *noun*
1 a part that sticks out from the trunk of a tree 2 a part of a railway or river or road that leads off from the main part 3 a part of a large organization

branch *verb*
to branch is to form a branch **to branch out** is to start doing something new

brand *noun*
a particular make or kind of goods • *Just get a cheap brand of tea.*

brand *verb*
to brand sheep or cattle is to mark them with a hot iron

brandish *verb*
to brandish something is to wave it about • *One of the guards stepped forward, brandishing his spear.*

brand new *adjective*
completely new

brandy *noun*
brandy is a kind of strong alcoholic drink

brass *noun*
1 brass is an alloy made from copper and zinc 2 brass also means the wind instruments made of brass, such as trumpets and trombones

brass trumpet

brave *adjective*
ready to face danger or suffering

brave *noun*
a Native American warrior

bravery *noun*
bravery is being brave
bravely *adverb*

brawl *noun*
a noisy fight or quarrel

bray *verb*
to bray is to make a noise like a donkey

brazen *adjective*
shameless or cheeky

breach *noun*
1 the breaking of an agreement or rule 2 a gap or broken place in something like a wall

bread *noun*
bread is food made by baking flour and water, usually with yeast

breadth *noun*
a thing's breadth is its width from side to side

break *verb* (**breaking, broke, broken**)
1 to break something is to make it go into several pieces by hitting it or dropping it 2 to break is to stop working properly • *I think my watch must have broken.* 3 to break a law or rule or promise is to fail to keep it or observe it 4 the weather breaks when it changes after being hot 5 waves break over rocks when they fall and froth over them 6 a boy's voice breaks when it starts to go deeper at about the age of 14 7 to break a record is to do better than the previous holder, for example in athletics **to break down** a machine or vehicle breaks down when it stops working properly **to break off** is to stop doing something for a time • *We broke off for lunch.*

to break out is to start and spread rapidly, like a disease or fighting **to break up 1** people break up when they leave one another after a long time together 2 is to finish school at the end of term

break *noun*
1 a broken place; a gap 2 a sudden dash or attempt to escape 3 a short rest from work

breakage *noun*
something that is broken
• *All breakages must be paid for.*

breakdown *noun*
1 a sudden failure to work, especially by a car • *We had a breakdown on the motorway.*
2 a period of mental illness caused by anxiety or depression

breaker *noun*
a wave breaking on the shore

breakfast *noun*
breakfast is the first meal of the day

breakthrough *noun*
an important discovery or step forward, for example in medical research

breast *noun*
1 one of the two parts on the front of a woman's body where milk is produced after she has had a baby 2 a person's or animal's chest

breaststroke *noun*
a stroke you use when swimming on your front, by pushing your arms forward and bringing them round and back

breath *noun* (*say* breth)
the air that you take into your lungs and send out again **to be out of breath** is to gasp for air after exercise

breathe *verb* (*say* breeth)
to breathe is to take air into your lungs through your nose or mouth and send it out again

breathless *adjective*
short of breath

breathtaking *adjective*
extremely beautiful or delightful

breech *noun*
the part of a gun barrel where the bullets are put in

breed *verb* (**breeding, bred**)
1 to breed is to produce offspring 2 to breed animals is to keep them in order to get young ones from them **breeder** *noun* someone who breeds animals

breed *noun*
a variety of similar animals

breeze *noun*
a gentle wind

a
b
c
d
e
f
g
h
i
j
k
l
m
n
o
p
q
r
s
t
u
v
w
x
y
z

breezy *adjective* (**breezier, breeziest**)
1 slightly windy 2 bright and cheerful

brevity *noun*
brevity is being brief or short • *I was surprised by the brevity of her answer.*

brew *verb*
1 to brew beer or tea is to make it 2 to be brewing is to start or develop • *Trouble is brewing.*

brewery *noun*
a place where beer is made

bribe *noun*
a bribe is money or a gift offered to someone to make them do something

bribe *verb*
to bribe someone is to give them a bribe **bribery** *noun* bribery is offering someone a bribe

brick *noun*
1 a small hard block of baked clay used in building 2 a rectangular block of something

bricklayer *noun*
a worker who builds with bricks

bridal *adjective*
to do with brides

bride *noun*
a woman on her wedding day

bridegroom *noun*
a man on his wedding day

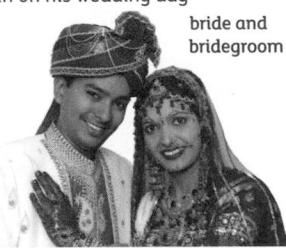

bride and bridegroom

bridesmaid *noun*
a girl or woman who helps the bride at her wedding

bridge *noun*
1 a bridge is a structure built over a river, railway, or road, to allow people to cross it 2 the bridge of a ship is the high platform above the deck, from where the ship is controlled 3 the bridge of your nose is the bony upper part of your nose 4 bridge is a card game rather like whist

bridle *noun*
the part of a horse's harness that fits over its head

bridle path *noun*
a path for people on horseback

brief *adjective*
lasting a short time or using only a few words **in brief** in a few words

briefcase *noun*
a flat case for keeping documents and papers in

briefs *plural noun*
short underpants

brigade *noun*
1 an army unit usually consisting of three battalions 2 a group of people in uniform, for example the fire brigade

bright *adjective*
1 giving out a strong light; shining 2 a bright colour is strong and vivid 3 clever • *He's a bright lad.* 4 cheerful

brighten *verb*
1 to brighten something is to make it brighter 2 to brighten is to become brighter

brilliance *noun*
1 brilliance is bright light • *the brilliance of the summer sky* 2 brilliance is also being very intelligent or clever

brilliant *adjective*
1 a brilliant person is very intelligent or clever 2 (*informal*) really good or enjoyable • *That was a brilliant film!* 3 very bright and sparkling

brim *noun*
1 the edge round the top of a container 2 the bottom edge of a hat that sticks out

brimming *adjective*
completely full
brimming over overflowing

brine *noun*
brine is salty water

bring *verb* (**bringing, brought**)
to bring someone or something is to make them come with you to a place **to bring someone up** is to look after them and educate them as a child **to bring something about** is to make it happen **to bring something up** is to mention it in a conversation

brink *noun*
the edge of a steep or dangerous place

brisk *adjective*
quick and lively

bristle *noun*
a short, stiff hair **bristly** *adjective* having lots of bristles

British *adjective*
to do with Great Britain

Briton *noun*
someone born in Great Britain

brittle *adjective* hard but likely to break or snap

broad *adjective*
1 wide and open • *They walked down a broad avenue.* 2 general, not detailed • *a broad outline*

broadband *noun*
a system for connecting computers to the Internet and sending information very quickly

broad bean *noun*
a large flat bean

broadcast *noun*
a radio or television programme

broadcast *verb*
to broadcast a radio or television programme is to transmit it or take part in it **broadcaster** *noun* a person who takes part in a radio or television programme

broaden *verb*
to broaden something is to make it broader

broadly *adverb*
in general terms • *They were broadly right.*

broccoli *noun* a vegetable with green or purple heads on green stalks

brochure *noun*
a booklet containing information, especially about a place

broke *adjective* (*informal*)
not having any money

broken *adjective*
1 broken English is English spoken with a strong foreign accent and lots of mistakes 2 a broken home is a home in which the parents have separated

bronchitis *noun* (say brong-**ky**-tiss)
bronchitis is a disease of the lungs

bronze *noun*
1 bronze is an alloy of copper and tin 2 bronze is also a yellowish-brown colour

brooch *noun* (*rhymes with* **coach**)
a piece of jewellery that can be pinned on to clothes

brooch

brood *noun*
a brood is a number of young birds hatched together

brood *verb*
1 birds such as chickens brood when they sit on eggs to hatch them **2** to brood over something is to keep on thinking and worrying about it

brook *noun*
a small stream

broom *noun*
1 a broom is a brush with a long handle, for sweeping **2** broom is a shrub with yellow, white, or pink flowers

broomstick *noun*
the handle of a broom

broth *noun*
broth is a thin kind of soup

brother *noun*
your brother is a man or boy who has the same parents as you

brother-in-law *noun*
a person's brother-in-law is the brother of their husband or wife, or the husband of their sister

brow *noun*
1 your brow is your forehead **2** your brows are your eyebrows **3** the brow of a hill is the top of it

brown *adjective*
of the colour of earth, wood, or toast

brown *noun*
a brown colour

Brownie *noun*
a junior member of the Guides

brownie *noun*
a small chocolate cake with nuts

browse *verb*
1 to browse is to read or look at something casually **2** animals browse when they feed on grass or leaves

bruise *noun*
a dark mark that appears on your skin when it is hit or hurt

bruise *verb*
to bruise your skin or a part of your body is to get a bruise on it

brunette *noun*
a woman with dark brown or black hair

brush *noun*
1 a tool with hairs or bristles for sweeping, painting, or arranging the hair **2** a fox's bushy tail

brush *verb*
1 to brush something is to use a brush on it • *Have you brushed your hair yet?* **2** to brush against someone is to touch them gently as you pass them

Brussels sprout *noun*
a green vegetable like a tiny cabbage

brutal *adjective*
savage and cruel **brutality** *noun*

brutality is savage cruelty **brutally** *adverb* with savage cruelty

brute *noun*
a cruel person

bubble *noun*
1 a thin transparent ball of liquid filled with air or gas **2** a small ball of air in a liquid or a solid

bubble *verb*
a liquid bubbles when it produces bubbles, as it does when it boils

bubbly *adjective* (**bubblier, bubbliest**)
1 full of bubbles, like fizzy water **2** a bubbly person is cheerful and lively

buccaneer *noun*
an old word for a pirate

buck *noun*
a male deer, rabbit, or hare

buck *verb*
a horse bucks when it jumps with its back arched

bucket *noun*
a container with a handle, for carrying liquids or something such as sand

buckle *noun*
a clip at the end of a belt or strap for fastening it

buckle *verb*
1 to buckle something is to fasten it with a buckle **2** to buckle is to bend or give way under a strain • *The arm of the crane was beginning to buckle.* **to buckle down** is to start work

bud *noun*
a flower or leaf before it has opened

Buddhism *noun* (*say* **buud**-izm)
Buddhism is a religion that started in Asia and follows the teachings of Buddha **Buddhist** *noun* someone who practises Buddhism

budding *adjective*
showing great promise • *The new class had several budding musicians.*

budge *verb*
to budge is to move slightly • *The door was stuck and wouldn't budge.*

budgerigar *noun*
(*say* **bud**-jer-i-gar) an Australian bird often kept as a pet in a cage

budget *noun*
1 the money someone plans to spend on something **2** a plan for earning and spending money

budgerigar

budget *verb*
to budget is to plan how much you are going to spend

budgie *noun*
(*informal*) a budgerigar

buffalo *noun* (**buffalo** or **buffaloes**)
a wild ox with long curved horns

buffer *noun*
something that softens a blow or collision, especially a device on a railway engine or wagon or at the end of a railway line

buffet *noun* (*say* **buu**-fay)
1 a cafe or place for buying drinks and snacks **2** a meal where guests serve themselves

bug *noun*
1 a tiny insect **2** (*informal*) a germ that causes illness • *I may have a tummy bug.* **3** (*informal*) a hidden microphone **4** a fault or problem in a computer program that stops it working properly

bugle *noun* (*say* **byoo**-gul)
a brass instrument like a small trumpet **bugler** *noun* someone who plays the bugle

build *verb* (**building, built**)
to build something is to make it by putting the parts together **to build something up** is to make it larger or stronger • *Regular exercise will build up your strength.* **to build up** is to become larger or stronger • *The traffic was starting to build up.*

build *noun*
your build is the shape of your body

builder *noun*
someone who puts up buildings

building *noun*
a building is a structure that someone has built, such as a house or a block of flats

bulb *noun*
1 the glass part of an electric light which glows when you switch it on **2** an onion-shaped root which grows into a plant or flower when it is put in the ground

bulge *noun*
a part that sticks out; a swelling

bulge *verb*
to bulge is to stick out or swell

bulk *noun*
1 a thing's bulk is its size, especially when it is large **2** the bulk of something is most of it • *He spends the bulk of his time on the computer.* **in bulk** in large quantities

bulky adjective (**bulkier, bulkiest**)
taking up a lot of space

bull noun
1 the male of the cattle family
2 a male seal, whale, or elephant

bulldozer noun
a heavy vehicle with a wide metal blade in front, used to clear or flatten land

bullet noun
a piece of shaped metal shot from a rifle or pistol

bulletin noun
a short announcement of news on radio or television

bullfight noun
in Spain, a public entertainment in which people challenge bulls, and sometimes kill them **bullfighter** noun someone who takes part in a bullfight

bullion noun
gold or silver in the form of bars

bullock noun
a young bull

bull's-eye noun
the centre of a target

bully verb (**bullies, bullying, bullied**)
to bully someone is to hurt or frighten them when they are weaker

bully noun (**bullies**)
someone who bullies people

bulrush noun
a tall reed which grows in water or on boggy land

bumble bee noun
a large kind of bee with a loud buzz

bump verb
to bump something is to knock against it accidentally **to bump into someone** (informal) is to meet them unexpectedly

bump noun
1 an accidental knock **2** a swelling or lump

bumper[1] noun
a bar along the front or back of a motor vehicle to protect it in collisions

bumper[2] adjective
unusually large or fine • We had a bumper crop of apples this year.

bumpy adjective (**bumpier, bumpiest**)
having lots of bumps

bun noun
1 a small round sweet cake **2** a round bunch of hair that some women make at the back of their head

bunch noun
a number of things joined or tied together, such as fruit or flowers or keys • He was eating a bunch of grapes.

bundle noun
a number of things tied or wrapped loosely together, such as clothes or papers

bundle verb
1 to bundle things together is to tie or wrap them loosely **2** to bundle someone into a room or car is to push them there hurriedly • They bundled him into the back of a taxi.

bung noun
a stopper for a bottle or barrel

bungalow noun
a house with all the rooms on one floor

bungle verb
to bungle something is to do it badly and clumsily

bunk or **bunk bed** noun
a single bed with another bed above it or below it

bunker noun
1 a container for storing fuel such as coal **2** a hollow filled with sand, made as an obstacle on a golf course **3** an underground shelter

bunny noun (**bunnies**)
(informal) a rabbit

bunsen burner noun
a gas burner with a flame you can adjust, used in laboratories

buoy noun (say boi)
a floating object in the sea, used as a marker or warning sign

buoyant adjective
able to float **buoyancy** noun buoyancy is being able to float

bur noun
part of a plant that clings to your clothes or hair

burden noun
1 a heavy load **2** something troublesome that you have to put up with

bureau noun (**bureaux**) (say bewr-oh) an office or department • They will tell you at the Information Bureau.

burger noun
a hamburger

burglar noun
someone who breaks into a building to steal things **burglary** noun burglary is the crime of stealing things from a building

burgle verb
to burgle someone is to steal from their house

burial noun
putting a dead body in a grave

burly adjective (**burlier, burliest**)
a burly person is big and strong

burn[1] verb (**burning, burnt** or **burned**)
1 to burn something is to damage or destroy it by fire or strong heat **2** to burn is to be damaged or destroyed by fire or heat **3** to be burning is to be on fire **4** to be burning is also to feel very hot

burn[1] noun
1 an injury or mark caused by fire or strong heat **2** the firing of a spacecraft's rocket

burn[2] noun
(in Scotland) a small stream

burner noun
the part of a lamp or cooker that forms the flame

burp verb
to burp is to make a noise through your mouth by letting air come up from your stomach

burp noun
the act or sound of burping

burrow noun
a hole dug by an animal such as a rabbit or fox

burrow verb
1 an animal burrows when it digs a burrow **2** to burrow is also to dig or search deeply • He burrowed in his pockets to find a pound coin.

burst verb (**bursting, burst**)
1 to burst is to break apart suddenly **2** to burst something is to make it break apart **3** to be bursting with energy or excitement is to have a lot of energy or to be very excited **to burst in** is to rush in noisily or clumsily **to burst into tears** is to suddenly start crying **to burst out laughing** is to start laughing noisily

burst noun
1 a split caused by something bursting • There's a burst in one of the pipes. **2** something short and quick • a burst of gunfire

bury verb (**buries, burying, buried**)
1 to bury something is to put it under the ground **2** to bury someone is to put them in a grave when they are dead

bus noun
a large road vehicle for carrying passengers

bush noun
1 a bush is a plant like a small tree with a lot of stems or branches **2** the bush is wild land, especially in Australia or Africa

bushy adjective (**bushier, bushiest**)
thick and hairy • His dad has bushy eyebrows.

busily *adverb*
in a busy way

business *noun* (*say* **biz**-niss)
1 a business is an organization that makes money by selling goods or services • *His uncle worked in a garage business.* **2** business is what an organization does to make money • *She has made a career in business.* **3** a person's business is what concerns them and no one else • *Mind your own business.* **4** a business is also an affair or subject • *I am tired of the whole business.*

busker *noun*
someone who plays music in the street, hoping for money from people passing by

bus stop *noun*
a place where a bus regularly stops

bust¹ *noun*
1 a sculpture of a person's head and shoulders **2** a woman's breasts

bust² *adjective* (*informal*) **1** broken • *My watch is bust.* **2** bankrupt

bustle *verb*
to bustle is to be in a hurry or rushing about busily

busy *adjective* (**busier, busiest**)
1 a busy person is one with a lot to do **2** a busy place is one with a lot going on **3** a busy telephone line is one that someone is already using

busybody *noun* (**busybodies**)
someone who interferes in other people's affairs

but *conjunction*
you use **but** to join two words or statements that say different or opposite things • *I wanted to go but I couldn't.*

but *preposition*
except • *There's no one here but me.*

butcher *noun*
someone who runs a shop that cuts and sells meat

butler *noun*
a male servant in charge of other servants in a large private house

butt¹ *noun*
1 the thicker end of a weapon or tool **2** a large barrel **3** someone people often make fun o • *James always seems to be the butt of your jokes.*

butt² *verb*
to butt someone is to hit them hard with your head **to butt in** is to interrupt suddenly or rudely

butter *noun*
butter is a fatty yellow food made from cream

butterfly *noun* (**butterflies**)
1 an insect with a thin body and large white or brightly coloured wings **2** a stroke you use when swimming on your front, by raising both arms together over your head

butterflies

butterscotch *noun*
butterscotch is a kind of hard toffee

buttocks *plural noun*
your buttocks are the part of the body on which you sit, your bottom

button *noun*
1 a flat plastic or metal disc sewn on clothes and passed through a buttonhole to fasten them **2** a small knob you press to work an electric device

button *verb*
to button clothes or to button up clothes is to fasten them with buttons

buttress *noun*
a support built against a wall

buy *verb* (**buying, bought**)
to buy something is to get it by paying for it • *I bought a coat yesterday.* **buyer** *noun* someone who buys something

buy *noun*
something you buy • *That was a good buy.*

buzz *noun*
a sharp humming sound, like bees make

buzz *verb*
to buzz is to make a buzzing sound

buzzard *noun*
a bird of prey like a large hawk

buzzard

buzzer *noun*
an alarm or signalling device that makes a buzzing noise

by *preposition, adverb*
1 near, close • *Sit by me.* **2** using; by means of • *I fixed the tyre by sticking on a patch.* **3** before • *Do your homework by tomorrow.* **4** past • *She went by the window.* • *I can't get by.* **by and large** mostly, on the whole **by the way** a phrase you use to begin a new topic

bye *noun*
a run scored in cricket when the batsman has not touched the ball

bye-bye *exclamation* (*informal*) goodbye

bypass *noun*
a road that takes traffic round the edge of a town or city rather than going through the centre

bystander *noun*
someone who sees something happening but takes no part in it

byte *noun*
(*in computing*) a unit that measures data or memory

Cc

c
1 short for Celsius or centigrade **2** 100 in Roman numerals

cab *noun*
1 a taxi **2** the place for the driver in a lorry, bus, train, or crane

cabbage *noun*
a large round green vegetable with layers of closely packed leaves

cabin *noun*
1 a hut or shelter **2** one of the small rooms on a ship for sleeping in **3** the part of an aircraft where the passengers sit

cabinet *noun*
1 a cupboard with shelves and doors, used for storing things **2** the group of chief ministers who run the government

cable *noun*
1 a thick rope, wire, or chain used for lifting heavy loads or tying up ships **2** a telegram sent overseas

cable television *noun*
a television system in which programmes are transmitted along underground cables into people's houses

cackle *noun*
1 a cackle is the clucking of a hen **2** a cackle is also a loud, silly laugh **3** cackle is stupid chattering

a
b
c
d
e
f
g
h
i
j
k
l
m
n
o
p
q
r
s
t
u
v
w
x
y
z

cactus noun (**cacti**)
a fleshy plant that is covered in prickles and grows in hot, dry places

caddie noun
someone whose job is to help a golfer by carrying the clubs and giving advice

cadet noun
a young person who is being trained for the armed forces or the police

cafe noun (say **kaf**-ay)
a place that sells hot and cold drinks and light meals

cafeteria noun (say kaf-e-**teer**-i-a)
a cafe where customers serve themselves from a counter

caffeine noun
caffeine is a substance in tea and coffee and some other drinks, which keeps you awake and makes you feel active

cage noun
an enclosure made of bars or wires, for keeping birds or animals so that they can't get away

cagoule noun
a lightweight waterproof jacket

cake noun
1 a sweet food made from a baked mixture of flour, eggs, fat, and sugar **2** something made into a lump rather like a cake, such as soap **a piece of cake** (informal) something very easy to do

caked adjective
covered with something that has dried hard, like mud

calamity noun (**calamities**)
a disaster **calamitous** adjective disastrous

calcium noun
a greyish-white element contained in teeth, bones, and lime

calculate verb
to calculate something is to work it out by arithmetic or with a calculator **calculation** noun something you work out by using numbers or other information

calculator noun
a machine for adding up figures and doing other calculations with numbers

calendar noun
a chart or display that shows the days of the year

calf¹ noun (**calves**)
1 a young cow or ox **2** a young seal, whale, or elephant

calf² noun (**calves**)
the back part of your leg below your knee

call noun
1 a shout or cry • They heard a call

for help. **2** a short visit • She decided to pay her father a call. **3** a telephone conversation with someone

call verb
1 to call is to shout out **2** to call someone is to telephone them • I'll call you at the weekend. **3** to call someone near you is to ask them to come to you **4** to call on someone is to visit them **5** to be called something is to have it as your name • His friend was called Damon. **6** to call something a certain thing is to describe it that way • You don't call that working, do you? **to call something off** is to cancel it

calling noun
someone's calling is their profession or trade

callipers plural noun
a device for measuring the width of tubes or of round objects

callous adjective
a callous person is very unkind and doesn't care about other people's feelings

calm adjective
1 quiet and still • a calm sea **2** someone is calm when they are not excited or agitated • Please keep calm. **calmly** adverb **calmness** noun

calorie noun
a unit for measuring the amount of heat or the energy produced by food

camcorder noun
a video camera that can record pictures and sound

camel noun
a large animal with a long neck and one or two humps on its back • Arabian camels have one hump, and Bactrian camels have two.

camera noun
a device for taking photographs, films, or television pictures

camouflage noun (say **kam**-o-flahzh)
a way of hiding things by making them look like part of their surroundings

camouflage verb
to camouflage something is to hide it by making it look like part of its surroundings

camp noun
a place where people live in tents or huts or caravans for a short time

camp verb
1 to camp or go camping is to have a holiday in a tent **2** to camp is also to put up a tent or tents • Let's camp here for the night. **camper** noun a person who goes to a camp

campaign noun
1 a planned series of actions, especially to get people to support you or become interested in something • a campaign for human rights **2** a series of battles in one area or with one aim

campaign verb
to campaign is to carry out a plan of action to raise people's interest in something such as a good cause • They are campaigning to stop the destruction of the rainforests.

campsite noun
a place for camping

campus noun
the buildings of a college or university and the land around them

can¹ verb (present tense **can**; past tense **could**)
1 to be able to do something or to know how to do it • Can you lift this stone? • They can speak French. **2** to be allowed to do something • Can I go home?

can² noun
a sealed metal container holding food or drink

can² verb (**canning, canned**)
to can food is to put it into cans and seal it

canal noun
a long channel specially dug and filled with water for boats to travel along

canary noun (**canaries**)
a small yellow bird that sings, often kept in a cage as a pet

cancel verb (**cancelling, cancelled**)
1 to cancel something planned is to say that it will not be done or not take place after all **2** to cancel an order or instruction is to stop it **3** to cancel a stamp or ticket is to mark it so that it cannot be used again

cancellation noun
something that someone has cancelled, especially a theatre or travel booking that can then be sold to someone else

canary

cancer noun
a serious disease in which a harmful growth forms in the body

candidate noun
1 someone who has applied for a job or position **2** someone who is taking an exam

candle noun
a stick of wax with a wick through it, giving light when it is burning

candlestick noun
a holder for a candle or candles

candy noun (**candies**)
1 candy is crystallized sugar
2 a candy is a sweet

candyfloss noun
candyfloss is a fluffy mass of sugar that has been spun into fine threads

cane noun
a cane is the hollow stem of a reed or tall grass

cane verb
to cane someone is to beat them with a cane

canine adjective
to do with dogs

cannibal noun
1 a person who eats human flesh
2 an animal that eats animals of its own kind **cannibalism** noun
cannibalism is eating other people, or animals of the same kind

cannon noun
a large gun that fires heavy balls made of metal or stone

cannon

cannonball noun
a heavy metal or stone ball fired from a cannon

cannot
can not • *I cannot believe it.*

canoe noun
a light narrow boat driven with paddles **canoeist** noun someone who uses a canoe

canopy noun (**canopies**)
a covering that hangs over something • *The larger trees form a canopy over the roof of the forest.*

can't
short for cannot • *We can't see them.*

canteen noun
a restaurant in a factory or office or

school, where the people working there can get a meal

canter verb
a horse canters when it goes at a gentle gallop

canvas noun
1 canvas is strong, coarse cloth
2 a canvas is a piece of this kind of cloth used for painting on

canyon noun
a deep valley with a river running through it

cap noun
1 a soft hat without a brim but often with a peak **2** a cover or top

cap verb (**capping, capped**)
1 to cap something is to cover it

capable adjective
able to do something **capability** noun being able to do something
capably adverb to do something capably is to do it well

capacity noun (**capacities**)
1 ability to do something • *He has a great capacity for work.* **2** the amount that something can hold

cape[1] noun
a piece of high land sticking out into the sea

cape[2] noun
a cloak

caper verb
to caper is to jump about playfully

capital noun
1 the capital of a country is the most important city in it
2 capital is money or property that can be used to make more wealth

capital letter noun
a large letter of the kind used at the start of a name or a sentence, such as A, B, C

capital punishment noun
capital punishment is when someone is killed as a punishment for a crime, such as murder or treason

capsize verb
to capsize is to overturn in a boat in the water

capsule noun
1 a hollow pill containing medicine
2 a small spacecraft that separates from a larger rocket

captain noun
1 an officer in charge of a ship or aircraft **2** an officer in the army or navy **3** the leader in a sports team

caption noun
the words printed beside a picture to describe it

captivate verb
to captivate someone is to charm them or make them interested

captivating adjective charming and attractive

captive noun
a prisoner

captive adjective
imprisoned; unable to escape

captivity noun
1 captivity is being held prisoner
2 an animal in captivity is one kept in a zoo or wildlife park rather than living in the wild

capture verb
to capture an animal or person is to catch or imprison them

capture noun
catching or imprisoning an animal or person

car noun
1 a motor vehicle for about four or five people **2** a railway carriage
• *Does the train have a buffet car?*

caramel noun
1 caramel is burnt sugar used to give a sweet taste to food
2 a caramel is a sweet made from butter, milk, and sugar

carat noun
1 a measure of weight for precious stones **2** a measure of the purity of gold

caravan noun
1 a vehicle towed by a car and used for living in, especially by people on holiday **2** a large number of people travelling together, especially across a desert

carbon noun
carbon is an element found in charcoal, graphite, diamonds, and other substances

carbon dioxide noun
a colourless gas made by humans and animals breathing

carbon monoxide noun
a colourless, poisonous gas found especially in the exhaust fumes of motor vehicles

carcass noun
the dead body of an animal or bird

card noun
1 card is thick stiff paper **2** a card is a folded piece of thick paper that you use to send greetings to someone, for example a birthday card **3** a card is also a playing card **4** a card is also a small piece of plastic that a bank or building society issues to a customer, with an electronic strip recording details of their account **cards** is a game with playing cards

cardboard noun
cardboard is thick stiff paper

a
b
c
d
e
f
g
h
i
j
k
l
m
n
o
p
q
r
s
t
u
v
w
x
y
z

cardigan noun
a knitted jumper fastened with buttons down the front

cardinal number noun
a number for counting things, for example 1, 2, 3

care noun
1 care is worry or trouble • *She was free from care.* **2** care is also serious thought or attention • *Take more care with your homework.* **3** care is also protection or supervision • *You can leave your dog in my care.* **to take care** is to be especially careful **to take care of someone or something** is to look after them • *Please could you take care of the cat while I'm away?*

care verb
to care about something or someone is to feel interested or concerned about them **to care for someone** is to look after them • *He cared for his wife when she was ill.* **to care for something** is to like it or want it • *I don't much care for fried food.*

career noun
a person's career is what they have been trained to do to earn a living and make progress during their lives

career verb
to career along or down somewhere is to rush along wildly

carefree adjective
not having any worries or responsibilities

careful adjective
making sure that you do something well without any mistakes and without causing any danger • *She is a careful driver.* • *He was careful to read the instructions first.*

carefully adverb
to do something carefully is to do it with a lot of care and attention

careless adjective
not taking care; clumsy **carelessly** adverb to do something carelessly is to do it without much care and make a lot of mistakes **carelessness** noun carelessness is not taking care

caress noun (say ka-**ress**)
a gentle and loving touch

caress verb
to caress someone is to touch them gently and fondly

caretaker noun
someone who looks after a large building such as a church or school

cargo noun
the goods carried in a ship or aircraft

caricature noun
a drawing or description of someone that exaggerates their features and makes them look funny or ridiculous

carnation noun
a garden flower with a sweet smell

carnival noun
a festival or celebration with a procession of people in fancy dress

carnivore noun
an animal that eats meat **carnivorous** adjective a carnivorous animal is one that eats meat

carol noun
a hymn or song that you sing at Christmas time

carpenter noun
someone who makes things, especially parts of buildings, out of wood **carpentry** making things from wood

carpet noun
a thick soft covering for a floor

carriage noun
1 a carriage is one of the separate sections of a train where passengers sit **2** a carriage is also a passenger vehicle pulled by horses

carriageway noun
the part of a road that vehicles travel on

carrier bag noun
a large bag for holding shopping

carrot noun
a long thin orange-coloured vegetable

carrots

carry verb (**carries, carrying, carried**)
1 to carry something is to lift it and take it somewhere **2** to carry something is also to have it with you • *He is carrying a gun.* **3** a sound carries when it can be heard a long way away **to be carried away** is to become very excited **to carry on** is to continue doing someth *ey carried on chatting.* **to carry something out** is to put it into practice • *The following night he carried out his plan.*

cart noun
a small vehicle for carrying loads

cart verb
(informal) to cart something somewhere is to carry or transport it, especially when it is heavy or tiring • *I've been carting these books around the school all afternoon.*

carthorse noun
a large heavy horse

cartilage noun (say **kar**-ti-lij)
cartilage is tough and flexible tissue attached to one of the bones in the nose or ear

carton noun
a lightweight cardboard or plastic box

cartoon noun
1 a drawing that is funny or tells a joke **2** a series of drawings that tell a story **3** an animated film **cartoonist** noun someone who draws cartoons

cartridge noun
1 a container holding film to be put into a camera or ink to be put into a pen **2** the case containing the explosive for a bullet or shell

cartwheel noun
a somersault done sideways, with your arms and legs spread wide

carve verb
1 to carve wood or stone is to make something artistic by cutting it carefully **2** to carve meat is to cut it into slices

cascade noun
a waterfall or a series of waterfalls

cascade verb
to cascade is to tumble down like the water in a waterfall

case[1] noun
1 a container **2** a suitcase

case[2] noun
1 an example of something existing or happening • *We've had four cases of chickenpox.* • *It's just a case of being patient.* **2** a crime or incident that the police or a lawcourt are investigating • *The next case was a murder.* **3** the facts or arguments used to support something • *She made a good case for getting some extra money.* **in any case** anyway **in case** because something may happen • *Take an umbrella in case it rains.*

cash noun
cash is coins and banknotes that you use to pay for something

cash verb
to cash a cheque is to exchange it for coins and banknotes

cash dispenser noun
a machine from which customers of a bank or building society can get money

cashier noun
someone in charge of the money in a bank, office, or shop

cash register noun
a machine that records and stores money received in a shop

casket noun
a small box for jewellery or other small objects

casserole noun
1 a covered dish in which food is cooked **2** the food cooked in a dish of this kind

cassette noun
a small sealed case containing recording tape or film

cast verb
1 to cast something is to throw it **2** to cast a vote is to make your vote in an election **3** to cast something made of metal or plaster is to make it in a mould **4** to cast a play or film is to choose the performers for it **to cast off** is to untie a boat and start sailing in it

cast noun
1 a shape you make by pouring liquid metal or plaster into a mould **2** the performers in a play or film

castanets plural noun
two pieces of wood or ivory held in one hand and clapped together to make a clicking sound, as in Spanish dancing

castaway noun
someone who has been left in a deserted place, especially after a shipwreck

castle noun
1 a large old building with heavy stone walls and battlements, made to protect people in it from attack **2** a piece in chess, also called a *rook*

castor noun (say **kah**-ster)
a small wheel on the leg of a piece of furniture

castor sugar noun
finely ground white sugar

casual adjective
1 not deliberate or planned • *It was just a casual remark.* **2** casual clothes are informal clothes that you wear for leisure time **3** not regular or permanent • *His dad was doing casual work.*
casually adverb

casualty noun (**casualties**)
someone killed or injured in war or in an accident

cat noun
1 a small furry animal, usually kept as a pet and known for catching mice **2** a larger member of the same family, for example a lion, tiger, or leopard

catalogue noun
a list of goods for sale or of books in a library

catamaran noun
a sailing boat with two hulls fixed side by side

catapult noun
a small weapon made from a forked stick with elastic attached to each fork, used for shooting pellets or small stones

catastrophe noun (say ka-**tas**-tro-fi)
a great or sudden disaster
catastrophic adjective absolutely disastrous or dreadful • *The tornado did catastrophic damage.*

catch verb (**catching, caught**)
1 to catch something is to get hold of it, for example a ball that is coming towards you **2** to catch an animal is to capture it and not let it escape **3** to catch someone is to discover them doing something wrong • *He was caught going home early.* **4** to catch an illness is to get it from someone else **5** to catch a bus or train is to get on it before it leaves **6** to catch something someone says is to manage to hear it • *I'm afraid I didn't catch your question.* **7** to catch your clothes is to get them entangled in something • *I've caught my sleeve on a bramble.* **to catch fire** is to start burning **to catch on** (*informal*) is to become popular, as a craze or fashion does **to catch someone out** is to show that they are wrong or mistaken **to catch up with someone** is to reach them when they have been ahead of you

catch noun
1 catching something • *Maya made a brilliant catch.* **2** something you catch • *They had a large catch of fish.* **3** a hidden difficulty or snag • *The car was so cheap there had to be a catch.* **4** a device for fastening a door or window

catchment area noun
the area in which pupils go to a particular school

catchphrase noun
a phrase that someone famous has used and a lot of people now use

catchy adjective (**catchier, catchiest**)
pleasant and easy to remember, like a tune

category noun (**categories**)
a group or division of similar people or things • *She was a runner-up in the 8-10 age category.*

cater verb
to cater for someone or something is to give them what they need • *The library caters for all ages.*

caterer noun
someone whose job is to provide food for people, especially at an important party or occasion

caterpillar noun
a long, creeping creature that turns into a butterfly or moth

cathedral noun
a large and important church in a major city, with a bishop in charge of it

Catholic adjective
belonging to the Roman Catholic Church

Catholic noun
a member of the Roman Catholic Church

cattle plural noun
cattle are cows and bulls and other large grass-eating animals

cauldron noun
a large round iron cooking pot used especially by witches in stories

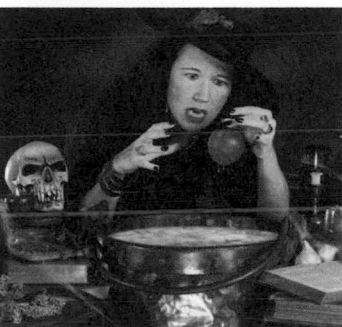

cauliflower noun
a kind of cabbage with a large head of white flowers

cause noun
1 what makes something happen, a reason • *The cause of the fire is still a mystery.* **2** the aim or purpose that a group of people are working for • *They were raising money for a good cause.*

cause verb
to cause something is to make it happen

caution noun
1 caution is being careful to avoid danger or mistakes **2** a caution is a warning

cautious adjective
careful to avoid a risk or difficulty
cautiously adverb

cavalry noun
soldiers who fight on horseback or in armoured vehicles

cave noun
a large hole in the side of a hill or cliff, or under the ground

a b **c** d e f g h i j k l m n o p q r s t u v w x y z

cave verb
to cave or go caving is to explore caves **to cave in** is to collapse

caveman or **cavewoman** noun (**cavemen** or **cavewomen**)
a person who lived in a cave in prehistoric times

cavern noun
a cave, especially a deep or dark cave

cavity noun (**cavities**)
a hollow or hole

CD
short for compact disc

CD-ROM
short for *compact disc read-only memory*, a system for storing information that can be viewed on a computer screen

cease verb
to cease doing something is to stop doing it

ceasefire noun
an agreement to stop using weapons, made by people who are fighting a war

cedar noun
an evergreen tree with hard sweet-smelling wood

ceiling noun (say **see**-ling)
the flat surface along the top of a room

celebrate verb
to celebrate a day or event is to do something special to show that it is important **celebration** noun
a party or other special event to celebrate something

celebrity noun (**celebrities**)
a famous person, especially in show business or on television

celery noun
a vegetable with crisp white or green stems

cell noun
1 a small room, especially in a prison 2 a tiny part of a living creature or plant 3 a device for producing electric current chemically

cellar noun
an underground room for storing things

cello noun (say **chel**-oh)
a large stringed musical instrument, which you play by placing it upright between the knees and using a bow **cellist** someone who plays the cello

cellulose noun
cellulose is a tissue that forms the main part of all plants and trees

Celsius adjective
using a scale for measuring temperature in which water freezes at 0 degrees and boils at 100 degrees

cement noun
1 cement is a mixture of lime and clay used in building to make floors and join bricks together 2 cement is also a strong glue

cemetery noun (**cemeteries**) (say sem-e-tr)i
a place where dead people are buried

censor verb
to censor films, plays, or books is to look at them to make sure that they are suitable for people to see, and to take out any parts that do not seem suitable **censorship** noun
the job or process of censoring films, plays, or books

census noun
an official count or survey of the number of people or the volume of traffic in a place

cent noun
a coin and unit of money in America and some other countries

centenary noun (**centenaries**)
the hundredth anniversary of something special or important

centigrade adjective
another word for Celsius

centimetre noun
one-hundredth of a metre, about four-tenths of an inch

centipede noun
a small, long creature with many pairs of legs

central adjective
1 at or near the centre of something 2 most important • *She will have a central role in our plans.* **centrally** adverb in a central position

central heating noun
central heating is a system of heating a building by sending hot water, hot air, or steam round it in pipes

centre noun
1 the middle of something 2 an important place • *Vienna is one of the great music centres of Europe.* 3 a building or place for a special purpose, such as a sports centre or a shopping centre

centurion noun
an officer in the ancient Roman army, originally commanding a hundred men

century noun (**centuries**)
1 a period of a hundred years 2 a hundred runs scored by one batsman in an innings at cricket

ceramics plural noun
ceramics is the art of making pottery

cereal noun
1 a grass that produces seeds which are used as food 2 a breakfast food made from seeds of this kind

ceremony noun (**ceremonies**) (say se-ri-mo-ni)
1 ceremony is the formal actions carried out at a wedding, funeral, or other important occasion 2 a ceremony is a formal event such as a wedding or funeral **ceremonial** adjective a ceremonial event or duty is one to do with a ceremony

certain adjective
1 something is certain when it is definitely true or is going to happen 2 you are certain about something when you know it is definitely true 3 known but not named • *A certain person was here this morning.* **for certain** definitely, for sure **to make certain** is to make sure

certainly adverb
as a fact, without any doubt • *They were certainly here last night.*

certainty noun (**certainties**)
1 a certainty is something that is sure to happen 2 certainty is being sure

certificate noun
an official document that records an important event or achievement, such as someone's birth or passing an exam

centurion

CFC
short for *chlorofluorocarbon*, a chemical that can damage the earth's ozone layer, and was once used in refrigerators and aerosols

chaffinch noun
a small bird

chain noun
1 a row of metal rings fastened together 2 a line of people 3 a connected series of things • *The story told of a strange chain of events.*

chair noun
a seat with a back for one person

chalk *noun*
1 a kind of soft white rock **2** a soft white or coloured stick of a similar rock, used for writing on blackboards **chalky** *adjective* white or powdery like chalk

challenge *verb*
to challenge someone is to demand that they perform some feat or take part in a fight **challenger** *noun* a person who makes a challenge, especially for a sports title

challenge *noun*
something difficult that someone has to do

chamber *noun*
1 (*old use*) a room **2** a hall used for meetings of a parliament or council

chameleon *noun*
(*say* ka-**mee**-li-on) a small lizard that can change the colour of its skin to match its surroundings and appear almost invisible

chameleon

champagne *noun*
(*say* sham-**payn**) a bubbly white French wine

champion *noun*
1 the person who has beaten all the others in a sport or competition **2** someone who supports a cause by fighting or speaking for it • *Martin Luther King was a champion of human rights.*

championship *noun*
a contest to decide who is the best player or competitor in a game or sport

chance *noun*
1 a chance is a possibility or opportunity • *This is your only chance to see them.* **2** chance is the way things happen accidentally • *It was pure chance that we met.* **by chance** accidentally, without any planning • *We found the place by chance.* **to take a chance** is to take a risk

chancellor *noun*
1 an important government or legal official **2** the chief minister of the government in some European countries

Chancellor of the Exchequer *noun*
the minister of the British government in charge of finances and taxes

chandelier *noun* (*say* shan-de-**leer**)
a light fitting that hangs from the ceiling and has a lot of bright bulbs

change *verb*
1 to change something or someone is to make them different **2** to change is to become different • *My gran said I'd changed since she'd last seen me.* **3** to change one thing for another is to exchange them • *I'm going to change my bike for a new one.* **4** to change money is to give coins or notes of small values in exchange for higher value money • *Can you change a £5 note?* **5** to change trains or buses is to get off one and get on another • *Change at York for the train to Durham.*

change *noun*
1 change is the process of changing **2** your change is the money you get back when you give more than the right money to pay for something **3** a change of clothes is a set of fresh clothes **to do something for a change** is to do it because it is different or unusual • *Let's walk home for a change.*

channel *noun*
1 a stretch of water joining two seas, like the English Channel between Britain and France **2** a television or radio station **3** a way for water to flow along **4** the part of a river or sea that is deep enough for ships to sail on

chant *noun*
a tune, especially one that is often repeated

chant *verb*
to chant words is to say them or call them out in a special rhythm

chaos *noun* (*say* **kay**-oss)
chaos is complete disorder or confusion • *The room was in chaos.*

chaotic *adjective* (*say* kay-**ot**-ik)
completely confused or in a mess

chap *noun*
(*informal*) a man or boy • *What a funny chap he is.*

chapatti *noun*
a flat thin cake of Indian bread made without yeast

chapel *noun*
1 a small church or part of a large church **2** a room in a large house, used for worship

chapped *adjective*
having rough, cracked skin

chapter *noun*
a section of a book

char *verb* (**charring, charred**)
to char something is to scorch it or blacken it with fire

character *noun*
1 the special nature and qualities of a person or thing **2** a person in a story or play

characteristic *noun*
something that makes a person or thing noticeable or different from others

characteristic *adjective*
typical, what you would expect of someone

charades *noun* (*say* sha-**rahdz**)
charades is a game in which people have to guess a word or the title of a book or film when other people act it out

charcoal *noun*
charcoal is a black substance made by burning wood slowly

charge *noun*
1 the price asked for something **2** an accusation that someone committed a crime • *He is facing three charges of burglary.* **3** an attack in a battle **4** the amount of an explosive needed to fire a weapon **5** the amount of an electric current **to be in charge of something or someone** is to be the one who decides what will happen to them

charge *verb*
1 to charge a price for something is to ask people to pay it **2** to charge someone is to accuse them of committing a crime **3** to charge in a battle is to rush to attack the enemy

chariot *noun*
a horse-drawn vehicle with two wheels, used in ancient times for fighting and racing **charioteer** *noun* someone who drove a chariot

charity *noun* (**charities**)
1 charity is giving money and help to other people **2** a charity is an organization that helps those in need **charitable** *adjective* kind and generous

charm *noun*
1 charm is being pleasant and attractive **2** a charm is a magic spell **3** a charm is also something small worn or carried to bring good luck

charm *verb*
1 to charm someone is to give them pleasure or delight **2** to charm someone is also to put a spell on them

charming *adjective*
pleasant and attractive

chart *noun*
1 a large plan or map **2** a diagram or list with information set out in columns or rows **3** a list of the most popular music sold

charter *noun*
an official document explaining people's rights or privileges

a b c d e f g h i j k l m n o p q r s t u v w x y z

charter *verb*
to charter an aircraft or vehicle is to hire it for a special journey

chase *verb*
to chase someone is to go quickly after them to try to catch them up

chase *noun*
a chase is when you chase someone

chassis *noun* (**chassis**)
(*say* **shass**-i) the frame and wheels of a vehicle, which support the body

chat *noun*
a friendly or informal talk with someone

chat *verb* (**chatting, chatted**)
to chat to someone is to talk to them in a friendly or informal way **chatty** *adjective* liking to chat to people in a friendly way

château *noun* (**châteaux**)
(*say* **shat**-oh)
a castle or large house in France

château

chatroom *noun*
a place on the Internet where people can have a conversation by sending messages to each other

chatter *verb*
1 to talk quickly or stupidly; to talk too much **2** to make a rattling noise
• *She couldn't stop her teeth from chattering.*

chauffeur *noun* (*say* shoh-**fer**)
someone who is paid to drive a large smart car for someone important

cheap *adjective*
1 low in price; not expensive **2** not well made or of good quality

cheat *verb*
1 to cheat someone is to trick them so they lose something **2** to cheat is to try to do well in an examination or game by breaking the rules

cheat *noun*
someone who cheats

check *verb*
1 to check something is to make sure that it is correct or all right
2 to check someone or something is to make them stop or slow down **to check on something or check up on something** is to look at it carefully to see if it is correct or suitable

check *noun*
1 a check is when you check something **2** check in chess is when the king is threatened by another piece **3** a check is a pattern of squares

checkmate *noun*
checkmate in chess is when one side wins by trapping the other side's king

checkout *noun*
the place where you pay for your shopping in a supermarket or a large shop

check-up *noun*
a careful check or examination by a doctor or dentist

cheek *noun*
1 the side of your face below your eye **2** being rude or impolite

cheeky *adjective*
rude or impolite, without being unpleasant or nasty **cheekily** *adverb* in a rude or cheeky way

cheer *noun*
a shout praising or supporting someone

cheer *verb*
1 to cheer someone is to support them by cheering **2** to cheer someone is to comfort or encourage them **to cheer someone up** is to make them more cheerful **to cheer up** is to become more cheerful

cheerful *adjective*
happy and bright

cheese *noun*
a white or yellow food made from milk. Cheese can be hard or soft. **cheesy** *adjective* tasting or smelling like cheese

cheetah *noun*
a large spotted animal of the cat family, which can run very fast

chef *noun* (*say* shef)
the chief cook in a hotel or restaurant

chemical *noun*
a substance used in or made by chemistry

chemical *adjective*
to do with chemistry or made by chemistry

chemist *noun*
1 someone who makes or sells medicines **2** an expert in chemistry

chemistry *noun*
the study of the way substances combine and react with one another

cheque *noun*
a written form instructing a bank to pay money out of an account

cherish *verb*
to cherish something is to look after it lovingly

cherry *noun* (**cherries**)
a small bright red fruit with a large stone

chess *noun*
a game for two players played with sixteen pieces each on a board of 64 squares

chest *noun*
1 a chest is a large strong box **2** your chest is the front part of your body between your neck and your waist

chess

chestnut *noun*
1 a hard brown nut **2** the tree that produces this kind of nut

chest of drawers *noun*
a piece of furniture with drawers for holding clothes

chew *verb*
to chew food is to grind it into pieces between your teeth **chewy** *adjective* chewy food is tough and needs a lot of chewing

chewing gum *noun*
a sticky flavoured gum for chewing

chick *noun*
a young bird

chicken *noun*
1 a chicken is a young hen **2** chicken is the meat of a hen used as food

chicken *adjective*
(*informal*) cowardly

chicken *verb*
to chicken out of something (*informal*) is to avoid it because you are afraid

chicken

chickenpox *noun*
a disease that produces red itchy spots on your skin

chief *noun*
1 a leader or ruler **2** the most important person, the boss

chief *adjective*
1 having the highest rank or power **2** most important

chiefly *adverb*
mainly, mostly • *Peter is the one who is chiefly to blame.*

chieftain *noun*
the chief of a tribe or clan

child noun (**children**)
1 a young person, a boy or girl
2 someone's son or daughter
• *Whose child is that?*

childhood noun
the time when you are a child

childish adjective
silly and immature • *Don't be childish!*

childminder noun
a person who is paid to look after
children while their parents are out
at work

childproof adjective
not able to be opened or operated
by small children • *The car has
childproof door locks.*

chill noun
1 chill is an unpleasant feeling of
being cold 2 a chill is a cold that
makes you shiver
chill verb
to chill something is to make it cold

chilli noun
the hot-tasting pod of a red pepper

chilly adjective
(**chillier,
chilliest**)
1 slightly cold
2 unfriendly • *They
went to see the head
and got a chilly reception.*

chillies

chime noun
a ringing sound made by a bell
chime verb
to chime is to make a ringing
sound • *The clock chimes every
quarter-hour.*

chimney noun
a tall pipe or passage that carries
away smoke from a fire

chimpanzee noun
an small African ape with black fur
and large eyes

chin noun
your chin is the part of your face
under your mouth

china noun
china is thin and delicate pottery

chink noun
1 a narrow opening • *He looked
through a chink in the curtains.*
2 a clinking sound • *They heard the
chink of coins.*

chip noun
1 a small piece of something
2 a place where a small piece
has been knocked off something
3 a small piece of fried potato
4 a small counter used in gambling
games 5 a silicon chip
chip verb
to chip something is to knock a small
piece off it by accident

chirp verb
to chirp is to make short sharp
sounds like a small bird

chisel noun
a tool with a sharp end for shaping
wood or stone
chisel verb (**chiselling, chiselled**)
to chisel wood or stone is to shape or
cut it with a chisel

chivalry noun
being ready to help people who are
less strong than you are **chivalrous**
adjective kind and helpful to people
who are less strong

chlorine noun
a chemical used to disinfect water

chlorophyll noun
the substance that makes plants green

chocolate noun
1 chocolate is a sweet brown food 2 a
chocolate is a sweet made of or covered
with chocolate 3 chocolate is also a
sweet powder used for making drinks

choice noun
1 choice is the process of choosing or
the power to choose • *I'm afraid we
have no choice.* 2 a choice is what
someone chooses • *Let me know
your choice of book.*

choir noun
a group of singers, especially in
a church

choke verb
1 to choke on something is to be
unable to breathe properly because
it is stuck in your throat 2 to choke
someone is to stop them breathing
properly 3 to choke something is to
block it up

cholera noun (say **kol**-er-a)
cholera is a severe infectious disease
that affects the intestines

cholesterol noun (say ko-**less**-te-rol)
cholesterol is a substance found in
the cells of your body which helps to
carry fat in the bloodstream

choose verb (**choosing, chose,
chosen**)
to choose something or someone is
to decide that you want them rather
than any of the others

choosy adjective (**choosier,
choosiest**)
(*informal*) a choosy person is fussy
and difficult to please

chop verb (**chopping, chopped**)
1 to chop something up is to cut
it into small pieces 2 to chop
something is to cut or hit it with
a heavy blow
chop noun
1 a chopping blow 2 a small thick
slice of meat

choppy adjective (**choppier,
choppiest**) a choppy sea is fairly
rough with lots of small waves

chopsticks plural noun
a pair of thin sticks used for eating
Chinese or Japanese food

choral adjective (say **kor**-al)
for a choir or chorus

chord noun (say kord)
a number of musical notes sounded
together

chore noun (say chor)
a boring or difficult task

chorister noun (say **kor**-is-ter)
someone who sings in a choir

chorus noun (say **kor**-us)
1 a group of people singing or
speaking together
2 a piece of music sung by a group
of people
3 the words repeated after every
verse of a song or poem

christen verb
to christen a child is to baptize it
and give it a name **christening**
noun the ceremony at which a child
is baptized

Christian noun
someone who believes in
Jesus Christ
Christian adjective
to do with Christ or Christians

Christianity noun
the religion of Christians

Christmas noun
the time of celebrating the birth of
Jesus Christ on 25 December

chrome or **chromium** noun
a shiny silvery metal

chromosome noun
in living things, the part of a cell that
contains the genes

chronic adjective
a chronic illness or problem is
one that lasts for a long time
chronically adverb to be
chronically ill is to have a
very long illness

chronicle noun
a list of events with their dates

chronological adjective
a chronological list of events is
arranged in the order in which
the events happened
chronologically adverb in the
order in which things happen

chrysalis noun
(say **kris**-a-lis)
the hard cover a caterpillar
makes round itself before it
turns into a butterfly or moth

chrysalis

chubby *adjective*
(**chubbier, chubbiest**)
plump and healthy

chuck *verb*
(*informal*) to chuck something is to throw it roughly • *He chucked a brick through the window.*

chuckle *verb*
to chuckle is to laugh quietly

chuckle *noun*
a quiet laugh

chum *noun*
(*informal*) a friend

chunk *noun*
a thick lump of something **chunky** *adjective* big and thick

church *noun*
1 a church is a building where Christians worship **2** a church is also a particular Christian religion, for example the Church of England

churchyard *noun*
the ground round a church, used as a graveyard

churn *noun*
1 a large container for milk **2** a machine for making butter

churn *verb*
to churn butter is to make it in a churn
to churn something out (*informal*) is to produce lots of it very quickly

chute *noun* (*say* shoot)
a steep channel for people or things to slide down

chutney *noun*
a spicy mixture of fruit and peppers in a sauce, eaten with meat or cheese

cigarette *noun*
a small, thin roll of shredded tobacco in thin paper for smoking

cinder *noun*
a small piece of coal or wood that is partly burned

cinema *noun*
a cinema is a place where people go to see films

circle *noun*
1 a round flat shape, the shape of a coin or wheel **2** a balcony in a cinema or theatre

circle *verb*
1 to circle is to move in a circle • *Vultures circled overhead.* **2** to circle a place is go round it • *The space probe circled Mars.*

circuit *noun* (*say* **ser**-kit)
1 a circular line or journey **2** a racecourse **3** the path of an electric current

circular *adjective*
round like a circle

circulate *verb*
to circulate is to move around and come back to the beginning • *Blood circulates in the body.*

circulation *noun*
1 the movement of blood around your body **2** the number of copies of each issue of a newspaper or magazine that are sold

circumference *noun*
the line or distance round a circle

circumstance *noun*
a circumstance is a fact or event that affects something • *He won under difficult circumstances.*

circus *noun*
an entertainment with clowns, acrobats, and sometimes animals, usually performed in a large tent

cistern *noun*
a water tank

citizen *noun*
a citizen of a place is someone who was born there or who lives there

citizenship *noun*
1 the citizenship of a country is the right to live there and be a citizen of it • *She has applied for American citizenship.* **2** citizenship is also the duties a person has when they are the citizen of a country • *The school has lessons in citizenship.*

citrus fruit *noun*
citrus fruits are juicy fruits with a tough skin, such as oranges, lemons, limes, and grapefruit

city *noun* (**cities**)
a large or important town

civic *adjective*
to do with a city or its citizens

civil *adjective*
1 to do with the citizens of a place **2** to do with the ordinary people and not those who are in the armed forces **3** a civil person is polite and courteous to other people

civilian *noun*
someone who is an ordinary citizen and not in the armed forces

civilization *noun*
a civilization is a society or culture at a particular time in history • *They were learning about the Bronze Age civilization.*

civilize *verb*
to civilize someone is to improve their education and manners

civil rights *plural noun*
people's civil rights are their rights as citizens to have freedom and fair treatment, and to vote in elections

civil service *noun*
the civil service is all the officials who do the work the government needs to do to run the country

civil war *noun*
a war fought between people of the same country, such as the English Civil War (1642–51) or the American Civil War (1861–65)

clad *adjective*
clothed or covered • *The story was about a knight clad in shining armour.*

claim *verb*
1 to claim something is to ask for it when you think it belongs to you • *You can claim the money for your train fare.* **2** to claim something is to state or assert it • *They claimed they had been at home all evening.*

claim *noun*
1 an act of claiming **2** something claimed

clam *noun*
a large shellfish

clams

clamber *verb*
to clamber is to climb up or over something difficult using your hands and feet • *We clambered over the slippery rocks.*

clammy *adjective* (**clammier, clammiest**)
damp and slimy

clamp *noun*
a device for holding things together

clamp *verb*
to clamp something is to fit a clamp on it

clan *noun*
a number of families with the same ancestor • *The Scottish clans include the Campbells and the MacDonalds.*

clang *verb*
to clang is to make a loud ringing sound

clap *verb* (**clapping, clapped**)
to clap is to make a noise by hitting the palms of your hands together, especially to show you like something

clap *noun*
1 a round of clapping, especially to show you like something • *They gave the winners a loud clap.* **2** a clap of

thunder is a sudden sound of loud thunder

clarify verb
(**clarifies, clarifying, clarified**)
to clarify something is to explain it and make it easier to understand
clarification noun clarification is making something clear and easier to understand

clarinet noun
a woodwind instrument with a low tone **clarinettist** noun someone who plays the clarinet

clarity noun
clarity is a clear quality
• They spoke with clarity.

clash verb
1 to clash is to make a loud sound like cymbals banging together 2 two events clash when they happen inconveniently at the same time • My favourite TV programmes clash at 8 o'clock tonight. 3 two or more people clash when they have a fight or argument • Gangs of rival supporters clashed outside the ground. 4 colours clash when they look ugly or unattractive together

clash noun
1 a clashing sound
2 a fight or argument

clasp verb
to clasp someone or something is to hold them tightly   clarinet

clasp noun
1 a device for fastening things 2 a tight grasp

class noun
1 a class is a group of similar people, animals, or things 2 a class is also a division according to how good or important something is • Send the letter by first class post. 3 a class is also a group of children or students who are taught together, or a lesson 4 class is a system of different ranks in society

class verb
to class things is to put them in classes or groups

classic noun
a book, film, or story that is well known and thought to be very good and important

classic adjective
1 a classic story is one that most people think is very good and

important 2 very typical or common
• They made the classic mistake of leaving things to the last moment.

classical adjective
1 to do with Greek and Latin literature 2 classical music is serious music, often written in the past and still played

classify verb (**classifies, classifying, classified**)
to classify things is to put them in classes or groups **classification** noun a system of classifying things or putting them into groups

classmate noun
your classmates are the people in the same class as you at school

classroom noun
a room where lessons are given at a school

clatter noun
a loud noise of things being rattled or banged

clatter verb
to clatter is to make a clatter

clause noun
1 (in grammar) a part of a sentence that has its own verb 2 a part of a contract, treaty, or law

claw noun
one of the hard sharp nails that some birds and animals have on their feet

clay noun
clay is a sticky kind of earth, and is used for making bricks and pottery

clean adjective
1 something is clean when it does not have any dirt or stains on it 2 fresh, not yet used • Start on a clean page. 3 not rude or offensive
• I hope your jokes are clean ones.

clean verb
to clean something is to make it clean

cleaner noun
1 someone who cleans rooms or offices 2 something used for cleaning **the cleaners** a firm which cleans clothes

cleanliness noun (say **klen**-li-nes)
the practice of keeping things clean

cleanly adverb
neatly, exactly • He cut the brick cleanly in two.

cleanse verb (say klenz)
to cleanse something is to clean it and make it pure **cleanser** noun something you use to make a thing clean

clear adjective
1 easy to see or hear or understand
• He spoke with a clear voice. 2 easy to see through • The window in the door has clear glass. 3 free from

things that get in the way or aren't wanted
• Make sure the table's clear for dinner.

clear adverb
1 clearly • Speak loud and clear.
2 completely • He got clear away.
3 at a distance from something
• You'd better stand clear of the gates.

clear verb
1 to clear something is to make it free of unwanted things • They cleared a space on the floor to sit on. 2 to clear is to become clearer
• After the storm, the sky slowly cleared. 3 to clear someone is to find out that they are not to blame for something people thought they had done 4 to clear something is to jump over it without touching it **to clear something out** is to empty or tidy it **to clear up** is to make things tidy

clearing noun
an open space in a wood or forest

clearly adverb
1 in a clear way • We could see the house clearly. 2 obviously • They were clearly going to win.

clef noun
a sign that shows the pitch of a stave in music

clench verb
to clench your teeth or fingers is to close them tightly

clergy plural noun
the clergy are the priests and other officials of a Christian Church
clergyman noun **clergywoman** noun

clerk noun (say klark)
someone who works in an office to keep records and accounts and file papers

clever adjective
quick to learn and understand things; skilful

cliché noun (say **klee**-shay)
a phrase that people use a lot, so that it doesn't mean very much

click noun
a short sharp sound • She heard a click as someone turned on the light.

client noun
someone who gets help or advice from a professional person such as a lawyer or architect; a customer

cliff noun
a steep rock face, especially on the coast

climate noun
the usual sort of weather in a particular area
climatic adjective to do with the climate

clef

climax *noun*
the most important or exciting part of a story or series of events

climb *verb*
1 to climb or climb up something is go up it 2 to climb down something is to go down it 3 to climb is to grow or rise upwards, like a tall plant or a building

climb *noun*
an act of climbing • *It's a long climb to the top of the hill.*

climber *noun*
someone who climbs hills and mountains for sport

cling *verb*
to cling to someone or something is to hold on tightly • *The child was clinging to its mother.*

clinic *noun*
a place where people see doctors for treatment or advice

clink *verb*
to clink is to make a short ringing sound, like a coin being dropped

clip *noun*
a fastener for keeping things together

clip *verb*
1 to clip things together is to fasten them with a clip 2 to clip something is to cut it with shears or scissors

cloak *noun*
a piece of outdoor clothing, usually without sleeves, that hangs loosely from your shoulders

cloakroom *noun*
1 a place where you can leave coats and bags while you are visiting a building 2 a lavatory

clock *noun*
an instrument that shows what the time is

clockwise *adverb, adjective*
moving round a circle in the same direction as the hands of a clock

clockwork *adjective*
worked by a spring which you wind up

clog *verb* (**clogging, clogged**)
to clog something is to block it up accidentally

clog *noun*
a shoe with a wooden sole

cloister *noun*
a covered path that is open on one side and goes round a courtyard or along the side of a cathedral or monastery

clone *noun*
an animal or plant made from the cells of another animal or plant

clone *verb*
to clone something is to produce a clone of it

close¹ *adjective* (say klohss)
1 near, either in time or place • *They were close to finding the answer.* • *The shops were quite close to their new house.* 2 careful and detailed • *Please pay close attention.* 3 tight; with little empty space • *They got the wardrobe in but it was a close fit.* 4 having a strong relationship • *The boys had been close friends for years.* 5 a close race or finish is one in which competitors are nearly equal at the end 6 stuffy; without fresh air • *It's very close in this room.*

close¹ *adverb* (say klohss)
at a close distance • *The children were following close behind.*

close¹ *noun* (say klohss)
1 a street that is closed at one end 2 an enclosed area, especially round a cathedral

close² *verb* (say klohz)
1 to close something is to shut it 2 to close an event or meeting is to finish it **to close down** is to stop doing business • *Several shops in the High Street have closed down recently.* **to close in** is to get nearer • *The police closed in around the house.*

closely *adverb* (say **klohss**-li)
1 carefully, with attention • *His friends were watching closely.* 2 tightly • *The box was closely packed with toys.*

close-up *noun* (say **klohss**-up)
a photograph or film taken at short range

clot *noun*
a mass of thick liquid like blood or cream that has become nearly solid

clot *verb* (**clotting, clotted**)
to clot is to form into clots, like blood or cream

cloth *noun*
1 cloth is material woven from wool, cotton, or some other fabric 2 a cloth is a piece of this material 3 a cloth is also a tablecloth

clothe *verb*
to clothe someone is to put clothes on them

clothes *plural noun*
clothes are the things you wear to cover your body

clothing *noun*
clothing is the clothes you wear

cloud *noun*
1 a mass of water vapour floating in the air 2 a mass of smoke or something else dense in the air

cloud *verb*
to cloud or cloud over is to become full of clouds • *In the afternoon the sky clouded over.*

cloudless *adjective* a cloudless sky does not have any clouds

cloudy *adjective* (**cloudier cloudiest**)
1 full of clouds 2 hard to see through • *The glass contained a cloudy liquid.*

clout *verb*
to clout someone is to give them a hard blow

clove *noun*
the dried bud of a tropical tree used as a spice, especially to flavour apples

clover *noun*
a small wild plant, usually with leaves in three parts

clown *noun*
1 a circus performer who dresses up and wears bright face paint and does silly things to make people laugh 2 an amusing or silly person

clown *verb*
to clown is to behave like a clown

clown

club *noun*
1 a heavy stick 2 a stick for playing golf 3 a group of people who meet together because they are interested in the same thing 4 a playing card with a black clover-leaf printed on it

club *verb* (**clubbing, clubbed**)
to club someone is to hit them hard with a heavy stick **to club together** is to join with other people in doing something, especially raising money

cluck *verb*
to cluck is to make a noise like a hen

clue *noun*
something that helps you to solve a puzzle or a mystery

clump *noun*
a cluster of trees or plants

clumsy *adjective* (**clumsier, clumsiest**)
a clumsy person is careless and awkward, and likely to knock things over or drop things

clumsily *adverb*
clumsiness *noun*

cluster *noun*
a group of people or things close together

clutch¹ *verb*
to clutch something or clutch at something is to grab hold of it

clutch¹ *noun*
1 a tight grasp **2** a device for disconnecting the engine of a motor vehicle from its gears and wheels

clutch² *noun*
a set of eggs in a nest

clutter *verb*
to clutter a place up is to make it untidy or messy

clutter *noun*
clutter is a lot of things left around untidily

cm
short for centimetre or centimetres

Co.
short for company

coach *noun*
1 a comfortable single-deck bus used for long journeys
2 a carriage of a railway train
3 a carriage pulled by horses
4 a person who trains or instructs people in a sport or skill

coach *verb*
to coach someone is to instruct or train them in a sport or skill

coal *noun*
coal is a hard black mineral used as fuel

coarse *adjective*
1 rough, not delicate or smooth
2 rude or offensive • *You have a very coarse sense of humour.*

coast *noun*
the seashore and the land close to it

coast *verb*
to coast is to ride downhill without using power • *They stopped pedalling and coasted down the slope.*

coastal *adjective*
by the coast or near the coast

coastguard *noun*
someone whose job is to keep watch on coasts

coastline *noun*
the edge of the land by the sea

coat *noun*
1 a piece of clothing with sleeves that covers most of the body and is worn outdoors over other clothes **2** a layer of paint

coat *verb*
to coat something is to cover it with a coating

coating *noun*
a covering or layer, especially of paint

coat of arms *noun*
a design on a shield or building, representing a historic family or town

coax *verb*
to coax someone is to persuade them gently or patiently

cobbler *noun*
someone whose job is to mend shoes

cobbles *plural noun*
cobbles are a surface of cobblestones on a road **cobbled** *adjective* paved with cobbles

cobblestone *noun*
a small smooth and rounded stone sometimes used in large numbers to pave roads in towns

cobra *noun* (*say* **koh**-bra)
a poisonous snake

cobweb *noun*
a net of thin sticky threads that spiders spin to catch insects

cock *noun*
a male bird, especially a male fowl

cock *verb*
1 to cock your eye or ear is to turn it in a particular direction
2 to cock a gun is to make it ready to fire

cockerel *noun*
a young male fowl

cockle *noun*
an edible shellfish

cockney *noun*
1 a cockney is someone born in the East End of London
2 cockney is a kind of English spoken by people from this part of London

cockpit *noun*
the place in an aircraft where the pilot sits

cockroach *noun*
a dark brown insect   cockroach

cocky *adjective*
(*informal*) conceite and cheeky

cocoa *noun*
1 a hot drink that tastes of chocolate
2 the powder from which you make this drink

coconut *noun*
a large round nut containing a milky juice, that grows on palm trees

cocoon *noun*
the covering round a chrysalis

cod *noun*
a large edible sea fish

code *noun*
1 a set of signs and letters for sending messages secretly
2 a set of rules • *the Highway Code* • *a code of behaviour*

code *verb*
to code a message is to use special signs and letters, so that other people cannot understand it

co-education *noun*
the teaching of boys and girls together
co-educational *adjective* a co-educational school or system is one that teaches boys and girls together

coffee *noun*
1 a hot drink made from the roasted and crushed beans of a tropical plant
2 the powder from which you make this drink

coffin *noun*
a long box in which a dead body is buried or cremated

cog *noun*
one of a number of pieces sticking out from the edge of a wheel and allowing it to drive another wheel

coil *noun*
a circle or spiral of rope or wire

coil *verb*
to coil something is to wind it into circles or spirals

coin *noun*
a piece of metal money

coin *verb*
to coin a new word is to invent it

coinage *noun*
a country's coinage is the system of money that it uses

coincide *verb*
to coincide is to happen at the same time as something else • *My birthday always seems to coincide with exams.*

coincidence *noun*
coincidence, or a coincidence, is when two things can happen by chance at the same time

coke *noun*
coke is a solid fuel made out of coal

cola *noun*
cola is a sweet brown fizzy drink

cold *adjective*
1 low in temperature, not hot or warm **2** a cold person is unfriendly and distant

cold *noun*
1 cold weather or temperature **2** a cold is an illness that makes your nose run and gives you a sore throat
coldly *adverb* to act coldly is to be very unfriendly
coldness *noun* coldness is being unfriendly

cold-blooded *adjective*
1 having blood that changes temperature according to the surroundings **2** cruel, ruthless

coleslaw *noun*
a salad made of chopped cabbage covered in mayonnaise

collaborate *verb*
people collaborate when they work together or share their information
collaboration *noun* working with someone or sharing information with them

collage *noun*
(*say* **kol**-ahzh or *say* kol-**ahzh**)
a picture made by arranging scraps of paper and other things on a card

collapse *verb*
1 to collapse is to fall or break into pieces because of too much weight 2 someone collapses when they fall from being very weak or ill

collapsible *adjective*
a collapsible piece of furniture or equipment can be folded up into a smaller space

collar *noun*
1 the part of a piece of clothing that goes round your neck 2 a band that goes round an animal's neck

colleague *noun*
someone's colleague is a person they work with

collect *verb*
1 to collect things is to get them together from various places, especially as a hobby • *She collects stamps, and I collect coins.* 2 to collect someone or something is to go and get them **collector** *noun* someone who collects things for a hobby

collection *noun*
1 things you have collected as a hobby 2 money given by people at a meeting or concert or service

college *noun*
a place where people continue to study after they have left school

collide *verb*
to collide with something is to hit it while moving • *The bicycle collided with the car.*

collision *noun*
a crash between moving vehicles • *There has been a collision on the motorway.*

colon *noun*
a punctuation mark (:) used to separate parts of a sentence or before items in a list

colonel *noun* (*say* ker-nel)
a senior army officer

colonial *adjective*
from or to do with a country's colonies abroad

colony *noun*
1 a country that another country governs and sends people out to live there 2 a group of people or animals living together

colossal *adjective*
huge, enormous

colours

colour *noun*
1 the quality of being red, green, blue, and so on, produced by rays of light of different wavelengths 2 the use of all colours, not just black and white • *Is this film in colour?* 3 the colour of someone's skin 4 a substance used to give colour to things

colour *verb*
to colour something is to give it a colour or colours with paints or crayons

colour-blind *adjective*
not able to see or distinguish between some colours, usually red and green

colourful *adjective*
1 having a lot of bright colours 2 lively • *The film was a colourful story of life on board a pirate ship.*

colt *noun*
a young male horse

column *noun*
1 a pillar 2 something long and narrow • *They could see a column of smoke in the distance.* 3 a strip of printing in a book or newspaper 4 a regular feature in a newspaper • *He always read the sports column.*

coma *noun* (*say* **koh**-ma)
someone is in a coma when they are unconscious for a long time

comb *noun*
1 a tool with teeth for making the hair tidy 2 the red, fleshy crest on a fowl's head

comb *verb*
1 to comb your hair is to tidy it with a comb 2 to comb an area is to search it carefully for something lost • *We combed the woods all day but couldn't find our dog.*

combat *noun*
a fight or contest

combat *verb*
to combat something bad or unpleasant is to fight it and try to get rid of it • *The police force combats crime.*

combination *noun*
1 combination is joining or mixing things 2 a combination is a group of things that have been joined or mixed together

combine *verb* (*say* kom-**byn**)
to combine things is to join them or mix them together

combine harvester *noun*
a machine that cuts and threshes the grain in the fields

combustion *noun*
combustion is what happens when something burns

come *verb* (**coming, came, come**)
1 to come is to move towards the person or place that is here, and is the opposite of **go** • *Do you want to come to my house?* • *Has that letter come yet?* 2 to come is also to occur or be present • *The pictures come at the end of the book.* to come about is to happen to come to something is to add up to it • *The bill came to £50.* to come true is to actually happen • *Their holiday was a dream come true.*

comedian *noun*
someone who entertains people with humour and jokes

comedy *noun* (**comedies**)
1 a comedy is a play or film that makes people laugh 2 comedy is using humour to make people laugh

comet *noun*
an object moving across the sky with a bright tail of light

comfort *noun*
1 comfort is a feeling of relief from worry or pain 2 your comforts are the things you have around you that you enjoy and that make life pleasant

comfort *verb*
to comfort someone is to make them feel happier when they are feeling sad or worried

comfortable *adjective*
1 pleasant to use or wear • *a comfortable chair* 2 free from worry or pain • *The nurse made the patient comfortable.*
comfortably *adverb*

comic *noun*
1 a children's magazine that has stories with pictures 2 a comedian

comical *adjective*
funny, making people laugh **comically** *adverb*

comic strip *noun*
a series of drawings that tell a story

comma *noun*
a punctuation mark (,) used to mark a pause in a sentence or between items in a list

command *noun*
1 a command is

comic

an instruction telling someone to do something **2** command is authority or control • *Who has command of these soldiers?* **3** a command of a subject is the skill or ability to understand it • *She has a good command of Spanish.*

command *verb*
1 to command someone is to tell them to do something **2** to command a group of people is to be in charge of them • *A centurion commanded a hundred soldiers.*

commander *noun*
someone who commands, especially a senior naval officer

commandment *noun*
a sacred command, especially one of the Ten Commandments of Moses

commando *noun*
a soldier trained for making dangerous raids

commemorate *verb*
to commemorate a past event is to do something special so that people remember it **commemoration** *noun*

commence *verb*
to commence something is to begin it **commencement** *noun* the beginning of something

comment *noun*
a remark or opinion

commentary *noun*
(**commentaries**) a description of an event by someone who is watching it, especially for radio or television

commentator *noun*
a person who gives a commentary, especially of a sports event

commerce *noun*
commerce is trade, or buying and selling goods

commercial *adjective*
1 connected with trade and making money **2** paid for by advertising • *a commercial radio station*

commercial *noun*
an advertisement, especially on television or radio

commit *verb* (**committing, committed**) to commit a crime is to do something against the law

commitment *noun*
1 commitment is being determined to do something **2** a commitment is something you have promised to do

committee *noun*
a group of people who meet to organize or discuss something

common *adjective*
1 ordinary or usual • *The dandelion is a common plant.* **2** happening or

used often • *Traffic jams are common where we live.* **3** shared by many people • *The story was common knowledge.* • *Music was their common interest.*

common *noun*
a piece of open land that anyone can use

commonplace *adjective*
ordinary, familiar

commonwealth *noun*
a group of countries cooperating together **the Commonwealth** an association of Britain and various other countries, such as Canada, Australia, and New Zealand

commotion *noun*
an uproar • *Suddenly he could hear a commotion in the kitchen.*

commune *noun*
a group of people who live in the same house and share the money and work

communicate *verb*
to communicate news or information is to pass it on to other people **communicative** *adjective* a communicative person is willing to talk to people and give them information

communication *noun*
1 communication is giving people useful information and telling them about things that have happened **2** a communication is a message or piece of information that someone gives you **3** communication is also a form of technology for passing on information, for example television and text messaging

Communion *noun*
Communion is the Christian ceremony in which holy bread and wine are given to worshippers

communism *noun*
communism is a political belief that everyone should share the wealth of a country and the state should control its industry and resources **communist** *noun* someone who believes in communism

community *noun* (**communities**)
the people living in one area

commuter *noun*
someone who travels to work every day by train or bus **commute** *verb* to commute is to travel to work every day

compact *adjective*
small and neat

compact disc *noun*
a small plastic and metal disc on which music or information is stored

as digital signals and is read by a laser beam. Usually called CD.

companion *noun*
a companion is someone who spends a lot of time with you **companionship** *noun* companionship is being with someone and enjoying their friendship

company *noun* (**companies**)
1 a company is a group of people, especially a business firm **2** company is having people with you • *Jill was lonely and longed for some company.* **3** a company is an army unit consisting of two or more platoons

comparatively *adverb*
in comparison, relatively • *They all went to bed comparatively late.*

compare *verb*
1 to compare things is to see how they are similar • *Compare your answers.* **2** to compare with something is to be as good as it • *Our football pitch cannot compare with Wembley Stadium.*

comparison *noun*
comparison, or a comparison, is thinking about several things and seeing how they are similar or different

compartment *noun*
a special place or section where you can put something • *The coach had a luggage compartment under the floor.*

compass *noun*
an instrument with a magnetized needle that shows which direction you are facing **compasses** or **pair of compasses** a device for drawing circles

compass

compassion *noun*
compassion is pity or mercy you show to people who are suffering **compassionate** *adjective* showing pity or mercy to people who are suffering

compatible *adjective*
1 people are compatible when they are able to live or exist together without trouble **2** machines and devices are compatible when they can be used together

compel *verb* (**compelling, compelled**)
to compel someone to do something is to force them to do it

compensate *verb*
to compensate someone is to give them something to make up for something they have lost or suffered **compensation** *noun* compensation is something given to someone to make up for a loss or injury

compete *verb*
to compete in a competition is to take part in it and try to win it

competent *adjective*
having the skill or knowledge to do something well • *He is not competent to teach French.* **competence** *noun* the ability to do something well

competition *noun*
a game or race in which you try to do better than other people **competitive** *adjective* a competitive person enjoys competing with other people **competitor** *noun* someone who competes in a game or race, or a rival in business

compile *verb*
to compile information is to collect and arrange it, especially in a book • *She compiled a collection of children's poems.* **compilation** *noun* a collection of information, stories, or poems that someone has compiled **compiler** *noun* someone who compiles something

complacent *adjective*
smugly satisfied with the way things are, without wanting to improve them

complain *verb*
to complain about something is to say that you are not pleased about it

complaint *noun*
1 you make a complaint when you are not pleased about something 2 you suffer from a complaint when you are slightly ill

complete *adjective*
1 having all its parts, with nothing missing • *I hope the tool kit is complete.* 2 finished, achieved • *By evening the jigsaw puzzle was complete.* 3 utter, total • *It came as a complete surprise.*

complete *verb*
to complete something is to finish it or make it complete **completion** *noun* the completing of something, the finish • *The work is nearing completion.*

completely *adverb*
totally, utterly • *You are completely wrong.*

complex *adjective*
difficult and complicated **complexity** *noun* being difficult or complicated

complex *noun*
a group of buildings, such as a sports centre

complexion *noun*
the colour or appearance of your skin

complicate *verb*
to complicate something is to make it difficult or awkward

complicated *adjective*
difficult to understand or cope with because it has so many parts or details

complication *noun*
a new problem that makes something else more difficult

compliment *noun*
words or actions that show you approve of a person or thing

complimentary *adjective*
1 praising someone or saying good things about them • *She liked Neil's work and was very complimentary about him.* 2 given to someone free of charge • *I enclose two complimentary tickets for our next production.*

component *noun*
one of the parts that a machine is made of

compose *verb*
1 to compose music or poetry is to write it 2 to be composed of several people or things is to be made up of them • *The class is composed of children up to the age of 8.* **composer** *noun* someone who writes music

composition *noun*
1 composition is composing or writing something 2 a composition is a piece of music or an essay

compost *noun*
compost is a mixture of decayed leaves, grass, and other natural refuse, and is used as manure

compost

compound¹ *noun*
1 a substance that is made of two or more parts or ingredients 2 (*grammar*) a word that is made from two or more other words, such as *bathroom* and *newspaper*

compound² *noun*
a fenced area containing buildings

comprehend *verb*
to comprehend something is to understand it

comprehension *noun*
1 comprehension is understanding 2 a comprehension is an exercise that tests or helps your understanding of a language

comprehensive school *noun*
a secondary school for children of all abilities

compress *verb*
1 to compress something is to press it or squeeze it together 2 to be compressed is to be forced into a small space **compression** *noun* compression is pressing or squeezing something

comprise *verb*
to comprise several people or things is to include them • *A football team comprises eleven players.*

compromise *verb*
(say **kom**-pro-myz)
to compromise is to accept less than you really wanted, especially so as to settle a disagreement

compromise *noun*
(say **kom**-pro-myz) accepting less than you really wanted

compulsory *adjective*
something is compulsory when you have to do it • *Wearing seat belts is compulsory.*

computer *noun*
an electronic machine that does word processing and rapid calculations, sorts data, and can control other machines

comrade *noun*
a friend or companion

comradeship *noun*
enjoying other people's company, friendship

con *verb*
(**conning, conned**)
(*informal*) to con someone is to swindle them

concave *adjective*
a concave surface is curved

like the inside of a circle or ball. The opposite of convex.

conceal verb
to conceal something is to hide it carefully or cleverly **concealment** noun concealment is hiding something carefully

conceit noun
conceit is thinking a lot about how clever or attractive you are **conceited** adjective a conceited person thinks a lot of themselves and is vain and proud

conceive verb
1 to conceive an idea or plan is to form it in your mind 2 a woman conceives when she becomes pregnant

concentrate verb
1 to concentrate on something is to think hard about it 2 to concentrate people or things is to bring them together in one place

concentrated adjective
a liquid is concentrated when it is made stronger by having water removed from it

concentration noun
concentration is thinking hard about something

concept noun
a new idea about something

conception noun
1 conception is forming an idea in your mind 2 conception is also when a woman becomes pregnant

concern verb
1 to concern someone is to be important or interesting to them 2 to concern something is to be about a particular subject • This story concerns a shipwreck. 3 to worry someone

concern noun
1 something that matters to someone • I think that is my concern. 2 a business

concerning preposition
on the subject of; in connection with • Do you have any information concerning his disappearance?

concert noun
a performance of music

concertina noun
a portable musical instrument that you squeeze to push air past reeds

concerto noun (say kon-**cher**-toh)
a piece of music for a solo instrument and an orchestra • a violin concerto

concise adjective
giving a lot of information in a few words

conclude verb
1 to conclude something is to end it 2 to conclude something is also to

decide about it • The jury concluded that he was not guilty.

conclusion noun
1 the ending of something 2 a decision that you reach after a lot of thought

concrete noun
cement mixed with water and gravel or sand and used in building

concussion noun
a temporary injury to the brain that is caused by a hard knock and leaves you feeling dizzy or unconscious

condemn verb
1 to condemn someone or something is to say that you strongly disapprove of them 2 to condemn criminals is to sentence them to a punishment • He was condemned to death. 3 to condemn a building is to declare that it is not fit to be used **condemnation** noun condemnation is saying that you blame someone or something or do not approve of them

condensation noun
drops of liquid formed from vapour that has condensed

condense verb
1 to condense a piece of writing is to make it shorter 2 to condense is to change into water or other liquid • Steam condenses on cold windows.

condition noun
1 the state in which a person or thing is • This bike is in good condition. 2 something that must happen if something else is to happen • Learning to swim is a condition of going sailing. • You can come on condition that you bring your sister too.

conduct verb (say kon-**dukt**)
1 to conduct someone is to lead or guide them 2 to conduct something is to organize it or carry it out • I decided to conduct a little experiment. 3 to conduct an orchestra or band is to direct it in a piece of music 4 to conduct electricity or heat is to allow it to pass along • Copper conducts electricity well.

conduct noun (say **kon**-dukt)
a person's conduct is their behaviour

conduction noun
the conducting of electricity or heat

conductor noun
1 someone who conducts an orchestra or band 2 something that conducts electricity or heat 3 someone who collects the fares on a bus or coach

cone noun
1 an object which is circular at one

end and pointed at the other end 2 an ice cream cornet 3 the fruit of a pine, fir, or cedar

confectionery noun
sweets that a shop sells

conference noun
a meeting for discussion

confess verb
to confess to something wrong or embarrassing is to admit that you have done it

confession noun
an act of admitting that you have committed a crime or done wrong • The burglar made a full confession.

confetti plural noun
tiny bits of coloured paper thrown at the bride and bridegroom after a wedding

confide verb
to confide in someone is to tell them a secret

confidence noun
1 you have confidence when you are sure that you are right or can do something 2 confidence in someone is trusting or believing them **in confidence** as a secret • He told me all this in confidence.

confident adjective
1 being sure that you are right or can do something 2 certain that something will happen • We are confident it will be an enjoyable day.

confidential adjective
information is confidential when it has to be kept secret **confidentially** adverb in confidence, as a secret

confine verb
1 to confine something is to restrict or limit it • Please confine your comments to points of fact. 2 to confine someone is to lock them up or shut them in a place **confinement** noun confinement is being locked up or shut in

confirm verb
1 to confirm something is to say that it is true or to show that it is true 2 to confirm an arrangement is to make it definite • Please write to confirm your order.

confirmation noun
a fact or piece of information that shows something is true or has happened • You will receive confirmation of your booking by email.

confiscate verb
to confiscate something is to take it away from someone as a punishment **confiscation** noun confiscation is taking something from someone as a punishment

conflict noun (say kon-flikt)
a fight or disagreement • the conflict in the Middle East • a conflict between the unions and the bosses

conflict verb (say kon-**flikt**)
two things conflict when they contradict or disagree with one another • The two accounts of the incident conflict.

conform verb
to conform is to follow other people's rules or ideas about something

confront verb
1 to confront someone is to challenge them face to face for a fight or argument • The police decided to confront the criminals there and then. 2 to confront a problem or difficulty is to deal with it firmly and positively **confrontation** noun meeting someone face to face for a fight or argument

confuse verb
1 to confuse someone is to make them puzzled or muddled 2 to confuse things is to mistake one thing for another **confusing** adjective difficult to understand, muddling **confusion** noun confusion is being confused or muddled

congratulate verb
to congratulate someone is to tell them how pleased you are about something they have done **congratulations** plural noun congratulations are words that tell someone how well they have done

congregation noun
the people who take part in a church service

congress noun
a large meeting or conference

Congress the parliament or government of the USA

conical adjective
shaped like a cone

conifer noun (say **kon**-i-fer)
an evergreen tree with cones **coniferous** adjective a coniferous tree has cones

conjunction noun
a word that joins other words and parts of a sentence, e.g. and, but, and whether

conjure verb
to conjure is to perform tricks that look like magic **conjurer** noun someone who performs magic tricks

conker noun
a hard and shiny brown nut that grows on

conkers

a horse chestnut tree **conkers** a game played with conkers threaded on pieces of string

connect verb
to connect things is to join them together

connection noun
1 a link between things 2 joining together

conquer verb
to conquer a people or country is to defeat them and take them over • William I conquered England. • He managed to conquer all his fears. **conqueror** noun someone who conquers a country and takes it over

conquest noun
a victory over another country or people

conscience noun (say **kon**-shens)
a feeling people have about what is right or wrong

conscientious adjective
(say kon-shee-**en**-shus) careful and hard-working **conscientiously** adverb

conscious adjective (say **kon**-shus)
1 awake and knowing what is happening 2 aware of something • Are you conscious of the danger you are in? 3 deliberate • She has made a conscious effort to improve. **consciously** adverb **consciousness** noun being aware of what is happening

conscription noun
conscription is a system of making young people join the army for a time

consecutive adjective
things are consecutive when they come one after another in a list or sequence

consent noun
consent is agreement or permission

consent verb
to consent to something is to agree to it or permit it

consequence noun
something which happens because of an event or action • His injury was the consequence of an accident. of no consequence not very important to take or suffer the consequences is to accept any unpleasant results from something you do **consequently** adverb as a result

conservation noun
conservation is keeping buildings and natural surroundings in a good state **conservationist**

noun someone who takes an interest in conservation

Conservative noun
someone who supports the Conservative Party, a British political party

conservative adjective
1 a conservative person doesn't like change and wants things to stay the same 2 a conservative estimate or guess is a careful or cautious one

conservatory noun (**conservatories**)
a room built on the back or side of a house, with glass walls and a glass roof

conserve verb
to conserve something is to keep it from being changed or spoilt

consider verb
1 to consider something is to think carefully about it 2 to consider something is also to believe it • We consider that people should be allowed to follow their own religion.

considerable adjective
large or important • The journey takes a considerable time. **considerably** adverb very much • Her new house is considerably larger.

considerate adjective
kind and thoughtful towards other people

consideration noun
1 consideration is careful thought or attention 2 a consideration is a serious thought or reason • Money is a major consideration in this plan. to take something into consideration is to think carefully about it when you are making a decision

considering preposition
in view of • The car goes well, considering its age.

consist verb
to consist of something is to be made from it • The meal consisted of pasta and cheese.

consistency noun (**consistencies**)
1 consistency is being the same 2 the consistency of a liquid is how thick it is

consistent adjective
1 always the same, regular 2 always acting in the same way **consistently** adverb in the same way, without changing • He consistently misspells 'accommodation'.

consolation noun
consolation is comfort or sympathy given to someone

console verb
to console someone is to give them comfort or sympathy

consonant noun
a letter that is not a vowel. The consonants in the English alphabet are b, c, d, f, g, h, j, k, l, m, n, p, q, r, s, t, v, w, x, y, z.

conspicuous adjective
something conspicuous stands out and is easy to see or notice

conspiracy noun (**conspiracies**)
a plot to do something bad or illegal **conspirator** noun someone who joins a conspiracy

constant adjective
1 not changing; continual **2** a constant person is loyal and faithful

constant noun
(in science and mathematics) a number or quantity that does not change **constancy** noun constancy is beng loyal and faithful **constantly** adverb continually, all the time • They are constantly complaining.

constellation noun
a group of stars that you can see in the sky at night

constellation

constipated adjective
someone is constipated when they cannot empty their bowels easily to get rid of the waste in their body **constipation** noun being constipated

constituency noun
(**constituencies**)
a district of the country that chooses its own Member of Parliament

constitute verb
to constitute something is to form it or make it up • 50 states constitute the USA.

constitution noun
1 the set of principles or laws by which a country is governed
2 a person's condition or state of health **constitutional** adjective to do with a constitution

construct verb
to construct something is to build it

construction noun
1 construction is the process

of building **2** a construction is something that someone has built

constructive adjective
helpful and positive • Their criticism was very constructive.

consult verb
to consult a person or book is to look for information or advice **consultation** noun a meeting with someone for information or advice

consultant noun
1 a person who provides professional advice **2** a senior hospital doctor

consume verb
1 to consume food or drink is to eat or drink it **2** to consume something is to use it up or destroy it • The building was consumed by fire.

consumer noun
someone who buys goods or services

consumption noun
the using up of food or fuel • The consumption of oil has increased.

contact noun
1 contact is touching someone or something **2** contact is also communication • I've lost contact with my uncle. **3** a contact is a person to communicate with
contact verb
to contact someone is to get in touch with them

contact lens noun
a small plastic lens worn against the eyeball instead of glasses

contagious adjective
(say kon-**tay**-jus)
you catch a contagious disease by having contact with people or things that are already infected with it

contain verb
to contain something is to have it inside • This book contains a great deal of information.

container noun
1 something that is designed to contain things **2** a large box-shaped container for taking goods abroad by sea

contaminate verb
to contaminate something is to make it dirty or impure **contamination** noun making something dirty or impure

contemplate verb
1 to contemplate something is to look hard at it or think about it **2** to contemplate doing something is to plan or intend to do it **contemplation** noun thinking hard and seriously about something

contemporary adjective
1 people or things are contemporary

when they belong to the same time • Florence Nightingale was contemporary with Queen Victoria. **2** modern or up to date • The shop sells contemporary furniture.

contempt noun
a feeling of strong disapproval when you despise someone or something **contemptible** adjective deserving contempt **contemptuous** adjective showing or feeling contempt

contend verb
1 to contend is to struggle or compete **2** to contend something is to state or claim it • We contend that the company was guilty of negligence. **contender** noun someone who takes part in a competition

content[1] noun (say **kon**-tent)
1 the amount of a substance that there is in something • Drink milk with a low fat content. **2** the content of a book, magazine, or piece of writing is what you read in it

content[2] adjective (say kon-**tent**)
happy and willing • Are you content to stay behind? **contentment** noun contentment is being happy

contented adjective (say kon-**tent**-id)
happy and satisfied • After his big dinner he looked very contented.

contents plural noun
(say **kon**-tents)
1 the contents of a box or other container are what is inside it **2** the contents of a book or magazine are the things you read in it

contest noun (say **kon**-test)
a competition
contest verb (say kon-**test**)
to contest something is to argue about it • After her death, relatives contested her will.

contestant noun (say kon-**test**-ant)
someone who takes part in a contest or competition

continent noun
one of the main masses of land in the world. The continents are Africa, Antarctica, Asia, Australia, Europe, North America, and South America. **the Continent** the mainland of Europe from the point of view of people living in Britain

continual adjective
happening repeatedly • I get fed up with his continual shouting. **continually** adverb repeatedly, often

continue verb
to continue something, or to continue to do something, is to go

on doing it **continuation** noun
continuing something

continuous adjective
going on all the time; without a break
• *We could hear a continuous hum
from the fridge.* **continuity** noun
the process of going on without any
breaks or changes **continuously**
adverb all the time

contour noun
1 the contour of something is its
shape or outline **2** a line on a map
joining points that are the same
height above sea level

contract noun (say kon-trakt)
a written legal agreement
contract verb (say kon-**trakt**)
1 to contract is to become smaller
• *Heated metal contracts as it cools.*
2 to contract to do something is to
make a contract about it
3 to contract an illness is to catch
it • *She contracted pneumonia.*
contraction noun contraction
is getting smaller or shorter

contradict verb
to contradict someone or something
is to say they are wrong or untrue
contradiction noun saying that
someone or something is wrong or
untrue **contradictory** adjective a
contradictory statement says
the opposite of what someone has
just said

contraption noun
a clumsy or strange-looking device
or machine

contrary adjective
1 (say **kon**-tra-ri) one thing is
contrary to another when they are
opposites or contradict one another
• *Contrary to popular belief, Viking
helmets didn't have horns.* **2** (say
kon-**trair**-i) someone who is contrary
is obstinate and difficult to deal with
• *Mary, Mary, quite contrary.* **on the
contrary** the opposite is true • *Are
you pleased? On the contrary, I'm
very annoyed.*

contrast verb (say kon-**trahst**)
1 to contrast two things is to show
they are different **2** one thing
contrasts with another when it is
clearly different
contrast noun (say **kon**-trahst)
a clear difference between things

contribute verb
1 to contribute to something is to
give money to help it **2** to contribute
to a result is to help cause it • *His
tiredness contributed to the accident.*
contribution noun money or
help that someone gives towards
something **contributor** noun
someone who gives money or help

control noun
1 control is the power to make
someone or something do what you
want **2** the controls of a machine are
the switches and levers that make
it work **to be in control** is to have
power or control over people or things
control verb (**controlling,
controlled**)
to control something or someone
is to have power over what they do
controller noun someone who
controls or organizes something

controversial adjective
a controversial action or statement
is one that is likely to cause people
to have strong opinions and disagree
about it

controversy noun (**controversies**)
(say kon-**tro**-ver-si or
say **kon**-trov-er-si)
a long argument or disagreement

conundrum noun
a riddle

convalescent adjective
recovering from an illness
convalescence noun a period
of recovery after an illness

convenience noun
1 convenience is usefulness
and comfort **2** a convenience is
something that is useful, such as
central heating **3** a convenience
is also a public lavatory **to do
something at your convenience** is
to do it when it suits you

convenient adjective
easy to use or reach **conveniently**
adverb in a convenient way

convent noun
a group of buildings where nuns live
and work

conventional adjective
done in the accepted way; usual,
traditional **conventionally** adverb
in a conventional way, traditionally

converge verb
to converge is to come together from
different directions • *The two roads
converge at the pub.* • *Thousands
of fans converged on the football
ground.*

conversation noun
when you talk to someone for a while
conversational adjective to do
with conversation, like conversation
• *Use a conversational style of writing.*

conversion noun
changing or converting something

convert verb (say kon-**vert**)
1 to convert something is to change it
so it is suitable for a new purpose **2** to
convert someone is to persuade them

to change their religion or beliefs
convert noun (say **kon**-vert)
someone who has changed their
beliefs **convertible** adjective
something is convertible when it can
be changed from one form or shape
to another

convex adjective
a convex surface is curved like
the outside of a circle or ball. The
opposite of concave.

convey verb
1 to convey someone or something is
to take them somewhere **2** to convey
a message or idea is to get someone
to understand it

convict noun (say **kon**-vikt)
a criminal in a prison
convict verb (say kon-**vikt**)
to convict someone of a crime is to
decide at their trial that they are
guilty of it and punish them

conviction noun
1 being convicted of a crime **2** being
convinced of something; a strong
opinion

convince verb
to persuade someone that something
is true or right

convoy noun
a group of ships or vehicles travelling
together

cook verb
to cook food is to make it ready to
eat by heating it
cook noun
someone who cooks, especially as
their job

cooker noun
a device with an oven and hotplates
for cooking food

cookery noun
the art or skill of cooking food

cool adjective
1 not very warm; fairly cold
2 a cool person is calm and not
easily excited **3** (*informal*) good or
fashionable • *He looks cool in those
glasses.* **coolly** adverb calmly
coolness noun
cool verb
1 to cool something is to make it cool
2 to cool is to become cool

coop noun
a cage for poultry

cooperate verb
to cooperate with people is to work
helpfully with them **cooperation**
noun when people work together
and help one another **cooperative**
adjective someone who is cooperative
is helpful and willing to do what
people ask them

coordinate verb (say koh-**or**-din-ayt) to coordinate people or things is to get them to work well together **coordination** noun the coordination of parts of your body, for example your hands and eyes, is making them help each other and work well together

cop verb (**copping, copped**) (informal) to cop something is to get or catch it, especially when you don't want it • Her brother copped most of the blame. to cop it is to get into trouble

cop noun (informal) a police officer

cope verb to cope with something awkward or difficult is to deal with it successfully

copper noun 1 copper is a reddish-brown metal used for making wire and pipes 2 a copper is a coin made of copper or bronze

copy noun (**copies**) 1 something made to look exactly like something else 2 something written out a second time 3 one example of a newspaper, magazine, or book that is made in large numbers • We each have a copy of 'Alice in Wonderland'.

copy verb (**copies, copying, copied**) 1 to copy something is to make a copy of it 2 to copy someone is to do the same as them 3 to copy a computer file or piece of text is to make another one exactly the same **copier** noun a machine for copying pages

coral noun coral is a hard substance made of the skeletons of tiny sea creatures

cord noun a cord is a piece of thin rope

cordial noun a sweet drink

corduroy noun (say **kor**-der-oi) thick cotton cloth with ridges along it

core noun the part in the middle of something

cork noun 1 cork is the lightweight bark of a kind of oak tree 2 a cork is a piece of this bark used to close a bottle

corkscrew noun 1 a device for removing corks from bottles 2 a spiral

cormorant noun a large black seabird

corn[1] noun grain • a field of corn

corn[2] noun a small, hard lump on your toe or foot

corner noun 1 the point where two lines, roads, or walls meet 2 a kick from the corner of a football field; a hit from the corner of a hockey field

corner verb 1 to corner someone is to trap them • The police cornered the escaped prisoner. 2 to corner is to go round a corner • The car cornered slowly and accelerated up the road.

cornet noun 1 a long cone-shaped biscuit open at the top for ice cream 2 a musical instrument like a trumpet

cornflakes plural noun toasted maize flakes eaten for breakfast

cornflour noun fine flour used for making puddings

corny adjective (**cornier, corniest**) (informal) a corny joke is one that is feeble and often repeated

coronation noun the ceremony of crowning a king or queen

coroner noun an official who holds an inquiry into the cause of an unnatural death

corporal noun a soldier just below sergeant in rank

corporation noun a group of people elected to govern a town

corps noun (say kor) 1 a large unit of soldiers 2 a special army unit • He is in the Medical Corps.

corpse noun a dead body

correct adjective 1 true or accurate; without any mistakes • Your answers are all correct. 2 proper, suitable • Is that the correct way to talk to your parents? **correctly** adverb to do something correctly is to do it the right way and without any mistakes

correct verb to correct a piece of work is to mark the mistakes in it, or to put them right

correction noun 1 correction is correcting something

coral

2 a correction is a change made to something in order to make it right

correspond verb 1 to correspond with something is to agree with it or match it • Your story corresponds with what I heard. 2 to correspond with someone is to exchange letters with them

correspondence noun 1 similarity or agreement 2 letters or writing letters

correspondent noun 1 someone who writes letters 2 a journalist who sends reports to a newspaper or TV or radio station • Julie is our Moscow correspondent.

corridor noun a long narrow passage from which doors open into rooms or compartments

corrode verb to corrode is to wear away by rust or chemical action **corrosion** noun corrosion is the process of corroding **corrosive** adjective a corrosive substance is likely to corrode

corrugated adjective shaped into folds or ridges • The roof was made of corrugated iron.

corrupt adjective a corrupt person is dishonest in carrying out their responsibilities or duties, for example by taking bribes

corrupt verb to corrupt someone is to make them dishonest, especially when they have important responsibilities

corruption noun corruption is dishonest behaviour by people who are in authority or have important responsibilities

cosmetics plural noun substances like lipstick and face powder, for making the skin or hair look attractive

cosmic adjective (say **koz**-mik) to do with the universe

cost verb to cost a certain amount is to have that amount as its price • The book only cost £5 last year.

cost noun what you have to spend to do or get something **at all costs** or **at any cost** no matter what the cost or difficulty may be

costly adjective (**costlier, costliest**) expensive

costume noun clothes, especially for a particular purpose or of a particular period

cosy *adjective* (**cosier, cosiest**)
warm and comfortable

cot *noun*
a baby's bed with high sides

cottage *noun*
a small house, especially in
the country

cottage cheese *noun*
soft white cheese made from
skimmed milk

cotton *noun*
1 a soft white substance covering
the seeds of a tropical plant 2 thread
made from this substance 3 cloth
made from cotton thread

couch *noun*
a long soft seat or sofa

cough *verb* (*say* kof)
to cough is to push air suddenly out
of your lungs with a harsh noise

cough *noun*
1 the action or sound of coughing 2 an
illness which makes you cough a lot

could
past tense of **can**[1]

council *noun*
a group of people chosen to organize
or discuss something, especially to
plan the affairs of a town

councillor *noun*
a member of a council

counsellor *noun*
someone who gives advice, especially
as their job

count[1] *verb*
1 to count is to use numbers to
find out how many people or things
there are in a place 2 to count or
count out is to say numbers in their
proper order 3 to count someone
or something is to include them in
a total • *There are 30 in the class,
counting the teacher.* 4 to count is to
have a particular value or
importance • *Playing well counts
a lot even if you lose.* to count on
someone or something is to rely on
them

count[1] *noun*
1 the total reached by counting
2 one of the things that someone is
accused of • *He was found guilty on
all counts.*

count[2] *noun*
a foreign nobleman

countdown *noun*
a counting down to 0, especially
before launching a rocket

counter *noun*
1 a long table where customers are
served in a shop or cafe 2 a small
plastic disc used in board games

counterfeit *adjective*
(*say* **kown**-ter-fit)
made as a copy of something real,
to deceive or swindle people • *They
were using counterfeit money.*

countess *noun*
the wife or widow of a count or earl; a
female earl

countless *adjective*
too many to count; very many

country *noun* (**countries**)
1 a country is a part of the world
where a particular nation of people
lives 2 the country is the countryside
• *I wish we lived in the country.*

countryside *noun*
an area with fields, woods, and
villages, away from towns

county *noun* (**counties**)
one of the areas that a country is
divided into, for example Kent in
England, Fife in Scotland, and Powys
in Wales

couple *noun*
a couple is two people or things

couple *verb*
to couple things is to join them
together

coupling *noun*
a link or fastening, especially for
vehicles

coupon *noun*
a piece of paper that gives you the
right to receive or do something

courage *noun*
the ability to be brave and overcome
your fear

courageous *adjective*
ready to face danger or pain

courgette *noun*
a kind of vegetable like a small
marrow

course *noun*
1 the direction in which something
moves along • *The ship's course was
to the west.* 2 a series of lessons or
exercises in learning something • *My
Mum's starting a cookery course at last.*
3 a part of a meal, such as the meat
course or the pudding course
4 a racecourse or golf course of course
naturally; certainly • *Of course they will
help us* . • *'Will you help us?' 'Of course!'*

court *noun*
1 a place where legal trials take
place; a lawcourt 2 an area marked
out for ball games like tennis or
netball 3 the place where a king or
queen lives 4 the people who are
usually at a king's or queen's court

court *verb*
to court someone is to try to win their
love or support

courteous *adjective* (*say* **ker**-ti-us)
friendly and polite towards other
people **courteously** *adverb*
courtesy *noun* courtesy is polite
behaviour towards other people

court martial *noun*
a trial of a soldier who is accused of
breaking a military law

courtship *noun*
courting someone, especially
a boyfriend or girlfriend

courtyard *noun*
a paved area surrounded by walls or
buildings

cousin *noun*
a son or daughter of your uncle or aunt

cove *noun*
a small bay

cover *verb*
1 to cover something is to put
something else over it to hide or protect
it 2 to cover a distance is to travel over it
• *We managed to cover ten miles a day.*
3 to cover a subject is to deal with it or
include it • *This book covers everything
you need to know about dinosaurs.* 4 to
cover something is to be enough money
for it • *I expect £2 will cover my fare.* to
cover something up is to make sure
no one knows about something wrong
or illegal

cover *noun*
1 a cover is something used for
covering something else; a lid or
wrapper 2 cover is a place where
someone can hide or take shelter

coverage *noun*
the amount of time or space given
to reporting an event on radio, or
broadcast in a newspaper

cow *noun*
a large female animal kept by
farmers for its milk and beef

coward *noun*
someone who has no courage
and runs away from danger and
difficulties **cowardice** *noun* being
a coward **cowardly** *adjective*
behaving like a coward

cowboy *noun*
a man who rides round looking after
the cattle on a large farm in America

coy *adjective*
pretending to be shy or modest
coyly *adverb*

crab *noun*   crab
a shellfish
with a
pair of
pincers
and four
pairs of
legs

crack *noun*
1 a line on the surface of something where it has broken but not come completely apart; a narrow gap • *There's a crack in this cup.* 2 a sudden sharp noise • *They heard the crack of a pistol shot.* 3 a sudden sharp blow • *He got a crack on the head.*

crack *verb*
1 to crack something is to make a crack in it 2 something cracks when it splits without breaking • *The plate has cracked.* 3 to crack is to make a sudden sharp noise 4 to crack a joke is to tell it

cracker *noun*
1 a decorated paper tube with a small gift inside it, which bangs when two people pull it apart 2 a thin crisp biscuit

crackle *verb*
to crackle is to make small cracking sounds, like a fire

cradle *noun*
a cot for a baby

craft *noun*
1 a craft is an activity which needs skill with the hands 2 a boat

craftsman or **craftswoman** *noun* (**craftsmen** or **craftswomen**)
someone who is skilled at making things with the hands **craftsmanship** *noun* the skill of a craftsman or craftswoman

crafty *adjective* (**craftier, craftiest**)
cunning and clever **craftily** *adverb* **craftiness** *noun*

crag *noun*
a steep piece of rough rock **craggy** *adjective* steep and rocky

cram *verb* (**cramming, crammed**)
1 to cram things is to force them into a small space 2 to cram is to study very hard for an examination

cramp *noun*
pain caused by a muscle tightening suddenly

cramped *adjective*
in a space that is too small or tight • *We felt very cramped sleeping three in the same room.*

crane *noun*
1 a machine for lifting and moving heavy objects 2 a large bird with long legs and neck

crane *verb*
to crane your neck is to stretch it so that you can see something

crane

crane-fly *oun* (**crane-flies**)
an insect with long thin legs

crank *noun*
1 an L-shaped rod used to turn or control something 2 a person with weird or unusual ideas

crank *verb*
to crank something like an engine is to turn it by using an L-shaped rod

cranny *noun* (**crannies**)
a crevice; a narrow hole or space

crash *noun*
1 the loud noise of something falling or breaking 2 a collision between road vehicles, causing damage

crash *verb*
1 to crash is to collide or fall violently 2 to crash a vehicle is to have a crash while driving it

crash helmet *noun*
a padded helmet worn by cyclists and motorcyclists

crate *noun*
a container in which goods are transported

crater *noun*
1 the mouth of a volcano 2 a hole in the ground made by a bomb

crave *verb*
to crave something is to want it very badly

crawl *verb*
1 to crawl is to move along on your hands and knees 2 to crawl is also to move slowly in a vehicle 3 to be crawling with something unpleasant is to be full of it or covered in it • *This room's crawling with cockroaches.*

crawl *noun*
1 a crawling movement 2 a powerful swimming stroke in which you bring each arm over your head in turn

crayon *noun*
a coloured pencil for drawing or writing

craze *noun*
a brief enthusiasm or fashion for something

crazy *adjective* (**crazier, craziest**)
mad or weird **crazily** *adverb* **craziness** *noun*

creak *noun*
a sound like the noise made by a stiff door opening

creak *verb*
to make a creak **creaky** *adjective* old and creaking

cream *noun*
1 the rich fatty part of milk 2 yellowish-white colour 3 a food containing or looking like cream 4 something that looks like cream, for example face cream **creamy** *adjective* smooth and thick like cream

crease *noun*
1 a line made in something by folding or pressing it 2 a line on a cricket pitch showing where the batsman should stand

crease *verb*
to crease something is to make a crease in it

create *verb*
to create something is to make it exist **creation** *noun* creating something **creator** *noun* someone who creates something

creative *adjective*
showing imagination and thought as well as skill • *The older children have started some creative writing.* **creativity** *noun* the ability to use the imagination to create things

creature *noun*
a living animal or person

crèche *noun* (*say* kresh)
a place where babies or small children are looked after while their parents are busy

credible *adjective*
able to be believed; trustworthy **credibility** *noun* being credible **credibly** *adverb* in a credible way

credit *noun*
1 honour or approval • *You have to give her credit for trying.* 2 someone who brings honour or approval • *He is a credit to his family.* 3 a system of allowing someone to pay for something later on • *Do you want cash now or can I have it on credit?* 4 an amount of money in an account at a bank or building society **credits** the list of people who have helped to produce a film, television programme, etc.

credit card *noun*
a card allowing someone to buy goods and pay for them later

creep *verb* (**creeping, crept**)
1 to creep is to move along with the body close to the ground 2 to creep about is to move quietly or secretly **to creep up on someone** is to go up to them quietly from behind

creeper *noun*
a plant that grows close to the ground or up walls

creepy *adjective* (**creepier, creepiest**)
(*informal*) weird and slightly frightening

cremate *verb*
to cremate a dead body is to burn it into fine ashes instead of burying it **cremation** *noun* the cremating of a dead body

crematorium *noun* (**crematoria**)
(*say* krem-a-**tor**-i-um)
a place where dead bodies are cremated

crêpe *noun* (*say* krayp)
1 cloth or paper with a wrinkled surface **2** a kind of thin French pancake

crescent *noun*
1 a narrow curved shape, pointed at both ends, like a new moon **2** a curved street

cress *noun*
a green plant used in salads and sandwiches

crest *noun*
1 a tuft of hair, feathers, or skin on an animal's head **2** the top of a hill or wave **3** a badge or emblem

crevasse *noun*
a deep crack in a glacier

crevice *noun*
a crack in rock or in a wall

crew *noun*
the people who work on a ship or aircraft

crib *noun*
1 a baby's cot **2** a framework containing fodder for animals **3** something copied

crib *verb* (**cribbing, cribbed**)
to crib someone else's work is to copy it

cricket¹ *noun*
a game played outdoors by two teams with a ball, two bats, and two wickets **cricketer** *noun* someone who plays cricket

cricket² *noun*
an insect like a grasshopper

cricket

crime *noun*
an act that breaks the law

criminal *noun*
someone who has committed one or more crimes

criminal *adjective*
to do with crime or criminals

crimson *noun, adjective*
a dark red colour

crinkle *verb*
to crinkle something is to crease or wrinkle it **crinkly** *adjective* full of creases, wrinkled

cripple *verb*
to cripple someone is to make them unable to walk properly

crisis *noun* (**crises**) (*say* **kry**-sis)
a difficult or dangerous time or situation

crisp *adjective*
1 very dry so that it breaks easily **2** firm and fresh • *I'd like a nice crisp apple.* **3** cold and frosty • *We woke up to a crisp winter morning.*

crisp *noun*
a thin fried slice of potato, sold in packets

criss-cross *adjective, adverb*
with crossing lines

critic *noun*
1 a person who criticizes someone or something **2** someone who gives opinions on books, plays, films, music, or other performances

critical *adjective*
1 criticizing **2** to do with critics or criticism **3** serious, reaching a crisis **critically** *adverb* in a critical way; seriously

criticism *noun* (*say* **krit**-i-**si**-zum)
an opinion or judgement about something, usually pointing out its faults

criticize *verb* (*say* **krit**-i-syz)
to criticize something or someone is to give an opinion pointing out their faults

croak *noun*
a deep sound, like a frog makes

croak *verb*
to make a croak

crochet *noun*
(*say* **kroh**-shay) a kind of needlework done with a hooked needle

crockery *noun*
dishes, plates, and cups and saucers used for eating

crocodile *noun*
a large reptile living in hot countries, with a thick skin, long tail, and huge jaws

croissant *noun* (*say* **krwa**-sahn)
a crescent-shaped roll of rich pastry, first made in France and usually eaten for breakfast

crook *noun*
1 (*informal*) someone who cheats or robs people; a criminal **2** a shepherd's or bishop's stick with a curved end

crook *verb*
to crook something is to bend it into a hook shape

crooked *adjective* (*say* **kruuk**-id)
1 bent or twisted **2** (*informal*) dishonest or criminal

crop *noun*
1 something grown for food, especially in a field • *They had a good crop of wheat last year.* **2** a riding whip with a loop instead of a lash

crop *verb* (**cropping, cropped**)
to crop something is to cut or bite the top off it • *They could see sheep in a field, cropping the grass.* **to crop up** is to happen or appear unexpectedly

cross *noun*
1 a mark or shape like + or x **2** an upright post with another post across it, used in ancient times for crucifixions **3** an animal produced by mixing one breed with another • *A mule is a cross between a donkey and a horse.* **the Cross** the cross on which Christ was crucified, used as a symbol of Christianity

cross *verb*
1 to cross something is to go across it • *She crossed the road to meet him.* • *A bit further on the road crossed a river.* **2** to cross your fingers or legs is to put one over the other **to cross something out** is to draw a line across something because it is unwanted or wrong

cross *adjective*
angry or bad-tempered **crossly** *adverb* angrily **crossness** *noun* being cross

crossbar *noun*
a horizontal bar between two upright bars

crossbow *noun*
a kind of bow used for shooting arrows, held like a gun and fired by pulling a trigger

cross-country *noun*
a running race through fields and country

crossing *noun*
a place where people can cross a road or railway

crossroads *noun*
a place where two or more roads cross one another

cross-section *noun*
a drawing of something as if it has been cut through

crossword *noun*
a puzzle with blank squares in which you put the letters of words worked out from clues

crotchet *noun* (*say* **kroch**-it)
a musical note equal to half a minim, written ♩

crouch *verb*
to crouch is to lower your body, with your arms and legs bent

crow *noun*
a large black bird

crow *verb*
1 to make a noise like a cock **2** to boast; to be proudly triumphant

crowbar *noun*
an iron bar used as a lever

crowd *noun*
a large number of people in one place

crowd *verb*
to crowd or crowd round is to form a crowd

crow

crowded *adjective*
having too many people or things • *The bus was a bit crowded, but we got on.*

crown *noun*
1 a crown is an ornamental headdress worn by a king or queen **2** the crown is the king or queen of a country • *This land belongs to the crown.* **3** the top of something, such as a hill or a person's head

crown

crown *verb*
1 to crown someone is to make them king or queen **2** to crown something is to form the top of it

crucial *adjective* (*say* **kroo**-shal)
extremely important

crucifix *noun*
a model of Christ on the Cross

crucify *verb* (**crucifies, crucifying, crucified**)
to crucify someone is to execute them by fixing their hands and feet to a cross and leaving them to die. The Romans used this method of executing criminals. **crucifixion** *noun* the execution of someone by crucifying them

crude *adjective*
1 natural; not purified • *The country exported crude oil.* **2** rough and simple • *They stayed in a crude hut in the mountains.* **3** rude

or dirty • *The boys were telling each other crude jokes.*

cruel *adjective* (**crueller, cruellest**)
causing pain and suffering to others • *They were ruled by a cruel tyrant.* **cruelly** *adverb* **cruelty** *noun* cruel acts or treatment

cruise *noun*
a holiday on a ship, usually visiting different places

cruise *verb*
1 to cruise is to sail or travel at a gentle speed **2** to cruise is also to have a cruise on a ship

crumb *noun*
a tiny piece of bread or cake

crumble *verb*
1 to crumble something is to break it into small pieces **2** to crumble is to be broken into small pieces • *The cliff was slowly crumbling into the sea.* **crumbly** *adjective* soft and likely to crumble

crumpet *noun*
a soft flat cake made with yeast, toasted and eaten with butter

crumple *verb*
1 to crumple something is to make it creased **2** to crumple is to become creased

crunch *noun*
the noise made by chewing hard food or walking on gravel

crunch *verb*
to crunch something is to chew or crush it with a crunch

crunchy *adjective* making a crunching sound

crusade *noun*
1 a military expedition to Palestine made by Christians in the Middle Ages **2** a campaign against something that you think is bad **crusader** *noun* someone who takes part in a crusade

crush *verb*
1 to crush something is to press it so that it gets broken or damaged **2** to crush an enemy is to defeat them

crush *noun*
1 a crowd; a crowded place **2** a fruit-flavoured drink **3** (*informal*) a sudden liking you have for someone

crust *noun*
1 the hard outside part of something, especially of a loaf **2** the rocky outer part of a planet

crustacean *noun*
(*say* krus-**tay**-shan)
a shellfish

crutch *noun*
a stick that fits under the arm, used as a support in walking

cry *verb* (**cries, crying, cried**)
1 to cry is to shout **2** to cry is also to let tears fall from your eyes

cry *noun*
1 a loud shout **2** a period of weeping

crypt *noun*
a large room underneath a church

crystal *noun*
1 a clear mineral rather like glass **2** a small solid piece of a substance with a symmetrical shape, such as snow and ice

crystallize *verb*
to crystallize is to form into crystals

cub *noun*
a young animal, especially a lion, tiger, fox, or bear **Cub** a junior Scout

cube *noun*
1 an object that has six square sides, like a box or dice **2** the result of multiplying something by itself twice • *The cube of 3 is 3 x 3 x 3 = 27.*

cube *verb*
1 to cube a number is to multiply it by itself twice • *4 cubed is 4 x 4 x 4 = 64.* **2** to cube something is to cut it into small cubes

cube root *noun*
a number that gives another number if it is multiplied by itself twice • *2 is the cube root of 8.*

cubic *adjective*
a cubic metre or foot is the volume of a cube with sides that are one metre or foot long

cubicle *noun*
a small division of a room

cuckoo *noun*
a bird that makes a sound like 'cuck-oo', and lays its eggs in other birds' nests

cucumber *noun*
a long green vegetable, eaten raw

cud *noun*
half-digested food that a cow brings back from its first stomach to chew again

cuddle *verb*
to cuddle someone is to put your arms closely round them and squeeze them in a loving way **cuddly** *adjective* a cuddly person is nice to cuddle

cue[1] *noun*
a word or signal that tells an actor when to start speaking or come on the stage

cue[2] *noun*
a long stick used to strike the ball in billiards or snooker

cuff *noun*
the end of a sleeve that fits round your wrist

a b c d e f g h i j k l m n o p q r s t u v w x y z

cuff verb
to cuff someone is to hit them with the hand

cul-de-sac noun
a street that is closed at one end

culprit noun
someone who is to blame for something

cultivate verb
to cultivate land is to grow crops on it **cultivation** noun

culture noun
1 culture is the development of the mind by education and learning 2 a culture is the customs and traditions of a people • *They were studying Greek culture.* **cultural** adjective to do with culture **cultured** adjective well educated and knowledgeable

cunning adjective
clever at deceiving people

cup noun
1 a small container with a handle, from which you drink liquid 2 a prize in the form of a silver cup, usually with two handles

cup verb
(**cupping, cupped**)
to cup your hands is to form them into the shape of a cup

cup

cupboard noun (say **kub**-erd)
a compartment or piece of furniture with a door, for storing things

curator noun (say kewr-**ay**-ter)
someone in charge of a museum or art gallery

curb verb
to curb a feeling is to hold it back or hide it • *You must curb your anger.*

curd noun
a thick substance formed when milk turns sour

curdle verb
to curdle is to turn sour and form into curds

cure verb
1 to cure someone who is ill is to make them better 2 to cure something bad is to stop it 3 to cure food is to treat it so as to preserve it • *Fish can be cured in smoke.*

cure noun
something that cures a person or thing • *They are still trying to find a cure for cancer.*

curfew noun
a time or signal after which people must stay indoors until the next day

curiosity noun (**curiosities**)
1 curiosity is being curious 2 a curiosity is something strange or interesting

curious adjective
1 wanting to find out about things 2 strange or unusual **curiously** adverb

curl noun
a curve or coil, especially of hair

curl verb
to curl is to form into curls **to curl up** is to sit or lie with your knees drawn up

curly adjective
full of curls

currant noun
1 a small black fruit made from dried grapes 2 a small juicy berry, or the bush that produces it

currency noun (**currencies**)
the money that is in use in a country • *You can pay with Russian currency.*

current noun
1 a flow of water or air 2 a flow of electricity through a wire

current adjective
happening or used now **currently** adverb now, at the moment • *The admission charge is currently £10.*

curriculum noun
the subjects that you study in a school

curry noun (**curries**)
food cooked with spices that make it taste hot

curse noun
1 a call or prayer for someone to be harmed or killed 2 something very unpleasant 3 an angry word or words

curse verb
to curse someone is to use a curse against them

cursor noun
a flashing signal showing your position on a computer screen

curtain noun
a piece of material hung at a window or door, or at the front of a stage

curtsy noun (**curtsies**)
a bow made by bending the knees, done by women as a mark of respect

curtsy verb (**curtsies, curtsying, curtsied**)
to curtsy is to make a curtsy

curve noun
a line that bends smoothly

curve verb
to curve is to bend smoothly

cushion noun
a fabric cover filled with soft material

so that it is comfortable to sit on or rest against

custard noun
a sweet yellow sauce eaten with puddings

custom noun
1 the usual way of doing things • *It is the custom to go on holiday in the summer.* 2 regular business from customers • *That rude man at the corner shop won't get my custom any more.* **customs** are the group of officials at a port or airport whose job is to check what goods people are bringing into the country

customary adjective
something that is customary is usually done or done according to a custom

customer noun
someone who uses a shop, bank, or business

cut verb (**cutting, cut**)
1 to cut something is to divide it or make a slit in it with a knife or scissors 2 to cut something like prices or taxes is to reduce them 3 to cut a pack of playing cards is to divide it 4 to cut a corner is to go across it rather than round it **to cut someone off** is to interrupt them • *She cut me off before I could finish my sentence.* **to cut something out** (informal) is to stop doing it • *Cut out the talking!*

cut noun
1 an act of cutting; the result of cutting • *Your hair could do with a cut.* 2 a small wound caused by something sharp

cute adjective
(informal) attractive in a quaint or simple way

cutlass noun
a short sword with a wide curved blade

cutlery noun
knives, forks, and spoons used for eating

cutlet noun
a thick slice of meat still on the bone

cutlery

cut-out noun
a design or shape cut out of paper or cardboard

cutting noun
1 something cut from a newspaper or magazine 2 a piece cut off a plant to grow as a new plant 3 a deep passage cut through high ground for a railway or road

cycle noun
1 a bicycle 2 a series of events that are regularly repeated • *Rainfall is part of the water cycle.*

cycle verb
to cycle is to ride a bicycle **cyclist** noun someone who rides a bicycle

cyclone noun
a strong wind rotating round a calm central area

cygnet noun (say **sig**-nit)
a young swan

cylinder noun
1 an object with straight sides and circular ends 2 part of an engine in which a piston moves

cylindrical adjective
shaped like a cylinder

cymbal noun
a cymbal is a round, slightly hollowed metal plate that you hit to make a ringing sound in music

cymbals

cynical adjective (say **sin**-ik-al)
thinking that nothing is good or worthwhile **cynic** noun someone who doubts that anything is good or worthwhile **cynicism** noun being cynical

cypress noun
an evergreen tree with dark leaves

Dd

dab noun a gentle touch with something soft
dab verb (**dabbing, dabbed**)
to dab something is to touch it gently with something soft • *I dabbed my eyes with a handkerchief.*

dabble verb
1 to dabble something is to splash it about in water 2 to dabble in something is to do it as a hobby or not very seriously • *She likes to dabble in photography.*

dad or **daddy** noun (**daddies**)
(informal) father

daddy-long-legs noun
a crane-fly

daffodil noun
a yellow flower that grows from a bulb

daft adjective
silly or stupid

dagger noun
a pointed knife with two sharp edges, used as a weapon

daily adjective, adverb
happening every day

dainty adjective (**daintier, daintiest**)
small and delicate **daintily** adverb **daintiness** noun

dairy noun (**dairies**)
a place where milk, butter, cream, and cheese are made or sold

daisy noun (**daisies**)
a small flower with white petals and a yellow centre

dale noun
a valley

dam noun
a wall built across a river to hold the water back
dam verb (**damming, dammed**)
to dam a river is to build a dam across it

damage verb
to damage something is to injure or harm it
damage noun
damage is injury or harm • *The storm caused a lot of damage.*

damn verb
to damn something is to say it is bad or wrong

damp adjective
slightly wet; not quite dry
damp noun
wetness in the air or on something

dampen verb
1 to dampen something is to make it damp 2 to dampen sound or noise is to make it softer

dance verb
to dance is to move about in time to music
dance noun
1 a piece of music or set of movements for dancing 2 a party or gathering where people dance
dancer noun someone who dances

dandelion noun
a yellow wild flower with jagged leaves

WORD ORIGIN

The word **dandelion** comes from the French words *dent-de-lion* meaning 'lion's tooth', because of the leaves having a jagged shape.

dandruff noun
dandruff is small white flakes of dead skin in a person's hair

danger noun
something that is dangerous

dangerous adjective
likely to harm you

dangle verb
to dangle is to swing or hang down loosely

dappled adjective
marked with patches of different colours

dare verb
1 to dare to do something is to be brave or bold enough to do it 2 to dare someone to do something is to challenge them to do it • *I dare you to climb that tree.*
dare noun
(informal) a challenge to do something risky

daredevil noun
a person who enjoys doing dangerous things

daring adjective
bold or brave

dark adjective
1 with little or no light 2 deep and rich in colour • *She wore a dark green coat.*
dark noun
1 dark or the dark is when there is no light • *Cats can see in the dark.* 2 dark is also the time when it becomes dark just after sunset • *Be home before dark.* **darkness** noun
darkness is when there is no light

darken verb
1 to darken something is to make it dark 2 to darken is to become dark • *The sky suddenly darkened.*

darling noun
someone who is loved very much

darn verb
to darn a hole is to mend it by sewing across it

dart noun
an object with a sharp point that you throw at a target called a dartboard in the game of **darts**

dash noun
1 a quick rush or a hurry • *They made a dash for the door.* 2 a dash of something is a small amount of it 3 a short line (–) used in writing or printing
dash verb
1 to dash somewhere is to rush there 2 to dash something is to hurl it and smash it • *In her anger she dashed the cup against the wall.*

dancer

a b c d e f g h i j k l m n o p q r s t u v w x y z

dashboard *noun*
a panel with dials and controls in front of the driver of a car

data *noun* (*say* **day**-ta)
data is pieces of information

database *noun*
a store of information held in a computer

date¹ *noun*
1 the day of the month, or the year, when something happens or happened 2 an appointment to go out with someone

date¹ *verb*
1 to date something that happened is to give it a date 2 to date from a time is to have existed from then • *The church dates from the 15th century.* 3 to date is also to seem old-fashioned • *Some fashions date very quickly.*

date² *noun*
a sweet brown fruit that grows on a palm tree

daughter *noun*
a girl or woman who is someone's child

dawdle *verb*
to dawdle is to walk or do something too slowly

dawn *noun*
the time of the day when the sun rises

dawn *verb*
1 to dawn is to begin to become light in the morning 2 something dawns on you when you begin to realize it

day *noun*
1 the 24 hours between midnight and the next midnight 2 the light part of the day 3 a period in time • *Write about what it was like in Queen Victoria's day.*

daybreak *noun*
the first light of day; dawn

daydream *verb*
to daydream is to have pleasant thoughts about things you would like to happen

daylight *noun*
1 the light of day 2 dawn • *They left before daylight.*

daze *noun*
to be in a daze is to be unable to think or see clearly

dazed *adjective*
someone is dazed when they can't think or see clearly

dazzle *verb*
a light dazzles you when it shines so brightly in your eyes that you are blinded for a moment

dead *adjective*
1 no longer alive 2 no longer working or active • *The phone went dead.* 3 a dead place is not at all lively • *This town is dead at the weekend.*

deaden *verb*
to deaden pain or noise is to make it weaker

dead end *noun*
a road or passage that is closed at one end

dead heat *noun*
a race in which two or more winners finish exactly together

deadline *noun*
the time by which you must finish doing something

deadly *adjective* (**deadlier, deadliest**)
likely to kill • *The liquid in the glass was a deadly poison.*

deaf *adjective*
unable to hear **deafness** *noun* being deaf

deafen *verb*
to be deafening is to be very loud • *The noise from the party upstairs was deafening.*

deal *verb* (**dealing, dealt**)
1 to deal in something is to buy and sell it • *He deals in scrap metal.* 2 to deal playing cards is to give them to players in a card game **to deal with someone or something** is to spend time doing what needs to be done • *I'll deal with you later.* **to deal with something** is to be concerned with it • *This book deals with cacti.*

deal *noun*
1 an agreement or bargain 2 someone's turn to give out playing cards • *Whose deal is it?* **a good deal** or **a great deal** a large amount

dealer *noun*
1 someone who buys and sells things 2 the person dealing at cards

dear *adjective*
1 loved very much 2 you use dear as the usual way of beginning a letter • *Dear Mary* 3 expensive

death *noun*
dying; the end of life

debate *noun*
a formal discussion about a subject

debate *verb*
to debate is to discuss or argue about something

debris *noun* (*say* **deb**-ree)
debris is scattered pieces that are left after something has been destroyed

debt *noun* (*say* det)
something that someone owes **to be in debt** is to owe money

début *noun*
(*say* **day**-bew or *say* **day**-boo)
someone's first public appearance as a performer

decade *noun*
a period of ten years

decathlon *noun* (*say* dek-**ath**-lon)
an athletics competition in which you take part in ten different events

decay *verb*
to decay is to rot or go bad

decay *noun*
decay is going bad or rotting

deceased *adjective* (*say* di-**seest**)
a formal word for dead

deceit *noun* (*say* di-**seet**)
deceit is telling lies or doing something dishonest **deceitful** *adjective* someone who is deceitful tells lies or does something dishonest **deceitfully** *adverb*

deceive *verb* (*say* di-**seev**)
to deceive someone is to make them believe something that is not true

December *noun*
the last month of the year

decent *adjective*
1 respectable and honest 2 of good enough quality • *Was it a decent film?* **decency** *noun* respectable and honest behaviour **decently** *adverb* in a respectable and honest way

deception *noun*
1 deception is making someone believe something that is not true 2 a deception is a trick or a lie

deceptive *adjective*
not what it seems to be • *The sunshine was deceptive and the wind made it very cold.*

decibel *noun*
a unit for measuring how loud a sound is

decide *verb*
1 to decide something is to make up your mind about it or make a choice 2 to decide a contest or argument is to settle it

deciduous *adjective*
a deciduous tree loses its leaves in autumn

decimal *adjective*
a decimal system uses tens or tenths to count things

decimal *noun*
a fraction with tenths shown as numbers after a dot (¼ is 0.25; 1½ is 1.5)

decimal point *noun*
the dot in a decimal fraction

decipher *verb* (*say* di-**sy**-fer)
to decipher writing is to work out what it means when it is in code or difficult to read

decision *noun*
a decision is what someone has decided

decisive *adjective*
1 ending or deciding something important • *The decisive battle of the war was fought here.* **2** a decisive person decides things quickly and firmly **decisively** *adverb*

deck *noun*
a floor on a ship or bus

deckchair *noun*
a folding chair with a seat of canvas or plastic material

declaration *noun*
an official or public statement

deckchair

declare *verb*
1 to declare something is to say it clearly and openly **2** a cricket team declares when it ends its innings before all the batsmen are out **to declare war** is to announce a state of war with another country

decline *verb*
1 to decline is to become weaker or smaller **2** to decline an offer is to refuse it politely

decode *verb*
to decode something written in code is to work out its meaning

decompose *verb*
to decompose is to decay or rot **decomposition** *noun* when something decays or rots

decorate *verb*
1 to decorate something is to make it look more beautiful or colourful **2** to decorate a room or building is to put fresh paint or paper on the walls **decorative** *adjective* colourful and pretty

decoration *noun*
1 decorations are the paint, wallpaper, and ornaments that make a place look more attractive **2** decoration is making something look more attractive or colourful

decorator *noun*
a person whose job is to paint rooms and buildings and to put up wallpaper

decoy *noun* (*say* **dee**-koi or *say* **di**-koi)
something used to tempt a person or animal into a trap

decrease *verb* (*say* di-**kreess**)
1 to decrease something is to make it smaller or less **2** to decrease is to become smaller or less

decrease *noun* (*say* **dee**-kreess)
the amount by which something decreases

decree *noun*
an official order or decision

decree *verb*
to decree something is to give an official order that it must happen

decrepit *adjective* (*say* dik-**rep**-it)
old and weak

dedicate *verb*
1 to dedicate yourself or your life to something is to spend all your time doing it • *She dedicated her life to nursing.* **2** to dedicate a book to someone is to name them at the beginning, as a sign of friendship or thanks

dedication *noun*
1 dedication is hard work and effort **2** a dedication is a message at the beginning of a book in which you name someone as a sign of friendship or thanks

deduce *verb*
to deduce a fact or answer is to work it out from what you already know is true • *She deduced from my smile that I had won the prize.*

deduct *verb*
to deduct an amount is to subtract it from a total • *His Dad deducted 50 pence from his pocket money for breaking a window.*

deduction *noun*
1 something that you work out by reasoning **2** an amount taken away from a total

deed *noun*
1 something that someone has done **2** a legal document that shows who owns something

deep *adjective*
1 going down or back a long way from the top or front **2** measured from top to bottom or from front to back • *The hole was two metres deep.* **3** intense or strong • *The room was painted a deep blue.* **4** a deep voice is very low in pitch **deeply** *adverb* very, extremely • *She was deeply upset.*

deepen *verb*
to deepen is to become deeper • *The pool deepened to 2 metres half way along.*

deer *noun*
a fast-running, graceful animal. The male has antlers.

deface *verb*
to deface something is to spoil its appearance by writing or drawing on it

defeat *verb*
to defeat someone is to beat them in a game or battle

defeat *noun*
1 defeat is losing a game or battle **2** a defeat is a lost game or battle

defect *noun* (*say* **dee**-fekt)
a flaw or weakness

defect *verb* (*say* di-**fekt**)
to defect is to desert a country or cause and join the other side **defection** *noun* when someone deserts a country or cause and joins the other side **defector** *noun* someone who defects

defective *adjective*
something is defective when it has flaws or faults or doesn't work properly

defence *noun*
1 something that protects you • *High walls were built around the city as a defence against enemy attacks.* **2** protecting yourself or a place from an attack or from criticism • *In her defence, she thought she was acting for the best.* **3** the players whose job is to stop the other team scoring in football and other games **defenceless** *adjective* someone who is defenceless can't protect themselves

defend *verb*
1 to defend someone or something is to protect them from an attack **2** to defend an idea, belief, or person is to argue in support of them **3** to defend an accused person is to try to prove that they are innocent **defender** *noun* someone who defends something

defendant *noun*
a person accused of something in a lawcourt

defensive *adjective*
1 used to defend something • *We need to take defensive measures.* **2** a defensive person is anxious about being criticized

defer *verb* (**deferring, deferred**)
to defer something is to put it off until later • *She deferred her departure until Saturday.*

defiant *adjective*
openly showing that you refuse to obey someone **defiance** *noun* when you openly show that you refuse to obey someone **defiantly** *adverb*

deficiency *noun* (**deficiencies**)
a lack or shortage **deficient** *adjective* to be deficient in something is not to have enough of it

define *verb*
1 to define a word is to explain what it means **2** to define an idea or problem is to show exactly what it is

definite *adjective*
fixed or certain • *Is it definite that we are going to move?*

definite article *noun*
the word **the**

definitely *adverb, exclamation*
certainly, without doubt • *We are definitely going to the party.*

definition *noun*
an explanation of what a word means

deflect *verb*
to deflect something that is moving is to make it go in a different direction **deflection** *noun* a deflection is a sudden change in direction of something that is moving

deforestation *noun*
the cutting down of a large number of trees in an area

deformed *adjective*
not properly shaped **deformity** *noun* a deformity is a part of someone's body that is deformed

defrost *verb*
1 to defrost a refrigerator or freezer is to remove the ice from it 2 to defrost frozen food is to thaw it out

deft *adjective*
skilful and quick **deftly** *adverb* in a skilful and quick way

defuse *verb*
1 to defuse a bomb is to remove its fuse so that it won't blow up 2 to defuse a situation is to make it less dangerous or tense

defy *verb* (**defies, defying, defied**)
1 to defy someone is to refuse to obey them 2 to defy something is to prevent it happening • *The door defied all attempts to open it.* 3 to defy someone to do something is to challenge them • *I defy you to find anything cheaper.*

degree *noun*
1 a unit for measuring temperature • *Water boils at 100 degrees centigrade, or 100°C.* 2 a unit for measuring angles • *There are 90 degrees (90°) in a right angle.* 3 the level or amount of something • *I agree with you to a large degree.* 4 an award to someone at a university or college who has successfully finished a course • *She has a degree in English.*

dehydrated *adjective*
dried up, with all the water removed **dehydration** *noun* someone suffers from dehydration when they lose too much water from their body

deity *noun* (**deities**)
(*say* **dee**-i-ti or **day**-i-ti) a god or goddess

dejected *adjective*
sad or depressed **dejection** *noun* dejection is being sad or depressed

delay *verb*
1 to delay someone is to make them late 2 to delay something is to put it off until later 3 to delay is to wait before doing something

delay *noun*
1 delaying or waiting • *Do it without delay.* 2 the period you have to wait when something happens late • *There will be a delay of 20 minutes.*

delete *verb*
to delete something is to cross it out or remove it **deletion** *noun* a deletion is something that has been crossed out or removed

deliberate *adjective*
(*say* di-**lib**-er-at)
1 done on purpose • *It was a deliberate lie.* 2 slow and careful • *He has a deliberate way of talking.* **deliberately** *adverb* to do something deliberately is to do it on purpose

delicacy *noun* (**delicacies**)
1 delicacy is being delicate 2 a delicacy is something small and tasty to eat

delicate *adjective*
1 fine and graceful • *The cloth had delicate embroidery.* 2 fragile and easily damaged 3 becoming ill easily 4 a delicate situation needs great care **delicately** *adverb*

delicatessen *noun*
a shop that sells cooked or prepared food such as meat and cheese

delicious *adjective*
tasting or smelling very pleasant **deliciously** *adverb* in a delicious way • *a deliciously creamy sauce*

delight *verb*
to delight someone is to please them a lot **delight** *noun* great pleasure **delightful** *adjective* giving great pleasure **delightfully** *adverb*

delinquent *noun*
a young person who breaks the law **delinquency** *noun* delinquency is criminal behaviour by young people

delirious *adjective*
1 in a confused state of mind because you are ill or have a high fever 2 extremely excited or enthusiastic **deliriously** *adverb* in a delirious way

degrees

deliver *verb*
1 to deliver letters, milk, or newspapers is to take them to a house or office 2 to deliver a speech or lecture is to give it to an audience 3 to deliver a baby is to help with its birth

delivery *noun* (**deliveries**)
1 delivery is when letters or goods are taken to a house or office 2 a person's delivery is the way they give a speech or lecture 3 giving birth to a baby

delta *noun*
a triangular area at the mouth of a river where it spreads into branches

deluge *noun*
1 a large flood 2 a heavy fall of rain 3 something coming in great numbers • *After the speech there was a deluge of questions.*

deluge *verb*
to be deluged with something is to get a huge amount of it • *We have been deluged with replies.*

de luxe *adjective*
of very high quality

demand *verb*
to demand something is to ask for it forcefully

demand *noun*
1 a demand is a very firm request for something 2 demand is a desire to have something • *There's not much demand for ice cream at this time of year.* **to be in demand** is to be wanted or popular

demanding *adjective*
1 asking for many things • *Toddlers can be very demanding.* 2 needing a lot of time or effort • *She has a demanding job.*

democracy *noun* (**democracies**)
1 democracy is government by leaders elected by the people 2 a democracy is a country governed in this way

democrat *noun*
a person who believes in or supports democracy

democratic *adjective*
a democratic idea or process is one that involves ordinary people and takes account of their views **democratically** *adverb* to do something democratically is to take account of ordinary people and their views

demolish *verb*
to demolish a building is to knock it down and break it up **demolition** *noun* the demolition of a building is when it is knocked down and broken up

demon *noun*
1 a devil or evil spirit 2 a fierce or forceful person

demonstrate *verb*
1 to demonstrate something is to show or prove it 2 to demonstrate is to take part in a demonstration **demonstrator** *noun*

demonstration *noun*
1 showing how to do or work something 2 a march or meeting to show everyone what you think about something
• *There will be a demonstration against the new motorway.*

den *noun*
1 the home of a wild animal • *a lion's den* 2 a hiding place, especially for children

denial *noun*
saying that something is not true

denim *noun*
strong cotton cloth, used to make jeans

denominator *noun*
the number below the line in a fraction
• *In ¼ the 4 is the denominator.*

denounce *verb*
to denounce someone or something is to speak strongly against them, or accuse them of something
• *They denounced him as a spy.*
denunciation *noun* denouncing someone or something

dense *adjective*
1 thick • *The fog was getting very dense.* 2 packed close together
• *They walked through a dense forest.*
3 (*informal*) stupid **densely** *adverb* thickly, close together • *a densely populated area*

density *noun* (**densities**)
1 how thick or tightly packed something is 2 (*in science*) the proportion of mass to volume
• *Water has greater density than air.*

dent *noun*
a hollow made in a surface by hitting it or pressing it

dent *verb*
to dent something is to make a dent in it

dental *adjective*
to do with the teeth or dentistry

dentist *noun*
a person who is trained to treat teeth, fill them or take them out, and fit false ones **dentistry** *noun* the work of a dentist

denture *noun*
a set of false teeth

deny *verb* (**denies, denying, denied**)
1 to deny something is to say that it is not true 2 to deny a request is to refuse it

deodorant *noun*
a powder or liquid that removes unpleasant smells

depart *verb*
to depart is to go away or leave
departure *noun* a departure is when someone or something leaves a place

department *noun*
one part of a large organization or shop

department store *noun*
a large shop that sells many different kinds of goods

depend *verb*
to depend on someone or something is to rely on them
• *We depend on you for help.*
to depend on something is to be decided or controlled by it • *Whether we can have a picnic depends on the weather.*

dependable *adjective*
that you can depend on; reliable

dependant *noun*
a person who depends on someone else, especially for money • *She has two dependants, a son and a daughter.*

dependent *adjective*
depending or relying on someone
• *He was dependent on his father.*
• *She has two dependent children.*
dependence *noun* dependence is being dependent on someone

depict *verb*
1 to depict something is to show it in a painting or drawing 2 to depict a scene is to describe it • *The story depicted a small village in Austria.*

deport *verb*
to deport someone is to send them out of a country **deportation** *noun* deportation is when someone is sent out of a country

deposit *noun*
1 an amount of money you pay into a bank 2 a sum of money paid as a first instalment 3 a layer of solid matter in or on the earth

deposit *verb*
1 to deposit something is to put it down somewhere 2 to deposit money is to pay it into a bank

depot *noun* (*say* **dep**-oh)
1 a place where things are stored 2 a place where buses or trains are kept and repaired

depress *verb*
to depress someone is to make them very sad

depressed *adjective*
someone who is depressed feels very sad and without hope

depression *noun*
1 a feeling of great sadness and hopelessness 2 a long period when there is less trade and business than usual and many people have no work 3 a shallow hollow or dip in the ground 4 an area of low air pressure which may bring rain

deprive *verb*
to deprive someone of something is to take it away from them • *Prisoners are deprived of their freedom.*

deprived *adjective*
without all the things you need to live a happy and comfortable life, like enough food and good housing

depth *noun*
how deep something is • *What is the depth of the river here?* **in depth** thoroughly **out of your depth** 1 in water that is too deep to stand in 2 trying to do something that is too difficult for you

deputy *noun* (**deputies**)
a person who acts as a substitute or chief assistant for someone and does that person's job when they are away

derail *verb*
a train is derailed when something causes it to leave the track

derby *noun* (**derbies**)
a sports match between two teams from the same city or area

derelict *adjective* (*say* **de**-re-likt)
abandoned and left to fall into ruin
• *The factory is now completely derelict.*

derision *noun*
scorn or ridicule • *They treated him with derision.*

derivation *noun*
where a word comes from

derive *verb*
to get something from another person or thing • *She derived a lot of pleasure from music.* • *Many English words are derived from Latin.*

derrick *noun*
1 a kind of large crane for lifting things 2 a tall framework that holds the machinery used for drilling an oil well

descant *noun*
a tune sung or played above another tune

descend *verb*
to descend something like a hill or staircase is to go down it **to be descended from someone** is to be in the same family as them but living at a later time

descendant noun
a person's descendants are the people who are descended from them

descent noun
a descent is a climb down, usually a hard or long one

describe verb
to describe something or someone is to say what they are like

description noun
1 description is saying what someone or something is like • She's a writer who's very good at description. **2** a description is something you write or say that describes what someone or something is like • He gave the police a description of the robbers.
descriptive adjective a descriptive word or piece of writing describes someone or something • a descriptive poem

desert noun (say **dez**-ert)
a large area of very dry, often sandy, land

desert verb (say di-**zert**)
to desert someone or something is to leave them without intending to return **deserter** noun a soldier who runs away from the army **desertion** noun desertion is when a soldier runs away from the army

deserted adjective
a place is deserted when there is nobody there

desert island noun
a tropical island where nobody lives

deserts plural noun (say di-**zerts**)
someone's deserts are what they deserve • He got his deserts.

deserve verb
to deserve something is to be worthy of it or to have a right to it **deservedly** adverb rightly, because it is deserved • This restaurant is deservedly popular.

design noun
1 the way that something is made or arranged **2** a drawing that shows how something is to be made **3** lines and shapes forming a pattern
design verb
to design something is to make a design or plan for it **designer** noun someone who designs things, especially clothes

desirable adjective
worth having or doing • It is desirable for you to come with us.

desire verb
to desire something is to want it very much

desire noun
a feeling of wanting something very much

desk noun
1 a piece of furniture with a flat top and drawers, used for writing, reading, or working at **2** a counter at which a cashier or receptionist sits

desktop adjective
small enough to use on a desk • I've bought a desktop computer.

desolate adjective
1 lonely and sad **2** a desolate place is empty, with no people living there • It was now a dark and desolate land. **desolation** noun feeling desolate

despair noun
despair is a complete loss of hope
despair verb
to despair is to lose hope completely

despatch noun (**despatches**), verb
a different spelling of dispatch

desperate adjective
1 extremely serious or hopeless • We were in a desperate situation. **2** ready to do anything to get out of a difficulty • There are three desperate criminals at large. **3** needing or wanting something very much • She was desperate to go home. **desperately** adverb seriously; recklessly **desperation** noun desperation is being desperate

despicable adjective
very unpleasant or evil

despise verb
to despise someone is to hate them and have no respect for them

despite preposition
in spite of • They went out despite the rain.

dessert noun
(say di-**zert**) dessert
fruit or a sweet food eaten at the end of a meal

destination noun
the place you are travelling to

destined adjective
intended by fate; meant to happen • They felt they were destined to win.

destiny noun (**destinies**)
your destiny is what is intended for you in the future; your fate • His destiny was to travel the world.

destroy verb
to destroy something is to ruin it or put an end to it **destruction** noun when something is destroyed **destructive** adjective causing a lot of damage

detach verb
to detach something is to remove it or separate it • Detach the coupon from the bottom of the page.

detached adjective
a detached house is one that is not joined to another house

detail noun
1 a small piece of information **2** a small part of a design or picture or piece of decoration **in detail** describing or dealing with everything fully

detain verb
1 to detain someone is to keep them in a place **2** to detain someone is also to keep them waiting • I'll try not to detain you for long.

detect verb
to detect something is to discover or notice it **detection** noun detection is detecting something **detector** noun a detector is a device that detects something

detective noun
a person, especially a police officer, who investigates crimes

detention noun
detention is when someone is made to stay in a place, especially made to stay late in school as a punishment

deter verb (**deterring, deterred**)
to deter someone is to put them off doing something

detergent noun
a kind of washing powder or liquid

deteriorate verb
to deteriorate is to become worse • The weather was starting to deteriorate. **deterioration** noun deterioration is when something becomes worse

determination noun
a strong intention to achieve something, even though it is difficult

determined adjective
having your mind firmly made up

deterrent noun
something that is meant to put people off doing something, such as a powerful weapon **deterrence** noun deterrence is being a deterrent

detest verb
to detest something is to dislike it very much **detestable** adjective horrid

detonate verb
to detonate a bomb is to make it explode **detonation** noun detonation is making a bomb explode **detonator** noun a device that makes a bomb explode

detour noun
a less direct route you use instead of the normal route

deuce noun
a tennis score when each player has 40 points and needs two more points in a row to win the game

devastate verb
to devastate a place is to ruin or destroy it, making it impossible to live in **devastation** noun devastation is destruction of a place

devastated adjective
someone is devastated when they are extremely shocked and upset

develop verb
1 to develop something is to make it bigger or better **2** to develop is to become bigger or better **3** to develop photographic film is to treat it with chemicals so that pictures appear on it

developing country noun
(**developing countries**)
a poor country that is building up its industry and trying to improve its living conditions

development noun
a development is something interesting that has happened • *Have there been any further developments since I last saw you?*

device noun
a piece of equipment used for a particular purpose **to leave someone to their own devices** is to leave them alone to do as they wish and not tell them what to do

devil noun
an evil spirit or person **devilish** adjective cruel or wicked, like a devil

devious adjective
1 using unfair and dishonest methods • *He got rich by devious means.* **2** not straight or direct • *The coach took us by a devious*

route to avoid the traffic jams.

devise verb
to devise a plan or idea is to think it up

devolution noun
handing over power from a central government to a local or regional government

devote verb
to devote yourself or your time to something is to spend all your time doing it • *They devote all their free time to sport.*

devoted adjective
loving and loyal • *They are devoted parents.* **devotion** noun great love or loyalty

devour verb
to devour something is to eat or swallow it greedily

devout adjective
deeply religious

dew noun
tiny drops of water that form during the night on the ground and other surfaces out of doors **dewy** adjective wet with dew or like dew

diabetes noun (say dy-a-**bee**-teez)
a disease in which there is too much sugar in a person's blood **diabetic** noun a person suffering from diabetes **diabetic** adjective suffering from diabetes

diabolical adjective
like a devil; very wicked

diagnose verb
to diagnose a disease is to find out what it is and what treatment is needed

diagnosis noun
a doctor makes a diagnosis when they decide what disease someone has

diagonal noun
a straight line joining opposite corners **diagonally** adverb across from one corner to another

diagram noun
a drawing or picture that shows the parts of something or how it works

dial noun
a circular piece of plastic or card with numbers or letters round it

dial verb
to dial a telephone number is to choose it by pressing numbered buttons

dialect noun
the form of a language used by people in one area of the country but not in the rest of the country

dialogue noun
talk between people, especially in a play, film, or book

diameter noun
1 a line drawn from one side of a circle to the other, passing through the centre **2** the length of this line

diamond noun
1 a very hard jewel that looks like clear glass **2** a shape which has four equal sides but which is not a square **3** a playing card with red diamond shapes on it

diamond

diarrhoea noun (say dy-a-**ree**-a)
an illness that makes you have to keep going to the toilet and the waste matter you empty from your bowels is very watery

diary noun (**diaries**)
a book with a separate space to write in for each day of the year, in which you write down what happens each day

dice noun (**dice**)
a small cube marked with one to six dots on each side, thrown to give a number in some games

dictate verb
1 to dictate something is to speak or read it aloud for someone else to write down **2** to dictate to someone is to give them orders in a bossy way **dictation** noun an exercise in writing down what someone reads out

dictator noun
a ruler who has complete power over the people of a country **dictatorship** noun a country ruled by a dictator

dictionary noun (**dictionaries**)
a book with words listed in alphabetical order, so that you can find out what a word means and how to spell it

die verb (**dying, died**)
to die is to stop living **to die down** is to gradually become less strong • *The wind died down at last.* **to die out** is to gradually disappear • *The tiger is beginning to die out.*

diesel noun
1 a diesel is an engine that works by burning oil in compressed air **2** diesel is fuel for this kind of engine

a b c d e f g h i j k l m n o p q r s t u v w x y z

diet noun
1 a diet is a choice of food that someone eats to be healthy or to lose weight • *The vet put the dog on a diet.* 2 someone's diet is the food they normally eat

diet verb
to diet is to keep to a special diet, especially in order to lose weight

differ verb
1 to differ from something is to be not the same as it 2 to differ is to disagree • *The two writers differ on this point.*

difference noun
1 the way in which something is different from something else 2 the amount between two numbers • *The difference between 8 and 3 is 5.*

different adjective
one person or thing is different from another when they are not the same **differently** adverb in a different way

difficult adjective
needing a lot of effort or skill; not easy

difficulty noun (**difficulties**)
1 difficulty is not being easy, trouble • *I had difficulty answering most of the questions.* 2 a difficulty is something that causes a problem • *She has learning difficulties.*

dig verb (**digging, dug**)
1 to dig soil or the ground is to break it up and move it 2 to dig a hole is to make it 3 to dig someone is to poke them • *He dug me in the ribs.* **digger** noun a machine for digging

dig noun
a sharp thrust or poke • *She gave me a dig in the ribs with her elbow.*

digest verb
to digest food is to soften and change it in the stomach and intestine so that the body can absorb it **digestible** adjective easy to digest **digestion** noun the way your body digests food

digestive adjective
to do with digesting food

digit noun (*say* **dij**-it)
1 any of the numbers from 0 to 9 2 a finger or toe

digital adjective
1 a digital clock or watch has a row of digits to indicate numbers 2 a digital computer or recording stores the data or sound as a series of binary digits

dignified adjective
having dignity

dignity noun
a calm and serious manner

dike noun
1 a long wall or embankment to hold

back water and prevent flooding 2 a ditch for draining water from land

dilemma noun
an awkward choice between two possible actions, either of which would cause difficulties

dilute verb
to dilute a liquid is to make it weaker by mixing it with water **dilution** noun diluting a liquid

dim adjective (**dimmer, dimmest**)
only faintly lit and difficult to see **dimly** adverb to see something dimly is to find it hard to see clearly

dim verb (**dimming, dimmed**)
a light dims when it becomes less bright • *As the curtain rose, the lights dimmed.*

dimension noun
1 a measurement such as length, width, area, or volume • *What are the dimensions of the box?* 2 size or extent

diminish verb
1 to diminish something is to make it smaller 2 to diminish is to become smaller

dimple noun
a small hollow on a person's cheek or chin

din noun
a loud noise

dine verb
to dine is to have dinner **diner** noun someone eating a meal in a restaurant or hotel

dinghy noun (**dinghies**) (*say* **ding**-i)
a kind of small boat

dingy adjective (**dingier, dingiest**) (*say* **din**-ji)
shabby and dirty-looking

dinner noun
the main meal of the day, eaten either in the middle of the day or in the evening

dinosaur noun
a prehistoric reptile, often of enormous size

dip verb (**dipping, dipped**)
1 to dip something is to put it into a liquid and then take it out again • *Dip the brush in the paint.* 2 to dip is to go or slope downwards • *The road dips steeply after the hill.* 3 to dip a vehicle's headlights is to lower the beam so that they do not dazzle other drivers

dinosaur

dip noun
1 a downward slope 2 a quick swim 3 a mixture into which things are dipped

diploma noun
a certificate awarded for skill in a particular subject

diplomacy noun
1 the business of keeping friendly with other nations 2 dealing with other people without upsetting or offending them

diplomatic adjective
1 to do with diplomacy 2 tactful and courteous **diplomat** noun someone who works in diplomacy **diplomatically** adverb in a tactful and courteous way

dire adjective
dreadful or serious • *The refugees are in dire need of food and shelter.*

direct adjective
1 as straight or quick as possible 2 frank and honest **directness** noun directness is being frank and honest

direct verb
1 to direct someone is to show them the way 2 to direct a film or play is to decide how it should be made or performed

direction noun
1 a direction is the way you go to get somewhere 2 direction is directing something **directions** information on how to use or do something or how to get somewhere

directly adverb
1 by a direct route • *Go directly to the shop.* 2 immediately • *I want you to come directly.*

director noun
1 a person who is in charge of something, especially one of a group of people managing a company 2 a person who decides how a film or play should be made or performed

directory noun (**directories**)
a book containing a list of people with their telephone numbers and addresses

dirt *noun*
earth or soil; anything that is not clean

dirty *adjective* (**dirtier, dirtiest**)
1 covered with dirt; not clean **2** rude or offensive **3** unfair or mean • *That was a dirty trick.* **dirtily** *adverb* **dirtiness** *noun*

disability *noun*
something that restricts someone's movements or senses

disabled *adjective*
having a disease or injury that restricts someone's movements or senses

disadvantage *noun*
something that hinders you or makes things difficult

disagree *verb*
1 to disagree with someone is to have or express a different opinion from them **2** to disagree with someone is also to have a bad effect on them • *Rich food disagrees with me.* **disagreement** *noun* when people don't agree about something or argue about it

disappear *verb*
1 to disappear is to become impossible to see; to vanish **2** to disappear is also to stop happening or existing • *Her nervousness soon disappeared.* **disappearance** *noun* a person's or thing's disappearance is when they disappear

disappoint *verb*
to disappoint someone is to fail to do what they want **disappointing** *adjective* causing someone to be disappointed **disappointment** *noun* a feeling of being disappointed

disapprove *verb*
to disapprove of someone or something is to have a bad opinion of them **disapproval** *noun* having a bad opinion

disaster *noun*
1 a very bad accident or misfortune, often one where many people are killed or injured **2** a complete failure • *The first night of the play was a disaster.* **disastrous** *adjective* causing great misfortune; going completely wrong **disastrously** *adverb*

disc *noun*
1 a round flat object **2** a round, flat piece of plastic on which sound or data is recorded; a CD

discard *verb*
to discard something is to throw it away

disciple *noun*
a follower of a political or religious leader

discipline *noun*
1 training people to obey rules and punishing them if they don't **2** the control you have over how you behave • *You need lots of discipline to learn the piano.*

disc jockey *noun*
someone who introduces and plays records on the radio or at a club

disclose *verb*
to disclose information or a secret is to tell someone about it **disclosure** *noun* disclosure is telling people information that is secret

disco *noun*
a place or party where music is played for dancing

discomfort *noun*
being uncomfortable

disconnect *verb*
to disconnect something is to break its connection or detach it **disconnection** *noun* disconnecting something

discontented *adjective*
unhappy and not satisfied **discontent** *noun* discontent is a feeling of being unhappy or not satisfied

discount *noun*
an amount by which a price is reduced

discourage *verb*
1 to discourage someone is to take away their enthusiasm or confidence **2** to discourage someone from doing something is to try to persuade them not to do it **discouragement** *noun* a feeling of being discouraged

discover *verb*
to discover something is to find it or learn about it, especially by chance or for the first time

discovery *noun* (**discoveries**)
1 finding or learning about something, especially by chance or for the first time • *Columbus is famous for the discovery of America.* **2** something that is found or learned about for the first time • *This drug was an important discovery in the history of medicine.*

discreet *adjective*
being careful in what you say and do, especially when you have a secret to keep **discreetly** *adverb*

discriminate *verb*
1 to discriminate between things is to notice the differences between them, or to prefer one thing to another **2** to discriminate between people is to treat them differently or unfairly because of their race, sex, or religion

discrimination *noun*
1 discrimination is treating people differently or unfairly because of their race, sex, or religion **2** discrimination is also the ability to notice the differences between things

discus *noun* (*say* **dis**-kuss)
a thick heavy disc thrown in an athletic contest

discuss *verb* (*say* dis-**kuss**)
to discuss a subject is to talk with other people about it or to write about it in detail

discussion *noun*
1 a conversation about a subject **2** a piece of writing in which the writer examines a subject from different points of view

disease *noun*
a disease is an illness or sickness **diseased** *adjective* someone or something is diseased when they have a disease

disembark *verb*
to disembark is to get out of a boat or aircraft

disgrace *noun*
1 disgrace is shame • *You have brought disgrace to your family.* **2** a disgrace is a person or thing that is so bad that people should feel ashamed • *This room is an absolute disgrace.* **disgraceful** *adjective* so bad that people should feel ashamed about it **disgracefully** *adverb*

disgrace *verb*
to disgrace someone or something is to bring them shame

disguise *verb*
to disguise someone or something is to make them look different so that other people won't recognize them

disguise *noun*
clothes or make-up you put on to change the way you look so that people won't recognize you

disguise

disgust *noun*
a strong feeling of dislike or contempt

disgust *verb*
to disgust someone is to make them feel disgust **disgusted** *adjective* disliking someone or something very much **disgusting** *adjective* very unpleasant; making you feel disgust

dish noun
1 a plate or bowl for food 2 food that has been prepared for eating

dish verb
to dish something out (informal) is to give it to people

dishonest adjective
not honest or truthful **dishonesty** noun dishonesty is being dishonest

dishwasher noun
a machine for washing dishes automatically

disinfect verb
to disinfect something is to treat it to kill all the germs in it

disinfectant noun
a liquid used to disinfect things

disintegrate verb
to disintegrate is to break up into small pieces
disintegration noun the disintegration of something is when it disintegrates

disinterested adjective
not favouring one side more than the other; impartial

disk noun
a disc, especially one used to store computer data

dislike verb
to dislike someone or something is not to like them

dislike noun
a feeling of not liking someone or something

dislocate verb
to dislocate a bone or joint in your body is to make it come out of its proper place by accident
dislocation noun dislocating something

dislodge verb
to dislodge something is to move it from its place

disloyal adjective
not loyal

dismal adjective
gloomy and sad
dismally adverb

dismantle verb
to dismantle something is to take it to pieces

dismay noun
a feeling of strong disappointment and surprise **dismayed** adjective disappointed and surprised

dismiss verb
1 to dismiss someone is to tell them that they have to leave, especially to leave their job 2 to dismiss an idea or suggestion is to reject it **dismissal** noun losing your job

dismount verb
to dismount is to get off a horse or bicycle

disobey verb
to disobey someone is to refuse to do what they tell you to do
disobedience noun disobedience is refusing to obey someone
disobedient adjective someone who is disobedient doesn't do what someone tells them to do

disorder noun
1 disorder is confusion or disturbance 2 a disorder is an illness
disorderly adjective behaving in a wild and noisy way

dispatch noun
a report or message

dispatch verb
1 to dispatch something or someone is to send them somewhere 2 to dispatch someone is to kill them

dispense verb
1 to dispense something is to give it out to people • The machine dispenses drinks and snacks. 2 to dispense medicine is to prepare it for patients **to dispense with something** is to do without it

disperse verb
1 to disperse people is to send them away in various directions • The police dispersed the crowd. 2 to disperse is to go off in various directions **dispersal** noun dispersal is when people go off in different directions

display verb
to display something is to arrange it so that it can be clearly seen

display noun
1 a show or exhibition 2 the showing of information on a computer screen

displease verb
to displease someone is to annoy them

disposable adjective
something that is disposable is made to be thrown away after it has been used

disposal noun
getting rid of something **at your disposal** ready for you to use

dispose verb
to dispose of something is to get rid of it

disprove verb
to disprove something is to prove that it is not true

dispute noun
a quarrel or disagreement

disqualify verb (**disqualifies, disqualifying, disqualified**)
to disqualify someone is to remove them from a race or competition

because they have broken the rules
disqualification noun when someone is disqualified

disregard verb
to disregard someone or something is to take no notice of them

disrespect noun
lack of respect; rudeness
disrespectful adjective showing disrespect **disrespectfully** adverb in a disrespectful way

disrupt verb
to disrupt something is to stop it running smoothly or throw it into confusion • Floods have disrupted local traffic. **disruption** noun when something stops running smoothly **disruptive** adjective causing so much disorder that a meeting or lesson can't continue

dissatisfied adjective
not satisfied or pleased
dissatisfaction noun dissatisfaction is being dissatisfied

dissect verb
to dissect something is to cut it up so that you can examine it **dissection** noun dissecting something

dissolve verb
1 to dissolve something is to mix it with a liquid so that it becomes part of the liquid 2 to dissolve is to melt or become liquid

dissuade verb
to dissuade someone is to persuade them not to do something

distance noun
the amount of space between two places or things **in the distance** a long way off but able to be seen

dissolve

distant adjective
1 far away 2 a person who is distant is not friendly or sociable

distil verb (**distilling, distilled**)
to distil a liquid is to purify it by boiling it and then letting it cool so that it becomes liquid again

distillery noun (**distilleries**)
a place where whisky and other alcoholic drinks are produced

distinct adjective
1 easily heard or seen; clear or definite • You have made a distinct improvement. 2 clearly separate or different • A rabbit is quite distinct from a hare.**distinctly** adverb clearly or noticeably

distinction noun
1 a distinction is a clear difference between two things **2** distinction is excellence or honour • *She is a writer of distinction.*

distinctive adjective
clearly different from all the others and easy to recognize or notice • *The school has a distinctive blue football strip.*

distinguish verb
1 to distinguish things is to notice the differences between them **2** to distinguish something is to see or hear it clearly

distinguished adjective
famous, successful, and much admired by other people • *There was a distinguished writer staying at the same hotel.*

distort verb
1 to distort something is to change it into a strange shape • *His face was distorted with anger.* **2** to distort facts is to change them so that they are untrue or misleading **distortion** noun distortion is distorting something

distract verb
to distract someone is to take their attention away from what they are doing • *Don't distract the bus driver.*
distraction noun
when you are distracted

distress noun
great sorrow, suffering or trouble
in distress a ship or plane is in distress when it is in difficulty and needs help

divers

distress verb
to distress someone is to make them feel very upset or worried

distribute verb
1 to distribute things is to give them out or deliver them • *The teacher distributed textbooks to the class.* **2** to distribute something is to share it among a number of people • *The money was distributed among all the local schools.* **3** to distribute something is also to spread or scatter it around • *Make sure your weight is evenly distributed.* **distribution** noun distribution is distributing things

district noun
part of a town or country

distrust noun
lack of trust; suspicion **distrustful** adjective not trusting people

distrust verb
to think that someone or something can't be trusted

disturb verb
1 to disturb someone is to interrupt them or spoil their peace **2** to disturb someone is also to worry or upset them **3** to disturb something is to move it from its right position **disturbance** noun a disturbance is something that disturbs someone

disused adjective
no longer used • *The house was next to a disused warehouse.*

ditch noun
a narrow trench to hold or carry away water

dither verb
to dither is to hesitate nervously

ditto noun
the same again. Ditto marks (") are sometimes used in lists or bills to show where something is repeated.

dive verb
1 to dive is to go into water head first **2** to dive is also to move downwards quickly • *The aeroplane then dived.*

diver noun
1 a swimmer who dives **2** someone who works under water using special breathing equipment

diverse adjective
very different from each other and of several different kinds • *He has a diverse collection of rocks.*
diversity noun diversity is variety

diversion noun
1 a different way for traffic to go when the usual road is closed **2** something amusing or entertaining

divert verb
1 to divert something is to change the direction it is moving in **2** to divert someone is to amuse or entertain them

divide verb
1 to divide something is to separate it into smaller parts or shares **2** (*in mathematics*) to divide a number by another number is to find out how many times the second number is contained in the first • *Divide six by two and you get three (6÷2 = 3).*

divine adjective
1 belonging to God or coming from God **2** like a god **3** (*informal*) excellent; extremely beautiful
divinity noun divinity is the fact of being a god or like God

division noun
1 the process of dividing numbers or things **2** one of the parts into which something is divided **divisible** adjective able to be divided exactly • *27 is divisible by 9.*

divorce noun
the legal ending of a marriage
divorce verb
a husband and wife divorce when they end their marriage by law

Diwali noun (*say* di-**wah**-li)
a Hindu festival held in October or November

DIY
short for do-it-yourself

dizzy adjective (**dizzier, dizziest**)
giddy and feeling confused **dizzily** adverb **dizziness** noun

DJ
short for disc jockey

do verb (**does, doing, did, done**)
1 to do something is to perform it or deal with it • *Are you doing your work?* • *I can't do this sum.* **2** to do well is to manage; to do badly is not to manage very well **3** you say that something will do when it is all right or suitable • *I'd really like some football boots but trainers will do.* **4** you also use **do** with other verbs in special ways • *Do you want this?* • *He does not want it.* • *I do like crisps.* • *We work as hard as they do.* **to do something up** is to fasten it • *Do up your coat.* **to do without something** is to manage without having it

docile adjective
gentle and obedient

dock[1] noun
a part of a harbour where ships are loaded, unloaded, or repaired
dock[1] verb
1 a ship docks when it comes into a dock **2** spacecraft dock when they join together in orbit
dock[2] noun
a place for the prisoner on trial in a lawcourt
dock[3] verb
to dock an animal's tail is to cut it short
dock[4] noun
a weed with broad leaves

docker noun
a person whose job is loading and unloading ships

doctor noun
a person trained to heal sick or injured people

document noun
1 an important written or printed piece of paper **2** something stored in a computer or on a disk, such as a piece of text or a picture

documentary noun
(**documentaries**)
a film or a television programme
that tells you about real events or
situations

dodge verb
to dodge something is to move
quickly to avoid it

dodge noun
a trick; a clever way of doing
something

dodgem noun
a small electrically driven car at a
funfair, in which you drive round an
enclosure, dodging and
bumping other cars

doe noun
a female deer, rabbit,
or hare

dog noun
a four-legged
animal that barks,
often kept as a pet

dogged
adjective (say
dog-id)
not giving up in
spite of difficulties;
obstinate **doggedly**
adverb

do-it-yourself
adjective
suitable for anyone
to make or use at home,
rather than paying for someone else
to do it

doldrums plural noun
the ocean regions near the equator,
where there is little or no wind **in the
doldrums** bored and unhappy

dole noun
(informal) money paid by the
government to unemployed people

doll noun
a toy model of a person, especially a
baby or child

dollar noun
a unit of money in the United States
and some other countries

dolphin noun
a sea mammal like a small whale
with a snout like a beak

dome noun
a roof shaped like the top half of a ball

domestic adjective
1 to do with the home **2** a domestic
animal is tame and kept at home

dominant adjective
most powerful or important
dominance noun being dominant

dominate verb
to dominate people is to control

dog

them by being the most powerful
domination noun dominating
people

domino noun (**dominoes**)
a small flat oblong piece of
wood or plastic with dots (1 to
6) or a blank space at each
end, used in the game of
dominoes

dominoes

donate verb
to donate something, especially
money, is to give it to a charity
or organization **donation** noun
a donation is something that is
donated

donkey noun (**donkeys**)
an animal that looks like a small
horse with long ears

donor noun
someone who gives something
• New blood donors are needed.

doodle noun
a quick drawing or scribble
doodle verb
to doodle is to draw a
doodle

doom noun
a grim fate like ruin or death
doom verb
to be doomed to something is to
have a grim fate you can't avoid

door noun
a movable panel that opens and
closes the entrance to a room,
building, or cupboard

doorway noun
the opening into which a door fits

dormitory noun (**dormitories**)
a room for several people to sleep in,
especially in a school

dose noun
the amount of a medicine that you
are meant to take at one time

dot noun
a tiny spot

dot verb (**dotting, dotted**)
to dot something is to mark
it with dots **dotted** adjective made
of dots • Write on the dotted line.

double adjective
1 twice as much or twice as many
2 having two of something • a
double-barrelled shotgun **3** suitable
for two people • a double bed

double noun
1 double is twice the amount or cost
2 a double is someone who looks
exactly like someone else **3** you play

doubles in tennis when you play with
someone else against another pair
of players

double verb
1 to double something is
to make it twice as big **2** to
double is to become twice
as big **to double up** is to
bend over because you are
in pain or laughing so much

double bass noun
a musical instrument with
strings, like a large cello

double-cross verb
to double-cross someone is to
cheat or betray them when you are
supposed to be supporting them

doubly adverb
twice as much • It's doubly
important that you should go.

doubt noun
not feeling sure about something

doubt verb
to doubt something is to feel unsure
about it • I doubt whether he is
telling the truth.

doubtful adjective
1 having doubts • She looked
doubtful. **2** making you feel doubt
• Their story was very doubtful.
doubtfully adverb

dough noun
a thick mixture of flour and water
used for making bread or pastry
doughy adjective thick and sticky
like dough

doughnut noun
a round or ring-shaped bun that has
been fried and covered with sugar

doughnuts

dove noun
a kind of pigeon, often used as a
symbol of peace

down[1] adverb, preposition
1 to or in a lower place • It fell down.
• Run down the hill. **2** along • Go
down to the shops.

down[2] noun
very soft feathers or hair • Ducks are
covered with down. **downy** adjective
covered in something very soft like
feathers or hair

downcast adjective
sad or dejected

downfall *noun*
1 a person's downfall is their ruin or fall from power 2 a heavy fall of rain or snow

downhill *adverb*
down a slope

downpour *noun*
a heavy fall of rain

downright *adjective, adverb*
very, completely • *I felt downright angry about it.*

downs *plural noun*
grass-covered hills • *Let's have a picnic on the downs.*

downstairs *adverb, adjective*
to or on a lower floor

downstream *adverb*
in the direction that a river or stream flows

downward or **downwards** *adverb*
towards a lower place

doze *verb*
to doze is to sleep lightly
dozy *adjective* feeling sleepy

dozen *noun*
a set of twelve

Dr
short for **Doctor**

drab *adjective* (**drabber, drabbest**)
1 dull and without colour • *His clothes were drab.* 2 dreary and uninteresting

draft *noun*
a rough plan for something you are going to write
draft *verb*
to draft something you are going to write is to make a rough plan of it

drag *verb* (**dragging, dragged**)
to drag something heavy is to pull it along
drag *noun*
(*informal*) something annoying or tedious

dragon *noun*
a winged lizard-like monster that breathes fire in stories

dragonfly *noun*
(**dragonflies**)
an insect with a long body and two pairs of transparent wings

dragonfly

drain *noun*
a pipe or ditch for taking away water or sewage
drain *verb*
1 to drain water is to take it away with drains 2 to drain is to flow or trickle away 3 to drain a glass or bottle is to empty liquid out of it 4 to drain someone is to exhaust them
drainage *noun* a system of drains

drama *noun*
1 drama is writing or performing plays 2 a drama is a play 3 a drama is also a series of exciting events

dramatic *adjective*
1 to do with drama 2 exciting and impressive • *A dramatic change has taken place.* **dramatically** *adverb*

dramatist *noun*
someone who writes plays

dramatize *verb*
1 to dramatize a story is to make it into a play 2 to dramatize an event is to exaggerate it • *Why do you always dramatize everything?* **dramatization** *noun* a dramatization is a play made from a story

drape *verb*
to drape something like cloth is to hang it loosely over something

drastic *adjective*
having a strong or violent effect **drastically** *adverb*

draught *noun* (*rhymes with* **craft**)
a current of cold air indoors **draughty** *adjective* a draughty room has lots of draughts

draughts *noun*
a game played with 24 round pieces on a chessboard

draw *verb* (**drawing, drew, drawn**)
1 to draw a picture or outline is to form it with a pencil or pen 2 to draw something is to pull it • *She drew her chair up to the table.* 3 to draw people is to attract them • *The fair drew large crowds.* 4 to draw is to end a game or contest with the same score on both sides • *They drew 2-2 last Saturday.* 5 to draw the curtains is to open or close them 6 to draw near is to come nearer • *The ship was drawing nearer.*
draw *noun*
1 a raffle or similar competition in which the winner is chosen by picking tickets or numbers at random 2 a game that ends with the same score on both sides 3 an attraction

drawback *noun*
a disadvantage

drawbridge *noun*
a bridge over a moat, hinged at one end so that it can be raised or lowered

drawer *noun*
a sliding box-like container in a piece of furniture

drawing *noun*
something you draw with a pencil or pen

drawing pin *noun*
a short pin with a large flat top that you use for fixing paper to a surface

dread *verb*
to dread something is to fear it very much
dread *noun*
great fear

dreadful *adjective*
very bad • *We've had dreadful weather.* **dreadfully** *adverb* very badly

dreadlocks *plural noun*
hair in long tightly-curled ringlets, worn especially by Rastafarians

dream *noun*
1 things you picture happening while you are sleeping 2 something you would like to do or have very much • *His dream is to be famous.* **dreamy** *adjective* like a dream; not real
dream *verb* (**dreaming, dreamt** or **dreamed**)
1 to dream is to have a dream 2 to dream is also to want something badly • *She dreams of being a ballet dancer.* 3 to dream something is to think it may happen • *I never dreamt she would leave.*

dreary *adjective* (**drearier, dreariest**)
1 dull or boring 2 gloomy **drearily** *adverb* **dreariness** *noun*

dredge *verb*
to dredge something is to drag it up, especially mud from the bottom of water **dredger** *noun* a machine for clearing mud from the bottom of a river

drench *verb*
to drench someone or something is to soak them • *They got drenched in the rain.*

dress *noun*
1 a dress is a woman's or girl's piece of clothing, having a top and skirt in one 2 dress is clothes or costume • *We have to wear fancy dress.*
dress *verb*
1 to dress is to put clothes on 2 to dress a wound is to put a bandage or plaster it

dresser *noun*
a sideboard with shelves at the top

a b c d e f g h i j k l m n o p q r s t u v w x y z

dressing *noun*
1 a sauce of oil, vinegar, and spices for a salad 2 a bandage or plaster used to cover a wound

dressing gown *noun*
a loose light indoor coat you wear over pyjamas or a nightdress

dribble *verb*
1 to dribble is to let saliva trickle out of your mouth 2 to dribble with a ball is to kick it gently as you run along, so that it stays close to your feet

drier *noun*
a device for drying hair or washing

drift *verb*
1 to drift is to be carried gently along by water or air 2 to drift is also to live casually or wander about without any real plan or purpose

drift *noun*
1 a mass of snow or sand piled up by the wind 2 the general meaning of what someone says • *Do you get my drift?*

drill *noun*
1 a tool for making holes 2 repeated exercises in military training, gymnastics, or sport 3 a set way of doing something • *Do you know the drill?*

drill *verb*
1 to drill a hole is to make a hole with a drill 2 to drill is to do repeated exercises

drink *verb* (**drinking, drank, drunk**)
1 to drink is to swallow liquid 2 to drink can also mean to have a lot of alcohol • *Don't drink and drive.* **drinker** *noun* someone who drinks

drink *noun*
1 a liquid for drinking 2 an alcoholic drink

drip *verb* (**dripping, dripped**)
1 to drip is to fall in drops 2 to drip is also to let liquid fall in drops • *The tap was dripping.*

drip *noun*
a falling drop of liquid

drive *verb* (**driving, drove, driven**)
1 to drive a vehicle is to operate it 2 to drive someone or something is to make them move • *The farmer was driving his herd across the road.* 3 to drive someone into a state or feeling is to force them into it • *That music is driving me mad!* **driver** *noun* someone who drives a vehicle

drive *noun*
1 a drive is a journey in a vehicle 2 drive is energy and enthusiasm 3 a drive is a road leading to a house

4 a drive is a powerful stroke of the ball in cricket, golf, and other games

drizzle *noun*
gentle rain

drizzle *verb*
to rain gently

drone *verb*
1 to make a low humming sound 2 to talk in a boring voice

drone *noun*
1 a droning sound 2 a male bee

droop *verb*
to droop is to hang down weakly

drop *noun*
1 a tiny amount of liquid 2 a fall or decrease • *There has been a sharp drop in prices.* **droplet** *noun* a small drop

drop *verb* (**dropping, dropped**)
1 to drop is to fall 2 to drop something is to let it fall 3 to drop is also to become less or lower • *The temperature suddenly dropped.* **to drop in** is to visit someone casually **to drop out** is to stop taking part in something

drought *noun* (*rhymes with* **out**)
a long period of dry weather

drown *verb*
1 to drown is to die from being under water and unable to breathe 2 to drown a person or animal is to kill them by forcing them to stay under water 3 to drown sounds is to make so much noise that they cannot be heard

drowsy *adjective* (**drowsier, drowsiest**)
sleepy **drowsily** *adverb* **drowsiness** *noun*

drug *noun*
1 a substance that kills pain or cures a disease 2 a substance that people take because it affects their senses or their mind. Some drugs cause addiction or are illegal.

drug *verb* (**drugging, drugged**)
to drug someone is to make them unconscious with drugs

drum *noun*
1 a musical instrument made of a cylinder with a thin skin stretched over one end or both ends 2 a cylindrical container • *There was a row of oil drums along the side of the road.*

drums

drum *verb* (**drumming, drummed**)
1 to drum is to play a drum or drums 2 to drum on something is to tap it repeatedly • *He drummed his fingers on the table.* **drummer** *noun* someone who plays the drums

drumstick *noun*
1 a stick used for hitting a drum 2 the lower part of a cooked bird's leg

drunk¹ *adjective*
not able to control your behaviour through drinking too much alcohol

drunk¹ *noun*
someone who is drunk **drunkard** *noun* a person who is often drunk

dry *adjective* (**drier, driest**)
1 not wet or damp 2 boring and dull • *The book I'm reading is rather dry.* 3 funny in a clever and sarcastic way • *He has a very dry sense of humour.* **drily** *adverb* you speak drily when you say something funny in a clever and sarcastic way **dryness** *noun*

dry *verb* (**dries, drying, dried**)
1 to dry is to become dry 2 to dry something is to make it dry

dry-cleaning *noun*
a method of cleaning clothes using chemicals rather than water

dual *adjective*
having two parts or aspects; double • *This building has a dual purpose.*

dual carriageway *noun*
a road with several lanes in each direction

dub *verb* (**dubbing, dubbed**)
1 to change or add new sound to the sound on a film • *It's a Japanese film but has been dubbed into English.* 2 to give someone a name or title

dubious *adjective*
1 feeling doubtful or uncertain • *I'm dubious about our chances of winning.* 2 probably not honest or not good

duchess *noun*
a duke's wife or widow

duck *noun*
1 a web-footed water bird with a flat beak 2 a batsman's score of nought at cricket

duck *verb*
1 to duck is to bend down quickly to avoid something 2 to duck someone is to push them under water quickly

duckling *noun*
a young duck

due *adjective*
1 expected to arrive • *The train is due in five minutes.* 2 needing to be paid • *Payment for the trip is due next week.* **due to something or someone**

because of something or someone
• *The traffic jam was due to an accident.*

due *adverb*
directly • *The camp is due north.*

duel *noun*
a fight between two people, especially with pistols or swords

duet *noun*
a piece of music for two players or two singers

duke *noun*
a member of the highest rank of noblemen

dull *adjective*
1 not bright or clear; gloomy • *It was a dull day.* **2** boring • *What a dull programme.* **3** not sharp • *I had a dull pain.* **dully** *adverb* **dullness** *noun*

duly *adverb*
rightly; as expected • *They promised to come, and later they duly arrived.*

dumb *adjective*
1 unable to speak; silent **2** (*informal*) stupid

dumbfounded *adjective*
unable to say anything because you are so astonished

dummy *noun* (**dummies**)
1 a large doll or model made to look like a human being; an imitation **2** an imitation teat for a baby to suck

dump *noun*
1 a place where something, especially rubbish, is left or stored **2** (*informal*) a place you don't like

dump *verb*
1 to dump something is to get rid of it when you don't want it **2** to dump something somewhere is to put it down carelessly

dumpling *noun*
a lump of boiled or baked dough, usually eaten with a stew

dumpy *adjective* (**dumpier, dumpiest**)
short and fat

dune *noun*
a hill of loose sand formed by the wind

dung *noun*
solid waste matter from an animal

dungarees *plural noun*
trousers with a piece in front covering your chest, held up by straps over your shoulders

dungeon *noun* (*say* **dun**-jon)
an underground prison cell

dunk *verb*
to dunk something is to dip it into a liquid

duo *noun*
a pair of people, especially playing music

duplicate *noun* (*say* **dew**-pli-kat)
something that is exactly the same as something else; an exact copy

duplicate *verb* (*say* **dew**-pli-kayt)
to duplicate something is to make an exact copy of it **duplication** *noun* making an exact copy of something

durable *adjective*
lasting and strong **durability** *noun* something has durability when it is strong and lasts a long time

duration *noun*
the time something lasts

during *preposition*
while something else is going on • *Let's meet in the cafe during the interval.*

dusk *noun*
the time of the day just after sunset when it is starting to get dark

dust *noun*
a fine powder made up of tiny pieces of dry earth or other material

dust *verb*
1 to dust things is to clear the dust off them **2** to dust something is to sprinkle it with dust or powder • *You can dust the cake with sugar.*

dustbin *noun*
a bin kept outside a house for rubbish

duster *noun*
a cloth for dusting things

dustman *noun* (**dustmen**)
a person whose job is to empty dustbins

dustpan *noun*
a pan into which you brush dust

dusty *adjective* (**dustier, dustiest**)
covered with or full of dust

dutiful *adjective*
doing your duty; obedient **dutifully** *adverb*

duty *noun* (**duties**)
1 your duty is what you have to do, because it is right or part of your job **2** a duty is a kind of tax

duvet *noun* (*say* **doo**-vay)
a kind of quilt used instead of other bedclothes

DVD *noun*
short for *digital video disc* or *digital versatile disc*, a disc on which large amounts of sound and pictures can be stored, especially films

dwarf *noun* (**dwarfs** or **dwarves**)
a very small person or thing

dwarf *verb*
to dwarf something is to make it seem very small • *The skyscraper dwarfs all the buildings round it.*

dwell *verb* (**dwelling, dwelt**) to dwell in a place is to live there **to dwell**

on something is to think or talk about it constantly

dwelling *noun*
a house or other place to live in

dwindle *verb*
to dwindle is to get smaller gradually • *Their food supplies were starting to dwindle.*

dye *verb*
to dye something is to change its colour by putting it in a special liquid

dye *noun*
a liquid used to dye things

dyke *noun*
another spelling of **dike**

dynamic *adjective*
energetic and active

dynamite *noun*
1 a powerful explosive **2** (*informal*) something that will make people angry or excited

dynamo *noun* (**dynamos**)
a machine that makes electricity

dynasty *noun* (**dynasties**)
(*say* **din**-a-sti) a series of kings and queens from the same family

dyslexia *noun* (*say* dis-**lek**-si-a)
special difficulty in being able to read and spell words **dyslexic** *adjective* someone is dyslexic when they have dyslexia

each *determiner, pronoun*
each person or thing in a group is every one of them when you think of them separately • *Each film lasts an hour.* • *You get ten marks for each of these questions.* • *We all knew each other.*

eager *adjective*
badly wanting to do something or to have something; enthusiastic **eagerly** *adverb* **eagerness** *noun*

eagle *noun*
a large bird of prey with strong eyesight

eagle

ear¹ noun
1 the part of your body that you hear with 2 an ear, or a good ear, for something is the ability to hear something clearly and understand it well • *She has an unusually good ear for music.*

ear² noun
the spike of seeds at the top of a stalk of corn

earache noun
a pain inside your ear

earl noun
a British nobleman

earlobe noun
the rounded part that hangs down at the bottom of your ear

early adverb, adjective (**earlier, earliest**)
1 arriving or happening before the usual or expected time • *Jane caught a bus and got home early.* 2 happening near the beginning • *The team was helped by an early goal.* • *The first murder comes early in the film.*

earn verb
1 to earn money is to get it by working for it 2 to earn a reward or praise is to do something good so that you deserve it

earnest adjective
serious about something you want to do or about something important **earnestly** adverb

earnings plural noun
earnings are money that someone earns

earphones plural noun
earphones are a set of two small flat speakers joined by a band that fits over your ears so that you can listen to music without other people hearing it

earring noun
an ornament worn on the ear

earshot noun
a sound is in earshot when it is close enough for you to be able to hear it

earth noun
1 the earth is the planet that we live on 2 earth is soil or the ground 3 an earth is a hole or burrow where a fox or badger lives you use **on earth** with words like *what, who,* and *where* to make the point stronger • *What on earth are you doing?*

earthly adjective
to do with life on earth

earthquake noun
a violent movement of part of the earth's surface caused by pressure that has built up underneath

earthworm noun
a common worm that is found in the soil

earwig noun
a crawling garden insect with pincers at the end of its body

ease noun
to do something with ease is to do it without any difficulty or trouble **to be at ease** is to be comfortable and relaxed • *She liked Tony and felt at ease with him.*

ease verb
1 to ease something unpleasant is to make it easier or less troublesome 2 a pain or problem eases when it becomes less severe or troublesome 3 to ease something is to move it gently into position

easel noun
a stand or frame for holding a blackboard or a painting

easily adverb
1 without difficulty; with ease • *Pencil marks can be easily rubbed out afterwards.* 2 by far • *This was easily the best victory of his career.* 3 very likely • *They could easily be wrong.*

east noun
1 the direction in which the sun rises 2 the part of a country or city that is in this direction

east adjective, adverb
1 towards the east or in the east 2 coming from the east • *An east wind made the day very cold.*

Easter noun
a Christian festival in spring, commemorating Christ's rising from the dead

eastern adjective
coming from or to do with the east

eastward or **eastwards** adjective, adverb
towards the east

easy adjective (**easier, easiest**)
something easy can be done or understood without trouble • *He started with easy questions.* • *The machine is easy to use.*

eat verb (**eating, ate, eaten**)
to eat food is to chew it and swallow it **to eat something up** or **eat something away** is to use it up or destroy it • *Acid rain has eaten away the forests.* • *The sun gradually ate up the mist.* • *Letter writing ate up most of her free time.*

eatable adjective
food is eatable when it is good and pleasant to eat

eaves plural noun
eaves are the overhanging edges of a roof

ebb noun
the movement of the tide when it is

going out **to be at a low ebb** is to be in a poor or weak condition

ebb verb
1 the tide ebbs when it goes away from the land 2 a good feeling ebbs or ebbs away when it becomes much weaker • *When he saw his opponent his courage ebbed away.*

ebony noun
ebony is a hard black wood

eccentric adjective (say ik-**sen**-trik) behaving strangely **eccentricity** noun strange or unusual behaviour

echo noun (**echoes**)
a second sound that you hear when the original sound bounces back off something solid such as walls or high rocks

echo verb
1 to echo is to make an echo 2 to echo something said is to repeat it

éclair noun (say ay-**klair**)
a finger-shaped cake of pastry with a cream filling

eclipse noun
the blocking of light from the sun or moon, causing a short period of darkness. An eclipse of the sun happens when the moon comes between the sun and the earth and blocks out the light from the sun; and an eclipse of the moon happens when the earth comes between the moon and the sun and casts a dark shadow on the surface of the moon.

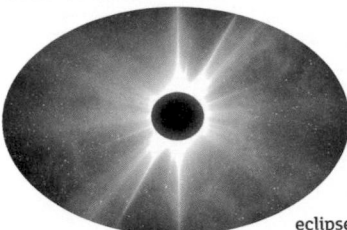

eclipse

ecology noun (say ee-**kol**-o-ji)
ecology is the study of living creatures and plants in their surroundings **ecological** adjective to do with ecology

economic adjective
(say eek-o-**nom**-ik or say ek-o-**nom**-ik)
1 to do with economics or the economy • *Coal no longer dominates the country's economic scene.* 2 making money, profitable • *It is not normally economic to get drinking water from the sea.*

economical adjective
(say eek-o-**nom**-ik-al)
using money and resources carefully **economically** adverb to do something economically is to use money and

resources carefully when you do it

economics noun
(say eek-o-**nom**-iks or say ek-o-**nom**-iks)
economics is the study of how money is used and how goods and services are provided and used

economist noun (say i-**kon**-o-mist)
someone who studies economics

economize verb (say i-**kon**-o-myz)
to economize is to use money more carefully

economy noun (**economies**)
(say i-**kon**-o-mi)
1 an economy is a country's or family's income and the way it is spent **2** economy is being careful with money **3** economies are ways of saving money

ecstasy noun (**ecstasies**)
a feeling of great delight or joy
ecstatic adjective delighted and joyful about something

eczema noun (say **ek**-si-ma)
eczema is a skin disease that causes rough itching patches

edge noun
1 the part along the side or end of something **2** the sharp part of a knife or other cutting device **to be on edge** is to feel nervous and irritable

edge verb
1 to edge is to move gradually and carefully • He edged a little closer to the door. **2** to edge something is to form a border to it • The lawn was edged with a brick path.

edgy adjective (**edgier, edgiest**)
nervous and irritable

edible adjective
an edible substance is one that you can eat, and is not poisonous

edit verb
1 to edit a book, newspaper, or magazine is to get it ready for publishing **2** to edit a film or tape recording is to choose parts of it and put them in the right order
editorial adjective to do with editing or editors

edition noun
1 the form in which something is published • There is a special illustrated edition of the book. **2** all the copies of a newspaper, magazine, or book issued at the same time

editor noun
1 someone who prepares a book, newspaper, or magazine for publishing **2** the person who manages a newspaper and is in charge of everything that is published in it

educate verb
to educate someone is to teach them and give them knowledge and skills

education noun
the process of teaching people and giving them knowledge and skills
educational adjective to do with learning or teaching

eel noun
a long thin fish that looks like a snake

eerie adjective
weird and frightening • It was dark outside and there was an eerie silence. **eerily** adverb in an eerie way • Her voice echoed eerily in the cold air. **eeriness** noun

effect noun
1 something that happens because of something else • The drink had a strange effect on Alice. **2** a general impression • The lights made a cheerful effect.

effective adjective
producing what you want; successful • The program is much more effective if it is linked to the Internet. **effectively** adverb **effectiveness** noun

effervescent adjective
(say ef-er-**vess**-ent) an effervescent liquid is fizzy and gives off bubbles
effervescence noun effervescence is being fizzy or effervescent

efficient adjective
doing work well; effective
efficiency noun efficiency is being efficient and doing work well
efficiently adverb

effort noun
1 effort is using energy or hard work **2** an effort is an attempt **effortless** adjective not needing much work or effort • The team won another effortless victory.

e.g.
for example • There are lots of ways of finding out, e.g. ask a teacher.

egg[1] noun
1 an oval or round object with a thin shell that birds, fish, reptiles, and insects lay, and in which their young develop **2** a hen's or duck's egg used as food

eggs

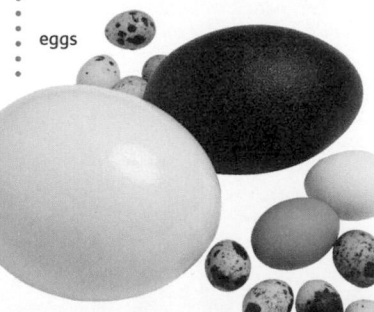

egg[2] verb
to egg someone on is to encourage them with taunts or dares • He didn't want to dance but his friends egged him on.

Eid noun (say eed)
a Muslim festival that marks the end of the fast of Ramadan

eiderdown noun (say **I**-der-down)
a quilt stuffed with soft material

eight noun
the number 8

eighteen noun
the number 18
eighteenth adjective, noun 18th

eighth adjective, noun
the next after the seventh **eighthly** adverb in the eighth place; as the eighth one

eighty noun (**eighties**)
the number 80
eightieth adjective, noun 80th

either determiner, pronoun
1 one or the other of two people or things • Either road will take us there. • Either of them might have seen the killer. **2** both of two things • The houses on either side were all boarded up.

either adverb
also; similarly • I don't like cabbage, and my brother doesn't either.

either conjunction
either ... or ... one thing or another, but not both • You can choose either a starter or pudding.

eject verb
1 to eject something is to send it out with force **2** to eject someone is to make them leave **ejection** noun ejection is ejecting something or someone

elaborate adjective
(say i-**lab**-er-at)
complicated or detailed

elastic noun
cord or material with strands of rubber in it so that it can stretch
elastic adjective
able to stretch and then return to its original shape or length

elated adjective
very pleased and excited

elbow noun
the joint in the middle of your arm, where it bends

elbow verb
to elbow someone is to push or prod them with your elbow

elder adjective
older • Josh is my elder brother.

elderly adjective
rather old

eldest *adjective*
oldest • *Their eldest son George was born in 1660.*

elect *verb*
to elect someone is to choose them by voting

election *noun*
the process of voting for people to be the government or to run an organization

electric or **electrical** *adjective*
to do with electricity, or worked by electricity **electrically** *adverb* by using electricity

electrician *noun*
someone whose job is to fit and repair electrical equipment

electricity *noun*
electricity is a kind of energy used to produce light and heat, and to make machines work

electrocute *verb*
to electrocute someone is to kill them when a large charge of electricity passes through them **electrocution** *noun* electrocution is electrocuting someone

electron *noun*
a particle of matter that is smaller than an atom and has a negative electric charge

electronic *adjective*
electronic equipment uses transistors and silicon chips which control electric currents **electronically** *adverb* by means of electronic devices

electronics *plural noun*
the use or study of electronic devices

elegant *adjective*
graceful and smart **elegance** *noun* elegance is being graceful and smart **elegantly** *adverb*

element *noun*
1 a substance that cannot be split up into simpler substances, for example copper and oxygen **2** a part of something **3** the elements of a subject are the basic facts to do with it, which you learn first **4** the elements are forces that make the weather, such as rain and wind **5** a wire or coil that gives out heat in an electric heater or cooker **to be in your element** is to be doing something you enjoy

elementary *adjective*
dealing with the simplest stages of something; easy

elephant *noun*
a very large animal found in Africa and India, with a thick grey skin, large ears, a trunk, and tusks

elevate *verb*
to elevate something is to lift it or raise it to a higher position

elevator *noun*
a lift for carrying people from one floor to another in a large building

eleven *noun*
1 the number 11 **2** a team of eleven people in cricket, football, and other sports **eleventh** *adjective, noun* 11th

elf *noun* (**elves**)
a tiny mischievous fairy in stories

eligible *adjective*
a person is eligible for something when they are qualified or suitable for it **eligibility** *noun* eligibility is being eligible for something

eliminate *verb*
to eliminate someone or something is to get rid of them **elimination** *noun* elimination is getting rid of someone or something

elk *noun* (**elk** or **elks**)
a large kind of deer

ellipse *noun*
an oval shape

elliptical *adjective*
oval-shaped

elm *noun*
a tall tree with large rough leaves

eloquent *adjective*
speaking well and expressing ideas clearly **eloquence** *noun* eloquence is speaking well and clearly

else *adverb*
besides; instead • *Nobody else knows.* **or else** otherwise • *Run or else you'll be late.*

elsewhere *adverb*
somewhere else

elude *verb*
to elude someone is to escape from them or avoid being caught by them

elusive *adjective*
difficult to find or catch • *Deer are elusive animals.*

email *noun*
1 email is a system of sending messages from one person to another, using computers, it is short for *electronic mail* **2** an email is a message sent this way

email *verb*
to email someone is to send them an email

embankment *noun*
a long wall or bank of earth that holds back water or supports a road or railway

embark *verb*
to embark is to go on board a ship **to embark on something** is to begin something important **embarkation** *noun* embarkation is going on board a ship

embarrass *verb*
to embarrass someone is to make them feel shy or awkward **embarrassment** *noun* embarrassment is feeling awkward or embarrassed

embassy *noun* (**embassies**)
a building where an ambassador from another country lives and has an office

embers *plural noun*
the embers of a fire are small pieces of coal or wood that keep glowing when the fire is going out

emblem *noun*
a symbol that stands for something • *The dove is an emblem of peace.*

embrace *verb*
to embrace someone is to hold them closely in your arms

embroider *verb*
to embroider cloth is to decorate it by stitching in designs or pictures **embroidery** *noun* embroidery is the art of embroidering

embroidery

embryo *noun* (**embryos**)
a baby or young animal that is growing in the womb

emerald *noun*
1 a green jewel **2** a bright green colour

emerge *verb*
to emerge is to come out or appear **emergence** *noun* the emergence of something is when it first appears

emergency *noun* (**emergencies**)
a sudden dangerous or serious

elephant

situation that needs to be dealt with very quickly

emigrant noun
someone who leaves their own country and goes to live in another country

emigrate verb
to emigrate is to leave your own country and go and live in another country **emigration** noun emigration is going to live in another country

eminent adjective
famous and respected • Britain's most eminent woman mountaineer died ten years ago. **eminence** noun eminence is being famous

emission noun
1 the action of sending something out 2 something that is emitted, for example smoke or fumes

emit verb (**emitting, emitted**)
to emit something such as smoke or fumes is to send it out

emotion noun
1 an emotion is a strong feeling in your mind, such as love or fear 2 emotion is being excited or upset • Tears of emotion flooded his eyes. **emotional** adjective showing emotion; to do with emotion **emotionally** adverb

emperor noun
the ruler of an empire

emphasis noun (**emphases**)
special importance given to something

emphasize verb
to emphasize something is to give it special importance, for example by saying it more loudly or by explaining it more fully

emphatic adjective
an emphatic statement or expression is one that you make very firmly or strongly • He agreed, with an emphatic nod of the head. **emphatically** adverb you say something emphatically when you are very firm and definite about it

empire noun
1 a group of countries ruled by one person or group of people 2 a large group of businesses or shops under the control of one person or group of people

employ verb
1 to employ someone is to pay them to work for you 2 to employ something is to use it

employee noun (say im-**ploi**-ee)
someone who works for another person or group of people

employer noun
a person or organization that has people working for them

employment noun
work for which you are paid

empress noun
a female emperor, or the wife of an emperor

empty adjective (**emptier, emptiest**)
an empty place or container has nothing or no one in it **emptiness** noun emptiness is being empty

empty verb (**empties, emptying, emptied**)
1 to empty something is to make it empty 2 to empty is to become empty • After the show the hall quickly emptied.

emu noun (say ee-mew)
a large Australian bird that cannot fly, like an ostrich but smaller

emulsion noun
1 emulsion is a creamy or slightly oily liquid 2 emulsion, or emulsion paint, a kind of water paint used for decorating buildings

emu

enable verb
to enable someone to do something is to make it possible for them • A calculator will enable you to multiply and divide quickly.

enamel noun
1 enamel is a shiny glassy substance that is baked on to metal or pottery to form a hard bright surface 2 enamel is also the hard shiny surface of teeth 3 an enamel paint is a hard glossy paint

enchant verb
1 to enchant someone is to delight or please them 2 to enchant someone is also to put a magic spell on them in stories **enchanted** adjective under a magic spell **enchanting** adjective beautiful or delightful **enchantment** noun a feeling of wonder or delight

enclose verb
1 to enclose an area is to put a fence or wall round it 2 to enclose something is to put it in an envelope or packet with a letter

enclosure noun
a piece of ground with a fence or wall round it

encore noun (say **on**-kor)
an extra item performed at a concert or show when the audience has

clapped or cheered the main items

encounter verb
1 to encounter someone is to meet them unexpectedly 2 to encounter something is to experience it • We have encountered a few problems.

encourage verb
1 to encourage someone is to give them confidence or hope • We were encouraged by your support. 2 to encourage someone to do something is to urge and help them to do it • They try to encourage schools to take part in these road safety schemes. **encouragement** noun encouragement is supporting someone or something in what they do • The crowd shouted their encouragement.

encyclopedia noun
a book or set of books containing a lot of information on a particular subject, or on many different subjects **encyclopedic** adjective an encyclopedic book is one that gives you a lot of information

end noun
1 the end of something is the last part of it or the point where it stops • Holly stood at the end of the pier. • This is the end of our journey. 2 an end is an aim or purpose • They used the money for their own ends. **on end 1** upright • His hair stood on end. 2 continuously • She spoke for two hours on end.

end verb
1 to end something is to finish it 2 to end is to finish

endanger verb
to endanger someone or something is to cause them danger, especially of being injured

endangered species noun
a type of animal or plant that has become so rare that it is in danger of becoming extinct

endeavour verb
to endeavour to do something is to try hard to do it

ending noun
the last part of something • They all wanted a story with a happy ending.

endless adjective
never stopping • Top athletes need endless training. **endlessly** adverb without ending

endure verb
1 to endure pain or suffering is to put up with it 2 to endure is to continue or last **endurance** noun endurance

a b c d e f g h i j k l m n o p q r s t u v w x y z

is suffering or putting up with something unpleasant

enemy noun (**enemies**)
1 someone who is opposed to someone else and wants to harm them 2 a nation or army that is at war with another country

energetic adjective
1 an energetic person has a lot of energy 2 an energetic activity needs a lot of energy • They then performed an energetic dance. **energetically** adverb with a lot of energy

energy noun (**energies**)
1 energy is the ability to do work or provide power, for example electrical energy 2 a person's energy is the strength they have to do things

enforce verb
to enforce a law or order is to make people obey it **enforcement** noun enforcement is making people obey laws

engage verb
1 to engage someone is to give them a job 2 to engage someone in conversation is to talk to them

engaged adjective
1 someone is engaged when they have promised to marry someone 2 a telephone line or lavatory is engaged when someone is already using it

engagement noun
1 a promise to marry someone 2 an appointment to meet someone or do something

engine noun
1 a machine that turns energy into motion 2 a vehicle that pulls a railway train

engineer noun
a person who designs and builds machines, roads, and bridges

engineering noun
engineering is the designing and building of machines, roads, bridges, and other large buildings

engrave verb
to engrave a surface is to carve figures or words on it **engraving** noun a print made by engraving a design

engine

engrossed adjective
to be engrossed in something is to concentrate on it and ignore other things around you • He was so engrossed in his work that he didn't hear her come in.

engulf verb
to engulf something is to flow over it and swamp it • The town was engulfed by smoke from a huge forest fire.

enjoy verb
1 to enjoy something is to get pleasure from it 2 to enjoy yourself is to have a good time **enjoyable** adjective able to be enjoyed; pleasant **enjoyment** noun enjoyment is a feeling of great pleasure

enlarge verb
to enlarge something is to make it larger **enlargement** noun enlargement is making something larger

enormous adjective
very large; huge **enormously** adverb hugely; a lot • I enjoyed the party enormously.

enough determiner, noun, adverb
as much or as many as you need or can cope with

enquire verb
to enquire about something is to ask for information about it • He enquired if I was well. **enquiry** noun a question that asks for information

enrage verb
to enrage a person or animal is to make them very angry

enrol verb (**enrolling, enrolled**)
to enrol in a society or class is to become a member of it **enrolment** noun enrolment is becoming a member or making someone a member

ensure verb
to ensure that something happens or has happened is to make sure of it • Please ensure that you leave the room tidy when you go.

entangle verb
to entangle something is to get it tangled or caught up **entanglement** noun entanglement is becoming tangled

enter verb
1 to enter a place is to come into it or go into it 2 to enter something in a list or book is to write or record it there 3 to enter data in a computer is to key it in 4 to enter for a competition or examination is to take part in it

enterprise noun
1 enterprise is being bold and adventurous 2 an enterprise is a difficult or important task or project

enterprising adjective
an enterprising person or activity is

one that is exciting or adventurous

entertain verb
1 to entertain someone is to amuse them or give them pleasure, as a singer or comedian does 2 to entertain people is to have them as guests and give them food and drink **entertainer** noun someone such as a singer or comedian who entertains people **entertainment** noun entertainment is something that entertains or amuses people

enthusiasm noun
1 enthusiasm is a feeling of excitement and interest you show for something 2 an enthusiasm is a strong liking or interest

enthusiastic adjective
full of enthusiasm • She is very enthusiastic about breeding mice. **enthusiastically** adverb

entire adjective
whole or complete • The entire school gathered in the field for a photograph. **entirely** adverb completely; in every way • The brothers look entirely different.

entitle verb
to entitle someone to something is to give them a right to it • The voucher entitles you to a free drink with your pizza. **entitlement** noun a right you have to something

entrance[1] noun (say en-transs)
1 the way into a place 2 coming into a room or on to a stage or arena • Everyone clapped when the clowns made their entrance.

entrance[2] verb (say in-trahnss)
to entrance someone is to delight or enchant them

entrant noun
someone who goes in for a competition or examination

entreat verb
to entreat someone is to ask them seriously or earnestly **entreaty** noun a serious or earnest request

entrust verb
to entrust someone with something, or to entrust something to someone, is to give it to them to look after

entry noun (**entries**)
1 an entrance 2 something written in a list or diary

envelop verb (say in-vel-op)
to envelop something is to cover or wrap it completely • The mountain was enveloped in mist.

envelope noun
(say en-ve-lohp or say on-ve-lohp)
a paper wrapper for a letter

envious *adjective*
you are envious of someone when they have something you would like to have too **enviously** *adverb*

environment *noun*
1 surroundings, especially as they affect people and other living things • *Some animals and plants can die out if their environment is damaged.* **2** the environment is the natural world of the land and sea and air **environmental** *adjective* to do with the environment

envy *noun*
an unhappy feeling you have when you want something that someone else has got

envy *verb* (**envies, envying, envied**) to envy someone is to be envious of them

epic *noun*
1 a story or poem about heroes **2** an exciting or spectacular film

epidemic *noun*
a disease that spreads quickly among the people of an area

epilepsy *noun*
epilepsy is a disease of the nervous system, which causes fits

epileptic *adjective*
to do with epilepsy • *an epileptic fit*
epileptic *noun*
someone who suffers from epilepsy

epilogue *noun* (*say* **ep**-i-log)
words written or spoken at the end of a story or a play

episode *noun*
1 one event that is part of a series of happenings or forms part of a story **2** one programme in a radio or television serial

epitaph *noun*
words written on a tomb or describing a person who has died

equal *adjective*
things are equal when they are the same in amount, size, or value
equal *noun*
a person or thing that is equal to another • *He treated everyone as equals.*
equal *verb* (**equalling, equalled**)
to equal something is to be the same in amount, size, or value

equality *noun*
equality is being equal

equalize *verb*
to equalize things is to make them equal

equally *adverb*
in the same way or to the same extent • *You are all equally to blame.*

equation *noun* (*say* i-**kway**-zhon)
(*in mathematics*) a statement that two amounts are equal, for example $3 + 4 = 2 + 5$

equator *noun* (*say* i-**kway**-ter)
an imaginary line round the earth at an equal distance from the North and South Poles **equatorial** *adjective* to do with the equator or near the equator

equestrian *adjective*
to do with horse-riding

equestrian

equilateral *adjective*
(*say* ee-kwi-**lat**-er-al)
an equilateral triangle has all its sides equal

equilibrium *noun* (**equilibria**)
(*say* ee-kwi-**lib**-ri-um)
equilibrium is a state of even balance

equinox *noun*
the time of year when day and night are equal in length (about 20 March in spring and about 22 September in autumn)

equip *verb* (**equipping, equipped**)
to equip someone or something is to supply them with what is needed • *Are you equipped for mountaineering?*

equipment *noun*
equipment is a set of things needed for a special purpose

equivalent *adjective*
things are equivalent when they are equal in value, importance, or meaning **equivalence** *noun* equivalence is being equivalent

era *noun* (*say* **eer**-a)
a long period of history

erase *verb*
1 to erase something written is to rub it out **2** to erase a recording on magnetic tape is to wipe it out **eraser** *noun* a piece of rubber or plastic for rubbing out writing

erect *adjective*
standing straight up
erect *verb*
to erect something is to set it up or build it **erection** *noun* something that has been built or erected

erode *verb*
to erode something is to wear it away • *Water has eroded the rocks.*

erosion *noun*
erosion is the wearing away of the earth's surface by the action of water and wind

errand *noun*
a short journey to take a message or fetch something

erratic *adjective* (*say* i-**rat**-ik)
not reliable or regular **erratically** *adverb*

error *noun*
a mistake **in error** by mistake

erupt *verb*
1 a volcano erupts when it shoots out lava **2** something powerful or violent erupts when it suddenly happens • *An argument erupted over a disputed goal.* **eruption** *noun* when a volcano erupts

escalate *verb*
to escalate is to become gradually greater or more serious • *The riots escalated into a war.* **escalation** *noun* when something becomes greater or more serious

escalator *noun*
a staircase with a revolving band of steps moving up or down

escape *verb*
1 to escape is to get free or get away **2** to escape something is to avoid it • *He escaped the washing-up.*
escape *noun*
an act or way of escaping • *What a lucky escape!* • *There was no escape.*

escort *noun* (*say* **ess**-kort)
1 a person or group who accompanies someone, especially to give protection **2** a group of vehicles, ships, or aircraft accompanying someone or something
escort *verb* (*say* i-**skort**)
to escort someone or something is to act as an escort to them

especially *adverb*
chiefly; more than anything else • *I like cheese, especially strong cheese.*

espionage *noun*
(*say* **ess**-pi-on-ahzh)
espionage is spying on other countries or people

essay *noun*
a short piece of writing on one subject

essence *noun*
1 the most important quality or ingredient of something **2** a concentrated liquid

essential *adjective*
something is essential when it is very important and you must have it or do it • *A car is essential in the country.* **essentially** *adverb* basically; in many ways • *The two stories are essentially the same.*

essential *noun*
something you must have or do • *I've made a list of some essentials to pack.*

establish *verb*
1 to establish a business, government, or relationship is to start it on a firm basis **2** to establish a fact is to show that it is true • *He managed to establish his innocence.*

establishment *noun*
1 a place where people do business **2** establishing something

estate *noun*
1 an area of land with a set of houses or factories on it **2** a large area of land belonging to one person **3** everything that a person owns when they die

estate agent *noun*
someone whose business is selling or letting buildings and land

estimate *noun* (*say* ess-ti-mat)
a rough calculation or guess about an amount or value

estimate *verb* (*say* ess-ti-mayt)
to estimate is to make an estimate

estimation *noun*
1 estimation is making a rough estimate **2** a person's estimation is their opinion • *It is very good in my estimation.*

estuary *noun* (**estuaries**)
(*say* ess-tew-er-i)
the mouth of a large river where it flows into the sea

etc.
short for *et cetera*

et cetera
and other similar things; and so on

etch *verb*
to etch a picture is to make it by engraving on a metal plate with an acid **etching** *noun* a picture made by engraving

eternal *adjective*
lasting for ever; not ending or changing **eternally** *adverb* for ever **eternity** *noun* eternity is time that goes on for ever

ethnic *adjective*
belonging to a particular national or racial group

eucalyptus *noun*
(*say* yoo-ka-lip-tus)
an evergreen tree from which an oil is obtained

euphemism *noun*
a word or phrase which is used instead of an impolite or less tactful one.'Pass away' is a euphemism for 'die'. **euphemistic** *adjective* using words that won't upset people

euro

euro *noun* (**euros** or **euro**)
the single currency introduced in the European Union in 1999

euthanasia *noun*
(*say* yooth-an-ay-zi-a)
euthanasia is causing someone to die gently and without pain when they are suffering from an incurable disease

evacuate *verb*
to evacuate people is to move them away from a dangerous place **evacuation** *noun* evacuation is moving people away, especially during a war or when there is a danger **evacuee** *noun* someone who is evacuated, especially during a war

evade *verb*
to evade someone or something is to make an effort to avoid them

evaporate *verb*
to evaporate is to change from liquid into steam or vapour **evaporation** *noun* when a liquid changes into steam or vapour

evasive *adjective*
trying to avoid answering something; not honest or straightforward

eve *noun*
the day or evening before an important day, for example New Year's Eve

even *adjective*
1 level and smooth **2** calm and stable • *He has a very even temper.* **3** equal • *The scores were even.* **4** able to be divided exactly by two • *6 and 14 are even numbers.* **to get even with someone** is to take revenge on them **evenly** *adverb* in an even way • *Spread the varnish evenly over the surface.* • *The money will be shared out evenly.* **evenness** *noun*

even *verb*
1 to even something is to make it even **2** to even or even out is to become even

even *adverb*
used to emphasize another word • *You haven't even started your work!* • *I ran fast, but she ran even faster.* **even so** although that is correct

evening *noun*
the time at the end of the day before night time

event *noun*
1 something that happens, especially something important **2** an item in an athletics contest • *The next event will be the long jump.*

eventful *adjective*
full of happenings, especially remarkable or exciting ones • *They had an eventful train journey across the USA.*

eventual *adjective*
happening at last or as a result • *Many failures preceded his eventual success.*

eventually *adverb*
finally, in the end • *We eventually managed to get the door open.*

ever *adverb*
1 at any time • *It's the best present I've ever had.* **2** always • *ever hopeful* **3** (*informal*) used for emphasis • *Why ever didn't you tell me?* **ever so** or **ever such** (*informal*) very much • *I'm ever so pleased.* • *She's ever such a nice girl.*

evergreen *adjective*
having green leaves all through the year

evergreen *noun*
an evergreen tree

everlasting *adjective*
lasting for ever or for a long time

every *determiner*
all the people or things of a particular kind; each • *Every child should learn to swim.* **every other** each alternate one; every second one • *Every other house had a garage.*

everybody *pronoun*
everyone

everyday *adjective*
happening or used every day; ordinary • *Everyday life has changed a lot in the last fifty years.*

everyone *pronoun*
every person; all people • *Everyone likes her.*

everything *pronoun*
all things; all • *Everything you need is here.*

everywhere *adverb*
in all places

evict *verb*
to evict someone is to make them move out of their house **eviction** *noun* making someone move out of their house

evidence *noun*
evidence is facts and information that give people reason to believe something

evident *adjective*
obvious; clearly seen • *It is evident that he is lying.* **evidently** *adverb* clearly; obviously • *His mother had evidently changed her mind.*

evil *adjective*
an evil person or action is one that is wicked and harmful

evil *noun*
something wicked or harmful

evolution *noun*
(*say* ee-vo-**loo**-shon)
the development of animals and plants over many centuries from earlier or simpler forms of life

evolve *verb*
to develop gradually or naturally

ewe *noun* (*say* yoo)
a female sheep

ewe

exact *adjective*
completely correct or accurate **exactly** *adverb* in an exact way; correctly **exactness** *noun* being correct

exaggerate *verb*
to exaggerate something is to make it seem bigger or better or worse than it really is **exaggeration** *noun* making something seem more than it really is

exam *noun*
(*informal*) an examination

examination *noun*
1 a test of someone's knowledge or skill **2** a close inspection of something

examine *verb*
to examine something is to look at it closely or in detail

examiner *noun*
a person who sets and marks an examination to test students' knowledge

example *noun*
1 a single thing or event that shows what others of the same kind are like

2 a person or thing that you should copy or learn from **for example** as an example

exasperate *verb*
to exasperate someone is to make them very annoyed **exasperation** *noun* a feeling of being very annoyed

excavate *verb*
to excavate a piece of land is to dig in it, especially in building or archaeology **excavation** *noun* digging in land **excavator** *noun* a machine that excavates

exceed *verb*
1 to exceed an amount or achievement is to be more than it or do better than it **2** to exceed a rule or limit is to go beyond it when you are not supposed to • *The driver was exceeding the speed limit.*

exceedingly *adverb*
extremely; very much

excel *verb* (**excelling, excelled**)
to excel at something is to be very good at it, and better than everyone else

excellent *adjective*
extremely good; of the best kind **excellence** *noun* excellence is being extremely good

except *preposition*
not including; apart from
• *Everyone got a prize except me.*

exception *noun*
1 something or someone that does not follow the normal rule **2** something that is left out

exceptional *adjective*
unusual • *She has exceptional skill.* **exceptionally** *adverb* to an unusual degree

excerpt *noun*
a piece taken from a book or story or film

excess *noun*
too much of something
• *We have an excess of food.*

excessive *adjective*
too much or too great **excessively** *adverb* too; by too much • *They are excessively greedy.*

exchange *verb*
to exchange something is to give it and receive something else for it

exchange *noun*
1 changing one thing for another **2** a place where telephone lines are connected to each other when a call is made **3** a place where company shares are bought and sold

excite *verb*
to excite someone is to make them eager and enthusiastic about

something • *The thought of the outing excited them.* **excitable** *adjective* easily excited

excitement *noun*
excitement is being excited

exclaim *verb*
to exclaim is to shout or cry out

exclamation *noun*
an exclamation is a word or phrase you say out loud that expresses a strong feeling such as surprise or pain

exclamation mark *noun*
the punctuation mark (!) placed after an exclamation

exclude *verb*
1 to exclude someone or something is to keep them out **2** to exclude something is to leave it out • *Do not exclude the possibility of rain.* **exclusion** *noun* exclusion is keeping someone or something out or leaving them out

exclusive *adjective*
1 not shared with others
• *Today's newspaper has an exclusive report about the match.*
2 allowing only a few people to be involved • *They joined an exclusive club.* **exclusively** *adverb*

excrete *verb*
to excrete is to pass waste matter out of your body **excretion** *noun* excreting waste matter

excuse *noun* (*say* **iks**-kewss)
a reason you give to explain why you have done something wrong

excuse *verb* (*say* iks-**kewz**)
1 to excuse someone is to forgive them **2** to excuse someone something is to allow them not to do it • *Please may I be excused swimming?* **excuse me** a polite apology for interrupting or disagreeing

execute *verb*
1 to execute someone is to put them to death as a punishment **2** to execute something is to perform or produce it • *She executed the somersault perfectly.* **execution** *noun* putting someone to death **executioner** *noun* someone who executes people

executive *noun*
a senior person in a business or government organization

exercise *noun*
1 exercise is using your body to make it strong and healthy **2** an exercise is a piece of work done for practice

exercise *verb*
1 to exercise is to do exercises
2 to exercise an animal is to give it exercise

a
b
c
d
e
f
g
h
i
j
k
l
m
n
o
p
q
r
s
t
u
v
w
x
y
z

exercise book noun
a book for writing in

exert verb
to exert oneself or one's ability is to make an effort to get something done • He exerted all his strength to bend the bar. **exertion** noun exertion is making a big effort

exhale verb
to exhale is to breathe out **exhalation** noun breathing out

exhaust noun
1 the waste gases from an engine 2 the pipe these gases are sent out through

exhaust verb
1 to exhaust someone is to make them very tired 2 to exhaust something is to use it up completely **exhaustion** noun great tiredness

exhibit verb
to exhibit something is to show it in public, especially in a gallery or museum

exhibit noun
something displayed in a gallery or museum

exhibition noun
a collection of things put on display for people to look at

exile verb
to exile someone is to send them away from their country

exile noun
1 exile is having to live away from your own country • He was in exile for ten years. 2 an exile is a person who is exiled

exist verb
1 to exist is to have life or be real • Do ghosts exist? 2 to exist is also to stay alive • They existed on biscuits and water.

existence noun
1 existing or being 2 staying alive • It was a real struggle for existence.

exit noun
1 the way out of a place 2 going out of a room or going off a stage or arena • They decided it was time for a quick exit.

exit verb
to exit is to leave a stage or arena

exotic adjective
unusual and colourful, especially because it comes from another part of the world

expand verb
1 to expand something is to make it larger 2 to expand is to become larger **expansion** noun expansion is becoming larger or making something larger

expanse noun
a wide area

expect verb
1 to expect something is to think that it will probably happen • I expect it will rain. 2 to be expecting someone is to be waiting for them to arrive 3 to expect something is to think that it ought to happen • She expects us to be quiet. **expecting** adjective a woman is expecting when she is pregnant

expectant adjective
full of expectation or hope

expectation noun
1 expecting something or being hopeful 2 something you hope to get

expedition noun
a journey made in order to do something • They are going on a climbing expedition.

expel verb (**expelling, expelled**)
1 to expel something is to send or force it out • The fan expels stale air and fumes. 2 to expel someone is to make them leave a school or country • He was expelled for bullying.

expenditure noun
expenditure is when you spend money or use effort • We must reduce our expenditure.

expense noun
the cost of doing something

expensive adjective
costing a lot of money

experience noun
1 experience is what you learn from doing and seeing things 2 an experience is something that has happened to you

experience verb
to experience something is to have it happen to you

experienced adjective
having skill or knowledge from much experience

experiment noun
a test made in order to study what happens **experimental** adjective something is experimental when it is being tried out to see how good or successful it is **experimentally** adverb as an experiment

experiment verb
to experiment is to carry out experiments **experimentation** noun doing experiments

expert noun
someone who has skill or special knowledge in something

expert adjective
having great knowledge or skill

expertise noun
expert ability or knowledge

expire verb
1 to expire is to come to an end or to

stop being usable • My bus pass has expired. 2 to expire is also to die **expiry** noun the time when something expires

explain verb
1 to explain something is to make it clear to someone else 2 to explain a fact or event is to show why it happens • That explains his absence.

explanation noun
something you say that explains something or gives reasons for it

explode verb
1 to explode is to burst or suddenly release energy with a loud bang 2 to explode a bomb is to set it off 3 to explode is to increase suddenly or quickly • The city's population exploded to 3 million in a year.

exploit noun (say **eks**-ploit)
a brave or exciting deed

exploit verb (say iks-**ploit**)
1 to exploit resources is to use or develop them 2 to exploit someone is to use them selfishly or unfairly **exploitation** noun exploitation is exploiting something or someone

explore verb
1 to explore a place is to travel through it to find out more about it 2 to explore a subject is to examine it carefully • We need to explore all the possibilities. **exploration** noun exploring a place **explorer** noun someone who explores a remote country to find out more about it

explosion noun
1 the exploding of a bomb or other weapon 2 a sudden or quick increase • There was a population explosion after the war.

explosive noun
a substance that can explode

explosive adjective
likely to explode; able to cause an explosion

export verb (say iks-**port**)
to export goods is to send them abroad to be sold **exporter** noun someone who exports goods

export noun (say **eks**-port)
something that is sent abroad to be sold

expose verb
1 to expose something is to reveal or uncover it 2 to expose someone is to show that they are to blame for something 3 to expose a photographic film is to let light reach it in a camera, so as to take a picture

exposure noun
1 exposure is being harmed by the weather when in the open without enough protection 2 an exposure is a single photograph or frame on a film

express *adjective*
going or sent quickly

express *noun*
a fast train stopping at only a few stations

express *verb*
to express an idea or feeling is to put it into words

expression *noun*
1 the look on a person's face that shows what they are thinking or feeling **2** a word or phrase **3** a way of speaking or performing music that expresses feelings **expressive** *adjective* an expressive look or statement is one that shows your feelings

expulsion *noun*
when someone is driven away or made to leave

exquisite *adjective*
very delicate or beautiful **exquisitely** *adverb*

extend *verb*
1 to extend is to stretch out **2** to extend something is to make it longer or larger **3** to extend a greeting or welcome is to offer it

extension *noun*
1 extension is extending or being extended **2** an extension is something added on, especially to a building **3** an extension is also an extra telephone in an office or house

extensive *adjective*
covering a large area • *The bomb caused extensive damage.* **extensively** *adverb* over a large area • *She travelled extensively*

extent *noun*
1 the area or length of something **2** an amount or level • *The extent of the damage was enormous.*

exterior *noun*
the outside of something

exterminate *verb*
to exterminate a people or breed of animal is to kill all the members of it **extermination** *noun* extermination is killing all the people or animals in a place

external *adjective*
outside **externally** *adverb* on the outside

extinct *adjective*
1 an animal or bird is extinct when there are no more examples of it alive like the dodo **2** a volcano is extinct when it is not burning or active any more

dodo

extinction *noun* when something no longer exists or is no longer active

extinguish *verb*
to extinguish a fire or light is to put it out **extinguisher** *noun* a device for putting out a fire

extra *adjective*
more than usual; added • *There is an extra charge for taking a bicycle on the train.*

extra *noun*
1 an extra person or thing **2** someone acting as part of the crowd in a film or play

extract *noun* (*say* **eks**-trakt)
1 a short piece taken from a book, play, or film **2** something obtained from something else • *a plant extract*

extract *verb* (*say* iks-**trakt**)
to extract something is to remove it or take it out of something else

extraction *noun*
1 a person's extraction is the place or people they come from • *She is of Indian extraction.* **2** extraction is taking something out

extraordinary *adjective*
unusual or very strange **extraordinarily** *adverb* in an extraordinary way

extraterrestrial *adjective*
existing in or coming from another planet

extraterrestrial *noun*
a living thing from another planet, especially in science fiction

extravagant *adjective*
spending or using too much of something **extravagance** *noun* extravagance is being extravagant **extravagantly** *adverb*

extreme *adjective*
1 very great or strong • *They were suffering from extreme cold.* **2** farthest away • *She lives in the extreme north of the country.*

extreme *noun*
1 something very great, strong, or far away **2** either end of something

extremely *adverb*
as much or as far as possible; very much • *They are extremely pleased.*

exuberant *adjective*
very cheerful or lively **exuberance** *noun* exuberance is being exuberant

eye *noun*
1 the organ of your body used for seeing **2** the small hole in a needle **3** the centre of a storm

eye *verb* (**eyeing, eyed**)
to eye someone or something is to look at them closely

eyeball *noun*
the ball-shaped part of your eye, inside your eyelids

eyebrow *noun*
the curved line of hair growing above each eye

eyelash *noun*
one of the short hairs that grow on your eyelids

eyelid *noun*
the upper or lower fold of skin that can close over your eyeball

eyesight *noun*
a person's eyesight is their ability to see

eyesore *noun*
something that is ugly to look at

eyewitness *noun*
someone who actually saw something happen, especially an accident or crime

F
short for Fahrenheit

fable *noun*
a short story which teaches a lesson about how people should behave, often with animals as characters

fabric *noun*
cloth

fabulous *adjective*
1 very great • *The prince enjoyed fabulous wealth.* **2** (*informal*) wonderful; marvellous **3** belonging to fables and myths and not to real life • *Dragons are fabulous creatures.*

face *noun*
1 the front part of your head **2** the look on your face • *She had a friendly face.* **3** the front or upper side of something • *Put the cards face down.* **4** a surface • *A cube has six faces.* **face to face** looking directly at someone **facial** *adjective* on or to do with your face • *He had some facial injuries.*

face *verb*
1 to face in a certain direction is to look there or have the front in that direction • *Please face the front.* • *The church faces the school.* **2** to face a problem or danger is to accept that you have to deal with it

facility *noun* (**facilities**)
(*say* fa-**sil**-i-ti)
something that helps you to do things • *The youth club has facilities for dancing and sport.*

fact *noun*
something that is true or certain **as a matter of fact** or **in fact** really

factor *noun*
1 something that helps to bring about a result or situation • *Hard work has been a factor in her success.* **2** a number by which a larger number can be divided exactly • *4 and 5 are factors of 20.*

factory *noun* (**factories**)
a large building where machines are used to make things in large quantities

factual *adjective*
based on or containing facts • *Write down a factual account of what happened.* **factually** *adverb*

fade *verb*
1 to fade is to lose colour, freshness, or strength **2** to fade or fade away is to disappear gradually

Fahrenheit *adjective*
(*say* **fa**-ren-hyt)
using a scale for measuring temperature that gives 32 degrees for freezing water and 212 degrees for boiling water

fail *verb*
1 to fail is to try to do something but not be able to do it **2** to fail an exam or test is not to pass it **3** to fail is also to become weak or useless or to come to an end • *The batteries are failing.* • *The crops failed last year.* **4** to fail to do something is not to do it when you should • *He failed to warn me of the danger.*

fail *noun*
not being successful in an examination • *She has five passes and one fail.* **without fail** definitely or always • *I'll be there without fail.*

failing *noun*
a fault or weakness

failure *noun*
1 failure is not being successful **2** a failure is someone or something that has failed

faint *adjective*
1 weak; not clear or distinct **2** nearly unconscious, often because you are exhausted or very hungry
faintly *adverb* weakly or not clearly
faintness *noun*

faint *verb*
to faint is to become unconscious for a short time

faint-hearted *adjective*
not having much courage or confidence

fair¹ *adjective*
1 right or just; honest • *It was a fair fight.* **2** light in colour • *The sisters both had fair hair.* **3** quite good • *We've got a fair chance of winning.* **4** weather is fair when it is fine and not raining **fairness** *noun* fairness is being fair

fair² *noun*
1 an outdoor entertainment with rides, amusements, and stalls. Fairs move from town to town.
2 an exhibition or market • *a craft fair*

fairground *noun*
a place where a fair is held

fairly *adverb*
1 quite or rather • *It is fairly hard.* **2** honestly; justly • *He promised to treat everyone fairly.*

fairy *noun* (**fairies**)
an imaginary small creature with wings and magic powers

fairy story or
fairy tale *noun*
(**fairy stories**)
a story about fairies or magic

faith *noun*
1 faith is strong belief or trust • *We have great faith in her.* **2** a faith is a religion

fairy

faithful *adjective*
loyal and trustworthy **faithfully** *adverb* **faithfulness** *noun*

fake *noun*
a copy of something made to deceive people into thinking it is real

fake *adjective*
not real or genuine • *fake diamonds*

fake *verb*
1 to fake something is to make it look real in order to deceive people **2** to fake something is also to pretend to have it • *He was always faking illness so he could miss games.*

falcon *noun*
a small kind of hawk **falconry** *noun* the sport of training falcons to hunt other birds

fall *verb* (**falling, fell, fallen**)
1 to fall is to come down quickly towards the ground **2** numbers or prices fall when they get lower or smaller **3** a city or stronghold falls when it is captured **4** soldiers fall when they die in battle **5** when silence falls it becomes quiet **6** to fall sick or ill is to become ill **7** a look or glance falls on someone when it is directed at them **to fall for someone** is to start loving them **to fall for something** is to be tricked into believing it **to fall in** is to collapse • *The roof fell in.* **to fall out** is to quarrel and stop being friends **to fall through** is to fail to happen • *Our plans have fallen through.*

fall *noun*
1 a time when a person or thing falls • *My grandma had a bad fall.* **2** (*in America*) autumn

fallout *noun*
fallout is radioactive dust that is carried in the air after a nuclear explosion

fallow *adjective*
land that is fallow has been ploughed but not sown with crops • *The field was left fallow every three years.*

falls *plural noun*
a waterfall

false *adjective*
1 untrue or incorrect
2 faked; not genuine
3 treacherous or deceitful **falsely** *adverb*

falsehood *noun*
1 falsehood is telling lies
2 a falsehood is a lie

falter *verb*
1 to falter is to hesitate when you move or speak **2** to falter is also to become weaker • *His courage began to falter.*

fame *noun*
fame is being famous
famed *adjective* a person or thing is famed when they are very well known

familiar *adjective*
1 well-known; often seen or experienced • *It was a familiar sight.* **2** knowing something well • *Are you familiar with this story?* **3** very friendly **familiarity** *noun* familiarity with something is being familiar with it

family *noun* (**families**)
1 parents and their children, sometimes including grandchildren and other relations **2** a group of animals, plants, or things that are alike in some way • *The tiger is a member of the cat family.*

family tree *noun*
a diagram showing how people in a family are related

famine *noun*
a severe shortage of food that causes many people to die

famished *adjective*
extremely hungry

famous *adjective*
known to a lot of people • *Her uncle is a famous scientist.*

fan¹ *noun*
a device for making the air move about, in order to cool people or things

fan

fan¹ *verb* (**fanning, fanned**)
to fan something is to send a draught of air at it • *She fanned her face with her hand.* **to fan out** is to spread out in the shape of a fan

fan² *noun*
an enthusiastic follower or supporter of someone or something

fanatic *noun* (*say* fa-**nat**-ik)
someone who is too enthusiastic about something **fanatical** *adjective* too enthusiastic about something **fanatically** *adverb*

fanciful *adjective*
imagined rather than based on facts or reason

fancy *noun* (**fancies**)
1 fancy is imagination **2** a fancy is a liking or desire for something

fancy *adjective* (**fancier, fanciest**)
decorated; not plain

fancy *verb* (**fancies, fancying, fancied**)
1 to fancy something is to want or like it • *Does anyone fancy an ice cream?* **2** to fancy something unusual is to imagine or think of it • *Just fancy him riding a horse!*

fancy dress *noun*
unusual costume that you wear to a party or dance, often to make you look like someone else

fanfare *noun*
a short burst of music, often with trumpets and to announce something

fang *noun*
a long, sharp tooth

fantastic *adjective*
1 strange or unusual • *The blocks of ice had been carved into the most fantastic shapes.* **2** (*informal*) excellent **fantastically** *adverb* strangely or unusually

fantasy *noun* (**fantasies**)
1 something pleasant that you imagine but isn't likely to happen • *His fantasy is to play football for England.* **2** a very imaginative story

far *adverb* (**farther, farthest**)
1 a long way • *We didn't go far.* **2** much; by a great amount • *She's a far better singer than I am.* **so far** up to now

far *adjective* (**farther, farthest**) distant; opposite • *She swam to the far side of the river.*

farce *noun*
1 a far-fetched or absurd kind of comedy **2** a series of ridiculous events • *The trial was a complete farce.* **farcical** *adjective* absurd and ridiculous

fare *noun*
the money you pay to travel on a bus, train, ship, or aircraft

fare *verb*
to fare is to get on or make progress • *How did you fare in your exam?*

farewell *exclamation*
goodbye

far-fetched *adjective*
unlikely to be true; difficult to believe

farm *noun*
1 an area of land where someone grows crops and keeps animals for food **2** the buildings on land of this kind

farm *verb*
to farm is to grow crops and raise animals for food

farmer *noun*
someone who owns or looks after a farm

farmyard *noun*
the open area surrounded by farm buildings

farther *adverb, adjective*
at or to a greater distance; more distant • *She lives farther from the school than I do.*

farthest *adverb, adjective*
at or to the greatest distance; most distant

fascinate *verb*
to fascinate someone is to attract or interest them very much **fascinating** *adjective* very interesting **fascination** *noun* a feeling of being fascinated; a great interest in something

fashion *noun*
1 the style of clothes or other things that most people like at a particular time **2** a way of doing something • *Please continue in the same fashion.*

fashion *verb*
to fashion something is to make it in a particular shape or style • *The ring had been fashioned from the finest gold.*

fashionable *adjective*
something is fashionable when it follows a style that is popular at a particular time

fast¹ *adjective*
1 moving or done quickly • *He's a fast runner.* **2** allowing fast movement • *This is a fast road.* **3** a watch or clock is fast when it shows a time later than the correct time **4** firmly fixed • *Make the boat fast.* **5** a fast colour is one that is not likely to fade

fast¹ *adverb*
1 quickly **2** firmly
fast asleep deeply asleep

fast² *verb*
to fast is to go without food

fasten *verb*
to fasten something is to join it firmly to something else **fastener** or **fastening** *noun* a device used to fasten something

fat *noun*
1 the white greasy part of meat **2** an oily or greasy substance used in cooking

fat *adjective* (**fatter, fattest**)
1 having a very thick round body **2** thick • *What a fat book!* **3** fat meat is meat with a lot of fat

fatal *adjective*
1 causing someone's death • *There has been a fatal accident on the motorway.* **2** likely to have bad results • *He then made a fatal mistake.* **fatally** *adverb* someone is fatally injured or wounded when they die as a result of their injuries

fate *noun*
1 a power that is thought to make things happen **2** someone's fate is what has happened or will happen to them

father *noun*
your male parent

father-in-law *noun*
the father of your husband or wife

fatigue *noun* (*say* fa-**teeg**)
1 extreme tiredness **2** weakness in metals, caused by stress **fatigued** *adjective* extremely tired

a b c d e f g h i j k l m n o p q r s t u v w x y z

fatten *verb*
1 to fatten something is to make it fat **2** to fatten is to become fat

fatty *adjective* (**fattier, fattiest**)
containing a lot of fat

fault *noun*
1 something wrong that spoils a person or thing; a flaw or mistake **2** the responsibility or blame for something • *It's my fault we are late.* **to be at fault** is to be in the wrong or responsible for a mistake **faultless** *adjective* something is faultless when it is perfect and has nothing wrong with it

fault *verb*
to fault something is to find faults in it

faulty *adjective* (**faultier, faultiest**)
having a fault or faults; not working properly

fauna *noun* (*say* **faw**-na)
the animals of an area or of a period of time

favour *noun*
1 a favour is something kind that you do for someone • *Will you do me a favour?* **2** favour is approval or goodwill • *The idea found favour with most people.* **to be in favour of someone or something** is to like or support them

favour *verb*
to favour someone or something is to like or support them, or prefer them to others

favourable *adjective*
1 helpful or advantageous **2** showing approval **favourably** *adverb*

favourite *adjective*
that you like best • *This is my favourite book.*

favourite *noun*
the person or thing that you like best • *This book is my favourite.*

favouritism *noun*
favouritism is when someone is unfairly kinder to one person than to others

fawn *noun*
1 a young deer **2** a light brown colour

fawn

fear *noun*
fear, or a fear, is a feeling that something unpleasant may happen

fear *verb*
1 to fear someone or something is to be afraid of them **2** to fear something is also to be anxious or sad about it • *I fear we may be too late.*

fearful *adjective*
1 frightened **2** (*informal*) awful or horrid • *They had a fearful quarrel.* **fearfully** *adverb*

fearless *adjective*
having no fear **fearlessly** *adverb*

fearsome *adjective*
frightening

feasible *adjective*
able to be done; possible or likely

feast *noun*
a large and splendid meal for a lot of people

feast *verb*
to feast is to have a feast

feat *noun*
something brave or difficult that you do

feather *noun*
a bird's feathers are the very light coverings that grow from its skin **feathery** *adjective* soft or light like feathers

feature *noun*
1 your features are the different parts of your face • *He has rugged features.* **2** an important or noticeable part of something; a characteristic **3** a newspaper article or television programme on a particular subject

feature *verb*
1 to feature something is to make it an important part of something **2** to feature in something is to be an important part of it • *Sport features a lot in the Sunday papers.*

February *noun*
the second month of the year

fed up *adjective*
(*informal*) depressed or unhappy

fee *noun*
a payment or charge

feeble *adjective*
weak; not having much strength or force • *He uttered a feeble cry.* **feebly** *adverb*

feed *verb*
1 to feed a person or animal is to give them food **2** to feed on something is to eat it • *Sheep feed on grass.* **3** to feed a machine is to put coins or other things into it

feed *noun*
1 a feed is a meal **2** feed is food for animals

feel *verb* (**feeling, felt**)
1 to feel something is to touch it to find out what it is like **2** to feel a feeling or emotion is to experience it • *I feel very angry about it.* **to feel like something** is to want it

feel *noun*
what something is like when you touch it • *Her dress has a funny feel about it.*

feeler *noun*
an insect's feelers are the two long thin parts that extend from the front of its body and are used for feeling

feeling *noun*
1 feeling is the ability to feel or touch things • *She lost the feeling in her right hand.* **2** feeling is also what a person feels in the mind, such as love or fear • *I have hurt her feelings.* **3** a feeling is what you think about something • *My feeling is that he's right.*

feline *adjective*
to do with cats; like a cat

fell¹
past tense of **fall** *verb*

fell² *verb*
1 to fell a tree is to cut it down **2** to fell someone is to knock them down

fell³ *noun*
a hill or area of wild hilly country in the north of England

fellow *noun*
1 a friend or companion; someone who belongs to the same group **2** (*informal*) a man or boy • *He's a clever fellow.*

fellow *adjective*
of the same group or kind • *She arranged a meeting with her fellow teachers.*

fellowship *noun*
1 fellowship is friendship **2** a fellowship is a group of friends; a society

felt¹
past tense and past participle of **feel**

felt² *noun*
thick woollen material

felt-tip pen or **felt-tipped pen** *noun*
a pen with a tip made of felt or fibre

female adjective
of the sex that can produce offspring
female noun
a female person or animal

feminine adjective
1 to do with women or like women; suitable for women 2 in some languages, belonging to the class of words that includes words referring to women **femininity** noun being feminine

feminist noun
someone who believes that women should have the same rights and opportunities as men **feminism** noun the belief that women should have the same rights and opportunities as men

fen noun
an area of low-lying marshy or flooded land

fence noun
a wooden or metal barrier round an area of land
fence verb
1 to fence something or to fence it in is to put a fence round it 2 to fence is to fight with long narrow swords called *foils*, as a sport **fencer** noun someone who fences **fencing** noun the sport of fighting with swords

fend verb
to fend for yourself is to take care of yourself **to fend someone or something off** is to keep them away from yourself when they are attacking you

fender noun
a low guard placed round a fireplace to stop coal from falling into the room

ferment verb
beer or wine ferments when it bubbles and changes chemically by the action of yeast or bacteria. This makes the sugar turn into alcohol. **fermentation** noun the process of fermenting

fern noun
a plant with feathery leaves and no flowers

ferocious adjective
fierce or savage **ferociously** adverb
ferocity noun fierceness

ferret noun
a small fierce animal with a long thin body, used for catching rabbits and rats

ferry noun
a boat that takes people or things across a river or other stretch of water
ferry verb (**ferries, ferrying, ferried**)
to ferry people or things is to take them from one place to another,

especially by boat or car

fertile adjective
1 land that is fertile is good for growing crops and plants 2 people or animals that are fertile can produce babies or young animals **fertility** noun being fertile

fertilize verb
1 to fertilize the soil is to add chemicals or manure to it so that crops and plants grow better to fertilize an egg or plant is to put sperm or pollen into it so that it develops its young or seeds **fertilization** noun fertilizing the soil or an egg or plant

fertilizer noun
chemicals or manure added to the soil to make crops and plants grow better

fervent adjective
very enthusiastic or passionate about something • *He is a fervent supporter of reform.* **fervently** adverb
fervour noun great enthusiasm or passion

festival noun
1 a time of celebration, especially for religious reasons 2 an organized set of concerts, shows, or other events, especially one that is arranged every year

festive adjective
to do with joyful celebrating **festivities** noun parties and other events held to celebrate something

fetch verb
1 to fetch something or someone is to go and get them 2 something fetches a particular price when it is sold for that price • *My old bike fetched £10.*

fête noun (say fayt)
an outdoor event with stalls, games, and things for sale, often held to raise money

fetters plural noun
fetters are chains put round a prisoner's ankles

feud noun (say fewd)
a bitter quarrel between two people or families that lasts a long time
feud verb
people feud when they keep up a quarrel for a long time

feudal adjective (say few-dal)
in the Middle Ages, the feudal system was a system in which people could farm land in exchange for working or fighting for the owner **feudalism** noun the feudal system

fever noun
1 a person has a fever when their body temperature is higher than usual because they are ill 2 fever is excitement or agitation

feverish adjective
1 someone is feverish when they have a slight fever 2 excited or frantic • *There was feverish activity getting the hall ready for the show.* **feverishly** adverb

few determiner
not many
few noun
a small number of people or things **a good few** or **quite a few** a fairly large number

fez noun (**fezzes**)
a tall round hat with a flat top and a tassel, worn by some men in Muslim countries

fez

fiancé noun
(say fee-**ahn**-say)
a woman's fiancé is the man who she is engaged to be married to

fiancée noun (say fee-**ahn**-say)
a man's fiancée is the woman who he is engaged to be married to

fiasco noun (**fiascos**)
(say fi-**ass**-koh)
a complete failure • *The party turned into a fiasco.*

fib noun
a lie about something unimportant
fib verb (**fibbing, fibbed**)
to fib is to tell a lie about something unimportant
fibber noun someone who tells fibs

fibre noun (say **fy**-ber)
1 a fibre is a very thin thread 2 fibre is a substance made up of thin threads 3 fibre is also a substance in food that helps you to digest it **fibrous** adjective made up of lots of fibres

fibreglass noun
a kind of lightweight plastic containing glass fibres

fickle adjective
someone is fickle when they often change their mind or do not stay loyal to one person or group

fiction noun
fiction is writings about events that have not really happened; stories and novels **fictional** adjective existing only in a story, not in real life

fictitious adjective
made up; not true

fiddle noun
1 a violin
2 (informal) a swindle

fiddle verb
1 to fiddle is to play the violin 2 to fiddle with something is to keep touching or playing with it with your fingers 3 (informal) to fiddle something is to be dishonest about it **fiddler** noun someone who plays the violin

fiddly adjective
(informal) awkward to use or do because it involves handling small objects • Making the model of the ship was quite a fiddly job.

fidelity noun (say fi-**del**-i-ti)
being faithful or loyal

fidget verb
to fidget is to make small restless movements because you are bored or nervous **fidgety** adjective someone is fidgety when they fidget a lot

field noun
1 a piece of land with crops or grass growing on it, often surrounded by a hedge or fence 2 an area of grass where people play a sport 3 a subject that someone is studying or interested in • The book describes important developments in the field of science. 4 all the people or animals that take part in a race

field verb
1 to field a ball in cricket or other games is to stop it or catch it 2 to be fielding in cricket is to be on the side that is not batting **fielder** noun a player who is fielding

fiend noun (say feend)
1 a devil or evil spirit 2 a wicked or cruel person

fiendish adjective
1 wicked or cruel 2 very difficult or complicated • That was a fiendish puzzle. **fiendishly** adverb to be fiendishly difficult or complicated is to be very difficult or complicated indeed

fierce adjective
1 angry and violent and likely to attack you 2 strong or intense • The heat from the fire was fierce. **fiercely** adverb **fierceness** noun

fiery adjective
1 full of flames or heat 2 easily made angry • He had a fiery temper.

fiddle

fifteen noun
the number 15 **fifteenth** adjective, noun 15th

fifth adjective, noun
the next after the fourth **fifthly** adverb in the fifth place; as the fifth one

fifty noun
the number 50 **fiftieth** adjective, noun 50th

fifty-fifty adjective, adverb
to share something fifty-fifty is to share it equally between two people or groups • Let's split the money fifty-fifty.

fig noun
a soft fruit full of small seeds

fight noun
1 a struggle against someone, using hands or weapons 2 an attempt to achieve or overcome something • We can all help in the fight against crime.

fight verb (**fighting, fought**)
1 to fight someone is to have a fight with them 2 to fight something is to try to stop it • They fought the fire all night.

fighter noun
1 someone who fights
2 a fast military plane that attacks other aircraft

fighter

figure noun
1 one of the symbols that stand for numbers, such as 1, 2, and 3 2 the shape of someone's body 3 a diagram or illustration in a book or magazine 4 a pattern or shape • He drew a figure of eight.

figure verb
1 to appear or take part in something • His name does not figure in the list of entrants. 2 to think that something is probably true • I figure the best thing to do is to wait. **to figure something out** is to work it out • Can you figure out the answer?

file¹ noun
a metal tool with a rough surface that you rub on things to make them smooth or shape them

file¹ verb
to file something is to make it smooth or shape it with a file

file² noun
1 a box or folder for keeping papers in 2 (in computing) a set of data that has been stored under one name in a computer **to walk in single file** is to walk one behind the other

file² verb
1 to file a paper or document is to put it in a box or folder 2 to file is to walk one behind the other

fill verb
1 to fill something is to make it full 2 to fill is to become full • The room was filling quickly. 3 to fill a tooth is to put a filling in it **to fill in a form** is to write answers to all the questions on it **to fill something up** is to fill it completely

fill noun
enough to make you full • Eat your fill.

fillet noun
a piece of fish or meat without bones

filling noun
1 a piece of metal put in a tooth to replace a decayed part 2 food you put inside a pie, sandwich, or cake

filling station noun
a place where petrol is sold

filly noun (**fillies**)
a young female horse

film noun
1 a series of moving pictures that tells a story, such as those shown in a cinema or on television 2 a roll or piece of thin plastic coated with a chemical that is sensitive to light, that you put in some cameras to take photographs 3 a very thin layer of something • The table was covered in a film of grease. **filmy** adjective thin and transparent

film verb
to film a book or story is to make a film of it

filter noun
a device for removing dirt or other unwanted things from a liquid or gas that passes through it

filter verb
1 to filter something is to pass it through a filter 2 to filter is to move gradually • People started to filter into the hall.

filth noun
disgusting dirt **filthy** adjective extremely dirty

fin noun
1 a thin flat part that sticks out from a fish's body and helps it to swim 2 a small part that sticks out from an aircraft or rocket and helps it to balance

final *adjective*
1 coming at the end; last 2 a decision is final when it puts an end to argument or doubt • *You must not go, and that's final!*

final *noun*
the last of a series of contests, that decides the overall winner

finale *noun* (say fin-**ah**-li)
the last part of a show or piece of music

finalist *noun*
a person or team taking part in a final

finally *adverb*
1 after a long time, at last • *We finally got there around midnight.* 2 as the last thing • *Finally, I would like to thank my parents.*

finance *noun*
1 finance is the business of using and looking after money 2 someone's finances are the amount of money or funds they have

finance *verb*
to finance something is to provide money for it

financial *adjective*
to do with money

finch *noun*
a small bird with a short thick beak

find *verb* (**finding, found**)
1 to find something is to see or get it by chance or by looking for it 2 to find something is also to learn it by experience • *He found that digging is hard work.* **to find someone out** is to discover them doing wrong **to find something out** is to get information about it **finder** *noun* someone who finds something

findings *plural noun*
things someone has found out

fine[1] *adjective*
1 of high quality; excellent 2 the weather is fine when it is sunny and not raining 3 very thin or delicate • *The curtains were made of a fine material.* 4 made of small particles • *The sand on the beach was very fine.* **finely** *adverb* into fine or small parts • *Slice the tomato finely.*

fine[2] *noun*
money that someone must pay as a punishment

fine[2] *verb*
to fine someone is to make them pay money as a punishment

finger *noun*
1 one of the long thin parts that stick out on your hand 2 something that is shaped like a finger

finger *verb*
to finger something is to touch it with your fingers

fingernail *noun*
the hard covering at the end of your finger

fingerprint *noun*
a mark made by the pattern of curved lines on the tip of your finger

fingerprint

finish *verb*
1 to finish something is to bring it to an end 2 to finish is to come to an end

finish *noun*
the end of something

fiord *noun* (say fi-**ord**)
in Norway, an inlet of the sea between high cliffs

fir *noun*
an evergreen tree with leaves like needles

fire *noun*
1 the flames, heat, and light that come from burning things 2 coal or wood burning in a grate or furnace to give heat 3 a device using electricity or gas to heat a room 4 the shooting of guns • *Hold your fire!* **to be on fire** is to be burning **to set fire to something** is to start it burning

fire *verb*
1 to fire a gun is to shoot it 2 (*informal*) to fire someone is to dismiss them from their job 3 to fire pottery or bricks is to bake them in an oven to make them hard

fire brigade *noun*
a team of people whose job is to put out fires and rescue people from fires

fire engine *noun*
a large vehicle that carries firefighters and equipment to fight fires

fire extinguisher *noun*
a metal cylinder containing water or foam for spraying over a fire to put it out

firefighter *noun*
someone whose job is to put out fires

fireplace *noun*
an open space for a fire in the wall of a room

fireproof *adjective*
something is fireproof when it can stand great heat without burning

fire station *noun*
the headquarters of a fire brigade

fireworks

firework *noun*
a cardboard tube containing chemicals that give off coloured sparks and lights and sometimes make loud noises

firm *noun*
a business organization • *She works for a clothing firm.*

firm *adjective*
1 fixed or solid so that it will not move 2 definite and not likely to change • *She has made a firm decision to go.* **firmly** *adverb* in a strong or definite way **firmness** *noun*

first *adjective*
1 coming before all others 2 the most important • *He plays football in the first team at school.*

first *adverb*
before everything else • *Finish your work first.*

first *noun*
a person or thing that is first **at first** at the beginning; to start with

first aid *noun*
simple medical treatment that is given to an injured person before a doctor comes

first-class *adjective*
1 belonging to the best part of a service • *Send the letter by first-class post.* 2 excellent

first-hand *adjective, adverb*
you get first-hand information directly, rather than from other people or from books

firstly *adverb*
as the first thing • *Firstly, let me tell you about our holiday.*

fish *noun* (**fish** or **fishes**)
an animal that lives and breathes in water

fish *verb*
to fish is to try to catch fish

fisherman *noun* (**fishermen**)
someone who tries to catch fish

fishmonger *noun*
a shopkeeper who sells fish

fishy *adjective* (**fishier, fishiest**)
1 smelling or tasting of fish 2 (*informal*) suspicious or doubtful • *His excuse was rather fishy.*

fist *noun*
a tightly closed hand with the fingers bent into the palm

fit[1] *adjective* (**fitter, fittest**)
1 healthy and strong because you get a lot of exercise 2 suitable or good enough • *It was a meal fit for a king.* 3 ready or likely • *They worked till they were fit to collapse.*

a b c d e f g h i j k l m n o p q r s t u v w x y z

fit¹ *verb* (**fitting, fitted**)
1 to fit someone or something is to be the right size and shape for them **2** to fit something is to put it into place • *We need to fit a new lock on the door.* **3** to fit something is to be suitable for it • *Her speech fitted the occasion perfectly.* **to fit in** is to be suitable for something • *Does this fit in with your plans?*

fit¹ *noun*
the way something fits • *The coat is a good fit.*

fit² *noun*
1 a sudden illness, especially one that makes you move violently or become unconscious **2** (*informal*) a sudden outburst • *He rushed off in a fit of rage.* **in fits and starts** in short bursts; now and then

fitness *noun*
being healthy and strong because of doing a lot of exercise

fitting *adjective*
suitable or proper

fitting *noun*
fittings are pieces of furniture or equipment in a room or building

five *noun*
the number 5

fix *verb*
1 to fix something is to join it firmly to something else or to put it where it will not move **2** to fix something is also to decide or settle it • *We have fixed a date for the party.* **3** to fix something that is broken is to mend it • *He's fixing my bike.* **to fix something up** is to arrange or organize something

fix *noun*
(*informal*) an awkward situation • *I'm in a fix.*

fixture *noun*
1 a sports event planned for a particular day **2** something fixed in its place, like a cupboard or a washbasin

fizz *verb*
1 to fizz is to make a hissing or spluttering sound **2** liquid fizzes when it produces a lot of small bubbles **fizzy** *adjective* a fizzy drink has a lot of bubbles

fizzle *verb*
to fizzle is to make a slight hissing sound **to fizzle out** is to end in a disappointing or unsuccessful way

flabby *adjective* (**flabbier, flabbiest**)
fat and soft; not firm

flag *noun*
a piece of material with a coloured pattern or shape on it, often used as the symbol of a country or organization

flag *verb* (**flagging, flagged**)
to flag is to become weak or droop

flagship *noun*
the main ship in a navy's fleet, which has the commander of the fleet on board

flagstone *noun*
a flat slab of paving stone

flake *noun*
1 a very light thin piece of something **2** a piece of falling snow **flaky** *adjective* like flakes, or likely to break into flakes

flake *verb*
to flake is to come off in light thin pieces **to flake out** (*informal*) is to faint or fall asleep

flame *noun*
a bright strip of fire that flickers and leaps

flame *verb*
to flame is to produce flames or become bright red

flamingo *noun* (**flamingos**)
a large wading bird with long legs, a long neck, and pale pink feathers

flammable *adjective*
that can be set alight

flan *noun*
a pie without any pastry on top

flank *noun*
the side of something, especially an animal's body or an army

flannel *noun*
1 a flannel is a piece of soft cloth you use to wash yourself **2** flannel is a soft woollen material

flap *noun*
1 a part that hangs down from one edge of something, usually to cover an opening **2** the action or sound of flapping

flap *verb* (**flapping, flapped**)
1 to flap something is to move it up and down or from side to side • *The bird flapped its wings.* **2** to flap is to wave about • *The sails were flapping in the breeze.*

flapjack *noun*
a cake made from oats and syrup

flare *verb*
1 to flare is to burn with a sudden bright flame **2** to flare up is to become suddenly angry **3** things flare when they get gradually wider

flare *noun*
1 a bright light fired into the sky as a signal **2** a gradual widening, especially in skirts or trousers

flash *noun*
1 a sudden bright burst of light **2** a device for making a brief bright light when you take a photograph **3** a

sudden display of anger or humour **in a flash** immediately or very quickly

flash *verb*
1 to flash is to make a sudden bright burst of light **2** to flash past or across is to approach and go past very fast • *The train flashed past into the distance.*

flashy *adjective* (**flashier, flashiest**)
showy and expensive

flask *noun*
1 a bottle with a narrow neck **2** a vacuum flask

flask

flat *adjective*
1 having no curves or bumps; smooth and level **2** spread out; lying at full length • *Lie flat on the ground.* **3** dull or uninteresting • *He spoke in a flat voice.* **4** a liquid is flat when it is no longer fizzy **5** a tyre is flat when it is punctured and has lost its air **6** below the proper musical pitch • *The clarinet was flat.* **flatness** *noun*

flat *adverb*
exactly and no more • *He won the race in ten seconds flat.* **flat out** as fast as possible • *They all worked flat out to get everything ready in time.*

flat *noun*
1 a set of rooms for living in, usually on one floor of a building **2** (*in music*) the note that is a semitone lower than the natural note; the sign (♭) that indicates this

flatly *adverb*
in a definite way, leaving no room for doubt • *They flatly refused to go.*

flatten *verb*
1 to flatten something is to make it flat **2** to flatten is to become flat

flatter *verb*
to flatter someone is to praise them

more than they deserve, often because you want to please them **flattery** noun too much praise

flavour noun
the taste and smell of something

flavour verb
to flavour something is to give it a particular taste and smell **flavouring** noun something added to food or drink to give it a particular flavour

flaw noun
a fault that stops a person or thing from being perfect • *The diamond had a flaw.* **flawed** adjective having a fault **flawless** adjective perfect, with no faults

flax noun
a plant that produces fibres from which cloth is made and seeds from which oil is obtained

flea noun
a small jumping insect that sucks blood

fled
past tense and past participle of **flee**

flee verb
to flee is to run away from something

flea

fleece noun
1 a sheep's fleece is the wool that covers its body **2** a piece of clothing made from a soft warm material **fleecy** adjective soft and warm like a fleece

fleet noun
a number of ships, aircraft, or vehicles owned by one country or company

fleeting adjective
very brief; passing quickly • *I caught a fleeting glimpse of him.*

flesh noun
the soft substance of the bodies of people and animals, made of muscle and fat **fleshy** adjective part of your body is fleshy when there is a lot of flesh on it

flex noun
flexible insulated wire for carrying an electric current

flex verb
to flex something is to move or bend it • *Try flexing your muscles.*

flexible adjective
1 easy to bend or stretch **2** able to be changed • *Our plans are flexible.* **flexibility** noun something that has flexibility can bend or stretch easily

flick noun
a quick light hit or movement

flick verb
to flick something is to hit or move it with a flick

flicker verb
to flicker is to burn or shine unsteadily

flight¹ noun
1 flight is the action of flying • *She looked up to see a flock of birds in flight.* **2** a flight is a journey in an aircraft or rocket **3** a flight is also a group of flying birds or aircraft **4** a flight of stairs is one set of stairs

flight² noun
running away; escape

flimsy adjective (**flimsier, flimsiest**)
light and thin; fragile

flinch verb
to flinch is to make a sudden movement because you are frightened or in pain

fling verb (**flinging, flung**)
to fling something is to throw it violently or carelessly

flint noun
1 flint is a very hard kind of stone **2** a flint is a piece of this stone or hard metal used to produce sparks

flip verb (**flipping, flipped**)
to flip something is to turn it over quickly • *We were flipping pancakes in the kitchen.*

flipper noun
1 a limb that water animals use for swimming **2** a flat rubber shoe shaped like a duck's foot, that you wear on your feet to help you swim

flit verb (**flitting, flitted**)
to flit is to fly or move lightly and quickly • *A moth flitted across the room.*

float verb
1 to float is to stay or move on the surface of a liquid or in the air **2** to float something is to make it stay on the surface of a liquid

float noun
1 a light object that is designed to float • *She learned to swim with the help of floats.* **2** a vehicle with a platform used for delivering milk or for carrying a display in a parade

flock noun
a group of sheep, goats, or birds

flock verb
to flock is to gather or move in a crowd

flog verb (**flogging, flogged**)
1 to flog someone is to beat them severely with a whip or stick **2** (*slang*) to flog something is to sell it

flood noun
1 a large amount of water spreading over a place that is usually dry **2** a great amount of something • *They received a flood of complaints.*

flood verb
1 to flood something is to cover it with a large amount of water **2** a river floods when it flows over its banks **3** to arrive in large amounts • *Offers of help came flooding in from all over the country.*

floodlight noun
a lamp that gives a broad bright beam, used to light up a public building or a sports ground at night **floodlit** adjective lit up by floodlights

floor noun
1 the part of a room that people walk on **2** all the rooms on the same level in a building • *The sports department is on the top floor.*

floorboard noun
one of the long flat boards in a wooden floor

flop verb (**flopping, flopped**)
1 to flop, or flop down, is to fall or sit down heavily **2** to flop is also to fall or hang loosely or heavily • *Her hair flopped over her eyes.* **3** (*informal*) to flop is to be a failure

flop noun
(*informal*) a failure or disappointment • *The play was a complete flop.*

floppy adjective (**floppier, floppiest**)
hanging loosely or heavily • *Our dog has huge floppy ears.*

flora noun (*say* flor-a)
the plants of an area or of a period of time

floral adjective
made of flowers or to do with flowers

florist noun
a shopkeeper who sells flowers

flounder verb
to flounder is to move or struggle clumsily because you are in difficulties • *For a moment the boy floundered about in the stream.*

flour noun
a fine powder made from corn or wheat and used for making bread, cakes, and pastry

flour

a b c d e f g h i j k l m n o p q r s t u v z

floury *adjective*
powdery like flour

flourish *verb*
1 to flourish is to grow or develop strongly; to be successful **2** to flourish something is to wave it about

flow *verb*
1 to flow is to move along smoothly, like a river does **2** to flow is also to hang loosely • *She had golden flowing hair.*

flow *noun*
a continuous steady movement of something

flower *noun*
1 the part of a plant from which the seed or fruit develops **2** a plant with a flower

flower *verb*
a plant flowers when it produces flowers

flowerpot *noun*
a pot in which plants are grown

flowerpots

flu *noun*
influenza

fluent *adjective*
skilful at speaking, especially a foreign language **fluency** *noun* skill at speaking a language **fluently** *adverb*

fluff *noun*
fluff is the small soft bits that come off wool and cloth **fluffy** *adjective* soft like fluff

fluid *noun*
a substance that flows easily, like liquids and gases

fluke *noun*
a success that you achieve by unexpected good luck

fluorescent *adjective*
a fluorescent light or lamp is one that produces a bright light by means of radiation

fluoride *noun*
a chemical that is added to water and toothpaste to help prevent tooth decay

flush[1] *verb*
1 to flush is to go slightly red in the face **2** to flush something is to clean or remove it with a fast flow of liquid

flush[1] *noun*
1 a slight blush **2** a fast flow of water

flush[2] *adjective*
level; without any part sticking out • *The doors are flush with the walls.*

flustered *adjective*
nervous and confused

flute *noun*
a musical instrument which you hold sideways across your mouth and play by blowing across a hole in it at one end

flutter *verb*
1 to flutter is to move with a quick flapping of wings • *A butterfly fluttered in through the window.*
2 to flutter is to move or flap quickly and lightly • *The flags fluttered in the breeze.*

fly *verb* (**flies, flying, flew, flown**)
1 to fly is to move through the air with wings or in an aircraft **2** to fly is also to wave in the air • *Flags were flying.* **3** to fly something is to make it move through the air • *They were flying model aircraft.* **4** to fly is to move or pass quickly • *The door flew open.* • *The weeks just flew by.*

fly *noun* (**flies**)
1 a small flying insect with two wings **2** the front opening of a pair of trousers

flying saucer *noun*
a saucer-shaped flying object believed to come from outer space, especially in science fiction stories

flyover *noun*
a bridge that carries one road over another

foal *noun*
a young horse

foam *noun*
1 a mass of tiny bubbles on a liquid **2** a spongy kind of rubber or plastic **foamy** *adjective* a foamy liquid produces a mass of tiny bubbles

foam *verb*
to foam is to form a mass of tiny bubbles

focus *noun* (**focuses** or **foci**)
1 the distance at which something appears most clearly to your eye or in a lens **2** the part of something that people pay most attention to **to be in focus** is to appear clearly and not blurred **to be out of focus** is to appear blurred

focus *verb*
1 to focus your eye or a camera lens is to adjust it so that objects appear clearly **2** to focus your attention on something is to concentrate on it

fodder *noun*
fodder is food for horses and farm animals

foe *noun*
(*old use*) an enemy

foetus *noun* (*say* fee-tus)
a developing embryo, especially an unborn human baby

fog *noun*
thick mist which makes it difficult to see **foggy** *adjective* it is foggy when there is a lot of fog

foil[1] *noun*
a very thin sheet of metal

foil[2] *noun*
a long narrow sword you use in fencing

foil[3] *verb*
to foil someone or something is to prevent them from succeeding • *Police foiled the kidnapping plan.*

fold[1] *verb*
1 to fold something is to bend it so that one part lies over another part **2** to fold is to bend or move in this way • *The table folds up when we are not using it.*

fold[1] *noun*
a line where something has been folded

fold[2] *noun*
an enclosure for sheep

folder *noun*
1 a folding cardboard or plastic cover you use to keep loose papers in **2** (*in computing*) a place where a set of files are grouped together in a computer

foliage *noun*
the leaves of a tree or plant

folk *plural noun*
people

folklore *noun*
old beliefs and legends

folk song *noun*
a song in the traditional style of a country

follow *verb*
1 to follow someone or something is to go or come after them, or to do something after they have **2** to follow someone's instructions or advice is to obey them **3** to follow a road or path is to go along it **4** to follow a sport or team is to take an interest in or support them • *Which football team do you follow?* **5** to follow someone is to understand them • *Do you follow me?* **6** to follow is to happen as a result • *Who knows what trouble may follow?*

follower *noun* a person who follows or supports someone or something

following *preposition*
after or as a result of • *Following the break-in we had new locks fitted.*

fond *adjective*
kind and loving • *She wished me a fond farewell.* to be fond of someone or something is to like them very much **fondly** *adverb* **fondness** *noun*

font *noun*
a stone or wooden basin in a church, to hold water for baptism

food *noun*
anything that a plant or animal can take into its body to make it grow or give it energy

food chain *noun*
a series of plants and animals, each of which is eaten as food by the one above in the series

fool *noun*
1 a silly or stupid person **2** a jester or clown • *Stop playing the fool.*
3 a pudding made of fruit mixed with custard or cream

fool *verb*
to fool someone is to trick or deceive them to fool about or fool around is to behave in a silly or stupid way

foolhardy *adjective* (**foolhardier, foolhardiest**)
bold but foolish; reckless **foolhardiness** *noun* being foolhardy

foolish *adjective*
stupid or unwise **foolishly** *adverb* **foolishness** *noun*

foolproof *adjective*
a plan or method is foolproof when it is easy to follow and can't easily go wrong

foot *noun*
1 the lower part of your leg below your ankle **2** the lowest part of something • *They met up at the foot of the hill.* **3** a measure of length, 12 inches or about 30 centimetres **on foot** walking

football *noun*
1 a game played by two teams which try to kick an inflated ball into their opponents' goal **2** the ball used in this game **footballer** *noun* someone who plays football

footing *noun*
your footing is the position of your feet when you are standing firmly on something • *He lost his footing and slipped.*

foot

footnote *noun*
a note printed at the bottom of the page

footpath *noun*
a path for people to walk along, especially one in the countryside

footprint *noun*
a mark made by a foot or shoe

footstep *noun*
the sound made each time your foot touches the ground when they are walking or running

for *preposition*
used to show **1** purpose or direction • *This letter is for you.* • *We set out for home.* • *Let's go for a walk.* **2** length of time or distance • *We've been waiting for hours.* • *They walked for three miles.* **3** price or cost • *She bought it for £2.* **4** an alternative • *New lamps for old!* **5** cause or reason • *He was rewarded for bravery.* • *I only did it for the money.* **6** support • *Are you for us or against us?* **for ever** always

for *conjunction*
because • *They paused, for they heard a noise.*

forbid *verb* (**forbidding, forbade, forbidden**)
1 to forbid someone to do something is to tell them that they must not do it **2** to forbid something is not to allow it • *Smoking is forbidden in this station.*

force *noun*
1 strength or power **2** (*in science*) an influence that pushes or pulls objects **3** an organized team of soldiers or police

force *verb*
1 to force someone to do something is to use your power or strength to make them do it
2 to force something is to break it open using your strength

forceful *adjective*
strong and effective **forcefully** *adverb*

forceps *plural noun* (*say* **for**-seps)
a pair of pincers or tongs that a dentist or surgeon uses

ford *noun*
a shallow place where you can wade or drive across a river

forecast *noun*
a statement about what is likely to happen, especially what the weather is likely to be

forecast *verb* (**forecasting, forecast** or **forecasted**)
to forecast something is to say what is likely to happen • *The weather report forecasts snow for tomorrow.*

forefinger *noun*
the finger next to your thumb

foregone conclusion *noun*
a result that is certain to happen

foreground *noun*
the part of a picture or view that is nearest to you

forehead *noun*
(*say* **for**-hed or *say* **fo**-rid)
the part of your face above your eyes

foreign *adjective*
belonging to or coming from another country

foreigner *noun*
a person from another country

foremost *adjective*
most important

forename *noun*
a person's first name

foresee *verb* (**foreseeing, foresaw, foreseen**)
to foresee something is to realize that it is likely to happen **foreseeable** *adjective* a foreseeable event is one that you should realize is likely to happen

foresight *noun*
the ability to realize that something is likely to happen in the future and prepare for it

forest *noun*
a large area of trees growing close together **forester** *noun* a worker in a forest

forestry *noun*
the science of planting forests and looking after them

foretell *verb* (**foretelling, foretold**)
to foretell something is to say it will happen

forever *adverb*
continually or always • *He is forever complaining.*

forfeit *noun*
something that you lose or have to pay as a penalty

forfeit *verb*
to forfeit something is to lose it as a penalty

forge *noun*
a place where metal is heated and shaped; a blacksmith's workshop

forge *verb*
1 to forge metal is to shape it by heating and hammering
2 to forge money or a signature is to copy it in order to deceive people

forgery *noun* (**forgeries**)
1 forgery is copying something in order to deceive people
2 a forgery is a copy of something made to deceive people

a
b
c
d
e
f
g
h
i
j
k
l
m
n
o
p
q
r
s
t
u
v
w
x
y
z

forget verb (**forgetting, forgot, forgotten**)
1 to forget something is to fail to remember it **2** to forget something is also to stop thinking about it • *Try to forget your worries.*

forgetful adjective
often forgetting things
forgetfulness noun

forget-me-not noun
a plant with small blue flowers

forgive verb (**forgiving, forgave, forgiven**)
to forgive someone is to stop being angry with them for something they have done **forgiveness** noun

fork noun
1 a small tool with prongs for lifting food to your mouth **2** a large tool with prongs used for digging or lifting things **3** a place where a road or river divides into two or more parts

fork verb
1 to fork something is to dig or lift it with a fork **2** to fork is to divide into two or more branches • *The tunnel suddenly forked into two.*

fork-lift truck noun
a truck with two metal bars at the front for lifting and moving heavy loads

forlorn adjective
looking sad and lonely

form noun
1 a form is a kind or type of thing • *What is your favourite form of transport?* **2** the form of something is its shape and general appearance • *They could see a shadowy form in front of them.* **3** a form is also a class in a school **4** a form is also a piece of paper with printed questions and spaces for the answers

fork-lift truck

form verb
1 to form something is to shape or make it **2** to form is to come into existence or develop • *Icicles formed on the window sill.*

formal adjective
1 strictly following the accepted rules or customs; not casual • *She has a formal manner and never calls me by my first name.* **2** official or ceremonial • *The formal opening of the bridge takes place tomorrow.*
formally adverb

formality noun (**formalities**)
1 formality is formal behaviour **2** a formality is something you do to obey a rule or custom

formation noun
1 the process of forming something • *This chapter is about the formation of ice crystals.* **2** something that is formed • *We were studying formations of rock.* **3** a special pattern or arrangement • *The aircraft were flying in formation.*

former adjective
earlier; in the past • *In former times the house had been an inn.* • *He is a former President of the US.* the former the first of two people or things just mentioned • *If it's a choice between a picnic or a swim I prefer the former.* See also **latter**

formerly adverb
once; previously

formidable adjective
(*say* for-**mid**-a-bul)
1 deserving respect because of being so powerful or impressive **2** very difficult to deal with or do • *This is a formidable task.*
formidably adverb something is formidably difficult when it is very difficult indeed

formula noun (**formulas** or **formulae**)
1 a set of chemical symbols showing what a substance consists of • H_2O is the formula for water. **2** a rule or statement expressed in symbols or numbers **3** a list of what you need to make something

forsake verb (**forsaking, forsook, forsaken**)
to forsake someone is to abandon them

fort noun
a building that has been strongly built against attack

forth adverb
forwards or onwards • *From that day forth they never fought again.*

fortification noun
a tower or wall that is built to help defend a place against attack

fortify verb (**fortifying, fortified**)
1 to fortify a place is to make it strong against attack **2** to fortify someone is to make them feel stronger • *A bowl of hot soup will fortify you.*

fortnight noun
a period of two weeks

fortnightly adverb every two weeks

fortress noun
a castle or town that has been strongly built against attack

fortunate adjective
lucky **fortunately** adverb luckily

fortune noun
1 fortune is luck or chance **2** a fortune is a large amount of money

fortune-teller noun
someone who tells you what will happen to you in the future

forty noun (**forties**)
the number 40
fortieth adjective, noun 40th

forward adjective
1 going towards the front **2** placed in the front **3** too eager or bold

forward adverb
forwards

forward noun
a player in an attacking position in a team at football, hockey, and other games

forwards adverb
to or towards the front; in the direction you are facing

fossil noun
the remains of a prehistoric animal or plant that has been in the ground for a very long time and become hardened in rock **fossilized** adjective a fossilized animal or plant has been formed into a fossil

fossil

foster verb
to foster someone is to look after someone else's child as if they were your own, but without adopting them

foster child noun
a child brought up by foster parents

foster parent noun
a parent who is fostering a child

foul adjective
1 disgusting; tasting or smelling unpleasant **2** breaking the rules of a game • *That was a foul shot.*
foulness noun

foul noun
an action that breaks the rules of a game

foul verb
to foul a player in a game is to commit a foul against them

found[1] *verb* (**founding, founded**)
to found an organization or society is to start it or set it up • *When was the hospital founded?*

foundation *noun*
1 a building's foundations are the solid base under the ground on which it is built **2** the basis for something **3** the founding of something

founder[1] *noun*
someone who founds something • *Guru Nanak was the founder of the Sikh religion.*

founder[2] *verb*
to founder is to fill with water and sink • *The ship foundered on the rocks.*

foundry *noun* (**foundries**)
a factory or workshop where metal or glass is made

fountain *noun*
an outdoor structure in which jets of water shoot up into the air

fountain pen *noun*
a pen that has a nib and can be filled with a cartridge or a supply of ink

four *noun*
the number 4 **to be on all fours** is to be on your hands and knees

fourteen *noun*
the number 14
fourteenth *adjective, noun* 14th

fourth *adjective, noun*
the next after the third **fourthly** *adverb* in the fourth place; as the fourth one

fowl *noun* (**fowl** or **fowls**)
a bird, such as a chicken or duck, that is kept for its eggs or meat

fox *noun*
a wild animal that looks like a dog with a long furry tail

fox *verb*
to fox someone is to puzzle them

foxglove *noun*
a tall plant with flowers like the fingers of gloves

foyer *noun* (*say* **foi**-ay)
the entrance hall of a cinema, theatre, or hotel

fraction *noun*
1 a number that is not a whole number, for example ½ and 0.5 **2** a tiny part or amount of something

fracture *verb*
to fracture something, especially a bone, is to break it

fracture *noun*
the breaking of something, especially a bone

fragile *adjective* (*say* **fra**-jyl)
easy to break or damage **fragility** *noun* being easy to break or damage

fragment *noun*
a small piece broken off something

fragrant *adjective* (*say* **fray**-grant)
having a sweet or pleasant smell
fragrance *noun* a sweet or pleasant smell

frail *adjective*
weak or fragile
frailty *noun* being weak or fragile

frame *noun*
1 a set of wooden or metal strips that fit round the outside of a picture or mirror to hold it **2** a rigid structure that supports something • *I've broken the frame of my glasses.* **3** a human body • *He has a small frame.* **your frame of mind** is the way you think or feel for a while • *Wait till he's in a better frame of mind.*

frame

frame *verb*
1 to frame a picture is to put a frame round it **2** (*informal*) to frame someone is to make them seem guilty of a crime by giving false evidence against them

framework *noun*
1 a structure that supports something **2** a basic plan or system

frank *adjective*
honest and saying exactly what you think • *I'll be frank with you.*
frankly *adverb* **frankness** *noun*

frank *verb*
to frank a letter or parcel is to mark it with a postmark

frantic *adjective*
wildly anxious or excited
frantically *adverb*

fraud *noun*
1 fraud is the crime of getting money by tricking people; a fraud is a swindle **2** a fraud is also someone who is not what they pretend to be
fraudulent *adjective* dishonest

fraught *adjective*
someone is fraught when they are tense and upset

frayed *adjective*
1 frayed material is worn and ragged at the edge • *Your shirt collar is frayed.* **2** tempers or nerves are frayed when people feel strained or upset • *Tempers were becoming frayed.*

freak *noun*
a very strange or unusual person, animal, or thing

freckle *noun*
a small brown spot on someone's skin **freckled** *adjective* covered in freckles

free *adjective*
1 able to do what you want to do or go where you want to go **2** not costing any money • *Entrance to the museum is free.* **3** available; not being used or occupied • *Is this seat free?* **4** not busy doing something • *Are you free tomorrow morning?* **5** generous • *She is very free with her money.* **to be free of something** is not to have it or be affected by it • *The roads are free of ice.* **freely** *adverb* to do something freely is to do it as you want, without anyone or anything stopping you

free *verb*
to free someone or something is to make them free **freedom** *noun* the right to go where you like or do what you like

freehand *adjective, adverb*
to draw something freehand is to do it without using a ruler or compasses

free-range *adjective*
1 free-range hens are allowed to move about freely in the open instead of being caged **2** free-range eggs are those laid by free-range hens

freewheel *verb*
to freewheel is to ride a bicycle without pedalling

freeze *verb*
1 to freeze is to turn into ice or another solid, or to become covered with ice • *The pond froze last night.* **2** to be freezing or to be frozen is to be very cold • *My hands are frozen.* **3** to freeze food is to store it at a low temperature to preserve it **4** a person or animal freezes when they suddenly stand still with fright

freezer *noun*
a large refrigerator for keeping food frozen

freezing point *noun*
the temperature at which a liquid freezes

freight *noun* (*say* frayt)
goods carried by road or in a ship or aircraft

frenzy *noun* (**frenzies**)
to be in a frenzy is to be wildly excited or angry about something **frenzied** *adjective* wildly excited or angry about something

a b c d e f g h i j k l m n o p q r s t u v w x y z

frequency *noun* (**frequencies**)
1 how often something happens
2 being frequent **3** the number of vibrations made each second by a wave of sound or light

frequent *adjective* (*say* **free**-kwent) happening often **frequently** *adverb* often

fresh *adjective*
1 newly made or produced; not old or used • *We need fresh bread.* **2** not tinned or preserved • *Would you like some fresh fruit?* **3** cool and clean • *It's nice to be in the fresh air.* **4** fresh water is water that is not salty **freshly** *adverb* newly or recently • *Here are some freshly made biscuits.* **freshness** *noun*

freshen *verb*
1 to freshen something is to make it fresh **2** to freshen is to become fresh

freshwater *adjective*
freshwater fish live in rivers or lakes and not the sea

fret *verb* (**fretting, fretted**)
to fret is to worry or be upset about something **fretful** *adjective* worried and upset

friar *noun*
a man belonging to a religious group that has vowed to live a life of poverty **friary** *noun* a place where friars live

friction *noun*
1 when one thing rubs against another **2** disagreement and quarrelling

Friday *noun*
the sixth day of the week

fridge *noun*
(*informal*) a refrigerator

friend *noun*
1 someone you like and who likes you **2** a helpful or kind person

friendly *adjective* (**friendlier, friendliest**)
kind and pleasant **friendliness** *noun*

friendship *noun*
friendship, or a friendship, is being friends with someone

frieze *noun* (*say* freez)
a strip of designs or pictures along the top of a wall

fright *noun*
a sudden feeling of fear

frighten *verb*
to frighten someone is to make them afraid

frightful *adjective*
awful; very great or bad • *It's a frightful shame.* **frightfully** *adverb* awfully or very • *I'm frightfully sorry.*

frill *noun*
a strip of pleated material used to decorate the edge of a dress or curtain **frilly** *adjective* decorated with frills

fringe *noun*
1 a straight line of short hair that hangs down over your forehead **2** a decorative edge of hanging threads on something like a piece of clothing or a curtain **3** the edge of something • *We walked around on the fringe of the crowd.* **fringed** *adjective* having a fringe

frisk *verb*
(*informal*) to frisk someone is to search them by moving your hands over their body

frisky *adjective* (**friskier, friskiest**)
playful or lively **friskily** *adverb* **friskiness** *noun*

fritter[1] *noun*
a slice of meat, potato, or fruit that is covered in batter and fried
fritter[2] *verb*
to fritter something or fritter it away is to waste it gradually • *He frittered all his money on comics.*

frivolous *adjective*
light-hearted and playful; not serious **frivolously** *adverb*

frizzy *adjective* (**frizzier, frizziest**)
frizzy hair has tight short curls

fro *adverb*
to and fro backwards and forwards

frog *noun*
a small jumping animal that can live both in water and on land **to have a frog in your throat** is to be hoarse

frolic *verb* (**frolicking, frolicked**)
to frolic is to spend time playing in a lively and cheerful way

from *preposition*
used to show **1** a beginning or starting point • *She comes from London.* • *Buses run from 8 o'clock.* **2** distance • *We are a mile from home.* **3** separation • *Get the gun from him.* **4** origin or source • *Get water from the tap.* **5** cause • *I suffer from headaches.* **6** difference • *Can you tell margarine from butter?*

front *noun*
1 the part of a person or thing that faces forwards • *The front of the house is blue.* **2** the part of a thing or place that is furthest forward • *Go to the front of the class.* **3** a wide road or path that runs alongside the seashore **4** the place where fighting is happening in a war • *More troops were moved to the front.* **in front** at or near the front

front *adjective*
placed at or near the front • *We sat in the front row.*

frontier *noun*
the boundary between two countries or regions

frost *noun*
1 powdery ice that forms on things in freezing weather **2** weather with a temperature below freezing point

frost *verb*
to frost up is to become covered with frost

frostbite *noun*
harm done to a person's body by very cold weather **frostbitten** *adjective* suffering from frostbite

frosty *adjective*
1 so cold that there is frost • *It was a frosty morning.* **2** unfriendly • *She gave us a frosty look.*

froth *noun*
a white mass of tiny bubbles on or in a liquid **frothy** *adjective* a frothy liquid has froth on top
froth *verb*
to froth is to form a froth

frown *verb*
to frown is to wrinkle your forehead because you are angry or worried
frown *noun*
the wrinkling of your forehead when you frown

friends

frog

fruit *noun*
1 the part of a tree or plant that contains the seeds and is often used as food, such as apples, oranges, and bananas 2 the good result of doing something • *He lived to see the fruits of his efforts.*

fruitful *adjective*
something is fruitful when it is successful or has good results • *Their talks were fruitful.* **fruitfully** *adverb*

fruitless *adjective*
something is fruitless when it is unsuccessful or has no results • *It was a fruitless search.* **fruitlessly** *adverb* without success

fruity *adjective* (**fruitier, fruitiest**)
tasting like fruit

frustrate *verb*
to frustrate someone is to prevent them from doing something or from succeeding in something, in a way that annoys them **frustration** *noun* the feeling of annoyance you have when you can't do what you want to do

fry *verb* (**fries, frying, fried**)
to fry food is to cook it in hot fat

frying pan *noun*
a shallow pan in which things are fried

fudge *noun*
a soft sweet made with milk, sugar, and butter

fuel *noun*
something that is burnt to make heat or power, such as coal and oil

fugitive *noun* (say few-ji-tiv)
a person who is running away from something, especially from the police

fulfil *verb* (**fulfilling, fulfilled**)
1 to fulfil something is to achieve it or carry it out • *She fulfilled her promise to come.* 2 to fulfil a prophecy is to make it come true **fulfilment** *noun* the feeling that you have achieved something

full *adjective*
1 containing as much or as many as possible • *The cinema was full.* 2 having many people or things • *You are full of ideas.* 3 complete • *Tell me the full story.* 4 the greatest possible • *They drove at full speed.* 5 fitting loosely; having many folds • *She's wearing a full skirt.* **in full** not leaving anything out **fully** *adverb* completely

full moon *noun*
the moon when you can see the whole of it as a bright disc

full stop *noun*
the dot used as a punctuation mark at the end of a sentence or an abbreviation

full-time *adjective, adverb*
you do something full-time when you do it for all the normal working hours of the day • *She has a full-time job.* • *She works full-time.*

fumble *verb*
to fumble is to handle or feel for something clumsily • *He fumbled in the dark for the light switch.*

fume *verb*
1 to fume is to give off strong-smelling smoke or gas 2 to be fuming is to be very angry

fumes *plural noun*
strong-smelling smoke or gas

fun *noun*
amusement or enjoyment **to make fun of someone or something** is to make them look silly or make people laugh at them

function *noun*
1 what someone or something does or ought to do • *The function of a doctor is to cure sick people.* 2 an important event or party 3 a basic operation of a computer or calculator

function *verb*
to function is to work properly or perform a function • *The chair also functions as a small table.*

fund *noun*
a fund is an amount of money collected or kept for a special purpose • *They started a fund for refugees.*

fundamental *adjective*
basic and necessary • *Let me explain the fundamental rules of the game.* **fundamentally** *adverb* basically

funeral *noun*
the ceremony where a person who has died is buried or cremated

fungus *noun* (**fungi**)
a plant without leaves or flowers that grows on other plants or on decayed material, such as mushrooms and toadstools

fungi

funnel *noun*
1 a tube that is wide at the top and narrow at the bottom, to help you pour things into bottles or other containers 2 a chimney on a ship or steam engine

funny *adjective* (**funnier, funniest**)
1 that makes you laugh or smile • *We heard a funny joke.* 2 strange or odd • *There's a funny smell in here.* **funnily** *adverb*

funnel

funny bone *noun*
part of your elbow which gives you a strange tingling feeling if you knock it

fur *noun*
1 the soft hair that covers some animals 2 animal skin with the hair on it, used for clothing; fabric that looks like animal skin with hair on it • *She was wearing a fur hat.*

furious *adjective*
very angry **furiously** *adverb*

furl *verb*
to furl a sail or flag or umbrella is to roll it up and fasten it

furnace *noun*
an oven in which great heat can be produced for making glass or heating metals

furnish *verb*
to furnish a room or building is to put furniture in it

furniture *noun*
tables, chairs, beds, cupboards, and other movable things that you need inside a building

furrow *noun*
1 a long cut in the ground made by a plough 2 a deep wrinkle on the skin

furry *adjective* (**furrier, furriest**)
1 soft and hairy like fur 2 covered with fur

further *adverb* and *adjective*
1 at or to a greater distance; more distant • *I can't walk any further.* 2 more • *We need further information.*

furthermore *adverb*
also; moreover

furthest *adverb* and *adjective*
at or to the greatest distance; most distant

furtive *adjective*
cautious, trying not to be seen • *He gave a furtive glance and helped himself to the biscuits.*

fury *noun* (**furies**)
violent or extreme anger

fuse[1] *noun*
a safety device containing a short piece of wire that melts if

b
c
d
e
f
g
h
i
j
k
l
m
n
o
p
q
r
s
t
u
v
w
x
y
z

too much electricity passes through it

fuse¹ *verb*
1 a piece of electrical equipment fuses when it stops working because a fuse has melted • *The lights have fused.* **2** to fuse things is to blend them together, especially through melting

fuse² *noun*
a device for setting off an explosive

fuselage *noun* (*say* **few**-ze-lah*zh*)
the main body of an aircraft

fuss *noun*
fuss, or a fuss, is unnecessary excitement or worry about something that is not important **to make a fuss of someone** is to pay a lot of attention to them in a kind way

fuss *verb*
to fuss is to be excited or worried about something that is not important

fussy *adjective* (**fussier, fussiest**)
worrying too much about something that is not important **fussily** *adverb* **fussiness** *noun*

futile *adjective* (*say* **few**-tyl)
useless or having no purpose **futility** *noun* being useless or having no purpose

futon *noun* (*say* **foo**-ton)
a seat with a mattress that you can roll out to form a bed

future *noun*
1 the time that will come **2** what is going to happen in the time that will come **in future** from now onwards

fuzzy *adjective* (**fuzzier, fuzziest**)
1 blurred or not clear **2** covered in something soft and hairy **fuzzily** *adverb* **fuzziness** *noun*

g
short for gram or grams

gabble *verb*
to gabble is to talk so quickly that it is difficult to hear the words

gable *noun*
the three-sided part of a wall between two sloping roofs

gadget *noun* (*say* **gaj**-it)
a small device or tool that helps you with a particular task

gag *noun*
1 something put over someone's mouth to stop them from speaking **2** (*informal*) a joke

gag *verb* (**gagging, gagged**)
to gag someone is to put a gag over their mouth

gain *verb*
1 to gain something is to get it when you did not have it before **2** a clock or watch gains when it goes ahead of the correct time **to gain on someone** is to come closer to them when you are following them

gain *noun*
something you have got that you did not have before; profit

gala *noun* (*say* **gah**-la)
1 a festival **2** a series of sports contests, especially in swimming

galaxy *noun* (**galaxies**) (*say* **gal**-ak-si)
a very large group of stars **galactic** *adjective* to do with a galaxy

gale *noun*
a very strong wind

gallant *adjective*
brave or courteous **gallantly** *adverb* **gallantry** *noun* gallantry is being gallant

galleon *noun*
a large Spanish sailing ship used in the 16th and 17th centuries

gallery *noun* (**galleries**)
1 a platform sticking out from the inside wall of a building **2** the highest set of seats in a cinema or theatre **3** a long room or passage **4** a building or room for showing works of art

galley *noun* (**galleys**)
1 an ancient type of long ship driven by oars **2** the kitchen in a ship

gallon *noun*
a measure of liquid, 8 pints or about 4.5 litres

gallop *noun*
1 the fastest pace that a horse can go **2** a fast ride on a horse

gallop *verb*
to gallop is to ride fast on a horse

gallows *plural noun*
gallows are a framework with a noose for hanging criminals

galore *adjective*
in large amounts • *There are bargains galore in the sale.*

gamble *verb*
to gamble is to play a betting game for money **gambler** *noun* someone who gambles

gamble *noun*
a risk • *We were taking a bit of a gamble on the weather being good.*

game *noun*
1 something that you can play, usually with rules **2** a section of a long game like tennis or whist **3** wild animals or birds hunted for sport or food **to give the game away** is to reveal a secret

gammon *noun*
gammon is a kind of ham or thick bacon

gander *noun*
a male goose

gang *noun*
1 a group of people who do things together **2** a group of criminals

gang *verb*
to gang up on someone is to form a group to fight them or frighten them

galleon

gangplank *noun*
a plank for walking on to or off a ship

gangster (*noun*)
a member of a gang of violent criminals

gangway *noun*
1 a gap left for people to move along between rows of seats or through a crowd **2** a movable bridge for getting on or off a ship

gaol *noun* and *verb*
a different spelling of jail

gaoler *noun*
a different spelling of **jailer**

gap *noun*
1 an opening or break in something **2** an interval

gape *verb*
1 to gape is to open your mouth wide **2** to gape is also to stare in amazement **gaping** *adjective* wide open • *There was now a gaping hole in the ice.*

garage *noun* (*say* **ga**-rah*zh* or *say* **ga**-rij)
1 a building for keeping motor vehicles in **2** a place where motor vehicles are serviced and repaired and where petrol is sold

garbage *noun*
garbage is household refuse or rubbish

garden *noun*
a piece of ground where flowers, fruit, or vegetables are grown

gardener noun
someone who looks after gardens, especially as a job

gardening noun
gardening is looking after a garden

gargle verb
to gargle is to wash your throat by holding liquid at the back of your mouth and breathing air through it

gargoyle noun
an ugly or comical carving of a face on a building, especially one that sticks out from a gutter and sends out rainwater through its mouth

garland noun
a wreath of flowers worn as a decoration

garlic noun
a plant with a bulb divided into sections (called cloves), which have a strong smell and taste and are used in cooking

garment noun
a piece of clothing

garnish verb
to garnish a dish of food is to decorate it with extra items such as salad

gas noun
1 a substance, such as oxygen, that can move freely and is not liquid or solid at normal temperatures **2** a gas that burns and is used for heating or cooking **gaseous** adjective in the form of a gas

gas verb (**gassing, gassed**)
to gas someone is to kill or injure them with a poisonous gas

gash noun
a long deep cut or wound

gasp verb
1 to gasp is to breathe in suddenly when you are shocked or surprised **2** to gasp is also to struggle to breathe when you are ill or tired **3** to gasp something is to say it in a breathless way

gate noun
1 a movable barrier, usually on hinges, used as a door in a wall or fence **2** a place where you wait before you board an aircraft **3** the number of people attending a football match

gateau noun (**gateaux** (say **gat**-oh))
a rich cream cake

gateway noun
an opening containing a gate

gather verb
1 to gather is to come together **2** to gather people or things is to collect them and bring them together **3** to gather a piece of information is to hear or read about it • *I gather you went to the same school as me?* **to gather speed** is to move gradually faster

gathering noun
an assembly or meeting of people; a party

gaudy adjective (**gaudier, gaudiest**)
very showy and bright

gauge noun (say gayj)
1 a measuring instrument, such as a fuel gauge **2** the distance between a pair of railway lines

gauge verb
to gauge something is to measure it or estimate it • *He looked down into the canyon, trying to gauge how deep it was.*

gaunt adjective
a gaunt person is thin and tired-looking

gauntlet noun
a glove with a wide covering for the wrist **to throw down the gauntlet** is to offer a challenge

gauze noun
gauze is thin transparent material

gaze verb
to gaze at something or someone is to look at them hard for a long time

gaze noun
a long steady look

GCSE
short for **General Certificate of Secondary Education**

gear noun
1 a gear is a set of toothed wheels working together in a machine, especially those connecting the engine to the wheels of a vehicle **2** gear is equipment or clothes • *He had left all his fishing gear behind by the river.* **in gear** with the gears connected **out of gear** with the gears no connected

Geiger counter noun
a device that detects and measures radioactivity

gel noun
gel is a substance like jelly, especially one used to give a style to hair

gelatine noun
gelatine is a clear tasteless substance used to make jellies

gem noun
1 a precious stone or jewel **2** an excellent person or thing • *Her auntie's a real gem.*

gender noun (say jen-der)
the group to which a noun or pronoun belongs in some languages (masculine, feminine, and neuter)

gene noun (say jeen)
the part of a living cell that controls which characteristics (such as the colour of your hair or eyes) you inherit from your parents

general adjective
1 to do with most people or things • *The general feeling is that we should go to the beach.* **2** not detailed or special • *The website has lots of general information on marine life.* **in general** usually; to do with most people

general noun
an army officer of high rank

general election noun
an election of Members of Parliament for the whole country

generally adverb
usually; to do with most people

generate verb
to generate something is to produce or create it

generation noun
1 a single stage in a family • *Three generations were included: children, parents, and grandparents.* **2** all the people born about the same time • *He was one of the most famous film stars of his generation.*

generator noun
a machine for producing electricity

generous adjective
ready to give or share what you have **generosity** noun being generous and ready to give a lot **generously** adverb

genetic adjective (say ji-**net**-ik)
to do with genes and with characteristics inherited from parents **genetically** adverb by means of genes

genetics plural noun
genetics is the study of genes and genetic behaviour

genie noun
a magical being in stories who can grant wishes

genie

genius noun
1 an unusually clever person **2** an unusually great ability or talent

a b c d e f g h i j k l m n o p q r s t u v w x y z

gentle *adjective*
kind and quiet; not rough or severe
gentleness *noun*
gently *adverb*

gentleman *noun* (**gentlemen**)
1 a man **2** a well-mannered or honest man • *He's a real gentleman.*

genuine *adjective*
1 something is genuine when it is real and not fake **2** a person is genuine when they are honest and sincere **genuinely** *adverb* really; in a genuine way

genus *noun* (**genera**)
(say **jee**-nus)
a group of similar animals or plants

geography *noun*
geography is the science or study of the world and its climate, peoples, and products **geographer** *noun* someone who studies geography **geographical** *adjective* a geographical area is a region of the earth that you can see on a map

geology *noun* (say ji-**ol**-o-ji)
geology is the study of the earth's crust and its layers **geologist** *noun* someone who studies geology **geological** *adjective* a geological era or period is a time in the past that you can see in the layers of the earth

geometry *noun*
geometry is the study of lines, angles, surfaces, and solids in mathematics **geometric** *adjective* a geometric shape or pattern has regular lines and angles **geometrical** *adjective*

gerbil *noun* (say **jer**-bil)
a small brown animal with long back legs

germ *noun*
a tiny living thing, especially one that causes a disease

germinate *verb*
a seed germinates when it starts growing and developing **germination** *noun* germination is the process of germinating

gesture *noun* (say **jes**-cher)
a movement or action which expresses what you feel

get *verb*
This word has many meanings, depending on the words that go with it **1** to get something is to obtain or receive it • *I got a new bike yesterday.* **2** to get (for example) angry or upset is to become angry or upset **3** to get to a place is to reach it • *We had to borrow money to get home.* **4** to get something (for example) on or off is take it on or off

• *I can't get my shoe on.* **5** to get (for example) a meal is to prepare it **6** to get an illness is to catch it • *I think she's got measles.* **7** to get someone to do something is to persuade or order them to do it • *Lara might get him to say yes.* **8** (*informal*) to get something is to understand it • *Do you get what I mean?* **to get by** is to manage **to get on** is to make progress, or to be friendly with someone **to get out of something** is to avoid having to do it **to get over something** is to recover from an illness or shock **to get your own back** is to have your revenge **to have got to do something** is to have no choice about it

getaway *noun*
an escape

geyser *noun*
(say **gee**-zer
or say **gy**-zer)
a natural spring that shoots up columns of hot water

ghastly *adjective*
horrible; awful

ghetto *noun* (say **get**-oh)
an area of a city, often a slum area, where a group of people live who are treated unfairly compared with other people

ghost *noun*
the spirit of a dead person seen by a living person **ghostly** *adjective* reminding you of a ghost • *The moon gave a ghostly light to the scene.*

ghoulish *adjective* (say **gool**-ish)
enjoying looking at things to do with death and suffering

giant *noun*
1 a creature in stories, like a huge man **2** something that is much larger than the usual size

giant *adjective*
huge

giddy *adjective*
feeling unsteady or dizzy **giddily** *adverb* **giddiness** *noun*

gift *noun*
1 a present **2** a talent • *She has a special gift for drawing.*

gifted *adjective*
a gifted person has a special talent or ability

gigantic *adjective*
huge; enormous

giggle *verb*
to giggle is to laugh in a silly way

giggle *noun*
1 a silly laugh **2** (*informal*) something amusing; a joke • *We did it for a giggle.* **the giggles** (*informal*) are a fit of giggling

gild *verb*
to gild something is to cover it with a thin layer of gold paint or gold

gills *plural noun*
the gills are the part of a fish's body that it breathes through

gimmick *noun*
something unusual done or used to attract people's attention

ginger *noun*
1 a hot-tasting tropical root, used as a flavouring for food **2** a reddish-yellow colour **gingery** *adjective*

gingerbread *noun*
a cake or biscuit flavoured with ginger

gingerly *adverb*
you do something gingerly when you do it carefully and cautiously because you are not sure about it • *She was walking very gingerly along the icy path.*

gingerbread

gipsy *noun*
a different spelling of **gypsy**

giraffe *noun*
a tall African animal with a very long neck

girder *noun*
a metal beam supporting part of a building or bridge

girl *noun*
1 a female child **2** a young woman **girlhood** *noun* the time when a woman was a girl **girlish** *adjective* looking or behaving like a girl

girlfriend *noun*
a person's female friend with whom they have a romantic relationship

girth *noun*
1 the measurement round something **2** a band fastened round a horse's belly to keep its saddle in place

gist *noun* (say jist)
the main points or general meaning of a speech or conversation

give *verb*
1 to give someone something is to let them have it • *She gave me a sweet.* **2** to give (for example) a laugh or shout is to laugh or shout out **3** to give a performance is to present or perform something • *They gave a concert to raise money.* **4** something gives if it bends or goes down under a strain • *Will this branch give if I sit on it?* **to give in** is to surrender **to give up** is to stop doing or trying something **to give way** is to break or collapse **giver** *noun* a person who gives something

given *adjective*
stated or agreed in advance • *Work out how much you can do in a given time.*

glacial *adjective* (*say* **glay**-shal) made of ice or formed by glaciers

glacier *noun* (*say* **glas**-i-er) a mass of ice moving slowly along a valley

glad *adjective*
happy and pleased **to be glad of something** is to be grateful for it **gladly** *adverb* you do something gladly when you are pleased to do it **gladness** *noun*

gladden *verb*
to gladden someone is to make them glad

gladiator *noun*
a man who fought with a sword or other weapons at public shows in ancient Rome

glamorous *adjective*
attractive and exciting

glamour *noun*
1 the glamour of something is what makes it attractive or exciting • *Just think of the glamour of competing in the Olympics.* **2** a person's glamour is their beauty or attractiveness • *Most of her clothes were chosen for comfort rather than glamour.*

glance *verb*
1 to glance at something is to look at it quickly **2** to glance off something is to hit it and slide off • *The ball glanced off his bat.*

glance *noun*
a quick look

gland *noun*
an organ of the body that separates substances from the blood, so that they can be used or passed out of the body

glare *verb*
1 to glare is to shine with a bright or dazzling light **2** to glare at someone is to look angrily at them

glare *noun*
1 a strong light **2** an angry stare

glaring *adjective*
1 very bright **2** very obvious and embarrassing • *Fortunately there were no glaring mistakes in their work.*

glass *noun*
1 glass is a hard brittle substance that lets light through **2** a glass is a container made of glass, for drinking out of **3** a glass is also a mirror or a lens

glassy *adjective* (**glassier, glassiest**)
like glass • *He gave a glassy stare.*

glasses *plural noun*
a frame holding two lenses that you wear over your eyes to improve your sight; spectacles

glaze *verb*
1 to glaze something is to cover or fit it with glass **2** to glaze pottery is to give it a shiny surface

glaze *noun*
a shiny surface

gleam *noun*
1 a beam of soft light, especially one that comes and goes **2** a clear sign of something • *She could see the gleam of excitement in his eyes.*

gleam *verb*
to gleam is to shine with beams of soft light

glee *noun*
glee is when you feel happy and excited about something **gleeful** *adjective* happy and excited **gleefully** *adverb*

glen *noun*
a narrow valley, especially in Scotland

glide *verb*
1 to glide is to fly or move smoothly **2** to glide is also to fly without using an engine

glider *noun*
an aircraft that does not use an engine and floats on air currents

glimmer *noun*
a faint light

glimmer *verb*
to glimmer is to shine with a faint light

glimpse *verb*
to glimpse something is to see it briefly

glimpse *noun*
a brief view of something

glint *verb*
to glint is to shine with a flash of light

glint *noun*
a brief flash of light

glisten *verb*
to glisten is to shine like something wet or oily

glitter *verb*
to glitter is to shine with tiny flashes of light

gloat *verb*
to gloat is to be pleased in an unkind way that you have succeeded or that someone else has been hurt or upset

global *adjective*
to do with the whole world **globally** *adverb* all over the world

global warming *noun*
the gradual increase in the average temperature of the earth's climate, caused by the greenhouse effect

globe

globe *noun*
1 a globe is something shaped like a ball, especially one with a map of the world on it **2** the globe is the world • *These stories come from all over the globe.*

gloom *noun*
gloom is a depressed condition or feeling

gloomy *adjective* (**gloomier, gloomiest**)
1 almost dark; not well lit **2** sad or depressed **gloomily** *adverb* **gloominess** *noun*

glorious *adjective*
splendid or magnificent

glory *noun* (**glories**)
1 glory is fame and honour **2** the glory of something is its splendour or beauty

gloss *noun*
the shine on a smooth surface

glossary *noun* (**glossaries**)
a list of words with their meanings explained

glossy *adjective*
smooth and shiny

glove *noun*
a covering for the hand, with a separate division for each finger

glow noun
1 a brightness and warmth without flames • *Her eyes glittered in the red glow of the fire.* 2 a warm or cheerful feeling • *Sarah felt a deep glow of satisfaction at her win.*

glow verb
to glow is to shine with a soft light

glower verb (*rhymes with* **flower**)
to glower is to stare with an angry look

glucose noun
glucose is a type of sugar found in fruits and honey

glue noun
glue is a thick liquid for sticking things together **gluey** adjective sticky like glue

glue verb
to glue something is to stick it with glue

glum adjective (**glummer, glummest**)
sad or depressed **glumly** adverb

glutton noun
someone who is greedy and enjoys eating too much **gluttonous** adjective greedy; eating too much **gluttony** noun when someone eats too much

gnarled adjective (*say* narld)
twisted and knobbly, like an old tree

gnash verb (*say* nash)
to gnash your teeth is to grind them together

gnat noun (*say* nat)
a tiny fly that bites

gnaw verb (*say* naw)
to gnaw something hard is to keep biting it

gnome noun (*say* nohm)
a kind of dwarf in fairy tales that usually lives underground

go verb (**going, went, gone**)
1 to go is to move or lead from one place to another • *Let's go in and see Mrs Cooper.* • *We'll have to go soon.* • *This road goes to Bristol.* 2 a machine or device goes when it is working • *My watch isn't going.* • *A car that doesn't go is not much use.* 3 you say that someone or something has gone when they are no longer there and you can't find them • *All her money had gone.* 4 **Go** also has many special uses shown in these examples • *The milk went sour.* • *The plates go on that shelf.* • *The party went well.* • *The gun went bang.* **to be going to do something** is to be ready to do it **to go in for something** is to take part in it **to go off** is to explode **to go off someone or something** is to stop liking them

to go on is to happen or continue • *What's going on?*

go noun (**goes**)
1 a go is a turn or try • *May I have a go?* 2 (*informal*) go is energy or liveliness • *She's full of go.* **on the go** always working or moving

goal noun (**goals**)
1 the two posts that the ball must go between to score a point in football, hockey, and other games 2 a point scored in football, hockey, netball, and other games 3 something that you try to do or to achieve • *Her goal is to become a pilot.*

goalkeeper noun
the player who guards the goal in football and hockey

goalpost noun
each of the upright posts of a goal in sports

goat noun
an animal with horns, belonging to the same family as sheep

gobble verb
to gobble something is to eat it quickly and greedily

goblet noun
a drinking glass with a long stem and a base

goblin noun
an evil or mischievous fairy in stories

WORD ORIGIN

The word **goblin** comes from an Old French word *gobelin*, which may be related to a Greek word *kobalos* meaning 'a mischievous goblin'.

God noun
the creator of the universe in Christian, Jewish, and Muslim belief

goddess noun
a female being that is worshipped

goggles plural noun
goggles are large glasses that you wear to protect your eyes, for example when you are swimming

gold noun
1 gold is a precious yellow metal 2 gold is also a bright yellow colour

golden adjective
1 made of gold 2 coloured like gold 3 precious or excellent • *It was a golden opportunity.*

goldfinch noun
a small, brightly-coloured bird with yellow feathers in its wings

goldfish noun (**goldfish**)
a small red or orange fish, often kept as a pet

golf noun
golf is an outdoor game played on a prepared course by hitting a small ball into a series of small holes, using a club **golfer** noun

gondola noun (*say* gon-do-la)
a boat with high pointed ends, used on the canals in Venice **gondolier** noun a person who moves a gondola along with a pole

gong noun
a large metal disc that makes a deep hollow sound when it is hit

good adjective (**better, best**)
1 of the kind that people like, want, or praise • *They wanted to have a good time.* 2 kind • *It was good of you to come.* 3 well-behaved • *Be a good boy.* 4 healthy; giving benefit • *Exercise is good for you.* 5 thorough; large enough • *Let's give it a good clean.*

good noun
1 something good or right • *Do good to others.* 2 benefit or advantage • *I'm telling you for your own good.* **for good** for ever **no good** useless

goodbye exclamation
a word you use when you leave someone or at the end of a telephone call

Good Friday noun
the Friday before Easter, when Christians remember Christ's death on the Cross

good-looking adjective
attractive or handsome

good-natured adjective
kind

goodness noun
1 goodness is being good 2 a thing's goodness is the good it does

goods plural noun
goods are things that people buy and sell

goodwill noun
goodwill is a kindly and helpful feeling towards people

gooey adjective
sticky or slimy

goose noun (**geese**)
a water bird with webbed feet, larger than a duck

gooseberry noun (**gooseberries**)
a small green fruit that grows on a prickly bush

goose pimples plural noun
goose pimples are lots of

tiny bumps you get on the skin when you are cold or afraid

gore *verb*
to gore a person or animal is to wound them savagely with a horn or tusk • *Several dogs had been gored by a wild boar.*

gorge *noun*
a narrow valley with steep sides

gorgeous *adjective*
magnificent; beautiful **gorgeously** *adverb*

gorilla *noun*
a large strong African ape

gorse *noun*
gorse is a prickly bush with small yellow flowers

gory *adjective* (**gorier, goriest**)
having a lot of blood and violence

gosling *noun*
a young goose

gospel *noun*
1 the gospel is the teachings of Jesus Christ **2** gospel is something you can safely believe • *You can take what she says as gospel.* **the Gospels** the first four books of the New Testament

gossip *verb*
to gossip is to talk a lot about other people

gossip *noun*
1 gossip is talk or rumours about other people **2** a gossip is someone who likes talking about other people

gouge *verb* (*say* gowj)
to gouge something is to press or scoop it out

govern *verb*
to govern a country or organization is to be in charge of it

government *noun*
the group of people who are in charge of a country

governor *noun*
someone who governs or runs a place

gown *noun*
a loose flowing piece of clothing

grab *verb* (**grabbing, grabbed**)
to grab something is to take hold of it firmly or suddenly

grace *noun*
1 grace is beauty, especially in movement **2** someone behaves with grace when they are kind and friendly to people

graceful *adjective*
beautiful and elegant in movement or shape **gracefully** *adverb*

gracious *adjective*
1 kind and pleasant to other people

2 merciful **graciously** *adverb* in a kind and generous way

grade *noun*
a step in a scale of quality, value, or rank

grade *verb*
to grade things is to sort or divide them into grades

gradient *noun* (*say* gray-di-ent)
1 a slope **2** the amount that a road or railway slopes

gradual *adjective*
happening slowly but steadily **gradually** *adverb* slowly or in stages

graduate *noun* (*say* grad-yoo-at)
someone who has a degree from a university or college

graffiti *plural noun*
(*say* gra-**fee**-tee)
graffiti is words or drawings scribbled on a wall

WORD ORIGIN

The word **graffiti** is the plural of an Italian word *graffito* meaning 'a scratch'.

grain *noun*
1 grain is cereals when they are growing or after they have been harvested **2** a grain is the hard seed of a cereal **3** a grain of something is a small amount of it • *The story had a grain of truth in it.* **4** the grain on a piece of wood is the pattern of lines going through it

gram *noun*
a unit of weight in the metric system, a thousandth of a kilogram

grammar *noun*
1 grammar is the rules for using words **2** a grammar is a book that gives the rules for using words **grammatical** *adjective* following the rules of grammar

grammar school *noun*
a kind of secondary school

grand *adjective*
1 great or splendid **2** a grand total is one that includes everything **grandly** *adverb* in a grand way

grandchild *noun* (**grandchildren**)
a child of a person's son or daughter. A girl is a **granddaughter** and a boy is a **grandson.**

grandfather *noun*
the father of a person's mother or father

grandfather clock *noun*
a clock in a tall wooden case

grandmother *noun*
the mother of a person's mother or father

grandparent *noun*
a grandmother or grandfather

grandstand *noun*
a building at a racecourse or sports ground, that is open at the front with rows of seats for spectators

granite *noun*
granite is a very hard kind of rock

grant *verb*
to grant someone something is to give or allow them what they have asked for **to take something for granted** is to assume that it is true or will happen

grant *noun*
a sum of money given for a special purpose

grape *noun*
a small green or purple fruit that grows in bunches on a vine

grapefruit *noun* (**grapefruit**)
a large round yellow citrus fruit with a soft juicy pulp

graph *noun*
a diagram that shows how two amounts are related

grapefruit

graphic *adjective*
1 short and lively • *He gave a graphic account of the journey.* **2** to do with drawing or painting • *She wants to be a graphic artist.* **graphically** *adverb* in a graphic way

graphics *plural noun*
graphics are diagrams, lettering, and drawings, especially pictures that are produced by a computer

graphite *noun*
graphite is a soft kind of carbon used for the lead in pencils

grapple *verb*
1 to grapple someone or grapple with someone is to fight them **2** to grapple something is to hold it tightly **3** to grapple with a problem is to try to deal with it

grasp *verb*
1 to grasp someone or something is to hold them tightly **2** to grasp something is to understand it

grasp *noun*
1 a firm hold **2** a person's grasp of a subject is how well they understand it

grass *noun*
1 grass is a green plant with thin stalks **2** a piece of grass is an area of ground covered with grass **grassy** *adjective* covered in grass

a
b
c
d
e
f
g
h
i
j
n
o
p
q
r
s
t
u
v
w
x
y
z

grasshopper noun
a jumping insect that makes a shrill noise

grate[1] noun
1 a metal framework that keeps fuel in the fireplace **2** a fireplace

grate[2] verb
1 to grate something is to shred it into small pieces **2** to grate is to make an unpleasant noise by rubbing something • *The chalk grated on the blackboard.*

grateful adjective
feeling glad that someone has done something for you **gratefully** adverb

grating noun
a framework of metal bars placed across an opening

gratitude noun
you show gratitude when you are grateful or thankful for something

grave[1] noun
the place where a dead body is buried

grave[2] adjective
serious or solemn • *We've had grave news.* **gravely** adverb • *The man nodded gravely.*

gravel noun
gravel is small stones mixed with coarse sand, used to make paths

gravestone noun
a stone monument over a grave

graveyard noun
a place where dead bodies are buried

gravity noun
1 gravity is the force that pulls all objects in the universe towards each other **2** the earth's gravity is the force that pulls everything towards itself **3** gravity is also the seriousness or importance of something

gravy noun
a hot brown sauce made from meat juices

graze verb
1 to graze is to feed on growing grass **2** to graze your skin is to scrape it slightly against something rough

graze noun
a sore place where skin has been scraped

grease noun
grease is thick fat or oil **greasy** adjective oily like grease

great adjective
1 very large **2** very important or distinguished • *She was a great writer.* **3** (*informal*) very good or enjoyable • *It's great to see you again.* **4** older or younger by one generation, as in *great-grandmother* and *great-grandson* **greatly** adverb
greatness noun

greed noun
greed is being greedy and wanting too much

greedy adjective (**greedier, greediest**)
wanting more food or money than you need **greedily** adverb

green adjective ●
1 of the colour of grass and leaves **2** concerned with protecting the natural environment

green noun
1 green is a green colour **2** a green is an area of grass

greenery noun
green leaves or plants

greenhouse noun
a glass building that is kept warm inside for growing plants

greenhouse effect noun
the warming of the earth's surface by gases (called **greenhouse gases**) such as methane and carbon dioxide, which trap heat in the earth's atmosphere

greet verb
1 to greet someone is to welcome them when they arrive • *His soft Moxie greeted him with a soft miaow.* **2** to greet something is to respond to it in a certain way • *They greeted the news with loud cheering.*

greeting noun
a greeting is the words or actions used to greet someone **greetings** are good wishes when you meet someone or talk to them

grenade noun
a small bomb, usually thrown by hand

grey adjective
of the colour between black and white, like ashes or dark clouds

grey noun ●
a grey colour

grid noun
a framework or pattern of bars or lines crossing each other

grief noun
grief is deep sadness or sorrow people feel when someone has died

grievance noun
something that people are unhappy or angry about

grieve verb
to grieve is to feel sad or sorrowful when someone has died

grill noun
1 a part of a cooker that sends heat downwards **2** grilled food **3** a grating

grill verb
1 to grill food is to cook it under a

grill 2 to grill someone is to question them closely and severely • *The police grilled him for several hours.*

grim adjective (**grimmer, grimmest**)
1 stern or severe **2** frightening or unpleasant • *They had a grim experience.* **grimly** adverb

grimace noun
a strange or twisted expression on your face

grime noun
grime is a layer of dirt on a surface **grimy** adjective very dirty

grin noun
a smile showing your teeth

grin verb
to grin is to smile showing your teeth

grind verb (**grinding, ground**)
1 to grind something is to crush it into a powder **2** to grind something hard is to sharpen or polish it by rubbing it on a rough surface **to grind to a halt** is to stop suddenly with a lot of noise **grinder** noun
something that grinds things

grip verb (**gripping, gripped**)
1 to grip something is to hold it tightly **2** a story, film, game, or other activity grips you when you find it very interesting or exciting

grip noun
1 a firm hold on something **2** a handle

grisly adjective (**grislier, grisliest**)
disgusting or horrible • *The book is full of scary villains and grisly murders.*

gristle noun
gristle is the tough rubbery part of meat **gristly** adjective gristly meat is tough and full of gristle

grit noun
1 grit is tiny pieces of stone or sand **2** a person's grit is their courage and determination to do something difficult **gritty** adjective rough like grit

grit verb (**gritting, gritted**)
1 to grit your teeth is to clench them tightly when in pain or trouble **2** to grit a road or path is to put grit on it

grizzly bear noun
a large bear of North America

groan verb
to groan is to make a long deep sound when in pain or distress

groan noun
a long deep sound of pain or distress

grocer noun
someone who keeps a shop that sells food, drink, and other goods for the house

grocery noun (**groceries**)
a grocer's shop **groceries** plural noun goods sold by a grocer

groin noun
the flat part where your thighs join the rest of your body

groom noun
1 someone whose job is to look after horses **2** a bridegroom

groom verb
1 to groom a horse or other animal is to clean and brush it **2** to groom the hair or a beard is to make it neat and trim

groove noun
a long narrow channel cut in the surface of something

grope verb
to grope for something is to feel about for it when you cannot see it

gross adjective
1 fat and ugly **2** having bad manners; crude or vulgar **3** very bad or shocking • *They showed gross stupidity.* **4** total, without anything taken off **grossly** adverb extremely or too much • *That's grossly unfair!*

gross noun
a gross is twelve dozen or 144

grotesque adjective (say groh-**tesk**)
strange and ugly **grotesquely** adverb

ground noun
1 the ground is the surface of the earth **2** a ground is a sports field

grounded adjective
1 aircraft are grounded when they are prevented from flying, for example because of the weather **2** (informal) someone is grounded when they are not allowed to go out

ground floor noun
in a building, the floor that is level with the ground

grounds plural noun
1 the reasons that explain or justify something • *There are grounds for suspecting that a crime has been committed.* **2** the gardens of a large house **3** bits of coffee at the bottom of a cup

group noun
a number of people, animals, or things that belong together in some way

group verb
to group people or things is to make them into a group

grouse noun
a large bird with feathered feet, that some people like to hunt as a sport

grove noun
a group of trees; a small wood

grovel verb (**grovelling, grovelled**)
1 to grovel is to crawl on the ground **2** to grovel is to be extremely humble and obedient towards someone, usually because you want something from them

grow verb (**growing, grew, grown**)
1 a person grows when they become bigger with age **2** a plant or seed grows when it develops in the ground **3** to grow something is to plant it in the ground and look after it • *She grows lovely roses.* **4** to grow is also to become • *By now it was growing dark on the moor.* • *He grew richer and richer.* **to grow out of something** is to become too big or too old for it **to grow up** is to become an adult **grower** noun someone who grows things

growl verb
to growl is to make a deep rough sound, like an angry dog

growl noun
a deep rough sound

grown-up noun
an adult

growth noun
1 growth is growing or development **2** a growth is something that has grown, especially something unwanted in the body such as a tumour

grub noun
1 a grub is a tiny creature that will become an insect; a larva **2** (slang) grub is food

grubby adjective (**grubbier, grubbiest**)
rather dirty

grudge noun
a dislike of someone because you think they have harmed you, or because you are jealous

grudge verb
to grudge someone something is to feel unwilling to let them have it **grudgingly** adverb you do something grudgingly when you don't really want to do it, and only do it because you have to

gruelling adjective
a gruelling test or journey or other experience is one that is very hard and tiring

gruesome adjective
horrible or disgusting to look at

gruff adjective
having a rough unfriendly voice or manner **gruffly** adverb

grumble verb
to grumble is to complain in a bad-tempered way **grumbler** noun someone who grumbles

grumpy adjective (**grumpier, grumpiest**)
bad-tempered **grumpily** adverb **grumpiness** noun

grunt verb
to grunt is to make a snorting sound like a pig

grunt noun
a snort like that of a pig

guarantee noun
a formal promise to do something, especially to repair something you have sold someone if it goes wrong

guarantee verb
to guarantee something is to make a promise to do it

guard verb
1 to guard something or someone is to keep them safe **2** to guard a prisoner is to prevent them from escaping **to guard against something** is to be careful to prevent it happening

guard noun
1 guard is protecting or guarding people or things • *Keep the prisoners under close guard.* **2** a guard is someone who protects or watches a person or place **3** a guard is also an official in charge of a railway train **4** a guard is a shield or device protecting people from the dangers of a fire or machinery **on guard** protecting; acting as a guard

guardian noun
1 someone who protects something **2** someone who is legally in charge of a child instead of the child's parents **guardianship** noun guardianship is being a guardian

guerrilla noun (say ge-**ril**-a)
a member of a small army or band that fights by means of surprise attacks

guess noun
an opinion or answer that you give without working it out in detail or being sure of it

guess verb
to guess is to make a guess

guest noun (say gest)
a person who is invited to a party or is staying at another person's house or at a hotel

guidance noun
guidance is giving help or information to someone, or telling them how to do something

guide noun
1 someone who shows people the way, helps them, or points out interesting sights **2** a book that tells you about a place

a b c d e f g h i j k l m n o p q r s t u v w x y z

Guide a member of the Girl Guides Association, an organization for girls

guide *verb*
to guide someone is to show them the way or help them do something

guide dog *noun*
a dog specially trained to lead a blind person

guidelines *plural noun*
guidelines are rules and information about how to do something

guillotine *noun* (*say* gil-o-teen)
1 a machine once used in France for beheading people **2** a device with a sharp blade for cutting paper

guilt *noun*
1 guilt is an unpleasant feeling you have when you have done something wrong **2** a person's guilt is the fact that they have done something wrong • *Everyone was convinced of his guilt.*

guilty *adjective* (**guiltier, guiltiest**)
1 someone is guilty when they have done wrong **2** someone feels guilty when they know they have done wrong

guinea pig *noun*
1 a small furry animal without a tail, kept as a pet **2** a person who is used in an experiment

guitar *noun*
a musical instrument played by plucking its strings
guitarist *noun* someone who plays the guitar

gulf *noun*
a large area of sea partly surrounded by land

gull *noun*
a seagull

gullet *noun*
the tube from the throat to the stomach

gullible *adjective*
someone is gullible when they can be easily fooled about something

gully *noun* (**gullies**)
a narrow channel that carries water

gulp *verb*
1 to gulp something is to swallow it quickly or greedily **2** to gulp is to make a loud swallowing noise, especially out of fear

gulp *noun*
a loud swallowing noise

gum¹ *noun*
the firm fleshy part of the mouth that holds the teeth

gum² *noun*
1 a sticky substance used as glue **2** chewing gum **gummy** *adjective* sticky like gum

gum² *verb* (**gumming, gummed**)
to gum something is to cover it or stick it with gum

gun *noun*
1 a weapon that fires shells or bullets from a metal tube **2** a pistol fired to signal the start of a race

gun *verb* (**gunning, gunned**)
to gun someone down is to shoot them with a gun

gunfire *noun*
gunfire is the firing of guns, or the noise they make

gunman *noun* (**gunmen**)
a man armed with a gun

gunpowder *noun*
gunpowder is a type of explosive

gurdwara *noun*
a building where Sikhs worship

gurgle *verb*
to gurgle is to make a bubbling sound • *Water gurgled down the pipe.*

guru *noun*
1 a Hindu religious teacher **2** a wise and respected teacher

Guru Granth Sahib *noun*
the holy book of the Sikh religion

gush *verb*
1 to gush is to flow quickly **2** to gush is also to talk quickly and with excitement

gust *noun*
a sudden rush of wind or rain **gusty** *adjective*

gut *noun*
the lower part of the digestive system; the intestine

gut *verb* (**gutting, gutted**)
1 to gut a dead fish or animal is to remove its insides before cooking it **2** to gut a place is to remove or destroy the inside of it • *The fire gutted the house.*

guts *plural noun*
1 the insides of a person or animal, especially the stomach and intestines **2** (*informal*) courage and determination

gutter *noun*
a long narrow channel at the side of a street or along the edge of a roof, to carry away rainwater

guy¹ *noun*
1 a figure in the form of Guy Fawkes, burnt on or near 5 November in memory of the Gunpowder Plot to blow up Parliament in 1605 **2** (*informal*) a man

guzzle *verb*
to guzzle food or drink is to eat or drink it greedily

gym *noun* (*say* jim) (*informal*)
1 a gym is a gymnasium **2** gym is gymnastics

gymkhana *noun* (*say* jim-kah-na)
a show of horse-riding contests and other events

gymnasium *noun*
a place equipped for gymnastics

gymnast *noun*
a person who does gymnastics

gymnastics *plural noun*
gymnastics are exercises and movements that show the body's agility and strength

gypsy *noun* (**gypsies**)
a member of a community of people, also called **travellers**, who live in caravans or similar vehicles and travel from place to place

gyroscope *noun*
a device used in navigation, that keeps steady because of a heavy wheel spinning inside it

gymnast

WORD ORIGIN

The word **gyroscope** comes from a Greek word *gyros* meaning 'a ring or circle'.

H h

habit *noun*
something that you do often and almost without thinking **habitual** *adjective* something is habitual when you do it regularly, as a habit **habitually** *adverb*

habitat *noun*
an animal's or plant's habitat is the place where it naturally lives or grows

hack *verb*
to hack something is to chop or cut it roughly

hacker *noun*
someone who uses a computer to get access to a company's or government's computer system without permission

hacksaw *noun*
a saw with a thin blade for cutting metal

haddock noun (**haddock**)
a sea fish used for food

hag noun
an ugly old woman

haggard adjective
looking ill or very tired

haggis noun
a Scottish food made from some of
the inner parts of a sheep mixed with
oatmeal

haggle verb
to haggle is to argue about a price or
agreement

haiku noun (**haiku**) (say **hy**-koo)
a Japanese short poem, with three lines
and 17 syllables in the pattern 5,7,5

hail¹ noun
frozen drops of rain

hail¹ verb
it hails or it is hailing when hail
falls

hail² verb
to hail someone is to call out or
wave to them to get their attention

hailstone noun
a piece of hail

hair noun
1 hair is the soft covering that grows
on the heads and bodies of people
and animals **2** a hair is one of the fine
threads that makes up this soft
covering

hairbrush noun
a brush for tidying your hair

haircut noun
cutting a person's hair when it
gets too long; the style into which
it is cut

hairdresser noun
someone whose job is to cut
and arrange people's hair

hair-raising adjective
terrifying or dangerous

hairstyle noun
a way or style of arranging your
hair

hairy adjective (**hairier, hairiest**)
having a lot of hair

Hajj noun
the Hajj is the journey to Mecca that
all Muslims try to make at least once
in their lives

hake noun (**hake**)
a sea fish used for food

halal adjective
halal meat is prepared according to
Muslim law

half noun (**halves**)
each of the two equal parts that
something is or can be divided into

half adverb
partly; not completely • *This meat is
only half cooked.*

half-hearted adjective
not very enthusiastic
half-heartedly adverb not very
enthusiastically

half-mast noun
a flag is at half-mast when it is
lowered to halfway down its flagpole,
as a sign that someone important
has died

half-term noun
a short holiday from school in the
middle of a school term

half-time noun
a short break in the middle of
a game

halfway adverb, adjective
at a point half the distance or
amount between two places or times

hall noun
1 a space or passage inside the
front door of a house **2** a very large
room for meetings, concerts, or other
large gatherings of people **3** a large
important building or house, such as
a town hall

hallo exclamation
a word used to greet someone or to
attract their attention

Hallowe'en noun
the night of 31 October, when people
used to think that ghosts and witches
might appear

hallucination noun
something you think you can
see or hear when it isn't really there

halo noun (**haloes**)
a circle of light, especially one shown
round the head of a saint or angel in
a painting

halt verb
to halt is to stop

halt noun
to call a halt is to stop something to
come to a halt is to stop

halter noun
a rope or strap put round a horse's
head so that it can be controlled

halve verb
1 to halve something is to divide it
into halves **2** to halve something is to
reduce it to half its size or amount
• *If the shop had another checkout it
would halve the queues.*

ham noun
ham is meat from a pig's leg

hamburger noun
a round flat cake of minced beef
that is fried and usually eaten in a
bread roll

hammer noun
a tool with a heavy metal head at the
end of a handle, used for hitting nails
in or beating out things

hammer verb
1 to hammer something is to
hit it with a hammer **2** to hammer
is to knock loudly • *We heard
someone hammering on the door.*
3 (*informal*) to hammer someone in
a game or contest is to defeat them
completely

hammock noun
a bed made of a strong net or piece
of cloth hung up above the ground
or floor

hamper¹ noun
a large box-shaped basket with
a lid

hamper² verb
to hamper someone or something is
to get in their way or make it difficult
for them to work

hamster noun
a small furry animal with cheek
pouches, often kept as a pet

hand noun
1 the part of your body at the end
of your arm **2** a pointer on a clock or
watch **3** the cards held by one player
in a card game **4** a worker, especially
a member of a ship's crew **5** side or
direction • *the right-hand side*
• *on the other hand* **at hand** near or
close by **to give someone a hand**
is to help them **on hand** ready and
available **to get out of hand** is to get
out of control

hand verb
to hand something to someone
is to give or pass it to them
something is handed down when it
is passed on from one generation to
the next

handbag noun
a small bag for holding money, keys,
and other personal items

handcuffs plural noun
a pair of metal rings joined by a
chain, used for locking a person's
wrists together

handful noun
1 as much as you can carry in
one hand **2** a small number of
people or things • *There were
only a handful of people in the
audience.* **3** (*informal*) a troublesome
person

handicap noun
a disadvantage

handicraft noun
artistic work done with your hands,
such as woodwork and pottery

a b c d e f g h i j k l m n o p q r s t u v w x y z

hang glider

handiwork *noun*
something you have done or made with your hands

handkerchief *noun*
(*say* **hang**-ker-cheef)
a square piece of material for wiping your nose

handle *noun*
the part of a thing by which you can hold or control it or pick it up
handle *verb*
1 to handle something is to touch or feel it with your hands **2** to handle a task or problem is to deal with it
• *I thought you handled the situation very well.*

handlebars *plural noun*
a bar with a handle at each end, used to steer a bicycle or motor cycle

handsome *adjective*
1 attractive or good-looking
2 large or generous • *They have made a handsome offer.*

handstand *noun*
an exercise in which you balance on your hands with your feet in the air

handwriting *noun*
writing done by hand; a person's style of writing **handwritten** *adjective* written by hand, not typed or printed

handy *adjective* (**handier, handiest**)
useful or convenient

hang *verb* (**hanging, hung**)
1 to hang something is to fix the top part of it to a hook or nail
• *Hang your coat on one of the pegs.* **2** something hangs when it is supported from the top and does not touch the ground • *The bat was hanging by its feet.* **3** to hang wallpaper is to paste it in strips on to a wall **4** to hang is to float in the air **5** (in this meaning, the past tense and past participle are **hanged**) to hang someone is to execute them by hanging them from a rope that tightens around their neck
• *He was hanged in 1950.* **to hang about** or **hang around** is to wait around doing nothing **to hang on** (*informal*) is to wait • *Hang on! I'm not ready yet.* **to hang on to**

something is to hold it tightly
to hang up is to end a telephone conversation

hangar *noun*
a large shed where aircraft are kept
hanger *noun*
a curved piece of wood, plastic, or wire with a hook at the top, that you use to hang clothes up on

hang glider *noun*
a frame like a large kite on which a person can glide through the air
hang gliding *noun* the sport of using a hang-glider

hanky *noun* (**hankies**)
(*informal*) a handkerchief

Hanukkah *noun*
A Jewish festival held in December

haphazard *adjective*
(*say* **hap**-haz-erd)
done or chosen at random, with no particular order or plan • *The books were arranged on the shelf in a haphazard way.* **haphazardly** *adverb*

happen *verb*
to happen is to take place or occur
to happen to do something is to do it by chance without planning it • *I happened to see him in the street.*

happening *noun*
something that happens; an unusual event

happy *adjective* (**happier, happiest**)
1 pleased or contented **2** satisfied that something is good • *My teacher is happy with my work this term.*
3 lucky or fortunate • *By a happy coincidence, we met Jenny in town.* **happily** *adverb* **happiness** *noun*

harass *verb* (*say* **ha**-ras)
to harass someone is to annoy or trouble them a lot
harassment *noun*

harbour *noun*
a place where ships can shelter or unload

hard *adjective*
1 firm or solid; not soft • *The ground was hard.* **2** difficult • *These sums are quite hard.* **3** severe or harsh • *There has been a hard frost.* **4** energetic; using great effort • *She is a hard worker.* **hard up** short of money
hardness *noun* being hard

hard *adverb*
1 with great effort • *We must work hard.* **2** with a lot of force • *It was raining hard.*

hardboard *noun*
stiff board made of compressed wood pulp

hard disk *noun*
a disk fitted inside a computer, able to store large amounts of data

harden *verb*
1 to harden is to become hard
• *Wait for the varnish to harden.* **2** to harden something is to make it hard • *What's the best way to harden a conker?*

hardly *adverb*
only just; only with difficulty
• *She was hardly able to walk.*

hardship *noun*
1 hardship is suffering or difficulty
2 a hardship is something that causes suffering

hardware *noun*
1 tools and other pieces of equipment you use in the house and garden
2 the machinery and electronic parts of a computer, not the software

hard-wearing *adjective*
able to stand a lot of wear

hardy *adjective* (**hardier, hardiest**) able to endure cold or difficult conditions

hare *noun*
a fast-running animal like a large rabbit

harm *verb*
to harm someone or something is to hurt or damage them

harm *noun*
injury or damage **harmful** *adjective* causing injury or damage **harmless** *adjective* safe; not at all dangerous

harmonica *noun*
a mouth organ

harmonious *adjective*
1 music is harmonious when it is pleasant to listen to **2** peaceful and friendly **harmoniously** *adverb* when people live or work harmoniously they do it in a friendly way without disagreeing

harmonize *verb*
to harmonize is to combine together in an effective or pleasant way

harmony *noun* (**harmonies**)
1 a pleasant combination of musical notes played or sung at the same time **2** agreement or friendship
• *They live in perfect harmony.*

harness *noun*
the straps put over a horse's head and round its neck to control it
harness *verb*
1 to harness a horse is to put a harness on it **2** to harness something is to control it and make use of it
• *They tried to harness the power of the wind to make electricity.*

harp noun
a musical instrument made of a frame with strings stretched across it that you pluck with your fingers **harpist** noun someone who plays the harp

harp

harp verb
to harp on about something is to keep on talking about it in an annoying way • *He keeps harping on about all the work he has to do.*

harpoon noun
a spear attached to a rope, fired from a gun to catch whales and large fish

harpsichord noun
a musical instrument like a piano but with the strings plucked and not struck

harsh adjective
1 rough and unpleasant **2** cruel or severe **harshly** adverb **harshness** noun

harvest noun
1 the time when farmers gather in the corn, fruit, or vegetables they have grown **2** the crop that is gathered in
harvest verb
to harvest crops is to gather them in

hassle noun
(*informal*) something that is difficult or causes problems

haste noun
hurry or speed **to make haste** is to hurry

hasten verb
1 to hasten is to hurry **2** to hasten something is to speed it up

hasty adjective (**hastier, hastiest**)
hurried; done too quickly • *a hasty decision* **hastily** adverb in a hurried way **hastiness** noun

hat noun
a covering for the head

hatch[1] noun
an opening in a floor, wall, or door, usually with a covering
hatch[2] verb
1 to hatch is to break out of an egg • *The chicks hatched this morning.*
2 to hatch an egg is to keep it warm until a young bird hatches from it
3 to hatch a plan is to form it

hatchet noun
a small axe

hate verb
to hate someone or something is to dislike them very much

hate noun
1 hate is a feeling of great dislike
2 (*informal*) a hate is someone or something that you dislike very much • *Sweetcorn is one of my hates.*

hateful adjective
hated; very nasty **hatefully** adverb

hatred noun (say **hay**-trid)
a strong feeling of great dislike

hat trick noun
getting three goals, wickets, or victories one after another

haughty adjective (**haughtier, haughtiest**) (say **haw**-ti)
proud of yourself and looking down on other people **haughtily** adverb **haughtiness** noun

haul verb
to haul something is to pull it using a lot of power or strength
haul noun
an amount that someone has won or gained • *The trawler brought home a large haul of fish.*

haunt verb
1 a ghost haunts a place or person when it appears often **2** an idea or memory haunts someone when they are always thinking of it **haunted** adjective a haunted place is one that people think is visited by ghosts

have verb (**has, having, had**)
This word has many meanings, depending on the words that go with it **1** to have something is to own or possess it • *We haven't any money.*
2 to have something in it is to contain it • *I thought this tin had biscuits in it.*
3 to have (for example) a party is to organize it **4** to have (for example) a shock or accident is to experience it • *I'm afraid she has had an accident.*
5 to have to do something is to be obliged or forced to do it • *We really have to go now.* **6** to have something (for example) mended or built is to get someone to mend or build it • *I'm having my watch mended.* **7** to have (for example) a letter is to receive it • *I had a letter from my cousin.* **8** The verb **have** can also be used to help make other verbs • *They have gone.* • *Has he seen my book?* • *We had eaten them.* **to have someone on** (*informal*) is to fool them

haven noun (say **hay**-ven)
1 a safe place **2** a harbour

hawk noun
a bird of prey with very strong eyesight and a hooked beak

hawthorn noun
a thorny tree with small red berries

hay noun
cut grass that is dried and used to feed to animals

hay fever noun
an allergy to pollen that makes you sneeze and makes your eyes water or itch

haystack noun
a large neat pile of stored hay

hazard noun
a risk or danger **hazardous** adjective dangerous or risky

haze noun
thin mist

hazel noun
1 a type of small nut tree **2** a nut from this tree **3** a light brown colour

hazy adjective (**hazier, haziest**)
1 misty • *hazy sunshine* **2** vague and unclear • *He has only a hazy memory of what happened.* **hazily** adverb **haziness** noun

he pronoun, noun
a male person or animal: used as the subject of a verb

head noun
1 the part of the body containing the brains, eyes, and mouth **2** brains or intelligence • *Use your head!* **3** the side of a coin on which someone's head is shown **4** a person • *It costs £10 per head.* **5** the top or front of something, such as a pin or nail **6** the person in charge • *She's the head of this school.* **to keep your head** is to stay calm **off the top of your head** (*informal*) without preparation or thinking carefully
head verb
1 to head a group or organization is to lead it or be the person in charge **2** to head a ball is to hit it with your head **3** to head in a particular direction is to start going there • *They headed for home.*

headache noun
1 a pain in your head that goes on hurting **2** (*informal*) a problem or difficulty

headdress noun
a decorative covering for the head

header noun
the act of hitting the ball with your head in football

heading noun
a word or words at the top of a piece of printing or writing

headlight noun
a strong light at the front of a vehicle

headline noun
a heading in a newspaper, printed in large type

a b c d e f g h i j k l m n o p q r s t u v w x y z

headlong *adverb, adjective*
1 falling with your head forward
2 in a hasty or thoughtless way • *He's always rushing headlong into trouble.*

head-on *adverb, adjective*
with the front parts hitting each other • *They had a head-on collision.*

headphones *plural noun*
a listening device that fits over the top of your head

headquarters *noun*
the place from which an organization is controlled

headteacher *noun*
the person in charge of a school

heal *verb*
1 to heal someone is to make them healthy 2 a wound or injury heals when it gets better • *The cut soon healed.* **healer** *noun* someone who heals people who are ill

health *noun*
how well or ill a person is • *His health is good for his age.*

health food *noun*
food that contains only natural substances and is thought to be good for your health

healthy *adjective* (**healthier, healthiest**)
1 free from illness; having good health 2 good for you • *Fresh air is healthy.* **healthily** *adverb* **healthiness** *noun*

heap *noun*
a pile, especially an untidy pile **heaps** (*informal*) a large amount • *We've got heaps of time.*

heap *verb*
1 to heap things is to pile them up 2 to heap something is to put large amounts on it • *She heaped his plate with food.*

hear *verb* (**hearing, heard**)
1 to hear is to take in sounds through your ears 2 to hear news or information is to receive it 3 you hear from someone when they write to you or phone you

hearing *noun*
1 the ability to hear 2 a chance to be heard • *Please give me a fair hearing.* 3 a trial in court

hearing aid *noun*
a device to help a partially deaf person to hear

hearse *noun*
a vehicle for taking a coffin to a funeral

heart *noun*
1 the part of the body inside your chest that pumps blood around your body 2 a person's feelings or emotions • *She has a kind heart.*

3 courage or enthusiasm • *We must take heart.* 4 the middle or most important part of something 5 a curved shape representing a heart, or a playing card with this shape on it **to break someone's heart** is to make them very unhappy **by heart** by using your memory

heart

heart attack *noun*
a sudden failure of the heart to work properly, causing pain and sometimes death

hearth *noun* (say harth)
the floor of a fireplace or the area near it

heartless *adjective*
cruel or without pity

hearty *adjective* (**heartier, heartiest**)
1 strong and healthy 2 enthusiastic or sincere • *Hearty congratulations!* 3 a hearty meal is large and filling **heartily** *adverb* **heartiness** *noun*

heat *noun*
1 being hot; great warmth 2 a race or contest to decide who will take part in the final

heat *verb*
1 to heat something, or heat something up, is to make it hot 2 to heat, or heat up, is to become hot

heater *noun*
a device for heating a place, especially a room or a car

heath *noun*
wild flat land often covered with heather or bushes

heather *noun*
a low bush with small purple, pink, or white flowers

heatwave *noun*
a long period of hot weather

heave *verb*
1 to heave something is to lift or move it with great effort 2 (*informal*) to heave something is to throw it **to heave a sigh** is to sigh deeply

heaven *noun*
1 the place where, in some religions, good people are thought to go when they die and where God and the

angels are thought to live 2 a very pleasant place or condition **the heavens** the sky

heavenly *adjective*
1 to do with the sky or in the sky 2 (*informal*) pleasing or delicious • *The cake is heavenly.*

heavy *adjective* (**heavier, heaviest**)
1 weighing a lot; hard to lift or carry 2 you talk about how heavy something is when you are talking about how much it weighs 3 strong or severe • *Heavy rain was falling.* 4 hard or difficult • *The climb up the hill was heavy going.* **heavily** *adverb* **heaviness** *noun*

Hebrew *noun*
the language of the ancient Jews, with a modern form used in Israel

hectare *noun* (say **hek**-tar)
a unit of area equal to 10,000 square metres or nearly 2½ acres

hectic *adjective*
very active or busy • *It's been a hectic morning.*

hedge *noun*
a row of bushes forming a barrier or boundary

hedgehog *noun*
a small animal covered with prickles

hedgerow *noun*
a row of bushes forming a hedge

heed *verb*
to heed something is to pay attention to it

heed *noun*
attention given to something **heedless** *adjective* taking no notice of something

heel *noun*
1 the back part of your foot 2 the part of a sock or shoe round or under the back part of your foot

hefty *adjective* (**heftier, heftiest**)
big and strong

heifer *noun* (say **hef**-er)
a young cow

height *noun*
1 how high someone or something is 2 a high place • *She's afraid of heights.* 3 the highest or most important part of something • *We shall be going at the height of the holiday season.*

heighten *verb*
1 to heighten something is to make it higher or more intense 2 to heighten is to become higher or more intense • *Their excitement heightened as the kick-off approached.*

heir noun (say air)
someone who inherits money or a title **heiress** noun a girl or woman who inherits money or a title

helicopter

helicopter noun
a kind of aircraft without wings, lifted by a large horizontal propeller on top

helium noun (say hee-li-um)
a colourless gas that is lighter than air and is sometimes used in balloons

hell noun
1 a place where, in some religions, wicked people are thought to be punished after they die and where the Devil is thought to live **2** a very unpleasant place or situation

hello exclamation
a word used to greet someone or to attract their attention

helm noun
the handle or wheel used to steer a ship

helmet noun
a strong hard hat or covering that you wear to protect your head

help verb
1 to help someone is to do something useful for them or make things easier for them **2** when you cannot help doing something, you cannot avoid doing it • I couldn't help sneezing. **3** to help someone to food is to give them some **helper** noun someone who helps another person

help noun
1 doing something useful for someone • Do you need any help? **2** someone who does something for someone • Thank you, you've been a great help.

helpful adjective
giving help; useful **helpfully** adverb

helping noun
a portion of food at a meal

helpless adjective
not able to do things or look after yourself **helplessly** adverb

hem noun
the edge of a piece of cloth that has been folded over and sewn down

hem verb (**hemming, hemmed**)
to hem material is to fold it over and sew down its edge
to hem someone in is to surround them and stop them moving

hemisphere noun
each half of the earth, above or below the equator • Australia is in the southern hemisphere.

hen noun
a female bird, especially a chicken

hence adverb
1 from this time on **2** therefore

her pronoun
a word used for she when it is the object of a verb, or when it comes after a preposition • I can see her. • He took the books from her.

her determiner
belonging to her • That is her book.

herald noun
1 an official who in the past used to make announcements or carry messages for a king or queen **2** someone or something that is a sign of things to come

herald verb
to herald something or someone is to say or show that they are coming

heraldry noun
the study of coats of arms **heraldic** adjective to do with heraldry

herb noun
a plant used for flavouring or for making medicines
herbal adjective made from herbs or using herbs

herbivore noun
an animal that only eats plants

herd noun
a large group of animals, especially cattle

herd verb
to herd animals or people is to gather them together or move them in a large group

here adverb
in or to this place **here and there** in various places or directions

hereditary adjective
passed down to a child from a parent

heredity noun (say hi-red-i-ti)
the passing down of characteristics from parents to children through their genes

heritage noun
things that have been passed from one generation to another; a country's history and traditions • Music is part of our cultural heritage.

hermit noun
someone who lives alone and keeps away from people, often for religious reasons

hero noun (**heroes**)
1 a man or boy who has done something very brave **2** the most important man or boy in a story, film, or play **heroic** adjective very brave, like a hero **heroically** adverb bravely **heroism** noun being a hero; great bravery

heroine noun
1 a woman or girl who has done something very brave **2** the most important woman or girl in a story, film, or play

heron noun
a wading bird with long legs and a long neck

herring noun (**herring** or **herrings**)
a sea fish that swims in large groups and is used for food

hers pronoun
belonging to her • Those books are hers.

herself pronoun
she or her and nobody else, used to refer back to the subject of a verb • She has hurt herself. **by herself** on her own; alone • She did the work all by herself.

hesitant adjective
being slow or uncertain when you speak or move **hesitantly** adverb

hesitate verb
to hesitate is to be slow or uncertain when you speak or move **hesitation** noun when you hesitate; a pause

hexagon noun
a flat shape with six sides **hexagonal** adjective having six sides

hibernate verb (say hy-ber-nayt)
animals hibernate when they sleep for a long time during cold weather **hibernation** noun hibernating

hiccup noun
a high gulping sound made when your breath is briefly interrupted

hiccup verb
to make this high gulping sound

hide verb (**hiding, hidden, hid, hidden**)
1 to hide is to get into a place where you cannot be seen or found • I hid behind a tree. **2** to hide someone or something is to keep them from being seen • The gold was hidden in a cave. **3** to hide information is to keep it secret • Are you hiding the truth from me?

hide-and-seek noun
a game in which one person looks for others who are hiding

hideous adjective
very ugly or unpleasant **hideously** adverb

a
b
c
d
e
f
g
h
i
j
k
l
m
n
o
p
q
r
s
t
u
v
w
x
y
z

hideout *noun*
a place where someone hides

hiding¹ *noun*
to go into hiding is to hide yourself so that people can't find you

hiding² *noun*
a thrashing or beating

hieroglyphics *plural noun*
(*say* hyr-o-**glif**-iks)
pictures or symbols used in ancient Egypt to represent words

high *adjective*
1 reaching a long way up • *They could see a high building.* **2** far above the ground or above sea level • *The clouds were high in the sky.* **3** measuring from top to bottom • *The post is two metres high.* **4** above average in amount or importance • *They are people of a high rank.* • *Prices are high.* **5** lively; happy • *They are in high spirits.* **6** a high note is one at the top end of a musical scale

high *adverb*
1 far above the ground or a long way up • *She jumped high into the air.* **2** at a high level • *The temperature is going to rise even higher this week.* **it is high time to do something** when you should do it at once • *It's high time you started work.*

high jump *noun*
an athletic contest in which competitors jump over a high bar

highland *adjective*
in the highlands; to do with the highlands

highlands *plural noun*
mountainous country, especially in Scotland **highlander** *noun* someone who lives in the highlands

highlight *noun*
the most interesting part of something • *We watched the highlights of the match on the TV.*

highlight *verb*
to highlight something is to draw attention to it

highly *adverb*
extremely • *He is highly amusing.* **to think highly of someone** is to admire them very much

Highness *noun*
a title of a prince or princess • *His Royal Highness, the Prince of Wales*

high-pitched *adjective*
high in sound

highway *noun*
an important road or route

highwayman *noun*
(**highwaymen**)
a man who in earlier times robbed travellers on highways

hijack *verb*
to hijack an aircraft or vehicle is to take control of it by force during a journey **hijacker** *noun* someone who hijacks an aircraft or vehicle

hike *noun*
a long walk in the countryside

hike *verb*
to hike is to go for a long walk in the countryside **hiker** *noun* someone who goes for long walks in the countryside

hilarious *adjective*
very funny **hilariously** *adverb* if something is hilariously funny it is extremely funny **hilarity** *noun* loud laughter

hill *noun*
a piece of ground that is higher than the ground around it **hillside** *noun* the side of a hill **hilly** *adjective* a hilly area has lots of hills

hilt *noun*
the handle of a sword or dagger **up to the hilt** completely

him *pronoun*
a word used for *he* when it is the object of a verb, or when it comes after a preposition • *I like him.* • *I gave it to him.*

himself *pronoun*
he or him and nobody else, used to refer back to the subject of a verb • *He has hurt himself.* **by himself** on his own; alone • *He did the work all by himself.*

hind¹ *adjective* (*say* hynd)
at the back • *The donkey had hurt one of its hind legs.*

hind² *noun* (*say* hynd)
a female deer

hinder *verb* (*say* **hin**-der)
to hinder someone is to get in their way, or to make it difficult for them to do something **hindrance** *noun* something that gets in your way, or makes it difficult for you to do something

Hindi *noun*
a language spoken in northern India

Hindu *noun*
someone who believes in **Hinduism**, one of the religions of India

hinge *noun*
a joining device on which a door, gate, or lid swings when it opens

hinged *adjective*
a hinged door, window, or lid is fixed on a hinge

hint *noun*
1 a slight indication or suggestion • *Give me a hint of what you want for your birthday.* **2** a useful piece of advice • *He was always giving us hints on model-making.*

hint *verb*
to hint is to suggest something without actually saying it • *She hinted that she'd like to have a puppy.*

hip *noun*
your hips are the bony parts at the side of your body between your waist and your thighs

hippo *noun* (**hippos**)
(*informal*) a hippopotamus

hippopotamus *noun*
a very large African animal that lives near water

hippopotamus

hire
verb
to hire something is to pay to use it for a time

hire *noun*
something is for hire when you can hire it

his *determiner*
belonging to him • *That is his book.*

hiss *verb*
to hiss is to make a sound like a continuous *s*, as some snakes do

historian *noun*
someone who writes or studies history

historic *adjective*
famous or important in history

historical *adjective*
1 to do with history **2** that really happened in the past • *The story is based on historical events.*

history *noun* (**histories**)
1 what happened in the past **2** the study of past events **3** a description of important events

hit *verb* (**hitting, hit**)
1 to hit someone or something is to come up against them with force, or to give them a blow **2** something hits you when you suddenly realize or feel it • *The answer suddenly hit me.* **3** to hit a place or people is to have a bad effect on them • *Famine hit the poorer countries.* **4** to hit a note is to reach it when you are singing **to hit it off with someone** is to get on well with them when you meet them **to**

hit on something is to think of an idea suddenly

hit noun
1 a knock or stroke 2 a shot that hits the target 3 a successful song or show

hitch verb
1 to hitch something is to tie it up with a loop 2 (informal) to hitch a lift is to hitchhike **to hitch something up** is to pull it up quickly or with a jerk • He hitched up his trousers.

hitch noun
a slight difficulty or delay

hitchhike verb
to hitchhike is to travel by getting lifts in other people's vehicles **hitchhiker** noun someone who hitchhikes

hitherto adverb
up to now

HIV
short for human immunodeficiency virus, a virus that weakens a person's resistance to disease and causes the disease Aids

hive noun
1 a beehive 2 a very busy place • The office was a hive of activity.

hoard noun
a hidden store of something valuable

hoard verb
to hoard things is to collect them and store them away **hoarder** noun someone who likes saving things and keeping them rather than throwing them out

hoarding noun
a tall fence covered with advertisements

hoarse adjective
having a rough or croaking voice • He was hoarse from shouting.

hoax noun
a trick played on someone in which they are told about something but it isn't true • The bomb scare was hoax.

hoax verb
to hoax someone is to trick them by telling them about something that isn't true

hobble verb
to hobble is to walk with unsteady steps, especially because your feet are sore

hobby noun (**hobbies**)
something that you enjoy doing in your spare time

hockey noun
an outdoor game played by two teams with long curved sticks and a small hard ball

hoe noun
a gardening tool with a long handle and a metal blade, used for scraping up weeds and making soil loose

hog noun
1 a male pig 2 (informal) a greedy person

hog verb (**hogging, hogged**)
(informal) to hog something is to take more than your fair share of it

Hogmanay noun
New Year's Eve in Scotland

hoist verb
to hoist something is to lift it up using ropes or pulleys

hold verb (**holding, held**)
1 to hold something is to have it in your hands 2 to hold something is also to possess it or be the owner of it • She holds the world high jump record. 3 to hold a party, meeting, or event is to organize it • The 2008 Olympic Games were held in Beijing. 4 a container holds an amount when that is what you can put in it • This jug holds a litre. 5 to hold someone or something is to support them • This plank won't hold my weight. 6 to hold someone is to keep them and stop them getting away • They held the thief until help arrived. 7 something like the weather holds when it stays the same • Will this good weather hold? 8 to hold an opinion is to believe it **hold it** (informal) stop; wait a minute **to hold on** (informal) is to wait • Hold on! I'm not ready yet. **to hold out** is to last or continue **to hold someone up** is to rob them with threats of force **to hold someone or something up** is to hinder or delay them • We were held up by the traffic.

hold noun
1 holding something • Don't lose hold of the rope. 2 the part of a ship where cargo is stored **to get hold of someone** is to make contact with them • I want to invite Jane to the party but I can't get hold of her. **to get or take hold of something** is to grasp it

hold-up noun
1 a delay 2 a robbery with threats or force

hole noun
1 a gap or opening made in something 2 an animal's burrow • a rabbit hole **holey** adjective full of holes

Holi noun
a Hindu festival held in the spring

holiday noun
a day or time when you do not go to work or school; a time when you go away to enjoy yourself **to be on holiday** is to be away from work or school enjoying yourself

hollow adjective
having an empty space inside; not solid

hollow verb
to hollow something is to make it hollow • We always hollow out a pumpkin at Halloween.

hollow noun
1 a hollow or sunken place 2 a small valley

holly noun
an evergreen bush with shiny prickly leaves and red berries

holster noun
a leather case for a pistol, usually attached to a belt

holy adjective (**holier, holiest**)
1 to do with God and treated with religious respect 2 a holy person is devoted to God or a religion **holiness** noun

home noun
1 the place where you live 2 the place where you were born or where you feel you belong 3 a place where people are looked after • She went to a home for the elderly. **to feel at home** is to feel comfortable and happy

home adverb
1 to or at the place where you live • Go home! • Is she home yet? 2 to the place aimed at • Push the bolt home. **to bring something home to someone** is to make them realize it

home verb
to home in on something is to aim for it

homeless adjective
not having a place to live

homely adjective
simple or ordinary

home-made adjective
made at home and not bought from a shop

homesick adjective
sad or upset because you are away from home **homesickness** noun the feeling of being homesick

homeward or **homewards** adverb
towards home

homework noun
school work that you have to do at home

honest adjective
truthful and able to be trusted; not stealing, cheating, or telling lies **honesty** noun being honest and truthful

honestly adverb
1 to say something honestly is to say it truthfully 2 to do something honestly is to do it without stealing or cheating

a b c d e f g h i j k l m n o p q r s t u v w x y z

honey *noun*
a sweet sticky food made by bees

honeycomb *noun*
a wax framework made by bees to hold their honey and eggs

honeycomb

honeymoon *noun*
a holiday that a newly-married couple spend together

honour *noun*
1 honour is great respect or reputation **2** an honour is something given to a person who deserves it because of the good work they have done **3** an honour is also something a person is proud to do • *It is an honour to meet you.*

honour *verb*
1 to honour someone is to show you respect them or to give them an honour **2** to honour a promise or agreement is to keep it

honourable *adjective*
someone is honourable when they can be trusted and always try to do the right thing **honourably** *adverb*

hood *noun*
1 a covering of soft material for the head and neck, usually part of a coat or sweatshirt **2** a folding roof or cover **hooded** *adjective* having or wearing a hood

hoof *noun* (**hoofs**)
the hard, bony part of the foot of horses, cattle, or deer

hook *noun*
a piece of bent or curved metal or plastic for hanging things on or catching hold of something **hooked** *adjective* having a curved shape like a hook

hook *verb*
1 to hook something is to fasten it with or on a hook **2** to hook a fish is to catch it with a hook

hooligan *noun*
a rough or noisy person

hoop *noun*
a large ring made of metal, wood, or plastic

hooray *exclamation*
a shout of joy or approval; a cheer

hoot *noun*
1 a sound like the one made by an owl or a car horn **2** a jeer

hoot *verb*
to hoot is to make a sound like an owl or a car horn

hooter *noun*
a horn or other device that makes a hoot

hop¹ *verb* (**hopping, hopped**)
1 to hop is to jump on one foot **2** animals hop when they move in jumps **3** (*informal*) to hop is also to move quickly • *Hop in and I'll give you lift.* **hop it** (*slang*) go away

hop¹ *noun*
a jump you make on one foot

hop² *noun*
a climbing plant used to give beer its flavour

hope *noun*
1 the feeling of wanting something to happen, and thinking that it will happen **2** a person or thing that makes you feel like this • *She is our big hope for a gold medal.*

hope *verb*
to hope for something is to want it and expect it to happen

hopeful *adjective*
1 having hope **2** likely to be good or successful • *The future did not seem very hopeful.*

hopefully *adverb*
1 in a hopeful way **2** I hope that … • *Hopefully we can all go to the sea tomorrow.*

hopeless *adjective*
1 without hope **2** very bad at something • *I'm hopeless at cricket.* **hopelessly** *adverb*

hopscotch *noun*
a game in which you hop into squares drawn on the ground

horde *noun*
a large group or crowd

horizon *noun* (*say* ho-**ry**-zon)
the line where the sky appears to meet the land or sea

horizontal *adjective*
(*say* ho-ri-**zon**-tal)
level or flat; going across from left to right **horizontally** *adverb* in a horizontal direction

hormone *noun*
a substance made in glands in the body and sent directly into the blood to make other organs work in special ways

horn *noun*
1 a kind of pointed bone that grows on the head of a bull, cow, ram, and other animals **2** a brass musical instrument that you blow **3** a device for making a warning sound

hornet *noun*
a large kind of wasp

horoscope *noun*
an astrologer's forecast of future events

horrible *adjective*
very unpleasant or nasty **horribly** *adverb*

horrid *adjective*
nasty or unkind

horrific *adjective*
shocking or terrifying **horrifically** *adverb*

horrify *verb* (**horrifying, horrified**)
to horrify someone is to make them feel shocked and disgusted

horror *noun*
1 horror is great fear or disgust **2** a horror is a person or thing you really dislike

horse *noun*
1 a four-legged animal used for riding on or pulling carts **2** a tall box that you jump over when you are doing gymnastics

horseback *noun*
to be on horseback is to be riding a horse

horse chestnut *noun*
a large tree that produces dark brown nuts called *conkers*

horsepower *noun* (**horsepower**)
a unit for measuring the power of an engine, equal to 746 watts

horseshoe *noun* (**horseshoes**)
a U-shaped piece of metal nailed as a shoe to a horse's hoof

hose *noun*
a long flexible tube through which liquids or gases can travel

hospitable *adjective*
welcoming to people; liking to give hospitality **hospitably** *adverb*

hospital *noun*
a place where sick or injured people are given medical treatment

hospitality *noun*
welcoming people and giving them food and entertainment

host¹ *noun*
someone who has guests and looks after them

host² *noun*
a large number of people or things

hostage *noun*
someone who is held prisoner until the people who are holding them get what they want

hostel *noun*
a building with rooms where students or other people can stay cheaply

hostess noun
a woman who has guests and looks after them

hostile adjective
1 unfriendly and angry • *The crowd outside was hostile.* **2** opposed to someone or something **hostility** noun unfriendliness and strong dislike

hot adjective (**hotter, hottest**)
1 having a high temperature; very warm **2** having a burning taste like pepper or mustard **3** excited or angry • *He has a hot temper.* **to be in hot water** (*informal*) is to be in trouble or difficulty

hot dog noun
a hot sausage in a bread roll

hotel noun
a building where people pay to stay for the night and have meals

hotly adverb
strongly or forcefully • *He hotly denied that he'd done it.*

hot-water bottle noun
a container that you fill with hot water to make a bed warm

hound noun
a dog used for hunting or racing
hound verb
to hound someone is to keep on chasing and bothering them • *The family was hounded by newspaper reporters.*

hour noun
1 one of the twenty-four parts into which a day is divided **2** a particular time • *Why are you up at this hour?*

hourglass noun
an old-fashioned device for telling the time, with sand running from one half of a glass container into the other through a narrow middle part

hourly adjective, adverb
every hour; done once an hour

house noun (*say* howss)
1 a building where people live, usually designed for one family **2** a building used for a special purpose • *They passed the opera house.* • *We visited the Houses of Parliament.* **3** one of the divisions in some schools for sports competitions and other events
house verb (*say* howz)
to house someone or something is to provide a house or room for them

household noun
all the people who live together in the same house

house-trained adjective
an animal that is house-trained is trained to be clean in the house

housewife noun (**housewives**)
a woman who stays at home to look after her children and do the housework rather than doing a paid job

housework noun
the work like cooking and cleaning that has to be done in a house

hover verb
1 to hover is to stay in one place in the air **2** to hover round someone is to wait near them to watch what they do

hovercraft noun (**hovercraft**)
a vehicle that travels just above the surface of water or land, supported by a strong current of air sent downwards by its engines

how adverb
1 in what way • *How did you do it?* **2** to what extent • *How much do you want?* **3** in what condition • *How are you?* **how about ...** would you like ... ? • *How about a game of football?* **how do you do?** a more formal greeting when you meet someone

however adverb
1 no matter how; in whatever way • *You will never catch him, however hard you try.* **2** nevertheless • *It was snowing; however, he went out.*
however conjunction
in any way • *You can do it however you like.*

howl noun
a long loud cry like an animal in pain
howl verb
to howl is to make a long loud cry like an animal in pain, or to weep loudly

HQ
short for headquarters

hub noun
the centre of a wheel

huddle verb
to huddle is to crowd together with other people for warmth or comfort

hue noun
a colour or tint

huff noun
to be in a huff is to be annoyed or offended

hug verb (**hugging, hugged**)
1 to hug someone is to clasp them tightly in your arms **2** to hug something is to keep close to it • *The ship hugged the shore.*
hug noun
clasping someone tightly in your arms

huge adjective
extremely large
hugely adverb greatly; very

hulk noun
1 the remains of an old decaying ship **2** a large clumsy person or thing
hulking adjective large, heavy, and clumsy

hull noun
the main part or framework of a ship

hum verb (**humming, hummed**)
1 to hum is to sing a tune with your lips closed **2** to hum is also to make a low continuous sound like a bee
hum noun
a humming sound

human noun
a man, woman, or child; a human being
human adjective
to do with humans

human being noun
a man, woman, or child; a human

humane adjective (*say* hew-**mayn**)
showing kindness and a wish to cause as little suffering or pain as possible **humanely** adverb in a way that causes as little suffering or pain as possible

humanity noun
1 all the people in the world **2** kindness and sympathy to other people

humble adjective
modest and not proud
humbly adverb

humid adjective (*say* hew-mid)
damp and warm in the air
humidity noun how damp it is in the air

humiliate verb
to humiliate someone is to make them feel ashamed or foolish in front of other people **humiliation** noun

humility noun
being humble

hummingbird noun
a small tropical bird that makes a humming sound by beating its wings rapidly

a b c d e f g h i j k l m n o p q

hummingbird

humorous *adjective*
amusing or funny

humour *noun*
1 being amusing; what makes people laugh **2** being able to enjoy things that are funny • *He has a good sense of humour.* **3** a person's mood • *Keep him in a good humour.*

humour *verb*
to humour someone is to keep them happy by doing what they want

hump *noun*
1 a rounded lump or mound **2** a lump on a person's back

hump *verb*
to hump something heavy is to carry it with difficulty on your back

hunch¹ *noun*
a feeling that you can guess what will happen • *I have a hunch that she won't come.*

hunch² *verb*
to hunch your shoulders is to bring them up and forward so that your back is rounded

hunchback *noun*
someone with a hump on their back **hunchbacked** *adjective* having a hunchback

hundred *noun*
the number 100
hundredth *adjective, noun* 100th

hundredweight *noun*
a unit of weight equal to 112 pounds or 50.8 kilograms

hunger *noun*
the feeling you get when you want or need to eat

hungry *adjective* (**hungrier, hungriest**)
you are hungry when you want or need to eat **hungrily** *adverb*

hunk *noun*
a large piece or chunk of something

hunt *verb*
1 to hunt animals is to chase and kill them for food or sport **2** to hunt for something is to look hard for it

hunt *noun*
1 a time when a group of people chase and kill animals for food or sport **2** a group of people who go hunting **3** a search

hunter or **huntsman** *noun*
someone who hunts for sport

hurdle *noun*
1 an upright frame that runners jump over in an athletics race **2** a problem or difficulty

hurl *verb*
to hurl something is to throw it as far as you can

hurrah or **hurray** *exclamation*
a shout of joy or approval; a cheer

hurricane *noun*
a severe storm with a strong wind

hurry *verb* (**hurries, hurrying, hurried**)
1 to hurry is to move or act quickly **2** to hurry someone is to try to make them be quick **hurriedly** *adverb* in a hurry • *We hurriedly got dressed.*

hurry *noun*
moving quickly; doing something quickly **in a hurry** hurrying or impatient • *They were in a hurry to catch their train.*

hurt *verb*
1 to hurt a person or animal is to harm them or cause them pain **2** part of your body hurts when you feel pain there **3** to hurt someone is also to upset them by doing or saying something unkind

hurt *noun*
pain or injury **hurtful** *adjective* a hurtful remark upsets someone because it is unkind

hurtle *verb*
to hurtle is to move quickly or dangerously • *A mass of snow and rocks hurtled down the mountain.*

husband *noun*
the man that a someone is married to

hush *verb*
to hush someone is to make them be quiet

hush *noun*
silence or quiet • *Let's have a bit of hush.*

husk *noun*
the dry outer covering of a seed

husky¹ *adjective* (**huskier, huskiest**)
you say a voice is husky when it is deep and rough • *She has a husky voice.* **huskily** *adverb* with a husky voice **huskiness** *noun*

husky² *noun* (**huskies**)
a large strong dog used in the Arctic for pulling sledges

hustle *verb*
1 to hustle is to hurry **2** to hustle someone is to push them rudely

hut *noun*
a small roughly made house or shelter

hutch *noun*
a box or cage for a rabbit or other pet animal

hybrid *noun*
an animal or plant that combines two different species • *A mule is a hybrid of a donkey and a mare.*

hydrant *noun*
an outdoor water-tap connected to the main water supply, for fixing a hose to

hydraulic *adjective*
worked by the movement of water or other liquid

hydroelectric *adjective*
using water-power to make electricity

hydrofoil *noun*
a boat designed to skim over the surface of the water

hydrogen *noun*
a very light gas which with oxygen makes water

hyena

hyena *noun* (say hy-**ee**-na)
a wild animal that looks like a wolf and makes a shrieking howl

hygiene *noun* (say **hy**-jeen)
keeping clean and healthy and free of germs

hygienic *adjective*
clean and healthy and free of germs **hygienically** *adverb*

hypermarket *noun*
a very large supermarket, usually outside a town

hyphen *noun*
a short dash used to join words or parts of words together, for example in *red-handed*

hypnosis *noun* (say hip-**noh**-sis)
to be under hypnosis is to be in a condition like a deep sleep in which a person follows the instructions of another person

hypnotism *noun* (say **hip**-no-tizm)
hypnotizing people **hypnotist** *noun* someone who hypnotizes people

hypnotize *verb*
to hypnotize someone is to put them to sleep by hypnosis

hypocrite *noun* (say **hip**-o-krit)
someone who pretends to be a better person than they really are **hypocrisy** *noun* being a hypocrite

hypocritical *adjective* someone is being hypocritical when they are pretending to be a better person than they really are

hypodermic *adjective* (*say* hy-po-**der**-mik) a hypodermic needle or syringe is one used to inject something under the skin

hypotenuse *noun* (*say* hy-**pot**-i-newz) the side opposite the right angle in a right-angled triangle

hypothermia *noun* a person suffers from hypothermia when they become so cold that their body temperature falls well below normal

hysteria *noun* wild uncontrollable excitement or emotion

hysterical *adjective* **1** extremely excited or emotional **2** (*informal*) very funny **hysterically** *adverb*

hysterics *plural noun* a fit of hysteria **to be in hysterics** (*informal*) is to be laughing a lot

I *pronoun* a word used by someone to speak about himself or herself

ice *noun* **1** ice is frozen water **2** an ice is an ice cream

ice *verb* **1** to ice or ice up is to become covered in ice **2** to ice a cake is to put icing on it

ice age *noun* a time in the past when ice covered large areas of the earth's surface

iceberg *noun* a large mass of ice floating in the sea, with most of it under water

ice cream *noun* **1** ice cream is a sweet creamy frozen food **2** an ice cream is a portion of this

ice hockey *noun* ice hockey is a game like hockey played on ice

ice cream

ice lolly *noun* (**ice lollies**) a piece of flavoured ice on a stick

ice-skating *noun* moving on ice wearing special boots with blades on the bottom

icicle *noun* a thin pointed piece of hanging ice formed from dripping water

icing *noun* a sugary substance for decorating cakes

icon *noun* **1** a small picture or symbol standing for a program on a computer screen **2** a painting of a holy person

ICT short for *information and communication technology*

icy *adjective* (**icier, iciest**) **1** an icy road has ice on it **2** an icy wind is very cold **3** very unfriendly; hostile • *He gave them an icy stare.* **icily** *adverb* in an unfriendly way

idea *noun* something that you have thought of; a plan **to have no idea** is to not know something

ideal *adjective* exactly what you want; perfect **ideally** *adverb* if things were perfect • *Ideally, I'd like to live by the sea.*

ideal *noun* something that is perfect or the best thing to have; a very high standard

identical *adjective* exactly the same • *Daniel and Sammy are identical twins.* **identically** *adverb* in exactly the same way • *They were identically dressed.*

identification *noun* **1** identification is any document, such as a passport, that proves who you are **2** identification is the process of discovering who someone is or what something is

identify *verb* (**identifies, identifying, identified**) to identify someone or something is to discover who or what they are • *The police have identified the car used in the robbery.*

identity *noun* (**identities**) who someone is or what something is • *Can you discover the identity of our mystery guest?*

idiom *noun* (*say* **id**-i-om) a phrase or group of words that together have a special meaning that is not obvious from the words themselves, for example *to be in hot water* means to be in trouble or difficulty

idiot *noun* (*informal*) a stupid or foolish person

idiotic *adjective* stupid or foolish **idiocy** *noun* foolish behaviour

idle *adjective* **1** a person is idle when they are lazy or doing nothing **2** a machine is idle when it is not being used **3** idle talk or gossip is talk that is silly or pointless

idle *verb* a machine or engine idles when it is working slowly **idly** *adverb* in a lazy way

idol *noun* **1** a famous person who is admired by a lot of people **2** a statue or image that people worship as a god

idolize *verb* to idolize someone is to admire them very much

i.e. short for the Latin *id est*, which means 'that is', used to explain something • *The world's highest mountain (i.e. Mount Everest) is in the Himalayas.*

if *conjunction* **1** on condition that • *I'll tell you what happened if you promise to keep it secret.* **2** although; even though • *I'll finish this job if it kills me!* **3** whether • *Do you know if lunch is ready?* **if only** ... I wish ... • *If only I could go with you!*

igloo *noun* a round house made of blocks of hard snow, built by the Inuit people of the Arctic

WORD ORIGIN

The word **igloo** comes from an Inuit word *iglu* meaning 'house'.

ignite *verb* **1** to ignite something is to set fire to it **2** to ignite is to catch fire

ignition *noun* **1** igniting **2** ignition is the system in a motor engine that starts the fuel burning

ignorant *adjective* not knowing about something; knowing very little **ignorance** *noun* someone shows ignorance when they don't know about something or know very little

ignore *verb* to ignore someone or something is to take no notice of them

ill *adjective* **1** not well; in bad health **2** bad or harmful • *There were no ill effects.*

illegal *adjective* something is illegal when it is against the law **illegally** *adverb*

illegible *adjective* (*say* i-**lej**-i-bul) illegible writing is not clear enough to read **illegibly** *adverb*

a b c d e f g h i j k l m n o p q r s t u v w x y z

illegitimate *adjective*
(*say* il-i-**jit**-i-mat)
(*old use*) someone is illegitimate when they are born to parents who are not married to each other

illiterate *adjective* (*say* i-**lit**-er-at)
unable to read or write
illiteracy *noun* illiteracy is not being able to read or write

illness *noun*
1 illness is being ill **2** an illness is something that makes people ill; a disease

illogical *adjective*
not logical or having any good reason
illogically *adverb* in a way that is not logical

illuminate *verb*
to illuminate a place or street is to light it up or decorate it with lights
illuminations *plural noun* lights put up to decorate a place or street

illusion *noun*
1 something that you think is real or happening but is not **2** an idea or belief you have that isn't true

illustrate *verb*
1 to illustrate something is to show it with pictures or examples **2** to illustrate a book is to put pictures in it

illustration *noun*
a picture in a book

illustrator *noun*
a person who produces the illustrations in a book

image *noun*
1 a picture or statue of a person or thing **2** what you see in a mirror or through a lens **3** a picture you have in your mind **4** the way that people think of a person or thing

imaginary *adjective*
not real; existing only in your mind

imagination *noun*
your ability to form pictures and ideas in your mind

imaginative *adjective*
showing that you are good at thinking of new and exciting ideas • *Her stories are always very imaginative.*

imagine *verb*
to imagine something or someone is to form a picture of them in your mind **imaginable** *adjective* that you can imagine

imam *noun*
a Muslim religious leader

imitate *verb*
to imitate someone or something is to do the same as them **imitation** *noun* copying someone or something **imitator** *noun* someone who copies

someone or something else

immature *adjective*
1 not fully grown or developed **2** behaving in a silly or childish way
immaturity *noun* being immature

immediate *adjective*
1 happening or done without any delay **2** nearest; with nothing or no one between • *The Smiths are our immediate neighbours.*

immediately *adverb*
without any delay; at once • *You must come immediately.*

immense *adjective*
huge **immensely** *adverb* extremely
immensity *noun* immensity is being immense

immerse *verb*
1 to immerse something is to put it completely into a liquid **2** to be immersed in something is to be very interested or involved in it **immersion** *noun* the immersion of something is when you put it into a liquid

immigrant *noun*
someone who has come into a country to live there

immigrate *verb*
to immigrate is to come into a country to live there **immigration** *noun* people coming into a country to live

immobile *adjective*
not moving **immobility** *noun* being immobile

immoral *adjective*
not following the usual standards of right and wrong **immorality** *noun* behaviour that does not follow the usual standards of right and wrong

immortal *adjective*
someone who is immortal lives for ever and never dies **immortality** *noun* living for ever

immune *adjective*
someone is immune to a disease if they cannot catch it **immunity** *noun* protection against a disease

immunize *verb*
to immunize someone is to make them safe from a disease, usually by giving them an injection

immunization *noun* immunization is immunizing someone

imp *noun*
1 a small devil **2** a naughty child
impish *adjective* naughty or mischievous

impact *noun*
1 the force of one thing hitting another **2** a strong influence or effect • *The Internet is having a big impact on our lives.*

impair *verb*
to impair something is to harm or weaken it • *The accident has impaired his health.*

impartial *adjective*
fair and not supporting one side more than the other • *A referee must be impartial.* **impartiality** *noun* someone shows impartiality when they are fair and do not support one side more than the other
impartially *adverb*

impatient *adjective*
annoyed because you can't wait for something to happen **impatience** *noun* annoyance because you can't wait for something to happen
impatiently *adverb*

imperative *adjective*
essential • *Speed is imperative.*

imperceptible *adjective*
too small or gradual to be noticed • *The change in the weather was imperceptible.* **imperceptibly** *adverb*

imperfect *adjective*
not perfect or complete
imperfection *noun* being imperfect

imperial *adjective*
belonging to an empire or its rulers

impersonal *adjective*
not showing friendly human feelings • *The letter was a bit impersonal.*

impersonate *verb*
to impersonate someone is to pretend to be them
impersonation *noun* an act in which you impersonate someone
impersonator *noun* a person who impersonates someone else

impertinent *adjective*
rude to someone and not showing them respect **impertinence** *noun* being impertinent

implement *noun*
a tool or device you use to do something

implication *noun*
1 an implication is something that someone suggests without actually saying it **2** an implication is also a possible effect or result

implore *verb*
to implore someone to do something is to beg them to do it

imply *verb* (**implies, implying, implied**)
to imply something is to suggest it without actually saying it • *Are you implying that I'm lazy?*

impolite *adjective*
not having good manners; not

respectful and thoughtful towards other people

import verb (say im-**port**)
to import goods is to bring them in from another country to sell them
importer noun
someone who imports goods

import noun (say **im**-port)
something brought in from another country to be sold

important adjective
1 needing to be taken seriously; having a great effect • *This is an important decision.* **2** an important person is powerful or influential
importance noun being important
importantly adverb seriously
• *Try to win the match but, more importantly, don't lose.*

impossible adjective
1 not possible **2** (informal) very annoying • *He is impossible!*
impossibility noun something that is not possible **impossibly** adverb

impostor noun
someone who is not what he or she pretends to be

impractical adjective
1 impractical people are not good at making or doing things
2 not likely to work or be useful
• *Their ideas are impractical.*

impress verb
1 to impress someone is to make them admire you **2** to impress something on someone is to make them realize or remember it

impression noun
1 a vague idea that you have about something • *I had the impression that he was waiting for me to speak.* **2** the effect that something has on your mind or feelings • *The book left a strong impression on me.* **3** an imitation of a person or a sound

impressive adjective
something is impressive when it makes you admire it **impressively** adverb

imprison verb
to imprison someone is to put them in prison **imprisonment** noun being put in prison

improbable adjective
unlikely **improbability** noun being improbable

improper adjective
1 not proper; wrong **2** rude or indecent

improve verb
1 to improve something is to make it better **2** to improve is to become better **improvement** noun
something that is better or makes a thing better

improvise verb
1 to improvise is to do something without any rehearsal or preparation, especially to play music without rehearsing **2** to improvise something is to make it quickly with what is to hand **improvisation** noun improvisation is improvising something

impudent adjective
not respectful; rude **impudence** noun being impudent

impulse noun
a sudden desire to do something

impulsive adjective
doing things suddenly without much thought **impulsively** adverb

impure adjective
not pure **impurity** noun something in a substance that makes it not pure

in preposition, adverb
1 showing position at or inside something • *They live in London.*
• *Please come in.* • *She fell in the water.* • *Then the others fell in.* **2** In also has some special uses, shown by the following examples • *We came in April.* • *I paid in cash.* • *The serial was in four parts.* • *He is in the army.* • *We knocked on the door but no one was in.* **in all** including everything • *The bill comes to £120 in all.* **to be in for something** is to be likely to get it
• *You're in for a shock.*

inability noun
inability is being unable to do something

inaccessible adjective
an inaccessible place is impossible to reach

inaccurate adjective
not accurate **inaccuracy** noun
inaccuracy is being inaccurate
inaccurately adverb

inactive adjective
not working or doing anything **inactivity** noun inactivity is being inactive

inadequate adjective
not enough **inadequacy** noun
inadequacy is being inadequate
inadequately adverb

inanimate adjective
(say in-**an**-im-at)
not living or moving

inappropriate adjective
not appropriate or suitable
inappropriately adverb

inaudible adjective
not able to be heard
inaudibly adverb so quietly that it cannot be heard

incapable adjective
not able to do something • *They are*

incapable of understanding the problem.

incapacity noun
incapacity is inability or disability

incense

incense noun (say **in**-senss)
incense is a substance that makes a spicy smell when it is burnt

incense verb (say in-**senss**)
to incense someone is to make them very angry

incentive noun
something that encourages a person to do something or to work harder

incessant adjective
going on without stopping, usually in an annoying way • *They were bothered by the incessant noise.*
incessantly adverb

inch noun
a measure of length, one twelfth of a foot or about 2½ centimetres

incident noun
an event, usually a strange or unusual one

incidental adjective
happening along with something else; not so important **incidentally** adverb by the way

incinerator noun
a bin or container for burning rubbish

inclination noun
a feeling that makes you want to do something • *He suddenly had an inclination to look through the keyhole.*

incline verb (say in-**klyn**)
to incline is to lean or bend **to be inclined to do something** is to feel like doing it • *I'm inclined to wait until later.*

incline noun (say **in**-klyn)
a slope

include verb
to include something or someone is to make or consider them as part of a group of things • *Did you include Peter in the party?* **inclusion** noun being included

inclusive adjective
including everything; including all the things mentioned • *We want to stay from Monday to Thursday inclusive.*

income noun
the money that a person earns regularly for their work

incompatible *adjective*
1 not able to live or exist together without trouble **2** machines and devices are incompatible when they cannot be used together

incompetent *adjective*
unable to do something properly **incompetence** *noun* the inability to do something properly **incompetently** *adverb*

incomplete *adjective*
not complete **incompletely** *adverb* not completely

incomprehensible *adjective*
not able to be understood

incongruous *adjective*
(*say* in-**kong**-roo-us) not suitable and out of place

inconsiderate *adjective*
not thinking of other people

inconsistent *adjective*
not consistent **inconsistency** *noun* being inconsistent **inconsistently** *adverb*

inconspicuous *adjective*
not easy to see or notice

inconvenient *adjective*
not convenient; awkward **inconvenience** *noun* when something is inconvenient • *Sorry for the inconvenience.*

incorporate *verb*
to incorporate something is to include it as a part of something else

incorrect *adjective*
not correct; wrong **incorrectly** *adverb* wrongly

increase *verb* (*say* in-**kreess**)
1 to increase something is to make it bigger **2** to increase is to become bigger **increasingly** *adverb* more and more • *They were becoming increasingly angry.*

increase *noun* (*say* **in**-kreess)
1 increasing **2** the amount by which something increases

incredible *adjective*
hard to believe; unbelievable **incredibly** *adverb*

incredulous *adjective*
finding it difficult to believe someone

incubate *verb*
to incubate eggs is to hatch them by keeping them warm **incubation** *noun* incubation is the hatching of eggs

incubator *noun*
1 a specially heated container for keeping newly born babies warm and well supplied with oxygen **2** a container for hatching eggs

indecent *adjective*
not decent; improper **indecency** *noun* **indecently** *adverb*

indeed *adverb*
used for emphasis • *He was very wet indeed.*

indefinite *adjective*
not definite; vague and unclear

indefinite article *noun*
the word *a* or *an*

indefinitely *adverb*
for an indefinite or unlimited time

independent *adjective*
1 free from the control of another person or country **2** not needing help from other people **independence** *noun* being independent **independently** *adverb* without help from other people

index *noun*
a list of names or topics, usually in alphabetical order at the end of a book

index finger *noun*
the finger next to the thumb

indicate *verb*
to indicate something is to point it out or show that it is there **indication** *noun* a sign of something

indicator *noun*
1 something that tells you what is happening **2** a flashing light on a vehicle, to show that it is turning left or right

indifferent *adjective*
1 you are indifferent to something when you have no interest in it at all **2** not very good; ordinary • *He is an indifferent tennis player.* **indifference** *noun* you show indifference when you have no interest at all in something **indifferently** *adverb*

indigestible *adjective*
not easy to digest

indigestion *noun*
indigestion is pain that you get when food is hard to digest

indignant *adjective*
angry at something that seems wrong or unjust **indignantly** *adverb* **indignation** *noun* indignation is a feeling of being indignant

indirect *adjective*
not direct or straight **indirectly** *adverb*

indispensable *adjective*
essential; that you have to have

indistinct *adjective*
not clear **indistinctly** *adverb*

individual *adjective*
1 of or for one person **2** single or separate **individually** *adverb* separately; one by one

individual *noun*
an individual is one person

indoctrinate *verb*
to indoctrinate someone is to fill their mind with particular ideas or beliefs, so that they accept them without thinking **indoctrination** *noun* indoctrination is indoctrinating someone

indoor *adjective*
placed or done inside a building • *We like indoor sports.*

indoors *adverb*
inside a building • *We'd better go indoors.*

induce *verb*
to induce someone to do something is to persuade them to do it **inducement** *noun* something given or done to persuade someone to do something

indulge *verb*
to indulge someone is to let them have or do what they want **to indulge in something** is to have or do something that you really like

indulgent *adjective*
kind and allowing people to do what they want **indulgence** *noun* indulgence is being indulgent

industrial *adjective*
to do with industry

industrious *adjective*
hard-working **industriously** *adverb*

industry *noun*
1 industry is making or producing goods to sell, especially in factories **2** an industry is a branch of this, such as the motor industry **3** industry is also working hard

ineffective *adjective*
not effective; not working well **ineffectively** *adverb*

inefficient *adjective*
not working well and wasting time or energy **inefficiency** *noun* being inefficient **inefficiently** *adverb*

inequality *noun* (**inequalities**)
inequality is not being equal

inevitable *adjective*
something is inevitable when it can't be avoided **inevitability** *noun* being inevitable **inevitably** *adverb*

inexhaustible *adjective*
that you cannot use up completely; never-ending

inexpensive *adjective*
not expensive; cheap **inexpensively** *adverb* cheaply

inexperience *noun*
inexperience is lack of experience **inexperienced** *adjective*

someone is inexperienced when they don't have much experience

inexplicable *adjective*
impossible to explain **inexplicably** *adverb* in a way that is impossible to explain

infallible *adjective*
1 never wrong **2** that never fails • *They have an infallible way of winning the lottery.* **infallibility** *noun* infallibility is being infallible **infallibly** *adverb*

infamous *adjective* (*say* **in**-fa-mus)
well-known for being bad or wicked **infamy** *noun* being infamous

infant *noun*
a baby or young child **infancy** *noun* the time when someone is a baby or young child

infantile *adjective*
childish and silly

infantry *noun*
infantry are soldiers trained to fight on foot

infect *verb*
to infect someone is to pass on a disease to them

infection *noun*
1 infection is infecting someone **2** an infection is an infectious disease

infectious *adjective*
1 an infectious disease is one that can spread from one person to another **2** something like laughter or fear is infectious when it spreads to other people

infer *verb* (**inferring, inferred**)
to infer something is to work it out from what someone says or does • *I inferred from his words that he did not really want to come.* **inference** *noun* something that you can work out from what someone says or does

inferior *adjective*
not as good or important as something else; lower in position or quality **inferiority** *noun* being inferior
inferior *noun*
a person who is lower in position or rank than someone else

inferno *noun* (**infernos**)
(*say* in-**fer**-noh) a fierce fire

infested *adjective*
a place is infested with (for example) insects or rats when it is full of them

infinite *adjective* (*say* **in**-fi-nit)
endless; too large to be measured or imagined **infinitely** *adverb* to an infinite extent

infinitive *noun* (*say* in-**fin**-i-tiv)
the basic form of a verb. In English it

often comes after *to*, as in *to go* and *to hit.*

infinity *noun* (*say* in-**fin**-i-ti)
infinity is an infinite number or distance

infirm *adjective*
someone is infirm when they are weak because they are ill or old **infirmity** *noun* being infirm

infirmary *noun* (**infirmaries**)
a place for sick people; a hospital

inflame *verb*
1 a part of the body is inflamed when it has become red and sore **2** to inflame someone is to make them angry

inflammable *adjective*
an inflammable material can be set alight

inflammation *noun*
a painful swelling or sore place on the body

inflate *verb*
1 to inflate something is to fill it with air or gas so that it swells up **2** a claim or statement is inflated when it is exaggerated **inflatable** *adjective* something is inflatable when it can be filled with air to make it swell up

inflation *noun*
inflation is a general rise in prices

inflexible *adjective*
that you cannot bend or change • *There are a lot of inflexible rules.* **inflexibility** *noun* being inflexible **inflexibly** *adverb*

inflict *verb*
to inflict something on someone is to make them suffer it • *She inflicted a severe blow on him.*

influence *noun*
the power to affect someone or something
influence *verb*
to influence someone or something is to have an effect on what they are or do • *The tides are influenced by the moon.*

influential *adjective*
having a big influence; important

influenza *noun* (*say* in-floo-**en**-za)
an infectious disease that causes fever, catarrh, and pain. It is more usually called **flu.**

inform *verb*
to inform someone of something is to tell them about it **to inform against or on someone** is to give information about them, especially to the police

informal *adjective*
not formal; casual and relaxed **informality** *noun* informality is being informal **informally** *adverb*

information *noun*
information is facts or what someone tells you

information technology *noun*
information technology is ways of storing, arranging, and giving out information, especially the use of computers and telecommunications

informative *adjective*
(*say* in-**form**-a-tiv) containing a lot of helpful information

informed *adjective*
you are informed about something when you know about it

informer *noun*
a person who tells the police about someone else

infrequent *adjective*
not frequent **infrequently** *adverb* only now and then

infuriate *verb*
to infuriate someone is to make them very angry

ingenious *adjective*
1 clever at doing things **2** cleverly made or done **ingeniously** *adverb* **ingenuity** *noun* cleverness or skill in doing things

ingot *noun*
a lump of gold or silver that has been cast in the form of a brick

ingots

ingratitude *noun*
ingratitude is not showing that you are grateful for something that someone has done for you

ingredient *noun* (*say* in-**greed**-i-ent)
1 one of the parts of a mixture **2** one of the things used in a recipe

inhabit *verb*
to inhabit a place is to live in it **inhabitant** *noun* one of the people who live in a place

inhale *verb*
1 to inhale is to breathe in **2** to inhale something is to breathe it in

inhaler *noun*
a device for taking medicine by inhaling it

inherit *verb*
1 to inherit money, property, or a title is to receive it when its previous owner dies **2** to inherit qualities or characteristics is to get them from your parents or ancestors **inheritance** *noun* something you inherit **inheritor** *noun* a person who inherits something

inhospitable *adjective*
(*say* in-hos-**pit**-a-bul *or say*
in-**hos**-pit-a-bul)
1 unfriendly to visitors **2** an
inhospitable place is difficult to live
in because it gives no shelter • *They
reached an inhospitable rocky island.*

inhuman *adjective*
cruel; without pity or kindness
inhumanity *noun* cruel behaviour

initial *noun*
the first letter of a word or name,
especially of someone's forename
initial *adjective*
first; of the beginning • *the initial
stages of the work* **initially** *adverb*
at the beginning

initiate *verb* (*say* in-**ish**-i-ayt)
1 to initiate something is to start
it **2** to initiate someone is to admit
them as a member of a society or
group, often with special ceremonies
initiation *noun* making someone a
new member of a society or group

initiative *noun* (*say* in-**ish**-a-tiv)
1 the action that starts something
• *She took the initiative in planning
the party.* **2** initiative is the ability or
power to start things or to get them
done on your own

inject *verb*
to inject someone is to put a medicine
or drug through their skin using
a hollow needle **injection** *noun*
injecting someone with medicine

injure *verb*
to injure someone is to harm or hurt
them

injury *noun* (**injuries**)
harm or damage done to someone

injustice *noun*
unfairness in the way
someone is treated

ink *noun*
ink is a black or coloured liquid
used for writing and printing **inky**
adjective inky fingers or pages are
covered in ink

inkling *noun*
a slight idea or suspicion • *I had an
inkling that we'd find them in here.*

inland *adverb*
away from the coast

inn *noun*
a hotel or public house, especially
in the country **innkeeper** *noun*
someone who runs an inn

inner *adjective*
inside; nearer the centre **innermost**
adjective furthest inside

innings *noun*
the time when a cricket team or
player is batting

innocence *noun*
1 when someone is not guilty of doing
something wrong **2** lack of experience
of the world and the evil things in it

innocent *adjective*
1 not guilty of doing something
wrong **2** not knowing much about
the world and the evil things in it
innocently *adverb*

innovation *noun*
1 innovation is inventing or using new
things **2** an innovation is something
new that you have just invented or
started using **innovative** *adjective*
new or original

innumerable *adjective*
too many to be counted

inoculate *verb*
to inoculate someone is to inject
them to protect them against
a disease **inoculation** *noun*
inoculation is being inoculated

input *noun*
what you put into something,
especially data put into a computer
input *verb* (**inputting, input**)
(*in computing*) to
input data or
programs is to put
them into a computer

inquest *noun*
an official investigation to
decide why someone died

insects

inquire *verb*
1 to inquire about something is
to ask about it **2** to inquire into
something is to make an official
investigation of it

inquiry *noun* (**inquiries**)
an official investigation

inquisitive *adjective*
always trying to find out things,
especially about other people
inquisitively *adverb*

insane *adjective*
not sane; mad **insanely** *adverb*
insanity *noun* insanity is being
insane

insanitary *adjective*
dirty and unhealthy

inscribe *verb*
to inscribe something is to write or
carve it on a surface

inscription *noun*
words written or carved on a
monument, stone, or coin, or written
in the front of a book

insect *noun*
a small animal with six legs and a
body divided into three parts

WORD ORIGIN

The word **insect** comes from a Latin word
insectum meaning 'cut up'.

insecticide *noun*
a poisonous chemical used for killing
insects

insecure *adjective*
1 not safe or protected properly
2 not feeling safe or confident
insecurely *adverb* not firmly or
safely **insecurity** *noun* insecurity
is not feeling safe or confident

insensitive *adjective*
not sensitive or thinking
about the feelings of other
people **insensitively** *adverb*
insensitivity *noun* being
insensitive

inseparable *adjective*
1 unable to be separated
2 people are inseparable when
they are very good friends and
always together • *The two girls were
inseparable during the summer.*
inseparably *adverb* two things are
inseparably linked when they are
so closely linked that they can't be
separated

insert *verb*
to insert something is to put it into
something else **insertion** *noun* the
insertion of something is when it is
inserted into something else

inside *noun*
1 the middle or centre of something;
the part nearest to the middle
2 (*informal*) your insides are your
stomach or abdomen **inside out**
with the inside turned so that it faces
outwards
inside *adjective*
placed on the inside of something
• *Stick the picture on an inside page.*
inside *adverb*, *preposition*
in or to the inside of something
• *Come inside.* • *It's inside that box.*

insignificant *adjective*
not important or influential
insignificance *noun* being
insignificant

insincere *adjective*
not sincere **insincerely** *adverb*
insincerity *noun* not being sincere

insist *verb*
to insist something is to be very firm
in saying it • *He insisted that he was
innocent.* **to insist on something** is
to demand it • *We insist on seeing
the manager.*

insistent *adjective*
insisting on doing or having
something **insistence** *noun* being
insistent

insolent *adjective*
very rude and insulting **insolence**
noun speaking to someone rudely
and without respect

insomnia noun (say in-**som**-ni-a)
insomnia is being unable to sleep

inspect verb
to inspect something or someone is
to look carefully at them, especially
to check them **inspection** noun a
close or careful look at something to
check it

inspector noun
1 someone whose job is to inspect
things or people **2** a police officer
next in rank above a sergeant

inspire verb
to inspire someone is to fill them with
ideas or enthusiasm **inspiration**
noun a person or thing that
encourages you and fills you with
ideas

install verb
to install something is to put it in
position ready for use • *We want to
install central heating.* **installation**
noun being installed

instalment noun
one of the parts into which something
is divided so that it is spread over a
period of time • *He is paying for his
bike in monthly instalments.* • *The
story was in three instalments.*

instance noun
an example **for instance** for example

instant adjective
1 happening immediately
• *It has been an instant success.*
2 that can be made very quickly
• *Do you like instant coffee?*

instant noun
a moment • *I don't believe it for an
instant.* **this instant** at once
• *Come here this instant!*

instantaneous adjective
happening or done in an
instant, or without any delay
instantaneously adverb in an
instant; immediately

instantly adverb
to do something instantly is to do it
without any delay

instead adverb
in place of something else; as a
substitute • *There were no potatoes,
so we had rice instead.*

instep noun
the top of your foot between the toes
and the ankle

instinct noun
a natural tendency to do or feel
something without being taught
• *Spiders spin webs by instinct.*
instinctive adjective done by
instinct **instinctively** adverb in an
instinctive way • *He knew instinctively
that something was wrong.*

institute noun
an organization set up to study
something or for some other purpose,
or the building used by it

institution noun
1 a large organization
2 something that is an established
habit or custom • *Going for a swim
on Sunday was a family institution.*

instruct verb
1 to instruct someone is to
teach them a subject or skill
2 to instruct someone is also
to give them information or orders

instruction noun
1 instruction is teaching a
subject or skill **2** an instruction
is an order or piece of information
• *Follow the instructions carefully.*

instrument noun
1 a device for making musical
sounds **2** a device for delicate or
scientific work

instrumental adjective
instrumental music uses musical
instruments without any singing

insufficient adjective not enough

insulate verb
to insulate something is to
cover it to stop heat, cold, or
electricity from passing in or
out **insulation** noun insulation
is insulating something

insult verb (say in-**sult**)
to insult someone is to speak or behave
in a rude way that offends them

insult noun (say **in**-sult)
a rude remark or action that offends
someone

insurance noun
a business agreement to receive
money or compensation if you suffer
a loss or injury, in return for a regular
payment called a premium

insure verb
to insure yourself or your goods is to
protect them with insurance

intact adjective
complete and undamaged • *Despite
the storm our tent was still intact.*

intake noun
the number of people or things taken
in • *The school had a high intake of
pupils this year.*

integer noun (say **in**-ti-jer)
a whole number, such as 0, 1, 24, and
not a fraction

integrate verb (say **in**-ti-grayt)
1 to integrate different things or
parts is to make them into a whole
2 to integrate people, especially of
different origins, is to bring them
together into a single community

integration noun integration is
being integrated

integrity noun (say in-**teg**-ri-ti)
integrity is being honest and
behaving well

intellect noun
the ability to think and work things
out with your mind

intellectual adjective
1 involving the mind and thinking
2 able to think effectively; keen to
study and learn **intellectually**
adverb

intellectual noun
an intellectual person

intelligence noun
your intelligence is your ability to
think and learn

intelligent adjective
good at thinking and learning
intelligently adverb

intelligible adjective
able to be understood
• *The message was barely intelligible.*
intelligibility noun being
intelligible **intelligibly** adverb in a
way that can be understood

intend verb
to intend to do something is to
have it in mind as a plan • *She was
intending to go swimming.*

intense adjective
1 very strong or great • *The heat was
intense.* **2** having or showing strong
feelings **intensely** adverb very
strongly **intensity** noun how
strong or great something is

intensive adjective
using a lot of effort; thorough
• *We have made an intensive
search.* **intensively** adverb

intent adjective
showing a lot of attention and
interest **to be intent on something**
is to be eager or determined to do
it **intently** adverb with a lot of
attention and interest

intent noun
a person's intent is what they intend
to do

intention noun
what you intend to do; a plan

intentional adjective
done on purpose; deliberate
intentionally adverb on purpose;
deliberately

interactive adjective
allowing information to be sent in
either direction, especially between a
computer system and its user

intercept verb
to intercept someone or something
is to stop them going from one place

to another **interception** noun
interception is intercepting someone
or something

interchange noun
a place where traffic moves from one
main road or motorway to another

interchangeable adjective
things are interchangeable when they
can be changed or swapped round

intercom noun
a device by which people in different
rooms or places can communicate
with one another

interest verb
to interest someone is to make them
want to look or listen or take part in
something

interest noun
1 interest is being interested
2 an interest is a thing that interests
you • *Jane's main interest is music.*
3 interest is also money a borrower
has to pay regularly for a loan

interfere verb
1 to interfere in something is to
become involved in it when it has
nothing to do with you **2** to interfere is
to get in the way • *I hope the weather
won't interfere with our picnic.*

interference noun
1 interfering in something
2 a crackling or distorting of a radio
or television signal

interior noun
the inside of something

interjection noun
an exclamation,
such as *oh!*

interlock verb
to interlock is
to fit into one
another • *The
gearwheels
interlocked.*

interlock

interlude noun
an interval

intermediate adjective
coming between two
things in place, order, or time

interminable adjective
(*say* in-**ter**-min-a-bul)
seeming to go on for ever
interminably adverb

internal adjective
of or in the inside of something
internally adverb on the
inside

international adjective
to do with more than one country
• *Interpol is an international police*

organization. **internationally**
adverb for or in more than one country

Internet noun
the Internet is a computer network
that allows people all over the world
to share information and send
messages

interpret verb
1 to interpret something is to explain
what it means **2** to interpret a foreign
language is to translate it into
another language **interpretation**
noun an explanation or translation
of something **interpreter** noun a
person who translates what someone
says into another language

interrogate verb
to interrogate someone is
to question them closely in order
to get information **interrogation**
noun when someone is interrogated

interrupt verb
1 to interrupt someone is to
stop them talking **2** to interrupt
something is to stop it continuing
interruption noun when someone
or something is interrupted

intersect verb
to intersect something is to cross or
divide it • *The cloth had a design of
intersecting lines.*

intersection noun
a place where lines or roads cross
each other

interval noun
a time between two events or
between two parts of a play or film **at
intervals** with some time or distance
between each one; not continuously

intervene verb
1 to intervene is to come between
two events • *During the intervening
years they went abroad.* **2** to
intervene in an argument or fight is
to interrupt it in order to stop it or
affect the result **intervention** noun
an intervention is when someone
intervenes in something

interview noun
a meeting with someone to ask them
questions or discuss something

interview verb
to interview someone is to have an
interview with them **interviewer**
noun a person who interviews
someone, especially on radio or
television

intestine noun
the long tube along which food
passes after leaving your stomach

intimate adjective (*say* in-ti-mat)
1 very friendly with someone
2 intimate thoughts are thoughts
that are private or personal

3 detailed • *They have an intimate
knowledge of the town.* **intimacy**
noun closeness or friendship
intimately adverb

intimidate verb
to frighten a person with threats into
doing something **intimidation**
noun intimidation is intimidating
someone

into preposition
1 to the inside of something
• *Go into the house.* **2 into** also has
some special uses, shown by the
following examples • *He got into
trouble.* • *She went into acting.*
• *3 into 12 goes 4 times.*

intolerable adjective
unbearable • *The noise outside was
intolerable.* **intolerably** adverb to
an intolerable degree

intolerant adjective
not willing to accept people or ideas
that are different in some way
intolerance noun intolerance
is being intolerant **intolerantly**
adverb

intonation noun
the way you use the pitch of your
voice to alter the meaning of what
you are saying, for example when
asking a question

intoxicate verb
a person is intoxicated when they are
drunk **intoxication** noun being drunk

intrepid adjective
brave or fearless
intrepidly adverb

intricate adjective
an intricate pattern or design is
detailed and complicated **intricacy**
noun intricacy is being intricate
intricately adverb

intrigue verb (*say* in-**treeg**)
to intrigue someone is to interest
them very much and make them
curious **intriguing** adjective very
interesting because it is unusual

introduce verb
1 to introduce someone is to make
them known to other people **2** to
introduce something is to get it into
general use **3** to introduce a radio or
television programme is to say a few
words to explain it

introduction noun
1 introducing someone or something
2 a piece at the beginning of a book,
explaining what it is about
introductory adjective coming at
the beginning of something

intrude verb
to intrude is to come in or
join in without being wanted

intrusion *noun* coming in where you are not wanted

intruder *noun*
someone who forces their way into a place where they are not supposed to be

intuition *noun* (*say* in-tew-**ish**-on) the power to know or understand things without having to think hard
intuitive *adjective* using intuition

invade *verb*
to invade a country or place is to attack and enter it **invaders** *plural noun* people who invade a place

invalid[1] *noun* (*say* in-va-leed or in-va-lid)
someone who is ill or weakened by a long illness
invalid[2] *adjective* (*say* in-**val**-id) not valid • *This passport is invalid.*

invaluable *adjective*
very valuable

invariable *adjective*
never changing; always the same **invariably** *adverb* always

invasion *noun*
when an army or a large number of people attack and enter a place

invent *verb*
1 to invent something is to be the first person to make it or think of it **2** to invent a story or excuse is to make it up **invention** *noun* something invented **inventor** *noun* a person who invents things

invertebrate *noun*
(*say* in-**vert**-i-brat)
an animal without a backbone, such as a worm or an amoeba

inverted commas *plural noun*
punctuation marks (" ") or (' ') that you put round spoken words and quotations

invertebrate

invest *verb*
to invest money is to use it to earn interest or make a profit **investor** *noun* someone who invests money

investigate *verb*
to investigate something or someone is to find out as much as you can about them • *Police are investigating the robbery* **investigation** *noun* a careful search for information

investigator *noun* a person who investigates someone or something

investment *noun*
1 money someone invests **2** something someone invests money in • *Houses are a safe investment.*

invincible *adjective*
not able to be defeated

invisible *adjective*
not visible; not able to be seen
invisibility *noun* being invisible
invisibly *adverb*

invitation *noun*
a request for someone to do something, such as come to a party

invite *verb*
to invite someone is to ask them to come to a party or do something special

inviting *adjective*
attractive or tempting
invitingly *adverb*

invoice *noun*
a bill that you get when someone has sold you something or done a job for you

involuntary *adjective*
not deliberate; done without thinking

involve *verb*
1 to involve something is to need it or result in it • *The job involved a lot of effort.* **2** to be involved in something is to take part in it • *The police think he may have been involved in the robbery.* **involvement** *noun* being involved in something

involved *adjective*
long and complicated

inward *adjective*
on the inside, or facing the inside
inward *adverb*
inwards

inwardly *adverb*
in your thoughts; privately
• *He kept his face severe but inwardly he was smiling.*

inwards *adverb*
towards the inside

iodine *noun*
(*say* I-o-deen or I-o-dyn)
iodine is a chemical used to kill germs

IQ *noun*
a measure of someone's intelligence, calculated from the results of a test.
IQ stands for *intelligence quotient.*

iris *noun*
1 the coloured part of your eyeball **2** a flower with long pointed leaves

iron *noun*
1 iron is a strong heavy metal

2 an iron is a device that you heat up and press on clothes to make them smooth **3** an iron is also a tool made of iron

iron *verb*
to iron clothes is to smooth them with an iron **to iron something out** is to solve a difficulty gradually and carefully

ironic or **ironical** *adjective*
(*say* I-**ron**-ik or *say* I-**ron**-ikal)
1 an ironic situation is strange because the opposite happens to what you might expect **2** you are being ironic when you say the opposite of what you mean
ironically *adverb*

irony *noun* (**ironies**) (*say* I-ro-ni)
1 irony is saying the opposite of what you mean in order to emphasize it or be funny, for example *What a lovely day* when it is pouring with rain **2** an irony is an unexpected or strange event or situation • *The irony is that she had sold all her jewels the day before the burglars broke in.*

irregular *adjective*
1 not regular; not usual
2 against the rules **irregularity** *noun* being irregular or unusual
irregularly *adverb*

irrelevant *adjective* (*say* i-**rel**-i-vant)
not relevant; not having anything to do with what is being discussed **irrelevance** *noun* something irrelevant

irresistible *adjective*
too strong or attractive or tempting to resist

irresponsible *adjective*
not thinking enough about the effects of your actions
irresponsibility *noun* someone shows irresponsibility when they act without thinking enough about the effects of their actions **irresponsibly** *adverb*

irreverent *adjective*
not respectful **irreverence** *noun* lack of respect **irreverently** *adverb*

irrigate *verb*
to irrigate land is to supply it with water so that crops can grow **irrigation** *noun* irrigating land

irritable *adjective*
easily annoyed; bad-tempered
irritability *noun* crossness; bad temper **irritably** *adverb*

irritate *verb*
1 to irritate someone is to annoy them **2** to irritate a part of your body is to make it itch or feel sore

a
b
c
d
e
f
g
h
i
j
k
l
m
n
o
p
q
r
s
t
u
v
w
x
y
z

irritation *noun*
1 irritation is being annoyed **2** an irritation is something that annoys you

Islam *noun* (say **iz**-lahm)
Islam is the religion of Muslims
Islamic *adjective* to do with Islam

island *noun*
a piece of land surrounded by water
islander *noun* someone who lives on an island

isle *noun*
an island

isolate *verb*
to isolate someone or something is to keep them apart from others
• *Patients with the disease need to be isolated.* **isolation** *noun* being isolated or alone

issue *verb*
1 to issue something is to send it or give it out to people • *They issued blankets to the refugees.* **2** to issue a book or piece of information is to publish it **3** to issue is to come out of something • *Smoke was issuing from the chimney.*

issue *noun*
1 an issue is a subject that people are discussing • *What are the most important issues?* **2** an issue of a magazine or newspaper is the edition sold on a particular day • *There's a good poster in this week's issue of my football magazine.*

it *pronoun*
1 the thing being talked about, used as the subject or object of a verb • *When the tree fell it hit the greenhouse.* **2** used to say things about the weather or the time • *It is raining.* • *Is it lunch time yet?*

italics *plural noun* (say it-**al**-iks)
letters printed with a slant, *like this*

itch *noun*
a tickling feeling in your skin that makes you want to scratch it **itchy** *adjective* a part of your body is itchy when it makes you want to scratch it

itch *verb*
a part of your body itches when it makes you want to scratch it

item *noun*
one thing in a list or group of things

itinerary *noun* (**itineraries**)
(say I-**tin**-er-er-i)
a list of places to be visited on a journey

its *determiner, pronoun*
of it; belonging to it • *The cat hurt its paw.*

it's
short for *it is* and (before a verb in the past tense) *it has* • *It's raining.* • *It's been raining.*

itself *pronoun*
it and nothing else, used to refer back to the subject of a verb
• *I think the cat has hurt itself.*
by itself on its own, alone • *The house stands by itself in a wood.*

ivory *noun*
the hard creamy-white substance that forms elephants' tusks

ivy *noun*
a climbing evergreen plant with shiny leaves

Jj

jab *verb* (**jabbing, jabbed**)
1 to jab someone or something is to poke them roughly **2** to jab something is to push it roughly into something else

jab *noun*
1 a quick hit with something pointed or a fist **2** (*informal*) an injection

jabber *verb*
to jabber is to chatter a lot or to speak quickly and not clearly

jack *noun*
1 a piece of equipment for lifting something heavy off the ground, especially a car **2** a playing card with a picture of a young man

jack *verb*
to jack something is to lift it with a jack

jackal *noun*
a wild animal rather like a dog

jacket *noun*
1 a short coat covering the top half of the body **2** a paper cover for a book

jackpot *noun*
an amount of prize money that increases until someone wins it

jade *noun*
jade is a hard green stone which is carved to make ornaments

jagged *adjective* (say **jag**-id)
having an uneven edge with sharp points

jaguar *noun*
a large fierce South American animal of the cat family rather like a leopard

jail *noun*
a prison

ivy

jail *verb*
to jail someone is to put them in prison

jailer *noun*
a person in charge of a jail

jam *noun*
1 a sweet food made of fruit boiled with sugar until it is thick **2** a lot of people or cars or other things crowded together so that it is difficult to move **to be in a jam** (*informal*) is to be in a difficult situation

jam *verb* (**jamming, jammed**)
1 to jam something is to make it stuck and difficult to move **2** to jam is to become stuck • *The door has jammed.* **3** to jam something is to push or squeeze it with force
• *I jammed on the brakes.*

jamboree *noun*
1 a large party or celebration **2** a rally of Scouts

jangle *verb*
to jangle is to make a harsh ringing sound

January *noun*
the first month of the year

jar¹ *noun*
a container made of glass or pottery

jar² *verb* (**jarring, jarred**)
1 to jar is to give you an unpleasant shock or jolt • *I jarred every bone in my body.* **2** to jar is also to make a harsh sound • *All that shrieking really jars on my ears.*

jaundice *noun*
jaundice is a disease that makes your skin turn yellow

jaunt *noun*
a short trip for fun

jaunty *adjective* (**jauntier, jauntiest**) lively and cheerful
jauntily *adverb* **jauntiness** *noun*

javelin *noun*
a light spear used for throwing in athletics competitions

jaw *noun*
1 one of the two bones that hold the teeth **2** the lower part of the face; the mouth and teeth of a person or animal **3** the part of a tool that grips something

jay *noun*
a noisy brightly-coloured bird

jazz *noun*
jazz is a kind of music with strong rhythm **jazzy** *adjective* bright and colourful

jealous *adjective*
1 unhappy or resentful because you feel that someone is better or luckier than you **2** upset because you think that someone you love is loved by someone else more **jealously** *adverb* **jealousy** *noun* the feeling of being jealous

jeans *plural noun*
casual trousers made of denim

Jeep *noun*
(*trademark*) a small strong vehicle that can be driven over rough ground

jeer *verb*
to jeer is to laugh rudely at someone and shout insults at them

jelly *noun* (**jellies**)
1 a soft sweet food with a fruit flavour **2** any soft slippery substance

jellyfish *noun* (**jellyfish**)
a sea animal with a body like jelly and tentacles that can sting

jellyfish

jerk *verb*
1 to jerk is to make a sudden sharp movement **2** to jerk something is to pull it suddenly

jerk *noun*
a sudden sharp movement

jerky *adjective* (**jerkier, jerkiest**)
moving with sudden sharp movements **jerkily** *adverb*

jersey *noun* (**jerseys**)
a pullover with sleeves

jest *noun*
a joke

jest *verb*
to jest is to make jokes to say something **in jest** is to be joking

jester *noun*
a professional entertainer at a royal court in the Middle Ages

jet¹ *noun*
1 a stream of liquid, gas, or flame forced out of a narrow opening **2** a narrow opening from which a jet comes out **3** an aircraft driven by jet engines

jet¹ *verb* (**jetting, jetted**)
1 to jet is to come out in a strong

stream **2** (*informal*) to jet around is to travel a lot in jet aircraft

jet² *noun*
1 a hard black mineral **2** a deep glossy black colour

jet engine *noun*
an engine that drives an aircraft forward by sending out a powerful jet of hot gas at the back

jetty *noun* (**jetties**)
a small pier or landing stage for boats

jewel *noun*
1 a precious stone **2** an ornament containing precious stones

jeweller *noun*
someone who sells or makes jewellery

jewellery *noun*
jewels or ornaments that people wear, such as rings and necklaces

Jewish *adjective*
being of Jewish faith; to do with Judaism

jig *noun*
a lively jumping dance

jig *verb* (**jigging, jigged**)
to jig is to move up and down with quick jerks

jigsaw *noun*
1 a jigsaw puzzle **2** a saw that can cut curved shapes

jigsaw puzzle *noun*
a puzzle made of differently shaped pieces that you fit together to make a picture

jingle *verb*
to jingle is to make a tinkling or clinking sound

jingle *noun*
1 a tinkling or clinking sound **2** a simple tune or song that is used in an advertisement

job *noun*
1 work that someone does regularly to earn a living • *He got a job as a postman.* **2** a piece of work that needs to be done • *We'll have tea when we've finished this job.* **3** (*informal*) a difficult task • *You'll have a job to lift that box.*

jockey *noun* (**jockeys**)
someone who rides horses in races

jodhpurs *plural noun*
(*say* jod-perz)
jodhpurs are trousers for riding a horse, fitting closely from the knee to the ankle

jog *verb* (**jogging, jogged**)
1 to jog is to run slowly, especially for exercise **2** to jog someone is to give them a slight knock or push **to**

jog someone's memory is to help them remember something **jogger** *noun* someone who goes jogging

join *verb*
1 to join things together, or join one thing to another, is to put or fix them together **2** two or more things join when they come together **3** to join a society or group is to become a member of it **to join in** is to take part in something

join *noun*
a place where things join

joiner *noun*
someone whose job is to make furniture and other things out of wood **joinery** *noun* the work of making furniture and other things out of wood

joint *noun*
1 a place where things are fixed together **2** the place where two bones fit together **3** a large piece of meat

joint *adjective*
shared or done by two or more people or groups • *The song was a joint effort.* **jointly** *adverb*

joist *noun*
a long beam supporting a floor or ceiling

joke *noun*
something that you say or do to make people laugh

joke *verb*
to joke is to make jokes, or to talk in a way that is not serious

joker *noun*
1 someone who makes jokes **2** an extra playing card with a picture of a jester on it

jolly *adjective*
happy and cheerful

jolly *adverb*
(*informal*) very • *It's jolly cold!*

jolt *verb*
1 to jolt something or someone is to hit them or move them suddenly and sharply **2** to jolt is to make a sudden sharp movement • *The bus jolted to a halt.*

jolt *noun*
1 a sudden sharp movement • *The plane landed with a jolt.* **2** a surprise or shock

jostle *verb*
to jostle someone is to push them roughly

jot *verb*
to jot something down is to write it quickly

journal *noun*
1 a newspaper or magazine **2** a diary

a
b
c
d
e
f
g
h
i
j
k
l
m
n
o
p
q
r
s
t
u
v
w
x
y
z

journalist *noun*
someone whose job is to write news stories for a newspaper or magazine or on television or radio **journalism** *noun* the job of writing news stories for a newspaper or magazine or on television or radio

journey *noun*
1 going from one place to another **2** the distance or time you take to travel somewhere • *The town is a day's journey away.*

journey *verb*
to journey is to go from one place to another

joust *verb*
to joust is to fight on horseback with lances, as knights did in medieval times

jovial *adjective*
cheerful and jolly **joviality** *noun* cheerfulness **jovially** *adverb*

joy *noun*
1 joy is great happiness or pleasure **2** a joy is something that gives happiness

joyful *adjective*
very happy **joyfully** *adverb*

joystick *noun*
1 (*informal*) the lever that controls the movement of an aircraft **2** a lever for controlling the cursor on a screen, especially in computer games

jubilant *adjective* (*say* joo-bi-lant)
very happy because you have won or succeeded **jubilantly** *adverb* **jubilation** *noun* rejoicing because you have won or succeeded

jubilee *noun*
a special anniversary of an important event. A **silver jubilee** is the 25th anniversary, a **golden jubilee** is the 50th anniversary, and a **diamond jubilee** is the 60th anniversary

Judaism *noun* (*say* joo-day-izm)
Judaism is the religion of the Jewish people

judge *noun*
1 someone who hears cases in a lawcourt and decides what should be done **2** someone who decides who has won a contest or competition **3** someone who is good at forming opinions or making decisions about things • *She's a good judge of musical ability.*

judge *verb*
1 to judge something is to act as judge in a law case or a competition **2** to judge an amount is to estimate or guess what it is **3** to judge something is to form an opinion about it

judgement *noun*
1 judgement is acting as judge for a law case or a contest **2** a judgement is the decision made by a lawcourt **3** judgement is also the ability to make decisions wisely **4** someone's judgement is their opinion • *In my judgement, you're making a big mistake.*

judo *noun* (*say* joo-doh)
judo is a Japanese form of unarmed combat for sport

jug *noun*
a container for pouring liquids, with a handle and lip

juggernaut *noun*
a very large articulated lorry

juggle *verb*
to juggle objects is to keep tossing and catching them so that you keep them moving in the air without dropping any **juggler** *noun* someone who juggles at a fair or circus

juice *noun*
the liquid from fruit, vegetables, or other food **juicy** *adjective* juicy fruit or meat is full of juice

jukebox *noun*
a machine that automatically plays a record of your choice when you put a coin in

July *noun*
the seventh month of the year

jumble *verb*
to jumble things is to mix them up in a confused way

jumble *noun*
a confused mixture of things; a muddle

jumble sale *noun*
a sale of second-hand clothes and other goods to raise money

jump *verb*
1 to jump is to move suddenly from the ground into the air **2** to jump a fence or other obstacle is to go over it by jumping **3** to jump up or out is to move quickly or suddenly • *He jumped out of his seat.* **4** to jump in or out of a vehicle is to get in or out quickly **to jump at something** (*informal*) is to accept it eagerly **to jump the queue** is to go in front of people before it is your turn

jump *noun*
1 a sudden movement into the air **2** an obstacle to jump over

jumper *noun*
a pullover with sleeves

junction *noun*
a place where roads or railway lines join

June *noun*
the sixth month of the year

jungle *noun*
a thick tangled forest, especially in tropical countries

junior *adjective*
1 younger **2** for young children • *She goes to a junior school.* **3** lower in rank or importance

junior *noun*
1 a younger person • *Peter is my junior.* **2** a person of lower rank or importance

junk[1] *noun*
useless or worthless things that should be thrown away • *The garage is full of junk.*

junk[2] *noun*
a Chinese sailing boat

junk food
food that contains a lot of sugar and starch and is not good for you

jury *noun*
a group of people (usually twelve) chosen to make a decision about a case in a lawcourt, especially whether a person accused of a crime is innocent or guilty **juror** *noun* a member of a jury

just *adjective*
1 fair and right; giving proper thought to everybody **2** deserved • *He got his just reward.* **justly** *adverb* in a just or fair way

just *adverb*
1 exactly • *It's just what I wanted.* **2** only; simply • *I just wanted another cake.* **3** barely; by only a short amount • *The ball hit her just below the knee.* **4** a short time ago • *They had just gone.* **5** now; immediately • *I'm just leaving.*

justice *noun*
1 justice is being just or having fair treatment **2** justice is also the actions of the law • *They were tried in a court of justice.*

justify *verb*
to justify something is to show that it is reasonable or necessary • *Do you think that you were justified in taking such a risk?* **justifiable** *adjective* easy to justify **justification** *noun* a good reason for doing something

jut *verb*
to jut, or to jut out, is to stick out

juvenile *adjective* (*say* joo-vi-nyl)
to do with young people

juvenile *noun*
a young person who is not yet an adult

Kk

kaleidoscope noun
(say kal-**I**-dos-kohp)
a tube that you look
through to see brightly-
coloured patterns which
change as you turn
the end of the tube

kangaroo noun
an Australian
animal that moves
by jumping on its
strong back legs

karaoke noun
(say ka-ri-**oh**-ki)
a party entertainment
in which people
sing songs with a
recorded background
played from a special
machine

karate noun (say ka-
rah-ti)
karate is a Japanese
method of
self-defence
using the
hands,
arms, and feet

kangaroo

kayak noun (say **ky**-ak)
a small canoe with a covering that
fits round the canoeist's waist

kebab noun
small pieces of meat or vegetables
grilled on a skewer

keel noun
the long piece of wood or metal along
the bottom of a boat
keel verb
to keel over is to fall sideways or
overturn

keen adjective
1 enthusiastic or eager • She is keen
on swimming. • We are keen to go.
2 strong or sharp • The knife had a
keen edge. • There was a keen wind.
keenly adverb a keenly fought
contest is one in which people are
competing very hard **keenness**
noun being keen

keep verb (**keeping, kept**)
1 to keep something is to have it and
not get rid of it **2** to keep something
in a place is to put it there when
you aren't using it **3** to keep (for
example) well or still is to continue
to be well or still **4** to keep someone
(for example) warm or happy is to

cause them to continue to be warm
or happy **5** something keeps when
it lasts without going bad • Will the
milk keep until tomorrow? **6** to keep
doing something is to continue to do
it • They kept laughing at her.
7 to keep your word or promise is to
honour it and not break it **8** to keep
animals or pets is to have them
and look after them **to keep
something up** is to continue
doing it • Keep up the good work!
to keep up with someone is to go
as fast as them
keep noun
1 someone's keep is the food or
money they need to live • They have
to earn their keep.
2 a keep is a strong tower in a
castle **for keeps** (informal) to
keep; permanently • Is this
football mine for keeps?

keeper noun
1 someone who looks after
the animals in a zoo **2** a
goalkeeper

keeping noun
something is in your keeping
when you are looking after
it • The diaries are in safe
keeping.

keg noun
a small barrel

kennel noun
a shelter for a dog

kerb noun
the edge of a pavement

kernel noun
the part inside the shell of a nut

ketchup noun
ketchup is a thick sauce made from
tomatoes

kettle noun
a container with a spout and handle,
used for boiling water in

key noun
1 a piece of metal shaped so that it
opens a lock **2** a small lever that you
press with your finger, on a piano or
keyboard **3** a device for winding up
a clock or clockwork toy **4** a scale of
musical notes • It is played in the key
of C major. **5** something that solves
a problem or mystery • Police think
they have found the key to the crime.

keyboard noun
a set of keys on a piano, typewriter,
or computer

keyhole noun
the hole through which you put a key
into a lock

kg
short for kilogram or kilograms

khaki noun (say **kah**-ki)
a dull yellowish-brown colour, often
used for army uniforms

kick verb
1 to kick someone or something is to
hit them with your foot **2** to kick is to
move your legs about vigorously **to
kick off** is to start a football match, or
(informal) to start doing something **to
kick someone out** is to get rid of them
to kick up a fuss or row (informal) is
to make a loud fuss or noise

kick noun
a kicking movement **to get a kick
out of something** (informal) is to
enjoy it very much

kick-off noun
the start of a football match

kid noun
1 a young goat
2 (informal) a child
kid verb (**kidding, kidded**)
(informal) to kid someone is to
deceive or tease them

kidnap verb (**kidnapping,
kidnapped**)
to kidnap someone is to capture
them by force, usually to get a
ransom **kidnapper** noun a person
who kidnaps someone

kidney noun (**kidneys**)
each of two organs in your body that
remove waste products from your
blood and send them as urine to your
bladder

kill verb
to kill a person or animal is to make
them die **killer** noun a person who
kills someone

kiln noun
an oven for hardening or drying
pottery or bricks

kilo noun
a kilogram

kilobyte noun
(in computing) a unit that measures
data or memory, equal to 1,024
bytes

kilogram noun
a unit of weight equal to
1,000 grams or about 2.2 pounds

kilometre noun
(say **kil**-o-mee-ter or say kil-**om**-i-ter)
a unit of length equal to 1,000
metres or about ²/₃ of a mile

kilowatt noun
a unit of electrical power equal to
1,000 watts

kilt noun
a kind of pleated skirt worn by men
as part of traditional Scottish dress
kilted adjective wearing a kilt

kin *noun*
a person's family or relatives **your next of kin** is your closest relative

kind¹ *noun*
a type or sort of something
• *What kind of food do you like?*

kind² *adjective*
helpful and friendly
kindness *noun*

kindergarten *noun*
(*say* **kin-der-gar-ten**)
a school or class for very young children

kind-hearted *adjective*
kind and generous

kindle *verb*
1 to kindle something is to get it to burn **2** to kindle is to start burning

kindly *adverb*
1 in a kind way • *He spoke kindly to the little boy.* **2** please • *Kindly close the door.*

kindly *adjective* (**kindlier, kindliest**)
kind • *She gave a kindly smile.*
kindliness *noun* kindliness is being kindly

king *noun*
1 a man who has been crowned as the ruler of a country **2** a piece in chess that has to be captured to win the game **3** a playing card with a picture of a king on it **kingly** *adjective* like a king

kingdom *noun*
a country that is ruled by a king or queen

kingfisher *noun*
a brightly-coloured bird that lives near water and catches fish

king-size or **king-sized** *adjective*
larger than the usual size

kink *noun*
a short twist in a rope, wire, or piece of hair

kiosk *noun* (*say* **kee-osk**)
1 a telephone box **2** a small hut or stall where you can buy newspapers, sweets, and drinks

kiss *noun*
touching someone with your lips as a sign of affection or greeting
kiss *verb*
to kiss someone is to give them a kiss

kingfisher

kit *noun*
1 equipment or clothes that you need to do a sport, a job, or some other activity **2** a set of parts sold to be fitted together to make something
• *a model aircraft kit*

kitchen *noun*
a room where food is prepared and cooked

kite *noun*
a light frame covered with cloth or paper that you fly in the wind at the end of a long piece of string

kitten *noun*
a very young cat

kitty¹ *noun* (**kitties**)
1 an amount of money that you can win in a card game **2** an amount of money that you put aside for a special purpose

kiwi *noun* (*say* **kee-wee**)
a New Zealand bird that cannot fly

kiwi fruit *noun*
a fruit with thin hairy skin, soft green flesh, and black seeds

km
short for kilometre or kilometres

knack *noun*
a special skill or talent • *There's a knack to putting up a deckchair.*

knapsack *noun*
a bag carried on the back by hikers or soldiers

knead *verb*
to knead dough is to press and stretch it with your hands, to make it ready for baking

knee *noun*
the joint in the middle of your leg

kneecap *noun*
the bony part at the front of your knee

kneel *verb* (**kneeling, knelt**)
to kneel is to bend your legs so you are resting on your knees

knickers *plural noun*
underpants worn by women or girls

knife *noun* (**knives**)
a cutting instrument made of a short blade set in a handle
knife *verb*
to knife someone is to stab them with a knife

knight *noun*
1 a man who has been given the honour that lets him put 'Sir' before his name **2** a warrior who had been given the rank of a nobleman, in the Middle Ages **3** a piece in chess, with a horse's head **knighthood** *noun* a man receives a knighthood when he is made a knight

knight *verb*
to knight someone is to make them a knight

knit *verb* (**knitting, knitted**)
to knit something is to make it by looping together threads of wool or other material, using long needles or a machine

knitting *noun*
1 knitting is the activity of making things by knitting **2** knitting is also something that is being made this way

knitting needle *noun*
a long large needle used in knitting

knob *noun*
1 the round handle of a door or drawer **2** a control to adjust a radio or television set **3** a lump of something **knobbly** *adjective* having a lumpy or bumpy surface

knock *verb*
1 to knock something is to hit it hard or bump into it • *Oops, I knocked the vase over.* **2** to knock is to hit something with your hand or fist
• *Who's knocking at the door?* **to knock someone out** is to hit them so that they become unconscious

knock *noun*
the act or sound of hitting something

knocker *noun*
a device for knocking on a door

knot

knockout *noun*
1 knocking someone out **2** a game or contest in which the loser in each round has to drop out

knot *noun*
1 a fastening made by tying or looping two ends of string, rope, or ribbon together **2** a round spot on a piece of wood where a branch once joined it **3** a unit for measuring the speed of ships and aircraft, 1,852 metres (or 2,025 yards) per hour **4** a knot of people is a small group of them standing close together

knot *verb* (**knotting, knotted**)
to knot something is to tie or fasten it with a knot

knotty *adjective*
1 full of knots **2** difficult or puzzling • *It's a knotty problem.*

know *verb* (**knowing, knew, known**)
1 to have something in your mind that you have learned or discovered • *Do you know the answer?* **2** to know a person or place is to recognize it or be familiar with it • *I've known him for years.*

knowledge *noun* (*say* **nol**-ij)
knowledge is what someone or everybody knows

knowledgeable *adjective* (*say* **nol**-ij-a-bul) knowing a lot about something **knowledgeably** *adverb*

knuckle *noun*
a joint in your finger

koala *noun* (*say* koh-**ah**-la)
a furry Australian animal that looks like a small bear

Koran *noun* (*say* kor-**ahn**)
the holy book of Islam, believed by Muslims to contain the words of Allah

kosher *adjective* (*say* **koh**-sher)
kosher food is food prepared according to Jewish religious law

kung fu *noun* (*say* kuung-**foo**)
kung fu is a Chinese method of self-defence rather like karate

L
short for learner

label *noun*
a piece of paper, cloth, or metal fixed on or beside something to show what it is or to give other information about it such as its price

label *verb* (**labelling, labelled**)
to label something is to put a label on it

laboratory *noun* (**laboratories**)
(*say* la-**bo**-ra-ter-i)
a room or building equipped for scientific work

laborious *adjective*
needing a lot of effort; very hard **laboriously** *adverb*

labour *noun*
1 labour is hard work **2** labour is also the movements of a woman's womb when a baby is born **Labour** the Labour Party, one of the main British political parties

labourer *noun*
someone who does hard work with their hands, especially outdoors

labyrinth *noun*
a complicated set of passages or paths; a maze • *She disappeared into the labyrinth of small streets.*

lace *noun*
1 lace is thin material with decorative patterns of holes in it **2** a lace is a piece of thin cord used to tie up a shoe or boot **lacy** *adjective* like lace or made of lace

lace *verb*
to lace up a shoe or boot is to fasten it with a lace

lack *noun*
there is a lack of something when there isn't any of it or there isn't enough of it • *The trip was cancelled because of lack of interest.*

lack *verb*
to lack something is to be without it • *He lacks courage.*

lacquer *noun*
lacquer is a kind of varnish

lacrosse *noun*
lacrosse is a game using a stick with a net on it (called a *crosse*) to catch and throw a ball

lad *noun*
a boy or young man

ladder *noun*
1 a device to help you climb up or down something, made of upright pieces of wood, metal, or rope with crosspieces called rungs **2** a run of damaged stitches in tights or a stocking

laden *adjective*
carrying a heavy load

ladle *noun*
a large deep spoon with a long handle, which you use for serving soup or other liquids

lady *noun* (**ladies**)
1 a polite name for a woman **2** a well-mannered woman, or a woman who is high up in society **Lady** the title of a noblewoman or the wife of a knight

ladybird *noun*
a small flying beetle, usually red with black spots

ladylike *adjective*
polite and quiet, as a lady is supposed to be

lag¹ *verb* (**lagging, lagged**)
to lag is to go too slowly and not keep up with others • *The little boy was lagging behind.*

ladybirds

lag² *verb* (**lagging, lagged**)
to lag pipes or boilers is to wrap them

with insulating material to keep in the heat

lager *noun* (*say* **lah**-ger)
a light beer

lagoon *noun*
a lake separated from the sea by sandbanks or reefs

lair *noun*
the place where a wild animal lives

lake *noun*
a large area of water completely surrounded by land

lama *noun*
a Buddhist priest or monk in Tibet and Mongolia

lamb *noun*
1 a lamb is a young sheep **2** lamb is the meat from young sheep

lame *adjective*
1 not able to walk normally **2** weak and not very convincing • *What a lame excuse.* **lamely** *adverb* **lameness** *noun*

lamp *noun*
a device for producing light from electricity, gas, or oil

lamp-post *noun*
a tall post in a street or public place, with a lamp at the top

lampshade *noun*
a cover for the bulb of an electric lamp, to soften the light

lance *noun*
a long spear once used by soldiers on horseback

land *noun*
1 land or the land is all the dry parts of the world's surface **2** land is an area of ground **3** a land is a country or nation

land *verb*
1 to land is to come down to the ground from the air • *Where did the arrow land?* **2** to land is also to arrive in a ship or aircraft **3** to land someone or something is to bring them to a place by means of a ship or aircraft

landing *noun*
the floor at the top of a flight of stairs

landlady *noun* (**landladies**)
1 a woman who owns a house or rooms that people can rent **2** a woman who looks after a pub

landlord *noun*
1 a person who owns a house or rooms that people can rent **2** a person who looks after a pub

landmark *noun*
an object on land that you can easily see from a distance

landowner *noun*
a person who owns a large amount of land

landscape noun
1 a view of a particular area of town or countryside 2 a picture of the countryside

landslide noun
a landslide is when earth or rocks slide down the side of a hill

lane noun
1 a narrow road, especially in the country 2 a strip of road for a single line of traffic 3 a strip of track or water for one runner or swimmer in a race

language noun
1 language is the use of words in speech and writing 2 a language is the words used in a particular country or by a particular group of people 3 a language is also a system of signs or symbols giving information, especially in computing

lanky adjective (**lankier, lankiest**)
awkwardly tall and thin **lankiness** noun

lantern noun
a transparent case for holding a light and shielding it from the wind

lap¹ noun
1 the flat area from the waist to the knees, formed when a person is sitting down 2 going once round a racecourse

lap¹ verb (**lapping, lapped**)
to lap someone in a race round a track is to be so far ahead of them that you pass them from behind

lap² verb (**lapping, lapped**)
1 to lap liquid is to drink it with the tongue, as a cat or dog does 2 waves lap when they make a gentle splash on rocks or the shore

lapel noun (say la-**pel**)
the flap folded back at each front edge of a coat or jacket

lapse noun
1 a slight mistake or fault 2 the passing of time • After a lapse of three months work began again.

lapse verb
1 to lapse into a state is to pass gradually into it • He lapsed into unconsciousness. 2 a contract or document lapses when it is no longer valid • My passport has lapsed.

laptop noun
a computer small enough to be held and used on your lap, especially while you are travelling

lard noun
lard is white greasy fat from pigs, used in cooking

larder noun
a cupboard or small room for storing food

large adjective
more than the ordinary or average size; big **to be at large** is to be free and dangerous • The escaped prisoners were still at large. **largeness** noun

largely adverb
mainly; mostly • His success is largely a matter of hard work.

lark¹ noun
a small sandy-brown bird; a skylark

lark² noun
(informal) something amusing; a bit of fun • They just did it for a lark.

lark² verb
to lark about is to have fun or play tricks

larva noun (**larvae**)
an insect in the first stage of its life, after it comes out of the egg

lasagne noun (say la-**zan**-ya)
lasagne is pasta in the form of flat sheets, cooked with minced meat or vegetables and a white sauce

laser noun (say **lay**-zer)
a device that makes a very strong narrow beam of light

lash noun
1 an eyelash 2 a stroke with a whip

lash verb
1 to lash someone or something is to hit them with a whip or like a whip • Rain lashed the window. 2 to lash something is to tie it tightly • During the storm they lashed the boxes to the mast. **to lash out** is to speak or hit out angrily

lass noun
a girl or young woman

lasso noun (**lassos**) (say la-**soo**)
a rope with a loop at the end which tightens when you pull the rope, used for catching cattle

last¹ adjective
1 coming after all the others; final • Try not to miss the last bus. 2 most recent or latest • Where were you last night?

last¹ adverb
at the end; after everything or everyone else • He came last in the race.

last¹ noun
a person or thing that is last • I think I was the last to arrive. **at last** finally; at the end

last² verb
1 to continue • The journey lasts for two hours. 2 to go on without being used up • Our supplies won't last much longer.

lastly adverb
in the last place; finally

latch noun
a small bar fastening a gate or door

late adjective, adverb
1 after the proper or expected time 2 near the end of a period of time • They came late in the afternoon. 3 recent • Have you heard the latest news? 4 no longer alive • They saw the tomb of the late king. **lateness** noun

lately adverb
recently • She has been very tired lately.

lathe noun (say layth)
a machine for holding and turning pieces of wood or metal while you shape them

lather noun
the thick foam you get when you mix soap with water

Latin noun
Latin is the language of the ancient Romans

latitude noun
the distance of a place north or south of the equator, measured in degrees

latter adjective
later • We'd like a holiday in the latter part of the year. **the latter** the second of two people or things just mentioned • If it's a choice between a picnic or a swim I prefer the latter. see also **former**

laugh verb
to laugh is to make sounds that show you are happy or that you think something is funny

laugh noun
1 the sound you make when you laugh 2 (informal) something that is fun or amusing • Yesterday's party was quite a laugh.

laughter noun
laughter is laughing or the sound of laughing

launch¹ verb
1 to launch a ship is to send it into the water for the first time 2 to launch a rocket is to send it into space 3 to launch a new idea or product is to make it available for the first time

launch¹ noun
the launching of a ship or spacecraft

launch² noun
a large motor boat

launderette noun
a shop with washing machines that people pay to use

laundry noun (**laundries**)
1 laundry is clothes to be washed **2** a laundry is a place where clothes are sent or taken to be washed

laurel noun
an evergreen bush with smooth shiny leaves

lava noun
lava is molten rock that flows from a volcano, or the solid rock formed when it cools

lavatory noun (**lavatories**)
a toilet

lavender noun
1 lavender is a shrub with pale purple flowers that smell very sweet **2** a pale purple colour

lavish adjective
1 generous • *They are lavish with their gifts.* **2** plentiful • *What a lavish meal!*

law noun
1 a rule or set of rules that everyone must keep **2** something that always happens, for example the law of gravity

lawcourt noun
a room or building where a judge and jury or a magistrate decide whether someone has broken the law

lawful adjective
allowed or accepted by the law
lawfully adverb

lawn noun
an area of mown grass in a garden

lawnmower noun
a machine you use for cutting grass

lawyer noun
a person whose job is to help people with the law

lax adjective
not strict; tolerant • *Discipline was very lax.*

lay verb (**laying, laid**)
1 to lay something somewhere is to put it down in a particular place or in a particular way **2** to lay a table is to arrange things on it for a meal **3** to lay an egg is to produce it **to lay someone off** is to stop employing them **to lay something on** is to supply or provide it **to lay something out** is to arrange or prepare it

layer noun
something flat that lies on or under something else • *The cake had a layer of icing on top and a layer of jam inside.*

layout noun
the arrangement or design of something

laze verb
to laze is to spend time in a lazy way

lazy adjective (**lazier, laziest**)
not wanting to work; doing as little as possible **lazily** adverb
laziness noun

lb.
short for pound or pounds in weight

lead¹ verb (**leading, led**)
(*say* leed)
1 to lead a person or animal is to guide them, especially by going in front **2** to lead an activity is to be in charge of it **3** to lead in a race or contest is to be winning it **4** a road or path leads somewhere when it goes in that direction • *This road leads to the beach.* **to lead to something** is to cause it • *Their carelessness led to the accident.*

lead¹ noun (*say* leed)
1 the first or front place or position • *Who's in the lead now?* **2** help or guidance • *Just follow my lead.* **3** a strap or cord for leading a dog **4** an electric wire • *Don't trip over that lead.*

lead² noun (*say* led)
1 lead is a soft heavy grey metal **2** a lead is the writing substance (graphite) in the middle of a pencil

leader noun
someone who leads or is in charge **leadership** noun the ability to be a good leader

leaf

leaf noun (**leaves**)
1 a flat and usually green growth on a tree or plant, growing from its stem **2** a page of a book **3** a very thin sheet of metal, such as gold leaf **4** a flap that makes a table larger **to turn over a new leaf** is to make a fresh start and improve your behaviour **leafy** adjective having a lot of leaves or trees

leaflet noun
a piece of paper printed with information

league noun (*say* leeg)
1 a group of teams that play matches against each other **2** a group of countries that have agreed to work together for a particular reason

leak noun
a hole or crack through which liquid or gas escapes **leaky** adjective a leaky pipe or tap has a leak

leak verb
1 something leaks when it lets something out through a hole or crack • *The sink is leaking.* **2** liquid or gas leaks out when it escapes from a container **leakage** noun an escape of liquid or gas from a container

lean¹ verb (**leaning, leaned** or **leant**)
1 to lean is to bend your body towards something or over it **2** to lean something is to put it into a sloping position • *Do not lean bicycles against the window.* **3** to lean against something is to rest against it

lean² adjective
1 lean meat has little fat
2 a lean person is thin

leap noun
1 a high or long jump **2** a sudden increase or advance

leap verb (**leaping, leapt** or **leaped**)
1 to leap is to jump high or a long way **2** to leap is also to increase or advance suddenly

leap year noun
a year with an extra day in it, on 29 February

learn verb
to learn something is to find out about it and gain knowledge or skill in it • *She's learning to play the guitar.*

learned adjective (*say* ler-nid)
clever and knowledgeable

learner noun
someone who is learning something, for example how to drive a car

lease noun
an agreement to let someone use a building or land for a fixed period in return for a payment

leash noun
a strap or cord for leading a dog

least determiner, adverb
smallest; less than all the others • *I'll get the least expensive bike.* • *I like this one least.* **at least** **1** not less than what is mentioned • *It will cost at least £50.* **2** anyway • *He's at home; at least I think he is.*

least noun
the smallest amount

leather noun
a strong material made from animals' skins **leathery** adjective tough, like leather

leave verb (**leaving, left**)
1 to leave a person, place, or group is to go away from them **2** to leave something is to let it stay where it is or remain as it is • *You can leave your bags by the door.* **3** to leave something to someone is to give it to them in a will **to leave something or**

a b c d e f g h i j k l m n o p q r s t u v w x y z

someone out is not to include them
to be left over is to remain when
other things have been used

leave *noun*
permission, especially to be away
from work

lecture *noun*
1 a talk about a subject to an
audience or a class **2** a long or
serious warning given to someone
• *We got a lecture about closing the
windows.*

lecture *verb*
to lecture is to give a lecture
lecturer *noun* someone who gives
a lecture

ledge *noun*
a narrow shelf

leek *noun*
a long green and white vegetable like
an onion with broad leaves

leer *verb*
to leer at someone is to look at them
in an unpleasant or evil way

left *adjective, adverb*
on or towards the west if you think of
yourself as facing north

left *noun*
the left side

left-hand *adjective*
on the left side of something

left-handed *adjective*
using the left hand more than
the right hand

leftovers *plural noun*
food that has not been eaten
by the end of a meal

leg *noun*
1 one of the parts of a human's or
animal's body on which they stand or
move **2** one of the parts of a pair of
trousers that cover your leg **3** each of
the supports of a chair or other piece
of furniture **4** one part of a journey
5 each of a pair of matches between
the same teams in a competition

legacy *noun* (**legacies**)
something given to someone in a will

legal *adjective*
1 allowed by the law **2** to do with the
law or lawyers **legality** *noun* the
legality of something is whether it is
legal or not **legally** *adverb*

legalize *verb*
to legalize something is to make it
legal

legend *noun* (*say* **lej**-end)
an old story handed down from the
past **legendary** *adjective* to do with
legends; very famous • *the legendary
knight Sir Galahad*

legible *adjective*
clear enough to read • *Make sure
your writing is legible.* **legibility**
noun how easily you can read
something **legibly** *adverb*

legion *noun*
1 a division of the ancient Roman
army **2** a group of soldiers, or men
who used to be soldiers

legitimate *adjective*
(*say* li-**jit**-i-mat)
1 allowed by a law or rule **2** (*old use*)
born of parents who were married to
each other **legitimacy** *noun*
whether or not something is allowed
by a law or rule **legitimately**
adverb

leisure *noun*
leisure is free time, when you can do
what you like

leisurely *adjective*
done with plenty of time, without
hurrying • *They took a leisurely stroll
down to the river.*

lemon *noun*
1 a yellow citrus fruit with a sour
taste **2** a pale yellow colour

lemon

lemonade *noun*
a drink with a lemon flavour

lend *verb* (**lending, lent**)
1 to lend something to someone
is to let them have it for a short time
2 to lend someone money is to give
them money which they must pay
back plus an extra amount called
interest

length *noun*
1 how long something is **2** a piece of
something cut from a longer piece,
for example rope, wire, or cloth **3** the
distance of a swimming pool from
one end to the other **at length** after
a while; eventually

lengthen *verb*
1 to lengthen something is to make
it longer **2** to lengthen is to become
longer

lengthy *adjective* (**lengthier,
lengthiest**)
going on for a long time
• *He gave a lengthy speech.*

lenient *adjective* (*say* **lee**-ni-ent)
not as strict as expected, especially
when punishing someone **leniency**
noun when someone is not as strict
as expected **leniently** *adverb*

lens *noun*
1 a curved piece of glass or plastic
used to focus the light in a camera
or a pair of glasses **2** the transparent
part of the eye, behind the pupil

Lent *noun*
Lent is a period of about six weeks
when some Christians give up
something they enjoy

lentil *noun*
a kind of small bean

leopard *noun* (*say* **lep**-erd)
a large spotted wild animal
of the cat family

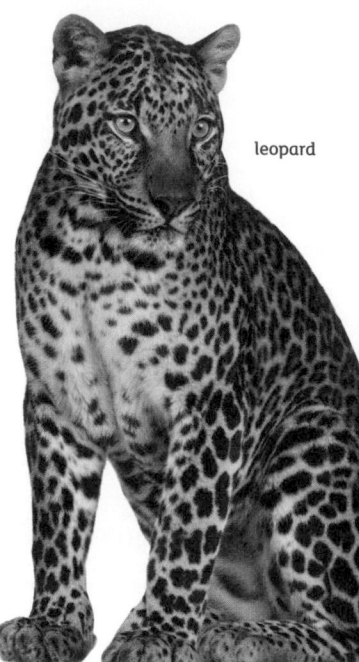

leopard

leotard *noun* (*say* **lee**-o-tard)
a close-fitting piece of clothing worn
by acrobats and dancers

less *determiner, adverb*
smaller; not so much • *Make less
noise.* • *It is less important.*

less *noun*
a smaller amount • *I have less than you.*

lessen *verb*
1 to lessen something is to make it
smaller or not so much **2** to lessen is
to become smaller or not so much

lesser *adjective*
the smaller or less great of two things
• *This is the lesser evil.*

lesson *noun*
1 the time when someone is teaching you 2 something that you have to learn 3 a passage from the Bible read aloud as part of a church service

let *verb* (**letting, let**)
1 to let someone do something is to allow them to do it 2 to let something happen is to cause it or not prevent it • *Don't let your bike slide into the ditch.* 3 to let a house or room or building is to allow someone to use it in return for payment 4 to let someone in or out is to allow them to go in or out **to let someone down** is to disappoint them **to let someone off** is to excuse them from a punishment or duty **to let something off** is to make it explode

lethal *adjective*
something that is lethal can kill you

let's *verb*
(*informal*) shall we? • *Let's go to the park.*

letter *noun*
1 one of the symbols used for writing words, such as a, b, or c 2 a written message sent to another person

letter box *noun*
a box or slot into which letters are delivered or posted

lettering *noun*
lettering is letters drawn or painted

lettuce *noun*
a green vegetable with crisp leaves used in salads

leukaemia *noun*
(*say* lew-**kee**-mi-a) a disease in which there are too many white cells in the blood

level *adjective*
1 flat or horizontal • *The ground is level near the house.* 2 at the same height or position • *Are these pictures level?* 3 equal or even • *After half an hour the scores were still level.*

level *verb* (**levelling, levelled**)
1 to level something is to make it flat or horizontal 2 to level, or to level out, is to become horizontal

level *noun*
1 height or position • *Fix the shelf at eye level.* 2 a standard or grade of achievement • *She has reached level 3 in gymnastics.* 3 a device that shows if something is horizontal

level crossing *noun*
a place where a road crosses a railway at the same level

lever *noun*
a bar that is pushed or pulled to lift something heavy, force something open, or make a machine work

liable *adjective*
1 likely to do or get something • *They are liable to forget things.* 2 responsible for something • *If there is any damage you will be liable.*

liar *noun*
someone who tells lies

liberal *adjective*
1 tolerant of other people's point of view 2 generous • *She is liberal with her money.* **liberally** *adverb* in large amounts or generously • *Pour the cream on liberally.*

liberate *verb*
to liberate someone is to set them free **liberation** *noun* setting someone free

liberty *noun* (**liberties**)
liberty is freedom

librarian *noun*
someone who looks after a library or works in one

library *noun* (**libraries**)
a place where books are kept for people to use or borrow

lice
plural of **louse**

licence *noun*
an official document allowing someone to do or use or own something

license *verb*
to license someone to do something is to give them a licence to do it • *We are not licensed to sell alcoholic drinks.*

lichen *noun* (*say* ly-ken)
a dry-looking plant that grows on rocks, walls, trees, and other surfaces

lick *verb*
to lick something is to move your tongue over it

lick *noun*
the act of moving your tongue over something

lid *noun*
1 a cover for a box or jar 2 an eyelid

lie¹ *verb* (**lying, lay, lain**)
1 to lie is to be in or get into a flat position, especially to rest with your body flat as it is in bed • *He lay on the grass.* • *The cat has lain here all night.* 2 to lie is also to be or remain a certain way • *The castle was lying in ruins.* • *The valley lay before us.*

lie² *verb* (**lying, lied**)
to lie is to say something that you know is not true

lie² *noun*
something you say that you know is not true

lieutenant *noun* (*say* lef-**ten**-ant)
an officer in the army or navy

life *noun* (**lives**)
1 a person's or animal's life is the time between their birth and death 2 life is being alive and able to grow 3 life is also all living things • *Is there life on Mars?* 4 life is also liveliness • *She is full of life.*

lifebelt *noun*
a large ring that will float, used to support someone's body in water

lifeboat *noun*
a boat for rescuing people at sea

life cycle *noun*
the series of changes in the life of a living thing • *The diagram shows the life cycle of a frog.*

lifeguard *noun*
someone whose job is to rescue swimmers who are in difficulty

life jacket *noun*
a special safety jacket that will help a person to float in water

lifeless *adjective*
1 without life 2 unconscious

lifelike *adjective*
looking exactly like a real person or thing

lifespan *noun*
how long a person or animal or plant lives

lifetime *noun*
the period of time during which someone is alive

lift *verb*
1 to lift something is to pick it up or move it to a higher position 2 to lift is to rise or go upwards • *The fog was beginning to lift.*

lift *noun*
1 a movement upwards 2 a device for taking people or goods from one floor to another in a building 3 a ride in someone else's car or other vehicle

lift-off *noun*
the vertical take-off of a rocket or spacecraft

light¹ *noun*
1 light is the form of energy that makes things visible, the opposite of darkness • *There was not enough light to see the garden.* 2 a light is something that provides light or a flame, especially an electric lamp • *Switch on the light.*

light¹ *adjective*
1 full of light; not dark

2 pale • *The house was painted light blue.*

light¹ *verb* (**lighting, lit** or **lighted**)
1 to light something is to start it burning **2** to light is to begin to burn • *The fire won't light.* **3** to light a place is to give it light • *The streets were lit by gaslamps.*

light² *adjective*
1 not heavy; weighing little **2** not large or strong • *There is a light wind.* **3** not needing much effort • *They were doing some light work in the garden.* **4** pleasant and entertaining rather than serious • *We prefer light music.* **lightly** *adverb* gently or only a little • *He kissed her lightly on the cheek.* • *It began to snow lightly.*

lighten *verb*
1 to lighten something is to make it lighter or brighter **2** to lighten is to become lighter

lighter *noun*
a device for lighting something like a cigarette or a fire

light-hearted *adjective*
1 cheerful; free from worry **2** not serious **light-heartedly** *adverb* **light-heartedness** *noun*

lighthouse *noun*
a tower with a bright light at the top to guide ships and warn them of danger

lightning *noun*
lightning is a flash of bright light in the sky during a thunderstorm

light year *noun*
the distance that light travels in one year (about 9.5 million million kilometres or 6 million million miles)

like¹ *verb*
to like someone or something is to think they are pleasant or satisfactory **should like** or **would like** to want • *I should like to see him.*

like² *preposition*
1 resembling; similar to; in the manner of • *She looks like her mother.* • *He cried like a baby.* **2** such as • *We need things like knives and forks.* **3** typical of • *It was like her to forgive him.*

likeable *adjective*
pleasant and easy to like

likely *adjective* (**likelier, likeliest**)
probable; expected to happen or to be true or suitable • *It's likely that it will rain this afternoon.*

likeness *noun*
a resemblance

likewise *adverb*
similarly; in the same way

liking *noun*
a feeling that you like something or someone • *She has a great liking for chocolate.* **to be to someone's liking** is to be what they like • *These shoes are not to my liking.*

lily *noun* (**lilies**)
a trumpet-shaped flower grown from a bulb

limb *noun*)
a leg or an arm

lime¹ *noun*
a green fruit like a small round lemon

lime

lime² *noun*
a tree with yellow blossom

lime³ *noun*
a white chalky powder used in making cement or as a fertilizer

limelight *noun*
to be in the limelight is to get a lot of publicity and attention

limerick *noun* (say **lim**-er-ik)
an amusing poem with five lines and a strong rhythm

limestone *noun*
limestone is rock from which lime (the chalky powder) is made, used in building and in making cement

limit *noun*
a line or point that you cannot or should not pass • *You must obey the speed limit.*

limit *verb*
to limit something or someone is to keep them within a limit • *You are limited to one choice each.* **limitation** *noun* something that limits what you can do

limited *adjective*
kept within limits; not great • *The choice was limited.*

limp¹ *verb*
to limp is to walk with difficulty because something is wrong with your leg or foot

limp¹ *noun*
a limping movement

limp² *adjective*
not stiff or firm; without much

strength • *He gave me a limp handshake.* **limply** *adverb* something hangs limply when it does so in a limp way • *Her hair hung limply over her forehead.*

limpet *noun*
a small shellfish that clings firmly to rocks

line¹ *noun*
1 a long thin mark made on a surface **2** a row or series of people or things **3** a length of something long and thin like rope, string, or wire **4** a number of words together in a play, film, poem, or song **5** a railway or a length of railway track **in line 1** forming a straight line **2** obeying or behaving well

line¹ *verb*
1 to line something is to mark it with lines **2** to line a place is to form an edge or border along it • *People lined the streets to watch the race.* **to line up** is to form lines or rows • *The children lined up in the playground.* **to line things up** is to set them up in a line or row

line² *verb*
to line material or a piece of clothing is to put a lining in it

linen *noun*
1 linen is cloth made from flax, used to make shirts, sheets, tablecloths, and so on **2** linen is also things made of this cloth

liner *noun*
a large passenger ship or aircraft

linesman *noun*
an official in football, tennis, and other games who decides whether the ball has crossed a line

linger *verb*
to linger is to stay for a long time or be slow to leave • *The smell of her perfume lingered in the room.*

linguist *noun*
an expert in languages, or someone who can speak several languages well **linguistic** *adjective* to do with languages

lining *noun*
a layer of material covering the inside of something

link *noun*
1 one of the rings in a chain **2** a connection between two things

link *verb*
to link things is to join them together **to link up** is to become connected

lino *noun*
lino is linoleum

linoleum *noun*
(*say* lin-**oh**-li-um)
linoleum is a stiff shiny floor covering

lint *noun*
lint is a soft material for covering wounds

lion *noun*
a large strong flesh-eating animal found in Africa and India

lioness *noun*
a female lion

lip *noun*
1 each of the two lips fleshy edges of the mouth
2 the edge of something hollow such as a cup or a crater **3** the pointed part at the top of a jug or saucepan, for pouring from

lip-read *verb*
to lip-read is to understand what someone is saying by watching the movements of their lips, not by hearing their voice

lipstick *noun*
a stick of a waxy substance for colouring the lips

liquid *noun*
a substance (such as water or oil) that can flow but is not a gas

liquid *adjective*
in the form of a liquid; flowing freely

liquidizer *noun*
a device for making food into a pulp or a liquid

liquor *noun* (*say* **lik**-er)
liquor is strong alcoholic drink

liquorice *noun say* **lik**-er-iss)
liquorice is a soft black sweet with a strong taste, which comes from the root of a plant

lisp *noun*
a way of speaking,in which *s* and *z* are pronounced like *th*

lisp *verb*
to lisp is to speak with a lisp

list¹ *noun*
a number of names or figures or items written or printed one after another

list¹ *verb*
to list things is to write or say them one after another

list² *verb*
a ship lists when it leans over to oneside in the water

listen *verb*
to listen to someone or something is to pay attention so that you can hear them • *Listen to me.* • *I like listening to music.* **listener** *noun* someone who is listening

literacy *noun* (*say* **lit**-er-a-si)
the ability to read and write

literal *adjective*
1 meaning exactly what it says **2** word for word • *Write out a literal translation.*

literally *adverb*
really; exactly as the words say • *The noise made me literally jump out of my seat.*

literary *adjective* (*say* **lit**-er-er-i)
to do with literature; interested in literature

literate *adjective* (*say* **lit**-er-at)
able to read and write

literature *noun*
literature is books or writings, especially the best or most famous

litmus *noun*
litmus is a blue substance used to show whether something is an acid or an alkali

litre *noun* (*say* **lee**-ter)
a measure of liquid, 1,000 cubic centimetres or about 1¾ pints

litter *noun*
1 litter is rubbish or untidy things left lying about **2** a litter is a number of young animals born to one mother at one time

litter *verb*
to litter a place is to make it untidy with litter

little *adjective* (**less** or **littler, least** or **littlest**)
1 small; not great or not much • *She brought a little boy.* • *We have very little time.* **2** a small amount of something • *Have a little sugar.* **little by little** gradually

little *adverb*
not much • *They go swimming very little now.*

live¹ *verb* (*rhymes with* **give**)
1 to live is to be alive **2** to live in a particular place is to have your home there • *She is living in Glasgow.* **3** to live in a certain way is to pass your life in that way • *He lived as a hermit.* **to live on something** is to have it as food or income • *The islanders lived mainly on fish.* • *No one can live on £50 a week.*

live² *adjective* (*rhymes with* **hive**)
1 alive **2** carrying electricity **3** broadcast while it is actually happening, not from a recording

livelihood *noun* (*say* **lyv**-li-huud)
a person's livelihood is the way in which they earn a living

lively *adjective* (**livelier, liveliest**)
full of life and energy; cheerful **liveliness** *noun*

liver *noun*
1 a large organ in the body that helps keep the blood clean **2** an animal's liver used as food

livestock *noun*
farm animals

livid *adjective*
1 very angry **2** of a dark blue-grey colour, like bruised skin

living *noun*
1 the way that a person lives • *They have a good standard of living.*
2 a means of earning money • *She makes a living selling jewellery.*

living room *noun*
a room for sitting and relaxing in

lizard *noun*
a reptile with a scaly skin, four legs, and a long tail

llama *noun* (*say* **lah**-ma)
a South American animal that has woolly fur and looks like a small camel without a hump

load *noun*
1 something large or heavy that has to be carried **2** (*informal*) a large amount • *It's a load of nonsense.*

load *verb*
1 to load something is to put things into it so they can be carried • *I'll go and load the back of the car.* **2** to load someone with something is to give them large amounts of it • *They loaded him with gifts.* **3** to load a gun is to put a bullet or shell into it **4** to load a machine is to put something into it, so that it can be operated **5** to load a computer is to enter programs or data on it

loaf¹ *noun* (**loaves**)
a shaped mass of bread baked in one piece

loaf² *verb*
to loaf or loaf about is to loiter or waste time **loafer** *noun* someone who loafs about

loan *noun*
something that has been lent to someone, especially money **on loan** being lent • *The books are on loan from the library.*

loan *verb*
to loan something is to lend it

loathe *verb* (*rhymes with* **clothe**)
to loathe something or someone is to dislike them very much

loathsome *adjective*
making you feel disgusted; horrible

lob *verb* (**lobbing, lobbed**)
to lob something is to throw or hit it high into the air

lobby *noun* (**lobbies**)
an entrance hall

a b c d e f g h i j k l m n o p q r s t u v w x y z

lobe noun
the rounded part at the bottom of your ear

lobster noun
a large shellfish with eight legs and two claws

lobster

local adjective
1 belonging to a particular place or area • *Where is your local library?*
2 affecting a certain part of the body • *You'll need a local anaesthetic.*
locally adverb nearby, in the area where you are • *Do you live locally?*

local noun
(*informal*) someone who lives in a particular district

locate verb
1 to locate something is to discover where it is • *I have located the fault.* 2 to be located in a place is to be situated there • *The cinema is located in the High Street.*

location noun
the place where something is • *What is the exact location of the submarine?* When a film is filmed **on location** it is filmed in natural surroundings, not in a studio.

loch noun
a lake in Scotland

lock¹ noun
1 a device for fastening a door or window or container, needing a key to open it 2 a section of a canal or river with gates at each end, so that the level of water can be raised or lowered to allow boats to pass from one level to another

lock¹ verb
1 to lock a door or window or lid is to fasten it with a lock
2 to lock something somewhere is to put it in a safe place that can be fastened with a lock
3 to lock is to become fixed in one place, or to jam

lock² noun
a few strands of hair formed into a loop

locker noun
a small cupboard for keeping things safe, often in a changing room

locket noun
a small case holding a photograph or lock of hair, worn on a chain round the neck

locomotive noun
a railway engine

locust noun
an insect like a large grasshopper, that flies in swarms which eat all the plants in an area

lodge noun
a small house, often at the entrance to a large house or building

lodge verb
1 to lodge is to become fixed or get stuck somewhere • *The ball lodged in the branches.* 2 to lodge somewhere is to stay there as a lodger

lodger noun
someone who pays to live in someone else's house

lodgings plural noun
a room or set of rooms that a person rents in someone else's house

loft noun
the room or space under the roof of a house

lofty adjective (**loftier, loftiest**)
1 high or tall 2 noble and proud • *They have lofty ideas.* **loftily** adverb

log noun
1 a large piece of a tree that has fallen or been cut down 2 a detailed record of what happens each day, especially on a journey or voyage

log verb (**logging, logged**)
to log information is to put it in a log **to log in** or **to log on** is to gain access to a computer **to log out** or **to log off** is to finish using a computer

logic noun
a way of thinking and working out ideas that makes sense

logical adjective
using logic or worked out by logic **logically** adverb

logo noun
a printed symbol used by a business company or other organization as its emblem

loiter verb
to loiter is to stand about not doing anything

lollipop noun
a hard sticky sweet on the end of a stick

lolly noun (**lollies**)
1 (*informal*) a lolly is a lollipop or an ice lolly 2 (*slang*) lolly is money

lone adjective
on its own; solitary • *a lone rider*

lonely adjective (**lonelier, loneliest**)
1 unhappy because you are on your own 2 far from other inhabited places; not often used or visited • *They passed through a lonely village.* **loneliness** noun

long¹ adjective
1 measuring a lot from one end to the other • *They walked up a long path.* 2 taking a lot of time • *I'd like a long holiday.*
3 measuring from one end to the other • *A cricket pitch is 22 yards long.*

long¹ adverb
1 for a long time • *Have you been waiting long?* 2 a long time before or after • *They left long ago.* **as long as** or **so long as** provided that; on condition that • *I'll come as long as I can bring my dog.*

long² verb
to long for something is to want it very much

longitude noun
(*say* **long**-i-tewd *or* **lon**-ji-tewd)
longitude is the distance of a place east or west, measured in degrees from an imaginary line that passes through Greenwich in London

long jump noun
an athletic contest of jumping as far as possible along the ground with one leap

long-sighted adjective
able to see things clearly when they are at a distance but not when they are close

look verb
1 to look is to use your eyes to see something, or to turn your eyes towards something 2 to look in a particular direction is to face it • *Look right and left before you cross.*
3 to look (for example) happy or sad is to appear that way **to look after something** or **someone** is to protect them or take care of them **to look down on someone** is to despise them **to look for something** or **someone** is to try to find them **to look forward to something** is to be waiting eagerly for it to happen **to look out** is to be careful **to look up to someone** is to admire or respect them

look *noun*
1 a look is the act of looking • *Take a look at this.* **2** the expression on someone's face • *She gave me a surprised look.* **3** the look of someone or something is their appearance • *I don't like the look of that dog.*

looking-glass *noun*
(*old use*) a glass mirror

lookout *noun*
1 a place from which you watch for something **2** someone whose job is to keep watch **3** watching or being watchful • *Keep a lookout for snakes.*

loom¹ *noun*
a machine for weaving cloth

loom² *verb*
to loom or loom up is to appear large and threatening • *An iceberg loomed out of the fog.*

loop *noun*
the shape made by a curve crossing itself; a piece of string, ribbon, or wire made into this shape

loop *verb*
to loop something is to make it into a loop

loophole *noun*
a way of getting round a law or rule without quite breaking it

loose *adjective*
1 not tight or firmly fixed • *a loose tooth* **2** not tied up or shut in • *The dog got loose.* **to be at a loose end** is to have nothing to do **to be on the loose** is to be free after escaping
loosely *adverb* in a way that is not firm or tight • *She tied the scarf loosely round her waist*

loosen *verb*
1 to loosen something is to make it loose **2** to loosen is to become loose

loot *noun*
loot is stolen things

loot *verb*
to loot a place is to rob it violently, especially during a war or riot **looter** *noun* someone who loots a place

lopsided *adjective*
uneven, with one side lower than the other • *She had a lopsided smile.*

lord *noun*
1 a nobleman, especially one who is allowed to use the title 'Lord' in front of his name **2** (*old use*) a master or ruler **Lord** a name used by Christians for God or Jesus Christ

lordly *adjective*
1 relating to a lord **2** proud; haughty

lorry *noun* (**lorries**)
a large motor vehicle for carrying goods

lose *verb* (**losing, lost**)
1 to lose something is to no longer have it, especially because you can't find it • *I've lost my hat.* **2** to lose a contest or game is to be beaten in it • *We lost last Friday's match.* **3** a clock or watch loses time when it gives a time that is earlier than the correct time **to lose your way** is not to know where you are
loser *noun* someone who loses a game, or who often loses or fails at things

loss *noun*
1 losing something **2** something you have lost **to be at a loss** is to be puzzled or unable to do something

lost *adjective*
1 not knowing where you are or not able to find your way • *I think we're lost.* **2** missing or strayed • *a lost dog*

lot *noun*
1 a lot is a large number of people or things **2** a lot can also mean very much • *Thanks a lot.* **to draw lots** is to choose one person or thing from a group by a method that depends on chance **the lot** or **the whole lot** everything

lotion *noun*
a liquid that you put on your skin to clean or soothe it

lottery *noun* (**lotteries**)
a game in which prizes are given to people who have winning tickets that are chosen by a draw

loud *adjective*
1 noisy; easily heard **2** bright or gaudy • *The room was painted in loud colours.* **loudly** *adverb* **loudness** *noun*

loudspeaker *noun*
the part of a radio or music system that produces the sound

lounge *noun*
a room in a house, hotel, or airport for sitting in and relaxing

lounge *verb*
to lounge is to sit or stand in a relaxed or lazy way

louse *noun* (**lice**)
a small insect that sucks the blood of humans or animals

love *noun*
1 love is a feeling of liking someone or something very much; great affection or kindness **2** someone's love is a person that they love **3** in games, love is a score of nothing **to be in love** is to love another person very deeply

love *verb*
to love someone or something

is to like them very much
lovable *adjective* easy to love
lovingly *adverb* in a way that shows love

lovely *adjective* (**lovelier, loveliest**)
1 beautiful **2** (*informal*) very pleasant or enjoyable **loveliness** *noun*

low¹ *adjective*
1 only reaching a short way up; not high **2** below average in amount or importance • *They are people of a low rank.* • *Prices are low.* **3** unhappy • *I'm feeling low.* **4** a low note is one at the bottom end of a musical scale

low² *verb*
to low is to make a sound like a cow

lower *verb*
1 to lower something is to move it down **2** to lower a sound is to make it less loud • *Please lower your voices.*

lowly *adjective* (**lowlier, lowliest**)
humble **lowliness** *noun*

loyal *adjective*
always true to your friends; faithful
loyally *adverb* in a faithful way
loyalty *noun* being true to your friends

lozenge *noun*
a small sweet tablet, especially one that contains medicine

lubricant *noun*
oil or grease for lubricating machinery

lubricate *verb*
to lubricate something like machinery is to put oil or grease on it so that it moves smoothly
lubrication *noun* putting oil or grease on something so that it moves smoothly

luck *noun*
1 luck is the way things happen by chance, without being planned **2** luck is also good fortune

luckily *adverb*
by a lucky chance; fortunately • *Luckily it stayed warm all day.*

lucky *adjective* (**luckier, luckiest**)
having or bringing good luck

ludicrous *adjective*
(*say* loo-di-krus)
extremely silly or absurd
ludicrously *adverb*

lug *verb* (**lugging, lugged**)
to lug something heavy is to carry it or drag it with difficulty

luggage noun
luggage is the suitcases and bags you take on a journey

lukewarm adjective
1 slightly warm **2** not very keen or enthusiastic • *They got a lukewarm response.*

lull verb
to lull someone is to soothe or calm them

lull noun
a short period of quiet or rest • *There was a lull in the fighting.*

lullaby noun (**lullabies**)
a song that you sing to send a baby to sleep

lumber verb
1 to lumber is to move along clumsily and heavily • *A black bear came lumbering through the woods.*
2 (*informal*) to lumber someone is to leave them with something unpleasant or difficult to do

lumberjack noun
someone whose job is to cut down trees and transport them

luminous adjective
(*say* **loo**-mi-nus)
shining or glowing in the dark **luminosity** noun luminosity is being luminous

lump noun
1 a solid piece of something **2** a swelling **lumpy** adjective having lots of lumps

lump verb
to lump different things together is to put them together in the same group

lunacy noun (**lunacies**)
(*say* **loo**-na-si)
lunacy is madness

lunar adjective
to do with the moon

lunatic noun (*say* **loo**-na-tik)
an insane person

lunch noun
a meal eaten in the middle of the day

lung noun
each of the two organs in your chest that you use for breathing

luggage

lunge verb
to lunge is to make a sudden movement forwards

lurch¹ verb
to lurch is to stagger or lean suddenly

lurch¹ noun
a sudden staggering or leaning movement

lurch² noun
to leave someone in the lurch is to desert them when they are in difficulty

lure verb
to lure a person or animal is to tempt them into a trap or difficulty

lurk verb
to lurk is to wait threateningly where you can't be seen

luscious adjective
(*say* **lush**-us)
tasting or smelling delicious • *The bushes were heavy with luscious fruit.*

lush adjective
growing thickly and healthily • *The moist climate helps to cover the countryside with lush grass.*

lustre noun (*say* **lus**-ter)
a thing's lustre is its brightness or brilliance **lustrous** adjective shining brightly

lute noun
a musical instrument rather like a guitar but with a deeper and rounder body. It was used a lot in the Middle Ages.

luxury noun (**luxuries**)
1 a luxury is something expensive that you enjoy but don't really need **2** luxury is having a very comfortable and expensive way of life • *They led a life of luxury.*
luxurious adjective very comfortable and expensive

lynch verb
to lynch someone is to execute them without a proper trial

lyre noun
an ancient musical instrument like a small harp

lyrical adjective
sounding like a song or a poem

lyrics plural noun
the words of a popular song

m
short for metre, metres, miles, or millions

mac noun
(*informal*) a mackintosh

macaroni noun
macaroni is pasta in the form of short tubes

WORD ORIGIN

The word **macaroni** comes from an Italian word *maccaroni*, which in turn comes from a Greek word *makaria* meaning 'food made from barley'.

machine noun
a piece of equipment made of moving parts that work together to do a job

machine gun noun
a gun that can keep firing bullets quickly one after another

machinery noun
1 machinery is machines generally • *farm machinery* **2** machinery is also the moving parts of a machine • *The lift's machinery is faulty.*

mackerel noun (**mackerel**)
a sea fish used as food

mackintosh noun
a raincoat

mad adjective (**madder, maddest**)
1 having something wrong with your mind; not sane **2** very foolish **3** very keen • *She's mad about rock music.*
4 (*informal*) very excited or annoyed **like mad** (*informal*) with great speed, energy, or enthusiasm **madness** noun

madam noun
a word sometimes used when speaking or writing politely to a woman, instead of her name • *Can I help you, madam?*

madden verb
to madden someone is to make them mad or angry

madly adverb
extremely; very much • *They are madly in love.*

magazine noun
1 a paper-covered publication with articles or stories, which comes out regularly **2** the part of a gun that holds the cartridges **3** a store for weapons and ammunition or for

explosives **4** a device that holds film for a camera or slides for a projector

maggot noun
the larva of some kinds of fly

magic noun
1 magic is the power to make impossible things happen **2** magic is also performing clever tricks

magical adjective
1 done by magic or as if by magic **2** wonderful; marvellous **magically** adverb by magic or as if by magic

magician noun
1 someone who does magic tricks **2** a man with magic powers; a wizard

magistrate noun
a judge in a local court who deals with some less serious cases

magnesium noun
magnesium is a silvery-white metal that burns with a very bright flame

magnet noun
a piece of metal that can attract iron or steel and that points north and south when it is hung in the air **magnetism** noun the attraction of a magnet

magnetic adjective
having or using the powers of a magnet

magnetize verb
to magnetize something is to make it into a magnet

magnificent adjective
1 looking splendid or impressive **2** excellent • We had a magnificent meal. **magnificence** noun being magnificent
magnificently adverb

magnify verb (**magnifies, magnified**)
to magnify something is to make it look bigger than it really is **magnification** noun magnification is making something look bigger than it really is

magnifying glass noun
a lens that magnifies things

magnitude noun
magnitude is how large or important something is

magpie noun (**magpies**)
a black and white bird with a long tail, which likes to collect bright objects

mahogany noun
(say ma-**hog**-a-ni)
mahogany is a hard brown wood used for making furniture

maid noun
1 a female servant in a hotel or private house **2** (old use) a girl

maiden noun
(old use) a girl

maiden name noun
a woman's family name before she gets married

maiden voyage or **maiden flight** noun
a ship's first voyage or an aircraft's first flight

mail[1] noun
1 mail is letters and parcels sent by post **2** mail is also electronic mail

mail[1] verb
to mail something is to send it by post or by electronic mail

mail[2] noun
armour made of metal rings joined together

maim verb
to maim someone is to injure them so badly that part of their body is damaged for life

main adjective
largest or most important

mains noun
the main pipe or cable in a system carrying water, gas, or electricity to a building

mainland noun
the mainland is the main part of a country or continent, not the islands around it

mainly adverb
chiefly or usually; almost completely

maintain verb
1 to maintain something is to keep it in good condition **2** to maintain a belief is to have it or state it • I maintain that animals should not be hunted. **3** to maintain someone is to provide money for them

maintenance noun
maintenance is keeping something in good condition

maize noun
maize is a tall kind of corn with large seeds

majestic adjective
stately and dignified **majestically** adverb

majesty noun (**majesties**)
1 the title of a king or queen **2** majesty is the quality of being stately and dignified

major adjective
more important; main • The

major roads are shown in red on the map.

major noun
an army officer above captain in rank

majority noun (**majorities**)
(say ma-**jo**-ri-ti)
1 the greatest part of a group of people or things; more than half • The majority of the class wanted a quiz. **2** the amount by which the winner in an election beats the loser • She had a majority of 25 over her opponent.

make verb (**making, made**)
1 to make something is to build or produce it • They are making a raft out of logs. **2** to make someone or something do something is to cause it to happen • The bang made him jump. **3** to make money is to get it or earn it • She makes £30,000 a year. **4** in a game, to make a score is to achieve it • He has made 20 runs so far. **5** to make a certain point is to reach it • The swimmer just made the shore. • Do you think we can make the 7 o'clock train? **6** to make something is to estimate it or reckon it • What do you make the time? **7** several numbers make a total when they add up to it • 4 and 6 make 10. **8** to make (for example) a suggestion or promise is to give it to someone **9** to make a bed is to tidy it or arrange it for use **to make someone's day** is to cause them to be happy or successful **to make do** is to manage with something that is not what you really want **to make for a place** is to go towards it **to make off** is to leave quickly **to make something** or **someone out** is to manage to see or hear or understand them **to make something up** is to invent a false story or excuse **to make up** is to be friendly again after a disagreement **to make up for something** is to give or do something in return for a loss or difficulty **to make up your mind** is to decide

make noun
a brand of goods; something made by a particular firm • What make of car is that?

make-believe noun
make-believe is pretending or imagining things

makeshift adjective
used because you have nothing better • We'll use the bed as a makeshift table.

maize

make-up noun
make-up is creams and powders for making your skin look beautiful or different

malaria noun (say ma-**lair**-i-a)
a tropical disease spread by mosquito bites, that causes fever

male adjective
of the sex that produces young by fertilizing the female's egg cells

male noun
a male person or animal

malevolent adjective
(say ma-**lev**-o-lent)
wanting to harm other people
malevolence noun malevolence is wanting to harm people
malevolently adverb

malice noun
malice is a desire to harm other people

malicious adjective
intending to do harm • He had a malicious glint in his eye.
maliciously adverb

mall noun
a large covered shopping centre

mallet noun
a large wooden hammer

malnutrition noun
malnutrition is bad health caused by not having enough food
malnourished adjective suffering from malnutrition

malt noun
malt is dried barley used in brewing and making vinegar

mammal noun
any animal of which the female gives birth to live young and can feed them with her own milk

mammoth noun
an extinct kind of hairy elephant with long curved tusks
mammoth adjective
huge

man noun (**men**)
1 a man is a grown-up male human being **2** a man is also any individual person • No man is perfect. **3** man is all the people in the world • Look what harm man is doing to the environment. **4** a man is one of the pieces used in a board game
man verb (**manning, manned**)
to man something is to supply people to work it • Man the pumps!

manage verb
1 to manage something is to be able to do it although it is difficult **2** to manage a shop or factory or other business is to be in charge of it

manageable adjective
able to be managed or done

management noun
1 management is being in charge of something **2** the management of a business is the people in charge of it

manager noun
a person who manages a business or part of it

manageress noun
a woman manager of a shop or restaurant

mane noun
the long hair along the back of the neck of a horse or lion

manger noun (say **mayn**-jer)
a trough in a stable for animals to feed from

mangle verb
to mangle something is to crush or twist it so it is badly damaged

mango noun (**mangoes**)
a juicy tropical fruit with yellow flesh

manhole noun
a hole, usually with a cover, through which a person can get into a sewer or boiler to inspect or repair it

mania noun
1 mania is violent madness **2** a mania is a strong enthusiasm • They have a mania for sport.

maniac noun
a person who acts in a violent and wild way

manic adjective
manic behaviour is busy and excited

manipulate verb
1 to manipulate something is to handle it skilfully **2** to manipulate someone is to get them to do what you want by treating them cleverly **manipulation** noun manipulating something or someone **manipulator** noun a person who manipulates something or someone

mankind noun
mankind is all the people in the world • This is a discovery for the good of all mankind.

manly adjective (**manlier, manliest**)
1 strong or brave **2** suitable for a man or like a man **manliness** noun

manner noun
the way that something happens or is done

manners plural noun
a person's manners are how they behave with other people; behaving politely

manoeuvre noun
(say ma-**noo**-ver)
a skilful or clever action

manoeuvre verb
1 to manoeuvre something is to move it skilfully into position **2** to manoeuvre is to move skilfully or cleverly **manoeuvrable** adjective easy to move into position

manor noun
a large important house in the country

mansion noun
a grand house

manslaughter noun
(say **man**-slaw-ter)
manslaughter is the crime of killing someone without meaning to

mantelpiece noun
a shelf above a fireplace

manual adjective
manual work is work you do with your hands; manual equipment is equipment used with your hands
manually adverb you do something manually when you use your hands to do it
manual noun
a handbook or book of instructions

manufacture verb
to manufacture things is to make them with machines, usually in a factory **manufacturer** noun a business that manufactures things

manure noun
animal dung added to the soil to make it more fertile

manuscript noun
something written or typed before it has been printed

many adjective (**more, most**)
large in number • There were many people at the party. • How many potatoes do you want?
many noun
a large number of people or things • Many of them wanted to stay.

Maori noun (say **mow**-ri)
1 a member of the aboriginal people of New Zealand **2** their language

map noun
a diagram of part or all of the earth's surface, showing features such as towns, mountains, and rivers
map verb (**mapping, mapped**)
to map an area is to make a map of it

maple noun
a tree with broad leaves

mar verb (**marring, marred**)
to mar something is to spoil it

marathon *noun*
a long-distance running race on roads, usually 26 miles (42 kilometres) long

marble *noun*
1 a marble is a small glass ball used in games **2** marble is a hard kind of limestone that is polished and used for building or sculpture

marbles

March *noun*
the third month of the year

march *verb*
1 to march is to walk with regular steps **2** to march someone is to make them walk somewhere • *He marched them up the hill.*

march *noun*
1 a march is a large group of people marching, sometimes to protest about something **2** a march is also a piece of music suitable for marching to

mare *noun*
a female horse or donkey

margarine *noun*
(*say* mar-ja-**reen**)
margarine is a soft creamy food used like butter, made from animal or vegetable fats

margin *noun*
1 the empty space between the edge of a page and the writing or pictures **2** the small difference between two scores or prices • *She won by a narrow margin.*

marine *adjective* (*say* ma-**reen**)
to do with the sea

marine *noun*
a soldier trained to serve on land and sea

marionette *noun*
a puppet that you work by strings or wires

mark *noun*
1 a spot, dot, line, or stain on something **2** a number or letter put on a piece of work to show how good it is **3** a special feature or sign of something • *They kept a minute's silence as a mark of respect.* **4** the place from which you start a race • *On your marks, get set, go!*

mark *verb*
1 to mark something is to put a mark on it **2** to mark a piece of work is to give it a number or letter to show how good it is **3** in football or hockey, to mark a player on the other team is to keep close to them to stop them getting the ball **4** to mark something said is to take note of it • *Mark my words!*

market *noun*
1 a place where things are bought and sold, usually from stalls in the open air **2** a demand for goods • *There is hardly any market for typewriters now.*

marksman *noun* (**marksmen**)
an expert in shooting at a target
marksmanship *noun* the skill of shooting at a target

marmalade *noun*
jam made from oranges or lemons

maroon *verb*
to maroon someone is to abandon them in a place far away from other people • *He was shipwrecked and marooned on a desert island.*

marquee *noun* (*say* mar-**kee**)
a large tent used for a party or exhibition

marriage *noun*
1 marriage is the state of being married **2** a marriage is a wedding

marrow *noun*
1 a marrow is a large green or yellow vegetable with a hard skin **2** marrow is the soft substance inside your bones

marry *verb* (**marries, marrying, married**)
1 to marry someone is to become their husband or wife **2** to marry two people is to perform a marriage ceremony

marsh *noun*
a low-lying area of very wet ground
marshy *adjective* marshy ground is low-lying and very wet

marshal *noun*
1 an official who supervises a contest or ceremony **2** a law officer in the USA

marshmallow *noun*
marshmallow is a soft spongy sweet

marsupial *noun*
(*say* mar-**soo**-pi-al)
an animal such as a kangaroo, wallaby, or koala. The female has a pouch for carrying her young.

martial arts *plural noun*
martial arts are fighting sports such as karate and judo

martyr *noun* (*say* **mar**-ter)
someone who is killed or suffers because of their beliefs **martyrdom** *noun* when someone is killed or suffers because of their beliefs

marvel *noun*
a wonderful thing

marvel *verb* (**marvelling, marvelled**)
to marvel at something is to be filled with wonder or astonishment by it

marvellous *adjective*
wonderful **marvellously** *adverb*

marzipan *noun*
marzipan is a soft sweet food made from almonds and sugar, sometimes put on the top of cakes

mascot *noun*
a person, animal, or object that people think will bring them good luck

masculine *adjective*
1 to do with men or like men; suitable for men **2** in some languages, belonging to the class of words that includes words referring to men **masculinity** *noun* being masculine

mash *verb*
to mash something is to crush it into a soft mass

mash *noun*
(*informal*) mashed potatoes

mask *noun*
a covering that you wear over your face to disguise or protect it

mask *verb*
1 to mask your face is to cover it with a mask **2** to mask something is to hide it

masks

mason *noun*
someone who builds or works with stone

masonry *noun*
masonry is the stone parts of a building

a b c d e f g h i j k l m n o p q r s t u v w x y z

Mass *noun*
the Communion service in a Roman Catholic church

mass *noun*
1 a large amount of something
2 a lump or heap 3 (*in science*) the amount of matter in an object, measured in grams
the masses the ordinary people

mass *verb*
to mass is to collect into a mass
• *People were massing in the square.*

massacre *verb* (*say* **mas**-a-ker)
to massacre people is to kill a large number of them

massacre *noun*
the killing of a large number of people

massage *verb* (*say* **mas**-ahzh)
to massage the body is to rub and press it to make it less stiff or less painful

massage *noun*
massaging someone's body

massive *adjective*
very big; large and heavy
massively *adverb* hugely

mast *noun*
a tall pole that holds up a ship's sails or a flag or aerial

master *noun*
1 a man who is in charge of something 2 a male teacher
3 someone who is very good at what they do, such as a great artist or composer 4 something from which copies are made **Master** (*old use*) a title put before a boy's name

master *verb*
1 to master a subject or skill is to learn it completely 2 to master a fear or difficulty is to control it • *She succeeded in mastering her fear of heights.*

mastermind *noun*
1 a very clever person 2 someone who organizes a scheme or crime

masterpiece *noun*
1 an excellent piece of work
2 someone's best piece of work

mastery *noun*
mastery is complete control or knowledge of something • *He has a complete mastery of the art of fencing.*

mat *noun*
1 a small piece of material that partly covers a floor 2 a small piece of material put on a table to protect the surface

match¹ *noun*
a small thin stick with a small amount of chemical at one end that gives a flame when rubbed on something rough

match² *noun*
1 a game or contest between two teams or players 2 one person or thing that is equal or similar to another • *Can you find a match for this sock?* 3 a marriage

match² *verb*
1 to match another person or thing is to be equal to them 2 one thing matches another when it goes well with it • *Your jacket matches your shoes.*

mate¹ *noun*
1 a friend or companion
2 one of a pair of animals that produce young together 3 one of the officers on a ship

mate¹ *verb*
animals mate when they come together in order to have offspring

mate² *noun*
checkmate in chess

material *noun*
1 anything used for making something else 2 cloth or fabric

maternal *adjective*
to do with a mother; motherly

maternity *noun*
maternity is having a baby; motherhood

mathematician *noun*
(*say* math-em-a-**tish**-an)
an expert in mathematics

mathematics *noun*
mathematics is the study of numbers, measurements, and shapes
mathematical *adjective*
to do with mathematics

maths *noun* (*informal*)
maths is mathematics

matinee *noun* (*say* **mat**-i-nay)
an afternoon performance at a theatre or cinema

matrimony *noun*
(*say* **mat**-ri-mo-ni)
matrimony is marriage
matrimonial *adjective* to do with marriage

matt *adjective*
not shiny • *The wall was decorated with matt paint.*

matted *adjective*
tangled

matter *noun*
1 something you need to think about or do • *It is a serious matter.* 2 a substance
• *Peat consists mainly of vegetable matter.* **a matter of fact** something true **no matter** it is not important **what's the matter?** what is wrong?

matter *verb*
to matter is to be important

mattress *noun*
a thick layer of soft or springy

material covered in cloth and used on a bed

mature *adjective*
1 fully grown or developed
2 behaving in a sensible adult manner **maturity** *noun* maturity is being fully grown or behaving in a sensible adult manner

mature *verb*
to become fully grown or developed

maximum *noun* (**maxima**)
the greatest number or amount possible • *The maximum is 10.*

maximum *adjective*
the greatest possible • *The maximum speed is 60 miles per hour.*

May *noun*
the fifth month of the year

may *verb* (past tense **might**)
1 may means to be allowed to • *May I have a sweet?* 2 may also means that something will possibly happen or has possibly happened • *He may come tomorrow.* • *He might have missed the train.*

maybe *adverb*
perhaps

mayonnaise *noun*
(*say* may-on-**ayz**)
mayonnaise is a creamy sauce made from eggs, oil, and vinegar, and used on salads

mayor *noun*
the person in charge of the council in a town or city

mayoress *noun*
a woman who is a mayor

maze *noun*
a complicated arrangement of paths or lines to follow your way through as a game or puzzle

me *pronoun*
a word used for *I*, usually when it is the object of a sentence, or when it comes after a preposition • *She likes me.* • *She gave it to me.*

meadow *noun*
a field of grass

meagre *adjective* (*say* **meeg**-er)
very little; barely enough • *They had already used up their meagre savings.*

meal *noun*
a meal is the food eaten at one time, such as breakfast, lunch, or dinner

mean¹ *verb* (**meaning, meant**)
1 to mean something is to have that as its explanation or equivalent, or to convey that as its sense • *What does this word mean?* 2 to mean to do something is to intend to do it
• *I meant to tell him, but I forgot.*

mean² *adjective*
1 not generous; selfish
• *What a mean man.* **2** unkind
or spiteful • *That was a
mean trick.* **meanly** *adverb*
meanness *noun*

mean³ *adjective*
(*in mathematics*) average
• *Work out the mean temperature.*

meaning *noun*
what something means
meaningless *adjective* having no
meaning or purpose

means *noun*
a means of doing something
is a way or method of doing it
by all means certainly **by means of
something** using something or with
something **by no means** not at all
means *plural noun*
money or other resources for doing
things

meantime *noun*
in the meantime meanwhile

meanwhile *adverb*
while something else is happening
• *I'll cut the cake up. Meanwhile, you
get the plates out.*

measles *plural noun*
measles is an infectious disease that
causes small red spots on the skin

measure *verb*
1 to measure something is to find
out how big it is **2** to measure (for
example) six feet is to be six feet long
measure *noun*
1 a unit used for measuring
something **2** a device used for
measuring **3** the size of something
4 something done for a particular
purpose; a law or rule • *We are
bringing in new measures to deal
with bullies.*

measurement *noun*
1 a measurement is the size or
length of something **2** measurement
is when you measure something

meat *noun*
meat is animal flesh that is cooked
as food **meaty** *adjective* full of meat
or like meat

mechanic *noun*
someone who maintains and repairs
machinery

mechanical *adjective*
1 to do with machines **2** done
without thinking about it
mechanically *adverb* you do
something mechanically when you
do it without thinking about it

mechanism *noun*
1 the moving parts of a machine
2 the way a machine works

medal

medal
noun
a piece of
metal shaped
likeba coin, star,
or cross, given to someone
for bravery or for achieving
something • *She won two
Olympic gold medals.*

medallist *noun*
a winner of a medal

meddle *verb*
to meddle in something is to
interfere in it **meddler** *noun*
someone who interferes with
something **meddlesome** *adjective*
always interfering

media *plural noun* (*say* **mee**-di-a)
the plural of **medium²**
the media newspapers, radio,
television and the Internet, which
provide information about current
events to the public

medical *adjective*
to do with the treatment of disease
medically *adverb*
by medical means

medicine *noun*
1 a medicine is a substance, usually
swallowed, used to try to cure an
illness **2** medicine is the treatment
of disease and injuries **medicinal**
adjective something is medicinal
when it helps to cure an illness

medieval *adjective*
(*say* med-i-**ee**-val)
to do with the Middle Ages

mediocre *adjective*
(*say* meed-i-**oh**-ker)
only fairly good **mediocrity** *noun*
being mediocre

meditate *verb*
to meditate is to think deeply
and seriously, usually in silence
meditation *noun*
when someone meditates

medium¹ *adjective*
average; of middle size
medium² *noun*
1 (**media**) a thing in which
something exists, moves, or is
expressed • *Air is the medium in
which sound travels.* • *Local radio is a
good medium for traffic information.*
2 (**mediums**) someone who claims
to communicate with the dead

meek *adjective*
quiet and obedient **meekly** *adverb*
quietly and obediently
meekness *noun*

meet *verb* (**meeting, met**)
1 to meet is to come together from

different places • *We all met in
London.* • *There is a statue where the
two roads meet.* **2** to meet someone
is to come face to face with them,
especially for the first time or by
an arrangement • *I met her at a
party.* • *I'll meet you at the
station.* **3** to meet a bill or
cost is to be able to pay it
• *He is finding it difficult to
meet all his debts.*

meeting *noun*
a time when people come
together for a special purpose,
often to discuss something

megabyte *noun*
(*in computing*) a unit that measures
data or memory, roughly equal to
one million bytes

megaphone *noun*
a funnel-shaped device for making
someone's voice
sound louder

melancholy *adjective*
sad and gloomy

mellow *adjective*
having a soft rich sound
or colour

melody *noun* (**melodies**)
a tune, especially one that is
pleasant to listen to **melodic**
adjective having a tune that is
pleasant to listen to

melon *noun*
a large juicy fruit with yellow or
green skin

melt *verb*
1 to melt something solid is to make
it liquid by heating it **2** to melt is
to become liquid by heating **3** to
melt, or to melt away, is to go away
or disappear slowly • *The crowd
gradually melted away.*

member *noun*
someone who belongs to a society or
group **membership** *noun* being a
member of a society or group

Member of Parliament *noun*
someone who has been elected by
the people of an area to speak for
them in Parliament

memorable *adjective*
1 worth remembering • *It was a
memorable holiday.* **2** easy to
remember • *He has a memorable
name.* **memorably** *adverb*

memorial *noun*
something set up to remind people of
a person or an event • *They passed a
war memorial in the High Street.*

memorize *verb*
to memorize something is to learn it
and remember it exactly

a
b
c
d
e
f
g
h
i
j
k
l
m
n
o
p
q
r
s
t
u
v
w
x
y
z

memory noun (**memories**)
1 memory is the ability to remember things 2 a memory is something that you remember, usually something interesting or special 3 a computer's memory is the part where information is stored **to do something in memory of someone** or **something** is to do it in order to remind people of a person or an event

menace verb
to menace someone is to threaten them with harm or danger

menace noun
1 something that threatens people with harm or danger 2 an annoying person or thing

mend verb
to mend something that is broken or damaged is to make it as good as it was before

menstruation noun
menstruation is the natural flow of blood from a woman's womb, normally happening every 28 days **menstrual** adjective to do with menstruation

mental adjective
1 to do with the mind • *mental arithmetic.* 2 (*informal*) mad or crazy **mentally** adverb in your head or mind

mention verb
to mention someone or something is to speak about them briefly

mention noun
when someone or something is mentioned • *Our school got a mention in the local paper.*

menu noun (**menus**)
(*say* **men**-yoo)
1 a list of the food that is available in a restaurant or served at a meal 2 (*in computing*) a list of possible actions, displayed on a screen, from which you choose what you want a computer to do

mercenary noun (**mercenaries**)
a soldier hired to fight for a foreign country

merchandise noun
merchandise is goods for buying or selling

merchant noun
someone involved in trade

merciful adjective
showing mercy
mercifully adverb

merciless adjective
showing no mercy; cruel
mercilessly adverb

mercury noun
mercury is a heavy silvery metal that is usually liquid, used in thermometers

mercy noun (**mercies**)
1 mercy is kindness or pity shown towards someone instead of harming them or punishing them 2 a mercy is something to be thankful for • *Thank God for small mercies.*

mere adjective
not more than • *He's a mere child.*

merely adverb
only; simply • *I was merely repeating what he told me.*

merge verb
1 to merge things is to combine or blend them 2 to merge is to be combined

meringue noun (*say* mer-**rang**)
a crisp cake made from the whites of eggs mixed with sugar and baked

merit noun
something that deserves praise • *I can see the merits of this argument.*

mermaid noun
in stories, a sea creature with a woman's body and a fish's tail instead of legs

merry adjective (**merrier, merriest**)
happy and cheerful **merrily** adverb **merriment** noun being happy and cheerful

merry-go-round noun
a large roundabout with horses and other things to ride on

mesh noun
mesh is material made like a net, with open spaces between the wire or threads

mess noun
1 something untidy or dirty 2 a difficult or confused situation 3 a place where soldiers or sailors eat their meals **to make a mess of something** is to do it very badly

mess verb
to mess about is to waste time behaving stupidly or doing things slowly • *Stop messing about and give me a hand.* **to mess something up** is to do it very badly

message noun
a piece of information that one person sends to another

messenger noun
someone who carries a message

messy adjective (**messier, messiest**)
1 untidy or dirty 2 difficult or complicated • *I'm afraid it's a messy situation.*
messily adverb

metal noun
a hard substance that melts when it is heated, such as gold, silver, copper, and iron **metallic** adjective like metal, especially sounding like it or shining like it

meteor noun (*say* **meet**-i-er)
a piece of rock or metal that moves through space and burns up as it enters the earth's atmosphere

meteorite noun
(*say* **meet**-i-er-ryt)
the remains of a meteor that has landed on the earth

meteorology noun
(*say* meet-i-er-**ol**-o-ji)
meteorology is the study of the weather **meteorological** adjective to do with meteorology **meteorologist** noun an expert on the weather

meter noun
a device for measuring something, especially for measuring how much of something has been used

method noun
a method is a way of doing something

methodical adjective
(*say* mi-**thod**-i-kal)
done carefully and in a logical way **methodically** adverb

meticulous adjective
very careful and precise **meticulously** adverb

metre noun (*say* **meet**-er)
1 the main unit of length in the metric system, equal to 100 centimetres or about 39½ inches 2 a particular type of rhythm in poetry

metric system noun
a measuring system based on decimal units (the metre, litre, and gram)

mew verb
to make a sound like a cat

miaow verb (*say* mee-**ow**)
to make a sound like a cat

microbe noun (*say* **my**-krohb)
a tiny organism that you need a microscope to see

microchip noun
a very small piece of silicon working as an electric circuit, used in computers

microchip

microphone *noun*
an electrical device that picks up sound waves for recording them or making them louder

microscope *noun*
(say **my**-kro-skohp)
a device with lenses that make tiny objects appear larger so you can study them

microscopic *adjective*
(say my-kro-**skop**-ik)
too small to be seen without a microscope; tiny

microwave *noun*
a kind of oven which heats things quickly by using energy in very short waves

microwave *verb*
to microwave food is to cook it in a microwave

mid *adjective*
in the middle of • *The holiday is from mid-July to mid-August.*

midday *noun*
the middle of the day; noon

middle *noun*
1 the middle of something is the place or part that is at the same distance from all its sides or edges or from both its ends **2** someone's waist

middle *adjective*
placed in the middle

middle-aged *adjective*
aged between about forty and sixty

Middle Ages *noun*
the period in history from about AD 1100 to 1500

Middle East *noun*
the countries to the east of the Mediterranean Sea, from Egypt to Iran

middle school *noun*
a school for children aged from about 9 to 13

midge *noun*
a small insect like a gnat

midnight *noun*
twelve o'clock at night

midst *noun*
to be in the midst of something is to be in the middle of it

midsummer *noun*
the middle of summer, when the days are longest

midway *adverb*
halfway

midwife *noun* (**midwives**)
a person trained to look after a woman who is giving birth to a baby

might[1]
past tense of **may**

might[2] *noun*
great power or strength

mighty *adjective* (**mightier, mightiest**) very strong or powerful
mightily *adverb* very much indeed
• *I was mightily relieved to see her.*

migraine *noun* (say **mee**-grayn)
a severe kind of headache

migrant *noun* (say **my**-grant)
1 a person who moves from one place to another, usually to find work **2** a bird or animal that moves from one region to another

migrate *verb* (say my-**grayt**)
1 to migrate is to move from one place to another, usually to find work **2** birds migrate when they fly to a warmer region for the winter
migration *noun* migrating to another country

mild *adjective*
gentle; not harsh or severe **mildly** *adverb* slightly • *She looked mildly surprised.* **mildness** *noun*

mile *noun*
a measure of distance, equal to 1,760 yards or about 1.6 kilometres

mileage *noun*
the number of miles you have travelled

milestone *noun*
1 a stone of a kind that used to be placed beside a road to mark the distance between towns **2** an important event in history or in a person's life

military *adjective*
to do with soldiers or the armed forces

milk *noun*
milk is a white liquid that female mammals produce in their bodies to feed to their young

milk *verb*
to milk a cow or other animal is to get milk from it

milkman *noun* (**milkmen**)
a person who delivers milk to people's houses

milkshake *noun*
a frothy drink of milk mixed with a sweet fruit flavouring

milky *adjective* (**milkier, milkiest**)
1 like milk; white **2** made with a lot of milk

mill *noun*
1 a building with machinery for grinding corn to make flour **2** a factory for making materials, such as a paper mill or a steel mill **3** a machine for grinding something such as coffee or pepper

mill *verb*
1 to mill something is to grind or crush it in a mill **2** people mill or mill about when they move in a confused crowd

millennium *noun*
a period of 1,000 years

miller *noun*
someone who runs a flour mill

milligram *noun*
one thousandth of a gram

millilitre *noun*
one thousandth of a litre

millimetre *noun*
one thousandth of a metre

million *noun*
a thousand thousands (1,000,000)
millionth *adjective, noun*
1,000,000th

millionaire *noun*
an extremely rich person who has at least a million pounds or dollars

mime *verb*
to mime is to tell a story by using movements of the body without speaking

mime *noun*
mime is the art of telling a story by using movements of the body without speaking

mimic *verb*
to mimic someone is to imitate them, especially to make people laugh
mimicry *noun* imitating someone to make people laugh
mimic *noun*
a person who is good at imitating other people

minaret *noun*
a tall tower on a mosque

WORD ORIGIN

The word **minaret** comes from an Arabic word *manara* meaning 'lighthouse'.

mince *noun*
mince is meat that has been cut up into very small pieces
mince *verb*
to mince food is to cut it up into very small pieces **mincer** *noun* a device for mincing food

mincemeat *noun*
mincemeat is a sweet mixture of currants, raisins, and chopped fruit, used in pies

mince pie *noun*
a pie containing mincemeat

mind *noun*
the ability of your brain to think, feel, understand, and remember; your thoughts and feelings **to change your mind** is to have a new opinion or make a different decision about something **to have a good mind to do something** is to intend to do it

a b c d e f g h i j k l m n o p q r s t u v w x y z

mind *verb*
1 to mind something is to be bothered or upset about it • *I don't mind missing the party.* **2** to mind someone or something is to look after them for a time • *He was minding the baby.* **3** to mind, or to mind out, is to be careful or watch out for something • *Mind you don't trip on the step.*

mindless *adjective*
done without thinking; stupid or pointless

mine¹ *adjective, pronoun*
belonging to me • *That book is mine.*

mine² *noun*
1 a place where coal, metal, or precious stones are dug out of the ground **2** a type of bomb hidden under the ground or in the sea that explodes when anything touches it

mine² *verb*
1 to mine something is to dig it from a mine **2** to mine a place is to lay explosives in it

minefield *noun*
an area where explosive mines have been laid

miner *noun*
someone who works in a mine

mineral *noun*
1 a hard substance that can be dug out of the ground, such as coal and iron ore **2** a cold fizzy drink

mineral water *noun*
mineral water is water that comes from a natural spring. It can be fizzy or still.

mingle *verb*
1 things mingle when they become mixed together **2** to mingle things is to mix or blend them

miniature *adjective*
(*say* **min**-i-cher)
very small; made in a much smaller size than usual

minibus *noun*
a small bus with seats for about ten people

minim *noun*
a musical note equal to two crotchets or half a semibreve, written h

minimum *noun* (**minima**)
the smallest number or amount possible • *We want the minimum of fuss.*

minimum *adjective*
least or smallest
• *The minimum charge is £5.*

minister *noun*
1 a member of the government who is in charge of a department **2** a member of the clergy

ministry *noun* (**ministries**)
1 a government department • *the Ministry of Defence* **2** the work of a minister in the church

mink *noun*
1 a mink is a small animal rather like a stoat **2** mink is this animal's valuable brown fur

minnow *noun*
a tiny freshwater fish

minor *adjective*
not very important, especially when compared to something else

minority *noun* (**minorities**)
(*say* myn-**o**-ri-ti)
1 the smaller part of a group of people or things • *There was a minority who wanted to leave.* **2** a small group that is different from others

minstrel *noun*
a travelling singer and musician in the Middle Ages

mint¹ *noun*
1 mint is a green plant with strong-smelling leaves used for flavouring **2** a mint is a sweet flavoured with peppermint

mint² *noun*
a place where a country's coins are made **to be in mint condition** is to be new, as if it had just been made

mint² *verb*
to mint coins is to make them

minus *preposition*
1 less; with the next number taken away • *Eight minus two equals six (8-2 = 6).* **2** less than zero • *The temperature is minus 5 degrees.*

minute¹ *noun* (*say* **min**-it)
1 one-sixtieth of an hour **2** (*informal*) a short time • *I'll be ready in a minute!*

minute² *adjective* (*say* my-**newt**)
1 tiny • *The insect was minute.* **2** very detailed • *He gave it a minute examination.* **minutely** *adverb* in a very detailed way

miracle *noun*
a wonderful or magical happening that cannot be explained **miraculous** *adjective* wonderful or magical **miraculously** *adverb*

mirage *noun* (*say* **mi**-rahzh)
something that seems to be visible but is not really there, like a lake in a desert

mirror *noun*
a sheet of glass painted with silver on the back so that it reflects things clearly

WORD ORIGIN

The word **mirror** comes from a Latin word *mirare* meaning 'to look at'.

mirth *noun*
mirth is laughter or cheerfulness

misbehave *verb*
to misbehave is to behave badly **misbehaviour** *noun* when someone behaves badly

miscarriage *noun*
a woman has a miscarriage when she gives birth to a baby before it is old enough to survive

miscellaneous *adjective*
(*say* mis-el-**ay**-ni-us)
a miscellaneous group is one that is made up of different kinds of thing

miscellany *noun* (**miscellanies**)
(*say* mis-**el**-an-ee)
a mixture of different things

mischief *noun*
mischief is naughty or troublesome behaviour

mischievous *adjective*
naughty or troublesome; full of mischief

miser *noun*
someone who stores money away and spends as little as they can **miserly** *adjective* hating to spend money

miserable *adjective*
1 very unhappy • *He felt miserable.* **2** unpleasant • *What miserable weather!* **miserably** *adverb*

misery *noun* (**miseries**)
1 misery is great unhappiness or suffering **2** (*informal*) a misery is someone who is always unhappy or complaining

misfire *verb*
1 a gun misfires when it fails to fire **2** a plan or idea or joke misfires when it goes wrong

misfit *noun*
someone who does not fit in well with other people

misfortune *noun*
1 a misfortune is an unlucky event or an accident **2** misfortune is bad luck

mishap *noun* (*say* **mis**-hap)
an unfortunate accident

misjudge *verb*
to misjudge someone or something is to form a wrong idea or opinion about them

mislay *verb* (**mislaying, mislaid**)
to mislay something is to lose it for a short time

mislead *verb*
to mislead someone is to give them a wrong idea or impression deliberately

misprint *noun*
a mistake in printing, such as a spelling mistake

Miss *noun*
a title you put before the name of a girl or unmarried woman

miss *verb*
1 to miss something is to fail to hit, reach, catch, see, hear, or find it
• *The bullet missed him by inches.*
• *I missed the last episode.* **2** to miss someone or something is to be sad because they are not with you • *I missed my sister when she was in hospital.* **3** to miss a train, bus, or plane is to arrive too late to catch it **4** to miss a lesson or other activity is to fail to attend it • *How many classes have you missed?* **5** to miss something is also to notice that it isn't where it should be • *When did you first miss your wallet?*

miss *noun*
not hitting, reaching, or catching something • *Was that shot a hit or a miss?*

missile *noun*
1 a weapon that is fired a long distance and explodes when it lands **2** an object thrown at someone

missing *adjective*
something is missing when it is lost or not in the proper place

mission *noun*
1 an important job that someone is sent to do or that someone feels they must do **2** a place or building where missionaries work

missionary *noun* (**missionaries**)
someone who goes to another country to spread a religious faith

misspell *verb* (**misspelling, misspelt** or **misspelled**)
to misspell a word is to spell it wrongly

mist *noun*
1 damp cloudy air like a thin fog **2** condensed water vapour on a window or mirror

mistake *noun*
something done or said wrongly

mistake *verb* (**mistaking, mistook, mistaken**)
to mistake one person or thing for another is to confuse them • *I'm sorry, I mistook you for someone else.*

mistaken *adjective*
to be mistaken is to be incorrect or wrong • *You are mistaken if you believe that.* **mistakenly** *adverb*

mistletoe *noun*
mistletoe is a plant with green leaves and white berries in winter

mistreat *verb*
to mistreat someone is to treat them badly or unfairly **mistreatment** *noun* treating someone badly or unfairly

mistress *noun*
1 a woman who is in charge of something **2** a woman who teaches in a school **3** the woman owner of a dog or other animal

mistrust *verb*
to mistrust someone or something is not to trust them

misty *adjective* (**mistier, mistiest**)
1 if it is misty outside there is a lot of mist **2** misty eyes are full of tears

misunderstand *verb* (**misunderstanding, misunderstood**)
to misunderstand something is to get a wrong idea or impression about it • *You misunderstood what I said.*
misunderstanding *noun* a wrong idea or impression

misuse *verb* (*say* mis-**yooz**)
to misuse something is to use it in the wrong way or treat it badly

misuse *noun* (*say* mis-**yooss**)
misuse is using something in the wrong way

mite *noun*
1 a tiny insect found in food **2** a small child

mitten *noun*
a kind of glove without separate parts for the fingers

mix *verb*
1 to mix different things is to stir or shake them together to make one thing **2** to mix is to get on well with other people • *She mixes well.* **to mix up people** or **things** is to confuse them **mixer** *noun* a machine for mixing food

mixed *adjective*
containing two or more kinds of things or people • *a bag of mixed nuts*

mixture *noun*
something made of different things mixed together

mix-up *noun*
a muddle or confused situation, especially one that ruins a plan

mm
short for millimetre or millimetres

moan *noun*
1 a long low sound, usually of suffering **2** a complaint or grumble

moan *verb*
1 to moan is to make a long low sound **2** to moan is also to complain or grumble

moat *noun*
a deep ditch round a castle, usually filled with water

mob *noun*
1 a large crowd of people who are hard to control **2** a gang

mob *verb* (**mobbing, mobbed**)
people mob someone when they crowd round them • *The singer was mobbed by her fans.*

mobile *adjective*
able to be moved or carried about easily **mobility** *noun* the ability to move easily from place to place

mobile *noun*
1 a decoration made to be hung up from threads so that it moves about in the air **2** (*informal*) a mobile phone

mobile phone *noun*
a telephone you can carry around with you

mock *verb*
to mock someone or something is to make fun of them **mockery** *noun* making fun of someone or something

mock *adjective*
not real or genuine • *They fought a mock battle.*

mode *noun*
the way that something is done
• *Flying is the fastest mode of transport.*

model *noun*
1 a small copy of an object
• *He makes models of aircraft.*
2 a particular version or design of something • *We saw the latest models at the motor show.*
3 someone who displays clothes by wearing them or who poses for an artist or photographer **4** someone or something worth copying or imitating

model *adjective*
1 being a small copy of something
• *I'd like a model railway.* **2** being a good example for people to follow
• *She was a model pupil.*

model *verb* (**modelling, modelled**)
1 to model something is to make it out of a material such as clay **2** to model one thing on another is to use the second thing as a pattern for the first • *The building is modelled on an Egyptian temple.* **3** to model, or to model clothes, is to work as an artist's model or a fashion model

modem *noun*
(*in computing*) a piece of equipment that links a computer to a telephone line

a b c d e f g h i j k l m n o p q r s t u v w x y z

moderate *adjective*
(*say* mod-er-at)
a moderate amount or level is not too little and not too much **moderately** *adverb* fairly but not very
moderation *noun* being moderate, not too little and not too much

modern *adjective*
belonging to the present day or recent times

modest *adjective*
1 not thinking or talking too much about how good you are
2 quite small in amount • *Their needs were modest.* **modestly** *adverb* **modesty** *noun* being modest

modify *verb* (**modifies, modifying, modified**) to modify something is to change it slightly **modification** *noun* a slight change in something

module *noun* (*say* mod-yool)
a separate section or part of something larger, such as a spacecraft or building

moist *adjective*
slightly wet

moisten *verb* (*say* moi-sen)
to moisten something is to make it slightly wet

moisture *noun*
moisture is tiny drops of water in the air or on a surface

mole *noun*
1 a small furry animal that digs holes under the ground
2 a small dark spot on the skin

molecule *noun* (*say* mol-i-kewl)
(*in science*) the smallest part into which a substance can be divided without changing its chemical nature; a group of atoms

molehill *noun*
a small pile of earth thrown up by a mole **to make a mountain out of a molehill** is to give something too much importance

mollusc *noun*
an animal with a soft body and usually a hard shell, such as a snail or an oyster

molten *adjective*
molten rock or metal has been made into liquid by great heat • *Molten lava flowed down the side of the volcano.*

moment *noun*
1 a very short period of time
• *Wait a moment.* **2** a particular time
• *At that moment, all the lights went out.* **at the moment** now

momentous *adjective*
(*say* moh-ment-us)
very important

momentum *noun*
(*say* moh-ment-um)
momentum is the force developed by something moving • *The stone gained momentum as it rolled down the hill.*

monarch *noun*
a king, queen, emperor, or empress ruling a country

monarchy *noun* (**monarchies**)
1 monarchy is rule by a monarch
2 a monarchy is a country ruled by a monarch

monastery *noun* (**monasteries**)
(*say* mon-a-ster-i)
a building where monks live and work **monastic** *adjective* to do with monks or monasteries

Monday *noun*
the second day of the week

money *noun*
money is coins and notes used by people to buy things

mongrel *noun* (*say* **mung**-rel)
a dog of mixed breeds

monitor *noun*
1 a device used for checking how something is working **2** a computer or television screen

monitor *verb*
to monitor something or someone is to watch or test them to see how they are working

monk *noun*
a member of a religious community of men

monkey *noun* (**monkeys**)
1 an animal with long arms, hands with thumbs, and a tail **2** a mischievous person, especially a child

monopolize *verb*
to monopolize something is to keep it to yourself without letting other people use it

monopoly *noun* (**monopolies**)
a situation where one person or group is the only one to sell something that people need

monotonous *adjective*
(*say* mon-ot-on-us)
boring because it does not change
• *This is monotonous work.*
monotonously *adverb* **monotony** *noun* when something is boring because it does not change; dullness

monsoon *noun*
a strong wind in and around the Indian Ocean, bringing heavy rain in summer

monster *noun*
a huge frightening creature

monstrous *adjective*
1 like a monster; huge **2** very shocking or cruel • *It was a monstrous crime.* **monstrosity** *noun* a monstrous thing

month *noun*
one of the twelve parts into which a year is divided

monthly *adjective, adverb*
something happens monthly when it happens every month

monument *noun*
a statue, building, or column put up to remind people of some person or event

moo *verb*
to make the sound of a cow

mood *noun*
the way someone feels at a particular time • *She is in a cheerful mood.*

moody *adjective* (**moodier, moodiest**)
1 gloomy or bad-tempered **2** likely to have sudden changes of mood
moodily *adverb* **moodiness** *noun*

moon *noun*
1 the natural satellite which orbits the earth and shines in the sky at night **2** a similar object which orbits another planet

moonlight *noun*
moonlight is the light reflected from the moon **moonlit** *adjective* a moonlit night is one that is lit by the moon

moor[1] *noun*
an area of rough land covered with bracken and bushes

moor[2] *verb*
to moor a boat is to tie it up to the land

moorhen *noun*
a small water bird

moose *noun* (**moose**)
a North American elk

mop *noun*
a piece of soft material on the end of a stick, used for cleaning floors or dishes

mop *verb* (**mopping, mopped**)
to mop something is to clean it with a mop **to mop something up** is to clear away spilt liquid

mope *verb*
to mope is to be miserable and not interested in doing anything

moped *noun* (*say* **moh**-ped)
a kind of small motorcycle with pedals

moral *adjective*
1 to do with people's behaviour and what is right and wrong
2 being or doing good and what is right • *We are expected to lead moral lives.* **morality** *noun* how moral

someone or something is **morally** *adverb*

moral *noun*
a lesson taught by a story or event

morale *noun* (*say* mo-**rahl**)
morale is confidence or courage

morals *plural noun*
standards of behaviour

morbid *adjective*
thinking about gloomy or unpleasant things such as death **morbidly** *adverb*

more *adjective*
greater in number or amount • *We need more money.* • *She is more beautiful.*

more *noun*
a larger number or amount • *I want more.*

more *adverb*
1 to a greater extent • *You must work more.* **2** again • *I'll tell you once more.* **more or less** almost; approximately • *I've more or less finished the work.* • *The repairs cost £100, more or less.*

morning *noun*
the early part of the day before noon or before lunchtime

morphine *noun* (*say* **mor**-feen)
morphine is a drug made from opium, used to relieve pain

morris dance *noun*
a traditional English dance performed by people in costume with ribbons and bells

Morse code *noun*
a code for sending messages by radio, using dots and dashes to represent letters and numbers

morsel *noun*
a small piece of food

mortal *adjective*
1 certain to die • *All men are mortal.* **2** causing death • *He received a mortal wound.* **mortality** *noun* being certain to die **mortally** *adverb* someone who is mortally wounded or ill is certain to die from their wounds or illness

mortar *noun*
1 mortar is a mixture of sand, cement, and water used in building to stick bricks together **2** a mortar is a small cannon

mortgage *noun* (*say* **mor**-gij)
an arrangement to borrow money to buy a house, repaid over many years

mortuary *noun* (**mortuaries**)
a place where dead bodies are kept before they are buried or cremated

mosaic *noun* (*say* moh-**zay**-ik)
a picture or design made from small coloured pieces of glass or stone

mosque *noun* (*say* mosk)
a building where Muslims worship

mosquito *noun* (**mosquitoes**)
(*say* mos-**kee**-toh)
an insect that sucks blood and carries disease

moss *noun*
a plant that grows in damp places and has no flowers
mossy *adjective* covered in moss

mosquito

most *adjective*
greatest in number or amount • *Most people came by bus.*

most *noun*
the greatest number or amount • *They've eaten most of the food.*

most *adverb*
1 more than any other • *I liked this book most.* **2** very; extremely • *It was most amusing.*

mostly *adverb*
mainly

motel *noun* (*say* moh-**tel**)
a hotel for people travelling by road, with parking near the rooms

moth *noun*
an insect rather like a butterfly, that usually flies around at night

mother *noun*
your female parent

mother-in-law *noun*
the mother of your husband or wife

motherly *adjective*
kind or tender like a mother

motion *noun*
a way of moving; movement

motionless *adjective*
not moving; still

motive *noun*
a person's motive is what makes them do something

motor *noun*
a machine that provides power to drive machinery

motorbike *noun*
(*informal*) a motorcycle

motorcycle *noun*
a two-wheeled vehicle with a petrol engine and a saddle for the rider
motorcyclist *noun* someone who rides a motorcycle

motorist *noun*
someone who drives a car

motorway *noun*
a wide road with two or more lanes for fast long-distance traffic

mottled *adjective*
marked with spots or patches of colour

motto *noun* (**mottoes**)
1 a short saying used as a guide for behaviour • *His motto was 'Do your best'.* **2** a short verse or riddle found inside a cracker

mould[1] *noun*
a mould is a container for making liquid things like jelly or plaster form a special shape when they harden

mould[1] *verb*
to mould something is to make it have a particular shape or character

mould[2] *noun*
mould is a furry growth that appears on some damp surfaces or stale food

mouldy *adjective* (**mouldier, mouldiest**)
something is mouldy when it has mould on it

moult *verb* (*say* mohlt)
animals or birds moult when they lose hair or feathers

mound *noun*
a pile of earth or stones; a small hill

mount *verb*
1 to mount a horse or bicycle is to get on it so that you can ride it **2** to mount is to increase in amount • *The excitement was mounting.* **3** to mount a picture or photograph is to put it in a frame or album in order to display it

mount *noun*
1 a mountain, especially in names such as *Mount Everest* **2** something on which a picture or photograph is mounted **3** an animal for someone to ride on

mountain *noun*
1 a very high hill **2** a large amount • *We've got a mountain of work to do.* **mountainous** *adjective* a mountainous place has a lot of mountains

mountaineer *noun*
someone who climbs mountains
mountaineering *noun* the sport of climbing mountains

mourn *verb*
to mourn is to be sad, especially because someone has died
mourner *noun* mourners are the people who go to a funeral, especially the family and friends of the person who has died

a b c d e f g h i j k l m n o p q r s t u v w x y z

mournful *adjective*
sad and sorrowful
mournfully *adverb*

mouse *noun* (**mice**)
1 a small animal with a long tail and a pointed nose **2** a small device that you move around with your hand to control the movements of a cursor on a computer screen

mousse *noun* (*say* mooss)
1 a creamy pudding flavoured with chocolate or fruit **2** a frothy creamy substance that you use to style your hair

moustache *noun*
(*say* mus-**tahsh**)
a strip of hair that a man grows above his upper lip

mouth *noun*
1 the part of the face that opens for eating and speaking **2** the place where a river flows into the sea **3** an opening or outlet

mouthful *noun*
an amount of food you put in your mouth

mouth organ *noun*
a small musical instrument you play by blowing and sucking while passing it along your lips

mouthpiece *noun*
the part of a musical instrument or other device that you put to your mouth

movable *adjective*
able to be moved

move *verb*
1 to move something is to take it from one place to another **2** to move is to go from one place to another **3** to move someone is to affect their feelings • *Their story moved us deeply.*

move *noun*
1 a movement **2** a player's turn in a game **to get a move on** (*informal*) is to hurry up **to be on the move** is to be moving or making progress

movement *noun*
1 movement is moving or being moved **2** a movement is a group of people working together to achieve something **3** a movement is also one of the main parts of a long piece of classical music such as a symphony

movie *noun*
a cinema film

moving *adjective*
making you feel strong emotion, especially sadness or pity

mow *verb* (**mowing, mowed, mown**)
to mow grass is to cut it with a machine **to mow people down** is to knock them down and kill them
mower *noun* a machine for mowing grass

MP
short for *Member of Parliament*

m.p.h.
short for *miles per hour*

Mr *noun* (*say* **mis**-ter)
a title you put before a man's name

Mrs *noun* (*say* **mis**-iz)
a title you put before a married woman's name

Ms *noun* (*say* miz)
a title you put before a woman's name, whether or not she is married

much *adjective*
existing in a large amount • *There is much work to do.*

much *noun*
a large amount of something
• *£5 is not very much.*

much *adverb*
greatly; considerably • *They came, much to my surprise.*

muck *noun*
1 muck is farmyard manure
2 (*informal*) muck is dirt or filth

muck *verb*
(*informal*) **to muck about** or **muck around** is to behave stupidly or idly **to muck something up** is to do it very badly

mucky *adjective* (**muckier, muckiest**)
dirty or messy

mud *noun*
mud is wet soft earth **muddy** *adjective* covered with mud

muddle *verb*
1 to muddle things is to mix them up **2** to muddle someone is to confuse them

muddle *noun*
a confusion or mess
• *I've got these papers in a bit of a muddle.*

mudguard *noun*
a curved cover fixed over a bicycle wheel to stop mud and water being thrown up on to the rider

muesli *noun*
(*say* **mooz**-li)
muesli is a breakfast food made of cereals, nuts, and dried fruit

muffle *verb*
1 to muffle something is to cover or wrap it to protect it or keep it warm **2** to muffle a sound is to make it quieter by covering the place that it is coming from

mug *noun*
a large cup, usually used without a saucer

mug *verb* (**mugging, mugged**)
to mug someone is to attack and rob them in the street **mugger** *noun* a person who attacks and robs someone in the street

muggy *adjective* (**muggier, muggiest**)
a muggy day is unpleasantly warm and damp

mule *noun*
an animal that is the offspring of a male donkey and a female horse

multiple *adjective*
having many parts

multiple *noun*
a number that can be divided exactly by another number
• *30 and 50 are multiples of 10.*

multiply *verb* (**multiplies, multiplying, multiplied**)
1 to multiply a number is to add it to itself a certain number of times • *Five multiplied by four equals twenty (5 x 4 = 20).* **2** to multiply is to increase or become many • *His doubts started to multiply.* **multiplication** *noun* multiplication is when you multiply numbers

multiracial *adjective*
(*say* mul-ti-**ray**-shal)
a multiracial area has people living there of many different races

multitude *noun*
a very large number of people or things

mum *noun*
(*informal*) mother

mumble *verb*
to mumble is to speak softly and unclearly

mummy *noun* (**mummies**)
in ancient Egypt, a dead body wrapped in cloth and treated with oils for burial

mummy

mumps *noun*
mumps is an infectious disease that makes your neck swell painfully

munch *verb*
to munch food is to chew it noisily

mural *noun*
a picture painted on a wall

murder *verb*
to murder someone is to kill them deliberately **murderer** *noun* someone who commits murder

murder *noun*
murder is the deliberate killing of someone

murky *adjective* (**murkier, murkiest**)
dark and gloomy

murmur *noun*
a low or soft continuous sound, especially of people speaking

murmur *verb*
to murmur is to speak softly with a low continuous sound

muscle *noun*
a bundle of fibres that can stretch or tighten to make a part of your body move

muscular *adjective*
having strong muscles

museum *noun*
a place where interesting old or valuable objects are displayed for people to see

mushroom *noun*
a fungus with a dome-shaped top, especially the kind that you can eat

music *noun*
1 music is pleasant or interesting sounds made by instruments or by the voice **2** music is also a system of printed or written symbols for making this kind of sound

musical *adjective*
1 to do with music **2** good at music or interested in it **musically** *adverb*

musical *noun*
a play or film with music and songs

musician *noun*
someone who plays a musical instrument, especially for a living

musket *noun*
an old type of rifle

Muslim *noun* (*say* **muuz**-lim)
someone who follows religious teachings of Muhammad, as set out in the Koran

muslin *noun*
fine cotton cloth

mussel *noun*
a black shellfish, often found sticking to rocks

must *verb*
a word used with another verb to show **1** that someone has to do something • *I must go home soon.* **2** that something is certain • *You must be joking!*

mustard *noun*
mustard is a yellow paste or powder used to give food a hot taste

muster *verb*
to muster something is to assemble or gather it together • *He put all the enthusiasm he could muster into his voice.*

musty *adjective* (**mustier, mustiest**)
smelling or tasting mouldy or stale **mustiness** *noun*

mute *adjective*
not speaking or able to speak **mutely** *adverb* without speaking

mutilate *verb*
to mutilate something is to damage it by breaking or cutting off part of it **mutilation** *noun* when someone damages something by breaking or cutting off part of it

mutiny *noun* (**mutinies**)
(*say* **mew**-tin-i)
a rebellion by sailors or soldiers against their officers **mutinous** *adjective* rebellious; taking part in a mutiny

mutiny *verb* (**mutinies, mutinying, mutinied**)
(*say* **mew**-tin-i)
to mutiny is to take part in a mutiny

mutter *verb*
to mutter is to speak in a low quiet voice that is difficult to understand

mutton *noun*
mutton is meat from an adult sheep

mutual *adjective*
(*say* **mew**-tew-al)
given or done to each other • *They have mutual respect for one another.* **mutually** *adverb* equally to two or more people • *Let's arrange a mutually convenient time to meet.*

muzzle *noun*
1 an animal's nose and mouth **2** a cover put over an animal's nose and mouth so that it cannot bite **3** the open end of a gun

muzzle *verb*
to muzzle an animal is to put a muzzle on it

my *determiner*
belonging to me • *This is my book.*

myself *pronoun*
me and nobody else, used to refer back to the person who is speaking • *I have hurt myself.* **by myself** on my own; alone • *I did the work all by myself.*

mysterious *adjective*
full of mystery; strange and puzzling **mysteriously** *adverb*

mystery *noun* (**mysteries**)
something strange or puzzling • *Exactly why the ship sank is a mystery.*

mystify *verb* (**mystifies, mystifying, mystified**)
to mystify someone is to puzzle them very much **mystification** *noun* mystification is being mystified

myth *noun*
1 an old story about gods and heroes in ancient times **2** an untrue story or belief • *It is a myth that carrots make you see better.*

mythical *adjective*
imaginary; only found in myths

mythology *noun*
mythology is a collection of myths or the study of myths **mythological** *adjective* mythological creatures or characters are found in myths

nab *verb* (**nabbing, nabbed**)
(*informal*) to nab someone is to catch or grab them

nag *verb* (**nagging, nagged**)
to nag someone is to keep criticizing them or complaining to them

nail *noun*
1 the hard covering on the end of one of your fingers or toes **2** a small, sharp piece of metal used to fix pieces of wood together

nail *verb*
to nail something is to fasten it with a nail or nails

naked *adjective* (*say* **nay**-kid)
without any clothes or coverings on **to look at something with the naked eye** is to look at it with your eyes without the help of a telescope or microscope **nakedness** *noun*

name *noun*
what you call a person or thing

name *verb*
1 to name someone or something is to give them a name **2** to name someone or something is to say what

they are called • *Can you name these plants?*

nameless adjective
1 not having a name **2** not named or identified • *The culprit shall be nameless.*

namely adverb
that is to say • *I will invite two friends, namely Vicky and Tom.*

nanny noun (**nannies**)
1 a woman whose job is to look after small children **2** (*informal*) a grandmother

nap noun
a short sleep

napkin noun
a piece of cloth or paper to keep your clothes clean or wipe your lips at meals

nappy noun (**nappies**)
a piece of cloth or a paper pad put round a baby's bottom

narrate verb
to narrate a story or experiences is to tell them to someone • *She narrated her adventures in South America.* **narration** noun telling a story

narrative noun
a story or account that someone tells

narrator noun
the person who is telling a story

narrow adjective
1 not wide **2** with only a small margin of error or safety • *We all had a narrow escape.* **narrowly** adverb only just • *She narrowly escaped injury.*

narrow-minded adjective
not liking or understanding other people's ideas or beliefs

nasal adjective
to do with the nose

nasty adjective (**nastier, nastiest**)
not pleasant; unkind **nastily** adverb **nastiness** noun

nation noun
1 a large number of people who have the same history, language, and customs, and live in the same part of the world • *The Czechs are a very musical nation.* **2** a country and the people who live there • *Athletes from 16 nations took part in the tournament.*

national adjective
belonging to a nation or country **nationally** adverb over the whole of a country

nationality noun (**nationalities**)
the nation someone belongs to • *What is her nationality?*

nationwide adjective, adverb
over the whole of a country

native noun
a person born in a particular place • *He is a native of Sweden.*

native adjective
of the country where you were born • *English is my native language.*

Native American noun
one of the original inhabitants of North or South America

Nativity noun (*say* na-**tiv**-i-ti)
the Nativity is the birth of Jesus Christ

natural adjective
1 made or done by nature, not by people or machines **2** normal; not surprising • *It was only natural that she was nervous.* **3** belonging to someone from birth • *He has plenty of natural ability.* **4** in music, not sharp or flat

natural noun
1 a natural note in music; a sign (♮) that shows a note is natural **2** someone who is naturally good at something • *She's a natural at juggling.*

natural history noun
natural history is the study of plants and animals

naturalist noun
someone who studies natural history

naturally adverb
1 in a natural way • *The gas is produced naturally.* **2** as you would expect • *Naturally I will pay your train fare.*

nature noun
1 nature is everything in the world that was not made by people, such as plants, animals, mountains, and rivers **2** a person's or thing's nature is the qualities or characteristics they have • *She has a loving nature.* **3** a nature is a kind or sort of thing • *He likes things of that nature.*

nature reserve noun
an area of land set aside to keep wild life

naughty adjective (**naughtier, naughtiest**)
not behaving as you should; disobedient or rude **naughtily** adverb **naughtiness** noun

nausea noun
nausea is a feeling of sickness or disgust **nauseous** adjective feeling sick

nautical adjective
to do with ships or sailors

naval adjective
to do with a navy

nave noun
the main central part of a church

navel noun
the small hollow at the front of your stomach, where the umbilical cord was attached

navigate verb
to navigate is to make sure that an aircraft, ship, or vehicle is going in the right direction **navigation** noun making sure that an aircraft, ship, or vehicle is going in the right direction **navigator** noun a person who navigates

navy noun (**navies**)
1 a fleet of ships and the people trained to use them **2** dark blue

near adverb, adjective
not far away **near by** at a place not far away • *They live near by.*

near preposition
not far away from something • *She lives near the town.*

near verb
to near a place is to come close to it • *The ships were nearing the harbour.*

nearby adjective
near; not far away • *We live in a nearby town.*

nearly adverb
almost • *It was nearly midnight.* **not nearly** not at all • *There is not nearly enough food.*

neat adjective
1 tidy and carefully arranged **2** skilfully done • *That was a neat goal.* **3** without water added • *They were drinking neat orange juice.* **neatly** adverb **neatness** noun

necessarily adverb
for certain; definitely • *It won't necessarily cost you a lot.*

necessary adjective
needed very much; essential

necessity noun (**necessities**)
1 necessity is need • *There is no necessity for you to come too.* **2** a necessity is something needed • *We have brought all the necessities for a picnic.*

neck noun
1 the part of the body that joins the head to the shoulders **2** a narrow part of something, especially of a bottle **to be neck and neck** is to be almost exactly together in a race or contest

neckerchief noun
a square of cloth worn round the neck, for example by Scouts and Cubs

necklace *noun*
a piece of jewellery you wear round your neck

nectar *noun*
nectar is a sweet liquid collected by bees from flowers

nectarine *noun*
a kind of peach with a smooth skin

need *verb*
1 to need something is to be without it when you should have it **2** to need to do something is to have to do it • *I needed to get a haircut.*

need *noun*
1 a need is something that you need **2** need is a situation in which something is necessary • *There's no need to shout.* **to be in need** is to need money or help **needless** *adjective* unnecessary

needle *noun*
1 a very thin pointed piece of metal used for sewing **2** something long, thin, and sharp, such as a knitting needle or a pine needle **3** the pointer of a meter or compass

needlework *noun*
needlework is sewing or embroidery

needy *adjective* (**needier, neediest**)
needy people are very poor and don't have what they need to live properly

negative *adjective*
1 a negative statement or answer is one that says 'no' **2** not definite or helpful **3** a negative number is one that is less than nought **4** a negative electric charge is one that carries electrons **negatively** *adverb*

negative *noun*
1 something that means 'no' **2** a photograph or film with the dark parts light and the light parts dark, from which prints are made

neglect *verb*
1 to neglect something or someone is to fail to look after them or deal with them **2** to neglect to do something is to fail to do it

neglect *noun*
neglect is failing to look after someone or do something

negotiate *verb*
(*say* nig-**oh**-shi-ayt)
1 to negotiate is to try to reach an agreement about something by discussing it **2** to negotiate an obstacle or difficulty is to get past it or over it **negotiation** *noun* negotiations are discussions people have to try to reach an agreement about something **negotiator** *noun* one of the people involved in negotiations

neigh *verb*
to make a high-pitched cry like a horse

neigh *noun*
the sound of a horse neighing

neighbour *noun*
someone who lives next door or near to you **neighbouring** *adjective* the neighbouring house or family is the one next door

neighbourhood *noun*
the area you live in

neighbourly *adjective*
someone is neighbourly when they are friendly and helpful to people who live near them

neither *determiner, pronoun*
(*say* **ny**-ther or *say* **nee**-ther)
not either • *Neither light was working.* • *Neither of them likes cabbage.*

neither *conjunction*
neither ... nor ... not one thing and not the other • *I neither know nor care.*

neon *noun* (*say* **nee**-on)
neon is a gas that glows when electricity passes through it, used in street lighting and signs

nephew *noun*
the son of a person's brother or sister

nerve *noun*
1 a nerve is one of the fibres inside your body that carry messages to and from your brain, so that parts of your body can feel and move **2** nerve is courage and calmness in a dangerous situation • *Don't lose your nerve.* **3** (*informal*) nerve is cheek or rudeness • *He had the nerve to ask for more.* **to get on someone's nerves** is to irritate them **nerves** nervousness • *I always suffer from nerves before an exam.*

nervous *adjective*
1 easily upset or agitated; timid **2** to do with the nerves **nervously** *adverb* in a way that shows you are nervous • *He smiled nervously.* **nervousness** *noun*

nest *noun*
1 the place where a bird lays its eggs and feeds its young **2** a warm place where some small animals live

nest *verb*
birds or animals nest when they make or have a nest • *Gulls were nesting on the cliffs.*

nestle *verb*
to nestle is to curl up comfortably

net *noun*
1 net is material made of pieces of thread, cord, or wire joined together in a criss-cross pattern with holes between **2** a net is a piece of this material • *a fishing net* **3** the net is the Internet

netball *noun*
netball is a game in which two teams try to throw a ball through a high net hanging from a ring

nettle *noun*
a wild plant with leaves that sting when you touch them

network *noun*
1 a criss-cross arrangement of lines **2** a system with many connections or parts, such as a railway or broadcasting or computer system

neuter *adjective* (*say* **new**-ter)
1 neither male nor female **2** in some languages, belonging to the class of words that are neither masculine nor feminine

neuter *verb* (*say* **new**-ter)
to neuter an animal is to remove its sexual organs so that it cannot breed

neutral *adjective* (*say* **new**-tral)
1 not supporting either side in a war or quarrel **2** not distinct or distinctive • *The room was painted in neutral colours.* **3** a neutral gear is one that is not connected to the driving parts of an engine **neutrality** *noun* neutrality is not supporting either side in a war or quarrel

neutralize *verb*
to neutralize something is to take away its use or effect

neutron *noun*
a particle of matter with no electric charge

never *adverb*
at no time; not ever; not at all

nevertheless *conjunction, adverb*
in spite of this; although that is a fact

new *adjective*
1 not existing before; just bought, made, or received • *Do you like my new shoes?* **2** different or unfamiliar • *They've moved to a new area.* **newly** *adverb* recently **newness** *noun*

newcomer *noun*
someone who has recently arrived in a place

new moon *noun*
the moon at the beginning of its cycle, when it appears as a thin crescent

a b c d e f g h i j k l m n o p q r s t u v w x y z

news *noun*
1 news is new information about people or recent events • *I've got some good news.*
2 news is also a radio or television report about important events

newsagent *noun*
a shopkeeper who sells newspapers and magazines

newspaper *noun*
1 a newspaper is a daily or weekly publication of large sheets of printed paper folded together, containing news reports and articles
2 newspaper is the paper these are printed on • *Wrap it in newspaper.*

newt *noun*
a small animal rather like a lizard, that lives near or in water

next *adjective*
the nearest; following immediately after

next *adverb*
1 in the nearest place 2 at the nearest time • *What comes next?*

nib *noun*
the pointed metal part at the end of a pen

nibble *verb*
to nibble something is to take small or gentle bites at it

nice *adjective*
pleasant or kind **nicely** *adverb* in a nice way • *Ask me nicely and I might say yes.*
niceness *noun*

nick *noun*
a small cut or notch **in the nick of time** only just in time

nick *verb*
1 to nick something is to make a small cut in it 2 (*slang*) to nick something is to steal it

nickel *noun*
a silvery-white metal

nickname *noun*
an informal name given to someone instead of their real name

nicotine *noun* (*say* **nik**-o-teen)
nicotine is a poisonous substance found in tobacco

niece *noun*
the daughter of a person's brother or sister

night *noun*
the time when it is dark, between sunset and sunrise

nightfall *noun*
nightfall is the time when it becomes dark just after sunset

nightingale *noun*
a small brown bird that sings sweetly

nightly *adjective*
happening every night

nightmare *noun*
1 a frightening or unpleasant dream 2 a terrifying experience
nightmarish *adjective* terrifying

nil *noun*
nothing • *We lost three-nil.*

nimble *adjective*
moving quickly or easily **nimbly** *adverb*

nine *noun*
the number 9

nineteen *noun*
the number 19
nineteenth *adjective, noun* 19th

ninety *noun*
the number 90
ninetieth *adjective, noun* 90th

ninth *adjective, noun*
the next after the eighth **ninthly** *adverb* in the ninth place; as the ninth one

nip *verb* (**nipping, nipped**)
1 to nip someone is to pinch or bite them sharply 2 (*informal*) to nip somewhere is to go quickly there • *I'll just nip into the supermarket.*

nip *noun*
1 a quick pinch or bite 2 a cold feeling • *There's a nip in the air.*

nipple *noun*
one of the two small parts that stick out at the front of a person's chest

nit *noun*
a louse or its egg

nitrogen *noun* (*say* **ny**-tro-jen)
nitrogen is a gas that makes up about four-fifths of the air

no *exclamation*
a word you use to refuse something or say that you don't agree

no *determiner, adverb*
not any • *We have no money.*
• *She is no better.*

nobility *noun*
1 the nobility is the nobles or the aristocracy 2 nobility is being noble

noble *adjective*
1 coming from the highest class in society; aristocratic 2 having a good and generous nature • *He is a noble king.* 3 grand or impressive • *It was a noble building.* **nobly** *adverb*

noble *noun*
a person who comes from a noble family, for example a duke or an earl

nobleman or **noblewoman**
noun (**noblemen** or **noblewomen**)
a man or woman from the highest class in society

nobody *pronoun*
no person; not anyone
• *Nobody knows.*

nocturnal *adjective*
(*say* nok-**ter**-nal)
happening or active at night
• *Badgers are nocturnal animals.*

nod *verb* (**nodding, nodded**)
to nod, or nod your head, is to move your head up and down as a way of agreeing with someone or as a greeting

noise *noun*
a loud sound, especially one that is unpleasant or unwanted

noisy *adjective*
making a lot of noise **noisily** *adverb*

nomad *noun* (*say* **noh**-mad)
a member of a tribe that moves from place to place **nomadic** *adjective* nomadic people move around from place to place

no man's land *noun*
the land between two armies in a war

nominate *verb*
to nominate someone is to suggest that they should be a candidate in an election or should be given a job or award **nomination** *noun* when someone is nominated for a job or award

none *pronoun*
not any; not one • *None of us went.*

none *adverb*
not at all • *He's none too pleased.*

nonetheless *conjunction, adverb*
in spite of this; nevertheless

non-existent *adjective*
not existing

non-fiction *noun*
writings that are not fiction; books about real things and true events

nonsense *noun*
1 nonsense is words that do not mean anything or make any sense 2 nonsense is also absurd or silly ideas or behaviour
nonsensical *adjective* not making any sense

non-stop *adverb, adjective*
1 not stopping • *They talked non-stop all morning.*
2 not stopping until the end of a journey • *There's a non-stop train to London.*

noodles *plural noun*
pasta made in narrow strips, used in soups and stir-fries

noon *noun*
twelve o'clock midday

noodles

no one *pronoun*
no person; not anyone

noose *noun*
a loop in a rope that gets smaller when the rope is pulled

nor *conjunction*
and not • *She cannot do it; nor can I.*

normal *adjective*
1 usual or ordinary • *It's normal to want a holiday.* **2** natural and healthy; not suffering from an illness **normality** *noun* a situation where things are normal

normally *adverb*
1 usually • *The journey normally takes an hour.* **2** in the usual way • *Just breathe normally.*

north *noun*
1 north is the direction to the left of a person facing east **2** north is also the part of a country or city that is in this direction
north *adjective, adverb*
1 towards the north or in the north **2** coming from the north • *A north wind was blowing.*

north-east *noun, adjective, adverb*
midway between north and east

northern *adjective*
from or to do with the north

northerner *noun*
someone who lives in the north of a country

northward or **northwards**
adjective, adverb
towards the north

north-west *noun, adjective, adverb*
midway between north and west

nose *noun*
1 the part of your face that you use for breathing and smelling **2** the front part of something, especially a vehicle or aircraft
nose *verb*
to nose forward or through is to make progress cautiously • *The ship nosed through the ice.*

nostalgia *noun* (*say* nos-**tal**-ja)
you feel nostalgia when you fondly remember something that made you happy in the past **nostalgic** *adjective* making you long for something in the past

nostril *noun*
each of the two openings in your nose

nosy *adjective*
(**nosier, nosiest**)
(*informal*) always wanting to know other people's business
nosiness *noun*

not *adverb*
a word you use to change the meaning of something to its opposite

notable *adjective*
remarkable or famous **notably** *adverb* especially or remarkably

notch *noun*
a small V-shaped cut or mark

note *noun*
1 something you write down as a reminder or help **2** a short letter **3** a single sound in music **4** a sound or tone that indicates something • *There was a note of anger in his voice.* **5** a piece of paper money • *Have you got a five-pound note?* **to take note of something** is to listen to it and understand it
note *verb*
to note something is to pay attention to it, or to write it down as a reminder or help

notebook *noun*
a book in which you write things down

notepaper *noun*
notepaper is paper for writing letters

nothing *noun*
nothing is not anything

notice *noun*
1 a notice is something written or printed and displayed for people to see **2** to take notice of something is to pay attention to it • *It escaped my notice.* **3** a warning that something is going to happen
notice *verb*
to notice something is to see it or become aware of it

noticeable *adjective*
easy to see or notice **noticeably** *adverb*

noticeboard *noun*
a board on which notices can be displayed

notion *noun*
an idea, especially one that is vague or uncertain • *The notion that the earth is flat was disproved long ago.*

notorious *adjective*
(*say* noh-**tor**-i-us)
well-known for doing something bad • *He was a notorious criminal.*
notoriety *noun* being well-known for doing something bad
notoriously *adverb*

nougat *noun* (*say* **noo**-gah)
nougat is a chewy sweet made from nuts and sugar or honey

nought *noun* (*say* nawt)
the figure 0

noun *noun*
a word that names a person, place, or thing

nourish *verb*
to nourish someone is to give them enough good food to keep them alive and well

nourishment *noun*
nourishment is the food someone needs to keep them alive and well

novel *noun*
a long story that fills a whole book
novel *adjective*
unusual • *What a novel idea.*

novelist *noun* (*say* **nov**-el-ist)
someone who writes novels

novelty *noun* (**novelties**)
1 novelty is being new or unusual • *The novelty of living in a cave soon wore off.* **2** a novelty is something new and unusual **3** a novelty is also a cheap toy or ornament

November *noun*
the eleventh month of the year

novice *noun*
a beginner

now *adverb*
1 at this time • *I am now living in Glasgow.* **2** without any delay • *Do it now!* **for now** until a later time • *Goodbye for now.* **now and again** or **now and then** occasionally; sometimes
now *conjunction*
since or as • *I do remember, now you mention it.*
now *noun*
this moment • *They should be home by now.*

nowadays *adverb*
at the present time

nowhere *adverb*
not anywhere; in no place or to no place

nozzle *noun*
the part at the end of a hose or pipe from which something flows

nuclear *adjective* (*say* **new**-kli-er)
1 to do with a nucleus, especially of an atom **2** using the energy that is created by the splitting of atoms • *nuclear weapons*

a b c d e f g h i j k l m n o p q r s t u v w x y z

nucleus noun (**nuclei**)
(say **new**-kli-us)
1 the central part of an atom or cell
2 the part in the centre of something, round which other things are grouped • *The queen bee is the nucleus of the hive.*

nude adjective
not wearing any clothes

nude noun
a nude person, especially in a work of art **nudity** noun nudity is not wearing any clothes

nudge verb
to nudge someone is to touch or push them with your elbow

nugget noun
a rough lump of gold from the ground

nuisance noun
an annoying person or thing

numb adjective
part of your body is numb when you can't feel anything in it **numbness** noun

number noun
1 a symbol or word that tells you how many of something there are **2** a quantity of people or things • *Do you know the number of bones in your body?* **3** a person's number is their telephone number **4** a song or piece of music

number verb
1 to number things is to count them or mark them with numbers • *Please number the pages of your essay.* **2** to number a certain amount is to reach it • *The crowd numbered 10,000.*

numeracy noun
numeracy is the ability to understand and work with numbers

numeral noun
a symbol or figure that stands for a number

numerical adjective
to do with numbers

numerous adjective
many • *There are numerous kinds of cat.*

nun noun
a member of a religious community of women

nurse noun
a person trained to look after people who are ill or injured

nurse verb
to nurse someone is to look after them when they are ill or injured

nursery noun (**nurseries**)
1 a place where young children are looked after or play **2** a place where young plants are grown and usually offered for sale

nursery rhyme noun
a simple poem or song that young children like

nursery school noun
a school for very young children

nurture verb
to nurture children is to look after them and educate them

nut noun
1 a fruit with a hard shell **2** the eatable part of this kind of fruit **3** a hollow piece of metal for screwing on to a bolt **nutty** adjective tasting of nuts or full of nuts

nutcrackers plural noun
pincers for cracking the shells of nuts

nutmeg noun
a hard seed that is made into a powder and used as a spice

nutrition noun
(say new-**trish**-on)
nutrition is the food someone needs to keep them alive and well

nutcrackers

nutritious adjective
(say new- **trish**-us)
nutritious food helps you to grow and keep well • *They ate a nutritious meal.*

nuzzle verb
to nuzzle someone is to rub gently against them with the nose, in the way that some animals do • *The kitten nuzzled her leg.*

nylon noun
nylon is a lightweight synthetic cloth or fibre

nymph noun
in myths, a young goddess who lives in trees or rivers or the sea

oak noun
a large tree that produces seeds called acorns

oar noun
a pole with a flat blade at one end, used for rowing a boat

oasis noun (say oh-**ay**-sis)
a fertile place with water and trees in a desert

oath noun
1 a solemn promise **2** a swear word

oats plural noun
a cereal used to make food for humans and animals

obedient adjective
doing what someone tells you to do; willing to obey **obedience** noun obedience is doing what you are told **obediently** adverb

obey verb
1 to obey someone is to do what they tell you **2** to obey a rule or law is to do what it says

object noun (say **ob**-jikt)
1 something that can be seen or touched **2** the purpose of something **3** (in grammar) the word naming the person or thing that the action of the verb affects, for example *him* in the sentence *I chased him.*

object verb (say ob-**jekt**)
to object to something or someone is to say that you do not like them or do not agree with them

objection noun
1 objection is objecting to something **2** an objection is a reason for objecting • *I have three objections to your plan.*

objective noun
what you are trying to reach or do; an aim

obligation noun
a duty

obligatory adjective
something is obligatory when you must do it because of a rule or law • *Games are obligatory.*

oblige verb
1 to oblige someone to do something is to force them to do it **2** to oblige someone is to help and please them • *Will you oblige me by closing the window?* **to be obliged to someone** is to be grateful to them for helping you

oblong noun ▄▄
a four-sided shape with right angles that is longer than it is wide
oblong adjective
having the shape of an oblong

obnoxious adjective
really horrible

oboe noun (say **oh**-boh)
a high-pitched woodwind instrument

oboist noun
a person who plays the oboe

obscure adjective
1 difficult to see or understand; very unclear **2** not well-known
obscurely adverb **obscurity** noun obscurity is being not well-known

observant adjective
quick at noticing things
observantly adverb

observation noun
1 observation is noticing or watching something carefully **2** an observation is a comment or remark • He made a few observations about the weather.

observatory noun (**observatories**) (say ob-**zerv**-a-ter-i)
a building equipped with telescopes for looking at the stars or weather

observe verb
1 to observe someone or something is to watch them carefully **2** to observe something is to notice it **3** to observe a law or custom is to obey it or keep it **4** to observe a fact is to state it • She observed that she did not like ice in her drinks.
observer noun someone who watches something

obsessed adjective
always thinking about something • He is obsessed with his work.
obsession noun something that you think about too much

obsolete adjective
not used any more; out of date

obstacle noun
something that gets in your way or makes it difficult for you to do something

obstinate adjective
not willing to change your ideas or ways, even though they may be wrong **obstinacy** noun obstinacy is being obstinate **obstinately** adverb

obstruct verb
to obstruct someone or something is to stop them from getting past, or to hinder them **obstruction** noun something causing a blockage

obtain verb
to obtain something is to get it or be given it **obtainable** adjective able to be bought or got

obtuse adjective
1 slow to understand; stupid **2** an obtuse angle is an angle of between 90 and 180 degrees **obtusely** adverb

obvious adjective
easy to see or understand

obviously adverb
it's obvious that; clearly • Obviously we don't want to lose.

occasion noun
1 the time when something happens • On this occasion we will not take any action. **2** a special event • The wedding was a marvellous occasion.

occasional adjective
happening from time to time, but not often and not regularly
occasionally adverb something happens occasionally when it happens from time to time

occupation noun
1 a person's occupation is their job or profession **2** the occupation of a country or territory is when an army captures it and stays there

occupy verb (**occupies, occupying, occupied**)
1 to occupy a place or building is to live in it **2** to occupy a space or position is to fill it **3** in a war, to occupy territory is to capture it and keep an army in it **4** to occupy someone is to keep them busy or interested

occur verb (**occurring, occurred**)
1 an event occurs when it happens or takes place • An earthquake occurred on the island in 1953. **2** something occurs when it exists or is found somewhere • These plants occur in ponds. **3** something occurs to you when it suddenly comes into your mind • Just then an idea occurred to me.

occurrence noun
something that happens or exists

ocean noun
1 the ocean is the area of salt water surrounding the land of the earth **2** an ocean is a large part of this water, such as the Pacific Ocean

o'clock adverb
used with numbers to show an exact hour • Lunch is at one o'clock.

octagon noun ●
a flat shape with eight sides
octagonal adjective having eight sides

octave noun
1 the interval between one musical note and the next note of the same name above or below it **2** these two notes played together

October noun
the tenth month of the year

octopus noun
a sea creature with eight arms (called tentacles)

WORD ORIGIN

The word **octopus** comes from a Greek word oktopous, which in turn comes from the words okto meaning 'eight' and pous meaning 'foot'.

odd adjective
1 strange or unusual **2** an odd number is one that cannot be divided by 2, such as 5 or 31 **3** left over or spare • I've got an odd sock. **4** of various kinds; occasional • He's doing odd jobs.
oddity noun something that is odd or strange **oddly** adverb
oddness noun

odds plural noun
1 the chances that something will happen **2** the proportion of money that you will win if a bet is successful • When the odds are 10 to 1, you will win £10 if you bet £1. **odds and ends** small things of various kinds

odour noun
a smell, usually an unpleasant one

of preposition
1 belonging to • She is the mother of the child. **2** coming from • He is a native of Italy. **3** about; concerning • Is there any news of your father? **4** from; out of • The house is built of stone.

off adverb
1 not on; away • His hat blew off. **2** not working or happening • The heating is off. • The match is off because of snow. **3** beginning to go bad • I think the milk is off.

off preposition
1 not on; away or down from • He fell off his chair. **2** not taking or wanting • She is off her food. **3** taken away from • There is £5 off the normal price.

offence noun
1 an offence is a crime or something illegal • When was the offence committed? **2** offence is a feeling of annoyance or hurt **to cause offence** is to hurt someone's feelings **to take offence** is to be upset by what someone has said or done

offend verb
1 to offend someone is to hurt their feelings or be unpleasant to them **2** to offend is to break a law or do something wrong **offender** noun someone who breaks a law or does something wrong

offensive adjective
1 insulting or causing offence **2** used for attacking • He was arrested for carrying an offensive weapon. **offensively** adverb

offer verb
1 to offer something is to hold it out so that someone can take it if they want it **2** to offer to do something is to say that you are willing to do it **3** to offer a sum of money is to say

how much you are willing to pay for something

offer *noun*
1 the action of offering something • *Thank you for your offer of help.*
2 an amount of money that you are willing to pay for something

offhand *adjective*
1 said without much thought
2 rude or abrupt

office *noun*
1 a room or building where people work, often at desks 2 a place where you can go for tickets, information, or some other purpose • *a lost property office* 3 an important job or position • *He was honoured to hold the office of President.*

officer *noun*
1 someone who is in charge of other people, especially in the armed forces 2 a policeman or policewoman

official *adjective*
1 done or said by someone with authority 2 connected with the job of someone in a position of authority • *The prime minister will make an official visit to Australia next month.*
officially *adverb*
official *noun*
someone who has power or makes decisions as part of their job

off-licence *noun*
a shop with a licence to sell alcoholic drinks for people to take away

offside *adjective*
(*in sport*) in a position which is not allowed by the rules

offspring *noun*
a child or young animal

often *adverb*
many times; in many cases

ogre *noun*
1 a cruel giant in stories
2 a frightening person

oil *noun*
1 an oil is a thick slippery liquid that does not mix with water 2 oil is a thick sticky liquid that is found underground and used to make petrol and other fuels and to keep machinery working smoothly
oil *verb*
to oil something is to put oil on it to make it work smoothly

oil painting *noun*
a painting done using paints made with oil

oil rig *noun*
a structure set up to support the equipment for drilling for oil

oil well *noun*
a hole drilled in the ground or under the sea to get oil

oily *adjective*
like oil or covered in oil

ointment *noun*
a cream that you put on sore skin and cuts

OK *adverb, adjective*
(*informal*) all right

old *adjective*
1 not new; born or made a long time ago 2 of a particular age • *I'm ten years old.* 3 former or original • *I liked my old school better than the one I go to now.*

old age *noun*
old age is the time when a person is old

old-fashioned *adjective*
of a kind that was usual a long time ago; out of date

olive *noun*
1 an evergreen tree with a small bitter fruit 2 the black or green fruit of this tree, used for eating and to make olive oil

olives

omelette *noun* (*say* **om**-lit)
eggs beaten together and fried, often with a filling or flavouring

omen *noun*
an event that some people see as a sign that something is going to happen

ominous *adjective*
suggesting that trouble is coming • *There was an ominous rumble from inside the tunnel.* **ominously** *adverb*

omission *noun*
something left out or not done

omit *verb* (**omitting, omitted**)
1 to omit something is to leave it out • *Several names have been omitted from the list.* 2 to omit to do something is to fail to do it • *I omitted to lock the back door.*

omnivorous *adjective*
an omnivorous animal is one that eats plants as well as meat

on *preposition*
1 at or over the top or surface of something • *Sit on the floor.*
2 at the time of • *Come on Monday.*
3 about; concerning • *We went to a talk on snakes.* 4 towards or near • *They advanced on the town.*
on *adverb*
1 so as to be on something • *Put your hat on.* 2 forwards • *Move on.* 3 working; in action • *Is the heater on?*

once *adverb*
1 at one time • *I once lived in Leeds.*
2 one time only• *I've only met him once.*
once *conjunction*
as soon as • *We can get out once I open this door.* **at once** immediately

one *noun*
the smallest whole number, 1
one *pronoun*
a person or thing on their own • *One likes to help.* • *One of my friends is ill.* **one another** each other
one *adjective*
single • *I have one packet left.*

oneself *pronoun*
one's own self; yourself • *One should not always think of oneself.*

one-way *adjective*
a one-way street is one where traffic is only allowed to go in one direction

onion *noun*
a round vegetable with a strong flavour

online *adjective, adverb*
connected to a computer

only *adjective*
being the one person or thing of a kind • *He's the only person we can trust.*
only *adverb*
no more than • *There are only three cakes.*
only *conjunction*
but then; however • *I want to come, only I'm very busy.*

onto *preposition*
to a position on • *They fell onto the floor.*

onward or **onwards** *adverb*
forward or forwards

ooze *verb*
a thick liquid oozes when it flows out slowly, especially through a narrow opening • *Blood oozed from his wound.*

opaque *adjective* (*say* oh-**payk**)
something that is opaque doesn't allow light through and so can't be seen through

open *adjective*
1 allowing people or things to pass through; not shut • *The door is open.* • *The bottles need to be open.* **2** not enclosed • *There were miles of open land.* **3** not folded; spread out • *She greeted us with open arms.* **4** honest; not secret or secretive • *They were quite open about what they had done.* **5** not settled or finished • *That is still an open question.* **in the open air** outdoors; not inside a house or building

open *verb*
1 to open something is to make it open **2** to open is to become open **3** to open is also to start • *The jumble sale opens at 2 o'clock.* **4** a shop opens when it starts business for the day • *What time do you open?*

opener *noun*
a device for opening a bottle or can

opening *noun*
1 a space or gap in something **2** the beginning of something

openly *adverb*
to do something openly is to do it for all to see, not secretly

open-minded *adjective*
ready to listen to other people's ideas and opinions; not having fixed ideas

opera *noun*
a form of drama in which the characters sing all or most of the words, with an orchestra **operatic** *adjective* to do with opera

operate *verb*
1 to operate something is to make it work **2** to operate is to work or be in action **3** to operate on someone is to perform a surgical operation on them

operation *noun*
1 something done to a patient's body by a surgeon to remove or repair a part of it **2** a carefully planned activity **to be in operation** is to be working • *The new rules are now in operation.*

operator *noun*
someone who works something, especially a telephone switchboard or exchange

opinion *noun*
what you think of something; a belief or judgement

opponent *noun*
someone who is against you in a contest, war, or argument

opportunity *noun*
a good time or chance to do something

oppose *verb*
to oppose someone or something is to be against them or disagree with them **to be opposed to something** is to disagree strongly with it • *We are opposed to parking in the town centre.*

opposite *adjective, adverb*
1 on the other side; facing • *She lives on the opposite side of the road to me.* • *I'll sit opposite.* **2** completely different • *They went in opposite directions.*

opposite *noun*
something that is completely different from something else • *'Happy' is the opposite of 'sad'.*

opposition *noun*
opposition is opposing something; resistance **the Opposition** the chief political party opposing the one that has formed the government

oppress *verb*
1 to oppress people is to govern them or treat them cruelly or unjustly **2** to oppress someone is to trouble them with worry or sadness **oppression** *noun* treating people cruelly or unjustly **oppressor** *noun* someone who treats people cruelly or unjustly

oppressive *adjective*
1 harsh and cruel • *He was an oppressive ruler.* **2** hot and tiring • *The weather can be very oppressive in July.*

opt *verb*
to opt for something or to do something is to choose it • *I opted for the cash prize.* • *We opted to go abroad.* **to opt out of something** is to decide not to join in with it

optical *adjective*
to do with sight or the eyes **optically** *adverb* as far as sight or the eyes are concerned

optician *noun* (say op-**tish**-an)
someone who tests your eyesight and makes and sells glasses and contact lenses

optimist *noun*
someone who usually expects things to turn out well **optimism** *noun* the feeling that things will turn out well

optimistic *adjective*
expecting things to turn out well **optimistically** *adverb*

option *noun*
1 one of the things that you can choose • *Your options are to travel by bus or by train.* **2** the right to choose; choice • *You have the option of staying.*

optional *adjective*
something is optional when you can choose whether to do it or not • *You have to study French, but German is optional.*

or *conjunction*
used to show that there is a choice or alternative • *Do you want a cake or a biscuit?*

oral *adjective*
1 spoken, not written **2** to do with the mouth or using your mouth **orally** *adverb* by speaking or using your mouth • *This medicine must not be taken orally.*

orange *noun*
1 a round juicy fruit with thick reddish-yellow peel **2** a reddish-yellow colour

orange *adjective* ●
reddish-yellow

orang-utan *noun*
(say o-**rang**-u-tan)
a large kind of ape found in Borneo and Sumatra

orbit *noun*
the curved path taken by something moving round a planet or other body in space

orbit *verb*
to orbit a planet or other body in space is to move round it • *The satellite orbited the earth.*

orchard *noun*
a piece of ground with fruit trees

orchestra *noun*
a group of musicians playing various instruments together **orchestral** *adjective* orchestral music is written to be played by an orchestra

orchid *noun* (say **or**-kid)
a type of brightly coloured flower

ordeal *noun*
a difficult or unpleasant experience

orchid

order *noun*
1 a command **2** a request for something to be supplied • *The waiter took our order.* **3** the way things are arranged • *The words are in alphabetical order.* **4** obedience or good behaviour • *Can we have some order please?* **5** tidiness or neatness **6** a group of religious monks, priests, or nuns **in order that** or **in order to** for the

purpose of **to be out of order** is to be broken or not working

order *verb*
1 to order someone to do something is to tell them to do it **2** to order something is to ask for it to be supplied to you

orderly *adjective*
1 arranged tidily or well; methodical **2** well-behaved; obedient

ordinary *adjective*
normal or usual; not special
ordinarily *adverb* normally or usually

ore *noun*
rock with metal in it, such as iron ore

organ *noun*
1 a musical instrument from which sounds are produced by air forced through pipes, played by keys and pedals **2** a part of your body which does a particular job, for example the liver which cleans the blood

organic *adjective*
1 organic food is grown or produced without using artificial chemicals **2** made by or found in living things

organism *noun*
a living animal or plant

organist *noun*
someone who plays the organ

organization *noun*
1 an organization is a group of people who work together to do something **2** organization is planning or arranging things such as getting people together to do something

organize *verb*
1 to organize people is to get them together to do something **2** to organize something is to plan or arrange it • *We organized a picnic.* **3** to organize things is to put them in order **organizer** *noun* someone who organizes something

oriental *adjective*
to do with the countries east of the Mediterranean Sea, especially China and Japan

orienteering *noun*
(*say* or-i-en-**teer**-ing)
orienteering is the sport of finding your way across rough country with a map and compass

origin *noun*
the start of something; the point where something began • *a book about the origins of life on earth*

original *adjective*
1 existing from the start; earliest • *They were the original inhabitants.*

2 new; not a copy or an imitation • *It is an original design.* **3** producing new ideas; inventive • *She was an original thinker.* **originality** *noun* originality is being original or inventive **originally** *adverb* in the beginning

originate *verb*
1 to originate something is to create it or develop it **2** to originate is to start in a certain way • *Supermarkets originated in America.* **originator** *noun* someone who originates something

ornament *noun*
an object you wear or display as a decoration
ornamental *adjective*
used to decorate something • *an ornamental fountain*

ornithology *noun*
(*say* or-ni-**thol**-o-ji)
ornithology is the study of birds
ornithological *adjective* to do with birds **ornithologist** *noun* a person who studies birds

orphan *noun*
a child whose parents are dead

orphanage *noun*
a home for orphans

orthodox *adjective*
having beliefs that are correct or generally accepted

ostrich *noun*
a large long-legged bird that can run fast but cannot fly

other
determiner
not the same as this; different • *Play some other tune.* • *Try the other shoe.* **every other day** every second day, for example Monday, Wednesday, and Friday **other than** except • *They have no belongings other than what they are carrying.* **the other day** or **the other week** a few days or weeks ago

ostrich

other *noun*
the other person or thing • *Where are the others?*

otherwise *adverb*
1 if you do not; if things happen differently • *Write it down, otherwise you'll forget it.* **2** in other ways • *It rained a lot but otherwise the holiday was good.* **3** differently • *We could not do otherwise.*

otter *noun*
an animal with thick fur, webbed feet, and a flat tail, that lives near water

otter

ought *verb*
used with other words to show
1 what you should or must do • *You ought to do your music practice.*
2 what is likely to happen • *With all these dark clouds it ought to rain.*

ounce *noun*
a unit of weight equal to $1/16$ of a pound or about 28 grams

our *determiner*
belonging to us • *This is our house.*

ours *pronoun*
belonging to us • *This house is ours.*

ourselves *pronoun*
us and nobody else, used to refer back to the subject of a *verb* • *We have hurt ourselves.* **by ourselves** on our own; alone • *We did the work all by ourselves.*

out *adverb*
1 away from a place or not in it; not at home **2** into the open or outdoors • *Are you going out today?* **3** not burning or working • *The fire has gone out.* **4** loudly • *She cried out.* **5** completely • *They were tired out.* **6** dismissed from a game • *Another batsman is out.*
to be out of something is to have no more of it left **out of date** old-fashioned; not used any more **out of doors** in the

open air **out of the way** remote or distant

outback *noun*
the remote inland areas of Australia

outbreak *noun*
the sudden start of a disease, war, or show of anger

outburst *noun*
the sudden beginning of anger or laughter

outcast *noun*
someone who has been rejected by family, friends, or society

outcome *noun*
the result of what happens or has happened

outcry *noun* (**outcries**)
a strong protest from many people • *There was an outcry over the rise in bus fares.*

outdated *adjective*
out of date

outdoor *adjective*
done or used outside • *You'll need your outdoor clothes.*

outdoors *adverb*
in the open air • *It is cold outdoors.*

outer *adjective*
nearer the outside; external

outer space *noun*
outer space is the universe beyond the earth's atmosphere

outfit *noun*
1 a set of clothes you wear together **2** a set of things you need for doing something

outgrow *verb* (**outgrowing, outgrew, outgrown**)
1 to outgrow something such as clothes or a habit is to grow too big or too old for them **2** to outgrow someone is to grow faster or taller than them

outing *noun*
a trip or short journey you make for pleasure

outlaw *noun*
a robber or bandit who is hiding to avoid being caught and is not protected by the law

outlaw *verb*
to outlaw something is to make it illegal

outlet *noun*
1 a way for something to get out • *The tank has an outlet at the bottom.* **2** a place to sell goods • *We need to find fresh outlets for our products.*

outline *noun*
1 a line round the outside of something; a line showing the shape of a thing **2** a summary

outline *verb*
1 to outline something is to draw a line round it to show its shape **2** to outline a story or account is to summarize or describe it briefly

outlook *noun*
1 a person's outlook is the way that they look at and think about things • *She has an odd outlook on life.*
2 what seems likely to happen in the future • *The outlook is bright.*

outnumber *verb*
to outnumber something else is to be greater in number than it • *The girls outnumber the boys in our team.*

outpatient *noun*
a patient who visits a hospital for treatment but does not stay there overnight

output *noun*
1 the amount produced, especially by a factory or business **2** information produced by a computer

output *verb*
to output information is to get it from a computer

outrage *noun*
1 outrage is the anger you feel when something shocking happens **2** an outrage is something very shocking or cruel

outrage *verb*
to outrage someone is to make them very shocked and angry

outrageous *adjective*
shocking or dreadful

outright *adverb*
1 completely • *We won outright.* **2** all at once; in one go • *They were able to buy their house outright.*

outside *noun*
the outer side or surface of a thing; the part furthest from the middle

outside *adjective*
1 on or coming from the outside **2** slight or remote • *There is an outside chance of snow.*

outside *adverb, preposition*
on or to the outside of something • *Go outside.* • *It's outside the house.*

outsider *noun*
1 someone who is not a member of a particular group of people **2** a horse or person that people think has no chance of winning a race or contest

outskirts *plural noun*
the parts on the outside edge of an area, especially of a town or city

outspoken *adjective*
speaking frankly even though it might offend people

outstanding *adjective*
1 extremely good or distinguished • *She is an outstanding athlete.*
2 not yet dealt with • *What are your outstanding debts?*

outward *adjective*
1 going outwards **2** on the outside

outwardly *adverb*
on the outside; for people to see • *They were outwardly calm.*

outwards *adverb*
towards the outside

outwit *verb* (**outwitting, outwitted**)
to outwit someone is to deceive or defeat them by being more clever

oval *adjective*
shaped like an egg or a number 0

oval *noun* ●
an oval shape

oven *noun*
a closed space, often part of a cooker, in which things are cooked or heated

over *adverb*
1 down or sideways; out and down from the top or edge
• *He fell over.* **2** across to a place
• *We walked over to the house.*
3 so that a different side shows
• *Turn the sheet over.* **4** finished
• *The lesson is over.* **5** left or remaining • *There are a few apples over.* **6** through or thoroughly • *Think it over.* **over and over** repeatedly; many times

over *preposition*
1 above or covering • *There's a light over the door.* • *I'll put a cloth over the table.* **2** across • *They ran over the road.* **3** more than • *The house is over a mile away.* **4** concerning; about • *They quarrelled over money.*
5 during • *We can talk over dinner.*

over *noun*
in cricket, a series of six balls bowled by one person

overall *adjective, adverb*
including everything; total
• *What is the overall cost?*

overalls *plural noun*
clothes that you wear over your other clothes to protect them when you are working

overboard *adverb*
to fall or jump overboard is to go over the side of a boat into the water

overcast *adjective*
covered with cloud • *The sky is grey and overcast.*

overcoat *noun*
a warm outdoor coat

overcome verb (**overcomes, overcoming, overcame, overcome**)
1 to overcome a problem or difficulty is to succeed in dealing with it or controlling it • *He overcame injury to win a gold medal.* **2** to be overcome by something is to become helpless from it • *She was overcome by the fumes.* **3** to overcome someone is to beat them

overdose noun
too large a dose of a drug or medicine

overdue adjective
something is overdue when it is later than it should be • *The train is overdue.*

overflow verb
to overflow is to flow over the edges or limits of something

overgrown adjective
a place is overgrown when it is thickly covered with weeds or unwanted plants

overhaul verb
to overhaul a machine or vehicle is to check it thoroughly and repair it if necessary

overhead adjective, adverb
above your head; in the sky

overhear verb
to overhear something is to hear it accidentally or without the speaker knowing

overlap verb (**overlapping, overlapped**)
one thing overlaps another when it lies across part of it • *The carpet overlapped the fireplace.*

overlook verb
not to notice it **2** to overlook a mistake or offence is not to punish it **3** to overlook a place is to have a view over it
• *The hotel overlooks the sea.*

overnight adverb, adjective
of or during a night • *We stayed overnight in a hotel.* • *There will be an overnight stop in Paris.*

overpower verb
to overpower someone is to defeat them because you are stronger
overpowering adjective very strong

overrun verb (**overrunning, overran, overrun**)
1 to overrun an area is to spread harmfully over it • *The place is overrun with mice.* **2** something overruns when it goes on longer than it should • *The programme overran by ten minutes.*

overseas adverb
abroad • *They travelled overseas.*

overseas adjective
from abroad; foreign • *We met some overseas students.*

oversight noun
a mistake you make by not noticing something

oversleep verb (**oversleeping, overslept**)
to sleep longer than you meant to

overtake verb (**overtaking, overtook, overtaken**)
to overtake a moving vehicle or person is to catch them up or pass them in the same direction

overthrow verb (**overthrowing, overthrew, overthrown**)
to overthrow a government is to remove it from power by force

overthrow noun
the overthrow of a government is when it is forced out of power

overtime noun
time someone spends working outside their normal hours

overture noun
a piece of music played at the start of a concert, opera, or ballet

overturn verb
1 to overturn something is to make it turn over or fall over **2** to overturn is to turn over • *The car went out of control and overturned.*

overweight adjective
too heavy

overwhelm verb
1 to overwhelm someone is to have a very strong effect on them • *I was overwhelmed by everyone's kindness.* **2** to overwhelm someone is to defeat them completely

owe verb
1 to owe something, especially money, is to have a duty to pay or give it to someone • *I owe you a pound.* **2** to owe something to someone is to have it thanks to them • *They owed their lives to the pilot's skill*
owing to something because of it • *The train was late owing to leaves on the line.*

owl noun
a bird of prey with large eyes and a short beak, usually flying at night

own adjective
belonging to yourself or itself **to get your own back** (*informal*) is to have your revenge **on your own** by yourself; alone• *I did it all on my own.* • *I sat on my own in the empty room.*

own verb
to own something is to have it as your property
to own up to something (*informal*) is to admit that you did it

owner noun
the person who owns something
ownership noun ownership is owning something

ox noun (**oxen**)
a male animal of the cow family, used for pulling loads

oxygen noun
oxygen is one of the gases in the air that people need to stay alive

oyster noun
a kind of shellfish whose shell sometimes contains a pearl

ozone noun
ozone is a strong-smelling gas that is a form of oxygen

ozone layer noun
a layer of ozone high in the atmosphere, which protects the earth from the sun's radiation

p
short for penny or pence

pace noun
1 one step in walking, marching, or running **2** speed • *He set a fast pace.*

pace verb
to pace is to walk up and down with slow or regular steps • *He was pacing across the room as he spoke.*

pacifist noun (say **pas**-i-fist)
someone who believes that war is always wrong **pacifism** noun the belief that war is always wrong

pacify verb (**pacifies, pacifying, pacified**) (say **pas**-i-fy)
to pacify someone is to calm them down

owl

pack *noun*
1 a bundle or collection of things wrapped or tied together 2 a set of playing cards 3 a strong bag carried on your back 4 a group of hounds, wolves, or other animals 5 a group of people, especially a group of Brownies or Cub Scouts

pack *verb*
1 to pack a suitcase or bag is to put things in it so that you can store them or take them somewhere 2 to pack a room or building is to fill it • *The hall was packed.*

package *noun*
1 a parcel or packet 2 a number of things offered or accepted together

package holiday *noun*
a holiday in which all the travel and accommodation is arranged and included in the price

packet *noun*
a small parcel

pad¹ *noun*
1 a number of sheets of blank or lined paper joined together along one edge 2 a piece of soft material used to protect or shape something 3 a piece of soft material that you wear to protect your leg in cricket and other games 4 a flat surface from which helicopters take off or rockets are launched

pad¹ *verb* (**padding, padded**)
to pad something is to put a piece of soft material on it or into it in order to protect or shape it

pad² *verb* (**padding, padded**)
to pad is to walk softly

padding *noun*
padding is soft material used to protect something or make it more comfortable

paddle *verb*
1 to paddle is to walk about with bare feet in shallow water 2 to paddle a boat is to move it along with a short oar

paddle *noun*
1 a time spent paddling in water 2 a short oar with a broad blade

paddock *noun*
a small field for keeping horses

paddy *noun* (**paddies**)
a field where rice is grown

padlock

padlock *noun*
a lock with a metal loop that you can use to fasten a gate or lock a bicycle

page¹ *noun*
a piece of paper that is part of a book or newspaper; one side of this piece of paper

page² *noun*
a boy who acts as an attendant or runs errands

pageant *noun* (*say* **paj**-ent)
1 a play or entertainment about historical events and people 2 a procession of people in costume

pageantry *noun* pageantry is elaborate display that is part of a ceremony or procession

pagoda *noun* (*say* pa-**goh**-da)
a Buddhist tower or Hindu temple in the Far East

pail *noun*
a bucket

pain *noun*
1 pain or a pain is an unpleasant feeling caused by injury or disease • *Are you in pain?* 2 pain is also mental suffering to take pains is to make a careful effort or take trouble over something

painful *adjective*
causing you pain • *My ankle is too painful to walk on.* **painfully** *adverb* to be (for example) painfully thin or painfully slow is to be extremely thin or slow

painstaking *adjective*
making a careful effort

paint *noun*
a liquid substance put on something to colour or cover it

paint *verb*
1 to paint something is to put paint on it 2 to paint a picture is to make it with paints 3 to paint someone or something is to make a picture of them using paint

paintbrush *noun*
a brush used in painting

paintbrushes

painter *noun*
1 an artist who paints pictures 2 a person whose job is painting walls and houses

painting *noun*
1 painting is using paints to make a picture • *She likes painting.* 2 a painting is a painted picture

pair *noun*
1 two things or people that go together or are the same kind • *I need a new pair of shoes.* 2 something made of two parts joined together • *Have you got a pair of scissors?*

palace *noun*
a large and splendid house where a king or queen or other important person lives

palate *noun* (*say* **pal**-at)
the roof of your mouth

pale *adjective*
1 almost white • *He had a pale face.* 2 not bright in colour; faint • *The sky was a pale blue.* **paleness** *noun*

palette *noun* (*say* **pal**-it)
a board on which an artist mixes colours

pallid *adjective*
pale, especially because of illness

palm *noun*
1 the inner part of your hand, between your fingers and wrist 2 a tropical tree with large leaves and no branches

paltry *adjective*
not very much or not very valuable • *His reward was a paltry 50 pence.*

pamper *verb*
to pamper someone is to go to a lot of trouble to make them feel comfortable and let them have whatever they want

pamphlet *noun*
a thin book with a paper cover

pan *noun*
1 a pot or dish with a flat base, used for cooking 2 something shaped like an open dish

pancake *noun*
a flat round cake of batter fried on both sides

panda *noun*
a large black and white bear-like animal found in China

pandemonium *noun*
you say there is pandemonium when there is a loud noise or disturbance • *Suddenly pandemonium broke loose.*

a b c d e f g h i j k l m n o p q r s t u v w x y z

A B C D E F G H I J K L M N O P Q R S T U V W X Y Z

pane *noun*
a sheet of glass in a window

panel *noun*
1 a long flat piece of wood, metal, or other material that is part of a door, wall, or piece of furniture **2** a group of people chosen to judge a competition or take part in a television quiz

pang *noun*
a sudden feeling of pain or strong emotion

panic *noun*
panic is sudden fear that makes you behave wildly **panicky** *adjective* feeling or showing panic

panic *verb* (**panicking, panicked**)
to panic is to be overcome with fear or anxiety and behave wildly

panorama *noun*
a view or picture of a wide area

pansy *noun* (**pansies**)
a small brightly-coloured garden flower

pant *verb*
you pant when you take short quick breaths, usually after running or working hard

panther *noun*
a leopard

pantomime *noun*
a Christmas show with dancing and songs, based on a fairy tale

pantry *noun* (**pantries**)
a cupboard or small room for storing food

pants *plural noun*
1 (*informal*) underpants or knickers **2** (*in America*) trousers

paper *noun*
1 paper is a thin substance made in sheets and used for writing or printing or drawing on, or for wrapping things **2** a paper is a newspaper **3** papers are documents

paper *verb*
to paper a wall or room is to cover it with wallpaper

paperback *noun*
a book with thin flexible covers

papier mâché *noun*
(*say* **pap**-yay **mash**-ay)
papier mâché is a mixture of paper pulp and glue you use to make models or ornaments

papyrus *noun* (**papyri**)
(*say* pa-**py**-rus)
papyrus is a kind of paper made from the stems of reeds, used in ancient Egypt

parable *noun*
a story told to teach people

something, especially one of the stories told by Jesus Christ

parachute *noun*
an umbrella-shaped device on which people or things can float slowly down to the ground from an aircraft **parachutist** *noun* someone who uses a parachute

parade *noun*
1 a line of people or vehicles moving forward through a place as a celebration **2** soldiers are on parade when they assemble for an inspection or drill

parade *verb*
1 to parade is to move forward through a place as a celebration **2** soldiers parade when they assemble for an inspection or drill

paradise *noun*
1 paradise is heaven or, in the Bible, the Garden of Eden **2** you can describe a wonderful or perfect place as a paradise

paraffin *noun*
paraffin is a kind of oil used as fuel

paragraph *noun*
one of the group of sentences that a piece of writing is divided into, beginning on **parallel** *adjective* parallel lines are lines that are the same distance apart for their whole length, like railway lines

parallelogram *noun*
a four-sided figure with its opposite sides parallel to each other and equal in length

paralyse *verb*
to paralyse someone is to make them unable to feel anything or to move

paralysis *noun* (*say* pa-**ral**-i-sis)
paralysis is the loss of the ability to move or feel anything

parapet *noun*
a low wall along the edge of a balcony, bridge, or roof

parasite *noun*
an animal or plant that lives in or on another and gets its food from it **parasitic** *adjective* a parasitic animal or plant lives as a parasite on another

parasol *noun*
a lightweight umbrella you use to shade yourself from the sun

paratroops *plural noun*
troops trained to be dropped from aircraft by parachute **paratrooper** *noun* a soldier in the paratroops

parcel *noun*
something wrapped up in paper for sending in the post

parched *adjective*
very dry or thirsty

parchment *noun*
parchment is a kind of heavy paper originally made from animal skins

pardon *verb*
to pardon someone is to forgive or excuse them

pardon *noun*
1 forgiveness; when someone is pardoned **2** used as an exclamation to mean 'I didn't hear or understand what you said', or 'I apologize'

parent *noun*
your parents are your father and mother **parental** *adjective* to do with parents

parish *noun*
a district that has its own church **parishoner** *noun* a person who regularly goes to a particular church

park *noun*
a large area with grass and trees, for public use

park *verb*
to park a vehicle is to leave it somewhere for a time

parliament *noun*
the group of people that make a country's laws **parliamentary** *adjective* to do with a parliament • *a parliamentary election*

parole *noun* (*say* pa-**rohl**)
parole is letting someone out of prison before they have finished their sentence, on condition that they behave well • *He was on parole.*

parrot *noun*
a brightly-coloured bird with a curved beak, that can learn to repeat words or sounds

parrot

parsley *noun*
parsley is a plant with crinkled green leaves used to flavour and decorate food

parsnip *noun*
a pale yellow vegetable

parson *noun*
a member of the Christian clergy, especially a vicar

part *noun*
1 some but not all of a thing or a number of things; anything that belongs to something bigger **2** the character played by an actor or actress; the words spoken by a character in a play • *She has a good part in the school play.*

part *verb*
1 to part people or things is to separate them or divide them **2** to part is to separate **3** to part hair is to divide it so that it goes in two different directions **to part with something** is to give it away or get rid of it

partial *adjective*
1 not complete or total • *There will be a partial eclipse of the sun.* **2** unfairly showing more support for one person or side than another **to be partial to something** is to like it **partially** *adverb* partly or not completely

participate *verb*
to participate in something is to take part in it **participant** *noun* someone who takes part in something **participation** *noun* taking part in something

participle *noun*
a word formed from a verb and used as part of the verb or as an adjective, for example 'going', 'gone', 'sailed', 'sailing'

particle *noun*
a very small piece or amount

particular *adjective*
1 only this one and no other; special; individual • *Are you looking for a particular book?* **2** fussy; hard to please • *He is very particular about his clothes.* **in particular** especially; chiefly **particularly** *adverb* you can say something is (for example) particularly good or useful when it is especially good or useful

parting *noun*
1 leaving or separation **2** the line where hair is combed in different directions

partition *noun*
a thin wall that divides a space into separate areas

partly *adverb*
not completely; in some ways

partner *noun*
1 one of a pair of people who do something together, especially dancing, running a business, or playing a game **2** someone's partner is the person they are married to or live with **partnership** *noun* partnership is being partners

part of speech *noun*
each of the groups (also called **word classes**) into which words can be divided in grammar: noun, adjective, verb, pronoun, adverb, preposition, conjunction, determiner

partridge *noun*
a bird with brown feathers that some people shoot as a sport

part-time *adjective, adverb*
working for only some of the normal hours

party *noun* (**parties**)
1 a time when people get together to enjoy themselves • *Come to my birthday party.* **2** a group of people working or travelling together • *They organized a search party.* **3** an organized group of people with similar political beliefs • *The Labour Party won the election.*

pass *verb*
1 to pass something or someone is to go past them **2** to pass in a certain direction is to move or go that way • *They passed over the bridge.* **3** to pass something to someone is to give it or hand it to them • *Can you pass the butter, please?* **4** to pass an examination is to be successful in it **5** to pass time is to use time doing something **6** to pass is to finish or no longer be there • *His opportunity passed.* **7** to pass a law or rule is to approve or accept it

pass *noun*
1 when a ball is kicked, hit, or thrown from one player to another in a game **2** a success in an examination • *She got several GCSE passes.* **3** a card or ticket that allows you to go in or out of a place

passage *noun*
1 a corridor or narrow space between two walls **2** a section of a piece of writing or music **3** a journey by sea or air **4** passing • *the passage of time*

passageway *noun*
a passage or way through, especially between buildings

passenger *noun*
someone who is driven in a car or travels by public transport

passer-by *noun* (**passers-by**)
someone who happens to be going past when something happens

passion *noun*
1 passion is strong feeling or emotion **2** a passion is a great enthusiasm for something

passionate *adjective*
full of passion or strong feeling **passionately** *adverb*

passive *adjective*
not active; not resisting or fighting against something **passively** *adverb*

Passover *noun*
Passover is a Jewish religious festival, celebrating the escape of the ancient Jews from slavery in Egypt

passport *noun*
an official document that allows you to travel abroad

passport

password *noun*
a secret word or phrase that you need to know to be allowed to go somewhere or to use a computer system

past *noun*
1 the time that has gone by • *Try to forget the past.* **2** the form of a verb used to describe an action that happened at a time before now, for example *came* in the sentence *My uncle came to visit us*

past *adjective*
of the time gone by • *He was thinking about his past achievements.*

past *preposition*
1 beyond • *Go past the school and turn right.* **2** later than • *It is past midnight.*

pasta *noun*
pasta is an Italian food made as a dried paste of flour, water, and often eggs, formed into various shapes such as spaghetti and lasagne

paste *noun*
a soft and moist or gluey substance

paste *verb*
to paste something is to stick it to a surface with paste

pastel *noun*
1 a crayon that is like a slightly greasy chalk **2** a light delicate colour

pasteurize *verb*
(*say* **pahs**-cher-ryz)
to pasteurize milk is to purify it by heating and then cooling it **pasteurization** *noun* the process of pasteurizing milk

pastime *noun*
something you do to pass time pleasantly; a hobby or game

past participle *noun*
a form of a verb used after *has, have, had, was, were,* to describe an action that happened at a time before now, for example *done, overtaken,* and *written*

pastry *noun* (**pastries**)
1 pastry is dough made from flour, fat, and water rolled flat and baked **2** a pastry is a cake made from this dough

pasture *noun*
land covered with grass where cattle, sheep, or horses can feed

pasty[1] *noun* (**pasties**)
(*say* **pas**-ti)
a pastry filled with meat and vegetables, like a small pie

pasty[2] *adjective* (**pastier pastiest**) (*say* **pay**-sti)
looking pale and unhealthy

pat *verb* (**patting, patted**)
to pat something or someone is to tap them gently with your open hand or with something flat

pat *noun*
a patting movement or sound **a pat on the back** congratulations or praise

patch *noun*
1 a piece of material put over a hole or damaged place **2** an area that is different from its surroundings • *We have a black cat with a white patch on its chest.* **3** a small area of land **4** a small piece of something • *There are patches of ice on the road.*

patch *verb*
to patch something is to put a piece of material on it to repair it **to patch something up** is to repair it roughly

patchwork *noun*
patchwork is small pieces of different cloth which are sewn together

patchy *adjective* (**patchier, patchiest**)
occurring in some areas but not others; uneven • *There may be some patchy rain.*

paternal *adjective*
to do with a father, or like a father

path *noun*
1 a narrow way to walk or ride along **2** the line along which something moves • *They were tracing the path of the meteor.*

pathetic *adjective*
1 sad and pitiful **2** sadly or comically weak or useless • *He made a*

pathetic attempt to climb the tree.
pathetically *adverb*

patience *noun* (*say* **pay**-shens)
1 patience is the ability to stay calm, especially when you have to wait for a long time **2** patience is also a card game that you play by yourself

patient *adjective* (*say* **pay**-shent)
1 able to wait for a long time without getting anxious or angry **2** able to bear pain or trouble **patiently** *adverb*

patient *noun* (*say* **pay**-shent)
a person who is getting treatment from a doctor or dentist

patio *noun* (**patios**)
(*say* **pat**-i-oh)
a paved area beside a house

WORD ORIGIN

The word **patio** is a Spanish word, and in Spanish it means 'a courtyard'.

---

patriot *noun* (*say* **pay**-tri-ot or *say* **pat**-ri-ot)
someone who loves and supports their country **patriotic** *adjective* loyal to your country **patriotism** *noun* patriotism is loving and supporting your country

patrol *verb* (**patrolling, patrolled**)
to walk or travel regularly round a place or a thing to guard it and make sure that all is well

patrol *noun*
1 a group of people or vehicles patrolling a place **2** a group of Scouts or Guides **to be on patrol** is to be patrolling a place

patron *noun* (*say* **pay**-tron)
1 someone who supports a person or cause with money or encouragement **2** a regular customer of a shop or business

patter *noun*
a series of light tapping sounds

patter *verb*
to patter is to make light tapping sounds • *The rain was pattering on the glass roof.*

pattern *noun*
1 a decorative arrangement of lines or shapes **2** a thing that you copy so that you can make something, such as a piece of clothing

pause *noun*
a short stop before continuing with something

pause *verb*
1 to pause is to make a short stop before continuing with something **2** to pause (for example) a film on television or CD player is to make it stop for a short time

pave *verb*
to pave a road or path is to put a hard surface on it **to pave the way** is to prepare for something

pavement *noun*
a path with a hard surface, along the side of a street

pavilion *noun*
a building at a sports ground for players and spectators to use

paw *noun*
an animal's foot

paw *verb*
an animal paws something when it touches or scrapes it clumsily with its paw

pawn *noun*
one of the sixteen pieces in chess that are at the front on each side and are the least valuable

pawn *verb*
to pawn something is to leave it with a pawnbroker in exchange for money • *He had to pawn his watch.*

pawnbroker *noun*
a shopkeeper who lends money to people in return for objects that they leave and which are later sold if the money is not paid back

pay *verb* (**paying, paid**)
1 to pay for something is to give money in return for it • *Have you paid for your lunch?* **2** to pay someone is to give them money for something they have done • *Wash my car and I'll pay you £5.* **3** to pay is to be profitable or worthwhile • *It pays to be honest.* **4** to pay (for example) attention or a compliment is to give someone your attention or make them a compliment **5** to pay for something you have done wrong is to suffer for it • *I'll make you pay for this!* **to pay someone back 1** is to pay money that you owe them **2** is to get revenge on them

pay *noun*
pay is the money you earn when you work

payment *noun*
1 payment is when you pay someone or are paid for something **2** a payment is money you pay

PC
short for *personal computer, police constable*

PE
short for *physical education*

pea *noun*
a small round green seed of a

climbing plant, growing inside a pod and used as a vegetable

peace noun
1 peace is a time when there is no war or violence • *At last the country was at peace.* 2 peace is also quietness and calm

peaceful adjective
1 quiet and calm
2 not involving violence **peacefully** adverb

peach noun
a soft round juicy fruit with a slightly furry skin and a large stone

peacock noun
a large male bird with a long brightly coloured tail that it can spread out like a fan. The female is called a *peahen.*

peak noun
1 the top of a mountain the highest or best point of something
• *Traffic reaches its peak at 5 o'clock.*
3 the part of a cap that sticks out in front **peaked** adjective a peaked hat or cap is one with a peak

peal verb
bells peal when they make a loud ringing sound

peal noun
a loud ringing sound made by bells

peanut noun
a small round nut that grows in a pod in the ground

pear noun
a juicy fruit that gets narrower near the stalk

pearl noun
a small shiny white ball found in the shells of some oysters and used as a jewel **pearly** adjective pearly white teeth are as white and shiny as a pearl

peasant noun
a person who works on the land, especially in poor areas of the world or in the Middle Ages **peasantry** noun the peasants of a region or country

peat noun
peat is rotted plant material that can be dug out of the ground and used as fuel or fertilizer

pebble noun
a small round stone found on the beach **pebbly** adjective a pebbly beach is one with lots of pebbles

peck verb
when a bird pecks something, it bites it or eats it with its beak

peck noun
1 a short sharp bite with a bird's beak 2 (*informal*) a quick kiss

peckish adjective
(*informal*) slightly hungry

peculiar adjective
strange or unusual **to be peculiar to someone** or **something** is to belong to a particular people or place
• *This species of bird is peculiar to Asia.* **peculiarly** adverb more than usually; strangely
• *He is peculiarly fond of brightly coloured socks.*

pedal noun
a lever that you press with your foot to operate a bicycle, car, or machine, or to play some musical instruments

pedal verb (**pedalling, pedalled**) to pedal is to push or turn the pedals of a bicycle or other device

pedestal noun
the base that supports a statue or pillar

pedestrian noun
someone who is walking in the street

pedigree noun
a list of a person's or animal's ancestors, especially to show how well an animal has been bred

peel noun
the skin of some fruit and vegetables

peel

peel verb
1 to peel a piece of fruit or a vegetable is to remove the peel or covering from it 2 to peel is to lose a covering or skin • *The paint on the walls was peeling.*

peep verb
1 to peep is to look quickly or secretly, or through a narrow opening 2 to peep or peep out is to come slowly or briefly into view • *The moon peeped out through the clouds.*

peep noun
a quick look

peer[1] verb
to peer at something or someone is to look at them closely or with difficulty

peer[2] noun
1 a nobleman or noblewoman 2 your peers are the people who are the same age as you

peg noun
a clip or pin for fixing things in place or for hanging things on

peg verb (**pegging, pegged**)
to peg something is to fix it with pegs • *We pegged out the tent.*

pelican noun
a large bird with a pouch in its long beak for storing fish

pellet noun
a tiny ball of metal, food, wet paper, or other substance

pelt[1] verb
1 to pelt someone with things is to throw a lot of things at them • *We pelted him with snowballs.* 2 it pelts down when it is raining very hard 3 to pelt is to run fast

pelt[2] noun
an animal skin, especially with the fur or hair still on it

pen[1] noun
a device with a metal point for writing with ink

pen[2] noun
an enclosure for cattle or other animals

penalize verb
1 to penalize someone is to punish them 2 in a game, to penalize someone is to award a penalty against them

penalty noun (**penalties**)
1 a punishment 2 a point or advantage given to one side in a game when a member of the other side breaks a rule

pence plural noun
pennies

pencil noun
a device for drawing or writing, made of a thin stick of graphite or coloured chalk inside a cylinder of wood or metal

pendulum noun
a weight hung at the end of a rod so that it swings to and fro, especially to keep a clock working

penetrate verb
to penetrate something is to find a way through it or into it **penetration** noun penetrating something

penfriend noun
someone in another country you write to, usually without meeting them

a b c d e f g h i j k l m n o p q r s t u v w x y z

penguin noun
an Antarctic sea bird that cannot fly but uses its wings as flippers for swimming

penguins

penicillin noun
penicillin is a drug that kills bacteria, used to cure infections

peninsula noun
a long piece of land that is almost surrounded by water

penis noun
the part of the body with which a male person or animal urinates and has sexual intercourse

penknife noun (**penknives**)
a small folding knife

penniless adjective
having no money; very poor

penny noun (**pennies** or **pence**)
a British coin worth a hundredth of a pound

pension noun
an income of regular payments made to someone who has retired or been widowed **pensioner** noun someone who is receiving a pension

pentagon noun
a flat shape with five sides

pentathlon noun
(say pent-**ath**-lon)
a sports competition that has five different events

people plural noun
1 people are human beings; men, women, and children **2** the people of a particular country or area are the men, women, and children who live there

people noun
a people is a community or nation • They are a peaceful people.

pepper noun
1 pepper is a hot-tasting powder used to flavour food
2 a pepper is a bright green, red, or yellow vegetable **peppery** adjective peppery food is hot-tasting like pepper

peppermint noun
1 peppermint is a kind of mint used for flavouring
2 a peppermint is a sweet flavoured with this mint

per preposition
for each • The charge is £2 per person.

perceive verb
to perceive something is to see or notice it or understand it

per cent adverb
for every hundred • We pay interest at 5 per cent (5%). • Fifty per cent of the pupils walk to school.

percentage noun
an amount or rate expressed as a proportion of 100

perceptible adjective
able to be seen or noticed
perceptibly adverb in a perceptible way • It was perceptibly warmer.

perception noun
perception is the ability to see, notice, or understand something

perceptive adjective
quick to notice or understand things • It was very perceptive of you to spot that.

perch[1] noun
a place where a bird sits or rests
perch[1] verb
to perch is to sit or stand on the edge of something or on something small • She was perched on a tall stool at the kitchen table.
perch[2] noun
a freshwater fish used for food

percussion noun
percussion is musical instruments that you play by hitting them or shaking them, such as drums and cymbals **percussionist** noun someone who plays percussion instruments

perennial adjective
lasting or occurring for many years • It is a perennial problem.
perennial noun
a plant that lives for many years **perennially** adverb year after year

perfect adjective (say **per**-fikt)
1 so good that it cannot be made any better; without any faults
2 complete • The man is a perfect

stranger. **perfection** noun when something is perfect
perfect verb (say **per**-fekt)
to perfect something is to make it perfect

perfectly adverb
1 completely • She stood perfectly still. **2** without any faults • The toaster works perfectly now.

perforate verb
to perforate something is to make tiny holes in it, especially so that it can be torn off easily **perforation** noun perforations are the tiny holes made in something so that it can be torn off easily

perform verb
1 to perform something is to present it in front of an audience • They performed a play in the school hall.
2 to perform something is also to carry it out or complete it • The surgeon performed the operation on Tuesday. **performer** noun someone who performs an entertainment

performance noun
the showing of something in front of an audience

perfume noun
1 a sweet-smelling liquid that people put on their skin
2 a sweet or pleasant smell

perhaps adverb
it may be; possibly

peril noun
peril is danger • She was in great peril. **perilous** adjective dangerous • It was a perilous climb. **perilously** adverb dangerously • We came perilously close to disaster

perimeter noun
(say per-**im**-it-er)
1 a boundary • A fence marks the perimeter of the airfield.
2 the distance round the edge of something

period noun
1 a length of time **2** the time every month when a woman or girl bleeds from her womb in menstruation

periodical noun
a magazine published regularly, for example once a month

periscope noun
a device with a tube and mirrors that lets you see things at a higher level, used for example in submarines

perish verb
1 to perish is to die or be destroyed • Many sailors perished in the shipwreck.
2 to perish is also to rot

The tyres have perished.
3 (*informal*) to be perished is to feel extremely cold • *I was perished after the long walk in the hills.*
perishable *adjective* perishable food is likely to go off quickly

permanent *adjective*
lasting for ever or for a long time • *Will there be any permanent damage?* **permanently** *adverb* for ever or for a long time

permission *noun*
you have permission to do something when you are allowed to do it

permissive *adjective*
letting people do what they wish; tolerant or liberal

permit *verb* (**permitting, permitted**) (*say* per-**mit**)
1 to permit someone to do something is to allow them to do it **2** to permit something is to allow it to be done

permit *noun* (*say* **per**-mit)
a written or printed statement that says you are allowed to do something

perpendicular *adjective*
standing upright, or at a right angle to a line or surface

perpetual *adjective*
lasting for ever or for a long time **perpetually** *adverb* continually

perplex *verb*
to perplex someone is to puzzle them very much **perplexity** *noun* feeling puzzled and confused

persecute *verb*
to persecute someone is to be continually cruel to them, especially because you disagree with their beliefs **persecution** *noun* when someone is being persecuted **persecutor** *noun* the person who is persecuting someone

persevere *verb*
to persevere is to go on with something even though it is difficult **perseverance** *noun* you show perseverance when you go on with something even though it is difficult

persist *verb*
1 to persist is to keep on firmly or obstinately doing something • *She persists in breaking the rules.* **2** to persist is also to last for a long time • *The rain persisted all afternoon.*

persistent *adjective*
1 refusing to give up **2** lasting for a long time • *The rain was persistent.* **persistence** *noun* you show persistence when you keep on doing

something without giving up **persistently** *adverb*

person *noun* (**people** or **persons**)
a human being; a man, woman, or child

personal *adjective*
1 belonging to, done by, or concerning a particular person • *The stars of the film will be making a personal appearance at the première.* **2** private • *I can't tell you about that because it's personal.*

personal computer *noun*
a small computer designed to be used by one person

personality *noun* (**personalities**)
1 your personality is your nature and character • *She has a cheerful personality.* **2** a well-known person • *There were several TV personalities at the party.*

personally *adverb*
1 in person; being actually there • *The head thanked me personally* **2** as far as I am concerned • *Personally, I'd rather stay here.*

personnel *noun* (*say* per-so-**nel**)
the personnel in a business or organization are the people who work there

perspective *noun*
1 perspective is the impression of depth and space in a picture or scene **2** your perspective on a situation is your point of view **in perspective** giving a balanced view of things • *Try to see the problem in perspective.*

perspire *verb*
to perspire is to sweat **perspiration** *noun* sweat

persuade *verb*
to persuade someone is to get them to agree about something or do something, by giving them reasons **persuasion** *noun* when you persuade someone to do or believe something **persuasive** *adjective* good at persuading people

pessimist *noun*
someone who usually expects things to turn out badly **pessimism** *noun* the feeling that things will turn out badly

pessimistic *adjective*
expecting things to turn out badly **pessimistically** *adverb*

pest *noun*
1 a destructive insect or animal, such as a locust or a mouse
2 an annoying person; a nuisance

pester *verb*
to pester someone is to annoy them with frequent questions or interruptions

pet *noun*
1 a tame animal that you keep at home **2** a person treated as a favourite • *She seems to be teacher's pet.*

petal *noun*
each of the separate coloured outer parts of a flower

petition *noun*
a written request for someone in authority to do something, usually signed by a large number of people

petrify *verb* (**petrifies, petrifying, petrified**)
to petrify someone is to make them so terrified that they cannot move or act

petrol *noun*
petrol is a liquid made from oil, used as a fuel for engines

petticoat *noun*
a piece of women's clothing worn under a skirt or dress

petty *adjective* (**pettier, pettiest**)
1 minor and unimportant • *There are some petty regulations.* **2** mean and selfish about small things **pettily** *adverb* **pettiness** *noun*

pew *noun*
one of the long wooden seats in a church

pewter *noun*
pewter is a grey alloy of tin and lead

pH *noun*
a measure of how much acid or alkali a solution contains. Acids have a pH between 0 and 7 and alkalis have a pH between 7 and 14.

phantom *noun*
a ghost

pharmacy *noun* (**pharmacies**)
a shop that sells medicines

phase *noun*
a stage in the progress or development of something

pheasant *noun* (*say* **fez**-ant)
a bird with a long tail that some people shoot as a sport

phenomenal *adjective*
(*say* fin-**om**-in-al)
amazing or remarkable

phenomenon *noun* (**phenomena**)
an event or fact, especially one that is remarkable or unusual

a
b
c
d
e
f
g
h
i
j
k
l
m
n
o
p
q
r
s
t
u
v
w
x
y
z

philosophical *adjective*
1 to do with philosophy **2** calmly accepting disappointment or suffering • *He was philosophical about losing.* **philosophically** *adverb*

philosophy *noun*
(**philosophies**) (*say* fil-**os**-o-fi)
1 philosophy is the study of what life and human behaviour is all about **2** a philosophy is a way of thinking or a system of beliefs
philosopher *noun* someone who studies philosophy

phobia *noun* (*say* **foh**-bi-a)
a great or unusual fear of something

phone *noun*
a telephone
phone *verb*
to phone someone is to telephone them

phone-in *noun*
a radio or TV programme in which people telephone the studio and take part in a discussion

phosphorescent *adjective*
shining or glowing in the dark
phosphorescence *noun*
phosphorescence is being phosphorescent

phosphorus *noun*
phosphorus is a yellowish substance that glows in the dark

photo *noun*
(*informal*) a photograph

photocopier *noun*
a machine that makes photocopies

photocopy *noun*
a copy of a document or page made by a machine that photographs it on special paper

photocopy *verb* (**photocopies, photocopying, photocopied**)
to photocopy a document is to make a copy of it with a photocopier

photograph *noun*
a picture made on film or digitally using a camera
photograph *verb*
to photograph someone or something is to take a photograph of them
photographer *noun* someone who takes photographs

photography *noun*
photography is taking photographs with a camera **photographic** *adjective* to do with photography

phrase *noun*
1 a group of words that do not make a complete sentence, for example *in the garden* in the sentence *The*

Queen was in the garden **2** a short section of a tune

physical *adjective*
1 to do with the body rather than the mind or feelings **2** to do with things you can touch or see **physically** *adverb* in a way that is connected with the body rather than the mind or feelings

physical education *noun*
physical education is gymnastics or other exercises that you do to keep your body healthy

physics *noun*
physics is the study of matter and energy, including movement, heat, light, and sound **physicist** *noun* an expert in physics

pianist *noun*
someone who plays the piano

piano *noun*
a large musical instrument with a row of black and white keys on a keyboard

piccolo *noun*
a small high-pitched flute

pick[1] *verb*
1 to pick something or someone is to choose them • *Pick a card from this pack.* **2** to pick flowers or fruit is to cut or pull them off the plant or tree **3** to pick someone's pocket is to steal from it **4** to pick a lock is to open it without using a key **5** to pick bits off or out of something is to pull them away from it **to pick on someone** is to keep criticizing or bothering them **to pick someone up** is to give them a lift in a vehicle **to pick something up 1** is to take it from the ground or a surface **2** is to collect it • *I'll pick up my bags from the station.*

pick[1] *noun*
1 a choice • *Take your pick.* **2** the best part of something

pick[2] *noun*
a pickaxe

pickaxe *noun*
a heavy pointed tool with a long handle, used for breaking up concrete or hard ground

picket *noun*
a group of workers on strike who try

to persuade other people not to go into the place where they work

pickle *noun*
a strong-tasting food made of vegetables preserved in vinegar
pickle *verb*
to pickle food is to preserve it in vinegar or salt water

pickpocket *noun*
a thief who steals from people's pockets or bags

picnic *noun*
a meal eaten in the open air away from home

picnic *verb* (**picnicking, picnicked**)
to picnic is to have a picnic
picnicker *noun* someone having a picnic

pictorial *adjective*
with or using pictures **pictorially** *adverb*

picture *noun*
1 a painting, drawing, or photograph **2** a film at the cinema **to be in the picture** is to know about something
picture *verb*
1 to picture someone or something is to show them in a picture **2** to picture someone or something in your mind is to imagine them

picturesque *adjective*
(*say* pik-cher-**esk**)
a picturesque place is attractive or charming • *We drove through a picturesque village.*

pie *noun*
a baked dish of meat or fruit covered with pastry

piece *noun*
1 a part of something; a bit **2** a work of art or writing or music • *They played a piece of piano music.* **3** one of the objects you use on a board to play a game • *You've dropped a chess piece.* **4** a coin • *a 20p piece* **piece by piece** gradually; one bit at a time
piece *verb*
to piece things together is to join them to make something

pier *noun*
a long structure built out into the sea for people to walk on

pierce *verb*
to pierce something is to make a hole through it

piercing *adjective*
1 a piercing sound is loud and high-pitched • *We heard a piercing shriek.* **2** something piercing seems to go right through you • *The wind was cold and piercing.*

piccolo

A
B
C
D
E
F
G
H
I
J
K
L
M
N
O
P
Q
R
S
T
U
V
W
X
Y
Z

pig *noun*
1 a fat animal with short legs and a blunt snout, kept for its meat
2 (*informal*) you can describe someone as a pig when they are greedy, dirty, or unpleasant

pigeon *noun*
a common grey bird with a small head and large chest

piggyback *noun*
a ride on someone's back

piglet *noun*
a young pig

pigment *noun*
a substance that colours something

pigmy *noun* (**pigmies**)
another spelling of **pygmy**

pigsty *noun* (**pigsties**)
1 a place for keeping pigs
2 (*informal*) you can describe a very untidy room or place as a pigsty

pigtail *noun*
a single plait of hair worn hanging at the back of the head

pike *noun*
1 a large fish that lives in rivers and lakes 2 a heavy spear

pilchard *noun*
a small sea fish

pile *noun*
a number of things on top of one another; a large amount of something

pile *verb*
to pile things is to put them into a pile

pilgrim *noun*
someone who goes on a journey to a holy place

pilgrimage *noun*
a journey to a holy place

pill *noun*
a small piece of medicine that you swallow

pillar *noun*
a tall stone post supporting part of a building

pillion *noun*
a seat for a passenger behind the driver's seat on a motorcycle

WORD ORIGIN

The word **pillion** comes from a Scottish Gaelic word meaning 'cushion'.

pillow *noun*
a cushion to rest your head on in bed

pillowcase *noun*
a cloth cover for a pillow

pilot *noun*
1 someone who flies an aircraft

2 someone who helps to steer a ship in and out of a port or through a difficult stretch of water

pilot *verb*
to pilot an aircraft is to be the pilot of it

pimple *noun*
a small round swelling on your skin
pimply *adjective* having pimples

pin *noun*
a short piece of metal with a sharp point and a rounded head, used to fasten pieces of paper or cloth together **pins and needles** a tingling feeling in the skin

PIN *noun*
personal identification number

pin *verb* (**pinning, pinned**)
to pin something is to fasten it with a pin

pincer *noun*
the claw of a shellfish such as a lobster

pincers *plural noun*
a tool for gripping and pulling things, especially for pulling out nails

pinch *verb*
1 to pinch something is to squeeze it tightly between two things, especially between the finger and thumb 2 (*informal*) to pinch something is to steal it

pinch *noun*
1 a firm squeezing movement 2 the amount you can pick up between the tips of your finger and thumb • *Take a pinch of salt.* **at a pinch** if it is really necessary

pine¹ *noun*
an evergreen tree with leaves shaped like needles

pine² *verb*
1 to pine for someone or something is to feel a strong longing for them 2 to pine, or pine away, is to become weak or ill through sorrow or yearning

pineapple *noun*
a large tropical fruit with yellow flesh and prickly leaves and skin

ping-pong *noun*
ping-pong is table tennis

pineapple

pink *adjective* ●
pale red

pink *noun*
1 a sweet-smelling garden flower
2 a pink colour

pint *noun*
a measure of liquid, an eighth of a gallon or about 568 millilitres

pioneer *noun*
one of the first people to go to a place or do something new

pious *adjective*
very religious or devout **piously** *adverb*

pip *noun*
a small hard seed of a fruit such as an apple, orange, or pear

pipe *noun*
1 a tube for carrying water, gas, or oil from one place to another 2 a short tube with a small bowl at one end, used to smoke tobacco 3 a musical instrument in the shape of a small tube

pipe *verb*
1 to pipe something is to send it along pipes or wires 2 to pipe is to play music on a pipe or the bagpipes **to pipe up** (*informal*) is to start saying something

pipeline *noun*
a pipe for carrying oil, water, or gas over a long distance

piper *noun*
someone who plays a pipe or the bagpipes

piping *adjective*
high-pitched; shrill
piping hot very hot, ready to eat

pirate *noun*
a sailor who attacks and robs other ships
piracy *noun*
piracy is robbing ships

pistol *noun*
a small gun held in the hand

piston *noun*
a disc that moves up and down inside a cylinder in an engine or pump

pit *noun*
1 a deep hole or hollow 2 a coal mine 3 the part of a race circuit where cars are refuelled and serviced during a race

pirate

pitch¹ *noun*
1 a pitch is a piece of ground marked out for cricket, football, or another game 2 pitch is how high or low a

voice or musical note is
3 the pitch of something is
also its intensity or strength
• *Excitement was at a high pitch.*

pitch¹ *verb*
1 to pitch something is to throw or
fling it **2** to pitch a tent is to set it
up **3** to pitch is to fall heavily • *He
tripped over the doorstep and pitched
forward.* **4** a ship pitches when it
moves up and down on a rough sea

pitch² *noun*
pitch is a black sticky substance like tar

pitch-black or **pitch-dark**
adjective
completely black or dark, with no
light at all

pitcher *noun*
a large jug, usually with
two handles

pitchfork *noun*
a large fork with two prongs
for lifting hay

pitfall *noun*
a hidden danger or difficulty

pitiful *adjective*
1 making you feel pity • *It was a
pitiful sight.* **2** inadequate; feeble
• *He made a pitiful attempt to make
us laugh.* **pitifully** *adverb*

pitiless *adjective*
having or showing no pity
pitilessly *adverb*

pitta bread *noun*
pitta bread is a flat, round piece of bread
that you can open and fill with food

pity *noun*
1 pity is the feeling of being sorry
because someone is suffering or in
trouble • *I feel pity for the homeless
people.* **2** a pity is something that
you regret • *It's a pity they can't
come.* **to take pity on someone** is to
help someone who is in trouble

pity *verb* (**pities, pitying, pitied**)
to pity someone is to feel sorry for
them

pivot *noun*
a point on which something turns or
balances

pixie or **pixy** *noun*
a small fairy or elf

pizza *noun* (*say* **peet**-sa)
an Italian food made as a layer
of dough covered with cheese,
vegetables, and spices and baked

placard *noun*
a large poster or notice, especially
one carried at a demonstration

place *noun*
1 a particular part of space,
especially where something belongs;
an area or position **2** a position in a

race or competition **3** a seat • *Save
me a place.* **in place** in the proper
position **in place of something** or
someone instead of them
out of place 1 in the wrong position
2 unsuitable • *Jeans and sandals are
out of place in a smart restaurant.* **to
take place** is to happen

place *verb*
to place something somewhere is to
put it in a particular place

placid *adjective*
calm and gentle; peaceful
• *a placid horse.* **placidly** *adverb*

plague *noun*
1 a dangerous illness that spreads
very quickly **2** a large number of
pests • *The crops were devastated by
a plague of locusts.*

plague *verb*
to plague someone is to pester or
annoy them continuously • *They
have been plagued with complaints.*

plaice *noun* (**plaice**)
a flat sea fish used for food

plain *adjective*
1 simple; not decorated **2** not pretty
3 easy to understand or see **4** frank;
straightforward • *I'll be quite plain
with you.* **plainness** *noun*

plain *noun*
a large area of flat country without
trees

plainly *adverb*
1 clearly or obviously
• *The clock tower was plainly visible
in the distance.* **2** simply • *She was
plainly dressed.*

plait *noun* (*say* plat)
a length of hair or rope made by
twisting several strands together

plait *verb* (*say* plat)
to plait hair or rope is to make it into
a plait

plan *noun*
1 a way of doing something
that you think out in advance
2 a drawing showing how the parts of
something are arranged **3** a map of a
town or district

plan *verb* (**planning, planned**)
1 to plan something is to think out
in advance how you are going to
do it **2** to plan to do something is
to intend to do it **planner** *noun*
someone who plans things

plane¹ *noun*
1 an aeroplane **2** a tool for making
wood smooth **3** a flat
or level surface

plane¹ *verb*
to plane wood is to smooth it with a
plane

plane² *noun*
a tall tree with broad leaves

planet *noun*
one of the bodies that move in an
orbit round the sun. The main planets
of the solar system are Mercury,
Venus, Earth, Mars, Jupiter, Saturn,
Uranus and Neptune.

plank *noun*
a long flat piece of wood

plankton *noun*
plankton is made up of tiny creatures
that float in the sea and lakes

plant *noun*
1 a living thing that grows out of the
ground, including flowers, bushes,
trees, and vegetables **2** a factory or
its equipment

plant *verb*
1 to plant something such as a tree
or flower is to put it in the ground to
grow **2** to plant something is also to
put it firmly in place • *He planted his
feet on the ground and took hold of
the rope.* **3** to plant something is to
secretly put it somewhere, usually to
cause trouble
• *A bomb was planted on a train.*

plantation *noun*
an area of land where a crop such as
tobacco, tea, or rubber is planted

plaque *noun* (*say* plak or plahk)
1 a plaque is a metal or porcelain
plate fixed on a wall as a memorial
or an ornament **2** plaque is a
substance that forms a thin layer
on your teeth, allowing bacteria to
develop

plaster *noun*
1 a plaster is a small covering you
put over your skin around a cut or
wound to protect it **2** plaster is a
mixture of lime, sand, and water,
used to cover walls and ceilings

plaster *verb*
1 to plaster a wall or ceiling is to
cover it with plaster **2** to plaster a
surface is to cover it thickly • *His clothes were
plastered with mud.* **plasterer** *noun*
someone who plasters walls and
ceilings

plastic *noun*
a strong light synthetic substance
that can be moulded into different
shapes

plastic *adjective*
made of plastic • *I need a
plastic bag.*

Plasticine *noun*
(*trademark*) Plasticine is a soft and
easily shaped substance used for
making models

plastic surgery *noun*
plastic surgery is work done by a surgeon to change or mend parts of someone's body

plate *noun*
1 a dish that is flat or almost flat, used for eating 2 a thin flat sheet of metal, glass, or other hard material 3 an illustration on a separate page in a book

plate *verb*
to plate metal is to cover it with a thin layer of gold, silver, tin, or other soft metal

plateau *noun* (**plateaux**)
(*say* **plat**-oh)
a flat area of high land

platform *noun*
1 a flat raised area along the side of the line at a railway station 2 a raised area for speakers or performers in a hall

platinum *noun*
platinum is a silver-coloured metal that does not lose its brightness

platoon *noun*
a small unit of soldiers

platypus *noun*
an Australian animal with a beak and feet like those of a duck

play *verb*
1 to play, or play a game, is to take part in a game or other amusement 2 to play music, or a musical instrument, is to make music or sound with it 3 to play a part in a film or play is to perform it 4 to play a disk is to put it in a machine and listen to it or watch it **to play about** or **around** is to have fun or be mischievous **to play someone up** is to tease or annoy them **player** *noun* someone who plays a game or a musical instrument

play *noun*
1 a play is a story acted on a stage or broadcast on radio or television 2 play is playing or having fun

playful *adjective*
1 wanting to play; full of fun 2 not serious **playfully** *adverb* **playfulness** *noun*

playground *noun*
a place out of doors where children can play

playgroup *noun*
a place where very young children can play together and are looked after by parents and other helpers

playing card *noun*
each of a set of cards (usually 52) used for playing games

playing field *noun*
a grassy field for outdoor games

playtime *noun*
the time when young schoolchildren go out to play

playwright *noun*
someone who writes plays

plea *noun*
1 a request or appeal 2 a statement of 'guilty' or 'not guilty' made in a lawcourt by someone accused of a crime

plead *verb*
to plead with someone is to beg them to do something **to plead guilty** or **not guilty** is to state in a lawcourt that you are guilty or not guilty of a crime

pleasant *adjective*
pleasing or enjoyable or friendly **pleasantly** *adverb* in a pleasant way • *I was pleasantly surprised.*

please *verb*
1 to please someone is to make them happy or satisfied 2 used when you want to ask something politely • *Please shut the door.*

pleasure *noun*
1 pleasure is a feeling of being pleased 2 a pleasure is something that pleases you **with pleasure** gladly; willingly

pleat *noun*
a fold made in cloth by pressing or sewing it **pleated** *adjective*

pledge *noun*
a solemn promise

pledge *verb*
to pledge something is to promise it

plentiful *adjective*
large in amount **plentifully** *adverb*

plenty *noun*
to have plenty of something is to have a lot of it or more than enough • *We have plenty of chairs.*

pliers *plural noun*
pincers with flattened jaws for gripping something or for breaking wire

plight *noun*
a difficult and sad situation • *They were stranded for several days before anyone knew of heir plight.*

plod *verb* (**plodding, plodded**)
to plod is to walk slowly and with heavy steps • *We plodded back through the rain.*

plop *noun*
the sound of something dropping into a liquid

plop *verb* (**plopping, plopped**)
to plop is to fall into a liquid with a plop

plot *noun*
1 a secret plan, especially to do something illegal or bad 2 what happens in a story, film, or play 3 a piece of land for a house or garden

plot *verb* (**plotting, plotted**)
1 to plot is to make a secret plan to do something 2 to plot a chart or graph is to make it, marking all the points on it **plotter** *noun* plotters are people who take part in a plot

plough *noun* (*say* plow)
a large farm tool pulled by a tractor or animal, used for turning over the soil

plough *verb*
to plough the soil is to turn it over with a plough

ploughman *noun* (**ploughmen**)
someone who uses a plough

pluck *verb*
1 to pluck a bird is to pull the feathers off it to prepare it for cooking 2 to pluck a flower or fruit is to pick it 3 to pluck something is to pull it or pull it out • *She plucked a book from the shelf.* 4 in music, to pluck a string is to pull it and let it go again **to pluck up courage** is to be brave and overcome fear

pluck *noun*
pluck is courage or bravery

plucky *adjective* (**pluckier, pluckiest**)
brave or courageous **pluckily** *adverb*

plug *noun*
1 something used to stop up a hole, especially in a sink or bath 2 a device that is used to connect a piece of electric equipment to a socket

plug *verb* (**plugging, plugged**)
1 to plug a hole is to stop it up 2 (*informal*) to plug an event or product is to publicize it **to plug something in** is to connect it to an electric socket with a plug

plum *noun*
a soft juicy red or purple fruit with a stone in the middle

plum

plumage noun (say **ploo**-mij)
a bird's plumage is its feathers

plumber noun
someone who fits and mends water pipes in a building

plumbing noun
1 plumbing is the work of a plumber 2 the plumbing in a building is all the water pipes and water tanks

plume noun
1 a large feather 2 something shaped like a feather • We saw a plume of smoke in the distance.

plump adjective
rounded or slightly fat

plump verb
to plump for something or someone is to choose them

plunder verb
to plunder a place or an enemy is to rob them violently, especially in a time of war or disorder **plunderer** noun someone who plunders a place

plunder noun
1 plunder is plundering a person or place 2 plunder is also goods taken by plundering

plunge verb
1 to plunge into water is to jump or dive into it with force 2 to plunge something into a liquid or something soft is to put it in with force

plunge noun
a sudden fall or dive

plural noun
the form of a word meaning more than one person or thing, such as cakes and children

plural adjective
in the plural; meaning more than one • 'Mice' is a plural noun.

plus preposition
with the next number or thing added • 2 plus 2 equals 4 (2 + 2 = 4).

p.m.
short for Latin post meridiem which means 'after midday'

pneumatic adjective
(say new-**mat**-ik)
filled with air or worked by compressed air • a pneumatic tyre • a pneumatic drill

pneumonia noun
(say new-**moh**-ni-a)
pneumonia is a serious disease of the lungs

poach verb
1 to poach food, especially fish or an egg taken out of its shell, is to cook it in or over boiling water 2 to poach animals is to hunt them illegally on someone else's land **poacher** noun

someone who hunts animals illegally on someone else's land

pocket noun
part of a piece of clothing shaped like a small bag, for keeping things in

pocket adjective
small enough to carry in your pocket • Use a pocket calculator.

pocket verb
to pocket something is to put it in your pocket

pocket money noun
pocket money is money given to a child to spend

pod noun
a long seed-container on a pea or bean plant

podgy adjective (**podgier, podgiest**)
short and fat

poem noun
a piece of writing arranged in short lines, often with a particular rhythm and sometimes rhyming

poet noun
someone who writes poetry

poetry noun
poetry is poems as a form of literature • Do you write poetry?

point noun
1 the narrow or sharp end of something • Don't hold the knife by its point. 2 a written dot • Put in a decimal point. 3 a single mark in a game or quiz • How many points did I get? 4 a particular place or time • They gave up at this point. 5 something that someone says during a discussion • That's a very good point. 6 a detail or special feature • He has some good points. 7 purpose or advantage • There's no point in hurrying. 8 the points on a railway line are the movable parts that allow trains to change from one track to another **to come to the point** is to mention the thing you really want to say

point verb
1 to point to something is to show where it is, especially by holding out your finger towards it 2 to point something is to aim it or direct it • She pointed a gun at us. **to point something out** is to show it or explain it

point-blank adjective, adverb
1 close to the target 2 directly and completely • He refused point-blank.

pointed adjective
having a point at the end

pointer noun
a stick or device you use to point at something

pointless adjective
something is pointless when it has no purpose or meaning **pointlessly** adverb

point of view noun (**points of view**)
a way of looking or thinking of something

poise noun
poise is a dignified and self-confident manner

poise verb
1 to poise something is to balance it or keep it steady 2 to be poised to do something is to be ready to do it

poison noun
a substance that can kill or harm living things if they eat or absorb it

poison verb
1 to poison someone is to kill or harm them with poison 2 to poison something is to put poison in it **poisoner** noun a person who kills someone using poison

poisonous adjective
1 a poisonous chemical, gas, or plant can kill or harm you if you swallow it or breathe it in 2 poisonous animals or insects can kill or harm you with poison if they bite you • a poisonous snake

poke verb
to poke something or someone is to push or jab them hard with your finger or a pointed object **to poke out** is to stick out

poke noun
a prod or jab

poker noun
1 a poker is a metal rod for stirring a fire 2 poker is a card game in which the players bet on who has the best cards

polar adjective
to do with the North or South Pole, or near one of them

polar bear noun
a powerful white bear living near the North Pole

pole[1] noun
a long thin piece of wood or metal

pole[2] noun
1 each of the two points on the earth that are furthest from the equator, the **North Pole** and the **South Pole** 2 each end of a magnet

pole vault noun
the pole vault is an athletic contest in which you jump over a high bar with the help of a long springy pole

police noun
the police are the people whose job

is to catch criminals and make sure
that people obey the law

policeman or
policewoman *noun*
(**policemen** or **policewomen**)
a man or woman member of the
police

police officer *noun*
a member of the police

policy *noun* (**policies**)
the aims or plans of a person or
group of people

polio *noun* (*say* **poh**-li-oh)
a disease that paralyses the body

polish *verb* (*say* **pol**-ish)
to polish something is to make its
surface shiny or smooth **to polish
something off** (*informal*) is to finish
it quickly

polish *noun* (*say* **pol**-ish)
1 polish is a substance used in
polishing **2** a polish is a shine got by
polishing • *He gave his shoes a good
polish.*

polite *adjective*
having good manners; respectful
and thoughtful towards other people
politely *adverb* **politeness** *noun*

political *adjective*
to do with the governing of a country
politically *adverb* in a way that is
to do with politics

politician *noun*
someone who is involved in politics

politics *noun*
politics is political matters;
the business of governing a country

poll *noun*
1 a round of voting at an election
2 a survey of what people think
about something

pollen *noun*
pollen is yellow powder found inside
flowers, containing male seeds for
fertilizing other flowers

pollinate *verb*
to pollinate a flower or plant is to
put pollen into it so that it becomes
fertilized
pollination *noun* the process of
pollinating a flower or plant

pollute *verb*
to pollute a place or thing is to make
it dirty or impure

pollution *noun*
pollution is the process of making the
air, water, and soil dirty or impure

polo *noun*
polo is a game rather like hockey,
with players on horseback using long
mallets

poltergeist *noun*
(*say* pol-ter-**gyst**)
a noisy mischievous ghost that
moves things or throws them
about

polygon *noun*
a figure or shape with many sides,
such as a hexagon or octagon

polythene *noun*
(*say* **pol**-i-theen)
polythene is a lightweight plastic
used to make bags and wrappings

pomp *noun*
pomp is the dignified and solemn
way in which an important ceremony
is carried out

pompous *adjective*
someone is being pompous when
they are thinking too much of their
own importance

pond *noun*
a small lake

ponder *verb*
to ponder something is to think
carefully and seriously about it

pony *noun*
a small horse

ponytail *noun*
a bunch of long hair tied at the back
of the head

poodle *noun*
a dog with long curly hair

pool¹ *noun*
1 a pond **2** a puddle **3** a swimming pool
pool² *noun*
1 a group of things shared by several
people **2** the fund of money that can
be won in a gambling game **3** pool
is a game similar to snooker but
played on a smaller table **the pools** a
system of gambling on the results of
football matches

poor *adjective*
1 having very little money
• *He came from a poor
family.* **2** not good or
adequate • *This is poor
work.* **3** unfortunate
• *Poor fellow!*

poorly *adverb*
not adequately; badly
• *She did poorly in the
test.*
poorly *adjective*
unwell • *I'm feeling poorly today.*

pop¹ *noun*
1 a pop is a small sharp bang
2 pop is a fizzy drink
pop¹ *verb* (**popping, popped**)
1 to pop is to make a small sharp
bang **2** (*informal*) to pop somewhere
is to go there quickly • *I'm just
popping out to the shops.* **3** to pop

something somewhere is to put it
there quickly • *Will you pop the
potatoes in the oven?*
pop² *noun*
pop is modern popular music

popcorn *noun*
a snack made from grains of maize
heated till they burst and form light
fluffy balls

Pope *noun*
the Pope is the leader of the Roman
Catholic Church

poppy *noun* (**poppies**)
a plant with large red flowers

popular *adjective*
liked or enjoyed by a lot of people
popularity *noun* being liked or
enjoyed by a lot of people

populated *adjective*
a place is populated when it has
people living there • *The land is
thinly populated.*

population *noun*
the population of a particular place is
all the people who live there; the total
number of people who live there
• *What's the population of London?*

porcelain *noun* (*say* **por**-se-lin)
porcelain is a fine kind of china

porch *noun*
a covered area in front of the door of
a building

porcupine *noun*
a small animal covered with long
prickles

WORD ORIGIN

The word **porcupine** comes from old
French words meaning 'prickly pig'.

porcupine

pore *noun*
one of the tiny openings in your skin
which sweat can pass through

pork *noun*
pork is meat from a pig

porous *adjective*
something is porous when it allows liquid or air to pass through • *Sandy soil is porous.*

porpoise *noun* (say **por**-pus)
a sea animal rather like a small whale

porridge *noun*
porridge is a food made by boiling oatmeal to make a thick paste

port¹ *noun*
1 a port is a harbour 2 a port is also a city or town with a harbour 3 port is the left-hand side of a ship or aircraft when you are facing forward

port² *noun*
port is a strong red Portuguese wine

portable *adjective*
able to be carried easily

portcullis *noun*
a heavy grating that can be lowered to block the gateway to a castle

porter *noun*
1 someone whose job is to carry luggage or goods 2 someone whose job is to look after the entrance to a large building

porthole *noun*
a small round window in the side of a ship or aircraft

portion *noun*
1 a part or share given to someone 2 an amount of food for one person

portly *adjective* (**portlier, portliest**)
rather fat

portrait *noun*
a picture of a person

portray *verb*
to portray something or someone is to describe or show them in a certain way • *The play portrays the king as a kind man.* **portrayal** *noun* how a person or thing is described or shown

pose *noun*
a way of standing or sitting for a portrait or photograph to be made of you • *Just hold that pose for a second.*

pose *verb*
1 to pose is to put your body into a special position
2 to pose someone is to put them in a particular position to be painted or photographed
3 to pose as someone is to pretend to be them
• *The man posed as a police officer.*
4 to pose a question or problem is to present it • *Icy weather always poses a problem to motorists.*

posh *adjective*
(*informal*) very smart or high-class • *They stayed at a posh hotel.* • *She spoke with a posh accent.*

position *noun*
1 the place where something is or should be 2 the way in which someone or something is placed or arranged • *He was sleeping in an uncomfortable position.* 3 a person's place in a race or competition 4 a regular job

positive *adjective*
1 sure or definite • *I am positive I saw him.* • *We need positive proof.* 2 agreeing or saying 'yes' • *We received a positive answer.* 3 a positive number is one that is greater than nought 4 a positive electric charge is one that does not carry electrons **positively** *adverb*

positive *noun*
a photographic print made from a negative, with light and dark parts as in real life

posse *noun* (say **poss**-i)
a group of people who help a sheriff in the USA

possess *verb*
to possess something is to own or have it **possessor** *noun* a person who owns or has something

possessed *adjective*
someone is possessed when they are behaving as if they are controlled by an outside force • *He fought like a man possessed.*

possession *noun*
something that you own

possessive *adjective*
you are being possessive when you want to get and keep things for yourself

possibility *noun* (**possibilities**)
1 possibility is being possible • *Is there any possibility of changing your mind?* 2 a possibility is something that is possible • *There are many possibilities.*

possible *adjective*
able to exist, happen, be done, or be used

possibly *adverb*
1 in any way • *That cannot possibly be right.* 2 perhaps • *I will arrive at six o'clock, or possibly earlier.*

post¹ *noun*
1 an upright piece of wood, concrete, or metal fixed in the ground 2 the starting point or finishing point of a race • *He was left at the post.*

post² *noun*
1 the post is the collecting and delivering of letters and parcels

2 post is letters and parcels carried by post; mail 3 a post is a collection or delivery of mail at a particular time • *The last post is at 4 p.m.*

post² *verb*
1 to post a letter or parcel is to send it to someone by post 2 to send a message to an Internet site to display information online

post³ *noun*
1 a regular job 2 the place where a sentry stands

post³ *verb*
to be posted somewhere is to be sent there for a time as part of your job

postage *noun*
postage is the cost of sending a letter or parcel by post

postal *adjective*
to do with the post; by post

postbox *noun*
a box into which you put letters to be sent by post

postcard *noun*
a card you can write on and post without an envelope

postcode *noun*
a group of letters and numbers put at the end of an address to help in sorting the post

poster *noun*
a large public notice having information or advertising something

postman *noun* (**postmen**)
someone who collects and delivers letters and parcels

postmark *noun*
an official mark stamped on something sent by post, showing when and where it was posted

post office *noun*
a place where you can post letters and parcels and buy stamps and other official documents

postpone *verb*
to postpone a meeting or event is to arrange for it to take place later than was originally planned • *The match has been postponed for two weeks.* **postponement** *noun* when something is arranged to take place later than was originally planned

posture *noun*
the way that a person stands, sits, or walks

posy *noun* (**posies**)
a small bunch of flowers

pot *noun*
1 a deep round container
2 a flowerpot **pots of money** (*informal*) a lot of money

pot verb (**potting, potted**)
1 to pot a plant is to put it into a flowerpot 2 to pot a ball in a game such as snooker or pool is to hit it into a pocket

potassium noun
potassium is a soft silvery-white metallic substance that living things need

potato noun (**potatoes**)
a vegetable that grows underground

potent adjective
powerful **potency** noun the potency of something is how powerful it is **potently** adverb

potential adjective
possible or capable of happening in the future • She is a potential star. **potentially** adverb as a possibility in the future • He is potentially one of our best players.

potential noun
to have potential is to be capable of becoming important or useful in the future

pothole noun
1 a deep natural hole in the ground 2 a hole in a road

potion noun (say **poh**-shon)
a drink containing medicine or poison

potter noun
someone who makes pottery

pottery noun (**potteries**)
1 pottery is pots, cups, plates, and other things made of baked clay 2 pottery is also the craft of making pottery

potty noun (**potties**)
(informal) a small bowl used by young children as a toilet

pouch noun
1 a small bag or pocket 2 a fold of skin in which a kangaroo keeps its young

poultry noun
poultry are birds such as chickens, geese, and turkeys, kept for their eggs and meat

pounce verb
to pounce on someone or something is to jump on them or attack them suddenly

pound¹ noun
1 a unit of money, in Britain equal to 100 pence 2 a unit of weight equal to 16 ounces or about 454 grams

pound² verb
1 to pound something is to hit it repeatedly to crush it 2 to pound, or pound along, is to walk with heavy steps 3 your heart is pounding when it beats heavily, making a dull thumping sound • My heart was pounding with the excitement.

pour verb
1 to pour a liquid is to make it flow out of a container 2 to pour is to flow in a large amount • Blood was pouring from the wound on her leg. 3 it is pouring when it is raining heavily 4 to pour in or out is to come or go in large numbers or amounts • After the programme, letters of complaint poured in. • The fans poured out of the stadium.

pout verb
you pout when you stick out your lips because you are annoyed or sulking

poverty noun
poverty is being poor

powder noun
1 a mass of tiny pieces of something dry, like flour or dust 2 make-up in the form of powder **powdery** adjective like powder

powder verb
to powder something is to put powder on it • She powdered her face. **powdered** adjective made into a powder • powdered milk

power noun
1 power is strength or great energy 2 power is also control over other people 3 the power to do something is the ability to do it • Humans have the power of speech. 4 a power is a powerful country 5 power is also electricity or another form of energy 6 (in mathematics) the power of a number is the result obtained by multiplying the number by itself one or more times • 27 is the third power of 3 ($3 \times 3 \times 3 = 27$). **powered** adjective a device is (for example) electric-powered or solar-powered when it is worked by electricity or by the sun's energy

powerful adjective
having a lot of power or influence **powerfully** adverb

powerless adjective
someone is powerless if they are unable to act or control things

power station noun
a building where electricity is produced

practical adjective
1 someone is practical when they are able to do or make useful things • She is a very practical person. 2 something is practical when it is likely to be useful • That is a practical idea. 3 concerned with doing or making things • He has had practical experience.

practical noun
a lesson or examination in which you actually do or make something rather than reading or writing about it

practical joke noun
a trick played on someone

practically adverb
1 in a practical way • He is practically skilled. 2 almost • It's practically ready now.

practice noun
1 practice is doing something often and regularly so that you get better at it • I must do my piano practice. 2 practice is also actually doing something rather than thinking or talking about it • It's time to put this theory of yours into practice. • I hope my plan works in practice. 3 a practice is the business of a doctor or lawyer

practise verb
1 to practise something is to do it often so that you get better at it 2 to practise an activity or custom is to do it regularly • She practises yoga. 3 to practise (for example) medicine or law is to work as a doctor or lawyer

prairie noun
a large area of flat grass-covered land in North America

praise verb
to praise someone or something is to say that they are good or have done well

praise noun
praise is words that praise someone or something

pram noun
a small open carriage for a baby, pushed by a person walking

prance verb
to prance is to jump about in a lively or happy way

prank noun
a trick played on someone for mischief

prawn noun
a shellfish like a large shrimp, used for food

pray verb
1 to pray is to talk to God 2 to pray is also to ask earnestly or hope for something • We are praying for good weather.

prayer noun
1 prayer is praying 2 a prayer is what you say when you pray

preach verb
to preach is to give a talk about religion or about right and wrong **preacher** noun someone who preaches

a
b
c
d
e
f
g
h
i
j
k
l
m
n
o
p
q
r
s
t
u
v
w
x
y
z

precarious adjective
(say pri-**kair**-i-us)
not at all safe or secure • That
vase is in a precarious position.
precariously adverb

precaution noun
something you do to prevent trouble
or danger in the future • I took the
precaution of bringing my umbrella.

precede verb
one thing precedes another when it
comes or goes in front of the other
thing • The film was preceded by a
short cartoon.

precinct noun (say **pree**-sinkt)
a part of a town where traffic is
not allowed • The town has a large
shopping precinct.

precious adjective
very valuable or loved

precipice noun
the steep face of a mountain or cliff

precise adjective
1 clear and accurate • I gave them
precise instructions. 2 exact • At that
precise moment, the doorbell rang.
precisely adverb accurately and
carefully **precision** noun being
exact or accurate

predator noun (say **pred**-a-ter)
an animal that hunts other animals
predatory adjective hunting other
animals

predict verb
to predict something is to say
that it will happen in the future
predictable adjective likely or
expected • His angry reaction was
predictable.
prediction noun something that
you predict

preen verb
a bird preens when it smoothes and
cleans its feathers using its beak

preface noun (say **pref**-ass)
an introduction at the beginning of
a book

prefect noun
an older pupil in some schools who is
given authority to help to keep order

prefer verb (**preferring,
preferred**)
to prefer one thing to another is to
like it better than the other thing
preference noun what you prefer

prefix noun
a group of letters joined to the front
of a word to change or add to its
meaning, as in disorder, overflow, and
unhappy

pregnant adjective
a pregnant woman has an unborn
baby growing inside

her womb **pregnancy** noun
a time of being pregnant

prehistoric adjective
belonging to a very long time ago,
before written records were kept
prehistory noun prehistoric times

prejudice noun
a prejudice is when you make
up your mind that you don't like
someone or something without a
good reason or without thinking
about it **prejudiced** adjective
having a prejudice

preliminary adjective
coming before something or
preparing for it

prelude noun (say **prel**-yood)
an introduction to a play,
poem, or event

premature adjective
happening or coming before the
proper time • a premature baby

première noun (say **prem**-yair)
the first public performance of
a play or showing of a film

premises plural noun
an organization's or business's
premises are the building and
land it uses

premium noun
(say **pree**-mi-um)
an amount paid regularly to
an insurance company

preparation noun
1 preparation is getting something
ready 2 preparations are things
you do in order to get ready for
something • We were making last-
minute preparations.

prepare verb
to prepare something is to get
it ready **to be prepared to do
something** is to be ready or willing
to do it

preposition noun
a word you put in front of a noun or
pronoun to show how the noun or
pronoun is connected with another
word, for example on in the sentence
Put the flowers on the table and with
in the sentence I'd like some sauce
with my food.

prescribe verb
to prescribe a medicine for a patient
is to instruct them to take it and give
them a prescription for it

prescription noun
a doctor's written order for a chemist
to prepare a medicine for a patient

presence noun
your presence somewhere is the fact
that you are there
• Your presence is expected.

in the presence of someone while
they are there, in the same place

present¹ adjective (say **prez**-ent)
1 in a particular place; here
• Nobody else was present.
2 existing or happening now
• Who is the present Queen?

present¹ noun (say **prez**-ent)
1 the present is the time now
• Our teacher is away at present.
2 the form of a verb that describes
something that is happening now,
for example likes in the sentence He
likes swimming.

present² noun (say **prez**-ent)
something that you give to someone
or receive from them

presents

present² verb (say pri-**zent**)
1 to present something to someone
is to give it to them, especially with
a ceremony • Who will present the
prizes this year? 2 to present a play
or other entertainment is to perform
it or arrange for it to be performed
3 to present a radio or television
programme is to introduce it to the
audience 4 to present something
you have done or made is to show it
formally to people • We are here to
present our latest products.

presentation noun
1 a formal talk showing or
demonstrating something
2 a ceremony in which someone is
given a gift or prize • I'd like to make
a little presentation.

presenter noun
someone who presents something,
especially a radio or television
programme

presently adverb
soon; in a while • They will be here
presently.

present participle noun
a form of a verb that ends in -ing and
describes something that is or was
happening, for example watching
in the sentences I am watching
television and They were watching
television.

preservative noun
a substance added to food to
preserve it

preserve *verb*
to preserve something is to keep it safe or in good condition
preservation *noun* preserving something

president *noun*
1 the head of a country that is a republic 2 the person in charge of a society, business, or club
presidency *noun* the job of being a president **presidential** *adjective* to do with a president

press *verb*
1 to press something is to push it firmly or squeeze it • *Press the red button.* 2 to press clothes is to make them flat and smooth with an iron 3 to press someone for something is to urge them to do or give it • *She's pressing me for a decision.*

press *noun*
1 the action of squeezing or pushing on something • *Give the bell another press.* 2 the press are newspapers and journalists 3 a machine for printing things

pressure *noun*
1 pressure is continuous pushing or squeezing • *Apply pressure to the cut to stop it bleeding.* 2 pressure is also the force with which a liquid or gas pushes against something 3 there is pressure on you when someone is trying to persuade or force you to do something

prestige *noun* (*say* pres-**teezh**)
prestige is the respect something has because it is important or of a high quality

presumably *adverb*
probably; I suppose

presume *verb*
1 to presume something is to suppose it • *I presumed that he was dead.* 2 to presume to do something is to dare to do it • *I wouldn't presume to advise you.*

pretence *noun*
a pretence is an attempt to pretend something

pretend *verb*
1 to pretend is to behave as if something untrue or imaginary is true 2 to pretend something is to claim it dishonestly • *They pretended they were policemen.*

pretty *adjective* (**prettier, prettiest**)
pleasant to look at or hear; attractive
prettily *adverb* **prettiness** *noun*
pretty *adverb* (*informal*) quite; moderately • *It's pretty cold outside.*

prevent *verb*
1 to prevent something is to stop it from happening or make it impossible 2 to prevent someone is to stop them from doing something
prevention *noun* stopping something bad from happening
preventive *adjective* meant to help prevent something • *preventive medicine*

preview *noun*
a showing of a film or play before it is shown to most people

previous *adjective*
coming before this; preceding
• *I was in London the previous week.*
previously *adverb* before or earlier

prey *noun* (*say* pray)
an animal that is hunted or killed by another animal for food

prey *verb* (*say* pray)
to prey on something is to hunt and kill an animal for food • *Owls prey on mice and other small animals.*

price *noun*
1 the amount of money for which something is sold
2 what you have to give or do to get something • *Giving up this land was a small price to pay for peace.* **at any price** at any cost **pricey** *adjective* expensive

priceless *adjective*
very valuable

prick *verb*
1 to prick something is to make a tiny hole in it 2 to prick someone is to hurt them with something sharp or pointed
to prick up your ears is to start listening suddenly

prickle *noun*
a sharp point on a plant or animal
prickly *adjective* covered in prickles or feeling like prickles

prickle *verb*
to prickle is to make your skin feel as though lots of little sharp points are sticking into it • *This jumper is prickling me.*

pride *noun*
1 pride is a feeling of being very pleased with yourself or with someone else who has done well
• *My heart swelled with pride.* 2 pride is also being too satisfied because of who you are or what you have done 3 a pride is something that makes you feel proud • *This stamp is the pride of my collection.* 4 a pride is also a group of lions

priest *noun*
1 a member of the clergy 2 someone who performs religious ceremonies; a religious leader

priesthood *noun* the position of being a priest

priestess *noun*
a female priest in a non-Christian religion

prim *adjective* (**primmer, primmest**)
liking things to be correct, and easily shocked by anything rude **primly** *adverb*

primary *adjective*
first; most important
primarily *adverb* mainly; most importantly

primary colour *noun*
one of the colours from which all other colours can be made by mixing: red, yellow, and blue (of paint), and red, green, and violet (of light)

primary school *noun*
a first school for children from the age of 5 onwards

prime *adjective*
1 chief or most important • *The weather was the prime cause of the accident.* 2 of the best quality

prime minister *noun*
the leader of a government

prime number *noun*
a number that can only be divided exactly by itself and the number one, for example 2, 3, 5, 7, and 11

primitive *adjective*
1 at an early stage of development or civilization
• *Primitive humans were hunters rather than farmers.* 2 basic or simple • *Our accommodation was fairly primitive.*

prince *noun*
1 the son of a king or queen
2 a man or boy in a royal family
princely *adjective* a princely sum is a large or generous amount of money

princess *noun*
1 the daughter of a king or queen 2 a woman or girl in a royal family 3 the wife of a prince

principal *adjective*
chief or most important • *Name the principal cities of Britain.*
principally *adverb* chiefly or mainly

principal *noun*
the head of a college or school

principle *noun*
1 a general rule or truth
• *She taught me the principles of geometry.* 2 someone's principles are the basic rules and beliefs they have about how they should behave
in principle in general, not in detail
• *I agree with your plan in principle.*

a b c d e f g h i j k l m n o p q r s t u v w x y z

print *verb*
1 to print words or pictures is to put them on paper with a machine
2 to print letters is to write them separately and not joined together
3 to print a photograph is to print it, usually on photographic paper

printing blocks

print *noun*
1 print is printed words or pictures 2 a print is a mark made by something pressing on a surface • *Her thumb left a print on the glass.* 3 a print is also a photograph made from a negative

printer *noun*
1 a machine that prints on paper from data in a computer
2 someone who prints books or newspapers

printout *noun*
the information printed on paper from data in a computer

priority *noun* (**priorities**)
(*say* pry-**o**-ri-ti)
1 a priority is something that is more urgent or important than other things and needs to be dealt with first • *Repairing the roof is a priority.* 2 priority is the right to go first or be considered before other things • *People in need of urgent medical help will have priority.*

prise *verb*
to prise something open is to force or lever it open • *He prised open the lid with a screwdriver.*

prism *noun*
a piece of glass that breaks up light into the colours of the rainbow

prison *noun*
a place where people are locked up as a punishment for crimes

prisoner *noun*
someone who is kept in a prison or who is a captive

privacy *noun*
privacy is being private or away from other people • *Our new garden fence will give us more privacy.*

private *adjective*
1 belonging to a particular person or group of people • *This is a private road.* 2 meant to be kept secret • *These letters are private.* 3 away from other people • *Is there a private place to swim?* **in private** where only particular people can see or hear; not in public **privately** *adverb* separately; not with other people • *Can we speak privately?*

private *noun*
a soldier of the lowest rank

privilege *noun*
a special right or advantage given to one person or group of people **privileged** *adjective* having special advantages that other people don't have

prize *noun*
something you get for winning a game or competition, or for doing well in an examination

prize *verb*
to prize something is to value it highly

probable *adjective*
likely to be true or to happen **probability** *noun* the probability of something is how likely it is to happen **probably** *adverb*

probation *noun*
probation is a time when someone is tried out in a new job to make sure they are suitable for the work **on probation** being supervised by a probation officer

probe *noun*
1 a long thin instrument used to look closely at something such as a wound 2 an investigation

probe *verb*
to probe is to investigate or look at something closely

problem *noun*
something that is difficult to answer or deal with

procedure *noun*
a fixed or special way of doing something

proceed *verb* (*say* pro-**seed**)
to proceed is to go on or continue

proceedings *plural noun*
things that happen; activities

proceeds *plural noun*
(*say* **proh**-seedz)
the proceeds of a sale or event are the money made from it

process *noun*
a series of actions for making or doing something **to be in the process of doing something** is to be in the middle of doing it

process *verb*
to process something is to treat it or deal with it by a process so that it can be used • *He took the film to the chemist to be processed.*

procession *noun*
a number of people or vehicles moving steadily forwards

proclaim *verb*
to proclaim something is to announce it officially or publicly **proclamation** *noun* a public announcement

prod *verb* (**prodding, prodded**)
to prod something or someone is to poke or jab them

produce *verb* (*say* pro-**dewss**)
1 to produce something is to make or create it 2 to produce something that is hidden or put away is to bring it out so that people can see it
3 to produce a play or film or other entertainment is to organize the performance of it

produce *noun*
(*say* prod-**yewss**)
produce is things produced, especially by farmers **producer** *noun* someone who produces a play or film

product *noun*
1 something someone makes or produces for sale 2 the result of multiplying two numbers • *12 is the product of 4 and 3.*

production *noun*
1 production is the process of making or creating something • *The factory is equipped for car production.* 2 a production is a version of a play or film

productive *adjective*
producing a lot of good or useful things **productivity** *noun* the rate at which someone works or produces things

profession *noun*
a type of work for which you need special knowledge and training, for example medicine, law, or teaching

professional *adjective*
1 doing a certain type of work to earn money • *He became a professional tennis player.* 2 to do with a profession 3 done with great skill and to a high standard **professionally** *adverb*

professional *noun*
someone doing a certain type of work to earn money

professor *noun*
a teacher of the highest rank in a university

proficient *adjective*
(*say* pro-**fish**-ent)
to be proficient at something is to

be able to do it well **proficiency** *noun* the ability to do something well **proficiently** *adverb*

profile *noun*
1 a person's profile is a side view of their face 2 a short description of a person's life or character

profit *noun*
1 the extra money you get by selling something for more than it cost to buy or make
2 an advantage or benefit

profit *verb*
to profit from something is to get an advantage from it

profitable *adjective*
making a profit; bringing in money

profound *adjective*
1 very deep or intense
• *His death had a profound effect on us all.* 2 showing or needing great knowledge or thought • *The poem she wrote was quite profound.*
profoundly *adverb*

program *noun*
a series of instructions for a computer to carry out

program *verb* (**programming, programmed**)
to program a computer is to prepare or control it by means of a program

programme *noun*
1 a show, play, or talk on radio or television 2 a list of a planned series of events 3 a leaflet or pamphlet that gives details of a play, concert, or other event

progress *noun* (*say* **proh**-gress)
1 progress is forward movement
• *The procession made slow progress.*
2 progress is also development or improvement • *You have made a lot of progress this term.*
progress *verb* (*say* pro-**gress**)
1 to progress is to move forward 2 to progress is also to develop or improve
progression *noun* when something develops or moves forward

prohibit *verb*
to prohibit something is to forbid it, especially by law • *Smoking is prohibited.* **prohibition** *noun* forbidding something

project *noun* (*say* **proj**-ekt)
1 a task in which you find out as much as you can about something and write about it
2 a plan or scheme
project *verb* (*say* pro-**jekt**)
1 to project is to stick out 2 to project your voice is to speak loudly and clearly so that it carries a long way 3 to project a picture or film is to

show it with a projector on a screen
projection *noun* 1 something that sticks out 2 showing a picture or film on a screen

projector *noun*
a machine for showing films or photographs on a screen

prologue *noun* (*say* **proh**-log)
an introduction to a poem or play or long story

prolong *verb*
to prolong something is to make it last longer

promenade *noun*
(*say* prom-en-**ahd**)
a wide path for walking beside the sea

prominent *adjective*
1 easily seen; standing out
• *She has prominent teeth.*
2 important **prominence** *noun* being prominent **prominently** *adverb*

promise *noun*
1 a promise is a statement that you will definitely do or not do something
2 something shows promise when it shows signs that it will be successful in the future

promise *verb*
to promise to do something is to say that you will definitely do it

promising *adjective*
likely to be good or successful • *We have several promising pupils.*

promote *verb*
1 to be promoted is to be given a more senior or more important job or rank 2 a sports team is promoted when it moves to a higher division or league 3 to promote a product or cause is to make people more aware of it • *He has done much to promote the cause of peace.*

promotion *noun*
1 promotion is when someone is given a more senior or more important job or rank
2 promotion is also when a sports team moves to a higher division or league
3 a promotion is a piece of publicity or advertising

prompt *adjective*
happening soon or without delay • *We need a prompt reply.*
promptly *adverb* without delay
prompt *verb*
1 to prompt someone to do something is to cause or encourage them to do it 2 to prompt an actor is to remind them of

their words if they forget them during a play

prone *adjective*
lying face downwards **to be prone to something** is to be likely to do it or suffer from it • *He is prone to lose his temper.*

prong *noun*
one of the pointed spikes at the end of a fork

pronoun *noun*
a word used instead of a noun, such as *he, her, it, them, those*

pronounce *verb*
1 to pronounce a word is to say it in a particular way
• *'Too' and 'two' are pronounced the same.* 2 to pronounce something is to declare it formally • *I now pronounce you man and wife.*

pronunciation *noun*
(*say* pro-**nun**-si-ay-shon)
the way a word is pronounced

proof *noun*
proof is a fact which shows that something is true or exists • *There is no proof that she stole the money.*
proof *adjective*
giving protection against something
• *They wore bullet-proof jackets.*

prop[1] *noun*
a support, especially one made of a long piece of wood or metal
prop[1] *verb* (**propping, propped**)
to prop something somewhere is to lean it there so that it doesn't fall over • *The ladder was propped up against the wall.*

prop[2] *noun*
a piece of furniture or other object used on stage in a theatre

propaganda *noun*
propaganda is information, especially false information, that is spread around to make people believe something

propel *verb* (**propelling, propelled**)
to propel something is to send it rapidly forward

propeller *noun*
a set of blades on a hub that spin round to drive an aircraft or ship

propeller

a b c d e f g h i j k l m n o p q r s t u v w x y z

proper *adjective*
1 suitable or right • *This is the proper way to hold a bat.* 2 respectable • *You must behave in a proper fashion.* 3 (*informal*) complete; real • *I haven't had a proper meal for days.* **properly** *adverb* in a way that is correct or suitable

proper noun *noun*
the name given to one person or thing, such as *Mary* and *Tokyo*, and usually written with a capital first letter

property *noun* (**properties**)
1 a person's property is a thing, or all the things, that belong to them 2 a property is buildings or land belonging to someone 3 a property is also a quality or characteristic that something has • *People thought the berries had healing properties.*

prophecy *noun* (**prophecies**)
(*say* **prof**-i-si)
something that someone has said will happen in the future

prophesy *verb* (**prophesies, prophesying, prophesied**)
(*say* prof-i-**sy**)
to prophesy something is to say that it will happen in the future

prophet *noun*
1 someone who makes prophecies 2 a religious teacher who is believed to speak the word of God **the Prophet** a name for Muhammad, the founder of the Muslim faith

prophetic *adjective*
saying or showing what will happen in the future

proportion *noun*
1 a fraction or share of something • *Water covers a large proportion of the earth's surface.* 2 the proportion of one thing to another is how much there is of one compared to the other • *What is the proportion of oil to vinegar in this salad dressing?* 3 the correct relationship between the size, amount, or importance of two things • *You've drawn the head out of proportion with the body.* **proportions** size or scale • *It is a ship of large proportions.*

proportional or **proportionate** *adjective*
in proportion; according to a ratio **proportionally, proportionately** *adverb* in proportion

proposal *noun*
1 a suggestion or plan 2 when someone asks another person to marry them

propose *verb*
1 to propose an idea or plan is to suggest it 2 to propose to someone is to ask them to marry you

proprietor *noun*
(*say* pro-**pry**-et-er)
the owner of a shop or business

propulsion *noun*
propulsion is propelling something or driving it forward

prose *noun*
prose is writing that is like ordinary speech, not poetry or verse

prosecute *verb*
to prosecute someone is to make them go to a lawcourt to be tried for a crime **prosecution** *noun* the process of prosecuting someone **prosecutor** *noun* an official who prosecutes people

prospect *noun* (*say* **pros**-pekt)
a possibility or hope; what may happen in the future • *There's not much prospect of the weather improving.*

prosper *verb*
to prosper is to be successful or do well

prosperous *adjective*
successful or rich **prosperity** *noun* being successful or rich

protect *verb*
to protect someone or something is to keep them safe **protection** *noun* keeping someone or something safe **protector** *noun* a person who protects someone or something

protective *adjective*
1 a person is protective when they want to protect someone or something 2 a thing is protective when it is meant to protect something

protein *noun* (*say* **proh**-teen)
protein is a substance found in some types of food which your body needs to help you grow and be healthy

protest *noun* (*say* **proh**-test)
something you say or do because you disapprove of someone or something

protest *verb* (*say* pro-**test**)
to protest about something is to say publicly that you think it is wrong **protester** *noun* someone who protests about something

Protestant *noun*
(*say* **prot**-is-tant)
a member of a western Christian Church other than the Roman Catholic Church

proton *noun*
a particle of matter with a positive electric charge

protractor *noun*
a device in the shape of a semicircle, used for measuring and drawing angles on paper

protractor

proud *adjective*
1 very pleased with yourself or with someone else who has done well • *I am proud of my sister.* 2 too satisfied because of who you are or what you have done • *They were too proud to ask for help.* **proudly** *adverb*

prove *verb*
1 to prove something is to show that it is true 2 to prove to be something is to turn out to be that way • *The forecast proved to be correct.*

proverb *noun*
a short well-known saying that gives advice or says something about life, for example *many hands make light work*

proverbial *adjective*
1 occurring in a proverb 2 familiar or well-known

provide *verb*
1 to provide something is to supply it 2 to provide for something is to prepare for it • *They have provided for all possible disasters.* **provided** or **providing** on condition; on condition that • *You can come providing you bring some food.*

province *noun*
a region or division of a country

provision *noun*
provision is providing something • *the provision of free meals for old people*

provisional *adjective*
arranged or agreed on for the time being, but not yet definite • *21 July is the provisional date for the summer fair.*

provisions *plural noun*
supplies of food and drink

provocative *adjective*
likely to make someone angry • *That was a provocative remark.*

provoke *verb*
1 to provoke someone is to deliberately make them angry 2 to provoke a feeling is to arouse or cause it • *His remarks provoked a great deal of criticism.* **provocation** *noun* saying or doing something to deliberately make someone angry

prow *noun*
the front end of a ship

prowl *verb*
to prowl is to move about quietly and secretly, as some animals do when

they are hunting **prowler** noun
someone who prowls threateningly

proximity noun
to be in the proximity of something is
to be near it

prudent adjective (say **proo**-dent)
wise and careful; not taking risks
prudence noun being wise and
careful **prudently** adverb

prune¹ noun
a dried plum

prune² verb
to prune a tree or bush is to cut off
unwanted parts from it

pry verb (**pries, prying, pried**)
to pry is to be nosy or inquisitive
about someone else's business

PS
something you write at the end
of a letter when you want to add
something else to it. **PS** is short for
Latin *post meridiem* which means
'after midday'.

psalm noun (say sahm)
a religious song from the Bible

pseudonym noun
(say **s'yoo**-do-nim)
a name used by an author instead of
their real name

psychiatrist noun
(say sy-**ky**-a-trist)
a doctor who treats mental illness

psychiatry noun
(say sy-**ky**-a-tree)
psychiatry is the treatment of mental
illness **psychiatric** adjective to do
with psychiatry

psychic adjective (say **sy**-kik)
someone is psychic when they can tell
the future or read other people's minds

psychologist noun
(say sy-**kol**-o-jist)
someone who studies how the mind
works

psychology noun
psychology is the study of the
mind and the way people behave
psychological adjective to do with
psychology

pub noun
(informal) a building where people
can buy and drink alcoholic drinks

puberty noun (say **pew**-ber-ti)
puberty is the time when a young
person starts to become an adult and
their body starts to change

public adjective
1 belonging to everyone or able to be
used by everyone • *I often use public
transport.* **2** to do with people in general
• *Newspapers can influence public
opinion.* **publicly** adverb in public

public noun
the public is people in general **in
public** openly; where anyone can see
or take part

publication noun
1 a publication is a book or
magazine that is printed and sold
2 publication is printing and selling
books or magazines

publicity noun
publicity is information or
advertising that makes people know
about someone or something

public school noun
a secondary school that charges fees

publish verb
1 to publish books or magazines is
to print and sell them **2** to publish
information is to make it known
publicly **publisher** noun a person
or company that publishes books or
magazines

puck noun
a hard rubber disc used in ice hockey

pudding noun
1 a hot sweet cooked food • *rice
pudding* **2** a savoury food made with
flour or suet • *Yorkshire pudding*
3 the sweet course of a meal • *What's
for pudding?*

puddle noun
a small pool, especially of rainwater

puff verb
1 to puff smoke or steam is to blow
it out **2** you puff when you breathe
with difficulty • *She was puffing
when she got to the top of the hill.*
3 to puff something, or to puff it out,
is to inflate or swell it • *He puffed out
his chest.*

puff noun
a small amount of breath, wind,
smoke, or steam
• *He vanished in a puff of smoke.*

puffin noun
a seabird
with a large
striped beak

puma

pull verb
1 to pull something is to get hold
of it and make it come towards you
or follow behind you **2** to pull is to
move with an effort • *She tried to
grab the boy but he pulled away.* **to
pull a face** is to twist your face into
a strange expression **to pull in 1** a
car pulls in when it stops at the side
of the road **2** a train pulls in when
it comes into a station and stops **to
pull out** is to decide to stop taking
part in something • *He had to pull
out of the race after he twisted his
ankle.* **to pull someone's leg** is to
tease them **to pull something off**
is to achieve it **to pull through** is to
recover from an illness **to pull up** is
to stop • *A car pulled up and two men
got out.* **to pull yourself together** is
to become calm or sensible

pull noun
a pull is an action of pulling
• *Give the handle a good pull.*

pulley noun (**pulleys**)
a wheel with a groove round it to take
a rope, used for lifting heavy things

pullover noun
a knitted piece of clothing for the top
half of your body, that you put on
over your head

pulp noun
a soft wet mass of something,
especially for making paper

pulpit noun
a raised platform in a church, from
which the priest or minister speaks
to the congregation

pulse¹ noun
1 your pulse is the regular beat
as your heart pumps your blood
through your arteries. You can feel
your pulse in your wrist or neck. **2** a
regular vibration or movement • *The
music had a throbbing pulse.*

pulse² noun
pulses are the edible seeds of certain
plants, such as peas, beans, and
lentils

puma noun
a large wild cat of
North America

a b c d e f g h i j k l m n o p q r s t u v w x z

pumice *noun* (say **pum**-iss)
pumice is a kind of soft sponge-like stone rubbed on hard surfaces to clean or polish them

pump *noun*
1 a device that forces air or liquid into or out of something, or along pipes **2** a lightweight shoe • *She took off her pumps.*

pump *verb*
to pump air or liquid is to force it into or out of something with a pump **to pump something up** is to fill something like a balloon or tyre with air or gas

pumpkin *noun*
a large round fruit with a hard yellow skin

pun *noun*
a joke made by using a word with two different meanings, or two words that sound the same, as in *Choosing where to bury him was a grave decision.*

punch[1] *verb*
1 to punch someone is to hit them with your fist **2** to punch a hole is to make a hole in something • *The guard checked and punched our tickets.* • *The builder punched a hole in the wall.*

punch[1] *noun*
1 a punch is a blow or hit with the fist **2** a punch is also a device for making holes in paper, metal, or other things

punch[2] *noun*
punch is a hot alcoholic drink

punchline *noun*
the last part of a joke or story, that makes it funny

punctual *adjective*
you are punctual when you arrive exactly on time, not late **punctuality** *noun* how punctual someone is **punctually** *adverb* in good time

punctuate *verb*
to punctuate a piece of writing is to put the commas, full stops, and other punctuation in it

punctuation *noun*
punctuation is the set of marks such as commas, full stops, and brackets put into a piece of writing to make it easier to understand

puncture *noun*
a small hole made in a tyre by accident

punish *verb*
to punish someone is to make them suffer in some way because they have done something wrong **punishment** *noun* a way of punishing someone

puny *adjective* (**punier, puniest**) (say **pew**-ni)
small and weak

pup *noun*
a puppy

pupa *noun* (**pupae**) (say **pew**-pa)
an insect at the stage of development between a larva and an adult insect; a chrysalis

pupil *noun*
1 someone who is being taught by a teacher **2** the opening in the centre of your eye

puppet *noun*
a kind of doll that can be made to move by fitting it over your fingers or hand or by pulling strings or wires attached to it

puppy *noun* (**puppies**)
a young dog

purchase *verb*
to purchase something is to buy it **purchaser** *noun* someone who buys something

purchase *noun*
1 a purchase is something you have bought **2** purchase is the fact of buying something • *Keep the receipt as proof of purchase.*

pure *adjective*
1 not mixed with anything else • *Use pure olive oil.* **2** clean or clear • *They washed in a pure cold mountain stream.*

purely *adverb*
only, simply • *They did it purely for the money.*

purify *verb* (**purifies, purifying, purified**)
to purify something is to make it pure **purification** *noun* purification is purifying something

purity *noun*
purity is the state of being pure

purple *noun* and *adjective* ●
a deep reddish-blue

purpose *noun*
the reason why you do something; what something is for **to do something on purpose** is to do it deliberately

purposely *adverb*
on purpose

purr *verb*
a cat purrs when it makes a gentle murmuring sound because it is pleased

purse *noun*
a small bag for holding money

pursue *verb*
1 to pursue someone or something is to chase them **2** to pursue an activity is to continue to do it or work at it • *She pursued her studies at college.*

pursuer *noun* a person who chases someone

pursuit *noun*
1 pursuit is the action of chasing someone **2** a pursuit is something you spend a lot of time doing

pus *noun*
pus is a thick yellowish substance produced in boils and other sore places on your body

push *verb*
1 to push something is to move it away from you by pressing against it **2** to push something is also to press it in • *Try pushing the button.*

push *noun*
a pushing movement

pushchair *noun*
a small folding chair with wheels, in which a child can be pushed along

puss *noun* (**pusses**)
(*informal*) a cat

put *verb* (**putting, put**)
1 to put something in a place is to move it there • *Put the shopping down here.* • *Where shall I put it?* **2** to put also means to affect someone or something in a particular way • *They've put me in a bad mood.* **3** to put an idea in a certain way is to express it in words of a special kind • *She put it very tactfully.* **to put someone off** is to make them less keen on something • *Seeing you eat so much has put me off my food.* **to put something off** is to decide to do it later instead of now • *We'll have to put off the party if you're ill.* **to put something on 1** is to switch on an electrical device, for example a light or a television **2** is to start wearing a piece of clothing • *I'll just put on my coat.* **to put something out** is to stop something like a fire or light from burning or shining **to put someone up** is to give them a place to sleep • *Can we put them up for the night?* **to put something up** is to raise it or make it upright • *Let's put up the tent.* **to put up with something** is to be willing to accept it without complaining

putty *noun*
putty is a soft paste that sets hard, used by builders to fit windows in their frames

puzzle *noun*
1 a tricky game that you have to solve **2** a difficult question; a problem

puzzle *verb*
1 to puzzle someone is to give them a problem that is hard to understand **2** to puzzle over something is to think hard about it

pygmy noun (**pygmies**)
(say **pig**-mi)
an unusually small person or animal

pyjamas plural noun
a loose lightweight set of jacket and
trousers that you wear in bed

pylon noun
a metal tower for supporting electric
cables

pyramid noun
1 an object with a square base
and four sloping sides coming to a
point **2** a massive ancient Egyptian
monument shaped like this

python noun
a large snake that crushes its prey

quack noun
the harsh loud sound made by a duck

quack verb
a duck quacks when it makes a harsh
loud sound

quad noun
(informal) **1** a quadrangle **2** a
quadruplet

quadrangle noun
a rectangular courtyard with large
buildings round it

quadrant noun
a quarter of a circle

quadrilateral noun
a flat shape with four straight sides

quadruple adjective
1 four times as much or as many
2 having four parts

quadruplet noun
each of four children born to the
same mother at one time

quail[1] noun
a bird that looks like a small
partridge

quail[2] verb
to quail is to feel or show fear

quaint adjective
attractive in an unusual or
old-fashioned way

quake verb
to quake is to tremble or shake

qualification noun
1 a skill or ability to do a job **2** an
examination you have passed or
a course you have completed that
shows you have a skill or ability

qualify verb (**qualifies,
qualifying, qualified**)
1 to qualify for something such as a
job is to be suitable for it or show you
have gained the abilities you need to
do it • She qualified as a doctor last
year. **2** to qualify for a competition is
to reach a high enough standard to
take part in it

quality noun (**qualities**)
1 the quality of something is how
good or bad it is **2** what something is
like • The paper had a shiny quality.

quantity noun
how much there is of something, or
how many things there are of one
sort

quarantine noun
(say **kwo**-ran-teen)
quarantine is a period when a person
or animal is kept apart from others to
prevent a disease from spreading

quarrel noun
a strong or angry argument

quarrel verb (**quarrelling,
quarrelled**)
to quarrel with someone is to argue
fiercely with them

quarrelsome adjective
fond of quarrelling or often
quarrelling

quarry noun (**quarries**)
1 a place where stone or slate is dug
out of the ground **2** an animal that is
being hunted

quart noun (say kwort)
a measure of liquid, a quarter of a
gallon or about 1.136 litres

quarter noun
1 each of four equal parts into which
something is divided or can be divided
2 three months, one-fourth of a year
• We get a phone bill every quarter. at
close quarters close together • They
fought at close quarters.

quarters plural noun
where someone lives for a time;
lodgings

quartet noun (say **kwor**-tet)
a group of four musicians or singers

quartz noun (say kworts)
quartz is a hard mineral, used in
making accurate electronic watches
and clocks

quaver verb
to quaver is to tremble
• He spoke in a quavering
voice.

quaver noun
1 a trembling sound
2 a musical note
equal to half a
crotchet, written ♪

quay noun (say kee)
a harbour wall or pier where ships
can be tied up for loading and
unloading

queasy adjective (**queasier,
queasiest**)
you feel queasy when you feel
slightly sick

queen noun
1 a woman who has been crowned as
the ruler of a country **2** a king's wife
3 a female bee or ant that produces
eggs **4** a piece in chess, the most
powerful on the board **5** a playing
card with a picture of a queen on it

queer adjective
1 strange or odd **2** ill or unwell
• I feel a bit queer.

quench verb
1 to quench your thirst is to drink
until you aren't thirsty any more **2** to
quench a fire is to put it out

query noun (**queries**)
(say **kweer**-i)
a question

query verb (**queries, querying,
queried**)
to query something is to question
whether it is true
or correct

quest noun
a long search, especially
for something precious or valuable

question noun
1 something you ask
• I will try to answer your question.
2 a problem or subject for discussion
to be out of the question is to
be impossible or not even worth
considering

question verb
1 to question someone is to ask them
questions **2** to be doubtful about it **questioner**
noun someone who asks a question

question mark noun
the punctuation mark (?) put at the
end of a question

quartz

a
b
c
d
e
f
g
h
i
j
k
l
m
n
o
p
q
r
s
t

questionnaire *noun*
(*say* kwes-chon-**air**)
a set of questions asked to get information for a survey

queue *noun* (*say* kew)
a line of people or vehicles waiting for something

queue *verb* (*say* kew)
people queue, or queue up, when they wait in a queue

quiche *noun* (*say* keesh)
an open tart with a savoury filling

quick *adjective*
1 taking only a short time
• *You were quick.* **2** done in a short time • *She gave a quick answer.*
3 able to learn or think fast **quickly** *adverb* in a short time; fast

quicken *verb*
1 to quicken something is to make it quicker • *She quickened her pace.*
2 to quicken is to become quicker

quicksand *noun*
quicksand is an area of loose wet sand that sucks in anything that falls into it

quiet *adjective*
1 silent **2** not loud • *He spoke in a quiet voice.*
3 calm and peaceful
• *They lead a quiet life.* **quietly** *adverb*

quiet *noun*
quiet is a time when it is calm and peaceful
• *Let's have a bit of quiet now.*

quieten *verb*
1 to quieten something or someone is to make them quiet **2** to quieten is to become quiet

quill *noun*
a pen made from a large feather

quilt *noun*
a thick soft cover for a bed

quintet *noun*
a group of five musicians or singers

quit *verb* (**quitting, quitted** or **quit**)
1 to quit something is to leave or abandon it **2** (*informal*) to quit doing something is to stop it • *Quit teasing him!*

quite *adverb*
1 rather or fairly • *He's quite a good swimmer.* **2** completely or entirely
• *I haven't quite finished.*

quiver[1] *verb*
to quiver is to tremble • *He was quivering with excitement.*

quiver[2] *noun*
a long container for arrows

quiz *noun*
a series of questions, especially as an entertainment or competition

quota *noun* (*say* kwoh-ta)
a fixed share or amount • *Each school has its quota of equipment.*

quotation *noun*
an interesting sentence or set of words taken from a book or speech

quotation marks *plural noun*
inverted commas, used to mark a quotation (" ")

quote *verb*
to quote words is to use them in a quotation

quotient *noun*
(*say* **kwoh**-shent)
the result of dividing one number by another • *The quotient of 12 divided by 3 is 4.*

quill

R r

rabbi *noun* (*say* **rab**-I)
a Jewish religious leader

rabbit *noun*
a furry animal with long ears that digs burrows

rabies *noun* (*say* **ray**-beez)
rabies is a fatal disease which causes madness in dogs and cats and can be passed to humans

raccoon *noun*
a small North American meat-eating animal with greyish-brown fur and a bushy, striped tail

rabbit

race[1] *noun*
a competition to be the first to reach a particular place or to do something

race[1] *verb*
1 to race someone is to have a race against them **2** to race is to move very fast • *The train raced along the track.* **racer** *noun* a competitor in a race

race[2] *noun*
a large group of people who have the same ancestors, and share certain physical features such as the colour of their skin and hair

racecourse *noun*
a place where horse races are run

racial *adjective*
to do with a person's race or with different races
racially *adverb*

racism *noun* (*say* **ray**-sizm)
racism is believing that one race of people is better than all the others and treating people unfairly because they belong to a different race
racist *noun* someone who practises racism
racist *adjective* showing racism

rack *noun*
1 a framework used as a shelf or container • *a plate rack*
2 an ancient device for torturing people by stretching them

rack *verb*
to rack your brains is to think hard to remember something or solve a problem

racket[1] *noun*
a bat with strings stretched across a frame, used in tennis and similar games

racket[2] *noun*
1 to make a racket is to make a loud noise **2** (*informal*) a dishonest way of making money

radar *noun* (*say* **ray**-dar)
radar is a system that uses radio waves to show the position of ships or aircraft which cannot be seen because of distance or poor visibility

radiant *adjective*
1 radiating light or heat **2** you can say someone is radiant when they look happy and beautiful **radiance** *noun* brightness
radiantly *adverb*

radiate *verb*
1 to radiate heat, light, or other energy is to send it out in rays
2 to radiate is to spread out like the spokes of a wheel • *The city's streets radiate from the central square.*

radiation *noun*
1 radiation is heat, light, or other energy given out by something
2 radiation is also energy or particles sent out by something radioactive

radiator *noun*
1 a device that gives out heat, especially a metal container through which steam or hot water flows **2** a device that cools a car's engine

radical *adjective*
1 thorough and complete; going right to the roots of something • *The new government made radical changes.* **2** wanting to make changes or reforms • *He is a radical politician.*
radically *adverb* to be radically different is to be completely different

radio *noun*
1 radio is sending or receiving sound by means of electrical waves **2** a radio is an apparatus for receiving broadcast sound programmes, or for receiving and sending messages

radioactive *adjective*
radioactive substances have atoms that break up and give out dangerous radiation **radioactivity** *noun* the state of being radioactive

radish *noun*
a small hard red vegetable with a hot taste, eaten raw in salads

radius *noun* (**radii**)
1 a straight line from the centre of a circle to the circumference **2** the length of this line

raffle *noun*
a way of raising money by selling numbered tickets, some of which win prizes

raffle *verb*
to raffle something is to give it as a prize in a raffle

raft *noun*
a floating platform of logs or barrels tied together

rafter *noun*
each of the long sloping pieces of wood that hold up a roof

rag *noun*
1 an old or torn piece of cloth **2** to be dressed in rags is to be wearing very old, torn clothes

rage *noun*
great or violent anger
rage *verb*
1 to rage is to be very angry **2** to rage is also to be violent or noisy • *The storm was raging outside.*

ragged *adjective* (*say* **rag**-id)
1 torn or frayed **2** wearing torn or old clothes • *a ragged beggar*

raid *noun*
1 a sudden attack **2** an unexpected visit from police to search a place or arrest people

raid *verb*
to raid a place is to make a raid on it **raider** *noun* raiders are people who attack a place in a raid

rail *noun*
1 a bar or rod that you can hang things on or that forms part of a fence or banisters **2** a long metal strip that is part of a railway track **by rail** on a train

railings *plural noun*
a fence made of metal bars

railway *noun*
1 a system of transport with trains running on rails **2** the parallel metal strips that trains travel on

rain *noun*
rain is drops of water that fall from the sky

rain *verb*
1 to fall as rain • *It is still raining.* • *Do you think it will rain this afternoon?* **2** to rain is to come down like rain • *After the explosion fragments of glass rained on them from above.* **3** to rain something is to send it down like rain • *They rained blows on him.*

rainbow *noun*
a curved band of colours that you can sometimes see in the sky when the sun shines through rain

raincoat *noun*
a waterproof coat

raindrop *noun*
a single drop of rain

rainfall *noun*
rainfall is the amount of rain that falls in a particular place or time

rainforest *noun*
a dense tropical forest in an area of very heavy rainfall

raise *verb*
1 to raise something is to move it to a higher place or to an upright position **2** to raise money is to succeed in collecting it • *They raised £1,000 for the appeal.* **3** to raise your voice is to speak loudly **4** to raise a subject or idea is to mention it for people to think about **5** to raise young children is to bring them up and educate them **6** to raise animals is to breed them

raisin *noun*
a dried grape

rake *noun*
a gardening tool with a row of short spikes fixed to a long handle

rake *verb*
to rake something is to move it or smooth it with a rake

rally *noun* (**rallies**)
1 a large public meeting **2** a competition to test skill in driving **3** a series of strokes and return strokes of the ball in tennis or squash

rally *verb* (**rallies, rallying, rallied**)
1 to rally people is to bring them together for a special effort **2** to rally, or rally round, is to come together to support someone **3** to rally is to recover after an illness or setback • *The team rallied when they realized they could win.*

ram *noun*
a male sheep

ram *verb* (**ramming, rammed**)
to ram something is to push one thing hard against another

Ramadan *noun* (*say* **ram**-a-dan)
Ramadan is the ninth month of the Muslim year, when Muslims do not eat or drink during the daytime

ramble *noun*
a long walk in the country

ramble *verb*
1 to ramble is to go for a long walk in the country **2** to ramble is also to say a lot without keeping to a subject **rambler** *noun* someone who goes rambling in the country

ramp *noun*
a slope joining two different levels

rampage *verb* (*say* **ram**-payj)
to rampage is to rush about wildly or violently

ranch *noun*
a large cattle-farm in America

random *noun*
at random by chance; without any purpose or plan
random *adjective*
done or taken at random • *They took a random sample.*

range *noun*
1 a collection of different things of the same type • *The shop sells a wide range of games and puzzles.* **2** the limits of something, from the highest to the lowest • *Most of the children here are in the 8–11 age range.* **3** a line of hills or mountains **4** the distance that a gun can shoot, or an aircraft can fly, or a sound can be heard **5** a place with targets for shooting practice **6** a kitchen fireplace with ovens

a
b
c
d
e
f
g
h
i
j
k
l
m
n
o
p
q
r
s
t
u
v
w
x
y
z

range *verb*
1 to range between two limits is to extend from one to the other • *Prices ranged from £1 to £50.* **2** to range people or things is to arrange them in a line • *Crowds were ranged along the streets, hoping to see the Queen go by.* **3** to range is to wander or move over a wide area • *Hens ranged all over the farm.*

Ranger *noun*
a senior member of the Guides

ranger *noun*
1 someone who looks after a park or forest **2** a mounted police officer in a remote area

rank *noun*
1 a position in a series of people or things • *He was promoted to the rank of captain.* **2** a line of people or things

rank *verb*
to rank is to have a certain rank or place • *She ranks among the greatest writers.*

ransack *verb*
to ransack a place is to search it thoroughly, looking for something to steal, and leave it in a mess

ransom *noun*
money paid so that someone who has been kidnapped can be set free **to hold someone to ransom** is to keep them prisoner and demand a ransom

rap *verb* (**rapping, rapped**)
to rap is to knock quickly and loudly

rap *noun*
1 a rap is a rapping movement or sound **2** rap is a kind of pop music in which you speak words rapidly in rhythm

rapid *adjective*
moving or working at speed **rapidity** *noun* speed **rapidly** *adverb* very quickly

rapids *plural noun*
part of a river where the water flows very fast over rocks

rare *adjective*
unusual; not often found or experienced • *She died of a rare disease.* **rarely** *adverb* not very often **rarity** *noun* something that is rare

rascal *noun*
a dishonest or mischievous person

rash¹ *adjective*
you are rash when you do something too quickly without thinking properly about it • *He tends to be rash.* • *It was a rash decision.* **rashly** *adverb*

rash² *noun*
an outbreak of red spots or patches on the skin

rasher *noun*
a slice of bacon

raspberry *noun* (**raspberries**)
a small soft red fruit

Rastafarian *noun*
(*say* ras-ta-**fair**-i-an)
a member of a religious group that started in Jamaica

rat *noun*
an animal like a large mouse

rate *noun*
1 how fast or how often something happens • *The train moved at a great rate.* **2** a charge or payment • *What is the rate for a letter to Italy?* **at any rate** anyway **at this rate** if this is typical or true

rate *verb*
to rate something or someone is to regard them in a certain way or as having a certain value • *Drivers rate the new car very highly.* • *He rated me among his best friends.*

rather *adverb*
1 slightly; somewhat • *It was rather dark.* **2** you would rather do one thing than another thing if you would prefer to do it • *I think I'd rather do this later.* **3** more truly or correctly • *He lay down, or rather fell, on the bed.*

ratio *noun* (**ratios**)
(*say* **ray**-shi-oh)
the relationship between two numbers; how many times one number goes into another • *In a group of 2 girls and 10 boys, the ratio of girls to boys is 1 to 5.*

ration *noun* (*say* **rash**-on)
the amount of something one person is allowed to have

ration *verb* (*say* **rash**-on)
to ration something is to give it out in fixed amounts because there is not a lot of it to share

rational *adjective*
(*say* **rash**-o-nal)
reasonable or sensible • *No rational person would do such a thing.* **rationally** *adverb*

rattle *verb*
1 to rattle is to make a series of short sharp hard sounds **2** to rattle something is to make it rattle

rattle *noun*
1 a rattling sound **2** a baby's toy that rattles when you shake it

rattlesnake *noun*
a poisonous American snake that makes rattling sounds with its tail

rave *verb*
1 to be raving is to be talking wildly **2** to rave about something is to talk very enthusiastically about it

rave *noun*
a big party held in a large building with loud electronic music to dance to

raven *noun*
a large black bird

ravenous *adjective*
(*say* **rav**-e-nus)
very hungry **ravenously** *adverb*

raven

ravine *noun*
(*say* ra-**veen**)
a very deep narrow gorge

ravioli *noun*
ravioli is small squares of pasta filled with meat and served with a sauce

raw *adjective*
1 raw food is not cooked **2** raw (for example) cotton or sugar is in its natural state before being processed • *What raw materials do you need?* **3** you can say someone is raw when they don't have any experience • *They are just raw beginners.* **4** with the skin removed • *He had a raw wound on his leg.* **5** cold and damp • *There was a raw wind.*

ray¹ *noun*
a thin line of light, heat, or other energy

ray² *noun*
a large sea fish with a flat body and a long tail

razor *noun*
a device with a very sharp blade, used for shaving

reach *verb*
1 to reach a place is to go as far as it and arrive there **2** to reach, or reach out, is to stretch out your hand to get or touch something **3** to reach something is to be long enough to touch it • *The carpet doesn't reach the wall.*

reach *noun*
1 the distance you can reach with your hand **2** a distance that you can easily travel • *I'd like to live within reach of the sea.*

react *verb*
to react is to act in response to another person or thing

rattle

reaction noun
what you feel or say or do when something happens, or when someone does something

reactor noun
an apparatus for producing nuclear power

read verb (**reading, read**)
1 to read something written or printed is to look at it and understand it or say it aloud
2 a gauge or instrument reads a certain amount when that is what it shows • *The thermometer reads 20°.*

reader noun
1 someone who reads **2** a book that helps you learn to read

readily adverb
1 willingly or eagerly • *She readily agreed to help.* **2** quickly and without any difficulty • *All the ingredients you need are readily available.*

reading noun
1 reading is the action of reading a book, magazine, or newspaper **2** a reading is an amount shown on a gauge or instrument

ready adjective (**readier, readiest**)
1 prepared so that you can do something straight away; able or willing to do something • *Are you ready to leave?* **2** prepared for use • *Is dinner ready?* **at the ready** ready for action or ready to be used
readiness noun readiness is being ready for something

real adjective
1 true or existing; not imaginary **2** genuine; not a copy • *Are those pearls real?*

realistic adjective
1 true to life • *It is a very realistic painting.* **2** seeing things as they really are • *She is realistic about her chances of winning.*
realistically adverb

reality noun (**realities**)
reality is what is real

realize verb
to realize something is to understand it or accept that it is true
realization noun when you realize something

really adverb
truly; certainly; in fact

realm noun (*say* relm)
1 a kingdom **2** an area of knowledge or activity

reap verb
1 to reap corn is to cut it down and gather it in when it is ripe **2** to reap a benefit is to gain it **reaper** noun someone who reaps corn

reappear verb
to reappear is to appear again
reappearance noun a time when someone or something appears again

rear[1] adjective
placed or found at the back • *I was looking out of the rear window.*

rear[1] noun
the back part of something

rear[2] verb
1 to rear young children or animals is to bring them up or help them grow **2** a horse or other animal rears, or rears up, when it rises up on its hind legs so that its front legs are in the air

reason noun
1 the reason for something is why it happens **2** reason is thinking in a clear and logical way • *He wouldn't listen to reason.*

reason verb
1 to reason is to think in a logical way **2** to reason with someone is to try to persuade them of something

reasonable adjective
1 sensible or logical **2** fair or moderate • *These are reasonable prices for what you get.*

reasonably adverb
1 in a reasonable way; sensibly • *They were behaving quite reasonably.* **2** fairly; somewhat • *She can swim reasonably well.*

reassure verb
to reassure someone is to take away their doubts or fears **reassurance** noun something you say that reassures someone

rebel verb (**rebelling, rebelled**) (*say* ri-**bel**)
to rebel is to refuse to obey someone in authority, especially the government

rebel noun (*say* **reb**-el)
someone who refuses to obey or fights against people who are in charge

rebellion noun
1 rebellion is when people refuse to obey or fight against people in charge **2** a rebellion is a fight against someone in authority, especially the government

rebellious adjective
someone is rebellious when they refuse to obey people in charge or are likely to rebel

rebound verb
to rebound is to bounce back after hitting something

rebuild verb (**rebuilding, rebuilt**)
to rebuild something is to build it again after it has been destroyed

recall verb
1 to recall someone or something is to remember them **2** to recall someone is to tell them to come back

recap verb (**recapping, recapped**)
(*informal*) to recap is to summarize what has been said

recapture verb
to recapture something or someone is to capture them again, especially after they have escaped

recede verb
1 to recede is to go back • *The floods have receded.* **2** a man's hair is receding when he starts to go bald at the front

receipt noun (*say* ri-**seet**)
a written statement saying that a payment has been received or goods have been delivered

receive verb
1 to receive something is to get it when it is given or sent to you **2** to receive visitors is to greet them formally • *The President was received at Buckingham Palace.*

receiver noun
1 the part of a telephone that you hold to your ear **2** a radio or television set

recent adjective
made or happening a short time ago
recently adverb
only a short time ago

receptacle noun
a container used for holding something

reception noun
1 the sort of welcome that someone gets • *We were given a friendly reception.* **2** a formal party to receive guests • *a wedding reception* **3** a place in a hotel or office where visitors report or check in **4** the quality of the signals your radio or television set receives • *We don't get good reception here.*

receptionist noun
someone in an office or hotel who deals with visitors and answers the telephone

recession noun
a time when a country is not trading well and a lot of people can't find jobs

recipe noun (say **ress**-i-pi)
a list of ingredients and instructions for preparing or cooking food

recital noun (say ri-**sy**-tal)
a performance of music or poetry by a small number of people

recite verb
to recite something such as a poem is to say it aloud

reckless adjective
someone is reckless when they do things without thinking or caring about what might happen **recklessly** adverb **recklessness** noun

reckon verb
1 to reckon something is to calculate or count it 2 to reckon something is to think it or have an opinion about it • I reckon it's about to rain.

recline verb
to recline is to lean or lie back

recognize verb
1 to recognize someone or something is to know who they are because you have seen them before 2 to recognize a fault or mistake is to admit to it • We recognize that we may have acted unfairly. **recognition** noun recognizing someone or something **recognizable** adjective able to be recognized

recoil verb
to recoil is to move backwards suddenly • He recoiled in horror.

recollect verb
to recollect something is to remember it **recollection** noun a memory of something; being able to remember something

recommend verb
1 to recommend something is to suggest it because you think it is good or suitable • I recommend the strawberry ice cream. 2 to recommend an action is to advise someone to do it • We recommend that you wear strong shoes on the walk. **recommendation** noun something that you recommend

reconcile verb
1 to be reconciled with someone is to become friendly with them again after quarrelling or fighting with them 2 you are reconciled to something when you are persuaded to put up with it • He soon became reconciled to wearing glasses. **reconciliation** noun becoming friendly with someone again after quarrelling or fighting with them

reconstruction noun
1 reconstruction is building something up again 2 a reconstruction is acting out an event that took place in the past • The police did a reconstruction of the bank robbery.

record noun (say **rek**-ord)
1 a disc with recorded sound on it 2 the best performance in a sport or the most remarkable event of its kind • She broke the record for swimming 100 metres. 3 a set of facts or information about something that you write down and keep • Keep a record of all the birds you see in the garden.

record verb (say ri-**kord**)
1 to record music or sound or a television programme is to store it on a tape or disc 2 to record things that have happened is to put them down in writing

records

recorder noun
1 a wooden musical instrument that you play by blowing into one end and covering holes with your fingers 2 a tape recorder, video recorder, or other machine for recording sounds and pictures

recount verb
to tell someone about something true that has happened • We recounted our adventures.

recover verb
1 to recover is to get better after being ill 2 to recover something is to get it back after losing it **recovery** noun getting better after being ill; getting something back after it was lost

recreation noun
something you do for fun or enjoyment **recreational** adjective to do with recreation

recorder

recruit noun
someone who has just joined the armed forces or a business or club

recruit verb
to recruit someone is to get them to join something you belong to

rectangle noun
a shape with four straight sides and four right angles **rectangular** adjective in the form of a rectangle

recuperate verb
to recuperate is to get better after you have been ill

recur verb
something recurs when it happens again **recurrence** noun a recurrence of something is when it happens again

recycle verb
to recycle waste material is to treat it so that it can be used again • Waste paper can be recycled to make cardboard.

red adjective (**redder, reddest**) ●
1 of the colour of blood 2 red hair is orangey-brown in colour **red** noun a red colour **to see red** is to become suddenly angry **redden** verb to redden is to become red • He reddened with embarrassment.

red-handed adjective
to catch someone red-handed is to catch them while they are actually committing a crime or doing something wrong

redhead noun
a person with reddish-brown hair

reduce verb
1 to reduce something is to make it smaller or less 2 to be reduced to something is to be forced to do it • He was reduced to asking for more money.

reduction noun
1 there is a reduction in something when it becomes smaller or less 2 the amount by which something is reduced • They gave us a reduction of £5.

redundant adjective
1 to be redundant is to be no longer needed 2 someone is made redundant when they lose their job because it is no longer needed **redundancy** noun when someone loses their job because it is no longer needed

reed noun
1 a plant that grows in or near water 2 a thin strip that vibrates to make the sound in some wind instruments,

such as a clarinet, saxophone, or oboe **reedy** *adjective* a reedy voice or sound is high and not very pleasant

reef *noun*
a line of rocks or sand just below the surface of the sea

reek *verb*
to reek is to have a strong unpleasant smell

reel *noun*
1 a round device on which cotton or thread is wound
2 a lively Scottish dance

reels

refer *verb* (**referring, referred**)
1 to refer to someone or something is to mention them or speak about them 2 to refer to (for example) a dictionary or encyclopedia is to look at it so that you can find something out 3 to refer a question or problem to someone else is to give it to them to deal with

referee *noun*
someone who makes sure that people keep to the rules of a game

referee *verb*
to referee a game is to act as referee in it

reference *noun*
1 a mention of something 2 a place in a book or file where information can be found 3 a letter or note about how well someone has done their work, used especially when they are applying for a job

reference book *noun*
a book that gives information, such as a dictionary or encyclopedia

referendum *noun*
(*say* ref-er-**en**-dum)
a vote on an important matter by all the people in a country

refill *verb*
to refill something is to fill it again

refill *noun*
a container used to replace something that has been used up • *My pen needs a refill.*

refine *verb*
to refine something is to purify or improve it

refined *adjective*
1 refined (for example) sugar or oil has been made pure by taking other substances out of it 2 someone is refined when they have good manners and are well educated

refinement *noun*
1 refinement is the process of refining something 2 a refinement is something special that improves a thing

refinery *noun* (**refineries**)
a factory for refining a product, such as oil

reflect *verb*
1 something reflects light or heat or sound when it sends them back from a surface 2 a mirror or other shiny surface reflects something when it forms an image of it 3 you reflect on something when you think seriously about it

reflection *noun*
the image you can see in a mirror or other shiny surface

reflex *noun* (*say* **ree**-fleks)
a movement or action that you do without any conscious thought

reform *verb*
1 to reform a person or thing is to improve them by getting rid of their faults 2 someone reforms when they improve their behaviour

reform *noun*
1 reform is changing something to improve it 2 a reform is a change in a system or law **reformer** *noun* someone who tries to change a system

refrain¹ *verb*
to refrain from something is to keep yourself from doing it • *Please refrain from talking.*

refrain² *noun*
the chorus of a song

refresh *verb*
to refresh someone who is tired is to make them feel fresh and strong again

refreshments *plural noun*
food and drink

refrigerator *noun*
a cabinet in which you can store food at a low temperature to keep it fresh

refuel *verb* (**refuelling, refuelled**)
to refuel a ship or aircraft is to supply it with more fuel

refuge *noun*
a place where someone can go to be safe from danger

refugee *noun* (*say* ref-yoo-**jee**)
someone who has had to leave their home or country because of war or persecution or disaster

refund *verb* (*say* ri-**fund**)
to refund money is to pay it back

refund *noun* (*say* **ree**-fund)
money that is paid back to you

refuse *verb* (*say* ri-**fewz**)
to refuse something, or to do something, is to say that you will not accept it or do it • *They refuse to help.* **refusal** *noun* when someone refuses something

refuse *noun* (*say* **ref**-yooss)
rubbish or waste material

regain *verb*
to regain something is to get it back

regard *verb*
1 to regard someone or something as something is to think of them in a certain way • *I regard her as a friend.*
2 to regard someone or something is also to look at them closely

regard *noun*
with regard to something about it; in connection with it

regarding *preposition*
to do with; about • *There are rules regarding use of the library.*

regardless *adjective, adverb*
paying no attention to something • *Buy it, regardless of the cost.* • *We asked her to stop, but she carried on regardless.*

regards *plural noun*
kind wishes you send in a message • *Give your parents my regards.*

regatta *noun* (*say* ri-**gat**-a)
a meeting for boat or yacht races

reggae *noun* (*say* **reg**-ay)
reggae is a West Indian style of music with a strong beat

regiment *noun*
a large army unit **regimental** *noun* to do with or belonging to a regiment

region *noun*
1 a part of a country 2 a part of the world • *These plants only grow in tropical regions.* **regional** *adjective* belonging to a particular region

a
b
c
d
e
f
g
h
i
j
k
l
m
n
o
p
q
r
s
t
u
v
w
x
y
z

register *noun*
an official list of names or information, especially of people present each day at a school

register *verb*
1 to register something or someone is to put their name on an official list **2** a gauge or instrument registers a certain amount when that is what it shows • *The thermometer registered 25°.* **3** to register a letter or parcel is to have it officially recorded for sending with special care **registration** *noun* making an official record of something

regret *noun*
you feel regret when you feel sorry or sad about something

regret *verb* (**regretting, regretted**) to regret something is to feel sorry or sad about it

regrettable *adjective*
you say something is regrettable when you wish it hadn't happened

regular *adjective*
1 always happening at certain times • *You need regular meals.* **2** even or symmetrical • *She has beautiful regular teeth.* **3** normal or correct • *Do you want a regular or large coffee?* **regularity** *noun* being regular **regularly** *adverb*

regulate *verb*
to regulate something is to adjust or control it

regulation *noun*
a regulation is a rule or law

rehearse *verb*
to rehearse (for example) a play or piece of music is to practise it before you perform it **rehearsal** *noun* when you practise something before performing it

reign *verb*
to reign is to rule as a king or queen

reign *noun*
the time when someone is king or queen

rein *noun*
a strap used by a rider to guide a horse

reindeer *noun*
a kind of deer that lives in Arctic regions

reinforce *verb*
to reinforce something is to strengthen it

reinforcement *noun*
a thing that strengthens something

reinforcements *plural noun* extra troops sent to strengthen a military force

reject *verb* (*say* ri-**jekt**)
1 to reject something or someone is to refuse to accept them • *They have rejected my offer of help.* **2** to reject something is to get rid of it • *Faulty parts are rejected at the factory.* **rejection** *noun* being rejected

reject *noun* (*say* **ree**-jekt)
a thing that is got rid of, especially because it is faulty or poorly made

rejoice *verb*
to rejoice is to be very happy or pleased

relate *verb*
1 things relate to each other when there is a connection between them **2** to relate one thing with another is to compare them **3** to relate a story is to tell it

related *adjective*
1 two people are related when they belong to the same family **2** two things are related when they are connected or linked in some way

relation *noun*
a relation is someone who is related to you

relationship *noun*
1 the way people or things are connected with each other **2** the way people get on with one another • *There is a good relationship between the teachers and the children.* **3** a close friendship or connection between two people

relative *noun*
your relatives are the people who are related to you

relative *adjective*
1 connected or compared with something **2** compared with the average • *They live in relative comfort.*

reindeer

relatively *adverb*
compared with other people or things; more or less • *Books are relatively cheap.*

relax *verb*
1 to relax is to become less anxious or worried **2** to relax is also to rest or stop working **3** to relax a part of you is to make it less stiff or tense • *Try to relax your arm.* **relaxation** *noun* relaxing

relay *verb*
to relay a message or broadcast is to pass it on

relay *noun*
1 a race between two teams in which each member of the team runs part of the distance **2** a fresh group taking the place of another • *The firemen worked in relays.*

release *verb*
1 to release something or someone is to set them free or unfasten them **2** to release a film or record is to make it available to the public

release *noun*
1 release is being released **2** a release is something released, especially a new film or record

relegate *verb* (*say* **rel**-i-gayt)
1 a sports team is relegated when it goes down into a lower division of a league **2** to relegate something is to put it into a lower group or position than before **relegation** *noun* when a sports team is relegated

relent *verb*
to relent is to be less angry or severe than you were going to be

relentless *adjective*
never stopping or letting up • *Their criticism was relentless.* **relentlessly** *adverb*

relevant *adjective*
(*say* **rel**-i-vant)
connected with what you are discussing or dealing with **relevance** *noun* the relevance of something is how relevant it is

reliable *adjective*
able to be trusted or depended on **reliability** *noun* how reliable something is **reliably** *adverb*

relic *noun*
something that has survived from an ancient time

relief *noun*
1 a good feeling you get because something unpleasant has stopped or is not going to happen • *It was such a relief when we reached dry land.* **2** relief is the ending or lessening of pain or

suffering **3** aid or help given to people in need • *The charity is involved in famine relief.* **4** relief is also a method of making a map or design that stands out from a flat surface • *The model shows hills and valleys in relief.*

relieve *verb*
to relieve pain or suffering is to end or lessen it

relieved *adjective*
feeling good because something unpleasant has stopped or is not going to happen

religion *noun*
what people believe about God or gods, and how they worship

religious *adjective*
1 to do with religion **2** believing in a religion

reluctant *adjective*
you are reluctant to do something when you don't want to do it
reluctance *noun* not wanting to do something
reluctantly *adverb* you do something reluctantly when you would prefer not to be doing it

rely *verb* (**relies, relying, relied**)
to rely on someone or **something** is to trust them or need them to help or support you

remain *verb*
1 to remain is to continue in the same place or condition • *It will remain cloudy all day.* **2** to remain is also to be left over • *A lot of food remained after the party.*

remainder *noun*
1 something left over **2** (*in mathematics*) the amount that is left over when you divide one number into another

remains *plural noun*
1 something left over **2** ruins or relics **3** a dead body

remark *verb*
to remark on something is to say something that you have thought or noticed

remark *noun*
something you say

remarkable *adjective*
so unusual or impressive that you notice or remember it **remarkably** *adverb* unusually or noticeably

remedy *noun* (**remedies**)
a cure for an illness or problem

remember *verb*
1 to remember something is to keep it in your mind, or bring it into your mind when you need to

2 to remember someone is to be thinking about them

remembrance *noun* you do something in remembrance of someone or something when you do it as a way of remembering them

remind *verb*
to remind someone is to help or make them remember something • *The girl in that painting reminds me of you.*
reminder *noun* something that makes you think about or remember a person or thing

remnant *noun*
a small piece of something left over

remorse *noun*
remorse is deep regret for something wrong you have done **remorseful** *adjective* feeling remorse

remote *adjective*
1 far away • *He lived on a remote island.* **2** unlikely or slight • *Their chances of winning were remote.*
remotely *adverb*
remoteness *noun*

remote control *noun*
1 remote control is controlling something from a distance, usually by means of radio or electricity **2** a remote control is a device for doing this

removal *noun*
removing or moving something

remove *verb*
to remove something is to take it away or take it off

rendezvous *noun* (**rendezvous**) (*say* ron-day-voo) an arrangement to meet someone

renew *verb*
to renew something is to make it as it was before or replace it with something new
renewal *noun* when something begins again or is replaced with something new

renewable *adjective*
able to be renewed or replaced; never completely used up • *Wind is a renewable source of energy.*

renowned *adjective*
famous • *She is renowned for her generosity.*

rent *noun*
a regular payment for using something, especially a house or flat

rent *verb*
to rent something is to pay money to use it

repair *verb*
to repair something is to mend it

repair *noun*
1 repair is mending something • *The car is in for repair.* **2** a repair is a mended place • *You can hardly see the repair.* **to be in good repair** is to be in good condition

repay *verb* (**repaying, repaid**)
1 to repay money is to pay it back **2** to repay someone's kindness is to do something for them in return
repayment *noun* paying money back

repeat *verb*
to repeat something is to say it or do it again

repeat *noun*
something that is repeated, especially a television programme

repeatedly *adverb*
several times; again and again

repel *verb* (**repelling, repelled**)
1 to repel someone or something is to drive or force them away or apart **2** to repel someone is to make them disgusted **repellent** *adjective* disgusting

repent *verb*
to repent is to be sorry for what you have done **repentance** *noun* repentance is being sorry for what you have done
repentant *adjective* sorry for what you have done

repetition *noun*
1 repeating or doing something again **2** something repeated

repetitive *adjective*
something is repetitive when it is repeated too much and so becomes boring

replace *verb*
1 to replace something is to put it back in its place **2** to replace someone or something is to take their place **3** to replace something is to put a new thing in the place of it • *I promise I'll replace the book I lost.*

replacement *noun*
1 replacement is when something or someone is replaced for another **2** a replacement is something used or given in place of another

replay *noun*
1 a football match played for a second time after the first match has ended in a draw **2** the playing or showing again of a recording

replica *noun* (*say* **rep**-li-ka)
an exact copy

reply *noun* (**replies**)
what you say or write when someone asks or says something

reply *verb* (**replies, replying, replied**)
to reply is to give a reply

report *verb*
1 to report something is to describe something that has happened or something you have studied **2** to report someone is to complain about them to those in charge of them **3** to report to someone is to tell them you have arrived or are available

report *noun*
1 a description or account of something **2** a regular statement of how someone has worked or behaved, especially at school **3** an explosive sound • *We heard the report of a gun.*

reporter *noun*
someone whose job is to collect news for a newspaper or for radio or television

represent *verb*
1 to represent something or someone is to be a picture or model or symbol of them • *The dotted lines represent county boundaries.*
2 to represent someone else is to speak or act on their behalf • *She was chosen to represent her school in the competition.*
representation *noun* a representation of a thing is something that shows or describes it

representative *noun*
a person who acts or speaks for other people

representative *adjective*
typical of a group

reprieve *noun* (*say* ri-**preev**)
someone is given a reprieve when their punishment is postponed or cancelled, especially the death penalty

reprieve *verb*
to reprieve someone is to cancel or postpone their punishment

reprimand *verb*
to reprimand someone is to scold them or tell them off

reprimand *noun*
a telling-off

reprisal *noun* (*say* ri-**pry**-zal)
an act of revenge

reproach *verb*
to reproach someone is to blame them for something and show you are disappointed with them

reproach *noun*
reproach is blame or criticism • *His behaviour was beyond reproach.*

reproduce *verb*
1 to reproduce something is to make it be heard or seen again • *CDs can reproduce sound.*
2 to reproduce something is also to copy it **3** animals and people reproduce when they produce offspring
reproductive *adjective* to do with producing offspring

reproduction *noun*
1 reproduction is the process of producing offspring **2** a reproduction is a copy of something

reptile *noun*
a cold-blooded animal that creeps or crawls, such as snakes and lizards

reptile

republic *noun*
a country ruled by a president and government that are chosen by the people

repulsive *adjective*
disgusting

reputation *noun*
what most people think about a person or thing • *He has a reputation for being honest.*

request *verb*
to request something is to ask politely or formally for it

request *noun*
what someone asks for

require *verb*
1 to require something is to need or want it **2** you are required to do something when you have to do it • *Pedestrians are required to walk on the pavements.* **requirement** *noun* something that is needed

rescue *verb*
to rescue someone is to save them from danger or capture

rescue *noun*
when someone is rescued **rescuer** *noun* a person who rescues someone

research *noun*
research is careful study or investigation to learn more about a subject
researcher *noun* someone who does research

resemblance *noun*
there is a resemblance between two or more things when they are similar

resemble *verb*
to resemble someone or something is to look or sound like them

resent *verb*
to resent something is to feel angry about it because you think it is unfair
resentful *adjective* angry about something that you think is unfair
resentment *noun* a feeling of resenting something

reservation *noun*
1 arranging for (for example) a restaurant table or seat on a train to be kept for you **2** an area of land kept for a special purpose **3** you have reservations about something when you feel doubtful or uneasy about it • *I had reservations about the excuses he made.*

reserve *verb*
to reserve something is to keep it or order it for a particular person or for a special use

reserve *noun*
1 a person kept ready to be used if necessary, especially an extra player in a sports team **2** an area of land kept for a special purpose • *This island is a nature reserve.*

reserved *adjective*
1 kept for someone • *These seats are reserved.* **2** someone is reserved when they are shy or unwilling to show their feelings

reservoir *noun* (*say* **rez**-er-vwar)
an artificial lake where water is stored

residence *noun*
a place where someone lives

resident *noun*
someone who lives in a particular place

resign *verb*
to resign is to give up your job or position **to resign yourself to something** is to accept a difficulty without complaining or arguing

resignation *noun*
1 resignation is accepting a difficulty without complaining **2** a resignation is a letter saying you are resigning a job or position

resin *noun* (*say* **rez**-in)
resin is a sticky substance that comes from plants or is made artificially

resist *verb*
1 to resist someone or something is to oppose them or try to stop them **2** you cannot resist something when you cannot stop yourself doing it • *I can't resist telling her what happened.* **resistance** *noun* fighting back or taking action against someone or something **resistant** *adjective* to be resistant to something is not to be affected or damaged by it

resolute *adjective*
(*say* **rez**-o-loot) determined or firm **resolutely** *adverb*

resolution *noun*
1 resolution is being determined or firm **2** a resolution is something you have decided to do

resolve *verb*
1 to resolve to do something is to decide to do it **2** to resolve doubts or disagreements is to deal successfully with them

resort *noun*
a place where people go for a holiday, especially by the sea **the last resort** the only thing you can do when everything else has failed

resort *verb*
to resort to something is to make use of it, especially when everything else has failed • *In the end they resorted to violence.*

resource *noun*
resources are things that you have and are able to use • *The land is rich in natural resources.*

respect *noun*
1 respect is admiration for someone's good qualities or achievements **2** respect is also consideration or concern • *Have respect for people's feelings.* **3** a respect is a detail or aspect • *In some respects, he is like his sister.* **with respect to something** concerning something

respect *verb*
to respect someone is to have respect for them

respectable *adjective*
1 a respectable person has good manners and character **2** something respectable is of a good size or standard **respectability** *noun* respectability is being respectable **respectably** *adverb* **respectful** *adjective* showing respect; polite **respectfully** *adverb*

respective *adjective*
belonging to each one of several • *We went to our respective rooms.*

respectively *adverb*
in the same order as the people or things already mentioned • *Emma and I went to London and Paris respectively.*

respiration *noun*
respiration is breathing **respiratory** *adjective* to do with breathing

respirator *noun*
a mask or machine for helping with people's breathing

respond *verb*
to respond to someone or something is to reply or react to them

response *noun*
how you reply or react to something

responsibility *noun* (**responsibilities**)
1 responsibility is being responsible for something **2** a responsibility is something for which you are responsible

responsible *adjective*
1 looking after something and likely to take the blame if anything goes wrong **2** able to be trusted **3** important and needing trust • *She has a responsible job.* **4** to be responsible for something is to be the cause of it • *Faulty wiring was responsible for the fire.* **responsibly** *adverb* in a way that shows you can be trusted

rest¹ *noun*
1 a time when you can sleep or relax **2** a support for something

rest¹ *verb*
1 to rest is to sleep or relax **2** to rest on or against something is to lean on it • *The ladder is resting against the wall.* **3** to rest something is to lean or support it somewhere • *Rest the ladder on the roof.*

rest² *noun*
the rest the part that is left; the others

restaurant *noun*
a place where you can buy a meal and eat it

restless *adjective*
you are restless when you can't relax or keep still **restlessly** *adverb* **restlessness** *noun*

restore *verb*
to restore something is to put it back as it was or make it new again **restoration** *noun* when something is put back as it was or made new again

restrain *verb*
to restrain someone or something is to hold them or keep them tightly controlled **restraint** *noun* self-control

restrict *verb*
to restrict someone or something is to keep them within certain limits or stop them from acting freely **restriction** *noun* something that restricts you

result *noun*
1 a thing that happens because something else has happened **2** the score or situation at the end of a game or competition or race **3** the answer to a sum or problem

result *verb*
to result is to happen as a result **to result in something** is to have it as a result • *The game resulted in a draw.*

retain *verb*
1 to retain something is to keep it • *Retain your tickets for inspection.* **2** to retain something is to hold it in place

retina *noun* (*say* **ret**-i-na)
a layer at the back of your eyeball that is sensitive to light

retire *verb*
1 someone retires when they give up regular work at a certain age **2** to retire is also to retreat or withdraw, or to go to bed • *He was so exhausted he had to retire from the race.* **retirement** *noun* the time when someone gives up regular work

retort *verb*
to retort is to reply quickly or angrily

a b c d e f g h i j k l m n o p q r s t u v w x y z

retort *noun*
a quick or angry reply

retrace *verb*
to retrace your steps is to go back the way you came

retreat *verb*
to retreat is to go back when you are attacked or defeated

retrieve *verb*
to retrieve something is to get it back or find it again **retrieval** *noun* retrieval is retrieving something

return *verb*
1 to return is to come or go back to a place 2 to return something is to give it or send it back

return *noun*
1 when you come back to a place 2 something that is given or sent back 3 a ticket for a journey to a place and back again • *Do you want a single or return?*

reunion *noun*
a meeting of people who have not met for some time

rev *verb* (**revving, revved**)
(*informal*) to rev an engine is to make it run quickly

reveal *verb*
to reveal something is to show it or make it known **revelation** *noun* a surprising fact that is made known

revenge *noun*
revenge is harming someone because they have done harm to you

revenue *noun* (say rev-e-nyoo)
revenue is money that a business or organization receives

revere *verb* (say ri-**veer**)
to revere someone or something is to respect them deeply or religiously

reverence *noun*
reverence is great respect or awe, especially towards God or holy things **reverent** *adjective* feeling or showing awe or respect

Reverend *noun*
the title of a member of the clergy • *This is the Reverend John Smith.*

reverse *noun*
1 the opposite way or side 2 the gear used to drive a vehicle backwards **in reverse** going in the opposite direction

reverse *verb*
1 to reverse something is to turn it round 2 to reverse is to go backwards in a vehicle 3 to reverse a decision is to change or cancel it **reversal** *noun* when something is reversed **reversible** *adjective* reversible clothing can be worn with either side on the outside

review *noun*
1 a published description and opinion of a product, book or film or play, or a piece of music 2 an inspection or survey of something

review *verb*
1 to review a book or play or film, or a piece of music, is to write a review of it 2 to review something is to inspect or survey it **reviewer** *noun* someone who writes a review

revise *verb*
1 before you do an examination, you revise when you go over work that you have already done 2 to revise something is to correct or change it

revision *noun*
a change or correction; learning work before you do an examination

revive *verb*
1 to revive something is to start using it again • *The village has revived a number of traditional customs.* 2 to revive someone is to make them conscious again after fainting

revival *noun* when something improves or becomes popular again

revolt *verb*
1 to revolt is to rebel 2 something revolts you when it disgusts or horrifies you **revolting** *adjective* very unpleasant or disgusting

revolt *noun*
a rebellion

revolution *noun*
1 a rebellion that overthrows the government 2 a complete change 3 one turn of a wheel or engine

revolutionary *adjective*
1 to do with a revolution 2 completely new or original

revolve *verb*
something revolves when it goes round in a circle

revolver *noun*
a pistol that has a revolving store for bullets so that it can be fired several times without having to be loaded again

reward *noun*
something given to a person in return for something they have done

reward *verb*
to reward someone is to give them a reward

rewarding *adjective*
satisfying and worth doing

rewrite *verb* (**rewriting, rewrote, rewritten**)
to rewrite something is to write it again or differently

rheumatism *noun*
(say **roo**-ma-tizm)
rheumatism is a disease that causes pain and stiffness in the joints and muscles

rhinoceros *noun* (**rhinoceroses** or **rhinoceros**)
(say ry-**noss**-er-os)
a large heavy animal with a horn or two horns on its nose

rhinoceros

rhombus *noun* ♦
a shape with four equal sides and no right angles, like a diamond on a playing card

rhubarb *noun*
rhubarb is a plant with pink or green stalks that you can cook and eat

rhyme *noun*
1 similar sounds in the endings of words, as in *bat* and *mat*, *batter* and *matter* 2 a short rhyming poem

rhyme *verb*
1 a poem rhymes when it has rhymes at the ends of its lines 2 one word rhymes with another word when it forms a rhyme with it • *Bat rhymes with hat.*

rhythm *noun*
a regular pattern of beats, sounds, or movements in music and poetry **rhythmic** or **rhythmical** *adjective* having a rhythm **rhythmically** *adverb*

rib *noun*
your ribs are the curved bones above your waist

ribbon *noun*
a strip of nylon, silk, or other material

ribbon

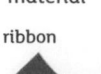

rice *noun*
rice is white seeds from a cereal plant, used as food

rich *adjective*
1 someone is rich when they have a lot of money or property 2 something is rich when it is full of goodness, quality, or strength • *Fruit is rich in vitamins.* 3 costly or luxurious • *The house has rich furnishings.* **richness** *noun*

riches *plural noun*
wealth

richly *adverb*
thoroughly, completely • *They richly deserved their punishment.*

rickety *adjective*
unsteady and likely to break or fall down • *a rickety chair*

rickshaw *noun*
a two-wheeled carriage pulled by one or more people, used in the Far East

WORD ORIGIN

The word **rickshaw** is from Japanese, and is a shorter form of *jinriksha* which means 'person-power vehicle'

ricochet *verb* (*say* rik-o-shay)
to ricochet is to bounce off something • *The bullets ricocheted off the wall.*

rid *verb* (**ridding, rid**)
to rid a person or place of something unwanted is to free them from it • *He rid the town of rats.* **to get rid of** something or someone is to cause them to go away • *I wish I could get rid of these spots.*

riddance *noun*
good riddance used to show that you are glad that something or someone has gone

riddle *noun*
a puzzling question, especially as a joke

ride *verb* (**riding, rode, ridden**)
1 to ride a horse or bicycle is to sit on it and be carried along on it 2 to ride is to travel in a vehicle **rider** *noun* someone who rides a horse

ride *noun*
a journey on a horse or bicycle, or in a vehicle

ridge *noun*
a long narrow part higher than the rest of something • *a mountain ridge*

ridicule *verb*
to ridicule someone or something is to make fun of them

ridiculous *adjective*
extremely silly or absurd **ridiculously** *adverb*

rifle *noun*
a long gun that you hold against your shoulder when you fire it

rift *noun*
1 a crack or split 2 a disagreement or a break in a friendship

rig *verb* (**rigging, rigged**)
1 to rig a ship is to fit it with rigging, sails, and other equipment 2 to rig an election or competition is to control the result dishonestly **to rig** something **up** is to make it quickly

rigging *noun*
rigging is the ropes that support a ship's masts and sails

right *adjective*
1 on or towards the east if you think of yourself as facing north 2 correct • *Is this sum right?* 3 fair or honest • *It's not right to cheat.*

right *adverb*
1 on or towards the right • *Turn right.* 2 completely • *Turn right round.* 3 exactly • *She stood right in the middle.* 4 straight; directly • *Go right ahead.* **right away** immediately

right *noun*
1 the right side 2 what is fair or just; something that people ought to be allowed • *They fought for their rights.* • *He had no right to talk to you like that.*

right *verb*
to right something is to put it right • *The fault might right itself.*

right angle *noun*
an angle of 90 degrees, like angles in a rectangle

rightful *adjective*
deserved or proper • *The bike was returned to its rightful owner.*

right-hand *adjective*
on the right side of something

right-handed *adjective*
using the right hand more than the left hand

rightly *adverb*
correctly or fairly

rigid *adjective* (*say* rij-id)
1 firm or stiff 2 strict or harsh • *The rules are rigid.* **rigidity** *noun* how rigid something is **rigidly** *adverb*

rim *noun*
the outer edge of a cup or wheel or other round object

rind *noun*
the tough skin on bacon, cheese, or fruit

ring[1] *noun*
1 something in the shape of a circle • *The children sat in a ring around the clown.* 2 a thin circular piece of metal you wear on a finger 3 the place where a boxing match or other contest is held 4 the space where a circus performs

ring[1] *verb*
to ring something is to put a ring round it • *Ring the answer that you think is the right one.*

ring[2] *verb* (**ringing, rang, rung**)
1 to ring a bell is to make it sound 2 a bell rings when it makes a clear musical sound 3 to ring someone is to telephone them • *She rang her brother last night.*

ring[2] *noun*
a ringing sound **to give someone a ring** (*informal*) is to telephone them

ringleader *noun*
someone who leads other people in doing wrong or in rebellion

ringlet *noun*
a long curled piece of hair

ringmaster *noun*
the person who is in charge of a performance in the circus ring

ring road *noun*
a road that takes traffic round a town rather than through it

rink *noun*
a place made for skating

rinse *verb*
to rinse something is to wash it in clean water without soap

rinse *noun*
a wash in clean water without soap

riot *noun*
wild or violent behaviour by a crowd of people in a public place

riot *verb*
people riot when they run wild and behave violently in a public place

rip *verb* (**ripping, ripped**)
to rip something is to tear it roughly

rip *noun*
a torn place

ripe *adjective*
ready to be harvested or eaten **ripeness** *noun*

ripen *verb*
1 to ripen something is to make it ripe 2 to ripen is to become ripe

a
b
c
d
e
f
g
h
i
j
k
l
m
n
o
p
q
r
s
t
u
v
w
x
y
z

ripple *noun*
a small wave on the surface of water

ripple *verb*
water ripples when it forms small waves on the surface

rise *verb* (**rising, rose, risen**)
1 to rise is to go upwards
• *Smoke was rising from the fire.*
• *The sun rises in the east.* **2** to rise is also to get larger or more • *Prices rose this year.* **3** a person rises when they get up from sleeping or sitting
• *They all rose as she came in.*
4 people rise, or rise up, when they rebel • *The army rose against the government.*

rise *noun*
1 an increase, especially in wages **2** an upward slope

risk *verb*
to risk something is to take a chance of damaging or losing it • *They risked their lives during the rescue.*

risk *noun*
a chance that something bad will happen • *There's a risk that the river might flood.* **risky** *adjective* dangerous; involving risk

robot

rite *noun*
a ceremony or ritual

ritual *noun*
a regular ceremony or series of actions

rival *noun*
a person or thing that competes with another or tries to do the same thing **rivalry** *noun* when two people compete against each other

rival *verb* (**rivalling, rivalled**)
to rival someone or something is to be as good as they are • *Nothing can rival the taste of home-made ice cream.*

river *noun*
a large natural stream of water that flows into the sea or into a lake

rivet *noun*
a strong metal pin for holding pieces of metal together

rivet *verb*
1 to rivet something is to fasten it with rivets **2** to rivet someone is to hold them still • *She stood riveted to the spot.* **3** to be riveted by something is to be fascinated by it
• *The children were riveted by his story.* **riveting** *adjective* fascinating; holding your attention

roam *verb*
to roam is to wander • *They roamed about the city.*

roar *noun*
a loud deep sound of the kind that a lion makes

roar *verb*
to roar is to make a loud deep sound

roast *verb*
1 to roast food is to cook it in an oven or over a fire **2** you say you are roasting when you are very hot

rob *verb* (**robbing, robbed**)
to rob someone or a place is to steal something from them
• *He robbed me of my watch.*
• *The bank's been robbed.*
robber *noun* someone who steals something
robbery *noun* when something is stolen

robe *noun*
a long loose piece of clothing

robin *noun*
a small brown bird with a red breast

robot *noun*
a machine that imitates the movements of a person or does the work of a person

robust *adjective*
tough and strong

rock¹ *noun*
1 a rock is a large stone **2** rock is a large mass of stone **3** rock is also a hard sweet usually shaped like a stick and sold at the seaside

rock² *verb*
1 to rock is to move gently backwards and forwards or from side to side **2** to rock something is to make it do this

rock² *noun*
rock music

rockery *noun* (**rockeries**)
part of a garden where people grow flowers between rocks

rocket *noun*
1 a firework that shoots high into the air **2** a pointed tube-shaped vehicle propelled into the air by hot gases, especially as a spacecraft or weapon

rocking chair *noun*
a chair which can be rocked by the person sitting in it

rock music *noun*
rock music is popular music with a heavy beat

rocky *adjective* (**rockier, rockiest**)
1 a rocky place is full of rocks
2 unsteady or shaky

rod *noun*
1 a long thin stick or bar **2** a rod with a line attached for fishing

rode
past tense of **ride** *verb*

rodent *noun*
an animal that has large front teeth for gnawing things, such as a rat, mouse, or squirrel

rodeo *noun* (**rodeos**)
(*say* roh-**day**-oh *or say* **roh**-di-oh)
a display or contest in which cowboys show their skills in riding and in controlling cattle

rogue *noun*
a dishonest or mischievous person
roguish *adjective* a roguish smile is a mischievous one

role *noun*
1 the part that an actor plays in a play, film, or story
2 the purpose something has
• *Computers have a role in language learning.*

roll *verb*
1 to roll is to move along by turning over and over, like a ball or wheel **2** to roll something is to make it do this **3** to roll something, or roll something up, is to form it into the shape of a cylinder or ball **4** to roll something soft is to flatten it by moving a round heavy object over it **5** a ship rolls when it sways from side to side **6** drums roll when they make a long rumbling sound

roll *noun*
1 a cylinder made by rolling something up **2** a small loaf of bread shaped like a bun **3** a list of names **4** the rumbling sound of drums or thunder

roller *noun*
a cylinder-shaped object, especially one used for flattening things

roller skate *noun*
roller skates are boots with two pairs of wheels fitted underneath, so that you can move smoothly over the ground

rolling pin *noun*
a heavy cylinder you roll over pastry to flatten it

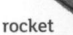
rocket

Roman Catholic *noun*
a member of the Church with the Pope in Rome at its head

romance *noun*
1 romance is experiences and feelings connected with love **2** a romance is a love affair or a love story

Roman numerals *plural noun*
letters that represent numbers, as used by the ancient Romans (compare *arabic figures*): I = 1, V = 5, X = 10, L = 50, C = 100, and M = 1000

romantic *adjective*
to do with love or romance
romantically *adverb*

romp *verb*
to romp is to play in a lively way

rompers *plural noun*
a piece of clothing for a young child, covering the body and legs

roof *noun*
1 the part that covers the top of a building, shelter, or vehicle **2** the upper part of your mouth

rook *noun*
1 a black bird that looks like a crow **2** a piece in chess, also called a castle

room *noun*
1 a room is a part of a building with its own walls and ceiling **2** room is space for someone or something
• *Is there room for me?*

roomy *adjective* (**roomier, roomiest**)
somewhere is roomy when there is plenty of room or space inside

roost *noun*
the place where a bird rests

root *noun*
1 the part of a plant that grows under the ground **2** a source or basis of something • *People say that money is the root of all evil.* **3** a number that gives another number when multiplied by itself • *9 is the square root of 81.* **to take root** is to grow roots or to become established • *The custom never took root in other countries.*

root *verb*
1 to root is to take root in the ground **2** to root someone is to fix them firmly • *Fear rooted him to the spot.* **to root something out** is to find it and get rid of it

rope *noun*
a strong thick cord made of strands twisted together **to show someone the ropes** is to show them how to do a job

rose *noun*
a scented flower with a long thorny stem

rosy *adjective* (**rosier, rosiest**)
1 pink **2** hopeful or cheerful
• *The future looks rosy.*

rot *verb* (**rotting, rotted**)
to rot is to go soft or bad so that it is useless
• *This wood has rotted.*

rot *noun*
rot is decay

rota *noun*
a list of tasks to be done and the people who have to do them

rotate *verb*
1 to rotate is to go round like a wheel **2** to rotate is to take turns at something • *The job of treasurer rotates.*

rotation *noun*
1 rotation, or a rotation, is when something goes round like a wheel **2** rotation is also taking turns to do something

rotor *noun*
the part of a machine that goes round, especially the large horizontal blade on top of a helicopter

rotten *adjective*
1 rotted or decayed
• *There was rotten fruit on the ground.*
2 (*informal*) nasty or very bad • *We had rotten weather.*

rotten

rough *adjective*
1 not smooth; uneven **2** violent; not gentle • *He is a rough boy* **3** not exact; done quickly • *It's only a rough guess.* **roughness** *noun*

roughen *verb*
to roughen something is to make it rough

roughly *adverb*
1 approximately; not exactly • *There were roughly a hundred people there.* **2** in a rough way; not gently • *She pushed him roughly out of the way.*

round *adjective*
1 shaped like a circle or ball or cylinder **2** a round trip is one that returns to the start

round *adverb*
1 in a circle or curve; by a longer route • *Go round to the back of the house.* **2** in every direction or to every person • *Hand the cakes round.* **3** in a new direction • *Turn your chair*

rose

round. **4** to someone's house or place of work • *Come round at lunchtime.*

round *preposition* **1** on all sides of • *We'll put a fence round the field.* **2** in a curve or circle about • *The earth moves round the sun.* **3** to every part of • *Show them round the house.*

round *noun*
1 each stage in a competition • *The winners go on to the next round.* **2** a series of visits or calls made by a doctor, postman, or other person **3** a whole slice of bread, or a sandwich made from two whole slices of bread **4** a shot or series of shots from a gun; a piece of ammunition **5** a song in which people sing the same words but start at different times

round *verb*
to round a place is to travel round it • *A large car rounded the corner.* **to round a number down** is to decrease it to the nearest lower number • *123.4 may be rounded down to 123.* **to round a number up** is to increase it to the nearest higher number • *123.7 may be rounded up to 124.* **to round something off** is to finish it to **round up people or things** is to gather them together

roundabout *noun*
1 a road junction at which traffic has to pass round a circular island **2** a merry-go-round

roundabout *adjective*
not using the shortest or most direct way • *We went by a roundabout route.*

rounders *noun*
rounders is a game in which players try to hit a ball and run round a circuit

roundly *adverb*
thoroughly or severely
• *We were roundly told off for being late.*

rouse *verb*
to rouse someone is to wake them up or make them excited

rout *verb* (say rowt)
to rout an enemy is to defeat them and chase them away

route *noun* (say root)
the way you have to go to get to a place

routine *noun* (say roo-teen)
a regular or fixed way of doing things

a b c d e f g h i j k l m n o p q r s t u v w x y z

rove *verb*
to rove is to roam or wander • *Her eyes roved around the classroom.*
rover *noun* someone who roves

row¹ *noun* (*rhymes with* **go**)
a line of people or things

row² *verb* (*rhymes with* **go**)
to row a boat is to use oars to make it move **rower** *noun* someone who rows a boat

row³ *noun* (*rhymes with* **cow**)
1 a great noise or disturbance
2 a noisy quarrel or argument

row³ *verb*
people row when they have a noisy argument

rowdy *adjective* (**rowdier, rowdiest**)
noisy and disorderly
rowdily *adverb* **rowdiness** *noun*

rowing boat *noun*
a small boat that you move forward by using oars

royal *adjective*
to do with a king or queen **royalty** *noun* the members of a royal family

rub *verb* (**rubbing, rubbed**)
to rub something is to move it backwards and forwards while pressing it on something else
• *He rubbed his hands together.* **to rub something off or out** is to make it disappear by rubbing it

rub *noun*
when you rub something
• *Give it a quick rub.*

rubber *noun*
1 rubber is a strong elastic substance used for making tyres, balls, hoses, and other things 2 a rubber is a piece of rubber or soft plastic for rubbing out pencil marks **rubbery** *adjective* soft and easy to stretch

rubbish *noun*
1 things that are not wanted or needed 2 nonsense

rubble *noun*
rubble is broken pieces of brick or stone

ruby *noun* (**rubies**)
a red jewel

rucksack *noun*
a bag with shoulder straps that you carry on your back

rudder *noun*
a flat hinged device at the back of a ship or aircraft, used for steering it

ruddy *adjective* (**ruddier, ruddiest**)
red and healthy-looking
• *He had a ruddy face.*

rude *adjective*
1 not polite; not showing respect for other people • *It was rude of me to push in.* 2 indecent or improper
• *a rude joke*
rudely *adverb* **rudeness** *noun*

ruffian *noun*
a rough violent person

ruffle *verb*
1 to ruffle something is to make it untidy or less smooth • *The bird ruffled its feathers.* 2 to ruffle someone is to annoy them or upset them

rug *noun*
1 a thick piece of material that partly covers a floor 2 a thick blanket

rugby or **rugby football** *noun*
rugby is a kind of football game using an oval ball that players may kick or carry

rugby ball

rugged *adjective* (*say* **rug**-id)
something rugged has a rough or uneven surface or outline
• *His face was rugged.* • *It has a rugged coastline.*

ruin *verb*
to ruin something is to spoil it or destroy it completely

ruin *noun*
1 a ruin is a building that has been so badly damaged that it has almost all fallen down 2 ruin is when something is ruined or destroyed to be in ruins is to be destroyed
• *My plans were in ruins.* **ruinous** *adjective* leading to ruin

rule *noun*
1 a rule is something that people have to obey
2 rule is ruling or governing • *The country used to be under French rule.* **as a rule** usually; normally

rule *verb*
1 to rule people is to govern them; to rule is to be a ruler 2 to rule something is to make a decision
• *The referee ruled that it was a foul.* 3 to rule a line is to draw a straight line with a ruler or other straight edge

ruler *noun*
1 someone who governs a country
2 a strip of wood, plastic, or metal with straight edges, used for measuring and drawing straight lines

ruler

ruling *noun*
a judgement or decision
• *I will give my ruling tomorrow.*

rum *noun*
rum is a strong alcoholic drink made from sugar cane

rumble *verb*
to rumble is to make a deep heavy sound like thunder
• *His stomach was rumbling.*

rumble *noun*
a long deep heavy sound
• *There was a rumble of thunder in the distance.*

rummage *verb*
to rummage is to turn things over or move them about while looking for something

rummy *noun*
rummy is a card game in which players try to form sets or sequences of cards

rumour *noun*
something that a lot of people are saying, although it may not be true

rump *noun*
the back part of an animal, above its hind legs

run *verb* (**running, ran, run**)
1 to run is to move with quick steps and with both feet off the ground for a time 2 to run is also to move or go or travel • *Tears ran down his cheeks.* 3 a tap or your nose runs when liquid flows from it 4 an engine or machine runs when it is working or functioning
• *The engine was running smoothly.* 5 to run something is to manage it or organize it • *She runs a corner shop.* 6 to run someone somewhere is to give them a lift there **to run a risk** is to take a chance **to run away** is to leave a place quickly or secretly **to run into someone** is to meet them unexpectedly **to run out of something** is to have used up a supply of it **to run someone over** is to knock them down with a car or bicycle

run *noun*
1 a spell of running • *Let's go for a run.* 2 a point scored in cricket or baseball 3 a series of damaged stitches in a pair of tights or other

piece of clothing **4** a continuous series of events • *They've had a run of good luck.* **5** a place with a fence round it for keeping animals to be **on the run** is to be running away, especially from the police

runaway *noun*
someone who has run away from home

rung *noun*
each of the short crossbars on a ladder

runner *noun*
1 a person or animal that runs in a race **2** the part of a sledge that slides along the ground

runner bean *noun*
a kind of climbing bean

runner-up *noun*
someone who comes second in a race or competition

runny *adjective* (**runnier, runniest**)
flowing or moving like liquid

runway *noun*
a long strip with a hard surface for aircraft to take off and land

rural *adjective*
to do with the countryside; in the country

rush¹ *verb*
1 to rush is to move or go very quickly • *When the doorbell rang I rushed to see who it was.* **2** to rush someone is to make them hurry • *I'm trying not to rush you.* **3** to rush someone is also to attack or capture them by surprise

rush¹ *noun*
a rush is a hurry • *I can't stop – I'm in a rush.*

rush² *noun*
rushes are plants with thin stems that grow in wet or marshy places

rusk *noun*
a kind of hard dry biscuit for babies to chew

rust *noun*
rust is a red or brown substance formed on metal that is exposed to air and dampness

rust *verb*
metal rusts when it develops rust

rustle *verb*
1 to rustle is to make a gentle sound like dry leaves being blown by the wind **2** to rustle horses or cattle is to steal them

rusty *adjective*
1 coated with rust **2** not as good as it used to be because you have not had enough practice • *My French is a bit rusty.*

rut *noun*
a deep groove made by wheels in

soft ground **to be in a rut** is to have a dull life with no changes

ruthless *adjective*
someone is ruthless when they are determined to get what they want and don't care if they hurt other people **ruthlessly** *adverb* **ruthlessness** *noun*

rye *noun*
rye is a cereal used to make bread and biscuits

Ss

sabbath *noun*
the sabbath is the weekly day for rest and prayer, Saturday for Jews, Sunday for Christians

sabotage *noun* (*say* sab-o-tahzh)
sabotage is deliberately damaging machinery or equipment

sabotage *verb*
to sabotage machinery or equipment is to deliberately damage it **saboteur** *noun* someone who commits sabotage

sac *noun*
any bag-like part of an animal or plant

sachet *noun* (*say* sash-ay)
a small sealed packet of something such as shampoo or sugar

sack *noun*
a large bag made of strong material **to get the sack** (*informal*) is to be dismissed from your job

sack *verb*
(*informal*) to sack someone is to dismiss them from their job

sacred *adjective*
to do with God or a god; holy

sacrifice *noun*
1 giving up a thing that you value so that something good may happen • *If you want to save some money you might have to make a few sacrifices.* **2** killing an animal or person as an offering to a god **sacrificial** *adjective* offered as a sacrifice

sacrifice *verb*
1 to sacrifice something is to give it up so that something good may happen **2** to sacrifice an animal or person is to kill them as an offering to a god

sad *adjective* (**sadder, saddest**)
unhappy; showing sorrow or causing it **sadly** *adverb* in a sad way • *He shook his head sadly.* **sadness** *noun*

sadden *verb*
something saddens you when it makes you sad or unhappy

saddle *noun*
1 a seat that you put on the back of a horse or other animal so that you can ride it **2** the seat of a bicycle

saddle *verb*
to saddle an animal is to put a saddle on its back

safari *noun* (*say* sa-**far**-i)
an expedition to see wild animals or hunt them

WORD ORIGIN

The word **safari** comes from an Arabic word *safara* meaning 'to travel'.

safari park *noun*
a large park where wild animals can roam around freely and visitors can watch them from their cars

safe *adjective*
1 free from danger; protected **2** not causing danger • *Drive at a safe speed.* **safely** *adverb* without risk or danger • *The plane landed safely.*

safe *noun*
a strong cupboard or box in which valuable things can be locked away to keep them safe

safeguard *noun*
something that protects you against danger

safeguard *verb*
to safeguard something is to protect it from danger

safety *noun* safety is being safe; protection • *We listened to a talk on road safety.*

safety belt *noun*
a belt to hold someone securely in a seat

safety pin *noun*
a curved pin made with a clip that closes to cover the point

sag *verb* (**sagging, sagged**)
something sags when it sinks slightly in the middle because something heavy is pressing on it

saga *noun*
a long story with many adventures

safety pins

sail *noun*
1 a large piece of strong cloth attached to a mast to make a boat move **2** a short voyage • *We went for a sail around the island.* **3** an arm of a windmill **to set sail** is to start on a voyage in a ship

sail *verb*
1 to sail somewhere is to travel there in a ship **2** a ship or boat sails when

a b c d e f g h i j k l m n o p q r s t u v w x y z

it starts out on a voyage • *What time does the ferry sail?* **3** to sail a ship or boat is to control it

sailor *noun*
1 a member of a ship's crew
2 someone who sails

saint *noun*
a holy or very good person **saintly** *adjective* very good or holy

sake *noun*
for the sake of something in order to do it or get it • *He'll do anything for the sake of money.* for someone's sake in order to help them or please them • *She went to a lot of trouble for his sake.*

salad *noun*
a mixture of vegetables eaten cold and often raw

salami *noun*
salami is a kind of strong spicy sausage

salary *noun*
a regular wage, usually paid every month

sale *noun*
1 the selling of something **2** a time when a shop sells things at reduced prices for sale or on sale able to be bought

salesperson *noun*
someone whose job is to sell things
salesman *noun*
saleswoman *noun*

saliva *noun* (*say* sa-ly-va)
saliva is the natural liquid in your mouth

salmon *noun* (**salmon**)
a large fish with pink flesh, used for food

salon *noun*
a room or shop where a hairdresser or a beauty specialist works

salt *noun*
salt is the white substance that gives sea water its taste and is used for flavouring food
salty *adjective* tasting of salt
salt *verb*
to salt food is to use salt to flavour or preserve it

salmon

salute *verb*
to salute is to raise your hand to your forehead as a sign of respect or greeting
salute *noun*
the act of saluting

salvage *verb*
to salvage something such as a damaged ship is to save or rescue it or parts of it

salvation *noun*
salvation is saving someone or something

same *adjective*
not different; exactly equal or alike • *We are the same age.* • *Look, these two leaves are exactly the same.*

samosa *noun*
a small case of crisp pastry filled with a mixture of spicy meat or vegetables

samosas

sample *noun*
a small amount that shows what something is like

sample *verb*
1 to sample something is to take a sample of it • *Scientists sampled the lake water.* **2** to sample something is also to try part of it • *She sampled the cake.*

sanctuary *noun* (**sanctuaries**)
1 a safe place, especially for someone who is being chased or attacked **2** a place where wildlife is protected • *We visited a bird sanctuary.*

sand *noun*
sand is the tiny grains of rock that you find on beaches and in deserts

sandal *noun*
a light shoe with straps that go round your foot

sandpaper *noun*
sandpaper is strong paper coated with hard grains, rubbed on rough surfaces to make them smooth

sandstone *noun*
sandstone is rock made of compressed sand

sandwich *noun*
slices of bread with meat, cheese, or some other filling between them

sandy *adjective*
(**sandier, sandiest**)
1 made of sand; covered with sand
2 sandy hair is yellowish-red

sane *adjective*
having a healthy mind; not mad

sanitary *adjective*
free from germs and dirt; hygienic

sanitation *noun*
sanitation is arrangements for drainage and getting rid of sewage

sanity *noun*
sanity is being sane

sap *noun*
sap is the juice inside a tree or plant
sap *verb* (**sapping, sapped**)
to sap someone's strength or energy is to use it up or weaken it gradually • *The heat had sapped all my energy.*

sapling *noun*
a young tree

sapphire *noun*
a bright blue jewel

sarcastic *noun*
you are being sarcastic when you mock someone or something by saying the opposite of what you mean • *She said she liked the music I was playing but I think she was being sarcastic.* **sarcastically** *adverb* **sarcasm** *noun* when someone is being sarcastic

sardine *noun*
a small sea fish, usually sold packed tightly in tins

sari *noun* (*say* sar-i)
a long length of cloth worn as a dress, especially by Indian women and girls

sash *noun*
a strip of cloth worn round the waist or over one shoulder

satchel *noun*
a bag you wear over your shoulder or on your back, especially for carrying books to and from school

satellite *noun*
1 a spacecraft sent into space to move in an orbit round a planet, in order to get and send information **2** a moon that moves in orbit round a planet

satellite dish *noun*
a dish-shaped aerial for receiving television signals sent by satellite

satellite television *noun* satellite television is television programmes that are broadcast using a satellite

satin *noun*
satin is a silky material that is shiny on one side

satire *noun*
1 satire is using humour or exaggeration to show the faults of a person or thing, especially the

government **2** a satire is a play or piece of writing that does this **satirical** *adjective* using satire to criticize someone **satirist** *noun* someone who writes satire

satisfaction *noun*
satisfaction is the feeling of being satisfied

satisfactory *adjective* good enough; acceptable **satisfactorily** *adverb* in a satisfactory way

satisfy *verb* (**satisfies, satisfying, satisfied**)
1 to satisfy someone is to give them what they need or want **2** to be satisfied is to be sure of something • *I am satisfied that you have done your best.*

saturate *verb*
to be saturated is to be soaking wet • *My clothes are saturated with rain.* **saturation** *noun* saturation is being saturated

Saturday *noun*
the seventh day of the week

sauce *noun*
a sauce is a thick liquid served with food to add flavour

saucepan *noun*
a metal cooking pan with a long handle

saucer *noun*
a small curved plate for a cup to stand on

saucy *adjective* (**saucier, sauciest**)
rude or cheeky

sauna *noun* (say **saw**-na *or say* **sow**-na) a room filled with steam where people sit and sweat a lot, used as a kind of bath

saunter *verb*
to saunter is to walk about in a leisurely way

sausage *noun*
a tube of edible skin or plastic stuffed with minced meat and other ingredients

savage *adjective*
wild and fierce; cruel **savagely** *noun* in a violent or cruel way **savagery** *noun* cruel and violent behaviour

savage *verb*
an animal savages someone when it attacks them and bites or scratches them fiercely

savannah *noun* (say sa-**van**-a) a grassy plain in a hot country, with few trees

save *verb*
1 to save someone or something is to free them from danger or harm **2** to save something, especially money, is

to keep it so that it can be used later **3** to save computer data is to instruct the computer to keep it on its hard disk **4** in football, to save a ball is to stop it going into your goal

savings *plural noun*
your savings are the money that you have saved

saviour *noun*
a person who saves someone

savoury *adjective*
savoury food is tasty but not sweet

saw *noun*
a tool with sharp teeth for cutting wood or other hard materials

saw *verb* (**sawing, sawed, sawn** *or* **sawed**)
to saw something is to cut it with a saw

sawdust *noun*
sawdust is powder that comes from wood when it is cut with a saw

saxophone *noun*
a wind instrument with a tube that curves upward with a wider opening

WORD ORIGIN

The word **saxophone** comes from the name of Adolphe Sax, a Belgian instrument-maker.

say *verb* (**saying, said**)
1 to say something is to make words with your voice **2** to say something is also to give information or instructions • *The notice said 'Keep Out'.*

saying *noun*
a well-known phrase or proverb

scab *noun*
a hard covering that forms over a cut or graze while it is healing

scabbard *noun*
a cover for a sword or dagger

scaffold *noun*
a platform on which criminals were executed in the past

scaffolding *noun*
scaffolding is a structure of poles and planks for workers to stand on when they are building or repairing a house

scald *verb*
to scald your skin is to burn it with very hot liquid or steam

scale¹ *noun*
1 a series of units or marks for measuring something • *This ruler has one scale in centimetres and another in inches.* **2** the relationship between the size of something on a map or model and the actual size of the thing in the real world • *The*

scale of this map is one inch to the mile. **3** a series of musical notes going up or down in a fixed pattern **4** the relative size or importance of something • *They love organizing parties on a massive scale.*

scale¹ *verb*
to scale something is to climb up it

scale² *noun*
one of the thin overlapping parts on the outside of fish, snakes, and other animals **scaly** *adjective* covered in scales

scales *plural noun*
a device for weighing things

scalp *noun*
the skin on the top of your head

scamper *verb*
to scamper is to run quickly with short steps

scampi *plural noun* scampi are large prawns eaten in batter or breadcrumbs

scan *verb* (**scanning, scanned**)
1 to scan something is to look at every part of it **2** to scan a piece of writing is to look over it quickly **3** to scan an area, or a part of the body, is to sweep a radar or electronic beam over it in order to find something **4** poetry scans when it has a fixed rhythm

scan *noun*
a search or examination using a scanner

saxophone

scandal *noun*
1 a scandal is a shameful or disgraceful action
2 scandal is gossip that damages someone's reputation

scandalous *adjective* shocking or disgraceful

scanner *noun*
1 a machine used to examine part of the body, using an electronic beam **2** a machine that converts print and pictures into data that can be read by a computer

scanty *adjective* (**scantier, scantiest**)
hardly big enough; small **scantily** *adverb* barely; just sufficiently

scapegoat *noun*
someone who gets all the blame for something that other people have done

scar *noun*
a mark left on your skin by a cut or burn after it has healed

scar *verb* (**scarring, scarred**)
an injury scars you when it leaves a permanent mark on your skin

scarce *adjective*
not enough to supply people • *Wheat was scarce because of the bad harvest.* to make yourself scarce (*informal*) is to go away or keep out of the way **scarcity** *noun* a shortage of something

scarcely *adverb*
hardly; only just • *She could scarcely walk.*

scare *verb*
to scare someone is to frighten them

scare *noun*
a scare is a fright • *You gave me quite a scare.*

scarecrow *noun*
a figure of a person dressed in old clothes, that farmers put in a field to frighten birds away from crops

scarf *noun* (**scarves**)
a strip of material that you wear round your neck or head

scarlet *adjective* ●
bright red

scary *adjective*
(**scarier, scariest**)
(*informal*)
frightening

scatter *verb*
1 to scatter things is to throw them in all directions
2 to scatter is to move quickly in all directions • *The crowd scattered when the police arrived.*

scavenge *verb*
an animal or bird scavenges when it eats dead animals that have been killed by another animal **scavenger** *noun* an animal or bird that scavenges

scene *noun*
1 the place where something happens • *Here is the scene of the crime.* 2 a part of a play or film 3 a view you can see 4 an angry or noisy outburst • *They made a scene about the money.*

scenery *noun*
1 scenery is the natural features of an area • *We were admiring the scenery.* 2 scenery is also the painted panels and other things put on a stage to make it look like a place

scent *noun* (*say* sent)
1 a pleasant smell or perfume
2 an animal's smell, that other

animals can follow **scented** *adjective* having a strong pleasant smell

scent *verb*
to scent something is to discover it by its scent

sceptic *noun* (*say* **skep**-tik)
someone who doesn't believe things easily or readily

sceptical *adjective*
(*say* **skep**-tik-al)
you are sceptical when you don't believe things easily or readily **scepticism** *noun* scepticism is not believing things easily or readily

schedule *noun* (*say* **shed**-yool)
a timetable of things that have to be done to be on schedule is to be on time; not late

scheme *noun*
a plan of what to do
  scheme *verb*
  to scheme is to make secret plans

scarf

schooner

scholar *noun*
1 someone who studies a subject thoroughly 2 someone who has been given a scholarship

scholarly *adjective*
showing knowledge and learning

scholarship *noun*
1 a scholarship is a grant of money given to someone for their education 2 scholarship is knowledge and learning

school[1] *noun*
1 a place where children go to be taught 2 the children who go there • *The whole school had a holiday.* 3 a place where you can learn a skill • *a driving school*

school[2] *noun*
a group of whales or fish swimming together

schoolchild *noun*
(**schoolchildren**)
a child who goes to school

schoolteacher *noun*
a teacher at a school

schooner *noun* (*say* **skoo**-ner)
a sailing ship with two or more masts

science *noun*
science is the study of objects and happenings in the world that can be observed and tested

WORD ORIGIN

The word **science** comes from a Latin word *scientia* meaning 'knowledge'

science fiction *noun*
science fiction is stories about imaginary worlds, especially in space and in the future

scientific *adjective*
1 to do with science 2 studying things carefully and logically

scientist *noun*
someone who studies science or is an expert in science

scissors *plural noun*
a cutting device made of two movable blades joined together

scoff *verb*
to scoff at someone or something is to make fun of them

scold *verb*
to scold someone is to tell them off harshly

scone *noun* (*say* skon or skohn)
a small plain cake, usually eaten with butter and jam

scoop *noun*
1 a deep spoon for serving soft food such as ice cream or mashed potato 2 a deep shovel 3 (*informal*) an important piece of news that one newspaper prints before all the others

scoop *verb*
to scoop something, or to scoop it out, is to take it out with a scoop or the palm of your hand

scooter *noun*
1 a simple type of bicycle for a child, with two wheels and a narrow platform. You stand on the platform and push on the ground with one foot. 2 a kind of motorcycle with small wheels

scope *noun*
1 an opportunity or possibility for something • *There is scope for improvement.* 2 what something deals with or includes • *That question doesn't come within the scope of this book.*

scorch *verb*
to scorch something is to make it go brown by slightly burning it

scorching *adjective*
very hot

score *noun*
1 the number of points or goals that are got in a game • *What's the score?* 2 (old use) a score is twenty • *He reached the age of four-score (= 80) years.*

score *verb*
1 to score a goal or point in a game is to get it 2 to score is to keep a count of the score in a game • *I thought you were scoring.* 3 to score a surface is to scratch it **scorer** *noun* someone who scores a goal or point

scorn *noun*
scorn is treating a person or thing with contempt

scorn *verb*
to scorn someone or something is to have contempt for them **scornful** *adjective* full of contempt and showing no respect **scornfully** *adverb*

scorpion *noun*
an animal related to the spider, with pincers and a poisonous sting in its curved tail

Scot *noun*
a person from Scotland

Scottish
adjective
to do with
Scotland   scorpion

scoundrel *noun*
a wicked or dishonest person

scour *verb*
1 to scour (for example) a pan or bath is to rub it hard with something rough until it is clean and bright 2 to scour an area is to search it thoroughly

Scout *noun*
a member of the Scout Association

scout *noun*
someone sent out ahead of a group in order to collect information

scowl *verb*
to scowl is to look bad-tempered

scowl *noun*
an angry look

scramble *verb*
1 to scramble is to move quickly and awkwardly • *We scrambled up the steep slope.* 2 to scramble eggs is to cook them by mixing them and heating them in a pan 3 to scramble for something is to struggle to do it or get it

scramble *noun*
1 a climb or walk over rough ground 2 a struggle to get something • *There was a scramble for the best seats.* 3 a motorcycle race across rough country

scrap¹ *noun*
1 a scrap is a small piece of something 2 scrap is rubbish, especially unwanted metal

scrap¹ *verb* (**scrapping, scrapped**)
to scrap something is to get rid of it when you do not want it

scrap² *noun*
(*informal*) a fight

scrap² *verb* (**scrapping, scrapped**)
to scrap is to fight or quarrel

scrape *verb*
1 to scrape something is to rub it with something rough, hard, or sharp 2 to scrape past or through is to only just get past or succeed • *She scraped through her exams.* 3 to scrape something together is to collect it with difficulty • *They scraped together enough money for a holiday.* **scraper** *noun* a device for scraping something clean

scrape *noun*
1 a scraping movement or sound 2 a mark made by scraping something 3 (*informal*) an awkward situation • *He's always getting into scrapes.*

scrappy *adjective*
done carelessly or untidily

scratch *verb*
1 to scratch a surface is to damage it by rubbing something sharp over it 2 you scratch your skin when you rub it with your fingers because it itches

scratch *noun*
1 a mark or cut made by scratching 2 the action of scratching • *I need to have a scratch.* **to start from scratch** is to begin at the very beginning **to be up to scratch** is to be up to the proper standard

scrawl *noun*
untidy writing • *Can you read my scrawl?*

scrawl *verb*
to scrawl something is to write it in a hurried or careless way

scream *noun*
a loud high-pitched cry of pain or fear or anger

scream *verb*
to scream is to make a loud high-pitched cry

screech *noun*
a harsh high-pitched sound • *There was a screech of tyres as the car sped off.*

screech *verb*
to screech is to make a harsh high-pitched sound

screen *noun*
1 a surface on which films or television programmes or computer data are shown 2 a movable panel used to hide or protect something 3 a windscreen

screen *verb*
1 to screen a film or television programme is to show it 2 to screen something is to hide it or protect it with a screen 3 to screen people is to test them to find out if they have a disease

screw *noun*
1 a metal pin with a spiral ridge round it, which holds things by being twisted into them 2 a propeller

screw *verb*
1 to screw something is to fix it with screws 2 to screw something in or on is to fit it by turning it • *Screw the lid on to the jar.* • *I screwed in the light-bulb.* **to screw something up** is to twist or squeeze it into a tight ball

screwdriver *noun*
a tool for putting in or taking out screws

scribble *verb*
to scribble is to write untidily or carelessly, or to make meaningless marks

script *noun*
1 the words of a play, film, or broadcast 2 handwriting 3 something you write, especially the answers you write to exam questions

scripture *noun*
the sacred writings of a religion, especially the Bible

scroll *noun*
a roll of paper or parchment with writing on it

scroll *verb*
you scroll up or down on a computer screen when you move the text up or down on the screen to see what comes before or after

scrounge *verb*
(*informal*) to scrounge something is to get it without paying for it • *He scrounged a meal from us.* **scrounger** *noun* someone who tries to get things without paying for them

scrub¹ *verb* (**scrubbing, scrubbed**)
to scrub something is to rub it with a hard brush

scrub¹ *noun*
the action of scrubbing • *You'll need to give your face a good scrub.*

scrub² *noun*
scrub is low trees and bushes, or land covered with them

scruffy *adjective* (**scruffier, scruffiest**)
shabby and untidy

scrum or **scrummage** *noun*
(in rugby football) a group of players from each side who push against each other and try to win the ball with their feet

scuba diving *noun*
scuba diving is swimming underwater, breathing air from a supply carried on your back

scuffle *noun*
a confused struggle or fight

scuffle *verb*
people scuffle when they fight in a confused way

sculptor *noun*
someone who makes sculptures

sculpture *noun*
1 a sculpture is something carved or shaped out of a hard material such as stone, clay, or metal 2 sculpture is the art or work of a sculptor

scum *noun*
scum is froth or dirt on the top of a liquid

scurry *verb*
to scurry is to run or hurry with short steps

scurvy *noun*
scurvy is a disease caused by lack of fresh fruit and vegetables

scuttle¹ *noun*
a container for coal, kept by a fireplace

scuttle² *verb*
to scuttle a ship is to sink it deliberately by making holes in the side or bottom

scuttle³ *verb*
to scuttle is to run with short quick steps

scythe *noun*
a tool with a long curved blade for cutting grass or corn

sea *noun*
1 the salt water that covers most of the earth's surface 2 a large lake or area of water, such as the Mediterranean Sea or the Sea of Galilee 3 a large area of something • I looked down at the sea of faces in the audience. at sea 1 on the sea 2 unable to understand something or cope with it • He's completely at sea in his new job.

seabed *noun*
the seabed is the bottom of the sea

seafaring *adjective, noun*
travelling or working on the sea

seafarer *noun* someone who travels or works at sea

seafood *noun*
seafood is fish or shellfish from the sea eaten as food

seagull *noun*
a sea bird with long wings

sea horse *noun*
a small fish that swims upright, with a head like a horse's head

sea horse

seal¹ *noun*
a furry sea animal that breeds on land

seal² *noun*
1 something designed to close an opening and stop air or liquid getting in or out 2 a design pressed into a soft substance such as wax or lead

seal² *verb*
to seal something is to close it by sticking two parts together • He sealed the envelope.

sea level *noun*
sea level is the level of the sea halfway between high and low tide • The mountain rises 1,000 metres above sea level.

sea lion *noun*
a large kind of seal. The male has a kind of mane.

seam *noun*
1 the line where two edges of cloth join together 2 a layer of coal in the ground

seaman *noun* (**seamen**)
a sailor

search *verb*
1 to search for something or someone is to look very carefully for them 2 to search a person or place is to look very carefully for something they may have **searcher** *noun* someone who is trying to find something or someone

search *noun*
1 a very careful look for someone or something 2 when you look for information in a computer database or on the Internet • Let's do a search for 'Roald Dahl'.

search engine *noun*
a computer program that helps you find information on the Internet

searchlight *noun*
a light with a strong beam that can be turned in any direction

seashore *noun*
the seashore is the land close to the sea

seasick *adjective*
someone is seasick when they are

sick because of the movement of a ship **seasickness** *noun* feeling sick

seaside *noun*
the seaside is a place by the sea where people go on holiday

season *noun*
1 one of the four main parts of the year: spring, summer, autumn, and winter 2 the time of year when a sport or other activity happens • When does the football season start?

season *verb*
to season food is to put salt, pepper, or other strong-tasting things on it to flavour it

seasonal *adjective*
happening only at certain times of the year • Fruit-picking is seasonal work.

seasoning *noun*
seasoning is something strong-tasting like salt and pepper, used to season food

season ticket *noun*
a ticket that you can use as often as you like for a certain period

seat *noun*
1 something used for sitting on 2 a place in parliament or on a council or a board of a business

seat *verb*
a place seats a certain number of people when it has that many seats for them • The stadium seats 50,000.

seat belt *noun*
a strap to hold a person securely in the seat of a vehicle or aircraft

seaweed *noun*
seaweed is plants that grow in the sea

secateurs *plural noun*
(say **sek-a-terz**)
a tool used for pruning plants

secluded *adjective*
a secluded place is away from large numbers of people; quiet and hidden • They found a secluded beach for their picnic. **seclusion** *noun* seclusion is being private or hidden

second *adjective, noun*
the next after the first to have second thoughts is to wonder whether your decision was really right

second *noun*
1 a very short period of time, one-sixtieth of a minute 2 a person or thing that is second 3 someone who helps a fighter in a boxing match or duel

second *verb*
to second a proposal or motion is to support it formally

secondary *adjective*
coming second; not original or essential • *This is of secondary importance.*

secondary school *noun*
a school for children more than about 11 years old

second-hand *adjective, adverb*
bought or used after someone else has used it • *He could only afford a second-hand car.*

secondly *adverb*
as the second thing • *Secondly, I'd like to thank my parents.*

secrecy *noun*
secrecy is being secret

secret *adjective*
1 that must not be told or shown to other people 2 that is not known by many people; hidden • *The house had a secret passage.* **secretly** *adverb* without telling other people

secret *noun*
something that is secret to do something in secret is to do it secretly

secretary *noun* (**secretaries**)
(*say* sek-re-tri)
someone whose job is to type letters, keep files, answer the telephone, and make business arrangements for a person or organization

secrete *verb* (*say* si-**kreet**)
to secrete a substance in the body is to release it • *Saliva is secreted in the mouth.* **secretion** *noun* a substance that is secreted

secretive *adjective*
(*say* **seek**-rit-iv)
liking or trying to keep things secret **secretively** *adverb* **secretiveness** *noun*

sect *noun*
a group of people who have special or unusual religious opinions or beliefs

section *noun*
a part of something • *Our school library has a large history section* • *The tail section of the plane broke off.*

sector *noun*
a part of an area or activity

secure *adjective*
1 firm and safe • *Is that ladder secure?* 2 made safe or protected from attack • *Check that all the doors and windows are secure.* **securely** *adverb*

secure *verb*
to secure something is to make it safe or firmly fixed

security *noun*
1 security is being secure or safe 2 security is also measures taken to prevent theft, spying, or terrorism

sedate *adjective* (*say* si-**dayt**)
calm and dignified **sedately** *adverb*

sedative *noun* (*say* sed-a-tiv)
a medicine that makes a person calm or helps them sleep

sediment *noun*
sediment is solid matter that settles at the bottom of a liquid

see *verb* (**seeing, saw, seen**)
1 to see something or someone is to use your eyes to notice them or be aware of them 2 to see someone is to meet or visit them • *See me after class.* 3 to see something is to understand it • *I see what you mean.* 4 to see someone as something is to imagine them being it • *Can you see yourself as a teacher?* 5 to see that something happens is to make sure of it • *See that the windows are shut.* 6 to see someone somewhere is to escort or lead them • *I'll see you to the door.* to see through something or someone is not to be deceived by them to see to something is to deal with it • *Can you see to the lunch?*

seed *noun*
a tiny part of a plant that can grow in the ground to make a new plant

seedling *noun*
a very young plant

seek *verb* (**seeking, sought**)
1 to seek a person or thing is to try to find them 2 to seek something is to try to achieve it • *She is seeking fame.*

seem *verb*
to seem to be something or to have some quality is to appear that way or give that impression • *They seem happy in their new house.*

seep *verb*
a liquid or gas seeps when it flows slowly through or into or out of something • *Water was seeping into the cellar.* **seepage** *noun* when something is seeping

see-saw *noun*
a plank balanced in the middle so that people can sit at each end and make it go up and down

seethe *verb*
1 a liquid seethes when it boils or bubbles 2 you are seething when you are very angry or excited

segment *noun*
a part that is cut off or can be separated from the rest

of something • *He ate a few segments of an orange*

segments

segregate *verb*
(*say* **seg**-ri-gayt)
to segregate people of different races or religions is to keep them apart and make them live separately **segregation** *noun* when people of different races or religions are kept apart and made to live separately

seize *verb* (*say* seez)
1 to seize someone or something is to take hold of them suddenly or firmly 2 to seize a place is to capture it using force to seize up is to become jammed or stuck

seizure *noun*
a seizure is a sudden attack of an illness

seldom *adverb*
not often
• *I seldom cry.*

select *verb*
to select a person or thing is to choose them carefully

select *adjective*
small and carefully chosen
• *They have a select group of friends.*

self *noun* (**selves**)
the type of person you are; your individual nature • *You'll soon be feeling your old self again.*

self-centred *adjective*
selfish; thinking about yourself too much

self-confident *adjective* confident in what you can do **self-confidence** *noun* being self-confident

self-conscious *adjective*
embarrassed or shy because you know people are watching you

self-control *noun*
self-control is the ability to control your own behaviour or feelings **self-controlled** *adjective* able to control your own behaviour or feelings

self-defence *noun*
1 you act in self-defence when you do something defending yourself against attack 2 self-defence is also skill in defending yourself if someone attacks you

c d e f g h i j k l m n o p q r s t u v w x y z

self-employed *adjective* someone who is self-employed works independently and not for an employer

selfish *adjective* having or doing what you want without thinking of other people **selfishly** *adverb* **selfishness** *noun*

selfless *adjective* thinking of other people rather than yourself; not selfish

self-service *adjective* a self-service shop or restaurant is one where customers serve themselves with goods and pay a cashier for what they have taken

sell *verb* (**selling, sold**) to sell goods or services is to offer them in exchange for money to sell out is to sell all your stock of something

semaphore *noun* semaphore is a system of signalling by holding flags out with your arms in positions to indicate letters of the alphabet

semaphore

semibreve *noun* (*say* **sem**-i-breev) the longest musical note normally used, written ○

semicircle *noun* ❭ half a circle **semicircular** *adjective* in the form of a semicircle

semicolon *noun* a punctuation mark (;), marking a more definite break in a sentence than a comma does

semi-detached *adjective* a semi-detached house is one that is joined to another house on one side

semi-final *noun* a match played to decide who will take part in the final **semi-finalist** *noun* a contestant in a semi-final

semitone *noun* half a tone in music

senate *noun* (*say* **sen**-at) **1** the governing council in ancient Rome **2** the higher-ranking section of the parliament in France, the USA, and some other countries **senator** *noun* a member of a senate

send *verb* (**sending, sent**) **1** to send something somewhere is to arrange for it to be taken there **2** to send someone somewhere is to tell them to go there to send for something or someone is to ask for them to come to you

senior *adjective* **1** older than someone else **2** higher in rank • *He is a senior officer in the navy.* **seniority** *noun* a person's seniority is how old or high in rank they are

senior *noun* someone is your senior when they are older or higher in rank than you are

senior citizen *noun* an elderly person, especially a pensioner

sensation *noun* **1** a feeling • *There's an itchy sensation in my leg.* **2** a very exciting event or the excitement caused by it • *The news caused a great sensation.*

sensational *adjective* causing great excitement or shock

sense *noun* **1** the ability to see, hear, smell, touch, or taste things **2** the ability to feel or appreciate something • *She has a good sense of humour.* **3** the power to think or make good judgements • *He hasn't got the sense to come in out of the rain.* **4** meaning • *The word 'set' has many senses.* to make sense is to have a meaning you can understand

sense *verb* **1** to sense something is to feel it or be aware of it • *I sensed that she did not like me.* **2** to sense something is also to detect it • *This device senses radioactivity.*

senseless *adjective* **1** stupid; not sensible • *I am sick of all this senseless fighting.* **2** unconscious • *He fell senseless to the ground.*

sensible *adjective* wise; having or showing good sense **sensibly** *adverb*

sensitive *adjective* **1** affected by the sun or chemicals or something else physical • *I have sensitive skin.* **2** easily offended or upset • *He's quite sensitive about being criticized.* **3** aware of other people's feelings **sensitively** *adverb* in a way that shows you are aware of other people's feelings **sensitivity** *noun* being sensitive; something you are sensitive about

sensor *noun* a device or instrument for detecting something physical such as heat or light

sentence *noun* **1** a group of words that express a complete thought and form a statement or question or command **2** the punishment given to a convicted person in a lawcourt

sentence *verb* to sentence someone is to give them a sentence in a lawcourt • *They were sentenced to two years in prison.*

sentiment *noun* **1** a sentiment is a feeling or opinion **2** sentiment is a show of feeling or emotion

sentimental *adjective* showing or making you feel emotion, especially too much sad emotion • *The film is a sentimental love story.* **sentimentality** *noun* sentimentality is being too sentimental **sentimentally** *adverb*

sentry *noun* (**sentries**) a soldier guarding something

separate *adjective* (*say* **sep**-er-at) **1** not joined to anything; on its own **2** not together; not with other people • *They lead separate lives.* **separately** *adverb* not together • *They arrived together but left separately.*

separate *verb* (*say* **sep**-er-ayt) **1** to separate things or people is to take them away from others **2** to separate is to become separate or move away from each other **3** two people separate when they stop living together as a couple **separation** *noun* when people are apart from each other

September *noun* the ninth month of the year

septic *adjective* a wound goes septic when it becomes infected with harmful bacteria

sequel *noun* (*say* **see**-kwel) a book or film that continues the story of an earlier one

sequence *noun* (*say* **see**-kwenss) a series of things coming in a particular order

sequin *noun* (*say* **see**-kwin) sequins are tiny bright discs sewn on clothes to decorate them

serene *adjective*
calm and peaceful **serenely** *adverb*
serenity *noun* serenity is being
calm and peaceful

sergeant *noun* (*say* **sar**-jent)
a soldier or police officer who is in
charge of others

serial *noun*
a story that is presented in separate
parts over a period,
for example week by week

series *noun* (**series**)
1 a number of things following
each other or connected with each
other 2 a set of television or radio
programmes with the same title

serious *adjective*
1 not funny; important • *We need a
serious talk.* 2 thoughtful or solemn
• *His face was serious.* 3 very bad
• *They've had a serious accident.*
seriously *adverb* **seriousness**
noun

sermon *noun*
a talk given by a preacher during a
religious service

serpent *noun*
a snake

servant *noun*
a person whose job is to work in
someone else's house

serve *verb*
1 to serve people in a shop is
to help them find the things they
want to buy 2 to serve food or drink
is to give it to people at a meal
3 to serve a person or organization
is to work for them 4 to serve is to
be suitable for a purpose • *This tree
stump will serve as a table.* 5 (*in
tennis*) to serve is to start play by
hitting the ball to your opponent
it serves you right you deserve it
server *noun* the player who starts
play by serving in tennis

serve *noun*
the action of serving in tennis

service *noun*
1 service is working for someone
or something • *He retired after
forty years' service.* 2 a service is
something that helps people or
supplies what they want • *There is
a good bus service into town.* 3 a
service is also a religious ceremony
in a church 4 a service, or dinner
service, is a set of plates and
crockery 5 a vehicle or machine
has a service when someone spends
time repairing and maintaining
it 6 (*in tennis*) a service is a serve
the services the armed forces of a
country

service *verb*
to service a vehicle or machine is to
check it and repair it if necessary

service station *noun*
a place beside the road where you
can buy petrol

serviette *noun*
a cloth or paper napkin that you can
wipe your hands and mouth on

session *noun*
1 a time spent doing a particular
thing • *They were in the middle of a
recording session.* 2 a meeting
or series of meetings • *The Queen
will open the next session of
Parliament.*

set *verb* (**setting, set**)
This word has many meanings,
depending on the words that go with
it: 1 to set something somewhere is
to put or place it there • *Set the vase
on the table.* 2 to set a device is to
make it ready to work • *Have you
set the alarm?* 3 to set is to become
solid or hard • *The jelly has set now.*
4 the sun sets when it goes down
towards the horizon at the end of
the day 5 to set someone doing
something is to start them doing
it • *The news set me thinking.* 6 to
set someone a task or problem is
to give it to them to do or solve •
I'd better set you some more work.
to set about something is to start
doing it to set off or set out is to
begin a journey to set something
out is to display it or make it known
• *She set out her reasons for leaving.*
to set something up is to place it in
position or get it started • *We want
to set up a playgroup.*

set *noun*
1 a group of people or things
that belong together 2 a radio or
television receiver 3 a series of
games in a tennis match 4 the
scenery or furniture on a stage or in
a film

setback *noun*
something that causes a difficulty
for a while

set square *noun*
a device in the shape of a right-angled
triangle, used for drawing parallel
lines and to draw angles

settee *noun*
a sofa

setting *noun*
1 the setting of a story is the place
and time in which it happens
2 the land and buildings around
something • *The house stood in a
rural setting.*

settle *verb*
1 to settle a problem, difficulty, or
argument is to solve it or decide
about it 2 to settle, or settle down, is
to become relaxed or make yourself
comfortable • *He settled down in
the armchair.* 3 to settle somewhere
is to go and live there • *The family
settled in Canada.* 4 something light
such as dust or snow settles when it
comes to rest on something
• *The dust was settling on the books.*
• *A bird flew down and settled on the
fence.* 5 to settle a bill or debt is to
pay it

settlement *noun*
1 a settlement is a group of
people or houses in a new area 2 a
settlement is also an agreement to
end an argument

settler *noun*
one of the first people to settle in a
new area

set-up *noun*
(*informal*) the way that something is
organized or arranged

seven *noun*
the number 7

seventeen *noun*
the number 17
seventeenth *adjective, noun* 17th

seventh *adjective, noun*
the next after the sixth **seventhly**
adverb in the seventh place; as the
seventh one

seventy *noun* (**seventies**)
the number 70
seventieth *adjective, noun*
70th

sever *verb*
to sever something is to cut or break
it off

several *adjective*
more than two but not many

severe *adjective*
1 strict or harsh; not gentle
or kind 2 very bad or serious
• *a severe cold* • *We're in
for some severe weather.* **severely**
adverb harshly or seriously
severity *noun* being severe,
or how severe something is

sew *verb* (**sewing, sewn** or
sewed) (*say* so)
1 to sew cloth or other soft material
is to use a needle and cotton to join
it or for it into clothing 2 to sew is
to work with a needle and
thread or with a sewing machine

sewage *noun* (*say* **soo**-ij)
sewage is waste matter
carried away in drains

a b c d e f g h i j k l m n o p q r s t u v w x y z

sewer *noun* (*say* soo-er)
an underground drain that carries away sewage

sex *noun*
1 a sex is each of the two groups, male or female, that people and animals belong to 2 sex is the physical act by which people and animals produce offspring **sexual** *adjective* to do with sex or the sexes

sexism *noun*
sexism is the unfair or offensive treatment of people of a particular sex, especially women **sexist** *adjective* offensive to people of a particular sex, especially women **sexist** *noun* someone who treats people of a particular sex, especially women, in an unfair or offensive way

shabby *adjective* (**shabbier, shabbiest**)
1 very old and worn • *She was wearing a shabby grey coat.*
2 mean or unfair • *What a shabby trick.* **shabbily** *adverb* **shabbiness** *noun*

shack *noun*
a roughly-built hut

shade *noun*
1 shade is an area sheltered from bright sunlight • *We sat down in the shade.* 2 a shade is a colour, or how light or dark a colour is 3 a shade is also a device that reduces or shuts out bright light

shade *verb*
1 to shade something or someone is to shelter them from bright light
2 to shade a drawing is to make parts of it darker than the rest **shading** *noun* the parts of a drawing that you make darker than the rest

shadow *noun*
1 a shadow is a dark shape that falls on a surface when something is between it and the light 2 shadow is an area that is dark because the light is blocked • *His face was in shadow.* **shadowy** *adjective* dark or hard to see

shadow *verb*
to shadow someone is to follow them secretly

shady *adjective* (**shadier, shadiest**)
1 giving shade • *We sat under a shady tree.* 2 situated in the shade • *Find a shady spot.*
3 dishonest or suspect • *He's always making shady deals.*

shaft *noun*
1 a long thin rod or straight part of

something 2 a deep narrow hole in a mine or building • *They found an old mine shaft.* • *a lift shaft* 3 a beam of light

shaggy *adjective*
(**shaggier, shaggiest**)
having long untidy hair

shake *verb* (**shaking, shook, shaken**)
1 to shake something is to move it quickly up and down or from side to side • *Have you shaken the bottle?*
2 to shake is to move in this way
3 to shake someone is to shock or upset them • *The news shook her.*
4 to shake is to tremble • *His voice was shaking.* to shake hands is to clasp someone's right hand as a greeting or as a sign that you agree

shake *noun*
a quick movement up and down or from side to side • *Give the bottle a shake.*

shaky *adjective* (**shakier, shakiest**)
shaking or likely to fall down **shakily** *adverb*

shall *verb* (past tense **should**)
used with *I* and *we* to refer to the future • *We shall arrive tomorrow.*
• *We told them we should arrive the next day.*

shallow *adjective*
not deep • *The stream is quite shallow here.* • *We were playing in the shallow end of the pool.*

sham *noun*
a person or thing that is not genuine or what they claim to be

shambles *noun*
a scene of confusion and chaos; a mess • *The rehearsal was a complete shambles.*

shame *noun*
1 shame is a feeling of great sorrow or guilt because you have done something wrong
2 you say something is a shame when it is something that you regret or are sorry about
• *What a shame you won't be able to come.*

shame *verb*
to shame someone is to make them feel ashamed

shameful *adjective* causing shame; disgraceful **shamefully** *adverb*

shameless *adjective*
feeling or showing no shame **shamelessly** *adverb*

shampoo *noun*
shampoo is liquid soap for washing things, especially your hair or a carpet

shampoo *verb*
to shampoo something is to wash it with shampoo

WORD ORIGIN

The word **shampoo** comes from a Hindi word *campo* meaning 'press!' (as an instruction).

shamrock *noun*
shamrock is a small plant rather like clover, with leaves divided in three

shandy *noun*
shandy is a mixture of beer with lemonade or another soft drink

shanty[1] *noun* (**shanties**)
a sailor's traditional song

shanty[2] *noun* (**shanties**)
a roughly-built hut

shape *noun*
1 the outline of something or the way it looks 2 something that has a definite or regular form, such as a square, circle, or triangle 3 the condition that something is in • *The garden isn't in very good shape.* to take shape is to start to develop properly

shape *verb*
to shape something is to give it a shape to shape up is to develop well

shapeless *adjective*
having no definite shape

share *noun*
1 one of the parts into which something is divided between several people or things 2 part of a company's money, lent by someone who is then given part of the profits in return

share *verb*
1 to share something, or share it out, is to divide it between several people or things 2 to share something is to use it when someone else is also using it • *She shared a room with me.*

shark *noun*
a large sea fish with sharp teeth

shark

sharp adjective
1 a sharp object has an edge or point that can cut or make holes • *This is a sharp knife.* 2 quick to learn or notice things • *She has sharp eyes.* • *It was sharp of you to spot that mistake.* 3 sudden or severe • *We came to a sharp bend in the road.* • *I felt a sharp pain in my side.* 4 slightly sour • *The apples taste sharp.* 5 above the proper musical pitch **sharply** adverb **sharpness** noun

sharp adverb
1 with a sudden change of direction • *Now turn sharp right.* 2 punctually; exactly • *Be there at six o'clock sharp.*

sharp noun
the note that is a semitone above a particular musical note; the sign that indicates this

sharpen verb
to sharpen something is to make it sharp or pointed **sharpener** noun a device for sharpening a pencil

shatter verb
1 to shatter is to break suddenly into lots of tiny pieces 2 to shatter something is to break it in this way 3 someone is shattered when they are very upset by something or very tired • *We were shattered by the news.*

shave verb
1 someone shaves when they scrape hair from their skin with a razor 2 to shave something is to cut or scrape a thin slice off it **shaver** noun an electric razor

shave noun
the act of shaving the face • *Dad was having a shave.* **a close shave** (*informal*) a narrow escape

shavings plural noun
thin strips that have been shaved off a piece of wood or metal

shawl noun
a large piece of material for covering the shoulders or wrapping a baby

she pronoun
a female person or animal: used as the subject of a verb

sheaf noun (**sheaves**)
1 a bundle of papers 2 a bundle of corn stalks tied together after reaping

shear verb (**shearing, sheared, shorn** or **sheared**)
to shear a sheep is to cut the wool from it **shearer** noun someone who shears sheep

shears plural noun
a tool like a very large pair of scissors for trimming grass and bushes or for shearing sheep

sheath noun
a cover for the blade of a sword or dagger

sheathe verb
to sheathe a sword is to put it into its sheath

shed¹ noun
a simply-made building used for storing things or sheltering animals, or as a workshop

shed² verb
(**shedding, shed**)
to shed something is to let it fall or flow • *The trees are shedding their leaves.* • *He was so badly hurt he was shedding blood.*

sheen noun
a soft shine on a surface

sheep noun
a grass-eating animal kept by farmers for its wool and meat

sheepdog noun
a dog trained to guard and control sheep

sheepish adjective
someone looks sheepish when they look shy or embarrassed **sheepishly** adverb

sheer adjective
1 complete or total • *There was a look of sheer misery on his face.* 2 extremely steep; vertical • *To the right of the road there was a sheer drop.* 3 sheer material is so thin that you can see through it

sheet noun
1 a large piece of light material put on a bed 2 a whole flat piece of paper, glass, or metal • *You will need two sheets of newspaper.* 3 a wide area of water, snow, ice, or flame

sheikh noun (say shayk)
the leader of an Arab tribe or village

shelf noun (**shelves**)
1 a flat piece of hard material fitted to a wall or in a piece of furniture so that you can put things on it 2 a flat level surface that sticks out from a cliff or under the sea

shell noun
1 the hard outer covering round a nut or egg, or round an animal such as a snail or tortoise 2 a metal case filled with explosive, fired from a large gun 3 the walls or framework of a building or ship

shell verb
1 to shell something is to take it out of its shell 2 to shell a building, ship, town, etc., is to fire explosive shells at it

shellfish noun
(**shellfish**)
a sea animal that has a shell

shells

shelter noun
1 a shelter is a place that protects people from danger or from the weather 2 shelter is being protected from danger or from the weather • *We found shelter from the rain.*

shelter verb
1 to shelter somewhere is to stay there because you are protected from danger or from the weather • *We sheltered under the trees.* 2 to shelter something or someone is to protect or cover them • *The hill shelters the house from the wind.*

shelve verb
1 to shelve something is to put it on a shelf or shelves 2 to shelve an idea or piece of work is to reject or postpone it

shepherd noun
someone whose job is to look after sheep

sherbet noun
a fizzy sweet powder or drink

sheriff noun
1 in the USA, the chief law officer in a county 2 the chief judge of a Scottish county

sherry noun
a kind of strong wine

shield noun
1 a large piece of metal or wood a person carries to protect their body in fighting 2 a design or trophy in the shape of a shield 3 a protection from harm • *The spacecraft's heat shield protects it as it enters the planet's atmosphere.*

shield verb
to shield someone or something is to protect them • *She shielded her eyes from the sun.*

shift noun
1 a change of position or condition 2 a group of workers who start work as another group finishes; the time when they work • *He's on the night shift this month.*

shift *verb*
1 to shift something is to move it
2 to shift is to change position

shilling *noun*
an old British coin that was worth a twentieth of a pound (now 5 pence)

shimmer *verb*
to shimmer is to shine with a quivering light • *The sea shimmered in the sunlight.*

shin *noun*
the front of your leg between your knee and your ankle

shine *verb* (**shining, shone** or, in 'polish' sense, **shined**)
1 to shine is to give out or reflect bright light 2 to shine a torch or light somewhere is to point the light in that direction 3 to shine something is to polish it • *Have you shined your shoes?* 4 to shine is to do well or be excellent • *He does not shine in maths.*

shine *noun*
1 shine is brightness 2 a shine is an act of polishing • *Give your shoes a good shine.*

shingle *noun*
shingle is pebbles on a beach

shiny *adjective* (**shinier, shiniest**)
bright or glossy

ship *noun*
a large boat, especially one that goes to sea

ship *verb* (**shipping, shipped**)
to ship something is to send it on a ship

shipwreck *noun*
1 when a ship is wrecked in a storm or accident at sea 2 the remains of a wrecked ship **shipwrecked** *adjective* left somewhere after your ship has been wrecked at sea

shipyard *noun*
a place where ships are built and repaired

shirk *verb*
you shirk a task or duty when you avoid doing it

shirt *noun*
a piece of clothing you wear on the top half of the body, with a collar and sleeves

shiver *verb*
you shiver when you tremble with cold or fear **shivery** *adjective* unable to stop yourself shivering

shiver *noun*
an act of shivering • *I felt a shiver down my spine.*

shoal *noun*
a large number of fish swimming together

shock¹ *noun*
1 a shock is a sudden unpleasant surprise 2 a shock is also a violent knock or jolt 3 shock is weakness caused by severe pain or injury 4 a shock, or electric shock, is a painful effect caused by a strong electric current passing through your body

shock¹ *verb*
1 to shock someone is to give them a shock 2 to shock someone is also to make them feel disgusted or upset

shock² *noun*
a shock of hair is a bushy mass of it

shocking *adjective*
1 horrifying or disgusting 2 very bad • *The weather's been shocking today.*

shoddy *adjective* (**shoddier, shoddiest**)
of poor quality; badly made • *This is shoddy work.*

shoe *noun*
1 a strong covering you wear on your foot 2 a horseshoe

shoelace *noun*
a cord for fastening a shoe

shoot *verb*
1 to shoot a gun or other weapon is to fire it 2 to shoot a person or animal is to fire a gun at them 3 to shoot somewhere is to move very fast • *The car shot past.* 4 (in football) to shoot is to kick or hit a ball at a goal 5 to shoot a film or scene is to film or photograph it • *The film was shot in Africa.*

shoot *noun*
a young branch or new growth of a plant

shooting star *noun*
a meteor

shop *noun*
a building where people buy things

shop *verb* (**shopping, shopped**)
to shop is to go and buy things at shops **shopper** *noun* someone who goes shopping

shopkeeper *noun*
someone who owns or looks after a shop

shoplifter *noun*
someone who steals from shops **shoplifting** *noun* stealing things from shops

shopping *noun*
1 shopping is buying things at shops • *I like shopping.* 2 shopping is also things that you have bought in shops • *Let me help you carry your shopping.*

shore *noun*
1 the seashore 2 the land along the edge of a lake

short *adjective*
1 not long; not lasting long • *I went for a short walk.* 2 not tall • *He is a short man.* 3 not sufficient; scarce • *Water is short.* 4 bad-tempered • *He was rather short with me.* 5 short pastry is rich and crumbly, and contains a lot of fat **for short** as a shorter form of something • *Joanna is called Jo for short.* **short for something** a shorter form of something • *Jo is short for Joanna.* **to be short of something** is to not have enough of it • *We seem to be short of chairs.* **shortness** *noun*

short *adverb*
1 before reaching the point aimed at • *My ball landed just short of the hole.* 2 suddenly • *The horse stopped short.*

shortage *noun*
there is a shortage when there is not enough of something

shipwreck

shortbread noun
shortbread is a rich sweet biscuit made with butter

shortcake noun
1 shortbread 2 a light cake usually served with fruit

shortcoming noun
a fault or weakness • *He has many shortcomings.*

short cut noun
a route or method that is quicker than the usual one

shorten verb
1 to shorten something is to make it shorter 2 to shorten is to become shorter

shorthand noun
shorthand is a set of special signs for writing words down as quickly as people say them

shortly adverb
soon • *I'll be there shortly.*

shorts plural noun
trousers with legs that stop at or above the knee

short-sighted adjective
1 unable to see things clearly when they are further away 2 not thinking enough about what may happen in the future

shot¹ noun
1 a shot is the firing of a gun or other weapon 2 shot is lead pellets fired from small guns 3 a good or bad shot is a person judged by their skill in shooting • *She is a great shot.* 4 a shot is a stroke in a game with a ball, such as tennis or snooker 5 a shot is also an injection 6 in photography, a shot is a photograph or filmed sequence 7 a shot is a heavy metal ball thrown as a sport 8 a shot at something is an attempt to do it • *Have a shot at this puzzle.*

shot² past tense and past participle of **shoot** verb

shotgun noun
a gun that fires small lead pellets

should verb
used to express 1 what someone ought to do • *You should have told me.* 2 what someone expects • *They should be here soon.* 3 what might happen • *If you should happen to see him, tell him to come.*

shoulder noun
the part of your body between your neck and your arm

shoulder blade noun
each of the two large flat bones at the top of your back

shout verb
to shout is to speak or call very loudly

shout noun
a loud cry or call

shove verb (say shuv)
to shove something is to push it hard

shovel noun (say **shuv**-el)
a tool like a spade with the sides turned up, for lifting and moving coal, earth, sand, snow, and other things

shovel verb (**shovelling, shovelled**)
to shovel (for example) earth or snow is to move it or clear it with a shovel

show verb (**showing, showed, shown**)
1 to show something is to let people see it • *She showed me her new bike.* 2 to show something to someone is to explain it to them • *Can you show me how to do it?* 3 to show someone somewhere is to guide or lead them there • *I'll show you to your seat.* 4 to show is to be visible • *That stain won't show.* to show off is to try to impress people to show something off is to be proud of letting people see it

show noun
1 an entertainment • *She loves TV game shows.* 2 a display or exhibition • *Have you been to the flower show?*

show business noun
show business is the entertainment business; the theatre, films, radio, and television

shower noun
1 a brief fall of light rain • *It's only a shower.* 2 a lot of small things coming or falling like rain • *They were met by a shower of stones.* 3 a device for spraying water to wash your body; a wash in this

shower verb
1 to shower is to fall like rain 2 to shower someone with things is to give a lot of them • *He showered her with presents.* 3 to shower is to wash under a shower

showery adjective
raining occasionally

showjumping noun showjumping is a competition in which riders make their horses jump over fences and other obstacles
showjumper noun someone who takes part in showjumping

show-off noun
someone who is trying to impress other people

showy adjective (**showier, showiest**)
likely to attract attention; bright or

highly decorated **showily** adverb **showiness** noun

shrapnel noun
shrapnel is pieces of metal scattered from an exploding shell

shred noun
1 a tiny strip or piece torn or cut off something • *His cloak had been ripped to shreds.* 2 a very small amount of something. • *There's not a shred of evidence for what you say.*

shred verb (**shredding, shredded**)
to shred something is to tear or cut it into tiny strips or pieces

shrew noun
a small animal rather like a mouse

shrewd adjective
having common sense and showing good judgement **shrewdly** adverb **shrewdness** noun

shriek noun
a shrill cry or scream

shriek verb
to shriek is to give a shrill cry or scream

shrill adjective
a shrill sound is very high and loud • *There was a shrill blast of the whistle.* **shrilly** adverb **shrillness** noun

shrimp noun
a small shellfish

shrine noun
an altar or chapel or other sacred place

shrink verb (**shrinking, shrank, shrunk**)
1 to shrink is to become smaller • *My dress has shrunk.* 2 to shrink something is to make it smaller, usually by washing it • *Their jeans have been shrunk.* 3 to shrink from something is to avoid it because you are afraid or embarrassed • *He shrank from meeting strangers.*

shrivel verb (**shrivelling, shrivelled**)
to shrivel is to become wrinkled and dry

shroud noun
a sheet in which a dead body is wrapped

shroud verb
to shroud something is to cover or conceal it • *The mountain was shrouded in mist.*

shrub noun
a bush or small tree

shrubbery noun (**shrubberies**)
an area where shrubs are grown

a b c d e f g h i j k l m n o p q r s t u v w x y z

shrug verb (**shrugging, shrugged**)
you shrug when you raise your shoulders slightly as a sign that you don't care or don't know

shrug noun
the act of shrugging

shrunken adjective smaller than it used to be because it has shrunk

shudder verb
you shudder when you shake because you are cold or afraid

shudder noun
the act of shuddering

shuffle verb
1 to shuffle is to drag your feet along the ground as you walk 2 to shuffle playing cards is to mix them by sliding them over each other several times

shuffle noun
the act of shuffling • Give the cards a quick shuffle.

shunt verb
to shunt a railway train or wagons is to move them from one track to another

shut verb (**shutting, shut**)
1 to shut a door or window, or a lid or cover, is to move it so that it blocks up an opening 2 to shut is to become closed • The door shut suddenly. to shut down is to stop work or business to shut up (informal) is to stop talking

shut adjective
closed • Keep your eyes shut.

shutter noun
1 a panel or screen that can be closed over a window 2 the device in a camera that opens and closes to let light fall on the film

shuttle noun
1 a train or bus or aircraft that makes frequent short journeys between two places 2 a space shuttle 3 the part of a loom that carries the thread from side to side

shuttlecock noun
a small rounded piece of cork or plastic with a ring of feathers fixed to it, that you use in the game of badminton

shuttlecock

shy adjective
timid and afraid to meet or talk to other people
shyly adverb **shyness** noun

sibling noun
your siblings are your brothers and sisters

sick adjective
1 ill or unwell • He looks after sick animals. 2 you feel sick when you feel that you are going to vomit; you are sick when you vomit to be sick of something or someone is to be tired of them or fed up with them

sicken verb
1 to sicken someone is to disgust them 2 to sicken is to start feeling ill

sickly adjective (**sicklier, sickliest**)
1 often ill; unhealthy • a sickly child 2 making people feel sick • The drink had a sickly taste.

sickness noun
an illness or disease

side noun
1 a flat surface, especially one that joins the top and bottom of something 2 a line that forms the edge of a shape • A triangle has three sides. 3 the outer part of something that is not the front or the back • The instructions are on the side of the box. 4 a position or space to the left or right of something • There's a window on either side of the door. 5 your sides are the parts of your body from your armpits to your hips • I've got a pain down my right side. 6 a group of people playing, arguing, or fighting against another group • They are on our side.

side verb
to side with someone is to support them in a quarrel or argument

sideboard noun
a long heavy piece of furniture with drawers and cupboards and a flat top

sideshow noun
a small entertainment forming part of a large show, especially at a fair

sideways adverb, adjective
1 to or from the side • Crabs walk sideways. 2 with one side facing forward • We sat sideways in the bus.

siding noun
a short railway line leading off the main line

siege noun (say seej)
when an army surrounds a place until the people inside surrender

sieve noun (say siv)
a device made of mesh or perforated metal or plastic, used to separate harder or larger parts from liquid or powder

sift verb
1 to sift a fine or powdery substance is to pass it through a sieve 2 to sift facts or information is to examine or select them

sigh noun
a sound you make by breathing out heavily when you are sad, tired, or relieved

sigh verb
to sigh is to make a sigh

sight noun
1 sight is the ability to see • She has very good sight. 2 a sight is something that you see • That sunset is a sight I'll never forget. 3 the sights of a place are the interesting places worth seeing there • Visit the sights of Paris. 4 a sight on a gun is a device that helps you to aim it to be in sight is to be able to be seen to be out of sight is to be no longer able to be seen

sight verb
to sight something is to see it or observe it

sightseeing noun
sightseeing is going round looking at interesting places **sightseer** noun someone who goes sightseeing

sign noun
1 a mark or symbol that stands for something • a minus sign 2 a board or notice that tells or shows people something 3 something that shows that a thing exists • There are signs of rust. 4 an action or signal giving information or a command • She made a sign to them to be quiet.

sign verb
1 you sign your name when you write your signature on something 2 to sign is to make a sign or signal • He signed to them to follow him. 3 to sign someone is to give them a contract for a job, especially in a professional sport • They have signed three new players.

signal noun
1 a device or gesture or sound or light that gives information or a message 2 a series of radio waves sent out or received

signal verb (**signalling, signalled**)
to signal to someone is to give them a signal

signature noun
your name written by yourself

significant adjective
something is significant when it has a meaning or importance **significance** noun the significance of something is

its meaning or importance

significantly *adverb* in a way that is important or has a meaning

signify *verb* (**signifying, signified**)
to signify something is to mean it or indicate it

signing or **sign language** *noun*
signing is a way of communicating by using movements of your hands instead of sounds, used by deaf people

sign language

signpost *noun*
a sign at a road junction showing the names and distances of the places that each road leads to

Sikh *noun* (*say* seek)
someone who believes in **Sikhism**, a religion of India having one God and some Hindu and Islamic beliefs

silence *noun*
silence is when no sound can be heard

silence *verb*
to silence someone or something is to make them silent

silencer *noun*
a device designed to reduce the sound made by an engine or a gun

silent *adjective*
without any sound; not speaking **silently** *adverb*

silhouette *noun* (*say* sil-oo-et)
a dark outline of something seen against a light background

silicon *noun*
silicon is a substance found in many rocks and used in making microchips

silk *noun*
1 silk is a fine soft thread produced by silkworms for making their cocoons **2** silk is also smooth shiny cloth made from this thread **silken** *adjective* made of silk **silky** *adjective* soft, smooth, and shiny like silk

silkworm *noun*
a kind of caterpillar that covers itself with a cocoon of fine threads when it is ready to turn into a moth

silk moth and cocoon

sill *noun*
a strip of stone or wood or metal underneath a window or door

silly *adjective* (**sillier, silliest**)
foolish or unwise **silliness** *noun*

silver *noun*
1 silver is a shiny white precious metal **2** silver is also coins made of this metal or a metal that looks like it **3** silver is also a greyish-white colour **silvery** *adjective* like silver • *the moon's silvery light*

similar *adjective* one thing is similar to another when it is like it in some ways but not exactly the same **similarity** *noun* the similarity between two things is the fact that they are similar **similarly** *adverb* in a similar way

simile *noun* (*say* sim-i-li)
a kind of expression in which you describe something by comparing it with something else, such as *bold as brass* or *as brave as a lion*

simmer *verb*
food simmers when it boils very gently over a low heat
to simmer down is to become calm after being anxious or angry

simple *adjective*
1 easy • *That's a simple question to answer.* **2** not complicated • *It was a simple plan, but it worked.* **3** plain • *She was wearing a simple dress.* **simplicity** *noun* how simple something is

simplify *verb* (**simplifies, simplifying, simplified**)
to simplify something is to make it simple or easy to understand **simplification** *noun* something that has been made simpler

simply *adverb*
1 in a simple way • *Explain it simply.* **2** completely • *It's simply delicious.* **3** only or merely • *It's simply a question of time.*

simulate *verb*
1 to simulate something is to reproduce the conditions for it • *The machine simulates a space flight.* **2** to simulate a feeling or state is to pretend to have it • *He simulated illness.* **simulation** *noun* when something is simulated or reproduced **simulator** *noun* a machine for reproducing the conditions for something, such as flying an aeroplane

simultaneous *adjective* (*say* sim-ul-tay-ni-us)
two things are simultaneous when they happen at the same time **simultaneously** *adverb* two things happen simultaneously when they happen at the same time

sin *noun*
something bad a person does that breaks a religious or moral law

sin *verb* (**sinning, sinned**)
to sin is to commit a sin **sinful** *adjective* guilty of sin **sinner** *noun* someone who sins

since *conjunction*
1 from the time when • *Where have you been since I last saw you?* **2** because • *Since we have missed the bus, we must walk home.*

since *preposition*
from a certain time • *I have been here since Christmas.*

since *adverb*
between then and now • *He has not been seen since.*

sincere *adjective*
you are being sincere when you mean what you say and express your true feelings • *I gave them my sincere good wishes.* **sincerely** *adverb* **sincerity** *noun* sincerity is being sincere

sinew *noun*
strong tissue that joins a muscle to a bone

sing *verb* (**singing, sang, sung**)
1 to sing is to make musical sounds with your voice **2** birds and insects sing when they make musical sounds **singer** *noun* someone who sings

singe *verb* (*say* sinj)
to singe something is to burn it slightly

single *adjective*
1 only one; not double **2** designed for one person • *The bedroom had two single beds.* **3** not married **4** for a journey in one direction only

single *noun*
1 a ticket for a journey you make to a place but not back again **2** a record or CD with one song or short piece of music on it **3** you play singles in tennis when you play against only one other person

single *verb*
to single someone out is to pick them from other people

single file

single file *noun*
in single file in a line, one behind the other

single-handed *adjective*
by your own efforts; without any help

single parent *noun*
a person who is bringing up a child or children without a partner

singular *noun*
the form of a word meaning only one person or thing, such as *cake* and *child*

singular *adjective*
1 in the singular; meaning only one • *'Mouse' is a singular noun.*
2 extraordinary • *She is a woman of singular courage.*

sinister *adjective*
looking or seeming evil or harmful

sink *verb* (**sinking, sank** or **sunk, sunk**)
1 to sink is to go under water • *The ship sank in a storm.* 2 to sink something is to make it go under water • *They fired on the ship and sank it.* 3 to sink, or to sink down, is to go or fall down to the ground • *He sank to his knees.* to sink in is to be gradually understood

sink *noun*
a fixed basin with taps to supply water

sinus *noun* (*say* **sy-nus**)
your sinuses are the hollows in the bones of your skull, connected with your nose • *My sinuses are blocked.*

sip *verb* (**sipping, sipped**)
to sip a drink is to drink it slowly in small mouthfuls

siphon *noun*
a bent tube used for taking liquid from one container to another at a lower level

siphon *verb*
to siphon liquid is to transfer it with a siphon

sir *noun*
1 a word sometimes used when speaking politely to a man, instead of his name • *Can I help you, sir?* 2 the title given to a knight • *Sir Francis Drake.*

siren *noun*
a device that makes a loud hooting or screaming sound, usually as a warning signal

sister *noun*
1 your sister is a woman or girl who has the same parents as you 2 a senior nurse in a hospital

sister-in-law *noun* (**sisters-in-law**)
a person's sister-in-law is the sister of their husband or wife, or the wife of their brother

sit *verb* (**sitting, sat**)
1 to sit is to rest on your bottom, as you do when you are on a chair 2 to sit someone, or to sit someone down, is to put them in a sitting position 3 to sit an exam or test is to take it 4 to sit somewhere is to be situated or positioned there • *The house sits on top of a hill.* 5 to sit for someone is to act as a babysitter **sitter** *noun* someone who is sitting; a babysitter

site *noun*
1 the place where something has been built or will be built • *They crossed a building site.* 2 a place used for something or where something happened • *We stayed at a camping site.* • *This is the site of a famous battle.*

sitting room *noun*
a room with comfortable chairs for sitting in

situated *adjective*
to be situated in a particular place or position is to be placed there • *They lived in a town situated in a valley.*

situation *noun*
1 a place or position; where something is 2 all the things that are happening to someone at a particular time; the way things are • *We're now in a difficult situation because we've run out of money.* 3 a job or employment

six *noun*
the number 6

sixteen *noun*
the number 16
sixteenth *adjective*, *noun* 16th

sixth *adjective*, *noun*
the next after the fifth
sixthly *adverb* in the sixth place; as the sixth one

sixty *noun* (**sixties**)
the number 60 **sixtieth** *adjective*, *noun* 60th

size *noun*
1 how big a person or thing is 2 the measurement something is made in • *I wear a size eight shoe.*

sizzle *verb*
to sizzle is to make a crackling and hissing sound • *The bacon sizzled in the pan.*

skate *noun*
1 a boot with a steel blade attached to the sole, used for sliding smoothly over ice 2 a roller skate

skate *verb*
to skate is to move around on skates
skater *noun* someone who skates

skateboard *noun*
a small board with wheels, used for standing and riding on as a sport

skeleton *noun*
the framework of bones in a person's or animal's body

sketch *noun*
1 a quick or rough drawing 2 a short amusing play

sketch *verb*
to sketch something or someone is to make a sketch of them

sketchy *adjective* (**sketchier, sketchiest**)
roughly drawn or described, without any detail • *Reports of what happened are sketchy at the moment.*

skeleton

skewer *noun*
a long wooden or metal or plastic pin that you push through meat to hold it together while it is being cooked

ski *noun* (*say* **skee**)
a long flat strip of wood or metal or plastic, fastened to each foot for moving quickly over snow

ski *verb* (**skiing, skied** or **ski'd**)
to ski is to travel on snow wearing skis
skier *noun* someone who skis

skid *verb* (**skidding, skidded**)
to skid is to slide accidentally, especially in a vehicle

skid *noun*
a skidding movement • *The car went into a skid on the icy road.*

skilful *adjective*
having or showing a lot of skill
skilfully *adverb*

skill noun
1 to do something with skill is to do it well 2 a type of work or ability that you learn through training and practice • *He's been learning some new football skills.* **skilled** adjective having a skill or skills

skim verb (**skimming, skimmed**)
1 to skim is to move quickly over a surface 2 to skim something is to remove it from the surface of a liquid, especially to take the cream off milk **skimmed** adjective skimmed milk has had the cream removed

skin noun
1 the outer covering of a person's or animal's body 2 the outer covering of a fruit or vegetable 3 a thin firm layer that has formed on the surface of a liquid

skin verb (**skinning, skinned**)
to skin something is to take the skin off it

skin diving noun
skin diving is swimming under water with flippers and breathing equipment but without a diving suit **skin diver** noun someone who goes skin diving

skinny adjective (**skinnier, skinniest**)
very thin

skip¹ verb (**skipping, skipped**)
1 to skip is to jump or move along by hopping from one foot to the other 2 to skip is also to jump with a skipping rope 3 to skip something is to miss it out or ignore it • *You can skip the last chapter.*

skip¹ noun
a skipping movement

skip² noun
a large metal container for taking away builders' rubbish

skipper noun
the captain of a ship or team

skipping rope noun
a length of rope, usually with a handle at each end, that you swing over your head and under your feet as you jump

skirt noun
a piece of clothing for a woman or girl that hangs down from her waist

skirt verb
to skirt something is to go round the edge of it

skittle noun
a piece of wood or plastic shaped like a bottle, that people try to knock down with a ball in a game of skittles

skull noun
the framework of bones in your head which contains your brain

skunk noun
a black and white furry animal from North America that can make an unpleasant smell

sky noun (**skies**)
the space above the earth, where you can see the sun, moon, and stars

skylark noun
a small brown bird that sings as it hovers high in the air

skylight noun
a window in a roof

skyscraper noun
a very tall building

slab noun
a thick flat piece of something hard

slack adjective
1 loose; not pulled tight • *The rope was slack.* 2 lazy; not busy or working hard **slackly** adverb **slackness** noun

slacken verb
1 to slacken something is to loosen it 2 to slacken is to become slower or less busy • *Her pace gradually slackened.*

slam verb (**slamming, slammed**)
1 to slam (for example) a door is to shut it hard or loudly 2 to slam something is to hit it with great force • *He slammed the ball into the net.*

slang noun
slang is a kind of colourful language that you use when speaking to your friends but not in writing or when you want to be polite

slant verb
to slant is to slope or lean

slant noun
a sloping or leaning position • *The caravan floor was at a slant.*

slap verb (**slapping, slapped**)
1 to slap someone is to hit them with the palm of your hand 2 to slap something somewhere is to put it there forcefully or carelessly • *We slapped paint on the walls.*

slap noun
to give someone a slap is to slap them

slapstick noun
slapstick is noisy lively comedy, with people hitting each other, throwing things, and falling over

slash verb
1 to slash something is to make large cuts in it 2 to slash prices or costs is to reduce them a lot

slash noun
1 a large cut 2 a sloping line (/) used to separate words or letters

slat noun
a thin strip of wood or plastic, usually arranged to overlap with others, for example in a blind or screen

slate noun
1 slate is a kind of grey rock that is easily split into flat plates 2 slates are flat pieces of this rock used to cover a roof **slaty** adjective like slate

slaughter verb (say **slor**-ter)
1 to slaughter an animal is to kill it for food 2 to slaughter people or animals is to kill a lot of them

slaughter noun
slaughter is the killing of a lot of people or animals

slave noun
a person who is owned by someone else and has to work for them without being paid

slave verb
to slave over something is to work very hard

slavery noun
slavery is being a slave or the system of having slaves

slay verb (**slaying, slew, slain**)
(old or poetical use) to slay someone is to kill them

sledge or **sled** noun
a vehicle for travelling over snow, with strips of metal or wood instead of wheels

sledgehammer noun
a very large heavy hammer

sleek adjective
smooth and shiny • *She has lovely sleek hair.*

sleep noun
1 sleep is the condition in which your eyes are closed, your body is relaxed, and your mind is unconscious • *You need some sleep.* 2 a sleep is a time when you are sleeping • *Did you have a good sleep?*

sleep verb (**sleeping, slept**)
to sleep is to have a sleep

sleeper noun
1 someone who is asleep • *I am a heavy sleeper.* 2 each of the wooden or concrete beams on which a railway line rests 3 a railway carriage equipped for sleeping in

sleeping bag noun
a warm padded bag for sleeping in, especially when you are camping

sleepless adjective
unable to sleep; without sleep • *We've had a sleepless night.*

a b c d e f g h i j k l m n o p q r s t u v w x y z

slime

sleepwalker *noun*
someone who walks around while they are asleep **sleepwalking** *noun* what a sleepwalker does

sleepy *adjective* (**sleepier, sleepiest**)
feeling tired and wanting to go to sleep **sleepily** *adverb* **sleepiness** *noun*

sleet *noun*
sleet is a mixture of rain with snow or hail

sleeve *noun*
the part of a piece of clothing that covers your arm **sleeveless** *adjective* not having sleeves

sleigh *noun* (*say* slay)
a large sledge pulled by horses

slender *adjective*
1 slim or thin **2** slight or small • *Their chances of winning are slender.*

slice *noun*
a thin flat piece cut off something
slice *verb*
to slice something is to cut it into slices

slick *adjective*
done quickly and in a clever way, without obvious effort
slick *noun*
a large patch of oil floating on water

slide *verb* (**sliding, slid**)
1 to slide is to move smoothly over a flat or polished or slippery surface • *She loved sliding down the bannister.* **2** to slide somewhere is to move there quickly or secretly • *The thief slid behind a bush.*
slide *noun*
1 a sliding movement **2** a structure for children to play on, with a smooth slope for sliding down **3** a type of photograph that lets light through and that can be shown on a screen **4** a small glass plate on which you can examine things under a microscope **5** a large decorative clip for keeping your hair tidy

slight *adjective*
very small; not serious or important

slightly
adverb
in a slight way; not seriously
• *They were slightly hurt.*

slim *adjective* (**slimmer, slimmest**)
1 thin and graceful **2** small; hardly enough • *We have a slim chance of winning.*

slim *verb* (**slimming, slimmed**)
to slim is to try to make yourself thinner, especially by dieting **slimmer** *noun* someone who is slimming

slime *noun*
slime is unpleasant wet slippery stuff • *There was slime on the pond.*
slimy *adjective* covered in slime

sling *verb* (**slinging, slung**)
1 to sling something somewhere is to throw it there roughly or carelessly • *You can sling your wet clothes into the washing machine.*
2 to sling something is also to hang it up or support it so that it hangs loosely • *He had slung the bag round his neck.*

sling *noun*
1 a piece of cloth tied round your neck to support an injured arm **2** a device for throwing stones

slink *verb* (**slinking, slunk**)
to slink somewhere is to move there slowly and quietly because you feel guilty or don't want to be noticed • *He slunk off to bed.*

slip *verb* (**slipping, slipped**)
1 to slip is to slide without meaning to or to fall over **2** to slip somewhere is to move there quickly and quietly • *He slipped out of the house before anyone was awake.* **3** to slip something somewhere is to put it there quickly without being seen • *She slipped the letter into her pocket.* **4** to slip something is to escape from it • *The dog slipped its leash.* **to slip up** to make a mistake

slip *noun*
1 an accidental slide or fall • *One slip and you could fall into the river.* **2** a small mistake **3** a small piece of paper **4** a piece of women's underwear like a thin dress or skirt **to give someone the slip** is to escape from them or avoid them

slipper *noun*
a soft comfortable shoe for wearing indoors

slippery *adjective*
smooth or wet so that it is difficult to stand on or hold

slit *noun*
a long narrow cut or opening
slit *verb* (**slitting, slit**)
to slit something is to make a slit in it

slither *verb*
to slither is to slip or slide along, often unsteadily • *The snake slithered away.* • *We were slithering around on the ice.*

sliver *noun* (*say* sli-ver)
a thin strip of wood, glass, or other material

slog *verb* (**slogging, slogged**)
1 to slog something is to hit it hard or wildly **2** to slog is to work hard • *I'm slogging away at my essay.* **3** to slog is also to walk with effort • *We slogged through the snow.*
slog *noun*
a piece of hard work or effort • *Climbing up that hill was a real slog.*

slogan *noun*
a short catchy phrase used to advertise something or to sum up an idea

slop *verb* (**slopping, slopped**)
1 to slop liquid is to spill it over the edge of its container **2** liquid slops when it spills in this way

slope *verb*
to slope is to go gradually downwards or upwards or to have one end higher than the other
slope *noun*
1 a sloping surface **2** the amount by which a surface slopes • *The hill has a slope of 30°.* **3** the side of a mountain

sloppy *adjective* (**sloppier, sloppiest**)
1 liquid and spilling easily **2** careless or badly done

• *Their work is sloppy.*
3 (*informal*) too sentimental or
romantic • *What a sloppy story.*
sloppily *adverb* **sloppiness** *noun*

slot *noun*
a narrow opening to put things through

sloth *noun* (*rhymes with* **both**)
1 sloth is laziness **2** a sloth is a long-
haired South American animal that
lives in trees and moves very slowly

slot machine *noun*
a machine that you work by putting
a coin in a slot

slouch *verb*
to slouch is to move or stand or sit
in a lazy way, especially with your
head and shoulders bent forwards

slovenly *adjective* (*say* **sluv**-en-li)
careless or untidy

slow *adjective*
1 not quick; taking more time than
usual **2** a clock or watch is slow
when it shows a time earlier than the
correct time

slow *adverb*
at a slow rate; slowly • *Go slow.*
slowly *adverb* at a slow rate or speed
slowness *noun* slowness is being slow

slow *verb*
1 to slow, or to slow down, is to go
slower **2** to slow something, or to
slow it down, is to make it go slower

sludge *noun*
sludge is thick sticky mud

slug *noun*
a small slimy animal like a snail
without its shell

slum *noun*
an area of dirty and crowded houses
in a city

slumber *noun*
slumber is peaceful sleep
slumber *verb*
to slumber is to sleep peacefully

slump *verb*
to slump is to fall heavily or suddenly

slush *noun*
slush is snow that is melting on the
ground **slushy** *adjective* slushy
snow is melting and wet

sly *adjective*
cunning or mischievous
slyly *adverb* **slyness** *noun*

smack *verb*
to smack someone is to slap them
with your hand, especially as a
punishment
smack *noun*
a slap with your hand

small *adjective*
not large; less than the
normal size

smart *adjective*
1 neat and well dressed
2 clever and quick-thinking
3 fast • *We'll need to walk at a smart
pace.* **smartly** *adverb*

smart *verb*
to smart is to feel a stinging pain

smarten *verb*
1 to smarten something or someone
is to make them smarter • *You need
to smarten yourself up a bit.* **2** to
smarten is to become smarter

smash *verb*
1 to smash is to break into pieces
noisily and violently; to smash
something is to break it in this way
2 to smash into something is to hit
it with great force • *The lorry left the
road and smashed into a wall.*

smash *noun*
1 the act or sound of smashing **2** a
collision between vehicles

smear *verb*
to smear something dirty or greasy
is to rub it thickly over
a surface
smear *noun*
a dirty or greasy mark made by
smearing

smell *verb* (**smelling, smelt** or
smelled)
1 you smell something when you
use your nose to sense it
2 to smell is to give out a smell • *The
cheese smells funny.*

smell *noun*
1 a smell is something you can
smell, especially something
unpleasant **2** smell is the ability to
smell things • *I have a good sense
of smell.*

smelly *adjective* (**smellier,
smelliest**)
having an unpleasant smell

smelt *verb*
to smelt ore is to melt it in order to
get metal from it

smile *noun*
an expression on your face that
shows you are pleased or amused,
with your lips stretched and turning
upwards at the ends

smile

smile *verb*
to smile is to give a smile

smith *noun*
someone who makes things
out of metal

smock *noun*
a loose piece of clothing like
a very long shirt

smog *noun*
smog is a mixture of smoke and fog

smoke *noun*
1 smoke is the grey or blue mixture
of gas and particles that rises from
a fire **2** to have a smoke is to spend
time smoking a cigarette • *He wants
a smoke.* **smoky** *adjective* full of
smoke

smoke *verb*
1 something smokes when it gives
out smoke • *The fire is smoking.*
2 someone is smoking when they
have a lit cigarette in their mouth
and are breathing in the smoke
from it **smoker** *noun* someone who
smokes cigarettes

smooth *adjective*
1 having an even surface without
any marks or roughness **2** a smooth
liquid or substance has no lumps in
it **3** moving without bumps or jolts
• *We had a smooth ride.* **4** not harsh;
flowing easily • *She spoke in a
smooth voice.* **smoothly** *adverb* in
a smooth way; evenly **smoothness**
noun

smooth *verb*
to smooth something is to make it
smooth and flat

smother *verb*
1 to smother someone is to cover
their face so that they can't breathe
2 to smother something is to cover
it thickly • *He brought in a cake
smothered in icing.* **3** to smother a
fire is to put it out by covering it

smoulder *verb*
to smoulder is to burn slowly without
a flame

smudge *noun*
a dirty or messy mark made by
rubbing something
smudge *verb*
to smudge paint or ink is to touch
it while it is still wet and make it
messy

smug *adjective* (**smugger,
smuggest**)
too pleased with yourself **smugly**
adverb **smugness** *noun*

smuggle *verb*
to smuggle something is
to bring it into a country secretly
and illegally **smuggler** *noun*
someone who smuggles goods

a b c d e f g h i j k l m n o p q r s t u v w x y z

snake

snack *noun*
a quick light meal

snag *noun*
an unexpected difficulty or obstacle

snag *verb* (**snagging, snagged**)
to snag something you are wearing is to catch it on something sharp

snail *noun*
a small animal with a soft body in a hard shell

snake *noun*
a reptile with a long narrow body and no legs

snap *verb* (**snapping, snapped**)
1 something snaps when it breaks suddenly with a sharp noise **2** an animal snaps when it bites suddenly or quickly • *The dog snapped at me.* **3** to snap something is to say it quickly and angrily • *There's no need to snap.* **4** to snap your fingers is to make a sharp snapping sound with them **5** to snap something or someone is to take a quick photograph of them

snap *noun*
1 a snap is the act or sound of snapping **2** a snap is also an informal photograph taken quickly **3** snap is a card game in which players shout 'Snap!' when they spot two similar cards

snappy *adjective* (**snappier, snappiest**)
quick and lively

snapshot *noun*
an informal photograph taken quickly

snare *noun*
a trap for catching animals

snare *verb*
to snare an animal is to catch it in a snare

snarl¹ *verb*
an animal snarls when it growls angrily

snarl¹ *noun*
a snarling sound

snarl² *verb*
to be snarled up is to become tangled or jammed • *The motorway was snarled up for several miles.*

snatch *verb*
to snatch something is to grab it quickly
• *He snatched the bag from me.*

sneak *verb*
to sneak somewhere is to move there quietly and secretly

sneak *noun*
(*informal*) a person who tells tales

sneaky *adjective*
dishonest or deceitful

sneer *verb*
to sneer is to speak or behave in a scornful way

sneeze *verb*
you sneeze when you push air through your nose suddenly and uncontrollably

sneeze *noun*
the action or sound of sneezing

sniff *verb*
1 to sniff is to make a noise by drawing air in through your nose **2** to sniff something is to smell it with a sniff

sniff *noun*
the action or sound of sniffing or smelling something

sniffle *verb*
to keep sniffing because you have a cold or are crying

snigger *verb*
to snigger is to give a quiet sly laugh

snigger *noun*
a quiet sly laugh

snip *verb* (**snipping, snipped**)
to snip something is to cut a small piece or pieces off it

snip *noun*
an act of snipping something

sniper *noun*
someone who shoots at people from a hiding place

snippet *noun*
a short piece of news or information

snivel *verb* (**snivelling, snivelled**)
to snivel is to cry or complain in a whining way

snob *noun*
someone who looks down on people who have not got wealth or power or particular tastes or interests
snobbery *noun* snobbery is being a snob **snobbish** *adjective* thinking or behaving like a snob

snooker *noun*
snooker is a game played with long sticks (called *cues*) and 22 coloured balls on a cloth-covered table

snoop *verb*
to snoop is to pry or try to find out about someone else's business
snooper or **snoop** *noun* someone who snoops

snore *verb*
to snore is to breathe noisily while you are sleeping

snorkel *noun*
a tube with one end above the water, worn by an underwater swimmer to get air

snort *verb*
to snort is to make a loud noise by forcing air out through your nose

snort *noun*
a snorting noise

snout *noun*
an animal's snout is the front part sticking out from its head, with its nose and mouth

snow *noun*
snow is frozen drops of water falling from the sky as small white flakes

snow *verb*
to fall as snow • *It was still snowing when they went out.* • *It might snow later.*

snowball *noun*
snow pressed into the shape of a ball for throwing

snowdrop *noun*
a small white flower that blooms in early spring

snowflake *noun*
a flake of snow

snowman *noun*
a figure of a person made of snow

snowplough *noun*
a vehicle with a large blade at the front for clearing snow from a road or railway track

snowstorm *noun*
a storm with snow falling

snowy *adjective* (**snowier, snowiest**)
1 with snow falling • *We're expecting snowy weather.* **2** covered with snow • *The roofs looked snowy.* **3** brightly white

snowman

snub *verb* (**snubbing, snubbed**)
to snub someone is to treat them in a scornful or unfriendly way

snug *adjective* (**snugger, snuggest**)
warm and cosy • *We found a snug corner by the fire.* **snugly** *adverb* in a snug way • *The little ones are tucked up snugly in bed.*

snuggle *verb*
to snuggle is to curl up in a warm comfortable place
• *She snuggled down in bed.*

so *adverb*
1 in this way; to such an extent • *Why are you so cross?* **2** very • *Cricket is so boring.* **3** also • *I was wrong but so were you.* **and so on** and other similar things • *They took food, water, spare clothing, and so on.* **or so** or about that number • *We need about fifty or so.* **so as to** in order to **so far** up to now **so what?** (*informal*) what does that matter?

so *conjunction*
for that reason • *It was dark, so we took a torch.*

soak *verb*
to soak someone or something is to make them very wet or leave them in water **to soak something up** is to take in a liquid in the way that a sponge does

soap *noun*
1 soap is a substance you use with water for washing and cleaning things **2** (*informal*) a soap is a soap opera **soapy** *adjective* full of soap or covered in soap

soap opera *noun*
a television serial about the ordinary life of a group of imaginary people

soar *verb*
1 to soar is to rise or fly high in the air **2** to soar is also to increase a lot • *Prices were soaring.*

sob *verb* (**sobbing, sobbed**)
to sob is to cry with gasping noises
sob *noun*
a sound of sobbing

sober *adjective*
1 not drunk **2** calm and serious • *She had a sober expression.* **3** not bright or showy • *The room was painted in sober colours.*

so-called *adjective*
having the name but perhaps not deserving it • *Even the so-called experts couldn't solve the problem.*

soccer *noun*
soccer is a game played by two teams which try to kick an inflated ball into their opponents' goal

sociable *adjective*
sociable people are friendly and like to be with other people
sociably *adverb*
sociability *noun*

social *adjective* (*say* soh-shal)
1 to do with people meeting one another in their spare time • *Let's join a social club.* **2** living in groups, not alone • *Bees are social insects.* **3** to do with society or a community • *They were writing a social history of the area.* **socially** *adverb* in your spare time, not at work

social media *noun*
websites and computer programmes that people use to communicate on the Internet

social work *noun*
social work is work helping people in a community who have problems **social worker** *noun* someone who has a job in social work

society *noun* (**societies**)
1 a society is a community of people; society is people living together in a group or nation **2** a society is also a group of people organized for a particular purpose • *He's joined a dramatic society.*

sock *noun*
a soft piece of clothing that covers your foot and the lower half of your leg **to pull your socks up** (*informal*) is to try to do better

socket *noun*
a device or hole that something fits into, especially the place where an electric plug is put to make a connection

soda *noun*
1 soda is a substance made from sodium **2** soda water

soda water *noun*
soda water is fizzy water used in drinks

sodium *noun* (*say* soh-di-um)
sodium is a soft silvery-white metal

sofa *noun*
a long soft seat with sides and a back

soft *adjective*
1 not hard or firm; easily pressed or cut into a new shape **2** smooth; not rough or stiff **3** gentle; not loud • *He spoke in a soft voice.* **softly** *adverb* in a gentle way; quietly
• *She closed the door softly behind her.* **softness** *noun*

soft drink *noun*
a drink that does not contain alcohol

soften *verb*
1 to soften something is to make it softer **2** to soften is to become softer

software *noun*
(*in computing*) software is programs and data, which are not part of the machinery (the *hardware*) of a computer

soggy *adjective* (**soggier, soggiest**)
very wet and soft

soil¹ *noun*
soil is the loose earth that plants grow in

soil² *verb*
to soil something is to make it dirty

solar *adjective*
to do with the sun or powered by the sun's energy

solar system *noun*   solar system
the solar system is the sun and the planets that revolve round it

solder *noun*
solder is a soft alloy that is melted to join pieces of metal together

solder *verb*
to solder two pieces of metal is to join them together with solder

soldier *noun*
a member of an army

sole¹ *noun*
1 the bottom part of a shoe or foot **2** a flat sea fish used for food

sole² *adjective*
single or only • *She was the sole survivor.* **solely** *adverb*

solemn *adjective*
serious and dignified **solemnity** *noun* solemnity is being solemn **solemnly** *adverb* in a serious and dignified way

solicitor *noun*
a lawyer who advises clients and prepares legal documents

a b c d e f g h i j p q r s t u v w x y z

solid *adjective*
1 keeping its shape; not a liquid or gas **2** not hollow; with no space inside • *These bars are made of solid steel.* **3** firm or strongly made • *The house is built on solid foundations.* **4** strong and reliable • *They gave solid support.* **solidly** *adverb* something is solidly built when it is firmly and strongly built; to rain solidly is to rain continuously **solidity** *noun* how solid something is

solid *noun*
1 a solid thing **2** a three-dimensional shape, such as a cube, sphere, or cone

solitary *adjective*
1 alone; on your own • *He lived a solitary life.* **2** single • *There was a solitary van in the car park.*

solitude *noun*
solitude is being on your own

solo *noun*
something sung or performed by one person alone

soloist *noun*
someone who plays or sings a solo

soluble *adjective*
a soluble substance is able to be dissolved

solution *noun*
1 the answer to a problem or puzzle **2** a liquid with something dissolved in it

solve *verb*
to solve a problem or puzzle is to find an answer to it

sombre *adjective*
gloomy or dark

some *determiner*
1 a few or a little • *I'd like some biscuits and some sugar.* **2** a certain amount of • *Would you like some cake?* **3** an unknown person or thing • *Some fool left the door open.*

some *pronoun*
a certain or unknown number or amount • *Some of them were late.*

somebody *pronoun*
someone; some person

somehow *adverb*
in some way • *We must finish the work somehow.*

someone *pronoun*
some person

somersault *noun*
(*say* sum-er-solt)
a movement in which you turn head over heels and land on your feet

something *pronoun*
a certain or unknown thing

sometime *adverb*
at some time • *I saw her sometime last year.*

sometimes *adverb*
at some times but not always • *We sometimes walk to school.*

somewhat *adverb*
to some extent; rather • *He was somewhat annoyed.*

somewhere *adverb*
in or to some place

son *noun*
a boy or man who is someone's child

sonar *noun*
sonar is a system using the echo from sound waves to locate objects underwater

song *noun*
1 a song is a tune with words for singing **2** a bird's song is the musical sounds it makes **3** song is singing • *He burst into song.*

songbird *noun*
a bird that sings sweetly

sonic *adjective*
to do with sound or sound waves

sonnet *noun*
a kind of poem with 14 lines

soon *adverb*
1 in a short time from now **2** not long after something • *She became ill, but was soon better.* **3** early or quickly • *You spoke too soon.* **as soon as** willingly • *I'd just as soon stay at home.* **sooner** or **later** at some time in the future

soot *noun*
soot is the black powder left by smoke in a chimney or on a building **sooty** *adjective* covered in soot

soothe *verb*
1 to soothe someone is to make them calm **2** to soothe a pain or ache is to make it hurt less

sophisticated *adjective*
(*say* sof-**iss**-ti-kay-tid)
1 someone is sophisticated when they are used to a fashionable or cultured life and have experienced a lot of different things **2** something is sophisticated when it is complicated and highly developed • *It is a sophisticated machine.* **sophistication** *noun* sophistication is being sophisticated

sopping *adjective*
very wet; soaked

soppy *adjective* (**soppier, soppiest**)
(*informal*) sentimental or silly

soprano *noun* (**sopranos**)
(*say* so-prah-noh)
a woman or young boy with a high singing voice

sorcerer *noun*
someone who can do magic **sorcery** *noun* magic or witchcraft

sorceress *noun*
a woman who can do magic

sore *adjective*
painful or smarting • *I've got a sore throat.* **soreness** *noun*

sore *noun*
a red and painful place on your skin

sorely *adverb*
seriously; very • *I was sorely tempted to run away.*

sorrow *noun*
sorrow is sadness or regret **sorrowful** *adjective* feeling sorrow **sorrowfully** *adverb*

sorry *adjective* (**sorrier, sorriest**)
1 you are sorry that you did something when you regret doing it or want to apologize • *I'm sorry I forgot to send you a birthday card.* **2** you feel sorry for someone when you feel pity for them or are sad that something bad has happened to them • *I'm sorry you've been ill.*

sort *noun*
a group of things or people that are similar; a kind • *What sort of fruit do you like?* **sort of** (*informal*) rather; to some extent • *I sort of wanted to go.*

sort *verb*
to sort things is to arrange them in groups or kinds **to sort something out** is to organize it or arrange it

SOS *noun*
an SOS is an urgent appeal for help from someone whose life is in danger

soul *noun*
a person's invisible spirit that some people believe goes on living after the body has died

sound¹ *noun*
1 sound is vibrations in the air that you can detect with your ear **2** a sound is something that you can hear

sound¹ *verb*
1 to sound is to make a sound • *The trumpets sounded.* **2** to sound something is to make a sound with it • *Don't forget to sound your horn.* **3** to sound a certain way is to give that impression when heard • *You sound in a good mood.* • *The car sounds as if it needs a service.*

sound² *verb*
to sound someone out is to try to find out what they think or feel about something

sound³ *adjective*
1 not damaged; in good condition
2 healthy **3** reasonable or correct
• *His ideas are sound.* **4** reliable
or secure • *They made a sound
investment.* **5** thorough or deep
• *She has a sound knowledge of
the subject.* • *I am a sound sleeper.*
soundly *adverb* thoroughly or
completely **soundness** *noun* being
reliable or sensible

sound effects *plural noun*
special sounds produced to make a
play or film more realistic

soundtrack *noun*
the sound or music that goes with a
film or television programme

soup *noun*
a liquid food made from vegetables
or meat

sour *adjective*
1 having a sharp taste like vinegar
or lemons **2** unpleasant or bad-
tempered **sourly** *adverb* **sourness**
noun

source *noun*
1 the place where something comes
from **2** the place where a river starts

south *noun*
1 the direction to the right of a
person facing east **2** the part of
a country or city that is in this
direction

south *adjective, adverb*
1 towards the south or in the south
2 coming from the south • *A south
wind was blowing.*

south-east *noun, adjective,
adverb*
midway between south and east

southern *adjective* (*say* **suth**-ern)
from or to do with the south

southerner *noun*
(*say* **suth**-er-ner)
someone who lives in the south of a
country

southward or **southwards**
adjective, adverb
towards the south

south-west *noun, adjective,
adverb*
midway between south and west

souvenir *noun* (*say* soo-ven-**eer**)
something that you buy or keep to
remind you of a person, place, or
event

sovereign *noun* (*say* **sov**-rin)
1 a king or a queen **2** an old British
gold coin that was worth £1

sow¹ *verb* (**sowing, sowed,
sown** or **sowed**)
(*rhymes with* **go**)
to sow seeds is to put them into the

ground so that they will grow into
plants

sow² *noun* (*rhymes with* **cow**)
a female pig

soya bean *noun*
a bean that is rich in protein, used to
make kinds of oil and flour

space *noun*
1 space is the whole area outside the
earth, where the stars and planets
are **2** space is also an area or volume
• *There isn't enough space for a car.*
3 a space is an empty area or gap
• *There is a space at the back of the
cupboard.* • *Leave a space for your
name and address.* **4** a space is also
a period of time • *They moved house
twice in the space of a year.*

space *verb*
to space things, or space things
out, is to arrange them with gaps or
periods of time between them

spacecraft *noun* (**spacecraft**)
a vehicle for travelling in outer space

spaceship *noun*
a spacecraft

space shuttle *noun*
a spacecraft that can travel into
space and return to earth

space station *noun*
a satellite which orbits the earth and
is used as a base by scientists and
astronauts

space station

spade *noun*
1 a tool with a long handle and a
wide blade for digging **2** a playing
card with black shapes like upside-
down hearts on it

spaghetti *noun* (*say* spa-**get**-i)
spaghetti is pasta made in long
strings

span *noun*
1 the length from one end
of something to the other
2 the distance between
the tips of your thumb
and little finger when
your hand is spread out
3 a part of a bridge
between two supports
4 a period of time

span *verb* (**spanning,
spanned**)
to span something is to
reach from one side or
end of it to the other
• *A wooden bridge
spanned the river.*

spaghetti

spank *verb*
to spank someone is to smack them
several times on the bottom as a
punishment

spanner *noun*
a tool for tightening or loosening
a nut

spar *verb* (**sparring, sparred**)
to spar is to practise boxing
• *He was my sparring partner.*

spare *verb*
1 to spare something is to afford it
or be able to give it to someone
• *Can you spare a moment?* **2** to
spare someone is to avoid harming
them or making them suffer
something unpleasant

spare *adjective*
1 not used but kept ready in case it
is needed; extra • *Where's the spare
wheel?* • *What do you do in your
spare time?* **2** thin or lean

spare *noun*
a spare thing or part • *The local
garage sells spares.*

spark *noun*
1 a tiny flash of electricity **2** a tiny
glowing piece of something hot

spark *verb*
to spark is to give off sparks

sparkle *verb*
to sparkle is to shine with a lot of
tiny flashes of bright light
• *The sea sparkled in the sunlight.*

sparkler *noun*
a firework that sparkles

sparrow *noun*
a small brown bird

sparse *adjective*
small in number or amount; thinly
scattered • *Vegetation on the
island is sparse.* **sparsely** *adverb* a
sparsely populated area is one with
only a few people

g
h
i
j
k
l
m
n
o
p
q
r
s
t
u
v
w
x
y
z

spatter *verb*
to spatter something is to splash it or scatter it in small drops or pieces • *The paint spattered all over the page.*

spatter

spawn *noun*
spawn is the eggs of frogs, fish, and other water animals

speak *verb* (**speaking, spoke, spoken**)
1 to speak is to say something • *I spoke to them this morning.* **2** to speak a language is to be able to talk in it • *Do you speak German?* to speak up is to say something more clearly or loudly

speaker *noun*
1 a person who is speaking or making a speech **2** the part of a radio, CD player, or computer that the sound comes out of

spear *noun*
a long pole with a sharp point, used as a weapon

spear *verb*
to spear something is to pierce it with a spear or something pointed

special *adjective*
1 different from other people or things; unusual **2** meant for a particular person or purpose • *You'll need special training.*

specialist *noun*
an expert in a particular subject

speciality *noun* (**specialities**)
something that you are especially good at doing

specially *adverb*
for a special purpose • *I came specially to see you.*

species *noun* (**species**)
(*say* spee-shiz)
a group of animals or plants that have similar features and can breed with each other

specific *adjective*
1 definite or precise **2** to do with a particular thing • *The money was given for a specific purpose.*

specifically *adverb*
1 in a special way or for a special purpose • *These scissors are designed specifically for left-handed people.* **2** clearly and precisely • *I specifically said we had to go.*

specify *verb* (**specifies, specifying, specified**)
to specify a person or thing is to name or mention them precisely • *The recipe specified brown sugar, not white.*

specimen *noun*
1 a small amount or sample of something **2** an example of one kind of plant, animal, or thing • *We saw a fine specimen of an oak.*

speck *noun*
1 a tiny piece of something **2** a tiny mark or spot

speckled *adjective*
covered with small spots

spectacle *noun*
1 an exciting sight or display **2** a ridiculous sight

spectacles *plural noun*
a pair of lenses in a frame, which you wear over your eyes to help improve your eyesight

spectacular *adjective*
exciting to see

spectator *noun*
a person who watches a game or show

spectre *noun* (*say* spek-ter)
a ghost

spectrum *noun* (**spectra**)
the band of colours like those in a rainbow

speech *noun*
1 speech is the ability to speak or a person's way of speaking **2** a speech is a talk given to a group of people

speechless *adjective*
unable to speak, especially because you are surprised or angry

speech marks *plural noun*
inverted commas, (" ") used to show that someone is speaking

speed *noun*
1 the speed of something is the rate at which it moves or happens **2** speed is being quick or fast at speed fast; quickly

speed *verb* (**speeding, sped or speeded**)
to speed is to go very fast or too fast • *Drivers can be fined for speeding.* to speed up is to become quicker to speed something up is to make it go or happen faster

speedboat *noun*
a fast motor boat

speedboat

speedometer *noun*
(*say* spee-**dom**-it-er)
a gauge in a vehicle that shows its speed

speedy *adjective*
(**speedier, speediest**)
quick or fast • *We need a speedy reply.* **speedily** *adverb* fast or quickly

spell[1] *verb* (**spelling, spelt or spelled**)
to spell a word is to give its letters in the right order

spell[2] *noun*
1 a period of time • *We're having a cold spell.* **2** a period of activity • *I must do a spell of work now.*

spell[3] *noun*
a set of words that is supposed to have magic power

spelling *noun*
1 the way in which letters are put together to form words **2** how well someone can spell • *Her spelling is poor.*

spend *verb* (**spending, spent**)
1 to spend money is to use it to pay for things **2** to spend time is to pass it doing something • *He spent the weekend painting his bedroom.* **3** to spend energy or effort is to use it up • *She spends all her spare energy on gardening.*

sphere *noun*
a perfectly round solid shape; a globe or ball **spherical** *adjective* shaped like a ball

spice *noun*
a strong-tasting substance used to flavour food, often made from the dried parts of plants **spicy** *adjective* having a strong flavour; full of spices

spider *noun*
a small animal with eight legs that spins webs to catch insects on which it feeds

spike *noun*
a pointed piece of metal; a sharp point **spiky** *adjective* full of spikes or sharp points • *She has short spiky hair.*

spill *verb* (**spilling, spilt or spilled**)
1 to spill something is to let it fall out of a container by accident • *Careful or you'll spill your juice.* **2** to spill is to fall out of a container • *The coins came spilling out.*

spill *noun*
when something gets spilt • *There's been an oil spill at sea.*

spin *verb* (**spinning, spun**)
1 to spin is to turn round and round quickly **2** to spin something is to make it spin **3** to spin is also to make pieces of wool or cotton into

thread by twisting them **4** to spin a web or cocoon is to make it out of threads • *The spider spun a web.*

spinach *noun*
spinach is a vegetable with dark green leaves

spindle *noun*
1 a thin rod on which you wind thread **2** a pin or bar that turns round, or on which something turns round

spine *noun*
1 the line of bones down the middle of your back **2** a sharp point on an animal or plant • *This cactus has sharp spines.* **3** the back part of a book where the pages are joined together **spinal** *adjective* to do with your spine **spiny** *adjective* covered in spines

spine-chilling *adjective* frightening and exciting • *We heard a spine-chilling ghost story.*

spinning wheel *noun*
a machine for spinning thread out of wool or cotton

spinster *noun*
a woman who has not married

spiral *adjective*
going round and round a central point, getting further from it with each turn
spiral *noun*
something with a spiral shape

spire *noun*
a tall pointed part on top of a church tower

spirit *noun*
1 a person's spirit is their soul or their deepest thoughts and feelings **2** a spirit is a ghost or other supernatural being **3** spirit is courage or liveliness **4** a person's spirits are their mood or the way they feel • *She was in good spirits after the exam.* **5** a spirit is also a strong alcoholic drink

spiritual *adjective*
1 to do with the human soul and with a person's deepest thoughts and feelings **2** to do with religious beliefs **spiritually** *adverb*
spiritual *noun*
a religious song originally sung by Black Americans

spit[1] *verb* (**spitting, spat**)
to spit is to shoot drops of liquid out of your mouth • *He spat into the basin.*
spit[1] *noun*
saliva that has been spat out
spit[2] *noun*
a long thin metal spike put through meat to hold it while it is roasted

spite *noun*
spite is a desire to hurt or annoy someone **in spite of something** although something has happened or is happening • *They went out in spite of the rain.* **spiteful** *adjective* wanting to hurt or annoy someone **spitefully** *adverb*

splash *verb*
1 to splash liquid is to make it fly about, as you do when you jump into water **2** to splash is to fly about in drops • *The water splashed all over me.* **3** to splash someone or something is to make them wet by sending drops of liquid towards them • *The bus splashed us as it went past.*
splash *noun*
the action or sound of splashing

splashdown *noun*
the landing of a spacecraft in the sea

splendid *adjective*
magnificent; very fine **splendidly** *adverb*

splendour *noun*
splendour is a brilliant display or appearance

splint *noun*
a straight piece of wood or metal that is tied to a broken arm or leg to hold it firm

splinter *noun*
a small sharp piece of wood or glass broken off a larger piece
splinter *verb*
to splinter is to break into splinters

split *verb* (**splitting, split**)
1 to split is to break into parts **2** to split something is to divide it into parts **to split up 1** is to divide into parts **2** is to separate after being together for some time
split *noun*
a crack or tear in something, where it has split

splutter *verb*
1 to splutter is to make a quick series of spitting or coughing sounds • *The smoke from the bonfire made him splutter.* **2** to splutter is also to speak quickly and unclearly

spoil *verb* (**spoiling, spoilt** or **spoiled**)
1 to spoil something is to damage it and so make it less good or useful • *The rain spoilt our holiday.* **2** to spoil someone is to make them selfish by always letting them have what they want

spoilsport *noun*
someone who spoils other people's fun

spoke *noun*
each of the rods or bars that go from the centre of a wheel to the rim

sponge *noun*
1 a lump of soft material containing lots of tiny holes, used for washing **2** a sea creature from which this kind of material is made **3** a soft lightweight cake or pudding
sponge *verb*
to sponge something is to wash it with a sponge

spongy *adjective* (**spongier, spongiest**)
soft and absorbent like sponge

sponsor *verb*
1 to sponsor someone is to promise to give them money if they do something difficult and give the money to charity **2** to sponsor something or someone is to provide money to support them
sponsor *noun*
someone who provides money to support a person or thing, or who supports someone who sets out to do something for charity **sponsorship** *noun* the money someone provides to support a person or thing

spontaneous *adjective* (*say* spon-**tay**-ni-us)
happening or done without being planned; not forced or suggested by someone else • *Everyone burst into spontaneous applause.* **spontaneously** *adverb* **spontaneity** *noun* behaving in a spontaneous way

spooky *adjective* (**spookier, spookiest**)
(*informal*) frighteningly strange; haunted by ghosts

spool *noun*
a rod or reel for winding on something such as thread or film or tape

spoon *noun*
a piece of metal or wood or plastic consisting of a small bowl with a handle, used for lifting food to your mouth or for stirring or measuring
spoon *verb*
to spoon something is to lift it or take it with a spoon

sport *noun*
1 a sport is a game that exercises your body, especially a game you play out of doors • *What sports do you play?* **2** sport is games of this sort • *Are you keen on sport?*

a b c d e f g h i j k l m n o p q r s t u v w x y z

sporting adjective
1 connected with sport
2 behaving fairly and unselfishly

sportsman or **sportswoman**
noun (**sportsmen** or
sportswomen)
a man or woman who takes part in sport

sportsmanship noun
sportsmanship is behaving fairly
and generously in sport

spot noun
1 a small round mark 2 a pimple
on your skin 3 a small amount of
something • We've had a spot of
bother 4 a place • This is a nice spot.
on the spot immediately; there and
then • We can repair your bike on
the spot.

spot verb (**spotting, spotted**)
1 to spot someone or something is to
notice them or see them • I suddenly
spotted my friend Alex in the crowd.
2 to be spotted is to be marked with
spots

spotless adjective
perfectly clean **spotlessly** adverb
to be spotlessly clean is to be
perfectly clean

spotlight noun
a strong light with a beam that
shines on a small area

spotty adjective
(**spottier, spottiest**)
marked with spots

spout noun
1 a pipe or opening from which
liquid can pour 2 a jet of liquid
spout verb
to spout is to come out in a jet of
liquid

sprain verb
you sprain your ankle or wrist when
you injure it by twisting it
sprain noun
an injury by spraining

sprawl verb
1 you sprawl when you sit or lie
with your arms and legs spread out
2 to be sprawled is to be spread out
loosely or untidily • There were
books and papers sprawled all over
the floor.

spray verb
to spray liquid is to scatter it in
tiny drops over something; to spray
something is to cover it with liquid
in this way
spray noun
1 tiny drops of liquid sprayed on
something 2 a device for spraying
liquid

spread verb (**spreading, spread**)
1 to spread something is to lay or

stretch it out to its full size
• The bird spread its wings and flew
away. 2 to spread something over
a surface is to make it cover the
surface • He spread a thick layer
of jam on his toast. 3 to spread
news or information is to make it
widely known 4 news or information
spreads when it becomes widely
known • The story spread quickly
round the village.

spread noun
1 something you can spread on
bread 2 (informal) a large meal

sprightly adjective (**sprightlier,
sprightliest**)
lively and energetic

spring noun
1 spring is the season of the year
when most plants start to grow,
between winter and summer 2 a
spring is a coil of wire that goes back
to its original shape when you bend
it or squeeze it and let it go
3 a spring is also a sudden
upward movement 4 a spring is also
a place where water rises out of the
ground and becomes a stream

spring verb (**springing, sprang,
sprung**)
1 to spring is to move quickly or
suddenly • He sprang to his feet. 2 to
spring, or spring up, is to develop or
come from something • This squabble
has sprung from a misunderstanding.
3 to spring something on someone is
to surprise them with it

springboard noun
a springy board from which people
jump or dive

springtime noun
springtime is the season of spring

springy adjective (**springier,
springiest**)
able to spring back to its original
position when you bend it or squeeze
it and let it go

sprinkle verb
to sprinkle liquid or powder
is to make tiny drops or
pieces of it fall on something
sprinkler noun a device for
sprinkling liquid

sprint verb
to sprint is to run very fast for a short
distance **sprinter** noun someone
who sprints
sprint noun
a short fast race

sprout verb
1 a plant sprouts when it starts to
produce leaves or shoots
2 to grow or start appearing

• Whiskers sprouted from his
ears and nose.
sprout noun
a green vegetable like a tiny
cabbage

spruce[1] noun
a kind of fir tree
spruce[2] adjective
neat and smart

spud noun
(informal) a potato

spur noun
a sharp spike that a rider wears
on the heel of their boot to urge a
horse to go faster on the spur of the
moment on an impulse; without
planning
spur verb (**spurring, spurred**)
to spur someone, or to spur someone
on, is to encourage them

spurt verb
a liquid spurts when it gushes
out or up • Blood was spurting from
the cut.
spurt noun
1 a jet of liquid 2 a sudden increase
in speed • He put on a spurt and
caught us up.

spy noun (**spies**)
someone who works secretly
to find out things about another
country or person
spy verb (**spies, spying,
spied**)
1 to spy is to be a spy or to watch
secretly • He was spying on us.
2 to spy someone or something
is to see them or notice them
• We spied a house in the
distance.

squabble verb
people squabble when they quarrel
about something unimportant
squabble noun
a minor quarrel or argument

squad noun
a small group of people working or
being trained together

squadron noun
part of an army, navy, or air force

squalid adjective
dirty and unpleasant • He lived in
a squalid little flat. **squalor** noun
squalor is being squalid • They lived
in squalor.

squander verb
to squander money or time is to
waste it

square noun ■
1 a shape with four equal sides and
four right angles 2 in a town, an area
surrounded by buildings 3 the result
of multiplying a number by itself
• 9 is the square of 3.

square *adjective*
1 shaped like a square **2** used for units of measurement that give an area, such as a square metre and a square foot. For example, a square metre is the size of a square with each side one metre long. **3** equal or even • *The teams are all square with six points each.* • *If you pay for lunch, we'll be square.*

square *verb*
1 to square a number is to multiply it by itself • *3 squared is 9.* **2** to square with something is to match it or agree with it • *His story doesn't square with yours.*

squarely *adverb*
directly or exactly • *The ball hit him squarely in the mouth.*

square root *noun*
the number that gives a particular number if it is multiplied by itself • *3 is the square root of 9.*

squash *verb*
1 to squash something is to squeeze it so that it loses its shape **2** to squash a person or thing into something is to force them into it when there is not much space • *We squashed ourselves into the minibus.*

squash *noun*
1 a squash is when people or things are pressed together because there is not enough space • *There was a tremendous squash outside the football ground.* **2** squash is a fruit-flavoured drink **3** squash is also a game played with rackets and a small ball in a special indoor court

squat *verb* (**squatting, squatted**)
1 to squat is to sit back on your heels **2** to squat in an unoccupied house is to live there without permission **squatter** *noun* someone who squats in a house

squat *adjective* (**squatter, squattest**)
short and fat

squaw *noun*
a Native American woman or wife

squawk *verb*
to squawk is to make a loud harsh cry

squawk *noun*
a loud harsh cry

squeak *verb*
to make a short high-pitched sound or cry

squeak *noun*
a short high-pitched sound or cry
squeaky *adjective* making squeaks • *a squeaky floorboard*

squeal *verb*
to squeal is to make a long shrill sound

squeal *noun*
a long shrill sound

squeeze *verb*
1 to squeeze something is to press it from opposite sides, especially so that you get liquid out of it **2** to squeeze somewhere is to force a way into or through a place or gap • *We squeezed into the car*
squeezer *noun* a device for squeezing fruit

squeeze *noun*
1 the action of squeezing **2** a tight fit • *We all got on the bus but it was a bit of a squeeze.*

squelch *verb*
to squelch is to make a sound like someone treading in thick mud

squelch *noun*
a squelching sound

squid *noun*
a sea animal with eight short arms and two long ones

squiggle *noun*
a short curly or wavy line

squint *verb*
1 to squint at something is to peer at it or look at it with half-shut eyes **2** to squint is to have eyes that look in different directions

squint *noun*
a fault in someone's eyesight that makes them squint

squire *noun*
1 the man who owns most of the land in a country district **2** in the Middle Ages, a young nobleman who served a knight

squirm *verb*
to squirm is to wriggle about, especially when you feel awkward or embarrassed

squirrel *noun*
a small animal with grey or red fur and a bushy tail, that lives in trees and eats nuts

squirt *verb*
to squirt something is to send it out in a strong jet of liquid; to squirt is to come out like this • *The orange juice squirted in his eye.*

St. *or* **St**
short for saint or street

stab *verb* (**stabbing, stabbed**)
to stab someone is to pierce or wound them with something sharp • *She stabbed him with a knife.*

stab *noun*
1 the action of stabbing **2** a sudden sharp pain

stability *noun*
stability is being stable or firm

stabilizer *noun*
a small extra wheel on a bicycle to make it stable

stable¹ *adjective*
steady or firmly fixed
stably *adverb*

stable² *noun*
a building where horses are kept

stack *noun*
1 a neat pile of things **2** a large amount of something • *I've got a stack of work to do.* **3** a single small chimney

stack *verb*
to stack things is to pile them up neatly

stadium *noun* (**stadiums** or **stadia**)
a large sports ground surrounded by seats for spectators

WORD ORIGIN

The word **stadium** comes from a Greek word *stadion*, which originally meant a measure of length of about 185 metres. This was the usual length of a race in an ancient stadium.

---

staff *noun*
1 the people who work in an office or shop **2** *the teachers in a school or college* **3** a thick stick for walking with

stag *noun*
a male deer

stage *noun*
1 a platform for performances in a theatre or hall **2** the point that you have reached in a process or journey • *The final stage is to paint the model.*

stage *verb*
1 to stage a performance is to present it on a stage **2** to stage an event is to organize it • *They decided to stage a protest.*

stagecoach *noun*
a kind of horse-drawn coach that used to travel regularly along the same route

stagger *verb*
1 to stagger is to walk unsteadily **2** to stagger someone is to amaze or shock them • *I was staggered at the price.* **3** to stagger events is to arrange them so that they do not all happen at the same time • *We stagger our holidays so that someone is always here*
staggering *adjective* very surprising or shocking

stagnant *adjective*
stagnant water is not flowin
or fresh • *The pond is stagnant.*

stain *noun*
a dirty mark that is difficult to
remove

stain *verb*
1 to stain something is to make a
stain on it • *The juice has stained my
dress.* **2** to stain material or wood is
to colour it

stainless steel *noun*
stainless steel is steel that does not
rust easily

stair *noun*
each of a series of steps that take
you from one floor to another in a
building

staircase *noun*
a set of stairs

stake *noun*
1 a thick pointed stick to be
driven into the ground
2 the thick post to which
people used to be tied for
execution by being burnt alive
3 an amount of money you bet on
something **to be at stake** is to be at
risk of being lost

stake *verb*
to stake money is to use it on a
bet **to stake a claim** is to claim
something or get a right to it

stalactite *noun*
a stony spike hanging like an icicle
from the roof of a cave

stalagmite *noun*
a stony spike standing like a pillar
on the floor of a cave

stale *adjective*
no longer fresh • *This bread has
gone stale.* • *The air in here smells
stale.*

stalk¹ *noun*
the main part of a plant, from which
the leaves and flowers grow

stalk² *verb*
to stalk a person or animal is to
follow or hunt them stealthily

stall¹ *noun*
1 a table or small open-fronted shop
where things are sold, usually in the
open air **2** a place for one animal in
a stable or shed

stall¹ *verb*
a vehicle stalls when the engine
stops suddenly • *The car stalled at
the traffic lights.*

stall² *verb*
to stall is to delay or hold things up
to give yourself more time

stallion *noun*
a male horse

stalls *plural noun*
the seats on the ground
floor of a theatre or cinema

stamen *noun*
(*say* **stay**-men)
the part of
a flower
that produces
pollen

stamina *noun*
(*say* **stam**-in-a)
stamina is the
strength and
energy you
need to keep
doing something
for a long time
• *Does she have the stamina
to run a marathon?*

stammer *verb*
to stammer is to keep
repeating the sounds
at the beginning of words

stammer *noun*
when someone
stammers a lot

stamp *noun*
1 a small piece of
gummed paper with
a special design on it,
which you stick on
a letter or parcel to
show you have paid
the postage **2** when you
bang your foot on the
ground **3** a small block
with raised letters for
printing words or marks
on something; the words or
marks made with this

stamp *verb*
1 to stamp is to bang your foot
heavily on the ground
2 to stamp an envelope or parcel is
to put a postage stamp on it
3 to stamp something
is also to put marks on it with
a stamp • *The librarian stamped my
books.*

stallion

stampede *noun*
a sudden rush
of animals
or people

stampede *verb*
animals or people
stampede when they
rush in a stampede

stand *verb* (**standing, stood**)
1 to stand is to be on your
feet without moving • *She stood
at the back of the hall.* **2** to stand
something somewhere is to put it
upright there • *Stand the vase on
the table.* **3** something stands
somewhere when that is where it is
• *The castle stood on the top of a hill.*
4 something stands when it stays
unchanged • *My offer still stands.*
5 to stand a difficulty or hardship is
to be able to bear it • *I can't stand
the heat.* **to stand by** is to be ready
for action **to stand for something
1** is to tolerate it or put up
with it • *She won't stand
for any arguments.* **2** is to
mean something • *'Dr' stands
for 'Doctor'.* **to stand in for
someone** is to take their
place **to stand out** is to be
clear or obvious **to stand
up** is to rise to your feet **to
stand up for someone** is
to support them or defend
them

stand *noun*
1 something made for
putting things on • *The statue
had fallen off its stand.* **2** a stall
where things are sold or displayed
3 a structure at a sports ground
with rows of seats for spectators
4 when someone resists an attack
or defends their opinion • *She was
determined to make a stand for her
rights.*

standard *noun*
1 how good something is • *They
reached a high standard of work.*

stamps

2 a thing used to measure or judge something else • *The metre is the standard for length.* **3** a special flag, especially one used by an army

standard *adjective*
of the usual or ordinary kind

standard of living *noun*
(**standards of living**)
the level of comfort and wealth that a person or country has

standstill *noun*
a complete stop • *The blizzard brought traffic to a standstill.*

stanza *noun*
a group of lines in a poem

staple¹ *noun*
1 a tiny piece of metal used to fasten pieces of paper together **2** a U-shaped nail **stapler** *noun* a machine for putting staples in paper

staple¹ *verb*
to fasten pieces of paper together with a staple

staple² *adjective*
main or normal • *Rice is the staple food in many countries.*

star *noun*
1 a large mass of burning gas that you see as a bright speck of light in the sky at night **2** a shape with five or six points **3** one of the main performers in a film or show; a famous entertainer **starry** *adjective* a starry sky or night is full of stars

star *verb* (**starring, starred**)
1 to star in a film or show is to be one of the main performers **2** a film or show stars someone when it has them as a main performer

starboard *noun*
starboard is the right-hand side of a ship or aircraft when you are facing forward

starch *noun*
1 starch is a white substance found in bread, potatoes, and other food, which is an important part of the human diet **2** starch is also a form of this substance used to stiffen clothes **starchy** *adjective* like starch, or containing starch

stare *verb*
to look hard at someone or something without moving your eyes

stare *noun*
a long fixed look
• *I gave him a hard stare*

starfish *noun*
(**starfish** or **starfishes**)
a sea animal shaped like a star with five points

starling *noun*
a noisy black or brown speckled bird

start *verb*
1 to start something is to take the first steps in doing it **2** to start, or start out, is to begin a journey **3** to start is also to make a sudden movement of surprise • *They all started at the noise outside.*

start *noun*
1 the act of starting • *We need to make an early start tomorrow.* **2** the point or place where something starts • *Go back to the start.* • *Saturday is the start of the new season.* **3** an advantage that someone starts with • *We gave the young ones 10 minutes' start.* **4** a sudden movement of surprise • *It gave me quite a start when the hooter sounded.*

startle *verb*
to startle a person or animal is to surprise or alarm them

starve *verb*
1 someone starves when they suffer or die because they do not have enough food **2** to starve someone is to make them suffer or die in this way • *The prisoners had been starved to death.* **3** (*informal*) to be starving is to be very hungry **starvation** *noun* when someone does not have enough food and so dies

state *noun*
1 the way that someone or something is, or the condition that they are in • *The room was in an untidy state.* **2** a nation or country **3** a division of a country • *the state of California* **4** you can refer to a government and its officials as the state to be in a state (*informal*) is to be upset

state *verb*
to state something is to say it clearly or formally

statement *noun*
1 words that state something **2** a formal account of something that happened • *A witness to the*

starfish

robbery has given a statement to the police. **3** a report made by a bank about the money in a person's account

statesman or **stateswoman** *noun* (**statesmen** or **stateswomen**)
someone who is important or skilled in governing a state

static *adjective*
not moving or changing

static electricity *noun* electricity which is present in something but does not flow as a current

station *noun*
1 a place where people get on or off trains or buses **2** a building for police, firemen, or other workers who serve he public **3** a place from which radio or television broadcasts are made

station *verb*
to station a person somewhere is to place them there for a particular purpose
• *He was stationed at the door to take the tickets.*

WORD ORIGIN

The word **station** comes from a Latin word *stare* meaning 'to stand', because a station was originally a place where someone stood.

stationary *adjective*
not moving; still
• *The car was stationary when the van hit it.*

stationery noun
stationery is paper, envelopes, and other things used for writing

statistic noun
a piece of information expressed as a number • These statistics show that the population has doubled. **statistical** adjective statistical information is expressed as numbers **statistically** adverb

statue noun
a model made of stone or metal to look like a person or animal

status noun
a person's status is their position or rank in relation to other people • What is her status in the company?

staunch adjective
firm and loyal • They are the team's most staunch supporters.

stave noun
a set of five lines on which music is written

stave verb
to stave something off is to keep something unwelcome away or delay it • I ate a banana to stave off my hunger.

stay verb
1 to stay somewhere is to continue to be there or to remain there 2 to stay somewhere or with someone is to spend time as a visitor • We stayed in a little hotel near the sea.

stay noun
a period of time spent somewhere • We didn't have time for a long stay.

steady adjective (**steadier, steadiest**)
1 not shaking or moving; firm 2 regular or constant; not changing much • They kept up a steady pace. **steadily** adverb in a steady way; gradually

steady verb
to steady something is to make it steady

steak noun
a thick slice of meat or fish

steal verb (**stealing, stole, stolen**)
1 to steal something is to take and keep it when it does not belong to you 2 to steal somewhere is to move there quietly without being noticed • He stole out of the room.

stealthy adjective (**stealthier, stealthiest**)
moving or doing something secretly and quietly so that you are not noticed
stealth noun stealth is being stealthy **stealthily** adverb

steam noun
steam is the gas or vapour that comes from boiling water **steamy** adjective full of steam

steam verb
1 to steam is to give out steam 2 to steam somewhere is to move using the power of steam • The boat steamed down the river. 3 to steam food is to cook it in steam • Let's have a steamed pudding. to steam up is to be covered with mist or condensation • The windows have steamed up.

steam engine noun
a railway engine driven by steam

steamer noun
a steamship

steamroller noun
a heavy vehicle with wide metal wheels, used to flatten surfaces when making roads

steamship noun
a ship driven by steam

steed noun
(old or poetical use) a horse

steel noun
steel is a strong metal made from iron and carbon **steely** adjective hard, cold, or grey like steel

steel verb
to steel yourself is to find the courage to do something difficult

steel band noun
a West Indian band of musicians who play instruments made from oil drums

steep adjective
rising or sloping sharply **steeply** adverb **steepness** noun

steeple noun
a church tower with a spire

steeplechase noun
a race across country or over hedges and fences

steer¹ verb
to steer a vehicle is to make it go in the direction you want

steer² noun
a young bull kept for its beef

steering wheel noun
a wheel for steering a vehicle

stem noun
1 the main long thin part of a plant above the ground, that the leaves and flowers grow from; a stalk 2 the thin part of a wine glass

stem verb (**stemming, stemmed**)
to stem from something is to start there or come from it • The problem stems from lack of money.

stench noun
a very unpleasant smell

stencil noun
a piece of card or metal or plastic with pieces cut out of it, used to produce a picture or design

step noun
1 a movement you make with your foot when you are walking, running, or dancing 2 the sound you make when you put your foot down to walk 3 each of the level surfaces on a stair or ladder 4 each of a series of actions • The first step is to make a plan. to watch your step is to be careful

step verb (**stepping, stepped**)
to step is to tread or walk to step something up is to increase it

stepchild noun
a child that someone's husband or wife has from an earlier marriage. A boy is a stepson and a girl is a stepdaughter.

stepfather noun
a man who is married to your mother but is not your own father

stepladder noun
a folding ladder with flat treads

stepmother noun
a woman who is married to your father but is not your own mother

stepping stone noun
stepping stones are a line of stones put in a river or stream to help people walk across

steps plural noun
a stepladder • Have you seen my steps?

stereo noun
a system for playing recorded music using two speakers to spread the sound

sterile adjective
1 clean and free from germs 2 not able to have children or young **sterility** noun sterility is being sterile

sterilize verb
1 to sterilize something is to make it free from germs 2 to sterilize a person or animal is to make them unable to bear young **sterilization** noun sterilization is sterilizing something or someone

sterling noun
sterling is British money • Tourists paid for their meals in sterling.

stern¹ adjective
strict and severe **sternly** adverb **sternness** noun

stern² *noun*
the back part of a ship

stethoscope *noun*
(*say* steth-o-skohp)
a device used by doctors for listening to a patient's heartbeat or breathing

stew *verb*
to stew food is to cook it slowly in liquid

stew *noun*
a dish of meat and vegetables cooked slowly in liquid

steward *noun*
1 a man whose job is to look after the passengers on a ship or aircraft **2** an official who looks after the arrangements at a public event

stewardess *noun*
a woman whose job is to look after the passengers on a ship or aircraft

stick¹ *noun*
1 a long thin piece of wood **2** a walking stick **3** the long piece of wood used to hit the ball in hockey, polo, or other ball games **4** a long thin piece of something • *I must get a stick of rock.*

stick² *verb* (**sticking, stuck**)
1 to stick something sharp into a thing is to push it in roughly or carelessly • *He stuck a pin in her finger.* **2** to stick things is to fasten or join them **3** something sticks when it becomes fixed or jammed • *The door keeps sticking.* **4** (*informal*) you can't stick something when you can't bear it • *I can't stick it any longer.* **to stick out** is to come out from a surface or be noticeable **to stick together** is to stay loyal to one another **to stick up for someone** (*informal*) is to support them or defend them **to be stuck with someone or something** (*informal*) is to be unable to avoid dealing with them

stick insects

sticker *noun*
a label or sign for sticking on something

stick insect *noun*
an insect with a long thin body that looks like a twig

stickleback *noun*
a small fish with sharp spines on its back

sticky *adjective*
(**stickier, stickiest**)
able or likely to stick to

things **stickiness** *noun*

stiff *adjective*
1 not able to bend or change its shape easily **2** difficult • *We had a stiff examination.* **3** formal; not friendly **4** strong or severe • *There's a stiff breeze outside.* **stiffly** *adverb*
stiffness *noun*

stiffen *verb*
1 to stiffen something is to make it stiff **2** to stiffen is to become stiff

stifle *verb*
1 to be stifled is to find it difficult or impossible to breathe **2** to stifle something is to stop it happening • *She stifled a yawn.*

stile *noun*
a set of steps or bars for people to climb over a fence or wall

still *adjective*
1 not moving **2** quiet and peaceful • *In the night, the streets are still.* **3** not fizzy **stillness** *noun* stillness is being quiet and not moving

still *adverb*
1 up to this or that time • *He was still there.* **2** even; yet; in a greater amount • *They wanted still more food.* **3** however • *They lost. Still, they have another game.*

still *verb*
to still something is to make it still

stilts *plural noun*
1 a pair of poles on which you can walk high above the ground **2** supports for a house built over water

stimulate *verb*
1 to stimulate someone is to make them excited or interested **2** to stimulate something is to encourage it to develop • *His new book stimulated an interest in wildlife.* **stimulation** *noun* being stimulated or excited

stimulus *noun*
something that encourages a thing to develop or produces a reaction

sting *noun*
1 the part of an insect or plant that can cause pain or a wound **2** a painful area or wound caused by an insect or plant

sting *verb* (**stinging, stung**)
1 an insect or plant stings you when it wounds or hurts you with a sting • *She was stung by a wasp.* **2** part of your body stings

when you feel a sharp or throbbing pain there • *My back is stinging from sunburn.*

stingy *adjective* (**stingier, stingiest**) (*say* stin-ji)
mean; not generous

stink *noun*
an unpleasant smell

stink *verb* (**stinking, stank** or **stunk, stunk**)
to stink is to have an unpleasant smell

stir *verb*
1 to stir something liquid or soft is to move it round and round, especially with a spoon **2** to stir is to move slightly or start to move after sleeping or being still • *She didn't stir all afternoon.* **to stir something up** is to excite or arouse it • *They are always stirring up trouble.*

stir *noun*
1 an act of stirring • *Give it a stir.* **2** a fuss or disturbance • *The news caused a stir.*

stirrup *noun*
a metal loop that hangs down on each side of a horse's saddle to support the rider's foot

stitch *noun*
1 a loop of thread made in sewing or knitting **2** a sudden pain in your side caused by running

stitch *verb*
to stitch something is to sew it with stitches

stoat *noun*
an animal rather like a weasel

stock *noun*
1 a stock of things is an amount of them kept ready to be sold or used **2** stock is a collection of farm animals, also called livestock **3** stock is a liquid used in cooking, made from the juices you get by stewing meat, fish, or vegetables **4** stock is also a number of a company's shares

stock *verb*
1 a shop stocks goods when it keeps a supply of them to sell **2** to stock a place is to provide it with a stock of things • *The explorers stocked their base camp with tinned food.* **to stock up** is to buy a large supply of something

stocking *noun*
a piece of clothing that covers the whole of someone's leg and foot

stocks *plural noun* a wooden framework with holes for

people's legs and arms, in which criminals were locked as a punishment in the past

stocky adjective (**stockier, stockiest**)
short and solidly built

stodgy adjective (**stodgier, stodgiest**)
thick and heavy; not easy to digest • *The pudding's very stodgy.*

stoke verb
to stoke a furnace or fire is to add fuel to it

stomach noun
1 the part of your body where food starts to be digested 2 the front part of your body that contains your stomach; your abdomen
stomach verb
to stomach something is to tolerate it or put up with it • *I can't stomach their awful jokes.*

stone noun (**stones** or, for the unit of weight, **stone**)
1 stone is the hard solid mineral of which rocks are made 2 a stone is a piece of this mineral 3 a stone is also a jewel 4 a stone is also the hard seed in the middle of some fruits, such as a cherry, plum, or peach 5 a stone is also a unit of weight equal to 14 pounds or about 6.35 kilograms • *She weighs 6 stone.*
stone verb
1 to stone someone is to throw stones at them 2 to stone fruit is to take the stones out of it

stone-deaf adjective
completely deaf

stony adjective (**stonier, stoniest**)
1 stony ground is full of stones 2 hard like stone 3 unfriendly or hostile • *Our question was met by a stony silence.*

stool noun
a small seat without a back

stoop verb
1 to stoop is to bend your body forwards and downwards 2 to stoop to doing something is to lower your standards of behaviour • *I didn't think he'd stoop to cheating.*

stop verb (**stopping, stopped**)
1 to stop something is to finish doing it, or make it finish 2 to stop is to be no longer moving or working or to come to an end 3 to stop something is to prevent it happening or continuing • *I must go out and stop that noise.* 4 to stop a hole or gap, or stop it up, is to fill it

5 to stop at a place is to stay there briefly
stop noun
1 when something stops or ends • *She brought the car to a stop.* 2 a place where a bus or train stops regularly

stopper noun
something that fits into the top of a bottle or jar to close it

stopwatch noun
a watch that you can start or stop, used for timing races

storage noun
storage is the storing of things

store verb
to store things is to keep them until they are needed
store noun
1 a place where things are stored 2 a supply of things kept for future use 3 a shop, especially a large one to be in store is to be waiting to happen soon • *There is a treat in store for you.*

storey noun (**storeys**)
one whole floor of a building

stork noun
a large bird with long legs and a long beak

storm noun
1 a period of bad weather with strong winds, rain or snow, and often thunder and lightning 2 a violent attack or outburst • *There was a storm of protest.*
storm verb
1 to storm is to move or shout angrily • *He stormed out of the room.* 2 soldiers or police storm a place when they attack it suddenly • *They stormed the castle.*

stormy adjective (**stormier, stormiest**)
1 likely to end in a storm • *The weather is stormy today* 2 loud and angry • *We had a stormy meeting.*

story noun (**stories**)
1 an account of real or imaginary events 2 (*informal*) a lie • *Don't tell stories!*

stout adjective
1 rather fat 2 thick and strong • *She carried a stout stick.*

3 brave • *The defenders put up a stout resistance.* **stoutly** adverb **stoutness** noun

stove noun
a device that produces heat for warming a room or cooking

stow verb
to stow something is to pack it or store it away to stow away is to hide on a ship or aircraft so that you can travel without paying

stowaway noun
someone who stows away on a ship or aircraft

straddle verb
1 to straddle something is to sit or stand with your legs either side of it 2 to straddle something is also to be built across it • *A long bridge straddles the river.*

straggle verb
1 to straggle is to walk too slowly and not keep up with the rest of a group 2 to straggle is also to grow or move in an untidy way • *Brambles straggled across the path.* **straggler** noun someone who does not keep up with the rest of a group
straggly adjective growing or hanging untidily

straight adjective
1 going continuously in one direction; not curving or bending 2 level • *Is this picture straight?* 3 tidy; in proper order 4 honest or frank • *Give me a straight answer.*
straight adverb 1 in a straight line • *Go straight on, then turn left.* 2 at once; directly • *I came straight here.*

straightaway adverb immediately; at once

straighten verb
1 to straighten something is to make it straight 2 to straighten is to become straight

straightforward adjective
1 easy to understand or do; not complicated 2 honest or frank

strain verb
1 to strain something is to stretch it or push it or pull it hard or too hard 2 to strain is to make a great effort to do something 3 to strain liquid is to put it through a sieve to take out any lumps or other things in it
strain noun
1 the strain on something is when

stork

it is stretched or pulled too hard • *The rope broke under the strain.* **2** a strain is an injury caused by straining **3** strain is the effect on someone of too much work or worry

strait *noun*
a narrow stretch of water connecting two seas

strand *noun*
1 each of the threads or wires twisted together to make a rope or cable **2** a lock of hair

stranded *adjective*
1 left on sand or rocks in shallow water • *We could see a stranded ship.* **2** left in a difficult or lonely position • *They were stranded in the desert.*

strange *adjective*
1 unusual or surprising **2** not known or experienced before **strangely** *adverb* in a strange way • *The house was strangely quiet.* **strangeness** *noun*

stranger *noun*
1 a person you do not know **2** a person who is in a place they do not know

strangle *verb*
to strangle someone is to kill them by pressing their throat so they can't breathe

strap *noun*
a flat strip of leather or cloth or plastic for fastening things together or holding them in place

strap *verb* (**strapping, strapped**)
to strap something is to fasten it with a strap or straps

strategy *noun* (**strategies**)
1 a strategy is a plan to achieve or win something **2** strategy is planning a war or military campaign **strategic** *adjective* done as part of a plan to achieve or win something

stratum *noun* (**strata**)
(*say* **strah**-tum)
a layer or level • *You can see several strata of rock in the cliffs.*

straw *noun*
1 straw is dry cut stalks of corn **2** a straw is a narrow tube that you can drink through

strawberry *noun* (**strawberries**)
a small red juicy fruit, with its seeds on the outside

stray *verb*
to stray is to wander or become lost

stray *adjective*
1 wandering around lost • *We found a stray cat.* **2** out of place; separated from all the others • *a stray hair*

stray *noun*
a stray dog or cat

streak *noun*
1 a long thin line or mark **2** a streak of something is a trace or sign of it • *He has a cruel streak.* **streaky** *adjective* marked with streaks

streak *verb*
1 to streak something is to mark it with streaks **2** to streak somewhere is to move there very quickly

stream *noun*
1 a narrow river or brook **2** a flow of liquid **3** a number of things moving in the same direction, such as traffic **4** a group in a school containing children of similar ability

stream *verb*
1 to stream is to move in a strong or fast flow • *Traffic streamed across the junction.* **2** to stream is also to produce a flow of liquid • *Blood was streaming from her cut hand.*

streamer *noun*
a long strip of paper or ribbon

streamers

streamlined *adjective*
a streamlined vehicle or object has a smooth shape that helps it to move easily through air or water

street *noun*
a road with houses beside it in a city or town

strength *noun*
1 strength is how strong a person or thing is **2** a person's strengths are their good points or the things they are good at • *Patience is your greatest strength.*

strengthen *verb*
1 to strengthen something or someone is to make them stronger **2** to strengthen is to become stronger

strenuous *adjective*
needing or using great effort and determination **strenuously** *adverb*

stress *noun*
1 a stress is a force or pressure that pulls or pushes or twists something **2** stress is the effect on someone of too much work or worry or pressure **3** stress is also the extra loudness or emphasis you give to a word or part of a word when you say it

stress *verb*
1 to stress a word or part of a word is to pronounce it with extra emphasis **2** to stress a point or idea is to emphasize it • *I must stress that this is an unusual problem.*

stretch *verb*
1 to stretch something is to pull it so that it becomes longer or wider **2** something stretches when it becomes longer or wider when it is pulled **3** you stretch, or stretch out, when you reach out with your arms or extend your arms and legs fully **4** to stretch somewhere is to extend or continue there • *The wall stretches all the way round the park.*

stretch *noun*
1 the action of stretching something • *I got up and had a good stretch.* **2** a continuous period of time or area of land or water

stretcher *noun*
a framework like a light folding bed with handles at each end, for carrying a sick or injured person

strew *verb* (**strewing, strewed, strewn** or **strewed**)
to strew things is to scatter them over a surface • *Flowers were strewn over the path.*

strict *adjective*
1 demanding that people obey rules and behave well • *The teachers are all fairly strict.* **2** complete or exact • *He's not really a hero in the strict sense of the word.* **strictly** *adverb* completely or exactly • *Taking photographs here is strictly forbidden.*

stride *verb* (**striding, strode, stridden**)
to stride is to walk with long steps

stride *noun*
a long step you take when walking or running

strike *verb* (**striking, struck**)
1 to strike something or someone is to hit them **2** to strike people or a place is to attack them suddenly • *A hurricane struck the village.* **3** to strike a match is to light it by rubbing it against something rough **4** a clock strikes (for example) seven

a b c d e f g h i j k l m n o p q r s t u v w x y z

when it rings seven chimes at seven o'clock **5** workers strike when they stop working as a protest **6** to strike oil or gold is to find it by drilling or mining **7** to strike someone in some way is to make them think that way • *The film struck me as rather violent.*

strike *noun*
1 a hit **2** when workers refuse to work, as a way of making a protest to **go on strike** is to stop working as a protest

striker *noun*
1 a worker who is on strike **2** in football, an attacking player who tries to score goals

striking *adjective*
so impressive, interesting, or attractive that you can't help noticing it

string *noun*
1 string is thin rope or cord for tying things; a string is a piece of thin rope **2** a string is a piece of stretched wire or nylon used in a musical instrument to make sounds **3** a string of things is a line or series of them • *There was a string of buses along the High Street.*

string *verb* (**stringing, strung**)
1 to string something is to hang it on a string **2** to string pearls or beads is to thread them on a string **3** to string a racket or musical instrument is to put strings on it

stringed *adjective*
in music, stringed instruments are ones that have strings, especially members of the violin family

strings *plural noun*
the stringed instruments in an orchestra

stringy *adjective* (**stringier, stringiest**)
1 long and thin like string **2** stringy meat contains tough fibres

strip¹ *verb* (**stripping, stripped**)
1 to strip something is to take a covering off it **2** to strip is to take all your clothes off **3** to strip someone of something is to take it away from them

strip¹ *noun*
the special outfit worn by a sports team

strip² *noun*
a long narrow piece of something

strip cartoon *noun*
a series of drawings telling a story; a comic strip

stripe *noun*
a long narrow band of colour
striped or **stripy** *adjective* having stripes

strive *verb* (**striving, strove, striven**)
to strive to do something is to try hard to do it

strobe *noun*
a light that flickers on and off continuously

stroke¹ *noun*
1 a hit or movement made by swinging your arm **2** a swimming style **3** a line drawn by a pen or brush **4** a sudden illness that often causes someone to be paralysed

stroke² *verb*
to stroke something is to move your hand gently along it

stroll *verb*
to stroll is to walk slowly

stroll *noun*
a short leisurely walk

strong *adjective*
1 having great power, energy, or effect **2** not easily broken or damaged • *The gate was held by a strong chain.* **3** having a lot of flavour or smell • *Do you like your tea strong?*

stronghold *noun*
a fortress or other place that is well defended

strongly *adverb*
1 in a strong way; with strength • *They fought back strongly.* **2** very much • *The room smelt strongly of perfume.*

structure *noun*
1 a structure is something that has been built or put together **2** a thing's structure is the way that it is built or made **structural** *adjective* to do with the way that something is built or made

struggle *verb*
1 to struggle is to move your body about violently while you are fighting or trying to get free **2** to struggle to do something is to make strong efforts to do it

struggle *noun*
1 fighting or trying to get free **2** a great effort

strum *verb* (**strumming, strummed**)
to strum a guitar is to sound it by running your finger across its strings

strut *verb* (**strutting, strutted**)
to strut is to walk proudly or stiffly

strut *noun*
1 a strutting walk **2** a bar of wood or

metal that strengthens a framework

stub *verb* (**stubbing, stubbed**)
you stub your toe when you knock it against something hard

stub *noun*
a short piece of something left after the rest has been used up or worn down

stubble *noun*
1 stubble is the short stalks of corn left in the ground after a harvest **2** stubble is also the short stiff hairs growing on a man's chin when he has not shaved

stubborn *adjective*
not willing to change your ideas or ways; obstinate **stubbornly** *adverb* **stubbornness** *noun*

stuck *adjective*
unable to move or make progress • *Is anyone stuck?*

stuck-up *adjective*
(*informal*) unpleasantly proud or snobbish

stud *noun*
a small metal button or knob fixed into something

student *noun*
someone who studies, especially at a college or university

studio *noun*
1 a place where radio or television broadcasts are made **2** a place where cinema or television films are made **3** the room where an artist or photographer works

studious *adjective*
fond of studying; studying hard **studiously** *adverb*

study *verb* (**studies, studying, studied**)
1 to study is to spend time learning about something **2** to study something is to look at it carefully

study *noun* (**studies**)
1 study is the process of studying **2** a study is a room used for studying or writing

stuff *noun*
1 stuff is a substance or material • *What's this stuff at the bottom of the glass?* **2** stuff is also a group of things or a person's possessions • *Will you move your stuff off the table?*

stuff *verb*
1 to stuff something is to fill it tightly, especially with stuffing • *She stuffed the turkey.* **2** to stuff one thing inside another is to push it in carelessly • *He stuffed the paper into his pocket.*

stuffing *noun*
1 stuffing is material used to fill the inside of something **2** stuffing is also a savoury mixture you put into meat or poultry before cooking it

stuffy *adjective* (**stuffier, stuffiest**)
1 a stuffy room is badly ventilated, without enough fresh air **2** formal and boring **stuffiness** *noun*

stumble *verb*
1 to stumble is to lose your balance or fall over something **2** to stumble when you are speaking is to make mistakes or hesitate to stumble across something or stumble on something is to find it by chance

stump *noun*
1 the bottom of a tree trunk left in the ground when the tree has fallen or been cut down **2** (*in cricket*) each of the three upright sticks of a wicket

stump *verb*
1 (*in cricket*) to stump the person batting is to get them out by touching the stumps with the ball when they are not standing in the correct place **2** something stumps you when it is too difficult for you • *The last question stumped everyone.*

stun *verb* (**stunning, stunned**)
1 to stun someone is to knock them unconscious **2** something stuns you when it shocks or

stumps

confuses you • *They were stunned by the news.*

stunt *noun*
1 something daring or dangerous done in a film or as part of a performance **2** something unusual done to attract publicity or attention

stupendous *adjective*
amazing; tremendous

stupid *adjective*
not sensible; not clever or thoughtful **stupidity** *noun* stupidity is being stupid **stupidly** *adverb*

sturdy *adjective* (**sturdier, sturdiest**)
strong and solid **sturdily** *adverb* **sturdiness** *noun*

stutter *verb*
to stutter is to keep repeating the sounds at the beginning of words
stutter *noun*
a habit of stuttering

sty[1] *noun* (**sties**)
a pigsty
sty[2] or **stye** *noun* (**sties** or **styes**)
a sore swelling on your eyelid

style *noun*
1 a style is the way that something is done, made, said, or written **2** style is being smart and elegant

stylish *adjective*
fashionable and smart **stylishly** *adverb*

subcontinent *noun*
a large area of land that forms part of a continent • *the Indian subcontinent*

subdue *verb*
1 to subdue someone is to overcome them or bring them under control **2** to subdue a person or animal is to make them quieter or gentler

subject *noun* (*say* **sub**-jikt)
1 the person or thing that is being talked or written about **2** something that you can study **3** (*in grammar*) the person or thing that is doing the action stated by the verb in a sentence, for example *dog* in the sentence *The dog chewed a bone.* **4** someone who must obey the laws of a particular ruler or government
subject *verb* (*say* sub-**jekt**)
to subject someone to something is to make them experience or suffer it • *They subjected him to a string of questions.*

submarine *noun*
a type of ship that can travel under water

submerge *verb*
1 to submerge is to go under water **2** to submerge something or someone is to put them under water

submit *verb* (**submitting, submitted**)
1 to submit to someone is to give in to them or agree to obey them **2** to submit something to someone is to hand it in or offer it to be judged or considered **submission** *noun* submission is submitting to someone **submissive** *adjective* willing to obey

subscribe *verb*
to subscribe to something is to pay money to receive it regularly or to be a member of a club or society **subscriber** *noun* someone who subscribes to something

subscription *noun*
money you pay to receive something regularly or to be a member of a club or society

subsequent *adjective*
coming later or after something else • *Subsequent events proved that she was right.* **subsequently** *adverb* later

subside *verb*
1 to subside is to sink • *After a few days the flood water began to subside.* **2** to subside is also to become quiet or normal • *The noise subsided after midnight.* **subsidence** *noun* when a building or piece of land sinks into the ground

subsidy *noun* (**subsidies**)
money paid to keep prices low or to support an industry or activity

subsidize *verb*
to subsidize someone or something is to help pay the cost of something

substance *noun*
something that you can touch or see; what something is made of

substantial *adjective*
1 large or important **2** strong and solid **substantially** *adverb* mostly • *This story is substantially true.*

substitute *verb*
to substitute one thing or person for another is to use the first one instead of the second • *In this recipe you can substitute oil for butter.* **substitution** *noun* when one thing or person is used instead of another
substitute *noun*
a person or thing that is used instead of another

subtle *adjective* (*say* **sut**-el)
1 slight and delicate • *This soup has a subtle flavour.* **2** clever but not obvious • *Your jokes are too subtle for*

a
b
c
d
e
f
g
h
i
j
k
l
m
n
o
p
q
r
s
t
u
v
w
x
y
z

me. **subtly** adverb in a subtle way
subtlety noun subtlety is being subtle or delicate

subtract verb
to subtract one amount from another is to take it away
• If you subtract 2 from 7, you get 5. **subtraction** noun the process of taking one amount from another

suburb noun
an area of houses on the edge of a city or large town **suburban** noun a suburban area or street is in a suburb

subway noun
an underground passage for pedestrians

succeed verb
1 to succeed is to do or get what you wanted or intended 2 to succeed someone is to be the next person to do what they did, especially to be king or queen

success noun
1 success is doing or getting what you wanted or intended 2 a success is a person or thing that does well
• The plan was a great success.

successful adjective
having success; doing well
successfully adverb

succession noun
1 a number of people or things coming one after another
• The cooks brought in a succession of dishes. 2 the right to be the next person to do something, especially becoming king or queen

successor noun
someone who has a position or does a job after someone else • The headteacher retired and handed over to her successor.

such adjective
1 of that kind; of the same kind
• Try not to think about such things. 2 so great or so much • That was such fun!

suck verb
1 to suck liquid or air is to take it in through your mouth • I sucked milk through a straw. 2 to suck something is to move it around inside your mouth so that you can taste it • She was sucking a sweet. 3 to suck something is also to draw it in or absorb it • The boat was sucked into the whirlpool. • He sucked in his cheeks.

suck noun
the action of sucking

suction noun
suction is the process of drawing in

liquid or air by creating a vacuum
• Vacuum cleaners work by suction.

sudden adjective
happening or done quickly and unexpectedly **suddenness** noun

suddenly adverb
quickly and unexpectedly

suds plural noun
froth on soapy water

sue verb
to sue someone is to start a claim in a lawcourt to get money from them

suede noun (say swayd)
suede is leather with one side soft and velvety

suffer verb
1 to suffer is to feel pain or misery 2 to suffer something unpleasant is to have to put up with it

suffering noun
suffering is pain or misery

sufficient adjective
enough • Have we sufficient food?
sufficiently adverb to a sufficient degree

suffix noun
a word or syllable joined to the end of a word to change or add to its meaning, as in forget*ful*, lion*ess*, and rust*y*

suffocate verb
1 to suffocate is to suffer or die because you cannot breathe 2 to suffocate someone is to kill them by stopping them breathing
suffocation noun suffocation is when someone dies because they cannot breathe

sugar noun
sugar is a sweet food obtained from the juices of various plants, such as sugar beet or sugar cane **sugary** adjective full of sugar; sweet

suggest verb
1 to suggest something is to mention it as an idea or possibility 2 to suggest something is also to give an idea or impression of something • Your smile suggests that you agree with me.

suggestion noun
something that you mention to someone as an idea or possibility

suicide noun
suicide is killing yourself deliberately • He committed suicide.
suicidal adjective wanting to commit suicide

suit noun
1 a matching set of jacket and trousers or jacket and skirt, that

are meant to be worn together 2 a set of clothing for a particular activity • He wore a diving suit. 3 each of the four sets in a pack of playing cards: spades, hearts, diamonds, and clubs

suit verb
1 to suit someone or something is to be suitable or convenient for them
• What time would suit you? 2 a piece of clothing or hairstyle suits you when it looks good on you

suitable adjective
satisfactory or right for a particular person, purpose, or occasion
suitability noun how suitable something is **suitably** adverb

suitcase noun
a container with a lid and a handle, for carrying your clothes and other things when you are travelling

suite noun (say sweet)
1 a set of rooms in a hotel 2 a set of matching furniture

suitor noun
a man who wants to marry a particular woman

sulk verb
to sulk is to be silent and bad-tempered because you are not pleased

sulky adjective (**sulkier, sulkiest**)
sulking or moody **sulkily** adverb
sulkiness noun

sullen adjective
silent and moody
sullenly adverb
sullenness noun

sulphur noun
sulphur is a yellow chemical used in industry and medicine

sultan noun
the ruler of certain Muslim countries

sultana noun
a raisin without seeds

sum noun
1 a total, or the amount you get when you add numbers together 2 a problem in arithmetic 3 an amount of money

sum verb (**summing, summed**)
to sum up is to give a summary at the end of a discussion or talk

summarize verb
to summarize something is to give a short statement of its main points

summary noun (**summaries**)
a short statement of the main points of something that someone has said or written

summer noun
the warm season between spring

and autumn **summery**
adjective like summer,
or suitable for summer

summertime *noun*
summertime is the
season of summer

summit *noun*
1 the top of a mountain or hill
2 a meeting between the leaders of
powerful countries

summon *verb*
to summon someone is to order
them to come or appear

sun *noun*
1 the star round which the earth
travels, and from which it gets
warmth and light 2 warmth and light
from the sun • *Shall we sit in the sun?*

sun *verb* (**sunning, sunned**)
to sun yourself is to warm yourself
in the sun

sunbathe *verb*
to sunbathe is to sit or lie in the sun
to get a suntan

sunburn *noun*
sunburn is the redness of the skin
someone gets if they are in the sun for
too long **sunburned** or **sunburnt**
adjective affected by sunburn

sundae *noun* (*say* **sun**-day)
a mixture of ice cream with fruit,
nuts, and cream

Sunday *noun*
the first day of the week

sundial *noun*
a device that shows
the time by a
shadow made
by the sun

sunflower *noun*
a tall flower
with a large
round yellow
head

sunglasses
plural noun
dark glasses you
wear to protect your
eyes from strong sunlight   sunflowers

sunlight *noun*
sunlight is light from the sun **sunlit**
adjective
lit by sunlight

sunny *adjective* (**sunnier,
sunniest**)
1 having a lot of sunshine
• *It's a sunny day.* 2 full of sunshine
• *What a sunny room.*

sunrise *noun*
sunrise is the time when the sun first
appears; dawn • *They left at sunrise.*

sunset *noun*
sunset is the time
when the sun sets

sunshade *noun*
a parasol or other device to protect
people from the sun

sunshine *noun*
sunshine is warmth and light that
come from the sun

sunstroke *noun*
sunstroke is an illness caused by
being in the sun for too long

suntan *noun*
a brown colour of the skin caused
by the sun **suntanned** *adjective*
having a suntan

super *adjective*
(*informal*) excellent or very good

superb *adjective*
magnificent or excellent **superbly**
adverb

superficial *adjective*
1 on the surface • *It's only a
superficial cut.* 2 not deep or
thorough • *His knowledge of French
is fairly superficial.* **superficially**
adverb

superintendent *noun*
1 someone who is in charge
2 a police officer above the
rank of inspector

superior *adjective*
1 higher or more important than
someone else 2 better than another
person or thing 3 showing that you
think you are better than other
people **superiority** *noun* being
better than something else;
behaviour that shows you
think you are better than
other people

superior *noun*
someone of higher rank
or position than another
person

supermarket *noun*
a large self-service shop
that sells food and other
goods

supernatural *adjective*
not belonging to the natural world
or having a natural explanation

supersonic *adjective*
faster than the speed of sound

superstition *noun*
a belief or action that is not based
on reason or evidence
• *It is a superstition that 13 is
an unlucky number.* **superstitious**
adjective believing in superstitions

supervise *verb*
to supervise someone or something
is to be in charge

of them **supervision** *noun*
being in charge of someone
or something **supervisor**
noun someone who supervises you

supper *noun*
a meal or snack that you eat
in the evening

supple *adjective*
able to bend easily; flexible,
not stiff **suppleness** *noun*
suppleness is being supple

supplement *noun*
1 something added as an extra
2 an extra section added to a book
or newspaper **supplementary**
adjective added as an extra

supply *verb*
1 to supply something is to
give or sell it to people who need it
2 to supply someone is to give them
what they need **supplier** *noun*
someone who supplies something

supply *noun*
1 a supply of something is an
amount of it kept ready to be used
when needed • *We keep a supply of
paper in the cupboard.* 2 supplies
are food, medicines, or equipment
needed by an army or an expedition
• *The truck was carrying medical
supplies.*

support *verb*
1 to support something is to hold
it so that it does not fall down 2 to
support someone or something is to
give them help or encouragement
3 to support a sports team is to like
them and want them to do well
• *Which football team do you
support?*

support *noun*
1 support is help or encouragement
• *You can rely on my support.*
2 something that holds another
thing up

supporter *noun*
someone who gives support,
especially to a sports team

suppose *verb*
to suppose something is to think
that it is likely or true to be
supposed to do something is to
have to do it as an order or duty

suppress *verb*
to suppress something is to keep
it hidden or stop it happening • *He
managed to suppress a smile.*
suppression *noun* suppression is
suppressing something

supreme *adjective*
highest or greatest; most important
supremacy *noun* having more

h
i
j
k
l
m
n
o
p
q
r
s
t
u
v
w
x
y
z

power or a higher position than anyone else

supremely *adverb* extremely

sure *adjective*
1 confident about something; having no doubts • *Are you sure you locked the door?* **2** very likely to happen or do something • *Don't worry, we're sure to win.* **3** completely true or known • *One thing is sure: she is not here at the moment.* **4** reliable • *Visiting places is a sure way of getting to know them.* **to make sure of something** is to find out that it is true or right

sure *adverb*
(*informal*) certainly; of course • *Sure I'll come with you.*

surely *adverb*
1 certainly or definitely
2 it must be true; I feel sure • *Surely I met you last year.*

surf *noun*
surf is the white foam of waves breaking on rocks or the seashore

surf *verb*
1 to surf is to go surfing
2 to surf the Internet is to browse through it

surface *noun*
1 the outside of something **2** each of the sides of something, especially the top part

surface *verb*
1 to surface is to come up to the surface from under water • *The submarine slowly surfaced.* **2** to surface a road or path is to give it a hard covering layer

surfboard *noun*
a board used in surfing

surfing *noun*
surfing is the sport of balancing yourself on a board that is carried towards the seashore by the waves **surfer** *noun* someone who goes surfing

surge *verb*
to surge is to move forwards or upwards like waves

surge *noun*
a sudden rush forward or upward

surgeon *noun*
a doctor who deals with disease or injury by cutting or repairing the affected parts of the body

surgery *noun* (**surgeries**)
1 a surgery is a building or room where a doctor or dentist sees patients
2 surgery is the time when patients can see a doctor or dentist • *Surgery will close at 6 o'clock today.*
3 surgery is also the work of a surgeon

surgical *adjective*
to do with a surgeon or surgery **surgically** *adverb* by means of surgery

surname *noun*
your last name, which you share with other members of your family

surpass *verb*
to surpass someone is to do better or be better than them

surplus *noun*
an amount left over after you have spent or used what you need

surprise *noun*
1 a surprise is something that you did not expect **2** surprise is the feeling you have when something unexpected happens

surprise *verb*
1 to surprise someone is to be a surprise to them **2** to surprise someone is also to catch or attack them unexpectedly

surrender *verb*
1 to surrender to someone is to stop fighting them and admit that you have been beaten **2** to surrender something to someone is to hand it over to them

surrender *noun*
when someone surrenders

surround *verb*
to surround someone or something is to be or come all round them

surroundings *plural noun*
the things or conditions around a person or place

survey *noun* (say ser-vay)
1 a general look at a topic or activity **2** a detailed inspection or examination of a building or area

survey *verb* (say ser-**vay**)
to survey something is to inspect it or make a survey of it

surveyor *noun*
someone whose job is to survey buildings and land

survive *verb*
1 to survive is to stay alive **2** to survive an accident or disaster is to remain alive in spite of it • *Only two people survived the car crash.* **3** to survive someone is to continue living after they have died **survival** *noun* survival is staying alive **survivor** *noun* someone who survives, especially after an accident or disaster

suspect *verb* (say su-**spekt**)
1 to suspect something unwelcome is to think that it is likely or possible
2 to suspect someone is to think that they have done something wrong or are not to be trusted

suspect *noun* (say **sus**-pekt)
someone who is thought to have done something wrong

suspend *verb*
1 to suspend something that is happening is to stop it for a time
2 to suspend someone is to take away their job or position for a time • *He was suspended from the team for bad behaviour.* **3** to suspend something is to hang it up

suspense *noun*
suspense is an anxious or uncertain feeling you have while you are waiting for something to happen or for news about something • *Don't keep us in suspense – who won?*

suspension *noun*
1 suspension is suspending something or someone **2** a vehicle's suspension is the set of springs and other devices that make the ride more comfortable

suspension bridge *noun*
a bridge supported by cables

suspicion *noun*
1 suspicion is feeling that someone has done something wrong or cannot be trusted **2** a suspicion is a slight or uncertain feeling about something or someone

suspicious *adjective*
1 making you suspect someone or something • *There are suspicious footprints along the path.*
2 suspecting someone or something • *I'm suspicious about what happened.* **suspiciously** *adverb*

sustain *verb*
1 to sustain something is to keep it going • *It's difficult to sustain such an effort.* **2** to sustain someone is to

give them energy or strength • *We'd packed sandwiches to sustain us on our walk.*

swagger *verb*
to walk or behave in a conceited way

swallow[1] *verb*
to swallow something is to make it go down your throat to swallow something up is to cover it or make it disappear • *He was soon swallowed up by the darkness.*

swallow[2] *noun*
a small bird with a forked tail and pointed wings

swamp *verb*
1 to swamp something is to flood it **2** to be swamped is to be overwhelmed with a large number of things • *They have been swamped with complaints.*

swamp *noun*
a marsh **swampy** *adjective* full of swamps

swan *noun*
a large white water bird with a long neck and powerful wings

swap *verb* (**swapping, swapped**)
(*informal*) to swap something is to exchange one thing for another • *After the game they swapped jerseys.*

swap *noun*
1 an act of swapping • *Let's do a swap.*
2 something you swap for something else

swarm *noun*
a large number of bees or other insects flying or moving about together

swarm *verb*
1 bees or other insects swarm when they move in a swarm
2 to be swarming is to be crowded with people • *The town is swarming with tourists in summer.*

swarm

swat *verb* (**swatting, swatted**)
(*say* swot)
to swat a fly or other insect is to hit or crush it **swatter** *noun* a device for swatting flies

sway *verb*
to sway is to move gently from side to side

swear *verb* (**swearing, swore, sworn**)
1 to swear is to make a solemn promise • *She swore to tell the truth.*
2 to swear someone to secrecy is to make them promise not to tell anyone **3** to swear is also to use very rude or offensive words

swear word *noun*
a word that is very rude or offensive, used especially by someone who is very angry

sweat *verb* (*say* swet)
you sweat when you give off moisture through the pores of your skin, especially when you are hot or doing exercise

sweat *noun* (*say* swet)
sweat is moisture that comes out of your skin when you sweat **sweaty** *adjective* covered or damp with sweat

sweater *noun* (*say* swet-er)
a jumper or pullover

sweatshirt *noun*
a thick cotton jersey

swede *noun*
a large kind of turnip with purple skin and yellow flesh

sweep *verb* (**sweeping, swept**)
1 to sweep a room or floor is to clean or clear it with a broom or brush • *He swept the floor.* **2** to sweep something away is to move or change it quickly • *The flood has swept away the bridge.* **3** to sweep somewhere is to go there swiftly or grandly • *She swept out of the room.* **sweeper** *noun* a machine for sweeping floors

sweep *noun*
1 a sweeping action or movement • *Give this room a sweep.* **2** someone who cleans out a chimney

sweet *adjective*
1 tasting of sugar or honey
2 very pleasant • *There was a sweet smell in the room.*
3 charming or delightful • *What a sweet little cottage.* **sweetly** *adverb* in a very pleasant way • *She smiled sweetly at him.* **sweetness** *noun* sweetness is tasting sweet

sweet *noun*
1 a small piece of sweet food made from sugar or chocolate **2** a pudding; the sweet course in a meal

sweetcorn *noun*
sweetcorn is the juicy yellow seeds of maize

sweeten *verb*
to sweeten something is to make it

sweet **sweetener** *noun* something used instead of sugar to make food or drink taste sweeter

sweetheart *noun*
a person you love very much

swell *verb* (**swelling, swelled, swollen** or **swelled**)
to swell is to get bigger or louder **swollen** *adjective* having swelled a lot • *My wrist is still very swollen where I bumped it.*

swell *noun*
the rise and fall of the sea's surface

swelling *noun*
a swollen place on your body

swelter *verb*
to swelter is to be uncomfortably hot

swerve *verb*
to swerve is to move suddenly to one side • *The car swerved to avoid the cyclist.*

swerve *noun*
a swerving movement

swift *adjective*
quick; moving quickly and easily **swiftly** *adverb* quickly **swiftness** *noun*

swift *noun*
a small bird rather like a swallow

swill *verb*
to swill something is to rinse or flush it

swill *noun*
swill is a sloppy mixture of waste food given to pigs

swim *verb* (**swimming, swam, swum**)
1 to swim is to move yourself through the water or to be in the water for pleasure
2 to swim a stretch of water is to cross it by swimming • *She has swum the Channel.* **3** to be swimming in liquid or with liquid is to be covered in it or full of it • *Their eyes were swimming with tears.*
4 your head swims when you feel dizzy

swim *noun*
a spell of swimming • *Let's go for a swim.*

swimmer *noun*
someone who swims • *Are you a good swimmer?*

swimming bath or **swimming pool** *noun*
a specially built pool with water for people to swim in

swimming costume *noun*
a piece of clothing for swimming in

swimsuit *noun*
a one-piece swimming costume

swindle *verb*
to swindle someone is to get money or goods from them dishonestly
swindler *noun* someone who swindles people
swindle *noun*
a trick to swindle someone

swine *noun* (**swine** or **swines**)
a pig

swing *verb* (**swinging, swung**)
1 to swing is to move to and fro or in a curve 2 to swing something is to turn it quickly or suddenly • *He swung the car round to avoid the bus.*
swing *noun*
1 a swinging movement
• *He took a swing at the ball.*
2 a seat hung on chains or ropes so that it can move backwards and forwards to be in full swing is to be full of activity or working fully

swipe *verb*
1 to swipe someone or something is to give them a hard hit 2 (*informal*) to swipe something is to steal it
3 to swipe a credit card is to pass it through a special reading device when you make a payment
swipe *noun*
a hard hit

swirl *verb*
to swirl is to move around quickly in circles; to swirl something is to make it do this • *The water swirled down the plug hole.*
swirl *noun*
a swirling movement

swish *verb*
to swish is to make a hissing or rustling sound
swish *noun*
a swishing sound

switch *noun*
1 a device that you press or turn to start or stop something working, especially by electricity 2 a sudden change of opinion or methods
switch *verb*
1 to switch a device on or off is to use a switch to make it work or stop working • *Shall I switch the light on?*
2 to switch something is to change it suddenly

switchboard *noun*
a place in a large building or organization where telephone calls are connected

swivel *verb* (**swivelling, swivelled**)
to swivel is to turn round

swoop *verb*
1 to swoop is to dive or come down suddenly • *The eagle swooped down on its prey.*

2 to swoop is also to make a sudden attack or raid
swoop *noun*
a sudden dive or attack

swop *verb* (**swopping, swopped**)
(*informal*) to swap

sword *noun* (*say* sord)
a weapon with a long pointed blade fixed in a handle

swot *verb*
(*informal*) to swot is to study hard
swot *noun*
(*informal*) someone who swots

sycamore *noun*
a tall tree with winged seeds

syllable *noun*
a word or part of a word that has one separate sound when you say it
• *'Cat' has one syllable, 'el-e-phant' has three syllables.*

syllabus *noun* (*say* sil-a-bus)
a list of things to be studied by a class or for an examination

symbol *noun*
1 a mark or sign with a special meaning 2 a thing that stands for something • *The crescent is a symbol of Islam.*

symbolic *adjective*
acting as a symbol of something
symbolically *adverb*
symmetrical *adjective*
(*say* sim-et-rik-al)
having two halves which are exactly the same but the opposite way round • *Wheels and butterflies are symmetrical.* **symmetrically** *adverb* in a symmetrical way
symmetry *noun* symmetry is the quality of being symmetrical

sympathetic *adjective*
feeling sympathy or understanding for someone **sympathetically** *adverb* in a way that shows you feel sympathy for someone • *She smiled at me sympathetically.*

sympathize *verb*
to sympathize with someone is to show or feel sympathy for them

sympathy *noun* (**sympathies**)
1 sympathy is the sharing or understanding of other people's feelings or opinions 2 sympathy is also the feeling of being sorry for someone's unhappiness or suffering

symphony *noun* (**symphonies**)
a long piece of music for an orchestra **symphonic** *adjective* to do with a symphony

symptom *noun*
something wrong with you that is a

sign that you have an illness • *Red spots are a symptom of measles.*

synagogue *noun* (*say* sin-a-gog)
a building where Jewish people meet to worship

WORD ORIGIN

The word **synagogue** comes from a Greek word *synagoge* meaning 'assembly'.

synonym *noun* (*say* sin-o-nim)
a word that means the same or nearly the same as another word, such as *big* and *large* **synonymous** *adjective* two words are synonymous when they have the same, or nearly the same, meaning

synthesizer *noun*
an electronic musical instrument that can make many different sounds

synthetic *adjective*
artificially made; not natural
synthetically *adverb*

syringe *noun*
a device with a tube and a long needle, used for sucking in liquid and giving injections

syrup *noun*
a thick sweet liquid
syrupy *adjective* thick and sticky like syrup

system *noun*
1 a set of parts or things or ideas that work together • *the digestive system* • *the Solar System* 2 a well-organized way of doing something • *We have a new system for taking books out of the library.*

systematic *adjective*
using a system; careful and well planned **systematically** *adverb*

tab *noun*
a small strip or flap that sticks out

tabby *noun* (**tabbies**)
a grey or brown cat with dark streaks in its fur

table *noun*
1 a piece of furniture with a flat top supported on legs
2 a list of facts or numbers arranged in rows and columns

tablecloth *noun*
a cloth for covering a table

tablespoon *noun*
a large spoon used for serving food

tablet *noun*
1 a pill 2 a flat piece of stone or wood with words carved or written on it 3 a small flat computer that you use by touching the screen

table tennis *noun*
table tennis is a game played on a table divided in the middle by a net, over which you hit a small ball with bats

tack *noun*
a short nail with a flat top **to change tack** or **to try a different tack** is to find a different way of doing something

tack *verb*
1 to tack something is to nail it with tacks 2 to tack material is to sew it together quickly with long stitches 3 to tack is to sail a zigzag course to get full benefit from the wind

tackle *verb*
1 to tackle a task is to start doing it 2 in football or hockey, to tackle a player is to try to get the ball from them or (in rugby) to bring them to the ground

tackle *noun*
1 tackle is equipment, especially for fishing 2 a tackle is when you tackle someone in football or rugby or hockey

tacky *adjective* (**tackier, tackiest**)
sticky or not quite dry • *The paint is still tacky.*

tact *noun*
tact is skill in not offending or upsetting people

tactful *adjective*
careful not to offend or upset people by saying something unkind **tactfully** *adverb* in a way that avoids offending or upsetting someone

tactics *plural noun*
someone's tactics are the methods they use to achieve or win something **tactical** *adjective* done to help you achieve or win something

tactless *adjective*
likely to offend or upset people by saying the wrong thing; having no tact **tactlessly** *adverb* in a way that offends or upsets someone

tadpole *noun*
a young frog or toad at a stage when it has an oval head and a long tail and lives in water

tag¹ *noun*
a label tied or stuck to something
tag¹ *verb* (**tagging, tagged**)
to tag something is to fix a tag or

label on it **to tag along** is to go along with other people
tag² *noun* tag is a game in which one person chases the others

tail *noun*
1 the part that sticks out from the rear end of the body of an animal or bird 2 the part at the end or rear of something, such as an aircraft 3 the side of a coin opposite the head **tailless** *adjective* not having a tail

tail *verb*
to tail someone is to follow them without them seeing you **to tail off** is to become less and less or smaller and smaller

tailback *noun*
a long line of traffic stretching back from an obstruction

tailor *noun*
someone whose job is to make clothes

take *verb* (**taking, took, taken**)
This word has many meanings, depending on the words that go with it: 1 to take something or someone is to get hold of them or bring them into your possession • *He took a cake from the plate.* • *Who do you think took the money?* • *They took many prisoners.* 2 to take someone or something somewhere is to carry or drive them there • *Shall I take you to the station?* • *Take this parcel to the post.* 3 to take something useful or pleasant is to make use of it • *Do you take sugar?* • *You must take a holiday this year.* • *Do take a seat.* 4 to take someone or something is to need them for a purpose • *It will take two people to lift the table.* 5 to take a piece of information is to make a note of it • *Take their names and addresses.* 6 to take a class for a subject is to teach it to them • *Who takes you for English?* 7 to take one number from another is to subtract it • *Take two from ten and you get eight.* 8 to take an exam or test is to do it • *I'm taking my maths exam today.* 9 to take a joke is to accept it well 10 to take a photograph or picture is to produce it with a camera **to take off** is to leave the ground at the beginning of a flight **to take part in something** is to share in doing it **to take place** is to happen **to take someone in** is to fool or deceive them **to take something off** is to remove it **to take something over** is to take control of it **to take something up** is to start doing it • *I've taken up yoga.*

takeaway *noun*
1 a place that sells cooked food for

customers to take away 2 a meal from a takeaway

takings *plural noun*
money that has been received by a shop

talcum powder or **talc** *noun*
talcum powder is a perfumed powder you put on your skin to dry it or make it smell pleasant

tale *noun*
a story

talent *noun*
a natural ability or skill to do something well • *She has a talent for singing.*
talented *adjective* good at doing something

talk *verb*
to talk is to speak or have a conversation **talker** *noun* someone who talks, especially someone who talks a lot

talk *noun*
1 a conversation or discussion 2 a lecture

talkative *adjective*
someone is talkative when they talk a lot

tall *adjective*
1 higher than the average • *They sat under a tall tree.*
2 measured from the bottom to the top • *The bookcase is two metres tall.*
a tall story is a story that is hard to believe

Talmud *noun*
a collection of writings on Jewish religious law

talon *noun*
a strong claw, especially on a bird of prey

tambourine *noun*
a round musical instrument like a small drum with metal discs fixed around the edge so that it jingles when you shake it or hit it

tambourine

tame *adjective*
1 a tame animal is one that is gentle and not afraid of people
2 something is tame when it is dull or uninteresting **tamely** *adverb* **tameness** *noun*
tame *verb*
to tame a wild animal is to make it used to being with people **tamer** *noun* someone who tames wild animals • *a lion-tamer*

tamper *verb*
to tamper with something is to interfere with it or change it so that it will not work properly

tan *noun*
1 a tan is a suntan 2 tan is a yellowish-brown colour
tan *verb* (**tanning, tanned**)
1 to tan your skin is to make it brown with a suntan 2 to tan the skin of a dead animal is to make it into leather

tandem *noun*
a bicycle for two riders, one behind the other

tang *noun*
a strong flavour or smell

tangent *noun* (*say* **tan**-jent)
a straight line that touches the outside of a curve or circle

tangerine *noun* (*say* tan-jer-**een**)
a kind of small orange

tangerine

WORD ORIGIN

The word **tangerine** is named after Tangier in Morocco, where the fruit originally came from.

tangle *verb*
1 you tangle something, or it tangles, when it becomes twisted or muddled • *My fishing line has tangled.* 2 something is tangled up when it is twisted together in an untidy mess • *These computer cables are all tangled up.*
tangle *noun*
a twisted or muddled mass of (for example) hair or wire

tank *noun*
1 a large container for a liquid or gas 2 a large heavy vehicle with guns, used in war

tankard *noun*
a large heavy mug for drinking from

tanker *noun*
1 a large ship for carrying oil 2 a large lorry for carrying a liquid

tantalize *verb*
to tantalize someone is to torment them by showing them something good that they cannot have

tantrum *noun*
an outburst of bad temper

tap[1] *noun* (**taps**)
a device for letting out liquid or gas in a controlled flow
tap[1] *verb* (**tapping, tapped**)
to tap a telephone is to fix a device to it so that you can hear someone else's conversation

tap[2] *noun*
1 a tap is a quick light hit, or the sound it makes • *I gave him a tap on the shoulder.* 2 tap is tap-dancing
tap[2] *verb* (**tapping, tapped**)
to tap someone or something is to give them a tap or gentle hit • *I tried tapping on the window.*

tap dancing *noun*
tap dancing is dancing in hard shoes that make sharp tapping sounds on the floor **tap dance** *noun* a dance of this kind
tap dancer *noun* someone who does tap-dancing

tape *noun*
1 tape is soft material such as cloth or paper or plastic in a thin strip; a tape is a piece of this 2 tape is also a narrow plastic strip coated with a magnetic substance and used for making recordings
tape *verb*
1 to tape something is to fasten it by sticking it or tying it with tape 2 to tape music or sound or a television programme is to record it on magnetic tape

tape measure *noun*
a long strip marked in centimetres or inches for measuring things

taper *verb*
something tapers when it gets narrower towards one end

tape recorder *noun*
a machine for recording music or sound on magnetic tape and playing it back **tape recording** *noun* a recording made with magnetic tape

tapestry *noun*
(**tapestries**) (*say* **tap**-i-stree)
a piece of strong cloth with pictures or patterns woven or embroidered on it

tapestry

tar *noun*
tar is a thick black sticky liquid made from coal or wood and used in making roads
tar *verb* (**tarring, tarred**)
to tar something is to cover it with tar

tarantula

tarantula *noun*
(*say* ta-ran-tew-la)
a large hairy poisonous spider found in warm countries

target *noun*
something that you aim at and try to hit or reach

tarmac *noun*
tarmac is a mixture of tar and broken stone, used for making a hard surface on roads and paths and open areas

tarnish *verb*
1 metal tarnishes when it becomes stained and less shiny 2 to tarnish something is to spoil it • *The scandal tarnished his reputation.*

tarpaulin *noun*
a large sheet of waterproof canvas

tart[1] *noun*
a pie containing fruit or jam
tart[2] *adjective* (**tarter, tartest**)
sour-tasting • *The apples are tart.*

tartan *noun*
a Scottish woollen cloth with a pattern of squares and stripes in different colours

task *noun*
a piece of work that needs to be done

tassel *noun*
a bundle of threads tied together at the top and used to decorate something

taste *verb*
1 to taste food or drink is to eat or drink a small amount to see what it is like **2** food or drink tastes a certain way when it has a particular flavour • *The milk tastes sour.*

taste *noun*
1 the taste of something is the flavour it has when you taste it • *The milk has a strange taste.* **2** taste is the ability to taste things **3** your tastes are the things you like or prefer • *What are your tastes in music?* **4** you show taste when you are able to choose things that are of good quality or go together well • *The way she dresses shows good taste.* **5** a taste is a tiny amount of food • *Can I have a taste of your pudding?*

tasteful *adjective*
showing good taste **tastefully** *adverb*

tasteless *adjective*
showing poor taste **tastelessly** *adverb*

tasty *adjective* (**tastier, tastiest**)
tasty food has a strong pleasant taste

tattered *adjective*
tattered clothing is badly torn and ragged

tatters *plural noun*
in tatters badly torn

tattoo¹ *noun*
a picture or pattern made on someone's skin with a needle and dye

tattoo¹ *verb* (**tattooing, tattooed**)
someone is tattooed when they have a tattoo on their skin

tattoo² *noun*
an outdoor entertainment including military music and marching

tatty *adjective* (**tattier, tattiest**)
shabby and worn

taunt *verb*
to taunt someone is to jeer at them or insult them

taunt *noun*
an insulting or mocking remark

taut *adjective*
stretched tightly **tautly** *adverb* **tautness** *noun*

tavern *noun*
(*old use*) an inn or pub

tax *noun* (**taxes**)
an amount of money that people and businesses have to pay to the government to pay for things like hospitals and schools

tax *verb*
1 to tax someone is to charge them a tax **2** to tax goods or someone's income is to put a tax on them • *The government taxes alcohol, tobacco, and petrol.* **taxation** *noun* money that has to be paid as taxes

taxi *noun*
a car with a driver which you can hire for journeys

taxi *verb*
an aircraft taxis when it moves slowly along the ground before taking off or after landing

tea *noun*
1 tea is a drink made by pouring hot water on the dried leaves of a shrub grown in Asia **2** tea is also the dried leaves of this shrub **3** tea is also a meal eaten in the late afternoon or early evening

tea

teabag *noun*
a small bag of tea for making tea in a cup

teach *verb* (**teaching, taught**)
1 to teach someone is to show them how to do something or give them knowledge about something **2** to teach a subject is to give lessons in it • *She taught us history last year.*

teacher *noun*
someone who teaches people at a school or college

tea cloth or **tea towel** *noun*
a cloth you use for drying washed dishes and cutlery

teak *noun*
teak is a hard strong wood from Asia

team *noun*
1 a set of players who form one side in a game or sport **2** a group of people who work together

teapot *noun*
a pot with a handle and spout, for making and pouring out tea

tear¹ *verb* (**tearing, tore, torn**)
(*say* tair)
1 to tear something is to make a split in it or to pull it apart **2** to tear something is also to pull or remove it with force • *He tore the picture off the wall.* **3** to tear is to become torn • *Paper tears easily.* **4** to tear somewhere is to move very quickly there • *He tore down the street.*

tear¹ *noun* (*say* tair)
a hole or split made by tearing something

tear² *noun* (*say* teer)
a drop of water that comes from your eye when you cry

tearful *adjective*
in tears; crying easily • *He suddenly became very tearful.* **tearfully** *adverb*

tease *verb*
to tease someone is to make fun of them and say things to make them annoyed

teaspoon *noun*
a small spoon for stirring drinks

teat *noun*
1 a nipple through which a baby drinks milk **2** the cap of a baby's feeding bottle

technical *adjective*
1 to do with technology or the way things work **2** using the words that only people who know a lot about a subject will understand • *This article is full of technical terms.* **technically** *adverb*

technician *noun*
someone whose job is to look after scientific equipment and do practical work in a laboratory

technique *noun* (*say* tek-**neek**)
a particular method of doing something skilfully

technology *noun* (**technologies**)
technology is using science and machines to help you make things and do things **technological** *adjective* to do with technology • *technological developments*

teddy bear *noun*
a soft furry toy bear, **Teddy** is a shortened form of the name *Theodore* and comes from the name of Theodore Roosevelt, who was the American president at the end of the 19th century and was a keen hunter of bears.

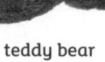
teddy bear

a
b
c
d
e
f
g
h
i
j
k
l
m
n
o
p
q
r
s
t
z

tedious adjective (say tee-di-us)
annoyingly slow or long; boring
tediously adverb **tediousness**
noun

tedium noun
tedium is a dull or boring time or
experience • He hated the tedium of
visiting his grandparents.

teem verb
1 to teem with something is to be
full of it • The river was teeming with
fish. **2** to teem, or teem down, is to
rain very hard

teenage or **teenaged** adjective in
your teens; to do with teenagers

teenager noun
a person in their teens

teens plural noun the time of your
life between the ages of 13 and 19
• They started playing chess in their
teens.

teetotal adjective
never drinking alcoholic drink
teetotaller noun someone who is
teetotal

telecommunications
plural noun
telecommunications is sending
news and information over long
distances by telephone, television,
radio, or the Internet

telegram noun
a message sent by telegraph

telegraph noun
is a way of sending messages by
using electric current along wires or
by radio

telepathy noun
(say til-ep-a-thee)
telepathy is understanding another
person's thoughts without them
speaking, writing, or making
gestures **telepathic**
adjective
able to know what
someone else is thinking

telephone noun
a device using electric wires
or radio to enable someone
to speak to another person who
is some distance away

telephone verb   telescope
to telephone
someone is to speak
to them by telephone

telescope noun
a tube with lenses at each
end, through which you can
see distant objects more
clearly because they
look closer and
larger

telescopic adjective
1 to do with telescopes **2** folding
into itself like a portable telescope
• a telescopic umbrella

teletext noun
teletext is a system for displaying
news and information on a
television screen

televise verb
to televise an event is to film it and
put it on television

television noun
1 television is a system using radio
waves to reproduce pictures on a
screen **2** a television, or a television
set, is a device for receiving these
pictures

tell verb (**telling, told**)
1 to tell something to someone
is to give them information by
speaking to them **2** to tell
someone to do something is to give
them instructions to do it
3 to tell is to reveal a secret
• Promise you won't tell. **4** to tell
something is to recognize it
• Can you tell the difference between
butter and margarine? to tell
someone off is to tell them severely
that they have done wrong to tell
tales is to report someone else's
bad behaviour

temper noun
1 a person's mood • He is in a good
temper. **2** an angry mood • She was
in a temper. to lose your temper is
to become very angry

temperature noun
1 the temperature of something
is how hot or cold it is **2** an
unusually high body temperature
• She's feverish and has a
temperature.

tempest noun
(old use) a violent storm

temple[1] noun
a building where a god is
worshipped

temple[2] noun
the part of your head
between your forehead
and your ear

tempo noun (**tempos**)
the tempo of a
piece of music is its
speed or rhythm

temporary adjective
only lasting or used for a
short time • They were using
a temporary classroom.
temporarily adverb
for a short time only

tempt verb
to tempt someone is to try to

make them do something, especially
something they ought not to do
temptation noun when someone
is being tempted **tempting**
adjective hard to resist

ten noun
the number 10

tenant noun
someone who rents a house or
building or a piece of land from
a landlord **tenancy** noun when
someone rents a house or building or
a piece of land

tend[1] verb
something tends to happen when it
is likely to happen or is what usually
happens • Prices tend to rise.

tend[2] verb
to tend something or someone is
to look after them • She tended her
little garden with care.

tendency noun
the way a person or thing is likely
to behave • She has a tendency to
be lazy.

tender adjective
1 not tough or hard; easy to chew
2 delicate or sensitive • These are
more tender plants. **3** gentle or
loving • She gave a tender smile.
tenderly adverb gently or lovingly
tenderness noun

tendon noun
a piece of strong tissue in the body
that joins a muscle to a bone

tennis noun
tennis is a game played with rackets
and a ball on a court with a net
across the middle

tenor noun
a male singer with a high voice

tenpin bowling noun
tenpin bowling is a game in which
you knock down sets of ten skittles
with a ball

tense[1] adjective
1 tightly stretched • tense muscles
2 to be tense is to be nervous and
not able to relax a tense situation
makes people feel nervous and
unable to relax **tensely** adverb

tense[2] noun
a form of a verb that shows when
something happens.
The past tense of come is
came and the present tense is
come

tension noun
1 tension is a feeling of anxiety or
nervousness about something about
to happen **2** tension is also how
tightly stretched a rope or wire is

tent *noun*
a shelter made of canvas or cloth supported by upright poles

tentacle *noun*
a long bending part of the body of an octopus and some other animals

tenth *adjective, noun*
the next after the ninth
tenthly *adverb* in the tenth place; as the tenth one

tepid *adjective*
tepid liquid is only slightly warm; lukewarm

term *noun*
1 a part of the year when a school or college does its teaching 2 a definite period • *He was sentenced to a term of imprisonment.* 3 a word or expression with a special meaning • *I don't understand these technical terms.* 4 the terms of an agreement are the conditions offered or agreed • *They won't agree to our terms.* to be on good or bad terms is to be friendly or unfriendly with someone

terminal *noun*
1 a building where passengers arrive or depart • *an airport terminal* 2 a place where a wire is connected to a battery or electric circuit 3 a computer keyboard and screen used for sending data to or from the main computer
terminal *adjective*
a terminal illness is one that cannot be cured and that the person will die from

terminate *verb*
you terminate something, or it terminates, when it ends or stops • *This train terminates here.*
termination *noun* ending or stopping something

terminus *noun* (**termini**)
the station at the end of a railway or bus route

termite *noun*
a small insect that eats wood and lives in large groups

termite mound

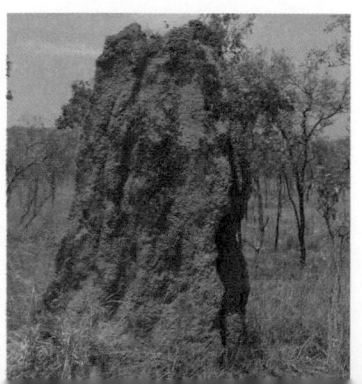

terrace *noun*
1 a row of houses joined together 2 a level area on a slope or hillside 3 a paved area beside a house

terrapin *noun*
a kind of small turtle that lives in water

terrible *adjective*
awful; very bad

terribly *adverb*
awfully; badly • *I'm terribly sorry I kept you waiting.* • *He was missing his parents terribly.*

terrific *adjective*
(*informal*) 1 very good or excellent • *That's a terrific idea.* 2 very great • *They went at a terrific speed.*
terrifically *adverb* very; greatly

terrify *verb* (**terrifies, terrifying, terrified**)
to terrify a person or animal is to make them very frightened

territory *noun* (**territories**)
an area of land, especially an area that belongs to a country or person
territorial *adjective* to do with territory

terror *noun*
terror is great fear

terrorism *noun* terrorism is the use of violence, such as setting off bombs, for political purposes **terrorist** *noun* someone who takes part in terrorism

terrorize *verb*
to terrorize someone is to terrify them with threats

test *noun*
1 a short set of questions to check someone's knowledge, especially in school 2 a medical examination • *Amy went to have an eye test.* 3 a trial or experiment to find out what something is like • *Tests have shown there is a high level of pollution in the water.* 4 (*informal*) a test match
test *verb*
1 to test someone is to give them a test 2 to test something is to use it so that you can find out whether it works properly or find out more about it

testament *noun*
1 a written statement 2 each of the two main parts of the Bible, the Old Testament and the New Testament

testify *verb* (**testifies, testifying, testified**)
to testify is to give evidence in a lawcourt

testimony *noun* (**testimonies**)
evidence; what someone testifies

test match *noun*
a cricket or rugby match between teams from different countries

test tube *noun*
a tube of thin glass closed at one end, used for experiments in chemistry

tether *verb*
to tether an animal is to tie it up so that it cannot move far
tether *noun*
a rope for tying an animal to be at the end of your tether is to be unable to stand something any more

text *noun*
1 the words of something printed or written 2 a text message
text *verb*
you text someone when you send them a text message

textbook *noun*
a book that teaches you about a subject

textiles *plural noun*
kinds of cloth; fabrics

text message *noun*
a written message sent using a mobile phone

texture *noun*
the way that the surface of something feels when you touch it • *Silk has a smooth texture.*

than *conjunction*
compared with another person or thing • *Claire is taller than David.*

thank *verb*
to thank someone is to tell them you are grateful for something they have given you or done for you
thank you words that you say when you thank someone

thankful *adjective*
feeling glad that someone has done something for you **thankfully** *adverb* used to show that you are pleased and relieved about something • *Thankfully no one was hurt.*

thanks *plural noun*
1 words that thank someone 2 (*informal*) a short way of saying 'Thank you' thanks to someone or something because of them • *Thanks to you, we succeeded.*

that *determiner*
the one there • *Whose is that book?*
that *conjunction*
used to introduce a fact or statement or result • *I hope that you are well.* • *Do you know that it is one o'clock?* • *The puzzle was so hard that no one could solve it.*

a b c d e f g h i j k l m n o p q r s t u v w x y z

that *pronoun*
1 the one there • *Whose book is that?*
2 which or who • *This is the book that I wanted.* • *Are you the person that I saw the other day?*

thatch *noun*
thatch is straw or reeds used to make a roof

thatch *verb*
to thatch a roof is to make it with straw or reeds

thaw *verb*
something thaws when it melts and is no longer frozen • *The snow was beginning to thaw.*

the *determiner* (called the *definite article*) a particular one; that or those

theatre *noun*
1 a building where people go to see plays or shows 2 a special room where you go to have an operation

theatrical *adjective*
to do with plays or acting

theft *noun*
theft is stealing

their *determiner*
belonging to them • *This is their house.*

theirs *pronoun*
belonging to them • *This house is theirs.*

them *pronoun*
a word used for *they* when it is the object of a verb, or when it comes after a preposition • *I like them.* • *I gave it to them.*

theme *noun*
1 a main idea or subject of something such as a book or speech 2 a short tune or melody

theme park *noun*
an amusement park with rides and activities connected with a special subject or theme

themselves *plural noun*
them and nobody else, used to refer back to the subject of a verb • *They have hurt themselves.* **by themselves** on their own; alone • *They did the work all by themselves.*

then *adverb*
1 at that time • *I lived in London then.* 2 after that; next • *Then they came home.* 3 in that case; therefore • *If you are going, then I can stay.*

theology *noun*
theology is the study of God and religion **theological** *adjective* to do with theology

theoretical *adjective*
based on theory and not on practice or experience **theoretically** *adverb* in theory

theory *noun*
1 a theory is an idea or set of ideas suggested to explain something 2 the theory of a subject is the ideas and principles behind it, rather than the practice **in theory** according to what should happen

therapy *noun* (**therapies**)
a way of treating an illness of the mind or the body, usually without using surgery or artificial medicines **therapist** *noun* an expert in therapy • *a speech therapist*

there *adverb*
1 in or to that place 2 a word that you say to call attention to someone or something or to refer to them • *There's a spider in the bath.* • *There has been a mistake.*

therefore *adverb*
for that reason; and so

thermal *adjective*
to do with heat; using heat

thermometer *noun*
a device for measuring temperature

thermostat *noun*
a device that automatically controls the temperature of a room or piece of equipment

thesaurus *noun*
(**thesauri** or **thesauruses**)
a kind of dictionary in which words with similar meanings are listed in groups together, instead of one long list in alphabetical order

these *determiner, pronoun*
the people or things here

they *pronoun*
1 the people or things that someone is talking about 2 people in general • *They say it's a very good film.*

thick *adjective*
1 measuring a lot from one side to the other • *He cut himself a thick slice of cake.* 2 measured from one side to the other • *The wall is ten centimetres thick.* 3 dense or closely packed together • *The town was in thick fog.* 4 not very runny • *I love thick gravy.* 5 (*informal*) stupid **thickly** *adverb* in thick pieces or in a deep layer **thickness** *noun* how thick something is

thicken *verb*
you thicken something, or it thickens, when it becomes thicker • *As he stirred the sauce, it started to thicken.*

thicket *noun*
a group of trees and shrubs growing close together

thief *noun* (**thieves**)
someone who steals things

thigh *noun*
the part of your leg above your knee

thimble *noun*
a metal or plastic cover that you put on the end of your finger to protect it when you are sewing

thin *adjective* (**thinner, thinnest**)
1 measuring a small amount from one side to the other 2 not fat 3 not dense or closely packed together 4 runny or watery **thinly** *adverb* in thin pieces or in a thin layer **thinness** *noun* thinness is being thin

thin *verb* (**thinning, thinned**)
1 to thin something, or thin something out, is to make it less thick or less crowded 2 to thin, or thin out, is to become less dense or less crowded • *The crowds had thinned by late afternoon.*

thing *noun*
an object; anything that can be touched or seen or thought about

think *verb* (**thinking, thought**)
1 to think is to use your mind 2 to think something is to have it as an idea or opinion • *I think that's a good idea.* 3 to be thinking of doing something is to be planning to do it **thinker** *noun* someone who thinks about things

third *adjective, noun*
the next after the second **thirdly** *adverb* as the third thing

third *noun*
each of three equal parts into which something can be divided

Third World *noun*
the poor or developing countries of Asia, Africa, and South and Central America

thirst *noun*
thirst is the feeling that you need to drink

thirsty *adjective*
(**thirstier, thirstiest**)
feeling that you need to drink

thirteen *noun*
the number 13
thirteenth *adjective, noun* 13th

thirty *noun* (**thirties**)
the number 30
thirtieth *adjective, noun* 30th

this *determiner, pronoun*
the one here • *Take this pen.* • *This is the one.*

thistle noun
a wild plant with prickly leaves and purple or white or yellow flowers

thorn noun
a sharp point growing on the stem of roses and other plants

thorny adjective (**thornier, thorniest**)

thistle

1 full of thorns; prickly 2 a thorny problem is a difficult one that causes argument or disagreement

thorough adjective
1 done properly and carefully • *This is a thorough piece of work.* 2 absolute or complete • *Everything was in a thorough mess.*
thoroughly adverb properly and carefully; completely
thoroughness noun doing things properly and carefully

those determiner, pronoun
the ones there • *Where are those cards?* • *Those are the ones I want.*

though conjunction
in spite of the fact that; even if • *It is not true, though he says it is.*

though adverb
however; all the same • *She's right, though.*

thought noun
1 a thought is something that you think; an idea or opinion 2 thought is thinking • *I'll give the matter some thought.*

thoughtful adjective
1 looking or sounding as if you are thinking a lot about something 2 thinking of other people and what they would like **thoughtfully** adverb **thoughtfulness** noun

thoughtless adjective
not thinking of other people and what they would like; inconsiderate **thoughtlessly** adverb **thoughtlessness** noun

thousand noun
the number 1,000 **thousandth** adjective, noun 1,000th

thrash verb
1 to thrash someone is to keep hitting them hard with a stick or whip 2 to thrash a person or team is to defeat them completely in a game or sport 3 to thrash, or thrash about, is to fling your arms and legs about wildly

thread noun
1 a long piece of cotton, wool, nylon, or other material used for sewing or weaving 2 a long thin piece of something 3 the spiral ridge round a screw or bolt

thread verb
1 to thread a needle is to put a thread through its eye 2 to thread a long and thin material is to put it through or round something 3 to thread a piece of string is to put beads on it

threadbare adjective
clothes are threadbare when they are worn thin with threads showing

threat noun
1 a warning that you will punish or harm someone if they do not do what you want 2 a danger

threaten verb
1 to threaten someone is to warn them that you will punish or harm them if they do not do what you want 2 to threaten is to be a danger to someone or something • *The quarrel threatened to turn violent.*

three noun
the number 3

three-dimensional adjective
having three dimensions: length, width, and height or depth

thresh verb
to thresh corn is to beat it so that you separate the grain from the husks

threshold noun
1 a slab of stone or board under the doorway of a building; the entrance 2 the beginning of something important • *We are on the threshold of a great discovery.*

thrift noun
thrift is being careful with money and not wasting it

thrifty adjective (**thriftier, thriftiest**)
careful with money and not wasting it **thriftily** adverb

thrill noun
1 a sudden feeling of excitement 2 something that gives you this feeling

thrill verb
something thrills you when it gives you a sudden feeling of excitement **thrilling** adjective very exciting

thriller noun
an exciting story or film, usually about crime

thrive verb
to thrive is to grow strongly or do well

throat noun
1 the front of your neck 2 the tube in your neck that takes food and air into your body

throb verb (**throbbing, throbbed**)
to throb is to beat or vibrate with a strong rhythm • *The ship's engines throbbed quietly.* • *He had a throbbing pain in his head.*

throb noun
a throbbing sound or feeling

throne noun
1 a special chair for a king or queen 2 the position of being king or queen • *The Prince of Wales is heir to the throne.*

throng noun
a large crowd of people

throttle verb
to throttle someone is to squeeze their throat and strangle them

throttle noun
a device to control the flow of fuel to an engine

through adverb and preposition
1 from one end or side to the other • *I can't get through.* • *Climb through the window.* 2 because of; by means of • *We'll do it through hard work.* 3 (informal) finished • *I'm through now.*

throughout preposition, adverb all the way through

throw verb (**throwing, threw, thrown**)
1 to throw something or someone is to send them through the air 2 to throw something somewhere is to put it there carelessly • *He came in and threw his coat on the chair.* 3 to throw a part of your body is to move it quickly • *She threw her head back and laughed.* 4 to throw someone into a certain state is to put them in that state • *We were thrown into confusion.* to throw something away is to get rid of it

throw noun
a throwing action or movement • *That was a good throw.*

thrush noun
a bird that has a white front with brown spots

thrust verb
to thrust something somewhere is to push it there with a lot of force • *He thrust his hands into his pockets.*

thud noun
the dull sound of something heavy falling

thud verb (**thudding, thudded**)
to fall with a thud

a b c d e f g h i j k l m n o p q r s t u v w x y z

thumb *noun*
the short thick finger at the side of each hand

thump *verb*
1 to thump someone or something is to hit them heavily 2 to thump is to make a dull heavy sound

thump *noun*
an act or sound of thumping

thunder *noun*
thunder is the loud rumbling noise that you hear with lightning during a storm

thunder *verb*
1 to thunder is to make the noise of thunder 2 someone thunders when they speak with a loud booming voice **thunderous** *adjective* extremely loud • *The curtain came down to thunderous applause.*

thunderstorm *noun*
a storm with thunder and lightning

Thursday *noun*
the fifth day of the week

thus *adverb*
1 in this way • *We did it thus.* 2 therefore • *Thus, we must try again.*

tick *noun*
1 a small mark (✓) made next to something when checking it as a sign that it is correct or has been done 2 each of the regular clicking sounds that a clock or watch makes

tick *verb*
1 to tick something is to mark it with a tick • *She ticked the correct answers.* 2 a clock or watch ticks when it makes regular clicking sounds **to tick someone off** (*informal*) is to scold them or tell them off

ticket *noun*
a piece of paper or card that allows you to do something such as see a show or travel on a bus or train

tickle *verb*
1 to tickle someone is to keep touching their skin lightly so that they get a tingling feeling that can make them laugh and wriggle 2 to tickle is to have a tickling or itching feeling • *My throat is tickling.* 3 to tickle someone is also to please or amuse them

tickets

ticklish *adjective*
someone is ticklish when they are likely to laugh or wriggle if they are tickled

tidal *adjective*
to do with tides or affected by tides

tidal wave *noun*
a huge sea wave moving with the tide

tiddler *noun*
(*informal*) a very small fish

tiddlywink *noun*
a small counter that you flip into a cup with another counter in the game of tiddlywinks

tide *noun*
the regular rising or falling of the sea, which usually happens twice a day

tide *verb*
to tide someone over is to give them what they need, especially money, for the time being

tidy *adjective* (**tidier, tidiest**)
1 a tidy place is neat and orderly, with things in the right place • *What a tidy room.* 2 a tidy person keeps things neat and in the right place 3 (*informal*) fairly large • *That's a tidy sum of money.* **tidily** *adverb* **tidiness** *noun*

tidy *verb* (**tidies, tidying, tidied**)
to tidy a place is to make it neat by putting things away in the right place

tie *verb* (**ties, tying, tied**)
1 to tie something is to fasten it with string, rope, or ribbon 2 to tie a knot or bow is to make one in a strip of material such as a ribbon 3 two players or teams tie when they finish a game or competition with an equal score or position

tie *noun*
1 a thin strip of material tied round the collar of a shirt with a knot at the front 2 the result of a game or competition in which two players or teams have the same position or score 3 one of the matches in a competition

tiger *noun*
a large wild animal of the cat family, with yellow and black stripes

tight *adjective*
1 fitting very closely or firmly fastened • *These shoes are a bit tight.* 2 fully stretched • *Is this string tight enough?* **tightly** *adverb* **tightness** *noun*

tight *adverb*
1 firmly • *Hold on tight.* 2 fully stretched • *Now pull the string tight.*

tighten *verb*
1 to tighten something is to make it tighter • *These screws need to be tightened.* 2 to tighten is to become tighter

tightrope *noun*
a tightly stretched rope above the ground, for acrobats to perform on

tights *plural noun*
a piece of clothing that fits tightly over the lower parts of the body including the legs and feet

tigress *noun*
a female tiger

tile *noun*
a thin piece of baked clay or other hard material used in rows to cover roofs, walls, or floors **tiled** *adjective* covered with tiles

till¹ *preposition, conjunction*
until

till² *noun*
a drawer or box for money in a shop; a cash register

till³ *verb*
to till soil or land is to plough it ready to grow crops

tiller *noun*
a handle used to turn a boat's rudder

tilt *verb*
1 to tilt is to slope or lean 2 to tilt something is to tip it or make it slope

tilt *noun*
a sloping position

timber *noun*
1 timber is wood used for building or making things 2 a timber is a beam of wood

time *noun*
1 time is a measure of the passing of years, months, days, and other units 2 you ask the

tiger

time when you want to know what point in the day it is, as shown on a watch or clock • *What's the time?* **3** a time is a particular moment or period of things existing or happening • *There was a time when I would have agreed with you.* • *Come back another time.* • *There were fields here in past times.* **4** a time is also an occasion • *This is the first time I've been here.* **5** a time is also a period for which something lasts • *She spent a long time in the library.* **6** time is the rhythm and speed of a piece of music **at times** or **from time to time** sometimes or occasionally **in time** or **on time** soon or early enough; not late • *Make sure you get to the station in time.* • *The train left on time.*

time *verb*
1 to time something is to measure how long it takes **2** to time an event or activity is to arrange the time when it will happen • *You timed your arrival perfectly.*

timer *noun*
a device for timing things

times *plural noun*
multiplied by • *5 times 3 is 15 (5 x 3 = 15).*

timetable *noun*
a list of the times when things happen, such as buses and trains leaving and arriving, and when school lessons take place

timid *adjective*
nervous and easily frightened **timidly** *adverb* **timidity** *noun* timidity is being timid

timing *noun*
timing is choosing the right time to do something • *Arriving at lunchtime was good timing.*

tin *noun*
1 tin is a soft white metal **2** a tin is a metal container for preserving food **tinned** *adjective* tinned food is preserved in a tin

tingle *verb*
part of your body tingles when you have a slight stinging or tickling feeling there • *The cold water made my skin tingle.*

tingle *noun*
a tingling feeling

tinker *verb*
to tinker with something is to try to mend or improve it, often without really knowing how to • *He loves tinkering with old clocks.*

tinker *noun*
(*old use*) someone who travelled around mending pots and pans

tinkle *verb*
something tinkles when it makes a gentle ringing sound

tinkle *noun*
a tinkling sound

tinny *adjective* (**tinnier, tinniest**)
a tinny sound is thin and high-pitched

tinsel *noun*
tinsel is strips of glittering material used for decoration

tint *noun*
a shade of a colour, especially a pale one

tint *verb*
to tint something is to colour it slightly

tiny *adjective*
very small

tip[1] *noun*
the part at the very end of something **tipped** *adjective* having a tip • *The parcel was tied in a ribbon tipped with gold.*

tip[2] *noun*
1 a small amount of money given to thank someone who has helped you **2** a quick piece of advice or useful information

tip[2] *verb* (**tipping, tipped**)
1 to tip someone is to give them a small amount of money to thank them for helping you **2** to tip someone or something is to name them as likely to win or succeed

tip[3] *verb* (**tipping, tipped**)
to tip something is to turn it upside down or tilt it • *She tipped the water out of the bucket.* • *He tipped his head back and laughed.*

tip[3] *noun*
1 a place where rubbish is left **2** a very untidy place

tiptoe *verb*
to tiptoe is to walk on your toes very quietly or carefully

tiptoe *noun*
on tiptoe walking or standing on your toes

tire *verb*
1 to tire someone is to make them tired **2** to tire is to become tired

tired *adjective*
feeling that you need to sleep or rest to be tired of something is to have had enough of it

tiresome *adjective*
annoying or tedious

tissue *noun*
1 tissue, or tissue paper, is thin soft paper **2** a tissue is a piece of this, especially one you use for blowing your nose **3** tissue is also

the substance of which an animal or plant is made

tit *noun*
a kind of small bird

title *noun*
1 the name of something such as a book, film, painting, or piece of music **2** a word that shows a person's position or profession, such as • *Sir, Lady, Dr, Mrs.*

titter *verb*
to titter is to giggle or laugh in a silly way

to *preposition*
1 towards • *They set off to London.* **2** as far as; so as to reach • *I am soaked to the skin.* **3** compared with; rather than • *She prefers cats to dogs.* **4** used with a verb to make an infinitive • *I want to see him.* **5** used to show purpose • *He does that to annoy us.*

to *adverb*
to the usual or closed position • *Push the door to.* **to and fro** backwards and forwards

toad *noun*
an animal like a large frog, that lives on land

toad

toadstool *noun*
a fungus that looks like a mushroom, and is often poisonous

toast *verb*
1 to toast food is to cook it by heating it under a grill or in front of a fire **2** to toast someone or something is to have a drink in their honour

toast *noun*
1 toast is toasted bread **2** a toast is when people are asked to toast someone or something with a drink • *Let's drink a toast to the bride and groom.*

toaster *noun*
an electrical device that makes toast

tobacco *noun*
tobacco is the dried leaves of certain plants used for smoking in cigarettes, cigars, or pipes

toboggan *noun*
a small sledge for sliding downhill **tobogganing** *noun* sliding downhill on a toboggan

today *noun*
this day • *Today is Monday.*

today *adverb*
1 on this day • *I saw him today* **2** nowadays • *Today we don't have slaves.*

toddler noun
a young child who is just learning to walk

toe noun
1 each of the five separate parts at the end of each foot **2** the part of a shoe or sock that covers your toes

toffee noun
1 toffee is a sticky sweet made from butter and sugar **2** a toffee is a piece of this

together adverb
with another person or thing; with each other • *They went to school together.* • *Now glue the two parts together.*

toil verb
1 to toil is to work hard **2** to toil is also to move slowly and with difficulty • *The old man toiled up the hill.*

toilet noun
1 a large bowl with a seat that you use for getting rid of waste from your body **2** a room with a toilet in it

token noun
1 a card or voucher that you can exchange for goods in a shop **2** a piece of metal or plastic you use instead of money to pay for something **3** a sign or signal of something • *Please accept these flowers as a small token of my gratitude.*

tolerable adjective
able to be tolerated; bearable

tolerant adjective
accepting or putting up with other people's behaviour and opinions when you don't agree with them **tolerance** noun being willing to accept other people's behaviour and opinions **tolerantly** adverb

tolerate verb
to tolerate something is to allow it or put up with it although you do not approve of it

toll¹ noun
1 a payment charged for using a bridge or road **2** an amount of loss or damage • *The death toll in the earthquake is rising.*

toll² verb
to toll a bell is to ring it slowly

tom or **tomcat** noun
a male cat

tomahawk noun
an axe used by Native Americans

tomato noun (**tomatoes**)
a soft round red fruit with seeds inside it, eaten as a vegetable

tomb noun (*say* toom)
a place where a dead body is buried; a grave

tomboy noun
a girl who enjoys rough noisy games and activities

tombstone noun
a memorial stone set up over a grave

tomorrow noun, adverb
the day after today

ton noun
1 a unit of weight equal to 2,240 pounds or about 1,016 kilograms **2** (*informal*) a large amount • *There's tons of room.*

tone noun
1 the nature or quality of a sound • *I didn't like the sound of his voice.* **2** a sound in music **3** a shade of a colour **4** the quality or character of something

tone verb
to tone something down is to make it softer or quieter to tone in is to blend or fit in well, especially in colour

tongs plural noun
a tool with two arms joined at one end, used to pick things up or hold them

tongue noun
1 the long soft part that moves about inside your mouth **2** a language **3** the flap of material under the laces of a shoe

tongue-tied adjective
to be tongue-tied is to feel too shy or embarrassed to speak

tongue-twister noun
a sentence or phrase that is very difficult to say

tonic noun
something that makes a person healthier or stronger

tonight adverb, noun
this evening or night

tonne noun
a unit of weight equal to 1,000 kilograms

tonsillitis noun
tonsillitis is a disease that makes your tonsils extremely sore

tonsils plural noun
your tonsils are the two small masses of soft flesh inside your throat

too adverb
1 also • *I'd like to come too.* **2** more than is wanted or allowed or wise • *The box is too small.* • *Don't drive too fast.*

tomatoes

tool noun
a device that you use to help you do a particular job, such as a hammer or saw

tooth noun (**teeth**)
1 each of the hard white bony parts that grow in your gums, used for biting and chewing **2** each in a row of sharp points on a saw or comb **toothed** adjective having teeth

toothache noun
toothache is a pain in one of your teeth

toothbrush noun
a small brush on a long handle, for brushing your teeth

toothpaste noun
toothpaste is a creamy paste for cleaning your teeth

top¹ noun
1 the highest part of something **2** the upper surface of something **3** the covering or stopper of a jar or bottle **4** a piece of clothing you wear on the upper part of your body

top¹ adjective
highest or most important • *We live on the top floor.* • *They were travelling at top speed.*

top¹ verb (**topping, topped**)
1 to top something is to put a top on it • *The cake was topped with icing.* **2** to top something is also to be at the top of it • *She tops the class in maths.* to top something up is to fill it to the top when it is already partly full

top² noun
a toy that can be made to spin on its point

top hat noun
a man's tall stiff black or grey hat worn with formal clothes

topic noun
a subject that you are writing or talking or learning about

topical adjective
to do with things that are happening or in the news now • *The film we saw was very topical.* **topicality** noun topicality is being topical **topically** adverb

topping noun
food that is put on the top of a cake, pudding, or pizza

topple verb
1 to topple, or topple over, is to fall over **2** to topple something is to make it fall over **3** to topple someone in power is to overthrow them

top secret adjective
extremely secret

topsy-turvy adverb, adjective
upside-down; in a muddle

torch noun
1 a small electric lamp that you hold in your hand **2** a stick with burning material on the end, used as a light

torment verb
1 to torment someone is to make them suffer or feel pain **2** to torment someone is also to keep annoying them deliberately **tormentor** noun the person who is tormenting someone

torment noun
torment is great suffering

tornado noun (**tornadoes**)
(say tor-**nay**-doh)
a violent storm or whirlwind

torpedo noun
(**torpedoes**)
a long tube-shaped missile sent under water to destroy ships and submarines

torpedo verb
to torpedo a ship is to attack it with a torpedo

torrent noun
a very strong stream or fall of water **torrential** adjective torrential rain pours down very heavily

torso noun (**torsos**)
the main part of the human body, not including the head, arms, or legs

tortoise noun (say tor-tus)
a slow-moving animal with a shell over its body

torture verb
to torture someone is to make them feel great pain, especially so that they will give information

torture noun
torture is something done to torture a person

toss verb
1 to toss something is to throw it into the air **2** to toss a coin is to throw it in the air and see which side is showing when it lands, as a way of deciding something **3** to toss is to move about restlessly in bed
• She was tossing and turning all night.

total noun
the amount you get by adding everything together

total adjective
1 including everything • What is the total amount? **2** complete; utter • There was total darkness outside. **totally** adverb completely
• Now I'm totally confused.

total verb (**totalling, totalled**)
1 to total something is to add it up **2** to total an amount is to reach it as a total • Sales totalled over £50,000 this month.

totem pole noun
a large pole carved or painted by Native Americans

totter verb
to totter is to walk unsteadily or wobble

toucan noun
a tropical bird with a large brightly-coloured beak

touch verb
1 you touch something when you feel it lightly with your hand or fingers **2** to touch something is to come into contact with it or hit it gently **3** to be touching something is to be next to it so that there is no space in between **4** to touch something is also to interfere or meddle with it
• Don't touch anything in this room. **5** to touch an amount is to just reach it
• His temperature touched 104 degrees. **6** to touch someone is to affect their emotions • We were deeply touched by his sad story.
to touch down is to land in an aircraft or spacecraft
to touch something up is to improve it by making small changes or additions

touch noun
1 a touch is an act of touching
• You can find any train timetable you want at the touch of a button.
2 touch is the ability to feel things by touching them **3** a touch is also a small thing that greatly improves something
• We're just putting the finishing touches to it.

totem pole

4 touch is also communication with someone • We have lost touch with them. **5** touch is also the part of a football or rugby pitch outside the playing area • He kicked the ball into touch.

touch and go adjective
uncertain or risky

touchy adjective
(**touchier, touchiest**)
easily or quickly offended

tough adjective
1 strong; hard to break or damage
• You'll need tough shoes for the climb. **2** tough food is hard to chew **3** rough or violent • The police were dealing with tough criminals.
4 firm or severe • It's time to get tough with football hooligans.
5 difficult • It was a tough decision.
toughly adverb **toughness** noun

toughen verb
to toughen someone or something, or toughen them up, is to make them tougher

tour noun
a journey in which you visit several places

tourist noun
someone who is travelling or on holiday abroad **tourism** noun travelling or being on holiday abroad

tournament noun
a competition in which there is a series of games or contests

tow verb (rhymes with **go**)
to tow a vehicle or boat is to pull it behind you in another vehicle
• They towed our car to a garage.

tow noun
an act of towing

towards or **toward**
preposition
1 in the direction of
• She walked towards the sea.
2 in relation to • He behaved kindly towards his children.
3 as a contribution to • Put the money towards a new bicycle.

towel noun
a piece of soft cloth that you use for drying yourself

tower noun
a tall narrow building or part of a building

a
b
c
d
e
f
g
h
i
j
k
l
m
n
o
p
q
r
s
t
u
v
w
x
y
z

tower verb
to tower above or over things is
to be much taller than them
• The skyscrapers towered above
the city.

tower block noun
a tall building containing offices or
flats

town noun
a place with many houses, shops,
schools, offices, and other buildings

town hall noun
a building with offices for the local
council and usually a hall for public
events

towpath noun
a path beside a canal or river

toxic adjective
poisonous

toy noun
something to play with

toy verb
to toy with an idea is to think about
it casually or idly

trace noun
1 a mark or sign left by a person or
thing • He vanished without a trace.
2 a very small amount of something
• They found traces of blood on the
carpet.

trace verb
1 to trace someone or something is
to find them after a search
• Police are trying to trace one of the
witnesses. **2** to trace a picture or map
is to copy it by drawing over it on thin
paper you can see through

track noun
1 a path made by people or animals
2 tracks are marks left by a person
or thing **3** a set of rails for trains or
trams to run on **4** a road or area of
ground prepared for racing
5 a metal belt used instead of
wheels on a heavy vehicle such as
a tank or tractor **6** one song or item
on a record or CD **to keep track of**
something or **someone** is to know
where they are or what they are
doing

track verb
to track a person or animal is to
follow them by following the signs
they leave **to track something down**
is to find it after it has been lost
tracker noun someone who
tracks people or animals

tracksuit noun
a warm loose suit of a
kind worn by athletes
for jogging and
warming up

tractor noun
a motor vehicle with
large rear wheels, used for pulling
farm machinery or heavy loads

trade noun
1 trade is the business of buying
or selling or exchanging things
2 a trade is a job or occupation,
especially a skilled craft

trade verb
to trade is to buy or sell or exchange
things **to trade something in** is to
give it towards the cost of something
new • He traded in his motorcycle
for a car. **trader** noun someone who
buys and sells things in trade

trademark noun
a symbol or name that only one
manufacturer is allowed to use

tradesman noun (**tradesmen**)
someone who sells or delivers
goods

trade union noun
an organization of workers in a
particular industry, set up to help
improve pay and work conditions

tradition noun
1 tradition is the passing down
of customs and beliefs from one
generation to the next **2** a tradition
is a custom or belief passed on in
this way

traditional adjective
1 passed down from one generation
to the next • It is a book of
traditional stories from all round the
world. **2** of a kind that has existed
for a long time • We go to a very
traditional school. **traditionally**
adverb

traffic noun
1 traffic is vehicles, ships, or aircraft
moving along a route **2** traffic is also
trade, especially in something illegal
or wrong • They were involved in
traffic in drugs.

traffic verb (**trafficking,**
trafficked)
to traffic in something is to trade in it
illegally

tractor

traffic lights plural noun
a set of coloured lights used to
control road traffic

traffic warden noun
an official whose job is to make
sure that vehicles are parked
legally

tragedy noun (**tragedies**)
1 a story or play with unhappy
events or a sad ending **2** a very sad
event

tragic adjective
1 very sad or distressing **2** to do
with tragedy **tragically** adverb
in a way that is very sad or
distressing

trail noun
1 a path or track through
the countryside or a forest
2 the scent and marks left behind
by an animal as it moves **3** marks
left behind by something that has
passed

trail verb
1 to trail an animal is to follow the
scent or marks it has left behind
2 you trail something, or it trails,
when it drags along the ground
behind you **3** to trail behind someone
is to follow them more slowly or at
a distance • A few walkers trailed
behind the others. **4** to trail is also to
hang down or float loosely • She wore
a long trailing scarf.

trailer noun
1 a truck or other container that is
pulled along by a car or lorry
2 a short film advertising a film or
television programme that will soon
be shown

train noun
1 a group of railway coaches or
trucks joined together and pulled
by an engine **2** a number of people
or animals moving along together,
especially in a desert • a camel train
3 a series of things • The train of
events began in London. **4** a long
part of a dress that trails behind on
the ground

train verb
1 to train someone is to give them
skill or practice in something
2 to train is to learn how to do a job
• He's training to be a doctor.
3 to train is also to practise for a
sporting event • She was training for
the race. **4** to train a plant is to make
it grow in a particular direction
• Roses can be trained up walls.
5 to train a gun is to aim it at a
target • He trained his rifle on the
bridge.

trainer noun
1 a person who trains people or

animals **2** a soft shoe with a rubber sole, worn for running and sport

traitor noun
someone who betrays their country or friends

tram noun
a passenger vehicle that runs along rails set in the road

tramp noun
1 a person without a home or job who walks from place to place **2** a long walk **3** the sound of heavy footsteps

tramp verb
1 to tramp is to walk with heavy footsteps **2** to tramp is also to walk for a long distance

trample verb
to trample something, or to trample on it, is to crush it by treading heavily on it

trampoline noun
(say **tramp**-o-leen)
a large piece of canvas joined to a frame by springs, used by gymnasts for jumping on

trance noun
a dreamy or unconscious state like sleep

tranquil adjective
quiet and peaceful **tranquility** noun being quiet and peaceful

tranquillizer noun
a drug used to make a person feel calm and relaxed

transaction noun
a piece of business that involves buying and selling something

transfer verb (**transferring, transferred**) (say trans-**fer**)
to transfer someone or something is to move them from one place to another

transfer noun
(say **trans**-fer)
1 the process of moving a person or thing from one place to another **2** a piece of paper with a picture or design that can be transferred to another surface by soaking or heating the paper

transform verb
to transform a person or thing is to change their form or appearance to something quite different • The caterpillar is transformed into a butterfly. **transformation** noun a complete change in the form or appearance of something

transfusion noun
putting blood taken from one person into another person's body

transistor noun
1 a tiny electronic device that controls a flow of electricity **2** a portable radio that uses transistors

transition noun
a change from one thing to another

translate verb
to translate something said or written in one language is to say or write it in another language **translation** noun something translated from another language **translator** noun someone who translates language

transmission noun
1 transmission is transmitting something **2** a transmission is a radio or television broadcast

transmit verb (**transmitting, transmitted**)
1 to transmit a broadcast or signal is to send it out **2** to transmit something is to send it or pass it from one person or place to another • We don't know how the disease is transmitted.

transmitter noun
a piece of equipment for transmitting radio or television signals

transparent adjective
something is transparent when you can see through it **transparency** noun how transparent something is

transplant verb
1 to transplant a body organ is to remove it from one person and put it in the body of a person who is ill **2** to transplant a plant is to move it from one place to another **transplantation** noun transplantation is transplanting something

transplant noun
1 when a body organ is removed from one person and put in another • a heart transplant **2** something that is transplanted

transport verb (say trans-**port**)
to transport people or things is to take them from one place to another

transport noun (say **trans**-port)
1 transport is the process of transporting people or things **2** transport is also vehicles used to do this

transporter noun
a heavy vehicle for transporting large objects, such as cars

trap noun
1 a device for catching and holding animals **2** a plan or trick to capture or cheat someone **3** a two-wheeled carriage pulled by a horse

trap verb (**trapping, trapped**)
1 to trap a person or animal is to catch them in a trap **2** to trap someone is to capture or cheat them **3** to be trapped is to be stuck in a dangerous situation you can't escape from • They were trapped in the burning building.

trapdoor noun
a door in a floor, ceiling, or roof

trapeze noun
a bar hanging from two ropes high above the ground, used as a swing by acrobats

trapezium noun
a four-sided figure that has only two parallel sides, which are of different length

trapper noun
someone who traps animals, especially for their fur

trash noun
trash is rubbish or nonsense **trashy** adjective worthless or rubbish

travel verb (**travelling, travelled**)
to travel is to go from one place to another

travel noun
travel is going on journeys • Do you enjoy travel?

travel agent noun
a person or business whose job is to arrange travel and holidays for people

traveller noun
1 someone who is travelling or who often travels **2** a person who lives in a vehicle and does not settle in one place

trawler noun
a fishing boat that pulls a large net behind it

tray noun
a flat piece of wood or metal or plastic, used for carrying food, cups, plates, and other household things

treacherous adjective
1 betraying someone; not loyal **2** dangerous or unreliable • It's been snowing and the roads are treacherous. **treacherously** adverb **treachery** noun doing something that betrays someone

treacle noun
treacle is a thick sweet sticky liquid made from sugar

tread verb (**treading, trod, trodden**)
to tread on something is to walk on it or put your foot on it

tread noun
1 the sound someone makes when they walk • *He had a heavy tread.*
2 the part of a staircase or ladder that you put your foot on 3 the part of a tyre that touches the ground

treason noun
treason is betraying your country

treasure noun
1 treasure is a collection of valuable things like jewels or money 2 a treasure is a precious thing

treasure

treasure verb
to treasure something is to think that it is very precious

treasure hunt noun
a game in which people try to find a hidden object

treasurer noun
an official who is in charge of the money of an organization or club

treasury (**treasuries**) noun
a place where treasure or money is stored **the Treasury** the government department in charge of a country's income

treat verb
1 to treat someone or something in a certain way is to behave towards them in that way • *She treats her friends very kindly.* 2 to treat a person or animal is to give them medical care • *He was treated for sunstroke.* 3 to treat something is to put it through a process to improve it • *The woodwork needs treating so that it doesn't rot.* 4 to treat someone is to pay for their food or drink or entertainment • *I'll treat you to an ice cream.*

treat noun
1 something special that gives someone pleasure 2 the act of treating someone by paying for them • *This is my treat.*

treatment noun
1 your treatment of someone is the way you treat them 2 treatment is medical care

treaty noun (**treaties**)
a formal agreement between two or more countries, for example to end a war

treble adjective
three times as much or three times as many

treble noun
1 treble the amount of something is three times as much or as many
2 a treble is a boy with a high singing voice

treble verb
1 to treble something is to make it three times as big
2 to treble is to become three times as big

tree noun
a tall plant with leaves, branches, and a thick wooden trunk

trek verb (**trekking, trekked**)
to trek is to make a long walk or journey

trek noun
a long walk or journey

trellis noun
a framework of crossing wooden or metal bars, used to support climbing plants

tremble verb
to tremble is to shake gently, especially because you are afraid

tremble noun
a trembling movement or sound

tremendous adjective
1 very large or very great • *There was a tremendous explosion.* 2 excellent **tremendously** adverb very much

tremor noun
1 a shaking or trembling
2 a small earthquake

trench noun
a long hole or ditch dug in the ground

trend noun
the general direction in which something is going or developing

trendy adjective
(*informal*) fashionable; trying to be up to date **trendily** adverb **trendiness** noun

trespass verb
to trespass is to go on someone's land or property without their permission • *The sign said 'No Trespassing'.* **trespasser** noun someone who is trespassing • *Trespassers will be prosecuted.*

trestle noun
each of a set of supports on which you place a board to make a table

trial noun
1 trying or testing something to see how well it works
2 the process of hearing all the evidence about a crime in a lawcourt to find out whether someone is guilty of it **by trial and error** by trying out different methods until you find one that works **on trial** being tried out, or being tried in a lawcourt

triangle noun
1 a flat shape with three straight sides and three angles 2 a musical instrument made from a metal rod bent into a triangle and played by striking it **triangular** adjective in the shape of a triangle

tribe noun
a group of families living together, ruled by a chief **tribal** adjective to do with tribes or a tribe • *a tribal leader*

tributary noun (**tributaries**)
a river or stream that flows into a larger river or a lake

tribute noun
something you say or do as a mark of respect or admiration for someone

trick noun
1 something done to deceive or fool someone 2 a clever or skilful action • *a card trick.* 3 the winning of one round of a card game such as whist

trick verb
to trick someone is to deceive or fool them **trickery** noun doing something to deceive or fool someone

trickle verb
liquid trickles when it flows slowly in small quantities

trickle noun
a slow gradual flow

tricky adjective (**trickier, trickiest**)
difficult or awkward • *There were a couple of tricky questions in the quiz.*

tricycle noun
a vehicle like a bicycle with three wheels

trifle noun
1 a pudding made of sponge cake covered with custard, fruit, and cream 2 something that has little importance or is very small

trifling adjective
very small or unimportant

trigger noun
a lever that is pulled to fire a gun

trillion noun
a million million (1,000,000,000,000), or sometimes a million million million (1,000,000,000,000,000,000)

trilogy noun
a group of three books or films about the same characters

trim adjective (**trimmer, trimmest**)
neat and tidy

trim verb
1 you trim something when you cut the edges or unwanted parts from it **2** to trim clothing is to decorate its edges • *The gown was trimmed with fur.*

trim noun
an act of trimming • *My hair needs a quick trim.*

trio noun
1 three people or things **2** a group of three musicians

trip verb (**tripping, tripped**)
1 to trip, or trip over, is to catch your foot on something and fall or stumble **2** to trip someone, or trip them up, is to make them fall or stumble **3** to trip, or trip along, is to move with quick gentle steps

trip noun
1 a short journey or outing **2** the action of tripping or stumbling

triple adjective
1 three times as much or three times as many **2** consisting of three parts or involving three people or groups

triple verb
to triple something is to make it three times as big

triple jump noun
an athletics event in which athletes try to jump as far as possible with a hop, step, and jump
triple jump

triplet noun
each of three children or animals born at the same time to the same mother

tripod noun (*say* try-pod)
a stand with three legs, for supporting a camera or other instrument

triumph noun
1 a triumph is a great success or victory **2** triumph is a feeling of victory or success • *They returned home in triumph.*

triumph verb
to triumph is to win or succeed

triumphant adjective
enjoying a victory or celebrating one **triumphantly** adverb

trivial adjective
not important or valuable **trivially** adverb
triviality noun triviality is being unimportant

troll noun
a creature in Scandinavian mythology, either a dwarf or a giant

trolley noun (**trolleys**)
1 a basket on wheels, used in supermarkets • *a shopping trolley* **2** a small table on wheels, used for serving food and drink

trombone noun
a large brass musical instrument with a sliding tube

troop noun
an organized group of people, especially soldiers or Scouts

troop verb
people troop when they move along in large numbers

troops plural noun
soldiers

trophy noun (**trophies**)
a cup or other prize you get for winning a competition

tropic noun
a line of latitude about 231/2° north of the equator (**Tropic of Cancer**) or about 231/2° south of the equator (**Tropic of Capricorn**) the tropics the hot regions between these two latitudes **tropical** adjective to do with the tropics or from the tropics

trot verb (**trotting, trotted**)
1 a horse trots when it runs gently without cantering or galloping **2** a person trots when they run gently with short steps

trot noun
a slow or gentle run

trouble noun
trouble is something that causes worry or difficulty **to be in trouble** is to be likely to get punished because of something you have done **to take trouble** is to take great care in doing something

trouble verb
1 to trouble someone is to cause them worry or difficulty **2** to trouble someone is also to bother or disturb them • *Sorry to trouble you, but can you spare a minute?* **3** to trouble to do something is to make an effort to do it • *Nobody troubled to ask us what we wanted.*

troublesome adjective
causing trouble or worry

trough noun (*say* trof)
a long narrow box for animals to eat or drink from

trousers plural noun
a piece of clothing worn over the lower half of your body, with two parts to cover your legs

trout noun (**trout**)
a freshwater fish

trowel noun
1 a tool for digging small holes or lifting plants **2** a tool with a flat blade for spreading cement or mortar

truant noun
a child who stays away from school without permission **to play truant** is to stay away from school without permission **truancy** noun being absent from school without permission

truce noun
an agreement to stop fighting for a while

truck noun
1 a lorry **2** an open railway wagon for carrying goods

trudge verb
to trudge is to walk slowly and heavily

true adjective
1 real or correct; telling what actually exists or happened • *This is a true story.* **2** genuine or proper • *He was the true heir.* **3** loyal and faithful • *You are a true friend.* **to come true** is to actually happen • *I hope your dreams come true.*

truly adverb
1 truthfully **2** sincerely or genuinely • *We are truly grateful.*

trump noun
a playing card of a suit that ranks above the others for one game or round of play • *Hearts are trumps this time.*

trump verb
to trump a card is to beat it by playing a trump

trumpet *noun*
a brass musical instrument with a narrow tube that widens at the end

trumpeter *noun*
someone who plays the trumpet

trumpet

trumpet *verb*
1 an elephant trumpets when it makes a loud sound **2** to trumpet something is to shout it out or announce it loudly

truncheon *noun*
a short thick stick carried as a weapon by a police officer

trundle *verb*
to trundle is to move along heavily, especially on wheels • *A lorry trundled across the bridge.*

trunk *noun*
1 the main stem of a tree **2** an elephant's long flexible nose **3** a large box with a hinged lid, for carrying or storing clothes and other things **4** the human body except for the head, legs, and arms

trunks *plural noun*
shorts worn by men and boys for swimming, boxing, and other activities

trust *verb*
1 to trust someone or something is to believe that they are good or truthful or reliable **2** to trust that something is so is to hope it • *I trust that you are well.* **to trust someone with something** is to let them use it or look after it

trust *noun*
1 trust is the feeling that a person or thing can be trusted **2** trust is also responsibility or being trusted • *Our pet dog was left in the trust of our next-door neighbour.*

trustworthy *adjective*
able to be trusted; reliable

trusty *adjective*
trustworthy or reliable

truth *noun*
truth is the quality of being true; the facts about something

truthful *adjective*
1 telling the truth • *They are truthful children.* **2** true • *They gave a truthful account of what happened.* **truthfully** *adverb* **truthfulness** *noun*

try *verb* (**tries, trying, tried**)
1 to try to do something is to make an effort to do it or to see if you can do it • *Try to keep still.* **2** to try something is to use it to see if it works or taste it to see if you like it

• *Try this can opener.* **3** to try someone in a lawcourt is to find out whether they are guilty of a crime, by hearing all the evidence about it **4** to try someone is also to annoy them over a long time • *You really do try me with your constant complaining.* **to try something on** is to put on clothes to see if they fit or look good **to try something out** is to use it to see if it works

try *noun* (**tries**)
1 a go at trying something; an attempt • *Have another try.* **2** (*in rugby football*) putting the ball down on the ground behind your opponents' goal to score points

T-shirt *noun*
a shirt or vest with short sleeves

tub *noun*
a round container for liquids or soft stuff such as ice cream

tuba *noun* (*say* **tew**-ba)
a large brass musical instrument that makes a deep sound

tube *noun*
1 a tube is a long thin hollow piece of material such as metal, plastic, rubber, or glass **2** a tube is also a long hollow container for something soft such as toothpaste **3** the tube is the underground railway in London • *She goes to work by tube.*

tuber *noun*
a thick rounded plant root or stem that produces buds

tubular *adjective*
shaped like a tube

tuck *verb*
to tuck something somewhere is to push a loose edge of it there so that it is tidy or hidden • *Now tuck in the flap of the envelope.* • *She tucked her hair under her cap.* **to tuck in** (*informal*) is to eat heartily **to tuck someone up** or **in** is to put the bedclothes snugly round them

Tuesday *noun*
the third day of the week

tuft *noun*
a bunch of soft or fluffy things such as threads, grass, hair, or feathers, held or growing together

tug *verb*
to tug something is to pull it hard

tug *noun*
1 a hard or sudden pull

2 a small powerful boat used for towing ships

tug-of-war *noun*
a contest between two teams pulling a rope from opposite ends

tulip *noun*
a large bright cup-shaped flower that grows on a tall stem from a bulb

tumble *verb*
to tumble is to fall over or fall down clumsily

tumbler *noun*
1 a drinking glass with no stem or handle **2** an acrobat

tummy *noun* (**tummies**)
(*informal*) your stomach

tumour *noun* (*say* **tew**-mer)
an abnormal growth on or in your body

tumultuous *adjective*
noisy and excited • *The teams came out to tumultuous applause.*

tuna *noun* (**tuna** or **tunas**)
(*say* **tew**-na)
a large sea fish used for food

tundra *noun*
tundra is a large area of flat land in cold regions (especially northern Canada and Siberia) with no trees and with soil that is frozen for most of the year

tune *noun*
a short piece of music; a pleasant series of musical notes **to be in tune** is to be at the correct musical pitch

tune *verb*
1 to tune a musical instrument is to adjust it to be in tune **2** to tune a radio or television is to adjust it to receive a particular broadcasting station **3** to tune an engine is to adjust it so that it works smoothly

tuneful *adjective*
having a pleasant tune **tunefully** *adverb*

tunic *noun* (*say* **tew**-nik)
1 a jacket that is part of some uniforms **2** a loose piece of clothing with no sleeves

tunnel *noun*
a passage made underground or through a hill

tunnel *verb* (**tunnelling, tunnelled**)
to tunnel is to make a tunnel

turban *noun*
a covering for the head made by wrapping a long strip of cloth round it, worn especially by Sikh, Hindu, or Muslim men

turbine *noun*
a machine or motor that is driven by a flow of water or gas

turbulent *adjective*
moving violently; heaving • *The seas in March can be turbulent.*
turbulence *noun* violent and uneven movement of air or water, causing aircraft and ships to be tossed about

turf *noun* (**turfs** or **turves**)
1 turf is short grass with the soil it is growing in **2** a turf is a piece of grass and soil cut out of the ground

turkey *noun* (**turkeys**)
a large bird kept for its meat

turkey

turmoil *noun*
turmoil is a great disturbance or confusion

turn *verb*
1 to turn is to move round or move to a new direction; to turn something is to make it move in this way **2** to turn (for example) pale is to change appearance and become pale **3** to turn into something is to change into it • *The frog turned into a prince.* **4** to turn something into something else is to change it • *You can turn milk into cheese.* **5** to turn a device on or off is to use a switch to make it work or stop working; to turn (for example) a radio or television up or down is to make it louder or softer **to turn out** is to happen a certain way • *The weather's turned out fine.* **to turn something down** is to refuse it **to turn something out** is to empty it **to turn up** is to appear or arrive suddenly or unexpectedly

turn *noun*
1 the action of turning; a turning movement • *Give the key three turns.* **2** a place where a road bends; a junction • *Take the next turn on the left.* **3** a task or duty that people do one after the other • *It's your turn to wash up.* **4** a short performance in a show **5** (*informal*) an attack of illness; a nervous shock • *It gave me a nasty turn.* **a good turn** is a favour you do for someone **in turn** first one and then the other; following one after another

turnip *noun*
a plant with a large round white root used as a vegetable

turnstile *noun*
a revolving gate that lets one person through at a time

turntable *noun*
a revolving platform or support, especially the part of a record player that you put the record on

turpentine *noun*
(*say* ter-pen-tyn)
turpentine is a kind of oil used to make paint thinner and to clean paintbrushes

turquoise *noun*
(*say* ter-kwoiz)
1 a sky-blue or greenish-blue colour **2** a blue jewel

turret *noun*
1 a small tower in a castle **2** a revolving structure containing a gun

turtle *noun*
a sea animal that looks like a tortoise **to turn turtle** is to capsize

tusk *noun*
one of a pair of long pointed teeth that stick out of the mouth of an elephant or walrus or boar

tussle *noun*
a hard struggle or fight
tussle *verb*
to tussle is to struggle or fight over something

tutor *noun*
a teacher who teaches one person or a small group at a time

TV
short for television

tweak *verb*
to tweak something is to twist it or pull it sharply

tweed *noun*
tweed is a thick rough woollen cloth

tweezers *plural noun*
a small tool for gripping or picking up small things like stamps and hairs

twelve *noun*
the number 12
twelfth *adjective, noun* 12th

twenty *noun*
the number 20
twentieth *adjective, noun* 20th

twice *adverb*
1 two times; on two occasions **2** double the amount

twiddle *verb*
to twiddle something is to turn it round or over and over in an idle way • *He was twiddling a knob on the radio.*

twig *noun*
a short thin piece from a branch of a tree

twilight *noun*
twilight is the time of dim light just after sunset

twin *noun*
each of two children or animals born at the same time from one mother

twine *noun*
twine is strong thin string

twinge *noun*
a sudden sharp pain or unpleasant feeling

twinkle *verb*
to twinkle is to sparkle or shine with flashes of bright light
twinkle *noun*
a twinkling light

twirl *verb*
to twirl is to turn round and round quickly; to twirl something is to make it do this
twirl *noun*
a twirling movement

twist *verb*
1 to twist something is to turn its ends in opposite directions **2** to twist is to turn round or from side to side • *The road twisted through the hills.* **3** to twist something is to bend it out of its proper shape • *My bicycle's front wheel is twisted.* • *I think I've twisted my ankle.*
twist *noun*
a twisting movement or action

twitch *verb*
to twitch is to jerk or move suddenly and quickly; to twitch something is to make it do this
twitch *noun*
a twitching movement

twitter *verb*
birds twitter when they make quick chirping sounds

two *noun*
the number 2 **to be in two minds** is to be undecided about something

type *noun*
1 a type is a group or class of similar people or things; a kind or sort • *What type of computer of you got?* **2** type is letters and figures designed for use in printing
type *verb*
to type something is to write it with a typewriter or computer

typewriter *noun*
a machine with keys that you press to print letters or figures on a sheet of paper **typewritten** *adjective* written with a typewriter

a b c d e f g h i j k l m n o p q r s t u v w x y z

typhoon *noun*
a violent tropical storm with strong winds and rain

typical *adjective*
1 usual or normal • *Her typical day would begin with a good breakfast.* 2 as you would expect from a particular person or thing • *She worked with typical thoroughness.* **typically** *adverb* usually

typist *noun*
a person who types, especially as their job

tyranny *noun* (**tyrannies**)
(*say* ti-ra-nee)
tyranny is a cruel or unjust way of ruling people **tyrannical** *adjective* a tyrannical ruler uses their power in a cruel or unjust way

tyrant *noun* (*say* ty-rant)
someone who rules people cruelly or unjustly

tyre *noun*
a covering of rubber fitted round the rim of a wheel to make it grip the road and run smoothly

Uu

udder *noun*
the bag-like part of a cow, goat, or ewe, from which milk is taken

UFO *noun*
short for *unidentified flying object*, a flying object that no one can explain

UFO

ugly *adjective* (**uglier, ugliest**)
1 not beautiful; unpleasant to look at 2 threatening or dangerous • *The crowd was in an ugly mood.* **ugliness** *noun*

ulcer *noun*
a sore on the inside or outside of your body

ultimate *adjective*
furthest in a series of things; final **ultimately** *adverb* finally or eventually

ultraviolet *adjective*
ultraviolet light is light beyond the violet end of the spectrum, that causes your skin to tan

umbilical cord *noun*
the tube through which a baby receives nourishment in the mother's womb, connected to the baby's navel

umbrella *noun*
a mushroom-shaped piece of cloth stretched over a folding frame, which you open to protect yourself from rain

WORD ORIGIN

The word **umbrella** comes from an Italian word *ombrella* meaning 'a little shade'.

umpire *noun*
someone who makes sure that people keep to the rules in cricket, tennis, and some other games

unable *adjective*
not able • *She was unable to hear.*

unanimous *adjective*
(*say* yoo-**nan**-i-mus)
a unanimous decision or vote is one where everyone agrees **unanimously** *adverb* with everyone agreeing • *She was elected unanimously.*

unarmed *adjective*
without weapons • *unarmed combat.*

unavoidable *adjective*
not able to be avoided; bound to happen **unavoidably** *adverb*

unaware *adjective*
not knowing about something • *She was unaware of the danger ahead.*

unawares *adjective* unexpectedly; without someone knowing • *His question caught me unawares.*

unbearable *adjective*
something is unbearable when it is so painful or unpleasant that you cannot bear or endure it **unbearably** *adverb* in an unbearable way • *It was unbearably hot.*

unbelievable *adjective*
1 difficult to believe 2 amazing **unbelievably** *adverb*

unblock *verb*
to unblock something is to clear it of a block or obstruction

uncalled for *adjective*
not justified or necessary • *Your rudeness is uncalled for.*

uncanny *adjective* (**uncannier, uncanniest**)
strange and mysterious • *There was an uncanny silence.*

uncertain *adjective*
1 not certain • *He is uncertain about what to do.* 2 not reliable • *The weather is uncertain at the moment.*

uncertainty *noun*
uncertainty is being uncertain about something

uncle *noun*
1 the brother of your father or mother 2 your aunt's husband

uncomfortable *adjective*
not comfortable **uncomfortably** *adverb*

uncommon *adjective*
not common; unusual

unconscious *adjective*
1 not awake or knowing what is happening around you because you have fainted or been knocked out 2 not aware of something • *I was unconscious of doing anything wrong.* **unconsciously** *adverb* without being aware of doing something **unconsciousness** *noun* being unconscious

uncontrollable *adjective* unable to be controlled **uncontrollably** *adverb*

uncouth *adjective* (*say* un-**kooth**)
rude and rough in manner

uncover *verb*
1 to uncover something is to take the cover or top off it 2 to uncover a secret or something unknown is to discover it • *The police have uncovered a huge fraud.*

undecided *adjective*
you are undecided about something when you have not made up your mind about it

undeniable *adjective*
impossible to deny; certainly true **undeniably** *adverb* something is undeniably true when it is certainly true

under *preposition*
1 lower than; below • *Hide it under the desk.* 2 less than • *They are under 5 years old.* 3 ruled or controlled by • *The army is under his command.* 4 in the process of; undergoing • *The road is under repair.* 5 using; moving by means of • *The machine moves under its own power.*

under *adverb*
in or to a lower place • *Slowly the diver went under.*

underarm *adjective, adverb*
with the arm kept below shoulder level and moving forward and upwards

undercarriage *noun*
an aircraft's undercarriage is its landing wheels and the parts that support them

underclothes *plural noun*
or **underclothing** *noun*
underwear

underdog *noun*
the person or team in a contest that
is expected to lose

underdone *adjective*
not properly done or cooked

underfoot *adverb*
1 on the ground where you are walking
• *It was slippery underfoot.* **2** under
someone's feet • *The flag fell to the
ground and was trampled underfoot.*

undergo *verb* (**undergoing,
underwent, undergone**)
to undergo something is to
experience something or have to do
it • *He underwent several operations
on his leg.*

undergraduate *noun*
a student at a university who has not
yet taken a degree

underground *adjective, adverb*
1 under the ground **2** done or
working in secret

underground *noun*
a railway that runs through tunnels
under the ground

undergrowth *noun* undergrowth
is bushes and other plants growing
closely under tall trees

underhand *adjective*
secret and deceitful

underline *verb*
1 to underline something you have
written is to draw a line under it
2 to underline a fact is to emphasize
it or show it clearly • *This accident
underlines the need to be careful all
the time.*

undermine *verb*
to undermine someone's efforts or
plans is to weaken them gradually

underneath *preposition, adverb*
below or beneath

underpants *plural noun*
a piece of men's underwear worn
under trousers

underpass *noun*
a place where one road or path goes
under another

underprivileged *adjective* people
who are underprivileged don't have
the same opportunities or standard
of living as most people

understand *verb*
(**understanding, understood**)
1 to understand something is to
know what it means or how it works
2 to understand something is also to
have heard about it • *I understand
you've not been well.* **3** to understand

someone is to know what they are
like and why they behave the way
they do **understandable** *adjective*
able to be understood; easy to
understand

understanding *noun*
1 understanding is the power to
understand or think; intelligence
2 an understanding is when
people have an agreement • *In the
end the two brothers came to an
understanding.* **3** understanding is
also sympathy or tolerance

understanding *adjective*
sympathetic and helpful • *He was
very understanding when I was ill.*

understudy *noun*
(**understudies**)
an actor who learns a part in a play
so that they can play the part if the
usual actor isn't able to perform

undertake *verb* (**undertaking,
undertook, undertaken**)
to undertake something is to agree
or promise to do it

undertaker *noun*
someone whose job is to arrange
funerals

undertaking *noun*
something that someone agrees to do

underwater *adjective*
placed or used or done below the
surface of water

underwater

underwear *noun*
underwear is clothes
you wear next to your skin, under
your main clothes

underworld *noun*
1 in legends, the underworld is the
place for the spirits of the dead; hell
2 the underworld is also people who
are regularly involved in crime

undesirable *adjective*
not wanted or liked

undeveloped *adjective*
not yet developed

undo *verb* (**undoing, undid,
undone**)
1 to undo something is
to unfasten or unwrap
it • *Can you undo
this knot?*

2 to undo something already
done is to cancel the effect of it
• *He has undone all our careful work.*

undoubted *adjective*
definite or certain **undoubtedly**
adverb certainly

undress *verb*
1 to undress is to take your clothes
off **2** to undress someone is to take
their clothes off

unearth *verb*
1 to unearth something is to dig it
up **2** to unearth something is also to
find it after searching for it

unearthly *adjective* supernatural;
strange and frightening

uneasy *adjective* (**uneasier,
uneasiest**)
anxious or worried **uneasily** *noun*
in a way that shows you are anxious
or worried

uneatable *adjective*
not fit for eating

unemployed *adjective*
to be unemployed is to be without a
job **unemployment** *noun* being
without a job; the number of people
without a job

uneven *adjective*
not level, flat, or regular • *The path
was uneven.* **unevenly** *adverb*
unevenness *noun*

unexpected *adjective*
not expected; surprising
unexpectedly *adverb* when you
are not expecting it

unfair *adjective*
not fair; unjust **unfairly** *adverb*
unfairness *noun*

unfaithful *adjective*
not faithful or loyal

unfamiliar *adjective*
not familiar

unfasten *verb*
to unfasten something is to open it
when it has been fastened

unfinished *adjective*
not finished

unfit *adjective*
1 someone is unfit when they are not
fit or fully healthy **2** to be unfit for
something is to be not suitable • *He
is unfit for the job.*

unfold *verb*
1 to unfold something is to open it
or spread it out • *She unfolded the
map.* **2** to unfold a story or plan is
to make it known gradually **3** a
story unfolds when it becomes
known gradually

unforgettable *adjective*
impossible to forget

a b c d e f g h i j k l m n o p q r s t u v w x y z

unforgivable *adjective*
not able to be forgiven

unfortunate *adjective*
1 unlucky **2** you say something is
unfortunate when you wish it hadn't
happened; regrettable • *It was an
unfortunate remark.*
unfortunately *adverb* used to say
you are sad about something
• *Unfortunately he wasn't able to
come to the party.*

unfriendly *adjective*
not friendly
unfriendliness *noun*

ungrateful *adjective*
not grateful
ungratefully *adverb*

unhappy *adjective* (**unhappier,
unhappiest**)
1 not happy or pleased**2** you say
something is unhappy when you
wish it hadn't happened; regrettable
• *It was an unhappy choice of words.*
unhappily *adverb* **unhappiness**
noun

unhealthy *adjective*
(**unhealthier, unhealthiest**)
1 not in good health **2** not good for
you • *She has an unhealthy diet.*

unheard-of *adjective*
never known or done before;
extraordinary

unicorn *noun* (*say* **yoo**-ni-korn)
an imaginary animal in stories, like
a horse with a long straight horn
growing out of the front of its head

unicorn

uniform *noun*
the special clothes worn by members
of an army or school or organization
uniform *adjective*
always the same; not changing
uniformly *adverb* in a way that
does not change

uniformity *noun*
uniformity is being uniform
or the same

unify *verb* (**unifies, unifying,
unified**)
to unify several things, especially
countries, is to join them into one thing;
to unify is to join together **unification**

noun when several things are joined
together into one thing

unimportant *adjective*
not important

uninhabited *adjective*
a place is uninhabited when there is
nobody living there

unintentional *adjective*
not done deliberately
unintentionally *adverb* by
accident; not on purpose

uninterested *adjective*
not interested

uninteresting *adjective*
not interesting

union *noun*
1 the joining of things together; a
united thing **2** a trade union

Union Jack *noun*
the flag of the United Kingdom

unique *adjective* (*say* yoo-**neek**)
something is unique when it is the
only one of its kind • *Everyone's
fingerprints are unique.* • *This jewel is
unique.* **uniquely** *adverb*
uniqueness *noun*

unisex *adjective*
designed to be suitable for either
men or women

unison *noun* (*say* **yoo**-ni-son)
in unison said or done by people
together at the same time

unit *noun*
1 an amount used in measuring or
counting, such as a centimetre or a
pound **2** a single person or thing **3** a
group of people or things that belong
together

unite *verb*
1 to unite several people or things is
to form them into one thing or group
2 people or things unite when they
join together

unity *noun* (**unities**)
unity is being united or having
agreement

universal *adjective*
including everyone and everything
universally *adverb* by everyone
• *This theory is now universally
accepted.*

universe *noun*
the universe is everything that exists,
including the earth and living things
and all the stars and planets

university *noun* (**universities**)
a place where people go to study for
a degree after they have left school

unjust *adjective*
not fair or just
unjustly *adverb*

unkind *adjective*
cruel and not kind **unkindly** *adverb*
unkindness *noun*

unless *conjunction*
except when; if not • *We cannot go
unless we are invited.*

unlike *preposition*
not like • *unlike me, she enjoys
sport.*

unlike *adjective*
not alike; different • *The two children
are very unlike.*

unlikely *adjective*
(**unlikelier, unlikeliest**)
not likely to happen or be true

unload *verb*
to unload a container or vehicle is to
take off the things it carried

unlock *verb*
to unlock a door or container
is to open it with a key

unlucky *adjective* (**unluckier,
unluckiest**)
not lucky **unluckily** *adverb*

unmistakable *adjective*
not likely to be mistaken for
something or someone else; clear
and definite **unmistakably**
adverb in a way that is unlikely to
be mistaken for something else • *His
accent was unmistakably French.*

unnatural *adjective*
not natural or normal **unnaturally**
adverb

unnecessary *adjective*
not needed **unnecessarily** *adverb*
when it is not needed

unoccupied *adjective*
a house is unoccupied when
it is empty, with no one living there

unpack *verb*
to unpack a suitcase or bag
is to take out the things in it

unpleasant *adjective*
not pleasant **unpleasantly** *adverb*
unpleasantness *noun*

unplug *verb* (**unplugging,
unplugged**)
to unplug an electrical device is to
disconnect it by taking its plug out of
the socket

unpopular *adjective*
not liked or enjoyed by people
unpopularity *noun* the fact that a
person or thing is unpopular

unravel *verb* (**unravelling,
unravelled**)
1 to unravel something is to unwind
it or disentangle it **2** to unravel a
problem or mystery is to investigate
it and solve it

unreal *adjective*
not real; existing only in the imagination

unreasonable *adjective*
not reasonable or fair

unrest *noun*
unrest is trouble caused by people feeling unhappy

unroll *verb*
to unroll something is to open it when it has been rolled up

unruly *adjective* (**unrulier, unruliest**) (*say* un-**roo**-lee)
badly behaved and difficult to control **unruliness** *noun*

unsafe *adjective*
not safe; dangerous

unscrew *verb*
to unscrew something is to undo it by turning it or by removing screws

unseen *adjective*
not seen or noticed • *He managed to slip out of the room unseen.*

unselfish *adjective*
not selfish; not thinking only about yourself **unselfishly** *adverb* **unselfishness** *noun*

unsightly *adjective*
not pleasant to look at; ugly

unsteady *adjective* (**unsteadier, unsteadiest**) shaking or wobbling or likely to fall **unsteadily** *adverb* **unsteadiness** *noun*

unsuccessful *adjective*
not successful
unsuccessfully *adverb*

unsuitable *adjective*
not suitable **unsuitably** *adverb*

unthinkable *adjective*
too bad or unlikely to be worth thinking about

untidy *adjective* (**untidier, untidiest**)
messy and not tidy
untidily *adverb* **untidiness** *noun*

untie *verb* (**unties, untying, untied**)
to untie something is to undo it when it has been tied

until *preposition, conjunction*
up to a particular time or event • *The shop is open until 8 o'clock.* • *We will stay with you until the train comes.*

untold *adjective*
too great to be counted or measured • *The hurricane caused untold damage.*

untrue *adjective*
not true

untruthful *adjective*
not telling the truth **untruthfully** *adverb*

unused *adjective* (*say* un-**yoozd**)
not yet used **unused to something** (*say* un-**yoost**) not familiar with something • *He is unused to eating meat.*

unusual *adjective*
different from what is usual or normal; strange or rare **unusually** *adverb*

unwanted *adjective*
not wanted

unwell *adjective*
not well; ill

unwilling *adjective*
you are unwilling to do something when you don't want to do it **unwillingly** *adverb* **unwillingness** *noun*

unwind *verb* (**unwinding, unwound**) (*rhymes with* **find**)
1 to unwind something is to unroll it
2 to unwind is to become unrolled
3 (*informal*) to unwind is also to relax after you have been working hard

unwrap *verb* (**unwrapping, unwrapped**)
to unwrap something is to take it out of its wrapping

unzip *verb* (**unzipping, unzipped**)
to unzip something is to undo it when it is zipped up

up *adverb*
1 in or to a standing or upright position • *Stand up.* **2** in or to a high or higher place or level • *Put it up on the shelf.* • *Prices are going up.*
3 completely • *Eat up your carrots.*
4 out of bed • *It's time to get up.*
5 finished • *Your time is up.*
6 (*informal*) happening
• *Something is up.* **ups and downs** changes of luck, sometimes good and sometimes bad **to be up to something** is to be doing something mysterious or suspicious • *What are they up to?* **up to date 1** modern or fashionable **2** having the latest information

up *preposition*
in or to a higher position on something • *Let's climb up the mountain.*

upbringing *noun*
your upbringing is the way you have been brought up

update *verb*
to update something is to bring it up to date

upgrade *verb*
to upgrade a machine is to improve it by installing new parts in it

upheaval *noun*
a sudden violent change or disturbance

uphill *adjective, adverb*
1 sloping upwards; going up a slope
2 difficult • *It was an uphill struggle.*

uphold *verb* (**upholding, upheld**)
to uphold a decision or belief is to support it or agree with it

upholstery *noun*
upholstery is covers and padding for furniture

upkeep *noun*
the upkeep of something is the cost of looking after it and keeping it in good condition

uplands *plural noun*
the highest part of a country or region

upon *preposition*
on

upper *adjective*
higher in position or rank

upright *adjective*
1 standing straight up; vertical
2 honest

upright *noun*
an upright post or support

uprising *noun*
a rebellion or revolt against the government

uproar *noun*
uproar is a loud or angry noise or disturbance • *The room was in uproar.*

upset *adjective* (*say* up-**set**)
unhappy or anxious about something

upset *verb* (**upsetting, upset**) (*say* up-**set**)
1 to upset someone is to make them unhappy or anxious **2** to upset something is to knock it over and spill its contents

upset *noun* (*say* **up**-set)
a slight illness • *He's got a stomach upset.*

upside down *adjective, adverb*
1 with the upper part underneath instead of on top; the wrong way up
2 in disorder or confusion • *The thieves turned the place upside down.*

upstairs *adverb, adjective*
to or on a higher floor in a house or other building

upstream *adjective, adverb*
in the direction opposite to the flow of a river or stream

uptight *adjective*
(*informal*) upset or nervous about something

up-to-date *adjective*
1 modern or fashionable
2 having the latest information

upward *adjective, adverb*
going towards what is higher

a
b
c
d
e
f
g
h
i
j
k
l
m
n
o
p
q
r
s
t
u
v
w
x
y
z

upwards *adverb*
towards what is higher

uranium *noun*
(*say* yoor-**ay**-ni-um)
uranium is a radioactive metal used as a source of atomic energy

urban *adjective*
to do with a town or city

Urdu *noun*
Urdu is a language related to Hindi, spoken in northern India and Pakistan

urge *verb*
1 to urge someone to do something is to try to persuade them to do it **2** to urge people or animals is to drive them forward

urge *noun*
a sudden strong desire or wish • *She felt an urge to go for a swim.*

urgent *adjective*
needing to be done or dealt with immediately **urgency** *noun* urgency is when something needs to be done or dealt with immediately **urgently** *adverb*

urinate *verb* (*say* **yoor**-i-nayt)
to urinate is to pass urine out of your body **urination** *noun* urination is passing urine

urine *noun* (*say* **yoor**-in)
urine is the waste liquid that collects in your bladder and is passed out of your body

urn *noun*
1 a large metal container with a tap, in which water is heated **2** a kind of large vase for holding the ashes of a person who has been cremated

us *pronoun*
a word used for *we*, usually when it is the object of a sentence, or when it comes after a preposition • *She likes us* • *She gave it to us.*

urn

usage *noun*
(*say* **yoo**-sij)
the way that something is used, especially the way that words and language are used

use *verb* (*say* yooz)
to use something is to perform an action or job with it • *Are you using my pen?* **used to** did in the past • *I used to live in Glasgow.* **to be used to something** or **someone** is to know them well or be familiar with them

• *We're used to hard work.* **to use something up** is to use all of it, so that none is left

use *noun* (*say* yooss)
1 the action of using something or being used **2** the purpose or value of something • *Can you find a use for this box?* • *This knife is no use to us.*

used *adjective* (*say* yoozd)
not new; second-hand
• *We're buying a used car.*

useful *adjective*
able to be used a lot or do something that needs doing **usefully** *adverb* **usefulness** *noun*

useless *adjective*
1 not having any use **2** (*informal*) not very good at something • *I'm useless at drawing.* **uselessly** *adverb* **uselessness** *noun*

user *noun*
someone who uses something

user-friendly *adjective* (**user-friendlier, user-friendliest**)
designed to be easy to use

usher *noun*
someone who shows people to their seats in a church or cinema or theatre

usher *verb*
to usher someone is to lead them in or out of a place

usherette *noun*
a woman who shows people to their seats in a cinema or theatre

usual *adjective*
as happens often or all the time; expected • *He sat in his usual chair by the fire.* • *She was late as usual.* **usually** *adverb* on most occasions; normally

utensil *noun*
(*say* yoo-**ten**-sil)
a tool or device, especially one you use in the house

utmost *adjective*
greatest • *Look after it with the utmost care.*

utter[1] *verb*
to utter something is to say it clearly, or to make a sound with your mouth • *He uttered a loud yell.* **utterance** *noun* something that someone says

utter[2] *adjective*
complete or absolute • *It was utter misery.* **utterly** *adverb* completely • *You look utterly ridiculous.*

vacancy *noun* (**vacancies**)
a job, or a room in a guest house, that is available and not taken

vacant *adjective*
1 empty; not filled or occupied
• *There were no vacant seats.*
2 not showing any expression
• *He gave a vacant stare.*

vacate *verb*
to vacate a place is to leave it empty

vacation *noun*
(*say* vay-**kay**-shon)
a holiday, especially between the terms at a university

vaccinate *verb* (*say* **vak**-si-nayt)
to vaccinate someone is to protect them from a disease by injecting them with a vaccine **vaccination** *noun* when you are vaccinated against a disease

vaccine *noun* (*say* **vak**-seen)
a type of medicine injected into people to protect them from disease

WORD ORIGIN
vacca meaning 'cow', because the first vaccine was taken from cows.

vacuum *noun*
a completely empty space; a space without any air in it

vacuum *verb*
to clean something using a vacuum cleaner

vacuum cleaner *noun*
an electrical device that sucks up dust and dirt from the floor

vacuum flask *noun*
a container with double walls that have a vacuum between them, for keeping liquids hot or cold

vagina *noun* (*say* va-**jy**-na)
the passage in a woman's female body that leads from the outside of her body to her womb

vague *adjective*
not definite or clear • *I only have a vague memory of his face.* **vaguely** *adverb* not clearly **vagueness** *noun*

vain *adjective*
1 too proud of yourself, especially of how you look **2** unsuccessful or useless • *They made vain attempts to save him.* **in vain** with no result;

without success • *I tried in vain to call for help.* **vainly** *adverb* without success

valentine *noun*
1 a card sent on St Valentine's Day (14 February) to someone you love
2 the person you send a valentine to

valentine card

valiant *adjective*
brave or courageous **valiantly** *adverb* in a brave or courageous way

valid *adjective*
able to be used or accepted; legal • *My passport is no longer valid.* **validity** *noun* the validity of something is the fact that it is acceptable or legal

valley *noun* (**valleys**)
an area of low land between hills

valour *noun*
valour is bravery, especially in a battle

valuable *adjective*
1 worth a lot of money 2 very useful or important • *She gave me valuable advice.*

valuables *plural noun*
things that are worth a lot of money

value *noun*
1 the amount of money that something could be sold for 2 how useful or important something is

value *verb*
1 to value something is to think that it is important or worth having • *I value her friendship.* 2 to value something is also to work out how much it could be sold for • *The estate agent is coming to value the house.*

valuation *noun* an estimate of what something is worth **valuer** *noun* someone who values something

vampire

valve *noun*
a device used to control the flow of gas or liquid

vampire *noun*
in stories, a creature that sucks people's blood

van *noun*
1 a small lorry with a covered area for goods at the back 2 a railway carriage used for goods or for the train's guard

vandal *noun*
someone who deliberately breaks or damages things, especially buildings

vandalism *noun*
doing deliberate damage to something, especially a building

vanilla *noun*
vanilla is a flavouring made from the pods of a tropical plant

vanish *verb*
to vanish is to disappear completely

vanity *noun*
vanity is being too proud of yourself, especially of how you look

vanquish *verb*
to vanquish someone is to win a victory over them

vapour *noun*
a visible gas, such as mist or steam, which some liquids and solids can be turned into by heat

variable *adjective*
able or likely to change

variation *noun*
1 a change in something • *There have been slight variations in temperature.* 2 a different form of something

varied *adjective*
of various kinds; full of variety • *She has varied interests.*

variety *noun*
1 a variety is a number of different kinds of the same thing • *There was a variety of cakes to choose from.*
2 a variety is a particular kind of something • *There are many rare varieties of butterfly.* 3 variety is a situation where things are not always the same • *We have a life full of variety.*

various *determiner*
1 of different kinds • *They came for various reasons.*
2 several • *We met various people.* **variously** *adverb* in several different ways

varnish *noun*
a liquid that dries to form a hard shiny surface on wood or other surfaces

varnish *verb*
to varnish wood or another surface is to put varnish on it

vary *verb* (**varies, varying, varied**)
1 to vary is to keep changing • *The weather varies a lot here.* 2 things vary when they are different from each other • *The cars are the same, although the colours vary.* 3 to vary something is to make changes to it

vase *noun* (*say* vahz)
a jar used for holding flowers or as an ornament

vast *adjective*
very large or wide **vastly** *adverb* greatly; very • *They are from vastly different backgrounds.* **vastness** *noun* being very large or wide

VAT
short for *value-added tax*, a tax on goods and services

vat *noun*
a very large container for holding liquid

vault *verb*
you vault something, or vault over it, when you jump over it, using your hands to support you or with the help of a pole

vault *noun*
1 a jump done by vaulting
2 an underground room for storing money and valuables

VDU
short for *visual display unit*

veal *noun*
veal is the meat from a calf

vector *noun*
(*in mathematics*) a quantity that has size and direction, such as velocity (which is speed in a certain direction)

Veda *plural noun*
the ancient writings of the Hindu religion

veer *verb*
to veer is to swerve or change direction suddenly • *The cyclist veered off to the left.*

vegan *noun* (*say* **vee**-gan)
someone who does not use or eat any products made from animals

vegetable *noun*
a plant that can be used as food

vegetarian *noun*
(*say* vej-i-**tair**-i-an)
someone who does not eat meat

vegetation *noun*
vegetation is plants that are growing

vehicle *noun*
a means of carrying people or things, especially on land. Cars, buses, trains, and lorries are vehicles.

veil *noun*
a piece of thin material to cover a woman's face or head **veiled** *adjective* covered with a veil; partially hidden

vein *noun*
1 your veins are the tubes in your body that carry blood towards your heart **2** a line or streak on a leaf or rock or insect's wing **3** a long deposit of a mineral in the middle of rock

velocity *noun* (**velocities**)
(*say* vil-**os**-i-tee)
velocity is speed in a particular direction

velvet *noun*
velvet is a soft material with short furry fibres on one side **velvety** *adjective* soft, like velvet

vendetta *noun*
a long-lasting quarrel or feud

WORD ORIGIN

Vendetta is an Italian word, which comes from a Latin word *vindicta* meaning 'vengeance'.

vending machine *noun*
a machine that you can buy food, drinks, or other things from, which you operate by putting in coins

venerable *adjective*
worthy of respect or honour because of being so old

venetian blind *noun*
a blind for a window, made of thin horizontal slats which you can move to control the amount of light that comes through

vending machine

vengeance *noun*
vengeance is harming or punishing someone because they have done harm to you **vengeful** *adjective* a vengeful person wants to punish someone who has harmed them

venison *noun*
venison is the meat from a deer

Venn diagram *noun*
(in mathematics) a diagram using circles to show how sets of things relate to one another

venom *noun*
1 venom is the poison of snakes **2** venom is also a feeling of bitter

hatred for someone **venomous** *adjective* poisonous

vent *noun*
an opening in something, especially to let out smoke or gas

ventilate *verb*
to ventilate a place is to let fresh air come into it and move around it **ventilation** *noun* letting fresh air move freely around a place **ventilator** *noun* a machine that breathes for someone in hospital

ventriloquist *noun*
(*say* ven-**tril**-o-kwist)
an entertainer who speaks without moving their lips, so that it looks as though a dummy is speaking **ventriloquism** *noun* what a ventriloquist does

venture *noun*
something new that you decide to do that is risky or daring

venture *verb*
to venture somewhere is to go there even though you know it might be difficult or dangerous • *Shall we venture out into the snow?*

veranda *noun* (*say* ver-**an**-da)
an open terrace with a roof along the outside of a house

verb *noun*
a word that shows what someone or something is doing, such as *be*, *go*, *sing*, *take*

verbal *adjective*
spoken rather than written • *We had a verbal agreement.* **verbally** *adverb* in spoken words, not in writing

verdict *noun*
the decision reached by a judge or jury about whether someone is guilty of a crime

verge *noun*
a strip of grass beside a road or path **on the verge of** about to do something • *She was on the verge of leaving.*

verge *verb*
to verge on something is to be nearly something • *His remark verged on the absurd.*

verify *verb* (**verifies, verifying, verified**)
to verify something is to find or show whether it is true or correct **verification** *noun* verification is verifying something

vermin *noun*
vermin are animals or insects that damage crops or food or carry disease, such as rats and fleas

verruca *noun* (**verrucas**)
(*say* ver-**oo**-ka)
a kind of wart on the sole of your foot

versatile *adjective*
(*say* **ver**-sa-tyl)
able to do or be used for many different things **versatility** *noun* versatility is being able to do or be used for many different things

verse *noun*
1 verse is writing in the form of poetry **2** a verse is a group of lines in a poem or song **3** a verse is also each of the short numbered sections of a chapter in the Bible

version *noun*
1 someone's account of something that has happened • *His version of the accident is different from mine.* **2** a different form of a thing • *I don't like their version of the song.*

versus *preposition*
against or competing with, especially in sport • *The final will be Brazil versus Germany.*

vertebra *noun* (**vertebrae**)
(*say* **ver**-ti-bra)
each of the bones that form your backbone

vertebrate *noun* (*say* **ver**-ti-brit)
an animal with a backbone

vertical *adjective*
going directly upwards, at right angles to something level or horizontal **vertically** *adverb* in a vertical direction

vertigo *noun*
vertigo is feeling dizzy because you are high up

very *adverb*
to a great amount; extremely • *It is very cold.*

very *adjective*
1 exact or actual • *That's the very thing we need!* **2** extreme • *We've reached the very end.*

Vesak *noun* (*say* **ves**-ak)
Vesak is an important festival of Buddhism, held in April to May

vessel *noun*
1 a boat or ship 2 a container for liquids 3 a tube inside an animal or plant, carrying blood or some other liquid

vest *noun*
a piece of underwear you wear on the top half of your body

vestment *noun*
a piece of outer clothing worn by the clergy or choir at a church service

vet *noun*
a person trained to treat sick animals

veteran *noun*
1 a person with long experience of something 2 a soldier who has returned from a war

veterinary *adjective* (*say* **vet**-rin-ree)
to do with the medical treatment of animals

veto *noun* (*say* **vee**-toh)
1 a refusal to let something happen 2 the right to stop something from happening

veto *verb* (**vetoes, vetoing, vetoed**)
to veto something is to refuse to let it happen

vex *verb*
to vex someone is to annoy or worry them **vexation** *noun* vexation is vexing someone

via *preposition* (*say* **vy**-a)
going through; stopping at • *This train goes from Edinburgh to London via York.*

viaduct *noun* (*say* **vy**-a-dukt)
a long bridge with many arches, carrying a road or railway over low ground

vibrate *verb*
to vibrate is to move quickly from side to side and with small movements • *Every time a train went past the walls vibrated.* **vibration** *noun* when something moves quickly from side to side and with small movements

vicar *noun*
a minister of the Church of England who is in charge of a parish

vicarage *noun*
the house of a vicar

vice[1] *noun*
1 a vice is a bad or evil habit

2 vice is evil or wickedness

vice[2] *noun*
a device with jaws for holding something tightly in place while you work on it

vice-president *noun*
a deputy to a president

vice versa *adverb*
(*say* vys-**ver**-sa)
the other way round • *'We need them and vice versa'* means *'We need them and they need us'.*

vicinity *noun* (**vicinities**)
the area near or surrounding a particular place • *Are there any parks in the vicinity?*

vicious *adjective* (*say* **vish**-us)
1 cruel and aggressive 2 severe or violent **viciously** *adverb* **viciousness** *noun*

victim *noun*
1 a person who suffers from something • *He is a polio victim.* 2 someone who is killed, injured, or robbed • *The murderer lay in wait for his victim.*

victimize *verb*
to victimize someone is to treat them unfairly

victor *noun*
the winner of a battle or contest

victory *noun* (**victories**)
winning a battle or contest or game **victorious** *adjective* someone is victorious when they win a battle or contest or game

video *noun* (**videos**) 1 a system of recording moving pictures and sound, especially as a digital file • *The accident was captured on video.* 2 a short film or recording that you can watch on a computer or mobile phone, especially over the Internet 3 a copy of a film or television programme that has been recorded

video *verb* (**videos, videoing, videoed**)
to record something on video

WORD ORIGIN

The word **video** comes from a Latin word *videre* meaning 'to see'. The *-o* ending is based on *audio* in *audiovisual*.

video recorder or **video cassette recorder** *noun*
a machine for recording television programmes and playing them back

videotape *noun*
videotape is magnetic tape used for video recording

view *noun*
1 what you can see from one place • *There's a fine view from the top of*

the hill. 2 someone's opinion • *She has strong views about smoking.* **on view** shown for people to see

view *verb*
1 to view something is to look at it carefully 2 to view something or someone in a certain way is to think about them in that way • *They seemed to view us with suspicion.*

viewer *noun*
someone who watches something, especially a television programme

vigilant *adjective* (*say* **vij**-i-lant)
someone is vigilant when they are watching carefully for something **vigilantly** *adverb* **vigilance** *noun* vigilance is watching carefully for something

vigorous *adjective*
full of strength and energy **vigorously** *adverb*

vigour *noun*
vigour is strength and energy

Viking *noun*
a Scandinavian pirate or trader in the 8th to 10th centuries

vile *adjective*
disgusting or bad • *What a vile smell.*

villa *noun*
a house, especially a large one in its own grounds, or one used for holidays abroad

village *noun*
a group of houses and other buildings in the country, smaller than a town **villager** *noun* someone who lives in a village

villain *noun*
a wicked person or criminal **villainous** *adjective* wicked **villainy** *noun* wicked behaviour

vine *noun*
a plant on which grapes grow

vinegar *noun*
vinegar is a sour liquid used to flavour food

vineyard *noun* (*say* **vin**-yard)
an area of land where vines are grown to produce grapes for making wine

vintage *noun*
1 all the grapes that are harvested in one season, or the wine made from them 2 the period from which something comes • *The furniture is of 1920s vintage.*

vinyl *noun* (*say* **vy**-nil)
vinyl is a kind of plastic

viola *noun* (*say* vee-**oh**-la)
a stringed instrument rather like a violin but slightly larger and with a lower pitch

blood vessels

a
b
c
d
e
f
g
h
i
j
k
l
m
n
o
p
q
r
s
t
u
v
w
x
y
z

violate verb
1 to violate a rule or law is to break it **2** to violate a person or place is to treat them without respect **violation** noun the breaking of a rule or law

violence noun
1 violence is when someone uses force to hurt or kill people **2** violence is also force that damages things • *We weren't prepared for the violence of the storm.* **violent** adjective using violence; strong and forceful **violently** adverb with violence or great force

violet noun
1 a bluish-purple colour **2** a small plant that usually has purple flowers

violin noun
a musical instrument with four strings, played with a bow

violin

violinist noun someone who plays a violin

VIP
short for *very important person*

viper noun
a small poisonous snake

virtual adjective
1 almost the same as the real thing • *His silence was a virtual admission of guilt.* **2** using virtual reality • *Click here to go on a virtual tour of the gallery.*

virtually adverb
in effect; nearly • *She comes here so often she's virtually a member of the family.*

virtual reality noun
virtual reality is an image or environment created by a computer that imitates the real world and that you can be part of

virtue noun
1 a virtue is a good quality in a person's character • *Honesty is a virtue.* **2** virtue is moral goodness **virtuous** adjective behaving in a very good way

virus noun (say **vy**-rus)
1 a microscopic creature that can cause disease **2** a disease caused by a virus • *The doctor said I had a virus.* **3** a hidden set of instructions in a computer program that is designed to destroy data

visa noun
an official mark put on someone's passport to show that the person has permission to enter a country

visibility noun
visibility is how far you can see clearly • *Visibility is down to 20 metres.*

visible adjective
able to be seen • *The ship was visible on the horizon.*

vision noun
1 vision is the ability to see **2** a vision is something that you see or imagine, especially in a dream **3** vision is also imagination and understanding • *They need a leader with vision.*

visit verb
to visit a place or person is to go to see them or stay there
visit noun
a short stay at a place or with a person
visitor noun
someone who is visiting or staying at a place

visor noun (say **vy**-zer)
the clear part of a helmet that closes over the face

visual adjective
to do with seeing; used for seeing **visually** adverb in a way that is connected with your ability to see

visual display unit noun
a screen on which a computer displays information

vital adjective
1 extremely important; essential • *It is vital that we get there on time.* **2** connected with life; needed in order to live **vitally** adverb

vitality noun
vitality is liveliness or energy

vitamin noun
each of several substances which are present in some foods and which you need to stay healthy

vivid adjective
bright and clear • *The colours are very vivid.* • *She gave a vivid description of the storm.* **vividly** adverb **vividness** noun

vixen noun
a female fox

vocabulary noun (**vocabularies**)
1 the vocabulary of a language is all the words used in it **2** a person's vocabulary is the words that they know and use

vocal adjective
to do with the voice; using your voice

vocation noun
a job or activity that you feel strongly you want to do

vodka noun
vodka is a strong alcoholic drink especially popular in Russia

voice noun
1 the sound you make when you speak or sing **2** the ability to speak or sing • *She has lost her voice.*

volcano noun (**volcanoes**)
a mountain with a hole at the top formed by molten lava which has burst through the earth's crust **volcanic** adjective caused or produced by a volcano

WORD ORIGIN

The word **volcano** is Italian and comes from Vulcan, the name of the Roman god of fire.

vole noun
a small animal rather like a rat

volley noun
1 a number of bullets or shells fired at the same time **2** in ball games, hitting or kicking the ball back before it touches the ground

volleyball noun
volleyball is a game in which two teams hit a large ball to and fro over a net with their hands

volt noun
a unit for measuring the force of an electric current

voltage noun
voltage is electric force measured in volts

volume noun
1 the amount of space filled by something **2** the strength

volca

or power of sound • *Turn down the volume!* **3** an amount • *The volume of traffic has increased.* **4** a book, especially one of a set

voluntary *adjective*
done or doing something because you want to, not for pay
voluntarily *adverb* because you want to

volunteer *verb*
1 to volunteer is to offer to do something that you do not have to do **2** to volunteer information or time is to provide it willingly without being asked for it • *Several people generously volunteered their time.*

volunteer *noun*
someone who volunteers to do something

vomit *verb*
to vomit is to bring food back from the stomach through your mouth

vote *verb*
1 to vote for someone or something is to show which you prefer by putting up your hand or making a mark on a piece of paper **2** to vote to do something is to say that you want to do it • *I vote we go away this weekend.*

vote *noun*
1 a way of choosing someone or something by getting people to put up their hand or make a mark on a piece of paper **2** a choice you make by voting **3** the right to vote

voter *noun*
someone who votes, especially in an election

voucher *noun*
a piece of paper showing that you are allowed to pay less for something or that you can get something in exchange

vow *verb*
to vow is to make a solemn promise to do something

vow *noun*
a solemn promise

vowel *noun*
any of the letters a, e, i, o, u, and sometimes y

voyage *noun*
a long journey by ship or in a spacecraft

vulgar *adjective*
rude; without good manners or good taste

vulgar fraction *noun*
a fraction shown by numbers above and below a line (such as ½ and ⅞), not a decimal fraction

vulnerable *adjective*
able to be harmed or attacked easily

vulture *noun*
a large bird that eats the flesh of dead animals

vulture

Ww

wad *noun*
a pad or bundle of soft material or pieces of paper

waddle *verb*
to waddle is to walk with short steps, rocking from side to side, like a duck

wade *verb*
to wade through water or mud is to walk through it

wafer *noun*
a thin kind of biscuit, often eaten with ice cream

waffle *noun*
1 a waffle is a crisp square pancake with a pattern of squares on it **2** waffle is talking for a long time without saying anything important or interesting

wag *verb* (**wagging, wagged**)
1 a dog wags its tail when it moves it quickly from side to side because it is happy or excited **2** you wag your finger when you move it up and down or from side to side

wag *noun*
a wagging movement

wage *noun* or **wages** *plural noun*
the money paid to someone for the job they do

wage *verb*
to wage a war or campaign is to fight it

wager *noun* (*say* **way**-jer)
a bet

wager *verb*
to wager someone is to make a bet with them

waggle *verb*
to waggle something is to move it quickly from side to side or up and down • *Can you waggle your ears?*

wagon *noun*
1 a cart with four wheels, pulled by a horse or ox **2** an open railway truck

wail *verb*
to wail is to make a long sad cry

wail *noun*
a sound of wailing

waist *noun*
the narrow part in the middle of your body

waistcoat *noun*
a close-fitting jacket without sleeves, worn over a shirt and under a jacket

wait *verb*
1 to wait, or to wait for someone or something, is to stay in a place or situation until something happens **2** to wait is also to be a waiter

wait *noun*
a time spent waiting • *We had a long wait for the bus.*

waiter *noun*
a man who serves people with food in a restaurant or hotel

waitress *noun*
a woman who serves people with food in a restaurant or hotel

wake¹ *verb* (**waking, woke, woken**)
1 you wake, or wake up, when you stop sleeping **2** to wake someone, or wake them up, is to make them stop sleeping • *You have woken the baby.*

wake² *noun*
the trail left on the water by a ship or boat

waken *verb*
to waken someone is to wake them

walk *verb*
to walk is to move along on your feet at an ordinary speed

wagon

a b c d e f g h i j k l m n o p q r s t u v w x y z

walk noun
1 a journey on foot 2 the way that someone walks • *He has a funny walk.* 3 a path or route for walking • *There are some lovely walks near here.*

walker noun
someone who goes for a walk, especially a long one

walkie-talkie noun
a small portable radio transmitter and receiver

walking stick noun
a stick a person carries or uses as a support while walking

wall noun
1 a structure built of brick or stone and forming one of the sides of a building or room, or going round a garden or other space 2 the outer surface of something, such as the stomach

wall verb
to wall something, or wall it in, is to surround or enclose it with a wall

wallaby noun (**wallabies**)
(*say* **wol**-a-bee)
a kind of small kangaroo

wallet noun
a small flat folding case for holding paper money, credit cards, and small documents

wallflower noun
a sweet-smelling garden plant

wallow verb
1 to wallow is to roll about in water or mud 2 to wallow in something is to get great pleasure from it • *They are wallowing in luxury.*

wallpaper noun
wallpaper is paper used to cover the walls of rooms

walnut noun
a kind of nut with a wrinkled surface

walrus noun
a large Arctic sea animal that looks like a large seal and has two long tusks

waltz noun
a dance with three beats to a bar

waltz verb
to waltz is to dance a waltz

wand noun
a short thin rod used by a magician, wizard, or fairy

wander verb
1 to wander is to go about without trying to reach a particular place 2 to wander, or wander off, is to stray or get lost • *Don't let the sheep wander.* **wanderer** noun someone who keeps travelling from place to place

wane verb
1 the moon wanes when its bright area gets gradually smaller 2 to wane is to become less or smaller or less strong • *His popularity was waning.*

want verb
1 to want something is to feel that you would like to have it or do it 2 to want something is also to need it • *Your hair wants cutting.*

want noun
1 a want is a wish to have something 2 want of something is a lack of it • *They died for want of water.*

wanted adjective
someone is wanted when they are being looked for by the police as a suspected criminal • *He was a wanted man.*

war noun
1 war is fighting between nations or armies; a war is a period of fighting 2 a war is also a serious struggle or effort against an evil such as crime or disease

warble verb
to warble is to sing gently, the way some birds do

warble noun
a warbling sound

ward noun
1 a long room with beds for patients in a hospital 2 a child looked after by a guardian 3 an area of a town or city represented by a councillor

ward verb
to ward something off is to keep it away • *He put his arms up to ward off the blows.*

warden noun
an official in charge of a hostel, college, or other building

warder noun
an official who guards prisoners in a prison

wardrobe noun
1 a cupboard to hang your clothes in 2 a stock of clothes or costumes

warehouse noun
a large building where goods are stored

wares plural noun
goods offered for sale

warfare noun
warfare is fighting or waging war

warhead noun
the part of a missile that explodes

warlike adjective
warlike people are fond of fighting or are likely to start a war

warm adjective
1 fairly hot; not cold or cool 2 warm clothes are thick and keep you warm 3 a warm person is enthusiastic or friendly • *They gave us a warm welcome.* 4 (*informal*) close to the right answer, or to something hidden • *You're getting warm now.*
warmly adverb

warm verb
1 to warm something or someone is to make them warm 2 to warm, or warm up, is to become warm
to warm up is to do gentle exercises to prepare yourself before playing sport

warm-blooded adjective
having blood that does not change temperature according to the surroundings

warmth noun
1 warmth is being warm or keeping warm • *The cattle huddled together for warmth.* 2 warmth is also being friendly and enthusiastic • *She was touched by the warmth of their welcome.*

warn verb
to warn someone is to tell them about a danger or difficulty that might affect them

warning noun
something that tells someone about a danger

warp verb (*say* worp)
to warp, or be warped, is to become bent or twisted out of shape because of dampness or heat

warrant noun
a document that gives the police the right to arrest someone or search a place

warren noun
a piece of ground where there are many rabbit burrows

warrior noun
someone who fights in battles; a soldier

warship noun
a ship designed for use in war

wart noun
a small hard lump on your skin

wary adjective (**warier, wariest**)
cautious and careful • *I gave the tiger a wary glance.*
warily adverb cautiously **wariness** noun

wash verb
1 to wash something is to clean it with water 2 you wash when you clean yourself with water 3 to wash is to flow over or against something • *Waves washed over the beach.*

4 to be washed somewhere is to be carried along by the force of moving water • *The boxes were washed overboard.* **to wash up** is to wash the dishes and cutlery after a meal

wash *noun*
1 the action of washing **2** the disturbed water behind a moving ship **3** a thin coating of colour or paint

washbasin *noun*
a small basin with taps, holding water for washing your hands and face

washer *noun*
a small ring of metal or rubber placed between two surfaces so that they fit tightly together

washing *noun*
washing is clothes that need to be washed or have been washed

washing-up *noun*
washing the dishes and cutlery after a meal; the things that need to be washed

wasp *noun*
a stinging insect with black and yellow stripes across its body

wastage *noun*
wastage is losing something by waste

waste *verb*
1 to waste something is to use more of it than you need to, or to use it without getting much value from it **2** to waste something is also to fail to use it • *You are wasting a good opportunity.* **to waste away** is to become thinner and weaker

waste *adjective*
1 left over or thrown away because it is not wanted • *What shall we do with all this waste paper?* **2** not used or usable • *We came to an area of waste land.*

waste *noun*
1 a waste is wasting something or not using it well • *It's a waste of time.* **2** waste is things that are not wanted or used **3** a waste is also an area of desert or frozen land • *We flew over the wastes of Alaska.*

wasteful *adjective*
wasting things or not using them well
wastefully *adverb*

watch *verb*
1 to watch someone or something is to look at them for some time **2** to watch, or watch out, is to be on guard or ready for something to happen • *Watch for the lights to change.* **3** to watch something is also to take care of it • *His job is to watch* the sheep. **to watch out** is to be careful about something **watcher** *noun* someone who watches something

watch *noun*
1 a device like a small clock, usually worn on a person's wrist **2** a period of being on guard or on duty

watchdog *noun*
a dog kept to guard buildings

watchful *adjective*
alert and watching carefully
watchfully *adverb* **watchfulness** *noun*

watchman *noun* (**watchmen**)
someone whose job is to guard a building at night

water *noun*
1 water is a transparent colourless liquid that falls as rain and is found in seas, rivers, and lakes **2** a water is a sea or lake **to pass water** is to urinate

water *verb*
1 to water a plant is to sprinkle water over it • *Have you watered the flowers?* **2** to water an animal is to give it water to drink **3** your eyes or mouth water when they produce tears or saliva • *The smell of toast makes my mouth water.*
to water something down is to dilute it or make it weaker

watercolour *noun*
1 a paint that can be mixed with water **2** a painting done with this kind of paint

watercress *noun*
a kind of cress that grows in water

waterfall *noun*
a place where a river or stream flows over a cliff or large rock

watering can *noun*
a container with a long spout, for watering plants

waterlogged *adjective* waterlogged ground is so wet it cannot soak up any more water

watermark *noun*
a faint design in some types of paper, which you can see if you hold it up to the light

waterproof *adjective*
able to keep water out • *a waterproof jacket*

water-skiing *noun*
the sport of skimming over the surface of water on flat boards (**water-skis**) while being towed by a motor boat

watertight *adjective*
1 made so that water cannot get into it **2** so carefully prepared that it has no mistakes or weaknesses • *He has a watertight alibi.*

waterway *noun*
a river or canal that ships or boats can travel on

waterworks *noun*
a place with pumping machinery for supplying water to a district

watery *adjective*
1 like water • *The paint is too watery.* **2** full of water • *You have watery eyes.*

watt *noun*
a unit of electric power

wave *verb*
1 to wave is to move your hand from side to side, usually to say hello or goodbye **2** you wave something, or it waves, when it moves from side to side or up and down • *Flags were waving in the wind.* **3** to wave hair is to make it curl

wave *noun*
1 a moving ridge on the surface of water, especially on the sea **2** a curling piece of hair **3** (*in science*) one of the to-and-fro movements in which sound and light and electricity travel **4** the action of waving your hand • *He gave us a little wave.* **5** a sudden increase in something strong • *She felt a wave of anger.*

wavelength *noun*
the size of a sound wave or electric wave

waver *verb*
1 to waver is to hesitate or be uncertain • *They wavered between two choices.* **2** to waver is also to be unsteady or move unsteadily

wavy *adjective* (**wavier, waviest**)
full of waves or curves

wax¹ *noun*
wax is a soft substance that melts easily, used for making candles, crayons, and polish **waxy** *adjective* looking or feeling like wax

wax¹ *verb*
to wax something is to cover it with wax

wax² *verb*
the moon waxes when its right area gets gradually larger

waxwork *noun*
a model made of wax, especially a full-size model of a person

way *noun*
1 how something is done; a method or manner **2** the way to a place is how you get there **3** a road or path leading from one place to another **4** a distance • *Is it a long way?* **5** a

a b c d e f g h i j k l m n o p q r s t u v w x y z

respect • *It's a good idea in some ways.* **6** a condition or state • *Things are in a bad way.* **to get your own way** is to make people let you have what you want **in the way** blocking your path so that you can't move or see properly **no way** (*informal*) that is impossible; that is not true

we *pronoun*
a word used by someone to mean 'I and someone else' or 'I and others'

weak *adjective*
1 without much strength or energy **2** easy to break, bend, or defeat **3** poor at doing something **weakly** *adverb* **weakness** *noun* weakness is being weak; a weakness is a fault you have or something you don't do well

weaken *verb*
1 to weaken something is to make it weaker **2** to weaken is to become weaker

weakling *noun*
a weak person

wealth *noun*
1 wealth is a lot of money or property **2** a wealth of something is a lot of it • *The book has a wealth of illustrations.*

wealthy *adjective* (**wealthier, wealthiest**)
someone is wealthy when they have a lot of money or property

weapon *noun*
something used to harm or kill people in a battle or fight

wear *verb* (**wearing, wore, worn**)
1 to wear something is to be dressed in it **2** to wear something is to damage it by rubbing or using it; to wear is to become damaged like this • *The carpet has worn thin.* **3** to last • *This cloth wears well.* **to wear off** is to become less strong or intense **to wear out** is to become weak or useless **to wear someone out** is to make them very tired

wear *noun*
1 wear is clothes • *Where can I find men's wear?* **2** wear is gradual damage done by rubbing or using something

weary *adjective* (**wearier, weariest**)
very tired **wearily** *adverb* in a way that shows you are very tired **weariness** *noun*

weasel *noun*
a small fierce animal with a slender body

weather *noun*
weather is the rain, snow, wind, sunshine, and temperature at a particular time or place **to be under the weather** is to feel ill or depressed

weather *verb*
1 to weather is to become worn because of being exposed to the weather **2** to weather something is to make it suffer the effects of the weather • *The wind and rain have weathered the cliffs.* **3** you weather a difficulty when you come through it successfully • *They weathered the storm.*

weathercock or **weathervane** *noun*
a pointer, often shaped like a cockerel, that turns in the wind and shows which way the wind is blowing

weave *verb* (**weaving, wove, woven**)
1 to weave material or baskets is to make them by crossing threads or strips over and under each other **2** to weave is to twist and turn • *He wove skilfully through the traffic.*
weaver *noun* someone who weaves material

web *noun*
1 a net of thin sticky threads that spiders spin to catch insects **2** something complicated • *We were caught up in a web of lies.* **3** a computer network, especially the Internet

webbed or **web-footed** *adjective*
webbed feet have toes joined by pieces of skin, as ducks' feet do

website *noun*
a place on the Internet where you can get information

wed *verb* (**wedding, wedded** or **wed**)
to wed someone is to marry them

wedding *noun*
the ceremony when two people get married

wedge *noun*
1 a piece of wood or metal or plastic that is thick at one end and thin at the other, pushed between things to force them apart or to hold them tight **2** something shaped like a wedge • *a wedge of cheese*

wedge *verb*
to wedge something is to hold it in place, especially with a wedge

Wednesday *noun*
the fourth day of the week

weed *noun*
a wild plant that grows where it is not wanted

weed *verb*
to weed the ground is to remove weeds from it

weedy *adjective* (**weedier, weediest**)
1 full of weeds **2** thin and weak

week *noun*
1 a period of seven days, especially from Sunday to the following Saturday **2** the part of the week that doesn't include the weekend

weekday *noun*
any day except Saturday and Sunday

weekend *noun*
Saturday and Sunday

weekly *adjective, adverb*
every week

weep *verb* (**weeping, wept**)
to weep is to cry or shed tears

weigh *verb*
1 to weigh something is to find out how heavy it is **2** to weigh a certain amount is to have that as its weight • *How much do you weigh?* **to weigh anchor** is to raise the anchor and start a voyage **to weigh something down** is to hold it down with something heavy **to weigh something up** is to think about it carefully before deciding what to do

weight *noun*
1 weight is the measure of how heavy something is **2** a weight is a piece of metal that you know the weight of, used on scales to weigh things **3** a weight is also a heavy object, used to hold things down

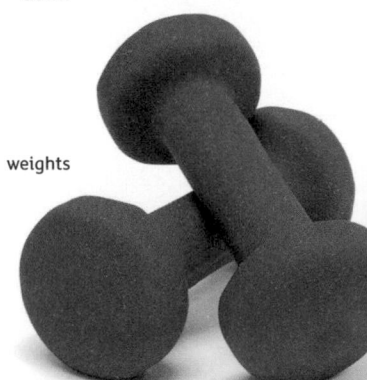

weights

weightless *adjective* astronauts are weightless when they float around because there is no gravity

weightlifting *noun*
weightlifting is the sport or exercise of lifting heavy weights

A B C D E F G H I J K L M N O P Q R S T U V W X Y Z

weighty *adjective* (**weightier, weightiest**)
1 heavy **2** important or serious • *These are weighty matters.*

weir *noun* (*say* weer)
a small dam across a river or canal to control the flow of water

weird *adjective* (*say* weerd)
very strange or unnatural
weirdly *adverb*
weirdness *noun*

welcome *noun*
a kind or friendly greeting or reception

welcome *adjective*
1 that you are glad to get or see • *This is a welcome surprise.*
2 allowed or free to do or take something • *You are welcome to use my bicycle.*

welcome *verb*
to welcome someone or something is to show that you are pleased when they arrive

weld *verb*
to weld pieces of metal or plastic together is to join them by using heat or pressure **welder** *noun* someone who welds things together

welfare *noun*
welfare is people's health, happiness, and comfort

well¹ *noun*
a deep hole dug or drilled to get water or oil out of the ground

well² *adverb* (**better, best**)
1 in a good or successful way • *He can play the piano quite well now.* **2** thoroughly • *Wash your hands well.* **3** actually; probably • *It may well be our last chance.* **as well** also
to be well off is to be fairly rich or fortunate

well² *adjective*
1 in good health • *She is not well.*
2 good or satisfactory • *All is well.*

well-being *noun*
well-being is health or happiness

wellington boots or **wellingtons** *plural noun*
rubber or plastic waterproof boots

WORD ORIGIN

The word **wellingtons** comes from the name of the Duke of Wellington, the British statesman and soldier who defeated Napoleon at the Battle of Waterloo in 1815.

wellington boots

well-known *adjective*
known to many people; famous

werewolf *noun* (**werewolves**)
in stories, a person who sometimes changes into a wolf

west *noun*
1 the direction where the sun sets
2 the part of a country or city that is in this direction

west *adjective, adverb*
1 towards the west or in the west
2 coming from the west • *There was a west wind blowing.*

western *adjective*
from or to do with the west

western *noun*
a film or story about American cowboys

westward or **westwards** *adjective, adverb*
towards the west

wet *adjective* (**wetter, wettest**)
1 covered or soaked in water or other liquid **2** not yet set or dry • *Watch out for wet paint.* **3** rainy • *It's been wet here all day.* **wetness** *noun*

wet *verb*
to wet something is to make it wet

wet suit *noun*
a rubber suit that clings to the skin, worn by skin divers and windsurfers to keep them warm and dry

whack *verb*
to whack someone or something is to hit them hard

whack *noun*
a hard hit or blow

whale *noun*
a very large sea animal **to have a whale of a time** (*informal*) is to enjoy yourself

whaling *noun*
whaling is hunting whales

wharf *noun*
(**wharves** or **wharfs**) (*say* worf)
a quay where ships are loaded or unloaded

what *determiner*
1 used to ask questions about something • *What kind of bike have you got?*
2 used to say how strange or great a person or thing is • *What a fool you are!*

what *pronoun*
1 what thing or things • *What did you say?* **2** the thing that • *This is what you must do.*

whatever *pronoun*
1 anything or everything • *Do whatever you like.* **2** no matter what • *I'll be there whatever happens.*

whatever *determiner*
of any kind or amount • *Get whatever help you can.*

wheat *noun*
wheat is a cereal plant from which flour is made

wheel *noun*
a round device that turns on an axle passing through its centre. Wheels are used to move vehicles or work machinery.

wheel *verb*
1 to wheel a bicycle or cart is to push it along on its wheels **2** to wheel is to move in a curve or circle • *The column of soldiers wheeled to the right.*

wheelbarrow *noun*
a small cart with one wheel at the front and two handles at the back

wheelchair *noun*
a chair on wheels for a person who cannot walk

wheeze *verb*
to wheeze is to make a whistling or gasping noise as you breathe

whales

whelk *noun*
a shellfish that looks like a snail

when *adverb*
at what time • *When can you come to tea?*

when *conjunction*
1 at the time that • *The bird flew away when I moved.* **2** because; considering that • *Why are you wearing a coat when it's so hot?*

whenever *conjunction*
at any time; every time
• *Whenever I see him, he's smiling.*

a b c d e f g h i j k l m v w x y z

where *adverb, conjunction*
1 in or to what place • *Where have you put the glue?* **2** in or to that place • *Leave it where it is.*

whereabouts *adverb*
roughly where; in what area • *Whereabouts is Timbuktu?*

whereabouts *noun*
the place where something is • *Have you any idea of her whereabouts?*

whereas *conjunction*
but on the other hand • *Some people like sailing, whereas others hate it.*

whereupon *adverb*
after that; and then

wherever *adverb, conjunction*
in or to whatever place; no matter where

whether *conjunction*
used to introduce more than one possibility • *I don't know whether they are here or not.*

whey *noun* (*say* way)
whey is the watery liquid left when milk forms curds

which *determiner*
what particular • *Which way did he go?*

which *pronoun*
1 what person or thing • *Which is your desk?* **2** the person or thing just mentioned • *Here's my book, which you asked me to bring.*

whichever *determiner, adjective* that or those which; any which • *Take whichever you like.*

whiff *noun*
a slight smell of something • *He caught a whiff of perfume as she walked past him.*

while *conjunction*
1 during the time that; as long as • *She was singing while she worked.* **2** but; although • *She is fair, while her sister is dark.*

while *noun*
a period of time • *We have waited all this while.*

while *verb*
to while away time is to pass it doing something leisurely

whilst *conjunction*
while

whim *noun*
a sudden desire to do or have something

whimper *verb*
to whimper is to cry with a low trembling voice

whimper *noun*
a sound of whimpering

whine *verb*
1 to whine is to make a long high piercing sound **2** to whine is also to complain in an annoying way

whine *noun*
a whining sound

whinny *verb* (**whinnies, whinnying, whinnied**)
a horse whinnies when it neighs gently

whip *noun*
a cord or strip of leather fixed to a handle and used for hitting people or animals

whip *verb* (**whipping, whipped**)
1 to whip a person or animal is to beat them with a whip **2** to whip cream is to beat it until it becomes thick and frothy **3** (*informal*) to whip something is to steal it **to whip something out** (*informal*) is to take it out quickly or suddenly **to whip something up** is to stir up people's feelings • *They quickly whipped up support for the idea.*

whirl *verb*
you whirl something round, or it whirls, when it turns or spins very quickly

whirl *noun*
when something turns or spins very quickly

whirlpool *noun*
a strong current of water going round in a circle and pulling things towards it

whirlpool

whirlwind *noun*
a very strong wind that whirls around or blows in a spiral

whirr *verb*
to whirr is to make a continuous buzzing sound

whirr *noun*
a continuous buzzing sound

whisk *verb*
1 to whisk cream or eggs is to beat them until they are thick or frothy **2** to whisk something somewhere is to move it there very quickly • *A waiter whisked away my plate.*

whisk *noun*
1 a device for whisking eggs or cream **2** a whisking movement

whisker *noun*
1 whiskers are the long stiff hairs on the face of a cat or other animal **2** you can refer to the hair growing on a man's face as his whiskers

whisky *noun*
a kind of very strong alcoholic drink

whisper *verb*
to whisper is to speak very softly or secretly

whisper *noun*
a very soft voice or sound

whist *noun*
whist is a card game for four people

whistle *verb*
1 you whistle when you make a shrill or musical sound by blowing through your lips **2** something whistles when it makes a shrill sound • *The kettle was whistling away.*

whistle *noun*
1 a whistling sound **2** a device that makes a shrill sound when you blow into it

white *adjective*
1 of the very lightest colour, like snow or milk **2** having light-coloured skin **3** white coffee is coffee with milk
whiteness *noun*

white *noun*
1 a white colour **2** the substance round the yolk of an egg, which turns white when it is cooked

whitewash *noun*
whitewash is a white liquid made from lime and chalk and painted on walls and ceilings

whitewash *verb*
to whitewash a wall or ceiling is to coat it with whitewash

whizz *verb*
1 to whizz is to move very quickly **2** to whizz is also to sound like something rushing through the air

who *pronoun*
1 which person or people • *Who threw that?* **2** the person or people spoken about • *These are the boys who did it.*

whoever *pronoun*
any person who • *Whoever comes is welcome.*

whole *adjective*
1 all of something; without anything missing • *Could you eat a whole pizza?* **2** not broken or damaged

whole *noun*
a complete thing; all the parts of something **on the whole** considering everything; mainly

wholefood *noun*
wholefood is food that has been produced without using artificial fertilizers

wholemeal *adjective*
wholemeal flour or bread is made from the whole grain of wheat

whole number *noun*
a number without a fraction

wholesale *adjective, adverb*
1 sold in large quantities to be sold again by others **2** on a large scale; including everybody or everything • *There has been wholesale destruction.*

wholesome *adjective*
healthy and good for you • *We all need wholesome food.*

wholly *adverb*
completely or entirely • *He's not wholly to blame.*

whom *pronoun*
a word used for who when it is the object of a verb or comes after a preposition, as in *the boy whom I saw* or *the boy to whom I spoke*

whooping cough *noun*
(*say* **hoop**-ing-kof)
whooping cough is an illness that makes you cough and gasp

who's
short for *who has* or *who is*

whose *adjective, pronoun*
1 belonging to what person • *Whose bike is that?* **2** of which; of whom • *The girl whose party we went to.*

why *adverb*
for what reason or purpose • *Why have you come?*

wick *noun*
the string that goes through the middle of a candle, which you light to give a flame

wicked *adjective*
1 very bad or cruel; doing things that are wrong **2** mischievous • *He gave a wicked smile.* **3** (*slang*) very fine or good • *That's a wicked goal!* **wickedly** *adverb* in a cruel or mischievous way **wickedness** *noun* doing bad things

wicker or **wickerwork** *noun* wicker or wickerwork is reeds or canes woven together to make baskets and furniture

wicket *noun*
1 in cricket, each set of three stumps with two bails on top of them **2** the part of a cricket ground between or near the wickets

wicketkeeper *noun*
the fielder in cricket who stands behind the batsman's wicket

wide *adjective*
1 measuring a lot from one side to the other • *The river was wide.* **2** from one side to the other • *The room is 4 metres wide.* **3** covering a large range • *She has a wide knowledge of birds.*

wide *adverb*
1 you are wide awake when you are completely or fully awake **2** to open or spread something wide is to open or spread it as far as possible **3** far from the target • *The shot went wide.*

widely *adverb*
commonly; among many people • *They are widely admired.*

widen *verb*
to widen something is to make it wider; to widen is to become wider

widespread *adjective*
existing or found in many places; common

widow *noun*
a woman whose husband has died

widower *noun*
a man whose wife has died

width *noun*
the width of something is how much it measures from one side to the other

wield *verb* (*say* weeld)
to wield a weapon or tool is to hold it and use it • *a picture of a knight wielding a sword*

wife *noun* (**wives**)
the woman that a man is married to

WORD ORIGIN

The word **wife** comes from an Anglo-Saxon word *wif* meaning 'woman'

wig *noun*
a covering of false hair worn on the head

wiggle *verb*
to wiggle something is to move it from side to side

wiggle *noun*
a wiggling movement

wigwam *noun*
the tent of a Native American

wild *adjective*
1 wild animals and plants live or grow in their natural state and are not looked after by people **2** wild land is in its natural state and has not been changed by people **3** not controlled; violent or angry • *His behaviour became more and more wild.* • *She went wild when she saw the mess.* **4** very foolish or unreasonable • *They do have wild ideas.* **wildly** *adverb* in a way that is not controlled • *My heart was beating wildly.* **wildness** *noun*

wild *noun*
animals live in the wild when they live in their natural environment

wilderness *noun*
an area of wild country; a desert

wildlife *noun*
wildlife is wild animals in their natural setting

wilful *adjective*
1 someone is wilful when they are determined to do exactly what they want • *What a wilful child.* **2** something is wilful when it is done deliberately • *This is wilful disobedience.* **wilfully** *adverb* **wilfulness** *noun*

will¹ *verb* (past tense **would**)
used to refer to the future • *I will be there at 12 o'clock.*

will² *noun*
1 will is the power to use your mind to decide and control what you do **2** someone's will is what they choose or want • *He was forced to write the letter against his will.* **3** someone's will to do something is their determination to do it • *She has a strong will to succeed.* **4** a will is a legal document saying what is to be done with someone's possessions after they die

willing *adjective*
ready and happy to do what is wanted • *Are you willing to help?* **willingly** *adverb* **willingness** *noun*

willow *noun*
a tree with long thin branches, often growing near water

wilt *verb*
a plant wilts when it loses freshness and droops

wily *adjective* (**wilier, wiliest**)
crafty or cunning **wiliness** *noun*

win *verb* (**winning, won**)
1 to win a contest or game or battle is to do better than your opponents **2** to win something is to get it by using effort or in a competition • *She won second prize.*

win *noun*
a success or victory

wince *verb*
to wince is to make a slight movement because you are in pain or embarrassed

winch *noun*
a device for lifting or pulling things, using a rope or cable that goes round a wheel or drum

winch *verb*
to winch something is to lift it or pull it with a winch

wind¹ *noun* (*rhymes with* **tinned**)
1 wind, or a wind, is a current of air **2** wind is gas in the stomach or intestines that makes you uncomfortable **3** wind is also breath used for a purpose, such as running **4** in an orchestra, the wind is the wind instruments

wind² *verb* (**winding, wound**) (*rhymes with* **find**)
1 something like a road or river winds when it twists and turns • *The river winds down the valley.* **2** to wind something is to wrap or twist it round something else • *She wound her scarf round her neck.* **3** to wind, or wind up, a watch or clock is to tighten its spring so that it works

windfall *noun*
1 a fruit blown down from a tree **2** a piece of unexpected good luck, especially a sum of money

wind instrument *noun*
a musical instrument played by blowing, such as a flute or clarinet

windmill *noun*
a mill with four long arms called *sails* which are turned by the wind

window *noun*
1 an opening in a wall or roof to let in light and air, usually filled with glass **2** (*in computing*) an area on a computer screen used for a particular purpose

windpipe *noun*
the tube through which air reaches your lungs

windscreen *noun*
the window at the front of a motor vehicle

windsurfing *noun*
windsurfing is surfing on a board

windmill

with a sail fixed to it

windsurfer *noun* someone who goes windsurfing

wires

windy *adjective*
with a lot of wind • *It's a windy day today.*

wine *noun*
an alcoholic drink made from grapes or other plants

wing *noun*
1 a bird's or insect's wings are the parts it uses for flying **2** an aircraft's wings are the long flat parts that stick out from its sides and support it in the air **3** a part of a building that is built at the side and is joined to the main part **4** each side of a theatre stage, out of sight of the audience **5** the part of a car's body above a wheel **6** each of the players in football and other ball games whose place is at the side of the field **on the wing** flying **to take wing** is to fly away **winged** *adjective* having wings • *Pegasus was a mythical winged horse.*

wingspan *noun*
the distance across the wings of a bird or aeroplane

wink *verb*
1 you wink when you close and open one of your eyes quickly **2** a light winks when it flickers or twinkles

wink *noun*
1 when you close and open one of your eyes quickly **2** a short period of sleep • *I didn't sleep a wink.*

winkle *noun*
a shellfish that is used for food

winner *noun*
1 a person who wins something **2** (*informal*) something very successful • *Her new book is a winner.*

winnings *plural noun*
the money someone wins in a game or by betting

winter *noun*
the coldest season of the year, between autumn and spring **wintry** *adjective* cold, like winter

wintertime *noun*
wintertime is the season of winter

wipe *verb*
to wipe something is to rub it gently to dry it or clean it **to wipe**

something out is to destroy it or cancel it • *He's wiped out his debt.*

wipe *noun*
when you wipe something • *Give it a quick wipe.*

wire *noun*
a thin length of metal used to carry electric current or for making fences

wire *verb*
to wire something, or wire it up, is to connect it with wires to carry electricity

wireless *adjective*
something that is wireless can send and receive signals without using wires • *You can get a wireless Internet connection for your computer.*

wireless *noun*
(*old use*) a radio set

wiring *noun*
wiring is the system of wires carrying electricity in a building or in a device • *The fire was caused by faulty wiring.*

wiry *adjective* (**wirier, wiriest**)
1 a wiry person is lean and strong **2** wiry hair is tough and stiff

wisdom *noun*
1 wisdom is being wise **2** wisdom is also wise sayings or writings

wisdom tooth *noun* (**wisdom teeth**)
a tooth that may grow at the back of your jaw much later than the other teeth

wise *adjective*
knowing or understanding many things and so able to make sensible decisions **wisely** *adverb* when it is the sensible thing to do • *He wisely decided to tell the truth.*

wish *verb*
1 to wish something, or wish to do something, is to think or say that you would like it **2** to wish someone something is to say that you hope they will get it • *They wished us luck.*

wish *noun*
1 something you want **2** when you wish for something • *Make a wish* • *We send you our best wishes.*

wishbone *noun*
a forked bone from the breast of a chicken or other bird

wisp *noun*
a thin piece or line of something light or fluffy, such as hair or smoke **wispy** *adjective* thin and fluffy

wistful *adjective*
thinking sadly about something you can no longer have **wistfully** *adverb*
wistfulness *noun*

wit *noun*
1 wit is intelligence or cleverness **2** wit is also a clever kind of humour **3** a wit is a witty person **to keep your wits about you** is to stay alert

witch *noun*
a woman who is believed to use magic

witchcraft *noun*
witchcraft is using magic, especially to make bad things happen

with *preposition*
there are many meanings, of which the most important are: **1** having • *I saw a man with a wooden leg.* **2** in the company of or accompanied by • *I came with a friend.* **3** using • *Hit it with a hammer.* **4** against • *They fought with each other.* **5** because of • *He shook with laughter.*

withdraw *verb* (**withdrawing, withdrew, withdrawn**)
1 to withdraw something is to take it away or take it back • *She withdrew her offer.* **2** to withdraw is to retreat or drop out of something • *The troops have withdrawn from the frontier.* • *His injury meant he had to withdraw from the race.*
withdrawal *noun* when someone withdraws something or withdraws from a place

wither *verb*
a plant withers when it shrivels or wilts

withhold *verb* (**withholding, withheld**)
to withhold something is to refuse to give it to someone • *He has withheld his permission.*

within *preposition, adverb*
inside; not beyond something • *Is the top shelf within your reach?*

without *preposition*
not having; free from • *It is difficult to live without money.*

withstand *verb* (**withstanding, withstood**)
to withstand something is to resist it or put up with it successfully • *The bridge is designed to withstand high winds.*

witness *noun*
1 a person who sees something happen and can describe it • *There were no witnesses to the accident.* **2** a person who gives evidence in a lawcourt

witty *adjective* (**wittier, wittiest**)
clever and amusing
wittily *adverb*

wizard *noun*
1 a man who has magic powers **2** a person who is very good at something • *He's a wizard on the accordion.* **wizardry** *noun* the clever and impressive things that a computer or other machine can do

wizard

wobble *verb*
to wobble is to move unsteadily from side to side
wobble *noun*
a wobbling movement
wobbly *adjective* moving unsteadily from side to side

woe *noun*
1 someone's woes are their troubles and misfortunes **2** woe is great sorrow **woeful** *adjective* very sad; very bad or serious **woefully** *adverb*

wok *noun*
a deep round-bottomed frying-pan used in Chinese cookery

wolf *noun*
a wild animal like a large fierce dog

woman *noun* (**women**)
a grown-up female human being

womb *noun* (*say* woom)
the part of a female's body where babies develop before they are born

wonder *verb*
1 to wonder about something is to be trying to decide about it or to be curious about it • *I wonder what we should do next.* • *I wonder what's for dinner.* **2** to wonder at something is to feel surprise and admiration about it

wonder *noun*
1 wonder is a feeling of surprise and admiration **2** a wonder is something that makes you feel surprised and admiring **no wonder** it is not surprising

wonderful *adjective*
marvellous or excellent
wonderfully *adverb* extremely; very well

won't
short for *will not*

wood *noun*
1 wood is the substance that trees are made of **2** a wood is a lot of trees growing together

wooded *adjective*
a wooded area is covered with growing trees

wooden *adjective*
made of wood

woodland *noun*
land covered with trees

woodlouse *noun* (**woodlice**)
a small crawling creature with seven pairs of legs, living in rotten wood or damp soil

woodpecker *noun*
a bird that taps tree trunks with its beak to find insects

woodwind *noun*
in an orchestra, the woodwind is the wind instruments that are usually made of wood or plastic, such as the clarinet and oboe

woodwork *noun*
1 woodwork is making things with wood **2** woodwork is also things made out of wood

woodworm *noun* (**woodworm** or **woodworms**)
the larva of a beetle that bores into wood

woody *adjective* (**woodier, woodiest**)
1 like wood or made of wood **2** full of trees

wool *noun*
1 wool is the thick soft hair of sheep or goats **2** wool is also thread or cloth made from this hair

woollen *adjective*
made of wool

a b c d e f g h i j k l m n o p q r s t u v w x y z

woolly *adjective* (**woollier, woolliest**)
1 covered with wool **2** made of wool or like wool **3** vague and not clear • *He has woolly ideas.* **woolliness** *noun*

word *noun*
1 a set of sounds or letters that has a meaning and is written with a space before and after it **2** a brief talk with someone • *Can I have a word with you?* **3** your word is when you promise to do something • *He gave me his word.* **4** a command or signal to do something • *Run when I give the word.* **5** a message or piece of news • *We sent word that we had arrived safely.*

word *verb*
to word something is to express it in words • *I'm not sure how to word this question.*

word class *noun*
each of the groups (also called **parts of speech**) into which words can be divided in grammar: noun, adjective, pronoun, adverb, preposition, conjunction, interjection

wording *noun*
the wording of something is the words used to say it

word processing *noun*
word processing is using a computer for writing and editing letters and documents, and for printing them out **word processor** *noun* a computer used for word processing

work *verb*
1 to work is to spend time doing something that needs effort or energy **2** to work is also to have a job or be employed • *She works in a bank.* **3** something works when it operates correctly or successfully • *Is the lift working?* **4** to work something is to make it act or operate • *Can you work the lift?* **5** to work loose is to become gradually loose • *The screw had worked loose.* **to work out** is to succeed or happen in a certain way • *Things have worked out well for her.* **to work something out** is to find the answer to it

work *noun*
1 work is something that you have to do that needs effort or energy • *Digging is hard work.* **2** a person's work is their job • *What work do you do?* **3** at school, your work is something you write or produce • *Please get on with your work quietly.* **4** a work is a piece of writing or music or painting • *The book has*

all the works of Shakespeare. **to be at work** is to be working

worker *noun*
1 someone who does work **2** a bee or ant that does the work in a hive or colony but does not produce eggs

workman *noun* (**workmen**)
a man who does manual work

workmanship *noun* workmanship is skill in making something

works *plural noun*
1 the moving parts of a machine **2** a factory or industrial site

worksheet *noun*
a sheet of paper with a set of questions about a subject for students

workshop *noun*
a place where things are made or mended

world *noun*
1 the world is the earth with all its countries and peoples **2** a world is a planet • *The film is about creatures from another world.* **3** everything to do with a particular subject or activity • *He knows a lot about the world of sport.*

worldly *adjective* (**worldlier, worldliest**)
1 to do with life on earth **2** only interested in money and possessions

worldwide *adjective, adverb*
over the whole world

World Wide Web *noun*
the system of keeping information on computers all over the world so that people can use it by using the Internet

worm *noun*
1 a small thin wriggling animal without legs, especially an earthworm **2** (*informal*) an unimportant or unpleasant person

worm *verb*
to worm your way somewhere is to move along slowly when people or things are in your way • *He wormed his way through the crowd.* **to worm something out of someone** is to get them to tell you something secret

worn *adjective*
damaged because it has been rubbed or used so much **to be worn out** is to be very tired

worry *verb* (**worries, worrying, worried**)
1 to worry is to feel anxious or troubled about something **2** to worry someone is to make them feel anxious or troubled about something **worried** *adjective* anxious or troubled about something **worrier** *noun* someone who worries a lot

worry *noun*
1 worry is worrying or being anxious **2** a worry is something that makes you anxious

worse *adjective, adverb*
more bad or more badly; less good or less well

worsen *verb*
1 to worsen is to become worse **2** to worsen something is to make it worse

worship *verb* (**worshipping, worshipped**)
1 to worship God or a god is to give them praise or respect **2** to worship someone is to adore them or have great respect for them **worshipper** *noun* someone who worships

worship *noun*
worship is worshipping; religious ceremonies or services

worst *adjective, adverb*
most bad or most badly; least good or least well

worth *adjective*
1 having a certain value • *This stamp is worth £100.* **2** deserving something; good or important enough for something • *That book is worth reading.*

worth *noun*
a thing's worth is its value or usefulness

worthless *adjective*
having no value; useless

worthwhile *adjective*
important or good enough to be worth doing

worthy *adjective* (**worthier, worthiest**)
deserving respect or support • *The sale is for a worthy cause.* **to be worthy of something** is to deserve or be good enough for something • *This charity is worthy of your support.* **worthily** *adverb* **worthiness** *noun* worthiness is being deserving or good enough for something

would *verb*
1 past tense of the verb will[1] • *We said we would do it.* • *He said he would come if he could.* **2** used in polite questions or requests • *Would you like some tea?*

wound *noun* (*say* woond)
an injury done to a part of a person's or animal's body, especially one in which the skin is cut

wound *verb*
to wound a person or animal is to give them a wound

wrap *verb* (**wrapping, wrapped**)
to wrap something is to put paper or some other covering round it

wrapper *noun*
a piece of paper or plastic that something is wrapped in

wrapping *noun*
wrapping is material used to wrap something, especially a present

wrath *noun* (*rhymes with* **cloth**)
(*old-fashioned use*) anger **wrathful** *adjective* angry

wreath *noun*
(*say* reeth)
flowers and leaves and branches bound together to make a circle

wreathe *verb* (*say* reeth)
to be wreathed in something is to be covered in it or decorated with it • *Her face was wreathed in smiles.*

wreck *verb*
to wreck something is to damage or ruin it so badly that it cannot be used again **wrecker** *noun* someone who wrecks something

wreck *noun*
a badly damaged ship or car

wreckage *noun*
wreckage is the pieces of something that has been wrecked

wren *noun*
a very small brown bird

wrench *verb*
to wrench something is to pull or twist it suddenly or violently • *He wrenched the door open.*

wrench *noun*
1 a wrenching movement **2** a tool for gripping and turning bolts or nuts

wrestle *verb*
1 to wrestle with someone is to fight them by grasping them and trying to throw them to the ground **2** to wrestle with a problem or difficulty is to struggle to solve it **wrestler** *noun* someone who wrestles for sport **wrestling** *noun*

wretch *noun*
someone who is unhappy poor, or disliked

wretched *adjective* (*say* rech-id)
1 poor and unhappy •*a wretched*

beggar **2** not satisfactory or pleasant • *This wretched car won't start.*

wriggle *verb*
to wriggle is to twist and turn your body **to wriggle out of something** is to avoid doing something you do not like

wriggle *noun*
a wriggling movement **wriggly** *adjective* wriggling a lot

wring *verb* (**wringing, wrung**)
1 to wring something wet, or to wring it out, is to squeeze or twist it to get the water out of it **2** to wring something is to squeeze it violently • *I'll wring your neck!* **wringing wet** very wet; soaked

wrinkle *noun*
1 wrinkles are the small lines and creases that appear in your skin as you get older **2** a small crease or line on the surface of something

wrinkle *verb*
something wrinkles when wrinkles appear in or on it **wrinkled** *adjective* wrinkled skin or clothing has wrinkles

wrist *noun*
the joint that connects your hand to your arm

wristwatch *noun*
a watch that you wear on your wrist

write *verb* (**writing, wrote, written**)
1 to write words or signs is to put them on paper or some other surface so that people can read them **2** to write a story or play or a piece of music is to be the author or composer of it **3** to write to someone is to send them a letter **to write something off** is to think it is lost or useless

writer *noun*
a person who writes; an author

writhe *verb* (*say* ryth)
to writhe is to twist your body about because you are in pain or discomfort

writing *noun*
1 writing is something you write **2** your writing is the way you write

wrong *adjective*
1 not fair or morally right • *It is wrong to cheat* **2** incorrect • *That's the wrong answer.* **3** not working properly • *There's something wrong with the engine.* **wrongly** *adverb* in a way that is unfair or incorrect

wrong *adverb*
wrongly • *You guessed wrong.*

wrong *noun*
something that is wrong **to be in the wrong** is to have done or said something wrong

wrong *verb*
to wrong someone is to do wrong to them

wry *adjective*
slightly mocking or sarcastic • *He gave a wry smile.*

Xmas *noun*
(*informal*) Christmas

X-ray

X-ray *noun*
a photograph of the inside of something, especially a part of the body, made by a kind of radiation that can pass through something solid

X-ray *verb*
to X-ray something is to make an X-ray of it

xylophone *noun*
(*say* **zy**-lo-fohn)
a musical instrument made of wooden bars of lengths, that you hit with small hammers

WORD ORIGIN

The word **xylophone** comes from Greek words *xylon* meaning 'wood' and *phone* meaning 'sound' (the same word as in telephone).

Yy

yacht *noun* (*say* yot)
1 a sailing boat used for racing or cruising
2 a private ship

yam *noun*
a tropical vegetable that grows underground

yank *verb*
to yank something is to pull it strongly and suddenly

yap *verb* (**yapping, yapped**)
a small dog yaps when it makes a shrill barking sound

yap *noun*
a shrill barking sound

yard[1] *noun*
a measure of length, 36 inches or about 91 centimetres

yard[2] *noun*
a piece of ground beside a building, or one used for a special purpose, such as a railway yard

yarn *noun*
1 yarn is thread spun by twisting fibres together
2 (*informal*) a yarn is a tale or story

yashmak *noun*
a veil covering most of the face, worn by some Muslim women

yawn *verb*
you yawn when you open your mouth wide and breathe in deeply because you are tired or bored

yawn *noun*
an act of yawning

year *noun*
the time that the earth takes to go right round the sun, about 3651/4 days or twelve months

yearly *adjective, adverb*
every year

yearn *verb*
to yearn for something is to long for it

yeast *noun*
yeast is a substance used in baking bread and in making beer and wine

yell *noun*
a loud cry or shout

yell *verb*
to yell is to cry or shout loudly

yellow *noun*
the colour of ripe lemons and buttercups

yellow *adjective*
1 yellow in colour
2 (*informal*) cowardly

yelp *verb*
to yelp is to make a shrill bark or cry, as a dog does when it is hurt

yelp *noun*
a yelping sound

yacht

yes *exclamation*
a word used for agreeing to
something

yesterday *noun, adverb*
the day before today

yet *adverb*
1 up to now; by this time
• *Has the postman called yet?*
2 eventually; still • *I'll get even with
him yet.* **3** in addition; even • *She
became yet more excited.*

yet *conjunction*
nevertheless • *It is strange, yet it is
true.*

yeti *noun* (**yetis**) (*say* **yet**-ee)
a very large hairy creature that
some people think lives in the
Himalayas

yew *noun*
an evergreen tree with red
berries and dark leaves like
needles

yield *verb*
1 to yield is to surrender or
give in • *He yielded to persuasion.*
2 to yield a crop or profit is to
produce it • *These trees yield good
apples.*

yield *noun*
an amount produced by something
• *What is the yield of wheat per acre?*

yodel *verb* (**yodelling,
yodelled**)
to yodel is to sing or shout with your
voice going rapidly from low to high
notes

yoga *noun*
yoga is a Hindu system of exercise
and meditation

yoghurt *noun* (*say* **yog**-ert)
yoghurt is milk made thick
by the addition of bacteria, giving it
a sharp taste

yoke *noun*
a curved piece of wood put across the
necks of animals pulling a cart

yoke *verb*
to yoke animals is to harness them or
link them by means of a yoke

yolk *noun*
(*rhymes with* **coke**)
the yellow part of an egg

Yom Kippur *noun*
the Day of Atonement, an important
Jewish religious festival

Yorkshire pudding *noun*
a pudding made of batter and
usually eaten with roast beef

you *pronoun*
1 the person or people someone
is speaking to • *Who are you?*
2 people; anyone • *You can never be
too sure.*

young *adjective*
having lived or existed only
a short time; not old

young *plural noun*
an animal's or bird's young
are its babies

youngster *noun*
a young person or child

your *determiner*
belonging to you

yours *pronoun*
belonging to you • *Is this
house yours?* **Yours faithfully,
Yours sincerely, Yours truly** formal
ways of ending a letter before you
sign it

yourself *pronoun* (**yourselves**)
you (referring to one person) and
nobody else, used to refer back to
the subject of a verb • *Have you hurt
yourself?* **by yourself** or **yourselves**
on your own • *Did you do the work all
by yourself?*

youth *noun*
1 youth is being young, or the time
when you are young **2** a youth is
a young man **3** youth also means
young people • *The youth of today
are much more serious.*
youthful *adjective* looking young
or behaving like a
young person

youth club *noun*
a club providing leisure activities for
young people

youth hostel *noun*
a hostel where young people
can stay cheaply when they
are on holiday

yo-yo *noun* (**yo-yos**)
a round wooden or plastic toy
that moves up and down on
a string which you hold

zany *adjective* (**zanier, zaniest**)
funny in a crazy kind of way

WORD ORIGIN

The word **zany** comes from the Italian
name Gianni, a shortening of Giovanni,
which is the name often used for 'clown' in
an old form of Italian comedy.

zap *verb* (**zapping, zapped**)
(*slang*) **1** to zap something or
someone is to attack or destroy
them, especially in a computer game
2 to zap between television channels
is to use a remote control to quickly
change from one to another **zapper**
noun a remote control for changing
television channels

zeal *noun*
zeal is enthusiasm or eagerness,
especially in doing what you believe
to be right

zealous *adjective* (*say* **zel**-us)
very enthusiastic or keen **zealously**
adverb very enthusiastically

zebra *noun*
an African animal like a
horse with black and white stripes

zebra crossing *noun*
part of a road marked with broad
white stripes for pedestrians to cross

zebra

zero *noun*
nought; the figure 0

WORD ORIGIN

The word **zero** comes from French, Italian, and Spanish words that in turn come from an Arabic word *sifr*.

zest *noun*
zest is great enjoyment or enthusiasm

zigzag *noun*
a line or route full of sharp turns from one side to the other

zigzag *verb* (**zigzagging, zigzagged**)
to zigzag is to move in a series of sharp turns from one side to the other

zinc *noun*
zinc is a white metal

zip *noun*
1 a zip, or zip fastener, is a device with two rows of small teeth that fit together, used to join two pieces of material **2** zip is liveliness or energy

zip *verb* (**zipping, zipped**)
1 to zip something, or zip it up, is to fasten it with a zip **2** to zip, or zip along, is to move quickly with a sharp sound

zodiac *noun* (*say* **zoh**-di-ak)
an area of the sky divided into twelve equal parts, called **signs of the zodiac**, each named after a constellation

zone *noun*
a district or area set aside for a particular use • *This is a no-parking zone.*

zoo *noun*
a place where wild animals are kept so that people can look at them or study them

zoology *noun* (*say* zoh-**ol**-o-jee)
zoology is the study of animals **zoological** *adjective* to do with zoology **zoologist** *noun* an expert in zoology

zoom *verb*
to zoom is to move very quickly, especially with a buzzing sound

zoom lens *noun*
a camera lens that you can use to make distant objects appear closer

zip

zoom lens

A B C D E F G H I J K L M N O P Q R S T U V W X Y Z

Oxford
Illustrated
Children's
Thesaurus

OXFORD
UNIVERSITY PRESS

footprints

butterfly

OXFORD
UNIVERSITY PRESS

Great Clarendon Street, Oxford OX2 6DP

Oxford University Press is a department of the University of Oxford.
It furthers the University's objective of excellence in research, scholarship,
and education by publishing worldwide in

Oxford   New York

Auckland   Cape Town   Dar es Salaam   Hong Kong   Karachi
Kuala Lumpur   Madrid   Melbourne   Mexico City   Nairobi
New Delhi   Shanghai   Taipei   Toronto

With offices in

Argentina   Austria   Brazil   Chile   Czech Republic   France   Greece
Guatemala   Hungary   Italy   Japan   Poland   Portugal   Singapore
South Korea   Switzerland   Thailand   Turkey   Ukraine   Vietnam

Oxford is a registered trade mark of Oxford University Press
in the UK and in certain other countries

© Oxford University Press 2010, 2017

Database right Oxford University Press (maker)

First published 2010
This edition 2017

British Library Cataloguing in Publication Data

Data available

ISBN: 978-0-19-911994-3

Oxford Illustrated Children's Dictionary & Thesaurus
2017 revised edition ISBN: 978-0-19-276394-5

1 3 5 7 9 10 8 6 4 2

Printed in China

treasure chest

owl

scorpion

core

balls

starfish

feet

lion

The Publishers would like to thank Shutterstock and
Wikipedia for permission to use their material. Every care has
been taken to trace copyright holders. However, if there have
been unintentional omissions or failure to trace copyright
holders, we apologize, and will, if informed, endeavour to
make corrections in any future edition.

How to Use your Thesaurus

numbered senses
show you when a word has more than one meaning

example sentences
show how you might use a word, each meaning has a separate example sentence

headwords
are words you look up, they are in alphabetical order

guide words
give the first and last word on the page

word class
tells you whether a word is a *noun*, *verb*, *adjective*, *adverb*, or *preposition*

alphabet tab
shows the letter of the alphabet

opposites
words that are opposite in meaning to the headword

word web panels
give lists of words related to a topic, useful for project work and story writing

labels
tell you that certain synonyms are formal or informal

synonyms
words that mean the same, or nearly the same, as the headword

overused word panels
offer more interesting words for common words like *nice*, *good*, or *bad*

writing tips panels
help you create more colourful descriptions

Sample page

beware → bird   17

2 *I had a cold, but I'm **better** now.*
recovered, cured, healed, improved, well

beware *verb*
Beware! There are thieves about.
be careful! watch out! look out! take care! be on your guard!
beware of
Beware of the bull.
watch out for, avoid, mind, heed, keep clear of

biased *adjective*
*A referee should not make a **biased** decision.*
prejudiced, partial, one-sided, partisan, unfair
OPPOSITE impartial

big *adjective*
*The giant owned three pairs of **big** boots.*
large, huge, great, massive, enormous, gigantic, colossal, mammoth
(*informal*) whopping, ginormous, humungous
OPPOSITE small, little, tiny

bit *noun*
1 *Mum divided the cake into eight **bits**.*
piece, portion, part, section, segment, share, slice

OVERUSED WORDS
Try to vary the words you use for **big**. Here are some other words you could use.
FOR A **big person** OR **big creature**
burly, giant, hefty, hulking, mighty, monstrous, towering *The mighty robot clanked as it moved.*
FOR A **big object**:
bulky, heavy, hefty, weighty *What could be inside that bulky envelope?*
FOR A **big room** OR **big box**
roomy, sizeable, spacious *Inside, the spaceship was surprisingly roomy.*
OPPOSITE cramped
FOR A **big distance**
immense, infinite, vast *A vast stretch of ocean lay before them.*
FOR A **big amount** OR **big helping**
ample, considerable, substantial *We each got an ample helping of porridge.*
OPPOSITE meagre, paltry
FOR A **big decision** OR **big moment**
grave, important, serious, significant *Yesterday was the most significant day in my short life.*
OPPOSITE unimportant, minor

WORD WEB

bird *noun*
A female bird is a **hen**.
A male bird is a **cock**.
A young bird is a **chick**, **fledgling**, or **nestling**.
A family of chicks is a **brood**.
A group of birds is a **colony** or **flock**.
A group of flying birds is a **flight** or **skein**.
A person who studies birds is an **ornithologist**.

SOME COMMON BRITISH BIRDS
blackbird, blue tit, bullfinch, bunting, chaffinch, crow, cuckoo, dove, greenfinch, jackdaw, jay, linnet, magpie, martin, nightingale, pigeon, raven, robin, rook, skylark, sparrow, starling, swallow, swift, thrush, tit, wagtail, waxwing, woodpecker, wren, yellowhammer

BIRDS OF PREY
buzzard, eagle, falcon, hawk, kestrel, kite, merlin, osprey, owl, sparrowhawk, vulture

FARM AND GAME BIRDS
chicken, duck, goose, grouse, partridge, pheasant, quail, turkey
Birds kept by farmers are called **poultry**.

SEA AND WATER BIRDS
albatross, auk, bittern, coot, cormorant, crane, curlew, duck, gannet, goose, guillemot, gull, heron, kingfisher, kittiwake, lapwing, mallard, moorhen, oystercatcher, peewit, pelican, penguin, puffin, seagull, snipe, stork, swan, teal

BIRDS FROM OTHER COUNTRIES
bird of paradise, budgerigar, canary, cockatoo, flamingo, humming bird, ibis, kookaburra, lovebirds, macaw, mynah bird, parakeet, parrot, toucan

BIRDS WHICH CANNOT FLY
emu, kiwi, ostrich, peacock, penguin

PARTS OF A BIRD'S BODY
beak, bill, claw, talon, breast, crown, throat, crest, feather, down, plumage, plume, wing

SOME TYPES OF BIRD HOME
nest, nesting box, aviary, coop, roost

SOUNDS MADE BY BIRDS
cackle, caw, cheep, chirp, chirrup, cluck, coo, crow, gabble, honk, peep, pipe, quack, screech, squawk, trill, tweet, twitter, warble
A turkey **gobbles**.
An owl **hoots**.

SPECIAL NAMES
A female peacock is a **peahen**.
A young duck is a **duckling**.
A young goose is a **gosling**.
A young swan is a **cygnet**.
An eagle's nest is an **eyrie**.
A place where rooks nest is a **rookery**.

WRITING TIPS
You can use these words to describe a **bird**.
1 TO DESCRIBE *how a bird moves*
circle, dart, flit, flutter, fly, glide, hop, hover, peck, perch, preen, skim, soar, swoop, waddle, wheel *A pair of swallows flitted among the rooftops.*

2 TO DESCRIBE *a bird's feathers*
bedraggled, downy, drab, fluffy, gleaming, iridescent, ruffled, smooth, speckled *The peacock displayed its iridescent tail.*

eagle

flamingo

lovebirds

owl

ostrich

a
b
c
d
e
f
g
h
i
j
k
l
m
n
o
p
q
r
s
t
u
v
w
x
y
z

What is a thesaurus for?

Here are three good reasons to use your thesaurus:

✓ **to find a more interesting word**
What words can you use besides *fly* for how a bird moves? Look up **bird** to find some other ways of describing how birds fly.

✓ **to find the right word**
What do you call a line of mountains? Look up **mountain** to find the answer.

✓ **to give you ideas for writing**
Imagine you are describing outer space. Look up **space** and **planet** for some ideas for the setting, and then look up **alien** for some ideas on what might be out there!

In this book you will find the following special panels:

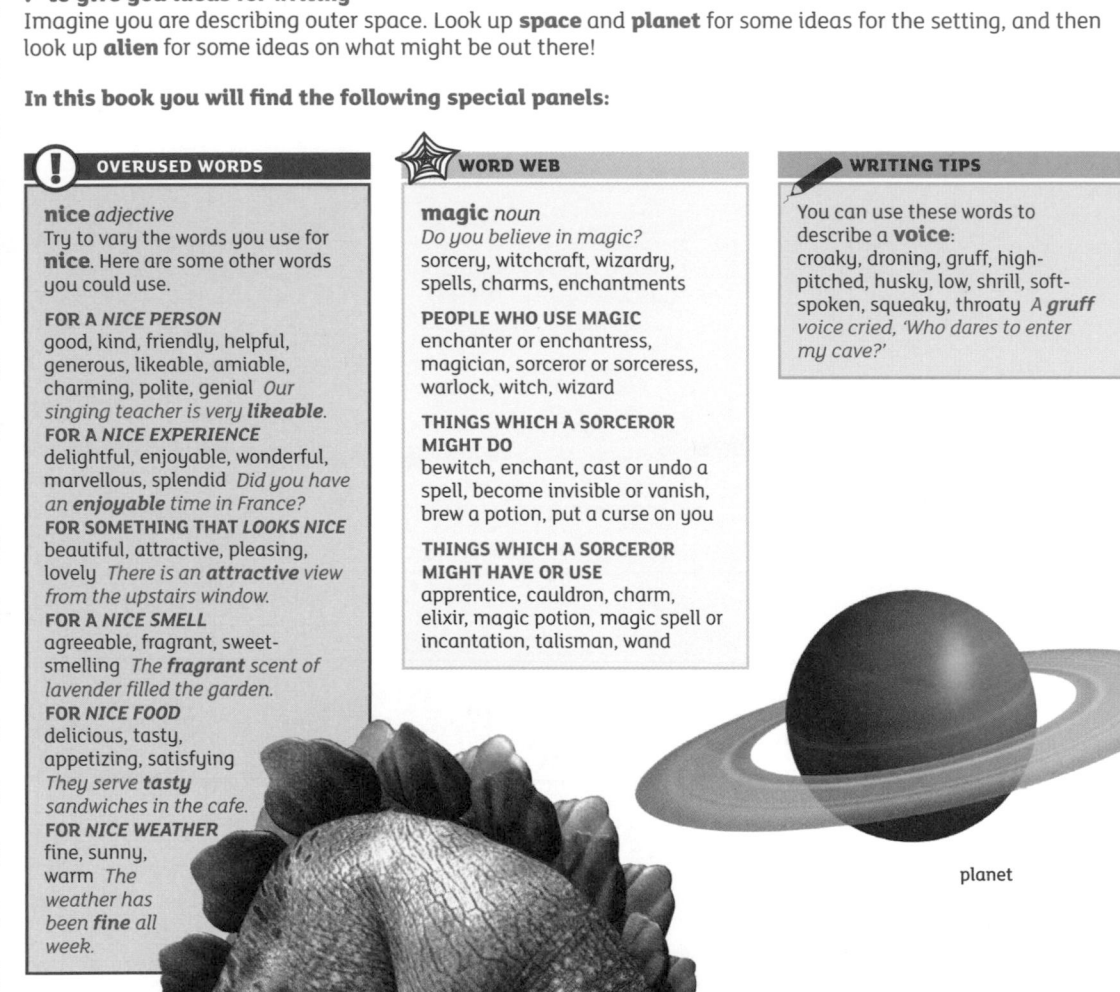

! **OVERUSED WORDS**

nice *adjective*
Try to vary the words you use for **nice**. Here are some other words you could use.

FOR A *NICE PERSON*
good, kind, friendly, helpful, generous, likeable, amiable, charming, polite, genial *Our singing teacher is very **likeable**.*

FOR A *NICE EXPERIENCE*
delightful, enjoyable, wonderful, marvellous, splendid *Did you have an **enjoyable** time in France?*

FOR SOMETHING THAT *LOOKS NICE*
beautiful, attractive, pleasing, lovely *There is an **attractive** view from the upstairs window.*

FOR A *NICE SMELL*
agreeable, fragrant, sweet-smelling *The **fragrant** scent of lavender filled the garden.*

FOR *NICE FOOD*
delicious, tasty, appetizing, satisfying *They serve **tasty** sandwiches in the cafe.*

FOR *NICE WEATHER*
fine, sunny, warm *The weather has been **fine** all week.*

🕸 **WORD WEB**

magic *noun*
Do you believe in magic?
sorcery, witchcraft, wizardry, spells, charms, enchantments

PEOPLE WHO USE MAGIC
enchanter or enchantress, magician, sorceror or sorceress, warlock, witch, wizard

THINGS WHICH A SORCEROR MIGHT DO
bewitch, enchant, cast or undo a spell, become invisible or vanish, brew a potion, put a curse on you

THINGS WHICH A SORCEROR MIGHT HAVE OR USE
apprentice, cauldron, charm, elixir, magic potion, magic spell or incantation, talisman, wand

---

✏ **WRITING TIPS**

You can use these words to describe a **voice**:
croaky, droning, gruff, high-pitched, husky, low, shrill, soft-spoken, squeaky, throaty *A **gruff** voice cried, 'Who dares to enter my cave?'*

---

planet

dinosaur

abandon *verb*
1 *The robbers **abandoned** the stolen car.*
leave, desert, forsake, leave behind, strand (*informal*) dump, ditch
2 *We **abandoned** our picnic because of the rain.*
cancel, give up, scrap, drop, abort, discard

ability *noun*
*Skin has a natural **ability** to heal itself.*
capability, competence, aptitude, talent, expertise, skill

able *adjective*
1 *Will you be **able** to come to my party?*
allowed, permitted, free, willing
OPPOSITE unable
2 *Penguins are very **able** swimmers.*
competent, capable, accomplished, expert, skilful, proficient, talented, gifted
OPPOSITE incompetent

abolish *verb*
*I wish someone would **abolish** homework!*
get rid of, do away with, put an end to, eliminate
OPPOSITE create

about *preposition*
*There are **about** two hundred children in the school.*
approximately, roughly, close to, around
to be about something
*The film is **about** a dog called Scruff.*
concern, deal with, involve

abrupt *adjective*
1 *The book came to a very **abrupt** end.*
sudden, hurried, hasty, quick, unexpected
OPPOSITE gradual
2 *The sales assistant had a very **abrupt** manner.*
blunt, curt, sharp, rude, gruff, impolite, tactless, unfriendly
OPPOSITE polite

absent *adjective*
*Why were you **absent** from school yesterday?*
away, missing
To be absent from school without a good reason is to **play truant**.
OPPOSITE present

absolute *adjective*
*The hypnotist asked for **absolute** silence.*
complete, total, utter, perfect

absolutely *adverb*
*This floor is **absolutely** filthy!*
completely, thoroughly, totally, utterly, wholly, entirely

abuse *verb*
1 *The rescued dog had been **abused** by its owners.*
mistreat, maltreat, hurt, injure, damage, harm, misuse
2 *The referee was **abused** by players from both teams.*
be rude to, insult, swear at (*informal*) call someone names

abuse *noun*
1 *They campaigned against the **abuse** of animals.*
mistreatment, misuse, damage, harm, injury
2 *A spectator yelled **abuse** at the referee.*
insults, name-calling, swear words

accelerate *verb*
*The bus **accelerated** when it reached the motorway.*
go faster, speed up, pick up speed
OPPOSITE slow down

accept *verb*
1 *I **accepted** the offer of a lift to the station.*
take, receive, welcome
OPPOSITE reject
2 *The club **accepted** my application for membership.*
approve, agree to, consent to
OPPOSITE reject
3 *Do you **accept** responsibility for the damage?*
admit, acknowledge, recognize, face up to
OPPOSITE deny
4 *They had to **accept** the umpire's decision.*
agree to, go along with, tolerate, put up with, resign yourself to

acceptable *adjective*
1 *Would a pound be **acceptable** as a tip?*
welcome, agreeable, appreciated, pleasant, pleasing, worthwhile
2 *She said my handwriting was not **acceptable**.*
satisfactory, adequate, appropriate, permissible, suitable, tolerable, passable
OPPOSITE unacceptable

accident *noun*
1 *There has been an **accident** at a fireworks display.*
misfortune, mishap, disaster, calamity, catastrophe

A person who is always having accidents is **accident-prone**.
2 *A motorway **accident** is causing traffic delays.*
collision, crash, smash
An accident involving a lot of vehicles is a **pile-up**.
A railway accident may involve a **derailment**.
3 *It was pure **accident** that led us to the secret passage.*
chance, luck, a fluke

accidental *adjective*
1 *The damage to the building was **accidental**.*
unintentional, unfortunate, unlucky
2 *The professor made an **accidental** discovery.*
unexpected, unforeseen, unplanned, fortunate, lucky, chance
OPPOSITE deliberate

account *noun*
1 *I wrote an **account** of our camping trip in my diary.*
report, record, description, history, narrative, story, chronicle, log
(*informal*) write-up
2 *Money was of no **account** to him.*
importance, significance, consequence, interest, value

accurate *adjective*
1 *The detective took **accurate** measurements of the room.*
careful, correct, exact, meticulous, minute, precise
OPPOSITE inexact, rough
2 *Is this an **accurate** account of what happened?*
faithful, true, reliable, truthful, factual
OPPOSITE inaccurate, false

accuse *verb*
accuse of
*Miss Sharp **accused** her opponent **of** cheating.*
charge with, blame for, condemn for, denounce for
OPPOSITE defend

ache *noun*
*The **ache** in my tooth is getting worse.*
pain, soreness, throbbing, discomfort, pang, twinge

achieve *verb*
1 *He **achieved** his ambition to play rugby for Wales.*
accomplish, attain, succeed in, carry out, fulfil
2 *The singer **achieved** success with her first album.*
acquire, win, gain, earn, get, score

achievement *noun*
*To climb Mount Everest would be an **achievement**.*
accomplishment, attainment, success, feat, triumph

a
b
c
d
e
f
g
h
i
j
k
l
m
n
o
p
q
r
s
t
u
v
w
x
y
z

act *noun*
1 *Rescuing the boy from the river was a brave **act**.*
action, deed, feat, exploit, operation
2 *The best **act** at the circus involved three clowns.*
performance, sketch, item, turn

act *verb*
1 *We must **act** as soon as we hear the signal.*
do something, take action
2 *Give the medicine time to **act**.*
work, take effect, have an effect, function
3 *Stop **acting** like a baby!*
behave, carry on
4 *I **acted** the part of a pirate in the play.*
perform, play, portray, represent, appear as

action *noun*
1 *The driver's **action** prevented an accident.*
act, deed, effort, measure, feat
2 *The fruit ripens through the **action** of the sun.*
working, effect, mechanism
3 *The film was packed with **action**.*
drama, excitement, activity, liveliness, energy, vigour, vitality

active *adjective*
1 *Mr Aziz is very **active** for his age.*
energetic, lively, dynamic, vigorous, busy
2 *My uncle is an **active** member of the football club.*
enthusiastic, devoted, committed, dedicated, hard-working
OPPOSITE inactive

activity *noun*
1 *The town centre was full of **activity**.*
action, life, busyness, liveliness, excitement, movement, animation
2 *My mum's favourite **activity** is gardening.*
hobby, interest, pastime, pursuit, job, occupation, task

actual *adjective*
*Did you see the **actual** crime?*
real, true, genuine, authentic
OPPOSITE imaginary, supposed

actually *adverb*
*What did the teacher **actually** say to you?*
really, truly, definitely, certainly, genuinely, in fact

adapt *verb*
1 *I'll **adapt** the goggles so that they fit you.*
alter, change, modify, convert, reorganize, transform
2 *Our family **adapted** quickly to life in the country.*
become accustomed, adjust, acclimatize

add *verb*
*The poet **added** an extra line in the last verse.*
join on, attach, append, insert
to add to
*The herbs **add to** the flavour of the stew.*
improve, enhance, increase
to add up
1 *Can you **add up** these figures for me?*
count up, find the sum of, find the total of
(*informal*) tot up
2 (*informal*) *Her story just doesn't **add up**.*
be convincing, make sense

additional *adjective*
*There are **additional** toilets downstairs.*
extra, further, more, supplementary

adequate *adjective*
1 *A sandwich will be **adequate**, thank you.*
enough, sufficient, ample
2 *Your work is **adequate**, but I'm sure you can do better.*
satisfactory, acceptable, tolerable, competent, passable, respectable

adjust *verb*
1 *You need to **adjust** the TV picture.*
correct, modify, put right, improve, tune
2 *She **adjusted** the central heating thermostat.*
alter, change, set, vary, regulate

admire *verb*
1 *I **admire** her skill with words.*
think highly of, look up to, value, have a high opinion of, respect, applaud, approve of, esteem
OPPOSITE despise
2 *The travellers stopped to **admire** the view.*
enjoy, appreciate, be delighted by

admit *verb*
*Did he **admit** that he told a lie?*
acknowledge, agree, accept, confess, grant, own up
OPPOSITE deny

adopt *verb*
1 *Our school has **adopted** a healthy eating policy.*
take up, accept, choose, follow, embrace
2 *We have **adopted** a stray kitten.*
foster, take in

adore *verb*
1 *Rosie **adores** her big sister.*
love, worship, idolize, dote on
2 (*informal*) *I **adore** chocolate milk shakes!*
love, like, enjoy
OPPOSITE hate, detest

adult *adjective*
*An **adult** zebra can run at 80km an hour.*
grown-up, mature, full-size, fully grown
OPPOSITE young, immature

advance *verb*
1 *As the army **advanced**, the enemy fled.*
move forward, go forward, proceed, approach, come near, press on, progress, forge ahead, gain ground, make headway, make progress
OPPOSITE retreat
2 *Mobile phones have **advanced** in the last few years.*
develop, grow, improve, evolve, progress

advantage *noun*
*We had the **advantage** of the wind behind us.*
assistance, benefit, help, aid, asset
OPPOSITE disadvantage, drawback

adventure *noun*
1 *He told us about his latest **adventure**.*
enterprise, exploit, venture, escapade
2 *They travelled the world in search of **adventure**.*
excitement, danger, risk, thrills

advertise *verb*
*We made a poster to **advertise** the cake sale.*
publicize, promote, announce, make known (*informal*) plug

advice *noun*
*The website gives **advice** on building a bird table.*
guidance, help, directions, recommendations, suggestions, tips, pointers

advise *verb*
1 *What did the doctor **advise**?*
recommend, suggest, advocate, prescribe
2 *He **advised** me to rest.*
counsel, encourage, urge

affect *verb*
1 *Global warming will **affect** our climate.*
have an effect or impact on, influence, change, modify, alter
2 *The bad news **affected** us deeply.*
disturb, upset, concern, trouble, worry

afford *verb*
*I can't **afford** a new bike just now.*
have enough money for, pay for, manage, spare

afraid *adjective*
1 *We felt **afraid** as we approached the haunted house.*
frightened, scared, terrified, petrified, alarmed, fearful, anxious, apprehensive
OPPOSITE brave

2 *Don't be **afraid** to ask questions.*
hesitant, reluctant, shy

age *noun*
*The book is set in the **age** of the Vikings.*
period, time, era, epoch, days

aggressive *adjective*
*Bats are not **aggressive** creatures.*
hostile, violent, provocative, quarrelsome, bullying, warlike
OPPOSITE friendly

agile *adjective*
*Mountain goats are extremely **agile**.*
nimble, graceful, sure-footed, sprightly, acrobatic, supple, swift
OPPOSITE clumsy, stiff

agony *noun*
*He screamed in **agony** when he broke his leg.*
pain, suffering, torture, torment, anguish, distress

agree *verb*
1 *I'm glad that we **agree**.*
be united, think the same, concur
OPPOSITE disagree
2 *I **agree** that you are right.*
accept, acknowledge, admit, grant, allow
OPPOSITE disagree
3 *I **agree** to pay my share.*
consent, promise, be willing, undertake
OPPOSITE refuse

agreement *noun*
1 *There was **agreement** on the need for longer holidays.*
consensus, unanimity, unity, consent, harmony, sympathy, conformity
OPPOSITE disagreement
2 *The two sides signed an **agreement**.*
alliance, treaty
An agreement to end fighting is an **armistice** or **truce**.
A business agreement is a **bargain**, **contract**, or **deal**.

aid *noun*
1 *We can climb out with the **aid** of this rope.*
help, support, assistance, backing, cooperation
2 *They agreed to send more **aid** to the poorer countries.*
donations, subsidies, contributions

aid *verb*
*The local people **aided** the police in their investigation.*
help, assist, support, back, collaborate with, cooperate with, contribute to, lend a hand to, further, promote, subsidize

---

WORD WEB

aircraft *noun*

aeroplane

SOME TYPES OF AIRCRAFT
aeroplane, airliner, airship, biplane, bomber, fighter, glider, helicopter, hot-air balloon, jet, jumbo jet, seaplane

PARTS OF AIRCRAFT
cabin, cargo hold, cockpit, engine, fin, flap, flight deck, fuselage, joystick, passenger cabin, propeller, rotor, rudder, tail, tailplane, undercarriage, wing

airship

PLACES WHERE AIRCRAFT TAKE OFF AND LAND
aerodrome, airfield, airport, airstrip, helipad, heliport, landing strip, runway

PEOPLE WHO FLY IN AIRCRAFT
pilot, aviator, balloonist, co-pilot, cabin crew, flight attendant, passengers

helicopter

---

aim *noun*
*What was the **aim** of the experiment?*
ambition, desire, dream, goal, hope, intention, objective, purpose, target, wish

aim *verb*
1 *She **aims** to be a professional dancer.*
intend, mean, plan, propose, want, wish, seek
2 *He **aimed** his bow and arrow at the target.*
point, direct, take aim with, line up, level, train, focus

air *noun*
1 *We shouldn't pollute the **air** we breathe.*
atmosphere
2 *This room needs some **air**.*
fresh air, ventilation
3 *There was an **air** of mystery about the place.*
feeling, mood, look, appearance, sense

aircraft *noun* see panel above

alarm *verb*
*The barking dog **alarmed** the sheep.*
frighten, startle, scare, panic, agitate, distress, shock, surprise, upset, worry
OPPOSITE reassure

alarm *noun*
1 *Did you hear the **alarm**?*
signal, alert, warning, siren
2 *The sudden noise filled me with **alarm**.*
fright, fear, panic, anxiety, apprehension, distress, nervousness, terror, uneasiness

---

alien *adjective*
1 *The desert landscape looked **alien** to us.*
strange, foreign, unfamiliar, different, exotic
OPPOSITE familiar
2 *They saw the lights of an **alien** spaceship.*
extraterrestrial

WORD WEB

alien *noun*
*I wrote a story about **aliens** from Mars.*
extraterrestrial, alien life-form, spaceman or spacewoman, starman or starwoman

AN ALIEN MIGHT BE
humanoid, insect-like, lizard-like, reptilian, intelligent, primitive, super-intelligent, telepathic

alien

BODY PARTS AN ALIEN MIGHT HAVE
antenna, blotches, scales, slime, sucker, tentacle, webbing

TRANSPORT AN ALIEN MIGHT USE
alien vessel, flying saucer, mothership, pod, spacecraft, spaceship, starship, time-machine, transporter beam

An alien might call someone from Earth an **Earthling**.

alive *adjective*
Fortunately, my goldfish was still **alive**.
living, live, existing, in existence, surviving, breathing, flourishing
OPPOSITE dead

allow *verb*
1 *They don't* **allow** *skateboards in the playground.*
permit, let, authorize, approve of, agree to, consent to, give permission for, license, put up with, stand, support, tolerate
OPPOSITE forbid
2 *Have you* **allowed** *enough time for the journey?*
allocate, set aside, assign, grant, earmark

all right *adjective*
1 *The survivors appeared to be* **all right**.
well, unhurt, unharmed, uninjured, safe
2 *The food in the hotel was* **all right**.
satisfactory, acceptable, adequate, reasonable, passable
3 *Is it* **all right** *to play music in here?*
acceptable, permissable

almost *adverb*
1 *I have* **almost** *finished the crossword.*
nearly, practically, just about, virtually, all but, as good as, not quite
2 **Almost** *a hundred people came to the concert.*
about, approximately, around

alone *adjective, adverb*
1 *Did you go to the party* **alone**?
on your own, by yourself, unaccompanied
2 *Zoe had no friends and felt very* **alone**.
lonely, friendless, isolated, solitary, lonesome, desolate

also *adverb*
We need some bread, and **also** *more butter.*
in addition, besides, additionally, too, furthermore, moreover

alter *verb*
They have **altered** *the route for the cycle race.*
change, adjust, adapt, modify, transform, amend, make different, revise, vary

always *adverb*
1 *The sea is* **always** *in motion.*
constantly, continuously, endlessly, eternally, for ever, perpetually, unceasingly
2 *This bus is* **always** *late.*
consistently, continually, invariably, persistently, regularly, repeatedly

amaze *verb*
It **amazes** *me to think that the Earth is billions of years old.*
astonish, astound, startle, surprise, stun, shock, stagger, dumbfound
(*informal*) flabbergast

amazed *adjective*
I was **amazed** *by the number of emails I received.*
astonished, astounded, stunned, surprised, dumbfounded, speechless, staggered
(*informal*) flabbergasted

amazing *adjective*
The Northern Lights are an **amazing** *sight.*
astonishing, astounding, staggering, remarkable, surprising, extraordinary, incredible, breathtaking, phenomenal, sensational, stupendous, tremendous, wonderful, mind-boggling

ambition *noun*
1 *She had great* **ambition** *when she was young.*
drive, enthusiasm, enterprise, push, zeal
2 *My* **ambition** *is to play tennis at Wimbledon.*
goal, aim, intention, objective, target, desire, dream, wish, hope, aspiration

ambitious *adjective*
1 *If you're* **ambitious**, *you will probably succeed.*
enterprising, enthusiastic, committed, go-ahead, keen
OPPOSITE unambitious
2 *I think your plan is too* **ambitious**.
grand, big, large-scale

amount *noun*
1 *I worked out the exact* **amount** *I'd need to buy the jacket..*
sum, total, whole
2 *There's a large* **amount** *of paper in the cupboard.*
quantity, measure, supply, volume, mass, bulk

amuse *verb*
I think this joke will **amuse** *you.*
make you laugh, entertain, cheer up, divert
(*informal*) tickle

amusing *adjective*
I didn't find his jokes very **amusing**.
funny, witty, humorous, comic, comical, hilarious, diverting, entertaining
OPPOSITE unamusing, serious

ancient *adjective*
1 *Does that* **ancient** *car still go?*
old, old-fashioned, antiquated, out of date, obsolete

2 *In* **ancient** *times, our ancestors were hunters.*
early, primitive, prehistoric, remote, long past, olden
The times before written records were kept are **prehistoric** *times.*
The ancient Greeks and Romans lived in **classical** *times.*
OPPOSITE modern

anger *noun*
I was filled with **anger** *when I read her letter.*
rage, fury, indignation
(*old use*) wrath, ire
An outburst of anger is a **tantrum** *or a* **temper**.

anger *verb*
His cruelty towards his dog **angered** *me.*
enrage, infuriate, incense, madden, annoy, irritate, exasperate, antagonize, provoke
(*informal*) make your blood boil, make you see red
OPPOSITE pacify

angry *adjective*
Miss Potts turns purple when she gets **angry**.
cross, furious, enraged, infuriated, irate, livid, annoyed, incensed, exasperated, fuming, indignant, raging, seething
(*informal*) mad
To become angry is to **lose your temper**.
OPPOSITE calm

animal *noun*
see panel opposite

announce *verb*
1 *The head* **announced** *that sports day was cancelled.*
declare, state, proclaim, report
2 *The DJ* **announced** *the next record.*
present, introduce, lead into

announcement *noun*
1 *The head reads the* **announcements** *in assembly.*
notice
2 *The prime minister issued an* **announcement**.
statement, declaration, proclamation, pronouncement
3 *I heard the* **announcement** *on TV.*
report, bulletin, news flash

annoy *verb*
1 *I was* **annoyed** *that I missed the bus.*
irritate, bother, displease, exasperate, anger, upset, vex, trouble, worry
OPPOSITE please
2 *Please don't* **annoy** *me while I'm working.*
pester, bother, harass, badger, nag, plague, trouble, try (*informal*) bug

WORD WEB

animal *noun*
*Wild **animals** roam freely in the safari park.*
creature, beast, brute
A word for wild animals in general is **wildlife**.
A scientific word for animals is **fauna**.

VARIOUS KINDS OF ANIMAL
amphibian, arachnid, bird, fish, insect, invertebrate, mammal, marsupial, mollusc, reptile, rodent, vertebrate

An animal that eats meat is a **carnivore**.
An animal that eats plants is a **herbivore**.
An animal that eats many things is an **omnivore**.
Animals that sleep most of the winter are **hibernating animals**.
Animals that are active at night are **nocturnal animals**.

SOME ANIMALS THAT LIVE ON LAND
aardvark, antelope, ape, armadillo, baboon, badger, bat, bear, beaver, bison, buffalo, camel, cheetah, chimpanzee, chinchilla, chipmunk, deer, dormouse, elephant, elk, fox, gazelle, gibbon, giraffe, gnu, gorilla, grizzly bear, hare, hedgehog, hippopotamus, hyena, jackal, jaguar, kangaroo, koala, lemming, lemur, leopard, lion, llama, lynx, mongoose, monkey, moose, mouse, ocelot, opossum, orang-utan, otter, panda, panther, platypus, polar bear, porcupine, rabbit, rat, reindeer, rhinoceros, skunk, squirrel, stoat, tapir, tiger, vole, wallaby, weasel, wildebeest, wolf, wolverine, wombat, yak, zebra

SOME ANIMALS THAT LIVE IN THE SEA
dolphin, porpoise, seal, sea lion, walrus, whale

SOME EXTINCT ANIMALS
dinosaur, dodo, quagga

gorilla

PARTS OF AN ANIMAL'S BODY
antler, claw, fang, foreleg, hind leg, hoof, horn, jaws, mane, muzzle, paw, snout, tail, trotter, tusk, whisker, fur, coat, fleece, hide, pelt

MALE AND FEMALE ANIMALS
A male elephant or whale is a **bull** and a female is a **cow**.
A male fox is a **dog** and a female is a **vixen**.
A male goat is a **billy goat** and a female is a **nanny goat**.
A male hare or rabbit is a **buck** and a female is a **doe**.
A male horse is a **stallion** and a female is a **mare**.
A female lion is a **lioness**.
A female pig is a **sow**.
A male sheep is a **ram** and a female is a **ewe**.
A female tiger is a **tigress**.
A male wolf is a **dog** and a female is a **bitch**.

✏️ **WRITING TIPS**

You can use these words to describe an **animal**.
TO DESCRIBE *HOW AN ANIMAL MOVES*
bound, creep, crouch, dart, gallop, gambol, leap, lumber, nuzzle, pad, paw, pounce, roam, scuttle, skip, slink, slither, spring, stamp, stampede, trot, waddle *The jaguar **padded** along silently.*
TO DESCRIBE *AN ANIMAL'S BODY*
agile, nimble, sinewy, wiry; lumbering, majestic, mighty, muscular, powerful *The cheetah stretched its long, **sinewy** body.*
TO DESCRIBE *AN ANIMAL'S SKIN OR COAT*
coarse, fluffy, furry, glistening, glossy, hairy, leathery, matted, prickly, scaly, shaggy, shiny, silky, sleek, slimy, slippery, smooth, spiky, thick, thorny, tough, wiry, woolly; mottled, piebald, spotted, striped *The otters' coats were **smooth** and **silky**.*

YOUNG ANIMALS
A young beaver is a **kit**.
A young fox or lion is a **cub**.
A young goat is a **kid**.
A young hare is a **leveret**.
A young horse is a **foal**, **colt** (male), or **filly** (female).
A young pig is a **piglet**.
A young otter or seal is a **pup**.
A young sheep is a **lamb**.

lemur

HOMES OF WILD ANIMALS
den, lair
A badger lives in a **sett**.
A beaver or otter lives in a **lodge**.
A fox lives in an **earth**.
A rabbit lives in a **burrow** or **warren**.
A squirrel lives in a **drey**.

SOUNDS MADE BY ANIMALS
bark, bay, bellow, buzz, gnash, growl, grunt, hiss, howl, jabber, purr, roar, snap, snarl, snort, snuffle, squeak, trumpet, whimper, whine, yap, yelp, yowl

A sheep **bleats**.
A donkey **brays**.
A frog **croaks**.
Cattle **low** or **moo**.
A cat **mews** or **miaows**.
A horse **neighs** or **whinnies**.

giraffe

zebra

lion

tortoise

skunk

annoying *adjective*
*My brother has a lot of **annoying** habits.*
irritating, exasperating, maddening, provoking, tiresome, trying, vexing, troublesome

answer *noun*
1 *Did you get an **answer** to your letter?*
reply, response, acknowledgement, reaction
A quick or angry answer is a **retort**.
2 *The **answers** to the quiz are on the next page.*
solution, explanation

answer *verb*
1 *You haven't **answered** my question.*
give an answer to, reply to, respond to, react to, acknowledge
2 *'I'm quite well,' I **answered**.*
reply, respond, return
To answer quickly or angrily is to **retort**.

anxious *adjective*
1 *Are you **anxious** about your exams?*
nervous, worried, apprehensive, concerned, uneasy, fearful, edgy, fraught, tense, troubled
(*informal*) uptight, jittery
OPPOSITE calm
2 *I'm **anxious** to do my best.*
eager, keen, impatient, enthusiastic, willing

apologize *verb*
*The ogre **apologized** for being rude.*
make an apology, say sorry, express regret, repent, be penitent

apparent *adjective*
*There was no **apparent** reason for the crash.*
obvious, evident, clear, noticeable, detectable, perceptible, recognizable, conspicuous, visible
OPPOSITE concealed

appeal *verb*
to appeal for
*The prisoners **appealed for** our help.*
request, beg for, plead for, cry out for, entreat, ask earnestly for, pray for
to appeal to
*That kind of music doesn't **appeal to** me.*
attract, interest, fascinate, tempt

appear *verb*
1 *Snowdrops **appear** in the spring.*
come out, emerge, become visible, come into view, develop, occur, show, crop up, spring up, surface
2 *Our visitors didn't **appear** until midnight.*
arrive, come, turn up
(*informal*) show up

3 *It **appears** that the baby is asleep.*
seem, look
4 *I once **appeared** in a musical.*
act, perform, take part, feature

appearance *noun*
1 *They were startled by the **appearance** of the ghost.*
approach, arrival, entrance, entry
2 *Mr Hogweed had a grim **appearance**.*
air, aspect, bearing, look

appetite *noun*
1 *When I was ill, I completely lost my **appetite**.*
hunger
2 *Explorers have a great **appetite** for adventure.*
desire, eagerness, enthusiasm, passion, keenness, wish, urge, taste, thirst, longing, yearning, craving, lust, zest

apply *verb*
1 *The nurse told me to **apply** the ointment generously.*
administer, put on, lay on, spread
2 *My brother has **applied** for a new job.*
make an application for, ask for, request
3 *The rules **apply** to all our members.*
be relevant, relate, refer
4 *The vet **applied** all her skill to save the animal's life.*
use, employ, exercise, utilize

appreciate *verb*
1 *He **appreciates** good music.*
enjoy, like, love
2 *I **appreciate** her good qualities.*
admire, respect, regard highly, approve of, value, esteem
OPPOSITE despise
3 *I **appreciate** that you can't afford much.*
realize, recognize, understand, comprehend, know, see
4 *Dad hopes that the value of our house will **appreciate**.*
grow, increase, go up, mount, rise

approach *verb*
1 *The lioness **approached** her prey.*
draw near to, move towards, come near to, advance on
2 *I **approached** the head to ask if we could have a party.*
speak to, contact, go to
3 *The volunteers **approached** their work cheerfully.*
begin, undertake, embark on, set about

approach *noun*
1 *We could hear the **approach** of heavy footsteps.*
arrival, advance, coming

2 *Dad made an **approach** to the bank manager for a loan.*
application, appeal, proposal
3 *I like her positive **approach**.*
attitude, manner, style, way
4 *The easiest **approach** to the castle is from the west.*
access, entry, entrance, way in

appropriate *adjective*
*It's not **appropriate** to wear jeans to a wedding.*
suitable, proper, fitting, apt, right, tactful, tasteful, well-judged
OPPOSITE inappropriate

approval *noun*
1 *We cheered to show our **approval**.*
appreciation, admiration, praise, high regard, acclaim, respect, support
OPPOSITE disapproval
2 *The head gave her **approval** to our plan.*
agreement, consent, authorization, assent, go-ahead, permission, support, blessing
OPPOSITE refusal

approve *verb*
*The head **approved** my request for a day off school.*
agree to, consent to, authorize, allow, accept, pass, permit, support, back
OPPOSITE refuse

approximate *adjective*
*What is the **approximate** length of the journey?*
estimated, rough, nexact, near
OPPOSITE exact

approximately *adverb*
*The film will finish at **approximately** five o'clock.*
roughly, about, around, round about, close to, nearly, more or less

area *noun*
1 *From the plane we saw a big **area** of desert.*
expanse, stretch, tract
A small area is a **patch**.
An area of water or ice is a **sheet**.
2 *I live in an urban **area**.*
district, locality, neighbourhood, region, zone, vicinity

argue *verb*
1 *You two are always **arguing** over something.*
quarrel, disagree, differ, fall out, fight, have an argument, squabble, wrangle, bicker
OPPOSITE agree
2 *We **argued** over the price of the cloth.*
bargain, haggle
3 *He **argued** that it was my turn to walk the dog.*
claim, assert, try to prove, maintain, reason, suggest

argument *noun*
1 *They was an **argument** over who should pay for the meal.*
disagreement, quarrel, dispute, row, clash, controversy, debate, difference, fight, squabble, altercation
2 *Did you follow the **argument** of the book?*
line of reasoning, theme, outline, gist

WORD WEB

armour *noun*
PARTS OF A MEDIEVAL KNIGHT'S ARMOUR
breastplate, cuirass (breast and back plate), gauntlet, greave (shin guard), habergeon (sleeveless coat), helmet, visor

Armour made of linked rings is **chain mail**. An outfit of armour is a **suit of armour**.

arrange *verb*
1 *The books are **arranged** in alphabetical order.*
sort, order, put in order, group, organize, categorize, classify, collate, display, sort out, set out, lay out, line up
2 *Do you need any help **arranging** the party?*
plan, organize, prepare, set up, see to

arrangement *noun*
1 *They have improved the **arrangement** of the garden.*
layout, organization, design, planning
2 *Did you change the **arrangement** of my books?*
order, grouping, display, distribution, spacing
3 *We have an **arrangement** to use the swimming pool.*
agreement, deal, bargain, contract, scheme

arrive *verb*
*When is the train due to **arrive**?*
appear, come, turn up, show up, get in
*When a plane arrives it **lands** or **touches down**.*
to arrive at
*We **arrived at** the castle before midnight.*
get to, reach

arrogant *adjective*
*His **arrogant** manner annoys me.*
boastful, conceited, proud, haughty, self-important, bumptious, pompous, snobbish, superior, vain
(*informal*) cocky, snooty, stuck-up
OPPOSITE modest

art *noun see panel below*

article *noun*
1 *Have you any **articles** for the jumble sale?*
item, object, thing
2 *Did you read my **article** in the magazine?*
essay, report, piece of writing

artificial *adjective*
1 *Organic gardeners don't use **artificial** fertilizers.*
man-made, synthetic, unnatural, manufactured
OPPOSITE natural
2 *She had an **artificial** flower in her buttonhole.*
fake, false, imitation, unreal, bogus, counterfeit
OPPOSITE genuine, real

ashamed *adjective*
*He was **ashamed** because of what he had done.*
sorry, remorseful, repentant, embarrassed, shamefaced, abashed, mortified, apologetic, penitent
(*informal*) red-faced
OPPOSITE unashamed, unrepentant

ask *verb*
1 *I **asked** them to be careful with the parcel.*
beg, entreat, appeal to, implore, plead with
2 *'Are you ready?' I **asked**.*
demand, enquire, inquire, query, question
3 *I'm going to **ask** you to my party.*
invite
(*formal*) request the pleasure of your company

asleep *adjective*
*I didn't hear the phone because I was **asleep**.*
sleeping, dozing, having a nap, napping
(*formal*) slumbering
*A patient asleep for an operation is **anaesthetized** or **under sedation**.*

WORD WEB

art *noun* and **artist** *noun*
SOME ARTISTS AND CRAFTSPEOPLE
animator, blacksmith, carpenter, cartoonist, designer, draughtsman, draughtswoman, embroiderer, engraver, goldsmith, graphic designer, illustrator, knitter, mason, painter, photographer, potter, printer, quilter, sculptor, silversmith, weaver

SOME ARTS AND CRAFTS
animation, basketry, batik, beadwork, carpentry, carving, collage, crochet, cross-stitch, decoupage, drawing, embroidery, enamelling, engraving, etching, graphics, illustration, jewellery, knitting, metalwork, modelling, mosaics, needlework, origami, painting, patchwork, photography, pottery, printing, quilting, screen printing, sculpture, sewing, sketching, spinning, stained glass, stamping, stencilling, tapestry, weaving, woodwork

artistic *adjective*
*Mum's flower arrangements are very **artistic**.*
creative, imaginative, aesthetic, attractive, beautiful, tasteful
OPPOSITE ugly

potter

photographer

a b c d e f g h i j k l m n o p q r s t u v w x y z

An animal asleep for the winter is *hibernating*.
OPPOSITE awake
to fall asleep *We waited until the giant **fell asleep**.*
drop off, doze, nod off
To fall asleep quickly is *to go out like a light*.

assemble *verb*
1 *A crowd **assembled** to watch the rescue.*
gather, come together, converge, accumulate, crowd together, flock together, meet, convene
OPPOSITE disperse
2 *We **assembled** our luggage at the front door.*
collect, gather, bring together, pile up, put together
3 *The general **assembled** his troops.*
round up, rally, muster

assembly *noun*
*There was a large **assembly** of people in the market square.*
gathering, meeting, crowd, throng
An assembly for worship is a *service*.
A large assembly to show support for something, often out of doors, is a *rally*.
An assembly to discuss political matters is a *council* or *parliament*.
An assembly to discuss and learn about a particular topic is a *conference* or *congress*.

assistance *noun*
1 *Do you need **assistance** with your luggage?*
help, aid, support, encouragement
2 *We bought new sports equipment with the **assistance** of a local firm.*
backing, collaboration, cooperation, sponsorship, subsidy, support

assistant *noun*
*The magician was training a new **assistant**.*
helper, partner, colleague, associate, supporter

assorted *adjective*
*I bought a bag of sweets with **assorted** flavours.*
various, different, mixed, diverse, miscellaneous, several

assortment *noun*
*There was an **assortment** of sandwiches to choose from.*
variety, mixture, selection, array, choice, collection, diversity

assume *verb*
1 *I **assume** you'd like some chocolate.*
suppose, presume, imagine, believe, guess, expect, gather, suspect, think
2 *The bandit **assumed** a disguise.*
put on, adopt, dress up in, wear

assure *verb*
*I **assure** you that I will take care of your dog.*
promise, give your word to

astonish *verb*
*It **astonished** us to learn that the house was haunted.*
amaze, astound, surprise, stagger, shock, dumbfound, leave speechless, startle, stun, take aback, take by surprise
(*informal*) flabbergast, take your breath away

astonishing *adjective*
*The volcano was an **astonishing** sight.*
amazing, astounding, staggering, remarkable, surprising, extraordinary, incredible, breathtaking, phenomenal, sensational, stupendous, tremendous, wonderful

athletic *adjective*
*You need to be **athletic** to run in a marathon.*
fit, active, energetic, strong, muscular, powerful, robust, sturdy, vigorous, well-built
(*informal*) sporty
OPPOSITE feeble, puny

🕸 **WORD WEB**

astronaut *noun*
*The **astronauts** climbed aboard the space shuttle.*
spaceman or spacewoman

THINGS AN ASTRONAUT MIGHT USE OR WEAR
spacesuit, jet pack, oxygen tank, gloves, helmet, moonboots or spaceboots, visor

PLACES AN ASTRONAUT MIGHT VISIT
alien planet, moonbase, spacelab, space shuttle, space station, starbase

atrocious *adjective*
*Everyone was shocked by the **atrocious** crime.*
wicked, terrible, dreadful, abominable, brutal, savage, barbaric, bloodthirsty, callous, cruel, diabolical, evil, fiendish, horrifying, merciless, outrageous, sadistic, terrible, vicious, villainous

attach *verb*
***Attach** this label to the parcel.*
fasten, fix, join, tie, bind, secure, connect, link, couple, stick, affix, add, append
OPPOSITE detach

attack *noun*
1 *The pirates' **attack** took us by surprise.*
assault, strike, charge, rush, raid, ambush, invasion, onslaught
An attack with big guns or bombs is a *blitz* or *bombardment*.
An attack by planes is an *air raid*.

satellite

2 *The newspaper published an attack on his character.*
criticism, outburst, abuse, tirade
3 *I had a sneezing attack in assembly.*
bout, fit, spasm
(*informal*) turn

attack verb
1 *The travellers were attacked by highwaymen.*
assault, beat up, mug, set on, assail
To attack someone else's territory is to **invade** or **raid** it.
To attack someone from a hidden place is to **ambush** them.
To attack the enemy with bombs or heavy guns is to **bombard** them.
To attack by rushing at the enemy is to **charge**.
To attack a place suddenly is to **storm** it.
If an animal attacks you, it might **savage** you.
2 *He attacked her reputation.*
abuse, criticize, denounce
OPPOSITE defend

attempt verb
They will attempt to reconstruct a Viking ship.
try, endeavour, strive, seek, aim, make an effort

attend verb
Are you going to attend the end-of-term concert?
go to, appear at, be present at
to attend to
1 *Please attend carefully to my instructions.*
listen to, pay attention to, follow carefully, heed, mark, mind, note, notice, observe, think about
2 *Who will attend to the washing up?*
deal with, see to
3 *The nurses attended to the wounded.*
take care of, care for, look after, help, mind, tend

attitude noun
I'm trying to take a more positive attitude to life.
outlook, approach, behaviour, stance, frame of mind, disposition, view, position, manner, mood

attract verb
1 *Do you think our exhibition will attract people?*
interest, appeal to, fascinate, tempt, entice
2 *Baby animals attract big crowds at the zoo.*
draw, pull in

attractive adjective
1 *Miranda was a very attractive young woman.*
beautiful, pretty, good-looking, handsome, gorgeous, glamorous, striking, fetching, charming, lovely, delightful, pleasing, fascinating, captivating, enchanting
OPPOSITE unattractive, repulsive
2 *There are some attractive bargains in the sale.*
appealing, agreeable, interesting, desirable, tempting, irresistible

authority noun
1 *I have the head's authority to go home early.*
permission, consent, approval
2 *The king had the authority to execute the prisoners.*
power, right, influence
3 *My uncle is an authority on steam trains.*
expert, specialist

automatic adjective
1 *We took our car through the automatic car wash.*
automated, mechanical, programmed, computerized
2 *My sneezing was an automatic response to the pepper.*
instinctive, involuntary, impulsive, spontaneous, reflex, natural, unconscious, unthinking

available adjective
1 *There are no more seats available.*
obtainable, free
2 *Is there a phone available in the library?*
accessible, ready, usable, at hand, handy, within reach, convenient

average adjective
It was an average kind of day at school.
everyday, ordinary, normal, typical, usual, regular, commonplace, familiar
OPPOSITE unusual, extraordinary

avoid verb
1 *The driver tried hard to avoid the collision.*
get out of the way of, avert, dodge, keep clear of, steer clear of, fend off, shun
2 *The outlaws avoided capture for months.*
elude, evade, run away from, escape from
3 *How did you manage to avoid the washing up?*
get out of, shirk

awake adjective
Hester lay awake all night worrying.
wide awake, restless, sleepless, conscious, astir

Not being able to sleep is to be suffering from **insomnia**.
OPPOSITE asleep

award noun
Kirsty got a national award for gymnastics.
prize, trophy, medal

aware adjective
aware of
The spy was aware of the dangers of the mission.
acquainted with, conscious of, familiar with, informed about
OPPOSITE ignorant of

awful adjective
1 *The weather was awful last weekend.*
bad, dreadful, terrible, appalling, dire, abysmal
(*informal*) rubbish, lousy
2 *The teacher complained about our awful behaviour.*
disgraceful, shameful, disobedient, naughty
3 *Cinderella's stepmother was an awful woman.*
unpleasant, disagreeable, nasty, horrid, detestable, unkind, unfriendly
4 *The country was shocked by the awful crime.*
horrifying, shocking, atrocious, abominable, outrageous
5 *I feel awful about forgetting your birthday.*
sorry, ashamed, embarrassed, guilty, remorseful

awkward adjective
1 *The parcel was an awkward shape.*
bulky, inconvenient, unmanageable, unwieldy
OPPOSITE convenient
2 *The giant was very awkward with his knife and fork.*
clumsy, unskilful, bungling
OPPOSITE skilful
3 *We found ourselves in a very awkward situation.*
difficult, troublesome, trying, perplexing, tough
OPPOSITE straightforward, easy
4 *Are you trying to be awkward?*
obstinate, stubborn, uncooperative, unhelpful, exasperating
OPPOSITE cooperative
5 *I felt awkward as I didn't know anyone at the party.*
embarrassed, uncomfortable, uneasy, out of place
OPPOSITE comfortable, at ease

a b c d e f g h i j k l m n o p q r s t u v w x y z

Bb

baby *noun*
infant, child
A baby who has just been born is a
newborn.
A baby just learning to walk is
a **toddler**.
The time when someone is a baby is
their **babyhood**.

babyish *adjective*
*My brother thinks that dolls are
babyish.*
childish, immature, infantile
OPPOSITE grown-up, mature

back *noun*
*We always sit at the **back** of the bus.*
end, rear, tail end
OPPOSITE front

back *adjective*
*The **back** door of the cabin was
locked.*
end, rear, tail
The back
legs of an
animal are
its **hind**
legs.
OPPOSITE
front

back *verb*
1 *A big lorry
was **backing**
into our driveway.*
go backwards, reverse
2 *I'm **backing** the blue team to
win the race.*
bet on, put money on
3 *The council is **backing** the
plan to build a skate park.*
support, sponsor, endorse

background *noun*
1 *I drew a mermaid
with the sea in the
background.*
OPPOSITE
foreground
2 *The first chapter
deals with the
background to the
war.*
circumstances of,
history of, lead-up to
3 *My mother's
family has a Swedish
background.*
tradition, upbringing,
ancestry

bad *adjective*
Try to vary the words you use for
bad. Here are some other words you
could use.

FOR A BAD PERSON
wicked, evil, cruel, malevolent,
malicious, vicious, villainous, mean,
nasty, beastly, monstrous, corrupt,
deplorable, detestable, immoral,
infamous, shameful, sinful *Gobo
was a **detestable** king who was
loathed by his subjects.*
A bad person is a **scoundrel**, **rogue**,
or **rascal**.
A bad character in a story or film is a
villain or (*informal*) **baddy**.
OPPOSITE good, virtuous
FOR A BAD ACCIDENT OR BAD ILLNESS
serious, severe, grave, distressing,
acute *Ingrid has a **severe** case of
chickenpox.*
OPPOSITE minor
FOR BAD BEHAVIOUR
naughty, mischievous, disobedient,
disgraceful, wrong *That
mischievous kitten drank my milk!*
OPPOSITE exemplary, angelic
FOR A BAD EXPERIENCE OR BAD NEWS
unpleasant, unwelcome,
disagreeable, horrible, awful,
terrible, dreadful, horrific, appalling,
shocking, hideous, disastrous,
ghastly, frightful, abominable,
diabolical
*The letter contained **disagreeable**
news.*
Another word for a bad experience is
an **ordeal**.
OPPOSITE good, excellent
**FOR A BAD HABIT OR SOMETHING
THAT IS BAD FOR YOU**
harmful, damaging, dangerous,
undesirable, detrimental, injurious
*Fizzy drinks can be **harmful** to your
teeth.*
FOR BAD WEATHER
harsh, hostile, unfavourable,
adverse, miserable
(*informal*) lousy *Penguins face
hostile weather in the Antarctic.*
OPPOSITE fine, favourable
FOR FOOD THAT HAS GONE BAD
mouldy, rotten, off, decayed, sour,
spoiled, rancid *The strawberries
have started to
go **mouldy**.*
OPPOSITE fresh
TO FEEL BAD ABOUT SOMETHING
guilty, ashamed, sorry, remorseful,
repentant *Scrooge feels **repentant**
by the end of the story.*
OPPOSITE unashamed, unrepentant

bad *adjective*
*This has been a **bad** week for all
of us.*
awful, horrible, terrible
OPPOSITE good, fine, excellent

bad-tempered *adjective*
*Trolls are always **bad-
tempered** before breakfast.*
cross, grumpy, irritable,
moody, quarrelsome,
fractious, ill-tempered,
short-tempered,
cantankerous,
crotchety,
snappy, testy,
sullen
OPPOSITE good-tempered,
cheerful

bag *noun*
*I put my wet clothes in
a plastic **bag**.*
sack, carrier, holdall, satchel,
handbag, shoulder bag
A bag you carry on your back is a
backpack or **rucksack**.

ball *noun*
*Wind the string into
a **ball**.*
sphere, globe, orb
A small ball of something
is a **pellet** or **globule**.

ban *verb*
*Skateboards are **banned** from the
playground.*
forbid, prohibit, bar,
exclude, outlaw
OPPOSITE allow, permit

band *noun*
1 *The king was
surrounded by a **band**
of courtiers.*
company, group, gang,
party, troop, crew
2 *I play piano in the
junior jazz **band**.*
group, ensemble,
orchestra
3 *The team captain wears
a red arm **band**.*
strip, stripe, ring, line, belt,
hoop

bang *noun*
1 *There was a loud **bang** as
the balloon burst.*
blast, boom, crash, thud, thump,
pop, explosion, report
2 *He got a **bang** on the head
from the low ceiling.*
bump, blow, hit,
knock, thump,
punch, smack, whack, clout
(*informal*) wallop

bang verb
*Miss Crabbit **banged** her fist on the desk and scowled.*
hit, thump, strike, bash, slam, wham

banish verb
*The king's brother was **banished** forever.*
exile, expel, deport, send away, eject

bank noun
1 *The temple was built on the **banks** of the River Nile.*
edge, side, shore, margin, brink
2 *We rolled our Easter eggs down a grassy **bank**.*
slope, mound, ridge, embankment

banquet noun
*There was a **banquet** on the queen's birthday.*
dinner, feast

bar noun
1 *Did you eat the whole **bar** of chocolate?*
block, slab, chunk, wedge
A bar of gold or silver is an **ingot**.
A bar of soap is a **cake**.
2 *The window had iron **bars** across it.*
rod, pole, rail, stake, beam, girder

bar verb
1 *Two athletes were **barred** from competing in the race.*
ban, prohibit, exclude, keep out
2 *A fallen tree **barred** our way.*
block, hinder, impede, obstruct, stop, check

bare adjective
1 *I put suncream on my **bare** arms and legs.*
naked, nude, exposed, uncovered, unclothed, undressed
2 *The wolf had a **bare** patch on its back.*
bald, hairless
3 *We slept outside on the **bare** mountain.*
barren, bleak, treeless
4 *Inside, the dungeon was cold and **bare**.*
empty, unfurnished, vacant
5 *There wasn't a **bare** patch of wall left.*
blank, plain, clear, empty
6 *There is only room to pack the **bare** essentials.*
basic, minimum

barely adverb
*We **barely** had time to get dressed.*
hardly, scarcely, only just

bargain noun
1 *We made a **bargain** with the captain to take us ashore.*
deal, agreement, promise, pact
2 *That camera you bought was a **bargain**.*
good buy, special offer
(*informal*) snip, steal

bargain verb
*He refused to **bargain** with the pirates for his life.*
argue, do a deal, haggle, negotiate

bark verb
*The guard dog began to **bark** fiercely.*
woof, yap, yelp, growl

barrel noun
*The smugglers carried **barrels** of gunpowder.*
cask, drum, tub, keg, butt

barrier noun
1 *Spectators were asked to stay behind the **barrier**.*
wall, fence, railing, barricade
A barrier across a road is a **roadblock**.
2 *His shyness was a **barrier** to making friends.*
obstacle, hurdle, drawback, handicap, hindrance, stumbling block

base noun
1 *The footprints stop at the **base** of the pyramid.*
bottom, foot
2 *The dolls' house comes with a wooden **base**.*
foundation, support
A base under a statue is a **pedestal** or **plinth**.
3 *The mountaineers returned to their **base**.*
headquarters, camp, depot

basic adjective
1 *These are the **basic** moves in ice-skating.*
main, chief, principal, key, central, essential, fundamental, crucial
2 *My knowledge of French is very **basic**.*
elementary, simple
OPPOSITE advanced

bathe verb
1 *It was too cold to **bathe** in the sea.*
swim, go swimming, splash about, take a dip
To walk about in shallow water is to **paddle**.
To walk through deep water is to **wade**.
2 *The nurse gently **bathed** the wound.*
clean, cleanse, wash, rinse

battle noun
*The **battle** between our countries raged for many years.*
fight, clash, conflict, action, engagement, hostilities, struggle

beach noun
*We found these shells on the **beach**.*
sands, seashore, seaside, shore

beam noun
1 *Wooden **beams** ran across the ceiling.*
bar, timber, joist, plank, post, rafter, boom, spar, strut, support
2 *A **beam** of sunlight entered the cave.*
ray, shaft, stream, gleam
A strong narrow beam of light used in various devices is a **laser**.

bear verb
1 *The rope won't **bear** my weight.*
carry, support, hold, take
2 *The messenger **bore** a letter from the king.*
bring, carry, convey, transport, take, transfer
3 *The gravestone **bears** an old inscription.*
display, show, have
4 *The stench in the cave was too much to **bear**.*
put up with, cope with, stand, suffer, tolerate, endure, abide
5 *The lioness has **borne** three cubs.*
give birth to

beast noun
*In the darkness, they heard a wild **beast** howl.*
animal, creature
You might call a large or frightening beast a **brute** or **monster**.

beat verb
1 *It's cruel to **beat** an animal with a stick.*
hit, strike, thrash, batter, whip, lash, flog
(*informal*) whack, wallop
2 *I **beat** my brother at chess for the first time.*
defeat, conquer, vanquish, win against, get the better of, overcome, overwhelm, rout, thrash, trounce
(*informal*) hammer
3 ***Beat** the eggs, milk, and sugar together.*
whisk, whip, blend, mix, stir
4 *Can you feel your heart **beating**?*
pound, thump, palpitate
to beat someone up
*The bully threatened to **beat me up**.*
assault, attack

a b c d e f g h i j k l m n o p q r s t u v w x y z

beat *noun*
1 *Can you feel the **beat** of your heart?*
pulse, throb
2 *Reggae music has a strong **beat**.*
rhythm, accent, stress

beautiful *adjective*
1 *The fairy queen looked **beautiful** by moonlight.*
attractive, good-looking, pretty, gorgeous, glamorous, radiant, elegant, enchanting, dazzling, stunning, magnificent, resplendent
A man who is pleasing to look at is **good-looking** or **handsome**.
OPPOSITE ugly, unattractive
2 *It was a **beautiful** day for a bicycle trip.*
fine, excellent, glorious, marvellous, sunny, superb, splendid, wonderful
OPPOSITE dull, gloomy, drab
3 *The Northern Lights are a **beautiful** sight.*
glorious, magnificent, picturesque, scenic, spectacular, splendid
4 *The nightingale has a **beautiful** song.*
harmonious, mellifluous, melodious, sweet-sounding
OPPOSITE grating

beckon *verb*
*The guard was **beckoning** me to approach.*
signal, gesture, motion, gesticulate

become *verb*
1 *I soon **became** frustrated with the video game.*
begin to be, turn, get
2 *Eventually, the tadpoles will **become** frogs.*
grow into, change into, develop into, turn into
3 *That style of hat **becomes** you.*
look good on, suit, flatter

bed *noun*
1 *The children slept on hard, wooden **beds**.*
bunk, mattress
A bed for a baby is a **cot**, **cradle**, or **crib**.
Two single beds one above the other are **bunk beds**.
A bed on a ship or train is a **berth**.
A bed made of net or cloth hung up above the ground is a **hammock**.
2 *We planted daffodils in the flower **beds**.*
plot, patch, border
3 *These creatures feed on the **bed** of the ocean.*
bottom, floor
OPPOSITE surface

beg *verb*
*He **begged** me not to let go of the rope.*
ask, plead with, entreat, implore, beseech

begin *verb*
1 *The hunters **began** their search at dawn.*
start, commence, embark on, set about
OPPOSITE end, finish, conclude
2 *When did the trouble **begin**?*
start, commence, arise, emerge, appear, originate, spring up
OPPOSITE end, stop, cease

beginning *noun*
*The house was built at the **beginning** of last century.*
start, opening, commencement, introduction, establishment, foundation, initiation, launch, dawn
The beginning of the day is **dawn** or **daybreak**.
The beginning of a journey is the **starting point**.
The beginning of a stream or river is the **origin** or **source**.
A piece of writing at the beginning of a book is an **introduction**, **preface**, or **prologue**.
A piece of music at the beginning of a musical or opera is a **prelude** or **overture**.
OPPOSITE end, conclusion

behave *verb*
*Our neighbour is **behaving** very strangely.*
act, react, perform
to behave yourself
*We promised to **behave ourselves** in the car.*
be good, be on your best behaviour

behaviour *noun*
*I give my puppy treats for good **behaviour**.*
actions, conduct, manners, attitude

belief *noun*
1 *She was a woman of strong religious **beliefs**.*
faith, principle, creed, doctrine
2 *It is my **belief** that he stole the money.*
opinion, view, conviction, feeling, notion, theory

believable *adjective*
*None of the characters in the book are **believable**.*
credible, plausible
OPPOSITE unbelievable, implausible

believe *verb*
1 *I don't **believe** anything he says.*
accept, have faith in, rely on, trust
OPPOSITE disbelieve, doubt
2 *I **believe** they used to live in Canada.*
assume, feel, know, presume, reckon, suppose, think

belong *verb*
1 *This ring **belonged** to my grandmother.*
be owned by

2 *Do you **belong** to the sports club?*
be a member of, be connected with

belongings *plural noun*
*Don't leave any **belongings** on the bus.*
possessions, property, goods, things

bend *verb*
*This drinking straw **bends** in the middle.*
curve, turn, twist, curl, coil, loop, arch, warp, wind
A word for things which bend easily is **flexible** or (informal) **bendy**.
OPPOSITE straighten
to bend down
*I **bent down** to tie my shoelaces.*
stoop, bow, crouch, duck, kneel

bend *noun*
*Watch out for the sharp **bend** in the road.*
curve, turn, angle, corner, twist, zigzag

bend

bent *adjective*
1 *After the crash, the car was a mass of **bent** metal.*
curved, twisted, coiled, looped, buckled, crooked, arched, folded, warped
(informal) wonky
2 *The witch had a **bent** back and walked with a stick.*
crooked, hunched, curved, arched, bowed

best *adjective*
1 *She is our **best** goalkeeper.*
top, leading, finest, foremost, supreme, star, outstanding, unequalled, unrivalled
OPPOSITE worst
2 *We did what we thought was **best**.*
most suitable, most appropriate

betray *verb*
1 *He **betrayed** us by telling the enemy our plan.*
be disloyal to, be a traitor to, cheat, conspire against, double-cross
Someone who betrays you is a **traitor**.
To betray your country is to commit **treason**.
2 *The look in her eyes **betrayed** her true feelings.*
reveal, show, indicate, disclose, divulge, expose, tell

better *adjective*
1 *Which of these songs do you think is **better**?*
superior, finer, preferable
2 *I had a cold, but I'm **better** now.*
recovered, cured, healed, improved, well

beware *verb*
Beware! There are thieves about.
be careful! watch out! look out! take care! be on your guard!
beware of
Beware of the bull.
watch out for, avoid, mind, heed, keep clear of

biased *adjective*
*A referee should not make a **biased** decision.*
prejudiced, partial, one-sided, partisan, unfair
OPPOSITE impartial

big *adjective*
*The giant owned three pairs of **big** boots.*
large, huge, great, massive, enormous, gigantic, colossal, mammoth
(*informal*) whopping, ginormous, humungous
OPPOSITE small, little, tiny

(!) OVERUSED WORDS

Try to vary the words you use for **big**. Here are some other words you could use.

FOR A *BIG PERSON* OR *BIG CREATURE*
burly, giant, hefty, hulking, mighty, monstrous, towering *The **mighty** robot clanked as it moved.*
FOR A *BIG OBJECT*
bulky, heavy, hefty, weighty *What could be inside that **bulky** envelope?*
FOR A *BIG ROOM* OR *BIG BOX*
roomy, sizeable, spacious *Inside, the spaceship was surprisingly **roomy**.*
OPPOSITE cramped
FOR A *BIG DISTANCE*
immense, infinite, vast *A **vast** stretch of ocean lay before them.*
FOR A *BIG AMOUNT* OR *BIG HELPING*
ample, considerable, substantial *We each got an **ample** helping of porridge.*
OPPOSITE meagre, paltry
FOR A *BIG DECISION* OR *BIG MOMENT*
grave, important, serious, significant *Yesterday was the most **significant** day in my short life.*
OPPOSITE unimportant, minor

WORD WEB

bird *noun*
A female bird is a **hen**.
A male bird is a **cock**.
A young bird is a **chick**, **fledgling**, or **nestling**.
A family of chicks is a **brood**.
A group of birds is a **colony** or **flock**.
A group of flying birds is a **flight** or **skein**.
A person who studies birds is an **ornithologist**.

SOME COMMON BRITISH BIRDS
blackbird, blue tit, bullfinch, bunting, chaffinch, crow, cuckoo, dove, greenfinch, jackdaw, jay, linnet, magpie, martin, nightingale, pigeon, raven, robin, rook, skylark, sparrow, starling, swallow, swift, thrush, tit, wagtail, waxwing, woodpecker, wren, yellowhammer

BIRDS OF PREY
buzzard, eagle, falcon, hawk, kestrel, kite, merlin, osprey, owl, sparrowhawk, vulture

FARM AND GAME BIRDS
chicken, duck, goose, grouse, partridge, pheasant, quail, turkey

Birds kept by farmers are called **poultry**.

SEA AND WATER BIRDS
albatross, auk, bittern, coot, cormorant, crane, curlew, duck, gannet, goose, guillemot, gull, heron, kingfisher, kittiwake, lapwing, mallard, moorhen, oystercatcher, peewit, pelican, penguin, puffin, seagull, snipe, stork, swan, teal

BIRDS FROM OTHER COUNTRIES
bird of paradise, budgerigar, canary, cockatoo, flamingo, humming bird, ibis, kookaburra, lovebirds, macaw, mynah bird, parakeet, parrot, toucan

flamingo

BIRDS WHICH CANNOT FLY
emu, kiwi, ostrich, peacock, penguin

eagle

PARTS OF A BIRD'S BODY
beak, bill, claw, talon, breast, crown, throat, crest, feather, down, plumage, plume, wing

SOME TYPES OF BIRD HOME
nest, nesting box, aviary, coop, roost

SOUNDS MADE BY BIRDS
cackle, caw, cheep, chirp, chirrup, cluck, coo, crow, gabble, honk, peep, pipe, quack, screech, squawk, trill, tweet, twitter, warble
A turkey **gobbles**.
An owl **hoots**.

SPECIAL NAMES
A female peacock is a **peahen**.
A young duck is a **duckling**.
A young goose is a **gosling**.
A young swan is a **cygnet**.
An eagle's nest is an **eyrie**.
A place where rooks nest is a **rookery**.

✏ WRITING TIPS

You can use these words to describe a **bird**.
1 TO DESCRIBE *HOW A BIRD MOVES*
circle, dart, flit, flutter, fly, glide, hop, hover, peck, perch, preen, skim, soar, swoop, waddle, wheel
*A pair of swallows **flitted** among the rooftops.*

2 TO DESCRIBE *A BIRD'S FEATHERS*
bedraggled, downy, drab, fluffy, gleaming, iridescent, ruffled, smooth, speckled *The peacock displayed its **iridescent** tail.*

lovebirds

ostrich

owl

bit *noun*
1 *Mum divided the cake into eight **bits**.*
piece, portion, part, section, segment,
share, slice
2 *These jeans are a **bit** long for me.*
a little, slightly, rather, fairly,
somewhat, quite

bite *verb*
1 *I **bit** a chunk out of my apple.*
munch, nibble, chew, crunch, gnaw,
(*informal*) chomp
2 *Take care. These animals can **bite**.*
nip, pinch, pierce, wound
When an animal tries to bite you it
snaps at you.
When an insect bites you it ***stings*** you.
A fierce animal ***mauls*** or ***savages***
its prey.

bitter *adjective*
1 *The medicine had a **bitter** taste.*
sour, sharp, acid, acrid, tart
OPPOSITE sweet
2 *His brother was still **bitter** about
the quarrel.*
resentful, embittered, disgruntled,
aggrieved
OPPOSITE contented
3 *The wind blowing in from the sea
was **bitter**.*
biting, cold, freezing, icy, piercing,
raw, wintry,
(*informal*) perishing
OPPOSITE mild

black *adjective, noun*
*The pony had a shiny **black** coat.*
coal-black, jet-black, pitch-black,
ebony, raven
You can also describe a black night
as ***pitch-dark***.
Someone in a bad mood is said to
look ***as black as thunder***.
Common similes are ***as black as
coal*** and ***as black as night***.

blame *verb*
*Don't **blame** me if you miss the bus.*
accuse, criticize, condemn, reproach,
scold

blank *adjective*
1 *There are no **blank** pages left in
my jotter.*
empty, bare, clean, plain, unmarked,
unused
2 *The old woman gave us a **blank** look.*
expressionless, faceless, vacant

blaze *noun*
*Firefighters fought the **blaze** for hours.*
fire, flames, inferno

blaze *verb*
*Within a few minutes the campfire
was **blazing**.*
burn brightly, flare up

bleak *adjective*
1 *The countryside was **bleak** and barren.*
bare, barren, desolate, empty,
exposed, stark

2 *The future looks **bleak** for the club.*
gloomy, hopeless, depressing,
dismal, grim, miserable
OPPOSITE promising

blend *verb*
1 ***Blend** the flour with a tablespoon
of water.*
beat together, mix, stir together,
whip, whisk
2 *The paint colours **blend** well with
each other.*
go together, match, fit, harmonize
OPPOSITE clash

blind *adjective*
*Polar bear cubs are born **blind**.*
sightless, unsighted, unseeing
A common simile is ***as blind as a
bat***.
OPPOSITE sighted, seeing
blind to
*The captain was **blind to** his own
faults.*
ignorant of, unaware of, oblivious to
OPPOSITE aware of

bliss *noun*
*Having a whole day off school was
sheer **bliss**.*
joy, delight, pleasure, happiness,
heaven, ecstasy
OPPOSITE misery

blob *noun*
*The alien left **blobs** of green slime on
the carpet.*
drop, lump, spot, dollop, daub,
globule

block *noun*
1 *A **block** of ice fell from the glacier.*
chunk, hunk, lump, piece
2 *There must be a **block** in the
drainpipe.*
blockage, jam, obstacle, obstruction

block *verb*
1 *A tall hedge **blocked** our view of
the house.*
obstruct, hamper, hinder, interfere
with
2 *A mass of leaves had **blocked** the
drain.*
clog, choke, jam, plug, stop up,
congest (*informal*) bung up

bloodthirsty *adjective*
*The **bloodthirsty** pirates rattled their
swords.*
brutal, cruel, barbaric, murderous,
inhuman, pitiless, ruthless, savage,
vicious

bloom *noun*
*The pear tree was covered in white
blooms.*
flower, blossom, bud

bloom *verb*
*The daffodils **bloomed** early this
year.*
blossom, flower, open
OPPOSITE fade

blot *noun*
*The old map was covered with ink
blots.*
spot, blotch, mark, blob,
splodge, smudge, smear, stain

blot *verb*
to blot something out
*The new tower block **blots out** the
view.*
conceal, hide, mask,
obliterate, obscure

blow *noun*
1 *He was knocked out by a **blow** on
the head.*
knock, bang, bash, hit, punch, clout,
slap, smack, swipe, thump
(*informal*) wallop, whack
2 *Losing the hockey match was a
terrible **blow**.*
shock, upset, setback,
disappointment, catastrophe,
misfortune, disaster, calamity

blow *verb*
*The wind was **blowing** from the east.*
blast, gust, puff, fan
To make a shrill sound by blowing is
to ***whistle***.

blunder *noun*
*Forgetting her birthday was a terrible
blunder.*
mistake, error, fault, slip, slip-up,
gaffe
(*informal*) howler

blunt *adjective*
1 *This pencil is **blunt**.*
dull, worn, unsharpened
OPPOSITE sharp, pointed
2 *Her reply to my question was very
blunt.*
abrupt, frank, direct, outspoken,
plain, tactless
OPPOSITE tactful

blurred *adjective*
*The background of the photograph is
all **blurred**.*
indistinct, vague, blurry, fuzzy, hazy,
out of focus
OPPOSITE clear, distinct

blush *verb*
*The actor **blushed** with
embarrassment.*
flush, go red, colour

boast *verb*
*The knight was always **boasting**
about his fencing skills.*
brag, show off, crow, gloat, swagger
(*informal*) blow your own
trumpet

boastful *adjective*
*Giants are **boastful** creatures
and brag about everything.*
arrogant, big-headed,
conceited, vain, bumptious
(*informal*) cocky, swanky
OPPOSITE modest, humble

WORD WEB

boat *noun*
*Several fishing **boats** were moored in the harbour.*
ship, craft, vessel

SOME TYPES OF BOAT OR SHIP
barge, canoe, catamaran, cruise liner, dhow, dinghy, dugout, ferry, freighter, gondola, hovercraft, hydrofoil, junk, launch, lifeboat, motor boat, oil tanker, paper boat, punt, raft, rowing boat, schooner, skiff, speedboat, steamship, tanker, trawler, tug, yacht

MILITARY BOATS OR SHIPS
aircraft carrier, battleship, destroyer, frigate, gunboat, minesweeper, submarine, warship

SOME BOATS USED IN THE PAST
brigantine, clipper, coracle, cutter, galleon, galley, man-of-war, paddle steamer, schooner, trireme, windjammer

kayak

The left-hand side of a boat is called *port*.
The right-hand side of a boat is called *starboard*.
A shed where boats are stored is a *boathouse*.

canoe

lifeboat

WORDS FOR PARTS OF A BOAT OR SHIP
boom, bridge, bulwark, cabin, crow's nest, deck, engine room, fo'c'sle or forecastle, funnel, galley, helm, hull, keel, mast, poop, porthole, propeller, quarterdeck, rigging, rudder, sail, tiller

SPECIAL NAMES
The front part of a boat is the *bow* or *prow*.
The back part of a boat is the *stern*.

yacht

cruise liner

dinghy

a b c d e f g h i j k l m n o p q r s t u v w x y z

A
B
C
D
E
F
G
H
I
J
K
L
M
N
O
P
Q
R
S
T
U
V
W
X
Y
Z

⭐ **WORD WEB**

body *noun*
The study of the human body is *anatomy*.
The main part of your body except your head, arms, and legs is your *trunk* or *torso*.
The shape of your body is your *build*, *figure*, or *physique*.
A person's dead body is a *corpse*.
The dead body of an animal is a *carcass*.

OUTER PARTS OF THE HUMAN BODY
abdomen, ankle, arm, armpit, breast, buttocks, calf, cheek, chest, chin, ear, elbow, eye, finger, foot, forehead, genitals, groin, hand, head, heel, hip, instep, jaw, knee, kneecap, knuckle, leg, lip, mouth, navel, neck, nipple, nose, pores, shin, shoulder, skin, stomach, temple, thigh, throat, waist, wrist

INNER PARTS OF THE HUMAN BODY
arteries, bladder, bowels, brain, eardrum, glands, gullet, gums, guts, heart, intestines, kidneys, larynx, liver, lung, muscles, nerves, ovaries, pancreas, prostate, sinews, stomach, tendons, tongue, tonsil, tooth, uterus, veins, windpipe, womb

bog *noun*
We felt our boots sinking into the **bog**.
swamp, quagmire, quicksand, fen

boisterous *adjective*
Baby dragons can be loud and *boisterous*.
lively, noisy, rowdy, unruly, wild, disorderly
OPPOSITE restrained, calm

bold *adjective*
1 *It was a **bold** move to attack the fortress.*
brave, courageous, daring, adventurous, audacious, confident, enterprising, fearless, heroic, valiant, intrepid, plucky
OPPOSITE cowardly
2 *The poster uses large letters in **bold** colours.*
striking, strong, bright, loud, showy, conspicuous, eye-catching, noticeable, prominent
OPPOSITE inconspicuous, subtle

bolt *verb*
1 *Did you remember to **bolt** the door?*
fasten, latch, lock, secure, bar
2 *The horses **bolted** when they heard the thunder.*
dash away, dart, flee, sprint, run away, rush off

3 *Don't **bolt** your food.*
gobble, gulp, guzzle, wolf down

book *verb*
1 *Have you **booked** a seat on the train?*
order, reserve
2 *I've **booked** the disco for the party.*
arrange, engage, organize

border *noun*
1 *The town is on the **border** between France and Germany.*
boundary, frontier
2 *I drew a thin line around the **border** of the picture.*
edge, margin, perimeter
A decorative border round the top of a wall is a *frieze*.
A border round the bottom of a skirt is a *hem*.
A decorative border on fabric is a *frill*, *fringe*, or *trimming*.

boring *adjective*
The film was so **boring** I fell asleep.
dull, dreary, tedious, tiresome, unexciting, uninteresting, dry, monotonous, uninspiring, insipid, unimaginative, uneventful, humdrum
OPPOSITE interesting, exciting

bossy *adjective*
Stop being so **bossy** towards your sister.
domineering, bullying, dictatorial, officious, tyrannical
An informal name for a bossy person is *bossy boots*.

bother *verb*
1 *Would it **bother** you if I played some music?*
disturb, trouble, upset, annoy, irritate, pester, worry, vex, exasperate
(informal) bug, hassle
2 *Don't **bother** to phone tonight.*
make an effort, take trouble, concern yourself, care, mind

bother *noun*
It's such a **bother** to remember the password.
nuisance, annoyance, irritation, inconvenience, pest, trouble, difficulty, problem
(informal) hassle

bottom *noun*
1 *We camped at the **bottom** of the mountain.*
foot, base
OPPOSITE top, peak
2 *The wreck sank to the **bottom** of the sea.*
bed, floor
OPPOSITE surface
3 *A wasp stung me on the **bottom**.*
backside, behind, buttocks, rear, rump, seat
(informal) bum

bottom *adjective*
I got the **bottom** mark in the test.
least, lowest
OPPOSITE top

bounce *verb*
The ball **bounced** twice before it reached the net.
rebound, ricochet, spring, leap

bound *verb*
The puppies **bounded** across the lawn.
leap, bounce, jump, spring, skip, gambol, caper, frisk

box *noun*
case, chest, crate, carton, packet
A small box for jewellery or treasure is a *casket*.
A large box for luggage is a *trunk*.

boy *noun*
lad, youngster, youth
(informal) kid

brain *noun*
You'll need to use your **brain** to solve this riddle.
intelligence, intellect, mind, reason, sense, wit

branch *noun*
1 *A robin perched on a **branch** of the tree.*
bough, limb
2 *I've joined the local **branch** of the Kennel Club.*
section, division, department, wing

branch *verb*
Follow the track until it **branches** into two.
divide, fork

brand *noun*
Which **brand** of ice cream do you like?
make, kind, sort, type, variety, label
The sign of a particular brand of goods is a *trademark*.

brave *adjective*
It was **brave** of you to save the cat from drowning.
courageous, heroic, valiant, fearless, daring, gallant, intrepid, plucky
A common simile is *as brave as a lion*.
OPPOSITE cowardly

bravery *noun*
The police dog was awarded a medal for **bravery**.
courage, heroism, valour, fearlessness, daring, nerve, gallantry, grit, pluck
(informal) guts, bottle
OPPOSITE cowardice

break *noun*
1 *Can you see any **breaks** in the chain?*
breach, crack, hole, gap, opening, split, rift, puncture, rupture, fracture, fissure

2 *Let's take a **break** for coffee.*
interval, pause, rest, lull,
time-out
(*informal*) breather

break *verb*
1 *The vase fell off the shelf and* ***broke***.
smash, shatter, fracture, chip, crack,
split, snap, splinter
(*informal*) bust
2 *The burglar was arrested for **breaking** the law.*
disobey, disregard, violate, flout
3 *In her last race, she **broke** the world record.*
beat, better, exceed, surpass, outdo

breathe *verb*
To breathe in is to ***inhale***.
To breathe out is to ***exhale***.
To breathe heavily when you have been running is to ***pant*** or ***puff***.
The formal word for breathing is ***respiration***.

breed *verb*
1 *Salmon swim upstream to **breed** every year.*
reproduce, have young, multiply,
procreate, spawn
2 *Bad hygiene **breeds** disease.*
cause, produce, generate, encourage,
promote, cultivate, induce

breed *noun*
*What **breed** of dog is that?*
kind, sort, type, variety
The evidence of how a dog has been bred is its ***pedigree***.

breezy *adjective*
*This morning the weather was bright and **breezy**.*
windy, blowy, blustery, gusty, fresh,
draughty

bridge *noun*
A bridge you can walk over is a ***footbridge***.
A bridge to carry water is an ***aqueduct***.
A long bridge carrying a road or railway is a ***viaduct***.

brief *adjective*
1 *We paid a **brief** visit to our cousins on the way home.*
short, quick, hasty, fleeting,
temporary
2 *Give me a **brief** account of what happened.*
short, concise, abbreviated,
condensed, compact, succinct

bright *adjective*
1 *We saw the **bright** lights of the town in the distance.*
shining, brilliant, blazing, dazzling,
glaring, gleaming
OPPOSITE dull, dim, weak

2 ***Bright*** *colours will make the poster stand out.*
strong, intense, vivid
Colours that shine in the dark are ***luminous*** colours.
OPPOSITE dull, faded, muted
3 *Her teachers thought she was very **bright**.*
clever, intelligent, gifted, sharp,
quick-witted
(*informal*) brainy
A common simile is ***as bright as a button***.
OPPOSITE stupid, dull-witted
4 *Miranda gave me a **bright** smile.*
cheerful, happy, lively, merry, jolly,
radiant
OPPOSITE sad, gloomy
5 *The day was cold, but **bright**.*
sunny, fine, fair, clear, cloudless
OPPOSITE dull, cloudy, overcast

brilliant *adjective*
1 *The fireworks gave off a **brilliant** light.*
bright, blazing, dazzling, glaring,
gleaming, glittering, glorious,
shining, splendid, vivid
OPPOSITE dim, dull
2 *Brunel was a **brilliant** engineer.*
clever, exceptional, outstanding,
gifted, talented
OPPOSITE incompetent, talentless
3 (*informal*) *I saw a **brilliant** film last week.*
excellent, marvellous, outstanding,
wonderful, superb
(*informal*) fantastic, fabulous

bring *verb*
1 *Can you **bring** the shopping in from the car?*
carry, fetch, deliver, bear, transport
2 *You can **bring** a friend to the party.*
invite, conduct, escort, guide, lead
3 *The war has **brought** great sorrow to our people.*
cause, produce, lead to, result in,
generate
to bring something about
*The new coach **brought about** some changes.*
cause, effect, create, introduce, be
responsible for
to bring someone up
*In the story, Tarzan is **brought up** by apes.*
rear, raise, care for, foster, look after,
nurture, educate, train
to bring something up
*I wish you hadn't **brought up** the subject of money.*
mention, talk about, raise, broach

brisk *adjective*
1 *Mr Hastie went for a **brisk** walk every evening.*
lively, fast-paced, energetic, bracing,

invigorating, vigorous, refreshing
OPPOSITE slow, leisurely
2 *The flower shop does a **brisk** trade around Easter.*
busy, lively, bustling, hectic
OPPOSITE quiet, slack, slow

broad *adjective*
1 *The streets in the city were **broad** and straight.*
wide, open, large, roomy, spacious,
vast, extensive
OPPOSITE narrow
2 *Just give me a **broad** outline of what happened.*
general, rough, vague, loose,
indefinite, imprecise
OPPOSITE specific, detailed

broken *adjective*
1 *Don't use that computer—it's **broken**.*
faulty, defective, damaged, out of
order
OPPOSITE working
2 *After losing all his money, Forbes was a **broken** man.*
crushed, defeated, beaten, spiritless

brush *verb*
1 *Jill spent ages **brushing** her hair for the party.*
groom, comb, tidy
2 *A bird **brushed** against my cheek as it flew past.*
touch, contact, rub, scrape

brutal *adjective*
*The bandits launched a **brutal** attack.*
savage, vicious, cruel, barbaric,
bloodthirsty, callous, ferocious,
inhuman, merciless, pitiless, ruthless,
sadistic
OPPOSITE gentle, humane

bubble *verb*
*A green liquid **bubbled** in the witch's cauldron.*
boil, seethe, gurgle, froth, foam

bubbly *adjective*
1 ***Bubbly*** *drinks get up my nose.*
fizzy, sparkling, effervescent
2 *Sophie has a bright and **bubbly** personality.*
cheerful, lively, vivacious, spirited,
animated

buckle *noun*
*The pirate wore a belt with a large silver **buckle**.*
clasp, fastener, fastening, clip, catch

buckle *verb*
1 *Please **buckle** your seat belts.*
fasten, secure, clasp, clip, do up,
hook up
2 *The bridge **buckled** when the giant stepped onto it.*
bend, warp, twist, crumple, cave in,
collapse

budge *verb*
The window was stuck and wouldn't **budge**.
give way, move, shift, stir

bug *noun*
1 *Birds help to control **bugs** in the garden.*
insect, pest
2 (*informal*) *I can't get rid of this stomach **bug**.*
infection, virus, germ, disease, illness
3 *There are a few **bugs** in the computer program.*
fault, error, defect, flaw
(*informal*) gremlin

build *verb*
*Dad is going to **build** a shed in the garden.*
construct, erect, put together, put up, set up, assemble
to build up
1 *I'm **building up** a collection of vinyl records.*
accumulate, assemble, collect, put together
2 *We felt the tension **building up** in the crowd.*
increase, intensify, rise, grow, mount up, escalate

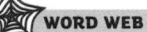

WORD WEB

building *noun*
*The new **building** will have seven storeys.*
construction, structure, dwelling
A person who designs buildings is an **architect**.

lighthouse

BUILDINGS WHERE PEOPLE LIVE
apartment, barracks, bungalow, castle, cottage, farmhouse, flat, fort, fortress, house, mansion, palace, skyscraper, tenement, terrace, tower, villa

BUILDINGS WHERE PEOPLE WORK
factory, garage, lighthouse, mill, shop, store, warehouse

BUILDINGS WHERE PEOPLE WORSHIP
abbey, cathedral, chapel, church, monastery, mosque, pagoda, shrine, synagogue, temple

OTHER TYPES OF BUILDING
cabin, cafe, cinema, college, gallery, hotel, inn, library, museum, observatory, police station, post office, power station, prison, pub or public house, restaurant, school, shed, theatre

build *noun*
*Charlotte was a girl of slender **build**.*
body, form, frame, figure, physique

bulge *noun*
*There was a large **bulge** in the robber's sack.*
bump, hump, lump, swelling, protuberance

bulge *verb*
*The creature had eyes which **bulged** out of its head.*
stick out, swell, puff out, protrude

bulky *adjective*
*The parcel is too **bulky** to go through the letterbox.*
big, large, hefty, substantial, sizeable, cumbersome, unwieldy
OPPOSITE small, compact

bully *verb*
*Some of the children were afraid of being **bullied**.*
persecute, torment, intimidate, terrorize, push around

bump *verb*
1 *The baby **bumped** his head on the table.*
hit, strike, knock, bang

PARTS YOU MIGHT FIND INSIDE A BUILDING
balcony, basement, cellar, conservatory, corridor, courtyard, crypt, dungeon, foyer, gallery, lobby, porch, quadrangle, room, staircase, veranda

PARTS YOU MIGHT FIND OUTSIDE A BUILDING
arch, balustrade, bay window, bow window, buttress, chimney, colonnade, column, dome, dormer window, drainpipe, eaves, foundations, gable, gutter, masonry, parapet, pediment, pillar, pipes, roof, tower, turret, vault, wall, window, windowsill

CASTLES AND FORTIFIED BUILDINGS
château, citadel, fort, fortress, motte and bailey, palace, stronghold, tower

PARTS OF A CASTLE
bailey, barbican, battlement, buttress, courtyard, donjon, drawbridge, dungeon, gate, gateway, keep, magazine, moat, motte, parapet, portcullis, postern, rampart, tower, turret, wall, watchtower
skyscraper

2 *My bicycle **bumped** up and down over the cobbles.*
bounce, shake, jerk, jolt
to bump into
1 *The taxi **bumped into** the car in front of it.*
collide with, bang into, run into, crash into
2 *I **bumped into** one of my friends in the bookshop.*
meet, come across, run into

bump *noun*
1 *We felt a **bump** as the plane landed.*
thud, thump, bang, blow, knock
2 *How did you get that **bump** on your head?*
lump, swelling, bulge

bumpy *adjective*
1 *The car jolted up and down on the **bumpy** road.*
rough, uneven, irregular, lumpy
OPPOSITE smooth, even
2 *We had a **bumpy** ride in a jeep over muddy tracks.*
bouncy, jerky, jolting, lurching, choppy

bunch *noun*
1 *The jailer jangled a **bunch** of keys.*
bundle, cluster, collection, set
2 *She picked a **bunch** of flowers.*
bouquet, posy, spray
3 (*informal*) *They're a friendly **bunch** of people.*
group, set, circle, band, gang, crowd

bundle *noun*
*I found a **bundle** of old newspapers.*
bunch, batch, pile, stack, collection, pack, bale

burn *verb*
1 *We could see the campfire **burning** in the distance.*
be alight, be on fire, blaze, flame, flare, flicker
To burn without flames is to **glow** or **smoulder**.
2 *The captain ordered them to **burn** the enemy ship.*
set fire to, incinerate, reduce to ashes
To start something burning is to **ignite**, **kindle**, or **light** it.
To burn something slightly is to **char**, **scorch**, or **singe** it.
To hurt someone with boiling liquid or steam is to **scald** them.
To burn a dead body is to **cremate** it.

To burn a mark on an animal is to **brand** it.

burst verb
*The balloon **burst** when my brother sat on it.*
puncture, rupture, break, give way, split, tear

bury verb
1 *The document was **buried** under a pile of old letters.*
cover, conceal, hide, secrete
2 *They say the old witch was **buried** in that graveyard.*
inter, entomb

bushy adjective
*The troll had **bushy** green eyebrows.*
hairy, thick, dense, shaggy, bristly

business noun
1 *My uncle runs a restaurant **business**.*
company, firm, organization
2 *The new bookshop does a lot of **business**.*
trade, trading, buying and selling, commerce
3 *What sort of **business** do you want to go into?*
work, job, career, employment, industry, occupation, profession, trade
4 *He left early to attend to some urgent **business**.*
matter, issue, affair, problem, point, concern, question

bustle verb
*Miss Flyte **bustled** about the kitchen making tea.*
rush, dash, hurry, scurry, scuttle, fuss

busy adjective
1 *Mum is **busy** making my birthday cake just now.*
occupied, engaged, employed, working, slaving away, beavering away
(*informal*) hard at it, up to your eyes
*A common simile is **as busy as a bee**.*
OPPOSITE idle
2 *Christmas is a very **busy** time for shops.*
active, hectic, frantic, lively
OPPOSITE quiet, restful
3 *Is the town always this **busy** on Saturdays?*
crowded, bustling, hectic, lively, teeming
OPPOSITE quiet, peaceful

buy verb
*I'm saving up to **buy** a skateboard.*
get, pay for, purchase, acquire
OPPOSITE sell

cabin noun
*The outlaws hid in a **cabin** in the woods.*
hut, shack, shed, lodge, chalet, shelter

cafe noun
*We had lunch in a **cafe** overlooking the river.*
cafeteria, coffee shop, tearoom, snack bar, buffet, canteen, bistro, brasserie

cage noun
A large cage or enclosure for birds is an **aviary**.
A cage or enclosure for poultry is a **coop**.
A cage or enclosure for animals is a **pen**.
A cage or box for a pet rabbit is a **hutch**.

calculate verb
*I **calculated** that it would take an hour to walk home.*
work out, compute, figure out, reckon, add up, count, total
To calculate something roughly is to **estimate**.

call noun
1 *We heard a **call** for help from inside the cave.*
cry, exclamation, scream, shout, yell
2 *Grandad made an unexpected **call**.*
visit, stop, stay
3 *There's not much **call** for suncream in winter.*
demand, need

call verb
1 *'Stop that racket!' **called** the janitor.*
cry out, exclaim, shout, yell
2 *It was too late at night to **call** my friends.*
phone, ring, telephone
3 *The headteacher **called** me to her office.*
summon, invite, send for, order
4 *The doctor **called** to see if I was feeling better.*
visit, pay a visit, drop in, drop by
5 *They **called** the baby Jessica.*
name, baptize, christen, dub
6 *What is your new book going to be **called**?*
name, title, entitle

calm adjective
1 *The weather was too **calm** to fly our kites.*
still, quiet, peaceful, tranquil, serene, windless
OPPOSITE stormy, windy

2 *The sea was **calm**, and we had a pleasant voyage.*
smooth, still, flat, motionless, tranquil
OPPOSITE rough, choppy
3 *I tried to stay **calm** before my judo exam.*
cool, level-headed, patient, relaxed, sedate, unemotional, unexcitable, untroubled
OPPOSITE anxious, nervous

cancel verb
*We had to **cancel** the race because of the weather.*
abandon, call off, scrap, drop
(*informal*) scrub, ditch, axe
To cancel something after it has already begun is to **abort** it.
To put something off until later is to **postpone** it.
To cancel items on a list is to **cross out**, **delete**, or **erase** them.

capture verb
1 *The bank robbers were **captured** by police this morning.*
catch, arrest, apprehend, seize, take prisoner
(*informal*) nab, nick
2 *The castle has never been **captured** by enemy forces.*
occupy, seize, take, take over, win

care noun
1 *The old wizard's face was full of **care**.*
worry, anxiety, trouble, concern, burden, responsibility, sorrow, stress
2 *I took great **care** with my handwriting.*
attention, concentration, thought, thoroughness, meticulousness
OPPOSITE carelessness
3 *Jake left his pet hamster in my **care**.*
charge, keeping, protection, safe keeping, supervision
to take care
*Please **take care** crossing the road.*
be careful, be on your guard, look out, watch out
to take care of someone or **something**
*My granny **takes care of** me after school.*
care for, look after, mind, watch over, attend to, tend

care verb
*Do you **care** which team wins the World Cup?*
mind, bother, worry, be interested, be troubled, be bothered, be worried
to care for someone or **something**
1 *The veterinary hospital **cares for** sick animals.*
take care of, look after, attend to, tend, nurse
2 *I don't really **care for** broccoli.*
like, be fond of, be keen on, love

career *noun*
Max had a successful **career** as a racing driver.
job, occupation, profession, trade, business, employment, calling

careful *adjective*
1 You must be more **careful** with your spelling.
accurate, conscientious, thorough, thoughtful, meticulous, painstaking, precise
OPPOSITE careless, inaccurate
2 Dad kept a **careful** watch on the bonfire.
attentive, cautious, watchful, alert, wary, vigilant
OPPOSITE careless, inattentive
to be careful
Please **be careful** with those scissors.
take care, be on your guard, look out, watch out

careless *adjective*
1 This is a very **careless** piece of work.
messy, untidy, thoughtless, inaccurate, slapdash, shoddy, scrappy, sloppy, slovenly
OPPOSITE careful, accurate
2 I was **careless** and cut my finger.
inattentive, thoughtless, absent-minded, heedless, irresponsible, negligent, reckless
OPPOSITE careful, attentive

carnival *noun*
The whole village comes out for the annual **carnival**.
fair, festival, fête, gala, parade, procession, show, celebration, pageant

carry *verb*
1 I helped Mum to **carry** the shopping to the car.
take, transfer, lift, fetch, bring, lug
2 Aircraft **carry** passengers and goods.
transport, convey
3 The rear axle **carries** the greatest weight.
bear, support, hold up
to carry on
We **carried on** in spite of the rain.
continue, go on, persevere, persist, keep on, remain, stay, survive
to carry something out
The soldiers **carried out** the captain's orders.
perform, do, execute, accomplish, achieve, complete, finish

carve *verb*
1 The statue was **carved** out of stone.
sculpt, chisel, hew
2 Mum **carved** the chicken for Sunday dinner.
cut, slice

case *noun*
1 I loaded my **case** into the boot of the car.
suitcase, trunk
A number of suitcases that you take on holiday is your **baggage** or **luggage**.
2 What's in those **cases** in the attic?
box, chest, crate, carton, casket
3 This has been a clear **case** of mistaken identity.
instance, occurrence, example, illustration
4 It was one of Sherlock Holmes's most famous **cases**.
inquiry, investigation
5 She presented a good **case** for abolishing hunting.
argument, line of reasoning

casual *adjective*
1 It was just a **casual** remark, so don't take it too seriously.
accidental, chance, unexpected, unintentional, unplanned
OPPOSITE deliberate
2 The restaurant had a **casual** atmosphere.
easy-going, informal, relaxed
OPPOSITE formal
3 The teacher complained about our **casual** attitude.
apathetic, careless, slack, unenthusiastic
OPPOSITE enthusiastic

catastrophe *noun*
The drought is a **catastrophe** for the farmers.
disaster, calamity, misfortune, mishap, tragedy

catch *verb*
1 My friends yelled at me to **catch** the ball.
clutch, grab, grasp, grip, hang on to, hold, seize, snatch, take
2 One of the anglers **caught** a fish.
hook, net, trap
3 The police hoped to **catch** the thief red-handed.
arrest, capture, corner
(informal) nab
4 I hope you don't **catch** my cold.
become infected by, contract, get
(informal) go down with
5 You must hurry if you want to **catch** the bus.
be in time for, get on

catch *noun*
1 The angler got a large **catch** of salmon.
haul
2 The car is so cheap that there must be a **catch**.
problem, obstacle, snag, difficulty, disadvantage, drawback, trap, trick

3 All the windows are fitted with safety **catches**.
fastening, latch, lock, bolt, hook

cause *noun*
1 What was the **cause** of the trouble?
origin, source, start
You can also talk about the **reasons** for the trouble.
2 You've got no **cause** to complain.
grounds, basis, motive
3 The sponsored walk is for a good **cause**.
purpose, object

cause *verb*
A single spark from the fire could **cause** an explosion.
bring about, create, generate, lead to, give rise to, result in, provoke, arouse

caution *noun*
1 We decided to proceed with **caution**.
care, attention, watchfulness, wariness, vigilance
2 The traffic warden let him off with a **caution**.
warning, reprimand, telling-off
(informal) ticking-off

cautious *adjective*
My grandad is a **cautious** driver.
careful, attentive, watchful, wary, vigilant, hesitant
OPPOSITE reckless

cease *verb*
The fighting **ceased** at midnight.
come to an end, end, finish, stop, halt
OPPOSITE begin

celebrate *verb*
1 Let's **celebrate**!
enjoy yourself, have a good time, be happy, rejoice
2 What shall we do to **celebrate** Granny's birthday?
commemorate, observe, keep

celebration *noun*
We had a big **celebration** for my cousin's wedding.
festivity, party, feast, festival, banquet, jamboree

celebrity *noun*
The awards were handed out by a TV **celebrity**.
famous person, personality, public figure, VIP, star, idol

cemetery *noun*
A famous author is buried in the local **cemetery**.
graveyard, burial ground, churchyard
A place where dead people are cremated is a **crematorium**.

central *adjective*
1 We are now in the **central** part of the building.
middle, core, inner, interior
OPPOSITE outer

2 *Who are the **central** characters in the story?*
chief, crucial, essential, fundamental, important, main, major, principal, vital
OPPOSITE unimportant

centre *noun*
*The library is in the **centre** of the town. The burial chamber is in the **centre** of the pyramid.*
middle, heart, core, inside, interior
The centre of a planet or a piece of fruit is the ***core***.
The centre of an atom or a living cell is the ***nucleus***.
The centre of a wheel is the ***hub***.
The point at the centre of a see-saw is the ***pivot***.
The edible part in the centre of a nut is the ***kernel***.
OPPOSITE edge, outside, surface

ceremony *noun*
1 *We watched the **ceremony** of the opening of parliament.*
rite, ritual, formalities
A ceremony where someone is given a prize is a ***presentation***.
A ceremony where someone is given a special honour is an ***investiture***.
A ceremony to celebrate something new is an ***inauguration*** or ***opening***.
A ceremony where someone becomes a member of a society is an ***initiation***.
A ceremony to make a church or other building sacred is a ***dedication***.
A ceremony to remember a dead person or a past event is a ***commemoration***.
A ceremony held in a church is a ***service***.
2 *They had a quiet wedding without a lot of **ceremony**.*
formality, pomp, pageantry, spectacle

certain *adjective*
1 *My mum was **certain** she would win the cookery competition.*
confident, convinced, positive, sure, determined
OPPOSITE uncertain
2 *We have **certain** proof that the painting is a forgery.*
definite, clear, convincing, absolute, unquestionable, reliable, trustworthy, undeniable, infallible, genuine, valid
OPPOSITE unreliable
3 *The damaged plane faced **certain** disaster.*
inevitable, unavoidable
OPPOSITE possible
4 *Her new book is **certain** to be a bestseller.*
bound, sure

chain *noun*
1 *The anchor was attached to a **chain**.*
One ring in a chain is a ***link***.
A chain used to link railway wagons together is a ***coupling***.

2 *The police formed a **chain** to keep the crowd back.*
line, row, cordon
3 *Holmes described the **chain** of events that led to the murder.*
series, sequence, succession, string

champion *noun*
1 *She is the current world **champion** at ice-skating.*
title-holder, prizewinner, victor, winner, conqueror
2 *Martin Luther King was a **champion** of civil rights.*
supporter, advocate, defender, upholder, patron, backer

championship *noun*
*Fifteen schools took part in the karate **championship**.*
competition, contest, tournament

chance *noun*
1 *They say there's a **chance** of rain later.*
possibility, likelihood, probability, prospect, danger, risk
2 *I haven't had a **chance** to reply yet.*
opportunity, time, occasion
3 *The director took a **chance** in hiring an unknown actor.*
gamble, risk
by chance
*I found the house quite **by chance**.*
by accident, accidentally, by coincidence
An unfortunate chance is ***bad luck*** or a ***misfortune***.
A fortunate chance is ***good luck*** or a ***fluke***.

change *verb*
1 *They've **changed** the programme for the concert.*
alter, modify, rearrange, reorganize, adjust, adapt, vary
2 *The town has **changed** a lot since Victorian times.*
alter, become different, develop, grow, move on
3 *Can I **change** these jeans for a bigger size, please?*
exchange, replace, switch, substitute (*informal*) swap
to change into
*Tadpoles **change into** frogs.*
become, turn into, be transformed into

change *noun*
*There has been a slight **change** of plan.*
alteration, modification, variation, difference, break
A change to something worse is a ***deterioration***.
A change to something better is an ***improvement*** or a ***reform***.
A very big change is a ***revolution*** or ***transformation*** or ***U-turn***.
A change in which one person or thing is replaced by another is a ***substitution***.

chaos *noun*
*After the earthquake, the city was in **chaos**.*
confusion, disorder, mayhem, uproar, tumult, pandemonium, anarchy, bedlam, muddle, shambles
OPPOSITE order

chaotic *adjective*
*Alice finds that life in Wonderland is **chaotic**.*
confused, disorderly, disorganized, muddled, topsy-turvy, untidy, unruly, riotous
OPPOSITE orderly, organized

chapter *noun*
*I read a **chapter** of my book last night.*
part, section, division
One section of a play is an ***act*** or ***scene***.
One part of a serial is an ***episode*** or ***instalment***.

character *noun*
1 *Her **character** is quite different from her sister's.*
personality, temperament, nature, disposition, make-up, manner
2 *Our neighbour is a well-known **character** in our street.*
figure, personality, individual, person
3 *Which **character** would you like to play in Peter Pan?*
part, role

charge *noun*
1 *The admission **charge** is five euros.*
price, rate
The charge made for a ride on public transport is the ***fare***.
The charge made to post a letter or parcel is the ***postage***.
A charge made to join a club is a ***fee*** or ***subscription***.
A charge made for certain things by the government is a ***duty*** or a ***tax***.
A charge made to use a private road, bridge, or tunnel is a ***toll***.
2 *The robbers face several criminal **charges**.*
accusation, allegation
3 *Many soldiers were killed in the **charge**.*
assault, attack, onslaught, raid
4 *My best friend left her hamster in my **charge**.*
care, keeping, protection, custody, trust
to be in charge of something
*An experienced sailor was **in charge of** the crew.*
manage, lead, command, direct, supervise, run

charge *verb*
1 *The library **charges** ten pence for a photocopy.*
ask for, make you pay
2 *A man has been **charged** with attempted robbery.*
accuse (of)

3 *The cavalry charged the enemy line.*
attack, assault, storm, rush

charm *verb*
Winnie the Pooh has charmed readers all over the world.
bewitch, captivate, delight, enchant, entrance, fascinate, please

charming *adjective*
We drove through some charming scenery.
delightful, attractive, pleasant, pleasing, likeable, appealing

chart *noun*
1 *The explorer stopped to consult his chart.*
map
2 *This chart shows the average rainfall for each month.*
diagram, graph, table

chase *verb*
The wolves chased a deer through the forest.
pursue, run after, follow, track, trail, hunt

chatty *adjective*
Frank is usually shy, but today he's quite chatty.
talkative, communicative
OPPOSITE silent

cheap *adjective*
1 *We got a cheap flight to London.*
inexpensive, affordable, bargain, cut-price, discount, reasonable
2 *These tyres are made from cheap rubber.*
inferior, shoddy, second-rate, worthless, trashy
(*informal*) tacky, tatty
OPPOSITE superior, good-quality

cheat *verb*
1 *She was cheated into buying a fake diamond ring.*
deceive, trick, swindle, double-cross, hoax
(*informal*) con, diddle, fleece, fool, rip off
2 *Anyone who cheats in the quiz will be disqualified.*
copy, crib

cheat *noun*
Don't trust him—he's a cheat.
cheater, deceiver, swindler, fraud, impostor, hoaxer

check *verb*
1 *Have you checked your work carefully?*
examine, inspect, look over, scrutinize
2 *The heavy snow checked their progress towards the Pole.*
hamper, hinder, block, obstruct, delay, hold back, slow, slow down, halt, stop

check *noun*
I need to run some checks on your computer.
test, examination, inspection, check-up

cheeky *adjective*
Don't be so cheeky!
disrespectful, facetious, flippant, impertinent, impolite, impudent, insolent, insulting, irreverent, mocking, rude, saucy, shameless
OPPOSITE respectful

cheer *verb*
1 *We cheered when our team scored a goal.*
clap, applaud, shout, yell
OPPOSITE jeer
2 *The good news cheered us.*
comfort, console, gladden, delight, please, encourage, uplift
OPPOSITE sadden

cheerful *adjective*
The sun was shining, and we set out in a cheerful mood.
happy, good-humoured, light-hearted, merry, jolly, joyful, joyous, glad, pleased, optimistic, lively, elated, animated, bright, buoyant, jovial, gleeful, chirpy
OPPOSITE sad

chest *noun*
I found some old books in a chest in the attic.
box, crate, case, trunk

chew *verb*
Are you still chewing that toffee?
eat, gnaw, munch

chief *noun*
The pirates chose Redbeard as their chief.
leader, ruler, head, commander, captain, chieftain, master, governor, president, principal
(*informal*) boss

chief *adjective*
1 *The chief ingredients in a trifle are jelly, custard, and cream.*
main, central, key, principal, crucial, basic, essential, important, vital, major, primary, foremost, fundamental, indispensable, necessary, significant, predominant, prominent
OPPOSITE unimportant, minor, trivial
2 *Albert was Queen Victoria's chief advisor.*
head, senior

child *noun*
1 *The book festival is aimed especially at children.*
boy or girl, infant, juvenile, youngster, youth, lad or lass
(*informal*) kid, tot, nipper
2 *How many children do you have?*
son or daughter, descendant, offspring

A child who expects to inherit a title or fortune from parents is an *heir* or *heiress*.
A child whose parents are dead is an *orphan*.
A child looked after by a guardian is a *ward*.

childish *adjective*
It's childish to make rude noises.
babyish, immature, juvenile, infantile
OPPOSITE mature

chilly *adjective*
1 *It's a chilly evening, so wrap up well.*
cold, cool, frosty, icy, crisp, fresh, raw, wintry
(*informal*) nippy
OPPOSITE warm
2 *The librarian gave me a very chilly look.*
unfriendly, hostile, unwelcoming, unsympathetic
OPPOSITE friendly

chip *noun*
1 *There were chips of broken glass on the pavement.*
bit, piece, fragment, scrap, sliver, splinter, flake, shaving
2 *This mug's got a chip in it.*
crack, nick, notch, flaw

chip *verb*
I chipped a cup while I was washing up.
crack, nick, notch, damage

choice *noun*
1 *My bike had a flat tyre, so I had no choice but to walk.*
alternative, option
2 *She wouldn't be my choice as team captain.*
preference, selection, pick, vote
3 *The greengrocer has a good choice of vegetables.*
range, selection, assortment, array, mixture, variety, diversity

choke *verb*
1 *This tie is so tight it's choking me.*
strangle, suffocate, stifle, throttle
2 *Thick fumes made the firefighters choke.*
cough, gasp

choose *verb*
1 *We had a show of hands to choose a winner.*
select, appoint, elect, vote for
2 *I chose the blue shoes to go with my dress.*
decide on, select, pick out, opt for, plump for, settle on, single out
3 *Lola chose to stay at home.*
decide, make a decision, determine, prefer, resolve

chop *verb*
1 *Chop the celery into large chunks.*
cut, split

2 *They **chopped** down the undergrowth to make a path.*
hack, slash
To chop down a tree is to **fell** it.
To chop off an arm or leg is to **amputate** it.
To chop a branch off a tree is to *lop* it.
To chop food into small pieces is to **dice** or **mince** it.

chunk *noun*
*I bit a **chunk** out of my apple.*
piece, portion, lump, block, hunk, slab, wedge

circle *noun*
1 *We arranged the chairs in a **circle**.*
ring, round, hoop, loop, band
A flat, solid circle is a **disc**.
A three-dimensional round shape is a **sphere**.
An egg shape is an **oval** or **ellipse**.
The distance round a circle is the **circumference**.
The distance across a circle is the **diameter**.
The distance from the centre to the circumference is the **radius**.
A circular movement is a **revolution** or **rotation**.
A circular trip round the world is a **circumnavigation**.
A circular trip of a satellite round a planet is an **orbit**.
2 *She has a wide circle of friends.*
group, set, crowd

city *noun*
The chief city of a country or region is the **metropolis**.
An area of houses outside the central part of a city is the **suburbs**.
A word meaning 'to do with a town or city' is **urban**.
A word meaning 'to do with a city and its suburbs' is **metropolitan**.

claim *verb*
1 *You can **claim** your prize for the raffle here.*
ask for, request, collect, demand, insist on
2 *The professor **claims** to be an expert on dinosaurs.*
declare, assert, allege, maintain, argue, insist

clap *verb*
1 *The audience **clapped** loudly at the end of the concert.*
applaud, cheer
2 *Suddenly, a hand **clapped** me on the shoulder.*
slap, hit, pat, smack

class *noun*
1 *There are 26 children in our class.*
form, set, stream
The other pupils in your class are your **classmates**.

2 *There are many different **classes** of plants.*
category, group, classification, division, set, sort, type, kind, species
3 *The ancient Romans divided people into social **classes**.*
level, rank, status

clean *adjective*
1 *Can you bring me a **clean** cup, please?*
spotless, washed, scrubbed, swept, tidy, immaculate, hygienic, sanitary
An informal word meaning 'very clean' is **squeaky-clean**.
A common simile is **as clean as a whistle**.
OPPOSITE dirty
2 *I began my diary on a **clean** piece of paper.*
blank, unused, unmarked, empty, bare, fresh, new
OPPOSITE used
3 *This plaster will keep the wound **clean**.*
sterile, sterilized, uninfected
4 *You can get **clean** water from this tap.*
pure, clear, fresh, unpolluted, uncontaminated
5 *The referee said he wanted a **clean** fight.*
fair, honest, honourable, sporting, sportsmanlike
OPPOSITE dishonourable

clean *verb*
1 *We **cleaned** the house from top to bottom. I tried to **clean** the mud off my boots.*
wash, wipe, mop, scour, scrub, polish, dust, sweep, vacuum, rinse, wring out, hose down, sponge, shampoo, swill
To clean clothes is to **launder** them.
OPPOSITE dirty, mess up
2 *The nurse **cleaned** the wound with an antiseptic wipe.*
cleanse, bathe, disinfect, sanitize, sterilize
OPPOSITE infect, contaminate

clear *adjective*
1 *We saw fish swimming in the **clear** pool.*
clean, pure, colourless, transparent
A common simile is **as clear as crystal**.
A simile which means the opposite is **as clear as mud**.
OPPOSITE opaque

2 *It was a beautiful **clear** day.*
bright, sunny, cloudless, unclouded
A clear night is a **moonlit** or **starlit** night.
OPPOSITE cloudy, overcast
3 *The instructions on the map were quite **clear**.*
plain, understandable, intelligible, lucid, unambiguous
OPPOSITE ambiguous, confusing
4 *The actor spoke his words with a **clear** voice.*
distinct, audible
A common simile is **as clear as a bell**.
OPPOSITE muffled
5 *The signature is not **clear**.*
legible, recognizable, visible
OPPOSITE illegible
6 *My camera takes nice **clear** pictures.*
sharp, well defined, focused
OPPOSITE unfocused
7 *Is your conscience is **clear**?*
innocent, untroubled, blameless
OPPOSITE guilty
8 *There's a **clear** difference between a male blackbird and a female.*
obvious, definite, noticeable, conspicuous, perceptible, pronounced
OPPOSITE imperceptible
9 *They made sure the road was **clear** for the ambulance.*
open, empty, free, passable, uncrowded, unobstructed
OPPOSITE congested

clear *verb*
1 *I **cleared** the weeds from the flower bed.*
get rid of, remove, eliminate, strip
2 *The plumber **cleared** the blocked drain.*
unblock, unclog, clean out, open up
To clear a channel is to **dredge** it.
3 *I **cleared** the misty windows.*
clean, wipe, polish
4 *If the fire alarm goes, **clear** the building.*
empty, evacuate
5 *The fog **cleared** slowly.*
disappear, vanish, disperse, evaporate, melt away
6 *The forecast said that the weather will **clear**.*
become clear, brighten, fair up
7 *He was **cleared** of all the charges against him.*
acquit, free, release
8 *The runners **cleared** the first hurdle.*
go over, get over, jump over, pass over, vault
to clear up
*Please **clear up** this mess before you go.*
clean up, tidy up, put right, put straight

climb

clever adjective
1 *Dr Hafiz is very **clever** and can read hieroglyphics.*
intelligent, bright, gifted, able, knowledgeable
(*informal*) brainy, smart
OPPOSITE unintelligent
An informal name for a clever person is a **brainbox**.
An uncomplimentary synonym is **clever clogs** or **smartypants**.
2 *The elves were very **clever** with their fingers.*
accomplished, capable, gifted, skilful, talented
If you are clever at a lot of things, you are **versatile**.
OPPOSITE unskilful
3 *They are **clever** enough to get away with it.*
quick, sharp, shrewd, smart
Uncomplimentary synonyms are **artful**, **crafty**, **cunning**, **wily**.
OPPOSITE stupid

climax noun
*The **climax** of the film is a stunning car chase.*
high point, highlight, peak, crisis
OPPOSITE anticlimax

climb verb
1 *It took us several hours to **climb** the mountain.*
ascend, clamber up, go up, scale
2 *The plane **climbed** into the clouds.*
lift off, soar, take off
3 *The road **climbs** steeply up to the castle.*
rise, slope
to climb down
3 *It's harder to **climb down** rock than to get up it.*
descend, get down from
*We all told him he was wrong, so he had to **climb down**.*
admit defeat, give in, surrender

cling verb
to cling to someone or **something**
1 *The baby koala **clung to** its mother.*
clasp, grasp, clutch, embrace, hug

2 *Ivy **clings to** the wall.*
adhere to, fasten on to, stick to

clip verb
1 *The sheets of paper were **clipped** together.*
pin, staple
2 *Dad **clipped** the hedges in the back garden.*
cut, trim
To cut unwanted twigs off a tree or bush is to **prune** it.

close adjective
1 *Our house is **close** to the shops.*
near, nearby, not far
To be actually by the side of something is to be **adjacent**.
OPPOSITE far, distant
2 *Anisha and I are **close** friends.*
intimate, dear, devoted, fond, affectionate
3 *The police made a **close** examination of the stolen car.*
careful, detailed, painstaking, minute, thorough
OPPOSITE casual

4 *It was an exciting race because it was so close.*
equal, even, level, well-matched
5 *Open the window—it's very **close** in here.*
humid, muggy, stuffy, clammy, airless, stifling, suffocating
OPPOSITE airy

close verb
1 *Don't forget to **close** the lid.*
shut, fasten, seal, secure
2 *The road has been **closed** to traffic for the parade.*
barricade, block, obstruct, stop up
3 *The band **closed** the concert with my favourite song.*
finish, end, complete, conclude, stop, terminate
(*informal*) wind up

clothes noun see panel above

cloudy adjective
1 *The day was cold and **cloudy**.*
dull, overcast, grey, dark, dismal, gloomy, sunless
OPPOSITE cloudless

🕸 WORD WEB

clothes plural noun
*What **clothes** are you taking on holiday?*
clothing, garments, outfits, dress, attire, garb, finery
(*informal*) gear, togs, get-up
A set of clothes to wear is a **costume**, **outfit**, or **suit**.
An official set of clothes worn for school or work is a **uniform**.

SOME ITEMS OF CLOTHING
blouse, caftan, camisole, chador or chuddar, dhoti, dress, dungarees, frock, gown, jeans, jersey, jodhpurs, jumper, kilt, kimono, leggings, miniskirt, pinafore, polo shirt, pullover, robe, sari, sarong, shirt, shorts, skirt, slacks, smock, suit, sweater, sweatshirt, trousers, trunks, T-shirt, tunic, waistcoat

OUTER CLOTHES
anorak, apron, blazer, cagoule, cape, cardigan, cloak, coat, dressing gown, duffel coat, fleece, gilet, hoodie, greatcoat, jacket, mackintosh, oilskins, overalls, overcoat, parka, poncho, raincoat, shawl, stole, tracksuit, windcheater

UNDERWEAR
boxer shorts, bra, briefs, crop top, drawers, knickers, pants, petticoat, slip, socks, stockings, tights, underpants, vest

CLOTHES FOR SLEEPING IN
nightdress or (*informal*) nightie, pyjamas

CLOTHES WORN IN THE PAST
corset, doublet, frock coat, gauntlet, ruff, toga

ACCESSORIES WORN WITH CLOTHES
belt, braces, cravat, earmuffs, glove, sash, scarf, shawl, tie

PARTS OF A GARMENT
bodice, button, buttonhole, collar, cuff, hem, lapel, pocket, seam, sleeve, waistband, zip

THINGS USED TO DECORATE CLOTHES
beads, frills, fringes, lace, ruffles, sequins, tassels

SOME KINDS OF HAT
balaclava, baseball cap, bearskin, beret, boater, bonnet, bowler, cap, deerstalker, fez, helmet, mitre, mortarboard, panama hat, skull cap, sombrero, sou'wester, stetson, sun-hat, tam-o'shanter, top hat, trilby, turban

✏ WRITING TIPS

You can use these words to describe **clothes**:
baggy, casual, chic, dowdy, drab, fashionable, fine, flashy, flattering, frilly, frumpy, glamorous, ill-fitting, loose, luxurious, old-fashioned, ornate, ragged, roomy, shabby, skimpy, smart, sporty, stylish, tattered or in tatters, threadbare, tight-fitting, trendy, worn

2 *We couldn't see any fish in the* ***cloudy*** *water.*
muddy, murky, hazy, milky
OPPOSITE clear, transparent

club *noun*
1 *The warrior brandished a wooden* ***club***.
stick, baton, truncheon
2 *Would you like to join our book* ***club***?
group, society, association, organization, circle, union

clue *noun*
1 *I don't know the answer. Can you give me a* ***clue***?
hint, suggestion, indication, pointer, tip, idea
2 *'This footprint is an important* ***clue***,' *said the detective.*
piece of evidence, lead

clumsy *adjective*
The ***clumsy*** *gnome was always breaking things.*
careless, awkward, ungainly, inept
An informal name for a clumsy person is ***butterfingers***.
OPPOSITE graceful

clutter *noun*
Clear up all this ***clutter***.
mess, muddle, junk, litter, rubbish, odds and ends

coach *verb*
He was ***coached*** *by a former champion.*
train, teach, instruct

coarse *adjective*
1 *The blanket was made of* ***coarse*** *woollen material.*
rough, harsh, scratchy, bristly, hairy
OPPOSITE soft
2 *We were shocked by their* ***coarse*** *table manners.*
rude, offensive, impolite, improper, indecent, crude, vulgar
OPPOSITE polite, refined

coat *noun*
1 *The detective was wearing a thick winter* ***coat***.
see **clothes** *panel opposite*
2 *The fox had a reddish brown* ***coat***.
hide, pelt, skin, fur, hair
A sheep's coat is a ***fleece***.
3 *The front door needs a* ***coat*** *of paint.*
layer, coating, covering

coat *verb*
We ate marshmallows ***coated*** *with chocolate.*
cover, spread, smear, glaze

coax *verb*
Sam ***coaxed*** *the hamster back into its cage.*
persuade, tempt, entice

coil *noun*
The snake twisted itself into a ***coil***.
spiral, twist, curl, twirl, screw, corkscrew, whirl, whorl, roll, scroll A coil of wool or thread is a ***skein***.

coil *verb*
The snake ***coiled*** *itself round a branch.*
curl, loop, roll, spiral, turn, twist, twirl, wind, writhe

cold *adjective*
1 *Wrap up warm in this* ***cold*** *weather.*
freezing, chilly, frosty, icy, raw, arctic, bitter, cool, crisp, snowy, wintry, (*informal*) perishing
A common simile is **as cold as ice**.
OPPOSITE hot, warm
2 *I tried to shelter from the* ***cold*** *wind.*
biting, bitter, keen, penetrating, piercing
3 *I was* ***cold*** *in spite of my woolly hat.*
freezing, frozen, chilly, chilled, shivering, shivery
To be so cold that you become ill is to suffer from ***hypothermia***.
OPPOSITE hot, warm
4 *The cyclops gave us a* ***cold*** *stare from his one eye.*
unfriendly, unkind, unfeeling, distant, cool, heartless, indifferent, reserved, stony, uncaring, unemotional, unsympathetic
OPPOSITE warm, friendly

collapse *verb*
1 *Many buildings* ***collapsed*** *in the earthquake.*
fall down, fall in, cave in, give way, crumple, buckle, disintegrate, tumble down
2 *Some of the runners* ***collapsed*** *in the heat.*
faint, pass out, fall over, keel over

collect *verb*
1 *Squirrels* ***collect*** *nuts for the winter.*
gather, accumulate, hoard, heap, pile up, store up, stockpile, amass
2 *A crowd* ***collected*** *to watch the fire.*
assemble, gather, come together, converge
OPPOSITE scatter, disperse
3 *We* ***collected*** *a large sum for charity.*
raise, take in
4 *She* ***collected*** *the car from the garage.*
fetch, get, obtain, bring
OPPOSITE drop off, hand in

collection *noun*
Would you like to see my fossil ***collection***?
assortment, set, accumulation, array, hoard, pile
A collection of books is a ***library***.
A collection of poems or short stories is an ***anthology***.

collide *verb*
to collide with *The runaway trolley* ***collided with*** *a wall.*
bump into, crash into, run into, smash into, hit, strike

collision *noun*
The ***collision*** *dented the front wheel of my bike.*
bump, crash, smash, knock, accident
A collision involving a lot of vehicles is a ***pile-up***.

colossal *adjective*
A ***colossal*** *statue towered above us.*
huge, enormous, gigantic, immense, massive, giant, mammoth, monumental, towering, vast
OPPOSITE small, tiny

✎ **WRITING TIPS**

colour *noun*
You can use these words to describe a **colour**.

TO DESCRIBE *A PALE COLOUR*
delicate, faded, light, muted, neutral, pastel, washed-out

TO DESCRIBE *A STRONG COLOUR*
bright, fluorescent, garish, loud, neon, vibrant, zingy

---

colourful *adjective*
1 *The rose garden is* ***colourful*** *in the summer.*
multicoloured, showy, vibrant, bright, brilliant, gaudy
OPPOSITE colourless
2 *The book gives a* ***colourful*** *account of life on an island.*
exciting, interesting, lively, vivid, striking, rich, picturesque
OPPOSITE dull

column *noun*
1 *The roof of the temple was supported by stone* ***columns***.
pillar, post, support, shaft
2 *A* ***column*** *of soldiers wound its way across the desert.*
line, file, procession, row, string
3 *I sometimes read the sports* ***column*** *in the newspaper.*
article, piece, report, feature

combine *verb*
1 *We* ***combined*** *our pocket money to buy a kite.*
put together, add together, join, merge, unite, amalgamate
OPPOSITE divide
2 ***Combine*** *the mixture with water to make a paste.*
mix, stir together, blend, mingle, bind
OPPOSITE separate

a b c d e f g h i j k l m n o p q r s t u v w x y z

come *verb*
1 *We expect our guests to **come** in the afternoon.*
arrive, appear, visit
OPPOSITE go
2 *When you hear a cuckoo, you know that summer is **coming**.*
advance, draw near
to come about
*Can you tell me how the accident **came about**?*
happen, occur, take place, result
to come across
*I **came across** an old friend of mine.*
find, discover, chance upon, meet, bump into
to come to
1 *Tell me when you **come to** the last chapter.*
reach, get to, arrive at
2 *What did the repair bill **come to**?*
add up to, amount to, total

comfort *noun*
1 *My teddy bear was a **comfort** to me when I was ill.*
reassurance, consolation, encouragement, support, relief
2 *If I had a million pounds, I could live in **comfort**.*
ease, luxury, contentment, well-being, prosperity, luxury, affluence

comfort *verb*
*The coach tried to **comfort** the team after they lost.*
cheer up, console, reassure, encourage, hearten, sympathize with, soothe

comfortable *adjective*
1 *The bed was so **comfortable** that Goldilocks fell fast asleep.*
cosy, snug, relaxing, easy, soft, warm, roomy, padded, plush (*informal*) comfy
OPPOSITE uncomfortable
2 *We'll need **comfortable** clothes for travelling.*
casual, informal, loose-fitting
3 *Our cat leads a **comfortable** life.*
contented, happy, pleasant, agreeable, well-off, prosperous, luxurious, affluent

command *noun*
1 *The general gave the **command** to attack.*
order, instruction, commandment, edict
2 *Captain Nemo has **command** of the whole crew.*
charge, control, authority (over), power (over), management, supervision
3 *My sister has a good **command** of Spanish.*
knowledge, mastery, grasp, understanding, ability (in), skill (in)

command *verb*
1 *The officer **commanded** his troops to fire.*
order, instruct, direct, tell, bid
2 *The captain **commands** the ship.*
control, direct, be in charge of, govern, head, lead, manage, administer, supervise

comment *noun*
*He made some nasty **comments** about his boss.*
remark, statement, observation, opinion, mention, reference
A hostile comment is a **criticism**.

commit *verb*
*The thieves were planning to **commit** another robbery.*
carry out, do, perform, execute

common *adjective*
1 *Colds are a **common** complaint in winter.*
commonplace, everyday, frequent, normal, ordinary, familiar, well known, widespread
OPPOSITE rare
2 *'Good morning' is a **common** way to greet people.*
typical, usual, regular, routine, standard, customary, conventional, habitual, traditional
OPPOSITE uncommon
3 *My friends and I have a **common** interest in music.*
shared, mutual, joint

commotion *noun*
*Football supporters were causing a **commotion** outside.*
disturbance, row, fuss, trouble, disorder, unrest, agitation, turmoil, uproar, racket, rumpus, upheaval, riot, fracas, furore, hullabaloo, brouhaha, pandemonium, bedlam

communicate *verb*
1 *Steve **communicated** his boredom with a yawn.*
express, make known, indicate, convey, disclose, announce, pass on, proclaim, publish, report
2 *Nowadays, we **communicate** by email.*
contact each other, correspond, be in touch

company *noun*
1 *My cousin works for a computer **company**.*
business, firm, corporation, organization, establishment
2 *Shrek shunned the **company** of other ogres.*
fellowship, companionship, friendship, society

compare *verb*
*Can you **compare** these sets of figures?*
contrast, juxtapose, relate, set side by side

to compare with
*This copy can't **compare with** the original painting.*
compete with, rival, emulate, equal, match

compete *verb*
*Five schools will be **competing** in the hockey tournament.*
participate, perform, take part, enter
to compete against
*We are **competing against** a strong team this week.*
oppose, play against, contend with

competent *adjective*
*You have to be a **competent** swimmer to join the club.*
able, capable, skilful, skilled, accomplished, proficient, experienced, expert, qualified, trained
OPPOSITE incompetent

competitor *noun*
*The **competitors** lined up for the start of the race.*
contestant, contender, challenger, participant, opponent, rival
People who take part in an exam are **candidates** or **entrants**.

complain *verb*
*Miss Grouch spent most of her life **complaining**.*
moan, protest, grumble, grouse, gripe, whinge, make a fuss
to complain about
*I wrote a letter **complaining about** the noise.*
protest about, object to, criticize, find fault with
OPPOSITE praise

complaint *noun*
1 *They received hundreds of **complaints** about the film.*
criticism, objection, protest, moan, grumble
2 *You have a nasty stomach **complaint**.*
disease, illness, ailment, sickness, infection
(*informal*) upset

complete *adjective*
1 *Your training as a witch is not yet **complete**.*
completed, ended, finished, accomplished, concluded
OPPOSITE unfinished
2 *Have you got a **complete** set of cards?*
whole, entire, full, intact
OPPOSITE incomplete
3 *My birthday party was a **complete** disaster.*
total, utter, sheer, absolute, thorough, downright, perfect, pure

complete verb
We have **completed** all the tasks on the sheet.
finish, end, conclude, carry out, perform

complex adjective
Defusing a bomb is a **complex** task.
complicated, difficult, elaborate, detailed, intricate, involved
(informal) fiddly
OPPOSITE simple

complicated adjective
The plot of the film is very **complicated**.
complex, intricate, involved, difficult, elaborate, convoluted
OPPOSITE simple, straightforward

compliments plural noun
It was nice to get **compliments** about my cooking.
praise, appreciation, approval, congratulations, tribute
Compliments which you don't deserve are **flattery**.
OPPOSITE insults

compose verb
Beethoven **composed** nine symphonies.
create, devise, produce, make up, think up, write
to be composed of
This quilt is **composed of** pieces of patchwork.
be made of, consist of, comprise

compulsory adjective
The wearing of seat belts is **compulsory**.
required, obligatory, necessary
OPPOSITE optional

conceal verb
1 The dog tried to **conceal** its bone.
hide, cover up, bury
2 We tried to **conceal** our hiding place.
disguise, mask, screen, camouflage, make invisible
3 Don't **conceal** the truth.
keep quiet about, keep secret, hush up, suppress

conceited adjective
He was so **conceited** when he won first prize!
boastful, arrogant, proud, vain, self-satisfied
(informal) big-headed, cocky
OPPOSITE modest

concentrate verb
I had to **concentrate** to hear what she was saying.
be attentive, think hard, focus

concern verb
1 This conversation doesn't **concern** you.
affect, involve, be important to, matter to, be relevant to, relate to

2 It **concerns** me that we are destroying the rain forests.
bother, distress, trouble, upset, worry

concern noun
1 My private life is no **concern** of theirs.
affair, business
2 Global warming is a great **concern** to us all.
worry, anxiety, fear
3 She's the head of a business **concern**.
company, firm, enterprise, establishment

concerned adjective
1 After waiting an hour, Julia began to feel **concerned**.
worried, bothered, troubled, anxious, upset, distressed
2 We're writing a letter to all those **concerned**.
involved, connected, related, affected

conclusion noun
1 The **conclusion** of the film was a bit puzzling.
close, end, finale, finish, completion, culmination
2 'What is your **conclusion**, Inspector?'
decision, judgement, opinion, verdict, deduction

condemn verb
1 The manager **condemned** the behaviour of the players.
criticize, disapprove of, denounce, deplore, reproach
OPPOSITE praise
2 The judge **condemned** the men to death.
sentence
OPPOSITE acquit

condition noun
1 Is your bike in good **condition**?
state, order, repair
2 A dog needs exercise to stay in good **condition**.
fitness, health, shape
3 It's a **condition** of membership that you pay a subscription.
requirement, obligation, term

confess verb
The goblin **confessed** that he had stolen the gold.
admit, own up to, acknowledge, reveal

confidence noun
1 We can face the future with **confidence**.
hope, optimism, faith
OPPOSITE doubt
2 I wish I had her **confidence**.
self-confidence, assurance, boldness, conviction

confident adjective
1 I am **confident** that we will win.
certain, sure, positive, optimistic
OPPOSITE doubtful
2 She is a **confident** sort of person.
self-confident, assertive, bold, fearless, unafraid

confirm verb
1 The strange events **confirmed** his belief in ghosts.
prove, justify, support, back up, reinforce
OPPOSITE disprove
2 I phoned to **confirm** my appointment at the dentist.
verify, make official
OPPOSITE cancel

confront verb
I decided to **confront** her and demand an apology.
challenge, stand up to, face up to
OPPOSITE avoid

confuse verb
1 I was **confused** by the directions on the map.
puzzle, bewilder, mystify, baffle, perplex
2 You must be **confusing** me with someone else.
mix up, muddle

confusion noun
1 There was great **confusion** when the lights went out.
chaos, commotion, fuss, uproar, turmoil, pandemonium, bedlam, hullabaloo
2 There was a look of **confusion** on her face.
bewilderment, puzzlement, perplexity

congratulate verb
We **congratulated** the winners.
praise, applaud, compliment
OPPOSITE criticize

connect verb
1 What's the best way to **connect** these wires?
join, attach, fasten, link, couple, fix together, tie together
OPPOSITE separate
2 The fingerprints **connected** him with the crime.
make a connection between, associate, relate

connection noun
There is a close **connection** between our two families.
association, relationship, link

conquer verb
1 Extra troops were sent to **conquer** the enemy forces.
beat, defeat, overcome, vanquish, get the better of, overwhelm, crush, rout
2 Gaul was **conquered** by Caesar.
seize, capture, take, win, occupy, possess

a b **c** d e f g h i j k l m n o p q r s t u v w x y z

conscientious *adjective*
Elves are very conscientious workers.
hard working, careful, dependable, reliable, responsible, dutiful, meticulous, painstaking, thorough
OPPOSITE careless

conscious *adjective*
1 *The patient was conscious throughout the operation.*
awake, alert, aware
OPPOSITE unconscious
2 *She made a conscious effort to improve her work.*
deliberate, intentional, planned
OPPOSITE accidental

consequence *noun*
1 *He drank the potion without thinking of the consequences.*
effect, result, outcome, sequel, upshot
2 *The loss of a few pence is of no consequence.*
importance, significance

consider *verb*
1 *The detective considered the problem carefully.*
think about, examine, contemplate, ponder on, reflect on, study, weigh up, meditate about
2 *I consider this to be my best work.*
believe, judge, reckon

considerate *adjective*
It was considerate of you to lend me your umbrella.
kind, kind-hearted, helpful, obliging, sympathetic, thoughtful, unselfish, caring, charitable, neighbourly
OPPOSITE selfish

consist *verb*
to consist of
1 *The planet consists largely of craters.*
be made of, be composed of, comprise, contain, include, incorporate
2 *His job consists mostly of answering the phone.*
involve

consistent *adjective*
1 *These plants need to be kept at a consistent temperature.*
steady, constant, regular, stable, unchanging
2 *Fortunately, our goalkeeper is a consistent player.*
predictable, dependable, reliable

console *verb*
He did his best to console me when my dog died.
comfort, soothe, sympathize with, support

conspicuous *adjective*
1 *The clock tower is a conspicuous landmark.*
prominent, notable, obvious, eye-catching, unmistakable, visible
2 *I had made some conspicuous mistakes.*
clear, noticeable, obvious, evident, glaring

constant *adjective*
1 *There is a constant noise of traffic on the motorway.*
continual, continuous, never-ending, non-stop, ceaseless, incessant, interminable, endless, everlasting, permanent, perpetual, unending, persistent, relentless
OPPOSITE changeable
2 *My dog has been my constant friend for many years.*
faithful, loyal, dependable, reliable, firm, true, trustworthy, devoted
OPPOSITE unreliable

construct *verb*
We constructed a tree-house in the back garden.
build, erect, assemble, make, put together, put up, set up
OPPOSITE demolish

consult *verb*
1 *You should consult the dentist about your sore tooth.*
ask, get advice from, speak to
2 *If you don't know how to spell a word, consult your dictionary.*
refer to

contact *verb*
I'll contact you when I have some news.
call, call on, get in touch with, notify communicate with, speak to, talk to, correspond with, phone, ring, write to

contain *verb*
1 *This box contains odds and ends.*
hold
2 *A dictionary contains words and definitions.*
include, incorporate, comprise, consist of

contemplate *verb*
1 *The princess contemplated herself in the mirror.*
look at, view, observe, survey, watch, stare at, gaze at
2 *The robbers contemplated what to do next.*
think about, consider, ponder, study, reflect on, weigh up, meditate about

contempt *noun*
The knight stared at his enemy with a look of contempt.
hatred, scorn, loathing, disgust, dislike, distaste
OPPOSITE admiration

contented *adjective*
After her meal, the cat looked very contented.
happy, pleased, content, satisfied, fulfilled, serene, peaceful, relaxed, comfortable, tranquil, untroubled
OPPOSITE discontented

contest *noun*
The tennis final was an exciting contest.
competition, challenge, fight, bout, encounter, struggle, game, match, tournament

contestant *noun*
There are twenty contestants in the spelling competition.
competitor, participant, player, contender

continual *adjective*
I get sick of their continual arguing.
constant, persistent, perpetual, repeated, frequent, recurrent, eternal, unending
OPPOSITE occasional

continue *verb*
1 *We continued our search until it got dark.*
keep up, prolong, sustain, persevere with, pursue
(*informal*) stick at
2 *This rain can't continue for long.*
carry on, last, persist, endure, keep on, go on, linger
3 *We'll continue our meeting after lunch.*
resume, proceed with, pick up

continuous *adjective*
We had continuous rain all through our holiday.
never-ending, non-stop, ceaseless, everlasting, incessant, unbroken, unceasing, uninterrupted
An illness which continues for a long time is a *chronic* illness.
OPPOSITE intermittent

contract *noun*
The actress has signed a contract for a new film.
agreement, deal, undertaking
A contract between two countries is an *alliance* or *treaty*.
A contract to end a dispute about money is a *settlement*.

contract *verb*
1 *Metal contracts when it gets colder.*
reduce, lessen, shrink, tighten
OPPOSITE expand
2 *The crew contracted a mysterious illness.*
catch, develop, get

contrast verb
1 *We were asked to* **contrast** *two of our favourite poems.*
compare, juxtapose, distinguish between
2 *Her handwriting* **contrasts** *with mine.*
clash, differ (from)

contrast noun
There is a sharp **contrast** *between the two paintings.*
difference, distinction, opposition
OPPOSITE similarity

contribute verb
Will you **contribute** *something to our charity collection?*
donate, give, provide
(*informal*) chip in
to contribute to
The sunny weather **contributed to** *our enjoyment.*
add to, help, aid, encourage, enhance

control noun
The captain had complete **control** *over the crew.*
authority, power, command, government, management, direction, leadership, guidance

control verb
1 *The government* **controls** *the country's affairs.*
be in control of, be in charge of, manage, run, command, direct, lead, guide, govern, administer, regulate, rule, superintend, supervise
2 *Can't you* **control** *that dog?*
manage, handle, restrain
3 *They built a dam to* **control** *the floods.*
check, curb, hold back, contain

convenient adjective
1 *Is there a* **convenient** *place to put my umbrella?*
suitable, appropriate, available, nearby, accessible
OPPOSITE inconvenient
2 *Mum has a* **convenient** *tool for opening jars.*
handy, helpful, useful, labour-saving, neat

conventional adjective
The **conventional** *way to greet someone is to shake hands.*
customary, traditional, usual, accepted, common, normal, ordinary, everyday, routine, standard, regular, habitual
OPPOSITE unconventional

conversation noun
An informal conversation is a **chat** *or* **gossip***.*
A more formal conversation is a **discussion***.*
A very formal conversation is a **conference***.*
Conversation in a play or novel is **dialogue***.*

WORD WEB

cook verb
To cook food for guests or customers is to **cater** for them.
Cooking as a business is **catering**.
The art or skill of cooking is **cookery**.

SOME WAYS TO COOK FOOD
bake, barbecue, boil, braise, brew, broil, casserole, deep-fry, fry, grill, poach, roast, sauté, simmer, steam, stew, toast

OTHER WAYS TO PREPARE FOOD
baste, blend, chop, dice, grate, grind, infuse, knead, liquidize, marinade, mince, mix, peel, purée, sieve, sift, stir, whisk

blender

SOME ITEMS THAT ARE USED FOR COOKING
baking tin or tray, barbecue, blender, bowl, carving knife, casserole, cauldron, chopping board, colander, cooker, dish, food processor, frying pan, grill, ladle, liquidizer, microwave, mincer, oven, pan, pot, rolling pin, saucepan, skewer, spatula, spit, strainer, toaster, whisk, wok, wooden spoon

---

convert verb
1 *We have* **converted** *our attic into a games room.*
change, adapt, alter, transform
2 *I never used to like football, but my cousin* **converted** *me.*
change someone's mind, persuade, convince, win over

convince verb
The prisoner **convinced** *them that he was innocent.*
persuade, assure, satisfy, make believe, win round

convincing adjective
I tried to think of a **convincing** *excuse.*
persuasive, believable, credible, plausible

cook verb see panel above

cool adjective
1 *The weather is* **cool** *for the time of year.*
chilly, coldish
OPPOSITE hot, warm
2 *Would you like a* **cool** *glass of lemonade?*
chilled, iced, refreshing
OPPOSITE hot
3 *Clifford remained* **cool** *when everyone else panicked.*
calm, level-headed, relaxed, unexcitable, unflustered
(*informal*) laid-back
A common simile is **as cool as a cucumber**.
OPPOSITE frantic
4 (*informal*) *Those trainers are really* **cool***!*
chic, fashionable, smart
(*informal*) trendy

cooperate verb
to cooperate with
The scouts **cooperated with** *each other to build a fire.*
work with or together with, collaborate with, aid, assist, support

cope verb
Shall I help you, or can you **cope** *on your own?*
manage, carry on, get by, make do, survive
to cope with
I can't **cope with** *all this homework!*
deal with, handle, manage, get through

copy noun
That isn't the original painting—it's a **copy***.*
replica, reproduction, duplicate, imitation, likeness
A copy made to deceive someone is a **fake** or a **forgery**.
A living organism which is identical to another is a **clone**.

copy verb
1 *I* **copied** *the poem into my notepad.*
duplicate, reproduce, write out
To copy something in order to deceive is to **fake** or **forge** it.
2 *My parrot can* **copy** *my voice.*
imitate, impersonate, mimic

core noun
It is very hot at the earth's **core***.*
centre, inside, middle, heart, nucleus

core

a b c d e f g h i j k l m n o p q r s t z

corner noun

1 *I'll meet you at the corner of the road.*
turn, turning, junction, crossroads, intersection
The place where two lines meet is an *angle*.

2 *I sat in a quiet corner and read her letter.*
alcove, recess, nook

correct adjective

1 *Your answers are all correct.*
right, accurate, exact, faultless

2 *I hope he has given us correct information.*
true, genuine, authentic, precise, reliable, factual

3 *What is the correct way to address this letter?*
proper, acceptable, regular, appropriate, suitable
OPPOSITE wrong

correct verb

1 *I have to correct my spelling mistakes.*
alter, put right, make better, improve

2 *Miss Nicol spent the day correcting exam papers.*
mark

correspond verb

to correspond with

1 *Her version of the story doesn't correspond with mine.*
agree with, match, be similar to, be consistent with, tally with

2 *Carol corresponds with a friend in Paris.*
write to, communicate with, send letters to

corrupt adjective

Corrupt officials had accepted millions of pounds in bribes.
dishonest, criminal, untrustworthy
(*informal*) bent, crooked
OPPOSITE honest

cost noun

The bill shows the total cost.
price, charge, amount, payment, fee, figure, expense, expenditure, tariff
The cost of travelling on public transport is the *fare*.

costume noun

The Irish dancers were wearing national costumes.
outfit, dress, clothing, suit, attire, garment, garb
(*informal*) get-up
A costume you dress up in for a party is *fancy dress*.
A set of clothes worn by soldiers or members of an organization is a *uniform*.

cosy adjective

It's good to feel cosy in bed when it's cold outside.
comfortable, snug, soft, warm, secure
OPPOSITE uncomfortable

count verb

1 *I'm counting the days until my birthday.*
add up, calculate, compute, estimate, reckon, figure out, work out, total

2 *It's playing well that counts, not winning.*
be important, be significant, matter

to count on

You can count on me to support you.
depend on, rely on, trust, bank on

country noun

1 *England and Wales are separate countries.*
nation, state, land, territory
A country ruled by a king or queen is a *kingdom*, *monarchy*, or *realm*.
A country governed by leaders elected by the people is a *democracy*.
A democratic country with a President is a *republic*.

2 *We went for a picnic in the country.*
countryside, landscape, outdoors, scenery
A word meaning 'to do with the country' is *rural* and its opposite is *urban*.
OPPOSITE town, city

courage noun

The rescue dogs showed great courage.
bravery, boldness, daring, fearlessness, nerve, pluck, valour, heroism, grit
(*informal*) guts
OPPOSITE cowardice

course noun

1 *The hot-air balloon was drifting off its course.*
direction, path, route, way, progress, passage

2 *The war changed the course of history.*
development, progression, sequence, succession

cover verb

1 *A coat of paint will cover the graffiti.*
conceal, disguise, hide, obscure, mask, blot out

2 *She covered her face with her hands.*
shield, screen, protect, shade, veil

3 *An encyclopedia covers many subjects.*
deal with, include, contain, incorporate

cover noun

1 *The cover of the book was torn.*
wrapper
A cover for a letter is an *envelope*.
A cover for a book is a *jacket*.
A cover to keep papers in is a *file* or *folder*.

2 *On the bare hillside, there was no cover from the storm.*
shelter, protection, defence, shield, refuge, sanctuary

covering noun

There was a light covering of snow on the hills.
coating, coat, layer, blanket, carpet, film, sheet, skin, veil

cowardly adjective

It was cowardly to run away.
timid, faint-hearted, spineless, gutless
(*informal*) yellow, chicken
OPPOSITE brave

cower verb

A frightened creature was cowering in the corner.
cringe, shrink, crouch, flinch, quail

crack noun

1 *There's a crack in this cup.*
break, chip, fracture, flaw, chink, split

2 *The outlaw hid in a crack between two rocks.*
gap, opening, crevice, rift, cranny

3 *The detective heard the crack of a pistol shot.*
bang, fire, explosion, snap, pop

4 *She gave the robber a crack on the head.*
blow, bang, knock, smack, whack

5 *I had a crack at writing a poem.*
try, attempt, shot, go

crack verb

A brick fell down and cracked the pavement.
break, fracture, chip, split, shatter, splinter

craft noun

1 *I'd like to learn the craft of weaving.*
art, skill, technique, expertise, handicraft

2 *All sorts of craft were in the harbour.*
boats, ships, vessels

crafty adjective

The evil sorceress had a crafty plan.
cunning, clever, shrewd, scheming, sneaky, sly, tricky, wily, artful

cram verb

1 *We can't cram any more people in—the car is full.*
pack, squeeze, crush, force, jam, compress

2 *My sister is cramming for her maths exam.*
revise, study
(*informal*) swot

cramped *adjective*
The seating on the train was a bit **cramped**.
confined, narrow, restricted, tight, uncomfortable, crowded
(*informal*) poky
OPPOSITE roomy

crash *noun*
1 *I heard a loud* **crash** *from the kitchen.*
bang, smash
2 *We saw a nasty* **crash** *on the motorway.*
accident, collision, smash, bump
A crash involving a lot of vehicles is a **pile-up**.
A train crash may involve a **derailment**.

crash *verb*
The car **crashed** *into a lamp post.*
bump, smash, collide, knock

crawl *verb*
I saw a caterpillar **crawling** *along a leaf.*
creep, edge, inch, slither, clamber

crawl

craze *noun*
This game is the latest **craze** *in the playground.*
fad, trend, vogue, fashion, enthusiasm, obsession, passion

crazy *adjective*
1 *The dog went* **crazy** *when it was stung by a wasp.*
mad, insane, frenzied, hysterical, frantic, berserk, delirious, wild
(*informal*) loopy, nuts
2 *It was a* **crazy** *idea to try to build a space rocket!*
absurd, ridiculous, ludicrous, daft, idiotic, senseless, silly, stupid, foolhardy, preposterous
(*informal*) bonkers, barmy, wacky
OPPOSITE sensible

create *verb*
1 *The cats were* **creating** *a racket outside.*
make, cause, produce
2 *We have* **created** *a website for our chess club.*
set up, start up, bring about, bring into existence, originate
You **write** a poem or story.
You **compose** music.
You **draw** or **paint** a picture.
You **carve** a statue.
You **invent** or **think up** a new idea.
You **design** a new product.
You **devise** a plan.
You **found** a new club or organization.
You **manufacture** goods.

You **generate** electricity.
You **build** or **construct** a model or a building.

creative *adjective*
My aunt is a very **creative** *person.*
artistic, imaginative, inventive, original, inspired
OPPOSITE unimaginative

creator *noun*
Walt Disney was the **creator** *of Mickey Mouse.*
inventor, maker, originator, producer, deviser
The creator of a design is an **architect** or **designer**.
The creator of goods for sale is a **manufacturer**.

creature *noun*
A wild-looking **creature** *emerged from the swamp.*
animal, beast, being

creep *verb*
1 *I watched the lizard* **creep** *back into its hiding place.*
crawl, edge, inch, slither, wriggle
2 *I* **crept** *out of bed without waking the others.*
move quietly, sneak, tiptoe, slip, slink, steal

creepy *adjective*
There were **creepy** *noises coming from the cellar.*
scary, frightening, eerie, ghostly, weird, sinister, uncanny, unearthly
(*informal*) spooky

crisis *noun*
The election result caused a **crisis** *in the country.*
emergency, problem, difficulty, predicament

crisp *adjective*
1 *Fry the bacon until it's* **crisp**.
crispy, crunchy, brittle
OPPOSITE soft, soggy, limp
2 *It was a* **crisp** *winter morning.*
cold, fresh, frosty

critical *adjective*
1 *Some people made* **critical** *comments about my hairstyle.*
negative, disapproving, derogatory, uncomplimentary, unfavourable
OPPOSITE complimentary
2 *This match is* **critical** *for our team's chances of success.*
crucial, important, vital, serious, decisive
OPPOSITE unimportant

criticize *verb*
She **criticized** *us for being so careless.*
blame, condemn, disapprove of, find fault with, reprimand, reproach, scold, berate
OPPOSITE praise

crooked *adjective*
1 *The wizard bent his wand into a* **crooked** *shape.*
bent, twisted, warped, knarled
OPPOSITE straight
2 (*informal*) *The* **crooked** *salesman was selling fake diamonds.*
criminal, dishonest, corrupt, illegal, unlawful
(*informal*) bent
OPPOSITE honest

cross *verb*
1 *There is a bus stop where the two roads* **cross**.
criss-cross, intersect
2 *You can* **cross** *the river at the footbridge.*
go across, pass over, traverse, ford, span

cross *adjective*
My mum will be **cross** *if we're late.*
angry, annoyed, upset, vexed, bad-tempered, ill-tempered, irritable, grumpy, testy, irate
OPPOSITE pleased

crouch *verb*
The outlaws **crouched** *silently in the bushes.*
squat, kneel, stoop, bend, duck, bob down, hunch, huddle

crowd *noun*
1 *A* **crowd** *of people waited outside the theatre.*
gathering, group, assembly, bunch, cluster, throng, mob, multitude, crush, horde, swarm
2 *There was a huge* **crowd** *for the tennis final.*
audience, spectators, gate, attendance

crowd *verb*
1 *People* **crowded** *on the pavement to watch the parade.*
gather, collect, assemble, congregate, mass, flock, muster
2 *Hundreds of people* **crowded** *into the hall.*
push, pile, squeeze, pack, cram, crush, jam, bundle, herd

crowd

crowded *adjective*
The shops are always **crowded** *at Christmas time.*
full, packed, teeming, swarming, overflowing, jammed, congested
OPPOSITE empty

a b c d e f g h i j k l m n o p q r s t u v w x y z

crude adjective
1 The refinery processes **crude** oil.
raw, natural, unprocessed, unrefined
OPPOSITE refined
2 We made a **crude** shelter out of twigs.
rough, clumsy, makeshift, primitive
OPPOSITE skilful
3 The teacher told them to stop using **crude** language.
rude, obscene, coarse, dirty, foul, impolite, indecent, vulgar
OPPOSITE polite

cruel adjective
I think hunting is a **cruel** way to kill animals.
brutal, savage, vicious, fierce, barbaric, bloodthirsty, barbarous, heartless, ruthless, merciless, inhuman, sadistic, uncivilized, beastly
OPPOSITE kind, humane, gentle

crumb noun
We put out some **crumbs** of bread for the birds.
bit, fragment, scrap, morsel

crumble verb
1 The walls of the castle were beginning to **crumble**.
disintegrate, break up, collapse, fall apart, decay, decompose
2 The farmer **crumbled** some bread into his soup.
crush, grind, pound, pulverize

crunch verb
1 The dog was **crunching** on a bone.
chew, munch, chomp, grind
2 I heard heavy footsteps **crunching** up the path.
crush, grind, pound, smash

crush verb
1 He **crushed** his anorak into his schoolbag.
squash, squeeze, mangle, pound, press, bruise, crunch, scrunch
To crush something into a soft mess is to **mash** or **pulp** it.
To crush something into a powder is to **grind** or **pulverize** it.
To crush something out of shape is to **crumple** or **smash** it.
2 Our soldiers **crushed** the attacking army.
defeat, conquer, vanquish, overcome, overwhelm, quash, trounce, rout

crush noun
There was a **crush** of people at the front gates.
crowd, press, mob, throng, jam, congestion

cry verb
1 Someone was **crying** for help from the burning house.
call, shout, yell, exclaim, roar, bawl, bellow, scream, screech, shriek

2 The baby started to **cry** when she dropped her toy.
sob, weep, bawl, blubber, wail, shed tears, snivel
When someone starts to cry, their eyes **well up with tears**.

cry noun
The wounded man let out a **cry** of pain.
call, shout, yell, roar, howl, exclamation, bellow, scream, screech, shriek, yelp

cuddle verb
My baby brother **cuddles** a teddy bear in bed.
hug, hold closely, clasp, embrace, caress, nestle against, snuggle against

cunning adjective
The pirates had a **cunning** plan to seize the ship.
clever, crafty, devious, wily, ingenious, shrewd, artful, scheming, sly, tricky

cup noun
A tall cup with straight sides is a **mug**.
A tall cup without a handle is a **beaker** or **tumbler**.
A decorative drinking cup is a **goblet**.

cure verb
1 These pills will **cure** your headache.
ease, heal, help, improve, make better, relieve
OPPOSITE aggravate
2 No-one can **cure** the problem with my computer.
correct, mend, sort, repair, fix, put an end to, put right

cure noun
I wish they could find a **cure** for colds.
remedy, treatment, antidote, medicine, therapy

curious adjective
1 We were all very **curious** about the secret chamber.
inquisitive, inquiring, interested (in), intrigued, agog
An uncomplimentary word is **nosy**.
OPPOSITE uninterested, indifferent
2 What is that **curious** smell?
odd, strange, peculiar, abnormal, queer, unusual, extraordinary, funny, mysterious, puzzling, weird

curl verb
1 The snake **curled** itself around a branch.
wind, twist, loop, coil, wrap, curve, turn, twine
2 Steam **curled** upwards from the cauldron.
coil, spiral, twirl, swirl, furl, snake, writhe, ripple

curl noun
The girl's hair was a mass of golden **curls**.
wave, ringlet, coil, loop, twist, roll, scroll, spiral

curly adjective
My new doll has **curly** black hair.
curled, curling, wavy, frizzy, crinkly, ringletted
OPPOSITE straight

current noun
The wooden raft drifted along with the **current**.
flow, tide, stream
A current of air is a **draught**.

current adjective
1 The shop sells all the **current** teenage fashions.
modern, contemporary, present-day, up to date, topical, prevailing, prevalent
OPPOSITE past, old-fashioned
2 Have you got a **current** passport?
valid, usable, up to date
OPPOSITE out of date
3 Who is the **current** prime minister?
present, existing
OPPOSITE past, former

curse noun
1 Long ago, a wizard put a **curse** on the family.
jinx, hex
2 When the gardener hit his finger, he let out a **curse**.
swear word, oath

curve noun
Try to draw a straight line without any **curves**.
bend, curl, loop, turn, twist, arch, arc, bow, bulge, wave
A curve in the shape of a new moon is a **crescent**.
A curve on a road surface is a **camber**.

curve verb
The road ahead **curves** round to the right.
bend, wind, turn, twist, curl, loop, swerve, veer, snake, meander

curved adjective
The wall was painted with a series of **curved** lines.
curving, curvy, curled, looped, coiled, rounded, bulging, bent, arched, bowed, twisted, crooked, spiral, winding, meandering, serpentine, snaking, undulating
A surface which is curved like the inside of a circle is **concave**.
A surface which is curved like the outside of a circle is **convex**.

custom noun
1 It's our **custom** to give presents at Christmas.
tradition, practice, habit, convention, fashion, routine, way

2 *The shop is having a sale to attract more **custom**.*
customers, buyers, trade, business

cut *verb*
1 *The woodcutter **cut** the tree trunk to make logs.*
chop, slit, split, chip, notch, axe, hack, hew, cleave
To cut off a limb is to **amputate** or **sever** it.
To cut down a tree is to **fell** it.
To cut branches off a tree is to **lop** them.
To cut twigs off a growing plant is to **prune** it.
To cut something up to examine it is to **dissect** it.
To cut stone to make a statue is to **carve** it.
To cut an inscription in stone is to **engrave** it.
2 *The cook **cut** the apples into small pieces.*
chop, slice, dice, grate, mince, shred
3 *I'm going to get my hair **cut** in the holidays.*
trim, clip, crop, snip, shave
To cut wool off a sheep is to **shear** it.
To cut grass is to **mow** it.
To cut corn is to **harvest** or **reap** it.
4 *Josh **cut** his foot on a sharp stone.*
gash, slash, nick, stab, pierce, wound
5 *This letter is too long—I'll need to **cut** it.*
shorten, condense, edit
6 *The shop has **cut** its prices by 10%.*
lower, reduce, decrease
If you cut something by half, you **halve** it.

cut *noun*
*I got a nasty **cut** when I was slicing bread.*
gash, wound, injury, nick, slash, scratch, slit, snip

damage *verb*
*Many books were **damaged** in the fire.*
harm, spoil, mar, break, impair, weaken, disfigure, deface, mutilate, scar
To damage something beyond repair is to **destroy**, **ruin**, or **wreck** it.
To damage something deliberately is to **sabotage** or **vandalize** it.

damp *adjective*
1 *Don't wear those clothes if they are **damp**.*
moist, soggy, clammy, dank

🕷 WORD WEB

dance *noun*
SOME KINDS OF DANCE OR DANCING
ballet, ballroom dancing, barn dance, belly-dancing, bolero, break-dancing, cancan, disco, flamenco, folk dance, Highland dancing, hornpipe, jazz dance, jig, jive dancing, limbo dancing, line-dancing, mazurka, morris dance, quadrille, reel, rumba, samba, Scottish country dancing, square dance, step dancing, street dance, tap dancing, tarantella

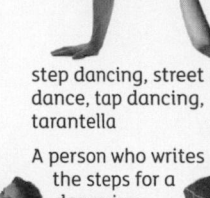
breakdancing

ballet

A person who writes the steps for a dance is a **choreographer**.

SOME BALLROOM DANCES
foxtrot, minuet, polka, quickstep, tango, waltz

GATHERINGS WHERE PEOPLE DANCE
ball, ceilidh, disco

flamenco

ballroom dancing

? *I don't like this **damp** weather.*
drizzly, foggy, misty, rainy, wet
Weather which is both damp and warm is **humid** or **muggy** weather.
OPPOSITE dry

dance *verb*
*I could have **danced** for joy.*
caper, cavort, frisk, frolic, gambol, hop about, jig about, jump about, leap, prance, skip, whirl

danger *noun*
1 *Who knows what **dangers** lie ahead?*
peril, jeopardy, trouble, crisis, hazard, menace, pitfall, threat, trap
OPPOSITE safety
2 *The forecast says there's a **danger** of frost.*
chance, possibility, risk

dangerous *adjective*
1 *We were in a **dangerous** situation.*
hazardous, perilous, risky, precarious, treacherous, unsafe, alarming, menacing
(*informal*) hairy
2 *The police arrested him for **dangerous** driving.*
careless, reckless
3 *A **dangerous** criminal had escaped from prison.*
violent, desperate, ruthless, treacherous
4 *It's wicked to empty **dangerous** chemicals into the river.*
harmful, poisonous, deadly, toxic
OPPOSITE harmless, safe

dangle *verb*
*There was a bunch of keys **dangling** from the chain.*
hang, swing, sway, droop, wave about, flap, trail

dare *verb*
1 *I wouldn't **dare** to make a parachute jump.*
have the courage, take the risk
2 *They **dared** me to climb the tree.*
challenge, defy

daring *adjective*
*It was a very **daring** plan.*
bold, brave, adventurous, courageous, fearless, intrepid, plucky, valiant
A daring person is a **daredevil**.
OPPOSITE timid

dark *adjective*
1 *It was a very **dark** night.*
black, dim, murky, shadowy, gloomy, dingy
OPPOSITE bright
2 *She wore a **dark** green coat.*
OPPOSITE pale, light

dash *verb*
1 *We **dashed** home because it was raining.*
hurry, run, rush, race, hasten, sprint, speed, tear, zoom
2 *She **dashed** her cup against the wall.*
throw, hurl, knock, smash

a b c d e f g h i j k l m n o p q r s t u v w x y z

data *plural noun*
*I entered all the **data** into the computer.*
information, details, facts
Data can be in the form of *figures*, *numbers*, or *statistics*.

dawn *noun*
1 *I was woken at **dawn** by the birds singing outside.*
daybreak, sunrise, first light
OPPOSITE dusk, sunset
2 *It was the **dawn** of the modern age.*
beginning, start, birth, origin

day *noun*
1 *Badgers sleep during the **day**.*
daytime
OPPOSITE night
2 *Things were different in my grandfather's **day**.*
age, time, era, epoch, period

dazed *adjective*
*He had a **dazed** expression on his face.*
confused, bewildered, muddled, perplexed

dazzle *verb*
1 *My eyes were **dazzled** by the bright lights.*
daze, blind
2 *The acrobats **dazzled** the audience with their skill.*
amaze, astonish, impress, fascinate, awe

dead *adjective*
1 *A **dead** fish floated by the side of the river.*
deceased, lifeless
Instead of 'the king who has just died', you can say 'the *late* king'.
A dead body is a *carcass* or *corpse*.
A common simile is *as dead as a doornail*.
OPPOSITE alive
2 *This battery is **dead**.*
flat, not working, worn out
3 *The town centre is **dead** at this time of night.*
dull, boring, uninteresting, slow
OPPOSITE lively

deadly *adjective*
*The witch gave her a **deadly** dose of poison.*
lethal, fatal, harmful, dangerous, destructive
OPPOSITE harmless

deafening *adjective*
*We complained about the **deafening** noise.*
loud, blaring, booming, thunderous, penetrating

deal *verb*
1 *Who is going to **deal** the cards?*
give out, distribute, share out
2 *My uncle used to **deal** in second-hand cars.*
do business, trade
to deal with something
1 *I can **deal with** this problem.*
cope with, sort out, attend to, see to, handle, manage, control, grapple with, look after, solve
2 *The book **deals with** the history of Rome.*
be concerned with, cover, explain about

deal *noun*
*She made a **deal** with the garage for her new car.*
arrangement, agreement, contract, bargain

dear *adjective*
1 *She is a very **dear** friend.*
close, loved, valued, beloved
OPPOSITE distant
2 *I didn't buy the watch because it was too **dear**.*
expensive, costly
(*informal*) pricey
OPPOSITE cheap

debate *noun*
*We had a **debate** about animal rights.*
discussion, argument, dispute
Something which people argue about a lot is a *controversy*.

debate *verb*
1 *We **debated** whether it is right to kill animals for food.*
discuss, argue
2 *I **debated** what to do next.*
consider, ponder, deliberate, weigh up, reflect on

decay *verb*
*Dead leaves fall to the ground and **decay**.*
decompose, rot, disintegrate, break down

decay

deceitful *adjective*
*Don't trust him—he's a **deceitful** person.*
dishonest, underhand, insincere, duplicitous, false, cheating, hypocritical, lying, treacherous, two-faced, sneaky
OPPOSITE honest

deceive *verb*
*The spy had been **deceiving** them for years.*
fool, trick, delude, dupe, hoodwink, cheat, double-cross, mislead, swindle, take in
(*informal*) con, diddle

decent *adjective*
1 *Do the decent thing and own up.*
honest, honourable
2 *My friend's jokes were not **decent**.*
polite, proper, respectable, fitting, acceptable, appropriate, suitable
OPPOSITE indecent
3 *I haven't had a **decent** meal for ages!*
satisfactory, agreeable, good, nice
OPPOSITE bad

decide *verb*
1 *We **decided** to finish our work instead of going out to play.*
choose, make a decision, make up your mind, opt, elect, resolve
2 *The referee **decided** that the player was offside.*
conclude, judge, rule
3 *The last lap **decided** the result of the race.*
determine, settle

decision *noun*
1 *Can you tell me what your **decision** is?*
choice, preference
2 *The judge announced his **decision**.*
conclusion, judgement, verdict, findings

decisive *adjective*
1 *A **decisive** piece of evidence proved that he was innocent.*
crucial, convincing, definite
OPPOSITE uncertain
2 *A referee needs to be **decisive**.*
firm, forceful, strong-minded, resolute, quick-thinking
OPPOSITE hesitant

declare *verb*
*He **declared** that he was innocent.*
announce, state, assert, make known, pronounce, proclaim, swear

decline *verb*
1 *Our enthusiasm **declined** as the day went on.*
become less, decrease, diminish, lessen, weaken, dwindle, flag, wane, tail off
OPPOSITE increase
2 *Why did you **decline** my invitation to lunch?*
refuse, reject, turn down
OPPOSITE accept

decorate *verb*
1 *We **decorated** the Christmas tree with tinsel.*
ornament, adorn, beautify, prettify, deck, festoon

To decorate a dish of food is to **garnish** it.
To decorate clothes with lace or ribbon is to **trim** them.
2 *Dad is going to* **decorate** *my bedroom next weekend.*
paint, paper, or wallpaper
(*informal*) do up, make over
3 *The firefighters were* **decorated** *for their bravery.*
award or give a medal to, honour, reward

decrease *verb*
1 *We* **decreased** *speed.*
reduce, cut, lower, slacken
2 *Our enthusiasm* **decreased** *as the day went on.*
become less, decline, decrease, diminish, lessen, weaken, dwindle, flag, wane, tail off, shrink, subside
OPPOSITE increase

dedicate *verb*
He **dedicates** *himself entirely to his art.*
commit, devote

deed *noun*
They thanked the rescue team for their heroic **deed**.
act, action, feat, exploit, effort, achievement

deep *adjective*
1 *The pond is quite* **deep** *in the middle.*
OPPOSITE shallow
2 *The letter expressed his* **deep** *regret.*
intense, earnest, genuine, sincere
OPPOSITE insincere
3 *Veronica fell into a* **deep** *sleep.*
heavy, sound
OPPOSITE light
4 *The actor spoke in a* **deep** *and sombre voice.*
low, bass
OPPOSITE high

defeat *verb*
The Greeks attacked and **defeated** *the Trojans.*
beat, conquer, vanquish, triumph over, win a victory over, overcome, overpower, crush, rout, trounce
To defeat someone in chess is to **checkmate** them.
To be defeated is to **lose**.

defeat *noun*
The team suffered a humiliating **defeat**.
failure, humiliation, rout, trouncing
OPPOSITE victory

defect *noun*
Cars are tested for **defects** *before they leave the factory.*
fault, flaw, imperfection, shortcoming, failure, weakness
A defect in a computer program is a **bug**.

defence *noun*
1 *What was the accused woman's* **defence**?
justification, excuse, explanation, argument, case
2 *The castle was built as a* **defence** *against enemy attack.*
protection, guard, safeguard, fortification, barricade, shield

defend *verb*
1 *They tried to* **defend** *themselves against the enemy.*
protect, guard, keep safe
OPPOSITE attack
2 *He gave a speech* **defending** *his actions.*
justify, support, stand up for, make a case for
OPPOSITE accuse

defiant *adjective*
The prisoner cursed with a **defiant** *look in his eye.*
rebellious, insolent, aggressive, challenging, disobedient, obstinate, quarrelsome, uncooperative, stubborn, mutinous
OPPOSITE submissive, compliant

definite *adjective*
1 *Is it* **definite** *that we're going to move?*
certain, sure, fixed, settled, decided
2 *The doctor saw* **definite** *signs of improvement.*
clear, distinct, noticeable, obvious, marked, positive, pronounced, unmistakable
OPPOSITE indefinite

definitely *adverb*
I'll **definitely** *phone you tomorrow.*
certainly, for certain, positively, surely, unquestionably, without doubt, without fail
OPPOSITE perhaps

defy *verb*
1 *The rebel army decided to* **defy** *the king.*
disobey, refuse to obey, resist, stand up to, confront
OPPOSITE obey
2 *I* **defy** *you to come up with a better idea.*
challenge, dare
3 *The jammed door* **defied** *our efforts to open it.*
resist, withstand, defeat, frustrate, beat

delay *verb*
1 *Don't let me* **delay** *you.*
detain, hold up, keep waiting, make late, hinder, slow down
2 *They* **delayed** *the race because of bad weather.*
postpone, put off, defer
3 *You'll miss the bus if you* **delay**.
hesitate, linger, pause, wait, dawdle, loiter

(*informal*) hang about or around, drag your feet

delay *noun*
There has been a **delay** *with the building work.*
hold-up, wait, pause

deliberate *adjective*
1 *That remark was a* **deliberate** *insult.*
intentional, planned, calculated, conscious, premeditated
OPPOSITE accidental, unintentional
2 *He walked with* **deliberate** *steps across the room.*
careful, steady, cautious, slow, unhurried
OPPOSITE hasty, careless

deliberately *adverb*
Did you say that **deliberately** *to hurt my feelings?*
on purpose, intentionally
OPPOSITE accidentally, unintentionally

delicate *adjective*
1 *The blouse has* **delicate** *embroidery on the cuffs.*
dainty, exquisite, intricate, neat
2 *Take care not to damage the* **delicate** *material.*
fragile, fine, flimsy, thin
3 **Delicate** *plants should be protected from frost.*
sensitive, tender
OPPOSITE tough, hardy
4 *The child was born with a* **delicate** *constitution.*
frail, weak, feeble, sickly, unhealthy
OPPOSITE strong
5 *The pianist's fingers had a* **delicate** *touch.*
gentle, light, soft

delicious *adjective*
The food at the banquet was **delicious**.
tasty, appetizing, mouth-watering, delectable
(*informal*) scrumptious, yummy
OPPOSITE horrible, disgusting

delight *noun*
Imagine my **delight** *when I saw my friend again!*
happiness, joy, pleasure, enjoyment, bliss, ecstasy

delight *verb*
The puppet show **delighted** *the children.*
please, charm, entertain, amuse, divert, enchant, entrance, fascinate, thrill
OPPOSITE dismay

delighted *adjective*
The **delighted** *crowd cheered the winners.*
pleased, happy, joyful, thrilled, ecstatic, elated, exultant

deliver verb
1 *Does anyone* **deliver** *mail to the island?*
convey, bring, hand over, distribute, present, supply, take round
2 *The head* **delivered** *a lecture on good behaviour.*
give, make, read out

demand verb
1 *I* **demanded** *a refund for my train fare.*
insist on, claim, call for, require, want
2 *'What do you want?'* **demanded** *a voice inside.*
ask, enquire, inquire

demand noun
1 *The king refused the* **demands** *of his people.*
request, claim, requirement
2 *There is not much* **demand** *for ice lollies in winter.*
need, call

demolish verb
They **demolished** *a building to make way for the road.*
destroy, flatten, knock down, level, pull down, tear down, bulldoze
OPPOSITE build, construct

demonstrate verb
1 *The teacher* **demonstrated** *how warm air rises.*
show, exhibit, illustrate
2 *Animal rights campaigners were* **demonstrating** *in the street.*
protest, march, parade

demonstration noun
1 *I watched a* **demonstration** *of the new computer game.*
show, display, presentation
2 *Everyone joined the* **demonstration** *against world poverty.*
protest, rally, march, parade
(*informal*) demo

den noun
We built a **den** *in the garden.*
hideout, shelter, hiding place, secret place
The den of a wild animal is its **lair***.*

dense adjective
1 *The accident happened in* **dense** *fog.*
thick, heavy
2 *A* **dense** *crowd waited in the square.*
compact, packed, solid
3 *I'm being rather* **dense** *today!*
stupid, slow

dent noun
There was a large **dent** *in the car door.*
indentation, depression, hollow, dip, dimple

deny verb
1 *The boy* **denied** *that he had stolen the money.*
reject, dispute, disagree with, contradict, dismiss, oppose
OPPOSITE admit, accept
2 *Her parents* **deny** *her nothing.*
refuse, deprive of, withhold
OPPOSITE give

depart verb
1 *What time is the train due to* **depart***?*
leave, set off, get going, set out, start, begin a journey
OPPOSITE arrive, get in
2 *It looks as if the robbers* **departed** *in a hurry.*
leave, exit, go away, retreat, withdraw, make off
(*informal*) clear off, scram, scarper
OPPOSITE arrive

depend verb
to depend on someone
I **depend on** *you to help me.*
rely on, count on, bank on, trust
to depend on something
My success will **depend on** *good luck.*
be decided by, rest on, hinge on

dependable adjective
Are these friends of yours **dependable***?*
reliable, trustworthy, loyal, faithful, trusty, honest, sound, steady
OPPOSITE unreliable

depressed adjective
After his friends left, he began to feel **depressed***.*
disheartened, dejected, discouraged, downcast, downhearted, unhappy, sad, low, gloomy, glum, melancholy, miserable, despondent, desolate, in despair
(*informal*) down
OPPOSITE cheerful

derelict adjective
They plan to pull down those **derelict** *buildings.*
dilapidated, crumbling, decrepit, neglected, deserted, abandoned, ruined

descend verb
1 *After admiring the view, we began to* **descend** *the mountain.*
climb down, come down, go down, move down
To descend through the air is to **drop** *or* **fall***.*
To descend through water is to **sink***.*
2 *The road* **descends** *gradually into the valley.*
drop, fall, slope, dip, incline
OPPOSITE ascend
to be descended from someone
She's **descended from** *a French family.*
come from, originate from

describe verb
1 *An eyewitness* **described** *how the accident happened.*
report, tell about, depict, explain, outline
2 *Friends* **described** *him as a quiet, shy man.*
portray, characterize, represent, present

description noun
1 *I wrote a* **description** *of our day at the seaside.*
report, account, story
2 *Write a* **description** *of your favourite character in the play.*
portrait, representation, sketch

descriptive adjective
The author writes in a very **descriptive** *style.*
expressive, colourful, detailed, graphic, vivid

desert verb
He **deserted** *his friends when they needed him most.*
abandon, leave, forsake, betray
(*informal*) walk out on
To desert someone in a place they can't get away from is to **maroon** *or* **strand** *them.*

deserted adjective
By midnight, the streets of the town were **deserted***.*
empty, unoccupied, uninhabited, vacant
OPPOSITE crowded

deserve verb
You **deserve** *a break after all your hard work.*
be worthy of, be entitled to, have earned, merit, warrant

design noun
1 *This is the winning* **design** *for the new art gallery.*
plan, drawing, outline, blueprint, sketch
A first example of something, used as a model for making others, is a **prototype***.*
2 *Do you like the* **design** *of this wallpaper?*
style, pattern, arrangement, composition

design verb
She **designs** *all her own clothes.*
create, develop, invent, devise, conceive, think up

desire verb
The magic mirror will show you what you most **desire***.*
wish for, long for, want, crave, fancy, hanker after, yearn for, pine for, set your heart on, have a yen for

desire noun
*My greatest **desire** is to swim with dolphins.*
wish, want, longing, ambition, urge, craving, fancy, hankering, yearning
A desire for food is **appetite** or **hunger**.
A desire for drink is **thirst**.
Excessive desire for money or other things is **greed**.

desolate adjective
1 *Jamie felt **desolate** when his goldfish died.*
depressed, dejected, miserable, sad, melancholy, hopeless, wretched, forlorn
OPPOSITE cheerful
2 *No-one wants to live in that **desolate** place.*
bleak, depressing, dreary, gloomy, dismal, cheerless, inhospitable, deserted, uninhabited, abandoned, godforsaken
OPPOSITE pleasant

despair noun
*The defeated knight was overcome by **despair**.*
depression, desperation, gloom, hopelessness, misery, anguish, dejection, melancholy, pessimism, wretchedness
OPPOSITE hope

desperate adjective
1 *The shipwrecked crew were in a **desperate** situation.*
difficult, critical, grave, serious, severe, drastic, dire, urgent, extreme
2 *The hills were home to a band of **desperate** outlaws.*
dangerous, violent, reckless

despise verb
*I **despise** people who cheat at cards.*
hate, loathe, feel contempt for, deride, have a low opinion of, look down on, scorn, sneer at
OPPOSITE admire

destiny noun
***Destiny** brought us together*
fate, fortune

destroy verb
1 *An avalanche **destroyed** the village.*
demolish, devastate, crush, flatten, knock down, level, pull down, shatter, smash, sweep away
2 *He tried to **destroy** the good work we had done.*
ruin, wreck, sabotage, undo

destruction noun
1 *The hurricane caused **destruction** all along the coast.*
devastation, damage, demolition, ruin, wrecking
OPPOSITE creation

2 *Global warming may cause the **destruction** of many animal species.*
elimination, annihilation, obliteration, extermination, extinction
OPPOSITE conservation

detach verb
*The camera lens can be **detached** for cleaning.*
remove, separate, disconnect, take off, release, undo, unfasten, part
To detach a caravan from a vehicle is to **unhitch** it.
To detach railway wagons from a locomotive is to **uncouple** them.
To detach something by cutting it off is to **sever** it.
OPPOSITE attach

detail noun
*Her account of what happened was accurate in every **detail**.*
fact, feature, particular, aspect, item, point, respect

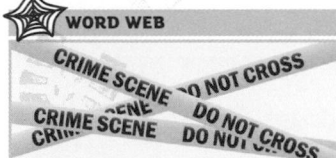

🕸 WORD WEB

detective noun
***Detective** Dewar solved the case of the stolen tiara.*
investigator, sleuth
(*informal*) private eye

THINGS A DETECTIVE MIGHT LOOK FOR
clues, evidence, eyewitness, fingerprints, footprints, murder weapon, tracks, criminal, crook, culprit, felon, suspect

THINGS A DETECTIVE MIGHT DO
analyse, comb (an area), deduce, deduct, detect, dig up, ferret out, follow a hunch, follow a lead or a tip-off, interrogate or question (a witness), investigate, pursue, shadow, solve (a case), stake out (a hiding place), tail or track down (a suspect)

An informal name for a story in which a detective solves a crime is a **whodunnit**.

deteriorate verb
1 *The queen's health had begun to **deteriorate**.*
worsen, decline, degenerate, get worse, go downhill
2 *The walls will **deteriorate** if we don't maintain them.*
decay, disintegrate, crumble
OPPOSITE improve

determination noun
*Marathon runners show great **determination**.*
resolve, commitment, will-power, courage, dedication, drive, grit, perseverance, persistence, spirit
(*informal*) guts

determined adjective
1 *Boudicca must have been a **determined** woman.*
resolute, decisive, strong-minded, assertive, persistent, tough, firm
OPPOSITE weak-minded
2 *I'm **determined** to finish the race.*
committed, resolved

detest verb
*I **detest** the smell of boiled cabbage.*
dislike, hate, loathe
Informal expressions are **can't bear** and **can't stand**.
OPPOSITE love

develop verb
1 *The zoo is **developing** its education programme.*
expand, extend, enlarge, build up, diversify
2 *Her piano playing has **developed** this year.*
improve, progress, evolve, advance, get better
3 *The plants will **develop** quickly in the spring.*
grow, flourish
4 *How did he **develop** that posh accent?*
get, acquire, pick up, cultivate

device noun
*The TV comes with a remote control **device**.*
tool, implement, instrument, appliance, apparatus, gadget, contraption
(*informal*) gizmo

devious adjective
1 *The mad professor had a **devious** plan to take over the world.*
cunning, deceitful, dishonest, furtive, scheming, sly, sneaky, treacherous, wily
2 *Because of the roadworks, we took a **devious** route home.*
indirect, roundabout, winding, meandering
OPPOSITE direct

a b c d e f g h i j k l m n o p q r s t u v w x y z

devoted *adjective*
*She's a **devoted** supporter of our team.*
loyal, faithful, dedicated, enthusiastic, committed
OPPOSITE apathetic

devour *verb*
*He **devoured** a whole plateful of sandwiches.*
eat, consume, guzzle, gobble up, gulp down, swallow
(*informal*) scoff, wolf down

diagram *noun*
*We drew a **diagram** of the life cycle of a frog.*
chart, plan, sketch, outline

diary *noun*
*I write all about my birthday party in my **diary**.*
journal, daily record
A diary describing a voyage or mission is a *log* or *logbook*.
A diary in which you insert pictures and souvenirs is a *scrapbook*.
A diary published on a website is a *blog*.

die *verb*
1 *My sister's hamster **died** last week.*
expire, pass away, perish
(*informal*) snuff it, kick the bucket, croak
To die of hunger is to *starve*.
2 *The flowers will **die** if they don't have water.*
wither, wilt, droop, fade
to die out
*When did the dinosaurs **die out**?*
become extinct, cease to exist, come to an end, disappear, vanish

differ *verb*
*The two men **differed** in their beliefs.*
disagree, conflict, argue, clash, contradict each other, oppose each other, quarrel
OPPOSITE agree
to differ from
*My style of painting **differs from** hers.*
be different from, contrast with

difference *noun*
1 *Can you see any **difference** between these two colours?*
contrast, distinction
OPPOSITE similarity
2 *This money will make a **difference** to their lives.*
change, alteration, modification, variation

different *adjective*
1 *We have **different** views about global warming.*
differing, contradictory, opposite, clashing, conflicting
2 *It's important that the teams wear **different** colours.*
contrasting, dissimilar, distinguishable
3 *The packet contains sweets of **different** flavours.*
various, assorted, mixed, several, diverse, numerous, miscellaneous
4 *Let's go somewhere **different** on holiday this year.*
new, original, fresh
5 *Everyone's handwriting is **different**.*
distinct, distinctive, individual, special, unique

difficult *adjective*
1 *This crossword is really **difficult**. We were faced with a **difficult** problem.*
hard, complicated, complex, involved, intricate, baffling, perplexing, puzzling
(*informal*) tricky, thorny, knotty
OPPOSITE simple
2 *It is a **difficult** climb to the top of the hill.*
challenging, arduous, demanding, taxing, exhausting, formidable, gruelling, laborious, strenuous, tough
OPPOSITE easy
3 *Mum says I was a **difficult** child when I was little.*
troublesome, awkward, trying, tiresome, annoying, disruptive, obstinate, stubborn, uncooperative, unhelpful
OPPOSITE cooperative

difficulty *noun*
1 *The explorers were used to facing **difficulty**.*
trouble, adversity, challenges, hardship
2 *There are some **difficulties** with your application.*
problem, complication, hitch, obstacle, snag

dig *verb*
1 *We spent the afternoon **digging** the garden.*
cultivate, fork over, turn over

2 *Rabbits **dig** holes in the ground.*
burrow, excavate, tunnel, gouge out, hollow out, scoop out
3 *Did you **dig** me in the back?*
poke, prod, jab

dignified *adjective*
*Lady Snodgrass was a very **dignified** old lady.*
refined, stately, distinguished, noble, sedate, solemn, proper, grave, grand, august
OPPOSITE undignified

dim *adjective*
1 *I could see the **dim** outline of a figure in the mist.*
indistinct, faint, blurred, fuzzy, hazy, shadowy, vague
OPPOSITE clear
2 *The light in the cave was rather **dim**.*
dark, dull, dingy, murky, gloomy
OPPOSITE bright

din *noun*
*I can't hear you because of that awful **din**!*
noise, racket, row, clatter, hullabaloo

dingy *adjective*
*How can we brighten up this **dingy** room?*
dull, drab, dreary, dowdy, colourless, dismal, gloomy, murky
OPPOSITE bright

✦ WORD WEB

dinosaur *noun*
SOME TYPES OF DINOSAUR
apatosaurus, archaeopteryx, brachiosaurus, diplodocus, gallimimus, iguanodon, megalosaurus, pterodactylus, stegosaurus, triceratops, tyrannosaurus rex, velociraptor

BODY PARTS WHICH A DINOSAUR MAY HAVE
dorsal plates, bony frill, fleshy fin, horn, wings, crest

A person who studies dinosaurs and other fossils is a *palaeontologist*.

dip verb
*I **dipped** my hand in the water.*
immerse, lower, plunge, submerge, dunk

dip noun
1 *There was a **dip** in the road ahead.*
hollow, hole, depression, slope
2 *It was so hot we decided to have a **dip** in the sea.*
swim, bathe

direct adjective
1 *It would be quicker to take the **direct** route.*
straight, shortest
OPPOSITE indirect
2 *Please give me a **direct** answer.*
straightforward, frank, honest, sincere, blunt, plain, outspoken, candid, unambiguous
OPPOSITE evasive

direct verb
1 *Can you **direct** me to the station?*
guide, point, show the way, give directions to
2 *A new manager has been apppointed to **direct** the company.*
manage, run, be in charge of, control, administer, superintend, supervise, take charge of
To direct an orchestra is to **conduct** it.
3 *The conductor **directed** us to begin playing.*
instruct, command, order, tell

dirt noun
1 *The floor was covered in **dirt**.*
filth, grime, mess, muck, mud, dust
2 *Chickens scratched about in the **dirt**.*
earth, soil, clay, loam, mud

dirty adjective
1 *Those **dirty** clothes need to be washed.*
unclean, filthy, grimy, grubby, soiled, stained, messy, mucky, muddy, sooty, foul
(*informal*) manky, grotty
OPPOSITE clean
2 *We refused to drink the **dirty** water.*
impure, polluted, murky, cloudy
OPPOSITE pure
3 *The other team used **dirty** tactics.*
unfair, dishonest, illegal, mean, unsporting
OPPOSITE honest
4 *The comedian used a lot of **dirty** words.*
rude,

offensive, coarse, crude, improper, indecent, obscene
OPPOSITE decent

disadvantage noun
*It's a **disadvantage** to be small if you play basketball.*
drawback, handicap, hindrance, inconvenience, downside, snag

disagree verb
*My sister and I often **disagree** about music.*
argue, differ, clash, quarrel, squabble, bicker, fall out
OPPOSITE agree
to disagree with
*He **disagrees with** everything I say.*
argue with, contradict, oppose, object to

disagreement noun
*We had a **disagreement** over who should pay for the meal.*
argument, dispute, difference of opinion, quarrel, row, clash, squabble, conflict
OPPOSITE agreement

disappear verb
1 *The markings will **disappear** as the chicks grow older.*
become invisible, vanish, fade, clear, disperse, dissolve
2 *The thief **disappeared** around the corner.*
run away, escape, flee, go away, withdraw
OPPOSITE appear

disappoint verb
*She didn't want to **disappoint** her fans by cancelling the show.*
let down, fail, dissatisfy, displease, upset
OPPOSITE please, satisfy

disappointed adjective
*I'm **disappointed** that you can't come to my party.*
saddened, unhappy, upset, let down, unsatisfied, displeased
OPPOSITE pleased, satisfied

disapprove verb
to disapprove of
*My aunt **disapproves of** watching television.*
object to, take exception to, dislike, deplore, condemn, criticize, denounce, frown on
(*informal*) take a dim view of
OPPOSITE approve of

discipline noun
***Discipline** is important in the army.*
order, control

discourage verb
1 *Don't let her criticism **discourage** you.*
demoralize, depress
(*informal*) put you off

2 *The burglar alarm will **discourage** thieves.*
deter, dissuade, prevent, restrain, stop, hinder

discover verb
*I **discovered** some old toys in the attic.*
find, come across, spot, stumble across, uncover
To discover something that has been buried is to **unearth** it.
To discover something that has been under water is to **dredge it up**.
To discover something you have been pursuing is to **track it down**.
OPPOSITE hide

discovery noun
*Scientists have made an exciting new **discovery**.*
find, breakthrough

discrimination noun
1 *She shows **discrimination** in her choice of music.*
good taste, good judgement
2 *The school has a policy against racial **discrimination**.*
prejudice, bias, intolerance, unfairness
Discrimination against people because of their sex is **sexism**.
Discrimination against people because of their race is **racism**.

discuss verb
*I **discussed** the idea with my parents.*
talk about, confer about, debate

discussion noun
*We had a lively **discussion** about pocket money.*
conversation, argument, exchange of views
*A formal discussion is a **conference** or **debate**.*

disease noun
*He suffers from a serious **disease**.*
illness, ailment, sickness, complaint, affliction
(*informal*) bug

disgrace noun
1 *He never got over the **disgrace** of being caught cheating.*
humiliation, shame, embarrassment, dishonour
2 *The way he treats it is a **disgrace**!*
outrage, scandal

disgraceful adjective
*We were shocked by her **disgraceful** behaviour.*
shameful, shocking, appalling, outrageous, scandalous
OPPOSITE honourable

disguise verb
*I tried to **disguise** my feelings.*
conceal, hide, cover up, camouflage, mask
to disguise yourself as
*The spy **disguised himself as** a hotel porter.*
dress up as, pretend to be

disguise noun
*I didn't recognize him in that **disguise**.*
costume, camouflage, make-up, mask

disgust noun
*The sight of the carcass filled me with **disgust**.*
repulsion, repugnance, distaste, dislike, horror, loathing, detestation
OPPOSITE liking

disgust verb
*The smell of rotten eggs **disgusts** me.*
repel, revolt, sicken, appal, offend, distress, shock, horrify
(*informal*) put you off, turn your stomach
OPPOSITE please

disgusting adjective
*The brew in the cauldron looked **disgusting**.*
repulsive, revolting, horrible, sickening, loathsome, nasty, repellent, repugnant, offensive, appalling, nauseating
(*informal*) yucky, icky, gross
OPPOSITE delightful, pleasing

dishonest adjective
1 *They were taken in by a **dishonest** salesman.*
deceitful, cheating, corrupt, disreputable, untrustworthy, immoral, lying, swindling, thieving
(*informal*) bent, crooked, dodgy, shady

2 *The author makes some **dishonest** claims.*
false, misleading, untruthful, fraudulent, devious

dishonesty noun
*The MP was accused of **dishonesty**.*
deceit, cheating, corruption, insincerity, lying, deviousness
(*informal*) crookedness
OPPOSITE honesty

disintegrate verb
*The cloth is so old that it's starting to **disintegrate**.*
break up, fall apart, break into pieces, crumble, decay, decompose

dislike noun
*His colleagues regarded him with intense **dislike**.*
hatred, loathing, detestation, disapproval, disgust, revulsion
OPPOSITE liking

dislike verb
*I **dislike** people who hunt wild animals.*
hate, loathe, detest, disapprove of
OPPOSITE like

disloyal adjective
*The rebels were accused of being **disloyal** to the king.*
unfaithful, treacherous, faithless, false, unreliable, untrustworthy
OPPOSITE loyal

dismal adjective
1 *How can we brighten up this **dismal** room?*
dull, drab, dreary, dingy, colourless, cheerless, gloomy, murky
OPPOSITE bright, cheerful
2 (*informal*) *It was a **dismal** performance by the home team.*
dreadful, awful, terrible, feeble, useless, hopeless
(*informal*) pathetic
OPPOSITE bright, cheerful

dismay noun
*We listened with **dismay** to the bad news.*
distress, alarm, shock, concern, anxiety, gloom

dismiss verb
1 *The teacher **dismissed** the class.*
send away, discharge, free, let go, release
2 *The firm **dismissed** ten workers.*
sack, give the sack, give notice to, make redundant
(*informal*) fire
3 *The weather was so bad that we **dismissed** the idea of having a picnic.*
discard, drop, reject

disobedient adjective
*She said she had never known such a **disobedient** child.*
naughty, badly behaved, undisciplined, uncontrollable, unmanageable, unruly, ungovernable, troublesome, defiant, disruptive, mutinous, rebellious, contrary
OPPOSITE obedient

disobey verb
1 *You will be penalized if you **disobey** the rules.*
break, ignore, disregard, defy, violate
2 *Soldiers are trained never to **disobey**.*
be disobedient, rebel, revolt, mutiny
OPPOSITE obey

display verb
*We planned the best way to **display** our work.*
demonstrate, exhibit, present, put on show, set out, show, show off
*To display something boastfully is to **flaunt** it.*

display noun
*We set out a **display** of our art work.*
exhibition, show, presentation, demonstration

disrespectful adjective
*She was very **disrespectful** towards her parents.*
rude, bad-mannered, insulting, impolite, insolent, cheeky
OPPOSITE respectful

disrupt verb
*Bad weather has **disrupted** the tennis tournament.*
interrupt, upset, interfere with, throw into confusion or disorder

dissatisfied adjective
*I was **dissatisfied** with my piano playing.*
displeased, disappointed, discontented, frustrated, annoyed
OPPOSITE satisfied

distance noun
*What is the **distance** from Earth to the Sun?*
measurement, space, extent, reach, mileage
*The distance across something is the **breadth** or **width**.*
*The distance along something is the **length**.*
*The distance between two points is a **gap** or **interval**.*

distant adjective
1 *I'd love to travel to **distant** countries.*
faraway, remote, out-of-the-way, inaccessible, exotic
OPPOSITE close

2 *His distant manner puts me off.*
unfriendly, unapproachable, formal, reserved, withdrawn, cool, haughty, aloof
OPPOSITE friendly

distinct adjective
1 *There is a distinct improvement in your handwriting.*
definite, evident, noticeable, obvious, perceptible
OPPOSITE imperceptible
2 *It was a small photo, but the details were quite distinct.*
clear, distinguishable, plain, recognizable, sharp, unmistakable, visible, well defined
OPPOSITE indistinct
3 *Organize your essay into distinct sections.*
individual, separate

distinguish verb
1 *It was impossible to distinguish one twin from the other.*
tell apart, pick out, discriminate, differentiate, make a distinction, decide
2 *In the dark we couldn't distinguish who was walking past.*
identify, tell, make out, determine, perceive, recognize, single out

distress verb
We could see that the bad news distressed her.
upset, disturb, trouble, worry, alarm, dismay, torment
OPPOSITE comfort

distribute verb
1 *The coach distributed water to the players at half-time.*
give out, hand round, circulate, dispense, issue, share out, take round
(*informal*) dish out, doll out
2 *Distribute the seeds evenly.*
scatter, spread, disperse

distrust verb
I distrusted the professor from the moment I met him.
doubt, mistrust, question, suspect, be suspicious or wary of, be sceptical about, feel uncertain or uneasy or unsure about
OPPOSITE trust

disturb verb
1 *Don't disturb the baby when she's asleep.*
bother, interrupt, annoy, pester
2 *They were disturbed by the bad news.*
distress, trouble, upset, worry, alarm, frighten
3 *Please don't disturb the papers on my desk.*
muddle, mix up, move around, mess about with

ditch noun
We dug a ditch to drain away the water.
trench, channel, drain, gully

dive

dive verb
1 *The mermaid dived into the water.*
plunge, jump, leap
A dive in which you land flat on your front is a *bellyflop*.
2 *The eagle dived towards its prey.*
pounce, swoop

divide verb
1 *We divided the class into two groups.*
separate, split, break up, move apart, part
OPPOSITE combine
2 *I divided the cake between my friends.*
distribute, share out, give out, allot, deal out, dispense
3 *Which way do we go? The path divides here.*
branch, fork
OPPOSITE converge

dizzy adjective
Going on a roundabout makes me feel dizzy.
dazed, giddy, faint, reeling, unsteady

do verb
1 *My friend always knows what to do in a crisis.*
act, behave, conduct yourself
2 *The vet has a lot of work to do this morning.*
attend to, cope with, deal with, handle, look after, perform, undertake
3 *It took me half an hour to do the washing-up.*
accomplish, achieve, carry out, complete, execute, finish
4 *I need to do all of these sums.*
answer, puzzle out, solve, work out
5 *Staring at the sun can do damage to your eyes.*
bring about, cause, produce, result in
6 *If you don't have lemonade, water will do.*
be acceptable, be enough, be satisfactory, be sufficient, serve

dock noun
A boat was waiting for us at the end of the dock.
harbour, quay, jetty, wharf, landing stage, dockyard, pier, port, marina

dodge verb
I just managed to dodge the snowball.
avoid, evade, side-step

dominate verb
The visiting team dominated the game.
control, direct, monopolize, govern, take control of, take over

donation noun
The museum relies on donations from the public.
contribution, gift, offering

done adjective
1 *All my thank-you letters are done.*
finished, complete, over
2 *The cake will be brown on top when it's done.*
cooked, ready

doomed adjective
The expedition was doomed from the start.
ill-fated, condemned, fated, cursed, jinxed, damned

door noun
A door in a floor or ceiling is a *hatch* or *trapdoor*.
The plank or stone underneath a door is the *threshold*.
The beam or stone above a door is the *lintel*.
The device on which most doors swing is the *hinge*.

dot noun
She was furious when she saw dots of paint on the carpet.
spot, speck, fleck, point, mark
The dot you always put at the end of a sentence is a *full stop*.
on the dot
(*informal*) *We left the house at nine o'clock on the dot.*
exactly, precisely

double adjective
You enter the room through a double set of doors.
dual, twofold, paired, twin, matching, duplicate

double noun
She's so like you—she's almost your double.
twin
(*informal*) lookalike, spitting image, dead ringer
A living organism created as an exact copy of another living organism is a *clone*.

doubt noun
1 *Have you any doubt about his honesty?*
distrust, suspicion, mistrust, hesitation, reservation, scepticism
OPPOSITE confidence

2 *There is no* **doubt** *that you will pass your exam.*
question, uncertainty, ambiguity, confusion
OPPOSITE certainty

doubt *verb*
There is no reason to **doubt** *her story.*
distrust, feel uncertain or uneasy or unsure about, question, mistrust, suspect, be sceptical about, be suspicious or wary of
OPPOSITE trust

doubtful *adjective*
He looked **doubtful***, but agreed to let us go.*
unsure, uncertain, unconvinced, hesitant, distrustful, sceptical, suspicious
OPPOSITE certain

doze *verb*
Dad often **dozes** *in the evening.*
rest, sleep, nod off
(*informal*) drop off

drab *adjective*
That dress is too **drab** *to wear to the party.*
dull, dingy, dreary, cheerless, colourless, dismal, gloomy, grey
OPPOSITE bright, cheerful

draft *noun*
I jotted down a **draft** *of my story.*
outline, plan, sketch, rough version

draft *verb*
I began to **draft** *my story.*
outline, plan, prepare, sketch, work out

drag *verb*
The tractor **dragged** *the car out of the ditch.*

pull, tow, tug, draw, haul, lug
OPPOSITE push

drain *verb*
1 *If they* **drain** *the marsh, lots of waterbirds will die.*
dry out, remove water from
2 *She* **drained** *the oil from the engine.*
draw off, empty
3 *The water slowly* **drained** *away.*
trickle, ooze, seep
4 *The tough climb* **drained** *my energy.*
use up, consume, exhaust

drastic *adjective*
After being without food for three days, the explorers needed to take **drastic** *action.*
desperate, extreme, radical, harsh, severe
OPPOSITE moderate

draw *verb*
1 *I* **drew** *some pictures of the flowers in our garden.*
sketch, trace, doodle
2 *I'm not very good at* **drawing** *faces.*
depict, portray, represent
3 *The horse was* **drawing** *a cart.*
pull, tow, drag, haul, tug, lug

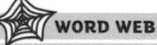

4 *We expect tomorrow's match to* **draw** *a big crowd.*
attract, bring in, pull in
5 *The two teams* **drew** *1–1.*
finish equal, tie
to draw near
As the spaceship **drew near***, I began to get nervous.*
approach, advance, come near

drawback *noun*
It's a **drawback** *to be small if you play basketball.*
disadvantage, difficulty, handicap, obstacle, inconvenience, hindrance, downside, snag

dread *noun*
Our teacher has a **dread** *of spiders.*
fear, horror, terror, phobia (about), anxiety (about)

dreadful *adjective*
1 *There has been a* **dreadful** *accident at sea.*
horrible, terrible, appalling, horrendous, distressing, shocking, upsetting, tragic, grim
2 *The weather at the weekend was* **dreadful***.*
bad, awful, terrible, abysmal, abominable, dire, foul, nasty
OPPOSITE good, pleasant

dream *noun*
A bad dream is a **nightmare***.*
A dreamlike experience you have while awake is a **daydream, fantasy,** *or* **reverie***.*
Something you see in a dream or daydream is a **vision***.*
The dreamlike state when you are hypnotized is a **trance***.*
Something you think you see that is not real is a **hallucination** *or* **illusion***.*

dreary *adjective*
1 *The newsreader had a very* **dreary** *voice.*
dull, boring, flat, tedious, unexciting, uninteresting
OPPOSITE lively
2 *When will this* **dreary** *weather end?*
depressing, dismal, dull, gloomy, cheerless, murky, overcast
OPPOSITE bright, sunny

dress *noun*
1 *What kind of* **dress** *are you wearing to the party?*
frock, gown
2 *The invitation said to wear casual* **dress***.*
clothes, clothing, outfit, costume, garments

🕷️ **WORD WEB**

dragon *noun*
A fearsome **dragon** *once lived in these hills.*

SOME WAYS TO DESCRIBE A DRAGON
ancient, fearsome, fiery, fire-breathing, mighty, monstrous, scaly

BODY PARTS A DRAGON MIGHT HAVE
claws, crest, forked tail or tongue, scales, spikes or spines, bat-like wings

A DRAGON'S SCALES MIGHT BE
dazzling, iridescent, patterned, shimmering

A DRAGON'S BREATH MIGHT BE
fiery, flaming, scorching, searing

THINGS A DRAGON MIGHT DO
breathe fire, puff smoke, roar, snort, change shape, fly, swoop

PLACES WHERE A DRAGON MIGHT LIVE
cave, den, lair

dress verb
1 *I helped to **dress** my little brother.*
clothe, put clothes on
OPPOSITE undress
2 *A nurse **dressed** my wound.*
bandage, put a dressing on, bind up

dribble verb
1 *Careful, the baby's **dribbling** on your jumper.*
drool
2 *Water **dribbled** out of the hole in the tank.*
drip, trickle, leak, ooze, seep

drift verb
1 *The boat **drifted** downstream.*
float, be carried, move slowly
2 *The crowd lost interest and **drifted** away.*
stray, wander, meander, ramble, walk aimlessly
3 *The snow will **drift** in this wind.*
pile up, accumulate, make drifts

drift noun
1 *The car was stuck in a snow **drift**.*
bank, heap, mound, pile, ridge
2 *Did you understand the **drift** of the speech?*
gist, main idea, point

drill verb
*It took a long time to **drill** through the wall.*
bore, penetrate, pierce

drink verb
To drink greedily is to **gulp**, **guzzle**, or **swig**.
To drink noisily is to **slurp**.
To drink a small amount at a time is to **sip**.
To drink with the tongue as a cat does is to **lap**.

drip noun
*Dad was worried by the **drips** of oil underneath the car.*
spot, dribble, splash, trickle

drip verb
*The oil **dripped** onto the garage floor.*
drop, leak, dribble, splash, trickle

drive verb
1 *The dog **drove** the sheep through the gate.*
direct, guide, herd
2 *I couldn't **drive** the spade into the hard ground.*
push, thrust, hammer, plunge, ram
3 *When can I learn to **drive** a car?*
control, handle, manage
4 *Lack of money **drove** him to steal.*
force, compel, oblige
to drive someone out
*The invading soldiers **drove** the people **out**.*
eject, expel, throw out
To drive people out of their homes is to **evict** them.

To drive people out of their country is to **banish** or exile them.

drive noun
1 *We went for a **drive** in the country.*
ride, trip, journey, outing, excursion, jaunt
2 *Have you got the **drive** to succeed?*
ambition, determination, keenness, motivation, energy, zeal

droop verb
*Plants tend to **droop** in dry weather.*
sag, wilt, bend, flop, be limp

drop noun
1 *Large **drops** of rain began to fall.*
drip, droplet, spot, bead, blob
2 *Could I have another **drop** of milk in my tea?*
dash, small quantity
3 *We expect a **drop** in the price of fruit in the summer.*
decrease, reduction, cut
4 *There's a **drop** of two metres on the other side of the wall.*
fall, descent, plunge

drop verb
1 *The hawk **dropped** onto its prey.*
descend, dive, plunge, swoop
2 *I **dropped** to the ground exhausted.*
collapse, fall, sink, subside, slump, tumble
3 *Why did you **drop** me from the team?*
omit, eliminate, exclude, leave out
4 *They **dropped** the plan for a new bypass.*
abandon, discard, reject, give up, scrap

drown verb
*The music from upstairs **drowned** our conversation.*
overwhelm, overpower, drown out

drowsy adjective
*If you feel **drowsy**, why not go to bed?*
sleepy, tired, weary

drug noun
*A new **drug** has been discovered for back pain.*
medicine, remedy, treatment
A drug which relieves pain is an **analgesic** or **painkiller**.
A drug which calms you down is a **sedative** or **tranquillizer**.
Drugs which make you more active are **stimulants**.

dry adjective
1 *Nothing will grow in this **dry** soil.*
arid, parched, moistureless, waterless, dehydrated, desiccated, barren
A common simile is **as dry as a bone**.
OPPOSITE wet

2 *He gave rather a **dry** speech.*
dull, boring, dreary, tedious, uninteresting
OPPOSITE interesting
3 *I can't understand his **dry** sense of humour.*
ironic, wry, witty, subtle

duck verb
*Oliver **ducked** to avoid the snowball.*
bend down, bob down, crouch, stoop

dull adjective
1 *I don't like **dull** colours.*
dim, dingy, drab, dreary, dismal, faded, gloomy, sombre, subdued
OPPOSITE bright, colourful
2 *The sky was **dull** that day.*
cloudy, overcast, grey, sunless, murky
OPPOSITE clear
3 *I heard a **dull** thud from upstairs.*
indistinct, muffled, muted
OPPOSITE distinct
4 *He's rather a **dull** student.*
stupid, slow, unintelligent, dim, unimaginative, dense, obtuse, (informal) thick
OPPOSITE clever
5 *The play was so **dull** that I fell asleep.*
boring, dry, monotonous, tedious, uninteresting, unexciting, lacklustre
A common simile is **as dull as ditchwater**.
OPPOSITE interesting

dumb adjective
1 *The spectators were struck **dumb** with amazement.*
If you do not speak, you are **mute** or **silent**.
If you cannot speak because you are surprised, confused, or embarrassed, you are **speechless** or **tongue-tied**.
If you find it hard to express yourself, you are **inarticulate**.
2 *(informal) He's too **dumb** to understand.*
stupid, unintelligent, dim, slow, dense, obtuse, (informal) thick

dump verb
1 *I decided to **dump** some of my old toys.*
get rid of, throw away, throw out, discard, dispose of, scrap
2 *Just **dump** your things in the bedroom.*
put down, set down, deposit, place, drop, throw down, tip

dusk noun
*Bats begin to emerge at **dusk**.*
twilight, nightfall, sunset, sundown
OPPOSITE dawn

duty noun
1 *I have a **duty** to help my parents.*
responsibility, obligation

a b c d e f g h i j k l m n o p q r s t u v w x y z

2 *I carried out my duties conscientiously.*
job, task, assignment, chore
3 *The government has increased the duty on petrol.*
charge, tax

dwindle *verb*
Our enthusiasm dwindled as the day went on.
become less, diminish, decline, decrease, lessen, subside, wane, weaken
OPPOSITE increase

dynamic *adjective*
The team has a new, dynamic captain.
energetic, lively, enthusiastic, vigorous, active, forceful, powerful
OPPOSITE apathetic

eager *adjective*
He is always eager to help.
keen, enthusiastic, desperate, anxious
OPPOSITE unenthusiastic

early *adjective*
1 *The bus was early today.*
ahead of time, ahead of schedule
OPPOSITE late
2 *The early computers were huge machines.*
first, old, primitive, ancient
OPPOSITE recent, new

earth *noun*
The earth was so dry that many plants died.
ground, land, soil
Rich, fertile earth is *loam*.
The top layer of fertile earth is *topsoil*.
Rich earth consisting of decayed plants is *humus*.
A heavy, sticky kind of earth is *clay*.

easy *adjective*
1 *Tonight's homework is really easy.*
undemanding, effortless, light
An informal word for an easy task is a *doddle*.
2 *The instructions were easy to understand.*
simple, straightforward, clear, plain, elementary
A common simile is *as easy as ABC*.
3 *Our cat has an easy life.*
carefree, comfortable, peaceful, relaxed, leisurely, restful, tranquil, untroubled
OPPOSITE difficult

eat *verb*
Hannah was eating a cheese sandwich.
consume, devour
(*informal*) scoff
When cattle eat grass they are *grazing*.
A person who eats a large amount is said to *eat like a horse*.
I was so hungry, I wolfed down a whole pizza.
bolt down, gobble, gulp, guzzle, gorge, polish off, wolf down
Rabbits like to chomp raw carrots.
chomp, crunch, gnash, gnaw, munch, slurp
Do you have any biscuits we could nibble?
nibble, peck, pick at or pick away at, taste
Mr Hogg was savouring a sausage roll.
relish, savour, tuck into
The guests will be dining in the great hall.
banquet, dine, feast

eccentric *adjective*
What is the reason for his eccentric behaviour?
odd, peculiar, strange, weird, abnormal, unusual, curious, unconventional, unorthodox, quirky, zany
(*informal*) way-out, dotty
OPPOSITE conventional, orthodox

echo *verb*
1 *The sound echoed across the valley.*
resound, reverberate
2 *'He's gone home.' 'Gone home?' she echoed.*
repeat, imitate, mimic

ecstatic *adjective*
Samantha was feeling ecstatic about her party.
elated, delighted, overjoyed, gleeful, joyful, blissful, rapturous, euphoric, exultant, delirious, fervent, frenzied

edge *noun*
The edge of a cliff or other steep place is the *brink*.

The edge of a cup or other container is the *brim* or *rim*.
The line round the edge of a circle is the *circumference*.
The line round the edge of any other shape is its *outline*.
The distance round the edge of an area is the *perimeter*.
The stones along the edge of a road are the *kerb*.
Grass along the edge of a road is the *verge*.
The space down the edge of a page is the *margin*.
The space round the edge of a picture is a *border*.
Something that fits round the edge of a picture is a *frame*.
The edge of a garment is the *hem*.
An edge with threads or hair hanging loosely down is a *fringe*.
The edge of a crowd also is the *fringe* of the crowd.
The area round the edge of a city is the *outskirts* or *suburbs*.
The edge of a cricket field is the *boundary*.
The edge of a football pitch is the *touchline*.

edge *verb*
1 *We edged away from the lion's den.*
creep, inch, move stealthily, steal, slink
2 *Her bonnet was edged with black lace.*
trim, hem

edgy *adjective*
Horses become edgy during thunderstorms.
nervous, restless, anxious, agitated, excitable, tense, jumpy, fidgety
(*informal*) uptight, jittery
OPPOSITE calm

educate *verb*
The job of a school is to educate young people.
teach, train, inform, instruct, tutor

eerie *adjective*
I heard some eerie sounds in the night.
strange, weird, uncanny, mysterious, frightening, creepy, ghostly, sinister, unearthly, unnatural
(*informal*) scary, spooky

effect *noun*
1 *The effect of eating too much was that I became fat!*
result, consequence, outcome, sequel, upshot
2 *Does this music have any effect on you?*
impact, influence
3 *The lighting gives an effect of warmth.*
feeling, impression, sense, illusion

efficient *adjective*
1 *An **efficient** worker can do the job in an hour.*
effective, competent, able, capable, proficient
2 *Dad tried to work out an **efficient** way of heating our house.*
economic, productive

effort *noun*
1 *A lot of **effort** went into making the film.*
work, trouble, exertion, industry, labour, toil
2 *She congratulated us on a good **effort**.*
attempt, try, endeavour, go, shot

elaborate *adjective*
*The plot of the book is so **elaborate** that I got lost halfway through.*
complicated, complex, detailed, intricate, involved, convoluted
OPPOSITE simple

elect *verb*
*We **elected** a new captain.*
vote for, appoint

elegant *adjective*
*She always wears **elegant** clothes.*
graceful, stylish, fashionable, chic, smart, tasteful, sophisticated
OPPOSITE inelegant

eliminate *verb*
*The government wants to **eliminate** crime.*
get rid of, put an end to
To be eliminated from a competition is to be **knocked out**.

embarrass *verb*
*Will it **embarrass** you if I tell people our secret?*
humiliate, distress, mortify, make you blush

embarrassed *adjective*
*Don't feel **embarrassed**—it happens to everyone!*
humiliated, ashamed, awkward, uncomfortable, bashful, distressed, flustered, mortified, self-conscious

embrace *verb*
1 *The mother gorilla **embraced** her baby.*
hug, clasp, cuddle, hold
2 *She's always ready to **embrace** new ideas.*
welcome, accept, adopt, take on

emerge *verb*
*He didn't **emerge** from his bedroom until ten o'clock.*
appear, come out

emergency *noun*
*Try to keep calm in an **emergency**.*
crisis, serious situation, danger, difficulty

emotional *adjective*
1 *He made an **emotional** farewell speech.*
moving, touching
2 *The music for the love scenes was very **emotional**.*
romantic, sentimental
3 *She's a very **emotional** woman.*
passionate, intense

emphasize *verb*
*She **emphasized** the important points.*
highlight, stress, focus on, dwell on, underline

empty *adjective*
1 *Please put the **empty** milk bottles outside the door.*
OPPOSITE full
2 *The house next to ours has been **empty** for weeks.*
unoccupied, uninhabited, vacant, deserted
OPPOSITE occupied
3 *After we put up our display, there was still some **empty** space on the wall.*
blank, bare, clear, unused

empty *verb*
1 ***Empty** the dirty water into the sink.*
drain, pour out
OPPOSITE fill
2 *The building **emptied** when the fire alarm went off.*
clear, evacuate, vacate
3 *Did you **empty** all the shopping out of the trolley?*
remove, unload

enchanting *adjective*
*The ballet dancers were **enchanting**.*
delightful, charming, appealing, attractive, bewitching, spellbinding

enchantment *noun*
1 *The forest had an air of **enchantment**.*
magic, wonder, delight, pleasure
2 *The witch recited an **enchantment**.*
spell, incantation

encourage *verb*
1 *We went to the match to **encourage** our team.*
inspire, support, motivate, cheer, spur on, egg on

embrace

2 *The poster **encourages** people to eat healthily.*
persuade, urge
3 *Is advertising likely to **encourage** sales?*
increase, boost, stimulate, further, promote, help, aid

encouraging *adjective*
*The results of the tests were **encouraging**.*
hopeful, positive, promising, cheering, reassuring, optimistic, favourable

end *noun*
1 *The fence marks the **end** of the garden.*
boundary, limit
2 *The **end** of the film was the most exciting part.*
ending, finish, close, conclusion, culmination
The last part of a show or piece of music is the **finale**.
A section added at the end of a letter is a **postscript**.
A section added at the end of a story is an **epilogue**.
3 *I was tired by the time we got to the **end** of the journey.*
termination, destination
4 *We arrived late and found ourselves at the **end** of the queue.*
back, rear, tail
5 *What **end** did you have in view when you started?*
aim, purpose, intention, objective, plan, outcome, result

end *verb*
1 *The meeting should **end** in time for lunch.*
finish, complete, conclude, break off, halt (*informal*) round off
2 *When did they **end** public executions?*
abolish, do away with, get rid of, put an end to, discontinue, eliminate
3 *The festival **ended** with a show of fireworks.*
close, come to an end, stop, cease, terminate, culminate, wind up

ending *noun*
*The **ending** of the film was the most exciting part.*
end, finish, close, conclusion, culmination, last part
The ending of a show or piece of music is the **finale**.

endless *adjective*
1 *Teachers need **endless** patience.*
unending, limitless, infinite, inexhaustible, unlimited
2 *There's an **endless** procession of cars along the main road.*
continual, continuous, constant, incessant, interminable, perpetual, unbroken, uninterrupted, everlasting, ceaseless

a b c d e f g h i j k l m n o p q r s t u v w x y z

endure *verb*
1 *She had to **endure** a lot of pain.*
bear, stand, suffer, cope with, experience, go through, put up with, tolerate, undergo
2 *These traditions have **endured** for centuries.*
survive, continue, last, persist, carry on, keep going

enemy *noun*
*They used to be friends but now they are bitter **enemies**.*
opponent, adversary, foe, rival
OPPOSITE friend, ally

energetic *adjective*
1 *She's a very **energetic** person.*
dynamic, spirited, enthusiastic, animated, active, zestful
OPPOSITE inactive, lethargic
2 *It was a very **energetic** exercise routine.*
lively, vigorous, brisk, fast, quick moving, strenuous
OPPOSITE slow-paced, sluggish

energy *noun*
1 *The dancers had tremendous **energy**.*
liveliness, spirit, vitality, vigour, life, drive, zest, verve, enthusiasm, dynamism
(*informal*) get-up-and-go, zip
OPPOSITE lethargy
2 *Wind power is a renewable source of **energy**.*
power, fuel

enjoy *verb*
*I really **enjoyed** the film.*
like, love, get pleasure from, be pleased by, admire, appreciate

enjoyable *adjective*
*It was an **enjoyable** party.*
pleasant, agreeable, delightful, entertaining, amusing
OPPOSITE unpleasant

enlarge *verb*
*The zoo is going to **enlarge** the lion enclosure.*
expand, extend, develop, make bigger
To make something wider is to **broaden** or **widen** it.
To make something longer is to **extend**, **lengthen**, or **stretch** it.
To make something seem larger is to **magnify** it.
OPPOSITE reduce

enormous *adjective*
***Enormous** waves battered the ship.*
huge, gigantic, immense, colossal, massive, monstrous, monumental, mountainous, towering, tremendous, vast
(*informal*) ginormous, humungous
OPPOSITE small

enough *adjective*
*Is there **enough** food for ten people?*
sufficient, adequate, ample

enquire *verb*
to enquire about
*I **enquired** about train times to Bristol.*
ask for, get information about, request, investigate

enter *verb*
1 *Silence fell as I **entered** the room.*
come in, walk in
To enter a place without permission is to **invade** it.
OPPOSITE leave
2 *The arrow **entered** his shoulder.*
go into, penetrate, pierce
3 *Can I **enter** my name on the list?*
insert, record, register, put down, set down, sign, write, inscribe
OPPOSITE cancel
4 *Our class decided to **enter** the competition.*
take part in, enrol in, sign up for, go in for, join in, participate in, volunteer for
OPPOSITE withdraw from

entertain *verb*
1 *The storyteller **entertained** us with scary ghost stories.*
amuse, divert, keep amused, make you laugh, please, cheer up
OPPOSITE bore
2 *You can **entertain** friends in the private dining room.*
receive, welcome, cater for, give hospitality to

entertainment *noun*
*Our hosts had arranged some **entertainment** for us.*
amusements, recreation, diversions, enjoyment, fun, pastimes

enthusiasm *noun*
1 *The young athletes showed plenty of **enthusiasm**.*
keenness, ambition, commitment, drive, zeal, zest
OPPOSITE apathy
2 *Collecting fossils is one of my **enthusiasms**.*
interest, passion, pastime, hobby, craze, diversion, fad

enthusiastic *adjective*
1 *He's an **enthusiastic** supporter of our local team.*
keen, passionate, avid, devoted, energetic, fervent, zealous
2 *The audience burst into **enthusiastic** applause.*
eager, excited, lively, vigorous, exuberant, hearty

entire *adjective*
*Donald spent the **entire** evening watching television.*
complete, whole, total, full

entirely *adverb*
*I'm not **entirely** sure that I agree with you.*
completely, absolutely, wholly, totally, utterly, fully, perfectly, quite

energy

entrance noun
1 *Please pay at the **entrance**.*
entry, way in, access, door, gate
When you go through the entrance to a building, you cross the **threshold**.
2 *I'll meet you in the **entrance**.*
entrance hall, foyer, lobby, porch
3 *Her sudden **entrance** took everyone by surprise.*
entry, arrival, appearance

entrance verb
*The crowd were **entranced** by the fireworks display.*
charm, delight, please, enchant

envious adjective
*He was **envious** of his brother's success.*
jealous, resentful

environment noun
*Animals should live in their natural **environment**, not in cages.*
habitat, surroundings, setting, conditions, situation
the environment
*We must do all we can to protect **the environment**.*
the natural world, nature, the earth, the world

envy noun
*I didn't feel any **envy**, even when I saw how rich she was.*
jealousy, resentment, bitterness

envy verb
*The evil queen **envied** Snow White's beauty.*
be jealous of, begrudge, grudge, resent

episode noun
1 *I paid for the broken window, and I want to forget the whole **episode**.*
event, incident, experience
2 *I missed last night's **episode** of 'Dr Who'.*
instalment, part

equal adjective
1 *Give everyone an **equal** amount.*
equivalent, identical, matching, similar, corresponding, fair
2 *The scores were **equal** at half-time.*
even, level, the same, square
To make the scores equal is to **equalize**.

equipment noun
*The shed is full of gardening **equipment**.*
apparatus, gear, kit, tackle, tools, implements, instruments, materials, machinery, paraphernalia, things
Computing equipment is **hardware**.

erase verb
*I **erased** the writing on the blackboard.*
delete, remove, rub out, wipe out, get rid of

erode verb
*The flood water **eroded** the river bank.*
wear away, eat away, destroy

errand noun
*I went on an **errand** to the corner shop.*
job, task, assignment, trip, journey

error noun
1 *The accident was the result of an **error** by the driver.*
mistake, fault, lapse, blunder
2 *I think there is an **error** in your argument.*
flaw, inaccuracy, misunderstanding, inconsistency
The error of leaving something out is an **omission** or **oversight**.

escape verb
1 *Why did you let him **escape**?*
get away, get out, run away, break free, break out
(*informal*) give you the slip
A performer who escapes from chains, etc., is an **escape artist** or **escapologist**.
2 *She always **escapes** the nasty jobs.*
avoid, get out of, evade, dodge, shirk

escape noun
1 *The prisoner's **escape** was filmed by security cameras.*
getaway, breakout, flight
2 *The explosion was caused by an **escape** of gas.*
leak, leakage, seepage

essential adjective
*Fruit and vegetables are an **essential** part of our diet.*
important, necessary, basic, vital, principal, fundamental, chief, crucial, indispensable

establish verb
1 *He plans to **establish** a new business.*
set up, start, begin, create, found, initiate, institute, introduce, launch, originate
2 *The police have not managed to **establish** his guilt.*
prove, show to be true, confirm, verify

estimate verb
*The builders **estimate** that the work will take four months.*
calculate, assess, work out, compute, count up, evaluate, judge, reckon, think out

eternal adjective
1 *The magic fountain was said to give **eternal** youth.*
everlasting, infinite, lasting, unending, timeless
Beings with eternal life are said to be **immortal**.
2 *I'm sick of your **eternal** quarrelling!*
constant, continual, never-ending, non-stop, persistent, perpetual, endless, ceaseless, incessant, unceasing

even adjective
1 *You need an **even** surface for ice skating.*
level, flat, smooth, straight
OPPOSITE uneven
2 *The runners kept up an **even** pace.*
regular, steady, unvarying, rhythmical, monotonous
OPPOSITE irregular
3 *Mr Lee has an **even** temper.*
calm, cool, placid, unexcitable
OPPOSITE excitable
4 *The scores were **even** at half time.*
equal, level, matching, identical, the same, square
OPPOSITE different
5 *2, 4, and 6 are **even** numbers.*
OPPOSITE odd

evening noun
*Towards **evening** it clouded over and began to rain.*
dusk, nightfall, sundown, sunset, twilight

event noun
1 *Her autobiography describes the main **events** of her life.*
happening, incident, occurrence
2 *There was an **event** to mark the launch of the new film.*
function, occasion, ceremony, entertainment, party, reception
3 *The World Cup is an important **event** for football fans.*
competition, contest, fixture, match, engagement, meeting, game, tournament

eventually adverb
*The journey took ages, but **eventually** we arrived safely.*
finally, at last, in the end, ultimately

evidence noun
*This piece of paper is **evidence** that he is lying.*
proof, confirmation
Evidence that someone accused of a crime was not there when the crime was committed is an **alibi**.
Evidence given in a law court is a **testimony**.
To give evidence in court is to **testify**.

evil adjective
1 *The charm was used to keep away **evil** spirits.*
malevolent, fiendish, diabolical
2 *Who would do such an **evil** deed?*
wicked, immoral, cruel, sinful, villainous, malicious, foul, hateful, vile
OPPOSITE good

evil noun
1 *The good witch tried to fight against **evil**.*
wickedness, badness, wrongdoing, sin, immorality, villainy, malevolence, malice

a b c d e f g h i j k l m n o p q r s t u v w x y z

2 *They had to endure the **evils** of famine and drought.*
disaster, misfortune, suffering, pain, affliction, curse

exact *adjective*
1 *I gave the police an **exact** account of what happened.*
accurate, precise, correct, true, faithful, detailed, meticulous, strict
2 *Is this an **exact** copy of the original document?*
identical, perfect, indistinguishable
OPPOSITE inaccurate

exaggerate *verb*
*He tends to **exaggerate** his problems.*
magnify, inflate, overdo, make too much of
OPPOSITE minimize

examination *noun*
1 *The results of the **examinations** will be announced next month.*
test, assessment
(*informal*) exam
2 *The judge made a thorough **examination** of the facts.*
investigation, inspection, study, analysis, survey, review, appraisal
3 *He was sent to hospital for an **examination**.*
check-up
A medical examination of a dead person is a *post-mortem*.

examine *verb*
1 *The judge **examined** the evidence.*
inspect, study, investigate, analyse, look closely at, pore over, scrutinize, probe, survey, review, weigh up, sift
2 *They were **examined** on their knowledge of history.*
question, interrogate, quiz
To examine someone rigorously is to *grill* them.

example *noun*
1 *Give me an **example** of what you mean.*
instance, illustration, sample, specimen, case
2 *She's an **example** to us all.*
model, ideal

excellent *adjective*
*That's an **excellent** idea!*
first-class, first-rate, outstanding, exceptional, remarkable, tremendous, wonderful, superb, great, fine, marvellous, superior, superlative, top-notch
(*informal*) brilliant, fantastic, terrific, fabulous, sensational, super
OPPOSITE bad, awful, second-rate

exceptional *adjective*
*It is **exceptional** to have such cold weather in June.*
unusual, extraordinary, uncommon, unexpected, amazing, rare, odd, peculiar, strange, surprising, special, abnormal, phenomenal, unheard-of, bizarre
OPPOSITE normal, usual

exchange *verb*
*The shop will **exchange** faulty goods.*
change, replace
To exchange goods for other goods without using money is to *barter*.
To exchange an old thing for part of the cost of a new one is to *trade it in*.
To exchange things with your friends is to *swap* or *swop* them.
To exchange players for other players in football, etc., is to *substitute* them.

excited *adjective*
*On Christmas Eve, my little brother was too **excited** to sleep.*
agitated, lively, enthusiastic, exuberant, thrilled, elated, eager, animated
OPPOSITE calm

excitement *noun*
*I could hardly bear the **excitement**!*
suspense, tension, drama, thrill

exciting *adjective*
*The last minutes of the match were the most **exciting** of all!*
dramatic, eventful, thrilling, gripping, sensational, stirring, rousing, stimulating, electrifying
OPPOSITE dull, boring

exclude *verb*
1 *Adults are **excluded** from joining our club.*
ban, bar, prohibit, keep out, banish, reject
2 *She had to **exclude** dairy products from her diet.*
leave out, omit

excuse *noun*
*What is your **excuse** for being so late?*
reason, explanation, defence, justification

excuse *verb*
*I can't **excuse** his bad behaviour.*
forgive, overlook, pardon
OPPOSITE punish
to be excused something
*May I **be excused** swimming?*
be exempt from, be let off, be released from

exercise *noun*
1 ***Exercise** helps to keep you fit.*
physical activity, working out, keep fit, training
2 *Doing **exercises** will improve your guitar playing.*
practice, training, drill

exercise *verb*
1 *If you **exercise** regularly, you will keep fit.*
keep fit, train, exert yourself
2 *I sometimes **exercise** our neighbour's dog.*
take for a walk, take out, walk
3 *We must **exercise** patience.*
show, use, apply, display, employ

exhausted *adjective*
*After a hard race, we lay **exhausted** on the grass.*
tired, weary, worn out, fatigued, breathless, gasping, panting
(*informal*) all in, done in, bushed, zonked

exhausting *adjective*
*Digging the garden is **exhausting** work.*
tiring, demanding, hard, laborious, strenuous, difficult, gruelling, wearisome
OPPOSITE easy

exhibition *noun*
*We went to see an **exhibition** of paintings by Picasso.*
display, show

expand *verb*
*Their computer business is **expanding** rapidly.*
increase, enlarge, extend, build up, develop, make bigger
To become larger is to *grow* or *swell*.
To become wider is to *broaden*, *thicken*, or *widen*.
To become longer is to *extend*, *lengthen*, or *stretch*.
OPPOSITE contract, reduce

expect *verb*
1 *I **expect** that it will rain today.*
anticipate, imagine, forecast, predict, foresee, prophesy
2 *She **expects** me to do everything for her!*
require, want, count on, insist on, demand
3 *I **expect** they missed the bus.*
believe, imagine, guess, suppose, presume, assume, think

expedition *noun*
An expedition into unknown territory is an *exploration*.
An expedition to carry out a special task is a *mission*.
An expedition to find something is a *quest*.
An expedition to worship at a holy place is a *pilgrimage*.
An expedition to see or hunt wild animals is a *safari*.

expel *verb*
1 *A fan **expels** the stale air and fumes.*
send out, force out

2 He was **expelled** from school.
dismiss, ban, remove, throw out, send away
To expel someone from their home is to **eject** or **evict** them.
To expel someone from their country is to **banish** or **exile** them.
To expel evil spirits is to **exorcise** them.

experience noun
1 Have you had any **experience** of singing in a choir?
practice, involvement, participation
2 I had an unusual **experience** today.
happening, event, occurrence, incident
An exciting experience is an **adventure**.
An unpleasant experience is an **ordeal**.

expert noun
He's an **expert** at chess.
specialist, authority, genius, wizard
(informal) dab hand, whizz

expert adjective
Only an **expert** sailor could cross the ocean.
brilliant, capable, clever, competent, experienced, knowledgeable, professional, proficient, qualified, skilful, skilled, specialized, trained
OPPOSITE amateur, unskilful

explain verb
1 The doctor **explained** the procedure carefully.
make clear, give an explanation of, clarify, describe
2 Can you **explain** your strange behaviour?
give reasons for, account for, excuse, make excuses for, justify

explode verb
1 The firework **exploded** with a bang.
blow up, make an explosion, go off, burst, shatter
2 The slightest movement might **explode** the bomb.
detonate, set off

explore verb
1 The spacecraft will **explore** the solar system.
search, survey, travel through, probe
2 We must **explore** all the possibilities.
examine, inspect, investigate, look into, research, analyse, scrutinize

WORD WEB

explorer noun
The **explorers** were looking for the legendary Lost City.
traveller, voyager, discoverer, wanderer

THINGS AN EXPLORER MIGHT FIND
catacombs, cave, cavern, chest, hieroglyphics, inscription, labyrinth, maze, mummy, parchment, pyramid, riddle, sarcophagus, seal, secret passage, skeleton, stone tablet, temple, tomb, treasure, tunnel, underground chamber

THINGS AN EXPLORER MIGHT USE OR CARRY
binoculars, chart, compass, machete, map, penknife, rope, rucksack, telescope, tent, torch, water bottle

explosion noun
The **explosion** rattled the windows.
blast, bang
An explosion from a volcano is an **eruption**.
An explosion of laughter is an **outburst**.
The sound of a gun going off is a **report**.

WORD WEB

expression noun
EXPRESSIONS YOU MIGHT SEE ON A FACE
beam, frown, glare, glower, grimace, grin, laugh, leer, long face, poker-face, pout, scowl, smile, smirk, sneer, wide-eyed look, wince, yawn

1 'Tickled pink' is a colloquial **expression**.
phrase, saying, term, wording
An expression that people use too much is a **cliché**.
2 Did you see her **expression** when I told her the news?
look, appearance, countenance, face

extra adjective
1 There is an **extra** charge for taking your bike on the train.
additional, further, added, supplementary, excess
2 There is **extra** food in the kitchen if you need it.
more, spare, surplus, reserve

extraordinary adjective
The astronauts saw many **extraordinary** sights.
amazing, astonishing, remarkable, outstanding, exceptional, incredible, fantastic, marvellous, miraculous, phenomenal, rare, special, strange, surprising, unheard of, unusual, weird, wonderful, abnormal, curious
OPPOSITE ordinary

extreme adjective
1 Polar bears can withstand **extreme** cold.
great, intense, severe, acute, excessive
2 She lives on the **extreme** edge of the town.
farthest, furthest

a b c d e f g h i j k l m n o p q r s t u v w x y z

F f

fabric noun
*This **fabric** will make a lovely dress for my doll.*
cloth, material, stuff
A plural word is **textiles**.

fabulous adjective
1 (*informal*) *We had a **fabulous** time at the party.*
excellent, first-class, marvellous, outstanding, superb, tremendous, wonderful
(*informal*) brilliant, fantastic, smashing
2 *Dragons are **fabulous** creatures.*
fictitious, imaginary, legendary, mythical

face noun
1 *We saw the anger in the witch's **face**.*
expression, features, look, countenance
2 *The **face** of the clock had been smashed.*
front

3 *A cube has six **faces**.*
side, surface

face verb
1 *Stand and **face** your partner.*
be opposite to, look towards
2 *The astronauts had to **face** many dangers.*
cope with, deal with, face up to, stand up to, tackle, meet, encounter, confront
OPPOSITE avoid

fact noun
*It is a **fact** that dodos are now extinct.*
reality, truth, certainty
OPPOSITE fiction

the facts
*The detective considered **the facts** in the case.*
details, particulars, information, data
Facts which are useful in trying to prove something are **evidence**.
Facts expressed as numbers are **statistics**.

factual adjective
*Anne Frank wrote a **factual** account of her life during the war*
real, true, truthful, accurate, authentic, faithful, genuine, objective, reliable
A film or story based on a person's life is **biographical**.

A film or story based on history is **historical**.
A film telling you about real events is a **documentary**.
OPPOSITE made-up, fictional

fade verb
1 *Sunlight has **faded** the curtains.*
make paler, bleach, blanch, whiten, dim
OPPOSITE brighten
2 *Those flowers will **fade** in a few days.*
wither, wilt, droop, flag, shrivel
OPPOSITE flourish
3 *Gradually, the light began to **fade**.*
weaken, decline, diminish, dwindle, fail, wane, disappear, melt away, vanish
OPPOSITE increase

fail verb
1 *Their plan to steal the crown jewels **failed** miserably.*
be unsuccessful, go wrong, fall through, founder, come to grief, miscarry
(*informal*) flop, bomb
OPPOSITE succeed
2 *The rocket engine **failed** before take-off.*
break down, cut out, give up, stop working

WRITING TIPS

face noun
You can use these words to describe a **face**.

TO DESCRIBE ITS SHAPE
flat, long, oval, round, rounded; lantern-jawed, square-jawed

TO DESCRIBE ITS FEATURES
chiselled, chubby, craggy, delicate, fine, gaunt, haggard, hollow, pinched, prominent, puffy, skeletal, sunken
*Their faces were **gaunt** and **pinched** from hunger.*

TO DESCRIBE ITS SKIN OR COLOUR
clear, dark, fair, flushed, freckled, fresh, glowing, healthy, rosy, ruddy, tanned; ashen, grey, leaden, pale, pallid, pasty, sallow, sickly, unhealthy, wan; flabby, saggy, shrivelled, weather-beaten, wizened, wrinkled, wrinkly; disfigured, pimply, pock-marked, scarred, spotty
*The old witch was **wizened** like a prune.*

TO DESCRIBE THE LOOK ON A FACE
cheeky, cheerful, radiant, sunny; grave, grim, serious; sulky, sullen, surly; blank, deadpan, faceless, impassive, unmoving, vacant *The guard stared ahead, his face **unmoving**.*

You can use these words to describe **eyes**:
beady, bulbous, bulging, deep-set, glassy, heavy-lidded, hooded, protuberant, saucer-like, sunken, cloudy, misty, moist, piercing, steely, tearful, watery *The monster had a single **bulging** red eye.*

You can use these words to describe a **nose**:
beak-like, bulbous, button, classical or Roman, crooked, pointed, snub, upturned *The troll had **bushy** eyebrows and a red, **bulbous** nose.*

3 *By late afternoon, the light had begun to* **fail**.
weaken, decline, diminish, dwindle, fade, get worse, deteriorate
OPPOSITE improve
4 *The professor* **failed** *to warn us of the danger.*
neglect, forget, omit
OPPOSITE remember
5 *I hope I don't* **fail** *my violin exam.*
OPPOSITE pass

failure noun
1 *The storm caused a power* **failure**.
breakdown, fault, malfunction, crash, loss, collapse, stoppage
2 *Their attempt to reach the North Pole was a* **failure**.
defeat, disappointment, disaster, fiasco
(informal) flop, wash-out
OPPOSITE success

faint adjective
1 *The details in the photograph are very* **faint**.
faded, dim, unclear, indistinct, vague, blurred, hazy, pale, shadowy, misty
OPPOSITE clear, distinct
2 *There was a* **faint** *smell of burning in the air.*
delicate, slight
OPPOSITE strong
3 *We heard a* **faint** *cry for help.*
weak, low, muffled, distant, hushed, muted, soft, thin
OPPOSITE loud
4 *Gordon was so hungry that he felt* **faint**.
dizzy, giddy, light-headed, unsteady, weak, exhausted, feeble
(informal) woozy

faint verb
The explorers nearly **fainted** *from exhaustion.*
become unconscious, collapse, pass out, black out
(old use) swoon

fair adjective
1 *I think the referee made a* **fair** *decision.*
just, proper, right, fair-minded, honest, honourable, impartial, unbiased, unprejudiced, disinterested
OPPOSITE unfair
2 *The twins both have* **fair** *hair.*
blond or blonde, light, golden, yellow
OPPOSITE dark
3 *Our team has a* **fair** *chance of winning the cup.*
reasonable, moderate, average, acceptable, adequate, satisfactory, passable, respectable, tolerable
4 *The weather should be* **fair** *today.*
dry, fine, sunny, bright, clear, cloudless, pleasant, favourable

fair noun
1 *My sister won a teddy at the* **fair**.
fairground, funfair, carnival, fête, gala

2 *Our school is holding a book* **fair** *next week.*
show, exhibition, display, market, bazaar

fairly adverb
1 *The competition will be judged* **fairly**.
honestly, properly, justly, impartially
2 *The ground is still* **fairly** *wet. I'm* **fairly** *certain that we are heading north.*
quite, rather, somewhat, slightly, moderately, up to a point, reasonably, tolerably
(informal) pretty

WORD WEB

fairy noun

THINGS A FAIRY MIGHT HAVE OR USE
fairy dust, lantern, wand, wings

A FAIRY'S WINGS OR CLOTHES MIGHT BE
diaphonous, feathery, glittering, glowing, gossamer, lustrous, sheer, sparkling, translucent, transparent

PLACES WHERE A FAIRY MIGHT LIVE
dell, glen, magic forest or tree, glade, mound, toadstool

SOME CREATURES LIKE FAIRIES
brownie, elf, imp, leprechaun, nymph, pixie, sprite

faithful adjective
My dog, Scruffy, is my **faithful** *friend.*
loyal, devoted, reliable, trustworthy, dependable, firm, constant, close
OPPOSITE unfaithful

fake noun
That's not a real Roman coin—it's a **fake**.
copy, imitation, reproduction, replica, forgery
(informal) phoney
An event which fakes a real event is a **hoax**, **sham**, or **simulation**.
A person who pretends to be another person is an **impostor**.

fake verb
The spy tried to **fake** *a foreign accent.*
imitate, copy, pretend, put on, reproduce, simulate
To fake someone's signature is to **forge** it.

fall verb
1 *The acrobat* **fell** *off a ladder and broke his leg.*
tumble, topple, crash down, pitch, plunge
2 *Snow was beginning to* **fall** *quite thickly.*
drop, come down, descend, rain down, plummet

3 *The level of the river had* **fallen** *since March.*
go down, subside, recede, sink, ebb
4 *The temperature in the cave* **fell** *to below freezing.*
go down, become lower, decrease, decline, lessen, diminish, dwindle
to fall in
The roof of the cabin **fell in** *during the storm.*
cave in, collapse, give way
to fall out
The twins are always **falling out** *with each other.*
argue, disagree, quarrel, squabble, bicker

fall noun
1 *Ellen had a* **fall** *and cut her knee.*
tumble
2 *We noticed a sharp* **fall** *in the temperature.*
drop, lowering
OPPOSITE rise
3 *There has been a* **fall** *in the price of coffee.*
decrease, reduction, decline
OPPOSITE increase
4 *This is a story about the* **fall** *of Troy.*
defeat, surrender

false adjective
1 *They gave us* **false** *information about the treasure.*
wrong, incorrect, untrue, inaccurate, mistaken, erroneous, faulty, invalid, misleading, deceptive
OPPOSITE correct
2 *The spy was travelling with a* **false** *passport.*
fake, bogus, sham, counterfeit, forged
OPPOSITE genuine, authentic
3 *Mrs Gummidge put in her* **false** *teeth.*
artificial, imitation
OPPOSITE real, natural
4 *The Black Knight turned out to be a* **false** *ally.*
unfaithful, disloyal, unreliable, untrustworthy, deceitful, dishonest, treacherous
OPPOSITE faithful, loyal

familiar adjective
1 *Seagulls are a* **familiar** *sight on the beach.*
common, everyday, normal, ordinary, usual, regular, customary, frequent, mundane, routine
OPPOSITE rare
2 *It seems a bit* **familiar** *to call her by her first name.*
informal, friendly, intimate, relaxed, close
OPPOSITE formal, unfriendly
to be familiar with something
Are you **familiar with** *the rules of chess?*
be acquainted with, be aware of, know

a b c d e f g h i j k l m n o p q r s t u v w x y z

family noun
Some members of my **family** live in New Zealand.
relations, relatives
An old-fashioned term for your family is your **kin**.
The official term for your closest relative is **next of kin**.
A group of related Scottish families is a **clan**.
A succession of people from the same powerful family is a **dynasty**.
In certain societies, a group of families living together is a **tribe**.
A single stage in a family is a **generation**.
The line of ancestors from which a family is descended is its **ancestry**.
A diagram showing how people in your family are related is a **family tree**.
The study of family history is **genealogy**.
A family of young birds is a **brood**.
A family of kittens or puppies is a **litter**.

MEMBERS OF A FAMILY MAY INCLUDE adopted child, aunt, brother, child, cousin, daughter, father, foster-child, foster-parent, grandchild, grandparent, guardian, husband, mother, nephew, niece, parent, sister, son, spouse, step-child, step-parent, uncle, ward, wife

family

famous adjective
Pele is a very **famous** football player.
well-known, celebrated, renowned, acclaimed, notable, prominent, distinguished, eminent
To be famous for doing something bad is to be **notorious**.
OPPOSITE unknown, obscure

fan noun
I used to be a **fan** of jazz music.
enthusiast, admirer, devotee, follower, supporter

fanatic noun
My brother is a rugby **fanatic**.
enthusiast, addict, devotee
(informal) freak, nut

fancy adjective
Alice bought a **fancy** hat for her friend's wedding.
elaborate, decorative, ornamental, ornate
OPPOSITE plain

fancy verb
1 What do you **fancy** to eat?
feel like, want, wish for, desire, prefer
2 I **fancied** I heard a noise downstairs.
imagine, think, believe, suppose

fantastic adjective
1 The story is full of **fantastic** creatures.
fanciful, extraordinary, strange, odd, weird, outlandish, far-fetched, incredible, imaginative
OPPOSITE realistic
2 (informal) We had a **fantastic** time at camp.
excellent, first-class, outstanding, superb, wonderful, tremendous, marvellous
(informal) brilliant, fabulous, smashing

fantasy noun
Rosie had a **fantasy** about being a mermaid.
dream, daydream, delusion, fancy

far adjective
1 The castle stood in the **far** north of the country.
distant, faraway, remote
2 The ferry took us to the **far** side of the river.
opposite, other

fascinate verb
We were **fascinated** by the inventor's workshop.
interest (in), engross, captivate, enthrall, absorb, beguile, entrance, attract, charm, enchant, delight
OPPOSITE bore

fashion noun
1 The Martians behaved in a peculiar **fashion**.
way, manner
2 Zoe dresses according to the latest **fashion**.
trend, vogue, craze, fad, style, look

fashionable adjective
Megan has a **fashionable** new hairstyle.
stylish, chic, up-to-date, popular, elegant, smart
(informal) trendy, hip, in
OPPOSITE unfashionable, out-of-date

fast adjective
The robber made a **fast** exit when he heard us coming.
quick, rapid, speedy, swift, brisk, hasty, hurried, high-speed, headlong, breakneck
(informal) nippy
Something which goes faster than sound is **supersonic**.
A common simile is **as fast as lightning**.
OPPOSITE slow, unhurried

farm noun
The formal word for farming is **agriculture**.
A farm which uses no artificial fertilizers or chemicals is an **organic farm**.
A very small farm is a **smallholding**.
A small farm growing fruit and vegetables is a **market garden**.
A small farm in Scotland is a **croft**.
A large cattle farm in America is a **ranch**.

combine harvester

740

fast adverb
1 Mr Toad was driving too **fast** in his motor car.
quickly, speedily, swiftly, rapidly, briskly
2 The boat was stuck **fast** on the rocks.
firmly, securely, tightly
3 Be quiet! The baby is **fast** asleep.
deeply, sound, completely

fasten verb
1 They **fastened** their ropes to the rock face.
tie, fix, attach, connect, join, link, bind, hitch, clamp, pin, clip, tack, stick

FARM BUILDINGS
barn, byre or cowshed, dairy, farmhouse, granary, milking parlour, outhouse, pigsty, stable

OTHER PARTS OF A FARM
barnyard or farmyard, cattle pen, fields, haystack, meadow, paddock, pasture, rick, sheep fold, silo

ITEMS OF FARM EQUIPMENT
baler, combine harvester, cultivator, drill, harrow, harvester, mower, planter, plough, tractor, trailer

PEOPLE WHO WORK ON A FARM
agricultural worker, (old use) dairymaid, farmer, farm labourer, ploughman, shepherd, stockbreeder, tractor driver

SOME FARM ANIMALS
bull, bullock, chicken or hen, cow, duck, goat, goose, horse, pig, sheep, turkey

Birds kept on a farm are *poultry*.
Animals kept for milk or beef are *cattle*.
Farm animals in general are *livestock*.
Birds kept on a farm are *poultry*.
Animals kept for milk or beef are *cattle*.
Farm animals in general are *livestock*.

tractor

**To fasten a boat is to *anchor* or *moor* it.
To fasten an animal is to *tether* it.**
2 They **fastened** the gate with a heavy chain.
secure, seal, lock, bolt, make fast

fat *adjective*
1 *You'll get **fat** if you eat too many crisps!*
overweight, obese, chubby, plump, podgy, dumpy, flabby, portly, stout, round, rotund
2 *The witch opened a big, **fat** book of spells.*
thick, bulky, chunky, weighty, substantial
OPPOSITE thin

fatal *adjective*
1 *The knight delivered a **fatal** wound to his enemy.*
deadly, lethal, mortal
A fatal illness is an *incurable* or *terminal* illness.
2 *Leaving the door unlocked was a **fatal** mistake.*
disastrous, catastrophic, dreadful, calamitous

fate *noun*
1 *The shipwrecked crew were in the hands of **fate**.*
fortune, destiny, providence, chance, luck

2 *The prisoner met with a terrible **fate**.*
death, end

fault *noun*
1 *This DVD has a **fault** in it.*
defect, flaw, malfunction, snag, problem, weakness
2 *It was my **fault** that we missed our bus.*
responsibility, liability

faulty *adjective*
*The TV was **faulty**, so we took it back to the shop.*
broken, not working, defective, out of order, unusable, damaged
OPPOSITE perfect

favour *noun*
1 *I asked my friend to do me a **favour**.*
good deed, good turn, kindness, service, courtesy
2 *The captain's plan found **favour** with most of the crew.*
approval, support, liking, goodwill
to be in favour of something
*We're all **in favour of** longer holidays.*
agree to, approve of, support, like the idea of

favourite *adjective*
*What is your **favourite** book?*
best-loved, preferred, treasured, dearest, special, top

A B C D E F G H I J K L M N O P Q R S T U V W X Y Z

fear *noun*
*When Garth heard the monster, he trembled with **fear**.*
fright, terror, horror, alarm, panic, dread, anxiety, apprehension, trepidation
A formal word for a special type of fear is **phobia**.
A fear of open spaces is **agoraphobia**.
A fear of spiders is **arachnophobia**.
A fear of enclosed spaces is **claustrophobia**.
A fear or dislike of foreigners is **xenophobia**.
OPPOSITE courage

fear *verb*
1 *My sister **fears** snakes and spiders.*
be frightened of, be afraid of, be scared of, dread
2 *I **fear** we may be too late.*
suspect, expect, anticipate

fearless *adjective*
*The **fearless** explorers entered the dark cave.*
brave, courageous, daring, heroic, valiant, intrepid, plucky
OPPOSITE cowardly

feast *noun*
*The king held a great **feast** to celebrate his birthday.*
banquet, dinner
(*informal*) spread

feat *noun*
*The trapeze artists performed many daring **feats**.*
act, action, deed, exploit, achievement, performance

feather *noun*
A large feather is a **plume**.
All the feathers on a bird are its **plumage**.
Soft, fluffy feathers are **down**.
A feather used as a pen is a **quill**.

feature *noun*
1 *The room has several unusual **features**.*
characteristic, detail, point, aspect, quality, peculiarity, trait, facet
A person's features are their **face**.
2 *There was a **feature** about our school in the newspaper.*
article, report, story, item, piece

feeble *adjective*
1 *The elderly knight looked tired and **feeble**.*
weak, frail, infirm, delicate, poorly, sickly, puny, weary, weedy
OPPOSITE strong, powerful
2 *I made a **feeble** attempt to stop the ball. Do you expect me to believe that **feeble** excuse?*
weak, poor, ineffective, inadequate, unconvincing, tame, flimsy, lame

feed *verb*
*We have enough sandwiches to **feed** six people.*
provide for, cater for, give food to, nourish
to feed on
*The leopard was **feeding on** its prey.*
eat, consume, devour

feel *verb*
1 *I **felt** the llama's soft, woolly fur.*
touch, caress, stroke, fondle
2 *It **feels** colder today.*
appear, seem, strike you as
3 *Older people tend to **feel** the cold.*
notice, be aware of, be conscious of, experience, suffer from
4 *I **feel** that it's time we made a start.*
think, believe, consider
to feel like
*Do you **feel like** going for a walk?*
fancy, want, wish for, desire

feel *noun*
*I love the **feel** of warm sand between my toes.*
feeling, sensation, touch

feeling *noun*
1 *The cat had lost all **feeling** in its paw.*
sense of touch, sensation, sensitivity
2 *I didn't mean to hurt your **feelings**.*
emotion, passion, sentiment
3 *I have a **feeling** that something is wrong.*
suspicion, notion, inkling, hunch, idea, impression, fancy, intuition

fence *noun*
*The mansion was surrounded by a tall **fence**.*
railing, barrier, wall, paling, stockade, hedge

ferocious *adjective*
*The mansion was guarded by a **ferocious** dog.*
fierce, fearsome, savage, wild, vicious, violent, bloodthirsty, brutal
OPPOSITE tame

fertile *adjective*
*The surrounding countryside was green and **fertile**.*
fruitful, productive, rich, fecund
OPPOSITE barren, sterile

festival *noun*
*The town holds a **festival** every summer.*
carnival, fiesta, fête, gala, fair, celebration, jamboree
A celebration of a special anniversary is a **jubilee**.

fetch *verb*
1 *I **fetched** the shopping from the car.*
get, bring, carry, collect, transfer, transport, convey, pick up, retrieve, obtain
2 *If we sell our car, how much will it **fetch**?*
make, raise, sell for, go for, bring in, earn

feud *noun*
*There has been a **feud** between our families for years.*
quarrel, dispute, conflict, hostility, enmity, rivalry, strife, antagonism
A feud that lasts a long time is a **vendetta**.

feverish *adjective*
1 *I felt **feverish** with the cold.*
When you are feverish you are **hot** and **shivery**.
With a bad fever you may become **delirious**.
2 *There was **feverish** activity in the kitchen.*
frenzied, frantic, frenetic, excited, agitated, hectic, busy, hurried, impatient, restless

fictional *adjective*
*Harry Potter is a **fictional** character.*
imaginary, made-up, invented, fanciful
OPPOSITE factual, real

fiddle *verb*
1 *Who's been **fiddling** with the DVD player?*
tinker, meddle, tamper, play about, mess about, twiddle
2 (*informal*) *Mr Filch had been **fiddling** the bank account for years.*
falsify, alter, rig
(*informal*) cook the books

fidget verb
*I begin to **fidget** when I'm bored.*
be restless, fiddle about, play about, mess about

field noun
1 *Cattle were grazing in the **field**.*
meadow, pasture
A small field for horses is a **paddock**.
An area of grass in a village is a **green**.
2 *The **field** is too wet to play football.*
ground, pitch, playing field
3 *Electronics is not my **field**.*
special interest, speciality, area of study

fierce adjective
1 *The travellers were killed in a **fierce** attack by armed bandits.*
vicious, ferocious, savage, brutal, violent, wild, cruel, merciless, ruthless, pitiless
2 *Our team will face **fierce** opposition in the final.*
strong, keen, eager, aggressive, competitive, passionate, relentless
3 *The explorers braved the **fierce** heat of the desert sun.*
blazing, intense, raging

fiery adjective
1 *It's best to avoid the **fiery** heat of the midday sun.*
blazing, burning, hot, intense, fierce, raging, flaming, red-hot, glowing
2 *My great aunt has always had a **fiery** temper.*
violent, passionate, excitable, angry, furious

fight noun
1 *The warriors faced each other for a **fight** to the death.*
Fighting is **combat** or **hostilities**.
A fight between armies is a **battle**.
A minor unplanned battle is a **skirmish**.
A series of battles is a **campaign** or **war**.
A minor fight is a **brawl**, **scrap**, **scuffle**, or **tussle**.
A fight arranged between two people is a **duel**.
2 *We support the **fight** to save the rainforest.*
campaign, crusade, struggle

fight verb
1 *Two seagulls were **fighting** over a scrap of bread.*
have a fight, scrap, scuffle, exchange blows, come to blows
2 *The two countries **fought** each other in the war.*
do battle with, wage war with, attack
Fighting with swords is **fencing**.
Fighting with fists is **boxing**.
Fighting in which you try to throw your opponent to the ground is **wrestling**.
Fighting sports such as karate and judo are **martial arts**.
3 *We will **fight** the decision to close our local library.*
protest against, oppose, resist, make a stand against, campaign against

figure noun
1 *Please write the **figure** '8' on the board.*
number, numeral, digit, integer
2 *Ballet dancers need to have a good **figure**.*
body, build, form, shape
3 *Inside the temple were several clay **figures**.*
statue, carving, sculpture

figure verb
*Donald Duck **figures** in cartoons.*
appear, feature, take part
to figure out
*We couldn't **figure out** what the riddle meant.*
work out, make out, understand, see

fill verb
1 *Dad **filled** the trolley with shopping.*
load, pack, stuff, cram, top up
To fill a tyre with air is to **inflate** it.
OPPOSITE empty
2 *What can I use to **fill** this hole?*
close up, plug, seal, block up, stop up
3 *Sightseers **filled** the streets.*
crowd, jam, block, obstruct
(*informal*) bung up

film noun
1 *There is a good **film** on TV tonight.*
movie, picture, video, DVD
A long film is a **feature film**.
A short excerpt from a film is a **clip**.
A script for a film is a **screenplay** and a writer of screenplays is a **screenwriter**.
A well-known film actor is a **film star**.
A theatre where films are shown is a **cinema**, **picture house**, or (American) **movie theatre**.
2 *There was a **film** of oil on the water.*
coat, coating, layer, covering, sheet, skin
A large patch of oil floating on water is a **slick**.

filthy adjective
*Those trainers are **filthy**!*
dirty, mucky, messy, grimy, grubby, muddy, soiled, stained
OPPOSITE clean

final adjective
1 *The **final** moments of the match were very tense.*
last, closing, concluding
OPPOSITE opening
2 *What was the **final** result?*
eventual, ultimate

finally adverb
*I've **finally** managed to finish my book.*
eventually, at last, in the end

find verb
1 *Did you **find** any fossils on the beach?*
come across, discover, see, spot, locate, encounter, stumble across, unearth
2 *The children never **found** the secret door again.*
trace, track down, recover, retrieve
OPPOSITE lose
3 *Did the doctor **find** what was wrong?*
detect, identify, diagnose, ascertain
4 *You will **find** that building a tree house is hard work.*
become aware, realize, learn, recognize, notice, observe

fine adjective
1 *The young musicians gave a **fine** performance.*
excellent, first-class, superb, good, splendid, admirable, commendable
OPPOSITE bad
2 *As the weather was **fine**, we took a picnic.*
sunny, fair, bright, clear, cloudless, pleasant
OPPOSITE dull
3 *Spiders spin very **fine** thread for their webs.*
delicate, fragile, thin, flimsy, slender, slim
OPPOSITE thick
4 *The desert dunes were made of **fine** sand.*
dusty, powdery
OPPOSITE coarse

finish verb
1 *When are you likely to **finish** your homework?*
complete, reach the end of, cease, round off
2 *The film should **finish** around nine o'clock.*
end, stop, conclude, terminate
(*informal*) wind up
3 *I've already **finished** my bag of crisps.*
consume, use up, get through, exhaust
(*informal*) polish off
OPPOSITE start

a
b
c
d
e
f
g
h
i
j
k
l
m
n
o
p
q
r
s
t
u
v
w
x
y
z

finish noun
*We stayed to watch the parade until the **finish**.*
end, close, conclusion, completion, result, termination
OPPOSITE start

fire noun
*The campers toasted marshmallows in the **fire**.*
blaze, flames, burning, combustion
A very big hot fire is an **inferno**.
An open fire out of doors is a **bonfire**.
An enclosed fire which produces great heat is a **furnace**.
An enclosed fire for cooking food is an **oven**.
An enclosed fire for making pottery is a **kiln**.
A team of people whose job is to put out fires is a **fire brigade**.
A member of a fire brigade is a **firefighter**.

fire verb
1 *The soldier aimed his rifle and **fired** two shots.*
shoot, discharge, let off, set off
To fire a missile is to **launch** it.
2 (informal) *Miss Stark **fired** her assistant for being late for work.*
dismiss, sack

firm noun
*Mr Perkins owns a **firm** that makes biscuits.*
company, business, organization, enterprise

firm adjective
1 *The surface of the planet was dry and **firm**.*
hard, solid, dense, compact, rigid, set
OPPOSITE soft
2 *Make sure the knots in the rope are **firm**.*
secure, tight, strong, stable, fixed, sturdy, steady
3 *Zelda had a **firm** belief in the power of magic.*
definite, certain, sure, decided, determined, resolute, unshakeable, unwavering
OPPOSITE unsure
4 *The two girls have become **firm** friends.*
close, devoted, faithful, loyal, constant, dependable, reliable

first adjective
1 *The **first** inhabitants of the area were Picts.*
earliest, original
2 *The **first** thing to do in an emergency is to keep calm.*
principal, key, main, fundamental, basic, chief

fit adjective
1 *Cinderella's gown was **fit** for a princess.*
suitable, appropriate, fitting, right, good enough, worthy (of)
OPPOSITE unsuitable
2 *I walk to school every day to keep **fit**.*
healthy, well, strong, robust
(old use) hale and hearty
A common simile is **as fit as a fiddle**.
OPPOSITE unhealthy
3 *After a long ride, the horses were **fit** to collapse.*
ready, liable, likely, about

fit verb
1 *We need to **fit** a new lock on the door.*
install, put in place, position
2 *This key doesn't **fit** the lock.*
*He **fits** the description of the wanted criminal.*
match, correspond to, go together with, tally with
3 *Her speech perfectly **fitted** the occasion.*
be suitable for, be appropriate to, suit

fix verb
1 *The soldier **fixed** a bayonet to the end of his rifle.*
fasten, attach, connect, join, link
2 *We **fixed** the tent poles in the ground.*
set, secure, make firm, stabilize
3 *Let's **fix** a time for the party.*
decide on, agree on, set, arrange, settle, determine, specify, finalize
4 (informal) *Dad says he can **fix** my bike.*
repair, mend, sort, put right

fix noun
(informal) *Can you help me? I'm in a **fix**.*
difficulty, mess, predicament, plight
(informal) jam, hole

fizzy adjective
*Could I have a bottle of **fizzy** water, please?*
sparkling, bubbly, effervescent, gassy, foaming
OPPOSITE still

flag noun
*The street was decorated with **flags** for the carnival.*
banner, pennant, streamer
The flag of a regiment is its **colours** or **standard**.
A flag flown on a ship is an **ensign**.
Decorative strips of small flags are **bunting**.

flap verb
*The sail **flapped** in the wind.*
flutter, sway, swing, wave about, thrash about

flash verb
*We saw a light **flash** from an upstairs window.*
shine, beam, blaze, flare, glare, gleam, glint, flicker, glimmer, sparkle

flash noun
*There were **flashes** of lightning in the sky.*
blaze, flare, beam, ray, shaft, burst, gleam, glint, flicker, glimmer, sparkle

flat adjective
1 *You need a **flat** surface to write on.*
even, level, smooth, plane
A common simile is **as flat as a pancake**.
OPPOSITE uneven
2 *I lay **flat** on the ground.*
horizontal, outstretched, spread out
To be lying face downwards is to be **prone**.
To be lying face upwards is to be **supine**.
OPPOSITE upright
3 *The robot spoke in a **flat**, electronic voice.*
dull, boring, lifeless, uninteresting, monotonous, tedious
OPPOSITE lively
4 *The front tyre of my bike was **flat**.*
deflated, punctured
OPPOSITE inflated
5 *Our request met with a **flat** refusal.*
outright, straight, positive, absolute, total, utter, point-blank

flatten verb
1 *We **flattened** the crumpled map on the desk.*
smooth, press, roll out, iron out
2 *The earthquake **flattened** several buildings.*
demolish, destroy, knock down, pull down, level
3 *The young plants were **flattened** by the rain.*
squash, crush, trample

flavour noun
1 *I don't like the **flavour** of raw onions.*
taste, tang
2 *Which **flavour** of ice cream do you like best?*
kind, sort, variety

flexible adjective
1 *I need a pair of trainers with **flexible** soles.*
bendable, supple, pliable, bendy, elastic, springy
OPPOSITE rigid, inflexible
2 *My working hours are very **flexible**.*
adjustable, adaptable, variable, open
OPPOSITE fixed

flicker *verb*
The candlelight **flickered** in the draught.
twinkle, glimmer, waver, flutter, blink, shimmer

flimsy *adjective*
1 The kite was so **flimsy** that it broke apart.
fragile, delicate, frail, brittle, weak, wobbly, shaky, rickety
OPPOSITE sturdy, robust
2 The fairy wore a dress of the **flimsiest** silk.
thin, fine, light, lightweight, floaty

flinch *verb*
He **flinched** as an arrow flew past his head.
back off, draw back, falter, recoil, shrink back, start, wince

fling *verb*
I **flung** a stone into the pond.
throw, cast, sling, toss, hurl, pitch (informal) chuck, bung

float *verb*
We watched the twigs **float** gently down the river.
sail, drift, glide, slip, slide, waft

flood *noun*
1 The **flood** of water swept away the bridge.
deluge, inundation, rush, torrent, spate
2 The restaurant has received a **flood** of complaints.
succession, barrage, storm, volley

flood *verb*
1 The river burst its banks and **flooded** the valley.
drown, swamp, inundate, submerge, immerse, engulf
2 We have been **flooded** with entries for our competition.
overwhelm, swamp, besiege

flop *verb*
1 I was so tired that I just **flopped** onto my bed.
collapse, drop, fall, slump
2 The plants will **flop** if you don't water them.
dangle, droop, hang down, sag, wilt
3 (informal) The first film **flopped**, but the sequel was a big hit.
be unsuccessful, fail, founder, fall flat

floppy *adjective*
The dog had long, **floppy** ears.
droopy, limp, saggy, soft
OPPOSITE stiff, rigid

flow *verb*
The rain water **flowed** along the gutter.
run, stream, pour, glide
To flow slowly is to **dribble**, **drip**, **ooze**, **seep**, or **trickle**.
To flow fast is to **cascade**, **gush**, or **sweep**.

flood

To flow with sudden force is to **spurt** or **squirt**.
To flow over the edge of something is to **overflow** or **spill**.
When blood flows from a wound, it **bleeds**.
When the tide flows out, it **ebbs**.

flow *noun*
1 It's hard work rowing against the **flow**.
current, tide, drift
2 There was a steady **flow** of water into the pond.
stream, flood, cascade, gush, rush, spate

fluffy *adjective*
Four **fluffy** ducklings were swimming in the pond.
feathery, downy, furry, fuzzy, hairy, woolly, shaggy, soft

flush *verb*
Rory **flushed** with embarrassment.
blush, go red, colour, redden, burn

flustered *adjective*
I get **flustered** when I have to read in assembly.
confused, upset, bothered, agitated, unsettled, ruffled
(informal) rattled
OPPOSITE calm

flutter *verb*
A moth **fluttered** about the light bulb.
flap, beat, flicker, quiver, tremble, vibrate

foam *noun*
The bath water was covered with pinkish **foam**.
bubbles, froth, suds, lather
Foam made by sea water is **surf** or **spume**.

foam *verb*
The mixture in the cauldron **foamed** and gurgled.
froth, bubble, fizz, boil, seethe, ferment, lather

fog *noun*
The top of the mountain was covered with **fog**.
Thin fog is **haze** or **mist**.
A thick mixture of fog and smoke is **smog**.

fold *verb*
Fold the paper along the dotted line.
bend, double over, crease, pleat

fold *noun*
She smoothed the soft **folds** of her dress.
crease, furrow, layer
A fold which is pressed into a garment is a **pleat**.

follow *verb*
1 Why does thunder always **follow** lightning?
come after, succeed, replace
OPPOSITE precede
2 I think that car is **following** us!
go after, chase, pursue, track, trail, tail, stalk, hunt, shadow
3 **Follow** this path until you reach the river.
go along, keep to
4 I **followed** the instructions on the packet.
carry out, comply with, heed, obey, observe
5 Which football team do you **follow**?
be a fan of, support
6 We found it hard to **follow** what the creature was saying.
understand, comprehend, grasp, take in, catch

fond *adjective*
1 Mrs Walker gave her pet poodle a **fond** kiss.
loving, tender, affectionate
2 Anna had a **fond** hope that she would become a film star.
foolish, silly, unrealistic, fanciful
to be fond of
I'm very **fond of** chocolate cake.
be keen on, be partial to, like, love

a b c d e f g h i j k l m n o p q r s t u v w x y z

food
see panel below

fool *noun*
*Only a **fool** would believe that ridiculous story.*
idiot, dope, ass, clown, halfwit, moron, dimwit, dunce, simpleton, blockhead, buffoon, clot, dunderhead, imbecile, (*informal*) twit, chump, nitwit, nincompoop

fool *verb*
*The spy **fooled** everyone with his disguises.*
deceive, trick, mislead, hoax, dupe, hoodwink
(*informal*) con, kid, have you on, take you in, pull the wool over your eyes

to fool about or **around**
*We were told not to **fool about** in the swimming pool.*
play about, mess about, misbehave

foolish *adjective*
*It would be **foolish** to stand too close to the lions.*
stupid, silly, idiotic, senseless, ridiculous, nonsensical, unwise, ill-advised, half-witted, unintelligent, absurd, crazy, mad, hare-brained
(*informal*) daft
OPPOSITE sensible

foot *noun*
1 *Rhona walked on the sand in her bare **feet**.*
The foot of an animal that has claws is a ***paw***.

The foot of a cow, deer, or horse is a ***hoof***.
A pig's foot is a ***trotter***.
A bird's feet are its ***claws***.
The feet of a bird of prey are its ***talons***.
2 *We set up camp at the **foot** of the mountain.*
base, bottom

football
see panel below

forbidden *adjective*
*Skateboarding is **forbidden** in the playground.*
banned, barred, prohibited, disallowed, outlawed
OPPOSITE allowed

force *noun*
1 *The firefighters had to use **force** to open the door.*
strength, power, might, muscle, vigour, effort, energy
2 *The **force** of the explosion broke all the windows.*
impact, effect, shock, intensity
3 *The soldiers are part of a peace-keeping **force**.*
group, unit, team, corps, army, troops

✷ WORD WEB

food *noun*
  *The banquet table was laid out with all kinds of **food**.*
  foodstuffs, rations, provisions, refreshments, eatables, nourishment, nutrition
  (*informal*) grub, nosh
The food that you normally eat or choose to eat is your ***diet***.
A diet which includes no meat is a ***vegetarian*** diet.
A diet which includes no animal products is a ***vegan*** diet.
Food which includes fish or shellfish is ***seafood***.
Foods made from milk, butter, cheese, or eggs are ***dairy foods***.
Food for farm animals is ***fodder***.

SOME TYPES OF SEAFOOD
bloater, bream, caviare, cod, crab, eel, haddock, halibut, herring, kipper, lobster, mackerel, monkfish, mussels, oysters, pilchard, plaice, prawn, salmon, sardine, scampi, sea bass, shrimp, sole, sprat, trout, tuna, whelks, whitebait, whiting

SOME DAIRY FOODS
butter, cheese, cream, curds, custard, eggs, ice cream, milk, yoghurt

FOODS MADE FROM FLOUR OR CEREALS
batter, biscuits, bread, bun, cornflakes, cracker, crispbread, muesli, noodles, oatcake, pancake, pastry, popcorn, porridge, ricecake, roll, scone, toast

SOME PREPARED DISHES OF FOOD
balti, bhaji, broth, casserole, chilli, chips, chop suey, chow mein, curry, dhal, fritters, goulash, houmous, hotpot, omelette, pakora, panini, pasta, pie, pizza, quiche, samosa, sandwich, soufflé, soup, stew, stir-fry, sushi

SOME PUDDINGS AND OTHER SWEET FOODS
brownie, cake, chocolate, flan, gateau, honey, jam, jelly, marmalade, marzipan, meringue, mousse, muffin, sponge, steamed pudding, sugar, tart, treacle, trifle

SOME FLAVOURINGS AND SAUCES FOR FOOD
chilli, chutney, French dressing, garlic, gravy, herbs, ketchup, mayonnaise, mustard, pepper, pickle, salsa, salt, spice, vinegar

Things like salt and pepper which you add to food are ***condiments*** or ***seasoning***.

✷ WORD WEB

football *noun*
Football is also known as ***soccer***.
Someone who plays football is a ***footballer***.
Football is played on a ***field*** or ***pitch*** in a ***ground***, ***park***, or ***stadium***.

MEMBERS OF A FOOTBALL TEAM
captain, defender, fullback, forward, goalkeeper or (*informal*) goalie, midfielder, striker, substitute, sweeper, winger

referee

force *verb*
1 *The slaves were **forced** to work in the mines.*
compel, make, order, require, oblige, pressurize, coerce
2 *The king **forced** a new law upon the country.*
impose, inflict
3 *The firefighters had to **force** the door.*
break open, burst open, prise open, smash, wrench
(*informal*) yank

foreign *adjective*
1 *Lots of **foreign** tourists visit Edinburgh in the summer.*
overseas, international
OPPOSITE native, domestic
2 *I like travelling to **foreign** countries.*
overseas, distant, faraway, exotic, remote, far-flung

forever *adverb*
*Timmy is **forever** complaining about something.*
constantly, continually, always, perpetually

forgery *noun*
*One of these paintings is a **forgery**.*
fake, copy, imitation, reproduction, replica
(*informal*) phoney

forget *verb*
1 *I **forgot** my toothbrush when I packed my suitcase.*
leave out, leave behind, overlook
2 *I **forgot** to switch off the computer.*
omit, neglect, fail

forgive *verb*
*Please **forgive** me for being so rude.*
excuse, pardon, let off, overlook, spare

form *noun*
1 *I made out the **form** of a man through the mist.*
shape, figure, outline, silhouette
2 *Ice is a **form** of water.*
kind, sort, type, variety
3 *My brother moves up into a higher **form** next term.*
class, year, grade, set

form *verb*
1 *The sculptor **formed** the clay into the shape of a bird.*
shape, mould, model, fashion, work, cast

2 *My friends and I have **formed** a chess club.*
set up, establish, found, create, start
3 *Icicles had **formed** on the roof of the cave.*
appear, develop, grow, emerge, take shape

formal *adjective*
1 *I was invited to the **formal** opening of the museum.*
official, ceremonial
2 *The letter was written in a very **formal** style.*
correct, proper, conventional, dignified, solemn
OPPOSITE informal, casual

fortune *noun*
1 *By good **fortune**, I stumbled across a secret doorway.*
chance, luck, accident, fate
2 *The millionairess left her **fortune** to charity.*
wealth, riches, possessions, property, assets, estate
(*informal*) millions

foul *adjective*
1 *The knight fainted at the **foul** smell of the dragon's breath.*
disgusting, revolting, repulsive, vile, rotten, stinking, offensive, unpleasant, loathsome, nasty, horrible
OPPOSITE pleasant
2 *The walls and floor of the dungeon were **foul**.*
dirty, unclean, filthy, mucky, messy
OPPOSITE clean, pure
3 *The player was sent off for using **foul** language.*
rude, offensive, insulting, abusive, improper, indecent, obscene

fragile *adjective*
*Fossil dinosaur bones are very **fragile**.*
breakable, delicate, frail, brittle, easily damaged, weak
OPPOSITE strong

frail *adjective*
1 *My grandad felt **frail** after his illness.*
weak, infirm, feeble
2 *That step-ladder looks a bit **frail**.*
flimsy, fragile, delicate, rickety, unsound
OPPOSITE strong, robust

frantic *adjective*
1 *I was **frantic** with worry when our kitten got lost.*
beside yourself, fraught, desperate, distraught, hysterical, worked up, berserk
2 *There was **frantic** activity on the day of the wedding.*
excited, hectic, frenzied, feverish, wild, mad

footballer

OTHER PEOPLE INVOLVED IN FOOTBALL
ballboy or ballgirl, coach, linesman, manager, referee

SOME MOVES A FOOTBALLER MIGHT MAKE
chip, dribble, dummy, header, kick, mazy run, miss, pass, score, shot, tackle, volley

SOME OTHER TERMS USED IN FOOTBALL
corner, crossbar, deflection, dugout, equalizer, extra time, final whistle, foul, free kick, goal, goalposts, half-time, kick-off, net, offside, penalty, penalty shootout, red or yellow card, sending off, throw-in

boots

corner flag

football

fraud noun
1 *The bank manager was found guilty of* **fraud**.
deceit, deception, dishonesty, swindling, cheating
2 *The prize draw was just a* **fraud**—*no-one won anything.*
swindle, trick, hoax, pretence, sham (*informal*) con, scam
(*informal*) con man, phoney

free adjective
1 *You are* **free** *to wander anywhere in the building.*
able, allowed, permitted, at liberty
OPPOSITE restricted
2 *After ten years in jail, the prisoners were* **free** *at last.*
freed, liberated, released, emancipated, at large, on the loose
A common simile is **as free as a bird**.
OPPOSITE imprisoned, enslaved
3 *I got a* **free** *drink with my sandwich.*
complimentary, free of charge, gratis, on the house
4 *Are you* **free** *this weekend?*
available, unoccupied
OPPOSITE busy, occupied
5 *The bathroom is* **free** *now.*
available, unoccupied, vacant, empty
OPPOSITE engaged

free verb
1 *The soldiers* **freed** *the prisoners of war.*
release, liberate, set free, deliver
To free slaves is to **emancipate** them.
To free prisoners by paying money to the captors is to **ransom** them.
OPPOSITE imprison
2 *We* **freed** *the dogs and let them run about.*
loose, turn loose, let go, untie, unchain
OPPOSITE confine

freedom noun
The animals have a lot of **freedom** *in the safari park.*
liberty, independence

freeze verb
1 *Water begins to* **freeze** *at 0°C.*
become ice, ice over, harden, solidify
2 *If you* **freeze** *food, you can store it for a long time.*
deep-freeze, chill, refrigerate

freezing adjective
It's **freezing** *cold outside in winter.*
chilly, frosty, icy, wintry, raw, bitter

frequent adjective
1 *I send* **frequent** *email messages to my friends.*
numerous, constant, continual, recurring, recurrent, repeated, countless
OPPOSITE infrequent

2 *Badgers are* **frequent** *visitors to the garden.*
regular, habitual, common, familiar, persistent
OPPOSITE rare

fresh adjective
1 *This pudding is made with* **fresh** *fruit.*
natural, raw, unprocessed
2 *The shop bakes* **fresh** *bread every day.*
new
OPPOSITE old, stale
3 *Sally went outside to get some* **fresh** *air.*
clean, cool, crisp, refreshing
OPPOSITE stuffy
4 *Have you put* **fresh** *sheets on the bed?*
new, clean, laundered, washed
OPPOSITE dirty
5 *Having a shower makes me feel nice and* **fresh**.
refreshed, revived, restored, invigorated
6 *We need some* **fresh** *ideas for our magazine.*
new, original, different, novel, innovative
OPPOSITE old

friend noun
I am inviting four **friends** *to my birthday party.*
companion, comrade
(*informal*) mate, pal, buddy, chum
A friend you play games with is a **playmate**.
A friend you work with or live with is your **partner**.
A friend you write to but don't normally meet is a **penfriend**.
A friend you know only slightly is an **acquaintance**.
OPPOSITE enemy

friendly adjective
1 *Our neighbour's pet dog is very* **friendly**.
affectionate, loving, good-natured, likeable, amiable, approachable, kind-hearted, kindly, amicable, genial, sociable, outgoing, sympathetic
2 *Those two are very* **friendly** *with each other.*
close, familiar, intimate
(*informal*) pally, chummy
3 *I like this cafe—it has a very* **friendly** *atmosphere.*
warm, welcoming, hospitable, cordial, neighbourly

fright noun
1 *The girl jumped up in* **fright** *and began to scream.*
fear, terror, alarm, horror, panic, dread

2 *The explosion gave us an awful* **fright**!
scare, shock, surprise, start, turn, jolt

frighten verb
Sorry—I didn't mean to **frighten** *you.*
scare, terrify, startle, alarm, shock, panic, petrify

frightened adjective
Mia always felt **frightened** *in the dark.*
afraid, scared, terrified, alarmed, fearful, panicky, petrified

frightening adjective
The ghost story she told was quite **frightening**.
terrifying, horrifying, scary, alarming, nightmarish, chilling, spine-chilling, hair-raising, bloodcurdling, chilling, eerie, sinister, fearsome
(*informal*) creepy, spooky

frisky adjective
The new lion cubs in the zoo are very **frisky**.
playful, lively, high-spirited, sprightly

frivolous adjective
Don't waste my time asking **frivolous** *questions.*
foolish, silly, ridiculous, shallow, superficial, pointless, unimportant, trivial, petty

front noun
1 *We stood at the* **front** *of the queue.*
head, start, beginning, lead, top
2 *The* **front** *of the house was painted white.*
face, facing, frontage, facade
The front of a ship is the **bow** or **prow**.
The front of a picture is the **foreground**.

front adjective
1 *The* **front** *runners came into sight round the corner.*
first, leading, most advanced
OPPOSITE back
2 *The horse had injured one of its* **front** *legs.*
fore
OPPOSITE back, rear, hind

frosty adjective
1 *It was a clear,* **frosty** *night.*
cold, crisp, icy, freezing, wintry
2 *The shopkeeper gave us a* **frosty** *stare.*
unfriendly, unwelcoming, cold, cool, stony

frown noun
On Christmas Eve, Scrooge had a **frown** *on his face.*
scowl, glare, grimace, glower, black look

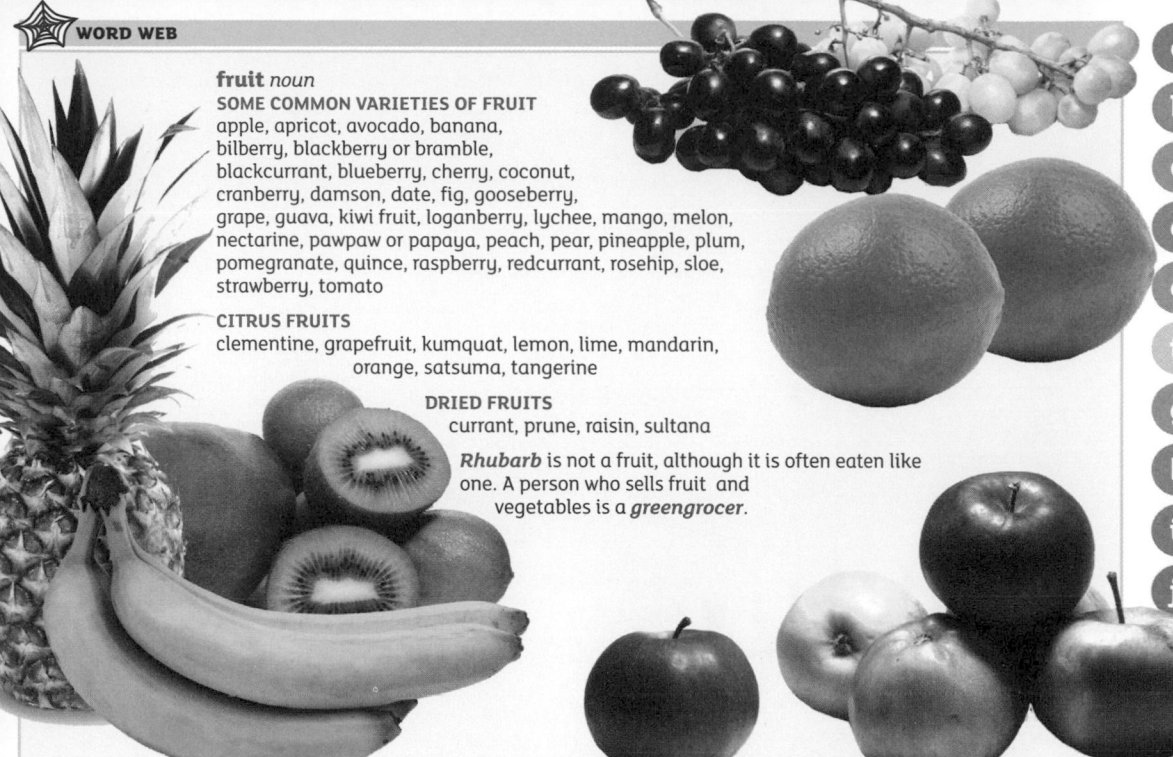

WORD WEB

fruit *noun*
SOME COMMON VARIETIES OF FRUIT
apple, apricot, avocado, banana,
bilberry, blackberry or bramble,
blackcurrant, blueberry, cherry, coconut,
cranberry, damson, date, fig, gooseberry,
grape, guava, kiwi fruit, loganberry, lychee, mango, melon,
nectarine, pawpaw or papaya, peach, pear, pineapple, plum,
pomegranate, quince, raspberry, redcurrant, rosehip, sloe,
strawberry, tomato

CITRUS FRUITS
clementine, grapefruit, kumquat, lemon, lime, mandarin,
orange, satsuma, tangerine

DRIED FRUITS
currant, prune, raisin, sultana

Rhubarb is not a fruit, although it is often eaten like
one. A person who sells fruit and
vegetables is a *greengrocer*.

---

frown *verb*
The witch **frowned** when her spell
didn't work.
scowl, glare, grimace, glower, knit
your brow, look sullen

fruit *noun see panel above*

frustrate *verb*
1 It was **frustrating** to have to wait
in the long queue.
exasperate, discourage, dispirit,
irritate
2 Our plan for the day was
frustrated by the weather.
block, foil, thwart, defeat, check,
hinder, prevent

full *adjective*
1 My suitcase is **full** to the brim.
filled, loaded, topped up
OPPOSITE empty
2 The shopping centre was **full** on
Saturday.
busy, crowded, jammed, packed,
crammed, congested
OPPOSITE empty
3 The detective gave a **full** account
of his findings.
complete, detailed, exhaustive
comprehensive, thorough,
OPPOSITE incomplete
4 The horses were galloping at **full**
speed.
top, maximum, greatest, highest
OPPOSITE minimum

fun *noun*
We had great **fun** at the beach on our
holiday.
amusement, diversion, enjoyment,
entertainment, games, jokes,
laughter, merriment, play, pleasure,
recreation, sport
to make fun of someone
It was cruel to **make fun of** her when
she fell over.
jeer at, laugh at, mock, ridicule,
taunt, tease

funny *adjective*
1 There are some very **funny** jokes
in the film.
amusing, humorous, comic, comical,
hilarious, witty, entertaining,
diverting
(*informal*) hysterical, priceless
OPPOSITE serious
2 There's a **funny** smell in here.
strange, odd, peculiar, curious,
puzzling, weird, queer, bizarre

furious *adjective*
The manager was **furious** when his
team lost.
angry, mad, enraged, infuriated,
incensed, livid, fuming, raging,
seething

furry *adjective*
A small, **furry** creature was curled
inside the box.
hairy, fleecy, woolly, fuzzy, downy,
feathery

fuss *noun*
There was a lot of **fuss** when the
queen arrived.
bother, commotion, excitement,
trouble, hullabaloo

fuss *verb*
Please don't **fuss**!
worry, fret, bother, get worked
up

fussy *adjective*
1 Our cat is **fussy** about her food.
finicky, hard to please, particular
(*informal*) choosy, picky
An informal name for a fussy person
is a **fusspot**.
2 I don't like clothes with **fussy**
designs.
fancy, elaborate, ornate, florid

future *noun*
She has a bright **future** as a tennis
player.
outlook, prospects
OPPOSITE past

fuzzy *adjective*
1 The TV picture has gone **fuzzy**.
blurred, bleary, unfocused, unclear,
indistinct, hazy, cloudy
OPPOSITE clear
2 Mia was wearing a **fuzzy**
cardigan.
fluffy, frizzy, furry, woolly,
fleecy

Gg

gadget noun
This torch is a handy little gadget.
tool, instrument, implement, device, contraption, gizmo

game noun
1 *My favourite game is hide-and-seek.*
amusement, pastime, sport, activity, recreation
2 *The big game is on this Saturday.*
match, contest, competition, tournament

cards

chess

gang noun
1 *The sea was swarming with gangs of pirates.*
group, band, crowd, pack, set, mob
2 *A gang of workmen dug a hole in the road.*
team, unit, crew, squad, party

gap noun
1 *The animals escaped through a gap in the fence.*
opening, space, hole, breach, break, crack, rift
2 *She returned to work after a gap of two years.*
break, interval, interruption, pause, lull

gate noun
People waited at the gate to be let in.
gateway, doorway, entrance, portal

gather verb
1 *A crowd gathered to watch the performers.*
assemble, collect, come together, congregate
OPPOSITE disperse
2 *The captain gathered her team to give them a talk.*
bring together, round up, muster
3 *We gathered daisies to make into chains.*
pick, pluck, collect, harvest

4 *I gather that you've been on holiday.*
understand, hear, learn, believe

general adjective
1 *There was a general air of gloom about the abbey.*
widespread, extensive, broad, sweeping, overall, prevalent
2 *I've only got a general idea of where we are.*
rough, approximate, indefinite, vague, loose

generous adjective
1 *It was generous of you to give me your seat.*
unselfish, charitable, kind-hearted
OPPOSITE selfish
2 *We each got a generous helping of ice cream.*
ample, large, lavish, plentiful
OPPOSITE meagre

genius noun
Nila is a genius at maths.
expert, master, mastermind, wizard, ace

gentle adjective
1 *The vet is very gentle with sick animals.*
kind, tender, good-tempered, humane
2 *Grasses swayed in the gentle breeze.*
light, slight, mild, soft, faint
OPPOSITE strong
3 *There is a gentle slope to the top of the hill.*
slight, gradual, easy
OPPOSITE steep

genuine adjective
1 *Is that a genuine diamond?*
real, actual, true, authentic
OPPOSITE fake
2 *Your friend seems like a very genuine person.*
honest, sincere, frank, earnest
OPPOSITE false

gesture noun
She opened her arms in a gesture of welcome.
sign, signal, motion, movement

get verb
1 *We're getting a goldfish for our class.*
acquire, obtain, buy, purchase
2 *Can you get me another blanket, please?*
bring, fetch, collect, pick up, retrieve
3 *Cara got a medal for swimming.*
receive, gain, earn, win, achieve
4 *What time did you get home?*
arrive at, reach, come to
OPPOSITE leave

5 *It was starting to get dark outside.*
become, grow, turn
6 *I got a stomach bug on holiday last year.*
catch, develop, pick up, come down with
7 *You'll never get Oscar to eat celery.*
persuade, urge, influence, coax
8 *I don't get the point of that film.*
understand, follow, comprehend, grasp
to get out of
My brother got out of doing the washing up.
avoid, evade, shirk
to get over
He hasn't got over the accident yet.
get better from, recover from, shake off, survive

ghastly adjective
The boy's face turned a ghastly shade of green.
appalling, awful, dreadful, frightful, grim, grisly, horrible, horrifying, shocking, monstrous, terrible

WORD WEB

ghost noun
Meldrop House was haunted by several ghosts.
spirit, spectre, phantom, ghoul, apparition, shade, wraith
(*informal*) spook
A ghost that makes a lot of noise is a poltergeist.

A GHOST OR GHOSTLY EXPERIENCE MIGHT BE
bloodcurdling, chilling, grisly, gruesome, hair-raising, macabre, nightmarish, spine-chilling, spine-tingling

THINGS A GHOST MIGHT DO
flit, float, glide, glow, haunt a person or place, hover, lurk, materialize, pass through walls, rattle chains, shimmer, vanish, waft

NOISES A GHOST MIGHT MAKE
cackle, clang, clank, creak, groan, hoot, howl, moan, screech, sigh, sob, wail

PLACES A GHOST MIGHT BE FOUND
catacombs, crypt, haunted house or mansion, graveyard, sepulchre, tomb, vault

OTHER THINGS THAT MIGHT BE IN A HAUNTED HOUSE
bats, candles, cellar, cobwebs, dungeon, gargoyle, mummy, owl, secret door or passage, skeleton, skull, trap door, turret

ghostly *adjective*
*The candlelight cast **ghostly** shadows on the wall.*
spectral, phantom, ghoulish, unearthly, eerie, sinister, uncanny
(*informal*) spooky, creepy

giant *adjective*
*A **giant** tree towered above us.*
gigantic, huge, enormous, massive, immense, mammoth, colossal, monstrous
OPPOSITE tiny

giddy *adjective*
*I felt **giddy** when I stood at the edge of the cliff.*
dizzy, faint, unsteady

gift *noun*
1 *I received some nice **gifts** on my birthday.*
present
2 *Elsa has a **gift** for music.*
talent, ability, flair, knack, genius

gigantic *adjective*
*The dragon reared its **gigantic** head.*
huge, giant, enormous, massive, colossal, immense, mammoth, monstrous
(*informal*) whopping, humungous
OPPOSITE tiny

giggle *verb*
*Ailsa and I couldn't stop **giggling**.*
snigger, titter, chuckle, laugh

girl *noun*
A synonym used in some parts of Britain is *lass*.
Old-fashioned words are *damsel*, *maid*, and *maiden*.

give *verb*
1 *Santa Claus **gave** each child a present.*
deal out, distribute, issue, supply, offer, present, hand over, pass, award
2 *Will you **give** something to our collection for charity?*
contribute, donate
3 *The giant **gave** a loud sneeze.*
utter, emit, let out
4 *We are **giving** a concert at the end of term.*
present, put on, lay on, organize, arrange

glimmer

5 *Will this branch **give** if I sit on it?*
collapse, give way, bend, break, buckle
to give in
*The boxer **gave in** after a long fight.*
surrender, yield, submit, quit
to give up
*He **gave up** trying to start the car.*
abandon, stop, cease, quit

glad *adjective*
*I'm **glad** to hear that you're feeling better.*
pleased, happy, delighted, thrilled
OPPOSITE sad

glance *verb*
*The bus driver **glanced** quickly at his watch.*
look quickly, peek, peep, glimpse

glare *verb*
*The troll **glared** at us from under his bushy eyebrows.*
stare, frown, scowl, glower

glare *noun*
1 *The **glare** of the lights dazzled me.*
dazzle, blaze, brightness, brilliance
2 *Miss Frump silenced the children with an angry **glare**.*
stare, scowl, glower, frown, nasty look

gleam *noun*
*I saw a **gleam** of moonlight between the clouds.*
glimmer, glint, flash, ray, shaft

gleam *verb*
*The lights **gleamed** on the water.*
glimmer, glint, glisten, shimmer, shine

glide *verb*
*The boat **glided** gently across the lake.*
move smoothly, slide, slip, drift, float, coast

glimmer *verb*
*The city lights **glimmered** in the distance.*
gleam, glint, glow, glisten, shimmer, flicker, blink

glimpse *verb*
*I **glimpsed** a deer running through the forest.*
catch sight of, spot, spy, sight

glimpse *noun*
*We caught a **glimpse** of a whale in the sea.*
peek, peep, glance, sighting, view

glint *verb*
*Sunlight **glinted** on the windows.*
flash, glitter, sparkle, twinkle

glisten *verb*
*The pavement **glistened** with frost.*
gleam, shine, glint, shimmer, glimmer

glitter *verb*
*The jewels **glittered** under the bright lights.*
sparkle, twinkle, shimmer, glimmer, glint, glisten, flash, shine

gloat *verb*
*He was **gloating** about winning the poetry prize.*
boast, brag, crow, show off

global *adjective*
*The Internet is a **global** network of computers.*
worldwide, international, universal

gloom *noun*
1 *We could hardly see in the **gloom** of the cave.*
darkness, dimness, shade, shadow, murk
The gloomy light late in the evening is *dusk* or *twilight*.
2 *There was an air of **gloom** in the abandoned tower.*
depression, sadness, unhappiness, melancholy, misery, despair

gloomy *adjective*
1 *It was cold and **gloomy** in the cellar.*
dark, dingy, dim, dismal, dreary, sombre, cheerless, murky, shadowy
OPPOSITE bright
2 *Eeyore was feeling **gloomy** again.*
depressed, sad, unhappy, glum, miserable, melancholy, low, downcast, dejected
(*informal*) down in the dumps
OPPOSITE cheerful

a b c d e f g h i j k l m n o p q r s t u v w x y z

glorious adjective
*Look at that **glorious** sunset!*
magnificent, splendid, stunning, spectacular, superb, wonderful, marvellous

glossy adjective
*The bear had a thick, **glossy** coat of black fur.*
shiny, sleek, silky, shining, gleaming, lustrous
OPPOSITE dull

glow noun
*The soft **glow** of burning candles lit the room.*
brightness, shine, gleam, radiance

glow verb
*The embers of the bonfire were still **glowing**.*
shine, gleam, burn
Something that glows in the dark is **luminous** or **phosphorescent**.

glum adjective
*Why are you looking so **glum**?*
depressed, sad, unhappy, gloomy, miserable, melancholy, low, downcast, dejected
OPPOSITE cheerful

gnarled adjective
*The branches of the tree were **gnarled** with age.*
bent, twisted, crooked, distorted, knobbly, knotty

gnaw verb
*The wolves **gnawed** at a pile of bones.*
chew, bite, nibble, munch

go verb
1 *A carriage was **going** slowly along the road.*
move, progress, proceed
2 *My granny has always wanted to **go** to China.*
travel, journey
3 *Some of the guests had already **gone**.*
leave, depart, get away, withdraw
4 *By morning, the ice had all **gone**.*
disappear, vanish
5 *The canal **goes** all the way from Inverness to Fort William.*
extend, lead, reach, stretch, run
6 *The mountaineer's face **went** blue with cold.*
become, turn, grow
7 *Is that old grandfather clock still **going**?*
function, operate, work, run
8 *Cups and saucers **go** on the bottom shelf.*
belong, be kept, be placed
9 *Time **goes** slowly when you're stuck indoors.*
pass, go by, elapse
to go back
*Sarah has **gone back** to the house.*
return, retreat, retrace your steps

to go off
1 *A bomb **went off** nearby.*
explode, blow up, detonate
2 *The milk will **go off** if it's not in the fridge.*
turn sour, go bad, rot
to go on
1 *What's **going on** over there?*
happen, occur, take place
2 *Please **go on** with your story.*
carry on, continue, keep going, proceed

go noun
*Would you like to have a **go** on my computer?*
try, turn, chance, opportunity
(*informal*) shot, bash, stab

goal noun
*The **goal** of the society is to protect wildlife.*
aim, ambition, intention, object, objective, purpose, target

gobble verb
*Ladybirds love to **gobble** greenfly.*
guzzle, gulp, bolt, devour

good adjective
see panel opposite
*That is a really **good** idea!*
excellent, fine, lovely, nice, wonderful
(*informal*) fantastic, great, super, cool
OPPOSITE bad

gorgeous adjective
*The gardens look **gorgeous** in the summer.*
beautiful, glorious, dazzling, stunning, splendid, superb, glamorous, handsome

gossip verb
*Two neighbours were **gossiping** over the fence.*
chatter, tell tales
(*informal*) natter

gossip noun
1 *Don't believe all the **gossip** you hear.*
chatter, rumour, hearsay, scandal
(*informal*) tittle-tattle
2 *Our next-door neighbour is a dreadful **gossip**.*
busybody, chatterbox, telltale, scandalmonger

govern verb
*The ancient Romans **governed** a vast empire.*
rule, run, administer, direct, command, manage, be in charge of

grab verb
*The cowboy **grabbed** the reins of the runaway horse.*
seize, grasp, catch, clutch, grip, get hold of, snatch

graceful adjective
*The gymnast made a **graceful** landing.*
elegant, beautiful, stylish, smooth, flowing, agile, nimble
OPPOSITE clumsy, graceless

grade noun
*My sister has reached the top **grade** in judo.*
class, standard, level, stage, rank, degree

gradual adjective
*There's been a **gradual** change in the weather.*
steady, slow, gentle, moderate, regular, even
OPPOSITE sudden

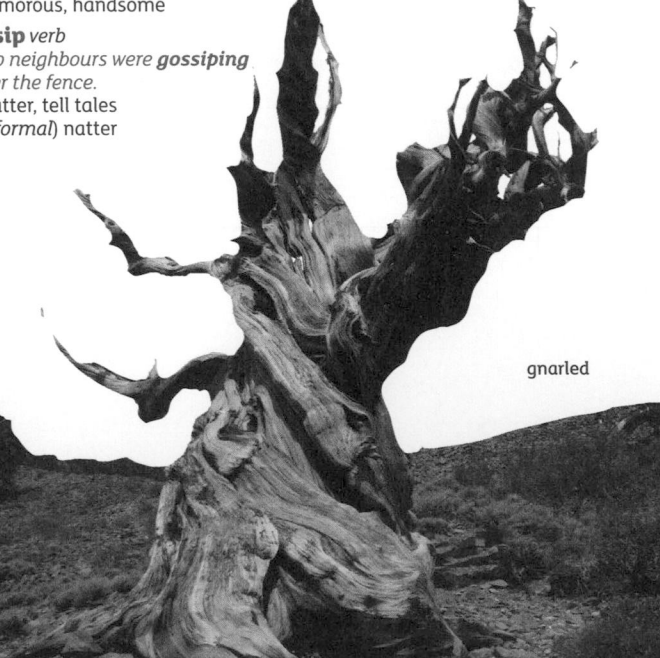

gnarled

grand adjective
1 The wedding was a **grand** occasion.
magnificent, splendid, stately, impressive, big, great, important, imposing
2 (informal) Keep going—you're doing a **grand** job!
excellent, fine, good, first-class

grapple verb
The guard **grappled** with the thief, but he got away.
struggle, wrestle, fight, tussle

grasp verb
1 The climber **grasped** the rope.
clutch, grab, grip, seize, catch, snatch, take hold of, hang on to
2 The ideas were quite difficult to **grasp**.
understand, comprehend, follow, take in

grateful adjective
I'm **grateful** for your help.
thankful, appreciative, obliged, indebted
OPPOSITE ungrateful

grave adjective
1 They looked **grave** when they heard the news.
grim, sad, serious, thoughtful
OPPOSITE cheerful
2 She made a **grave** mistake.
crucial, important, serious, vital
OPPOSITE trivial

graze verb
I **grazed** my knee falling off my bike.
scrape, cut, scratch, scuff

great adjective
1 The inventor had made a **great** discovery.
important, significant, major, leading, noteworthy
OPPOSITE insignificant, minor
2 Mozart was a **great** composer.
famous, notable, celebrated, eminent, distinguished, outstanding, brilliant
3 Their voices echoed round the **great** hall.
big, huge, large, enormous, vast, immense, gigantic, extensive, cavernous
OPPOSITE small
4 Beth took **great** care over her knitting.
considerable, extreme, exact
OPPOSITE little
5 (informal) That is a **great** idea!
very good, excellent, marvellous, outstanding, superb, tremendous, wonderful

(informal) brilliant, fantastic, super, smashing, terrific
OPPOSITE bad, awful

greed noun
The king wanted more gold to satisfy his **greed**.
avarice, selfishness, hunger, craving, gluttony

greedy adjective
1 The boys were so **greedy** that they ate all the cakes.
gluttonous
(informal) piggish
A common simile is **as greedy as a pig**.
2 Mr Skimp is very **greedy** with his money.
selfish, miserly, tight-fisted, grasping

greet verb
My aunt **greeted** us with a friendly wave.
welcome, hail, receive, salute

grey adjective
1 The old wizard had a bushy **grey** beard.
silver, silvery, grizzly, hoary, whitish
2 The mother's face was **grey** with worry.
ashen, pale, leaden, wan
3 The day began cold and **grey**.
dull, cloudy, overcast

grief noun
He couldn't hide his **grief** at his friend's death.
sorrow, sadness, mourning, anguish, unhappiness, distress, heartache
OPPOSITE joy

grieve verb
The family is still **grieving** over her death.
mourn, lament, sorrow, weep
OPPOSITE rejoice

grim adjective
1 The judge wore a **grim** expression on his face.
stern, severe, harsh, bad-tempered, sullen
OPPOSITE cheerful
2 The detective made the **grim** discovery of the body.
unpleasant, horrible, dreadful, terrible, hideous, shocking, gruesome, grisly
OPPOSITE pleasant

grimy adjective
Don't wipe those **grimy** feet on the carpet!
dirty, filthy, grubby, mucky, soiled
OPPOSITE clean

grin noun, verb
Mark arrived with a silly **grin** on his face.
smile, beam, smirk
A large grin is a **broad**, **wide**, or **cheesy** grin.

! OVERUSED WORDS

good adjective
Try to vary the words you use for **good**. Here are some other words you could use.

FOR A *GOOD PERSON*
honest, worthy, honourable, moral, decent, virtuous, noble, kind, humane, charitable, merciful *The **virtuous** knight defeated the evil queen.*
OPPOSITE evil, wicked
A good character in a story or film is a **hero** or **heroine** or (informal) **goody**.

FOR *GOOD BEHAVIOUR*
well-behaved, obedient, angelic, exemplary *The twins are surprisingly **well-behaved**.*
A common simile is **as good as gold**.
OPPOSITE naughty, disobedient

FOR A *GOOD FRIEND*
true, loyal, loving, reliable, trusty, trustworthy *My dog, Rusty, is a **loyal** companion.*

FOR A *GOOD FEELING* OR *GOOD MOOD*
happy, cheerful, light-hearted, positive, contented *Mr Fox was in a **cheerful** mood after his tea.*

FOR A *GOOD EXPERIENCE* OR *GOOD NEWS*
pleasant, enjoyable, delightful, agreeable, pleasing

OPPOSITE unpleasant, disagreeable
*The girls had an **enjoyable** time at the party. The letter contained some **pleasing** news.*

FOR A *GOOD PERFORMER* OR *GOOD WORK*
capable, skilful, clever, able, talented, competent, commendable, sound *My friend, Chris, is a **talented** dancer.*
OPPOSITE poor, awful

FOR *GOOD FOOD* OR A *GOOD MEAL*
delicious, healthy, nourishing, nutritious, tasty, well-cooked, wholesome, substantial, hearty *The crew ate a **hearty** breakfast together.*

FOR A *GOOD EXCUSE* OR *GOOD REASON*
acceptable, valid, proper, satisfactory, legitimate *I hope you have a **valid** excuse for being late.*
OPPOSITE poor, unacceptable

FOR *GOOD TIMING*
convenient, suitable, fortunate, appropriate, opportune *Is this a **convenient** time for a chat?*
OPPOSITE inconvenient, unsuitable

FOR *GOOD WEATHER*
fine, favourable *We are hoping for **fine** weather tomorrow.*
OPPOSITE harsh, adverse

a b c d e f g h i j k l m n o p q r s t u v w x y z

grind verb
1 *Grind the spices into a fine powder.*
crush, pound, powder, pulverize, mill
2 *This tool is used for grinding knives.*
sharpen, file, hone, whet

grip verb
1 *Grip the handle tightly.*
grasp, seize, clutch, clasp, hold
2 *The audience was gripped by the film.*
fascinate, engross, absorb, enthrall

grisly adjective
We found the grisly remains of a dead sheep.
gruesome, gory, ghastly, hideous, nasty, revolting, sickening

groan verb
The wounded soldier groaned with pain.
cry out, moan, sigh, wail

gross adjective
1 *That is a gross exaggeration!*
extreme, glaring, obvious, sheer, blatant, outright
2 *Most ogres have gross table manners.*
offensive, rude, coarse, vulgar

ground noun
1 *I planted some seeds in the ground.*
earth, soil, land
2 *The ground was too wet to play on.*
field, pitch, park, stadium, arena

group noun
1 *Japan consists of a group of islands.*
collection, set, batch, cluster, clump
2 *A group of children was waiting at the bus stop.*
crowd, bunch, gathering, band, body, gang

grow

3 *The book group meets once a month.*
club, society, association, circle
4 *We sorted the fossils into different groups.*
category, class, type, kind, sort

grow verb
1 *I've grown an inch taller since last summer.*
get bigger, put on growth, spring up, sprout
2 *The number of children in the school has grown.*
increase, develop, enlarge, expand, build up
OPPOSITE decrease
3 *Our neighbour grows orchids in her greenhouse.*
cultivate, produce, raise, farm
4 *It is growing dark outside.*
become, get, turn

growth noun
There's been a growth of interest in golf for kids.
increase, rise, spread, expansion, development, enlargement

grubby adjective
My hands were grubby from working in the garden.
dirty, filthy, grimy, messy, mucky, soiled
OPPOSITE clean

gruesome adjective
The battlefield was a gruesome sight.
grisly, gory, ghastly, hideous, monstrous, revolting, sickening, appalling, dreadful, frightful, shocking, abominable

gruff adjective
The ogre spoke in a gruff voice.
harsh, rough, hoarse, husky, throaty

grumble verb
You're always grumbling about the weather!
complain, moan, groan, protest, whine, gripe

grumpy adjective
Marge was grumpy because she had a headache.
bad-tempered, cross, irritable, testy, tetchy, cantankerous (informal) grouchy
OPPOSITE good-humoured

guard verb
The cave was guarded by a one-eyed giant.
protect, defend, stand guard over, patrol, safeguard, shield, watch over

guard noun
A guard was on duty at the gate.
sentry, sentinel, warder, lookout, watchman

guess verb
1 *There was a prize for guessing the weight of the cake.*
estimate, judge, work out, gauge, predict, reckon
2 *I guess you must be tired after your journey.*
suppose, imagine, expect, assume, think

guest noun
We are having guests for tea on Sunday.
visitor, caller, company

guide noun
1 *Our guide showed us around the zoo.*
courier, escort, leader, chaperon
2 *We bought a useful guide to the city.*
guidebook, handbook, manual

guide verb
The explorers used the stars to guide them at night.
direct, lead, steer, conduct, escort, show the way

guilty adjective
1 *The prisoner was found guilty of the crime.*
responsible, to blame, at fault, in the wrong, liable
OPPOSITE innocent
2 *You have a guilty look on your face!*
ashamed, guilt-ridden, remorseful, sorry, conscience-stricken, repentant, shamefaced, sheepish
OPPOSITE unrepentant

gulp verb
Peter gulped down the cake in one go.
swallow, bolt, gobble, guzzle, devour

gush noun
There was a gush of water from the pipe.
rush, stream, torrent, rush, cascade, flood, jet, spout, spurt

gush verb
Water gushed from the broken pipe.
rush, stream, flow, pour, flood, spout, spurt, squirt

guzzle verb
The seagulls guzzled all the bread.
gobble, gulp, bolt, devour

Hh

habit noun
1 It's her **habit** to go for a walk each morning.
custom, practice, routine, rule
2 My dog has a **habit** of scratching his ear.
mannerism, way, tendency, inclination, quirk

haggard adjective
The warriors looked **haggard** after the battle.
drawn, gaunt, thin, pinched, wasted, shrunken, wan
OPPOSITE healthy

haggle verb
The men **haggled** over the price of the gems.
bargain, negotiate, argue, wrangle

✎ WRITING TIPS

hair noun
You can use these words to describe **hair**.

TO DESCRIBE ITS COLOUR
auburn, blond (male) or blonde (female), brunette, carroty, dark, fair, flaxen, ginger, grey, grizzled, hoary, mousy, platinum blonde, raven, red, silver

TO DESCRIBE HOW IT LOOKS OR FEELS
bushy, coarse, curly, dishevelled, fine, frizzy, glossy, greasy, lank, limp, ringletted, shaggy, shiny, silky, spiky, straggly, straight, stringy, tangled, thick, tousled, tuggy, unkempt, wavy, windswept, wispy The elderly knight had a **grizzled, straggly** beard.

hairy adjective
Mammoths were like elephants with thick **hairy** coats.
shaggy, bushy, bristly, woolly, fleecy, furry, fuzzy, long-haired, hirsute

hall noun
1 The **hall** was full for the concert.
assembly hall, auditorium, concert hall, theatre
2 You can use the coat stand in the **hall**.
entrance hall, hallway, lobby, foyer

halt verb
1 The car **halted** at the red light.
stop, come to a halt, draw up, pull up, wait

2 A traffic jam **halted** the traffic.
stop, check, obstruct
3 Work **halted** when the whistle went.
end, cease, terminate, break off
OPPOSITE start, go

hand verb
The postman **handed** me several letters.
give, pass, present, offer, deliver

handle verb
1 Please don't **handle** the exhibits.
touch, feel, hold, stroke, fondle, finger, grasp
2 The referee **handled** the game well.
manage, control, conduct, deal with, cope with, tackle

handsome adjective
1 Prince Charming was very **handsome**.
attractive, good-looking, nice-looking, gorgeous
(informal) dishy
OPPOSITE ugly, unattractive
2 They sold their house for a **handsome** profit.
big, large, substantial, sizeable
OPPOSITE slight

handy adjective
1 This **handy** gadget is for peeling potatoes.
useful, helpful, convenient, practical
OPPOSITE awkward
2 I always keep my umbrella **handy**.
accessible, available, close at hand, nearby, ready
OPPOSITE inaccessible

hang verb
1 A monkey was **hanging** from the tree branch.
dangle, be suspended, swing, sway
2 The dog had hair **hanging** down over his eyes.
droop, drape, flop, trail, cascade
3 I **hung** the picture on the wall.
fix, attach, fasten, stick, peg
4 Smoke **hung** in the air.
float, hover, drift, linger, cling
to hang about or **around**
Don't **hang about**, we'll miss the bus.
delay, dawdle, linger, loiter
to hang on
(informal) Try to **hang on** a bit longer.
carry on, continue, stay, remain, persist, keep going, persevere
to hang on to something
1 **Hang on to** the rope.
hold, grip, grasp
2 **Hang on to** your bus ticket.
keep, retain, save

happiness noun
The bride's face glowed with **happiness**.
joy, joyfulness, delight, jubilation, pleasure, contentment, gladness, cheerfulness, merriment, ecstasy, bliss
OPPOSITE sorrow

happy adjective
1 The girls look really **happy** in the photograph.
cheerful, joyful, jolly, merry, light-hearted, contented, gleeful, delighted
OPPOSITE unhappy, sad
2 Sandy was **happy** when she won first prize.
thrilled, ecstatic, elated, overjoyed
(informal) over the moon, thrilled to bits, tickled pink
3 They spent a **happy** summer on the island.
enjoyable, joyous, glorious, blissful, heavenly, idyllic

harbour noun
Several yachts were tied up in the **harbour**.
port, dock, mooring, quay, pier, wharf

hard adjective
1 The ground was **hard** and covered with frost.
solid, firm, dense, compact, rigid, stiff
OPPOSITE soft
2 The climber gave the rope a **hard** pull.
strong, forceful, heavy, powerful, violent
OPPOSITE light
3 Digging the tunnel was **hard** work.
tough, gruelling, strenuous, tiring, exhausting, laborious, backbreaking
OPPOSITE easy
4 None of us could solve the **hard** riddle.
difficult, complicated, complex, intricate, perplexing, puzzling, baffling, knotty, thorny
OPPOSITE simple

hard adverb
1 Ros is working **hard** at learning French.
strenuously, energetically, diligently, keenly, intently
2 It has been raining **hard** all afternoon.
heavily, steadily
(informal) cats and dogs

hardly adverb
I could **hardly** see in the fog.
barely, scarcely, only just, with difficulty

harm verb
1 His captors didn't **harm** him.
hurt, injure, ill-treat, wound

a b c d e f g h i j k l m n o p q r s t u v w x y z

2 *Too much direct sunlight may* **harm** *this plant.*
damage, spoil, ruin

harm *noun*
I didn't mean to cause him any **harm***.*
damage, hurt, injury, pain
OPPOSITE benefit

harmful *adjective*
Junk food can be **harmful** *to your health.*
damaging, dangerous, destructive, injurious, unhealthy
OPPOSITE harmless, beneficial

harmless *adjective*
1 *You can drink the potion—it is quite* **harmless***.*
safe, non-toxic, innocuous
OPPOSITE harmful, dangerous
2 *It was just a bit of* **harmless** *fun.*
innocent, inoffensive

harsh *adjective*
1 *The trumpet sounded loud and* **harsh***.*
rough, rasping, grating, jarring, shrill, raucous
OPPOSITE soft, gentle
2 *We blinked in the* **harsh** *light.*
bright, brilliant, dazzling, glaring
OPPOSITE soft, subdued
3 *The rescue team braved the* **harsh** *weather.*
severe, strict, cruel, hard, tough, bleak
OPPOSITE mild
4 *The coach had some* **harsh** *words to say.*
strong, sharp, unkind, unfriendly

hasty *adjective*
1 *The robbers made a* **hasty** *exit.*
fast, hurried, quick, sudden, swift, rapid, speedy
OPPOSITE slow
2 *The king regretted his* **hasty** *decision.*
rash, reckless, impatient, foolhardy, thoughtless
OPPOSITE careful

hate *verb*
1 *Eddie* **hates** *broccoli and peas.*
dislike, detest, despise, loathe
2 *I* **hate** *to bother you.*
be sorry, be reluctant, regret

have *verb*
1 *I* **have** *my own CD player.*
own, possess
2 *Our house* **has** *three bedrooms.*
consist of, comprise, include, incorporate
3 *We are* **having** *a barbecue at the weekend.*
hold, organize, provide, host, throw
4 *Dad* **had** *trouble finding a place to park.*
experience, go through, meet with, run into, face, suffer

5 *The girls* **had** *a great time at the party.*
experience, enjoy
6 *The BBC has* **had** *lots of email messages.*
receive, get, be given, be sent
7 *Sharon* **had** *the last toffee.*
take, consume, eat
8 *One of the giraffes has* **had** *a baby.*
give birth to, bear, produce
9 *I* **have** *to be home by six o'clock.*
must, need to, ought to, should

hazy *adjective*
1 *The things in the distance were rather* **hazy***.*
blurred, misty, unclear, dim, faint
2 *He's only got a* **hazy** *knowledge of history.*
uncertain, vague

head *noun*
1 *My dad hit his* **head** *on the attic ceiling.*
skull, crown
(*informal*) nut
2 *Can you add up these figures in your* **head***?*
brain, mind, intellect, intelligence
3 *There is a new* **head** *of the music department.*
chief, leader, manager, director, controller
(*informal*) boss
4 *The girls waited at the* **head** *of the queue.*
front, lead, top
OPPOSITE back, rear

head *verb*
The professor was chosen to **head** *the expedition.*
lead, be in charge of, direct, command, manage, oversee, supervise
to head for
At the end of the day we **headed for** *home.*
go towards, make for, aim for

heal *verb*
1 *It took two months for my leg to* **heal** *properly.*
get better, mend, recover
2 *Part of a vet's job is to* **heal** *sick animals.*
cure, make better, treat, restore

health *noun*
The puppies are in excellent **health***.*
condition, fitness, shape, strength, vigour, wellbeing

healthy *adjective*
1 *Neil has always been a* **healthy** *child.*
well, fit, strong, sturdy, vigorous, robust
(*informal*) in good shape
OPPOSITE ill
2 *Porridge makes a very* **healthy** *breakfast.*
health-giving, wholesome, invigorating
OPPOSITE unhealthy

heap *noun*
There was an untidy **heap** *of clothes on the floor.*
mound, pile, stack, mountain, collection, mass

heap *verb*
We **heaped** *up all the rubbish in the corner.*
pile, stack, collect, bank, mass

hear *verb*
1 *Did you* **hear** *what she said?*
catch, listen to, make out, pick up, overhear, pay attention to
A sound that you can hear is **audible***.*
A sound that you cannot hear is **inaudible***.*
2 *Have you* **heard** *the news?*
be told, discover, find out, learn, gather

heart *noun*
1 *Have you no* **heart***?*
compassion, feeling, sympathy, tenderness, affection, humanity, kindness, love
2 *The hotel is located right in the* **heart** *of the city.*
centre, middle, hub
3 *They tried to get to the* **heart** *of the problem.*
core, essence

heat *noun*
1 *The cat basked in the* **heat** *of the fire.*
warmth, hotness, glow
2 *Last summer, the* **heat** *made me feel ill.*
hot weather, high temperatures, closeness
A long period of hot weather is a **heatwave***.*

heave *verb*
The men **heaved** *the sacks onto a lorry.*
haul, drag, pull, draw, tow, tug, hoist, lug, lift, raise, throw

heavy *adjective*
1 *The box was too* **heavy** *for me to lift.*
weighty, massive, dense, bulky
2 *Digging the garden is* **heavy** *work.*
hard, tough, gruelling, back-breaking, strenuous
3 *This book makes* **heavy** *reading.*
serious, intense, demanding
4 *The rain has caused* **heavy** *flooding.*
severe, extreme, torrential
5 *Both sides suffered* **heavy** *losses in the battle.*
large, substantial, considerable
6 *A* **heavy** *mist hung over the landscape.*
dense, thick

hectic *adjective*
The days before the wedding were **hectic**.
busy, frantic, feverish, frenzied, chaotic, (*informal*) manic
OPPOSITE quiet, leisurely

help *noun*
1 *Thank you for your* **help**.
aid, assistance, support, guidance, cooperation, advice
OPPOSITE hindrance
2 *Would a torch be of any* **help** *to you?*
use, benefit

help *verb*
1 *Could you please* **help** *me with my luggage?*
aid, assist, cooperate with
(*informal*) give a hand to
2 *The Red Cross is an organization that* **helps** *people in need.*
be helpful to, support, serve, stand by
3 *This medicine will* **help** *your cough.*
make better, cure, ease, relieve, improve
OPPOSITE aggravate, worsen
4 *I can't* **help** *coughing.*
stop, avoid, prevent, refrain from

helpful *adjective*
1 *The staff were friendly and* **helpful**.
obliging, cooperative, kind, considerate, thoughtful, sympathetic
OPPOSITE unhelpful
2 *The shop assistant gave us some* **helpful** *advice.*
useful, valuable, worthwhile, beneficial, profitable
OPPOSITE worthless

helpless *adjective*
Kittens are born blind and **helpless**.
powerless, weak, feeble, dependent, defenceless, vulnerable
OPPOSITE independent, strong

heroic *adjective*
The firefighters made a **heroic** *effort to put out the blaze.*
bold, brave, courageous, daring, fearless, noble, selfless, valiant
OPPOSITE cowardly

hesitate *verb*
I **hesitated** *for a moment before ringing the doorbell.*
pause, delay, wait, hold back, dither, falter, waver
(*informal*) think twice

hidden *adjective*
1 *The giant kept his gold* **hidden** *in a wooden chest.*
concealed, out of sight, unseen, invisible, covered, disguised
OPPOSITE visible
2 *There's a* **hidden** *message in the riddle.*
secret, mysterious, obscure, coded, cryptic
OPPOSITE obvious

hide *verb*
1 *Quick!—someone's coming—we'd better* **hide**.
go into hiding, take cover, take refuge, keep out of sight, lie low, go to ground
2 *They* **hid** *the jewels in a secret drawer.*
conceal, secrete, bury
(*informal*) stash
OPPOSITE expose
3 *The clouds* **hid** *the sun.*
blot out, cover, screen, shroud, veil, mask
OPPOSITE uncover
4 *I tried to* **hide** *my feelings.*
disguise, keep secret, suppress, camouflage, cloak
OPPOSITE show

hide

hideous *adjective*
The troll had a **hideous** *grin on his face.*
repulsive, revolting, ugly, grotesque, monstrous, ghastly, gruesome, horrible, appalling, dreadful, frightful
OPPOSITE beautiful

high *adjective*
1 *The castle was surrounded by a* **high** *wall.*
tall, towering, elevated, lofty
OPPOSITE low
2 *Sir Grinalot was a knight of* **high** *rank and status.*
senior, top, leading, important, prominent, powerful
OPPOSITE low, junior
3 *House prices are very* **high** *at the moment.*
expensive, dear, costly, excessive
OPPOSITE low
4 *A* **high** *wind was blowing.*
strong, powerful, forceful, extreme
OPPOSITE gentle
5 *The pixie spoke in a* **high** *squeaky voice.*
high-pitched, sharp, shrill, piercing
A high singing voice is **soprano** or **treble**.
OPPOSITE deep

hilarious *adjective*
The boys thought the cartoon was **hilarious**.
funny, amusing, comical
(*informal*) hysterical

hill *noun*
1 *From the top of this* **hill** *you can see for miles.*
mount, peak, ridge
A small hill is a **hillock** or **mound**.
The top of a hill is the **summit**.
2 *Jenny pushed her bike up the steep* **hill**.
slope, rise, incline, ascent, gradient

hinder *verb*
The snowstorm **hindered** *the rescue attempt.*
hamper, hold up, obstruct, impede, slow down, stand in the way of, restrict, handicap
OPPOSITE help

hint *noun*
1 *I don't know the answer—can you give me a* **hint**?
clue, indication, sign, suggestion, inkling
2 *The magazine offers handy* **hints** *for decorating.*
tip, pointer

hint *verb*
Mum **hinted** *that we might be getting a puppy.*
give a hint, suggest, imply, indicate

hit *noun*
1 *Matt got a nasty* **hit** *on the head.*
bump, blow, bang, knock, whack
A hit with your fist is a **punch**.
A hit with your open hand is a **slap** or **smack**.
A hit with a bat or club is a **drive**, **stroke**, or **swipe**.
2 *Their new album was an instant* **hit**.
success, triumph
(*informal*) winner

hit *verb*
1 *Auntie Flo* **hit** *the burglar on the head with her umbrella.*
strike, knock, bang, bash, thump, bump, crack, rap, slam, swipe, slog, cuff
(*informal*) whack, wham, wallop, sock, clout, clobber, belt, biff
(*old use*) smite
To hit with your fist is to **punch**.
To hit with the palm of your hand is to **slap** or **smack**.
To punish someone by hitting them is to **beat** them.
To hit someone with a stick is to **club** them.
To hit your toe on something is to **stub** it.
To kill an insect by hitting it is to **swat** it.
To hit something repeatedly is to **batter**, **buffet**, or **pound** it.

a b c d e f g h i j k l m n o p q r s t u v w x y z

To hit something gently is to **tap** it.
2 The drought has **hit** many farms in the area.
affect, damage, harm, hurt

hoard noun
Hamish keeps a **hoard** of sweets in his desk.
cache, store, stock, supply, pile, stockpile
A hoard of treasure is a **treasure trove**.

hoard verb
Squirrels **hoard** nuts for the winter.
store, collect, gather, save, put by, pile up, stockpile
(informal) stash away

hoard

hoarse adjective
Mr Barker's voice was **hoarse** from shouting.
rough, harsh, husky, croaky, throaty, gruff, rasping, gravelly

hobby noun
My favourite **hobby** is snorkelling.
pastime, pursuit, interest, activity, recreation

hold verb
1 Please **hold** the dog's lead.
clasp, grasp, grip, cling to, hang on to, clutch, seize
2 Can I **hold** the baby?
embrace, hug, cradle
3 They **held** the suspect until the police arrived.
confine, detain, keep
4 Will the ladder **hold** my weight?
bear, support, carry, take
5 If our luck **holds**, we could reach the final.
continue, last, carry on, persist, stay
6 She **holds** strong opinions.
believe in, maintain, stick to
to hold out
1 The robot **held out** one of his arms.
extend, reach out, stick out, stretch out
2 Our supplies won't **hold out** much longer.
keep going, last, carry on, continue, endure
to hold something up
1 Please **hold up** your hand.
lift, put up, raise
2 The accident **held up** the traffic.
delay, hinder, slow down

hole noun
1 The meteor created a massive **hole** in the ground.
pit, hollow, crater, dent, depression, cavity, chasm, abyss
2 The rabbits escaped through a **hole** in the fence.
gap, opening, breach, break, cut, slit, gash, split, tear, vent

hollow adjective
Tennis balls are **hollow**.
empty, unfilled
OPPOSITE solid

hollow noun
The ball rolled into a **hollow** in the ground.
dip, dent, depression, hole, pit, crater
A hollow between two hills is a **valley**.

holy adjective
1 The pilgrims knelt to pray in the **holy** shrine.
sacred, blessed, revered
2 The pilgrims were **holy** people.
religious, spiritual, devout, pious, godly, saintly

home noun
The hurricane forced people to flee their **homes**.
house, residence, dwelling, abode, lodging
A home for the sick is a **convalescent home** or **nursing home**.
A place where a bird or animal lives is its **habitat**.

honest adjective
1 He's an **honest** boy, so he gave the money back.
good, honourable, law-abiding, moral, trustworthy, upright, virtuous
OPPOSITE dishonest
2 Please give me your **honest** opinion.
sincere, genuine, truthful, direct, frank, candid, plain, straightforward, unbiased
OPPOSITE insincere

honour noun
1 Her success brought **honour** to the school.
credit, good reputation, good name, respect, praise, acclaim
2 It's an **honour** to meet you.
privilege, distinction

honour verb
The winners were **honoured** at a special ceremony.
praise, celebrate, salute, give credit to, pay tribute to, glorify

honourable adjective
1 The knight was an **honourable** man.
good, honest, sincere, noble, principled, moral, righteous, trustworthy, upright, virtuous, worthy, decent, fair, trusty
2 It was an **honourable** thing to do.
noble, admirable, praiseworthy, decent

hop verb
The goblins **hopped** about in excitement.
jump, leap, skip, spring, prance, caper, bound, dance

hope verb
I **hope** to see you again soon.
wish, trust, expect, look forward

hope noun
1 Her dearest **hope** was to see her family again.
ambition, dream, desire, wish
2 There's **hope** of better weather tomorrow.
prospect, expectation, likelihood

hopeful adjective
1 I am feeling **hopeful** about tomorrow's match.
optimistic, confident, positive, expectant
OPPOSITE pessimistic
2 The future is beginning to look more **hopeful**.
promising, encouraging, favourable, reassuring
OPPOSITE discouraging

hopeless adjective
1 The shipwrecked crew were in a **hopeless** situation.
desperate, wretched, beyond hope
OPPOSITE hopeful
2 I'm **hopeless** at ice-skating.
bad, poor, incompetent
(informal) useless, rubbish
OPPOSITE good, competent

horrible adjective
What a **horrible** smell!
awful, terrible, dreadful, appalling, unpleasant, disagreeable, offensive, objectionable, disgusting, repulsive, revolting, horrendous, horrid, nasty, hateful, odious, loathsome, beastly, ghastly
OPPOSITE pleasant

horrific adjective
The film has some **horrific** scenes of battle.
horrifying, terrifying, shocking, gruesome, dreadful, appalling, ghastly, hideous, atrocious, grisly, sickening

horrify verb
*We were **horrified** by the sight of the monster.*
appal, shock, terrify, scare, frighten, alarm, sicken, disgust

horror noun
1 *Ingrid screamed in **horror** when she saw the snake.*
terror, fear, fright, alarm, dread
2 *The film depicts the full **horror** of war.*
awfulness, hideousness, gruesomeness, ghastliness, frightfulness

hostile adjective
*The warriors shook their weapons in a **hostile** manner.*
aggressive, antagonistic, unfriendly, unwelcoming, warlike, malevolent
OPPOSITE friendly

hot adjective
1 *The weather has been **hot** this summer.*
warm, balmy, blazing, roasting, scorching, blistering, sweltering, stifling
OPPOSITE cold, cool
2 *Careful—the soup's really **hot**.*
burning, boiling, baking hot, piping hot, scalding, searing, sizzling, steaming
OPPOSITE cold, cool
3 *I like curry, but only if it's not too **hot**.*
spicy, peppery, fiery
OPPOSITE mild
4 *My sister, Diana, has a **hot** temper.*
fierce, fiery, violent, passionate, raging, angry, intense
OPPOSITE calm, mild

WORD WEB

house noun
WORDS FOR THE PLACE YOU LIVE IN
abode, dwelling, home, lodging, quarters, residence

BUILDINGS WHERE PEOPLE LIVE
apartment, bungalow, chalet, cottage, council house, croft, detached house, farmhouse, flat, hovel, hut, igloo, lodge, manor, manse, mansion, rectory, semi-detached house, shack, shanty, tenement, terraced house, thatched house, vicarage, villa

hover verb
1 *A flock of seagulls **hovered** overhead.*
fly, flutter, float, hang, drift
2 *He **hovered** outside the room, afraid to knock.*
linger, pause, wait about, hesitate, dally, loiter, dither
(*informal*) hang about

hover

howl verb
1 *The injured boy **howled** in pain.*
cry, yell, scream, yelp, shriek, wail
2 *They heard wolves **howling** in the night.*
bay, yowl

huddle verb
*The penguins **huddled** together to get warm.*
crowd, gather, flock, cluster, squeeze, pack, nestle, cuddle, snuggle
OPPOSITE scatter

hug verb
*Ellie was **hugging** her favourite teddy bear.*
cuddle, clasp, embrace, cling to, hold close, squeeze

huge adjective
*Elephants are **huge** animals.*
enormous, gigantic, massive, colossal, giant, immense, vast, mighty, mammoth, monumental, hulking, great, big, large
(*informal*) whopping, ginormous, humungous
OPPOSITE small, little, tiny

hum verb
*We heard insects **humming** in the air.*
buzz, drone, murmur, purr, whirr

humble adjective
1 *The gentle giant was both **humble** and kind.*
modest, meek, unassuming, polite, respectful, submissive
OPPOSITE proud
2 *Hansel and Gretel lived in a **humble** cottage.*
simple, modest, plain, ordinary, commonplace, lowly
OPPOSITE grand

humid adjective
*I don't like this **humid** weather.*
muggy, clammy, close, sticky, steamy, sweaty
OPPOSITE fresh

humiliate verb
*He **humiliated** her in front of her friends.*
embarrass, disgrace, shame, make ashamed, humble, crush, degrade
(*informal*) put you in your place, take you down a peg

humour noun
1 *I liked the **humour** in the film.*
comedy, wit, amusement, jokes

2 *The ogre was in a very bad **humour**.*
mood, temper, disposition, frame of mind, spirits

hunger noun
*After a week without food, the crew were faint with **hunger**.*
lack of food, starvation, famine
Bad health caused by not having enough food is **malnutrition**.

hungry adjective
*Our dog always seems to be **hungry**.*
starving, famished, ravenous
(*informal*) peckish

hunt noun
*Police have begun the **hunt** for clues.*
search, quest, chase, pursuit (of)

hunt verb
1 *Some Native Americans tribes used to **hunt** buffalo.*
chase, pursue, track, trail, hound, stalk
An animal which hunts other animals for food is a **predator**.
2 *I **hunted** in the attic for our old photos.*
search, seek, look, rummage, ferret, root around

hurry verb
1 *If you want to catch the bus, you'd better **hurry**.*
be quick, hasten, make speed
(*informal*) get a move on, step on it
OPPOSITE dawdle
2 *Alice saw the White Rabbit **hurrying** past.*
rush, dash, fly, speed, hurtle, scurry
OPPOSITE amble, stroll

hurt verb
1 *Be careful not to **hurt** yourself with the scissors.*
harm, injure, damage, wound, maim
To hurt someone deliberately is to **torment** or **torture** them.
2 *My feet **hurt**.*
be sore, be painful, ache, throb, sting, smart
3 *Your letter **hurt** me deeply.*
upset, distress, offend, grieve

hurtful adjective
*That was a very **hurtful** remark.*
upsetting, unkind, cruel, mean, painful, spiteful, nasty

hut noun
*The walkers came across a **hut** in the forest.*
shed, shack, cabin, den, shelter, shanty, hovel

hysterical adjective
1 *The fans became **hysterical** when the band appeared.*
crazy, frenzied, mad, delirious, raving, wild, uncontrollable
2 (*informal*) *We laughed at the **hysterical** jokes in the film.*
hilarious, funny, amusing, comical

a
b
c
d
e
f
g
h
i
j
k
l
m
n
o
p
q
r
s
t
u
v
w
x
y
z

ice hockey

WORD WEB

ice noun
WAYS TO DESCRIBE ICE
brittle, cracked, frozen solid, glacial, glassy, gleaming, glinting, hard, packed, slippery or (informal) slippy, smooth, treacherous

THINGS YOU MIGHT DO ON ICE
glide, skate, skid, slide, slip, slither

SPORTS THAT ARE PLAYED ON ICE
curling, figure skating, ice skating, ice hockey, speed skating

Ice sports are played on an **ice rink**.

icy adjective
1 You need to dress warmly in **icy** weather.
cold, freezing, frosty, wintry, arctic, bitter, biting
2 **Icy** roads are dangerous.
frozen, slippery, glacial, glassy (informal) slippy

idea noun
1 I've got a great **idea**!
plan, scheme, proposal, suggestion, inspiration
2 She has some funny **ideas** about life.
belief, notion, opinion, view, theory, concept, conception, hypothesis
3 What's the main **idea** of this poem?
point, meaning, intention, thought
4 Give me an **idea** of what you are planning.
clue, hint, inkling, impression

ideal adjective
It's **ideal** weather for a picnic.
perfect, excellent, the best, faultless, suitable

identical adjective
The twins were wearing **identical** clothes.
matching, similar, alike, indistinguishable
OPPOSITE different

identify verb
1 The police asked if I could **identify** the thief.
recognize, name, distinguish, pick out, single out

2 The doctor couldn't **identify** what was wrong.
diagnose, discover, spot (informal) put a name to

idiotic adjective
That was an **idiotic** thing to do.
stupid, silly, foolish, unwise, senseless, ridiculous, half-witted, unintelligent, crazy, mad, hare-brained (informal) daft
OPPOSITE sensible

idle adjective
1 The ogre was an **idle**, foul-smelling creature.
lazy, indolent, slothful, work-shy
OPPOSITE hard-working
2 The computers lay **idle** all week.
inactive, unused, inoperative
OPPOSITE busy, active

idol noun
1 The floor of the temple was littered with broken **idols**.
god, deity, image, statue
2 He was a pop **idol** of the fifties.
star, celebrity, icon, pin-up, favourite

ignorant adjective
Trolls are often described as **ignorant** creatures.
uneducated, simple, stupid

ignore verb
Ignoring the weather, Lynn went for a walk.
disregard, take no notice of, overlook, neglect, spurn, snub
(informal) turn a blind eye to

ill adjective
1 I missed school for a week when I was **ill**.
sick, unwell, poorly, sickly, ailing, infirm, unfit, indisposed, diseased, infected, nauseous, queasy, off colour, peaky
(informal) under the weather
OPPOSITE healthy, well
2 Did the plants suffer **ill** effects in the frost?
bad, harmful, adverse, damaging
OPPOSITE good

illegal adjective
Stealing is **illegal**.
unlawful, against the law, banned, prohibited, criminal, forbidden, wrong
OPPOSITE legal

illustrate verb
1 I used some photos to **illustrate** my story.
depict, picture, portray
2 The accident **illustrates** the importance of road safety.
show, demonstrate, make clear

illustration noun
1 I like cookery books with lots of **illustrations**.
picture, photograph, drawing, sketch, diagram
2 I'll give you an **illustration** of what I mean.
example, instance, demonstration, specimen

image noun
1 The film contained frightening **images** of war.
picture, portrayal, depiction, representation
2 The temple contained **images** of the gods.
figure, idol, statue, carving
3 You can see your **image** in the mirror.
reflection, likeness

imaginary adjective
The story takes place in an **imaginary** universe.
imagined, non-existent, unreal, made up, invented, fanciful, fictitious, fictional
OPPOSITE real

imagination noun
Use your **imagination** to draw an alien spaceship.
creativity, inventiveness, ingenuity, inspiration, originality, vision, artistry, fancy

imaginative adjective
Roald Dahl wrote highly **imaginative** stories.
creative, inventive, inspired, original, artistic, fanciful, ingenious, clever
OPPOSITE unimaginative, dull

imagine verb
1 **Imagine** what it would be like to visit Mars.
picture, visualize, pretend, think up, dream up, fancy, conjure up
2 I **imagine** you'd like something to eat.
suppose, assume, presume, believe, guess

imitate verb
Parrots can **imitate** the human voice.
copy, reproduce, mimic, mirror, echo, simulate, impersonate, follow, match
(informal) send up, take off

imitation noun
This is an **imitation** of a Viking helmet.
copy, replica, reproduction, duplicate
An imitation made to deceive someone is a **fake** or a **forgery**.

immediate adjective
1 Please can I have an **immediate** reply.
instant, instantaneous, prompt, speedy, swift, urgent, quick, direct
(informal) snappy
OPPOSITE slow

2 *Are you friends with your*
immediate neighbours?
closest, nearest, adjacent, next
OPPOSITE distant

immediately *adverb*
You must fetch a doctor immediately!
at once, now, straight away, right
away, instantly, promptly, directly

immense *adjective*
The giant wiggled one of his
immense toes.
huge, great, massive, enormous,
colossal, vast, giant, gigantic,
mighty, mammoth, monumental
(*informal*) whopping, ginormous,
humungous
OPPOSITE tiny

immoral *adjective*
It would be immoral to steal the money.
wrong, wicked, bad, sinful, dishonest,
corrupt
OPPOSITE moral, right

immortal *adjective*
The ancient Greeks believed their
gods were immortal.
undying, ageless, eternal, everlasting
OPPOSITE mortal

impact *noun*
1 *The crater was caused by the*
impact of a meteor.
crash, collision, smash, blow, bump,
bang, knock, jolt
2 *Computers have a big impact*
on our lives.
effect, influence

impatient *adjective*
1 *As time went on, Henry grew more*
and more impatient.
restless, agitated, anxious, fidgety,
irritable, snappy, testy, jumpy, edgy
OPPOSITE patient
2 *The crowd were impatient for the*
show to begin.
anxious, eager, in a hurry, keen
(*informal*) itching

important *adjective*
1 *The World Cup is an important*
sporting event.
major, significant, big, central,
momentous, outstanding, historic
2 *I have some important business*
to attend to.
serious, urgent, pressing, weighty,
vital, essential, crucial
3 *The prime minister is an*
important person.
prominent, powerful, influential,
notable, eminent, distinguished

impossible *adjective*
We used to think that space travel
was impossible.
impractical, unthinkable, unrealistic,
unachievable, unworkable, out of the
question
OPPOSITE possible

impact

impress *verb*
Frank impressed the coach with his
football skills.
make an impression on, influence,
leave its mark on, stick in your mind

impression *noun*
1 *I had the impression that*
something was wrong.
feeling, idea, sense, notion,
suspicion, hunch
2 *The film made a big impression*
on them.
effect, impact, influence, mark
3 *My sister does a good impression*
of the Queen.
imitation, impersonation
(*informal*) send-up

impressive *adjective*
The film includes some impressive
special effects.
striking, effective, powerful, remarkable,
spectacular, exciting, inspiring
OPPOSITE unimpressive, uninspiring

imprison *verb*
The thief was imprisoned for two years.
send to prison, jail, lock up,
incarcerate, confine, detain
(*informal*) put away, send down, put
under lock and key
OPPOSITE liberate

improve *verb*
1 *Her work improved this term.*
get better, advance, progress,
develop, move on
OPPOSITE deteriorate
2 *Has he improved since his illness?*
get better, recover, recuperate, pick
up, rally, revive
OPPOSITE get worse
3 *How can I improve this story?*
make better, enhance, refine, amend,
revise, correct, upgrade

improvement *noun*
1 *Your handwriting shows signs of*
improvement.
getting better, advance, progress,
development, recovery, upturn

2 *The author made some*
improvements to the book.
amendment, correction, revision,
modification, enhancement

impulsive *adjective*
She regretted her impulsive decision
to dye her hair.
hasty, rash, reckless, sudden,
spontaneous, thoughtless,
unthinking, impetuous
OPPOSITE deliberate

inaccurate *adjective*
That spelling of my surname is
inaccurate.
wrong, incorrect, mistaken, false,
inexact, untrue
OPPOSITE accurate

inadequate *adjective*
They had brought an inadequate
supply of matches.
insufficient, not enough, limited,
scarce, scanty, meagre
OPPOSITE adequate

incident *noun*
There was an amusing incident
at school this morning.
event, happening, occurrence,
episode, affair

include *verb*
Does the cost include postage
and packing?
contain, incorporate, comprise,
involve, take in, allow for, take into
account, cover
OPPOSITE exclude

inconsiderate *adjective*
It's inconsiderate to play the radio
so loudly.
selfish, unthinking, thoughtless, rude,
insensitive, tactless, unkind, uncaring
OPPOSITE considerate

inconvenient *adjective*
The guests arrived at an
inconvenient moment.
awkward, difficult, unsuitable,
unfortunate, untimely, inopportune
OPPOSITE convenient

a
b
c
d
e
f
g
h
i
j
k
l
m
n
o
p
q
r
s
t
u
v
w
x
y
z

increase *verb*
1 *They've **increased** the size of the tennis courts.*
make bigger, enlarge, expand, develop, add to, widen, broaden
2 *She **increased** the cooking time in the recipe.*
extend, lengthen, prolong
3 *The police **increased** their efforts to find the murderer.*
intensify, step up
4 *Will you be **increasing** the bus fares?*
put up, raise
5 *Can you **increase** the volume of the TV?*
turn up, amplify, boost
6 *The number of cars on the roads continues to **increase**.*
grow, mount, go up, rise, soar, build up, escalate, multiply

incredible *adjective*
1 *Do you expect us to believe that **incredible** story?*
unbelievable, unlikely, improbable, far-fetched, absurd, implausible
OPPOSITE credible
2 *The Forth Bridge is an **incredible** feat of engineering.*
extraordinary, amazing, astounding, magnificent, marvellous, spectacular

independent *adjective*
1 *My granny is a very **independent** person.*
free, liberated, self-sufficient, self-reliant
OPPOSITE dependent
2 *Luxembourg is an **independent** country.*
autonomous, self-governing
3 *We need an **independent** opinion on the matter.*
impartial, neutral, objective, unbiased
OPPOSITE biased

indifferent *adjective*
1 *I felt **indifferent** as I watched the game.*
uninterested, detached, uncaring, unenthusiastic, unmoved, uninvolved, unconcerned
OPPOSITE enthusiastic
2 *The food in the restaurant was **indifferent**.*
mediocre, ordinary, unexciting, average
OPPOSITE excellent

indignant *adjective*
*The player was **indignant** when he was sent off.*
annoyed, angry, cross, affronted, offended, outraged, piqued

indirect *adjective*
*The bus took an **indirect** route into town.*
roundabout, winding, meandering, rambling, zigzag
OPPOSITE direct

individual *adjective*
*Her singing has an **individual** style.*
characteristic, distinct, distinctive, special, unique, personal, singular

inevitable *adjective*
*If it rains, it is **inevitable** that the pitch will get wet.*
certain, sure, definite, unavoidable, inescapable

infect *verb*
*A virus may have **infected** the water supply.*
contaminate, pollute, poison

infection *noun*
*The **infection** spread rapidly.*
disease, virus, contagion, contamination

infectious *adjective*
*Chickenpox is highly **infectious**.*
contagious, catching

inferior *adjective*
1 *The clothes were of **inferior** quality.*
poor, bad, second-rate, mediocre, cheap, shoddy
2 *Officers can give orders to those of **inferior** rank.*
lesser, lower, junior, subordinate

infinite *adjective*
*You need **infinite** patience to train a puppy.*
endless, limitless, unlimited, boundless, never-ending, unending, inexhaustible
OPPOSITE finite

influence *noun*
*Rock music had a big **influence** on her life.*
effect, impact, power, dominance, guidance, authority, control

influence *verb*
*The money he was offered **influenced** his decision.*
affect, have an effect on, direct, guide, control, motivate

inform *verb*
*Please **inform** us if you move house.*
tell, let you know, notify, advise

informal *adjective*
1 *The party will be a very **informal** event.*
casual, relaxed, easygoing, friendly, homely, natural
2 *Emails are usually written in an **informal** style.*
colloquial, familiar, chatty, personal

information *noun*
*There is more **information** on our website.*
details, particulars, facts, data, advice, guidance, knowledge
(*informal*) info

inhabit *verb*
*People **inhabited** the caves thousands of years ago.*
live in, occupy, dwell in, reside in, populate, settle in

initiative *noun*
*You must use your **initiative** on the treasure hunt.*
resourcefulness, inventiveness, originality, enterprise

injure *verb*
*Was anyone **injured** in the accident?*
hurt, harm, wound
To injure someone causing permament damage is to **maim** them.

innocent *adjective*
1 *The jury found the man **innocent**.*
guiltless, blameless, free from blame
OPPOSITE guilty
2 *Baby tigers look so **innocent**.*
angelic, harmless, faultless, virtuous, pure, simple, inexperienced, naïve
OPPOSITE wicked

inquire *verb*
to inquire into
*Detectives are **inquiring into** the robbery.*
look into, investigate, examine, explore

insane *adjective*
1 *It was rumoured that the king had gone **insane**.*
mentally ill, mad, crazy, deranged, demented, disturbed, unhinged
(*informal*) off your head, out of your mind
OPPOSITE sane
2 *It would be **insane** to swim in the sea in January!*
crazy, mad, daft, senseless, stupid, foolish, idiotic
OPPOSITE sensible, wise

WORD WEB

insect *noun*
SOME TYPES OF INSECT
ant, aphid, bee, beetle, bluebottle, bumble-bee, butterfly, cicada, cockroach, crane fly or daddy-long-legs, cricket, dragonfly, earwig, firefly, flea, fly, glow-worm, gnat, grasshopper, greenfly, hornet, horsefly, ladybird, locust, louse, mantis, mayfly, midge, mosquito, moth, stick insect, termite, tsetse fly, wasp, weevil

LIFE STAGES OF SOME INSECTS
caterpillar, chrysalis, grub, larva, maggot, pupa

PARTS OF INSECTS' BODIES
head, thorax, abdomen, antennae, legs, wings

SOME CREATURES
SIMILAR TO INSECTS
centipede, earthworm, mite, slug, spider, woodlouse, worm

insensitive *adjective*
I'm sorry if my comments were **insensitive**.
thoughtless, tactless, unfeeling, uncaring, unsympathetic, callous
OPPOSITE sensitive

inside *noun*
The **inside** *of the nest was lined with feathers.*
interior, inner surface, centre, core, heart, middle
OPPOSITE outside

insignificant *adjective*
The author made a few **insignificant** *changes.*
unimportant, minor, trivial, negligible, slight, meaningless
OPPOSITE significant

insincere *adjective*
The butler welcomed us with an **insincere** *smile.*
false, pretended, hypocritical, dishonest, deceitful, deceptive, lying
(*informal*) two-faced
OPPOSITE sincere

insist *verb*
Griselda **insisted** *that she was not a witch.*
declare, state, assert, maintain, stress, emphasize, swear, vow, claim
to insist on
The magician **insisted on** *silence before he began.*
demand, require

inspect *verb*
They **inspected** *the damage done by the storm.*
check, examine, investigate, look over, study, survey, scrutinize

inspire *verb*
The crowd **inspired** *the team to play well.*
motivate, prompt, stimulate, encourage, stir, arouse, spur on

instant *adjective*
Gardeners don't expect **instant** *results.*
immediate, quick, rapid, fast, prompt, snappy, speedy, swift, direct

instant *noun*
The shooting star was gone in an **instant**.
moment, second, split second, flash
(*informal*) tick, jiffy

instinct *noun*
The detective always followed his own **instincts**.
impulse, inclination, intuition, hunch, feeling, urge

instruct *verb*
1 *All the staff are* **instructed** *in first aid.*
teach, train, coach, tutor
2 *The police officer* **instructed** *the cars to wait.*
tell, order, direct, command

instructions *plural noun*
Please follow the **instructions** *carefully.*
directions, guidelines, orders, commands

instrument *noun*
Dentists use special **instruments** *to check your teeth.*
tool, implement, utensil, appliance, device, gadget, contraption

insult *verb*
He was **insulted** *not to be invited to the wedding.*
offend, outrage, be rude to, hurt, injure, slight, snub

insult *noun*
It is considered an **insult** *to refuse a gift.*
rudeness, offence, affront, slight, slur, snub

insulting *adjective*
She made an **insulting** *comment about my clothes.*
offensive, rude, impolite, derogatory, scornful
OPPOSITE complimentary

intelligent *adjective*
The aliens from Planet Zog are highly **intelligent**.
clever, bright, smart, quick, sharp, perceptive, shrewd, able, brilliant, rational, thinking
(*informal*) brainy
OPPOSITE unintelligent, stupid

intense *adjective*
1 *I felt a sudden,* **intense** *pain in my chest.*
extreme, acute, severe, sharp, great, strong, violent
OPPOSITE slight, mild
2 *The contest aroused* **intense** *feelings.*
deep, passionate, powerful, strong, profound
OPPOSITE mild

interest *verb*
Politics doesn't **interest** *me at all.*
appeal to, stimulate, attract, capture your imagination, excite, fascinate, absorb
OPPOSITE bore

interest *noun*
1 *The dog showed no* **interest** *in the bone.*
curiosity, attention, concern, involvement
2 *The information was of no* **interest** *to anyone.*
importance, significance, consequence, value

3 *My* **interests** *include judo and playing the trombone.*
hobby, pastime, pursuit, activity, diversion

interesting *adjective*
Everyone wanted to hear about our **interesting** *adventures.*
fascinating, absorbing, enthralling, intriguing, engrossing, stimulating, riveting, gripping, entertaining diverting
OPPOSITE boring, dull

interfere *verb*
to interfere in
Don't **interfere in** *other people's affairs.*
intervene in, intrude in, meddle in, pry into, encroach on, butt in on
to interfere with
The bad weather **interfered with** *our plans.*
hamper, hinder, get in the way of, obstruct

international *adjective*
Interpol is an **international** *police organization.*
global, worldwide, intercontinental

interrupt *verb*
1 *Please don't* **interrupt** *while I am speaking.*
intervene, interject, break in, butt in, cut in
2 *Heavy rain* **interrupted** *the tennis match.*
stop, suspend, disrupt, break off, cut short

interruption *noun*
He wrote for an hour without any **interruption**.
break, pause, stop, gap, halt, disruption, suspension

interval *noun*
1 *There will be a short* **interval** *after the first act.*
break, pause, wait, delay, lapse, lull
Another word for an interval in a play or film is **interlude** or **intermission**.
An interval in a meeting is a **recess**.

a b c d e f g h i j k l m n o p q r s t u v w x y z

An interval when you take a rest is a **breather** or **breathing space**.
2 There were signs at regular **intervals** along the road.
space, gap, distance

interview verb
He **interviewed** the author about her new book.
question, talk to, interrogate, examine

intimate adjective
1 They have been **intimate** friends for years.
close, cherished, dear, friendly, informal
OPPOSITE distant
2 The newspaper printed **intimate** details about her life.
personal, private, confidential, secret

intriguing adjective
The results of the experiment are **intriguing**.
interesting, attractive, fascinating, captivating, beguiling

introduce verb
1 Let me **introduce** you to my friend.
present, make known
2 The director stood up to **introduce** the film.
give an introduction to, announce, lead into
3 They are **introducing** a new bus service next year.
set up, start, begin, create, establish, initiate, bring in

introduction noun
Something which happens as an introduction to a bigger event is a **prelude**.
An introduction to a book is a **preface**.
An introduction to a play is a **prologue**.
A piece played as an introduction to a concert or opera is an **overture**.

invade verb
The Vikings **invaded** many parts of Europe.
attack, enter, occupy, overrun, march into, raid

invent verb
James Dewar **invented** the thermos flask.
create, devise, think up, conceive, design, originate

inventor noun
James Dewar was the **inventor** of the thermos flask.
creator, designer, originator, discoverer

investigate verb
Police are **investigating** the cause of the accident.
examine, explore, inquire into, look into, study, consider, follow up, probe, research, scrutinize
(informal) go into

investigation noun
An **investigation** showed how the accident happened.
examination, inquiry, inspection, study, review, survey

invisible adjective
The wizard was **invisible** when he wore his magic cloak.
out of sight, unseen, unnoticed, hidden, concealed, covered, obscured, camouflaged, disguised, undetectable, unnoticeable, inconspicuous
OPPOSITE visible

invite verb
Our neighbours **invited** us round for tea.
ask, request your company, welcome, summon

involve verb
1 My job **involves** a lot of travel.
include, comprise, require, demand, necessitate, mean
2 Protecting the environment **involves** us all.
affect, concern, interest, touch

involved adjective
1 The film has a long and **involved** plot.
complex, complicated, elaborate, intricate, confusing, difficult, convoluted
OPPOSITE simple
2 Are you **involved** in the theatre?
concerned, participating, engaged, caught up, mixed up

irregular adjective
1 The bricks were arranged in an **irregular** pattern.
varying, erratic, haphazard, random, unpredictable, fitful
OPPOSITE regular
2 It is highly **irregular** to eat pizza with a spoon!
abnormal, unusual, exceptional, unconventional, improper
OPPOSITE normal

irresponsible adjective
It's **irresponsible** to drive too fast.
reckless, rash, thoughtless, inconsiderate, uncaring, unthinking, negligent
OPPOSITE responsible

irritable adjective
After a bad night, he woke in an **irritable** mood.
bad-tempered, grumpy, short-tempered, cross, impatient, snappy, touchy, testy, prickly, peevish
(informal) stroppy, shirty
OPPOSITE good-humoured, cheerful

irritate verb
The noise from next door began to **irritate** me.
annoy, bother, exasperate, anger, provoke, madden, vex
(informal) get on your nerves, bug

isolated adjective
They sheltered in an **isolated** cave in the mountains.
remote, out-of-the-way, secluded, outlying, inaccessible, cut off, deserted
OPPOSITE accessible

issue verb
1 They **issued** blankets to the refugees.
give out, distribute, supply
2 They have **issued** a new set of stamps.
bring out, put out, produce, publish, release, circulate, print
3 Green smoke **issued** from the dragon's nostrils.
come out, emerge, appear, flow out, gush, erupt

issue noun
1 The new **issue** of the magazine comes out this week.
edition, number, instalment, copy
2 They print stories about local **issues** in the magazine.
matter, subject, topic, affair, concern, question, problem

itch noun
1 I had an annoying **itch** on my foot.
tickle, tingling, prickle
2 Olga had a great **itch** to travel.
desire, longing, urge, wish, yearning, ache, impulse

item noun
1 I bought a few **items** in the jumble sale.
thing, object, article
2 There was an **item** about our school in the paper.
article, piece, report, feature

jab *verb*
*A passer-by **jabbed** me in the ribs.*
poke, prod, elbow, nudge, stab, thrust

jagged *adjective*
*This dinosaur had **jagged** teeth.*
rough, uneven, ragged, spiky,
toothed, serrated
OPPOSITE smooth

jam *noun*
1 *We got stuck in a **jam** on the
motorway.*
traffic jam, hold-up, tailback,
blockage
2 (*informal*) *I'm in a bit of a **jam**.*
difficulty, mess, predicament, plight
(*informal*) fix, tight corner

jam *verb*
1 *Someone had **jammed** the door
open.*
prop, wedge, stick
2 *The roads are **jammed** at rush
hour.*
block, clog, obstruct, congest
(*informal*) bung up
3 *I **jammed** my things into a
backpack.*
cram, pack, stuff, squeeze, squash,
crush, ram, crowd

jangle *verb*
*Silver bracelets **jangled** on her wrists.*
jingle, chink, clink, tinkle

jealous *adjective*
*Cinderella's sisters were **jealous**
of her beauty.*
envious, resentful, grudging

jeer *verb*
*Some of the audience whistled and
jeered.*
boo, hiss, sneer, taunt, mock, scoff,
ridicule
OPPOSITE cheer

jerk *verb*
*The rider **jerked** on the horse's reins.*
pull, tug, yank, pluck, wrench, tweak

jerky *adjective*
*The stagecoach drew to a **jerky** halt.*
jolting, jumpy, shaky, bouncy,
bumpy, uneven
OPPOSITE steady

jet *noun*
*A **jet** of water shot high in the
air.*
spout, spurt, squirt, gush, stream,
fountain

jingle *verb*
*Some coins **jingled** in his back
pocket.*
jangle, chink, clink, tinkle

job *noun*
1 *My sister wants a **job** as a TV reporter.*
post, position, profession, occupation,
employment, trade, work, career
The job you particularly want to do is
your **mission** or **vocation**.
2 *Whose **job** is it to do the washing-
up?*
duty, task, assignment, chore, errand

jog *verb*
1 *He **jogs** round the park every
morning.*
go jogging, run, trot
2 *A boy sitting next to me **jogged**
my elbow.*
nudge, prod, jolt, knock, bump, jar,
jostle
3 *The photograph may **jog** her
memory.*
prompt, stir, arouse, set off, stimulate

join *verb*
1 *Our families **joined** together to
buy the present.*
combine, come together, merge,
unite, amalgamate
OPPOSITE separate
2 ***Join** one piece of rope to the other.*
connect, fasten, attach, fix, link, put
together, tack on
OPPOSITE detach
3 *The two roads **join** here.*
meet, merge, converge
OPPOSITE divide
4 *I **joined** the crowd going into the
cinema.*
follow, go with, tag along with
OPPOSITE leave
5 *We have **joined** a local sports club.*
become a member of, enrol in, sign
up for
To join the army is to **enlist**.
OPPOSITE leave, resign from

join *noun*
*If you look hard, you can still see
the **join**.*
joint, connection, link, mend, seam

joint *adjective*
*The preparation of the meal was a
joint effort.*
combined, shared, common,
communal, cooperative, united,
collective, mutual
OPPOSITE individual

joke *noun*
*Do you know any good **jokes**?*
jest, quip, crack, witticism, wisecrack
(*informal*) gag

joke *verb*
*Those two are always laughing and
joking.*
jest, clown, have a laugh, make jokes

jolly *adjective*
*We had a **jolly** time on holiday.*
cheerful, merry, happy, joyful,
pleasant, enjoyable
OPPOSITE gloomy

jolt *verb*
*The car **jolted** over the bumps in the
road.*
jerk, jog, bump, bounce, shake,
shudder

journey *noun*
*On their **journey**, the astronauts will
pass the Moon.*
voyage, trip, expedition, travels, tour,
route

joy *noun*
*I remember the sheer **joy** of scoring
a goal!*
happiness, joyfulness, delight,
cheerfulness, gladness, mirth, glee,
jubilation, gaiety, rejoicing, bliss,
ecstasy, elation
OPPOSITE sorrow

joyful *adjective*
*The wedding was a **joyful** occasion.*
happy, cheerful, merry, joyous, jolly,
jovial, good-humoured
OPPOSITE sad

judge *verb*
1 *The umpire **judged** that the ball
was out.*
rule, decide, decree, adjudicate
2 *Who's **judging** the flower show
this year?*
decide on, assess, evaluate, appraise
3 *He **judged** the coin to be about
1000 years old.*
reckon, suppose, consider, gauge,
guess, estimate

judgement *noun*
1 *What is the **judgement** of the
court?*
decision, finding, ruling, verdict,
decree
2 *His comments show a lack of
judgement.*
wisdom, common sense,
understanding, discrimination
3 *In my **judgement**, you're making
a big mistake.*
opinion, view, belief, assessment,
estimate

jumble *noun*
*There was a **jumble** of clothes on the
floor.*
mess, muddle, clutter, chaos,
confusion, disorder

jumble *verb*
*Please don't **jumble** the pages.*
muddle, mix up, mess up,
disorganize, shuffle
OPPOSITE arrange

jump *verb*
1 *Suddenly a rabbit **jumped** in front
of us.*
leap, spring, bound, bounce, hop
When a cat jumps it **pounces**.
2 *All the horses **jumped** the first
hurdle.*
leap over, vault, clear

a
b
c
d
e
f
g
h
i
j
k
l
m
n
o
p
q
r
s
t
u
v
w
x
y
z

A B C D E F G H I J K L M N O P Q R S T U V W X Y Z

3 *The loud bang made them all jump.*
start, flinch, jolt

jump *noun*
*With a **jump**, the grasshopper landed on the leaf.*
leap, spring, bound, vault, hop

junk *noun*
*The garage is full of old **junk**.*
rubbish, clutter, garbage, jumble, trash, waste, scrap, odds and ends

just *adjective*
*It was a **just** punishment, considering the crime.*
fair, fitting, appropriate, deserved, proper, reasonable, justified
OPPOSITE unjust, unfair

keen *adjective*
1 *Rhona is a **keen** hockey player.*
enthusiastic, eager, fervent, avid, devoted, committed, motivated
A common simile is **as keen as mustard**.
OPPOSITE unenthusiastic
2 *A carving knife should have a **keen** edge.*
sharp, razor-sharp, cutting
OPPOSITE blunt
3 *Owls must have **keen** eyesight.*
sharp, acute, piercing
OPPOSITE poor
4 *A **keen** wind was blowing from the east.*
bitter, cold, icy, penetrating
OPPOSITE mild

keep *verb*
1 *Let's **keep** the rest of the cake for later.*
save, conserve, preserve, retain, hang on to, hold on to, guard, store
2 *Please **keep** still.*
stay, remain
3 *A man in the audience **kept** coughing.*
persist in, go on, carry on, continue
4 *You're late. What **kept** you?*
delay, detain, hold up, keep waiting
5 *Where do you **keep** the knives and forks?*
store, house, put, stow
6 *Will the milk **keep** until tomorrow?*
last, be usable, stay good
7 *It costs money to **keep** a pet.*
support, maintain, provide for, pay for
to keep something up
Keep up the good work!
carry on, continue, maintain

key *noun*
*Have you found the **key** to the riddle?*
answer, solution, explanation, clue

kick *noun*
1 *He gave the television a kick.*
hit, boot, blow
2 *(informal) Some people might get a kick out of crossing the Atlantic in an old bath.*
thrill, excitement, (informal) buzz

kick *verb*
1 *Merv kicked the ball out*
boot, hit, drive, send, punt, heel
2 *(informal) I kicked my bad habit.*
give up, quit, break, abandon, cease, desist from

kidnap *verb*
*In the story, a boy is **kidnapped** by bandits.*
abduct, capture, seize, carry off, snatch

kill *verb*
*A person was **killed** in the explosion.*
(informal) bump off, do away with (old use) slay
To kill someone deliberately is to **murder** them.
To kill large numbers of people is to **massacre** or **slaughter** them.

To kill someone as a punishment is to **execute** them or **put them to death**.
To kill someone for political reasons is to **assassinate** them.

kind *noun*
*What **kind** of music do you like to play?*
sort, type, variety, style, category, class, set

kind *adjective*
*It was very **kind** of you to help me.*
kind-hearted, caring, good-natured, kindly, affectionate, warm, genial, loving, sweet, gentle, lenient, amiable, friendly, generous, sympathetic, thoughtful, obliging, considerate, understanding, compassionate, unselfish, giving, gracious, merciful, benevolent, charitable, humane, neighbourly
OPPOSITE unkind

kit *noun*
*I've forgotten my games **kit**.*
gear, outfit, equipment, paraphernalia, tools, tackle

knack *noun*
*George has a **knack** for taking photographs.*
skill, talent, gift, flair

⊕ **WORD WEB**

knight *noun*
THINGS A MEDIEVAL KNIGHT MIGHT WEAR OR CARRY
armour, baldric (leather belt), coat of arms, falcon or hawk, lance, mace (metal club), pennant, shield, surcoat, sword, tabard, tunic

A fight between knights on horseback was a *joust*.
A series of sporting contests between knights was a *tournament*.
A boy training to be a knight was first a *page* and then a *squire*.
An expedition made by a knight was a *quest*.

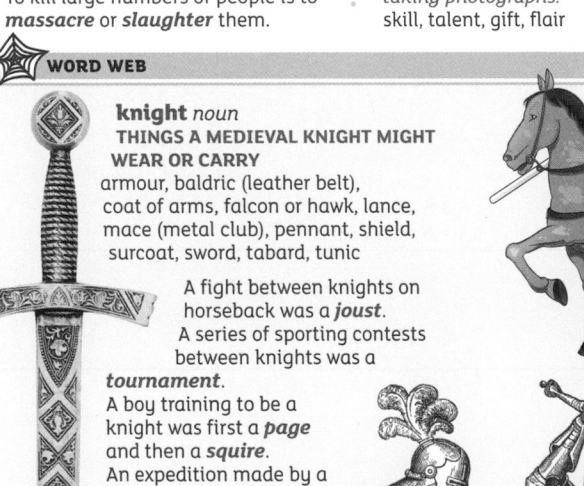

knock verb
*I **knocked** my head as I came out of the car.*
bump, bang, hit, strike, thump
(informal) bash

knot verb
*The sailors **knotted** the two ropes together.*
tie, bind, fasten, join, entwine, lash
OPPOSITE untie

know verb
1 *Do you **know** how to mend a puncture?*
understand, have knowledge of, comprehend
2 *As soon as she saw the unicorn, she **knew** what it was.*
recognize, realize, appreciate, be aware of
3 *Do you **know** Stewart well?*
be acquainted with, be familiar with, be a friend of

knowledge noun
1 *She has a good **knowledge** of Italian.*
understanding, grasp, command, familiarity (with)
2 *An encyclopedia contains a lot of **knowledge**.*
information, data, facts, learning, know-how, wisdom, scholarship

label noun
*The washing instructions are on the **label**.*
tag, ticket, sticker

lack noun
*The judge dismissed the case because of a **lack** of evidence.*
absence, shortage, scarcity, want
*A general lack of food is a **famine**.*
*A general lack of water is a **drought**.*
OPPOSITE abundance

lack verb
*The game **lacked** excitement.*
be short of, be without, want, need, require, miss

lag verb
*One runner was **lagging** behind the others.*
straggle, trail, fall behind, drop behind, dawdle, linger, loiter

lake noun
*We rowed across the **lake**.*
pond, pool
(Scottish) loch
*A salt-water lake is a **lagoon**.*

*A lake used to supply water is a **reservoir**.*

land noun
1 *The castle is surrounded by several acres of **land**.*
grounds, estate, property
2 *The **land** here is good for growing strawberries.*
ground, soil, earth
3 *China is a **land** with an ancient history.*
country, nation, state, region, territory

land verb
1 *The plane **landed** exactly on time.*
touch down, arrive
OPPOSITE take off
2 *The ship will **land** at Dover.*
dock, berth, come ashore
3 *How did these papers **land** on my desk?*
arrive, turn up, end up, wind up, settle

landscape noun
*We sat on the hill and admired the **landscape**.*
countryside, scenery, view, scene, outlook, prospect

lap noun
1 *My cat, Snowy, likes to sit on my **lap**.*
knees, thighs
2 *The cars were on the last **lap** of the race.*
circuit, round, loop

large adjective
1 *Elephants are **large** animals.*
big, huge, enormous, colossal, giant, gigantic, immense, great, massive, bulky, heavy, hefty, weighty, mighty, towering
(informal) whopping, ginormous
2 *The cook gave me a **large** helping of pudding.*
ample, generous, plentiful, abundant, lavish
3 *Is this room **large** enough for dancing in?*
spacious, roomy, sizeable
4 *The gales caused damage over a **large** area.*
wide, broad, extensive, widespread, vast
5 *The meeting was attended by a **large** number of people.*
considerable, substantial

last adjective
1 *Z is the **last** letter of the alphabet.*
final, closing, concluding, terminating, ultimate
OPPOSITE first
2 *Did you see the **last** Harry Potter film?*
latest, most recent
OPPOSITE next

last noun
at last
*The holidays are here **at last**!*
finally, eventually, in the end

late adjective
1 *The bus is **late**.*
delayed, overdue
OPPOSITE early, punctual, on time
2 *Mr Pettigrew showed us a portrait of his **late** wife.*
dead, deceased, departed, former

lately adverb
*There has been a lot of snow **lately**.*
recently, latterly, of late

later adverb
*I'm busy now, but I'll phone you **later**.*
afterwards, in a while, subsequently, next

laugh verb
1 *The childen **laughed** when the clown fell over.*
chuckle, chortle, giggle, titter, burst out laughing, roar or scream with laughter, roll or fall about laughing, guffaw
(informal) have hysterics, be in stitches
2 *It's rude to **laugh** at his way of singing.*
make fun of, mock, ridicule, scoff at, tease, deride

laughter noun
*We heard bursts of **laughter** coming from the kitchen.*
laughing, amusement, hilarity, mirth, merriment

lavish adjective
*The king put on a **lavish** feast for his birthday.*
generous, extravagant, sumptuous, luxurious, opulent, grand, abundant, copious, plentiful, bountiful
OPPOSITE meagre, paltry

law noun
*A law passed by parliament is an **act**.*
*A proposed law to be discussed by parliament is a **bill**.*
*The laws of a game are **regulations** or **rules**.*
*A regulation which must be obeyed is a **commandment**, **decree**, **edict**, or **order**.*

lay verb
1 *He **laid** the parchment carefully on his desk.*
put down, set down, place, position, spread, deposit, leave
2 *Please **lay** the table for dinner.*
set out, arrange

layer noun
1 *The walls needed two **layers** of paint.*
coat, coating, covering, thickness, film, sheet, skin

a b c d e f g h i j k l m n o p q r s t u v w x y z

2 *You can see various **layers** of rock in the cliff.*
seam, stratum

laze *verb*
*We spent the day **lazing** in the garden.*
be lazy, idle, loaf, lounge, lie about, relax, loll

lazy *adjective*
*My **lazy** little brother stayed in bed all day!*
idle, inactive, lethargic, slack, slothful, indolent
An informal name for a lazy person is **lazybones**.

lead *verb*
1 *The rescuers **led** the climbers to safety.*
guide, conduct, escort, usher, steer, pilot, shepherd
OPPOSITE follow
2 *Dr Martez will **lead** the expedition to Peru.*
be in charge of, direct, command, head, manage, supervise
3 *The British cyclist **led** from the start of the race.*
be in front, be in the lead, head the field
4 *The animals in the zoo **lead** a peaceful life.*
have, pass, spend, experience

lead *noun*
1 *The team followed the captain's **lead**.*
example, guidance, leadership, direction
2 *The Australian swimmer is in the **lead**.*
first place, front position
3 *Don't trip over the electrical **lead**.*
cable, flex, wire

leader *noun*
*The **leader** of the pirates was Captain Cutlass.*
head, chief, commander, ruler, captain, director, principal
(*informal*) boss
The leader of a group of wrongdoers is the **ringleader**.

leak *verb*
1 *The juice had **leaked** all over my schoolbag.*
escape, drip, seep, ooze, trickle
2 *Details of a secret plan were **leaked** to the newspaper.*
reveal, disclose, make known, pass on, give away, let out

lean *verb*
1 *I **leaned** against the wall.*
recline, rest, prop yourself, support yourself
2 *The yacht **leaned** to one side in the wind.*
slope, tilt, tip, incline, slant, list, bank

leap *verb*
*The dog **leaped** in the air to catch the ball.*
jump, spring, bound, vault

learn *verb*
1 *We are **learning** about the Vikings this term.*
discover, find out, gather, grasp, pick up
2 *I've got to **learn** the words of this song.*
learn by heart, memorize, master

learner *noun*
*This swimming class is for **learners** only.*
beginner, starter, novice
Someone learning things at school or college is a **pupil** or **student**.
Someone learning a trade is an **apprentice** or **trainee**.

leave *verb*
1 *Do you have to **leave** now?*
go, go away, depart, withdraw, take your leave, go out, set off, say goodbye
(*informal*) take off, disappear
OPPOSITE arrive
2 *The doctor **left** the room in a hurry.*
exit, go out of, depart from, quit, vacate
OPPOSITE enter
3 *Don't **leave** me here on my own!*
abandon, desert, forsake
4 *The crew **left** the sinking ship.*
evacuate, get out of
5 *My sister has **left** her job at the bank.*
give up, quit, resign from
(*informal*) walk out of
6 ***Leave** the milk bottles by the front door.*
place, position, put down, set down, deposit
7 *Lady Bigwig **left** all her money to charity.*
bequeath, hand down, will, endow

lecture *noun*
1 *There is a **lecture** about dinosaurs at the museum today.*
talk, lesson, speech, address
2 *The teacher gave us a **lecture** on how to behave.*
reprimand, warning
(*informal*)
telling off

ledge *noun*
*The climbers rested on a **ledge** of rock.*
shelf, projection
A ledge under a window is a **windowsill**.

leg *noun*
1 *Boris fell and bruised his **leg**.*
For parts of your body, see **body.**
2 *The rowers completed the first **leg** of the race.*
part, stage, section, phase, stretch

legal *adjective*
*Is it **legal** to park here on Sundays?*
lawful, legitimate, permissible, permitted, allowed
OPPOSITE illegal

legend *noun*
*I like reading **legends** about ancient heroes.*
myth, story, folk tale, fairy tale, fable, tradition

leisure *noun*
*Grandad has plenty of **leisure** since he retired.*
free time, spare time, relaxation, recreation, rest

lend *verb*
*Can you **lend** me some money until the weekend?*
loan, advance, let you have
OPPOSITE borrow

length *noun*
1 *My heart sank when I saw the **length** of the queue.*
extent, size
2 *We only had to wait a short **length** of time.*
space, period, stretch

lengthen *verb*
1 *Is it possible to **lengthen** these curtains?*
extend, make longer, increase, stretch
2 *The days **lengthen** in spring.*
draw out, get longer, stretch out

lenient *adjective*
*The teacher was **lenient** and let us off.*
easygoing, soft-hearted, tolerant, forgiving, indulgent, kind, merciful
OPPOSITE strict

lesson *noun*
*My piano **lesson** is on Friday afternoon.*
class, period, tutorial, instruction

let *verb*
1 *Abby's parents let her go to the party.*
allow, give permission to, permit, consent to, agree to
OPPOSITE forbid
2 *Our friends are letting their house for the summer.*
lease, rent out, hire out

lethal *adjective*
This bottle contains a lethal potion.
deadly, fatal, mortal, poisonous

level *adjective*
1 *You need a level field for playing rounders.*
even, flat, horizontal, smooth
OPPOSITE uneven
2 *At half-time the scores were level.*
equal, even, the same, matching
(*informal*) neck-and-neck

level *noun*
1 *The water had reached a high level.*
height
2 *The lift takes you up to the sixth level.*
floor, storey, tier
3 *What level have you reached in judo?*
grade, standard, stage, rank, degree

lid *noun*
Can you help me get the lid off this jar?
cap, cover, covering, top

lie *noun*
He accused the newspaper of printing lies.
deceit, falsehood, dishonesty
(*informal*) fib
OPPOSITE truth

lie *verb*
1 *It's twelve o'clock and he's still lying in bed!*
recline, stretch out, lounge, sprawl, rest
To lie face down is to be **prone**.
To lie face upwards is to be **supine**.
2 *The castle lies in a valley.*
be sited, be situated, be located, be found
3 *I don't trust her—I think she's lying.*
deceive someone, bluff
(*informal*) fib

life *noun*
1 *My hamster, Fluffy, leads a very easy life.*
existence, being, way of life
2 *Our lives depended on finding water.*
survival
3 *You seem to be full of life today!*
energy, liveliness, vigour, vitality, spirit, sprightliness, animation
4 *I'm reading a life of Elvis Presley.*
life story, autobiography, biography

lift *verb*
1 *The removal men lifted the piano carefully.*
pick up, raise, elevate, pull up, hoist
2 *The plane lifted off the ground.*
rise, ascend, soar

✏ WRITING TIPS

light

light *noun*
You can use these words to describe **light**.
TO DESCRIBE *HOW LIGHT APPEARS*
bright, brilliant, harsh, luminous, lustrous, strong; diffused, dim, muted, soft, warm
***LIGHT* MAY:**
beam, blaze, dazzle, flash, flicker, glare, gleam, glimmer, glint, glisten, glitter, glow, shimmer, shine, sparkle, twinkle

---

light *adjective*
1 *The artist worked in a light and airy studio.*
bright, well-lit, illuminated
OPPOSITE dim, gloomy
2 *She was wearing light blue jeans.*
pale
OPPOSITE dark
3 *The parcel looks big, but it is quite light.*
lightweight, portable, weightless, slight
A common simile is *as light as a feather*.
OPPOSITE heavy
4 *A light wind rippled the surface of the water.*
gentle, faint, slight
OPPOSITE strong
5 *We had a light meal before we went out.*
small, modest, simple, insubstantial
OPPOSITE heavy, substantial

light *verb*
1 *We lit the candles on my birthday cake.*
ignite, kindle, set alight, set fire to, switch on
OPPOSITE extinguish
2 *The fireworks lit the sky.*
light up, brighten, illuminate, shed light on, shine on
OPPOSITE darken

like *verb*
1 *Lauren likes her new puppy more than anything.*
admire, adore, be attached to, be fond of, care for, cherish, esteem, hold dear, love
(*informal*) have a soft spot for
2 *Alex likes chocolate cake very much. What sort of films do you like?*
appreciate, be interested in, be keen on, be partial to, delight in, enjoy, prefer, relish
OPPOSITE dislike

likely *adjective*
It's likely that the shop will be closed tomorrow.
probable, expected, anticipated, predictable, foreseeable
OPPOSITE unlikely

limit *noun*
1 *There is a limit of twenty pupils for this class.*
maximum, restriction, threshold, ceiling, cut-off point
A limit on time is a **deadline** or **time limit**.
2 *The fence marks the limit of the school grounds.*
border, boundary, edge, perimeter, frontier

limit *verb*
I had to limit the invitations to my party.
put a limit on, restrict, control, ration

limp *adjective*
The leaves on the plant are looking limp.
drooping, floppy, sagging, wilting, soft, flabby, slack
OPPOSITE rigid

line *noun*
1 *I drew a pencil line across the page.*
stroke, rule, underline, stripe, streak, band, bar, dash
A line that is cut into a surface is a **groove**, **score**, or **scratch**.
A line on a person's skin is a **wrinkle**.
A deep groove or wrinkle is a **furrow**.
A line on fabric is a **crease**
2 *There was a long line of people waiting at the bus stop.*
queue, row, file, column, rank, procession, chain
A line of police officers forming a barrier is a **cordon**.
A line of schoolchildren walking in pairs is a **crocodile**.
3 *The clothes were drying on the washing line.*
cord, rope, string, thread, wire, cable, flex, lead

a b c d e f g h i j k l m n o p q r s t u v w x y z

linger *verb*
1 *The smell of burning wood **lingered** in the air.*
continue, remain, stay, last, persist
OPPOSITE disappear
2 *Don't **linger** outside in this cold weather.*
hang about, wait about, loiter, dawdle, dally, delay
OPPOSITE hurry

link *noun*
*The two schools have close **links** with each other.*
relationship, association, connection, bond, tie

link *verb*
*They **linked** the trailer to the tractor.*
attach, connect, fasten, join, couple
OPPOSITE separate

list *noun*
A list of people's names is a **roll** or **register**.
A list of people who have tasks to do is a **rota**.
A list of books in the library or of goods for sale is a **catalogue**.
A list of topics mentioned in a book is an **index**.
A list of things to choose from is a **menu**.
A list of things to do or remember is a **checklist**.

list *verb*
*I helped to **list** the books in the library.*
record, write down, catalogue, index, register

listen *verb*
to listen to something
*The spy **listened** carefully **to** the instructions.*
pay attention to, take notice of, attend to, heed
To listen secretly to a private conversation is to **eavesdrop**.

little

litter *noun*
*The street was covered with **litter**.*
rubbish, waste, refuse, garbage, junk, clutter, mess, odds and ends

little *adjective*
1 *The camera is so **little** it will fit in your pocket.*
compact, mini, miniature, minute, petite, small, tiny
(*informal*) teeny (*Scottish*) wee
OPPOSITE big, large
2 *My granny lived in India when she was **little**.*
small, young
OPPOSITE big, old

live *adjective*
*The fishermen caught a **live** octopus in their nets.*
alive, living, breathing
OPPOSITE dead

live *verb*
*Will these plants **live** through the winter?*
stay alive, survive, exist, flourish, last, continue, remain
OPPOSITE die

lively *adjective*
1 *The toddlers were in a **lively** mood.*
active, energetic, animated, spirited, boisterous, excited, vivacious, sprightly, frisky, chirpy, perky
OPPOSITE inactive
2 *The city centre is always **lively** at night.*
busy, bustling, crowded, exciting, buzzing
OPPOSITE quiet, dead

living *adjective*
1 *Miss Millicent had no **living** relatives.*
alive
OPPOSITE dead
2 *There are no dinosaurs still **living**.*
existing, surviving
OPPOSITE extinct

living *noun*
1 *He makes a **living** from painting.*
income, livelihood
2 *What does she do for a **living**?*
job, occupation, profession, trade, career

load *noun*
1 *Camels can carry heavy **loads**.*
burden, weight
2 *The lorry delivered its **load** to the supermarket.*
cargo, consignment, goods, freight

load *verb*
1 *We **loaded** the suitcases into the car.*
pack, pile, heap, stow
2 *He arrived **loaded** with shopping bags.*
weigh down, burden, saddle

loathe *verb*
*My brother **loathes** the colour pink.*
hate, detest, dislike, despise
OPPOSITE love, adore

local *adjective*
*Our **local** shop delivers newspapers.*
neighbourhood, nearby, neighbouring

lock *noun*
1 *There was a heavy **lock** on the lid of the chest.*
fastening, clasp, padlock, bolt, latch
2 *The princess cut a **lock** from her hair.*
tress, curl, tuft

lock *verb*
*Make sure you **lock** the door when you go out.*
fasten, secure, bolt, close, shut, seal

logical *adjective*
*The robot always gave a **logical** answer.*
rational, reasonable, sensible, sound, valid, intelligent, clear, lucid, methodical, systematic
OPPOSITE illogical

lone *adjective*
*A **lone** rider galloped past.*
single, solitary, unaccompanied, isolated

lonely *adjective*
1 *Cara felt **lonely** while her friends were away.*
alone, friendless, lonesome, solitary, abandoned, neglected, forlorn, forsaken
2 *The climbers sheltered in a **lonely** hut.*
deserted, isolated, remote, secluded, out-of-the-way

long *adjective*
*It seemed a **long** time before the bus came.*
lengthy, prolonged, extended, extensive, long-lasting
OPPOSITE short

long *verb*
to long for something
*I'm **longing for** a drink.*
yearn for, crave, want, wish for, desire, fancy, hunger for, pine for, hanker after, itch for
(*informal*) be dying for

look *verb*
1 *If you **look** carefully, you'll see an owl in the tree.*
watch, observe, view, regard, keep your eyes open
2 *My pet snake **looks** a bit hungry.*
appear, seem
3 *The secret agent **looked** at her watch.*
glance, glimpse, peek, peep

4 *The fossil hunters **looked** at the rocks.*
stare, peer, study, scrutinize, examine, inspect, take a good look at
5 *The grumpy knight **looked** at his servant.*
glare, glower, grimace, frown, scowl
To look steadily is to **gaze**.
To look quickly is to **glance, glimpse, peek** or **peep**.
To look in amazement is to **gape**.
To look over a wide area is to **scan** or **survey** it.

look *noun*
1 *Did you have a **look** at what she was wearing?*
glance, glimpse, peep, sight, view
2 *The guard had an unfriendly **look**.*
appearance, bearing, manner, air, expression, face

loop *noun*
*Make a **loop** in the string and then tie a knot.*
coil, hoop, circle, ring, noose, bend, curl, kink, twist

loop *verb*
*The cowboy **looped** the reins round a fence post.*
coil, wind, curl, bend, turn, twist

loose *adjective*
1 *Some of the cobbles on the road are **loose**.*
insecure, unfixed, movable, unsteady, shaky, wobbly
OPPOSITE firm, secure
2 *The fire was started by a **loose** wire.*
disconnected, unattached, detached
3 *These jeans are **loose** around the waist.*
slack, baggy, roomy, loose-fitting
OPPOSITE tight
4 *The chickens wander **loose** about the farm.*
free, at large, at liberty, on the loose, unconfined, unrestricted
OPPOSITE confined

loot *noun*
*The thieves buried their **loot** in a safe place.*
haul, plunder, takings

loot *verb*
*Rioters **looted** the shops.*
raid, ransack, rob, steal from, pillage, plunder

lose *verb*
1 *Debbie has **lost** one of her gloves.*
be unable to find, mislay, misplace
OPPOSITE find
2 *Unfortunately, we **lost** the game on Saturday.*
be defeated, get beaten, suffer a defeat
OPPOSITE win

lot *noun*
*We are having another **lot** of visitors this weekend.*
group, batch, set, crowd, collection

a lot of
*My brother needs **a lot of** help with his spelling.*
a large amount of, a good or great deal of, plenty of

lots of
*There are **lots of** toys to choose from in the shop.*
a great number of, many, numerous, plenty (of)
(*informal*) loads of, tons of, masses of, oodles of, hundreds of

loud *adjective*
*The whole house was kept awake by the **loud** music.*
noisy, blaring, booming, deafening, rowdy, resounding, thunderous, penetrating, piercing
A noise which is loud enough to hear is **audible**.
OPPOSITE quiet, soft

love *noun*
*She often mentions her **love** of the outdoors.*
liking, passion, fondness, affection, devotion, admiration, adoration
(*informal*) soft spot (for)

love *verb*
1 *They **love** each other and want to get married.*
be in love with, care for, adore, cherish, hold dear, treasure, worship, idolize
A relationship between two people who love each other is a **romance**.
2 *My friend, Dot, **loves** knitting.*
like, have a passion for, be fond of, be partial to, enjoy

lovely *adjective*
1 *Jemma is a **lovely** girl.*
charming, delightful, lovable, likeable, dear, sweet, enchanting, endearing
2 *It's a **lovely** day for a bicycle trip.*
fine, glorious
3 *The girls had an **lovely** time camping*
pleasant, pleasing, enjoyable
OPPOSITE nasty
4 *The roses look **lovely** in that vase.*
appealing, attractive, beautiful, pretty

low *adjective*
1 *The garden is surrounded by a **low** wall.*
short, shallow, sunken
2 *They were soldiers of **low** rank in the army.*
junior, inferior, lowly, modest, humble
3 *We spoke in **low** whispers.*
quiet, soft, muted, subdued, muffled
4 *The tuba plays **low** notes.*
bass, deep
OPPOSITE high

lower *verb*
1 *The supermarket **lowered** its prices.*
reduce, cut, bring down, decrease, lessen
(*informal*) slash
2 *Please **lower** the volume of your radio.*
quieten, turn down
3 *At the end of the Olympic Games, they **lower** the flag.*
take down, let down, dip

loyal *adjective*
*Sir Valiant had always been a **loyal** knight.*
true, trusty, faithful, steadfast, reliable, dependable, devoted, constant, sincere
OPPOSITE disloyal

luck *noun*
1 *He found the secret entrance by **luck**.*
accident, chance, coincidence, fluke, fate, destiny
2 *She had a bit of **luck** today.*
good fortune, success

lucky *adjective*
1 *I got the right answer by a **lucky** guess.*
accidental, chance, unintentional, unplanned
2 *Some **lucky** person won a million pounds.*
fortunate, favoured, successful

luggage *noun*
*The **luggage** can go in the boot of the car.*
baggage, cases, suitcases, bags

lump *noun*
1 ***Lumps** of sticky clay stuck to his boots.*
chunk, piece, cluster, clump, wad, mass, hunk, wedge, block
A round lump of something is a **ball**.
A lump of gold is a **nugget**.
A lump of earth is a **clod**.
A lump of blood is a **clot**.
2 *I could feel a **lump** where I'd bumped my head.*
bump, swelling, bulge, protrusion

lunge verb
Robin **lunged** at the sheriff with his sword.
thrust, charge, rush, dive, pounce, throw yourself

lurch verb
1 The bus passengers **lurched** from side to side.
reel, sway, rock, stagger, stumble, totter
2 The ship **lurched** as the waves pounded it.
pitch, roll, heave, lean, list

lure verb
Spiders **lure** insects into their webs.
attract, entice, tempt, coax, draw, invite, persuade
Something used to lure an animal into a trap is **bait**.

lurk verb
The jaguar **lurked** in wait for its prey.
skulk, loiter, prowl, crouch, hide, lie in wait, lie low

lush adjective
Rainforests have **lush** vegetation.
rich, dense, thick, rampant, abundant

luxurious adjective
The dress was trimmed with **luxurious** lace.
grand, lavish, lush, rich, expensive, costly, deluxe, plush, magnificent, splendid, sumptuous
OPPOSITE simple, austere

luxury noun
The millionaire lived a life of **luxury**.
affluence, wealth, richness, splendour, comfort, ease
OPPOSITE poverty

machine noun
Do you know how this **machine** works?
apparatus, appliance, device, engine, contraption

mad adjective
1 You must be **mad** to go out on a day like this.
crazy, daft, insane, senseless, stupid, foolish, idiotic
(informal) out of your mind, potty, nuts
OPPOSITE sensible, wise
2 The emperor was **mad** with rage.
angry, furious, beside yourself, frenzied, hysterical
3 (informal) Sandra is **mad** about horses.
enthusiastic, fanatical, passionate

magazine noun
I bought a **magazine** to read on the train.
journal, periodical, paper, comic

magic adjective
1 My uncle taught me some **magic** tricks.
conjuring
2 The castle was surrounded by a **magic** spell.
magical, supernatural

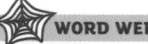
WORD WEB

magic noun
Do you believe in magic?
sorcery, witchcraft, wizardry, spells, charms, enchantments

PEOPLE WHO USE MAGIC
enchanter or enchantress, magician, sorceror or sorceress, warlock, witch, wizard

THINGS WHICH A SORCEROR MIGHT DO
bewitch, enchant, cast or undo a spell, become invisible or vanish, brew a potion, put a curse on you

THINGS WHICH A SORCEROR MIGHT HAVE OR USE
apprentice, cauldron, charm, elixir, magic potion, magic spell or incantation, talisman, wand

magician noun
1 The **magician** pulled a scarf out of his hat.
conjuror
2 King Arthur was helped by the **magician**, Merlin.
sorcerer, witch, wizard

magnificent adjective
1 The mountain scenery was **magnificent**.
beautiful, glorious, splendid, spectacular, impressive, majestic
2 The film star lived in a **magnificent** house.
grand, imposing, stately
(informal) posh
3 That was a **magnificent** meal!
excellent, first-class, marvellous, superb
(informal) fabulous, fantastic

magnify verb
Objects are **magnified** through binoculars.
enlarge, make larger
(informal) blow up
OPPOSITE reduce, minimize

main adjective
1 What was the **main** point of the story?
central, chief, most important, basic, essential, fundamental, primary, predominant
2 This is the **main** shopping area in the town.
major, principal, biggest, foremost, largest, leading, prime
OPPOSITE minor, unimportant

mainly adverb
Chimpanzees eat **mainly** fruit and vegetables.
largely, mostly, chiefly, principally, predominantly, primarily

maintain verb
1 The referee tried to **maintain** order.
keep, preserve
2 A team of gardeners **maintain** the grounds.
look after, take care of, keep in order
3 He still **maintains** that he's innocent.
claim, declare, assert, insist, state, contend

major adjective
1 There are delays on all the **major** roads into the city.
chief, principal, primary, leading
2 Writing her first novel was a **major** achievement.
big, great, considerable, significant, important
OPPOSITE minor

make verb
1 We **made** a shelter out of leaves and branches.
build, construct, assemble, put together, produce, manufacture
2 Those two are always **making** trouble.
cause, bring about, give rise to, provoke

3 *They made me captain.*
appoint, elect, nominate
4 *They've made the attic into a games room.*
change, turn, convert, modify, transform, alter
5 *She'll make a good actress when she's older.*
become, grow into, turn into, change into
6 *We can't make her go if she doesn't want to.*
force, compel, order
7 *He made a lot of money last year.*
gain, get, obtain, acquire, receive, earn, win
8 *The ship finally made land.*
reach, arrive at, get to, get as far as
9 *What time do you make it?*
calculate, estimate, reckon
10 *2 and 2 make 4.*
add up to, come to, total
11 *I'll make you an offer for your old bike.*
propose, suggest
12 *Have you made your bed this morning?*
arrange, tidy
to make someone or something out
I can't make out why everything went wrong.
understand, work out, comprehend, fathom, make sense of
to make up
I made up a new flavour of ice cream.
create, invent, think up, concoct

make noun
What make of computer do you have?
brand, model, label

man noun
A polite word for a man is **gentleman**.
Informal words are **bloke**, **chap**, **fellow**, and **guy**.
A married man is a **husband**.
A man who has children is a **father**.
An unmarried man is a **bachelor**.
A man whose wife has died is a **widower**.
A man on his wedding day is a **bridegroom**.
A man who is engaged to be married is a **fiancé**.
Words for a young man are **boy**, **lad**, and **youth**.

manage verb
1 *His eldest son manages the business now.*
be in charge of, run, direct, lead, control, govern, rule, supervise, oversee, preside over

2 *I can't manage any more work this week.*
cope with, deal with, take on, carry out
3 *We'll have to manage without the car.*
cope, make do, get along, get by

manner noun
1 *They did the work in an efficient manner.*
way, style, fashion, method
2 *I was put off by her frosty manner.*
behaviour, conduct, attitude, disposition, air, look, bearing
manners
Trolls have no manners at all!
politeness, courtesy, graces

manufacture verb
The factory manufactures pine furniture.
make, build, assemble, fabricate

many adjective
I've been on an aeroplane many times.
a lot of, plenty of, numerous, frequent, countless, innumerable, untold
(*informal*) umpteen, lots of
OPPOSITE few

map noun
The travel agent gave us a free map of Paris.
chart, diagram, plan
A book of maps is an **atlas**.
A person who draws maps is a **cartographer**.

march verb
The brass band marched down the High Street.
parade, file, troop, stride, pace

mark noun
1 *There were muddy paw marks all over the kitchen floor.*
spot, stain, blemish, blotch, blot, smear, smudge, streak
A mark left by a pen or pencil is a **scribble**.
A mark left by fingers is a **fingermark**.
A mark on your skin that you are born with is a **birthmark**.
2 *They stood in silence as a mark of respect.*
sign, token, indication, symbol, emblem
3 *What mark did you get in the spelling test?*
score, grade

mark verb
1 *Please be careful not to mark the photographs.*
stain, smudge, dirty, blot
2 *The teacher had a pile of essays to mark.*
correct, grade, assess

marry verb
In what year did your grandparents marry?
get married, wed
(*informal*) tie the knot, get hitched
A couple who have promised to marry are **engaged** to each other.
A man who is engaged to be married is a **fiancé** and the woman he is engaged to is his **fiancée**.

marsh noun
Wading birds are found in coastal marshes.
swamp, bog, wetland, marshland, fen

marvel verb
to marvel at
The crowd marvelled at the juggler's skill.
admire, wonder at, be amazed by, be astonished by

marvellous adjective
1 *The professor showed us his marvellous inventions.*
amazing, remarkable, extraordinary, incredible, miraculous, astonishing, phenomenal
OPPOSITE ordinary
2 *We had a marvellous day at the zoo.*
excellent, superb, tremendous, wonderful, splendid
(*informal*) brilliant, fantastic, terrific, super, smashing
OPPOSITE bad, awful

mash verb
Mash the potatoes until they're smooth.
crush, pound, pulp, smash, squash
To make something into powder is to **grind** or **pulverize** it.

mask verb
The entrance was masked by an overhanging tree.
conceal, hide, cover, obscure, screen, veil, shroud, camouflage

mass noun
She sifted through the mass of papers on her desk.
heap, pile, mound, stack, collection, quantity, accumulation
(*informal*) load

master noun
1 *We played a game in which I was master of the castle.*
lord, ruler, governor, chief
2 *Sherlock Holmes was a master of disguises.*
expert (at), genius, ace, wizard

master verb
1 *Have you mastered chess yet?*
grasp, learn, understand
(*informal*) get the hang of, get to grips with

a b c d e f g h i j k l m n o p q r s t u v w x y z

2 *I've managed to **master** my fear of heights.*
overcome, conquer, defeat, triumph over, get the better of, control, curb, subdue, tame

match noun
*The semi-final was a really exciting **match**.*
game, contest, competition, fixture, tournament, tie

match verb
*Does this tie **match** my shirt?*
go with, suit, fit with, blend with, tone in with
OPPOSITE contrast with

material noun
1 *I'm collecting **material** for the school magazine.*
information, facts, data, ideas, notes
2 *The cleaning **materials** are in the cupboard.*
stuff, substances, things
3 *The kite is made of lightweight **material**.*
cloth, fabric

matter noun
1 *The manager will deal with this **matter**.*
affair, concern, issue, business, situation, incident, subject, topic, thing
2 *Peat consists mainly of plant **matter**.*
material, stuff, substance
3 *What's the **matter** with the car?*
problem, difficulty, trouble, worry

matter verb
*Will it **matter** if I'm late?*
be important, count, make a difference

mature adjective
1 *The zoo has two **mature** gorillas.*
adult, fully grown, well developed
OPPOSITE young
2 *He acts very **mature** for his age.*
grown-up, responsible, sensible
OPPOSITE immature, childish

mean adjective
1 *Scrooge was too **mean** to buy any presents.*
selfish, miserly, uncharitable
(*informal*) stingy, tight-fisted, penny-pinching
OPPOSITE generous
2 *That was a **mean** trick to play.*
unkind, unpleasant, nasty, spiteful, vicious, cruel, malicious
OPPOSITE kind

mean verb
1 *A red traffic light **means** that cars have to stop.*
indicate, signify, denote, express, imply, convey, communicate, stand for, symbolize
2 *I **mean** to get better at swimming this year.*
intend, plan, aim, propose, want

meaning noun
*What is the **meaning** of this riddle?*
sense, significance, explanation, interpretation, definition

measure verb
***Measure** the height of the wall.*
calculate, gauge, assess, survey
To measure the weight of something is to **weigh** it.

measure noun
*They are taking **measures** to improve the park.*
step, action, course, procedure, means

medium adjective
*The man was of **medium** height.*
average, middle, middling, standard, moderate, normal

meek adjective
*Koalas look **meek**, but they have fierce claws.*
gentle, mild, tame, submissive, modest, docile, quiet, humble
OPPOSITE aggressive

meet verb
1 *I **met** an old friend at the party.*
come across, encounter, run into, see
(*informal*) bump into
2 *My parents **met** me at the station.*
greet, pick up, welcome
3 *We're **meeting** outside the cinema at eight.*
gather, assemble, collect, muster, rally
4 *The two roads **meet** here.*
come together, merge, connect, join, cross, intersect

meeting noun
*The bandits held a **meeting** to discuss their plan.*
gathering, assembly, council, forum, congress, conference
A large outdoor public meeting is a **rally**.
A formal meeting with a king or queen is an **audience**.

melt verb
*The ice began to **melt** in the sun.*
thaw, soften, unfreeze
To melt frozen food is to **defrost** it.
To melt ore to get metal from it is to **smelt** it.
Rock or metal that has melted through great heat is **molten**.
OPPOSITE freeze

mend verb
*Workmen were **mending** the pavement.*
fix, repair, put right, restore, renovate, patch

mention verb
1 *Please don't **mention** the idea to anyone.*
refer to, speak about, touch on, hint at

2 *You **mentioned** that you spoke Japanese.*
say, remark, reveal, disclose
(*informal*) let out
3 *The director **mentioned** all the cast.*
name, acknowledge, list

mercy noun
*The evil queen showed no **mercy**.*
compassion, humanity, sympathy, pity, leniency, kindness, charity
OPPOSITE cruelty

merge verb
1 *They plan to **merge** the two schools.*
join together, combine, integrate, put together, unite, amalgamate
2 *Two streams **merge** here to form a river.*
come together, converge, join, meet
OPPOSITE separate

merry adjective
*The postman was whistling a **merry** tune.*
cheerful, happy, jolly, bright, joyful, light-hearted, lively, spirited
OPPOSITE gloomy

mess noun
1 *Please clear up this **mess**.*
muddle, untidiness, chaos, disorder, confusion, clutter, jumble, litter, dirt
(*informal*) shambles
2 *Zoe made a **mess** of her audition.*
disaster, botch
(*informal*) hash

mess verb
to mess about
*We spent the day **messing about** on the beach.*
play about, fool around, lounge about
(*informal*) muck about
to mess things up
*I hope you haven't **messed up** my room.*
confuse, mix up, muddle, jumble, make a mess of, tangle
to mess something up
*I think I **messed up** my interview.*
bungle, botch
(*informal*) make a hash of

message noun
Did you get my message?
note, letter, text, email

messy adjective
My bedroom is really messy!
muddled, untidy, disorderly, chaotic,
dirty, filthy, grubby, mucky
(*informal*) higgledy-piggledy
OPPOSITE neat

method noun
*My granny has a secret method for
making jam.*
technique, way, procedure, process
A specially skilful method for doing
something is a **knack**.

middle adjective
The middle lane is reserved for buses.
central, inner, inside, midway

middle noun
*A scarecrow stood in the middle
of the field.*
centre, core, heart, midpoint
The middle of a wheel is the **hub**.
The middle part of an atom or cell is
the **nucleus**.

mighty adjective
The dragon let out a mighty roar.
powerful, forceful, vigorous, ferocious,
violent, great, enormous, hefty
OPPOSITE weak

mild adjective
1 *He's a mild person who never
complains.*
amiable, docile, easygoing, gentle,
good-tempered, harmless, kind,
lenient, merciful, placid, soft-hearted
2 *The weather has been mild for this
time of year.*
pleasant, warm, temperate
OPPOSITE severe

mind noun
1 *Her mind was as sharp
as ever.*
brain, intelligence, intellect, head,
sense, understanding, wits,
judgement, mental powers,
reasoning
2 *Are you sure you won't change
your mind?*
wishes, intention, fancy, inclination,
opinion, outlook, point of view

mind verb
1 *Will you mind my bag for a
minute?*
guard, look after, watch, care for
(*informal*) keep an eye on
2 *Mind the step.*
look out for, watch out for,
beware of, pay attention to,
heed, note
3 *They won't mind if
I'm late.*
bother, care, worry, be
upset, take offence,
object, disapprove

mingle verb
*The secret agent mingled with the
crowd.*
mix in, circulate, blend, combine,
merge, fuse

miniature adjective
*A piccolo looks like a miniature
flute.*
tiny, minute, diminutive, small-scale,
baby, mini

minor adjective
I only had a minor part in the play.
small, unimportant, insignificant,
inferior, subordinate, trivial, petty
OPPOSITE major

minute adjective
You can hardly see the minute crack.
tiny, minuscule, microscopic,
negligible
OPPOSITE large

miraculous adjective
*The patient made a miraculous
recovery.*
amazing, astonishing, astounding,
extraordinary, incredible, marvellous,
unbelievable, wonderful, mysterious,
inexplicable

misbehave verb
*My puppy has been misbehaving
again!*
behave badly, be naughty, be
disobedient, get up to mischief
OPPOSITE behave

miserable adjective
1 *You look miserable—what's the
matter?*
sad, unhappy, sorrowful, gloomy,
glum, downhearted, despondent,
dejected, depressed, melancholy,
mournful, tearful
OPPOSITE cheerful, happy
2 *The poor animals lived in
miserable conditions.*
distressing, uncomfortable, wretched,
pitiful, pathetic, squalid
OPPOSITE comfortable

misery noun
*The slaves must have led a
life of misery.*
sadness, sorrow, unhappiness,
grief, distress, despair, anguish,
wretchedness, suffering, torment,
heartache, depression
OPPOSITE happiness

misfortune noun
I heard about her family's misfortune.
bad luck, trouble, hardship, adversity,
affliction, setback, mishap
OPPOSITE good luck

misleading adjective
*The directions he gave were quite
misleading.*
confusing, unreliable, deceptive,
ambiguous, unclear

miss verb
1 *I missed the bus.*
be too late for
2 *The arrow missed the target.*
fall short of, go wide of
3 *If we leave now, we should miss
the traffic.*
avoid
4 *I missed dad when he was in
hospital.*
long for, yearn for, pine for
to miss something out
*I missed out the boring bits of the
story.*
leave out, omit, ignore, overlook,
skip

mission noun
1 *Her mission in life was to help
those in need.*
aim, purpose, objective, task, job,
campaign
2 *The astronauts are on a mission
to Mars.*
expedition, journey, voyage,
exploration

mist noun
We drove slowly through the mist.
fog, haze, cloud, drizzle

mistake noun
*This piece of writing is full of
mistakes.*
error, inaccuracy, blunder, slip, slip-
up, lapse
A spelling mistake is a **misspelling**.
A mistake where something is left
out is an **omission**.
A mistake in a printed book is
a **misprint**.

misty adjective
1 *If it's misty outside, take
a torch.*
foggy, hazy
2 *I can't see through the misty
window.*
steamy, cloudy, smoky, opaque

mix verb
Mix the ingredients in a bowl.
combine, blend, mingle
to mix something up
Please don't mix up my DVDs.
muddle, jumble, confuse
To mix up playing cards is to **shuffle**
them.

mixed adjective
Add a teaspoon of mixed herbs.
assorted, various, different,
miscellaneous
OPPOSITE separate

mixture noun
1 *Put the cake mixture in a baking
tin.*
mix, blend, combination
A mixture of metals is an **alloy**.
A mixture of two different species of
plant or animal is a **hybrid**.

a b c d e f g h i j k l m n o p q r s t u v w x y z

2 *There's an odd* **mixture** *of things in the drawer.*
assortment, collection, variety, jumble
A confused mixture is a **mishmash**.

moan *verb*
1 *The wounded warrior* **moaned** *in pain.*
cry, groan, sigh, wail, howl, whimper
2 *Ned's always* **moaning** *about the food.*
complain, grumble, grouse, whine
(*informal*) whinge

mob *noun*
An angry **mob** *stormed the gates of the castle.*
crowd, horde, throng, mass, rabble, gang, pack, herd, bunch

mock *verb*
It was mean of them to **mock** *his singing.*
jeer at, laugh at, make fun of, scoff at, sneer at, ridicule, scorn, deride
(*informal*) take the mickey out of

monster

model *noun*
1 *I'm building a* **model** *of a space rocket.*
copy, replica, toy
2 *This is the latest* **model** *of skateboard.*
design, type, version
3 *She's a* **model** *of good behaviour.*
example, ideal

moderate *adjective*
Her first book was a **moderate** *success.*
average, fair, modest, medium, reasonable, passable, tolerable
OPPOSITE exceptional

modern *adjective*
1 *All the equipment in their kitchen was* **modern**.
up to date, contemporary, advanced, the latest
OPPOSITE out of date
2 *She always dresses in* **modern** *clothes.*
fashionable, stylish, modish
(*informal*) trendy, hip
OPPOSITE old-fashioned

modest *adjective*
1 *He's very* **modest** *about his success.*
humble, quiet, reserved, shy, bashful, coy
OPPOSITE conceited
2 *There has been a* **modest** *increase in sales.*
moderate, reasonable, average, medium

moist *adjective*
1 *The walls of the dungeon were* **moist**.
damp, wet, watery, clammy, dank
2 *Tropical plants grow well in a* **moist** *atmosphere.*
humid, muggy, steamy, rainy

moisture *noun*
There is still a lot of **moisture** *on the ground.*
wetness, dampness, damp, dew, condensation, humidity

moment *noun*
1 *I'll be ready in a* **moment**.
minute, second, instant, flash
(*informal*) jiffy, tick
2 *It was a great* **moment** *in the history of space travel.*
time, occasion, period

money *noun*
How much **money** *do you have with you?*
cash, currency, funds, finance
(*informal*) dough, dosh
A large amount of money is a **fortune**, **riches**, or **wealth**.

monster *noun*
A sea **monster** *reared its head above the waves.*
beast, giant, ogre, brute

monstrous *adjective*
1 *The town was engulfed by a* **monstrous** *wave.*
huge, gigantic, enormous, immense, massive, colossal, great, hulking, mighty, towering, vast
2 *The nation was shocked by the* **monstrous** *crime.*
horrifying, shocking, wicked, evil, hideous, horrible, terrible, atrocious, dreadful, gruesome, outrageous, scandalous

mood *noun*
What sort of **mood** *is he in today?*
temper, humour, state of mind, disposition

moody *adjective*
She's been **moody** *and withdrawn for weeks.*
sulky, sullen, grumpy, bad-tempered, temperamental, touchy, miserable, gloomy, glum
OPPOSITE cheerful

WORD WEB

moon *noun*
FORMS IN WHICH WE SEE THE MOON
crescent moon, full moon, new moon; moonbeam, moonlight

THINGS YOU MIGHT FIND OR DO ON THE MOON
crater, moon dust, moon rock, moonscape, moonwalk

A word meaning 'to do with the Moon' is **lunar**.

moral *noun*
The **moral** *of this story is that crime doesn't pay.*
lesson, message, meaning

more *adjective*
The soup needs **more** *pepper.*
extra, further, added, additional
OPPOSITE less

mostly *adverb*
I spend my money **mostly** *on books and music.*
mainly, largely, chiefly, primarily, generally, usually, normally, typically, principally, predominantly

motive *noun*
The police can find no **motive** *for the crime.*
cause, motivation, reason, purpose, grounds

mould *verb*
The sculptor **moulded** *the figures from clay.*
shape, form, fashion, model, cast

mouldy *adjective*
All I found in the fridge was some **mouldy** *cheese.*
rotten, rotting, decaying, musty, damp

mound *noun*
1 *Her desk was covered with* **mounds** *of paper.*
heap, pile, stack, mass
2 *There used to be a castle on top of that* **mound**.
hill, hillock, rise, hump
An ancient mound of earth over a grave is a **barrow**.

mountain *noun*
see panel opposite

mourn *verb*
He was still **mourning** *the loss of his friend.*
grieve for, lament for

move *noun*
1 *Don't make a* **move**!
movement
2 *The spy was watching their every* **move**.
action, step, deed, manoeuvre
3 *Is it my* **move** *next?*
turn, go, chance, opportunity

move verb

to move from one place to another
carry, remove, transfer, transport, shift
*They **shifted** the piano into the front room.*

to move from a position
go, leave, depart, quit, budge
*The camel stared and refused to **budge**.*

to move restlessly
toss, turn, stir, twist, shake, fidget, twitch, flap
*Please stop **twitching** in your seat.*

to move from side to side
sway, swing, wave, wag, wiggle
*The knight **swung** a sword above his helmet.*

to move along
travel, walk, proceed
*Few people **travel** on these roads after dark.*

to move along quickly
hurry, dash, race, run, rush, hasten, hurtle, career, fly, speed, sweep, shoot, zoom
*A boy went **careering** past on a scooter.*

to move along slowly
amble, stroll, saunter, dawdle, crawl, drift
*Gerald the tortoise **sauntered** down the path.*

to move towards something
advance, approach, come, proceed, progress
*The lookout saw a pirate ship **approaching**.*

to move back or move away
back, retreat, reverse, withdraw

🕷 WORD WEB

mountain noun
The top of a mountain is the **peak** or **summit.**
A line of mountains is a **range.**
A long, narrow mountain is a **ridge.**
A mountain with a hole at the top caused by an eruption is a **volcano.**
An area of land with many mountains is said to be **mountainous.**

THINGS YOU MIGHT SEE ON OR NEAR A MOUNTAIN
avalanche, boulder, cave, cliff, crag, crevice, glacier, gorge, ledge, mountain pass, mountain stream, precipice, rocks, slope, valley or *(Scottish)* glen

SOME WORDS TO DESCRIBE A MOUNTAIN
barren, craggy, forbidding, jagged, lofty, massive, misty, rocky, rugged, snow-capped, soaring, towering, treacherous

---

*The serpent **retreated**, hissing, into its lair.*

to move downwards
drop, descend, fall, sink, swoop
*A pair of vultures **swooped** down from the sky.*

to move upwards
rise, ascend, climb, mount, soar, arise
*A hot-air balloon **mounted** into the air.*

movement noun
1 *The robot made a sudden, jerky **movement**.*
motion, move, action, gesture
2 *She was involved in the peace **movement**.*
organization, group, party, campaign

moving adjective
*The story was so **moving** that I started to cry.*
emotional, inspiring, stirring, touching
(informal) tear-jerking

muck noun
*They cleared the **muck** out of the stable.*
dirt, filth, grime, mud, sludge, dung, manure

mud noun
*The tractor left a trail of **mud** on the road.*
dirt, muck, mire, sludge, clay, soil

muddle noun
1 *There was a **muddle** over the date of the party.*
confusion, misunderstanding
(informal) mix-up
2 *There was a **muddle** of clothes on the floor.*
jumble, mess, tangle

muddle verb
1 *Who **muddled** the papers on my desk?*
mix up, mess up, disorder, jumble up, shuffle, tangle
OPPOSITE tidy
2 *They got **muddled** and took the wrong turning.*
confuse, bewilder, puzzle, perplex

muffled adjective
*They heard **muffled** voices from the next room.*
faint, indistinct, unclear, muted, deadened
OPPOSITE clear

muggy adjective
*The weather is often **muggy** before a storm.*
humid, close, clammy, sticky, moist, damp, oppressive
OPPOSITE fresh

mumble verb
*We couldn't hear the actor as he was **mumbling**.*
mutter, talk indistinctly

munch verb
*Kim sat **munching** popcorn all through the film.*
chew, crunch

murky adjective
*A creature loomed out of the **murky** waters of the loch.*
dark, clouded, cloudy, dim, dull, dingy, gloomy, grey, foggy, misty
OPPOSITE clear

murmur verb
*We heard voices **murmuring** in the room above.*
mutter, mumble, whisper

music noun
see panel on following page

musical adjective
*Helena has a very **musical** voice.*
tuneful, melodic, melodious, harmonious, sweet-sounding

musty adjective
*There was a **musty** smell in the cellar.*
damp, dank, mouldy, stale, stuffy, airless
OPPOSITE fresh

mutter verb
*The goblin sat **muttering** to himself in the corner.*
mumble, murmur, whisper

mysterious adjective
*They uncovered a **mysterious** sign on the wall.*
strange, puzzling, baffling, mystifying, perplexing, obscure, unexplained, incomprehensible, inexplicable, curious, weird

mystery noun
*What really happened was a **mystery**.*
puzzle, riddle, secret

music noun
see panel on following page

⭐ WORD WEB

music *noun*

VARIOUS KINDS OF MUSIC
blues, classical music, country and western, dance music, disco music, folk music, gospel, hip hop, jazz, orchestral music, pop music, punk, ragtime, rap, reggae, rock, soul, swing

TYPES OF MUSICAL COMPOSITION
anthem, ballad, carol, concerto, folk song, fugue, hymn, lullaby, march, melody, musical, opera, operetta, sonata, song, symphony, tune

FAMILIES OF MUSICAL INSTRUMENTS
brass, keyboard, percussion, strings, woodwind

STRINGED INSTRUMENTS THAT CAN BE PLAYED WITH A BOW
cello, double bass, viola, violin or fiddle

STRINGED INSTRUMENTS PLAYED BY PLUCKING OR STRUMMING
banjo, cittern, guitar, harp, lute, lyre, mandolin, sitar, ukulele, zither

BRASS INSTRUMENTS
bugle, cornet, euphonium, flugelhorn, French horn, trombone, trumpet, tuba

OTHER INSTRUMENTS PLAYED BY BLOWING
bagpipes, bassoon, clarinet, cor anglais, flute, harmonica or mouth organ, oboe, piccolo, recorder, saxophone

KEYBOARD INSTRUMENTS
accordion, harmonium, harpsichord, keyboard, organ, piano, synthesizer

PERCUSSION INSTRUMENTS
bass drum, bongo drum, castanets, cymbals, drum, glockenspiel, gong, kettledrum, maracas, marimba, rattle, snare drum, tabor, tambour, tambourine, timpani, tom-tom, triangle, tubular bells, vibraphone, xylophone

PEOPLE WHO PLAY VARIOUS INSTRUMENTS
bugler, cellist, clarinettist, drummer, fiddler, flautist, guitarist, harpist, lutenist, oboist, organist, percussionist, pianist, piper, timpanist, trombonist, trumpeter, violinist

SOME OTHER MUSICIANS
accompanist, composer, conductor, instrumentalist, singer, vocalist

GROUPS OF MUSICIANS
band, choir or chorus, duet or duo, ensemble, group, orchestra, quartet, quintet, trio

TERMS USED IN MUSIC
chord, counterpoint, discord, harmony, melody, note, octave, pitch, rhythm, scale, semitone, tempo, theme, tone, tune

NAMES OF NOTES AND SIGNS IN WRITTEN MUSIC
clef, crotchet, flat, key signature, minim, natural, quaver, semibreve, semiquaver, sharp, stave, time signature

violin

accordion

saxophone

guitar

drums

nag verb
He was always **nagging** her to work harder.
badger, pester, scold

naked adjective
He walked **naked** into the bathroom.
bare, nude, unclothed, undressed
OPPOSITE clothed

name noun
The official names you have are your **first names** or **forenames**, and **surname**.
Names a Christian is given at baptism are **Christian names**.
A false name is an **alias**.
A name people use instead of your real name is a **nickname**.
A false name an author uses is a **pen name** or **pseudonym**.
The name of a book or film is its **title**.

name verb
The zoo **named** the new lion cubs, Kiara and Kovu.
call
To name someone at the ceremony of baptism is to **baptize** or **christen** them.

nap noun
Granny always takes a **nap** on Sunday afternoons.
rest, sleep, doze, lie-down, siesta
(informal) snooze, forty winks

narrow adjective
The rabbit squeezed through a **narrow** opening in the fence.
thin, slender, slim
OPPOSITE wide

nasty adjective
1 Ogres have a thoroughly **nasty** temper.
unkind, unpleasant, unfriendly, disagreeable, objectionable, odious, mean, malicious, cruel, spiteful, vicious
2 A **nasty** smell wafted from the laboratory.
unpleasant, offensive, disgusting, repulsive, revolting, horrible, foul, rotten, sickening
OPPOSITE agreeable, pleasant
3 The weather suddenly turned **nasty**.
unpleasant, rough, stormy, squally

national adjective
The programme will be broadcast on **national** television.
nationwide
OPPOSITE local

natural adjective
1 Karen has a **natural** gift for music.
born, inborn, instinctive, intuitive, native
2 It's only **natural** to be nervous before an exam.
normal, common, understandable, reasonable, predictable
OPPOSITE unnatural

nature noun
1 I like TV programmes about **nature**.
natural history, wildlife
2 The old sheepdog has a very kind **nature**.
character, disposition, personality, manner
3 I collect coins, medals, and things of that **nature**.
kind, sort, type, description, variety

naughty adjective
The puppies were quite **naughty** when they were young.
bad, badly behaved, disobedient, mischievous, uncontrollable, unmanageable, troublesome, unruly
OPPOSITE well behaved

near adjective
1 We get on well with our **near** neighbours.
next-door, nearby, close, adjacent, surrounding
2 My birthday is **near**.
approaching, coming
(informal) round the corner
3 We sent cards to all our **near** relatives.
close, dear, familiar, intimate
OPPOSITE distant

nearly adverb
Thank goodness, it's **nearly** dinner time!
almost, practically, virtually, just about, approaching

neat adjective
1 Please leave the room as **neat** as possible.
clean, orderly, tidy, uncluttered, immaculate
(informal) spick and span
2 Craig always looks **neat** in his school uniform.
smart, elegant, spruce, trim
3 Her handwriting is very **neat**.
precise, skilful, well-formed
OPPOSITE untidy

necessary adjective
The recipe lists all the **necessary** ingredients.
essential, required, needed, needful, compulsory, obligatory, unavoidable
OPPOSITE unnecessary

need noun
There's a **need** for more shops in our area.
call, demand, requirement

need verb
1 I **need** a pound coin for the locker.
require, want, be short of, lack
2 The charity **needs** our support.
depend on, rely on

neglect verb
She's been **neglecting** her work.
forget, ignore, overlook, abandon, disregard, pay no attention to, shirk

nervous adjective
She always feels **nervous** before an exam.
anxious, worried, apprehensive, concerned, uneasy, fearful, edgy, fraught, tense, troubled
(informal) uptight, jittery
OPPOSITE calm

neutral adjective
A referee has to be **neutral**.
impartial, unbiased, unprejudiced, even-handed
OPPOSITE biased, prejudiced

new adjective
1 Start on a **new** sheet of paper.
clean, fresh, unused, brand-new
Something new and unused is **in mint condition**.
2 They went to the motor show to see the **new** models.
latest, current, modern, recent, up-to-date
3 They've found a **new** bug in the computer program.
additional, extra, unexpected, unfamiliar
4 Haven't you got any **new** ideas?
fresh, original, novel, innovative, creative, different
OPPOSITE old

news noun
What's the latest **news**?
information, word, report, bulletin
(old use) tidings

next adjective
1 He lives in the house **next** to the chip shop.
adjacent, closest, nearest
OPPOSITE distant
2 If you miss this bus, you can catch the **next** one.
following, subsequent
OPPOSITE previous

nice adjective
see panel on following page
1 That's not a very **nice** thing to say!
pleasant, agreeable
OPPOSITE nasty
2 There is a **nice** distinction between borrowing and stealing.
delicate, fine, precise, subtle

night noun
Badgers usually come out at **night**.
night-time, dark
Animals which are active at night are **nocturnal** animals.

a b c d e f g h i j k l m n o p q r s t u v w x y z

OVERUSED WORDS

nice *adjective*
Try to vary the words you use for **nice**. Here are some other words you could use.

FOR A *NICE PERSON*
good, kind, friendly, helpful, generous, likeable, amiable, charming, polite, genial *Our singing teacher is very **likeable**.*
FOR A *NICE EXPERIENCE*
delightful, enjoyable, wonderful, marvellous, splendid *Did you have an **enjoyable** time in France?*
FOR SOMETHING THAT *LOOKS NICE*
beautiful, attractive, pleasing, lovely *There is an **attractive** view from the upstairs window.*
FOR A *NICE SMELL*
agreeable, fragrant, sweet-smelling *The **fragrant** scent of lavender filled the garden.*
FOR *NICE FOOD*
delicious, tasty, appetizing, satisfying *They serve **tasty** sandwiches in the cafe.*
FOR *NICE WEATHER*
fine, sunny, warm *The weather has been **fine** all week.*

noble *adjective*
1 *The knight belonged to an ancient **noble** family.*
aristocratic, high-born, upper-class
2 *The rescuers were congratulated for their **noble** efforts.*
brave, heroic, courageous, honourable, worthy, virtuous, gallant
OPPOSITE cowardly, unworthy

nod *verb*
*Simon **nodded** his head in agreement.*
bob, bow, dip, lower

noise *noun*
*Where is that dreadful **noise** coming from?*
din, racket, row, uproar, commotion, tumult, hullabaloo, pandemonium

noisy *adjective*
1 *The people next door were playing **noisy** music.*
loud, blaring, booming, deafening, ear-splitting, thunderous
2 *The children are very **noisy** this morning.*
rowdy, raucous, chattering, talkative

nonsense *noun*
*Stop talking **nonsense**!*
rubbish, drivel, balderdash, piffle, gibberish, claptrap, gobbledegook (*informal*) rot, tripe, twaddle

normal *adjective*
1 *He had a **normal** kind of day at work.*
average, common, customary, familiar, habitual, ordinary, predictable, regular, routine, standard, typical, unsurprising, usual
2 *No **normal** person would sleep on a bed of nails.*
healthy, rational, reasonable, sane
OPPOSITE abnormal

nosy *adjective (informal)*
*Stop being so **nosy** and asking all these questions!*
inquisitive, curious, prying, snooping, intrusive
An informal name for a nosy person is a **nosy parker**.

note *noun*
1 *I sent a **note** thanking him for the present.*
message, letter, communication
2 *There was a **note** of anger in her voice.*
sound, tone, feeling, quality
note *verb*
1 *The detective **noted** the address on a scrap of paper.*
jot down, make a note of, write down, record, scribble
2 *Did you **note** what she was wearing?*
notice, see, take note of, pay attention to, heed, mark, observe

nothing *noun*
*Four minus four equals **nothing**.*
nought, zero
In cricket a score of nothing is a **duck**; in tennis it is **love**, and in football it is **nil**.

notice *noun*
*Someone put up a **notice** about the meeting.*
sign, advertisement, placard, poster, warning
to take notice of something
*They **took** no **notice of** the warning.*
heed, pay attention to
notice *verb*
1 *Did you **notice** what he was wearing?*
note, see, take note of, pay attention to, heed, mark, observe
2 *I **noticed** a funny smell in the room.*
become aware of, detect

now *adverb*
1 *My cousins are **now** living in Melbourne.*
at present, at the moment, currently, nowadays
2 *I'll give them a ring **now**.*
immediately, at once, straight away, without delay, instantly

nudge *verb*
*She **nudged** me with her elbow.*
poke, prod, shove, bump, jog, jolt

nuisance *noun*
*The traffic noise is a real **nuisance**.*
annoyance, irritation, inconvenience, bother, menace, pest, drawback

numb *adjective*
*My toes are **numb** with cold.*
unfeeling, deadened, frozen, insensitive, paralysed
OPPOSITE sensitive

number *noun*
1 *Add the **numbers** together to get the answer.*
figure, numeral
Any of the numbers from 0 to 9 is a **digit**.
A negative or positive whole number is an **integer**.
An amount used in measuring or counting is a **unit**.
2 *A large **number** of people applied for the job.*
amount, quantity, collection, crowd
3 *The band played some well-known **numbers**.*
song, piece, tune

obedient *adjective*
*The dog seems very **obedient**.*
well-behaved, disciplined, manageable, dutiful, docile
OPPOSITE disobedient

obey *verb*
1 *The dog **obeyed** his owner's commands.*
follow, carry out, execute, implement, observe, adhere to, heed
2 *The soldiers **obeyed** without question.*
do what you are told, take orders, be obedient, conform
OPPOSITE disobey

object *noun*
1 *We saw some strange **objects** in the museum.*
article, item, thing
2 *What is the **object** of this exercise?*
point, purpose, aim, goal, intention, objective
object *verb*
to object to something
*Several residents have **objected to** the plan.*
complain about, be opposed to, disapprove of, take exception to, protest against
OPPOSITE accept, agree to

observant adjective
If you're **observant**, you might see a fox tonight.
alert, attentive, sharp-eyed, vigilant, watchful
OPPOSITE inattentive

observation noun
1 They took him to hospital for **observation**.
study, watching, scrutiny
2 The detective made an interesting **observation**.
comment, remark, statement

observe verb
1 Astronomers **observed** the eclipse last night.
watch, look at, view, study
2 I have **observed** a change in his behaviour.
notice, note, see, detect, spot, discern, perceive, witness
3 It's important to **observe** the rules.
follow, abide by, adhere to, heed, keep to, obey
4 My friend **observed** that I had grown taller.
mention, say, comment, remark, declare

obsession noun
Football is Frank's **obsession**.
passion, fixation, addiction, mania

obstacle noun
1 They drove around the **obstacles** in the road.
obstruction, barrier, barricade
2 His age proved to be an **obstacle**.
problem, difficulty, hindrance, hurdle, snag, catch

obvious adjective
1 It was silly to make so many **obvious** mistakes.
glaring, noticeable, pronounced
2 The castle is an **obvious** landmark.
conspicuous, notable, prominent, visible
OPPOSITE inconspicuous
3 It was **obvious** that the woman was a spy.
clear, evident, apparent, plain, undeniable, unmistakable
OPPOSITE hidden

occasion noun
1 I've been to Italy on several **occasions**.
time, moment, instance, opportunity, chance
2 The wedding was a happy **occasion**.
affair, event, happening, incident, occurrence

occasional adjective
The weather forecast said there would be **occasional** showers.
intermittent, odd, scattered, irregular, infrequent
OPPOSITE frequent, regular

occasionally adverb
The dragon **occasionally** lifted its head and roared.
sometimes, now and again, once in a while, every so often
OPPOSITE frequently, often

occupation noun
1 He's not happy with his present **occupation**.
job, post, employment, profession, trade, work
2 Vita's favourite **occupation** is reading.
activity, hobby, pastime, pursuit

occupy verb
1 They **occupy** the house next door.
live in, reside in, dwell in, inhabit
2 The rebel army **occupied** the town.
capture, seize, take over, conquer, invade

occur verb
1 She told us what had **occurred**.
happen, take place, come about, arise
2 The disease only **occurs** in certain plants.
develop, crop up, turn up

odd adjective
1 Her behaviour seemed very **odd**.
strange, unusual, abnormal, peculiar, curious, puzzling, queer, unconventional, eccentric, funny, weird
OPPOSITE normal
2 He could only find a couple of **odd** socks.
left over, single, spare
3 He does **odd** jobs to earn money.
occasional, casual, irregular, various

offend verb
I hope my letter didn't **offend** you.
give or cause offence to, insult, upset, hurt your feelings, anger, displease, annoy, affront, disgust, vex

offensive adjective
1 The gas produces an **offensive** smell.
unpleasant, repellent, disgusting, revolting, nasty
OPPOSITE pleasant
2 He apologized for his **offensive** remarks.
insulting, impolite, rude, abusive

offer verb
1 A reward was **offered** for the capture of the outlaws.
propose, put forward, suggest, make available
2 He **offered** to help with the washing-up.
volunteer

offer noun
Their **offer** of help was gratefully received.
proposal, suggestion

often adverb
It **often** rains in April.
frequently, regularly, repeatedly, time after time, many times, again and again, constantly

old adjective
1 The **old** Norman church is to be restored.
ancient, historic, original
2 I put on **old** jeans to do some gardening.
worn, scruffy, shabby, threadbare
OPPOSITE new
3 The museum has a display of **old** computers.
old-fashioned, out of date, antiquated, early, obsolete
Things which are valuable because they are old are **antique**.
OPPOSITE up to date, current, modern

old-fashioned adjective
That hairstyle is quite **old-fashioned** now.
out of date, outdated, outmoded, antiquated
OPPOSITE modern, up to date

omit verb
1 His article was **omitted** from the magazine.
exclude, leave out, miss out, cut, eliminate, overlook, skip
2 Don't **omit** to turn off the lights.
forget, fail, neglect

ooze verb
The filling started to **ooze** out my sandwich.
leak, seep, escape, dribble, drip

open adjective
1 The puppy escaped through the **open** door.
unlocked, unfastened, ajar, gaping
OPPOSITE closed
2 The jam jar had been left **open**.
uncovered, unsealed
3 There is a view of **open** country from the back window.
clear, unrestricted, unenclosed, extensive
OPPOSITE enclosed
4 He was **open** about what he had done wrong.
frank, honest, sincere, straightforward, candid
OPPOSITE deceitful
5 The captain faced **open** rebellion from the crew.
unconcealed, undisguised, obvious, plain
OPPOSITE concealed

a b c d e f g h i j k l m n o p q r s t u v w x y z

A B C D E F G H I J K L M N O P Q R S T U V W X Y Z

open verb
1 *Please **open** the door.*
unfasten, unlock, unbolt
2 *I can't wait to **open** my birthday presents!*
undo, unwrap, untie, unseal
To open an umbrella is to **unfurl** it.
To open a wine bottle is to **uncork** it.
To open a map is to **unfold** or **unroll** it.
3 *The jumble sale **opens** at 10 a.m.*
begin, start, commence
(*informal*) get going

opening noun
1 *The sheep got out through an **opening** in the fence.*
gap, hole, breach, break, split
2 *The film has a very dramatic **opening**.*
beginning, start, commencement
3 *We are invited to the **opening** of the new sports centre.*
launch, initiation

opinion noun
*What was your honest **opinion** of the film?*
view, judgement, impression, belief, attitude, point of view, thought, conclusion, assessment, notion, feeling, idea

opportunity noun
1 *There were few **opportunities** to relax.*
chance, occasion, moment, time
2 *The job offers a good **opportunity** for a keen young person.*
opening
(*informal*) break

oppose verb
*Many people **opposed** the building of the new road.*
object to, disapprove of, be against, be hostile towards, argue against, fight against, attack, resist
OPPOSITE support, defend

opposite adjective
1 *They have **opposite** views about politics.*
contrasting, conflicting, contradictory, opposed, opposing, different, contrary
OPPOSITE similar
2 *My friend lives on the **opposite** side of the road.*
facing

opposite noun
*She says one thing and does the **opposite**.*
contrary, reverse, converse

optimistic adjective
*She's **optimistic** about her chances of success.*
hopeful, positive, confident, expectant, cheerful, buoyant
OPPOSITE pessimistic

ordeal noun
*The shipwrecked sailor told us about his **ordeal**.*
suffering, troubles, trial, anguish, torture, nightmare

order noun
1 *The captain gave the **order** to abandon ship.*
command, instruction, direction
2 *I've put in an **order** for the new book.*
request, demand, reservation, booking
3 *The police restored **order** after the riot.*
peace, calm, control, quiet, harmony, law and order
4 *The books are arranged in alphabetical **order**.*
arrangement, sequence, series, succession
5 *She keeps her bike in good **order**.*
condition, state

order verb
1 *She **ordered** them to be quiet.*
command, instruct, require, tell
2 *He **ordered** the new magazine.*
request, reserve, apply for, book

ordinary adjective
1 *It was just an **ordinary** sort of day.*
normal, typical, usual, customary, habitual, everyday
2 *This is more than just an **ordinary** robot.*
standard, average, common, conventional, regular
3 *It was a very **ordinary** game.*
mediocre, unexceptional, run-of-the-mill, routine

organize verb
1 *It took her ages to **organize** the party.*
coordinate, plan, make arrangements for, see to, set up, run
2 *The librarian has to **organize** the books in the library.*
arrange, put in order, classify, sort out, tidy up

original adjective
1 *The settlers drove out the **original** inhabitants.*
earliest, first, initial, native, aboriginal
2 *The story was very **original**.*
inventive, new, novel, creative, fresh, imaginative, unusual, unconventional
3 *Is that an **original** work of art or a copy?*
genuine, real, authentic, unique

ornament noun
*A few **ornaments** will make the room more attractive.*
decoration, adornment, trinket, bauble

outrageous adjective
1 *The behaviour of the trolls was **outrageous**.*
disgraceful, scandalous, shocking, atrocious, appalling, monstrous, shameful
2 *They charge **outrageous** prices at that shop.*
excessive, unreasonable

outside adjective
*Lookouts were stationed on the **outside** wall of the castle.*
exterior, external, outer

outside noun
*Insects have their skeletons on the **outside** of their bodies.*
exterior, shell, surface
OPPOSITE inside

outstanding adjective
1 *She will be an **outstanding** tennis player in a few years.*
excellent, exceptional, superb, extraordinary, superlative, brilliant, great, fine, distinguished, celebrated, remarkable, superior, striking, notable
OPPOSITE ordinary
2 *There are still some **outstanding** bills to pay.*
overdue, unpaid, owing

overcome verb
*He managed to **overcome** his fear of flying.*
conquer, defeat, master, get the better of

overpowering adjective
*I felt an **overpowering** urge to giggle.*
overwhelming, powerful, strong, compelling, irresistible, uncontrollable

overtake verb
*We **overtook** the car in front.*
pass, leave behind, pull ahead of, outstrip

own verb
*It was the first bike she had **owned**.*
be the owner of, have, possess
to own up to
*No one **owned up to** breaking the window.*
confess to, admit to, tell the truth about
(*informal*) come clean about

order

pace *noun*
1 *Move forward two **paces**.*
step, stride
2 *The front runner set a fast **pace**.*
rate, speed
A formal word is **velocity**.

pack *noun*
*There were four candles in each **pack**.*
package, packet, bundle,
bale

pack *verb*
1 *She **packed** her suitcase and
called a taxi.*
fill, load up
2 *I forgot to **pack** my hairdryer.*
stow away, wrap up
3 *They tried to **pack** too many
passengers onto the train.*
cram, crowd, squeeze, stuff, jam,
wedge

page *noun*
1 *Several **pages** have been torn out
of this book.*
sheet, leaf
2 *He wrote two **pages** of notes.*
side

pain *noun*
*Dirk felt a sudden jabbing **pain** in
his foot.*
anguish, suffering
A dull pain is an **ache** or **soreness**.
Severe pain is **agony**, **torment**,
or **torture**.
A slight pain is **discomfort**.
A slight pain which doesn't last long
is a **twinge**.
A sudden pain is a **pang** or **stab**.
Pain in your head is a **headache**.
Pain in your teeth is **toothache**.

painful *adjective*
1 *My shoulder is still really **painful**.*
sore, aching, tender, hurting,
smarting, stinging, throbbing
2 *The conversation brought back
many **painful** memories.*
unpleasant, upsetting, distressing,
disagreeable, traumatic

paint *verb*
1 *The bedroom walls were **painted**
green.*
colour, decorate
2 *Samantha **painted** the flowers in
bright colours.*
depict, portray, represent

painting *noun*
A picture painted on a wall is a
fresco or a **mural**.
A picture painted by a famous artist
of the past is an **old master**.

pair *noun*
A pair of people who go out together
are a **couple**.
Two people who sing or play music
together are a **duet**.
Two people who work together are
partners or a **partnership**.
Two babies born together are **twins**.

pale *adjective*
1 *Are you all right? You're looking a
little **pale**.*
white, pallid, pasty, wan, ashen,
sallow, anaemic
To go pale with fear is to **blanch**.
OPPOSITE ruddy, flushed
2 *That shade of pink is too **pale**.*
light, pastel, faded, faint, dim,
bleached, colourless
OPPOSITE bright

panic *noun*
*People fled the streets in **panic**.*
alarm, fright, terror, frenzy, hysteria

panic *verb*
*If a fire starts, don't **panic**!*
be alarmed, take fright, become
hysterical
(*informal*) lose your head, get in a
flap
To panic is also to be **panic-stricken**.

pant *verb*
*Some of the runners were **panting** by
the last lap.*
breathe quickly, gasp, wheeze, puff

paper *noun*
1 *She started her diary on a fresh
sheet of **paper**.*
A piece of paper is a **leaf** or a **sheet**.
2 *The doctor had some important
papers to sign.*
document, deed, certificate
3 *The story made the front page of
the local **paper**.*
newspaper, journal
(*informal*) rag

parade *noun*
A circus **parade** passed along the
street.
procession, march, spectacle, show,
display
A parade of vehicles or people or
horseback is a **cavalcade**.
A parade of people in costume is a
pageant.

parcel *noun*
*The postman delivered a bulky **parcel**.*
package, packet

pardon *verb*
*The king decided to **pardon** the
prisoners.*
release, free, set free, let off, spare,
excuse, forgive
To pardon someone who is condemned
to death is to **reprieve** them.

part *noun*
1 *All the **parts** of the engine are now
working properly.*
bit, component, constituent
2 *I only saw the first **part** of the
programme.*
section, piece, portion, element
3 *Which **part** of the business do they
own?*
branch, department, division
4 *Granny lives in another **part** of
the town.*
area, district, region, neighbourhood,
sector
5 *He's just right to act the **part** of
Peter Pan.*
character, role

part *verb*
1 *It was the first time she'd been
parted from her parents.*
separate, divide, remove
OPPOSITE join
2 *They exchanged a final kiss before
parting.*
go away, leave, depart, say goodbye
OPPOSITE meet

mural

a b c d e f g h i j k l m n o p q r s t u v w x y z

particular *adjective*
1 *The tickets must be used on a **particular** day.*
specific, certain, distinct, definite, exact
2 *She took **particular** care not to damage the parcel.*
special, exceptional, unusual, extreme, marked, notable
3 *The cat's very **particular** about his food.*
fussy, finicky, hard to please
(informal) choosy, picky

partner *noun*
*The two women have been business **partners** for years.*
colleague, associate, ally
In marriage, your partner is your **spouse** or your **husband** or **wife**.
An animal's partner is its **mate**.

party *noun*
1 *We had a class **party** at the end of term.*
celebration, festivity, function, gathering, reception
(informal) get-together, do
2 *A **party** of tourists was going round the museum.*
group, band, crowd, gang

pass *verb*
1 *We watched the parade as it **passed**.*
go by, move past
2 *She tried to **pass** the car in front.*
overtake, go ahead of
3 *We **passed** over the bridge.*
go, advance, proceed, progress
4 *Could you **pass** me the sugar, please?*
hand, give, deliver, offer, present
5 *Do you think you will **pass** your music exam?*
be successful in, get through, succeed in
6 *How did you **pass** the time on holiday?*
spend, use, occupy, fill, while away
7 *Three years **passed** before we met again.*
go by, elapse
8 *The pain will soon **pass**.*
go away, come to an end, disappear, fade

pass *noun*
*We had a **pass** to get into the concert for free.*
permit, licence, ticket

passage *noun*
1 *A secret **passage** led from the chamber to the outside.*
passageway, corridor, tunnel
2 *The guards forced a **passage** through the crowd.*
path, route, way
3 *Our homework is to choose a favourite **passage** from a book.*
episode, excerpt, extract, piece, quotation, section

4 *He hadn't changed, despite the **passage** of time.*
passing, progress, advance

passion *noun*
1 *'Romeo and Juliet' is a story of youthful **passion**.*
love, emotion
2 *She has a **passion** for sports.*
enthusiasm, eagerness, appetite, desire, craving, urge, zest, thirst, mania

passionate *adjective*
1 *The captain gave a **passionate** speech before the battle.*
emotional, intense, moving, heartfelt
OPPOSITE unemotional
2 *He is a **passionate** follower of football.*
eager, keen, avid, enthusiastic, fanatical, fervent
OPPOSITE apathetic

past *noun*
*In the **past**, things were different.*
past times, old days, olden days, days gone by
The study of what happened in the past is **history**.
The things and ideas that have come down to us from the past are our **heritage** or **traditions**.
OPPOSITE future

past *adjective*
*Things were very different in **past** centuries.*
earlier, former, previous, old
OPPOSITE future

pat *verb*
*Andy **patted** the Shetland pony on the head.*
tap, touch, stroke, pet
To touch something quickly and lightly is to **dab** it.
To stroke someone with an open hand is to **caress** them.

patch *verb*
*I need some material to **patch** my jeans.*
mend, repair
Another way to mend holes in clothes is to **darn** them or **stitch** them up.

path *noun*
*Please keep to the **path** as you walk through the gardens.*
pathway, track, trail, footpath, walk, walkway, lane
A path for horse-riding is a **bridleway**.
A path by the side of a road is a **pavement**.
A path above a beach is an **esplanade** or **promenade**.
A path along a canal is a **towpath**.
A path between buildings is an **alley**.

pathetic *adjective*
1 *The abandoned kittens were a **pathetic** sight.*
moving, touching, pitiful, distressing, heartbreaking, sad, sorry
2 *The goalie made a **pathetic** attempt to stop the ball.*
hopeless, useless, weak, feeble, inadequate, incompetent

patience *noun*
*She waited with great **patience** for an hour.*
calmness, tolerance, self-control, endurance, restraint, perseverance, persistence, resignation
OPPOSITE impatience

patient *adjective*
1 *The nurse was very **patient** with the children.*
calm, composed, even-tempered, easygoing, tolerant, lenient, mild, quiet, uncomplaining, resigned, long-suffering
2 *It took hours of **patient** work to restore the painting.*
persevering, persistent, unhurried, untiring, steady, determined
OPPOSITE impatient

pause *noun*
*There was a **pause** while the singers got their breath back.*
break, gap, halt, rest, lull, stop, wait, interruption, stoppage
A pause in the middle of a performance is an **interlude** or **interval**.
A pause in the middle of a cinema film is an **intermission**.

pause *verb*
1 *The stranger **paused** at the door before knocking.*
hesitate, wait, delay, hang back
2 *The cyclists **paused** to let the others catch up.*
halt, stop, rest, take a break, break off

pay *verb*
1 *How much did you **pay** for your new bike?*
spend, give out, hand over
(informal) fork out
2 *Who's going to **pay** the bill?*
pay off, repay, settle, clear, refund
3 *They had to **pay** for all the damage they caused.*
compensate, pay back
4 *I'll make you **pay** for this!*
suffer

pay *noun*
*We should get an increase in **pay** next year.*
wages, salary, income, earnings
A payment you get for doing a single job is a **fee**.

peace noun
1 *After the war there was a period of* **peace**.
agreement, harmony, friendliness
2 *She enjoys the* **peace** *of the countryside*.
calmness, peacefulness, quiet, tranquillity, stillness, serenity, silence

peaceful adjective
They enjoyed a **peaceful** *day fishing*.
calm, quiet, relaxing, tranquil, restful, serene, undisturbed, untroubled, gentle, placid, soothing, still
OPPOSITE noisy, troubled

peak noun
1 *The* **peak** *of the mountain was covered in snow*.
summit, cap, crest, crown, pinnacle, top, tip, point
2 *She is at the* **peak** *of her career as an athlete*.
top, height, highest point, climax

peculiar adjective
1 *What's that* **peculiar** *smell?*
strange, unusual, odd, curious, extraordinary, abnormal, funny, weird, bizarre
OPPOSITE ordinary
2 *He recognized her* **peculiar** *way of writing*.
characteristic, distinctive, individual, particular, personal, special, unique, identifiable

people plural noun
1 *How many* **people** *are you inviting?*
persons, individuals
People as opposed to animals are **humans** or **human beings** or **mankind**.
2 *The government is elected by the* **people** *of the country*.
population, citizens, the public, society, nation, race

perceptive adjective
It was very **perceptive** *of you to spot my mistake*.
observant, clever, sharp, shrewd, quick, alert
OPPOSITE unobservant

perfect adjective
1 *Each petal on the flower was* **perfect**.
faultless, flawless, ideal, intact, undamaged, complete, whole
2 *The dress is a* **perfect** *fit*.
exact, faithful, precise, accurate, correct
OPPOSITE imperfect
3 *I received a letter from a* **perfect** *stranger*.
complete, total, absolute, utter

perform verb
1 *Is this your first time* **performing** *on stage?*
act, appear, play, dance, sing

2 *The children* **performed** *a play about Cinderella*.
present, stage, produce, put on
3 *Soldiers are expected to* **perform** *their duty*.
do, carry out, execute, fulfil
To perform a crime is to **commit** a crime.

performance noun
1 *Tonight's* **performance** *is already sold out*.
show, production, presentation
2 *He congratulated the players on their outstanding* **performance**.
effort, work, endeavour, exertion, behaviour, conduct

permanent adjective
1 *Sugar can do* **permanent** *damage to your teeth*.
lasting, long-lasting, long-term, everlasting, enduring
2 *Traffic noise is a* **permanent** *problem in the city centre*.
never-ending, perpetual, persistent, chronic, perennial
3 *She has been offered a* **permanent** *job in the firm*.
stable, steady, fixed, lifelong

permission noun
They had the teacher's **permission** *to leave*.
consent, agreement, approval
(*informal*) go-ahead

permit verb
The council doesn't **permit** *fishing in the lake*.
allow, consent to, give permission for, authorize, license, grant, tolerate, admit
permit noun
You need a **permit** *to fish in the river*.
licence, pass, ticket

persecute verb
People were **persecuted** *for their religious beliefs*.
oppress, discriminate against, harass, intimidate, bully, terrorize, torment

persevere verb
The rescuers **persevered** *despite the bad weather*.
continue, carry on, keep going, persist
(*informal*) keep at it, stick at it
OPPOSITE give up

person noun
Not a single **person** *has replied to my email*.
individual, human being, character, soul

personal adjective
1 *The book is based on the writer's* **personal** *experience*.
own, individual, particular
2 *The contents of the letter are* **personal**.
confidential, private, secret, intimate

personality noun
Like all ogres, he has an ugly **personality**.
character, nature, disposition, temperament, make-up

persuade verb
I **persuaded** *my friend to join the choir*.
convince, coax, induce
To persuade someone to do something is also to **talk them into** doing it.
OPPOSITE dissuade

persuasive adjective
She used some very **persuasive** *arguments*.
convincing, effective, sound, strong, forceful, compelling, valid
OPPOSITE unconvincing

pessimistic adjective
The players are **pessimistic** *about their chances of winning*.
negative, unhopeful, gloomy, despairing, resigned, cynical
OPPOSITE optimistic

pester verb
Please don't **pester** *me while I'm busy!*
annoy, bother, trouble, harass, badger, hound, nag
(*informal*) bug

petrified adjective
Jack stood **petrified** *as the monster lumbered towards him*.
terrified, horrified, terror-struck, paralysed, frozen

phase noun
Going to school is the start of a new **phase** *in your life*.
period, time, stage, step

phone verb
I'll **phone** *you later this evening*.
telephone, call, ring, dial

photograph noun
I put my holiday **photographs** *in an album*.
photo, snap or snapshot, shot
The photographs you get when a film is processed are **prints**.
A photograph on the original film from which a print is made is a **negative**.
A photograph for projecting onto a screen is a **slide** or **transparency**.

pick verb
1 *They've* **picked** *the players for the hockey team*.
choose, select, decide on, settle on, opt for, single out
2 *Irene* **picked** *some flowers from the garden*.
gather, collect, cut
3 *I* **picked** *an apple off the tree*.
pluck, pull off, take

a b c d e f g h i j k l m n o p q r s t u v w x y z

to pick up
1 *He was too weak to **pick up** the box.*
lift, raise, hoist
2 *I'll **pick up** some milk on the way home.*
get, collect, fetch

picture *noun*
1 *There's a **picture** of a pyramid in this book.*
illustration, image, print
A picture which represents a particular person is a ***portrait***.
A picture which represents the artist himself or herself is a ***self-portrait***.
A picture which represents a group of objects is a ***still life***.
A picture which represents a country scene is a ***landscape***.

Pictures on a computer are ***graphics***.
2 *Mum took some **pictures** of us building a sandcastle.*
photograph, snapsot, snap

picture *verb*
1 *The girl is **pictured** against a background of flowers.*
depict, illustrate, represent, show, portray
2 *Can you **picture** what the world will be like in 100 years?*
imagine, visualize

piece *noun*
1 *They collected **pieces** of wood to build a raft.*
bar, block, length, stick, chunk, lump, hunk, bit, chip, fragment, particle, scrap, shred
2 *I've only got two **pieces** of chocolate left.*

bit, portion, part, section, segment, share, slice
3 *I've lost one of the **pieces** of the jigsaw.*
part, element, unit, component, constituent
4 *There's a **piece** about our school in the local paper.*
article, item, report, feature

pierce *verb*
*The arrow had **pierced** the knight's armour.*
enter, go through, make a hole in, penetrate, bore through
To pierce a hole through paper is to ***punch*** a hole or ***perforate*** it.
To pierce a hole in a tyre is to ***puncture*** it.
To pierce someone with a spike is to ***impale*** or ***spear*** them.

WORD WEB

pirate *noun*
*The ship was overrun by bloodthirsty **pirates**.*
buccaneer, marauder

THINGS YOU MIGHT FIND ON A PIRATE SHIP
barrels, cabin, crow's nest, deck, hammock, lantern, mast, plank, pirate flag, rigging, sail, treasure chest, wheel

telescope

A pirate flag is a ***Jolly Roger*** or ***skull-and-crossbones***.
A pirate ship might sail on the ***high seas*** or the ***Spanish Main***.

PEOPLE YOU MIGHT FIND ON A PIRATE SHIP
cabin boy or girl, captain, captives, cook, crew, first mate, lookout, stowaway

PIRATE TREASURE MIGHT CONTAIN
doubloons or ducats, gold bullion, pieces of eight
Goods or treasure seized by pirates is ***booty***.

WEAPONS A PIRATE MIGHT USE
cannon, cutlass, dagger, gunpowder, musket, pistol

OTHER THINGS A PIRATE MIGHT WEAR OR CARRY
bandanna or kerchief, bottle of rum, breeches, cocked hat, earrings, eye patch, hook, parrot or cockatoo, pigtail, sea chart, spyglass or telescope, treasure map, wooden leg or peg leg

SOME WORDS TO DESCRIBE A PIRATE
barbaric, black-hearted, bloodthirsty, cut-throat, daring, dastardly, fearless, heartless, lawless, merciless, murderous, pitiless, ruthless, savage, swashbuckling, vengeful, vicious, villainous

hat

parrot

dagger

musket

Jolly Roger

treasure map

treasure

pile *noun*
1 *Where did this **pile** of rubbish come from?*
heap, mound, mountain, stack, hoard, mass, quantity, collection, assortment
2 *I've still got **piles** of homework to do.*
plenty, a lot, a great deal (*informal*) lots, masses

pile *verb*
***Pile** everything in the corner and we'll sort it out later.*
heap, stack, collect, gather, assemble, hoard
to pile up
*The bills are beginning to **pile up**.*
build up, mount up, accumulate

pillar *noun*
*The roof was supported by tall **pillars**.*
column, pier, post, prop, support

pinch *verb*
1 *The baby **pinched** my arm and wouldn't let go.*
nip, squeeze, press, tweak, grip
2 (*informal*) *Who **pinched** my calculator?*
steal, take, snatch, pilfer (*informal*) nick, swipe, make off with

pipe *noun*
*The water flows away along this **pipe**.*
tube
A pipe used for watering the garden is a **hose**.
A pipe in the street which supplies water for fighting fires is a **hydrant**.
A pipe which carries oil, etc., over long distances is a **pipeline**.
The system of water pipes in a house is the **plumbing**.

pirate *noun*
see panel on previous page

pity *noun*
*The pirates showed no **pity** towards the captives.*
mercy, compassion, sympathy, humanity, kindness, concern, feeling
OPPOSITE cruelty
a pity
*It's **a pity** that you have to leave so early.*
a shame, unfortunate, bad luck

pity *verb*
*We **pitied** anyone who was caught up in the storm.*
feel sorry for, feel for, sympathize with, take pity on

place *noun*
1 *This is a good **place** to park.*
site, venue, spot, location, position, situation
2 *They are looking for a quiet **place** to live.*

area, district, locality, neighbourhood, region, vicinity
3 *Save me a **place** on the bus.*
seat, space

place *verb*
1 *The hotel is **placed** next to the beach.*
locate, situate, position, station
2 *You can **place** your coats on the bed.*
put down, set down, leave, deposit, lay (*informal*) dump, plonk

plain *adjective*
1 *The furniture in the room was very **plain**.*
simple, modest, basic, unelaborate
OPPOSITE elaborate
2 *Some people say she looks **plain** compared with her sister.*
unattractive, ordinary
OPPOSITE attractive
3 *It is **plain** to me that you are not interested.*
clear, evident, obvious, apparent, unmistakable
OPPOSITE unclear
4 *She told us what she thought in very **plain** terms.*
direct, frank, blunt, outspoken, honest, sincere, straightforward
5 *We need to wear a **plain** t-shirt for sports.*
unpatterned, self coloured

plan *noun*
1 *The captain explained her **plan** to the rest of the team.*
idea, proposal, scheme, strategy, project, suggestion, proposition
A plan to do something bad is a **plot**.
2 *They looked at the **plans** for the new sports centre.*
design, diagram, chart, map, drawing, blueprint

plan *verb*
1 *The outlaws **planned** an attack upon the sheriff.*
scheme, design, devise, work out, formulate, prepare, organize
To plan to do something bad is to **plot**.
2 *What do you **plan** to do next?*
aim, intend, propose, mean

WORD WEB

planet *noun*
*The new space probe will travel to far-off **planets**.*
world

THE PLANETS OF THE SOLAR SYSTEM (IN ORDER FROM THE SUN) ARE
Mercury, Venus, Earth, Mars, Jupiter, Saturn, Uranus, Neptune.

The path followed by a planet is its **orbit**.
Minor planets orbiting the sun are **asteroids**.

Something which orbits a planet is a **satellite**.

The earth's large satellite is the **Moon**.

WRITING TIPS

You can use these words to describe an **alien planet**
Earth-like, gaseous, inhospitable, uninhabitable

TO DESCRIBE ITS *SURFACE*
barren, desolate, dusty, frozen, icy, molten, rocky, volcanic

TO DESCRIBE ITS *ATMOSPHERE OR AIR*
airless, noxious, poisonous, thin, unbreathable

play *noun*
1 *There was a good **play** on TV last night.*
drama, performance, production
2 *It is important to balance work and **play**.*
playing, recreation, amusement, fun, games, sport

play *verb*
1 *The children went out to **play**.*
amuse yourself, have fun, romp about
2 *Do you like **playing** basketball?*
take part in, participate in, compete in

3 *We are **playing** the home team next week.*
compete against, oppose, challenge, take on
4 *Mira **played** the piano at the school concert.*
perform on
5 *My sister **played** Goldilocks in the school **play**.*
act, take the part of, portray, represent

playful adjective
*The kittens were in a **playful** mood.*
lively, spirited, frisky, mischievous, roguish, impish, joking, teasing
OPPOSITE serious

plead verb
to plead with
*The children **pleaded with** the witch to let them go.*
beg, entreat, implore, appeal to, ask, request, petition

pleasant adjective
1 *The owner of the shop is always **pleasant** to us.*
kind, friendly, likeable, charming, amiable, amicable, cheerful, genial, good-natured, good-humoured, approachable, hospitable, welcoming
2 *We spent a very **pleasant** evening playing cards.*
pleasing, enjoyable, agreeable, delightful, lovely, entertaining

pleased adjective
*Why do you look so **pleased** today?*
contented, delighted, elated, glad, grateful, happy, satisfied, thankful, thrilled
OPPOSITE annoyed

pleasure noun
1 *Mrs Ramsay gets a lot of **pleasure** from her garden.*
delight, enjoyment, happiness, joy, satisfaction, comfort, contentment, gladness
Very great pleasure is **bliss** or **ecstasy**.
2 *He talked about the **pleasures** of living in the country.*
joy, comfort, delight

plenty noun
*Don't buy any milk—there's **plenty** in the fridge.*
a lot, a large amount, an abundance, a profusion
A lot more than you need is a **glut** or **surplus**.
OPPOSITE scarcity
plenty of
*We've still got **plenty of** time.*
a lot of, lots of, ample, abundant
(informal) loads of, masses of, tons of

plot noun
1 *Guy Fawkes was part of a **plot** against the government.*
conspiracy, scheme, secret plan

2 *It was hard to follow the **plot** of the film.*
story, storyline, narrative, thread
3 *They bought a **plot** of ground to build a new house.*
area, piece, lot, patch
A plot of ground for growing flowers or vegetables is an **allotment**.
A large plot of land is a **tract** of land.

plot verb
1 *The gang were **plotting** a daring bank raid.*
plan, devise, concoct, hatch
(informal) cook up
2 *They were accused of **plotting** against the queen.*
conspire, intrigue, scheme

plump adjective
*The goblin was short and **plump**, with pointy ears.*
chubby, dumpy, fat, tubby, podgy, round, stout, portly
OPPOSITE skinny

plunge verb
1 *One by one, the girls **plunged** into the pool.*
dive, jump, leap, throw yourself
2 *As the wind died down, the kite **plunged** to the ground.*
drop, fall, pitch, tumble, plummet, swoop
3 *I **plunged** my hand in the cold water.*
dip, lower, sink, immerse, submerge
4 *Finn **plunged** his spear into the dragon's throat.*
thrust, stab, push, stick, shove, force

point noun
1 *Be careful—that knife has a very sharp **point**.*
tip, end, spike, prong
2 *The stars looked like **points** of light in the sky.*
dot, spot, speck, fleck
3 *He marked on the map the exact **point** where the treasure lay.*
location, place, position, site
4 *At that **point** the rain started to come down.*
moment, instant, time
5 *I agree with your last **point**.*
idea, argument, thought
6 *His sense of humour is one of his good **points**.*
characteristic, feature, attribute
7 *There is no **point** in phoning at this hour.*
purpose, reason, aim, object, use, usefulness
8 *I think I missed the **point** of that film.*
meaning, essence, core, gist

point verb
1 *She **pointed** the way.*
draw attention to, indicate, point out, show, signal
2 *Can you **point** me in the right direction for the station?*
aim, direct, guide, lead, steer

pointless adjective
*It's **pointless** to argue with him— he's so stubborn.*
useless, futile, vain
OPPOSITE worthwhile

poisonous adjective
*Some of those mushrooms may be **poisonous**.*
toxic, venomous, deadly, lethal

poke verb
*Someone **poked** me in the back with an umbrella.*
prod, dig, jab, stab, thrust
to poke out
*The kitten's head was **poking out** of the basket.*
stick out, project, protrude

pole noun
*Four **poles** marked the corners of the field.*
post, bar, rod, stick, shaft
A pole that you use when walking or as a weapon is a **staff**.
A pole for a flag to fly from is a **flagpole**.
A pole to support sails on a boat or ship is a **mast** or **spar**.
A pole with a pointed end to stick in the ground is a **stake**.
Poles which a circus entertainer walks on are **stilts**.

polish verb
*Beeswax is used to **polish** furniture.*
rub down, shine, buff, burnish, wax

polish noun
*The silverware had been cleaned to give it a good **polish**.*
shine, sheen, gloss, lustre, sparkle, brightness, glaze, finish

point

polite adjective
*My aunt is always **polite** to visitors.*
courteous, well-mannered, respectful, civil, well-behaved, gracious, gentlemanly or ladylike, chivalrous, gallant
OPPOSITE rude, impolite

pollute verb
*The river has been **polluted** by chemicals.*
contaminate, infect, poison

poor adjective
1 *You can't afford luxuries if you're **poor**.*
impoverished, poverty-stricken, penniless, needy, badly off, hard-up
OPPOSITE rich

2 *His handwriting is very* **poor**.
bad, inferior, inadequate,
incompetent, unsatisfactory, shoddy,
weak, worthless
OPPOSITE good, superior
3 *They pitied the* **poor** *animals
standing in the rain*.
unlucky, unfortunate, pitiful,
wretched
OPPOSITE lucky

popular adjective
1 *Disney has made a lot of* **popular**
children's films.
well-liked, well-loved, celebrated,
favourite
OPPOSITE unpopular
2 *Rollerblades are very* **popular** *just
now*.
fashionable, widespread, current, in
demand
(*informal*) trendy
OPPOSITE unpopular

port noun
*A large cruise ship sailed into
the* **port**.
harbour, dock, anchorage
*A harbour for yachts and pleasure
boats is a* **marina**.

portrait noun
There's a **portrait** *of the Queen on
every stamp*.
picture, image, likeness,
representation
*A portrait which shows a side view of
someone is a* **profile**.
*A portrait which shows just the
outline of someone is a* **silhouette**.
*A portrait which exaggerates some
aspect of a person is a* **caricature**.

portrait

posh adjective (*informal*)
We went to a **posh** *restaurant for a
treat*.
smart, stylish, high-class, elegant,
fashionable, up-market, luxurious,
luxury, deluxe, plush
(*informal*) classy, swanky, swish,
snazzy

position noun
1 *Mark the* **position** *on the map*.
location, place, point, spot, site,
whereabouts
2 *He shifted his* **position** *to avoid
getting cramp*.
pose, posture, stance
3 *Losing all her money put her in
a difficult* **position**.
situation, state, condition,
circumstances
4 *A referee should adopt a neutral*
position.
opinion, attitude, outlook, view
5 *Being a head teacher is an
important* **position**.
job, post, appointment, function

positive adjective
1 *The detective was* **positive** *that the
cook was lying*.
certain, sure, convinced, assured,
confident
OPPOSITE uncertain
2 *Miss Andrews made some* **positive**
comments on my singing.
helpful, useful, worthwhile,
beneficial, constructive
OPPOSITE negative

possible adjective
1 *Is it* **possible** *that life exists on
other planets?*
likely, probable, conceivable, credible
2 *It wasn't* **possible** *to shift the
piano*.
feasible, practicable, practical

post noun
1 *The farmer put up some* **posts** *for
a new fence*.
pole, pillar, shaft, stake, support, prop
2 *The* **post** *was delivered late*.
mail, letters, delivery
3 *Are you thinking of applying for
the* **post**?
job, position, situation, appointment,
vacancy

post verb
1 *Did you* **post** *those letters?*
mail, send, dispatch
2 *The names of the winners will be*
posted *on the noticeboard*.
display, put up, announce,
advertise

postpone verb
They **postponed** *the match because
of bad weather*.
put off, defer, delay
*To stop a game or meeting that
you intend to start again later is to*
adjourn *or* **suspend** *it*.

potion noun
A magic **potion** *was brewing in the
wizard's cauldron*.
drug, medicine, mixture

potion

pounce verb
to pounce on
The cat **pounced on** *the mouse*.
jump on, leap on, spring on, swoop
down on, lunge at, ambush, attack

pour verb
1 *Water* **poured** *through the hole*.
flow, run, gush, stream, spill, spout
2 *I* **poured** *some milk into my cup*.
tip, serve

power noun
1 *They were amazed by the* **power** *of
the robot*.
strength, force, might, energy
2 *The storyteller has the* **power** *to
enthrall an audience*.
skill, talent, ability, competence
3 *A policeman has the* **power** *to
arrest someone*.
authority, right
4 *The empress had* **power** *over
all the people*.
authority, command, control,
dominance, domination

powerful adjective
1 *Sir Joustalot was the most*
powerful *knight in the
kingdom*.
influential, leading, commanding,
dominant, high-powered
2 *The wrestler had a* **powerful**
punch.
strong, forceful, hard, mighty,
vigorous, formidable, potent
3 *He used some* **powerful**
arguments.
strong, convincing, effective,
persuasive, impressive

practical adjective
1 *I'll ask Katie what to do—she is
always very* **practical**.
down-to-earth, matter-of-fact,
sensible, level-headed
OPPOSITE impractical
2 *The robbers' plan was not very*
practical.
workable, realistic, sensible, feasible,
viable, achievable
OPPOSITE impractical
3 *Do you have any* **practical**
experience of childminding?
real, actual, hands-on
OPPOSITE theoretical

a b c d e f g h i j k l m n o p q r s t u v w x y z

practice noun
1 *We have extra football **practice** this week.*
training, exercises, preparation, rehearsal, drill
2 *Is it the **practice** amongst ogres to eat grubs for breakfast?*
custom, habit, convention, routine
in practice
*What will the plan involve **in practice**?*
in effect, in reality, actually, really

practise verb
1 *My piano teacher asked me to **practise** for longer.*
do exercises, rehearse, train, drill
To practise just before the start of a performance is to **warm up**.
2 *My sister wants to **practise** veterinary medicine.*
do, perform, carry out, put into practice, follow, pursue

praise verb
*The critics **praised** the actress for her outstanding performance.*
commend, congratulate, applaud, admire, compliment, pay tribute to (*informal*) rave about
OPPOSITE criticize

praise noun
*She received a lot of **praise** for her painting.*
approval, admiration, compliments, congratulations, applause

prance verb
*Milly started **prancing** about in a silly way.*
dance, skip, hop, leap, romp, cavort, caper, frolic, gambol

precious adjective
1 *Her most **precious** possession was an old photograph.*
treasured, cherished, valued, prized, dearest, beloved
2 *The throne glittered with **precious** gems and gold.*
valuable, costly, expensive, priceless
OPPOSITE worthless

precise adjective
1 *Can you tell me the **precise** time, please?*
exact, accurate, correct, true, right
OPPOSITE rough
2 *The map gave **precise** directions for finding the treasure.*
careful, detailed, specific, particular, definite
OPPOSITE vague

predict verb
*You can't **predict** what may happen in the future.*
forecast, foresee, foretell, prophesy

prefer verb
*Would you **prefer** juice or lemonade?*
rather have, go for, opt for, plump for, choose, fancy

prejudice noun
*The school has a policy against racial **prejudice**.*
bias, discrimination, intolerance, narrow-mindedness, bigotry
Prejudice against other races is **racism**.
Prejudice against other nations is **xenophobia**.
Prejudice against the other sex is **sexism**.
OPPOSITE fairness, tolerance

prepare verb
*The museum staff are **preparing** for the new exhibition.*
get ready, make arrangements for, organize, plan, set up
To prepare for a play is to **rehearse**.
To prepare to take part in a sport is to **train**.

present adjective
1 *Is everyone **present**?*
here, in attendance, at hand
2 *Who is the **present** world chess champion?*
current, existing

present noun
*What would you like for your birthday **present**?*
gift (*informal*) prezzie

present verb
1 *The head **presents** the prizes on sports day.*
award, hand over
2 *Our class is **presenting** a play about the Vikings.*
put on, perform, stage, mount
3 *Dr Smart **presented** her amazing invention to the world.*
put forward, show, display, exhibit, make known

press verb
1 ***Press** the fruit through a sieve to get rid of the seeds.*
push, force, squeeze, squash, crush, shove, cram, compress
2 *She **pressed** her blouse for the party.*
iron, flatten, smooth
3 *Our friends **pressed** us to stay a bit longer.*
beg, urge, entreat, implore

press noun
1 *We read about the competition in the **press**.*
newspapers, magazines
2 *The **press** came to the opening of the new arts centre.*
journalists, reporters, the media

pressure noun
1 *The nurse applied **pressure** to the wound.*
force, compression, squeezing, weight, load
2 *In the final, the home team were under a lot of **pressure**.*
stress, strain, tension

presume verb
*I **presume** you'd like something to eat.*
assume, take it, imagine, suppose, think, believe, guess

pretend verb
*She's not really crying—she's only **pretending**.*
put on an act, bluff, fake, sham, pose (*informal*) kid, put it on

pretend adjective
*That's not a real spider—it's just a **pretend** one!*
fake, false, artificial, made-up
OPPOSITE real

pretty adjective
*The doll was dressed in a **pretty** blue outfit.*
attractive, beautiful, lovely, nice, pleasing, charming, dainty, picturesque, quaint (*informal*) cute
A common simile is **as pretty as a picture**.
OPPOSITE ugly

prevent verb
1 *The driver could do nothing to **prevent** the accident.*
stop, avert, avoid, head off
2 *The police **prevented** an attempted bank raid.*
block, foil, frustrate, thwart
3 *There's not much you can do to **prevent** colds.*
stave off, ward off

price noun
*What is the **price** of a return ticket to Sydney?*
cost, amount, figure, expense, payment, sum, charge, rate
The price you pay for a journey on public transport is a **fare**.
The price you pay to send a letter is the **postage**.
The price you pay to use a private road, bridge, or tunnel is a **toll**.

priceless adjective
*The museum contained many **priceless** antiques.*
precious, rare, valuable, costly, expensive, dear

prick verb
*Jamie burst the balloon by **pricking** it with a pin.*
pierce, puncture, stab, jab, perforate

prickly adjective
*Holly leaves are very **prickly**.*
spiky, spiny, thorny, bristly, sharp, scratchy

A B C D E F G H I J K L M N O P Q R S T U V W X Y Z

pride noun
1 Mr Dodds takes great **pride** in his garden.
satisfaction, pleasure, delight
2 The medal winner was a source of great **pride** to his family.
self-esteem, self-respect, dignity, honour
3 **Pride** comes before a fall.
arrogance, conceit, bigheadedness, vanity, snobbery
OPPOSITE humility

prim adjective
Aunt Jemima is always very **prim** and proper.
prudish, strait-laced, formal, demure

prisoner noun
The **prisoner** tried to escape from jail.
convict, captive, inmate
A person who is held prisoner until some demand is met is a **hostage**.

private adjective
1 Everything I write in my diary is **private**.
secret, confidential, personal, intimate
Secret official documents are **classified** documents.
2 Can we go somewhere a little more **private**?
quiet, secluded, hidden, concealed

prize noun
Our team won first **prize** in the relay race.
award, reward, trophy
Money that you win as a prize is your **winnings**.
Prize money that keeps increasing until someone wins it is a **jackpot**.

prize verb
Chrissie **prized** her grandmother's ring above all else.
treasure, value, cherish, hold dear, esteem, revere
OPPOSITE dislike

probable adjective
A burst pipe was the most **probable** cause of the flood.
likely, feasible, possible, predictable, expected
OPPOSITE improbable

problem noun
1 Our maths teacher set us a difficult **problem**.
puzzle, question
(informal) brainteaser, poser
2 I'm having a **problem** with my computer.
difficulty, trouble, snag, worry
(informal) headache

procession noun
The **procession** made its way slowly down the hill.
parade, march, column, line

prod verb
Someone **prodded** me in the back with an umbrella.
poke, dig, jab, nudge, push

production noun
1 **Production** at the factory has increased this year.
output
2 We went to see a **production** of 'The Sound of Music'.
performance, show

programme noun
1 We worked out a **programme** for sports day.
plan, schedule, timetable
A list of things to be done at a meeting is an **agenda**.
2 There was a really good **programme** on TV last night.
broadcast, show, production, transmission

progress noun
1 I traced their **progress** on the map.
journey, route, movement, travels
2 I'm not making much **progress** learning Dutch.
advance, development, growth, improvement, headway
An important piece of progress is a **breakthrough**.

progress verb
Work on the new building is **progressing** well.
proceed, advance, move forward, make progress, make headway, continue, develop, improve
(informal) come along

prohibit verb
Skateboarding is **prohibited** in the school grounds.
ban, forbid, outlaw, rule out, veto
OPPOSITE permit, allow

project noun
1 We did a history **project** on the Victorians.
activity, task, assignment, piece of research
2 There is a **project** to create a bird sanctuary in the area.
plan, proposal, scheme

project verb
1 A narrow ledge **projects** from the cliff.
extend, protrude, stick out, jut out, overhang
2 The lighthouse **projects** a beam of light.
cast, shine, throw out

promise noun
1 We had **promises** of help from many people.
assurance, pledge, guarantee, commitment, vow, oath, word of honour
2 That young pianist shows **promise**.
potential, talent

promise verb
Dad **promised** that we'd go camping this summer.
assure someone, give your word, guarantee, swear, take an oath, vow

promote verb
1 Gareth has been **promoted** to captain.
move up, advance, upgrade, elevate
2 The singer is here to **promote** her new CD.
advertise, publicize, market, push, sell (informal) plug
3 The school is trying to **promote** healthy eating.
encourage, foster, advocate, back, support

prompt adjective
I received a **prompt** reply to my email.
punctual, quick, rapid, swift, immediate, instant
OPPOSITE delayed

prompt verb
Having a dog **prompted** her to take more exercise.
cause, lead, induce, motivate, stimulate, encourage, provoke

proof noun
There is no **proof** that he is a secret agent.
evidence, confirmation

proper adjective
1 The nurse showed them the **proper** way to tie a bandage.
correct, right, accurate, precise, true, genuine
OPPOSITE wrong, incorrect
2 It's only **proper** that he should pay for the broken window.
fair, just, fitting, appropriate, deserved, suitable
OPPOSITE inappropriate
3 It's not **proper** to speak with your mouth full.
decent, respectable, tasteful
OPPOSITE rude

property noun
1 This office deals with lost **property**.
belongings, possessions, goods

a
b
c
d
e
f
g
h
i
j
k
l
m
n
o
p
q
r
s
t
u
v
w
x
y
z

2 *The website lists **property** that is for sale in the city.*
buildings, houses, land, premises
3 *Many herbs have healing **properties**.*
quality, characteristic, feature, attribute, trait

protect *verb*
1 *A sentry was posted outside to **protect** the palace.*
defend, guard, safeguard, keep safe, secure
2 *I wore a hat to **protect** myself from the sun.*
shield, shade, screen, insulate

protest *noun*
1 *There were **protests** at the plan to close the cinema.*
complaint, objection
A general protest is an **outcry**.
2 *Some streets will be closed for a **protest** in the city centre.*
demonstration, march, rally
(*informal*) demo

protest *verb*
*We wrote a letter **protesting** about the closure of the cinema.*
complain, make a protest, object (to), take exception (to), express disapproval (of)

proud *adjective*
1 *Jennie's father was very **proud** when she passed her music exam.*
delighted (with), pleased (with)
A common simile is **as proud as a peacock**.
2 *He's too **proud** to mix with the likes of us!*
conceited, big-headed, arrogant, vain, haughty, self-important, snobbish, superior
(*informal*) stuck-up
OPPOSITE humble

prove *verb*
*The evidence will **prove** that he is innocent.*
confirm, demonstrate, establish, verify
OPPOSITE disprove

provide *verb*
1 *We'll **provide** the juice if you bring the sandwiches.*
bring, contribute, arrange for, lay on
To provide food and drink for people is to **cater** for them.
2 *The ski centre can **provide** you with boots and skis.*
supply, equip, furnish

provoke *verb*
1 *Don't do anything to **provoke** the lions!*
annoy, irritate, anger, incense, infuriate, exasperate, tease, taunt, goad
(*informal*) wind up
OPPOSITE pacify

2 *The referee's decision **provoked** anger from the crowd.*
arouse, produce, prompt, cause, generate, induce, stimulate, spark off, stir up, whip up

prowl *verb*
*Guard dogs **prowled** about the grounds of the palace.*
roam, slink, sneak, creep, steal

public *adjective*
1 *The **public** entrance is at the front of the gallery.*
common, communal, general, open, shared
OPPOSITE private
2 *The name of the author is now **public** knowledge.*
well-known, acknowledged, published, open, general, universal
OPPOSITE secret

publish *verb*
1 *The magazine is **published** every week.*
issue, print, produce, bring out, release, circulate
2 *When will they **publish** the results?*
announce, declare, disclose, make known, make public, report, reveal
To publish information on radio or TV is to **broadcast** it.

pudding *noun*
*Do you want any **pudding**?*
dessert, sweet
(*informal*) afters

puff *noun*
1 *A **puff** of wind caught his hat.*
gust, breath, flurry
2 *A **puff** of smoke rose from the chimney.*
cloud, whiff

puff *verb*
1 *The dragon **puffed** green smoke from its nostrils.*
blow out, send out, emit, belch
2 *By the end of the race I was **puffing**.*
breathe heavily, pant, gasp, wheeze
3 *The sails **puffed** out as the wind rose.*
become inflated, billow, swell

pull *verb*
1 *She **pulled** her chair nearer to the desk.*
drag, draw, haul, lug, trail, tow
OPPOSITE push
2 *Be careful—you nearly **pulled** my arm off!*
tug, rip, wrench, jerk, pluck

prowl

to pull out
1 *The dentist **pulled out** one of his teeth.*
extract, take out, remove
2 *He had to **pull out** of the race.*
back out, withdraw, retire
to pull up
*The bus **pulled up** at the traffic lights.*
draw up, stop, halt

pump *verb*
*The fire brigade **pumped** water out of the cellar.*
drain, draw off, empty
To move liquid from a higher container to a lower one through a tube is to **siphon** it.

punch *verb*
1 *Mrs Rafferty **punched** the robber on the nose.*
jab, poke, prod, thump
2 ***Punch** a hole through the card.*
bore, pierce

punish *verb*
*Those responsible for the crime will be **punished**.*
penalize, discipline, chastise

pupil *noun*
*There are 33 **pupils** in our class.*
schoolchild, student, learner, scholar
Someone who follows a great teacher is a **disciple**.

pure *adjective*
1 *The bracelet is made of **pure** gold.*
authentic, genuine, real
2 *He was talking **pure** nonsense.*
complete, absolute, utter, sheer, total
3 *All our dishes are made from **pure** ingredients.*
natural, wholesome
4 *They swam in the **pure**, clear water of the lake.*
clean, fresh, unpolluted
OPPOSITE impure

purpose noun
1 *Have you got a particular* **purpose** *in mind?*
intention, aim, end, goal, target, objective, outcome, result
2 *What's the* **purpose** *of your invention?*
point, use, usefulness, value

push verb
1 *We* **pushed** *our way through the crowd.*
shove, thrust, force, propel, barge, elbow, jostle
OPPOSITE pull
2 *Pete* **pushed** *his things into a bag.*
pack, press, cram, crush, compress, ram, squash, squeeze
3 *They* **pushed** *him to work even harder.*
pressurize, press, drive, urge, compel, bully
(*informal*) lean on

put verb
1 *You can* **put** *your schoolbags in the corner.*
place, set down, leave, deposit, dump, stand
2 *The dog* **put** *its head on my lap.*
lay, lean, rest
3 *I'll* **put** *some pictures on the wall.*
attach, fasten, fix, hang
4 *Where are they planning to* **put** *the car park?*
locate, situate
5 *I'm not sure of the best way to* **put** *this.*
express, word, phrase, say, state
to put someone off
The colour of the food **put** *me* **off** *eating.*
deter, discourage, distract
to put something off
They **put off** *their journey because of the fog.*
delay, postpone, defer
to put something out
The firefighters quickly **put out** *the blaze.*
extinguish, quench, smother
to put something up
1 *It doesn't take long to* **put up** *the tent.*
set up, construct, erect
2 *I'm going to buy a new bike before they* **put up** *the price.*
increase, raise

to put up with something
I don't know how you **put up with** *that noise.*
bear, stand, tolerate, endure

puzzle noun
Has anyone managed to solve the **puzzle**?
question, mystery, riddle, conundrum, problem
(*informal*) brainteaser, poser

puzzle verb
1 *Phil was* **puzzled** *by the mysterious message.*
confuse, baffle, bewilder, bemuse, mystify, perplex, fox
2 *We* **puzzled** *over the problem for hours.*
ponder, think, meditate, worry, brood

puzzled adjective
Why are you looking so **puzzled**?
confused, baffled, bewildered, mystified, perplexed

quaint adjective
They stayed in a **quaint** *thatched cottage.*
charming, picturesque, sweet, old-fashioned, old-world

quake verb
The ground **quaked** *with the thud of the giant's footsteps.*
shake, shudder, tremble, quiver, shiver, vibrate, rock, sway, wobble

quality noun
1 *We only use ingredients of the highest* **quality**.
grade, class, standard
2 *The most obvious* **quality** *of rubber is that it stretches.*
characteristic, feature, property, attribute, trait

quantity noun
1 *She receives a huge* **quantity** *of fan mail every week.*
amount, mass, volume, bulk, weight
(*informal*) load

quay

2 *We recycled a large* **quantity** *of empty bottles.*
number
When you add up numbers, you get a **sum** *or* **total**.

quarrel noun
We have **quarrels**, *but really we are good friends.*
argument, disagreement, dispute, difference of opinion, row, squabble, clash, tiff
Continuous quarrelling is **strife**.
A long-lasting quarrel is a **feud** *or* **vendetta**.
A quarrel in which people become violent is a **brawl** *or* **fight**.

quarrel verb
The twins **quarrelled** *over who should sit in the front.*
disagree, argue, row, squabble, bicker, clash, fight, fall out
to quarrel with something
I can't **quarrel with** *your decision.*
disagree with, object to, take exception to, oppose

quay noun
The ship unloaded its cargo onto the **quay**.
dock, harbour, pier, wharf, jetty, landing stage

quest noun
The knights set out on a **quest** *to find the enchanted tower.*
search, hunt, expedition, mission

question noun
1 *Does anyone have any* **questions**?
enquiry, query, problem
A question which someone sets as a puzzle is a **brain-teaser** *or* **conundrum** *or* **riddle**.
A series of questions asked as a game is a **quiz**.
A set of questions which someone asks to get information is a **questionnaire** *or* **survey**.

a
b
c
d
e
f
g
h
i
j
k
l
m
n
o
p
q
r
s
t
u
v
w
x
y
z

queue

2 *There's some* **question** *over the player's fitness.*
uncertainty, doubt, argument, debate, dispute

question verb
1 *The detective decided to* **question** *the suspect.*
ask, examine, interview, quiz, interrogate
To question someone intensively is to **grill** them.
2 *He* **questioned** *the referee's decision.*
challenge, dispute, argue over, quarrel with, object to, query

queue noun
There was a **queue** *of people outside the cinema.*
line, file, column, string
A long queue of traffic on a road is a **tailback**.

queue verb
Please **queue** *at the door.*
line up, form a queue

quick adjective
1 *You'd better be* **quick**—*the bus leaves in 10 minutes.*
fast, swift, rapid, speedy, hasty
(*informal*) nippy
A common simile is **as quick as a flash**.
OPPOSITE slow
2 *Do you mind if I make a* **quick** *phone call?*
short, brief, momentary, immediate, instant, prompt, snappy
OPPOSITE long, lengthy
3 *She's very* **quick** *at mental arithmetic.*
bright, clever, sharp, acute, alert
(*informal*) on the ball
OPPOSITE slow

quiet adjective
1 *The deserted house was still and* **quiet**.
silent, noiseless, soundless
A common simile is **as quiet as a mouse**.
OPPOSITE noisy
2 *The children spoke in* **quiet** *whispers.*
hushed, low, soft
Something that is so quiet that you can't hear it is **inaudible**.
OPPOSITE loud
3 *Amy has always been a* **quiet** *child.*
shy, reserved, subdued, placid, uncommunicative, retiring, withdrawn
OPPOSITE talkative
4 *We found a* **quiet** *place for a picnic.*
peaceful, secluded, isolated, restful, tranquil, calm, serene
OPPOSITE busy

quite adverb
Take care how you use **quite**, as the two senses are almost opposites.
1 *The two puppies have* **quite** *different personalities.*
completely, totally, utterly, entirely, absolutely, wholly
2 *They played* **quite** *well, but far from their best.*
fairly, reasonably, moderately, rather

quiz noun
Our class took part in a general knowledge **quiz**.
test, competition, questionnaire, exam, examination

race noun
1 *We had a* **race** *to see who was the fastest runner.*
competition, contest, chase
A race to decide who will take part in the final is a **heat**.
2 *We belong to different* **races** *but we're all humans.*
nation, people, ethnic group

race verb
1 *We* **raced** *each other to the end of the road.*
have a race with, run against, compete with
2 *She had to* **race** *home because she was late.*
run, rush, dash, hurry, sprint, fly, tear, whizz, zoom

racket noun
Please stop making that awful **racket**!
noise, row, din, commotion, disturbance, uproar, rumpus

ragged adjective
They met a traveller wearing **ragged** *clothes.*
tattered, tatty, threadbare, torn, frayed, patched, ripped, shabby, worn out

raid noun
The enemy **raid** *caught them by surprise.*
attack, assault, strike, onslaught, invasion, blitz

raid verb
1 *Long ago, Vikings* **raided** *the towns on the coast.*
attack, invade, ransack, plunder, loot, pillage
Someone who raids ships at sea is a **pirate**.
Someone who raids and steals cattle is a **rustler**.
2 *Police* **raided** *the house at dawn.*
descend on, rush, storm, swoop on

rain noun   rain
A formal word for rain is **precipitation**.
The rainy season in south and southeast Asia is the **monsoon**.
When there is no rain for a long time you have a **drought**.

raise verb
1 **Raise** *your hand if you need help.*
hold up, put up, lift
2 *The box was too heavy for him to* **raise**.
lift, pick up, elevate, hoist, jack up
3 *The Post Office is* **raising** *the price of stamps.*
increase, put up
4 *The runners hope to* **raise** *£1000 for charity.*
collect, gather, take in, make
5 *He* **raised** *some objections to the plan.*
bring up, mention, put forward, present, introduce
6 *The doctor didn't want to* **raise** *their hopes.*
encourage, build up, arouse
7 *It's hard work trying to* **raise** *a family.*
bring up, care for, look after, nurture, rear

ram verb
The car skidded and **rammed** *into a lamp-post.*
bump, hit, strike, crash into, collide with, smash into

random adjective
They picked a **random** *selection of pupils.*
arbitrary, chance, haphazard, casual, unplanned
OPPOSITE deliberate

range noun
1 *There is a* **range** *of mountains to the south.*
chain, line, row, series, string
2 *Supermarkets sell a wide* **range** *of goods.*
variety, assortment, selection, choice, spectrum
3 *The shop caters for all age* **ranges** *from toddlers to teenagers.*
span, scope

range verb
1 Prices **range** from five to twenty euros.
vary, differ, extend, fluctuate
2 Rows of jam jars were **ranged** on the shelf.
arrange, order, lay out, set out, line up
3 Wild deer **range** over the hills.
wander, ramble, roam, rove, stray

rapid adjective
The cyclists set off at a **rapid** pace.
fast, quick, speedy, swift, brisk
OPPOSITE slow

rare adjective
1 These flowers are now very **rare** in the wild.
uncommon, unusual, infrequent, scarce, sparse
OPPOSITE common
2 He has a **rare** ability to make people laugh.
exceptional, remarkable, special

rarely adverb
Our next-door neighbour **rarely** goes out.
seldom, infrequently, hardly ever
OPPOSITE often

rash adjective
Don't make any **rash** promises.
reckless, foolhardy, hasty, hurried, impulsive, unthinking
OPPOSITE careful

rate noun
1 The cyclists were pedalling at a furious **rate**.
pace, speed
2 What's the usual **rate** for washing a car?
charge, cost, fee, payment, price, figure, amount
rate verb
How do you **rate** their chance of winning?
judge, regard, consider, estimate, evaluate

rather adverb
1 It's **rather** chilly today.
quite, fairly, moderately, slightly, somewhat, a bit, a little
2 I'd **rather** not go out tonight.
preferably, sooner

rave verb
1 Connie **raved** about the film she saw last week.
be enthusiastic, talk wildly
2 The head **raved** on about their bad behaviour.
shout, rage, storm, yell, roar

raw adjective
1 **Raw** vegetables are supposed to be good for you.
uncooked
OPPOSITE cooked

2 The factory imports a lot of **raw** materials from abroad.
crude, natural, unprocessed, untreated
OPPOSITE manufactured, processed
3 Her knee felt **raw** after she fell off her bike.
red, rough, sore, tender, inflamed
4 There was a **raw** wind blowing from the east.
bitter, cold, chilly, biting, freezing, piercing

ray noun
A **ray** of light shone into the dark cave.
beam, shaft, stream

reach verb
1 They hoped to **reach** Oxford by lunch time.
arrive at, go as far as, get to, make
2 The appeal fund has **reached** its target.
achieve, attain
3 I'm not tall enough to **reach** the top shelf.
get hold of, grasp, touch
to reach out
Reach out your hands.
extend, hold out, put out, stick out, stretch out

reach noun
1 The shelf was just within his **reach**.
grasp
2 The shops are within easy **reach**.
distance, range

react verb
How did he **react** when he read the letter?
respond, behave, answer, reply

reaction noun
What was her **reaction** when you said you were sorry?
response, answer, reply

read verb
They couldn't **read** the doctor's handwriting.
make out, understand, decipher
To read through something very quickly is to **skim through** it.
To read here and there in a book is to **dip into** it.
To read something intently is to **pore over** it.

ready adjective
1 When will tea be **ready**?
prepared, set, done, available, in place
OPPOSITE not ready
2 He's always **ready** to help.
willing, glad, pleased, happy, keen, eager
OPPOSITE reluctant

real adjective
1 History is about **real** events.
actual, true, factual, verifiable
OPPOSITE fictitious, imaginary
2 The necklace was made from **real** rubies.
authentic, genuine, bona fide, natural
OPPOSITE artificial, fake
3 She doesn't often show her **real** feelings.
true, honest, sincere, genuine, heartfelt
OPPOSITE insincere

realistic adjective
1 The portrait of the artist is very **realistic**.
lifelike, true to life, faithful, convincing, recognizable
2 It's not **realistic** to expect a puppy to be quiet.
feasible, practical, sensible, possible, workable

realize verb
It took him a long time to **realize** what she meant.
understand, appreciate, grasp, comprehend, recognize, see
(informal) catch on to, twig

really adverb
1 Are you **really** going to Peru?
actually, definitely, truly, in fact, certainly, genuinely, honestly
2 I saw a **really** good film last night.
very, extremely, exceptionally

reasonable adjective
1 That's a **reasonable** plan.
sensible, intelligent, rational, logical, sane, sound
OPPOSITE irrational
2 They bought the house for a **reasonable** price.
fair, acceptable, average, moderate, respectable, normal, proper
OPPOSITE excessive

reassure verb
The doctor **reassured** her that the wound was not serious.
calm, comfort, encourage, hearten, give confidence to
OPPOSITE threaten

rebel verb
The king feared that the people would **rebel**.
revolt, rise up
To rebel against the captain of a ship is to **mutiny** and someone who does this is a **mutineer**.
OPPOSITE obey

rebellion noun
The protest soon became a widespread **rebellion**.
revolt, revolution, uprising, resistance
A rebellion on a ship is a **mutiny**.

a b c d e f g h i j k l m n o p q r s t u v w x y z

A B C D E F G H I J K L M N O P Q **R** S T U V W X Y Z

recent *adjective*
We watch the news to keep up with **recent** *events.*
current, up-to-date, contemporary, new, the latest, fresh

recite *verb*
Zoe **recited** *a poem she had written.*
say aloud, read out, narrate

reckless *adjective*
A man has been charged with **reckless** *driving.*
careless, irresponsible, mindless, thoughtless, negligent, foolhardy, rash, wild
OPPOSITE careful

reckon *verb*
1 *I tried to* **reckon** *how much she owed me.*
calculate, work out, add up, figure out, assess, estimate
2 *Do you* **reckon** *it's going to rain?*
think, believe, guess, imagine, feel

recognize *verb*
1 *I didn't* **recognize** *her with her new haircut.*
identify, know, distinguish, make out, recall, recollect, remember
2 *He refused to* **recognize** *that he was to blame.*
acknowledge, admit, accept, grant, concede, confess, realize

recommend *verb*
1 *The doctor* **recommended** *a complete rest.*
advise, counsel, propose, suggest, advocate, prescribe, urge
2 *The restaurant was* **recommended** *by a friend of mine.*
approve of, endorse, praise, commend

record *noun*
The zookeepers keep a **record** *of the animals' diet.*
account, report
A record of daily events is a **diary** *or* **journal***.*
The record of a voyage at sea or in space is the **log***.*

The record of what happened at a meeting is the **minutes**.
A record of people's names is a **register**.
Records consisting of historical documents are **archives**.

record *verb*
1 *The concert is being* **recorded** *by the BBC.*
tape, video
2 *She* **recorded** *our interview in a notebook.*
write down, note, set down, put down, enter

recover *verb*
1 *It took a long time to* **recover** *after my illness.*
get better, heal, improve, recuperate, pick up, mend,
come round, pull through,
revive, rally
2 *The police have* **recovered** *the stolen vehicles.*
get back, retrieve, reclaim, repossess, find, trace

recycle *verb*
You can **recycle** *glass by putting it in the bottle bank.*
reuse, reprocess, salvage, use again

red *adjective*
1 *I chose a* **red** *ribbon for my doll.*
Something which is rather red is **reddish**.
A common simile is **as red as a beetroot**.
2 *My nose and cheeks were* **red** *with cold.*
flushed, glowing, rosy, ruddy, blushing
3 *Her eyes were* **red** *from lack of sleep.*
bloodshot, inflamed, red-rimmed
4 *The fairy queen had flaming* **red** *hair.*
ginger, auburn, coppery
(*informal*) carroty

reduce *verb*
She's **reduced** *the amount of sugar in her diet.*
decrease, lessen, lower, cut, cut back, slash
To reduce something by half is to **halve** it.
To reduce the width of something is to **narrow** it.
To reduce the length of something is to **shorten** or **trim** it.
To reduce speed is to **decelerate**.
To reduce the strength of a liquid is to **dilute** it.
OPPOSITE increase

refer *verb*
The shop assistant **referred** *me to another department.*
hand over, pass on, direct, send
to refer to
1 *Please don't* **refer to** *this matter again.*
mention, speak of, make reference to, allude to, bring up
2 *If you can't spell a word,* **refer to** *a dictionary.*
look up, consult, go to, turn to

reflect *verb*
1 *Cat's-eyes* **reflect** *the light from car headlights.*
send back, throw back, shine back
2 *Their success* **reflects** *their hard work.*
show, indicate, demonstrate, exhibit, reveal
to reflect on
We need time to **reflect on** *what to do next.*
think about, contemplate, consider, ponder, mull over

refuse *verb*
1 *Why did you* **refuse** *my offer of help?*
decline, reject, turn down, say no to
OPPOSITE accept
2 *They were* **refused** *permission to enter the building.*
deny, deprive of
OPPOSITE allow

region *noun*
1 *The Arctic and Antarctic are polar* **regions**.
area, place, land, territory, part of the world
2 *There are two local radio stations serving this* **region**.
area, district, neighbourhood, locality, vicinity, zone

regret *verb*
She **regretted** *her decision to leave Ireland.*
be sorry for, repent, feel sad about

regular *adjective*
1 *Signs are placed at* **regular** *intervals along the cycle path.*
evenly spaced, fixed
OPPOSITE irregular, uneven

recycle

2 *The drummer kept up a **regular** rhythm.*
constant, consistent, steady, uniform, unvarying
A common simile is **as regular as clockwork**.
OPPOSITE erratic
3 *Is this your **regular** route to school?*
normal, usual, customary, habitual, ordinary, routine
OPPOSITE unusual
4 *Craig is a **regular** customer at the sweet shop.*
frequent, familiar, persistent
OPPOSITE rare, unusual

rehearse *verb*
*We had to **rehearse** the scene again.*
go over, practise, try out

reign *verb*
*Which British monarch **reigned** the longest?*
be king or queen, be on the throne, govern, rule

reject *verb*
1 *At first, she **rejected** their offer of help.*
decline, refuse, turn down, say no to
2 *As we picked the berries, we **rejected** any bad ones.*
discard, get rid of, throw out, scrap

rejoice *verb*
*The people **rejoiced** when the wicked queen died.*
celebrate, delight, be happy, exult
OPPOSITE grieve

relate *verb*
1 *Do you think the two crimes are **related**?*
connect, link, associate
2 *The travellers **related** the story of their adventures.*
tell, narrate, report, describe
relate to
*The letter **relates to** your great grandfather.*
be about, refer to, have to do with, concern

relationship *noun*
1 *There is a **relationship** between your diet and health.*
connection, link, association, bond
The relationship between two numbers is a **ratio**.
2 *The twins have a close **relationship**.*
friendship, attachment, understanding

relax *verb*
1 *I like to **relax** by listening to music.*
unwind, rest, take it easy
2 *This exercise will **relax** your shoulder muscles.*
loosen, ease
OPPOSITE tighten
3 *He **relaxed** his hold on the dog's leash.*
slacken, loosen, ease, lessen, reduce
OPPOSITE tighten

relaxed *adjective*
*They liked the **relaxed** atmosphere of village life.*
informal, casual, carefree, leisurely, easygoing, peaceful, restful, unhurried, calm
(*informal*) laid-back
OPPOSITE tense, stressful

release *verb*
1 *The prisoners were **released** early.*
free, let go, discharge, liberate, set free
To release slaves is to **emancipate** them.
OPPOSITE imprison
2 *The dog was tied up—who **released** him?*
let loose, set loose, unfasten, unleash, untie
3 *The band will **release** their new single in April.*
issue, publish, put out

relevant *adjective*
1 *The detective noted everything that was **relevant** to the case.*
applicable, pertinent, appropriate, suitable, significant, related, connected
2 *Don't interrupt unless your comments are **relevant**.*
to the point

reliable *adjective*
1 *The king summoned his most **reliable** knights.*
faithful, dependable, trustworthy, loyal, constant, devoted, staunch, true
2 *The secret agent always sent **reliable** information.*
dependable, valid, trustworthy, safe, sound, steady, sure

relieve *verb*
*The doctor said the pills would **relieve** the pain.*
ease, help, lessen, diminish, relax, soothe, comfort

religious *adjective*
1 *The choir sang a selection of **religious** music.*
sacred, holy, divine
OPPOSITE secular
2 *My grandparents were very **religious**.*
devout, pious, reverent, spiritual, godly
OPPOSITE ungodly

reluctant *adjective*
*The old woman was **reluctant** to open the door.*
unwilling, hesitant, slow, grudging, half-hearted, resistant
OPPOSITE eager

rely *verb*
*Are you sure that we can **rely** on their help?*
depend on, count on, have confidence in, trust
(*informal*) bank on

remain *verb*
1 *The boys were told to **remain** behind after school.*
stay, wait, linger
(*informal*) hang about
2 *It will **remain** warm and sunny all weekend.*
continue, persist, keep on, carry on
3 *Little **remained** of the house after the fire.*
be left, survive

remains *plural noun*
*They cleared away the **remains** of the picnic.*
remnants, leftovers, leavings, fragments, traces, scraps, debris
The remains at the bottom of a cup are **dregs**.
Remains still standing after a building has collapsed are **ruins**.
Historic remains are **relics**.

remarkable *adjective*
1 *He described his **remarkable** escape from the island.*
amazing, extraordinary, astonishing, memorable, wonderful, incredible, unforgettable, breathtaking
2 *The young violinist shows **remarkable** skill for her age.*
exceptional, notable, noteworthy, striking, outstanding, impressive, phenomenal

remember *verb*
1 *Can you **remember** what she looked like?*
recall, recollect, recognize, place
2 *He was trying to **remember** his lines for the play.*
learn, memorize, keep in mind
OPPOSITE forget
3 *My granny likes to **remember** the old days.*
reminisce about, think back to

remind *verb*
***Remind** me to buy a newspaper.*
prompt, jog your memory
to remind you of something
*What does this tune **remind** you of?*
make you think of, take you back to

remote *adjective*
1 *The tour will explore a **remote** part of Brazil.*
distant, faraway, isolated, cut-off, inaccessible, out-of-the-way, unfrequented
OPPOSITE accessible
2 *The chances of us winning are **remote**.*
poor, slender, slight, small, faint, doubtful
OPPOSITE likely

a b c d e f g h i j k l m n o p q r s t u v w x y z

remove verb
1 *Please **remove** your rubbish.*
clear away, take away
2 *The rowdy passengers were **removed** from the bus.*
throw out, turn out, eject, expel
(*informal*) kick out
To remove people from a house where they are living is to **evict** them.
To remove a monarch from the throne is to **depose** him or her.
3 *The author decided to **remove** the last paragraph.*
cut out, delete, erase, get rid of, do away with, eliminate
4 *The dentist **removed** my bad tooth.*
extract, pull out, take out, withdraw
5 *The divers slowly **removed** their wetsuits.*
take off, peel off, strip off, shed, cast off

renew verb
1 *The church roof has been completely **renewed**.*
repair, renovate, restore, replace, rebuild, reconstruct, revamp, refurbish, overhaul
(*informal*) do up
2 *You must **renew** your passport before you go abroad.*
bring up to date, update

repeat verb
1 *The parrot **repeated** everything he said.*
say again, copy, duplicate, reproduce, echo
2 *The actors had to **repeat** the opening scene.*
do again, redo

replace verb
1 *The spy carefully **replaced** the missing document.*
put back, return, restore, reinstate
2 *Who will **replace** the head teacher when she retires?*
follow, succeed, take over from, take the place of
3 *I need to **replace** one of the tyres on my bike.*
change, renew

reply noun
*He has received no **replies** to his email.*
response, answer, reaction, acknowledgement
An angry reply is a **retort**.

reply verb
to reply to
*She took a long time to **reply to** my letter.*
answer, respond to, give a reply to, react to, acknowledge

report verb
1 *The newspapers **reported** what happened.*
give an account of, record, state, describe, announce, publish

2 *We were told to **report** to reception when we arrived.*
present yourself,
make yourself known, check in
3 *If you cause any damage, I'll **report** you to the police.*
complain about, inform on, denounce

report noun
*There was a **report** in the paper about the crash.*
account, record, story, article, description

reporter noun
*The film star was being interviewed by a TV **reporter**.*
journalist, correspondent

represent verb
1 *The picture **represents** an ancient legend.*
depict, illustrate, portray, picture, show, describe
2 *A dove is often said to **represent** peace.*
stand for, symbolize
3 *He appointed a lawyer to **represent** him.*
speak for

⊛ WORD WEB

reptile noun
SOME ANIMALS WHICH ARE REPTILES
alligator, chameleon, crocodile, gecko, iguana, lizard, slow-worm, snake, terrapin, tortoise, turtle
A reptile found in myths and legends is the **basilisk**.

repulsive adjective
*We were put off eating by the **repulsive** smell.*
disgusting, revolting, offensive, repellent, disagreeable, foul, repugnant, obnoxious, sickening, hateful, hideous, horrible, loathsome, objectionable, vile
OPPOSITE attractive

reputation noun
*The singer's **reputation** spread throughout the world.*
fame, celebrity, name, renown, eminence, standing, stature

request verb
*She has **requested** a transfer to a different job.*
ask for, appeal for, apply for, beg for, call for, entreat, implore, invite, pray for, seek

request noun
*They have ignored our **request** for help.*
appeal, plea, entreaty, call, cry

crocodile

A request for a job or membership is an **application**.
A request signed by a lot of people is a **petition**.

require verb
1 *They **require** a draw to win the championship.*
need, must have
2 *Visitors are **required** to sign the register.*
instruct, oblige, request, direct, order, command

rescue verb
1 *A helicopter was sent to **rescue** the trapped climbers.*
free, liberate, release, save, set free
To rescue someone by paying money is to **ransom** them.
2 *The divers **rescued** some items from the sunken ship.*
retrieve, recover, salvage

reserve verb
1 *The astronauts had to **reserve** fuel for the return voyage.*
keep, put aside, set aside, save, preserve, retain, hold back
2 *Have you **reserved** your seats on the train?*
book, order, secure

reserve noun
1 *The climbers kept a **reserve** of food in their base camp.*
stock, store, supply, hoard, stockpile
A reserve of money is a **fund** or **savings**.
2 *They put him down as a **reserve** for Saturday's game.*
substitute, standby, stand-in, replacement
Someone who can take the place of an actor is an **understudy**.
3 *The wildlife **reserve** has a new baby rhino.*
reservation, park, preserve, sanctuary

resign verb
*The manager of the football team was forced to **resign**.*
leave, quit, stand down, step down, give in your notice
When a monarch resigns from the throne, he or she **abdicates**.

lizard

tortoise

resist verb
1 *They were too weak to resist the sorcerer's magic.*
stand up to, defend yourself against, withstand, defy, oppose, fend off
OPPOSITE yield to, surrender to
2 *I couldn't resist having another piece of chocolate.*
avoid, hold back from, refuse
OPPOSITE give in, accept

resources plural noun
1 *The country is rich in natural resources.*
materials, raw materials, reserves
2 *The library has limited resources for buying CDs.*
funds, money, capital, assets, means, wealth

respect noun
1 *Her colleagues have the deepest respect for her.*
admiration, esteem, regard, reverence, honour
2 *Have some respect for other people's feelings.*
consideration, sympathy, thought, concern
3 *In some respects, he's a better player than I am.*
way, point, aspect, feature, characteristic, detail, particular

respect verb
1 *Everyone respects her for her courage.*
admire, esteem, revere, honour, look up to, value
OPPOSITE scorn, despise
2 *She tried to respect the wishes of her dead husband.*
obey, follow, observe, adhere to, comply with
OPPOSITE ignore

respectable adjective
1 *He came from a very respectable family.*
decent, honest, upright, honourable, worthy
2 *I finished the race in a respectable time.*
reasonable, satisfactory, acceptable, passable, adequate, fair, tolerable

respond verb
to respond to
He didn't respond to my question.
reply to, answer, react to, acknowledge

response noun
Did you get a response to your letter?
reply, answer, reaction, acknowledgement
An angry response is a *retort*.

responsible adjective
1 *Parents are legally responsible for their children.*
in charge
OPPOSITE not responsible

2 *He's a very responsible sort of person.*
reliable, sensible, trustworthy, dependable, conscientious, dutiful, honest
OPPOSITE irresponsible
3 *Looking after people's money is a responsible job.*
important, serious
4 *Who is responsible for all this mess?*
to blame, guilty (of), at fault

rest noun
1 *The actors had a short rest in the middle of the rehearsal.*
break, breather, breathing-space, pause, respite, lie-down, nap
2 *The doctor said the patient needed complete rest.*
relaxation, leisure, inactivity, ease, quiet, time off
the rest
Take a few sweets now, but leave the rest for later.
the remainder, the surplus, the others, the remains

rest verb
1 *I think we should stop and rest for a while.*
have a rest, lie down, relax, lounge, have a nap
2 *Rest the ladder against the wall.*
lean, prop, stand, place, support

restless adjective
The animals became restless during the storm.
agitated, nervous, anxious, edgy, fidgety, excitable, jumpy, jittery
OPPOSITE relaxed

result noun
1 *The water shortage is a result of a long drought.*
consequence, effect, outcome, sequel (to), upshot
The result of a game is the *score*.
The result of a trial is the *verdict*.
2 *If you multiply 9 by 12, what is the result?*
answer, product

result verb
The bruising on his leg resulted from a bad fall.
come about, develop, emerge, happen, occur, follow, ensue, take place, turn out
to result in
Severe flooding resulted in chaos on the roads.
cause, bring about, give rise to, lead to, develop into

snake

retreat verb
1 *The army retreated to a safe position.*
move back, draw back, fall back, withdraw, retire
To retreat in a shameful way is to *run away* or (informal) *turn tail*.
2 *The snail retreated into its shell.*
shrink back, recoil

retrieve verb
I had to climb the fence to retrieve our ball.
get back, bring back, fetch, recover, rescue, salvage

return verb
1 *We hope to return to Paris next summer.*
go back, revisit
2 *My husband returns on Friday.*
get back, come back, come home
3 *I returned the book to its rightful owner.*
give back, restore
4 *Faulty goods may be returned to the shop.*
send back, take back
5 *Please return the money I lent you.*
give back, repay, refund
6 *We hoped that the fever would not return.*
happen again, recur

reveal verb
1 *The spy refused to reveal his real identity.*
declare, disclose, make known, confess, admit, announce, proclaim, publish, tell
2 *She swept aside the curtain to reveal a secret door.*
uncover, unveil, expose

revenge noun
He sought revenge for the killing of his brother.
reprisal, vengeance
to take revenge on someone
He declared that he would take revenge on them all.
get even with, repay
(informal) get your own back on

review noun
1 *They are carrying out a review of after-school clubs.*
study, survey, examination, inspection
2 *We had to write reviews of our favourite books.*
report, criticism, appraisal, critique

a b c d e f g h i j k l m n o p q r s t u v w x y z

review *verb*
*The judge began to **review** the evidence.*
examine, go over, study, survey, consider, assess, appraise, evaluate, weigh up

revise *verb*
1 *We **revised** the work we did last term.*
go over, review, study
2 *The new evidence forced me to **revise** my opinion.*
change, modify, alter, reconsider, re-examine
3 *The last chapter has been **revised** by the author.*
correct, amend, edit, rewrite, update

revive *verb*
1 *The patient **revived** slowly after the operation.*
come round, come to, recover, rally, wake up
2 *A cold drink will **revive** you.*
refresh, restore, invigorate, bring back to life, revitalize

revolt *verb*
1 *The people **revolted** against the cruel king.*
rebel, riot, rise up
To revolt on a ship is to **mutiny**.
2 *They were **revolted** by the stench in the dungeon.*
disgust, repel, sicken, nauseate, offend, appal

revolting *adjective*
*What is that **revolting** smell?*
disgusting, foul, horrible, nasty, loathsome, offensive, obnoxious, repulsive, repugnant, sickening, nauseating, vile, unpleasant
OPPOSITE pleasant, attractive

revolution *noun*
1 *The **revolution** brought in a new government.*
rebellion, revolt, uprising
2 *Computers brought about a **revolution** in the way people work.*
change, transformation, shift
3 *We have to understand orbits, **rotations** and **revolutions** of planets.*
rotation, turn, circuit, cycle

revolve *verb*
*She told me her life **revolves** around ponies.*
rotate, turn
To revolve quickly is to **spin** or **whirl**.
To move round something is to **circle** or **orbit** it.

reward *noun*
*There is a **reward** for finding the missing cat.*
prize, bonus, payment, award, decoration
OPPOSITE punishment

reward *verb*
1 *The firefighters were **rewarded** for their bravery.*
honour, decorate
2 *She was generously **rewarded** for her work.*
compensate, repay

rhythm *noun*
*We tapped our feet to the **rhythm** of the music.*
beat, pulse
The speed or type of rhythm of a piece of music is the **tempo**.
The type of rhythm of a piece of poetry is its **metre**.

rich *adjective*
1 *They must be **rich** to live in a castle.*
wealthy, affluent, prosperous, well-off, well-to-do
OPPOSITE poor
2 *The palace was full of **rich** furnishings.*
expensive, costly, luxurious, sumptuous, opulent, lavish, splendid, ornate
3 *The dancer wore a dress of a **rich** red colour.*
deep, strong, vivid, intense

rickety *adjective*
*Take care—that ladder looks **rickety**.*
shaky, unsteady, unstable, wobbly, flimsy
OPPOSITE solid

riddle *noun*
*They had to solve the **riddle** to find the treasure.*
puzzle, mystery, question, conundrum, problem

ride *verb*
*My little brother is learning to **ride** a bike.*
control, handle, manage, steer
ride *noun*
*They took us for a **ride** in their new car.*
drive, run, journey, trip
(*informal*) spin

ridiculous *adjective*
1 *My little sister looked **ridiculous** in high-heeled shoes.*
silly, stupid, foolish, daft, absurd, funny, laughable
2 *That is a **ridiculous** price for a pair of trainers!*
ludicrous, senseless, nonsensical, preposterous, outrageous, absurd, unreasonable, crazy

right *adjective*
1 *Put up your hand if you got the **right** answer.*
correct, accurate, true, exact
OPPOSITE wrong
2 *She was waiting for the **right** moment to tell him.*
proper, appropriate, fitting, suitable, ideal
OPPOSITE wrong

3 *It's not **right** to steal.*
fair, honest, decent, just, honourable, lawful, moral, upright, virtuous, ethical
OPPOSITE wrong

right *noun*
1 *The cafe is on the **right** along the High Street.*
OPPOSITE left
2 *People have the **right** to walk across the common.*
freedom, liberty
3 *You don't have the **right** to tell me what to do.*
authority, power

ring *noun*
1 *The children danced around in a **ring**.*
circle, round, loop, circuit
2 *The wooden barrel had metal **rings** round it.*
band, hoop

ring *verb*
1 *The whole area was **ringed** by a high fence.*
surround, encircle, enclose, circle
2 *The doorbell **rang**.*
chime, peal, toll, jangle, tinkle, sound, buzz
3 *Ring me tomorrow evening.*
phone, call, telephone, ring up
(*informal*) give a buzz

riot *noun*
*The police moved in to stop the **riot**.*
commotion, disorder, disturbance, turmoil, uproar, uprising
riot *verb*
*The crowds were **rioting** in the streets.*
run riot, run wild, run amok, rampage, revolt, rise up, rebel

ripe *adjective*
*Some of the plums on the tree are **ripe** now.*
mature, ready to eat
To become ripe is to **ripen**.

rise *verb*
1 *The kite **rose** high into the air.*
climb, mount, fly up, ascend, soar
When a plane rises into the air, it **takes off**.
When a rocket rises into the air, it **lifts off**.
OPPOSITE descend
2 *The outer wall of the castle **rose** before us.*
tower, loom, reach up, stick up
3 *House prices **rose** again last year.*
go up, increase
OPPOSITE fall
4 *The audience **rose** and applauded wildly.*
stand up, get up
OPPOSITE sit

rise *noun*
There will be a rise in temperature over the next few days.
increase, jump
OPPOSITE fall

risk *verb*
1 *If you place a bet, you risk losing the money.*
chance, dare, gamble, venture
2 *The firefighter risked his life to save them.*
endanger, put at risk, jeopardize, hazard

risk *noun*
1 *All outdoor activities carry an element of risk.*
danger, hazard, peril
2 *The forecast says there's a risk of snow.*
chance, likelihood, possibility

risky *adjective*
Cycling on icy roads is risky.
dangerous, hazardous, perilous, unsafe
OPPOSITE safe

rival *noun*
He has no serious rival for the championship.
competitor, adversary, challenger, opponent, contender, contestant

river *noun*
A small river is a **stream** or **rivulet** or (Scottish) **burn**.
A small river which flows into a larger river is a **tributary**.
The place where a river begins is its **source**.
The place where a river goes into the sea is its **mouth**.
A wide river mouth is an **estuary** or (Scottish) **firth**.
The place where the mouth of a river splits before going into the sea is a **delta**.
A river of ice is a **glacier**.

river

roar *noun, verb*
The dragon lifted its mighty head and roared.
bellow, cry, yell, bawl, howl, thunder

rob *verb*
The thieves planned to rob several banks in the city.
steal from, break into, burgle, hold up, raid, loot, ransack, rifle

rock *verb*
1 *I rocked the baby's cradle to and fro.*
sway, swing
2 *The ship rocked in the storm.*
roll, toss, lurch, pitch, tilt, reel

rod *noun*
The framework is held together by steel rods.
bar, rail, pole, strut, shaft, stick, spoke, staff

role *noun*
1 *Who is playing the lead role in the play?*
character, part
2 *Each player has an important role in the team.*
job, task, function, position

roar

roll *verb*
1 *The wheels of the carriage began to roll.*
move round, turn, revolve, rotate, spin, twirl, whirl
2 *Roll the paper around your finger.*
curl, wind, wrap, twist, coil
To roll up a sail on a yacht is to **furl** it.
3 *Roll the pastry into a large circle.*
flatten, level out, smooth
4 *The ship rolled about in the storm.*
pitch, rock, sway, toss, wallow, lurch

romantic *adjective*
1 *The film had a very romantic ending.*
sentimental, emotional, tender (informal) soppy, mushy
2 *The life of an explorer sounds very romantic.*
exotic, glamorous, exciting

room *noun*
1 *How many rooms are there in your house?*
An old word for room is **chamber**.
2 *Is there room in the car for another suitcase?*
space, capacity

root *noun*
We need to get to the root of the problem.
origin, source, cause, basis, starting point

rope *noun*
The sailors threw a rope to the men in the water.
cable, cord, line
The ropes that support a ship's mast and sails are the **rigging**.
A rope with a loop at one end used for catching cattle is a **lasso**.

rot *verb*
The wooden fence had begun to rot.
decay, decompose, become rotten, crumble, disintegrate
If metal rots it is said to **corrode**.
If rubber rots it is said to **perish**.
If food rots it is said to **go bad** or **putrefy**.

rotten *adjective*
1 *The window frame is rotten.*
decayed, decaying, decomposed, crumbling, disintegrating
Rotten metal is **corroded** or **rusty** metal.
OPPOSITE sound
2 *The fridge smelled of rotten eggs.*
bad, mouldy, mouldering, foul, putrid, smelly
OPPOSITE fresh
3 *(informal) The weather has been rotten all week.*
bad, unpleasant, disagreeable, awful, abysmal, dreadful, nasty (informal) lousy
OPPOSITE good

rough *adjective*
1 *A rough track led to the farm.*
bumpy, uneven, irregular, rocky, stony, rugged, craggy, jagged
OPPOSITE even, smooth
2 *The sea was rough and the boat lurched from side to side.*
stormy, turbulent, heaving
If the sea is rough with small waves it is said to be **choppy**.
OPPOSITE calm
3 *The woman wore a rough woollen cloak.*
coarse, harsh, scratchy, bristly
OPPOSITE soft
4 *The prisoners had suffered rough treatment.*
harsh, severe, cruel, hard, tough, violent
OPPOSITE gentle, mild
5 *I had only a rough idea of where we were.*
approximate, vague, inexact, imprecise, hazy
OPPOSITE exact
6 *Our guide made a rough sketch of the route.*
quick, hasty, crude, basic
OPPOSITE detailed, careful

round *adjective*
Holly bushes have small round berries.
rounded, spherical
A flat round shape is **circular**.

round *noun*
Our team got through to the second round of the competition.
stage, heat, bout, contest, game

round *verb*
The motorbike rounded the corner at top speed.
go round, travel round, turn
to round something off
They rounded the evening off with some songs.
bring to an end, conclude, end, finish, complete
to round up people or **things**
The captain rounded up his players.
assemble, gather, bring together, collect, muster, rally

a b c d e f g h i j k l m n o p q r s t u v w x y z

routine noun
1 *Brushing my teeth is part of my morning* **routine**.
pattern, procedure, way, custom, habit, practice, order
2 *The ice-skaters practised their new* **routine**.
act, programme, performance, number

row noun
1 *The gardener planted the vegetables in* **rows**. (rhymes with *go*)
column, line, string, series, sequence
A row of people waiting for something is a **queue**.
A row of people walking behind each other is a **file**.
A row of soldiers standing side by side on parade is a **rank**.
2 *The class next door was making a terrible* **row**. (rhymes with *cow*)
noise, racket, din, commotion, disturbance, uproar, rumpus
3 *One of the pirates had a* **row** *with the captain*. (rhymes with *cow*)
argument, fight, quarrel, squabble, disagreement, dispute

rowdy adjective
Later in the evening, the party became **rowdy**.
noisy, unruly, wild, disorderly, boisterous, riotous
OPPOSITE quiet

rub verb
1 *Kathy* **rubbed** *her sore elbow*.
stroke, knead, massage
2 *I* **rubbed** *some suncream on my arms*.
spead, smooth, smear, apply (to)
3 *These boots are* **rubbing** *against my ankles*.
graze, scrape, chafe
4 *She* **rubbed** *the mirror until it gleamed*.
polish, wipe, shine, buff
to rub something out
Can you **rub out** *those pencil marks?*
erase, wipe out, delete, remove

rubbish noun
1 *Mike took the* **rubbish** *out to the bin*.
refuse, waste, trash, garbage, junk, litter, scrap
2 *Don't talk* **rubbish**!
nonsense, drivel, balderdash, piffle, gibberish, claptrap, gobbledegook (*informal*) rot, tripe, twaddle

rude adjective
1 *It's very* **rude** *to talk with your mouth full*.
impolite, discourteous, disrespectful, impertinent, impudent, insolent, offensive, insulting, bad-mannered, ill-bred

To be rude to someone is to **insult** or **snub** them.
To be rude about sacred things is to be **blasphemous** or **irreverent**.
OPPOSITE polite
2 *Some of the jokes in the film are rather* **rude**.
indecent, improper, offensive, coarse, crude
OPPOSITE decent, clean

ruin verb
The storm had **ruined** *the farmer's crops*.
damage, destroy, spoil, wreck, devastate, demolish, lay waste, shatter

ruin noun
When they lost the match, it was the **ruin** *of their dream*.
collapse, failure, breakdown
Financial ruin is **bankruptcy**.

ruins
Archaeologists have discovered the **ruins** *of a Roman fort*.
remains, remnants, fragments

rule noun
1 *Players must stick to the* **rules** *of the game*.
law, regulation, principle
A set of rules is a **code**.
2 *The country was formerly under French* **rule**.
control, authority, command, power, government, reign

rule verb
1 *The Romans* **ruled** *a vast empire*.
command, govern, control, direct, lead, manage, run, administer
2 *Queen Victoria continued to* **rule** *for many years*.
reign, be ruler
3 *The umpire* **ruled** *that the batsman was out*.
judge, decree, pronounce, decide, determine, find

rumour noun
There was a **rumour** *that the queen was a witch in disguise*.
gossip, hearsay, talk
(*informal*) tittle-tattle

run verb
1 *We* **ran** *as fast as our legs could carry us*.
race, sprint, dash, tear, bolt, career, speed, hurry, rush, streak, fly, whiz, zoom, scurry, scamper, scoot
To run at a gentle pace is to **jog**.
When a horse runs, it **gallops**, **canters**, or **trots**.
2 *Tears* **ran** *down the mermaid's cheeks*.

stream, flow, pour, gush, flood, cascade, spill, trickle, dribble, leak
3 *That old sewing machine still* **runs** *well*.
function, operate, work, go, perform
4 *My uncle* **runs** *a restaurant in Leeds*.
manage, be in charge of, direct, control, supervise, govern, rule
5 *The High Street* **runs** *through the city centre*.
pass, go, extend, stretch, reach
to run away or **off**
The thieves **ran off** *when they heard footsteps*.
bolt, fly, flee, escape, take off, hurry off
(*informal*) make off, clear off, scarper
to run into
1 *Guess who I* **ran into** *the other day?*
meet, come across, encounter
(*informal*) bump into
2 *A cyclist skidded and* **ran into** *a tree*.
hit, collide with

run noun
1 *She goes for a* **run** *in the park every morning*.
A fast run is a **dash**, **gallop**, **race**, or **sprint**.
A gentle run is a **jog**.
2 *We went for a* **run** *in the car*.
drive, journey, ride
3 *They've had a* **run** *of good luck recently*.
sequence, stretch, series

runny adjective
This custard is too **runny**.
watery, thin, liquid, fluid
OPPOSITE thick

rush verb
I **rushed** *home with the good news*.
hurry, hasten, race, run, dash, fly, bolt, charge, shoot, speed, sprint, tear, zoom
When cattle or other animals rush along together they **stampede**.

rush noun
1 *We've got plenty of time, so what's the* **rush**?
hurry, haste, urgency
2 *There was a sudden* **rush** *of water*.
flood, gush, spurt, stream, spate

ruthless adjective
The pirates launched a **ruthless** *attack*.
cruel, brutal, bloodthirsty, barbaric, heartless, pitiless, merciless, callous, ferocious, fierce, savage, vicious, violent
OPPOSITE merciful

runny

S s

sack *verb*
*The manager threatened to **sack** the whole team.*
dismiss, discharge
(*informal*) fire, give you the sack

sad *adjective*
*Mia felt **sad** when her best friend moved away.*
unhappy, sorrowful, miserable, depressed, downcast, downhearted, despondent, crestfallen, dismal, gloomy, glum, blue, low, dejected, forlorn, desolate, doleful, wretched, woeful, woebegone, tearful, heartbroken, broken-hearted
If you are sad because you are away from home, you are **homesick**.
OPPOSITE happy

sadden *verb*
*The news of her friend's illness **saddened** her.*
distress, upset, depress, grieve, disappoint
(*informal*) break your heart
OPPOSITE cheer up

safe *adjective*
1 *The kitten was found **safe** and well in a neighbour's garden.*
unharmed, unhurt, uninjured, undamaged, sound, intact
(*informal*) in one piece
OPPOSITE hurt, damaged
2 *They felt **safe** indoors as the storm raged outside.*
protected, guarded, defended, secure
OPPOSITE vulnerable
3 *The secret code is in **safe** hands.*
reliable, trustworthy, dependable
4 *Is the tap water **safe** to drink?*
harmless, uncontaminated, innocuous
OPPOSITE dangerous

safety *noun*
*You must wear a seat belt for your own **safety**.*
protection, security, well-being
OPPOSITE danger

sail *verb*
*We **sailed** to Norway rather than going by air.*
travel by ship
To have a holiday sailing on a ship is to **cruise**.
To begin a sea voyage is to **put to sea** or **set sail**.

same *adjective*
the same
1 *Each pirate was given **the same** ration of rum.*
equal, identical, equivalent

2 *Everyone in the choir wore **the same** outfit.*
matching, similar, alike, uniform
3 *Her feelings remain **the same**.*
unaltered, unchanged, constant
OPPOSITE different

sarcastic *adjective*
*He made a **sarcastic** remark about my hat.*
mocking, satirical, ironical, sneering, taunting

satisfaction *noun*
*He gets a lot of **satisfaction** from growing vegetables.*
happiness, pleasure, enjoyment, contentment, fulfilment, sense of achievement, pride
OPPOSITE dissatisfaction

satisfactory *adjective*
*I'm afraid this work is not **satisfactory**.*
acceptable, adequate, passable, good enough, tolerable, competent
(*informal*) all right, up to scratch
OPPOSITE unsatisfactory

satisfy *verb*
*Nothing **satisfies** him—he's always complaining.*
please, content, make you happy
To satisfy your thirst is to **quench** or **slake** it.
OPPOSITE dissatisfy

savage *adjective*
1 *The invaders launched a **savage** attack on the town.*
vicious, cruel, barbaric, brutal, bloodthirsty, pitiless, ruthless, merciless, inhuman
OPPOSITE humane
2 *A **savage** beast lived in the cave.*
untamed, wild, ferocious, fierce
OPPOSITE domesticated

save *verb*
1 *They managed to **save** most of the books from the fire.*
rescue, recover, retrieve, salvage
2 *The knight pledged to **save** the princess from the witch's curse.*
protect, defend, guard, shield, preserve
3 *She **saved** him from making a fool of himself.*
stop, prevent, deter
4 *I **saved** you a piece of cake.*
keep, reserve, set aside, hold on to
5 *If you share a car, then you can **save** petrol.*
be sparing with, conserve, use wisely

say *verb*
1 *He found it hard to **say** what he meant.*
express, communicate, put into words, convey
2 *I would like to **say** a few words before we start.*
utter, speak, recite, read

a b c d e f g h i j k l m n o p q r s t u v w x y z

saying noun
'Many hands make light work' is a common **saying**.
expression, phrase, motto, proverb, catchphrase
An overused saying is a **cliché**.

scan verb
1 The lookout **scanned** the horizon, hoping to see land.
search, study, survey, examine, scrutinize, stare at, eye
2 I **scanned** through some magazines in the waiting room.
skim, glance at, flick through

scandal noun
1 The waste of food after the party was a **scandal**.
disgrace, embarrassment, shame, outrage
2 Some newspapers like to publish the latest **scandal**.
gossip, rumours, dirt

scar noun
The warrior had a **scar** across his forehead.
mark, blemish, wound

scar verb
The injuries he received **scarred** him for life.
mark, disfigure, deface

scarce adjective
Water is very **scarce** in the desert.
hard to find, in short supply, lacking, sparse, scanty, rare, uncommon
(informal) thin on the ground
OPPOSITE plentiful

scarcely adverb
She was so tired that she could **scarcely** walk.
barely, hardly, only just

scare noun
The explosion gave them a nasty **scare**.
fright, shock, alarm

scare verb
My brother tried to **scare** us by making ghost noises.
frighten, terrify, petrify, alarm, startle, panic
OPPOSITE reassure

scared adjective
When she heard the footsteps, Lily was too **scared** to move.
frightened, terrified, petrified, horrified, alarmed, fearful, panicky

scary adjective (informal)
I had to close my eyes at the **scary** bits in the film.
frightening, terrifying, horrifying, alarming, nightmarish, fearsome, chilling, spine-chilling, hair-raising, bloodcurdling, chilling, eerie, sinister

scatter verb
1 She **scattered** the seeds on the ground.
spread, sprinkle, sow, strew, throw about, shower
OPPOSITE collect
2 The animals **scattered** when the children ran towards them.
break up, separate, disperse, disband
OPPOSITE gather

scene noun
1 The police arrived quickly at the **scene** of the crime.
location, position, site, place, situation, spot
2 They were rehearsing a **scene** from the play.
episode, part, section, act
3 I gazed out of the window at the moonlit **scene**.
landscape, scenery, view, sight, outlook, prospect, spectacle, setting, backdrop
4 He didn't want to create a **scene** in the restaurant.
fuss, commotion, disturbance, quarrel, row

scenery noun
We admired the **scenery** from the top of the hill.
landscape, outlook, prospect, scene, view, panorama

scent noun
Rowena loves the **scent** of roses.
smell, fragrance, perfume, aroma

schedule noun
The athletes had a rigorous training **schedule**.
programme, timetable, plan, calendar, diary
A schedule of topics to be discussed at a meeting is an **agenda**.
A schedule of places to be visited on a journey is an **itinerary**.

scheme noun
They worked out a **scheme** to raise some money.
plan, proposal, project, procedure, method, system

scheme verb
The smugglers were **scheming** against each other.
plot, conspire, intrigue

scold verb
He **scolded** the paper boy for being late.
reprimand, reproach, tell off
(informal) tick off

scorch verb
The dragon's breath **scorched** the wizard's beard.
burn, singe, sear, blacken, char

scorch

score noun
We added up each other's **scores**.
marks, points, total
The final score is the **result**.

score verb
1 How many goals did you **score**?
win, get, make, gain, earn
2 Some lines were **scored** into the bark of the tree.
cut, gouge, mark, scrape, scratch

scorn noun
She dismissed my suggestion with **scorn**.
contempt, derision, disrespect, mockery, ridicule
OPPOSITE admiration

scowl verb
The witch **scowled** under her floppy black hat.
frown, glower

scramble verb
1 The smugglers escaped by **scrambling** over the rocks.
clamber, climb, crawl, scrabble
2 The children **scrambled** to get the best seats.
push, jostle, struggle, fight, scuffle

scrap noun
1 They fed the **scraps** of food to the birds.
bit, piece, fragment, morsel, crumb, speck, particle
2 He took a pile of **scrap** to the tip.
rubbish, waste, junk, refuse, litter
Scraps of cloth are **rags** or **shreds**.
3 (informal) There was a **scrap** between the two gangs.
fight, brawl, scuffle, tussle, squabble

scrap verb
The author **scrapped** the last paragraph.
discard, throw away, abandon, cancel, drop, give up
(informal) dump

scrape verb
1 She **scraped** her knee when she fell over.
graze, scratch, scuff
2 I tried to **scrape** the mud off my trainers.
rub, scour, scrub, clean

scratch verb
1 Someone **scratched** the side of the car.
mark, score, scrape, gouge, graze
2 The cat tried to **scratch** her.
claw

scratch noun
Who made this **scratch** on the side of the car?
gash, groove, line, mark, scrape

scream noun, verb
*A woman ran out of the house
screaming. We heard a woman's
scream in the distance.*
shriek, screech, shout, yell, cry, bawl,
howl, wail, squeal, yelp

scribble verb
*He **scribbled** his phone number on a
scrap of paper.*
scrawl, jot down, dash off, write
To scribble a rough drawing,
especially when you are bored, is to
doodle.

scrub verb
*She **scrubbed** the floor clean.*
rub, brush, clean, wash, scour

scruffy adjective
*Magnus wore an old jumper and
scruffy jeans.*
untidy, messy, ragged, tatty,
tattered, worn-out, shabby
OPPOSITE smart

WORD WEB

sea noun
The very large seas of the world
are called **oceans**.
An area of sea partly enclosed by
land is a **bay** or **gulf**.
A wide inlet of the sea is a **sound**.
A wide inlet where a river joins the
sea is an **estuary**, or in Scotland
a **firth**.
A narrow stretch of water linking
two seas is a **strait**.
The bottom of the sea is the
seabed.
The land near the sea is the **coast**
or the **seashore**.
Creatures that live in the sea are
marine creatures.

THINGS YOU MIGHT SEE ON THE SEA
breaker, iceberg, sea spray, surf,
swell, waves; boat, cruise ship,
ocean liner, yacht

SOME CREATURES THAT
LIVE IN THE SEA
dolphin, eel, fish, killer whale,
octopus, porpoise, seahorse,
seal, sea lion, shark, squid,
stingray, turtle, whale

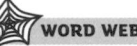
starfish

sculpture noun
*The temple was full of marble
sculptures.*
carving, figure, statue

WORD WEB

*We explored the **seashore**, looking
for shells and fossils.*
seaside, beach, shore, coast

THINGS YOU MIGHT SEE ON THE
SEASHORE
cave, cliff, coral reef, driftwood,
dunes, lighthouse, mudflats,
pebbles, rock pool, rocks, sand,
seashell, seaweed, shingle

CREATURES THAT LIVE ON THE
SEASHORE
barnacle, clam, cockle, coral,
crab, cuttlefish, jellyfish, limpet,
mussel, oyster, prawn, razor shell,
sea anemone, sea bird, seagull,
sea urchin, shrimp, sponge,
starfish, whelk

*If it's sunny tomorrow, we might
go to the **seaside**.*
beach, sands, seashore

THINGS YOU MIGHT SEE AT THE
SEASIDE
beach huts, funfair, harbour, ice-
cream van, jetty, pier, promenade

A town where you go to have fun
by the sea is a **seaside resort**.

THINGS YOU MIGHT TAKE TO THE
SEASIDE
beach ball, bucket and spade,
deckchair, fishing net, snorkel,
sunglasses, sunhat, sunshade,
suncream, surfboard, surfsuit,
swimming costume, towel,
windbreak

THINGS YOU MIGHT DO AT THE
SEASIDE
ball games, beachcombing,
building sandcastles, collecting
shells, fishing, paddling, scuba
diving, snorkelling, sunbathing,
surfing, swimming, water-skiing,
windsurfing

WRITING TIPS

You can use these
words to describe the
sea.

TO DESCRIBE A CALM SEA
calm, crystal clear, glassy,
sparkling, tranquil, unruffled

TO DESCRIBE A ROUGH SEA
choppy, raging, rough,
stormy, tempestuous,
turbulent, wild
WAVES ON THE SEA MIGHT
billow, break, crash, heave,
pound, roll, surge, swell,
tumble, wash

crab

lighthouse

seaweed

shell

fish

seal *verb*
*The entrance to the burial chamber had been **sealed**.*
close, fasten, shut, lock, secure
To seal a leak is to **plug** it or **stop** it.

search *verb*
1 *He was **searching** for the book he had lost.*
hunt, look, seek
To search for gold or some other mineral is to **prospect**.
2 *The police **searched** the house but didn't find anything.*
explore, scour, ransack, rummage through, comb
3 *Security staff **searched** all the passengers.*
check, inspect, examine, scrutinize
(*informal*) frisk

search *noun*
*After a long **search**, she found her keys.*
hunt, look, check
A long journey in search of something is a **quest**.

season *noun*
*The hotels are full during the holiday **season**.*
period, time

seat *noun*
*We found two empty **seats** at the back of the cinema.*
chair, place
A long seat for more than one person is a **bench**.
A long wooden seat in a church is a **pew**.
A seat on a bicycle or horse is a **saddle**.
A special seat for a king or queen is a **throne**.

second *adjective*
*Would anyone like a **second** helping of pudding?*
another, additional, extra, further

second *noun*
1 *The magic potion only takes a **second** to work.*
instant, moment, flash
(*informal*) jiffy, tick
2 *Inga was **second** in the cross-country race.*
runner-up

second *verb*
*We need someone to **second** the proposal.*
back, support

secret *adjective*
1 *The spy managed to get hold of a **secret** document.*
confidential, classified, restricted
(*informal*) hush-hush
2 *The detectives are part of a **secret** operation.*
undercover, covert
3 *The things I write in my diary are **secret**.*
private, confidential, personal, intimate
4 *The cook showed us a **secret** passageway into the castle.*
hidden, concealed, disguised

secretive *adjective*
*Why is she being so **secretive** about her past?*
uncommunicative, tight-lipped, reticent, reserved, mysterious, quiet
(*informal*) cagey
OPPOSITE communicative, open

section *noun*
*The website has a special **section** aimed at children.*
part, division, sector, portion, segment, bit, fragment
A section of a book is a **chapter**.
A section from a piece of classical music is a **movement**.
A section taken from a book or a long piece of music is a **passage**.
A section of a journey is a **stage**.

seat

secure *adjective*
1 *The ladder was not very **secure**.*
steady, firm, solid, fixed, fast, immovable
2 *She is still trying to find a **secure** job.*
permanent, regular, steady
3 *They bolted the doors to make the castle **secure**.*
safe, guarded, protected, defended

see *verb*
1 *If you look closely, you might **see** a dragonfly.*
catch sight of, spot, notice, observe, make out, distinguish, note, perceive, recognize, sight, spy
To see something briefly is to **glimpse** it.
To see an accident or some unusual event is to **witness** it.
2 *Did you **see** the news yesterday?*
watch, look at, view
3 *You may **see** me in my office after work.*
go to, report to
4 *I didn't expect to **see** you here!*
meet, run into, encounter
(*informal*) bump into
5 *Will we have time to **see** them on the way home?*
visit, call on, drop in on
6 *I **see** what you mean.*
understand, appreciate, comprehend, follow, grasp, realize, take in
7 *I find it hard to **see** him in the role of Peter Pan.*
imagine, picture, visualize
8 *Please **see** that the windows are shut.*
make sure, make certain, ensure
9 *I'll **see** what I can do.*
think about, consider, ponder, reflect on, weigh up
10 *I'll **see** you to the door.*
conduct, escort, accompany, guide, lead, take

seem *verb*
*Everything **seems** to be all right. She is far more friendly than she **seems**.*
appear, look, give the impression of being

seize *verb*
1 *The climber stretched out to **seize** the rope.*
grab, catch, snatch, take hold of, grasp, grip, clutch
2 *The police **seized** the robbers as they left the bank.*
arrest, capture
(*informal*) collar, nab
To seize someone's property as a punishment is to **confiscate** it.
To seize someone's power or position is to **usurp** it.
To seize an aircraft or vehicle during a journey is to **hijack** it.

seldom *adverb*
*It **seldom** rains in the desert.*
rarely, infrequently
OPPOSITE often

select *verb*
*They had to **select** a new captain.*
choose, pick, decide on, opt for, settle on, appoint, elect

selection *noun*
*The shop has a wide **selection** of rollerskates.*
choice, range, variety, assortment

selfish *adjective*
*He's so **selfish** that he kept all the chocolate to himself.*
greedy, mean, miserly, grasping, self-centred, thoughtless
OPPOSITE unselfish, generous

sell *verb*
*The corner shop **sells** newspapers and sweets.*
deal in, trade in, stock, retail
Uncomplimentary synonyms are **peddle** and **hawk**.
OPPOSITE buy

send *verb*
1 *I **sent** each of my friends a postcard.*
post, mail, dispatch

2 They plan to **send** a rocket to Mars.
launch, propel, direct, fire, shoot
to send for someone
I think we should **send for** a doctor.
call, summon, fetch
to send something out
The device was **sending out** weird noises.
emit, issue, give off, discharge

sensational adjective
1 The newspaper printed a **sensational** account of the murder.
shocking, horrifying, startling, lurid
2 (informal) Did you hear the **sensational** result of yesterday's match?
amazing, extraordinary, remarkable, fantastic, spectacular, stupendous

sense noun
1 A baby learns about the world through its **senses**.
Your five senses are **hearing**, **sight**, **smell**, **taste**, and **touch**.
2 A drummer needs to have a good **sense** of rhythm.
awareness, consciousness, perception, feeling (for)
3 If you had any **sense** you'd stay at home.
common sense, intelligence, wisdom, wit, brains
4 The **sense** of the word is not clear.
meaning, significance, import
to make sense of something
They couldn't **make sense of** the garbled message.
understand, make out, interpret, follow

sense verb
1 He **sensed** that she didn't like him.
be aware, realize, perceive, feel, guess, notice, suspect
2 The device **senses** any change of temperature.
detect, respond to

sensible adjective
1 It would be **sensible** to wait until the weather improves.
wise, intelligent, shrewd, rational, reasonable, careful, prudent, logical, sane, sound
OPPOSITE stupid
2 You will need **sensible** shoes for the hiking trip.
comfortable, practical
OPPOSITE impractical

sensitive adjective
1 She has **sensitive** skin which gets sunburnt.
delicate, tender, fine, soft
2 Take care what you say—he's very **sensitive**.
easily offended, easily upset, touchy
3 She's very **sensitive** towards other people.
tactful, considerate, thoughtful, sympathetic, understanding

sentimental adjective
1 He gets **sentimental** looking at old photographs.
emotional, nostalgic, tearful
2 I hate **sentimental** messages on birthday cards.
romantic, tender
(informal) soppy, mushy

separate adjective
1 The zoo kept the male lions **separate** from the cubs.
apart, separated, distinct, independent
OPPOSITE together
2 They slept in **separate** rooms.
different, detached, unattached
OPPOSITE attached, joined

separate verb
1 The sheepdog **separated** the sheep from the lambs.
cut off, divide, fence off, isolate, keep apart, remove, segregate, set apart, take away
To separate something which is connected to something else is to **detach** or **disconnect** it.
To separate things which are tangled together is to **disentangle** them.
OPPOSITE combine, mix
2 They walked along together until their paths **separated**.
split, branch, fork
OPPOSITE merge
3 Her friend's parents have **separated**.
split up, break up, part company
To end a marriage legally is to **divorce**.

series noun
1 We had to answer a **series** of questions in our exam.
succession, sequence, string, set, chain, train
2 Are you watching the new **series** on TV?
serial

serious adjective
1 His **serious** expression told them something was wrong.
solemn, sombre, unsmiling, grave, grim
OPPOSITE cheerful
2 She is writing a **serious** book about global warming.
learned, intellectual, scholarly
(informal) heavy
OPPOSITE light
3 Are you **serious** about wanting to learn to ski?
sincere, genuine, in earnest
4 This hospital ward is for people with **serious** injuries.
severe, acute, critical, bad, terrible, appalling, dreadful, major, grave
OPPOSITE minor, trivial

servant noun
This part of the house was where the **servants** lived.
attendant, retainer, helper, domestic, manservant, maid
The chief manservant in a private house is a **butler**.
The servant of a medieval knight was a **page** or **squire**.

serve verb
1 The shopkeeper was busy **serving** customers.
help, assist, aid
2 When everyone had sat down they **served** the first course.
give out, dish up, pass round, distribute

service noun
1 The genie bowed and said he was glad to be of **service**.
help, assistance, aid, use, usefulness, benefit
2 Their marriage **service** was held in the local church.
ceremony, ritual, rite
A service in church is a meeting for **worship**.
3 Mum says her car needs a **service**.
a check-over, maintenance, servicing

service verb
The garage **serviced** her car.
maintain, check, repair, mend, overhaul

set verb
1 The removal men **set** the piano on the floor.
place, put, stand, position
2 I helped Dad to **set** the table.
arrange, lay, set out
3 Have they **set** a date for the wedding yet?
appoint, specify, name, decide, determine, choose, fix, establish, settle
4 The jelly will **set** quicker in the fridge.
become firm, solidify, harden, stiffen
5 The sun was just beginning to **set**.
do down, sink
to set off
1 The knights **set off** on their quest.
depart, get going, leave, set out, start out
2 The burnt toast **set off** the smoke alarm.
activate, start, trigger
to set something out
The information is clearly **set out** on the page.
lay out, arrange, display, present
to set something up
They're trying to **set up** an after-school club.
establish, create, start, begin, introduce, organize

a b c d e f g h i j k l m n o p q r **s** t u v w x y z

A B C D E F G H I J K L M N O P Q R S T U V W X Y Z

set *noun*
1 *There is a* **set** *of measuring spoons in the drawer.*
collection, batch, kit
2 *Our class painted the* **set** *for the play.*
scenery, setting

setting *noun*
The house stood in a rural **setting**.
surroundings, location, place, position, site, background

settle *verb*
1 *The brothers tried to* **settle** *their differences.*
resolve, sort out, deal with, end
2 *The cat had just* **settled** *on the sofa.*
sit down, relax, rest
3 *A robin* **settled** *on a nearby branch.*
land, alight
4 *The family is planning to* **settle** *in Canada.*
emigrate (to), move (to), set up home
5 *You can see lots of fish when the mud* **settles**.
sink to the bottom, clear, subside
6 *We'll* **settle** *the hotel bill in the morning.*
pay, clear, square
to settle on
Have you **settled on** *a date for the wedding?*
agree on, decide on, choose, name, fix

severe *adjective*
1 *The jailer was very* **severe** *with the prisoners.*
harsh, strict, hard, stern
OPPOSITE lenient
2 *The traffic warden gave him a* **severe** *look.*
unkind, unsympathetic, disapproving, grim
OPPOSITE kind
3 *Ruby has a* **severe** *case of chickenpox.*
bad, serious, acute, grave
OPPOSITE mild
4 *The Arctic has a* **severe** *climate.*
extreme, tough, harsh, hostile
A severe frost is a **sharp** *frost.*
Severe cold is **intense** *cold.*
A severe storm is a **violent** *storm.*

shabby *adjective*
The witch disguised herself in a **shabby** *cloak.*
ragged, scruffy, tattered, worn, worn-out, threadbare, frayed, tatty, seedy, dingy
OPPOSITE smart

shade *noun*
1 *They sat in the* **shade** *of a chestnut tree.*
shadow
2 *The porch had a* **shade** *to keep out the sun.*
screen, blind, canopy
A type of umbrella used as a sun shade is a **parasol**.
3 *The bathroom walls are a pale* **shade** *of blue.*
hue, tinge, tint, tone, colour

shade *verb*
Wearing a cap will **shade** *your eyes from the sun.*
shield, screen, protect, hide, mask

shadow *noun*
Her face was deep in **shadow**.
shade, darkness, gloom

shadow *verb*
The detective was **shadowing** *the suspect.*
follow, pursue, tail, stalk, track, trail

shady *adjective*
1 *They found a* **shady** *spot under a tree.*
shaded, shadowy, sheltered, dark, sunless
OPPOSITE sunny
2 *He took part in some* **shady** *business deals.*
dishonest, disreputable, suspicious, dubious, suspect, untrustworthy, (*informal*) fishy, dodgy
OPPOSITE honest

shaggy *adjective*
Llamas have long **shaggy** *coats.*
bushy, woolly, fleecy, hairy, thick

shake *verb*
1 *The hurricane made the whole house* **shake**.
quake, shudder, shiver, rock, sway, totter, wobble, quiver, vibrate, rattle
2 *He was so upset that his voice was* **shaking**.
tremble, quaver
3 *The giant* **shook** *his fist and growled angrily.*
wave, brandish, flourish, wag, waggle, joggle
4 *They were* **shaken** *by the terrible news.*
shock, startle, distress, upset, disturb, alarm, frighten

shaky *adjective*
1 *Be careful— the table is rather* **shaky**.
unsteady, wobbly, insecure, rickety, flimsy, weak
2 *He was so nervous that his hands were* **shaky**.
shaking, trembling, quivering
3 *He spoke in a* **shaky** *voice.*
quavering, faltering, nervous, tremulous
OPPOSITE steady

shame *noun*
The guilty man hung his head in **shame**.
disgrace, dishonour, humiliation, embarrassment, guilt
a shame
It's **a shame** *that you can't stay for longer.*
a pity, unfortunate

shape *verb*
The potter **shaped** *the clay into a tall vase.*
form, mould, fashion
To shape something in a mould is to **cast** *it.*

share *noun*
Each of the pirates got a **share** *of rum.*
ration, allowance, portion, quota, helping, division, part
(*informal*) cut

share *verb*
The robbers **shared** *the loot between them.*
divide, split, distribute, allot, allocate, deal out, ration out

shatter *verb*
1 *The ball* **shattered** *a window.*
break, smash, destroy, wreck
2 *The windscreen* **shattered** *when a stone hit it.*
break, splinter, disintegrate

shed *noun*
They kept their lawnmower in the garden **shed**.
hut, shack, outhouse

shed *verb*
A lorry **shed** *its load on the motorway.*
drop, let fall, spill, scatter

sheer *adjective*
1 *The story he told was* **sheer** *nonsense.*
complete, total, utter, absolute, pure
2 *Don't try to climb that* **sheer** *cliff.*
vertical, perpendicular

sheet *noun*
1 *She started her diary on a fresh* **sheet** *of paper.*
page, leaf, piece
2 *The pond was covered with a thin* **sheet** *of ice.*
layer, film, covering, surface
3 *The glazier came to fit a new* **sheet** *of glass.*
panel, pane, plate

shaggy

shelf *noun*
*She put the books back on the **shelf**.*
ledge, rack
A shelf above a fireplace is a **mantelpiece**.

shelter *noun*
*They reached **shelter** just before the storm broke.*
cover, protection, safety, refuge, sanctuary

shelter *verb*
1 *The hedge **shelters** the garden from the wind.*
protect, screen, shield, guard, defend, safeguard
2 *We **sheltered** from the rain under the trees.*
hide, take refuge

shield *noun*
*The trees act as an effective wind **shield**.*
screen, barrier, defence, guard, protection
The part of a helmet that shields your face is the **visor**.

shield *verb*
*The mother bear **shielded** her cubs from danger.*
protect, defend, guard, safeguard, keep safe, shelter

shift *verb*
1 *I need some help to **shift** the furniture.*
move, rearrange, reposition
2 *It was hard work **shifting** the mud off the tyres.*
remove, dislodge, budge

shine *verb*
1 *A light **shone** from an upstairs window.*
beam, glow, blaze, glare, gleam
2 *He **shines** his shoes every morning.*
polish, rub, brush

shiny *adjective*
*She polished the mirror until it was **shiny**.*
shining, bright, gleaming, glistening, glossy, polished, burnished, lustrous
OPPOSITE dull

ship *noun*
Ships that travel long distances at sea are **ocean-going** or **seagoing** ships.
People who work on ships at sea are **nautical** or **seafaring** people.

shiver *verb*
*Ali waited outside, **shivering** with cold.*
tremble, quiver, shake, shudder, quake

shock *noun*
1 *The news of his death came as a great **shock**.*
blow, surprise, fright, upset
2 *People felt the **shock** of the explosion miles away.*
bang, impact, jolt
3 *The driver involved in the accident was in a state of **shock**.*
distress, trauma

shock *verb*
*The whole town was **shocked** by the news.*
horrify, appal, startle, alarm, stun, stagger, shake, astonish, astound, surprise, dismay, upset
A formal synonym is **traumatize**.

shoot *verb*
1 *Robin Hood **shot** an arrow into the air.*
fire, discharge, launch, aim
2 *It is now illegal to hunt and **shoot** tigers.*
fire at, hit, open fire on, gun down
3 *They watched the racing cars **shoot** past.*
race, speed, dash, rush, streak, hurtle, fly, whiz, zoom
4 *Part of the film was **shot** in Canada.*
film, photograph

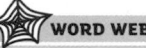

WORD WEB

shop *noun*
VARIOUS TYPES OF SHOP
boutique, corner shop, department store, hypermarket, market, shopping arcade, shopping centre, shopping mall, supermarket

SPECIALIST SHOPS
antique shop, baker, bookshop, butcher, cheesemonger, chemist, clothes shop, confectioner, delicatessen, DIY or do-it-yourself shop, fishmonger, florist, garden centre, greengrocer, grocer, haberdasher, health-food shop, ironmonger, jeweller, music shop, newsagent, off-licence, pharmacy, post office, shoe shop or shoemaker, stationer, toyshop, watchmaker

PEOPLE WHO WORK IN SHOPS
cashier, salesman or saleswoman, shop assistant, shopkeeper or storekeeper

short *adjective*
1 *They live a **short** distance from the shops.*
little, small
OPPOSITE long
2 *It was a very **short** visit.*
brief, quick, fleeting, hasty, temporary
OPPOSITE long
3 *The troll was very **short** and fat.*
small, tiny, little, squat, dumpy, diminutive, petite
OPPOSITE tall

4 *The supply of water was getting **short**.*
low, meagre, scant, limited, inadequate, insufficient
OPPOSITE plentiful
5 *There is no need to be **short** with me!*
abrupt, rude, sharp, curt, impolite, snappy
OPPOSITE patient, polite

shortage *noun*
*The **shortage** of water is worrying.*
scarcity, deficiency, lack, want, dearth
A shortage of water is a **drought**.
A shortage of food is a **famine**.

shorten *verb*
*She had to **shorten** the essay because it was too long.*
cut down, reduce, cut, trim, abbreviate, abridge, condense, compress, curtail
OPPOSITE lengthen

shot *noun*
1 *I heard a noise like the **shot** of a pistol.*
bang, blast, crack
2 *The striker had an easy **shot** at the goal.*
hit, strike, kick
3 *The photographer took some unusual **shots**.*
photograph, picture, snap, snapshot
4 *(informal) We each had a **shot** at solving the riddle.*
try, go, attempt
(informal) bash

shout *verb*
*The ogre was **shouting** and stamping with rage.*
call, cry out, bawl, yell, bellow, roar, howl, yelp, scream, screech, shriek
OPPOSITE whisper

shove *verb*
*A man ran past and **shoved** me to the side.*
push, thrust, force, barge, elbow, jostle, shoulder

shopping

show verb
1 *My uncle **showed** us his coin collection.*
present, reveal, display, exhibit
2 *The photo **shows** my grandparents on holiday.*
portray, picture, depict, illustrate, represent
3 *The dance tutor **showed** them what to do.*
explain to, make clear to, instruct, teach, tell
4 *The evidence **shows** that he was right.*
prove, demonstrate
5 *A nurse **showed** them into the waiting room.*
direct, guide, conduct, escort, usher
6 *The signpost **shows** the way.*
indicate, point out
7 *His vest **showed** through his shirt.*
be seen, be visible, appear
to show off
*Walter is always **showing off**.*
boast, brag, crow, gloat, swagger
(*informal*) blow your own trumpet
A person who shows off is a **show-off**.

show noun
1 *There is a **show** of artwork at the end of term.*
display, exhibition, presentation
2 *There's a good **show** on at the theatre.*
performance, production, entertainment

shriek noun, verb
*'Quick!' **shrieked** Alice. 'Open the door!'*
cry, scream, screech, shout, howl, bawl, squeal, wail, yell

shrill adjective
*They heard the **shrill** sound of a whistle.*
high, high-pitched, piercing, sharp, screechy
OPPOSITE low, soft

shrink verb
*My jeans have **shrunk** in the wash.*
become smaller, contract   shrivel
OPPOSITE expand

shrivel verb
*The plants **shrivelled** in the heat.*
wilt, wither, droop, dry up, wrinkle, shrink

shudder verb
*They **shuddered** with fear when they heard the creature roar.*
tremble, quake, quiver, shake, shiver

shuffle verb
1 *She **shuffled** along the corridor in her slippers.*
shamble, scuffle, hobble, scrape
2 *Did you remember to **shuffle** the cards?*
mix, mix up, jumble

shut verb
*Please **shut** the door behind you.*
close, fasten, seal, secure, lock, bolt, latch
To shut a door with a bang is to **slam** it.
to shut someone up
*He had been **shut up** in a dungeon for five years.*
imprison, confine, detain
shut up
(*informal*) *I wish those people behind us would **shut up**!*
be quiet, be silent, stop talking, hold your tongue

shy adjective
*The little girl was too **shy** to say anything.*
bashful, timid, coy, reserved, hesitant, self-conscious, inhibited, modest
OPPOSITE bold

sick adjective
1 *Katie is off school because she's **sick**.*
ill, unwell, poorly, sickly, ailing, indisposed, off colour, peaky
OPPOSITE healthy
2 *The sea was rough and the cabin boy felt **sick**.*
nauseous, queasy
to be sick of
*I'm **sick of** this miserable weather!*
be fed up with, be tired of, have had enough of

side noun
1 *A cube has six **sides**.*
face, surface
2 *The path runs along the **side** of the field.*
edge, border, boundary, fringe, perimeter
The side of a page is the **margin**.
The side of a road is the **verge**.
3 *I could see both **sides** of the argument.*
point of view, view, angle, aspect
4 *The football club has a strong **side** this year.*
team

sight noun
1 *Weasels have sharp **sight** and excellent hearing.*
eyesight, vision
2 *The woods in autumn are a lovely **sight**.*
spectacle, display, show, scene

3 *By the third day, the ship was in **sight** of land.*
view, range
4 *We went to London to see the **sights**.*
attraction, landmark

sign noun
1 *A **sign** pointed to the exit.*
notice, placard, poster, signpost
The sign belonging to a particular business or organization is a **logo**.
The sign on a particular brand of goods is a **trademark**.
2 *The witch gave no **sign** that she was angry.*
indication, clue, hint, warning
3 *The guard gave us a **sign** to pass through the gates.*
signal, gesture, cue, reminder

sign verb
1 *Please **sign** your name on the form.*
write, inscribe
2 *The club **signed** a new player last week.*
take on, engage, recruit, enrol

signal noun
*The spy waited for the **signal** that all was clear.*
sign, indication, prompt, cue
A signal that tells you not to do something is a **warning**.

signal verb
*The pilot **signalled** that he was going to descend.*
give a sign or signal, gesture, indicate, motion

significant adjective
1 *The book describes the **significant** events of last century.*
important, major, noteworthy, influential
2 *Global warming is having a **significant** effect on wildlife.*
noticeable, considerable, perceptible, striking

silence noun
*There was **silence** while we sat the exam.*
quiet, quietness, hush, stillness, calm, peace
OPPOSITE noise

silence verb
*He **silenced** the audience by ringing a gong.*
deaden, muffle, quieten, suppress
To silence someone by putting something in or over their mouth is to **gag** them.

silent adjective
1 *At night, the desert was cold and **silent**.*
quiet, noiseless, soundless, still, hushed
Something you can't hear is **inaudible**.
A common simile is **as silent as the grave**.
OPPOSITE noisy

2 Morris kept **silent** throughout the meeting.
quiet, speechless, mute
(*informal*) mum
To be too shy to speak is to be **tongue-tied**.
OPPOSITE talkative

silly *adjective*
It was **silly** of me to lock myself out of the house.
foolish, stupid, idiotic, senseless, thoughtless, brainless, unwise, unintelligent, half-witted, harebrained, scatterbrained
(*informal*) daft
OPPOSITE sensible

similar *adjective*
The puppies are **similar** in appearance.
alike, identical, indistinguishable, matching, the same
OPPOSITE dissimilar, different
similar to
The new book is **similar to** the previous one.
alike, close to, comparable to
OPPOSITE unlike, different from

similarity *noun*
It's easy to see the **similarity** between the twins.
likeness, resemblance
OPPOSITE difference

simple *adjective*
1 Can you answer this **simple** question?
easy, elementary, straightforward
OPPOSITE difficult
2 The help file is written in **simple** language.
clear, plain, uncomplicated, understandable, intelligible
OPPOSITE complicated
3 The girl wore a **simple** cotton dress.
plain, undecorated
OPPOSITE elaborate
4 He enjoys **simple** pleasures like walking and gardening.
ordinary, unsophisticated, humble, modest, homely
OPPOSITE sophisticated

sincere *adjective*
Please accept my **sincere** apologies.
genuine, honest, true, truthful, real, earnest, wholehearted, frank
OPPOSITE insincere

single *adjective*
1 We saw a **single** house high on the moors.
solitary, isolated
When only a single example of something exists, it is **unique**.
2 Miss Dempster was quite content to stay **single**.
unmarried
An unmarried man is a **bachelor**.
An unmarried woman is a **spinster**.

sinister *adjective*
He looked up with a **sinister** smile on his face.
menacing, threatening, malevolent, evil, disturbing, unsettling, eerie
(*informal*) creepy

sink *verb*
1 The ship hit the rocks and **sank**.
go down, become submerged, founder, capsize
To let water into a ship to sink it deliberately is to **scuttle** it.
2 The sun began to **sink** below the horizon.
drop, fall, descend, subside, dip
When the sun sinks to the horizon it **sets**.

sit *verb*
1 Rachel **sat** on the sofa reading a magazine.
have a seat, settle down, rest, perch
To sit on your heels is to **squat**.
To sit to have your portrait painted is to **pose**.
2 My brother is **sitting** his driving test next week.
take
(*informal*) go in for

site *noun*
This is the **site** of an ancient burial ground.
location, place, position, situation, setting, plot

situation *noun*
1 The house is in a pleasant **situation**.
location, locality, place, position, setting, site, spot
2 I found myself in an awkward **situation**.
position, circumstances, condition, state of affairs
A bad situation is a **plight** or **predicament**.

size *noun*
1 What **size** is the garden?
dimensions, proportions, area, extent
2 They were amazed by the sheer **size** of the pyramids.
scale, magnitude, immensity

sketch *noun*
1 She drew a quick **sketch** of her cat.
drawing, picture, outline
A sketch you do while you think of other things is a **doodle**.
2 The actors performed a comic **sketch**.
scene, turn, routine

sketch *verb*
He **sketched** a rough design for the poster
draw, draft, outline, rough out

skid *verb*
The postman **skidded** on the icy pavement.
slide, slip

skilful *adjective*
Dickens was a **skilful** writer.
expert, skilled, accomplished, able, capable, talented, brilliant, clever, masterly, deft
If you are skilful at a lot of things, you are **versatile**.
OPPOSITE incompetent

skill *noun*
It takes a lot of **skill** to build a boat.
expertise, ability, aptitude, capability, competence, accomplishment, talent, proficiency, deftness

skim *verb*
The stone **skimmed** across the surface of the pond.
glide, slide, skid, slip
to skim through
Luke **skimmed through** the newspaper.
scan, look through, skip through, flick through

skin *noun*
The cave people were dressed in animal **skins**.
coat, fur, hide, pelt
The type of skin you have on your face is your **complexion**.
Skin on fruit or vegetables is **peel** or **rind**.
Skin that might form on top of a liquid is a **coating**, **film**, or **membrane**.

skinny *adjective*
A **skinny** girl in bare feet answered the door.
thin, lean, bony, gaunt, lanky, scrawny, scraggy
OPPOSITE plump

skip *verb*
1 The children **skipped** along the pavement.
hop, jump, leap, bound, caper, dance, prance
2 I **skipped** the boring bits in the book.
pass over, miss out, ignore, omit, leave out

slant *verb*
Her handwriting **slants** backwards.
lean, slope, tilt, incline, be at an angle

slant *noun*
The floor of the caravan was at a **slant**.
slope, angle, tilt, incline, gradient
A slant on a damaged ship is a **list**.
A slanting line joining opposite corners of a square, etc., is a **diagonal**.
A surface slanting up to a higher level is a **ramp**.

slap *verb*
*He **slapped** his hand against his thigh and laughed.*
smack, strike, spank, hit, clout
(*informal*) whack

slaughter *noun*
*The battle ended in terrible **slaughter**.*
bloodshed, killing, massacre, butchery

sleek *adjective*
*Otters have **sleek** coats.*
smooth, glossy, shiny, silky, soft, velvety
OPPOSITE coarse

sleep *verb*
*The baby is **sleeping** in the next room.*
be asleep, take a nap, doze
(*informal*) snooze
To go to sleep is to **drop off** or **nod off**.

sleep *noun*
*Mr Khan had a short **sleep** after lunch.*
nap, rest, doze, catnap
(*informal*) snooze, forty winks, shut-eye
An afternoon sleep is a **siesta**.
The long sleep some animals have through the winter is **hibernation**.

sleepy *adjective*
*The giant was usually **sleepy** after dinner.*
drowsy, tired, weary, heavy-eyed, lethargic, ready to sleep
(*informal*) dopey
OPPOSITE wide awake

slender *adjective*
1 *The ballerina had a **slender** figure.*
slim, lean, slight, graceful, trim, svelte
OPPOSITE fat
2 *The spider dangled on a **slender** thread.*
thin, fine, fragile, delicate
OPPOSITE thick
3 *They only had a **slender** chance of winning.*
poor, slight, slim, faint, negligible, remote
OPPOSITE good
4 *The team won by a **slender** margin.*
narrow, small, slim
OPPOSITE wide

slice *verb*
To slice meat is to **carve** it.

slide *verb*
*I like **sliding** down the chute in the playground.*
glide, skid, slip, slither

slight *adjective*
1 *There's a **slight** problem with the computer.*
minor, unimportant, insignificant,

slither

negligible, superficial, trifling, trivial
OPPOSITE important
2 *The fairy was a **slight** creature, barely two inches tall.*
delicate, fragile, frail, slender, slim, small, spare, thin, tiny
OPPOSITE stout

slim *adjective*
1 *A tall, **slim** figure appeared out of the fog.*
graceful, lean, slender, spare, thin, trim
OPPOSITE fat
2 *Their chances of winning are **slim**.*
faint, poor, slight, slender, negligible, remote
OPPOSITE good
3 *They won by a **slim** margin.*
narrow, small, slender
OPPOSITE wide

slimy *adjective*
*The floor of the tunnel was covered with **slimy** mud.*
slippery, slithery, sticky, oozy
(*informal*) gooey, icky

sling *verb*
*Robin Hood **slung** his quiver over his shoulder.*
throw, cast, fling, hurl, pitch, heave, toss, lob
(*informal*) chuck

slink *verb*
*The spy **slunk** away without being seen.*
slip, sneak, steal, creep, edge, sidle

slip *verb*
1 *The paper boy **slipped** on the ice.*
skid, slither, skate
2 *The lifeboat **slipped** into the water.*
glide, slide
3 *Marion **slipped** out while everyone was talking.*
sneak, steal, slink, tiptoe, creep, edge, sidle

slippery *adjective*
*Take care—the floor is **slippery**.*
slithery, slippy, smooth, glassy
A surface slippery with frost is **icy**.
A surface slippery with grease is **greasy** or **oily**.
A common simile is **as slippery as an eel**.

slit *noun*
*The archers shot arrows through the **slits** in the castle wall.*
opening, chink, gap, slot, split, tear, cut

slither *verb*
*The rattlesnake **slithered** through the long grass.*
slide, slip, glide, slink, snake

slope *verb*
*The beach **slopes** gently down to the sea.*
fall or rise, incline, bank, shelve

slope *noun*
1 *It was hard work pushing my bike up the **slope**.*
hill, rise, bank, ramp
An upward slope is an **ascent**.
A downward slope is a **descent**.
2 *Rain runs down the roof because of the **slope**.*
incline, slant, tilt, gradient

sloppy *adjective*
1 *For breakfast, there was a bowl of steaming, **sloppy** porridge.*
runny, slushy, watery, liquid, wet
(*informal*) gloopy
2 *His handwriting is very **sloppy**.*
untidy, messy, careless, slovenly, slapdash, slipshod

slot *noun*
*To use the phone, put a coin into the **slot**.*
slit, chink, hole, opening

slouch *verb*
*Enid sat at her desk, **slouched** over the computer.*
hunch, stoop, slump, droop, flop

slow *adjective*
1 *Tortoises move at a **slow** but steady pace.*
unhurried, leisurely, gradual, plodding, dawdling, sluggish
2 *They took the train to London, followed by a **slow** bus journey.*
lengthy, prolonged, drawn-out, tedious
3 *The prisoner was **slow** to answer.*
hesitant, reluctant, tardy

slow *verb*
to slow down
***Slow down**—you're driving too fast!*
go slower, brake, reduce speed
OPPOSITE accelerate

sly *adjective*
The chess player knew several **sly** moves.
crafty, cunning, artful, clever, wily, tricky, sneaky, devious, furtive, secretive, stealthy, underhand
A common simile is **as sly as a fox**.
OPPOSITE straightforward

smack *verb*
He **smacked** the other player on the head by accident.
slap, strike, hit, cuff
(*informal*) whack

small *adjective*
1 Moles have incredibly **small** eyes and ears.
little, tiny, minute, compact, miniature, microscopic, minuscule, mini, baby
(*informal*) teeny, titchy, dinky
(*Scottish*) wee
OPPOSITE big, large
2 A **small** elf was standing on a toadstool.
little, short, petite, slight, dainty, diminutive
(*informal*) pint-sized
OPPOSITE big, tall, large
3 For breakfast there was stale bread with a **small** scraping of butter.
meagre, inadequate, insufficient, paltry, scanty, stingy, skimpy
(*informal*) measly
OPPOSITE large, generous, ample
4 The writers made some **small** changes to the script.
minor, unimportant, insignificant, trivial, trifling, negligible
OPPOSITE major, substantial

smart *adjective*
1 Everyone looked **smart** at the wedding.
elegant, well-dressed, well-groomed, stylish, spruce, fashionable, chic, neat, trim
To make yourself smart is to **smarten up**.
OPPOSITE scruffy
2 They booked a table in a very **smart** restaurant.
fashionable, high-class, exclusive, fancy
(*informal*) posh
3 The detective made a very **smart** move.
clever, ingenious, intelligent, shrewd, crafty
OPPOSITE stupid
4 The cyclists set off at a **smart** pace.
fast, quick, rapid, speedy, swift, brisk
OPPOSITE slow

smart *verb*
The smoke from the barbecue made our eyes **smart**.
hurt, sting, prick, prickle, tingle

smash *verb*
A vase fell off the table and **smashed** to pieces on the floor.
break, crush, shatter, crack
When wood smashes it **splinters**.
To smash something completely is to **demolish** or **destroy** or **wreck** it.
to smash into
A lorry had **smashed into** the side of a bus.
crash into, collide with, bang into, bump into

smear *verb*
The chef **smeared** butter over the cooking dish.
spread, wipe, plaster, rub, dab, smudge, daub

smell *noun*
1 The air was filled with the **smell** of roses.
scent, aroma, perfume, fragrance
2 The **smell** of mouldy cheese was unbearable.
odour, stench, stink, reek, whiff
(*informal*) pong, niff

smell *verb*
1 I could **smell** something baking in the oven.
scent, sniff
(*informal*) get a whiff of
2 After walking all day, my feet were beginning to **smell**.
stink, reek
(*informal*) pong

✎ WRITING TIPS

You can use these words to describe **how something smells**.

TO DESCRIBE SOMETHING WHICH SMELLS GOOD
fragrant, aromatic, perfumed, scented, sweet-smelling *The garden was planted with **sweet-smelling** herbs.*

TO DESCRIBE SOMETHING WHICH SMELLS BAD
smelly, stinking, evil-smelling, foul-smelling, musty, odorous, reeking, rotten, fetid, foul
(*informal*) stinky, pongy, whiffy
*The witch stirred the **evil-smelling** brew.*

---

smile *verb*
The stranger **smiled** and introduced himself.
grin, beam
To smile in a silly way is to **simper**.
To smile in a self-satisfied way is to **smirk**.
To smile in an insulting way is to **sneer**.

smoke *noun*
Puffs of green **smoke** came from the dragon's nostrils.
fumes, gas, steam, vapour
The smoke given out by a car is **exhaust**.
A mixture of smoke and fog is **smog**.

smooth *adjective*
1 This part of the road is **smooth** and good for cycling.
flat, even, level
OPPOSITE uneven
2 In the early morning, the lake was perfectly **smooth**.
calm, still, unruffled, undisturbed, glassy
OPPOSITE rough
3 Otters have **smooth** and shiny coats.
silky, sleek, velvety
OPPOSITE coarse
4 The journey by train is very quick and **smooth**.
comfortable, steady
OPPOSITE bumpy
5 Stir the cake mixture until it is **smooth**.
creamy, flowing, runny
OPPOSITE lumpy

smooth *verb*
Charlotte stood up and **smoothed** her dress.
flatten, level, even out
To smooth cloth you can **iron** or **press** it.
To smooth wood you can **plane** or **sand** it.

smother *verb*
1 Pythons **smother** their prey to death.
suffocate, choke, stifle
2 The pudding was **smothered** with cream.
cover, coat

smudge *noun*
There were **smudges** of ink all over the page.
smear, blot, streak, stain, mark

smudge *verb*
Don't **smudge** the icing on the cake!
smear, blur, streak

snap *verb*
1 A twig **snapped** under one of my boots.
break, crack
2 The dog **snapped** at the postman's ankles.
bite, nip
3 Mr Baker was in a bad mood and **snapped** at everyone.
snarl, bark

snatch *verb*
The thief **snatched** the jewels and ran off.
grab, seize, grasp, pluck, wrench away, wrest away

a b c d e f g h i j k l m n o p q r s t u v w x y z

sneak verb
*I managed to **sneak** in without anyone seeing.*
slip, steal, creep, slink, tiptoe, sidle, skulk

sneaky adjective
*That was a really **sneaky** trick.*
sly, underhand, cunning, crafty, devious, furtive, untrustworthy
OPPOSITE honest

sneer verb
to sneer at
*He **sneered at** my first attempts to ice-skate.*
make fun of, mock, ridicule, scoff at, jeer at, deride

snobbish adjective
*She's far too **snobbish** to mix with us.*
arrogant, pompous, superior, haughty
(*informal*) stuck-up, snooty, toffee-nosed
OPPOSITE humble

snoop verb
*They caught a man **snooping** round the office.*
sneak, pry, poke, rummage, spy

snub verb
*She **snubbed** the neighbours by not inviting them to the party.*
insult, offend, be rude to, brush off
(*informal*) put down

snug adjective
*Lucy was tucked up **snug** in bed.*
cosy, comfortable, warm, relaxed
(*informal*) comfy
A common simile is **as snug as a bug in a rug**.
OPPOSITE uncomfortable

soak verb
1 *Days of rain had **soaked** the cricket pitch.*
wet thoroughly, drench, saturate
2 *Leave the beans to **soak** in water overnight.*
steep, immerse, submerge

soaking adjective
*My socks are absolutely **soaking**!*
wet through, drenched, dripping, wringing, saturated, sodden, sopping, soggy
Ground that has been soaked by rain is **waterlogged**.

soar verb
*The seagull spread its wings and **soared** into the air.*
climb, rise, ascend, fly, wing

sob verb
*Tina threw herself on the bed, **sobbing** loudly.*
cry, weep, bawl, blubber, shed tears, snivel

soft adjective
1 *The kittens can only eat **soft** food.*
pulpy, spongy, squashy
(*informal*) squidgy
OPPOSITE hard, dry
2 *My head sank into the **soft** pillow.*
supple, pliable, springy, yielding, flexible
OPPOSITE firm, rigid
3 *The rabbit's fur felt very **soft**.*
smooth, silky, sleek, velvety, downy, feathery
OPPOSITE coarse
4 *A **soft** breeze stirred the leaves.*
gentle, light, mild, delicate
OPPOSITE rough, strong
5 *The smugglers spoke in **soft** whispers.*
quiet, low, faint
OPPOSITE loud
6 *It was hard to see clearly in the **soft** light.*
subdued, muted, pale, dim, low
OPPOSITE bright, dazzling
7 *You are being too **soft** with that puppy.*
lenient, easygoing, tolerant, indulgent
OPPOSITE strict, tough

soft

soggy adjective
1 *The pitch was **soggy** after all the rain.*
wet, drenched, soaked, saturated, sodden, waterlogged
2 *The bread in my sandwich had become **soggy**.*
moist, soft, pulpy, squelchy
(*informal*) squidgy

solemn adjective
1 *The butler always had a **solemn** expression on his face.*
serious, grave, sober, sombre, unsmiling, glum
OPPOSITE cheerful
2 *The coronation was a **solemn** occasion.*
formal, dignified, grand, stately, majestic, pompous
OPPOSITE frivolous

solid adjective
1 *A cricket ball is **solid**.*
OPPOSITE hollow
2 *The water turned into **solid** ice.*
hard, firm, dense, compact, rigid, unyielding
A common simile is **as solid as a rock**.
OPPOSITE soft
3 *The bars of the climbing frame are quite **solid**.*
firm, robust, sound, strong, stable, sturdy
OPPOSITE weak, unstable

4 *The crown was made of **solid** gold.*
pure, genuine
5 *He got **solid** support from his team-mates.*
firm, reliable, dependable, united, unanimous
OPPOSITE weak, divided

solve verb
*The professor was trying to **solve** an ancient riddle.*
interpret, explain, answer, work out, find the solution to, unravel, decipher

soothing adjective
*They played **soothing** music.*
calming, relaxing, restful, peaceful, gentle, pleasant

sore adjective
*My feet are still **sore** from the walk.*
painful, aching, hurting, smarting, tender, sensitive, inflamed, raw, red

sorrow noun
1 *He felt great **sorrow** at leaving his children behind.*
sadness, unhappiness, misery, woe, grief, anguish, despair, distress, heartache, heartbreak, melancholy, gloom, depression, desolation, wretchedness
Sorrow because of someone's death is **mourning**.
Sorrow at being away from home is **homesickness**.
OPPOSITE happiness
2 *She expressed her **sorrow** for what she had done.*
regret, remorse, repentance, apologies

sorry adjective
1 *Scott said he was **sorry** for losing my football.*
apologetic, regretful, remorseful, ashamed (of), repentant
OPPOSITE unapologetic
2 *We felt **sorry** for the villagers who had lost their homes.*
sympathetic, pitying, understanding, compassionate
OPPOSITE unsympathetic

sort noun
*What **sort** of music do you like?*
kind, type, variety, form, nature, style, genre, category, order, class
A sort of animal is a **breed** or **species**.

sort verb
*The books are **sorted** according to their subjects.*
arrange, organize, class, group, categorize, classify, divide
OPPOSITE mix

to sort something out
*They managed to **sort out** their disagreement.*
settle, resolve, clear up, cope with, deal with

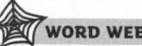
WORD WEB

sound noun
*We heard the **sound** of footsteps approaching.*
noise, tone
A loud, harsh sound is a **din** or **racket**.

SOUNDS MADE BY PEOPLE
bawl, bellow, boo, boom, cackle, chortle, clap, croak, cry, gasp, groan, gurgle, hiccup, hiss, howl, hum, moan, murmur, puff, scream, shout, shriek, sigh, sing, sniff, snore, snort, sob, splutter, stammer, stutter, wail, wheeze, whimper, whine, whisper, whistle, whoop, yell, yodel

SOUNDS MADE BY THINGS
bang, blare, beep, bleep, boom, buzz, chime, chink, chug, clang, clank, clash, clatter, click, clink, clunk, crack, crackle, crash, creak, crunch, ding, drone, drum, fizz, grate, gurgle, jangle, jingle, patter, peal, ping, plop, pop, purr, putter, rattle, ring, rumble, rustle, scrunch, sizzle, slam, snap, squeak, squelch, swish, throb, thud, thunder, tick, ting, tinkle, twang, whirr, whoosh, whistle, whiz, zoom

WRITING TIPS

You can use these words to describe a **sound**.

TO DESCRIBE A *PLEASANT SOUND*
dulcet, harmonious, mellifluous, melodious, sweet *I heard the **sweet** strains of a harp playing.*

TO DESCRIBE AN *UNPLEASANT SOUND*
grating, harsh, jarring, piercing, rasping, raucous, shrill, thin, tinny
*A **raucous** fight was going out outside.*

sound adjective
1 *The walls of the fortress seemed **sound**.*
firm, solid, stable, safe, secure, intact, undamaged
OPPOSITE unsound, unstable
2 *She gave us some **sound** advice.*
good, sensible, wise, reasonable, trustworthy
OPPOSITE unwise
3 *The travellers returned safe and **sound**.*
strong, well, fit, healthy
OPPOSITE weak, unfit

sour adjective
1 *These apples are a bit **sour**.*
tart, bitter, sharp, acid
OPPOSITE sweet
2 *The guard opened the door with a **sour** look on his face.*
cross, bad-tempered, grumpy, disagreeable, peevish

space noun
1 *There wasn't much **space** to move about.*
room, freedom, scope
2 *He peered through the tiny **space** in the curtains.*
gap, hole, opening, break
A space without any air in it is a **vacuum**.
A space of time is an **interval** or **period**.
3 *The astronauts will spend ten days in **space**.*
outer space

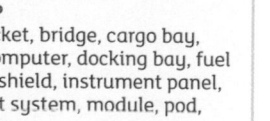
WORD WEB

space noun
Everything that exists in space is the **universe** or **cosmos**.
Distances in space stretch to **infinity**.
Travel to other planets is **interplanetary** travel.
Travel to other stars is **interstellar** travel.
Travel to other galaxies is **intergalactic** travel.
A traveller in space is an **astronaut**.
In stories, beings from other planets are **aliens** or **extraterrestrials**.

NATURAL OBJECTS FOUND IN SPACE
asteroid, black hole, comet, constellation, galaxy, meteor, meteorite, Milky Way, moon, nebula, nova, planet, red dwarf, red giant, shooting star, solar system, star, sun, supernova

WORDS TO DO WITH TRAVEL IN SPACE
blast-off, countdown, launch, mission, orbit, re-entry, rocket, satellite, spacecraft,

spare verb
1 *Can you **spare** any money for a good cause?*
afford, part with, give, provide, do without
2 *Gretel begged the witch to **spare** her brother.*
show mercy to, pardon, reprieve, let off, release, free

spare adjective
1 *The **spare** tyre is in the boot.*
additional, extra, reserve, standby
2 *Have you any **spare** change?*
leftover, surplus, odd, remaining, unused, unwanted

spark noun
*There was a **spark** of light as he struck the match.*
flash, gleam, glint, flicker, sparkle

satellite

spaceship, space shuttle, space station, spacesuit, spacewalk

A robot spacecraft is a **probe**.
A vehicle which can travel on the surface of a planet is a **buggy** or **rover**.

THINGS YOU MIGHT FIND ON A SPACESHIP
booster rocket, bridge, cargo bay, capsule, computer, docking bay, fuel tank, heat shield, instrument panel, life-support system, module, pod, solar panel

THINGS A SPACESHIP MIGHT DO
blast off, burn up, drift off-course, land, lift off, malfunction, orbit, re-enter the earth's atmosphere, splash down, touch down

shuttle

meteor

a
b
c
d
e
f
g
h
i
j
k
m
p
q
r
s
t
u

sparkle verb
The diamond ring **sparkled** in the sunlight.
glitter, glisten, glint, twinkle

speak verb
The robot opened its mouth and began to **speak**.
communicate, express yourself, say something, talk, utter

special adjective
1 Are you keeping the champagne for a **special** occasion?
important, significant, memorable, noteworthy, momentous, exceptional, extraordinary, out-of-the-ordinary
OPPOSITE ordinary
2 My granny has her own **special** way of making porridge.
unique, individual, characteristic, distinctive, different, peculiar
3 You need a **special** camera to film underwater.
particular, specific, proper, specialized

speck noun
She brushed a **speck** of dust from her shoes.
bit, dot, spot, fleck, grain, particle, trace, mark

spectacle noun
The fireworks for Diwali will be a great **spectacle**.
display, show, performance, exhibition, extravaganza

spectacular adjective
1 The acrobats gave a **spectacular** performance.
dramatic, exciting, impressive, thrilling, magnificent, sensational
2 The tulips are **spectacular** at this time of year.
eye-catching, showy, splendid, breathtaking, colourful

spectator noun
The spectators at a show are the **audience**.
The spectators at a football match are the **crowd**.
A person watching TV is a **viewer**.
If you see an accident or a crime you are an **eyewitness** or **witness**.
If you just happen to see something going on you are a **bystander** or **onlooker**.

speech noun
1 His **speech** was slurred and he looked tired.
speaking, talking, articulation, pronunciation
2 She was invited to give an after-dinner **speech**.
talk, address, lecture, oration
A talk in church is a **sermon**.
Speech between actors in a play is **dialogue**.

A speech delivered by a single actor is a **monologue**.

speed noun
1 Could a spaceship travel faster than the **speed** of light?
pace, rate
A formal synonym is **velocity**.
The speed of a piece of music is its **tempo**.
To increase speed is to **accelerate**.
To reduce speed is to **decelerate**.
2 They finished clearing up with amazing **speed**.
quickness, rapidity, swiftness
OPPOSITE slowness

speed verb
The skiers **sped** down the mountain.
race, rush, dash, dart, hurry, hurtle, career, fly, streak, tear, shoot, zoom, zip

spell noun
1 A magic **spell** had turned the knight into a toad.
charm, incantation
Making magic spells is **sorcery**, **witchcraft**, or **wizardry**.
2 We're hoping for a **spell** of dry weather.
period, interval, time, stretch, run

spend verb
1 Have you **spent** all your pocket money already?
pay out, use up, get through, exhaust
(informal) fork out, shell out
To spend money unwisely is to **fritter** or **squander** it.
2 She **spends** a lot of time working in the garden.
pass, occupy, fill
To spend time doing something useless is to **waste** it.

spill verb
1 Katie **spilled** her juice all over the table.
overturn, upset, tip over
2 Milk **spilled** onto the floor.
overflow, pour, slop, slosh, splash
3 The treasure chest fell open, **spilling** gold coins everywhere.
shed, tip, scatter, drop

spin verb
The rear wheels of the jeep **spun** round.
turn, rotate, revolve, whirl, twirl

spine noun
1 Your **spine** runs down the middle of your back.
backbone, spinal column
The bones in your spine are your **vertebrae**.
2 A porcupine has sharp **spines**.
needle, quill, point, spike, bristle

spirit noun
1 He carried a charm to keep evil **spirits** away.
ghost, ghoul, phantom, spectre, demon
2 The orchestra played the piece with great **spirit**.
energy, liveliness, enthusiasm, vigour, zest, zeal, fire
3 There is a real **spirit** of cooperation in the team.
feeling, mood, atmosphere

spiteful adjective
He made some really **spiteful** comments.
malicious, malevolent, ill-natured, hostile, venomous, vicious, nasty, unkind
OPPOSITE kind

splash verb
1 The bus **splashed** water over us.
shower, spray, spatter, sprinkle, squirt, slop, slosh, spill
(informal) splosh
2 The children **splashed** about in the playing pool.
paddle, wade, dabble, bathe

splendid adjective
1 There was a **splendid** banquet on the eve of the wedding.
magnificent, lavish, luxurious, impressive, imposing, grand, great, dazzling, glorious, gorgeous, elegant, rich, stately, majestic
2 That's a **splendid** idea!
excellent, first-class, admirable, superb, wonderful, marvellous

splinter verb
The glass **splintered** into pieces.
shatter, smash, fracture, chip, crack, split

split verb
1 He **split** the log in two.
chop, cut up, crack open, splinter
2 He **split** his trousers climbing over the fence.
rip open, tear
3 The pirates **split** the gold between them.
distribute, share out
4 The path **splits** here.
branch, fork, separate
to split up
The search party decided to **split up**.
break up, part, separate, divide
If a married couple splits up, they may **divorce**.

split noun
He had a **split** in the seat of his trousers.
rip, tear, slash, slit

spoil *verb*
1 *Bad weather **spoiled** the holiday.*
ruin, wreck, upset, mess up, mar, scupper
2 *The grafitti **spoils** the look of the new building.*
damage, harm, hurt, disfigure, deface
3 *His parents have **spoiled** him since he was a baby.*
indulge, pamper, make a fuss of

sport *noun*
see panel below

spot *noun*
1 *There were several **spots** of paint on the carpet.*
mark, stain, blot, blotch, smudge, dot, fleck, speck
Small brown spots on your skin are **freckles**.
A small dark spot on your skin is **a mole**.
A mark you have had on your skin since you were born is a **birthmark**.
A small round swelling on your skin is a **pimple**.
A lot of spots is a **rash**.
2 *We felt a few **spots** of rain.*
drop, blob, bead
3 *Here's a nice **spot** for a picnic.*
place, position, location, site, situation, locality

spot *verb*
1 *Nina **spotted** her friend in the crowd.*
see, sight, spy, catch sight of, notice, observe, make out, recognize, detect
2 *The tyres were **spotted** with mud.*
mark, stain, blot, spatter, fleck, speckle, mottle

sprawl *verb*
1 *We **sprawled** on the lawn.*
flop, lean back, lie, loll, lounge, recline, relax, slouch, slump, spread out, stretch out
2 *New houses have started to **sprawl** across the countryside.*
spread, stretch

spray *verb*
*A passing bus **sprayed** mud over us.*
shower, spatter, splash, sprinkle, scatter

spread *verb*
1 *I **spread** the map on the table.*
lay out, open out, fan out, unfold, unfurl, unroll
2 *The milk spilled and **spread** all over the floor.*
expand, extend, stretch, broaden, enlarge, swell
3 *The school website is a good way of **spreading** news.*
communicate, circulate, distribute, transmit, make known, pass on, pass round
4 *She **spread** jam on a piece of toast.*
smear
5 *He **spread** the seeds evenly over the ground.*
scatter, strew

spring *verb*
*Suddenly a rabbit **sprang** over the fence.*
jump, leap, bound, hop, vault
When a cat springs at a mouse, it **pounces**.
to spring up
*Weeds **spring up** quickly in damp weather.*
appear, develop, emerge, shoot up, sprout

sprinkle *verb*
*She **sprinkled** flakes of chocolate over the cake.*
scatter, shower, spray, dust, powder

spurt *verb*
*Water **spurted** from the hole in the pipe.*
gush, spout, shoot out, stream, squirt, jet

WORD WEB

sport *noun*
*I enjoy playing **sport** at the weekend.*
exercise, games

American football

TEAM SPORTS INCLUDE
American football, baseball, basketball, bowls, cricket, football or soccer, hockey, lacrosse, netball, polo, rounders, rugby, volleyball, water polo

INDIVIDUAL SPORTS INCLUDE
angling, archery, athletics, badminton, billiards, boxing, bowling, canoeing, climbing, croquet, cross-country running, cycling, darts, diving, fencing, golf, gymnastics, horse racing, jogging, judo, karate, motor racing, mountaineering, orienteering, pool, rowing, sailing, show jumping, snooker, squash, surfing, swimming, table tennis, tae kwon do, tennis, waterskiing, weightlifting, windsurfing, wrestling

WINTER SPORTS INCLUDE
bobsleigh, curling, ice hockey, ice skating, skiing, snowboarding, speed skating, tobogganing

PEOPLE WHO TAKE PART IN SPORT
athlete, coach, competitor, player, sportsman or sportswoman

PLACES WHERE SPORT TAKES PLACE
arena, field, ground, park, pitch, pool, ring, rink, run, slope, stadium, track

boxing

SOME ATHLETIC EVENTS
cross-country, decathlon, discus, heptathlon, high jump, hurdles, javelin, long jump, marathon, pentathlon, pole vault, relay race, running, shot, sprinting, steeplechase, triathlon, triple jump

snowboarding

tennis

baseball

basketball

spy noun
The **spy** was on a top-secret mission.
agent, secret agent
The work of a spy is **spying** or **espionage**.
A spy who works for two rival countries or organizations is a **double agent**.
An informal name for a spy who works undercover is a **mole**.

THINGS A SPY MIGHT DO
adopt a disguise or cover, assume a secret identity, carry out a secret mission, crack or decipher a code, gather intelligence, keep someone under surveillance, report to headquarters, uncover an enemy agent, work undercover

THINGS A SPY MIGHT USE OR CARRY
coded message, false passport, hidden camera or microphone, listening device, motion detector, night-vision goggles, password, torch, walkie talkie

A SPY'S MISSION MIGHT BE
clandestine, covert, secret, stealthy, surreptitious, top-secret, undercover, informal cloak-and-dagger, hush-hush

squabble verb
The twins are always **squabbling** in the car.
argue, fight, quarrel, bicker, wrangle

squash verb
1 My sandwich got **squashed** at the bottom of my schoolbag.
crush, flatten, press, compress, mangle
To squash food deliberately is to **mash** or **pulp** or **purée** it.
2 We **squashed** our sleeping bags into our rucksacks.
squeeze, stuff, force, cram, pack, ram

squat verb
We **squatted** on the ground to watch the puppet show.
crouch, sit

squat adjective
The alien had a **squat** little body on three short legs.
dumpy, stocky, plump, podgy, portly

squeeze verb
1 She **squeezed** the water out of the sponge.
press, wring, compress, crush

2 Five of us **squeezed** into the back of the car.
squash, cram, crowd, stuff, push, ram, shove, wedge
3 Holly **squeezed** her sister affectionately.
clasp, hug, embrace, cuddle
To squeeze something between your thumb and finger is to **pinch** it.

squeeze

squirt verb
My little brother made the tap water **squirt** all over me.
spurt, spray, gush, spout, shoot, jet

stab verb
1 He **stabbed** the sausage with his fork.
spear, jab, pierce, impale
2 She **stabbed** a finger at him.
stick, thrust, push, jab

stab noun
Jake felt a sudden **stab** of pain in his chest.
pang, prick, sting

stable adjective
1 The ladder doesn't look very **stable**.
steady, secure, firm, fixed, solid, balanced
OPPOSITE wobbly, shaky

2 He's been in a **stable** relationship for years.
steady, established, lasting, durable, strong
OPPOSITE temporary

stack noun
There were **stacks** of books all over the floor.
pile, heap, mound, tower
Another word for a stack of hay is a **rick** or **hayrick**.

stack verb
Stack the papers on the desk.
gather, assemble, collect, heap up, pile up

staff noun
There was a party at the hospital for all the **staff**.
workers, employees, personnel, workforce, team
The staff on a ship or aircraft are the **crew**.

stage noun
1 They went up on the **stage** to collect their prizes.
platform
2 The final **stage** of the journey was made by coach.
leg, step, phase, portion, stretch
3 At this **stage** in her life, she wants to try something new.
period, point, time, juncture

stagger verb
1 The wounded knight **staggered** and fell.
reel, stumble, lurch, totter, sway, falter, waver, wobble
2 We were **staggered** at the size of the pyramid.
amaze, astonish, astound, surprise, flabbergast, stupefy, startle, stun

stain noun
There were several coffee **stains** on the tablecloth.
mark, spot, blot, blotch, blemish, smear, smudge

stain verb
Her trainers were **stained** with mud.
discolour, mark, soil, dirty, blacken, tarnish

stale adjective
The bread had gone **stale**.
dry, hard, old, mouldy, musty
OPPOSITE fresh

stalk verb
1 The cheetah **stalked** its prey.
hunt, pursue, track, trail, follow, shadow, tail
2 Miss Foster turned and **stalked** out of the room.
stride, strut

stammer verb
Angela went red and started **stammering**.
stutter, falter, stumble, splutter

stamp verb
1 He **stamped** on the flower by mistake.
step, tread, trample
2 The librarian **stamped** my library book.
mark, print
To stamp a postmark on a letter is to **frank** it.
To stamp a mark on cattle with a hot iron is to **brand** them.

stand verb
1 The newborn pup was too weak to **stand**.
get to your feet, get up, rise
2 They **stood** the ladder against the wall.
put, place, set, position, station, erect
3 The offer still **stands**.
remain valid, be unchanged, continue
4 I can't **stand** the smell any longer.
bear, abide, endure, put up with, tolerate, suffer
to stand for something
1 She won't **stand for** any nonsense.
put up with, tolerate, accept, allow, permit
2 What do these initials **stand for**?
mean, indicate, signify, represent
to stand out
Among all the photographs, this one really **stood out**.
catch your eye, stick out, be prominent
to stand up for someone
He always **stands up for** his friends.
support, defend, side with, speak up for
(informal) stick up for

standard noun
1 Their writing is of a very high **standard**.
grade, level, quality
2 He considered the book good by any **standard**.
guidelines, ideal, measurement, model
3 The soldiers carried their **standard** proudly.
colours, flag, banner

standard adjective
The teacher showed us the **standard** way to write a letter.
normal, usual, common, conventional, typical, customary, accepted, approved, established, orthodox, regular, traditional
OPPOSITE abnormal

star noun
1 Astronomers study the **stars**.
A word meaning 'to do with stars' is **stellar**.
A night sky in which you can see stars is **starry** or **star-studded**.
A mark in the shape of a star in a piece of writing is an **asterisk**.
2 Several Hollywood **stars** attended the premiere of the film.
celebrity, idol, superstar

stare verb
The guard **stared** straight ahead, not blinking.
gaze, gape, peer, look
to stare at someone
The wolf was **staring** hungrily **at** us.
gaze at, gawp at, goggle at, eye, ogle, scrutinize, watch
To stare angrily at someone is to **glare** at them.

start verb
1 The new course will **start** in the autumn.
begin, commence
(informal) get going, get cracking, kick off
OPPOSITE finish, end
2 We are planning to **start** a book club.
create, set up, establish, found, institute, originate, introduce, initiate, open, launch
OPPOSITE close
3 The horses **started** when the gun went off.
jump, flinch, jerk, twitch, recoil, wince

start noun
1 Try not to miss the **start** of the film.
beginning, opening, introduction, commencement
OPPOSITE end, close, finish
2 She has been with the theatre company right from the **start**.
beginning, outset, creation, inception, birth, dawn, launch
3 The explosion gave us all a nasty **start**.
jump, jolt, shock, surprise

startle verb
The sudden noise **startled** the deer.
alarm, panic, frighten, scare, make you start, make you jump, surprise, take you by surprise

starving adjective (informal)
What's for dinner? I'm **starving**!
hungry, famished, ravenous
To be slightly hungry is to be **peckish**.

state noun
1 The roof of the cottage is in a bad **state**.
condition, shape
The state of a person or animal is their **fitness** or **health**.

2 He gets into a terrible **state** before an exam.
panic, fluster
(informal) flap
3 The queen is the head of **state**.
country, nation

state verb
Her passport **states** that she is an Australian citizen.
declare, announce, report, say, proclaim, pronounce, communicate

stay verb
1 Can you **stay** there while I park the car?
wait, hang about, remain
OPPOSITE leave, depart
2 We tried to **stay** warm by stamping our feet.
keep, carry on being, continue
3 Do you plan to **stay** in America for long?
live, reside, dwell, lodge, settle, stop

stay noun
Our friends came for a short **stay**.
visit, stopover, holiday, break

steady adjective
1 You need a **steady** hand to be a surgeon.
stable, balanced, settled, secure, fixed, firm, fast, solid
A common simile is **as steady as a rock**.
OPPOSITE unsteady, shaky
2 The plants need a **steady** supply of water.
continuous, uninterrupted, non-stop, consistent
OPPOSITE intermittent
3 The runners kept up a **steady** pace.
regular, constant, even, smooth, rhythmic, unvarying
OPPOSITE irregular

steal verb
1 The thieves **stole** several valuable paintings.
rob, thieve, take, lift, make off with
(informal) pinch, nick, swipe, snaffle
2 The children **stole** quietly upstairs.
creep, sneak, tiptoe, slip, slink

steep *adjective*
The bus inched its way slowly up the **steep** *slope.*
abrupt, sudden, sharp
A cliff or drop which is straight up and down is **sheer** or **vertical**.
OPPOSITE gradual, gentle

steer *verb*
She **steered** *the car into the parking space.*
direct, guide
To steer a vehicle is to **drive** it.
To steer a boat is to **navigate** or **pilot** it.

step *noun*
1 *The baby took her first* **steps** *yesterday.*
footstep, pace, stride
2 *Be careful not to trip on the* **step**.
doorstep, stair
A set of steps going from one floor of a building to another is a **staircase**.
A folding set of steps is a **stepladder**.
The steps of a ladder are the **rungs**.
3 *The first* **step** *in making a cake is to weigh the ingredients.*
stage, phase, action

step *verb*
Don't **step** *in the puddle!*
put your foot, tread, walk, stamp, trample
to step something up
They have **stepped up** *security at the airport.*
increase, intensify, strengthen, boost

stern *adjective*
The coach gave each of the players a **stern** *look.*
disapproving, unsmiling, severe, strict, hard, harsh, grim
OPPOSITE lenient

stick
noun
1 *They collected* **sticks** *to make a fire.*
twig, branch, stalk
2 *The elderly patient walked with a* **stick**.
cane, rod, staff, pole
A stick used by a conductor is a **baton**.

A stick carried by a police officer is a **truncheon**.
A magic stick used by a witch or fairy is a **wand**.

stick *verb*
1 *He* **stuck** *his fork into the potato.*
poke, prod, stab, thrust, dig, jab
2 *She tried to* **stick** *the broken pieces of china together.*
glue, paste, cement, bond, join, fasten
3 *The stamp wouldn't* **stick** *to the envelope.*
adhere, attach, cling
4 *The wheels of the caravan* **stuck** *fast in the mud.*
jam, wedge, become trapped
to stick out
The shelf **sticks out** *too far.*
jut out, poke out, project, protrude
to stick up for someone
(informal) She **stuck up for** *him when he was in trouble.*
support, defend, side with, stand up for, speak up for

sticky *adjective*
1 *Someone had left a blob of* **sticky** *toffee on the chair.*
tacky, gummy, gluey
(informal) gooey, icky
2 *I don't like hot* **sticky** *weather.*
humid, muggy, clammy, close, steamy, sultry
OPPOSITE dry

stiff *adjective*
1 *Stir the flour and water to a* **stiff** *paste.*
firm, hard, solid
A common simile is **as stiff as a poker**.
OPPOSITE soft
2 *He mounted the picture on* **stiff** *card.*
rigid, inflexible, thick
OPPOSITE pliable
3 *Her muscles were* **stiff** *after the long walk.*
aching, achy, painful, taut, tight
OPPOSITE supple
4 *The team will face* **stiff** *competition in the final.*
strong, powerful, tough, difficult
OPPOSITE easy

5 *His* **stiff** *manner made him hard to talk to.*
unfriendly, cold, formal, awkward, wooden
OPPOSITE relaxed
6 *The judge imposed a* **stiff** *penalty.*
harsh, severe, strict, hard
OPPOSITE lenient
7 *A* **stiff** *breeze was blowing.*
strong, brisk, fresh
OPPOSITE gentle

stifle *verb*
1 *We were almost* **stifled** *by the fumes from the exhaust pipe.*
choke, suffocate, smother
To kill someone by stopping their breathing is to **strangle** or **throttle** them.
2 *She tried to* **stifle** *a yawn.*
suppress, muffle, hold back, repress, restrain

still *adjective*
1 *The prisoner sat* **still** *and said nothing.*
motionless, unmoving, stationary, static, inert
2 *It was a beautiful* **still** *evening.*
calm, peaceful, quiet, tranquil, serene, hushed, silent, noiseless, windless

sting *verb*
The smoke made our eyes **sting**.
smart, hurt, prick, prickle, tingle

stingy *adjective (informal)*
He's too **stingy** *to give anyone a birthday card.*
mean, miserly, selfish, uncharitable
(informal) tight-fisted, penny-pinching
OPPOSITE generous

stink *verb*
The dungeon **stank** *of unwashed bodies.*
reek, smell

stink *noun*
The mouldy cheese gave off a dreadful **stink**.
odour, stench, reek, bad smell

stir *verb*
1 *Stir the mixture until it is smooth.*
mix, beat, blend, whisk
2 *The giant* **stirred** *in his sleep.*
move slightly, shift, toss, turn
to stir something up
The bandits were always **stirring up** *trouble.*
arouse, encourage, provoke, set off, trigger, whip up

stir *noun*
The news caused quite a **stir**.
fuss, commotion, excitement, hullabaloo

stomach *noun*
He rolled over and lay on his **stomach**.
belly, gut, paunch
(informal) tummy

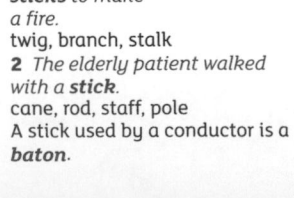

steps

The part of the body that contains the stomach is the **abdomen**.

stone noun
*The columns of the temple were carved from **stone**.*
A large lump of stone is a **rock**.
A large rounded stone is a **boulder**.
Small rounded stones are **pebbles**.
A mixture of sand and small stones is **gravel**.
Pebbles on the beach are **shingle**.
Round stones used to pave a path are **cobbles**.

stoop verb
*We had to **stoop** to go through the tunnel.*
bend, duck, bow, crouch

stop verb
1 *I'll go into town when the rain **stops**.*
end, finish, cease, conclude, terminate
OPPOSITE start
2 *Can you **stop** talking for a minute?*
give up, cease, suspend, quit, leave off, break off
(*informal*) knock off, pack in
OPPOSITE continue, resume
3 *Guards, **stop** that man!*
hold, detain, seize, catch, capture, restrain
4 *You can't **stop** me from going.*
prevent, obstruct, bar, hinder
5 *How do you **stop** this machine?*
turn off, immobilize
6 *The bus will **stop** at the school gates.*
come to a stop, halt, pull up, draw up
7 *If you tighten the valve, it will **stop** the leak.*
close, plug, seal, block up, bung up

stop noun
1 *Everything suddenly came to a **stop**.*
end, finish, conclusion, halt, standstill
2 *They drove down through France, with a short **stop** in Paris.*
break, pause, stopover, rest

store verb
*Squirrels need to **store** food for the winter.*
save, set aside, stow away, hoard, reserve, stockpile
(*informal*) stash

store noun
1 *The building is now used as a grain **store**.*
storeroom, storehouse, repository, vault
A store for food is a **larder** or **pantry**.
A store for weapons is an **armoury** or **arsenal**.
2 *He kept a large **store** of wine in the cellar.*
hoard, supply, quantity, stock, stockpile, reserve
3 *He's the manager of the local grocery **store**.*

storm noun
1 *Crops were damaged in the heavy **storms**.*
squall, blizzard, gale, thunderstorm, hurricane, typhoon
An old word for storm is **tempest**.
When a storm begins to develop it is **brewing**.
2 *Plans to close the library caused a **storm** of protest.*
outburst, outcry, uproar, clamour

storm verb
*The soldiers **stormed** the castle.*
charge at, rush at

stormy adjective
1 *It was a dark, **stormy** night.*
blustery, squally, tempestuous, wild, windy, rough, choppy, gusty, raging
OPPOSITE calm
2 *Fighting broke out at the end of a **stormy** meeting.*
bad-tempered, quarrelsome, turbulent, violent

stout adjective
1 *The doctor was a **stout** man with grey hair.*
fat, plump, chubby, dumpy, tubby, portly, stocky, beefy, burly
OPPOSITE thin
2 *You will need a pair of **stout** walking boots.*
strong, sturdy, tough, robust, sound, substantial
OPPOSITE weak
3 *The enemy put up a **stout** resistance.*
brave, courageous, spirited, plucky, determined, staunch, resolute, firm
OPPOSITE cowardly

straight adjective
1 *They walked in a **straight** line.*
direct, unswerving
A common simile is **as straight as an arrow**.
OPPOSITE crooked
2 *It took a long time to get the room **straight**.*
neat, orderly, tidy
OPPOSITE untidy
3 *She found it difficult to get a **straight** answer from him.*
honest, plain, frank, straightforward
OPPOSITE indirect, evasive

strain verb
1 *The dog was **straining** at its lead.*
pull, tug, stretch, haul
2 *People were **straining** to see what was going on.*
struggle, strive, make an effort, try, attempt
3 *Take it easy and don't **strain** yourself.*
weaken, exhaust, wear out, tire out, tax

strain noun
*The **strain** of her job was making her ill.*
stress, tension, worry, anxiety, pressure

stranded adjective
1 *A whale lay **stranded** on the beach.*
run aground, beached, marooned
2 *He was **stranded** in London without any money.*
abandoned, deserted, helpless, lost, stuck
(*informal*) high and dry

strange adjective
1 *A **strange** thing happened this morning.*
funny, odd, peculiar, unusual, abnormal, curious, extraordinary, remarkable, singular, uncommon
OPPOSITE ordinary, everyday
2 *Did you hear **strange** noises in the night?*
mysterious, puzzling, baffling, mystifying, perplexing, bewildering, inexplicable
3 *The professor showed us his **strange** inventions.*
weird, eccentric, peculiar, bizarre
(*informal*) oddball, wacky
4 *I find it hard to get to sleep in a **strange** bed.*
unfamiliar, unknown, new, alien
OPPOSITE familiar

strangle verb
*The victim had been **strangled**.*
throttle

strap noun
*The trunk was fastened with a leather **strap**.*
belt, band

stray verb
*Some sheep had **strayed** onto the road.*
wander, drift, roam, rove, straggle, meander, ramble

stretch

streak noun
1 *The horse had a white **streak** on his muzzle.*
band, line, stripe, strip, smear, stain
2 *There is a **streak** of meanness in his character.*
element, trace

streak verb
1 *Rain had begun to **streak** the window.*
smear, smudge, stain, line
2 *A group of motorbikes **streaked** past.*
rush, speed, dash, fly, hurtle, flash, tear, zoom

stream noun
1 *The climbers dipped their feet in a cool mountain **stream**.*
brook, rivulet
(*Scottish*) burn
2 *The raft was carried along with the **stream**.*
current, flow, tide
3 *A **stream** of water poured through the hole.*
cataract, flood, gush, jet, rush, torrent
4 *The museum had a steady **stream** of visitors.*
series, string, line, succession

stream verb
*Warm sunlight **streamed** through the window.*
pour, flow, flood, issue, gush, spill

strength noun
1 *Hercules was said to have enormous **strength**.*
power, might, muscle, brawn, toughness, force, vigour
2 *The main **strength** of the team is in scoring goals.*
strong point, asset, advantage
OPPOSITE weakness

strengthen verb
1 *Regular exercise **strengthens** your muscles.*
make stronger, build up, toughen, harden
2 *Concrete was used to **strengthen** the tunnel.*
fortify, reinforce, bolster, prop up

stress noun
1 *The hospital staff were working under a lot of **stress**.*
strain, pressure, tension, worry, anxiety
2 *My piano teacher puts great **stress** on the need to practise.*
emphasis, importance, weight

stress verb
*She **stressed** the need for absolute secrecy.*
emphasize, draw attention to, highlight, underline

stretch verb
1 *He **stretched** the rubber band until it snapped.*
expand, extend, draw out, pull out, elongate, lengthen
2 *She **stretched** her arms wide.*
extend, open out, spread out
3 *The road **stretched** into the distance.*
continue, extend

stretch noun
1 *He had a two-year **stretch** in the army.*
spell, period, time, stint
2 *There are often accidents on this **stretch** of road.*
section, length, piece
3 *It's a beautiful **stretch** of countryside.*
area, tract, expanse, sweep

strict adjective
1 *The club has **strict** rules about who can join.*
rigid, inflexible
(*informal*) hard and fast
OPPOSITE flexible
2 *The sergeant was known for being **strict** with his men.*
harsh, severe, stern, firm
OPPOSITE lenient
3 *He used the word in its **strict** scientific sense.*
exact, precise, correct
OPPOSITE loose

stride noun
*The robot took two **strides** forward.*
pace, step

strike verb
1 *Roy **struck** his head on the low ceiling.*
bang, bump, hit, knock, thump, collide with
(*informal*) wallop, whack
2 *The enemy could **strike** again at any time.*
attack

striking adjective
*The most **striking** feature of the mermaid was her iridescent tail.*
conspicuous, noticeable, prominent, remarkable, memorable, extraordinary, outstanding, impressive
OPPOSITE inconspicuous

string noun
1 *She tied some **string** round the parcel.*
rope, cord, twine
2 *They have received a **string** of complaints.*
series, succession, chain, sequence

string *verb*
We **strung** the fairy lights on the Christmas tree.
hang, arrange, thread

strong

strip *verb*
1 Lottie **stripped** the paper off her present.
peel, remove
OPPOSITE cover, wrap
2 He **stripped** and got into the bath.
get undressed, undress
OPPOSITE dress

strip *noun*
In front of the house was a narrow **strip** of grass.
band, length, ribbon, piece, bit

stripe *noun*
The tablecloth was white with blue **stripes**.
line, strip, band, bar

stroke *noun*
1 He split the log with a single **stroke**.
blow, hit, action, movement, effort
2 She added a few quick pencil **strokes** to her drawing.
line, mark

stroke *verb*
Jess was curled up on the sofa, **stroking** the cat.
pat, caress, rub, touch, fondle, pet

stroll *verb*
The children **strolled** quietly home.
walk slowly, amble, saunter

strong *adjective*
1 Crocodiles have **strong** jaws
powerful, muscular, mighty, well-built, beefy, brawny, burly, strapping
OPPOSITE weak, puny
2 The tent is made from **strong** material.
robust, sturdy, tough, hard-wearing, durable, stout, substantial
OPPOSITE thin, flimsy
3 The fugitive was caught in the **strong** beam of a searchlight.
bright, brilliant, dazzling, glaring
OPPOSITE weak, pale
4 I smelt the **strong** aroma of roasting coffee.
overpowering, pronounced, pungent, piquant
OPPOSITE faint, slight
5 The police have **strong** evidence of his guilt.
convincing, persuasive, effective, sound, solid, valid
OPPOSITE weak, feeble, flimsy
6 Zelda takes a **strong** interest in fashion.
enthusiastic, keen, passionate, fervent, avid, zealous
OPPOSITE slight

struggle *verb*
1 The captives **struggled** to get free.
strain, strive, wrestle, writhe about, tussle, fight, battle
2 The expedition had to **struggle** through a snowstorm.
stagger, stumble, flounder, labour

struggle *noun*
The rebels surrendered without a **struggle**.
fight, battle, combat, clash, contest

stubborn *adjective*
She's too **stubborn** to admit that she was wrong.
obstinate, pig-headed, strong-willed, uncooperative, inflexible, wilful
A common simile is **as stubborn as a mule**.
OPPOSITE compliant

stuck-up *adjective (informal)*
Nobody likes Ernest—he's so **stuck-up**.
arrogant, conceited, haughty, proud, snobbish, superior
(informal) snooty, toffee-nosed
OPPOSITE humble

study *verb*
1 He went to university to **study** medicine.
learn about, read, research into
2 The spy **studied** the document carefully.
examine, inspect, analyse, investigate, look closely at, scrutinize, survey
3 She has to **study** for her exams.
revise, cram
(informal) swot

stuff *noun*
1 What's that sticky **stuff** on the carpet?
matter, substance
2 You can put your **stuff** in one of the lockers.
belongings, possessions, things, gear

stuff *verb*
1 We managed to **stuff** everything into the boot of the car.
pack, push, shove, squeeze, ram, compress, force, cram, jam
2 The cushions are **stuffed** with foam rubber.
fill, pad

stuffy *adjective*
1 Open a window—it's **stuffy** in here.
airless, close, muggy, humid, stifling, musty, unventilated
OPPOSITE airy
2 I found the book a bit **stuffy**.
boring, dull, dreary, pompous, stodgy
OPPOSITE lively

stumble *verb*
1 He **stumbled** on a tree root and twisted his ankle.
trip, stagger, totter, flounder, lurch

2 The actress **stumbled** over her words.
stammer, stutter, falter, hesitate
to stumble across something
I **stumbled across** some old photos.
come across, encounter, find, unearth, discover

stun *verb*
1 The pilot was alive but **stunned**.
daze, knock out, knock senseless, make unconscious
2 The whole town was **stunned** by the news.
amaze, astonish, astound, shock, stagger, stupefy, bewilder, dumbfound

stupid *adjective*
1 Trolls are often very **stupid**.
foolish, unintelligent, dense, dim, dim-witted, brainless, dumb, slow, thick, feeble-minded, half-witted, simple, simple-minded, dopey, dull
2 It would be **stupid** to go snowboarding without a helmet.
senseless, mindless, idiotic, unwise, foolhardy, silly, daft, crazy, mad
OPPOSITE intelligent

sturdy *adjective*
1 Shetland ponies are short and **sturdy**.
stocky, strong, robust, athletic, brawny, burly, healthy, hefty, husky, muscular, powerful, vigorous, well-built
OPPOSITE weak
2 She bought some **sturdy** walking boots.
durable, solid, sound, substantial, tough, well made
OPPOSITE flimsy

stutter *verb*
He tends to **stutter** when he's nervous.
stammer, stumble, falter

style *noun*
1 I don't like that **style** of jeans.
design, pattern, fashion
2 The book is written in an informal **style**.
manner, tone, way, wording
3 The actress always dresses with great **style**.
elegance, stylishness, taste, sophistication

subject *noun*
1 Do you have any strong views on the **subject**?
matter, issue, question, point, theme, topic
2 Her passport shows that she is a British **subject**.
citizen, national

subtle *adjective*
1 There was a **subtle** smell of roses in the air.
faint, slight, mild, delicate

a b c d e f g h i j k l m n o p q r s t u v w x y z

2 *His jokes are too **subtle** for most people.*
ingenious, sophisticated
3 *I tried to give her a **subtle** hint.*
gentle, tactful, indirect

subtract *verb*
*If you **subtract** 5 from 20, you will have 15 left.*
take away, deduct, remove
OPPOSITE add

succeed *verb*
1 *You have to work hard if you want to **succeed**.*
be successful, do well, prosper, flourish, thrive
(*informal*) make it
2 *Everyone hoped that the plan would **succeed**.*
be effective, produce results, work
(*informal*) catch on
OPPOSITE fail
3 *Edward VII **succeeded** Queen Victoria.*
come after, follow, take over from, replace

success *noun*
1 *She talked about her **success** as an actress.*
achievement, attainment, fame
2 *They congratulated the team on their **success**.*
victory, win, triumph
3 *The **success** of the mission depends on the astronauts.*
effectiveness, successful outcome, completion

successful *adjective*
1 *She owns a very **successful** chain of restaurants.*
thriving, flourishing, booming, prosperous, profitable, popular
2 *The supporters cheered the **successful** team.*
winning, victorious, triumphant
OPPOSITE unsuccessful

suck *verb*
to suck something up
*A sponge will **suck up** water.*
soak up, draw up, absorb

sudden *adjective*
1 *Maria felt a **sudden** urge to burst into song.*
unexpected, unforeseen, impulsive, rash, quick
OPPOSITE expected
2 *The bus came to a **sudden** halt.*
abrupt, sharp, swift
OPPOSITE gradual

suffer *verb*
1 *He **suffers** terribly with his back.*
feel pain, hurt
2 *He will **suffer** for his crime.*
be punished, pay

3 *The home team **suffered** a humiliating defeat.*
experience, undergo, go through, endure, stand, bear, tolerate

suffocate *verb*
*The firefighters were nearly **suffocated** by the fumes.*
choke, stifle
To stop someone's breathing by squeezing their throat is to **strangle** or **throttle** them.
To stop someone's breathing by covering their nose and mouth is to **smother** them.

suggest *verb*
1 *Mum **suggested** going to the zoo.*
propose, advise, advocate, recommend
2 *Her comments **suggest** that she's not happy.*
imply, hint, indicate, signal

suggestion *noun*
*They didn't like his **suggestion**.*
proposal, plan, idea, proposition, recommendation

suit *verb*
1 *Would it **suit** you to stay here overnight?*
be convenient for, be suitable for, please, satisfy
OPPOSITE displease
2 *His new haircut doesn't **suit** him.*
look good on, become, flatter

suitable *adjective*
1 *Please wear clothes **suitable** for wet weather.*
appropriate, apt, fitting, suited (to), proper, right
OPPOSITE unsuitable
2 *Is this a **suitable** time to have a chat?*
convenient, acceptable, satisfactory
OPPOSITE inconvenient

sulk *verb*
*I was **sulking** because I wasn't allowed to play outside.*
be sullen, mope, brood, pout

sulky *adjective*
*Ron had turned into a **sulky** teenager.*
moody, sullen, brooding, moping, mopey

summarize *verb*
*Can you **summarize** the main points of the story?*
sum up, outline, review
(*informal*) recap

summary *noun*
*We each wrote a **summary** of the poem.*
synopsis, précis, outline

summon *verb*
*The king **summoned** his knights from far and wide.*
call, send for, order to come, bid to come

To ask someone politely to come is to **invite** them.

sunny *adjective*
*It was a beautiful **sunny** day.*
fine, clear, cloudless
OPPOSITE cloudy

sunrise *noun*
*The magic spell wears off at **sunrise**.*
dawn, daybreak
OPPOSITE sunset

sunset *noun*
*They arranged to meet in the churchyard at **sunset**.*
sundown, dusk, twilight, evening, nightfall
OPPOSITE sunrise

superb *adjective*
*Brazil scored another **superb** goal.*
excellent, outstanding, exceptional, remarkable, impressive, magnificent, marvellous, splendid, tremendous, wonderful
(*informal*) brilliant, fantastic, terrific, fabulous, sensational, super

supervise *verb*
*Children must be **supervised** by an adult in the park.*
oversee, superintend, watch over, be in charge of, be responsible for, direct, manage
To supervise candidates in an exam is to **invigilate**.

supple *adjective*
*The moccasins are made of **supple** leather.*
flexible, pliable, soft
OPPOSITE stiff, rigid

supply *verb*
*The art shop can **supply** you with brushes and paints.*
provide, equip, furnish

supply *noun*
*They had a good **supply** of fuel for the winter.*
quantity, stock, store, reserve
supplies
*We bought **supplies** for the camping trip.*
provisions, stores, rations, food, necessities

support *noun*
1 *She thanked them for their **support**.*
assistance, backing, aid, cooperation, encouragement, help
A support for a shelf is a **bracket**.
A support built against a wall is a **buttress**.
A support for someone with an injured leg is a **crutch**.
A bar of wood or metal supporting a framework is a **strut**.
A support put under a board to make a table is a **trestle**.

2 *The cinema was reopened with **support** from local businesses.*
donations, contributions, sponsorship

support *verb*
1 *The rope couldn't **support** his weight.*
bear, carry, stand, hold up
2 *The beams **support** the roof.*
prop up, strengthen, reinforce
3 *His friends **supported** him when he was in trouble.*
aid, assist, help, back, encourage, stand by, stand up for, rally round
4 *She had to work to **support** her family.*
maintain, keep, provide for
5 *He **supports** several local charities.*
donate to, contribute to, give to
6 *Which team did you **support** in the World Cup?*
be a supporter of, follow

supporter *noun*
1 *The home **supporters** cheered their team.*
fan, follower
2 *She is a well-known **supporter** of animal rights.*
champion, advocate, backer, defender

suppose *verb*
1 *I **suppose** you want to borrow some money.*
expect, presume, assume, guess, believe, think
2 *Suppose a spaceship landed in your garden!*
imagine, pretend, fancy
to be supposed to do something
*The bus is **supposed to** leave at 9 o'clock.*
be meant to, be due to, be expected to, ought to

sure *adjective*
1 *I'm **sure** that I'm right.*
certain, convinced, confident, definite, positive
OPPOSITE unsure, uncertain
2 *He's **sure** to phone tonight.*
bound, certain
OPPOSITE unlikely

surface *noun*
1 *The **surface** of Mars is barren and rocky.*
exterior, outside
*The surface of something may be covered with a **crust** or **shell** or **skin**.*
*A thin surface of expensive wood on furniture is a **veneer**.*
OPPOSITE centre
2 *A dice has dots on each **surface**.*
face, side
OPPOSITE inside

3 *Oil floated on the **surface** of the water.*
top
OPPOSITE bottom

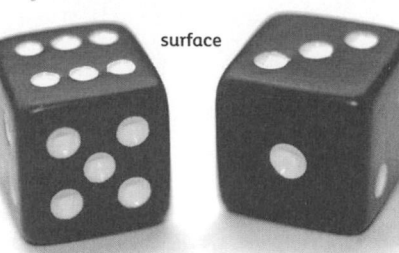

surface

surge *verb*
1 *Massive waves **surged** around the tiny raft.*
rise, roll, swirl, heave, billow
2 *The crowd **surged** forward.*
rush, push, sweep

surprise *noun*
*The news that Sara was married came as a **surprise**.*
amazement, astonishment, revelation, shock, wonder
(*informal*) bombshell

surprise *verb*
1 *I was **surprised** by how well she could sing*
amaze, astonish, astound, stagger, startle, stun, take aback, take by surprise, dumbfound
(*informal*) bowl over, flabbergast
2 *He **surprised** the burglars as they came through the window.*
discover, come upon, catch unawares, catch offguard, catch red-handed

surprised *adjective*

surprising *adjective*
*There are a **surprising** number of errors in the book.*
amazing, astonishing, astounding, extraordinary, remarkable, incredible, staggering, startling, stunning, unexpected
OPPOSITE predictable

> ✏ **WRITING TIPS**
>
> **SOMEONE WHO *FEELS SURPRISED* MIGHT**
> have eyes bulging out of their head, have eyes on the end of stalks, jump out of their skin, stare wide-eyed
>
> **SOMETHING WHICH *SURPRISES YOU* MIGHT**
> knock you for six, knock your socks off, knock you sideways, make your eyes pop

surrender *verb*
1 *The band of outlaws refused to **surrender**.*
admit defeat, give in, yield, submit, capitulate
2 *Please **surrender** your ticket to the driver.*
give, hand over

surround *verb*
1 *The garden was **surrounded** by a stone wall.*
enclose, fence in, wall in
2 *The pack of wolves **surrounded** its prey.*
encircle, ring, hem in, besiege

surroundings *plural noun*
*The hotel is set in very pleasant **surroundings**.*
setting, location, environment

survey *noun*
*They did a **survey** of local leisure facilities.*
review, investigation, study
*A survey to count the population of an area is a **census**.*

survey *verb*
1 *You can **survey** the whole valley from the top of the tower.*
view, look over, look at, observe
2 *They **surveyed** the damage done by the storm.*
inspect, examine, scrutinize, study

survive *verb*
1 *He managed to **survive** alone on the island for six months.*
stay alive, last, live, keep going, carry on, continue
OPPOSITE die
2 *Will the birds **survive** this cold weather?*
endure, withstand, live through, weather

suspect *verb*
1 *The police **suspected** his motives.*
doubt, mistrust, have suspicions about
2 *I **suspect** that the shop will be closed on Sundays.*
expect, imagine, presume, guess, sense, fancy

suspend *verb*
1 *The meeting was **suspended** until the next day.*
adjourn, break off, discontinue, interrupt
2 *For the party, we **suspended** balloons from the ceiling.*
hang, dangle, swing

suspense *noun*
*The film was a thriller, full of action and **suspense**.*
tension, uncertainty, anticipation, expectancy, drama, excitement

a b c d e f g h i j k l m n o p q r **s** t u v w x y z

suspicion noun
*I have a **suspicion** that he is lying.*
feeling, hunch, inkling, intuition,
impression

suspicious adjective
1 *There is something about
him which makes me
suspicious.*
doubtful, distrustful, mistrustful,
unsure, uneasy, wary
OPPOSITE trusting
2 *What do you make of his
suspicious behaviour?*
questionable, suspect, dubious,
shady
(*informal*) fishy

swagger verb
*The lead actor **swaggered** about
on stage.*
strut, parade

swallow verb
*The bread was so dry that it was hard
to **swallow**.*
gulp down
to swallow something up
*As it climbed higher, the
rocket was **swallowed up** by the
clouds.*
envelop, engulf, cover over, absorb

swamp verb
A huge wave threatened to swarm
***swamp** the ship.*
overwhelm, engulf, inundate,
flood, submerge

swamp noun
*Much of the land near the coast
is **swamp**.*
marsh, bog, mire, fen, quicksand,
quagmire

swap or **swop** verb
*We **swapped** seats so I could sit in
the aisle.*
change, exchange, switch,
substitute

swarm verb
*Hundreds of people **swarmed**
around the film star.*
crowd, flock
to swarm with
*The garden is **swarming** with ants.*
be overrun by, be crawling
with, be infested with, teem
with

sway verb
*The tall grass **swayed** in the breeze.*
wave, swing, rock, bend, lean

swear verb
1 *The knight **swore** that he
would protect the unicorn.*
pledge, promise, vow, give
your word, take an oath
2 *The player **swore** when he
bashed his knee.*
curse

sweat verb
*He **sweats** a lot in hot weather.*
perspire

sweep verb
1 *She **swept** the floor with an
old broom.*
brush, clean, dust
2 *The bus **swept** past.*
shoot, speed, zoom

sweet adjective
1 *The pudding is too **sweet** for me.*
sickly, sugary, sweetened, syrupy
OPPOSITE acid or bitter or savoury
2 *The **sweet** smell of roses filled the
room.*
fragrant, pleasant
OPPOSITE foul
3 *Fergus heard the **sweet** sound of
a harp.*
melodious, pleasant, soothing,
tuneful
OPPOSITE ugly
4 *What a **sweet** little cottage!*
attractive, charming, dear, lovely,
pretty, quaint
OPPOSITE unattractive

swerve verb
*The car **swerved** to avoid a
hedgehog.*
turn aside, veer, dodge,
swing

swift adjective
1 *They set off at a **swift** pace.*
fast, quick, rapid, speedy, brisk,
lively
2 *She received a **swift** reply
to her email.*
quick, fast, immediate, instant,
prompt, speedy, snappy

swing verb
1 *A glass chandelier **swung**
from the ceiling.*
hang, dangle, sway,
flap, wave about
2 *She **swung** round
when I called her name.*
turn, twist, veer, swerve

swirl verb
*Clouds of dust **swirled** up in the
desert wind.*
spin, twirl, whirl, churn

switch verb
1 *Please remember to **switch** off
the light.*
turn
2 *The teams will **switch** ends at
half-time.*
change, swap, exchange, shift

swoop verb
*The owl **swooped** and
caught the mouse.*
dive, drop, plunge, plummet,
descend, pounce

symbol noun
*The dove is a **symbol** of
peace.*
sign, emblem, image
*The symbols we use in
writing are **characters** or
letters.*
*The symbols used in ancient
Egyptian writing were **hieroglyphics**.*
*The symbol of a club or school is
their **badge**.*
*The symbol of a firm or organization
is their **logo**.*

symbol

sympathetic adjective
*They were **sympathetic** when my
mother was ill.*
understanding, compassionate,
concerned, caring, comforting, kind,
supportive
OPPOSITE unsympathetic

sympathize verb
to sympathize with
*We **sympathized with** those who
had lost their homes.*
be sympathetic towards,
be sorry for, feel for, commiserate
with

sympathy noun
*Did you feel any **sympathy**
for the characters in the
story?*
understanding, compassion,
pity, fellow-feeling,
tenderness

system noun
1 *The city has an archaic transport
system.*
organization, structure, network,
framework
(*informal*) set-up
2 *Do you understand the new
cataloguing **system**?*
procedure, process, scheme,
arrangement, method, routine

tactful *adjective*
*She gave him a **tactful** reminder about her birthday.*
subtle, discreet, diplomatic, sensitive, thoughtful
OPPOSITE tactless

take *verb*
1 *Naomi **took** her sister's hand.*
clutch, clasp, take hold of, grasp, grip, seize, snatch, grab
2 *The soldiers **took** many prisoners.*
catch, capture, seize, detain
3 *Someone has **taken** my pen.*
steal, remove, make off with
(*informal*) swipe, pinch
4 *The guide will **take** you to the edge of the forest.*
conduct, escort, lead, accompany
5 *The bus **took** us right to the station.*
bring, carry, convey, transport
6 *It'll **take** two people to lift that table.*
need, require
7 *The caravan can **take** six people.*
hold, contain, accommodate, have room for
8 *He couldn't **take** the heat of the midday sun.*
bear, put up with, stand, endure, tolerate, suffer, stomach
9 *He **took** their names and addresses.*
make a note of, record, write down
10 *The magician asked me to **take** a card.*
pick, choose, select

tame

11 ***Take** 2 from 8 and you get 6.*
subtract, take away, deduct

talent *noun*
*She has a great **talent** for music.*
gift, ability, aptitude, skill, flair, knack
Unusually great talent is ***genius***.

talented *adjective*
*He's a very **talented** dancer.*
gifted, able, accomplished, capable, skilled, skilful, clever, brilliant
If you are talented in several ways, you are ***versatile***.

talk *verb*
1 *Doug was trying to teach his parrot to **talk**.*
speak, say things, communicate, express yourself
2 *The two old friends had a lot to **talk** about.*
discuss, converse, chat, chatter, gossip
(*informal*) natter

talk *noun*
1 *I need to have a **talk** with you soon.*
conversation, discussion, chat
The talk between characters in a story is the ***dialogue***.
2 *There is a **talk** about Egyptian art at lunchtime.*
lecture, presentation, speech, address
A talk in church is a ***sermon***.

talkative *adjective*
*You're not very **talkative** this morning.*
chatty, communicative, vocal, forthcoming, articulate
An informal name for a talkative person is a ***chatterbox***.

tall *adjective*
1 *Jasmine is **tall** for her age.*
big
OPPOSITE short
2 *Singapore has many **tall** buildings.*
high, lofty, towering, soaring, giant
Buildings with many floors are ***high-rise*** or ***multi-storey*** buildings.
OPPOSITE low

tame *adjective*
1 *The guinea pigs are **tame** and used to people.*
domesticated, broken in, docile, gentle, obedient, manageable
OPPOSITE wild
2 *The film seems very **tame** nowadays.*
dull, boring, tedious, bland, unexciting, uninteresting
OPPOSITE exciting

tamper *verb*
to tamper with something
*Someone has been **tampering with** the lock.*
meddle with, tinker with, fiddle about with, interfere with

tap *verb*
*Someone **tapped** three times on the door.*
knock, rap, strike

tape *noun*
*The stack of old letters was tied up with **tape**.*
ribbon, braid, binding

target *noun*
1 *Her **target** was to swim thirty lengths.*
goal, aim, objective, intention, purpose, hope, ambition
2 *She was the **target** of his jokes.*
object, victim, butt

task *noun*
1 *The robot was given a number of **tasks** to do.*
job, chore, exercise, errand
2 *The soldiers' **task** was to capture the hill.*
assignment, mission, duty, undertaking

taste *verb*
1 ***Taste** the soup to see if it needs salt.*
sample, try, test, sip
2 *The curry **tastes** quite mild.*

taste *noun*
1 *I love the **taste** of ginger.*
flavour
2 *May I have a **taste** of the cheese?*
mouthful, bite, morsel, nibble, bit, piece, sample
3 *Her **taste** in clothes is a bit odd.*
choice, preference, discrimination, judgement

tasteless *adjective*
1 *He apologized for making a **tasteless** remark.*
crude, tactless, indelicate, inappropriate
OPPOSITE tasteful
2 *The sprouts were overcooked and **tasteless**.*
flavourless, bland, insipid
OPPOSITE flavourful

tasty *adjective*
*That pie was very **tasty**.*
delicious, appetizing
OPPOSITE unappetizing

taunt *verb*
*The gladiator **taunted** his opponent.*
barrack, insult, jeer at, laugh at, make fun of, mock, ridicule, sneer at

taut *adjective*
*Make sure the rope is **taut**.*
tight, tense, stretched
OPPOSITE slack

taut

teach verb
*My dad is **teaching** me to play the guitar.*
educate, inform, instruct
To teach people to play a sport is to **coach** or **train** them.
To teach one person at a time or a small group is to **tutor** them.

teacher noun
*We have a new ballet **teacher**.*
tutor, instructor, trainer
Someone who teaches you to play a sport is a **coach**.
In the past, a woman who taught children in a private household was a **governess**.

team noun
*She's been picked for the junior hockey **team**.*
side

tear verb
1 *The tree branch **tore** a hole in our kite.*
rip, snag, gash, shred, split, slit
2 *He **tore** home to watch his favourite TV programme.*
run, rush, dash, hurry, race, sprint, speed

tear noun
*There was a **tear** in one of the sails.*
cut, rip, rent, split, gash, hole, opening, slit, gap

tease verb
*They **teased** him about his new haircut.*
taunt, make fun of, poke fun at, mock, ridicule, laugh at

tell verb
1 ***Tell** us what you can see.*
describe, explain, reveal, report, say, state
2 ***Tell** me when you are ready.*
let you know, inform, notify, announce, communicate
3 *He **told** them to stop making so much noise.*
order, command, direct, instruct
4 *We **told** each other scary ghost stories.*
narrate, relate
5 *He **told** me he would buy the tickets.*
assure, promise
6 *She couldn't **tell** where she was in the dark.*
make out, recognize, identify, perceive

tear

7 *Can you **tell** one twin from the other?*
distinguish, separate
to tell someone off
*She **told them off** for being late.*
scold, reprimand, reproach
(*informal*) tick off

temper noun
1 *Mr Black had been in a bad **temper** all morning.*
mood, humour, state of mind
2 *The chef is always flying into a **temper**.*
rage, fury, fit of anger, tantrum
to lose your temper
*When she **loses her temper**, her cheeks go red.*
get angry, get annoyed, fly into a rage

temporary adjective
*They made a **temporary** shelter for the night.*
makeshift, provisional
OPPOSITE permanent

tempt verb
*Can I **tempt** you to have more pudding?*
coax, entice, persuade, attract
To tempt someone by offering them money is to **bribe** them.
To tempt an animal into a trap is to **lure** it.

tender adjective
1 *Frost may damage **tender** plants.*
delicate, fragile
OPPOSITE hardy, strong
2 *Cook the meat slowly until it is **tender**.*
soft, succulent, juicy
OPPOSITE tough
3 *The bruise is still **tender**.*
painful, sensitive, sore
4 *She gave him a **tender** smile.*
affectionate, kind, loving, caring, warm-hearted, compassionate, sympathetic, fond
OPPOSITE uncaring

tense adjective
1 *The muscles in her shoulders were **tense**.*
taut, tight, strained, stretched
2 *The crowd were **tense** as they waited to hear the results.*
anxious, nervous, apprehensive, edgy, on edge, fidgety, jumpy, jittery
(*informal*) uptight
3 *It was an extremely **tense** moment for all of us.*

nerve-racking, stressful, worrying
OPPOSITE relaxed

tension noun
*The **tension** of waiting was almost unbearable.*
stress, strain, anxiety, nervousness, suspense, worry

terrible adjective
*We heard there had been a **terrible** accident.*
awful, dreadful, horrible, appalling, shocking, ghastly, horrific, frightful

terrific adjective (*informal*)
1 *The footprint of the yeti was a **terrific** size.*
big, huge, immense, enormous, giant, gigantic, colossal, massive
2 *She's a **terrific** tennis player.*
excellent, first-class, first-rate, superb, marvellous, wonderful
(*informal*) brilliant, fantastic, fabulous

terrify verb
*The dogs were **terrified** by the thunder.*
frighten, scare, startle, alarm, panic, horrify, petrify

terror noun
*Her eyes filled with **terror** as she described the ghost.*
fear, fright, horror, panic, alarm, dread

test noun
*How did you do in the maths **test**?*
exam, examination, assessment, appraisal, evaluation
A set of questions you answer for fun is a **quiz**.
A test for a job as an actor or singer is an **audition**.
A test to find the truth about something is an **experiment** or **trial**.

test verb
1 *I made an appointment to have my eyes **tested**.*
examine, check, evaluate, assess, screen
2 *He is **testing** a new formula for invisibile ink.*
experiment with, try out, trial

thankful adjective
to be thankful for something
*We were **thankful for** her help.*
grateful for, appreciative of, pleased about, relieved about
OPPOSITE ungrateful

thanks *plural noun*
*She sent them a card to show her **thanks**.*
gratitude, appreciation

theme *noun*
*What is the **theme** of the poem?*
subject, topic, idea, gist, argument

theory *noun*
1 *The detective has a **theory** about the case.*
explanation, hypothesis, view, belief, idea, notion, suggestion
2 *She bought a book about musical **theory**.*
laws, principles, rules

thick

thick *adjective*
1 *The Roman wall was about 2 metres **thick**.*
wide, broad
OPPOSITE thin
2 *The cabin was made from **thick** logs of wood.*
stout, chunky, heavy, solid, substantial
OPPOSITE thin, slender
3 *The explorers hacked their way through the **thick** jungle.*
dense, close, compact
4 *His boots got stuck in a **thick** layer of mud.*
deep, heavy
OPPOSITE thin, shallow
5 *The guide spoke with a **thick** Polish accent.*
heavy, noticeable
OPPOSITE slight
6 *(informal) Fortunately, the giant was rather **thick**.*
stupid, brainless, foolish
OPPOSITE intelligent

thief *noun*
*The police managed to catch the **thief**.*
robber
Someone who steals from people's homes is a *burglar* or *housebreaker*.
Someone who steals from people in the street is a *pickpocket*.
Someone who steals from shops is a *shoplifter*.
Someone who used to steal from travellers was a *highwayman*.

thin *adjective*
1 *The prisoners were dreadfully **thin**.*
lean, skinny, bony, gaunt, spare, slight, underweight
Someone who is thin and tall is *lanky*.
Someone who is thin but strong is *wiry*.
Someone who is thin but attractive is *slim* or *slender*.

thin

Thin arms or legs are *spindly*.
A common simile is *as thin as a rake*.
OPPOSITE fat
2 *The fairy wore a **thin** cloak of spider's silk.*
fine, light, delicate, flimsy, sheer, wispy
A thin line is a *fine* or *narrow* line.
A thin book is a *slim* book.
OPPOSITE thick
3 *The icing should be **thin** enough to spread.*
runny, watery
OPPOSITE thick

thing *noun*
1 *What's that green **thing** on the floor?*
item, object, article
2 *We had a lot of **things** to talk about.*
matter, affair, detail, point, factor
3 *A lot of **things** had happened since we spoke.*
event, happening, occurrence, incident
4 *I have only one **thing** left to do.*
job, task, act, action
things
*Put your **things** in one of the lockers.*
belongings, possessions, stuff, equipment, gear

think *verb*
1 ***Think** before you do anything rash.*
consider, contemplate, reflect, deliberate, reason
To think hard about something is to *concentrate* on it.
To think quietly and deeply about something is to *meditate*.
To keep thinking anxiously about something is to *brood* on it.
2 *Do you **think** this is a good idea?*
believe, feel, consider, judge, conclude
3 *What do you **think** this ring is worth?*
reckon, suppose, imagine, estimate, guess, expect
to think about something
*I need some more time to **think** about it.*
consider, reflect on, ponder, muse on, mull over
to think something up
*They **thought up** a good plan.*
invent, make up, conceive, concoct, devise

thirsty *adjective*
*They were **thirsty** after their long walk.*
dry, parched
If someone is ill through lack of fluids, they are *dehydrated*.

thorough *adjective*
1 *The doctor gave him a **thorough** examination.*
comprehensive, full, rigorous, careful, methodical, systematic, meticulous, painstaking, conscientious
OPPOSITE superficial
2 *He's made a **thorough** mess of things!*
complete, total, utter, absolute, downright

thought *noun*
1 *She gave a lot of **thought** to the problem.*
consideration, deliberation, study
2 *The detective spent some time in **thought**.*
thinking, contemplation, reflection, meditation
3 *What are your **thoughts** on modern art?*
opinion, belief, idea, notion, conclusion

thoughtful *adjective*
1 *Mr Levi had a **thoughtful** expression on his face.*
pensive, reflective, absorbed, preoccupied
OPPOSITE blank, vacant
2 *She added some **thoughtful** comments in the margin.*
well-thought-out, careful, conscientious, thorough
OPPOSITE careless
3 *It was very **thoughtful** of you to visit me in hospital.*
caring, considerate, kind, friendly, good-natured, unselfish
OPPOSITE thoughtless

thoughtless *adjective*
*It was **thoughtless** of him to mention her dead husband.*
inconsiderate, insensitive, uncaring, unthinking, negligent, ill-considered, rash
OPPOSITE thoughtful

thrash *verb*
1 *The rider **thrashed** and spurred his horse to go faster.*
hit, beat, whip, flog
(informal) whack, wallop
2 *The crocodile **thrashed** its tail in the mud.*
swish, flail, jerk, toss
3 *(informal) The visitors **thrashed** the home side 6–0.*
beat, defeat, trounce

threat *noun*
1 *She made a **threat** about phoning the police.*
warning
2 *Earthquakes are a constant **threat** in California.*
danger, menace, hazard, risk

a b c d e f g h i j k l m n o p q r s t u v w x y z

threaten *verb*
1 *The bandits **threatened** him when he tried to escape.*
make threats against, menace, intimidate, terrorize, bully, browbeat
2 *The forecast **threatened** rain.*
warn of
3 *Wild tigers are **threatened** with extinction.*
endanger, put at risk

thrill *noun*
*Kim loves the **thrill** of rock climbing.*
adventure, excitement, sensation, tingle
(*slang*) buzz, kick

thrill *verb*
*The thought of seeing a real shark **thrilled** him no end.*
excite, exhilerate, electrify, rouse, stir, stimulate
OPPOSITE bore

thrilled *adjective*
*I was **thrilled** to be invited to the wedding.*
delighted, pleased, excited, overjoyed, ecstatic

throb *verb*
*She could feel the blood **throbbing** through her veins.*
beat, pound, pulse, pulsate

throw *verb*
1 *I **threw** some bread into the pond for the ducks.*
fling, cast, pitch, sling, toss
(*slang*) bung, chuck
To deliver the ball in cricket or rounders is to **bowl**.
To throw the shot in athletics is to **put** the shot.
To throw something high in the air is to **lob** it.
To throw something heavy is to **heave** it.
To throw something with great force is to **hurl** it.
If someone throws a lot of things at you, they **pelt** you.
2 *The horse **threw** its rider.*
throw off, shake off, dislodge

thrill

to throw away
*We **threw away** a pile of old junk.*
get rid of, dispose of, discard, scrap
(*informal*) dump, ditch

thrust *verb*
1 *Drew **thrust** his hands into his pockets.*
push, force, shove
2 *The bandit **thrust** at him with a dagger.*
lunge, jab, prod, stab, poke

thump *verb*
*'Silence!' he rasped, **thumping** his fist on the table.*
bang, bash, pound, hit, strike, knock, rap
(*informal*) whack, wham

tidy *adjective*
*I like to keep my office **tidy**.*
neat, orderly, uncluttered, trim, smart, spruce, straight
OPPOSITE untidy

tie *verb*
1 *Zoe **tied** a pink ribbon round the parcel.*
bind, fasten, hitch, knot, loop, secure
To tie up a boat is to **moor** it.
To tie up an animal is to **tether** it.
OPPOSITE untie
2 *The two teams are still **tied**.*
be equal, be level, draw

tight *adjective*
1 *The lid was too **tight** for him to unscrew.*
firm, fast, secure
If it is so tight that air cannot get through, it is **airtight**.
If it is so tight that water cannot get through, it is **watertight**.
OPPOSITE loose
2 *They squeezed into the **tight** space.*
cramped, compact, small, narrow, poky, snug
OPPOSITE spacious
3 *Make sure that the ropes are **tight**.*
taut, tense, stretched, rigid
A common simile is **as tight as a drum**.
OPPOSITE slack

tighten *verb*
1 *She **tightened** her grip on his hand.*
increase, strengthen, tense, stiffen
2 *You need to **tighten** the guy ropes.*
make taut, pull tighter, stretch
3 *He tried to **tighten** the screw.*
make tighter, screw up
OPPOSITE loosen

tilt *verb*
*The caravan **tilted** to one side.*
lean, incline, tip, slant, slope, angle
When a ship tilts to one side, it **lists**.

time *noun*
1 *Is this a convenient **time** to talk?*
moment, occasion, opportunity
2 *Autumn is my favourite **time** of the year.*
phase, season
3 *He spent a short **time** living in China.*
period, while, term, spell, stretch
4 *Shakespeare lived in the **time** of Elizabeth I.*
era, age, days, epoch, period
5 *Please try to keep **time** with the music.*
tempo, beat, rhythm
on time
*Please try to be **on time**.*
punctual, prompt

time

timid *adjective*
*At first, the mermaid was too **timid** to say anything.*
shy, bashful, modest, nervous, fearful, shrinking, retiring, sheepish
A common simile is **as timid as a mouse**.
OPPOSITE brave, confident

tiny *adjective*
*The ladybird was so **tiny** that you could hardly see it.*
little, minute, miniature, microscopic, minuscule
(*informal*) teeny, titchy
OPPOSITE big, large

tip *noun*
1 *The **tip** of his nose felt cold.*
end, point
The tip of an ink pen is the **nib**.
2 *The **tip** of the mountain was covered in snow.*
cap, peak, top, summit, pinnacle, crown
3 *He gave them some useful **tips** on first aid.*
hint, piece of advice, suggestion, clue, pointer
4 *They took a load of rubbish to the **tip**.*
dump, rubbish heap

tip *verb*
1 *The caravan* **tipped** *to one side.*
lean, tilt, incline, slope, slant
When a ship tips slightly to one side, it **lists**.
When a ship tips right over, it **capsizes**.
2 *Sophie* **tipped** *the box of crayons onto the table.*
empty, turn out, dump, unload
to tip over
He **tipped** *the milk jug* **over** *by accident.*
knock over, overturn, topple, upset

tired *adjective*
Have a lie down if you're **tired**.
exhausted, fatigued, weary, worn out, listless, sleepy, drowsy
(*informal*) all in
to be tired of something
I'm **tired of** *watching TV.*
bored with, fed up with, sick of
If you are not interested in anything, you are **apathetic**.

title *noun*
1 *She couldn't think of a* **title** *for the story.*
name, heading
The title above a newspaper story is a **headline**.
A title or brief description next to a picture is a **caption**.
2 *The form asks you to fill in your name and* **title**.
form of address, designation, rank
The ordinary title used before a man's name is **Mr**.
The ordinary title used before a woman's name is **Miss** or **Mrs** or **Ms**.
A polite way to address someone whose name you don't know is **sir** or **madam**.

tolerant *adjective*
Molly was very **tolerant** *towards other people.*
understanding, easygoing, open-minded, sympathetic, charitable, forgiving, lenient, indulgent, long-suffering
OPPOSITE intolerant

tolerate *verb*
1 *He won't* **tolerate** *sloppy writing.*
accept, permit, put up with
2 *Cactus plants can* **tolerate** *extreme heat.*
bear, endure, stand, abide, suffer, stomach
(*informal*) stick

tomb *noun*
Inside the **tomb** *were several ancient skeletons.*
burial chamber, crypt, grave, mausoleum, sepulchre, vault

An underground passage containing several tombs is a **catacomb**.
A tomb is often marked by a **tombstone**, **gravestone**, or **headstone**.

tone *noun*
1 *There was an angry* **tone** *to her voice.*
note, sound, quality, intonation, manner
2 *The room is painted in subtle* **tones**.
colour, hue, shade, tint
3 *Eerie music created the right* **tone** *for the film.*
feeling, mood, atmosphere, spirit, effect

✏ WRITING TIPS

tooth *noun*
You can use these words to describe **teeth** or **jaws**
jagged, serrated, razor-sharp, needle-sharp, pincer-like
***TEETH* MAY**
bite, chew, grind, munch, chomp, gnash, snap, tear, rip, puncture

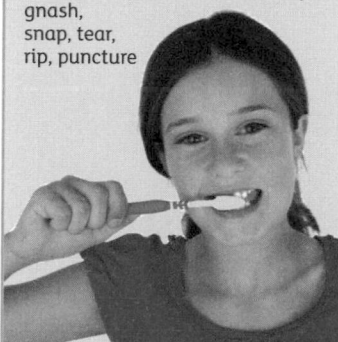

---

top *noun*
1 *They climbed to the* **top** *of the hill.*
peak, summit, tip, crown, crest, head
OPPOSITE bottom, base
2 *The desk* **top** *was covered with newspapers.*
surface
3 *The* **top** *of the jar was screwed on tightly.*
lid, cap, cover, covering

top *adjective*
1 *Their office is on the* **top** *floor.*
highest, topmost, uppermost, upper
OPPOSITE bottom, lowest
2 *She got* **top** *marks in her exam.*
most, best, highest
3 *The skiers set off at* **top** *speed.*
greatest, maximum
4 *He is one of Europe's* **top** *chefs.*
best, leading, finest, foremost, principal, superior
OPPOSITE junior

top *verb*
1 *Mum* **topped** *the cake with fudge icing.*
cover, decorate, garnish, crown
2 *The athlete is hoping to* **top** *her personal best.*
beat, better, exceed, outdo, surpass

topic *noun*
What was the **topic** *of the conversation?*
subject, talking-point, issue, matter, question

topical *adjective*
The website often discusses **topical** *issues.*
current, recent, up-to-date

toss *verb*
1 *He* **tossed** *a coin into the wishing-well.*
throw, cast, hurl, fling, pitch, sling
(*informal*) chuck
2 *Let's* **toss** *a coin to see who'll go first.*
flip, spin
3 *The little boat* **tossed** *about in the storm.*
lurch, pitch, roll, heave, rock, bob
4 *She* **tossed** *and turned, unable to get to sleep.*
thrash about, flail, writhe, wriggle

total *noun*
A **total** *of 15 million people live in Tokyo.*
sum, whole, entirety, amount

total *adjective*
1 *The bill shows the* **total** *amount due.*
full, complete, whole, entire
2 *The party was a* **total** *disaster.*
complete, utter, absolute, thorough, downright, sheer

total *verb*
The donations **total** *almost 300 euros.*
add up to, amount to, come to, make

touch *verb*
1 *Some animals don't like to be* **touched**.
feel, handle, stroke, fondle, caress, pat, pet
2 *The car just* **touched** *the gatepost.*
brush, graze, contact
3 *The speed of the racing car* **touched** *200 miles per hour.*
reach, rise to
4 *I was* **touched** *by the poem that she wrote.*
move, affect, stir

touch *noun*
1 *I felt a light* **touch** *on my arm.*
pat, stroke, tap, caress, contact
2 *There's a* **touch** *of frost in the air.*
hint, trace, suggestion

a b c d e f g h i j k l m n o p q r s t u v w x y z

touchy adjective
Be careful what you say—he's very **touchy**.
easily offended, sensitive, irritable, quick-tempered

tough adjective
1 You'll need **tough** shoes for hiking.
strong, sturdy, robust, durable, stout, hard-wearing, substantial
Common similes are **as tough as nails** and **as tough as old boots**.
OPPOSITE flimsy
2 The meat was very **tough**.
chewy, leathery, rubbery
OPPOSITE tender
3 They played against **tough** opposition.
strong, stiff, powerful, resistant, determined, stubborn
OPPOSITE weak, feeble
4 The police deal with some **tough** criminals.
rough, violent, vicious, hardened
5 It was a **tough** job to clean the oven.
demanding, laborious, strenuous, gruelling, tiring, exhausting
OPPOSITE easy
6 The crossword puzzle was too **tough** for him.
difficult, hard, puzzling, baffling, knotty, thorny
OPPOSITE easy

tower noun
A small tower on a castle or other building is a **turret**.
A church tower is a **steeple**.
The pointed structure on a steeple is a **spire**.
The top part of a steeple with a bell is a **belfry**.
The tall tower of a mosque is a **minaret**.

tower verb
to tower above something
The castle **towers above** the village.
rise above, stand above, dominate, loom over

Eiffel Tower

trace noun
1 The burglar left no **trace** of his presence.
evidence, sign, mark, indication, hint, clue, track, trail
A trace left by an animal might be its **footprint** or **scent** or **spoor**.
2 They found **traces** of blood on the carpet.
tiny amount, drop, spot

trace verb
She is trying to **trace** her distant ancestors.
track down, discover, find, uncover, unearth

track noun
1 A rough **track** leads past the farm.
path, pathway, footpath, trail
2 They followed the deer's **tracks** for miles.
footprint, footmark, trail, scent
3 They are laying the **track** for a new railway.
line, rails
4 The athletes are warming up on the **track**.
racetrack, circuit, course

track verb
Astronomers are **tracking** the path of the comet.
follow, trace, pursue, chase, tail, trail, hunt, stalk
to track someone or something down
They **tracked down** the owner of the car.
find, discover, trace, hunt down, sniff out, run to ground

tradition noun
It's a **tradition** to sing 'Auld Lang Syne' on New Year's Eve.
custom, convention, habit, routine, fashion

traditional adjective
1 The African drummers wore **traditional** costumes.
national, regional, historical

2 They chose to have a **traditional** wedding.
conventional, customary, established, time-honoured, habitual, typical, usual

tragedy noun
The accident at sea was a terrible **tragedy**.
disaster, catastrophe, calamity, misfortune

tragic adjective
He died in a **tragic** accident.
catastrophic, disastrous, calamitous, terrible, appalling, dreadful, unfortunate, unlucky

trail noun
1 We walked along a **trail** through the woods.
path, pathway, track, route
2 The police were on the **trail** of the bank robbers.
track, chase, hunt, pursuit
The trail left in the water by a ship is its **wake**.

trail verb
1 The detective **trailed** the suspect all day.
follow, chase, tail, track, pursue, shadow, stalk, hunt
2 She **trailed** her suitcase behind her.
pull, tow, drag, draw, haul
3 He is already **trailing** behind the front runners.
fall behind, lag, straggle, dawdle

train verb
1 He **trains** the football team every Saturday.
coach, instruct, teach, tutor
2 They are **training** hard for the Commonwealth Games.
practise, exercise, prepare yourself, (informal) work out

tramp verb
They **tramped** across the muddy fields.
march, hike, trek, trudge, plod, stride

trample verb
Don't **trample** the flowers!
crush, flatten, squash, tread on, walk over, stamp on

transfer verb
Some paintings have been **transferred** to the new gallery.
move, remove, shift, relocate, convey, hand over

transform verb
They **transformed** the attic into an office.
change, alter, turn, convert, adapt, modify

transmit verb
1 The spy **transmitted** her messages in code.
send, communicate, relay, emit, broadcast

bicycle

transport noun
TRANSPORT BY AIR
aeroplane, airship, helicopter, hot-air balloon

TRANSPORT BY ROAD
bicycle, bus, car, coach, horse, jeep, lorry, minibus, taxi, van

hot-air balloon

TRANSPORT BY RAIL
monorail, train, tram, underground

TRANSPORT BY WATER
barge, boat, canoe, ferry, punt, raft, ship, yacht

coach

VEHICLES WHICH CARRY PEOPLE
bus, cab, camper, car or motorcar, caravan, coach, jeep, minibus, minicab, people carrier, rickshaw, taxi, train, tram, trolleybus

OLD HORSE-DRAWN VEHICLES
carriage, cart, chariot, coach, gig, stagecoach, trap, wagon

VEHICLES USED FOR WORK
ambulance, bulldozer, dustcart, fire-engine, hearse, HGV or heavy goods vehicle, horsebox, lorry, milkfloat, removal van, pick-up truck, police car, steamroller, tank, tanker, tractor, truck, van

boat

VEHICLES WHICH TRAVEL ON SNOW OR ICE
sled or sledge, sleigh, skidoo, snowplough, toboggan

tram

To transmit a programme on radio or TV is to **broadcast** it.
OPPOSITE receive
2 Can the disease be **transmitted** to humans?
pass on, spread, carry

transparent adjective
The box had a **transparent** lid.
clear
(informal) see-through
Something which is not fully transparent, but allows light to shine through, is **translucent**.

trap noun
1 The animal was caught in a **trap**.
snare, net, noose, booby trap
2 The police set up a **trap** to catch the robbers.
ambush

trap verb
They tried to **trap** the mouse.
capture, catch, snare, corner

travel verb
She prefers to **travel** to work by bus.
go, journey, move along, proceed, progress

VARIOUS WAYS TO TRAVEL
cruise, cycle, drive, fly, go by rail, hike, hitch-hike, motor, pedal, ramble, ride, roam, row, sail, tour, trek, voyage, walk, wander

When birds travel from one country to another they **migrate**.
When people travel to another country to live there they **emigrate**.

PEOPLE WHO TRAVEL AS A WAY OF LIFE
itinerant, nomad, traveller

OTHER PEOPLE WHO TRAVEL
astronaut, commuter, cyclist, driver or motorist, explorer, hitch-hiker, holidaymaker, motorcyclist, passenger, pedestrian, pilot or aviator, rambler or walker, sailor, tourist

A person who travels to a religious place is a **pilgrim**.
A person who travels illegally on a ship or plane is a **stowaway**.
A person who likes travelling round the world is a **globetrotter**.

---

tread verb
Please **tread** carefully.
step, walk, proceed
to tread on
Don't **tread on** the wet cement!
walk on, step on, stamp on, trample, crush, squash

treasure noun
The **treasure** was buried somewhere on the island.
hoard, riches, wealth, fortune
A hidden store of treasure is a **cache**.

treasure verb
She **treasures** the photograph of her grandmother.
cherish, prize, value

treat verb
1 The old woman had always **treated** him kindly.
behave towards, deal with
2 She is being **treated** for minor injuries.
give treatment to

To treat a wound is to **dress** it.
To treat an illness or wound successfully is to **cure** or **heal** it.

treatment noun **1** The hospital is for the **treatment** of sick animals.
care, nursing, healing
2 He is trying a new **treatment** for back pain.
remedy, therapy, medication
Emergency treatment at the scene of an accident is **first aid**.
3 The sculpture has been damaged by careless **treatment**.
handling, use, care, management

tremble verb
The little fairy was **trembling** with cold.
shake, shiver, quake, quiver, shudder

tremendous adjective
1 They heard a **tremendous** roar issue from the cave.
big, enormous, great, huge, immense, massive, mighty, fearful
2 Winning the cup was a **tremendous** achievement.
marvellous, magnificent, wonderful, superb, terrific, sensational, spectacular, stupendous, extraordinary, outstanding

trend noun
1 There is a general **trend** towards healthier eating.
tendency, movement, shift, leaning
2 This type of computer game is the latest **trend**.
fashion, style, craze, fad, vogue

trial noun
1 Scientists are conducting **trials** on a new space probe.
test, experiment

2 *The **trial** will be heard in a crown court.*
case, hearing
*A military trial is a **court martial**.*

trick noun
1 *Stephie played a **trick** on her brother.*
joke, practical joke, prank
*Tricks which a magician performs are **conjuring tricks**.*
2 *The Trojans never guessed that the wooden horse was a **trick**.*
deception, pretence, fraud, cheat, hoax
(informal) con

trick verb
*He **tricked** them into believing he was a police officer.*
deceive, dupe, fool, hoodwink, cheat, swindle
(informal) con

trickle verb
*Water **trickled** from the tap.*
dribble, drip, leak, seep, ooze
OPPOSITE gush

tricky adjective
*There were a couple of **tricky** questions in the exam.*
difficult, complicated, awkward, intricate, involved, ticklish
OPPOSITE straightforward, easy

trip noun
*They went on a **trip** to the seaside.*
journey, visit, outing, excursion, jaunt, expedition

trip verb
*He **tripped** on the loose carpet.*
catch your foot, stumble, fall, slip, stagger

trivial adjective
*Don't bother me with **trivial** details.*
unimportant, minor, insignificant, trifling, negligible, petty, silly, slight, frivolous
OPPOSITE important

trouble noun
1 *The family has had a lot of **trouble** recently.*
difficulty, hardship, suffering, unhappiness, distress, misfortune, pain, sadness, sorrow, worry
2 *The police dealt with **trouble** in the crowd.*
disorder, unrest, disturbance, commotion, fighting, violence
3 *The **trouble** with this computer is that it's very slow.*
problem, difficulty, disadvantage, drawback
to take trouble
*He **took trouble** to remember all our names.*
bother, make an effort, take pains

trouble verb
1 *What's **troubling** you?*
distress, upset, bother, worry, concern, pain, torment, vex
2 *I don't want to **trouble** her if she's busy.*
disturb, interrupt, bother, pester
3 *Nobody **troubled** to tidy up the room.*
bother, make an effort, take trouble

true adjective
1 *Do you think the newspaper report is **true**?*
accurate, correct, right, factual, authentic, undeniable
OPPOSITE untrue, false
2 *This is a **true** copy of my birth certificate.*
genuine, real, actual, faithful, exact
OPPOSITE false
3 *Esther has always been a **true** friend.*
faithful, loyal, constant, devoted, sincere, steady, trustworthy, dependable, reliable
OPPOSITE unreliable

trust verb
*I **trusted** her to keep my identity a secret.*
rely on, depend on, count on, bank on, believe in, be sure of, have confidence in, have faith in

trust noun
1 *The director has **trust** in her acting ability.*
belief, confidence, faith
2 *They put their lives in the **trust** of the pilot.*
responsibility, safe-keeping, hands

truth noun
1 *The detective doubted the **truth** of her story.*
accuracy, authenticity, correctness, genuineness, reliability, truthfulness, validity
OPPOSITE inaccuracy or falseness
2 *Are you sure you're telling the **truth**?*
facts
OPPOSITE lies

truthful adjective
1 *She is normally a **truthful** person.*
honest, frank, sincere, straight, straightforward, reliable, trustworthy
2 *He gave a **truthful** answer.*
accurate, correct, proper, right, true, valid
OPPOSITE dishonest

try verb
1 *I'm going to **try** to beat my dad at chess.*
aim, attempt, endeavour, make an effort, strive, struggle
2 *Would you like to **try** a larger size?*
test, try out, evaluate, experiment with

try noun
1 *We may not succeed, but it's worth a **try**!*
attempt, effort, go, shot
2 *Would you like a **try** of my mango smoothie?*
trial, test, taste

trying adjective
*The way he keeps asking questions is very **trying**.*
tiresome, irritating, annoying, wearing, wearisome

tuck verb
*He **tucked** his t-shirt into his jeans.*
push, insert, stuff

tug verb
1 *It annoys me when my brother **tugs** my hair.*
pull, yank, jerk, pluck, wrench
2 *We **tugged** the sledge up the hill.*
drag, pull, tow, haul, lug, draw, heave

tune noun
*Can you play the **tune** to 'Happy Birthday'?*
melody, song, air, theme

turn verb
1 *A wheel **turns** on its axle.*
go round, revolve, rotate, roll, spin, swivel, pivot, twirl, whirl
2 *The van **turned** into a side street.*
change direction, corner
To turn unexpectedly is to **swerve** or **veer** off course.
If you turn to go back in the direction you came from, you **do a U-turn**.
If marching soldiers change direction, they **wheel**.
3 *He **turned** a curious shade of green.*
become, go, grow
4 *They **turned** the attic into a spare bedroom.*
convert, adapt, change, alter, modify, transform, develop
to turn something down
*She **turned down** the offer of a part in the play.*
decline, refuse, reject
to turn something on or **off**
*He **turned on** the radio.*
switch on or off
to turn out
*Everything **turned out** well in the end.*
end up, come out, happen, result
to turn over
*The boat **turned over**.*
capsize, overturn, turn upside down, flip over, keel over
to turn up
*A friend **turned up** unexpectedly.*
arrive, appear, drop in

turn noun
1 She gave the handle a **turn**.
twist, spin, whirl, twirl
A single turn of wheel is a **revolution**.
The process of turning is **rotation**.
2 The house is just past the next **turn** in the road.
bend, corner, curve, angle, junction
A sharp turn in a country road is a **hairpin bend**.
3 It's your **turn** to do the washing up.
chance, opportunity, occasion, time, slot, go
4 (informal) Seeing the skeleton gave her quite a **turn**.
fright, scare, shock, start, surprise

twinkle verb
The stars **twinkled** in the sky.
sparkle, shine, glitter, glisten, glimmer, glint

twist verb
1 She **twisted** a bandage round her wrist.
wind, loop, coil, curl, entwine
2 **Twist** the handle to open the door.
turn, rotate, revolve, swivel
3 The road **twists** through the hills.
wind, weave, curve, zigzag
4 He **twisted** and turned in his sleep.
toss, writhe, wriggle
5 I tried to **twist** the cap off the bottle.
unscrew
6 Heat can **twist** metal out of shape.
bend, buckle, warp, crumple, distort

twisted adjective
The trunk of the olive tree was **twisted** with age.
knarled, warped, buckled, misshapen, deformed

twitch verb
The dog **twitched** in his sleep.
jerk, jump, start, tremble

type noun
1 What **type** of films do you like to watch?
kind, sort, variety, category, class, genre
2 The book was printed in large **type**.
print, lettering, letters, characters

typical adjective
1 The weather is **typical** for this time of year.
normal, usual, standard, ordinary, average, predictable, unsurprising
OPPOSITE unusual
2 The pointed arch is **typical** of Gothic architecture.
characteristic, representative
OPPOSITE uncharacteristic

Uu

ugly adjective
1 The princess had to kiss a fat, **ugly** toad.
grotesque, hideous, unattractive, repulsive, revolting, monstrous
OPPOSITE beautiful
2 The room was filled with **ugly** furniture.
unattractive, unsightly, displeasing, tasteless, horrid, nasty
OPPOSITE beautiful
3 The crowd was in an **ugly** mood.
unfriendly, hostile, menacing, threatening, angry, dangerous
OPPOSITE friendly

unavoidable adjective
The accident was **unavoidable**.
inevitable, bound to happen, certain, destined

unaware adjective
unaware of
They were **unaware of** the dangers that lay ahead.
ignorant of, oblivious to, unconscious of

unbearable adjective
The stench in the cave was **unbearable**.
unendurable, intolerable, impossible to bear

unbelievable adjective
1 The account of the UFO sighting was **unbelievable**.
unconvincing, unlikely, far-fetched, improbable, incredible
2 She scored an **unbelievable** goal.
amazing, astonishing, extraordinary, remarkable, sensational, phenomenal

uncertain adjective
1 I was **uncertain** what to do next.
unsure, doubtful, in two minds, unclear
2 They are facing an **uncertain** future.
indefinite, unknown, undecided, unpredictable

uncomfortable adjective
1 She complained that her shoes were **uncomfortable**.
restrictive, cramped, hard, stiff, tight, tight-fitting
2 He spent an **uncomfortable** night sleeping on the floor.
restless, troubled, disagreeable, uneasy

ugly

unconscious adjective
1 The patient had been **unconscious** for two days.
If you are unconscious because of a hit on the head, you are **knocked out**.
If you are unconscious for an operation, you are **anaesthetized**.
If you are unconscious because of an accident or illness, you are **in a coma**.
2 She's **unconscious** of the effect she has on other people.
ignorant, unaware
3 They laughed at her **unconscious** slip of the tongue.
accidental, unintended, unintentional
OPPOSITE conscious
unconscious of
He's **unconscious of** all the trouble he's caused.
unaware of, ignorant of, oblivious to

uncover verb
1 Archaeologists have **uncovered** two more skeletons.
dig up, unearth, expose, reveal, show, disclose

a b c d e f g h i j k l m n o p q r s t u v w x y z

To uncover your body is to *strip* or *undress*.
2 He **uncovered** the truth about his family's past.
detect, discover, come across
OPPOSITE cover up, hide

understand *verb*
1 I don't **understand** what you mean.
comprehend, grasp, follow, see, take in, realize, appreciate, recognize, work out, fathom
2 Can you **understand** this writing?
read, interpret, make out, make sense of
To understand something in code is to *decode* or *decipher* it.
3 I **understand** they're moving to Sydney.
believe, hear

understanding *noun*
1 The robot has limited powers of **understanding**.
intelligence, intellect, sense, judgement
2 The course will increase your **understanding** of science.
appreciation, awareness, knowledge, comprehension, grasp
3 The two sides reached an **understanding**.
agreement, deal, settlement, arrangement, accord
4 She treats her patients with **understanding**.
sympathy, compasssion, consideration

undo *verb*
1 I'll have to **undo** this row of knitting.
unfasten, untie, unravel, loosen, release
To undo stitching is to *unpick* it.
2 Sue **undid** the wrapping on the parcel.
open, unwrap, unfold, unwind, unroll, unfurl
3 The good witch tried to **undo** the spell.
reverse, cancel out, wipe out

unemployed *adjective*
Since the factory closed, he has been **unemployed**.
out of work, jobless
(*informal*) on the dole
To be unemployed because there is not enough work to do is to be *redundant*.
OPPOSITE employed, working

uneven *adjective*
1 The ground was very **uneven** in places.
rough, bumpy, rutted
OPPOSITE smooth

uncover

2 Their performance has been **uneven** this season.
erratic, inconsistent, irregular, variable, unpredictable
OPPOSITE consistent
3 It was a very **uneven** contest.
one-sided, unbalanced, unequal, unfair
OPPOSITE balanced

unexpected *adjective*
Her reaction was totally **unexpected**.
surprising, unforeseen, unpredictable, unplanned
OPPOSITE expected

unfair *adjective*
1 Do you think that the umpire's decision was **unfair**?
unjust, unreasonable, wrong, one-sided, imbalanced, impartial, biased
OPPOSITE fair, just
2 I felt that her criticism of my work was **unfair**.
undeserved, unmerited, uncalled-for, unjustified
OPPOSITE fair, deserved

unfamiliar *adjective*
The astronauts looked on an **unfamiliar** landscape.
stange, unusual, curious, novel, alien
unfamiliar with
They were **unfamiliar with** the local customs.
unaccustomed to, unused to, unaware of

unfortunate *adjective*
1 The **unfortunate** couple had lost all their possessions.
unlucky, poor, unhappy, hapless, wretched, ill-fated
2 The goalkeeper made one **unfortunate** error.
disastrous, calamitous, unwelcome
OPPOSITE fortunate, lucky

3 He made an **unfortunate** remark about her cooking.
regrettable, inappropriate, tactless, unsuitable, untimely

unfriendly *adjective*
The housekeeper greeted us with an **unfriendly** glare.
unwelcoming, inhospitable, unsympathetic, unkind, impolite, uncivil, unhelpful, hostile, cold, cool, distant, standoffish, aloof, unsociable, unneighbourly
OPPOSITE friendly, amiable

unhappy *adjective*
You look **unhappy**—what's the matter?
brokenhearted, dejected, depressed, desolate, despairing, dismal, distressed
(*informal*) down, downcast, downhearted, forlorn, gloomy, glum, grave, heartbroken, in low spirits, miserable, regretful, sad, sorrowful, sorry, tearful, troubled, upset, wistful, woeful, wretched
OPPOSITE happy

unhealthy *adjective*
1 One of the calves has been **unhealthy** since birth.
unwell, ill, sick, diseased, infirm, sickly, poorly, weak, delicate, feeble, frail
OPPOSITE healthy, strong
2 He eats an **unhealthy** diet of junk food.
unwholesome, unnatural, harmful, unhygienic
OPPOSITE healthy, wholesome

unhelpful *adjective*
The shop assistant was most **unhelpful**.
uncooperative, unfriendly, inconsiderate, reluctant to help
OPPOSITE helpful

unimportant adjective
*Don't worry about **unimportant** details.*
insignificant, minor, trivial, trifling, irrelevant, secondary, slight, small, negligible, worthless, petty
OPPOSITE important

unique adjective
*Each person's fingerprints are **unique**.*
distinctive, different, individual, special, peculiar
(*informal*) one-off

unite verb
1 *King Bluetooth **united** the kingdoms of Denmark and Norway.*
combine, join, merge, link, integrate, unify, amalgamate, bring together
OPPOSITE separate
2 *People of all ages **united** to celebrate Chinese New Year.*
collaborate, cooperate, join forces
To unite to do something bad is to **conspire**.
OPPOSITE compete

unkind adjective
*It was a thoughtless and **unkind** remark.*
callous, hard-hearted, cruel, thoughtless, heartless, uncaring, unfeeling, inconsiderate, unsympathetic, unfriendly, uncharitable, harsh, mean, nasty, selfish, spiteful, vicious, malicious
OPPOSITE kind

unknown adjective
1 *The letter was in an **unknown** hand.*
unidentified, unrecognized
OPPOSITE known
2 *The author of the story is **unknown**.*
anonymous, nameless, unnamed, unspecified
OPPOSITE named
3 *The explorers entered **unknown** territory.*
unfamiliar, alien, foreign, undiscovered, unexplored, uncharted
OPPOSITE familiar
4 *The part was played by an **unknown** actor.*
little known, unheard of, obscure
OPPOSITE famous

unlikely adjective
*No-one believed her **unlikely** excuse.*
unbelievable, unconvincing, improbable, implausible, incredible, far-fetched
OPPOSITE likely

unlucky adjective
1 *Some people think that 13 is an **unlucky** number.*
unfavourable, ill-omened, ill-starred, jinxed

2 *By an **unlucky** chance, their plan was discovered.*
unfortunate, unwelcome, untimely

unnecessary adjective
*I'm deleting any **unnecessary** files from my computer.*
inessential, non-essential, uncalled for, unwanted, excessive, superfluous, surplus, extra, redundant
OPPOSITE necessary

unpleasant adjective
1 *Mr Smallweed was a thoroughly **unpleasant** man.*
disagreeable, unfriendly, unkind, bad-tempered, nasty, malicious, spiteful, hateful
2 *Being lost in the jungle had been an **unpleasant** experience.*
uncomfortable, disagreeable, awful
3 *The smell from the drain was very **unpleasant**.*
disgusting, foul, repulsive, revolting, horrible, horrid, repellent, offensive, objectionable

unpopular adjective
*The new manager was **unpopular** at first.*
disliked, hated, despised, unloved
OPPOSITE popular

untidy adjective
1 *Our house is the one with the **untidy** garden.*
messy, disorderly, cluttered, jumbled, tangled, littered, chaotic
(*informal*) higgledy-piggledy, topsy-turvy
2 *His work was **untidy** and full of mistakes.*
careless, disorganized, slapdash
(*informal*) sloppy
3 *She arrived looking **untidy** and flustered.*
dishevelled, bedraggled, rumpled, unkempt, scruffy, slovenly

unusual adjective
1 *The weather was **unusual** for the time of year.*
abnormal, out of the ordinary, exceptional, remarkable, extraordinary, odd, peculiar, singular, strange, unexpected, irregular, unconventional, unheard-of
OPPOSITE ordinary
2 *Ebenezer is an **unusual** name.*
uncommon, rare, unfamiliar
OPPOSITE common

upset verb
1 *Something in the letter had **upset** her.*
distress, trouble, disturb, displease, unsettle, offend, dismay, grieve, fluster, perturb
2 *Bad weather **upset** the train timetable.*
disrupt, interfere with, interrupt, affect, throw out

3 *The baby **upset** a whole bowl of cereal.*
knock over, spill, tip over, topple
4 *A fallen tree branch **upset** the canoe.*
overturn, capsize

urge verb
*He **urged** her to reconsider her decision.*
advise, counsel, appeal to, beg, implore, plead with, press
To urge someone to do something is also to **advocate** or **recommend** it.
OPPOSITE discourage

urge noun
*I had a sudden **urge** to burst into song.*
impulse, compulsion, longing, wish, yearning, desire, itch
(*informal*) yen

urgent adjective
1 *She had **urgent** business in New York.*
pressing, immediate, essential, important, top-priority
OPPOSITE unimportant
2 *He spoke in an **urgent** whisper.*
anxious, insistent, earnest

use verb
1 *She **used** a calculator to add up the figures.*
make use of, employ, utilize
To use your knowledge is to **apply** it.
To use your muscles is to **exercise** them.
To use a musical instrument is to **play** it.
To use an axe or sword is to **wield** it.
To use people or things selfishly is to **exploit** them.
2 *Can you show me how to use the photocopier?*
operate, work, handle, manage
3 *You've **used** all the hot water.*
use up, go through, consume, exhaust, spend

use noun
1 *Would these books be any **use** to you?*
help, benefit, advantage, profit, value
2 *A sonic screwdriver has many **uses**.*
function, purpose, point

useful adjective
1 *A flask is **useful** for keeping food warm.*
convenient, handy, effective, efficient, practical
2 *The website offers some **useful** advice.*
good, helpful, valuable, worthwhile, constructive, invaluable
OPPOSITE useless

a
b
c
d
e
f
g
h
i
j
k
l
m
n
o
p
q
r
s
t
u
v
w
x
y
z

useless adjective
1 *This old vacuum cleaner is* **useless**.
ineffective, inefficient, impractical, unusable
OPPOSITE useful, effective
2 *Her advice was completely* **useless**.
worthless, unhelpful, pointless, futile, unprofitable, fruitless
OPPOSITE useful
3 *(informal)* *I'm* **useless** *at drawing.*
bad, poor, incompetent
(informal) rubbish, hopeless
OPPOSITE good

usual adjective
1 *I'll meet you at the* **usual** *time.*
normal, customary, familiar, habitual, regular, standard
2 *It's* **usual** *to knock before entering.*
common, accepted, conventional, traditional

vacant adjective
1 *The house over the road is still* **vacant**.
unoccupied, uninhabited, deserted
OPPOSITE occupied
2 *The receptionist gave me a* **vacant** *stare.*
blank, expressionless, mindless, absent-minded, deadpan
OPPOSITE alert

vague adjective
1 *The directions she gave me were rather* **vague**.
indefinite, imprecise, broad, general, ill-defined, unclear, woolly
OPPOSITE exact, detailed

2 *A* **vague** *shape could be seen through the mist.*
blurred, indistinct, obscure, dim, hazy, shadowy
OPPOSITE definite

vain adjective
1 *The duchess was* **vain** *about her appearance.*
arrogant, proud, conceited, haughty, self-satisfied
OPPOSITE modest
2 *He made a* **vain** *attempt to tidy the room.*
unsuccessful, ineffective, useless, worthless, fruitless, futile, pointless
OPPOSITE successful

valuable adjective
1 *Apparently the painting is very* **valuable**.
expensive, costly, dear, precious, priceless
2 *He gave her some* **valuable** *advice.*
useful, helpful, constructive, good, worthwhile, invaluable
OPPOSITE worthlessNotice that invaluable is not the opposite of **valuable**.

value noun
1 *The house has recently increased in* **value**.
price, cost, worth
2 *He stressed the* **value** *of taking regular exercise.*
advantage, benefit, merit, use, usefulness, importance

value verb
1 *He had always* **valued** *her advice.*
appreciate, respect, esteem, have a high opinion of, set great store by
To value something highly is to **prize** or **treasure** it.

2 *A surveyor was sent to* **value** *the house.*
price, cost, rate, evaluate, assess

vanish verb
With a flick of his wand, the wizard **vanished** *into thin air.*
disappear, go away, fade, dissolve, disperse
OPPOSITE appear

vanity noun
His **vanity** *is such that he never admits he's wrong.*
arrogance, pride, conceit, self-esteem, self-importance

variety noun
1 *The centre offers a* **variety** *of leisure activities.*
assortment, mixture, array
2 *The supermarket has over thirty* **varieties** *of pasta.*
kind, sort, type, make, brand
A variety of animal is a **breed** or **species**.
3 *There is not much* **variety** *in her choice of words.*
variation, change, difference, diversity

vast adjective
1 *The miser accumulated a* **vast** *fortune.*
large, huge, enormous, great, immense, massive
2 *A* **vast** *stretch of water lay between them and dry land.*
broad, wide, extensive, sweeping

version noun
1 *The two newspapers gave different* **versions** *of the accident.*
account, description, story, report

view

2 *It's an English **version** of a French play.*
adaptation, interpretation
A version of something which was originally in another language is a **translation**.
3 *A new **version** of the computer game will be released in May.*
design, model, form, variation

very *adverb*
*Carl is a **very** talented juggler.*
extremely, highly, enormously, exceedingly, truly, intensely, especially, particularly, remarkably, unusually, uncommonly, outstandingly, really
(*informal*) terribly
OPPOSITE slightly

vibrate *verb*
*I pulled a lever and the whole engine began to **vibrate**.*
shake, shudder, tremble, throb, judder, quake, quiver, rattle

vicious *adjective*
1 *This was once the scene of a **vicious** murder.*
brutal, barbaric, violent, bloodthirsty, cruel, merciless, pitiless, ruthless, callous, inhuman, malicious, sadistic, atrocious, barbarous, murderous, villainous, wicked
2 *Male baboons can be **vicious** if provoked.*
fierce, ferocious, violent, savage, wild

victory *noun*
*Hannibal won several **victories** over the Romans.*
win, success, triumph
OPPOSITE defeat

view *noun*
1 *There's a good **view** from the top of the hill.*
outlook, prospect, scene, panorama, scenery
2 *What are your **views** on animal testing?*
opinion, thought, attitude, belief, conviction, idea, notion

view *verb*
1 *Thousand of tourists come to **view** Niagara Falls each year.*
look at, see, watch, observe, regard, contemplate, gaze at, inspect, survey, examine, eye
2 *Wanda **viewed** her cousin with extreme dislike.*
think of, consider, regard

vile *adjective*
1 *The professor gave us a **vile** concoction to drink.*
disgusting, repulsive, revolting, foul, horrible, loathsome, offensive, repellent, sickening, nauseating
OPPOSITE pleasant

2 *Murder is a **vile** crime.*
dreadful, despicable, appalling, contemptible, wicked, evil

villain *noun*
*Detectives are on the trail of an infamous **villain**.*
criminal, offender, rogue, wrongdoer
An informal word for the villain in a story is **baddy**.
OPPOSITE hero

violence *noun*
1 *The marchers protested against the use of **violence**.*
fighting, might, war, brute force, barbarity, brutality, cruelty, savagery
OPPOSITE non-violence, pacifism
2 *The **violence** of the storm uprooted trees.*
force, power, strength, severity, intensity, ferocity, fierceness, fury, rage
OPPOSITE gentleness, mildness

violent *adjective*
1 *There were **violent** clashes in the streets.*
aggressive, forceful, rough, fierce, frenzied, vicious, brutal
OPPOSITE gentle, mild
2 *The bridge was washed away in a **violent** storm.*
severe, strong, powerful, forceful, raging, tempestuous, turbulent, wild
OPPOSITE weak, feeble

visible *adjective*
*There were no **visible** signs that the door had been forced.*
noticeable, obvious, conspicuous, clear, distinct, evident, apparent, perceptible, recognizable, detectable
OPPOSITE invisible

visit *verb*
*They're **visiting** friends in Toronto for a few days.*
call on, come to see, drop in on, go to see, pay a call on, stay with

visit *noun*
1 *My grandmother is coming for a **visit**.*
call, stay
2 *We are planning a short **visit** to Paris.*
trip, excursion, outing

visitor *noun*
1 *They've got some Polish **visitors** staying with them.*
guest, caller
2 *Rome welcomes millions of **visitors** every year.*
tourist, holidaymaker, sightseer, traveller

vivid *adjective*
1 *Gaugin often painted in **vivid** colours.*
bright, colourful, strong, intense, vibrant, dazzling, brilliant, glowing, striking, showy

2 *He gave a **vivid** description of his travels in Mexico.*
lively, clear, powerful, evocative, imaginative, dramatic, lifelike, realistic, graphic
OPPOSITE dull

voice *noun*
*The robot spoke with a slow, metallic **voice**.*
speech, tone, way of speaking

✏️ **WRITING TIPS**

You can use these words to describe a **voice**:
croaky, droning, gruff, high-pitched, husky, low, shrill, soft-spoken, squeaky, throaty *A **gruff** voice cried, 'Who dares to enter my cave?'*

---

voluntary *adjective*
*She does **voluntary** work for a charity.*
optional, unpaid
OPPOSITE compulsory

vomit *verb*
*The smell made him want to **vomit**.*
be sick, heave, retch
(*informal*) throw up

vote *verb*
*Everyone has a right to **vote** in the election.*
cast your vote
to vote for someone or **something**
*I haven't decided who to **vote for**.*
choose, opt for, nominate, elect

vote

vote *noun*
*The results of the **vote** will be known tomorrow.*
ballot, election, poll, referendum

vulgar *adjective*
1 *The new colour scheme just looks **vulgar** to me.*
tasteless, unsophisticated, cheap, tawdry
(*informal*) tacky
OPPOSITE tasteful
2 *The book sometimes uses **vulgar** language.*
indecent, offensive, rude, coarse
OPPOSITE decent

a b c d e f g h i j k l m n o p q r s t u v w x y z

Ww

wail *verb*
Upstairs, the baby began to **wail**.
cry, howl, bawl, cry, moan, shriek

wait *verb*
Please **wait** *here until I get back.*
remain where you are, stay, stop, rest, pause, linger
(*informal*) hang about or around, hold on

wait *noun*
There was a long **wait** *before the show began.*
interval, pause, delay, hold-up

wake, **waken** *verbs*
1 *Hagor the giant* **woke** *from a deep sleep.*
awake, awaken, become conscious, come round, rise, arise, stir, wake up
2 *The alarm clock* **woke** *me at 6 a.m.*
rouse, arouse, awaken, disturb

walk *verb*
1 *I* **walked** *down the lane, humming a tune.*
amble, crawl, creep, dodder, pace, plod, saunter, step, stroll, wander
2 *A squat little troll* **walked** *towards the forest.*
hobble, limp, lope, lurch, shamble, shuffle, stagger, stumble, toddle, totter, waddle
3 *The robot* **walked** *its way up the stairs.*
clump, pound, stamp, traipse, tramp, trudge, wade
4 *The burglar* **walked** *away into the shadows.*
mince, pad, patter, prowl, slink, stalk, steal, tiptoe
5 *Captain Flint* **walked** *on board the ship.*
march, parade, stride, strut, swagger, trot
6 *They are planning to* **walk** *across the Himalayas.*
hike, trek, ramble
7 *The children* **walked** *into the classroom.*
file, troop

walk *noun*
1 *We went for a* **walk** *in the country.*
stroll, saunter, ramble, hike, trek, tramp, trudge
2 *There are some lovely* **walks** *through the forest.*
path, route

wander *verb*
1 *Sheep* **wandered** *about the hills.*
stray, roam, rove, range, ramble, meander, travel, walk

2 *We must have* **wandered** *off the path.*
stray, turn, veer, swerve

want *verb*
1 *He desperately* **wants** *to win a medal.*
wish, desire, long, hope
2 *Gayle had always* **wanted** *a pony of her own.*
wish for, desire, fancy, crave, long for, yearn for, hanker after, pine for, set your heart on, hunger for, thirst for
3 *That floor* **wants** *a good scrub.*
need, require

war *noun*
The **war** *between the two countries lasted many years.*
fighting, warfare, conflict, strife, hostilities

warm *adjective*
1 *It was a* **warm** *September evening.*
Weather which is unpleasantly warm is **close** or **sultry**.
Water or food which is only just warm is **lukewarm** or **tepid**.
A common simile is **as warm as toast**.
OPPOSITE cold
2 *Sandy put on a* **warm** *jumper.*
cosy, thick, woolly
OPPOSITE thin
3 *The fans gave the singer a* **warm** *welcome.*
friendly, warm-hearted, welcoming, kind, affectionate, genial, amiable, loving, sympathetic
OPPOSITE unfriendly

warm *verb*
She sat by the fire, **warming** *her hands and feet.*
heat, make warmer, thaw out
OPPOSITE chill

warn *verb*
The guide **warned** *us to keep to the path.*
advise, caution, alert, remind
To warn people of danger is to **raise the alarm**.

warning *noun*
1 *There was no* **warning** *of the danger ahead.*
sign, signal, indication, advance notice
2 *The traffic warden let him off with a* **warning**.
caution, reprimand

wash *verb*
1 *It took Rapunzel a long time to* **wash** *her hair.*
clean
To wash something with a cloth is to **mop**, **sponge**, or **wipe** it.
To wash something with a brush is to **scrub** it.
To wash something in clean water is to **rinse**, **sluice**, or **swill** it.

To wash yourself all over is to **bath** or **shower**.
2 *Waves* **washed** *over the beach.*
flow, splash

waste *verb*
Let's not **waste** *any more time.*
squander, misuse, throw away, fritter away
OPPOSITE save

waste *noun*
A lot of household **waste** *can be recycled.*
rubbish, refuse, trash, garbage, junk, litter
Waste food is **leftovers**.
Waste metal is **scrap**.

wasteful *adjective*
It's **wasteful** *to cook more food than you need.*
extravagant, uneconomical, prodigal, lavish, spendthrift
OPPOSITE economical, thrifty

watch *verb*
1 *I could sit and* **watch** *the sea for hours.*
gaze at, look at, stare at, view, contemplate
2 *Watch how the batsman holds the bat.*
observe, take notice of, keep your eyes on, pay attention to, attend to, heed, note
3 *Could you* **watch** *my bag for a few minutes?*
keep an eye on, keep watch over, guard, mind, look after, safeguard, supervise, tend

> ✏️ **WRITING TIPS**
>
> **water** *noun*
> You can use these words to describe **how water moves**:
> bubble, cascade, dribble, drip, flood, flow, froth, gurgle, gush, jet, ooze, overflow, ripple, roll, run, seep, shower, spill, spatter, splash, spout, spray, sprinkle, spurt, squirt, stream, surge, sweep, swirl, swish, trickle, well up

wave *verb*
1 *The tall grass* **waved** *in the breeze.*
move to and fro, sway, swing, flap, flutter
2 *I tried to get their attention by* **waving** *a newspaper.*
shake, brandish, flourish, twirl, wag, waggle, wiggle

wave *noun*
1 *We watched the* **waves** *break on the shore.*
breaker, roller, billow
A very small wave is a **ripple**.
A huge wave caused by an earthquake is a **tidal wave** or **tsunami**.

A number of white waves following each other is **surf**.
The top of a wave is the **crest** or **ridge**.
2 *A **wave** of anger spread through the crowd.*
surge, outbreak

wavy *adjective*
*The mermaid combed her long **wavy** hair.*
curly, curling, rippling, winding, zigzag
OPPOSITE straight

way *noun*
1 *Can you show me the **way** to the bus station?*
direction, route, road, path
2 *Is your house a long **way** from here?*
distance, journey
3 *This is the best **way** to make porridge.*
method, procedure, process, system, technique
4 *What a childish **way** to behave!*
manner, fashion, style
5 *In some **ways**, the brothers are very alike.*
respect, particular, feature, detail, aspect
6 *Things are in a bad **way**.*
state, condition

weak *adjective*
1 *The footbridge was old and **weak** in places.*
fragile, flimsy, rickety, shaky, unsound, unsteady, unsafe, decrepit
2 *The patient was too **weak** to walk very far.*
feeble, frail, ill, sickly, infirm, delicate, puny
3 *The nobles plotted against the **weak** king.*
timid, spineless, ineffective, powerless, useless
4 *The film was fun, but the plot was a bit **weak**.*
feeble, lame, unsatisfactory, unconvincing
5 *He asked for a mug of **weak** tea.*
watery, diluted, tasteless, thin
(*informal*) wishy-washy
OPPOSITE strong

weakness *noun*
1 *He pointed out the **weakness** in their plan.*
fault, flaw, defect, imperfection, weak point
2 *Eve has a **weakness** for toffee apples.*
liking, fondness (*informal*) soft spot

wealthy *adjective*
*They say that he comes from a very **wealthy** family.*
rich, well-off, affluent, prosperous, moneyed, well-to-do
(*informal*) flush, loaded
OPPOSITE poor

wear *verb*
1 *Can I **wear** my new dress to the party?*
dress in, be dressed in, have on
2 *The rug in the hallway is starting to **wear**.*
fray, wear away, wear out
3 *Those tyres have **worn** well.*
last, endure, survive

weather *noun see panel opposite*

weird *adjective*
1 *Weird noises have been heard in the tower at midnight.*
eerie, ghostly, unearthly, mysterious, uncanny, unnatural
(*informal*) spooky, creepy
OPPOSITE ordinary, natural
2 *My big sister has a **weird** taste in music.*
strange, odd, peculiar, bizarre, curious, quirky, eccentric, outlandish, unconventional, unusual
(*informal*) wacky, way-out
OPPOSITE conventional

welcome *noun*
*The landlady gave us a friendly **welcome**.*
greeting, reception
welcome *adjective*
1 *A cup of tea would be very **welcome**.*
pleasant, pleasing, agreeable, appreciated, desirable, acceptable
OPPOSITE unacceptable
2 *You're **welcome** to use my bike.*
allowed, permitted, free
OPPOSITE forbidden
welcome *verb*
*An elderly butler **welcomed** us at the door.*
greet, receive, meet, hail

well *adverb*
1 *The whole team played **well** on Saturday.*
ably, skilfully, expertly, effectively, efficiently, admirably, marvellously, wonderfully
OPPOSITE badly
2 *It's cold outside, so you'd better wrap up **well**.*
properly, suitably, correctly, thoroughly, carefully
3 *I know her brother **well**.*
closely, intimately, personally
well *adjective*
*Mrs Orr looks surprisingly **well** for her age.*
healthy, fit, strong, sound, robust, vigorous, lively, hearty
OPPOSITE ill

well-known *adjective*
*A **well-known** athlete will open the new sports shop.*
famous, celebrated, prominent, notable, renowned, distinguished, eminent
OPPOSITE unknown, obscure

WORD WEB

weather *noun*
The typical weather in a particular area is the **climate**.
A person who studies and forecasts the weather is a **meteorologist**.

SOME TYPES OF WEATHER
fog: mist, (Scottish) haar, haze, smog; ice and snow: blizzard, frost, hail, ice, sleet, snowstorm
light rain: drizzle, shower
heavy rain: cloudburst, deluge, downpour, monsoon, torrent sun: drought, heatwave, sunshine
storm: squall, tempest light wind: breeze, gust strong wind: cyclone, gale, hurricane, tornado, typhoon, whirlwind

WRITING TIPS

You can use these words to describe **weather**.

TO DESCRIBE CLOUDY WEATHER
dull, grey, overcast, sunless

TO DESCRIBE COLD WEATHER
arctic, bitter, chilly, frosty, icy, nippy, perishing, raw, snowy, wintry

TO DESCRIBE SNOW
crisp, powdery, slushy
TO DESCRIBE HOT WEATHER:
baking, humid, melting, roasting, sizzling, sticky, sultry, sweltering

TO DESCRIBE STORMY WEATHER
rough, squally, tempestuous, turbulent, violent, wild
THUNDER MAY:
boom, crash, resound, roar, rumble

TO DESCRIBE SUNNY WEATHER
bright, cloudless, fair, fine, springlike, summery, sunny, sunshiny

TO DESCRIBE WET WEATHER
damp, drizzly, raining cats and dogs, showery, spitting, torrential
RAIN MAY:
lash or pelt down, pour, teem
(*informal*) bucket, tip down

TO DESCRIBE WINDY WEATHER
biting, blowy, blustery, breezy, gusty
WIND MAY:
batter, blast, buffet, howl, moan, wail

wet *adjective*
1 *Archie took off his **wet** clothes and had a hot bath.*
damp, soaked, soaking, drenched, dripping, sopping, wringing wet
2 *The pitch was too **wet** to play on.*
waterlogged, saturated, sodden, soggy, dewy, muddy, boggy
3 *Take care—the paint is still **wet**.*
runny, sticky, tacky
4 *It was cold and **wet** all afternoon.*
rainy, showery, pouring, drizzly, misty

whip *verb*
1 *The jockey **whipped** his horse to make it go faster.*
beat, hit, lash, flog, thrash
2 ***Whip** the cream until it is thick.*
beat, whisk

whirl *verb*
*The snowflakes **whirled** in the icy wind.*
turn, twirl, spin, twist, circle, spiral, reel, pirouette, revolve, rotate

whisper *verb*
*What are you two **whispering** about?*
murmur, mutter, mumble
OPPOSITE shout

whole *adjective*
1 *I haven't read the **whole** book yet.*
complete, entire, full, total, unabbreviated
OPPOSITE incomplete
2 *The dinosaur skeleton appears to be **whole**.*
in one piece, intact, unbroken, undamaged, perfect
OPPOSITE broken, in pieces

wicked *adjective*
1 *Cinderella had a **wicked** stepmother.*
evil, cruel, vicious, villainous, detestable, mean, corrupt, immoral, sinful, foul, vile
OPPOSITE good, virtuous
2 *They hatched a **wicked** scheme to take over the world.*
evil, fiendish, malicious, malevolent, diabolical, monstrous, deplorable, dreadful, shameful
3 *The goblin had a **wicked** grin on his face.*
mischievous, playful, impish, naughty

wide *adjective*
1 *The hotel is close to a **wide** sandy beach.*
broad, expansive, extensive, large, spacious
OPPOSITE narrow
2 *She has a **wide** knowledge of classical music.*
comprehensive, vast, wide-ranging, encyclopedic
OPPOSITE limited

wield *verb*
*The lumberjack was **wielding** his axe.*
brandish, flourish, hold, use

wild *adjective*
1 *I don't like seeing **wild** animals in captivity.*
undomesticated, untamed
OPPOSITE tame
2 *The hedgerow was full of **wild** flowers.*
natural, uncultivated
OPPOSITE cultivated
3 *To the west is a **wild** and mountainous region.*
rough, rugged, uncultivated, uninhabited, desolate
OPPOSITE cultivated
4 *The crowd were **wild** with excitement.*
riotous, rowdy, disorderly, unruly, boisterous, excited, noisy, uncontrollable, hysterical
OPPOSITE calm, restrained
5 *The weather looked **wild** outside.*
blustery, windy, gusty, stormy, turbulent, tempestuous
OPPOSITE calm

willing *adjective*
1 *She is always **willing** to help.*
eager, happy, pleased, ready, prepared
2 *I need a couple of **willing** volunteers.*
enthusiastic, helpful, cooperative, obliging
OPPOSITE unwilling

wilt *verb*
*The flowers **wilted** in the heat.*
become limp, droop, flop, sag, fade, shrivel, wither
OPPOSITE flourish

win *verb*
1 *Who do you think will **win**?*
come first, be victorious, succeed, triumph, prevail
To win against someone is also to **beat**, **conquer**, **defeat** or **overcome** them.
OPPOSITE lose
2 *She **won** first prize in the poetry competition.*
get, receive, gain, obtain, secure
(*informal*) pick up, walk away with

wind *verb*
1 *She **wound** the wool into a ball.*
coil, loop, roll, turn, curl
2 *The road **winds** up the hill.*
bend, curve, twist and turn, zigzag, meander

wink

windy *adjective*
*It was a cold, **windy** day.*
breezy, blustery, gusty, squally, stormy
OPPOSITE calm

wilt

wink *verb*
*The lights **winked** on and off.*
flash, flicker, sparkle, twinkle

winner *noun*
*The **winner** was presented with a silver cup.*
victor, prizewinner, champion, conqueror
OPPOSITE loser

wipe *verb*
*I **wiped** the table with a cloth.*
rub, clean, polish, mop, swab, sponge
to wipe something out
*Pompeii was **wiped out** by the eruption of Mount Vesuvius.*
destroy, annihilate, exterminate, get rid of

wire *noun*
*Several **wires** protruded from the robot's head.*
cable, lead, flex
A system of wires is **wiring**.

wise *adjective*
1 *The soothsayer was very old and **wise**.*
sensible, reasonable, intelligent, perceptive, knowledgeable, rational, thoughtful
2 *I think you made a **wise** decision.*
good, right, proper, sound, fair, just, appropriate
OPPOSITE foolish

wish *noun*
*Her dearest **wish** was to travel to the Amazon.*
desire, want, longing, yearning, hankering, craving, urge, fancy, hope, ambition
(*informal*) yen

wish *verb*
*I **wish** that everyone would sit still for a minute!*
If you wish something would happen, you can say that you **want** or **would like** it to happen.

wither *verb*
*The flowers had **withered** and died.*
shrivel, dry up, shrink, wilt, droop, sag, flop
OPPOSITE flourish

witness *noun*
*A **witness** said that the car was going too fast.*
bystander, observer, onlooker, eyewitness, spectator

witty adjective
He gave a **witty** account of his schooldays.
humorous, amusing, comic, funny
OPPOSITE dull

wizard noun
1 The **wizard** cast a spell over the whole palace.
magician, sorcerer, enchanter
2 My sister is a **wizard** with computers.
expert, specialist, genius
(informal) whizz

wobble verb
1 The cyclist **wobbled** all over the road.
sway, totter, tetter, waver, rock
2 The jelly **wobbled** as I carried the plate.
shake, tremble, quake, quiver, vibrate

wobbly adjective
1 The baby giraffe was a bit **wobbly** on its legs.
shaky, tottering, unsteady
2 This chair is a bit **wobbly**.
loose, rickety, rocky, unstable, unsafe

woman noun
A polite word for a woman is **lady**.
A married woman is a **wife**.
A woman who has children is a **mother**.
An unmarried woman is a **spinster**.
A woman whose husband has died is a **widow**.
A woman on her wedding day is a **bride**.
A woman who is engaged to be married is a **fiancée**.
Words for a young woman are **girl** and **lass**.
Old words for a young woman are **maid** and **maiden**.

wonder noun
The sight of the Taj Mahal filled them with **wonder**.
admiration, awe, reverence, amazement, astonishment

wonder verb
I **wonder** why she left in such a hurry.
be curious about, ask yourself, ponder, think about

wonderful adjective
1 It's **wonderful** what computers can do these days.
amazing, astonishing, astounding, incredible, remarkable, extraordinary, marvellous, miraculous, phenomenal
2 We had a **wonderful** time at the party.
excellent, splendid, great, superb, delightful
(informal) brilliant, fantastic, terrific, fabulous, super
OPPOSITE ordinary

wood noun
1 All the furniture in the room was made of **wood**.
timber, lumber, planks, logs
2 We followed a nature trail through the **wood**.
woodland, woods, forest, trees

word noun
1 What's the French **word** for 'birthday'?
expression, term
All the words you know are your **vocabulary**.
2 You gave me your **word**.
promise, assurance, guarantee, pledge, vow
3 There has been no **word** from him for several weeks.
news, message, information

work noun
1 Digging the garden involves a lot of hard **work**.
effort, labour, toil, exertion
2 Do you have any **work** to do this weekend?
task, assignment, chore, job, homework, housework
3 What kind of **work** does she do?
occupation, employment, job, profession, business, trade, vocation

work verb
1 She's been **working** in the garden all day.
be busy, exert yourself, labour, toil, slave
2 He **works** in the bookshop on Saturdays.
be employed, have a job, go to work
3 My watch isn't **working**.
function, go, operate
4 Is the TV easy to **work**?
operate, run, use, control, handle

world noun
1 Antarctica is a remote part of the **world**.
earth, globe
2 Scientists are searching for life on other **worlds**.
planet

worried adjective
You look **worried**. Is something the matter?
anxious, troubled, uneasy, distressed, disturbed, upset, apprehensive, concerned, bothered, tense, strained, nervous
OPPOSITE relaxed

worry verb
1 There's no need to **worry**.
be anxious, be troubled, be disturbed, brood, fret

2 It **worried** her that he hadn't replied to her letter.
trouble, distress, upset, concern, disturb

worry noun
1 He's been a constant source of **worry** to her.
anxiety, distress, uneasiness, vexation
2 I don't want to add to your **worries**.
trouble, concern, burden, care, problem

worthwhile adjective
It may be **worthwhile** to get a second opinion.
helpful, useful, valuable, beneficial, profitable
OPPOSITE useless

wound noun
He is being treated in hospital for a head **wound**.
injury, cut, gash, graze, scratch, sore

wound verb
The fox was **wounded** in the leg and bleeding.
injure, hurt, harm

wrap verb
1 She **wrapped** the presents in shiny gold paper.
cover, pack, enclose, enfold, swathe
To wrap water pipes is to **insulate** or **lag** them.
2 The mountain was **wrapped** in mist.
cloak, envelop, shroud, surround, hide, conceal

world

wreck verb
1 His bicycle was **wrecked** in the accident.
demolish, destroy, crush, smash, shatter, crumple
2 The injury **wrecked** her chances of becoming a dancer.
ruin, spoil

wreckage noun
Divers have discovered the **wreckage** of an old ship.
debris, fragments, pieces, remains
The wreckage of a building is **rubble** or **ruins**.

wriggle verb
The prisoner managed to **wriggle** out of his bonds.
twist, writhe, squirm, worm your way

wrinkle noun
The old hag's face was covered in **wrinkles**.
crease, fold, furrow, line, ridge, crinkle, pucker, pleat
A small hollow on someone's skin is a **dimple**.

wrinkle verb
The creature **wrinkled** its nose and sniffed.
pucker up, crease, crinkle, crumple, fold
OPPOSITE smooth

write verb
1 My granny **wrote** a diary when she was a girl.
compile, compose, draw up, set down, pen
To write letters or emails to people is to **correspond** with them.
To write a rough version of a story is to **draft** it.
2 He **wrote** his address on the back of an envelope.
jot down, note, print, scrawl, scribble

To write on a document or surface is to **inscribe** it.
To write your signature on something is to **autograph** it.

writer noun
A person who writes books is an **author**.
A person who writes novels is a **novelist**.
A person who writes plays is a **dramatist** or **playwright**.
A person who writes scripts for films or television is a **scriptwriter** or **screenwriter**.
A person who writes poetry is a **poet**.
A person who writes about someone else's life is a **biographer**.
A person who writes for newspapers is a **correspondent**, **journalist**, or **reporter**.
A person who writes music is a **composer**.

writing noun
1 Can you read the **writing** on the envelope?
handwriting
Untidy writing is a **scrawl** or **scribble**.
The art of beautiful handwriting is **calligraphy**.
2 The **writing** on the stone was very faint.
inscription
3 (often plural) She introduced me to the **writings** of Roald Dahl.
literature, works

 WORD WEB

writing noun
VARIOUS FORMS OF WRITING AND LITERATURE
autobiography, biography, children's literature, comedy, crime or detective story, diary, drama or play, essay, fable, fairy story or fairy tale, fantasy, fiction, film or TV script, folk tale, ghost story, historical fiction, history, journalism, legend, letters or correspondence, lyrics, myth, newspaper article, non-fiction, novel, parody, philosophy, poetry or verse, prose, romance, satire, science fiction or sci-fi, spy story, thriller, tragedy, travel writing, western

wrong adjective
1 It was **wrong** to take the book without asking.
bad, dishonest, irresponsible, immoral, sinful, wicked, criminal, unfair, unjust

2 His calculations were all **wrong**.
incorrect, mistaken, inaccurate
3 Did I say the **wrong** thing?
inappropriate, unsuitable, improper
4 There's something **wrong** with the TV.
faulty, defective, not working, out of order
OPPOSITE right
to go wrong
The professor's plan began to **go wrong**.
fail, backfire
(informal) flop, go pear-shaped
OPPOSITE succeed

yell verb
I **yelled** to attract their attention.
call out, cry out, shout, bawl, bellow

young adjective
1 A lot of **young** people went to the concert.
youthful, juvenile
OPPOSITE older, mature
2 I think this book is a bit **young** for you.
childish, babyish, immature, infantile
OPPOSITE adult, grown-up
A young person is a **child** or **youngster**.
A young adult is an **adolescent** or **youth**.
A very young child is a **baby** or **infant**.
A young bird is a **chick**, **fledgling**, or **nestling**.
Young fish are **fry**.
A young plant is a **cutting** or **seedling**.
A young tree is a **sapling**.

young plural noun
The mother bird returned to feed her **young**.
offspring, children, young ones, family
A family of young birds is a **brood**.
A family of young cats or dogs is a **litter**.

zero noun
Four minus four makes **zero**.
nothing, nought
A score of zero in football is **nil**; in cricket it is a **duck**, and in tennis it is **love**.